# THE OXFORD HANDBOOK OF

# THE COLD WAR

# THE OXFORD HANDBOOK OF

# THE COLD WAR

*Edited by*

## RICHARD H. IMMERMAN

*and*

## PETRA GOEDDE

OXFORD
UNIVERSITY PRESS

# OXFORD

UNIVERSITY PRESS

Great Clarendon Street, Oxford, OX2 6DP,
United Kingdom

Oxford University Press is a department of the University of Oxford.
It furthers the University's objective of excellence in research, scholarship,
and education by publishing worldwide. Oxford is a registered trade mark of
Oxford University Press in the UK and in certain other countries

British Library Cataloguing in Publication Data
Data available

ISBN 978–0–19–923696–1

**Printed in Great Britain by
Clays Ltd, St Ives plc**

*To our many colleagues everywhere*

# ACKNOWLEDGMENTS

As editors, we first and foremost must acknowledge our contributors. Completing a volume comprised of more than thirty chapters, all written by separate authors, requires collaboration and cooperation. We could not have asked for more of either. Of course we are even more grateful for each of their efforts to remain within the word limits we imposed, without sacrificing any quality.

We also thank our British friends at Oxford University Press. Christopher Wheeler, the publisher at OUP, convinced us we could pull this *Handbook* together, and we would enjoy the experience. He was right on both counts. Along the way, we received invaluable assistance from Natasha Knight, Jenny Townshend, and Rachel Platt. It took all three to keep track of and post and repost on our very own website our multiple drafts, especially the multiple final drafts. We are not exactly sure what job description accompanies Matthew Cotton's title of Assistant Commissioning Editor. We are sure that no one did more to shepherd the manuscript through to completion, and never once did he lose patience with us. Emma Barber continually allowed us to include revisions long after the schedule allowed, as should a helpful production editor. As for Virginia Williams, our copy editor, we doubt she ever sleeps. We know she does not take off weekends.

Finally we must express our deepest appreciation to our families. This volume took some half-dozen years to complete. They lived with it throughout, including those times when we probably spent more time with the manuscripts, and each other, than we did with them. So thank you Marion, Morgan, Tyler, and at least for the end game, Fred and Anna; and Drew, Kai, Elena, and Noah.

Richard Immerman and Petra Goedde
Philadelphia, PA

# CONTENTS

## PART III  WAGING THE COLD WAR

## PART IV CHALLENGING THE COLD WAR PARADIGM

## PART V THE END OF THE COLD WAR

# List of Maps and Illustrations

# ABBREVIATIONS

| | |
|---|---|
| ACP | African, Caribbean, and Pacific Group of States |
| ADB | Asian Development Bank |
| AEC | Atomic Energy Commission |
| AID | Agency for International Development |
| AIOC | Anglo-Iranian Oil Company |
| ALSC | African Liberation Support Committee |
| ANC | African National Congress |
| ASEAN | Association of Southeast Asian Nations |
| BIT | bilateral investment agreements |
| CALCAV | Clergy and Laymen Concerned About Vietnam |
| CARIFTA | Caribbean Free Trade Association |
| CCF | Congress for Cultural Freedom |
| CCP | Chinese Communist Party |
| CDP | Community Development Program |
| CEDAW | Convention on the Elimination of all forms of Discrimination against Women |
| CENTO | Central Treaty Organization |
| CERD | Committee on the Elimination of Racial Discrimination |
| CGPM | General Conference on Weights and Measures |
| CHR | Commission on Human Rights |
| CIA | Central Intelligence Agency |
| CIS | Commonwealth of Independent States |
| CMEA | Council for Mutual Economic Assistance |
| CND | Campaign for Nuclear Disarmament |
| CNI | Committee for Nuclear Information |
| COCOM | Coordinating Committee for Multilateral Export Controls |
| Comecon | Council for Mutual Economic Assistance |
| COMSAT | Communication Satellite Corporation |
| CPM | Communist Party of Malaya |
| CPSU | Communist Party of the Soviet Union |
| CSCE | Conference on Security and Cooperation in Europe |
| CSCRQ | Central Standing Commission on Religious Questions |
| CSSR | Czechoslovak Socialist Republic |
| CSW | Commission on the Status of Women |
| CUC | Committee for Peasant Unity |
| DIA | Defense Intelligence Agency |

| | |
|---|---|
| DMZ | (Korean) Demilitarized Zone |
| DPRK | Democratic People's Republic of Korea |
| dwt | deadweight tons |
| ECE | Economic Commission for Europe |
| ECOSOC | Economic and Social Council (UN) |
| EDC | European Defense Community |
| EEC | European Economic Community |
| END | European Nuclear Disarmament |
| ERP | European Recovery Program |
| EU | European Union |
| FAO | Food and Agriculture Organization |
| FBI | Federal Bureau of Investigation |
| FCDA | Federal Civil Defence Administration |
| FDI | foreign direct investments |
| FLN | National Liberation Front (Algeria) *(Front de Libération Nationale)* |
| FNLA | National Front for the Liberation of Angola *(Frente Nacional de Libertaçäo de Angola)* |
| FRELIMO | Front for the Liberation of Mozambique *(Frente de Libertaçäo de Moçambique)* |
| FRG | Federal Republic of Germany |
| GATT | General Agreement on Tariffs and Trade |
| GDR | German Democratic Republic |
| GNP | gross national product |
| HUAC | House Un-American Activities Committee |
| IAU | International Astronomical Union |
| IBRD | International Bank for Reconstruction and Development |
| ICBM | intercontinental-range ballistic missile |
| ICC | International Criminal Court |
| ICCPR | International Covenant on Civil and Political Rights |
| ICERD | International Convention on the Elimination of Racial Discrimination |
| ICESCR | International Covenant on Economic, Social, and Cultural Rights |
| ICP | Iraqi Communist Party |
| ICT | information and communications technology |
| IFAD | International Fund for Agricultural Development |
| IFR | International Fellowship of Reconciliation |
| ILO | International Labour Organization |
| IMF | International Monetary Fund |
| INF | intermediate-range nuclear forces |
| INGO | international nongovernmental organization |
| INTELSAT | International Telecommunication Satellite Organization |
| IRBM | intermediate-range ballistic missiles |
| IRF | International Road Federation |

| | |
|---|---|
| ISI | Inter-Services Intelligence |
| ISO | International Organization for Standardization |
| ITU | International Telecommunications Union |
| IUCN | International Union for the Conservation of Nature |
| IWY | International Women's Year |
| KOR | Workers' Defense Committee (Poland) |
| LAFTA | Latin American Free Trade Association |
| LDP | Liberal Democratic Party (Japan) |
| LMG | League of the Militant Godless |
| LNHO | League of Nations Health Organization |
| LOP | League for the Protection of Nature *(Liga Ochrony Przyrody)* |
| MAD | mutual assured destruction |
| MLF | multilateral (nuclear) force |
| MNF | most favored nation |
| MPLA | Popular Movement for the Liberation of Angola *(Movimento Popular de Libertação de Angola)* |
| MRBM | medium-range ballistic missile |
| NAACP | National Association of Colored People |
| NAFTA | North American Free Trade Agreement |
| NAM | Non-Aligned Movement |
| NATO | North Atlantic Treaty Organization |
| NGO | nongovernmental organization |
| NICs | newly industrializing countries |
| NIEs | National Intelligence Estimates |
| NNC | National Negro Congress |
| NSDD | National Security Decision Directives |
| OAS | Organization of American States |
| OAU | Organization of African Unity |
| ODA | Overseas Development Aid |
| OECD | Organisation for Economic Co-operation and Development |
| OIHP | Office International d'Hygiène Publique |
| OPEC | Organization of Petroleum Exporting Countries |
| PASB | Pan American Sanitary Bureau |
| PKI | Indonesian Communist Party |
| PL | Public Law |
| PLO | Palestine Liberation Organization |
| PRC | People's Republic of China |
| RSFSR | Russian Soviet Federative Socialist Republic |
| SADF | South African Defence Force |
| SALT | Strategic Arms Limitation Talks |
| SANE | Sane Nuclear Policy |
| SDF | Self-Defense Force (Japan) |

| | |
|---|---|
| SDI | Strategic Defense Initiative |
| SEATO | South East Asia Treaty Organization |
| SEU | Social-Ecological Union |
| SI | International System of Units |
| SIOP | Single Integrated Operational Plan |
| SIPRI | Stockholm International Peace Research Institute |
| SLBM | submarine- launched ballistic missile |
| SPC | Soviet Peace Committee |
| SPD | (West German) Social Democratic Party |
| SWANU | South West Africa National Union |
| SWAPO | South West Africa People's Organization |
| TWh | terawatt |
| TNC | transnational corporations |
| UCC | Universal Copyright Convention |
| UCS | Union of Concerned Scientists |
| UDHR | Universal Declaration of Human Rights |
| UNCTAD | United Nations Conference on Trade and Development |
| UNDP | United Nations Development Program |
| UNEP | UN Environment Program |
| UNESCO | United Nations Educational, Scientific, and Cultural Organization |
| UNHCR | United Nations High Commissioner for Refugees |
| UNIDO | United Nations Industrial Development Organization |
| UNITA | National Union for the Total Independence of Angola (*União Nacional para a Independência Total de Angola*) |
| UNRRA | United Nations Relief and Rehabilitation Administration |
| UNRWA | United Nations Relief and Works Agency for Palestine Refugees in the Near East |
| USIA | United States Information Agency |
| VCP | Vietnamese Communist Party |
| WEU | Western European Union |
| WFDY | World Federation of Democratic Youth |
| WFTU | World Federation of Trade Unions |
| WHO | World Health Organization |
| WILPF | Women's International League for Peace and Freedom |
| WPC | World Peace Council |
| WRI | War Resisters' International |
| WTO | World Trade Organization |
| ZANU | Zimbabwe African National Union |
| ZAPU | Zimbabwe African People's Union |

# List of Contributors

**Ang Cheng Guan** is Head of Humanities and Social Studies Education, National Institute of Education Nanyang Technological University, Singapore.

**Antony Best** is a Senior Lecturer in International History at the London School of Economics.

**Roland Burke** is Lecturer in World History at La Trobe University and an Australian Research Council research fellow.

**Campbell Craig** is Professor of International Politics at Aberystwyth University.

**Prasenjit Duara** is Raffles Professor of Humanities and Director of the Asia Reseach Institute at the National University of Singapore.

**Christopher Endy** is Professor of History at California State University, Los Angeles.

**Andreas Etges** is Professor of North American History at Freie Universität, Berlin.

**Cary Fraser**, a historian of international relations, is the President of the University of Belize in Central America.

**Philipp Gassert** is Professor of Transatlantic History at the University of Augsburg, Germany.

**Petra Goedde** is Associate Professor of History at Temple University.

**Nicholas Guyatt** is Lecturer in History at the University of York.

**Richard H. Immerman** is Professor and Edward J. Buthusiem Distinguished Faculty Fellow in History, and Marvin Wachman Director of the Center for the Study of Force and Diplomacy at Temple University.

**Akira Iriye** is Charles Warren Professor of American History, Emeritus, Harvard University.

**Ian Jackson**, formerly a Senior Lecturer in International Relations and American Foreign Policy at De Montfort University, Leicester, UK, is a barrister-at-law.

**Barbara Keys** is Senior Lecturer in History at the University of Melbourne.

**Dianne Kirby** is Reader in History at the University of Ulster.

**Klaus Larres** is the Richard M. Krasno Distinguished Professor in History and International Affairs at the University of North Carolina, Chapel Hill and a Senior Fellow at Johns Hopkins University's School of Advanced International Studies.

**Helen Laville** is a Senior Lecturer in American History at the University of Birmingham, UK.

**Hyung-Gu Lynn** is the AECL/KEPCO Chair in Korean Research at the Institute of Asian Research, University of British Columbia, and the Editor of *Pacific Affairs*.

**Rana Mitter** is Professor of the History and Politics of Modern China at the University of Oxford.

**Vladimir O. Pechatnov** is Professor and Head of the Department of European and American Studies at Moscow State Institute of International Relations and Distinguished Scholar of the Russian Federation.

**Brenda Gayle Plummer** is Professor of History and Afro-American Studies at the University of Wisconsin, Madison.

**John Prados** is a Senior Fellow of the National Security Archive in Washington, DC.

**Andrew J. Rotter** is Charles Dana Professor of History at Colgate University.

**Amy L. Sayward** is Professor of History at Middle Tennessee State University.

**Elizabeth Schmidt** is Professor of History at Loyola University, Maryland.

**Lars Schoultz** is William Rand Kenan, Jr., Professor of Political Science at the University of North Carolina at Chapel Hill.

**Naoko Shibusawa** is Associate Professor of History and American Studies at Brown University.

**Robert Mark Spaulding** is Professor of History at the University of North Carolina, Wilmington.

**Bernd Stöver** is Professor of History at the University of Potsdam, Germany.

**David R. Stone** is Pickett Professor of Military History at Kansas State University.

**Richard P. Tucker** is Adjunct Professor in the School of Natural Resources and Environment, University of Michigan.

**Penny Von Eschen** is Professor of History and American Culture at the University of Michigan.

**Geoffrey Warner** is a former Fellow of Modern History at Brasenose College, University of Oxford.

**Salim Yaqub** is Associate Professor of History and Director of the Center for Cold War Studies and International History at the University of California, Santa Barbara.

**Vladislav Zubok** is Professor of History at Temple University.

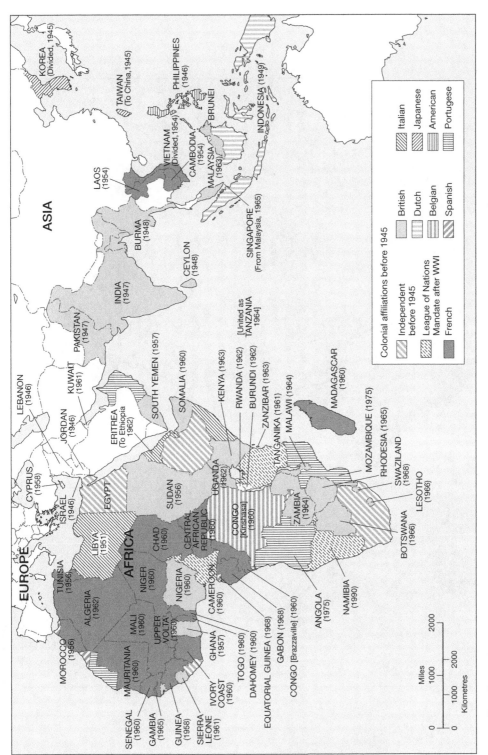

**MAP 1** Decolonization

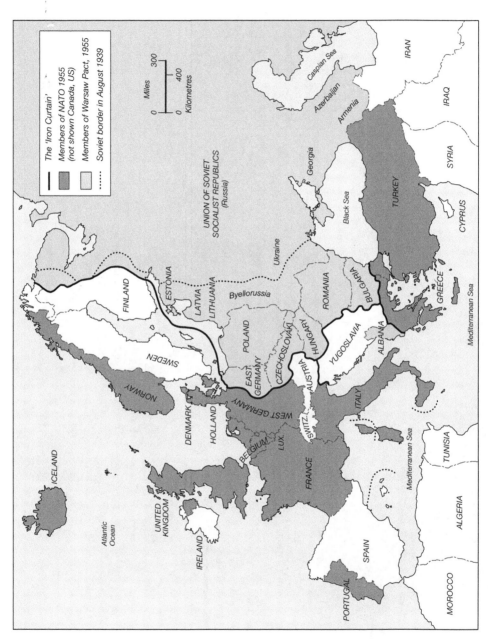

MAP 2 Cold War Europe, 1949

The 'Iron Curtain'

Members of NATO 1955
(not shown Canada, US)

Members of Warsaw Pact, 1955

Soviet border in August 1939

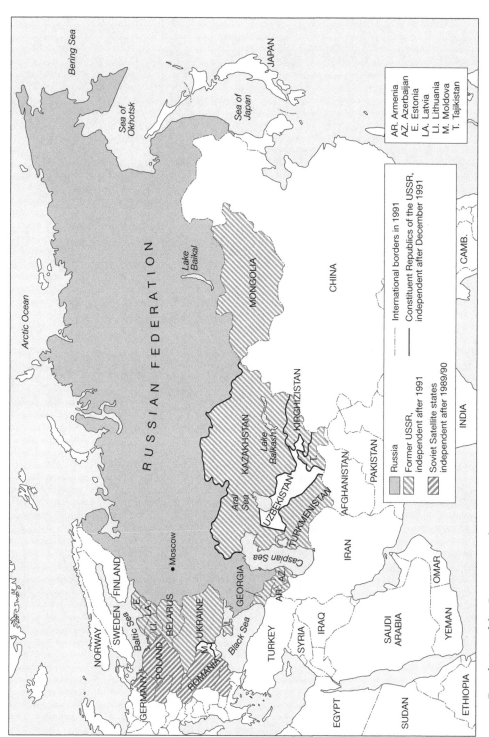

**MAP 3** Dissolution of the Communist Bloc

Legend:

AR. Armenia
AZ. Azerbaijan
E. Estonia
LA. Latvia
LI. Lithuania
M. Moldova
T. Tajikistan

International borders in 1991
Constituent Republics of the USSR, independent after December 1991

Russia
Former USSR, independent after 1991
Soviet Satellite states independent after 1989/90

RUSSIAN FEDERATION

Arctic Ocean
Bering Sea
Sea of Okhotsk
Sea of Japan
JAPAN
Lake Baikal
• Moscow
MONGOLIA
CHINA
KAZAKHSTAN
Lake Balkash
KIRGHIZISTAN
Aral Sea
UZBEKISTAN
TURKMENISTAN
Caspian Sea
AFGHANISTAN
PAKISTAN
INDIA
CAMB.
Black Sea
GEORGIA
AR. AZ.
IRAN
TURKEY
SYRIA
IRAQ
SAUDI ARABIA
OMAR
YEMEN
EGYPT
SUDAN
ETHIOPIA
NORWAY
SWEDEN
FINLAND
Baltic Sea
E.
LA.
LI.
GERMANY
POLAND
BELARUS
UKRAINE
M.
ROMANIA

# CHAPTER 1

········································································

# INTRODUCTION

········································································

## RICHARD H. IMMERMAN AND PETRA GOEDDE

FEW if any historical subjects over the past five decades have generated a voluminous scholarly literature of such high quality as that on the cold war. Particularly since the Soviet-American conflict's end in 1989, historians, political scientists, and their colleagues from multiple other disciplines from across the world have scrutinized previously inaccessible documents, whether declassified in the United States, the United Kingdom, or elsewhere in the "West," or made available in once-thought forever closed Soviet, Eastern European, Chinese, and Third World archives, to explore the impact of the cold war on a global scale. The outpouring of new scholarship precipitated by the end of the cold war and demise of the Soviet Union since 1990 did not generate a consensus on traditional questions such as the causes and consequences of the cold war. Although fundamental debates that drove various historiographies perhaps became less vitriolic, they remain robust and illuminating. Yet the remarkable diversity, originality, and increasing breadth of the new literature, particularly the myriad studies exploring the ways in which countries on the periphery in Latin America, Asia, the Middle East, and Africa shaped and were shaped by the conflict, have significantly enriched the field. As a result of the expansion in geographic, methodological, and archival inquiry, students and scholars alike have gained a far deeper and nuanced understanding of the extent and limits of the cold war era.

This *Handbook* offers a wide-ranging reassessment of the cold war based on innovative conceptual frameworks that have evolved incrementally over time in the field of international history. The cold war was a distinct period in 20th-century history that cannot be wished away, although some have tried. Yet albeit distinct, the cold war must be understood and evaluated within the broader context and contours of global political, economic, social, and cultural developments, some of which preceded the cold war and some of which persist to the present day and doubtless will continue into the future.

This contextualization of the cold war does not imply that the superpower rivalry between the United States and the Soviet Union has lost its significance. The chapters in this volume universally take note of the centrality of this rivalry, as they should. The cold war, nevertheless, can no longer be owned by either one or both of these countries' historical memory or historiography alone. It must be appreciated as global history, and as global history it reveals nuances, idiosyncrasies, and complexities obscured by more traditional accounts. The essays in this *Handbook*, accordingly, embed the cold war in national and transnational developments that were autonomous of, if almost invariably affected by, the particular policies and crises that represent milestones in the conventional historiography of the cold war. Those independent developments include global transformations in areas such as human rights, economic and cultural globalization, environmental transformations, and long-standing ethnic, religious, sectarian, and parallel conflicts with roots that extend back decades in time and anticipate end points that have yet to be reached.

Because of the volume's broad writ and our vision, we have not structured it along conventional chronological lines, nor did we solicit essays that focused on particular way stations and watershed moments throughout the history of the cold war. There are no chapters, for example, on the Iran, Greek, Berlin, Suez, Offshore Islands, Cuban missile crises, or multiple other crises that punctuate the historiography; SALT I, SALT II, START, or other arms control negotiations and treaties; the Marshall Plan, NATO, NSC-68, the New Look, or Détente; or even the wars in Korea, Vietnam, Iraq, and Afghanistan. The volume's goal is not to provide new answers to the questions scholars have addressed all these many years, although on occasion it does. Accordingly, only indirectly do the authors engage such questions as what year marks the cold war's onset, whether there was a first and second cold war, and what if any opportunities were missed to end the cold war earlier, and how responsibility or "blame" for the start, expansion, and continuation of the cold war should be apportioned.

Instead, organized thematically, the volume offers innovative essays on conceptual frameworks, regional perspectives, cold war instruments, and cold war challenges. The result is a rich and diverse assessment of the ways in which the cold war should be positioned within the broader context of the "long twentieth century." The individual chapters in this volume evaluate both the extent and the limits of the cold war's reach into world history. Rather than differentiate among the three levels of analysis, they synthesize them. Rather than distinguish between national and international histories, they merge them. Some of the essays call into question orthodox ways of ordering the cold war chronology, others present new insights into the global dimension of the conflict, still others reveal dynamics and phenomena obscured or even made invisible by traditional research strategies. Exploiting fully the archival trail but at the same time consciously taking a step back from it, they do not advance a single new mode of analysis; they should be read as welcome voices in the current and very healthy conversation about how most effectively and comprehensively to approach and understand this rich and complex period in global history.

Readers can thus acquire an awareness of the spectrum of approaches to the era from an outstanding variety of scholars trained in different historical sub-disciplines as well as steeped in different national historiographies. What is more, the essays not only encourage but also challenge readers to adopt a wider lens in their assessments of the period. This means without denying the salience of the state, moving beyond the nation state framework to situate processes of change within broader if less clearly identified or definable spaces. Those include local, regional, and global responses to the threat of nuclear war; the impact of decolonization; the rise of human rights; the concern for the environment; and comparable transnational concerns. In this regard the volume is positioned at the intersection of boundaries that divide many cold war histories and historians.[1]

Even though each essay offers a unique perspective on the cold war, all have been guided by three fundamental precepts. First, authors stress the global dimensions of the cold war. Some move the story beyond the US-Soviet rivalry to highlight the agency of other, primarily elite actors, among them Eastern and Western European leaders, alliance partners in the cold war system, and the leaders of non-aligned nations. Others give prominence to non-state actors in the international arena, including international organizations, activists, and intellectuals. Still others highlight transnational processes and developments that almost certainly would have occurred absent the cold war, but nonetheless were powerfully affected by cold war structures, products, and outcomes. There is no question that the cold war influenced economic, technological, environmental, and demographic changes as well as long-term processes such as decolonization, environmental transformation, and globalization. The challenge is to detect and document how, when, and why it influenced them.

A second precept guiding the essays is the effort to transcend the strict separation of the political, economic, ideological, and cultural aspects of the cold war. Even though the chapters emphasize one or another of the above considerations, they make clear important linkages among them. These essays thus mark an important step toward a global synthesis of the cold war. In other words, rather than continuing to argue along the lines of a causal hierarchy with either strategic/geopolitical, economic, or cultural factors trumping the others, the premise of the *Handbook* is that future scholarship will not so much present a competitive laundry list of the different influences on and drivers of the cold war as accept and recognize the reciprocal relationship among them.

The third precept underscores the synergy between domestic and international developments. Social, political, and economic transformations within a particular country affected the ways in which it acted in the international arena, and transformations in world affairs, in turn, affected domestic policies. Where appropriate, authors stress the ways internal political, economic, social, and cultural dynamics influenced political leaders' and populations' approach to the challenges of the cold war. By the same token, they analyze the ways in which cold war dynamics affected domestic policy, society, and culture. This synergy between international and domestic developments transcended the level of policy-making. For instance, the American civil rights movement was first and foremost a domestic event, precipitated by demands for racial justice in the American South and ultimately on the national level. But, as recent scholarship shows, civil rights activists drew significant parallels between their own struggle for racial equality and the struggle for decolonization in Africa. In addition, inspired by the decolonization movements in Africa, they utilized the platform of international organizations, such as the United Nations, to draw attention to their national campaign.[2] Likewise, the social protest movements of the 1960s were at once local and global, committed with equal intensity to improving the living and learning conditions at particular universities and supporting national liberation movements in the Third World.[3] The boundary between national and international environmental organizations was porous virtually from the start.[4] The list goes on.

The essays at once address discreet aspects of the cold war and find connections among them through overlapping themes and developments. Collectively they liberate the cold war from the bipolar perspective without denying or minimizing the vital significance of that conflict. They succeed in contextualizing the cold war within global developments, such as modernization, globalization, and decolonization. While key moments in the formation, progression, and demise of the cold war still have a place in each specific essay, they make no claims to serving as the sole or even preferred way to narrate and analyze the cold war. These watersheds still comprise the scaffolding that makes the cold war such an extraordinary era in modern history, but by themselves they cannot adequately explain the varied transformations of this period. By calling attention to forces that run broader and deeper than the sum of these cold war conflicts, we can better understand the complexity and multi-dimensional facets of the period.

These broader forces can significantly alter our interpretation of the cold war's transformative moments and on occasion even lead us to new key moments that had previously been ignored. A global perspective reorders as well as reassigns the key way stations of the cold war. For instance, the question of the origins of the cold war, one of the core questions of cold war historiography, held significance primarily for Eastern and Western Europe, the Soviet Union, and the United States. At the nexus between war and peace, between salvaging what was left of the war-ravaged European continent and creating a postwar world governed by a global rule of law and a clearly defined set of principles of peaceful coexistence, the United States and the Soviet Union became increasingly distrustful of each other's motives and intentions for the postwar period. Even though the leaders of the main wartime alliance, Winston Churchill, Joseph Stalin, and Franklin Delano Roosevelt, had first at Tehran and then at Yalta agreed on the general principles of the postwar world, their alliance proved fragile. Once the common enemy Nazi Germany had been vanquished, deeper fissures and the legacy of mutual distrust resurfaced. On the Soviet side, of course, this distrust was strengthened by the American refusal to share the secret of the atomic bomb with the Soviet Union or to place control over this powerful weapon with an international body, such as the United Nations.[5]

Many leading scholars of the cold war see this as a key moment in the deterioration of the US-Soviet relationship, and the contributors to this volume do not overlook it. Yet collectively the chapters provide evidence that it alone cannot explain the origins of the global cold war. They likewise demonstrate that the immediate postwar period can and should not be reduced to explaining the origins of the cold war. Indeed, a number of the chapters suggest alternative historical moments that deserve equal attention as shapers of the postwar international order.[6]

In doing so they are widening and to an extent repaving a road previously rarely taken by cold war historians but currently being travelled by scholarly pioneers. Among the alternative key moments that have largely been overshadowed by the scholarly focus on the origins of the cold war was the founding of the United Nations in October 1945. The United Nations Charter formulated a framework for international peace and security as well as a pledge for the defense of human rights. Alluding to the atrocities suffered in the recent world wars, the charter's preamble declared the United Nations' determination "to save succeeding generations from the scourge of war, which twice in our lifetime has brought untold sorrow to mankind, and to reaffirm faith in fundamental human rights, in the dignity and worth of the human person, in the equal rights of men and women and of nations large and small, and to establish conditions under which justice and respect for the obligations arising from treaties and other sources of international law can be maintained, and to promote social progress and better standards of life in larger freedom."[7]

Both the United States and the Soviet Union signed the Charter and became founding members of the United Nations, along with forty-nine other nations from Europe, Asia, Africa, and Latin America. This demonstration of global unity was as real as the growing friction among the principal wartime allies. But rather than reconcile these contradictory narratives, historians for a long time dismissed one of them as a fleeting moment of idealism and privileged the other as what really mattered. In the literature, the founding of the UN was soon overwhelmed by the attention to contemporaneous events more aligned with the cold war narrative that rested on such pillars as the crises in Iran and Greece; the futility of the negotiations at the meetings of the Council of Foreign Ministers at London, Moscow, and Paris; the abortive Baruch Plan to regulate and internationalize atomic energy (proposed at the UN, no less); and George Kennan's "Long Telegram," Winston's Churchill's Iron Curtain Speech, Stalin's Election Speech, and the pronouncement of the Truman Doctrine.

In recent years, however, cold war historians have begun to consider the history of human rights and the work of international non-governmental organizations as integral to the history of the global cold war.[8] Even though the superpower conflict severely limited and at times circumscribed the United Nations' ability to influence international relations, it nonetheless constituted a vital forum within the broader framework of global networks. Throughout the cold war, the United Nations Security Council and its General Assembly served as sounding boards that reflected the tension that existed between the spirit of internationalism and the bipolarity of the East-West conflict.

Two key events early in the cold war illustrate the entanglement of the UN in the increasingly tense East-West confrontation. The first was the Berlin blockade of 1948–9, which ended what little remained of the postwar cooperation among the four occupation powers of Germany and sealed the division of Germany into a Soviet controlled socialist East and a democratic West allied with the United States, Great Britain, and France. The source of the conflict had been the Western allies' unilateral decision to institute a currency reform in the Western parts of Germany, a move that each of the occupying powers recognized would ruin the financial viability of the Eastern sector of

Berlin, jointly administered by all four allied powers, and by extension the Soviet controlled occupation zone in East Germany. When the Soviet Union responded to the currency reform with a blockade of all traffic to and from Berlin, which of course was
located within the Soviet zone of occupation, the US military responded with an airlift
of vital goods to the Western sectors of the city. But no less importantly, albeit often
neglected in the literature, the United States appealed to the United Nations in an effort
to force an end to the blockade. The negotiations in the Security Council dragged on
into the spring of 1949, when the Soviet Union gave up its blockade. To be sure, it was the
success of the airlift and not the UN Security Council that ultimately prompted the
Soviet Union to back down. Nonetheless, the United Nations provided the central forum
for the expression and eventual resolution of the international dispute.

Two years later, the United States and its Allies again appealed to the United Nations
to force a withdrawal of North Korean forces from South Korea. UN Security Council
Resolution 83 in the summer of 1950 recommended military assistance to South Korea.
Protesting the UN membership's refusal to recognize the People's Republic of China as
the legitimate representative of China, the Soviet Union had been absent from the
Security Council when that body passed the Korea resolution, and it did not officially
get involved in the conflict (suffice it to say, it did lend unofficial support to the North
Koreans).

The United States, on the other hand, furnished the vast majority of the UN force and
led the military campaign against North Korea. China, however, which had turned communist in 1949, did engage the US-led UN forces, when, in the fall of 1950, General
Douglas MacArthur crossed the 38th parallel into North Korea and threatened to move
further into Chinese territory. The UN resolution, which authorized the international
military action against the North Korean aggressor, the UN participation in brokering
the cease-fire in the summer of 1953, and the role UN forces played in helping guard the
demilitarized zone separating North from South Korea at the 38th parallel, gave the
organization a prominent position in international affairs.[9]

We bring attention to the role of the United Nations in the Berlin Blockade and
Korean War not for the purpose of replacing the conventional story. That story is central
to the history of the cold war era. Rather, the aim is to supplement it by adding an additional layer, a layer that provides new insights even as it complicates the sequence of
events. Similarly, the expansion of the cold war to the periphery in the late 1940s and
especially the 1950s offers opportunities to explore alternative ways to appreciate salient
dimensions of key moments in cold war history.

The traditional narrative focused on the incentives for both the Soviet Union and the
United States to carry the cold war conflict into Asia, Latin America, the Middle East,
and Africa.[10] From the United States vantage point, the expansion was a result of the perceived need to secure strategic outposts and resources, successive American administrations' fear that the Soviets would exploit vulnerable emerging nations, and the
domino-theory like thinking that posited that a Soviet beachhead could not be contained. From the Soviet vantage point, engagement in the so-called "Third World"
offered the opportunity to advance the communist narrative of anti-imperialism,

anti-colonialism, peaceful co-existence, and social justice against what looked like the latest installment in the Western world's grab for yet more territory, resources, and markets. Scholars exploring the Soviet and American side of the cold war in the Third World offered keen insights into the incentives, processes, and consequences of the cold war expansion, which did much to clarify our understanding of this period.[11]

Again, this narrative is unassailable. When exploring the cold war from the vantage point of the periphery, nevertheless, additional historical transformations come into sharper relief, chief among them the struggle for decolonization. To be sure, the cold war significantly shaped the emerging countries' paths to independence in the 1950s and 1960s. It offered anti-colonial political activists powerful arguments in favor of independence and leverage to negotiate the terms of that independence. Still, rather than pitting one cold war camp against the other, most countries in the colonial world tried to forge a path of non-alignment. For them, the cold war rivalry between the two superpowers offered not just opportunities, but potential pitfalls as well.

These dynamics emerge much more vividly when taking into account events like the 1955 Bandung conference, where Asian and African nations as well as leaders from colonies on the verge of independence sought closer economic and political cooperation and a common strategy to fight colonialism and imperialism. The conference signaled the global South's effort to stake out a position of autonomy and strength in the cold war conflict without committing to one side or the other. One of the major results of the conference, the declaration of self-determination as the first right, underscored the claim to independence, both from the former colonial powers and from the influence and pressure of the two cold war camps.[12]

The Third World's interest in non-alignment did not mean a policy of non-engagement with cold war countries, nor did it prevent the practice of playing the superpowers off against each other in order to achieve maximum political benefits. To the contrary, one of the most skilled practitioners of this political maneuvering, able to take the greatest possible advantage from the cold war rivalry, was the Egyptian leader Gamal Abdel Nasser. He sought funds from both the Soviet Union and the United States to support a large construction project, the building of the Aswan dam to regulate the Nile River. He also struck an arms deal with Czechoslovakia, which set him on a collision course with the United States. Intricately interwoven with the Suez Crisis of 1956, one of the seminal moments in traditional accounts of the cold war in the Middle East, Nasser's skillful dealings with both superpower rivals and his eventual success in securing financial support from the Soviet Union for the dam project show that, even for leading figures in the non-alignment movement, siding with one side or another for short-term strategic objectives could be useful.[13] Contemporaries of Nasser who sought to follow suit, such as Cambodia's Norodom Sihanouk and Indonesia's Sukarno, were far less successful.[14]

Moving beyond the US-Soviet cold war framework also reveals new fissures within each of the ideological blocs as well as new connections among domestic, regional, and geopolitical developments. Those include a greater emphasis on the Sino-Soviet split, but also the internal challenges to the cold war order in both the Soviet and the Western orbit. Historians of cold war communism have long stressed the importance of the ideological and political disagreements between Chinese and Soviet communists, but did not identify the rift as a substantial challenge to the cold war order. But it is vitally important to recognize the multiple subtle linkages that existed and expanded between the domestic desire for reform in each of the two camps and the evolution of the international objective of reducing political-military tensions through a policy of détente. For instance, we now understand the Chinese opening to the United States in the late 1960s in the context of the domestic dissident movements in Eastern Europe, particularly the Prague Spring of 1968.[15]

Likewise, the Federal Republic of Germany's Chancellor Willy Brandt's Ostpolitik in the early 1970s, often framed as a local or regional response to the US-Soviet policy of détente, had its roots in the early 1960s' increasing disillusionment with the inflexible and ossified policies of the Konrad Adenauer government, as well as the increasingly vocal grassroots student movements that challenged the political status quo in West Germany. The proximity of the West German state to the Iron Curtain as well as the absence of official relations with East Germany provided additional incentives for the Social Democratic opposition to propose solutions to the cold war stalemate. The story of the emergence of détente has been well researched, but only recently have scholars begun to connect the political to the social and cultural story of the 1960s, and domestic to transnational upheavals in the cold war order.[16] Drawing these connections was from its inception integral to this volume.

Recent historiographical developments have added more nuance and new perspectives to recognized milestones of the cold war. But they also reveal new plotlines that had remained obscured by the focus on the cold war strategic, economic, political, and ideological contest. Chief among these is the struggle toward the creation of a global human rights regime. Because most efforts in this direction were continuously thwarted by flare-ups in cold war confrontations or received only lip-service, and lukewarm lip-service at that, from the Soviet Union, the United States, and their respective allies, the efforts of rights activists have been pushed to the sidelines of the historical narrative of the cold war. However, prompted by a moment of supreme optimism for a fresh and decisive role for the United Nations after the end of the cold war, rights activists as well as their chroniclers discovered the potential of human rights as both a political cause and historical subject. Hence events like the crafting and signing of the Human Rights Declaration in 1948, the emergence and proliferation of non-governmental human rights organizations, the Helsinki accords of 1977, as well as the series of UN sponsored women's rights conferences since 1975, gained new prominence as salient moments in cold war history. What emerged then in the 1990s and 2000s was a history rich in alternative moments and milestones, rich also in exposing missed opportunities and failed efforts, yet nonetheless a history that needs to be taken into account as both a complement and counter-narrative to the dominant story of cold war confrontations.[17]

Another development that emerged boldly only after the end of the cold war was the attention paid to the history of globalization. It became a political buzz-word of the 1990s, associated with neo-liberalism, neo-imperialism, and neo-colonialism. Yet globalization also matured into a concept that attracted a wide variety of academic scholars from disciplines as diverse as economics, anthropology, sociology, political science, history, communications, and cultural studies. The academic exploration of the concept thus offered a welcome opportunity for trans-disciplinary synthesis that had eluded the academy for decades.

Most scholars now agree that once the political polarity is stripped away from the term "globalization," what is revealed is a long-term process that preceded the cold war; transformed and was transformed by the cold war; and continued at accelerated speed after the cold war. For cold war scholars the challenge thus becomes to determine precisely how the cold war altered the course of political, economic, and cultural globalization, whether it halted or simply redirected the trajectory of increasing international connectivity and exchange, and how these long-term processes of globalization might have altered or possibly even contributed to the demise of the cold war.[18]

The same can be said for the environment, religion, and other "challenges to the cold war paradigm" that appear in this volume in juxtaposition with chapters on geopolitics, economics, and culture; the US-Soviet relationship and the cold war and the Middle East; the nuclear revolution and international institutions; and race and gender. The chapters do not speak with one voice, nor do they achieve a consensus let alone unanimity on the best and definite way to approach the history of the cold war. But that was never the objective behind bringing together this set of international scholars in a single collection. Rather, these chapters can and should be read as a conversation among experts in the field, each with a unique set of skills and perspective, in which the reader can play an active and independent part. Offering new, stimulating, and provocative avenues for future research, the essays represent the state of the field in historical scholarship on the cold war, bringing new insights to familiar topics and breaking ground on new ones. The cold war ended more than two decades ago; it will take decades more to take the full measure of it. While that process began almost as soon as the cold war originated, and it has benefited over the years from contributions from the likes of Herbert Feis and D.F. Fleming, Walter LaFeber and John Lewis Gaddis, Melvin Leffler and Michael Hogan, Odd Arne Westad and Robert J. McMahon, and so many, many more distinguished scholars, it has a long way to go. The intention of this volume is to both lay a foundation and serve as a catalyst for this continuing endeavor. It will be exciting.

## NOTES

1. For the boundaries and debates, see Matthew Connelly, Robert J. McMahon, Katherine A.S. Sibley, Thomas Borstelmann, Nathan Citino, and Kristin Hoganson, "SHAFR and the World," *Passport* (September 2011), 4–16.
2. Mary L. Dudziak, *Cold War Civil Rights: Race and the Image of American Democracy.* (Princeton, NJ: Princeton University Press, 2000); Dudziak, *Exporting American Dreams: Thurgood Marshall's African Journey* (New York: Oxford University Press, 2008); Thomas Borstelmann, *The Cold War and the Color Line: Race Relations and American Foreign Policy* (Cambridge, MA: Harvard University Press, 2001). Brenda Gayle Plummer, *Rising Wind: Black Americans and US Foreign Affairs, 1935–1960* (Chapel Hill, NC:

University of North Carolina Press, 1996). Carol Anderson, *Eyes Off the Prize: the United Nations and the African American Struggle for Human Rights, 1945–1955* (Cambridge and New York: Cambridge University Press, 2003); Penny Von Eschen, *Race against Empire: Black Americans and Anticolonialism, 1937–1957* (Ithaca, NY: Cornell University Press, 1997); Von Eschen, *Satchmo Blows Up the World: Jazz Ambassadors Play the Cold War* (Cambridge, MA: Harvard University Press, 2004); Kevin Gaines, *African Americans in Ghana: Black Expatriates and the Civil Rights Era* (Chapel Hill, NC: University of North Carolina Press, 2007).

3. Martin Klimke, *The Other Alliance: Student Protest in West Germany and the United States in the Global Sixties* (Princeton, NJ: Princeton University Press, 2009); Jeremi Suri, *Power and Protest: Global Revolution and the Rise of Détente* (Cambridge, MA: Harvard University Press, 2003), 216–26; Carole Fink, Philipp Gassert, and Detlef Junker (eds.), *1968: The World Transformed* (Washington, DC: The German Historical Institute, 1998).

4. Christof Mauch, Nathan Stoltzfus, and Douglas R. Weiner (eds.), *Shades of Green: Environmental Activism around the Globe* (Lanham, MD: Rowman & Littlefield, 2006).

5. The literature of the break-up of the Grand Alliance is far too extensive to cite. For a recent book that presents an original argument, see Frank Costigliola, *Roosevelt's Lost Alliances: How Personal Politics Helped Start the Cold War* (Princeton, NJ: Princeton University Press, 2011).

6. See in particular the chapters in this volume on "Historicizing the Cold War" by Akira Iriye and on "Human Rights" by Barbara Keys and Roland Burke.

7. Preamble of the United Nations charter accessed at <http://www.un.org/en/documents/charter/>.

8. Paul Kennedy, *The Parliament of Man: The Past, Present and Future of the United Nations* (New York: Random House, 2006); Mark Mazower, *No Enchanted Palace: The End of Empire and the Ideological Origins of the United Nations* (Princeton, NJ: Princeton University Press, 2009); Akira Iriye, *Global Community: The Role of International Orgainzations in the Making of the Contemporary World* (Berkeley, CA: University of California Press, 2002); Samuel Moyn, *The Last Utopia: Human Rights in History* (Cambridge, MA: Harvard University Press, 2010); Roland Burke, *Decolonization and the Evolution of International Human Rights* (Philadelphia: University of Pennsylvania Press, 2010).

9. See in particular William Stueck, *The Korean War: An International History* (Princeton, NJ: Princeton University Press, 1997).

10. Gordon H. Chang, *Friends and Enemies: The United States, China, and the Soviet Union, 1948–1972* (Stanford, CA: Stanford University Press, 1990); Marc Gallicchio, *The Scramble for Asia: US Military Power in the Aftermath of the Pacific War* (Lanham, MD: Rowman and Littlefield, 2008); Odd Arne Westad, *Cold War and Revolution: Soviet-American Rivalry and the Origins of the Chinese Civil War* (New York: Columbia University Press, 1987); Greg Grandin, *Empire's Workshop: Latin America, The United States, and the Rise of the New Imperialism* (New York: Holt Paperbacks, 2007); Hal Brands, *Latin America's Cold War* (Cambridge, MA: Harvard University, 2010); Stephen G. Rabe, *The Killing Zone: The United States Wages Cold War in Latin America* (New York: Oxford University Press, 2011); Lawrence Freedman, *A Choice of Enemies: America Confronts the Middle East* (New York: Public Affairs, 2008); Douglas Little, *American Orientalism: The United States and the Middle East since 1945* (Chapel Hill, NC: University of North Carolina Press, 2002); Salim Yaqub, *Containing Arab Nationalism: The Eisenhower Docrine and the Middle East* (Chapel

Hill, NC: University of North Carolina Press, 2004); Thomas Borstelmann, *Apartheid's Reluctant Uncle: The United States and Southern Africa in the Early Cold War* (New York: Oxford University Press, 1993); Piero Gleijeses, *Conflicting Missions: Havana, Washington, and Africa, 1959–1976* (Chapel Hill, NC: University of North Carolina Press, 2002).

11. Odd Arne Westad, *The Global Cold War: Third World Interventions and the Making of Our Times* (Cambridge and New York: Cambridge University Press, 2005).

12. Burke, *Decolonization and the Evolution of Human Rights*; Moyn, *The Last Utopia*; Christopher J. Lee (ed.), *Making the World After Empire: The Bandung Moment and its Political Afterlives* (Athens, OH: Ohio University Press, 2010); Seng Tan and Amitav Acharya (eds.), *Bandung Revisited: The Legacy of the 1955 Asian-African Conference for International Order* (Singapore: NUS Press, 2008).

13. Nigel Ashton, *Eisenhower, Macmillan, and the Problem of Nasser: Anglo-American Relations with Arab Nationalism* (New York: Macmillan, 1997); Ray Takeyh, *The Origins of the Eisenhower Doctrine: The US, Britain, and Nasser's Egypt, 1953–1957* (New York: Palgrave Macmillan, 2000); Yaqub, *Containing Arab Nationalism*.

14. Narodom Sihanouk, *My War with the CIA: The Memoirs of Prince Norodom Sihanouk* (New York: Pantheon, 1973); Franklin B. Weinstein, *Indonesian Foreign Policy and the Dilemma of Dependence* (London: Equinox Publishing, 2007).

15. Chen Jian, *Mao's China and the Cold War* (Chapel Hill, NC: University of North Carolina Press, 2001).

16. Suri, *Power and Protest*.

17. Akira Iriye, Petra Goedde, and William I. Hitchcock (eds.), *The Human Rights Revolution: An International History* (New York: Oxford University Press, 2011). See also the chapters in this volume on "Human Rights" by Barbara Keys and Roland Burke, and "Gender and Women's Rights in the Cold War" by Helen Laville.

18. See for example the recent prize-winning article, Andrew McKevitt, "'You Are Not Alone': Anime and the Globalizing of America," *Diplomatic History* 34 (November 2010): 893–921. Interdisciplinary works on globalization include Arjun Appadurai, *Modernity at Large: Cultural Dimensions of Globalization* (Minneapolis and London: University of Minnesota Press, 1996); Appadurai, *Globalization* (Durham, NC: Duke University Press, 2000); Joseph E. Stiglitz, *Globalization and its Discontents* (New York: W.W. Norton, 2002); George Ritzer (ed.), *The Blackwell Companion to Globalization* (Malden, MA and Oxford: Blackwell, 2007).

# PART I

## CONCEPTUAL FRAMEWORKS

CHAPTER 2

..................................................................................................

# HISTORICIZING THE COLD WAR

..................................................................................................

## AKIRA IRIYE

HISTORICIZING a historical event entails the question of chronology. In order to establish a periodizing scheme for understanding the history of the cold war, we have to ask some fundamental questions in interpreting the history of the world after the Second World War and the place of the cold war in that history. Does a chronology that centers on the vicissitudes of the cold war trump other ways of comprehending post-1945 history? To the extent that the cold war was just one development, however important, in international affairs, what place should we assign it in the history of the world after the war? If the world has changed significantly during the second half of the 20th century and into the 21st, what part did cold war history play in the story?

To assign the central role to the cold war in periodizing post-Second World War history is to consider geopolitics the key to recent history. Historians of international relations usually establish their chronologies in terms of wars. The history of the 20th century thus is schematized by way of the origins of the Great War, the First World War, the interwar period, the coming of the Second World War, the transition from that war to the cold war, the "high" cold war, détente, a new cold war, the ending of the cold war, and possibly yet another new cold war that may be lurking in the background. Such privileging of wars and conflicts makes sense if one is writing a history of geopolitics or geostrategy, because these subjects by definition are concerned with national security, balance of power, and related issues, and the cold war is indeed comprehensible in such frameworks. In this essay, however, I argue that if the subject is to be historicized, we must broaden our perspective and relativize, as it were, the geopolitical story against the background of many other stories that comprise history.

It is imperative to recognize, first of all, that while conflict is an important theme in the history of international relations, one must not forget other themes that coexist with, and sometimes even supersede, conflict. International cooperation is one obvious example. Nations do not merely prepare for the next war. They also choose not to preoccupy themselves with conflictual issues, envisaging their roles in the drama of "the rise and fall of the great powers," but instead to establish various frameworks for international cooperation and coexistence. A regional community is a good example. The European Union does not exist in order to prepare for war; its fundamental objective is to avoid conflict among its member states and to promote their mutual wellbeing. Likewise, nations establish intergovernmental organizations such as the United Nations in order to prevent war and, if it should nevertheless occur, to contrive a solution to bring about its termination.

The examples of the European Union and the United Nations also remind us that nations are interested in far more than national security and power. Both these institutions have championed the cause of human rights, not just national rights and interests. In addition, the UN has promoted such objectives as the eradication of communicable diseases, the protection of the natural environment, and the promotion of dialogue among civilizations. Neither diseases nor civilizations are national entities, and for that reason quite often they supersede narrowly defined national concerns. So does the ecological system. Human rights, in contrast to national rights, refer to the prevention of discrimination on account of racial, religious, and other distinctions. The idea of human rights has as its basis a conception of human beings as indivisible, as humanity. Civilizations may divide humanity, but it is also possible to speak of civilization in the singular, referring to ways in which human beings behave toward one another.

Whether speaking of diseases, civilizations, environmentalism, or human rights, one realizes that these subjects are not just of international significance, in the sense of nations cooperating with one another to deal with them. At a more fundamental level, they are inherently of transnational character, in that national distinctions are irrelevant because these phenomena transcend, cross, and in the process subvert national boundaries. The strengthening of transnational forces may, then, limit the utility of the international relations perspective in comprehending world history. Rather, transnational themes may have to be introduced into the picture inasmuch as they have their own identities and separate chronologies.

The distinction between international and transnational affairs, however, may be blurred, as is most unambiguously evident in economic transactions. The movement of capital, goods, and labor is both an international and transnational phenomenon. Trade, investment, and migration take place across nations and are regulated by states. At the same time, commercial, financial, and migratory transactions frequently defy state authority and produce consequences beyond its control. The phenomenon known as globalization is a good example. Initially promoted by states in order to further their trade, shipping, and investment activities abroad, globalization in time came to integrate individuals and private firms into the world economic order as global players. Nations became less and less relevant units in a globalizing world, although international organizations such as the World Trade Organization (WTO) and International Monetary Fund (IMF) remained important so as to ensure that globalization would not cause unanticipated disruptions across borders.

Accordingly, a chronology that prioritizes the cold war is a partial one and explains little about non-geopolitical aspects of international relations or about transnational movements. These latter were not sub-themes in the overarching history of the cold war. On the contrary, it can even be argued that the cold war was a minor theme in the broader history of globalization or of such other themes as environmentalism and human rights.

At the same time, there is also the national story, quite apart from the geopolitical drama. In addition to the obvious fact that each actor in the drama defined its own approach and sought to establish a relationship between the cold war and domestic politics and society, the post-Second World War era saw the emergence of a large number of post-colonial nations. This latter phenomenon cannot be viewed as having been merely a byproduct of the superpower conflict. After all, anti-imperialism and anti-colonialism had been a major force in world affairs from the late 19th century onward. The cold war neither subverted nor controlled it. Rather, decolonization and nation-building were stories with an integrity of their own.

Viewed within such a framework, the cold war emerges as having been but a fraction of world history, a history of the world that consists of national, international, and transnational phenomena. Particularly after the Second World War, non-geopolitical developments became so powerful that to give the cold war the privilege of defining the postwar chronology would be a grave distortion of history.

Nevertheless, the cold war was a reality and must somehow be put in the context of recent history. How should one do so? One may discuss the place of geopolitics in the post-1945 chronology and contextualize it in terms of other, arguably more significant, developments. In order to do so, the following discussion divides the post-Second World War years into three sub-periods: 1945–70, 1970–90, and 1990 to the present.

# 1945–1970

Usually considered in terms of the origins and development of the cold war, this quarter-century should also be seen as a major landmark in the history of decolonization. That history went back to the late 19th century and had been accelerated after the First World War, but in 1939 most of the world's empires still remained. Once war came, however, the struggle for independence gained fresh momentum as its leaders sought to take advantage of the global conflict to gain freedom for their people. By 1960 most countries in the Middle East, South Asia, Southeast Asia, and East Asia had gained independence or at least autonomy so that more than one-half of the UN's total membership of around one hundred consisted of newly independent nations. Only Africa remained still under colonial control, but its various regions, too, would achieve independence during the 1960s so that by the early 1970s most colonial areas in the world would have disappeared.

This was a momentous development. The age of imperialism that had begun in the last decades of the 19th century and had underlain international affairs for nearly a century was finally coming to an end. Compared to this story, the cold war drama paled in

significance. The cold war initially and primarily concerned the Western powers (including the Soviet Union), and to that extent it was a traditional game of power politics. As
had always happened after a major war, the victors fought over spoils of war.

The years immediately after the Second World War were in this sense not substantially different from earlier postwar years like the 1820s or the 1920s. The two principal
powers that successfully fought the Axis, the United States and the Soviet Union, clashed
over such issues as the occupation of Germany and the extent of Soviet military presence in Eastern Europe. In time it might have been expected that the two powers would
come at least to some provisional agreement about their respective spheres of influence—as they in a sense did after the early 1960s. In any event the Soviet-American
confrontation at its inception largely concerned Europe and was thus more of an intra-
Western civil war than a global conflict.

The bilateral tensions in Europe developed into a wider and nearly global confrontation when the rest of the world transformed themselves into post-colonial states. China,
for a long time a "semi-colony," was now an independent nation, having regained territory lost to Japan since the 1890s. Still, it took four years of civil war before a central government, which declared itself a people's republic and promptly tied itself to the Soviet
Union through a treaty of alliance, was established. Korea, liberated from nearly forty
years of Japanese colonial rule, was likewise divided by regional contenders for power
who were unable to unify the peninsula. When the communists in the north attempted a
final assault on the south in June 1950, it provoked an immediate US reaction, thus producing the first "hot war" in the cold war era. The Korean War was fundamentally a civil
war that turned into an international conflict because the United States and the Soviet
Union both saw it as the beginning of a more serious global conflict. By then, many formerly European colonies and protectorates in Asia and the Middle East had gained
independence. Some post-colonial states chose to tie themselves to one side or the other
in the global cold war, while others remained neutral, declaring themselves to be "Third
World" countries. It is doubtful that the cold war would have come to embrace the non-
Western parts of the world if colonialism had not ended. Put another way, it is possible
to see the cold war as a footnote in the longer and ultimately more consequential story of
decolonization.

Decolonization, however, was only one of the developing themes in world history in
the middle of the 20th century. Internationalism, in the sense of cooperation and coexistence among nations, reached a high point in the immediate aftermath of the Second
World War, as exemplified by the founding of the United Nations. Although the UN did
not always function as smoothly as might have been hoped for, its presence throughout
the cold war was a powerful reminder that sovereign states, of which there was an
increasing number, were sometimes ready to negotiate their differences and to pool
their resources, mental as well as material, to achieve common objectives. The history of
the UN did not parallel that of the cold war because the organization was interested in
much more than geopolitical issues. Indeed, it was quite powerless to deal with them,
precisely because internationalism is inherently incompatible with geopolitics. Rather,
we should focus on non-geopolitical aspects of the activities by the UN and many other

international organizations. Of such activities, those concerned with human rights stand out because the postwar years saw the international codification of the idea.

Human rights, not national rights, were now conceptualized as a valid, universal notion. Earlier, national self-determination had been the principal language to promote the idea of freedom and justice among colonial people, but that idea had not included the equality of the sexes or races. By elevating human rights as an idea applying to all humans, through the 1948 universal declaration and subsequent resolutions, the UN as well as its member states and many non-governmental organizations were accepting as axiomatic the idea that there were human beings before racial, national, gender, and other categories divided them into separate units and created cleavages. The civil rights movement, in the United States and elsewhere, now merged into the global movement for protection and promotion of human rights. There is little question, therefore, that such global vocabulary was at variance with the language of the cold war. Not only did the cold war divide the world into two camps, but within each camp there were clear violations of human rights. The suppression of freedom in Soviet-bloc nations was a glaring violation of human rights, but so were the remaining racial segregation in the West and non-democratic government among some US allies in the cold war.

Rather than arguing that the cold war justified such oppression, or that human rights became part of an ideology for each side in executing the global struggle, it would make more sense to say that human rights ultimately trumped the geopolitical confrontation by spreading waves of freedom and democratization throughout the world. Particularly during the 1960s, when anti-establishment forces across the globe erupted against the waging of the cold war by both the United States and the Soviet Union, they ignited movements for change, both domestically and internationally. The waning of the cold war after the late 1960s is inseparable from this phenomenon. In other words, the cold war can be considered to have been a footnote to human rights history, not the other way round. The ending of the cold war in the late 1980s was as much a story of human rights as of geopolitics.

Another key development in post-1945 history was globalization, or, more precisely, re-globalization. Historians date the origins of economic globalization variably. Some point to the "discovery" of the Western Hemisphere around 1500, but most prefer to choose the period from the middle to the last decades of the 19th century as the time when the pace of global economic interconnections accelerated through new communications and transportation technology that vastly facilitated the exchange of goods, capital, and labor. That story, however, met with a serious reversal during and immediately after the Great War, ushering in a period of what some economic historians call de-globalization. In the second half of the 1920s, it seemed as if this temporary setback was going to be reversed so that the world economy would regain the globalizing momentum of the pre-1914 days. Such did not prove to be the case because of the severe impact of the world economic crisis that began in 1929 and the international conflict that followed.

In that broad perspective the Second World War was both a culmination of the process of de-globalization as well as the beginning of the renewed efforts toward re-globalization. The United States was a factor in the former phenomenon, and it played the key role in the latter. Reversing its trade protectionism, immigration restriction, and other nationalistic policies, the nation entered (and ended) the war determined to reintegrate the world economy through international cooperation. The resulting Bretton Woods system was a major landmark in bringing about re-globalization. The story of post-1945 globalization has not yet ended. Starting from the establishment of international organizations such as the International Monetary Fund and the World Bank as well as agreements like the General Agreement on Tariffs and Trade, the United States and other countries have continued to seek to broaden the scope of global interdependence, which now covers transnational movements of capital, currencies, and labor.

Like human rights, globalization is a major phenomenon of 20th-century history, especially of the post-Second World War years. How might we link this story to the history of the cold war? Again like the case of human rights, it would be best to consider the cold war a footnote to the history of globalization. To be sure, the Bretton Woods system was pursued energetically by the United States and its allies, while the Soviet-bloc nations remained outside the system. Through the 1970s, there is little doubt that, thanks to the internationalist framework provided by Bretton Woods arrangements, US allies in Europe as well as Japan rapidly recovered from the devastations caused by the war and began to achieve phenomenal rates of economic growth, thus ensuring their domestic stability and ideological orientation toward the United States. "The West" became synonymous with prosperity as well as democracy and served as the principal agent of globalization. Because the United States remained the superior economic power, globalization at that time appeared to enhance the prestige of "the American way of life," a formidable ideological weapon in waging cold war. In contrast, the pace of growth in the "Eastern bloc" fell behind, although the Soviet Union and its allies continued to argue that the socialist system of production and distribution would ultimately prove more beneficial to the people. Moreover, the US side in the cold war made use of the World Bank to provide assistance to post-colonial states so as to promote their "development" and thus to prevent them from falling to Soviet or Chinese influence. In some such way, globalization became incorporated into the story of the cold war.

Such an equation, however, needs to be put in context. Globalization, after all, implies the interconnectedness and interdependence of all countries and regions of the world, whereas cold war geopolitics assumes a divided world in a global struggle for power. A divided world is incompatible with a globalized world. Had there been no cold war, the Soviet Union, China, and their allies would have been integrated into the world economy, precisely as they have since the 1980s. The United States instituted a system of stringent control over East-West economic relations, and the movement of goods, capital, and people across the divide, while never totally absent, was severely restricted. Likewise on the Soviet side; Moscow and Beijing disdained bourgeois capitalism and boasted of their ability to achieve economic gains without having to borrow from, or deal with, the West. Ultimately, such restrictionism on both sides gave way to integration, demonstrating that globalization proved to be a more influential force than geopolitics in shaping contemporary history.

The twenty-five year period after the Second World War, then, had abundant themes, of which the bipolar geopolitical confrontation was just one, and certainly not the key to all others. However, in one respect the cold war did leave a major imprint on contemporary history: the development of nuclear technology and armament. The US-USSR confrontation was of grave seriousness to the whole of humankind because the superpowers chose to acquire huge arsenals of nuclear weapons that threatened to destroy the entire world, human civilization, and the natural habitat. It has been argued that the cold war never developed into a third world war because both sides understood such consequences and adopted the strategy of mutually assured destruction so as to prevent nuclear war. That is debatable. What is not is that the use of nuclear weapons in local conflicts, if not against the major cold war rival, was actually contemplated, and the United States and the Soviet Union continued to expand their respective stockpiles of nuclear bombs and missiles. By the time the nuclear powers agreed to sign a non-proliferation treaty (1968) in order to prevent the spread of these weapons elsewhere, it was too late. France and China had already developed them, and others were just as eager to join the "nuclear club."

It is, of course, impossible to say whether or not there would have been a cold war if nuclear bombs had not been devised. But there is little doubt that these weapons contributed to creating a feeling of unprecedented fear not only on the part of the people directly involved in the bilateral confrontation but also throughout the whole world.

That is why protest movements against nuclear weapons became such a potent, global force during the cold war. An important episode in the long history of peace movements, the anti-bomb initiative became bound up with other phenomena that gained momentum after the Second World War: human rights and environmentalism. Nuclear armaments, in particular atmospheric testing, violated human rights in that they caused damage to people's health through radioactive agents that fell from the "mushroom clouds." Such "ashes of death" fell on all living things regardless of their location. Why should the vast majority of humankind suffer the consequences of the nuclear powers' militarization? Such awareness led people all over the world to organize movements against nuclear testing and, ultimately, against nuclear armament itself. Citizens in the United States and its allies also became involved, in many instances protesting against their own governments' nuclear strategy. Women were particularly active because of their concern with the effects of atmospheric testing upon babies and children. "End the arms race, not the human race" became a slogan among anti-bomb activist women in the United States.

Thus it is possible to see that even the military technology aspect of the cold war became bound up with the overall human rights movement after the Second World War. While the cold war may have ended, nuclear armaments have not, nor have movements against them. In such a long perspective, the cold war may be seen as a catalyst that triggered both nuclear proliferation and a global anti-nuclear movement.

The ban-the-bomb movement was also a part of the rising movement to protect the natural environment, for nuclear testing, whether in the atmosphere or underground, damaged the earth's habitat just as industrial waste and urban pollution did.

In combination such "modern" developments, whether military or economic, destroyed the ecological system that had sustained life on earth for millennia. Awareness of environmental degradation grew significantly during the 1950s because of nuclear fallout, but became intertwined with concerns over industrialization and urbanization in the subsequent decades. Although global environmentalism became active only after 1970, here again it is possible to put the cold war in the context of the history of the environment and of environmentalism.

That history has been bound up both with wars and with peace. Wars, whether hot or cold, devastate the natural habitat. The use of "Agent Orange," a toxic gas that damaged humans during the Vietnam War, also wreaked havoc with the forests and rice paddies of Indochina. The demilitarized zone dividing North from South Korea, on the one hand, became a haven for endangered species because they are safe from nuclear fallout.[1] On the other hand, this same haven is under threat from industrialization, indicating that peace, not simply war, can cause environmental hazards. In any event, in the long story of efforts to protect the natural environment, nuclear technology played a key, but not the only, role. If the history of the cold war is inseparable from that of nuclear armament, then, neither can it be treated separately from the story of global environmentalism.

What these observations suggest is that a chronology that prioritized the cold war is a misleading way to understand post-Second World War history. It makes just as much sense to periodize the post-1945 years in terms of the history of decolonization, internationalism, human rights, economic globalization, or environmentalism. Did these phenomena have anything in common so that there could be an overarching chronology of which these may be comprehended as subsidiary chronologies? This is one of the most interesting questions that historians can ponder.

## 1970–1990

In examining the above question, the decades after 1970 serve clearly to historicize the cold war, subordinating it to other developments that may be understood as aspects of the overall phenomenon of globalization. As noted above, economic globalization has a long history, and the years between 1945 and 1970 may be comprehended as a period of re-globalization. Developments after the early 1970s indicated that re-globalization had been successfully accomplished and that the process of more full-fledged globalization than earlier—more global and more extensive—had begun. To put it succinctly, non-geopolitical forces grew in importance in contrast to geopolitical developments.

To be sure, many historians still cling to a cold war-centric chronology of world history for the 1970s and the 1980s. For them, the US-USSR détente that began in the early 1970s was followed by a renewed crisis, "the second cold war" according to some writers, toward the end of the decade, which grew ominous in the early 1980s—until, all of a sudden, the cold war collapsed as a framework of international relations, leading ultimately to the break-up of the mighty Soviet empire.

That such a chronology is superficial becomes obvious as soon as we recall other non-geopolitical developments of the 1970s like the 1970 observance of the first "Earth Day," the 1971 collapse of the dollar that had sustained the Bretton Woods system, the 1972 UN conference on the environment, another 1972 landmark in the form of terrorist attacks on Israeli athletes at the Munich Olympics, the 1973 and 1978 oil shocks, the 1975 Helsinki Accords on human rights, the 1978 launching of "modernization" programs by the People's Republic of China, the 1980 announcement by the World Health Organization that by 1979 smallpox had been finally eradicated, or the fact that by the end of the decade most of Africa had come to consist of independent nations. While these were not necessarily interrelated phenomena, their combined impact was to demonstrate the growing importance of non-geopolitical (economic, social, cultural) phenomena in world affairs. Virtually all these developments may be put in the frameworks of internationalism and globalization. The decades of the 1970s and the 1980s showed that internationalism and globalization proved more enduring than cold war geopolitics.

An example like smallpox eradication fits nowhere in the history of the cold war, but who is to say that it was of less importance than the geopolitical drama in the annals of human history? The disease that had killed more people than all the wars of the century combined had been a target of cooperative international efforts, going back to the League of Nations' campaign during the 1920s, but the movement became more concerted after the Second World War. It was promoted by the United States and the Soviet Union, among others, all of whom worked together in Africa and elsewhere to eradicate the disease.[2] The successful consummation of the campaign was a tribute to the spirit of internationalism. It was also an aspect of the history of globalization in that public health endeavors were becoming more and more global in scope and that in an age when national barriers were steadily coming down through economic globalization, internationalism was achieving major successes.

It is true that economic globalization encountered a serious setback in 1971 when President Richard Nixon announced that the United States was "de-coupling" the dollar from gold, thus undermining the basis of the Bretton Woods system that had been based on the principle of stable rates of exchange among major currencies, all linked to the dollar that in turn had a fixed value in terms of gold. In the sense that this episode and the subsequent devaluation of the dollar against other major currencies amounted to indicating the passing of US hegemony in international commercial and financial transactions, it might seem that the process of re-globalization that had hinged on the economic strength and political commitment of the United States was coming to an end. The Bretton Woods system that had been dependent on the strong dollar did not disappear, but it was now to be necessarily reshaped so that other countries would play more active roles than in the past. Such developments did not mean that globalization itself was jeopardized. Rather, participation by other countries and regions of the world made globalization more truly global.

This can be seen most clearly in the fact that the 1971 "Nixon shock" was soon followed by the 1973 "oil shock," entailing the decision by the recently formed Organization of Petroleum Exporting Countries (OPEC) to triple (and even quadruple) the price of crude oil. This heralded the arrival of the oil-producing countries, particularly in the Middle East, as important players in the international economy. Even the United States and the wealthier nations of Europe as well as Japan were not immune from the devastating impact of OPEC's action, and "oil dollars" began to constitute a new source of liquid capital that would seek its investment opportunities elsewhere, not the least in the advanced countries. Moreover, the European Community, formally established in 1973 with Great Britain now joining its European neighbors in the regional economic order, produced a powerful economic bloc that would challenge US supremacy in international trade and investments. In the meantime, Japan and its Asian neighbors ("the little dragons" such as South Korea, Taiwan, Hong Kong, and Singapore) also emerged as key players in the world economy as they successfully weathered the disarray in the international currency market caused by the two "shocks."

It should also be noted that, as A. G. Hopkins has argued, with most former colonies having become independent states by the 1970s, globalization now entered the phase of "post-colonial globalization," involving all parts of the globe in world economic transactions.[3] Any country and any individual could now play a role in the global economy as participants in what economic historians call a "neo-liberal market" which they date from around 1973.[4] But the most conspicuous aspect of the new, more global globalization was the phenomenal growth in the number of multinational corporations, namely transnational, non-territorial firms that roamed throughout the world in search of cheaper resources and labor as well promising mass markets. While there were at most 1,000 such enterprises before 1970, their number expanded to over 10,000 by the end of the decade.

The process of post-1970 globalization became even more pronounced during the 1980s. The People's Republic of China, the world's most populous nation, now opened itself to global economic forces, with the post-Mao leadership determined to undertake economic modernization through globalization. Foreign investments began to be welcomed; Chinese officials, intellectuals, and business people visited abroad in increasing numbers to establish networks that would help integrate the nation into the world economy; and the Communist Party undertook extensive programs for building infrastructures such as highways and ports to facilitate trade, as well as for remodeling the country's educational system so as to produce scientists and engineers who would be able to compete in the world market in addition to contributing to modernization at home.

In the meantime, the United States and its wealthier economic partners continued to take steps to bring about the liberalization of the currency market. Among the most important was the Plaza Accord of 1985, so called because it resulted from a meeting of the finance ministers and central bank directors of the United States, Britain, France, Germany, and Japan who met in the Plaza Hotel, New York, to devalue the dollar still further and opened the way to reduce dramatically regulations that had hindered a free flow of money across national borders. The resulting financial liberalization was a major episode in the history of globalization, for it enabled anyone anywhere to play the game of currency exchange.

Given such momentous developments in the international economic scene, it would seem to be extremely parochial to periodize the history of the 1970s and the 1980s simply in terms of what happened in US-Soviet relations. Why "the second cold war" of the late 1970s into the early 1980s should suddenly have led to the ending of the cold war only a few years afterwards could never be explained solely in the framework of geopolitics. Although historians continue to dwell on such issues as the stationing of Soviet missiles in Eastern Europe, the countermeasures taken by NATO, and Ronald Reagan's devotion to the Strategic Defense Initiative as having been critical in defining the international relations of the 1980s, their significance would seem to pale in comparison with a single event, the Plaza Accord, in defining the history of the last decades of the 20th century and indeed of the first years of the 21st.

There were equally remarkable developments in the non-economic sphere during the 1970s and the 1980s, all of which may be grasped within the framework of the newer phase of globalization. Ironically, economic globalization became coupled with global environmentalism, and the latter owed its inspiration to a considerable extent to the awareness of the hazards of rapid industrialization and urbanization. Even as the nations of the world focused on economic development and expansion, individuals, non-governmental organizations, and even governments began to question the wisdom of unlimited growth that was doing so much damage to the natural environment. Per capita incomes were increasing rapidly in many parts of the world, enabling individuals to travel and consume to an extent never before possible. Earth Day, observed worldwide in 1970, issued a first warning against consumerism that was spreading across national boundaries. And global environmentalism became an international movement when the UN convened the first conference on "the human environment" in Stockholm in 1972. Out of the conference the UN Environmental Program was created, which would continue to sponsor international conferences designed to stop the uncontrolled exploitation of the earth's resources and to limit environmental damage due to pollution from factories, automobiles, and even homes.

It was no accident that during the 1970s the term "human security" began to be used, first at the United Nations Development Program (UNDP) and then gaining currency in scholarly circles. Going beyond the conventional notion of national security, the new concept indicated awareness that ultimately humans must learn to live with one another and with other species so that they would maintain the ecological system that had sustained civilization for so long. The popularity of concepts like "human community" and "planet earth" suggests that during the 1970s and subsequently, the common destiny of humankind came to be stressed, joining or even superseding the traditional notions of national security and national interests. In this context, the 1987 Montreal Protocol for the protection of the ozone layer must be considered just as significant a landmark in the history of the 1980s as the Reykjavik meeting by President Reagan and Chairman Gorbachev in the same year that produced the strategic arms limitation agreement.

One of the notable developments in connection with the environmental movement was that it was promoted primarily by private, non-governmental organizations. During the 1970s and the 1980s, many such organizations were established—for instance,

Friends of the Earth, Greenpeace—to promote the cause of environmentalism. Indeed, the remarkable growth of non-governmental organizations was one of the most dramatic developments of these decades. Although private associations to promote certain causes (anti-slavery, educational exchange, etc.) had existed for a long time, relatively few of them had reached across national boundaries, to turn themselves into international non-governmental organizations (INGO). Their number is estimated to have been around 3,000 in 1970, but they increased to over 13,000 by 1984.[5] That fact alone marks the 1970s as having been a significant turning point in recent history, for it suggests that non-state actors were increasing in number and assertiveness in national and international affairs. This was the decade when the idea of "planet earth," which had emerged in the 1960s, came to be widely accepted as a definition of human existence, implying that people living on the globe shared the same destiny, even the same identity. Whereas they had tended to be divided by national identities, each subordinate to state authority, they would also be united across national boundaries simply by virtue of being together on the "spaceship earth."

The growth of INGOs was another manifestation of such consciousness, for these entities revealed that men and women in many countries could unite to promote their shared objectives, be they environmental protection, human rights, or humanitarian causes. Nations and states would remain, but they would not monopolize human agendas or policy decisions. Indeed, the relative decline in the state's functions, even in its authority, was the other side of the coin of the same phenomenon. During the 1970s and the 1980s, the state's role and power were complemented, sometimes challenged, by transnational advocacy groups intent on redefining human agendas to go beyond nation-centric concerns.

This was also the moment when, as can be seen in the term "Reagan revolution" or "Thatcherism," political leaders in the United States and other advanced industrial nations began emphasizing the idea of "small government" in which the state's functions would be limited primarily to national security and public order, leaving to the private sector issues such as social welfare and medical care. The ideology of "neo-conservatism" and "neo-liberalism" sustained such reconceptualization. While the cold war may have intensified as a result of the renewed emphasis on national security, which justified continued defense spending and arms augmentation, the development of civil society had the opposite effect, for it was not limited to already democratic states but became particularly notable in countries hitherto ruled by authoritarian regimes, especially in Eastern Europe but also in Latin America and elsewhere. Gorbachev-initiated reforms ("perestroika" and "glasnost") were nothing if not a recognition of the need to foster non-state initiatives within a socialist nation. The eroding of the cold war in the late 1980s would make no sense unless it was put in such a context.

Another aspect of the phenomena of internationalism and globalization was the renewed eagerness on the part of non-state actors, now more determined and self-confident than earlier, to promote dialogue among national, religious, and cultural divides. The age that popularized the notion of planet earth not surprisingly persuaded people everywhere to see excessive nationalism as a major threat to the global community and to consider non-national entities such as religion, ethnicity, and language as increasingly important sources of identity. Globalization did not obliterate such identities; if anything, the seemingly monolithic force of economic and technological globalization was provoking a self-conscious assertiveness on the part of religious, ethnic, and linguistic groups to insist on their autonomy as a critical element in establishing individual identity. All the more reason, then, to promote dialogue among these groups so as not to splinter the globe in the age of globalization.

The language of common humanity underlay the renewed interest in this cause. At a conference of Western and non-Western intellectuals in Bellagio, Italy, in 1972, for instance, the participants spoke of "a growing network of individuals concerned with the improvement of long-term cultural relations among people and countries who wish to transcend the barriers—political, military, or ideological—which often distort or handicap the fulfillment of human relationships."[6] Such language echoed the by-then globally shared conception of humanity. It was logical, therefore, that the decade of the 1970s witnessed the mushrooming of INGOs oriented toward the promotion of human rights. The UN General Assembly had already during the 1960s passed a number of resolutions to elaborate on and implement the 1948 Universal Declaration of Human Rights. But during the subsequent decade non-state actors became actively involved in the cause, especially with respect to the rights of women, children, the handicapped, the poor, the illiterate, and all those whose humanity had not been fully recognized by separate states. Even in the geopolitical realm, the 1975 Helsinki Accords established human rights as a cardinal principle in great-power relations, a sure sign that the cold war was steadily changing its character. In such a context, the alleged "new cold war" of the late 1970s into the early 1980s would seem to have been but a sideshow. To prioritize such a development would be to place an emphasis on a traditional theme in global development that was fast losing its centrality as a definer of an age.

That during the 1980s the promotion of human rights became an even more global phenomenon than hitherto may be linked to the globalization of information technology. It was during the last two decades of the century that the Internet came to be available to individuals and groups far beyond its original users, the military, and communication across borders was immensely facilitated by the steadily spreading electronic mail system. An inevitable consequence was the dissemination and exchange of information and ideas with people in all parts of the world regardless of their national affiliation. Such landmarks as the democratization of Eastern European countries, the Tiananmen demonstrations in Beijing in June 1989, and the fall of the Berlin Wall toward the end of the year were all interrelated thanks to the new technology. Although Eastern European civil societies did not develop uniformly, nor did the demonstrations in China bear immediate fruit, they were key developments in the history of human rights, a history that has not ended. Even if the chronology of the cold war may be said to have come to its conclusion in 1989 or shortly thereafter, a chronology of world history that gives due regard to the subject of human rights would attribute a different significance to the 1980s, not as the presumed termination of a geopolitical struggle but as an important chapter in an unfinished story.

# 1990 TO THE PRESENT

If the cold war is defined as a struggle for power between the United States and the Soviet Union, it by definition came to an end with the collapse of the latter in 1991. However, if the cold war is taken to mean a chapter in the drama of "the rise and fall of the great powers," obviously it has not ended. The US-USSR cold war may soon be replaced by a struggle for power between the United States and Russia, or China, or another contender for global power. However, the key to understanding international affairs since the 1990s is not to be preoccupied with geopolitical affairs to the exclusion of other, far more significant developments, but to consider to what extent the world has continued to be transformed. In particular, how have forces of economic and technological globalization continued to shape human lives? Have there been further significant developments in environmental protection, human rights, cultural dialogue, disease prevention, and other spheres that had become major themes in world history during the 1970s and the 1980s?

These are important questions, but since this essay is limited to the objective of historicizing the cold war, I shall focus on the ways in which historians since the 1990s have developed a more global understanding of the history of the second half of the 20th century, a perspective in which the history of the cold war may appear different from more conventional narratives. In the historical literature nothing is more striking than the sudden and also growing popularity of world history, now often called global history or transnational history. This phenomenon, too, may be related to the development of globalization as a major force in world history in the last decades of the 20th century.

However, it is important to note the gap between the momentum for globalization that grew during the 1970s and the historiography that would seem to have lagged behind. Even though global moments had arrived, historians were slow to recognize them. Historiography lagged behind history. But by the early 1990s historians were finally recognizing the need to go beyond national narratives in understanding the past and to consider phenomena and themes that cut across national boundaries. The rising popularity of world and global history ensured that the basically Euro-centric narrative of modern history as consisting of national experiences would be supplemented, if not entirely replaced, by a less parochial perspective, a world view that took account of all regions and people in establishing a chronology. A growing number of scholars were likewise intent upon going beyond the conventional framework of international history understood as interrelations among nation states and to consider such transnational phenomena as encounters among religions, ethnicities, and races, migrations, diasporic communities, stateless refugees, environmental degradation, and diseases.

In the perspectives of world, global, or transnational history, power-political relations among some countries ("the great powers") constituted but one theme that needed to be put in the context of worldwide economic, social, or cultural developments. Historians were now eager to examine themes and devise chronologies that did not depend on a teleology that tended to privilege the modern West or established chronologies in terms of international affairs but instead to explore comparisons and connections across regional and civilizational divides. Christopher Bayly, Andre Gunder Frank, A. G. Hopkins, Patrick Manning, Bruce Mazlish, and others spearheaded the movement to de-nationalize and de-territorialize the study of the past. Because war, including the cold war, is defined by national and territorial entities, it is not surprising that the new world or global history moved in the direction of human or transnational history.

Historicizing the cold war, then, in the new historiographic perspective, means something significantly different from what it would be in a more geopolitically focused account. We are now in a position to understand the cold war not just in the framework of international relations and national strategies but also in that of global social, economic, and cultural developments. In that larger framework, it must be said that the winners in the cold war were not particular nations, for all nations began to lose their centrality during the decades that witnessed the growth of globalizing forces. Rather, the real winners were the non-national, transnational forces that united and integrated nations and peoples, forces that were often submerged under the dictates of geopolitics but that proved far more enduring as agents of historical transformation. That transformation has entailed the growing diversification as well as interdependence of the human community. The cold war, it would seem, contributed to neither of these themes, and to that extent it was a counter-historical event.

To go back to the questions posed at the beginning of this essay, a cold-war-centered chronology clearly misses other developments in 20th-century history that had their own chronologies: globalization, decolonization, human rights, environmentalism, and others. To take just one example, if globalization were to be viewed as having been a key theme in recent history, its chronology would have to start at least from the late 19th century. Even if we were to limit ourselves to the cold war era, roughly speaking from the end of the Second World War to the early 1990s, we would first periodize the era of US-led multilateralism (known as the Bretton Woods system) that spanned the years between 1944 and 1971. Then after a brief period of international economic and financial disarray, lasting between 1971 and the early 1980s, we could postulate the period between 1985 and 2007 as the age of far more global globalization than ever before. Whether this period of unparalleled globalization came to a grinding halt in 2008 due to the worldwide financial crisis and steep economic downturn, and how to characterize the post-2008 phase of world history would be questions that future historians would need to ponder.

What is the relationship between the two chronologies, one defined by the history of the cold war and the other by globalization? Unless we merge the two into one comprehensive chronology in which major episodes in both of these dramas are put together—such a master chronology would be just a listing of dates, not a historical narrative—we would have to take note of the two chronologies as parallel developments. But if we do not stop there, which would be tantamount to saying both were of equal significance, we might decide to subordinate one of the two chronologies to the other. I have argued that globalization was a far more significant and enduring historical development than the cold war, in other words that worldwide, transnational, and socioeconomic phenomena that made up the theme of globalization have played a much more crucial role in defining the contemporary world than the story of "the rise and fall of the great powers" of which the cold war was one of the major plots after the Second World War.

Others might disagree and insist that it was the cold war that promoted globalization so that the latter theme should be seen as a sub-plot of the former. Many writers still take that view, arguing that the United States and its allies, in contrast to their cold war adversaries, supported economic and financial multilateralism and therefore that the ending of the cold war had the effect of bringing the former antagonists into the global market place. I would reverse the equation and suggest that it was globalization that affected the history of the cold war by creating networks of interdependence across national boundaries and generating transnational forces that questioned the legitimacy of a national policy, whether in Washington or in Moscow, that continued to build up a huge nuclear arsenal for a war neither of them sought, and also by enhancing the relative power and influence of Europe, the Middle East, and other regions of the world vis-à-vis that of the two superpowers.

If we add, besides globalization, other, no less significant developments like decolonization and human rights, the place of the cold war in contemporary history would further diminish. Of course, one could so define the cold war as to include all those non- geopolitical developments—or even consider these other themes as aspects of the geopolitical drama. To the extent that geopolitics entails the question of the disposition of power, and if power may be construed as political, economic, technological, cultural, and even psychological in addition to being military and strategic, then obviously everything under the sun is geopolitical. But that would not help much in understanding the place and role of the cold war in the history of the world in the second half of the 20th century. To say that power is everything is really to say nothing. Power, whatever it entails, will need to be disaggregated. At least, it would make more sense to distinguish nation-centric conceptions of power from the power of non-state and transnational entities and forces, including business enterprises, non-governmental organizations, ethnic affiliations, and religions. Their activities steadily came to affect, at times even to overshadow, the behavior of nations, including the cold war protagonists. In the final analysis, then, to historicize the cold war may be part of a larger project, to historicize the nation state.

## Notes

1. Lisa M. Brady, "Life in the DMZ: Turning a Diplomatic Failure into an Environmental Success," *Diplomatic History* 32–4 (September 2008), 585–611.
2. See Erez Manela, "Smallpox," in Akira Iriye and Pierre Yves Saunier, eds., *Palgrave Dictionary of Transnational History* (Basingstoke, UK: Palgrove Macmillan, 2009).
3. A. G. Hopkins, "Rethinking Decolonization," *Past and Present*, no. 200 (August 2008), 211–47.

4. Robert Skidelsky, "The Growth of a World Economy," in Michael Howard and Wm. Roger Louis, eds., *The Oxford History of the Twentieth Century* (New York: Oxford University Press, 1998).
5. See Akira Iriye, *Global Community: The Role of International Organizations in the Making of the Contemporary World* (Berkeley: University of California Press, 2002), chapter 5.
6. Hazen Foundation, "Reconstituting the Human Community" (New Haven, 1972), p. 5.

## SELECT BIBLIOGRAPHY

Borstelmann, Tim. *The Cold War and the Color Line: American Race Relations in the Global Arena.* Cambridge, MA: Harvard University Press, 2001.
Connelly, Matthew. *Fatal Misconception: The Struggle to Control World Population.* Cambridge, MA: Harvard University Press, 2008.
Conway, Martin, and Kiran Klaus Patel, eds. *Europeanization in the Twentieth Century: Historical Approaches.* Houndsmills, Basingstoke, Hampshire: Palgrave Macmillan 2010.
Engerman, David, Nils Gilman, Mark Haefele, and Michael E. Latham, eds. *Staging Growth: Modernization, Development, and the Global Cold War.* Amherst, MA: University of Massachussetts Press, 2003.
Iriye, Akira, Petra Goedde, and William Hitchcock, eds. *The Human Rights Revolution: An International History.* New York: Oxford University Press, 2012.
McNeill, John R. *Something New Under the Sun: An Environmental History of the Twentieth-Century World.* New York: W.W. Norton, 2001.
Moyn, Samuel. *The Last Utopia: Human Rights in History.* Cambridge, MA: Harvard University Press, 2010.
Snyder, Sarah. *Human Rights Activism and the End of the Cold War: A Transnational History of the Helsinki Network.* New York: Cambridge University Press, 2011.

# CHAPTER 3

## IDEOLOGY, CULTURE, AND THE COLD WAR

### NAOKO SHIBUSAWA[1]

MICHAEL H. Hunt begins *Ideology and US Foreign Policy* (1987) by writing: "This is a little book about a big and slippery subject: the place of ideology in US foreign policy. It ventures into a complicated realm where conceptual confusion often reigns."[2] The same can be said of this little essay about ideology and culture during the cold war. "Confusion often reigns" not only because the terms are amorphous concepts, but also because scholars, including those within the same discipline, have defined "ideology" and "culture" differently. Let us then clarify what we mean by "culture"; we must understand this term before we define "ideology."

As James Cook and Lawrence Glickman note in their introduction to *The Cultural Turn in US History*, even self-identified historians of US culture do not adhere to the same definition of culture.[3] Among historians of American foreign relations, many use the word "culture" primarily in the anthropological sense, as a people's "common set of beliefs, customs, values, and rituals."[4] From this definition comes both the general notion that different peoples have their own distinct "culture" and the more specific idea of national cultures whose members share a "consciousness" or "*mentalités*" about geography, belonging, history, and practices.[5] Akira Iriye—a pioneer in emphasizing culture in studying foreign relations—argues that if all nations can be seen as embodiments of separate cultures, it is reasonable and proper to think of "international relations [as] intercultural relations." He points out that nations and peoples deal with each other not only in terms of political, strategic, or material interests, but also through their respective cultures.[6]

While recognizing the merits of this anthropologically-inspired definition of culture, I follow the definition of culture as a discursive system. Discourse here refers not simply to speech or written communication, but broadly to the sets of signifying practices through which people know and understand the world. Through the circulation of ideas, people determine what they accept to be true and valid, or reject as false and illegitimate. Considering culture as discourse allows us to better comprehend how power, culture, and knowledge-production are interdependent. Discursive analysis, in other words, is an effort to probe the limits and boundaries of what we know, as well as to pay attention to our subjectivity. We must consider how our personal backgrounds, experiences, and beliefs shape both the boundaries of our knowledge and influence what we seek to research. Defining culture as a discursive system thus means trying to consider our historical subjects' epistemologies, as well as our own: how did they know what they know, and how do *we* know what *we* know? This line of inquiry can yield new insights by leading us a step further to ask: how do our own epistemologies as privileged scholars limit our ability to understand others, especially disempowered others, on their own terms?[7]

With the above in mind, we can see that scholarship is rarely neutral, that knowledge establishes and sustains hierarchies because those who have it hold an advantage over those who lack it. This is a major insight of postcolonial theorists such as Edward W. Said, who built upon Michel Foucault's analysis of discourse. Said argued that the colonial powers gained, maintained, and justified their dominance over the colonized through their "superior" knowledge. This meant not only deploying technical, scientific, or administrative knowledge, but also gathering and controlling knowledge about the colonized, including the willful erasure of native histories and cultures/discourses.[8] Sharing a methodology with post-structural/postmodern theorists, postcolonial theorists also focus on the production of knowledge through textual analyses. They diverge in purpose, however, from theorists like Foucault and Jean-François Lyotard. While the latter have criticized modernism's faith in linear progress, rational planning, and empirically derived truth as fictions that originated during the Enlightenment, postcolonial scholars like Said have felt that they cannot afford the luxury of this postmodernist stance of rejecting notions of "progress," given the continued suffering in what we now call the Global South.[9] Indeed, postcolonial thinkers like Samir Amin castigate postmodernism as the intellectual "accessory" of neoliberalism—merely "satisfied with showing complexity and pluralism rather than offering a critique of a system that continues to ravage peoples, cultures, resources, and places." Postcolonial scholars thus charge that postmodernism encourages an engagement with theory as an end in itself, rather than mobilizing efforts to achieve social and economic justice.[10]

Framing an essay on the cold war with the definitions and priorities of postcolonial scholars makes sense if we remember that the "hot wars" of the period were fought primarily in the former colonies. It is in this context of competition for "hearts and minds" that we can more precisely define ideology and its relationship to culture. Odd Arne Westad characterizes the cold war as an ideological struggle for competing visions of modernity.[11] This is not to gainsay or minimize the material or strategic interests in the conflict, nor to deny the existence of variation in approaches, strategies, and goals within each so-called bloc. General statements can nonetheless be made without mistaking the participants as monolithic camps. One side—for its own security and self-validation—promoted socialist development as the path for nations to gain wealth, power, security, and justice. In order to do the same, the other side promoted liberal development through Rostovian "stages of growth." Ideology provided the *raison d'être* for both sides, but American politicians and leaders during the cold war were loath to say that they operated with an ideology. To them, "ideology" was a pejorative, synonymous with Marxism, "a system of wrong, false, distorted or otherwise misguided beliefs."[12] What they themselves believed, Americans labeled simply as common sense or the Truth.

Especially since the cold war's end, American students of US foreign relations have begun to recognize that Americans are not immune to ideological thinking, that ideology shapes what passes for common sense. Scholars have come to understand ideological thinking as a characteristic of all peoples rather than an unfortunate flaw of enemies.[13] With this insight, scholars such as Michael Latham have been able to define "modernization" as an ideology, following Hunt's definition of ideology as an "interrelated set of convictions or assumptions that reduces the complexity of a particular slice of reality to easily comprehensible terms and suggests an appropriate way of dealing with that reality."[14]

Ideologies in this context are the varying and dynamic beliefs that enable the elite to exercise control with the consent of the ruled through what Antonio Gramsci called cultural hegemony. By cultural hegemony Gramsci meant the everyday narratives and ideas that make sociopolitical hierarchies and economic inequities appear natural and commonsensical. These naturalized narratives are not static, and they do not represent a conspiracy by ruling elites to hoodwink the poor and disempowered. Instead, they are deeply held beliefs shared by many within a society, regardless of socio-economic status. They ultimately benefit the ruling elites, but the leaders themselves find the ideologies compelling because they cannot be "beyond" ideologies any more than they can be beyond their own cultures.[15] Dominant ideologies, then, are a subset of culture, or a discursive system. This culture or discursive system shifts as a small number of counterhegemonic narratives succeed in challenging the veracity and "common sense" of dominant ideologies.[16]

Space does not permit a wider discussion of this dynamism, and we will therefore focus on hegemonic ideologies defined by cultural historian Susan Smulyan as "the ideas that serve the powerful" and help them retain their power.[17] I argue that we can understand the function of hegemonic ideologies during the cold war most clearly by further analyzing how the ideology of modernization determined who was ready for self-rule. Rather than showing how "modernization" was applied to a variety of locales, I explore modernization's intellectual antecedents and offer some concluding remarks about its continuities.[18] Both David Ekbladh and Nils Gilman have suggested that modernization was a cold war variant of notions about "development" that predated and outlasted the conflict.[19] What they point out has been echoed by both Akira Iriye and Prasenjit Duara, who suggest in this volume that the salient features of the cold war that are compelling to study today cannot be limited, indeed properly studied or understood, solely within the years 1945–89.

Therefore, this essay on "culture and ideology" during the cold war is informed by a postcolonial perspective and examines the ongoing process of reproducing hegemonic knowledge. The narratives that have shaped and buttress US policy derive from a longer genealogy of western imperialism that continues today. My objective is to show how notions of modernity—especially in rationalizing capability of self-rule—took shape during the Enlightenment, inflected cold war policies, and continue to do so in our contemporary moment. I will emphasize continuities over time, but do so without the intention of ignoring or denying historic specificity. Ideologies are neither monolithic nor unchanging.[20] At stake in highlighting the continuities is a better understanding of the intellectual scaffolding on which state powers built their comprehension of geopolitics and strategies to achieve or maintain cultural, economic, and political, hegemony—that is, their ability to set the standards or rules which others must adhere to or resist. A variety of ideologies regarding race, gender, and maturity were involved in this process, as well as other narratives about revolution, political economy, and religion. I argue that the staying power of ideologies derives from their personification into binary, anthropomorphic figures. This is how an entire country could be depicted and acted upon as if it were a singular, developing human being.

## THE ORIGINS OF MODERNITY

If competing notions of modernity provided the ideological framework for the cold war, we must discuss briefly the origins of "modernity." Since Christians in Europe during the fifth century began using the term "modern" to distinguish their era from those of the pagan, pre-Christian era, the concept has been used to differentiate the present times from the past. The term "modernity," however, dates to the late 18th and early 19th centuries and signifies both a rupture with the past and expectations for the future. According to Jürgen Habermas, the "project of modernity" emerged with Enlightenment thinkers and their efforts to develop objective scientific methods of inquiry; to discern universal foundations in law and morality; and to foster "autonomous art." Enlightenment thinkers believed that the accumulation of this knowledge, along with "the rational organization of social relations" and rational modes of thought, would liberate humans from arbitrary abuses of power, superstitions, and myths. The "project of modernity" promised that "the arts and sciences would not merely promote the control of the forces of nature, but also further the understanding of self and nature, the progress of morality, justice in social institutions, and even human happiness."[21] In short, modernity functioned as ideology since it provided prescription, as well as description.

Although the concept of "modernity" emerged during the late 18th and early 19th centuries, the origins of what we recognize as the "modern era" came centuries earlier. Habermas, referring to Hegel, posits that the modern era began with "three monumental events around the year 1500": (1) European contact with the western hemisphere, (2) the Renaissance, and (3) the Reformation.[22] These "three monumental events," moreover, were not discrete but interrelated phenomena, as scholars today are increasingly beginning to realize. For instance, Europeans developed the scientific method as they sought to understand, control, and extract resources from their overseas colonies. Historian Antonio Barrera-Osorio has demonstrated that the absence of flora, fauna, and other features of the "New World" in classical scientific texts encouraged Spanish colonials to innovate empiricist methods that became the basis of the scientific revolution.[23] Scholars of Spanish America, moreover, also predate the origins of a universalist project to the "long sixteenth century" when the Spaniards attempted to Christianize the *indios* in the "new world."[24] Thus modernity has been coterminous with western imperialism. Empiricism, scientific systems of knowledge, and projects of "civilizing" the natives developed in tandem with and in the service of imperialism.[25]

Also with the advent of the modern era came the new notion that some people were primitive or underdeveloped. As Walter D. Mignolo points out, differentiating peoples according to chronology was unknown in medieval Europe. During the medieval era, moreover, "Europe" was not considered a coherent geopolitical and cultural entity, and the peoples living there saw themselves as inhabiting Christendom. Differences among people—Christians, non-Christians—were defined spatially or geographically. Non-Christians—whether Jews in their midst or the Muslim "infidels" living beyond the borders of Christendom—were seen as residing in different spheres of belief.[26] After coming to the western hemisphere, Christians/Europeans noted differences with Amerindians, but they had not yet conceptualized a theory that categorized the indigenous as underdeveloped. These notions of chronological lag became more fully formed with secularizing impulses of the Enlightenment, after which religious difference no longer remained *the* central factor differentiating peoples.[27] The thinkers of Enlightenment innovated the idea of universal and linear development from a supposed state of brute primitivism to one characterized by refinement, socio-economic structures, and wealth created through private property.[28] At this moment of European colonization and Enlightenment theorization, the colonized became seen as less developed or behind in time in comparison with those of European descent. Just prior to and during the Enlightenment (17th–18th centuries), colonized peoples and imported slave labor from Africa were being racialized in increasingly rigid and totalizing ways.

Therefore, differences since this imperial/modern age were measured not only geographically across space, but also chronologically across time or "development."[29] Western imperialists began to see existing and potential colonies as pre-modern places in their contemporary world that needed to be brought forcibly into the modern world with their intervention and guidance. This concept rested on the notion that some people (whites) were considered more "developed," advanced, or capable than others (non-whites). But conveniently, the less advanced were deemed capable of the sort of menial labor required for colonial enterprises; in fact, they were seen as fit only for such type of work. This sort of logic allowed John Locke to expound on the "natural rights of man" and yet invest in the slave-trading Royal Africa Company. Slavery existed prior to this time, of course. Africans enslaved Africans, and Europeans enslaved Europeans. But the modern era of European overseas imperialism created the permanent, hereditary system of slavery by using a random (but useful) physical marker to separate free from unfree labor. Thus the "modern/colonial world was founded and sustained through a geopolitical [and economic] organization of the world that, in the last analysis, consisted of an ethnoracial foundation."[30] A central feature of racialization was to confer or deny power, wealth, land, and/or opportunities.

# READINESS FOR SELF-RULE

Postcolonial critics have not ignored the liberating promises of modernity, among them self-determination and freedom from arbitrary and oppressive rule. In fact, their criticism comes from how most in the Global South have been largely denied these promises. This denial of political freedom and economic justice has been possible with a series of rationalizations that have been sustained in one form or another since the age of Enlightenment. Espousal of the "natural rights of man" did not hamper racial colonialization, because westerners simply invented a range of rationalizations as to why some did not meet the qualifications of manhood. Or, to put it another way, they came up with reasons as to why some humans weren't really adults capable of self-rule or ready to appreciate the social and political freedoms promised by modernity.

Apart from race, two other criteria to rate readiness for self-rule were also biologically based: gender and maturity. By virtue of their gender, of course, women did not fit into the category of "all men." But why gender was and continues to be the basis for exclusion and disempowerment is less apparent. To talk about gender does not mean a focus on women as subjects per se, but the perceived differences between the males and females beyond biological differences. This perception of difference has been common throughout many societies and eras—so common that the differences appear innate rather than as a consequence of socialization. Magnifying the supposed differences in temperament and thus ability between the genders signified relationships of power, as Joan Scott pointed out.[31] Thus power differences among nations have often been expressed through gendered references implying weakness, dependence, emotionality, and irrationality on one side and strength, rationality, discipline on the other.

Gender is a malleable ideology—indeed this versatility is what gives any ideology its resilience and utility. Pundits and policymakers have frequently resorted to gendered metaphors to explain differentials in power and to argue for the subjugation of or guidance to another people. For example, the feminized rendering of occupied Germany by Americans after World War II was relatively brief in comparison to American notions of a feminized Japan or an effeminate India that predated the war and continued throughout the 20th century.[32] By virtue of being non-western, the latter two nations were and are often orientalized as being feminine in culture—and, by extension, as a people. Scholars who have expanded Said's original thesis with a gendered analysis have demonstrated that gendered visions underlay notions about the exoticism (and eroticism) of the "Other."[33]

Just as importantly, a gendered perspective frames what pundits and policymakers have thought not only of other peoples, but also of themselves. Thus those who advocated war with Spain in 1898 derided William McKinley as an old woman when he hesitated about entering the conflict, while sixty years later, the Kennedy and Johnson administrations favored "toughness" with disastrous consequences in Vietnam.[34] At the same time, the gendered self-image included a conviction that one's own society treated women better than other "less advanced" peoples. This notion can be seen in the Americas as early as Cabeza de Vaca's observation in the 16th century that the *indios* worked their women too hard, but it was often repeated during the cold war and beyond regarding Asian men's treatment of Asian women.[35] Since the end of the cold war the trend is visible in American popular discourse about Muslim societies.[36] This gendered rationale helped justify wars on Iraq and Afghanistan, and has tragically brought more suffering, particularly upon Afghani women.[37]

Likewise, the ideology of maturity has helped to deny self-determination, usually to non-whites. Analogies corresponding to the natural life cycle have long been used as conceptual devices to justify political privilege and dominance. "Maturity" signified ability, wisdom, and self-control and entitlement to status and power. Colonial powers have used the rhetoric of maturity to justify their rule over non-white peoples. Images of the Filipinos, Cubans, Hawaiians, or Puerto Ricans as babies—often squalling—or as students in a classroom led by "Uncle Sam" were abundant in American media at the turn of the 20th century.[38] In the words of William Howard Taft, the first governor-general of the Philippines, "our little brown brothers," would require "fifty or one hundred years" of US supervision "to develop anything resembling Anglo-Saxon political principles and skills."[39] This practice of depicting colonized or otherwise disempowered peoples as immature or even helpless "dependents" needing the firm hand of American guidance continued into the 20th century and beyond (see Figures 3.1 and 3.2).

Unlike race or gender, however, immaturity could be a transitional stage, not a permanent fate. After World War II, when the United States focused on exerting hegemonic power without formal colonial structures, it took more seriously its and other imperial-

FIGURE 3.1 "Not Yet Ready to Walk Alone"

Source: Jacksonville (Florida) Times, February 1949.

**FIGURE 3.2** "Iraq's Baby Steps"

Source: Ventura County Star, February 2005. Courtesy of Ventura County Star.

ist powers' previously false promises to bestow freedom when the natives "grew up." American policymakers and media justified its occupation of Japan as necessary because the Japanese were "not yet ready to walk alone." Still, they were not expected to be under direct American "tutelage" forever, and indeed, after seven years of occupation, the Japanese regained their national sovereignty. Contrasting sharply with permanent colonial paternalism, this "liberal paternalism" was selectively applied during the postwar period—again, according to a perceived sliding scale of readiness for self-rule.[40]

The ideologies of race, gender, and maturity were and are mutually reinforcing. Stereotypes or notions about women, non-whites, and children not only overlapped, but also provided rationales for the others. Women were considered weak, weepy, and emotional like children. Children enjoyed frivolities and were fey like women. Non-whites were deemed undisciplined, unschooled, and ignorant like children. Children were portrayed as "little savages" (and literally believed to be so, according to turn-of-the-century recapitulation theory).[41] On the other side of the binary, then, were notions of white adult men being cool, levelheaded, responsible decision-makers. The interlocking characteristic of the ideologies explains their strength and, indeed, can add up to a simplified worldview that bifurcates people into those who should be in control and those who should be controlled.

# Development, civilization, and American exceptionalism

Also constituting this simplified, binary worldview have been other ideologies in addition to those based on biological differences discussed thus far. These include nationalism and fear of revolutions, as Hunt discusses in *Ideology and US Foreign Policy*, as well as free trade, Christianity, and western civilization or modernity.[42] That free trade and Christianity can be seen as an "interrelated set of convictions" about how to understand and act in the world is self-evident and need not be explained further here.[43] Western civilization or modernity functions as an ideology because it assumes that western civilization is the historical apex of human achievement in the arts, the academy, jurisprudence, governance, economic productivity, civic institutions, and society. It is the universal standard to which all other peoples should aspire—and, indeed, be helped to do so under the direction and mentorship of westerners. This ideology, from which modernization theory sprang, has deep historical roots that date, as discussed, to the period of European overseas imperialism.[44] Notions about development intrinsic to the ideology of civilization, moreover, have underlain the nationalist narrative of the United States: American exceptionalism. It is through the prism of this teleological narrative of destiny and progress that Americans—both leaders and the broad public—have understood their nation's ascendancy to power and global role.

The ideology of American exceptionalism explained to Americans why they were particularly suited, even destined, to be world leaders, but that they must be ever vigilant in maintaining their fitness. American exceptionalism held that America was founded by healthy, young, vital, and hardworking people who freed themselves from the shackles of European/British imperialism and acquired control of a largely empty continent that was abundant in natural resources. This settler-colonial narrative dates to the 1780s and 1790s when it offered an attractive national identity to counteract the centripetal forces pulling apart the new nation after the successful revolution. The American Revolution became not simply the action of aggrieved provincials, but "a shot heard around the world"—the first sound in a noble fight for human liberty. Over time, "Americans—white Americans especially—came to see the founding of free and equal people as their calling in the world."[45] But Americans also believed that this exemplary status had to be maintained—through constant movement, said Frederick Jackson Turner in 1893—lest they lapse into senescence and enervation. Thus, John Foster Dulles stated in 1950: "There may come a time in the life of a people when their work of creation ends. That hour has not struck for us. We are still vital and capable of great endeavor. Our youth are spirited, not soft or fearful."[46] Dulles' statements demonstrate that notions about the developmental lifespan of civilizations were also gendered and raced.[47] The "spirited" and "not soft," youth Dulles invoked were of a specific gender and race, not to mention age. Such notions help explain why, a decade later, Sargent Shriver and the Kennedy administration fretted about American youth and believed that the Peace Corps would help young Americans experience the "frontier" life-style and retain what Theodore Roosevelt had called "the barbarian virtues" at the turn of the century.[48] Stemming from Jeffersonian republican fears of "overdevelopment" and effeminization of American society, preserving "vitality" and "vigor" (usually at the expense of the indigenous) remained a concern among policymakers since "the closing of the frontier."[49]

Thus the existential stakes in spreading the "blessings of our liberty"—i.e., spreading US liberal economic systems and/or democratic institutions, especially to "Third

World" natives—made the struggle with the Soviet Union especially charged ideologic-ally. The struggle symbolized not only the opposition of capitalism and communism but also competing exceptionalist claims.[50] Marxism and liberalism, both economic and political, came from the same Enlightenment lineage. As such, adherents saw their chosen way as universal and following a single trajectory of development over time. Although W. W. Rostow meant his "Non-Communist Manifesto" to be the antithesis of Marx's, they both believed that there existed a singular model of economic growth towards modernity.[51] The Soviets and the Americans disagreed, of course, over whether capitalism or socialism was the final epoch of history or the best way to attain "modern-ity." Yet both modernization theory and Marxist theory were universalist, secular, devoted to science, and materialist. Both held that "men" could shape the world, and both believed that democracy was best protected and run by elites—whether they be John F. Kennedy and the "best and the brightest" or Nikita Khrushchev and the Communist Party. Moreover, they purported to champion anti-colonial struggles and racial equality, a claim the United States became better at arguing as the civil rights movement gained victories. Likewise, both the Americans and the Soviets viewed national governments that either disagreed or resisted their particular favored path to modernity—communist or liberal capitalist—as problems to be solved either through appeasement or elimination.[52]

The "tragedy of American diplomacy" according to William Appleman Williams was that the exceptionalist narrative undermined US commitment to democracy and self-determination for the "Others." He recognized that Americans had a deep-felt commit-ment to democracy and wished to share this system with the world, but that by also insisting that other people attain and practice democracy in ways sanctioned by the United States, Americans undermined the very principle of self-determination they sought to promote. This has meant either overthrowing or trying to overthrow "unco-operative" national leaders—including those that were popularly elected—and often installing undemocratic leaders whose policies aligned with the interests of the United States. American leaders were not always comfortable with the choices they had made, but not uncomfortable enough to undo their decisions. JFK stated that while a best case scenario for a Third World country was "a decent democracy," he believed that if the United States were not given that choice, "a Trujillo regime" had to be supported in order to prevent "a Castro regime." And although the US State Department "blanched" at the bloodshed and sheer violence of their brutal clients in Guatemala, they still did not rec-ommend a policy change.[53]

Modernization theory failed to acknowledge what the peoples of Guatemala and else-where knew from experience: exploitation from imperialism and capitalism. The word "justice" does not appear in Rostow's "The Stages of Economic Growth."[54] The theory denied the historical relationship between poorer and richer countries, and instead looked at each state as if it were hermeneutically sealed in order to determine when it was ready for "take-off." Modernization theory was thus compatible with authoritarian governance by drawing on a paternalist and racist rhetoric that categorized non-whites as children, needing a firm strongman to maintain order.[55] And the grinding poverty and cycles of violent political unrest undergirded American perceptions that nations of the Third World/Global South needed guidance by the "advanced" nations.

The continued poverty and "instability" persist as a legacy of colonialism, but in ways that appeared to reaffirm the notions of the western and/or wealthy, industrial powers that the decolonized are not yet ready for self-rule. In *The Wretched of the Earth*, Frantz Fanon explained that intractable problems ensue after the achievement of state independence because the native leadership ended up reinforcing existing hierarchies, sans the top colonialist layer. Natives (often interracial *mestizos*), who were given a slightly privileged place in the colonial order, were the technicians, the teachers, the clerks, and the other low to middling functionaries that made the colony run smoothly. They lacked the education, training, and most certainly the capital resources to run a successful business enterprise—especially a new one based on a more equitable model. They therefore simply repeated or tried to reproduce the same productive models from the colonial days, and thus failed to diversify the economy, going by what had always worked in their experience. Moreover, the new nation was now shut out from the reliable, if dependent and peripheral, position in the colonial power's economic system.[56] Some, like Haiti, were impoverished by having to pay an indemnity at gunpoint to its former colonial overlords for the losses they incurred with Haitian independence. Haitian scholar Alex Dupuy has pointed out that, as a result of colonialism's social and economic relations and structures, the new Haitian elites were thus unable to maintain the plantation system, much less create an industrial infrastructure. Moreover, the ruling elites were not a homogeneous monolith, but fragmented groups, constantly in competition, creating and perpetuating instability and authoritarian rule.[57]

Because most American policymakers have not been fully cognizant of the deep historical—and man-made—roots of such poverty and cycles of violence, they have not trusted the colonized or decolonized to handle liberalism, either economic or political. American leaders, and most American citizens, believe that economic liberalism (the capitalist system) best fostered political liberalism (democracy), and vice versa. The tricky question has always been: which one should come first? Lack of confidence in the colonized/recently decolonized non-white peoples—and a healthy dose of vested material interests—has meant that US policy almost invariably supports efforts to ensure that economic liberalism is fostered and maintained, oftentimes at the expense of political liberalism. And the rationale to prioritize economic liberalism over political liberalism has posited the former as a necessary developmental step: economic liberalism (or "free trade," or "globalization") will bring investment; investments will create jobs; the jobs will make the people industrious and create a strong civic society; the existence of a strong civic society will lay the foundation for democracy. But forgotten or neglected in this logical scheme is that nothing requires these jobs to be good jobs, with worker safety, good wages, and worker benefits—elements all necessary for a strong civic society by creating a sizeable and prosperous middle class. Moreover, as we know, efforts to make the jobs into good jobs were and continue to be brutally suppressed.[58] Therefore, an essential link from capital investment to democracy has often been missing. As workers of the Global South have been telling us, democracy is needed first to ensure democracy and the establishment of democratic institutions. We in the Global North cannot seem to hear this message sufficiently, if at all.

This essay has argued that ideological narratives, including nationalist founding myths, must be considered in order to understand the worldviews that guided and continue to guide policy. This belief that America still serves as a beacon to the world is manifest in the inaugural address of President Barack Obama:

> And so, to all other peoples and governments who are watching today, from the grandest capitals to the small village where my father was born: know that America is a friend of each nation and every man, woman and child who seeks a future of peace and dignity, and we are ready to lead once more.[59]

Obama's address is a paean to American exceptionalism. The theme of "only in America" resounded in Obama's addresses and in media commentaries leading up to the election and inauguration.[60] To the surprise of country music fans who recalled George W. Bush using the same song in 2004, Obama chose Brooks and Dunn's song, "Only in America" to close his DNC nomination acceptance speech.[61] For a presidential nominee committed to uniting a "blue and red America"—and trying to get elected—this strategy made sense. As the new president, however, he spoke to the wider, global audience and said: "To the people of poor nations, we pledge to work alongside you to make your farms flourish and let clean waters flow; to nourish starved bodies and feed hungry minds."[62]

Every president since Truman has made a similar commitment. Some may argue that certain administrations were more sincere in this commitment than others. As Williams recognized, the impulse to help others spoke to a generosity among Americans, though this quality has hardly been exclusive to Americans. What has been unique is the global reach or hegemonic power of the United States. There have always been dissidents and moments of greater dissidence. Yet the majority of Americans have tended to see their hegemony as benevolent. It is a conviction that comes from an exceptionalist ideology about the nation's historic mission in the world. And it helps to explain how US policymakers and pundits can moralize and dictate to poorer countries to embrace free trade when the United States and Europe have more protectionist measures on their agricultural products than the entire Global South combined.[63]

After 9/11, Americans became more aware of a global current of hostility directed toward them. Uninformed of cold war history, many remain confused as to why this might be so. Or perhaps informed by a cold war history that focuses largely on the struggle with the Soviet Union, they forget the violence unleashed during this period on the peoples of the poorer and poorest nations on earth. And they do not understand the patterns of colonialism predating the cold war that created the "Third World." To be sure, some Americans are quite aware and critical of the US foreign policies that propel the current grievances.[64] Yet many Americans persist in thinking otherwise—that it might be "a clash of civilizations" or perhaps something intrinsic to the United States. Obama reinforced this stance by pronouncing also at his inaugural address: "We will not apologize for our way of life nor will we waver in its defense." Saying that the United States will be steadfast in defending the "American way of life"—a familiar phrase from the Cold

War—continues to deflect attention from actual US policies in the world. What's best for America or, more accurately, for some Americans, has not been what's best for most people in America or the world. Most Americans do not know this or, perhaps, do not want to know this. It does not fit the stories we have been telling about ourselves.

## Notes

1. Many thanks to Richard H. Immerman, Petra Goedde, Cindy Franklin, and Michael Sherry for their extraordinary patience, sharp insights, and last minute interventions. All errors and faults are mine, of course.

2. Michael H. Hunt, *Ideology and US Foreign Policy* (New Haven: Yale University Press, 1987), xi.

3. James W. Cook and Lawrence B. Glickman, "Twelve Propositions for a History of US Cultural History," in James W. Cook, Lawrence B. Glickman, and Michael O'Malley, eds., *The Cultural Turn in US History: Past, Present, and Future* (Chicago: University of Chicago Press, 2008), 3–57.

4. Cook and Glickman, "Twelve Propositions," 12. Cook and Glickman helpfully point out six broad definitions of culture that, in addition to the anthropological sense, cultural historians have used, sometimes in combination. The other five: (1) artistic expression; (2) the larger matrix of commercial institutions and structures in which artistic forms are produced and consumed; (3) any social or institutional sphere in which collective forms of meaning are made, enforced, and contested; (4) a semiotic or discursive system; and (5) transnational or global circulation. See pp. 10–14.

5. Rather than see cultures as "internally coherent units, different and irreconcilable with each other," as Margaret Mead, Ruth Benedict, and others once did, since the 1980s the majority of anthropologists understand culture "as being perpetually in process, shaped by human interactions and societal interactions." Keith Brown, "Samuel Huntington, Meet the Nuer," in Catherine Besteman and Hugh Gusterson, eds., *Why America's Top Pundits are Wrong: Anthropologists Talk Back* (Berkeley: University of California Press, 2005), 44.

6. Akira Iriye, "Culture and International History," in Michael J. Hogan and Thomas G. Paterson, *Explaining the History of American Foreign Relations*, 2nd ed. (Cambridge: Cambridge University Press, 2004), 243–4. See also: Akira Iriye, *Across the Pacific; an Inner History of American-East Asian Relations* (New York: Harcourt, Brace & World, 1967); Akira Iriye, *Power and Culture: The Japanese-American War, 1941–1945* (Cambridge, MA: Harvard University Press, 1981).

7. To ask this question is not suggesting that only people with the same ethnic, racial, or social status can study each other. Instead, it asks scholars to pay attention to their presumptions about their subjects and requires them to be self-consciously aware of the intimate connection between knowledge and power. Gayatri Chakravorty Spivak, "Can the Subaltern Speak?: Speculations on Widow Sacrifice," *Wedge* 7/8 (Winter/Spring 1985): 120–30.

8. Edward W. Said, *Orientalism*, 1st ed. (New York: Pantheon Books, 1978).

9. "Afterword," in *Orientalism* (1978 reprint, New York: Vintage, 1994), 348–52. See also: Said, *Representations of the Intellectual: The 1993 Reith Lectures* (New York: Pantheon, 1994).

10. Samir Amin, *The Liberal Virus: Permanent War and the Americanization of the World* (New York: Monthly Review Press, 2004), especially pp. 19–20. See also: David Harvey, *The*

*Condition of Postmodernity: An Enquiry into the Origins of Cultural Change* (Cambridge, MA: Wiley-Blackwell, 1989).

11. Odd Arne Westad, *The Global Cold War: Third World Interventions and the Making of Our Times* (Cambridge: Cambridge University Press, 2005).

12. Teun A. van Dijk, *Ideology: A Multidisciplinary Approach* (London: Sage, 1998), 1–2.

13. See the works of the anthropologists cited above and the works of cognitive linguist George Lakoff: with Mark Johnson, *Metaphors We Live By* (Chicago: University of Chicago Press, 1980) and *Moral Politics: How Liberals and Conservatives Think*, 2nd ed. (Chicago: University of Chicago Press, 2002).

14. Hunt, *Ideology*, xi; Michael E. Latham, *Modernization as Ideology: American Social Science and "Nation Building" in the Kennedy Era* (Chapel Hill, NC: University of North Carolina Press, 2000). See also: David C. Engerman, Nils Gilman, Mark H. Haefele, and Michael E. Latham, eds., *Staging Growth: Modernization, Development, and the Global Cold War* (Amherst, MA: University of Massachusetts Press, 2003); David C. Engerman, *Modernization from the Other Shore: American Intellectuals and the Romance of Russian Development* (Cambridge, MA: Harvard University Press, 2003); Nils Gilman, *Mandarins of the Future: Modernization Theory in Cold War America* (Baltimore: Johns Hopkins University Press, 2007); David Ekbladh, *The Great American Mission: Modernization and the Construction of an American World Order* (Princeton, NJ: Princeton University Press, 2009).

15. What Gramcsi called "cultural hegemony" is not equivalent to political scientist Joseph Nye's notion of "soft power." As Randolph B. Persaud has pointed out, "soft power" is a purely utilitarian tool—as if cultural hegemonic power is "something done to others, out there in the wider world," rather than an ongoing process that describes the way the United States or any state functions. Nye's advocacy of "soft power" is a strategy for those who want to rally, maintain, and even further American power abroad. Randolph B. Persaud, "Shades of American Hegemony: The Primitive, the Enlightened, and the Benevolent," *Connecticut Journal of International Law* (Spring 2004): 268–70.

16. For example, feminists and women's rights advocates pushed the discourse such that it is now "common sense" that women are capable of more responsibilities and skills than in the past.

17. Susan Smulyan, *Popular Ideologies: Mass Culture at Mid-Century* (Philadelphia: University of Pennsylvania Press, 2007), 13–14.

18. cf., David C. Engerman, ed., "Special Forum: Modernization as a Global Project," *Diplomatic History* 23:3 (June 2009).

19. David Ekbladh, H-Diplo Article Review on "Special Forum: Modernization as a Global Project," *Diplomatic History* 23:3 (June 2009), No. 238-A, July 29, 2009, accessed at <http://www.h-net.org/~diplo/reviews/PDF/AR238-A.pdf>; Nils Gilman, H-Diplo Article review, No. 238-B, accessed at <http://www.h-net.org/~diplo/reviews/PDF/AR238-B.pdf>.

20. See the argument in Kevin Hoskins' "The Wages of Empire: Working-Class Americans, 'Cuba Libre,' and US Imperialism" (Ph.D. diss., Brown University, 2012).

21. Jürgen Habermas, "Modernity: an Unfinished Project," in Maurizio Passerin d'Entrèves and Seyla Benhabib, eds., *Habermas and the Unfinished Project of Modernity* (Cambridge, MA: MIT Press, 1997), 39, 45.

22. Habermas credits Hegel (1770–1830) as being "the first philosopher to develop a clear concept of modernity." In contrast, Walter D. Mignolo insists that Hegel "was a regional historian who presented his work as universal history" that "became identified with modernity

and with European Enlightenment." Jürgen Habermas, *The Philosophical Discourse of Modernity* (Cambridge, MA: MIT Press, 1996), 5; Walter D. Mignolo, *The Darker Side of the Renaissance: Literacy, Territoriality, & Colonization*, 2nd ed. (Ann Arbor, MI: University of Michigan Press, 2003), 427–8.

23. Antonio Barrera-Osorio, *Experiencing Nature: The Spanish American Empire and The Early Scientific Revolution* (Austin, TX: University of Texas Press, 2006).

24. Scholars of Spanish America find that they must challenge a northern European bias in English-language historiography. See Jorge Cañizares-Esguerra, *Puritan Conquistadors: Iberianizing the Atlantic, 1550–1700* (Palo Alto, CA: Stanford University Press, 2006); Walter D. Mignolo, "Coloniality of Power and Subalternity," in Ileana Rodríguez, ed., *The Latin American Subaltern Studies Reader* (Durham, NC: Duke University Press, 2001), 432; Immanuel Wallerstein and Anibal Quijano's "Americanity as a Concept, or the Americas in the Modern World-System," *International Social Science Journal* 44 (1992), 549–57.

25. See also: Jorge Cañizares-Esguerra, *Nature, Empire, And Nation: Explorations of the History of Science in the Iberian World* (Palo Alto, CA: Stanford University Press, 2006).

26. Mignolo, *Darker Side of the Renaissance*, ch. 5.

27. Walter D. Mignolo, "The *Enduring* Enchantment: (Or the Epistemic Privilege of Modernity and Where to Go from Here)," *South Atlantic Quarterly* 101:4 (2002): 927–54.

28. George C. Caffentzis, "On the Scottish Origins of 'Civilization'" in Silvia Federici, *Enduring Western Civilization: The Construction of the Concept of Western Civilization and its "Others"* (Westport, CT: Praeger Paperback, 1995), 29.

29. The time/space connection was also foundational to republican ideology, which drew from Enlightenment notions of societies as organic entities with a lifespan. See Drew R. McCoy, *The Elusive Republic: Political Economy in Jeffersonian America* (1980; repr. Chapel Hill, NC: The University of North Carolina Press, 1996).

30. Mignolo, "The *Enduring* Enchantment," 935.

31. Joan W. Scott, "Gender: A Useful Category of Historical Analysis," *American Historical Review* 91, no. 5 (December 1986): 1053–75.

32. See Petra Goedde, *GIs and Germans: Culture, Gender, and Foreign Relations, 1945–1949* (New Haven, CT: Yale University Press, 2003); Naoko Shibusawa, *America's Geisha Ally: Reimagining the Japanese Enemy* (Cambridge, MA: Harvard University Press, 2006); Andrew J. Rotter, *Comrades at Odds: The United States and India, 1947–1964* (Ithaca, NY: Cornell University Press, 2000).

33. For example: Reina Lewis, *Gendering Orientalism: Race, Femininity and Representation* (London: Routledge, 1995); Meyda Yegenoglu, *Colonial Fantasies: Towards a Feminist Reading of Orientalism* (Cambridge: Cambridge University Press, 1998); Mari Yoshihara, *Embracing the East: White Women and American Orientalism* (New York: Oxford University Press, 2002); Rana Kabbani, *Imperial Fictions: Europe's Myths of Orient* (London: Saqi Books, 2008); Mary Roberts, *Intimate Outsiders: The Harem in Ottoman and Orientalist Art and Travel Literature* (Durham, NC: Duke University Press, 2008).

34. Kristin L. Hoganson, *Fighting for American Manhood: How Gender Politics Provoked the Spanish-American and Philippine-American War* (New Haven, CT: Yale University Press, 1998); Robert D. Dean, *Imperial Brotherhood: Gender and the Making of Cold War Foreign Policy* (Amherst, MA: University of Massachusetts Press, 2001).

35. Álvar Núñez Cabeza De Vaca, *Chronicle of the Narvaez Expedition*, Harold Augenbraum, ed. and Fanny Bandelier, trans. (1542; repr. New York: Penguin Classics, 2002); Katharine H. S. Moon, *Sex Among Allies* (New York: Columbia University Press, 1997); Ji-Yeon Yuh,

*Beyond the Shadow of Camptown: Korean Military Brides in America* (New York: NYU Press, 2004); Dorinne Kondo, *About Face: Performing Race in Fashion and Theater* (New York: Routledge, 1997); Shibusawa, *America's Geisha Ally*.

36. Kelly Shannon, "Veiled Intentions: Islam, Global Feminism, and US Foreign Policy since the late 1970s" (Ph.D. diss., Temple University, 2010).
37. RAWA, the Revolutionary Association of the Women of Afghanistan, a group formed to broadcast the misogynistic abuses of the Taliban, argue that the presence of US forces worsened the safety of Afghani women. See: <http://www.rawa.org/index.php>, accessed March 23, 2010. Iraqi feminist Yanar Mohammed likewise argues that the Obama administration has not improved the dire straits in which Iraqi women find themselves, and that the re-imposition of *sharia* law in Iraq diminished the minimal rights women enjoyed under Saddam. <http://www.democracynow.org/2010/3/19/seven_years_of_war_on_anniversary>, accessed March 29, 2010.
38. See the cartoons from the era of the Philippine-American War collected in Abe Ignacio et al., *The Forbidden Book* (San Francisco, CA: T'Boli, 2004).
39. Quoted in Stuart Creighton Miller, *Benevolent Assimilation: The American Conquest of the Philippines, 1899–1903* (New Haven, CT: Yale University Press, 1984), 134.
40. Shibusawa, *America's Geisha Ally*, ch. 2. Nonetheless, American policymaking elites selectively applied liberal paternalism.
41. Gail Bederman, *Manliness and Civilization: A Cultural History of Gender and Race in the United States, 1880–1917* (Chicago, IL: University of Chicago Press, 1996).
42. I am not discussing the notion of "alternative modernities" because I am not convinced that the western, universalist bias can be eliminated by this concept.
43. For further discussion on religion, see Dianne Kirby's chapter in this volume.
44. For further discussion of western civilization as an ideology, see Federici, *Enduring Western Civilization*.
45. Joyce Appleby, "Recovering America's Historic Diversity: Beyond Exceptionalism," *Journal of American History* 79 (September 1992): 419–31.
46. Shibusawa, *America's Geisha Ally*, quote on p. 90.
47. Bederman, *Manliness & Civilization*.
48. Dean, *Imperial Brotherhood*; Fritz Fischer, *Making Them Like Us: Peace Corps Volunteers in the 1960s* (Washington, DC: Smithsonian Institution Press, 1998).
49. See McCoy, *Elusive Republic*.
50. Westad, *Global Cold War*, 39.
51. W.W. Rostow, *The Stages of Economic Growth: A Non-Communist Manifesto* (Cambridge, IL: Cambridge University Press, 1960).
52. For instance, the two rival powers either supported or attacked, either directly or covertly, the governments of Cuba, Guatemala, Chile, Nicaragua, North or South Vietnam, North or South Korea, South Africa, Ethiopia, Somalia, Iraq, Iran, and Afghanistan. See Westad, *Global Cold War*.
53 Greg Grandin, *The Last Colonial Massacre: Latin America in the Cold War* (Chicago IL: University of Chicago Press, 2004).
54. W.W. Rostow, "The Stages of Economic Growth," *The Economic History Review* 12:1 (1959): 1–16.
55. David F Schmitz, *Thank God They're on Our Side: The United States and Right-Wing Dictatorships, 1921–1965* (Chapel Hill, NC: University of North Carolina Press, 1999); Schmitz, *The United States and Right-Wing Dictatorships, 1965–1989* (Cambridge: Cambridge University Press, 2006).

56. Frantz Fanon, *The Wretched of the Earth*, trans. by Richard Philcox (1961 repr.; New York: Grove Press, 2005), 97–144.
57. Alex Dupuy, *Haiti in The World Economy: Class, Race, and Underdevelopment since 1700* (Boulder, CO: Westview Press, 1989).
58. Aviva Chomsky, *Linked Labor Histories: New England, Colombia, and the Making of a Global Working Class* (Durham, NC: Duke University Press, 2008). For instance, in 2008, seventy-six trade unionists were murdered worldwide, with forty-nine in Colombia alone. Gustavo Capdevila, "Labor: Colombia Still Leads in Trade Unionist Murders," Inter Press Service/Global Information Network (IPS/GIN) wire, June 10, 2009, found at: <http://www.globalinfo.org/eng/reader.asp?ArticleId=65408>, accessed June 22, 2009.
59. "Barack Obama's Inaugural Address," *New York Times*, January 20, 2009, sec. US/Politics, <http://www.nytimes.com/2009/01/20/us/politics/20text-obama.html>, accessed June 22, 2009.
60. During his speech on race given on March 18, 2008, Obama asserted that "in no other country on Earth is my story even possible." The text of the speech can be found at: <http://www.msnbc.msn.com/id/23690567/>, accessed June 22, 2009. David Berreby reminds us, however, that other nations have elected heads of state from "stigmatized ethnic minorities or 'foreign' enclaves," including: Britain, Peru, India, and Kenya. Berreby, "Only in America? The wrongheaded American belief that Barack Obama could only happen here," *Slate Magazine*, posted November 17, 2008, <http://www.slate.com/id/2204822/>, accessed June 22, 2009.
61. "Obama Uses Brooks & Dunn's 'Only in America' to Close Convention Speech | CMT Blog," posted August 28, 2008, <http://blog.cmt.com/2008-08-29/obama-uses-brooks-dunns-only-in-america-to-close-convention-speech/>, accessed June 22, 2009.
62. Obama inaugural address.
63. Persaud, "Shades of American Hegemony," 273. See also: Ha-Joon Chang, *Bad Samaritans: The Myth of Free Trade and the Secret History of Capitalism* (London: Bloomsbury Press, 2007).
64. For instance, see Mahmood Mamdani, *Good Muslim, Bad Muslim: America, the Cold War, and the Roots of Terror* (New York: Pantheon Books, 2004). Even Osama bin Laden cited US policies—support for "Israeli tanks in Palestine," the World War II bombing of Japan, and economic sanctions on Iraq that starved millions of children. See Osama bin Laden, "Speech on September 11 Attacks," October 7, 2001, reprinted in Joanne Meyerowitz, ed., *History and September 11th: Critical Perspectives on the Past* (Philadelphia, PA: Temple University Press, 2003), 244–5.

## Select Bibliography

Appleby, Joyce. "Recovering America's Historic Diversity: Beyond Exceptionalism," *Journal of American History* 79 (September 1992): 419–31.

Barrera-Osorio, Antonio. *Experiencing Nature: The Spanish American Empire and the Early Scientific Revolution*. Austin, TX: University of Texas Press, 2006.

Bederman, Gail. *Manliness and Civilization: A Cultural History of Gender and Race in the United States, 1880–1917*. Chicago: University of Chicago Press, 1996.

Chomsky, Aviva. *Linked Labor Histories: New England, Colombia, and the Making of a Global Working Class*. Durham, NC: Duke University Press, 2008.

Cook, James W. and Lawrence B. Glickman and Michael O'Malley, eds. *The Cultural Turn in US History: Past, Present, and Future.* Chicago, IL: University of Chicago Press, 2008.

Dupuy, Alex. *Haiti in The World Economy: Class, Race, and Underdevelopment since 1700.* Boulder, CO: Westview Press, 1989.

Engerman, David C. and Nils Gilman, Mark H. Haefele, and Michael E. Latham, eds. *Staging Growth: Modernization, Development, and the Global Cold War.* Amherst, MA: University of Massachusetts Press, 2003.

Fanon, Frantz. *The Wretched of the Earth,* trans. by Richard Philcox. 1961; New York: Grove Press, 2005.

Federici, Silvia. *Enduring Western Civilization: The Construction of the Concept of Western Civilization and its "Others."* Westport, CT: Praeger Paperback, 1995.

Habermas, Jürgen. *The Philosophical Discourse of Modernity.* Cambridge, MA: MIT Press, 1996.

Hunt, Michael H. *Ideology and US Foreign Policy.* New Haven, CT: Yale University Press, 1987.

Latham, Michael E. *Modernization as Ideology: American Social Science and "Nation Building" in the Kennedy Era.* Chapel Hill, NC: University of North Carolina Press, 2000.

Mamdani, Mahmood. *Good Muslim, Bad Muslim: America, the Cold War, and the Roots of Terror.* New York: Pantheon Books, 2004.

McCoy, Drew R. *The Elusive Republic: Political Economy in Jeffersonian America.* 1980; Chapel Hill, NC: University of North Carolina Press, 1996.

Mignolo, Walter D. *The Darker Side of the Renaissance: Literacy, Territoriality, & Colonization,* 2nd ed. Ann Arbor, MI: University of Michigan Press, 2003.

Mignolo, Walter D. "The *Enduring* Enchantment: (Or the Epistemic Privilege of Modernity and Where to Go from Here)," *South Atlantic Quarterly* 101:4 (2002): 927–54.

Rostow, W.W. *The Stages of Economic Growth: A Non-Communist Manifesto.* Cambridge: Cambridge University Press, 1960.

Said, Edward W. *Orientalism.* 1978 reprint; New York: Vintage, 1994.

Said, Edward W. *Representations of the Intellectual: The 1993 Reith Lectures.* New York: Pantheon, 1994.

Shibusawa, Naoko. *America's Geisha Ally: Reimagining the Japanese Enemy.* Cambridge, MA: Harvard University Press, 2006.

Smulyan, Susan. *Popular Ideologies: Mass Culture at Mid-Century.* Philadelphia, PA: University of Pennsylvania Press, 2007.

Westad, Odd Arne. *The Global Cold War: Third World Interventions and the Making of Our Times.* Cambridge: Cambridge University Press, 2005.

# CHAPTER 4

# ECONOMICS AND THE COLD WAR

IAN JACKSON

In comparison to the political, diplomatic, and security aspects of post-1945 international relations, the economic factors behind the cold war have received scant treatment in the literature. This is surprising given the centrality of economics in the ideological conflict between Western capitalism and Soviet communism. While economists have analyzed the dynamics of the cold war, their approach has been ahistorical. Yet, there are only a handful of works on economics written by cold war historians. Indeed, at the time of this writing a thorough overview of the economic dimension of the cold war remains to be written.[1] The nature of the subject appears to have proved a major deterrent for historians. To the untrained eye, economic history can be a highly technical, complex, and esoteric discipline. The primary source material, moreover, requires a working knowledge of key macroeconomic concepts and principles.

Exacerbating the problem is the strict division of labor between historians in the writing of the cold war. The orthodox school and the postrevisionists have concentrated on those aspects of the cold war concerned with security and geopolitics, while economics has been the domain of revisionist scholars. There has been little or no dialogue between the two approaches. In fact, as this chapter will elucidate, a more rounded and sophisticated understanding of the cold war can be gleaned from an awareness of the interplay of economics, security, diplomacy, and the other factors that underpinned the East-West confrontation.

This chapter does not purport to offer a definitive survey of economics and the cold war. Rather, it focuses on four themes in the literature, thereby providing a synthesis of current research and suggesting new avenues of scholarly inquiry. The four themes are as follows. First, the chapter provides a brief survey of the historiographic debates on the role of economic factors in the cold war. Second, it explores the nature and scope of the conflict between the rival economic systems of Western capitalism and Soviet communism. Third, the chapter evaluates recent research on the efficacy of the strategic embargo employed by the Western states against the communist nations. Finally, it examines the impact of economic issues on the ending of the cold war.

# HISTORIOGRAPHICAL DEBATES

Historians have long debated the role played by economic factors in the origins, course, and end of the cold war. In the formative accounts of the conflict, written in the 1950s and 1960s, one can discern two divergent perspectives in the literature. The orthodox school was concerned primarily with describing and explaining the response of American officials to the breakdown in relations with the Soviet Union and the ensuing confrontation with Moscow. Orthodox historians, for the most part, largely ignored economic issues in their narratives save for occasional references to the economic and military assistance programs of the Franklin Roosevelt and Harry S. Truman administrations. The focus of this orthodox school was on national security, the international balance of power, and diplomacy.[2] Unlike the orthodox perspective, revisionist scholars placed economic considerations at the center of their analysis. Drawing on the insights developed by Charles A. Beard, they argued that since the late nineteenth century the United States had been engaged in a crusade to achieve global economic dominance. Successive generations of American leaders pursued foreign policies based on the principles of the "Open Door" and economic expansionism. The rapid industrialization and unprecedented growth of the American economy necessitated a strategy designed to seek out new foreign outlets for US goods in order to alleviate domestic short-term economic and political crises created by overproduction and market saturation. As the United States became the most powerful state after the Second World War, this quest for global economic predominance intensified.[3]

In the mid-1980s Michael J. Hogan proposed a corporatist synthesis for understanding US foreign policy during the cold war. Corporatism drew on the research of scholars of American foreign relations in the 1920s and historians concerned with the interaction of functional groups such as organized labor, business, and agriculture in the organization and development of the US economy in the 20th century.[4] Hogan, influenced by the earlier research of Thomas McCormick,[5] argued that postwar American officials were concerned with building a global order along the lines of the corporatist model that had emerged in the United States during the New Deal era. The establishment of the Bretton Woods institutions and the creation of an international trade regime under American leadership not only helped to formalize economic cooperation between nations, but also became integral facets of a global corporatist order.[6] In his notable study of the Marshall Plan, Hogan demonstrates how the United States strove to export the ideas of the New Deal coalition overseas, especially to war-ravaged Western Europe.[7] Critics of corporatism, however, charged that the model could only be applied to specific periods in American history such as the 1920s and could therefore not realize Hogan's ambitions for a comprehensive synthesis for explaining US foreign policy during the cold war.[8] The corporatist approach, moreover, downplayed critical geopolitical security considerations.

Economic factors lie at the heart of Thomas J. McCormick's more recent attempt to explain post-1945 international relations from the perspective of American dominance of the international system.[9] McCormick's modified world systems theory of US foreign relations was inspired by the writings of the eminent sociologist, Immanuel Wallerstein. One can also see the influence of revisionism on McCormick's work, especially that of William Appleman Williams.[10] In short, McCormick's framework for analysis acknowledged the existence of both a global economy governed by the imperatives of the international system and an inter-state system underpinned by nationalist impulses. The chief objective of US hegemony during the cold war, McCormick maintained, was to reduce the underlying tensions of economic internationalism and political nationalism that characterized these two systems after the Second World War.

How did the United States achieve its hegemonic objectives? According to McCormick, hegemony endowed Washington with the twin roles of world banker and global policeman. Containment of the Soviet Union thus provided the rationale, and facilitated winning the support of the American public and Congress, for US intervention in the core and periphery. Perhaps the greatest achievement of American hegemony, in McCormick's eyes, was the integration of West Germany and Japan into the world system. These two potential challengers to US hegemony were, in effect, rendered dependent on Washington for economic assistance, secure access to global resources, and military protection. McCormick judged US hegemony to be successful in the early postwar decades. This was a golden age of capitalism marking the economic revival of Japan and Western Europe.

The long slump beginning in the 1970s, however, precipitated the demise of US hegemony. This was inevitable, McCormick concluded, as Washington began to feel the effects of imperial over-stretch after the Vietnam War. Together with the loss of its competitive edge in world markets to Japan and Western Europe, overspending on military production hastened the economic decline of the United States at home as the government failed to allocate adequate capital expenditure and invest in research and development in the civilian goods sector. By the end of the cold war, Washington was forced to address its declining competitive position and substantially cut back its political and military obligations overseas. Far from being a winner in the cold war, McCormick finds that the United States was a major economic loser.[11] But as a later section in this chapter will illustrate, this evaluation of the end of the cold war has been disputed by historians.

McCormick has made a valuable contribution to cold war historiography. He provided the first truly global analysis of the dynamics of the cold war system and underscored the importance of the economic dimension of foreign policy. McCormick also highlighted the geopolitical tensions created by the accentuation of the economic gap between the rich industrial countries and the poorer less-developed regions of Africa, Asia, and Latin America in his analysis of "core-periphery" relations. In this regard his pioneering research presages recent interest among scholars in the role of globalization and the history of the cold war. The world systems perspective, however, while offering a valuable prism through which to view post-1945 international relations, has tended toward economic reductionism. In other words, the approach has prioritized economic factors at the expense of important diplomatic and security dimensions.

## COMPETING GLOBAL ECONOMIC ORDERS

The cold war economy that emerged after the Second World War consisted of three central features. First, like the East-West political and military confrontation, it pitted two rival economic systems against each other. The two economic systems were radically different in terms of character and design. The Western capitalist order under the leadership of the United States was based on cooperation, compromise, and shared mutual interests. By contrast the Soviets' communist bloc was founded on coercion, control, and dependency. Whereas the Western model sought to create an open, multilateral world economy, the Soviet economic order shunned international trade and foreign investment in favor of a closed, state-controlled autarkic system.

Second, despite combining to defeat Nazi Germany, the Soviet Union and its capitalist allies discontinued their cooperative relationship after the Second World War. While the United States had provided $11 billion to Moscow through its lend-lease program during the war, the Soviet Union was refused further economic assistance after 1945 and subsequently excluded from (although ostensibly invited to join) the Marshall Plan. The resulting division of Europe and partition of Germany led to the outbreak of a political and economic cold war between the former allies.

Third, both the West and the Soviet bloc experienced high levels of economic success during the early postwar decades. Capitalism enjoyed a "golden era" in the 1950s and 1960s; the communist nations registered unprecedented economic growth rates that surpassed those of their counterparts in the West. However, both economic models experienced painful periods of adjustment and decline in the 1970s and 1980s. The West suffered from spiraling levels of inflation together with negative economic growth following the collapse of the postwar international financial arrangements; the Soviet Union and its satellite states encountered an array of shortcomings and inadequacies in the command economy model.[12]

The bedrock on which the Western economic order was built was the Bretton Woods financial system. Conceived in 1944, the Bretton Woods arrangements were designed to produce international financial stability, foster an open, multilateral trade system, and allow governments autonomy to pursue national economic goals such as full employment and social welfarism. They established the International Monetary Fund (IMF) and the International Bank for Reconstruction and Development (IBRD, later renamed the World Bank) as global financial institutions. Given its vast economic and financial power, the United States was to play the titular role in the new monetary and trade arrangements.[13] Currencies were tied to the dollar, which was in turn linked to gold at

$35 an ounce. The United States would act as world banker, enabling countries to redeem gold in return for their excess dollars. Thus, the dollar became the leading medium of exchange, bestowing on Washington the responsibility for ensuring the smooth operation of the international payments system. In essence, this mirrored the security commitment the United States assumed as the leader of the Western alliance over the course of the cold war.[14]

The Bretton Woods system did not become fully operational until the mid-1950s. This was due to the perilous economic state of Western Europe and Japan after the devastation wrought by the Second World War. In the short term the United States was forced to abandon its objective of establishing a multilateral economic system in order to address the pressing problems of its allies.[15] The regional strategy it adopted was two-fold. First, Washington strove to plug the "dollar gap" with Western Europe and Japan. Governments were provided with much needed currency to purchase essential raw materials and manufacturing goods from the United States with a view to stimulating economic recovery and reducing chronic payments deficits. Second, American officials reasoned that the economic rejuvenation of its allies would not only strengthen the capitalist system, but also act to curb Soviet expansion in Europe and Southeast Asia. Western Europe and Japan recovered sufficiently to enable the Bretton Woods system to begin to function in the late 1950s. While the Bretton Woods era only lasted a decade, it produced international financial stability, high levels of domestic growth, and a previously unheralded explosion in global trade.[16]

Just as soon as the Bretton Woods system had begun to function effectively, nevertheless, it began to encounter difficulties. Undoubtedly, the chief problem with the system concerned the role played by the dollar as the linchpin of the international financial arrangements. By the late 1950s the dollar gap had been replaced by a dollar glut. As countries started to run sizable payments surpluses on an annual basis, they sought to diversify their monetary reserves by redeeming gold from the United States in exchange for dollars. American officials began to worry not only about the increasing gold drain, but also about the impact overseas military expenditure and international liabilities were having on the balance of payments position of the United States. The dual challenges of the gold drain and persistent payments deficits were threats to Washington's position as international banker, the dollar as global reserve currency, and ultimately the Western capitalist order. From a position of dominating the world economy in the early postwar period, the United States now found itself hamstrung by the burdens of international financial leadership.[17] Contrary to the arguments advanced by the world systems perspective, the Bretton Woods era demonstrated the limits that the global financial system imposed on American power. Far from exercising hegemony in the world economy in the 1960s, Washington was engaged in fighting a rearguard action to preserve the crumbling edifice of Bretton Woods and maintaining costly American defense commitments overseas.[18]

By the late 1960s the United States was in an economic and security quandary caused by its leadership of the Western capitalist order. While allies dependent on American military assistance in the struggle against global communism, Western Europe and

Japan became economic rivals of the United States in the 1970s and 1980s. Recognizing the shift in economic power in the world economy, President Richard Nixon ended the Bretton Woods arrangements by devaluing the dollar and closing the gold window in August 1971. This action liberated the United States from its financial obligations and paved the way for an international monetary order which allowed currencies to float freely against each other. [19]

By contrast the Soviet-led communist economic order evolved in a more piecemeal fashion. As noted above, the Marshall Plan was pivotal in dividing Europe and triggering the ensuing conflict between East and West. Stalin refused to participate in the program and compelled Poland and Czechoslovakia to withdraw from negotiations with the United States regarding economic assistance. The Soviet Union signed a number of bilateral barter agreements with its neighbors and extracted war reparations from Hungary and Romania. During 1945–6 the barter agreements yielded the Soviet Union raw materials, equipment, and heavy machinery to the value of $15–20 billion over the course of a decade.[20] Along with the deep penetration and exploitation of the Eastern European economies, Stalin wanted to consolidate his dominance over the region by creating a ring of satellite states that would act as a defensive buffer against encirclement by the Western capitalist states. Over the course of the cold war, the Soviet Union confined its international economic activity to its Eastern European sphere of influence. In response to the American-led campaign to restrict East-West trade, Moscow sought to build commercial bridges in the developing world. As the cold war thawed in the 1960s and 1970s, the Kremlin also engaged in trade with several Western nations. Frustrated by the East-West trade embargo and anxious to avail themselves of Eastern European markets, West Germany and the Scandinavian countries initiated lucrative commercial contacts with the Warsaw Pact membership.[21]

The command economy model, which had first been instituted in the Soviet Union in the 1920s, was geared toward heavy industrialization and military production. Eschewing free enterprise and the private sector, the command economy model empowered the state to organize, manage, and direct economic activity. Central bureaucracies staffed by state officials under the direction of the Communist Party allocated resources, and labor, and operated the key economic and financial sectors of the economy including banking, trade, and transport. The central bureaucracy was divided into a number of distinct departments each responsible for the regulation of an aspect of the economy. Each ministry, moreover, was responsible for setting and achieving the growth targets set out in the national five year plans, monitoring the development of industries within the sector and allotting sufficient resources and labor for realizing the objectives of the broader national plan.

During the cold war the Soviet Union devoted the bulk of its resources and labor to the goals of rapid industrialization and conventional and nuclear military production at the expense of agriculture and civilian goods. Stalin and his successors perceived themselves to be in an ideological conflict with the capitalist states and strove to record higher growth rates than their counterparts in the West and defeat the United States in the nuclear arms race. The Eastern European satellite states specialized in different sectors of industrial production such as iron, steel, chemicals, and electronics. In each case they were contributing primarily to the development of the Soviet war machine.[22]

Initially, the Soviet command economy yielded spectacular growth rates. It has been estimated that by 1970 the Soviet bloc was responsible for 30 percent of total world industrial output. Most strikingly, the Soviet Union and its Eastern European allies achieved growth rates that were not only comparable with those of the West but in many instances surpassed the levels of the capitalist nations.[23] The Soviet economic model, nonetheless, had within it the seeds of its own destruction. By the 1970s the exclusive concentration on heavy industry and preoccupation with the superpower arms race had taken its toll on the centrally-planned economies. With military expenditure in the region of 15 percent of GNP (gross national product), the industrial, manufacturing, and agricultural sectors were critically short of investment.[24] Agriculture was the hardest hit and suffered a precipitous decline across the region. Inefficient state farms were unable to produce the high levels of production required by the central bureaucracies to feed the population. Shortages were also evident in the consumer and civilian goods sector.[25] Although the Soviet Union had achieved nuclear parity with the United States by the early 1970s, it was apparent that this effort had put a heavy strain on the Soviet economy. The relaxation of cold war tensions as a result of détente between the superpowers promised a greater liberalization of East-West trade and a potential lifeline for the Soviet economic model. East-West trade, however, merely highlighted the deficiencies of the command economy model, as Soviet bloc countries became reliant on borrowing from Western banks and their imports failed to keep pace with exports. High indebtedness and debilitating trade deficits had the effect of stalling the growth of the Eastern European economics in the late 1970s.[26]

While the cold war era was dominated by the East-West rivalry, a substantial number of "Third World" or developing countries pursued an alternative economic model. This third way approach encompassed political non-alignment and economic self-sufficiency.[27] Eschewing both Western capitalism and the Soviet command model, nations from Latin America, post-colonial Africa, and Asia erected barriers to trade and closed their economies to foreign capital and investment. Inspired by import-substituting industrialization first practiced in Latin America in the 1930s, developing countries concentrated their resources on the creation of indigenous industries producing goods for the home market, nurtured by state subsidies and protected from the vagaries of international trade.[28] In the short term this approach proved successful, and many developing countries recorded impressive economic growth rates, witnessed a noticeable improvement in living standards, and experienced rapid industrialization. As Jeffrey Frieden has written, "import substitution appeared a successful economic concomitant to national political independence" for the Third World.[29]

Economic success, however, was short-lived. Almost as soon as developing world economies prospered, the inherent flaws in the import-substituting industrialization model became apparent.[30] Plagued by persistent balance-of-payments deficits, budget shortfalls, and spiraling inflation, the more developing world countries industrialized, the more they became reliant on imports. Far from eliminating the need for foreign trade, Third World countries were forced to buy essential imports of raw materials and machinery which their national economies could not produce. In order to pay for these imports they needed to increase exports. Although some finance was made available through loans from the IBRD and foreign aid, the developing world governments did not have an adequate supply of hard currency to pay for imports. Consequently, their economies lurched from one financial crisis to another. Astronomical inflation made goods and basic foodstuffs highly expensive, depressing living standards and resulting in debilitating poverty for millions of people. Despite economic autarky, the Third World was not immune from the effect of the global recession and oil shocks that engulfed the capitalist world in the 1970s. Although a handful of newly industrializing countries (NICs) in Southeast Asia were able to survive through export-orientated strategies, the majority of the developing world suffered as the North-South economic divide widened. There was an attempt to extract concessions from the West in the form of a G-77 of Third World nations manifesto demanding technology transfer, financial aid, and industrial market access.[31] These requests, however, fell on deaf ears. Together with the East-West strategic competition, the latter decades of the cold war were defined by a North-South conflict with an economic impact more devastating and far-reaching than that of the superpower confrontation. Neither the United States nor the Soviet Union would win the battle for the hearts and minds of the Third World.

## THE ECONOMIC COLD WAR

Having considered the structures of the Western and Soviet-led economic orders, this section examines the interaction between the two blocs during the cold war. Because the issue of economic warfare is discussed in a subsequent chapter in this volume, only a short summary of recent scholarship outlining pertinent themes in the literature is presented here.

From the outset, there was general consensus within the Western alliance that the restriction of strategic exports to the Soviet Union was desirable from the standpoint of the cold war.[32] Both the United States and its allies believed that a strategic embargo would help to maintain Western military superiority over the Soviet Union and delay Moscow's program of military production. The Western Europeans, however, clashed with Washington over the contents of the strategic embargo. They wanted the international export control lists administered by the East-West trade group, CG-COCOM, to be limited solely to goods of strategic value. The United States, on the other hand, understood strategic goods to include items of potential "dual purpose" value to the Soviet bloc. Dual-purpose goods could be used both in civilian and military production. The European objection to the control of dual-purpose goods rested squarely on the conviction that for the purposes of economic recovery Western Europe needed access to Eastern European markets for raw materials and foodstuffs.

The literature on COCOM has underscored the important role played by the Western European governments in moderating American economic defense objectives. From the inception of the strategic embargo, Britain in particular was keen to limit the scope of the export control program to items of a strictly military nature. While supporting the strategic aims of the embargo, London steadfastly opposed restrictions on civilian trade with Eastern Europe throughout the 1940s and 1950s. As the cold war appeared to thaw in the early 1950s, Prime Minister Winston Churchill stepped up the campaign for the liberalization of commercial East-West trade and collaborated with President Dwight D. Eisenhower to push through a wholesale revision of the international export control lists in August 1954. The August 1954 revisions removed from the lists many of the dual-purpose items that had been a major bone of contention between the United States and its allies. For many of the Western European governments, however, this radical over-haul of the strategic embargo was unsatisfactory, and COCOM remained a source of friction in the Western alliance for the remainder of the cold war.[33]

The Western allies were at even greater odds over trade with the People's Republic of China (PRC). In tandem with COCOM, a multilateral body known informally as CHINCOM had been formed in the early 1950s to monitor and restrict strategic exports to the PRC. The CHINCOM lists imposed a much more stringent embargo than those of COCOM. The so-called "China differential" proved an intractable source of tension between the allies, especially after the August 1954 revisions of the COCOM lists. It was not until November 1957 that European and Japanese will prevailed in CHINCOM. Prodded by Parliament and domestic business groups, Prime Minister Macmillan uni-laterally declared that his government would no longer recognize the China differential. Following Macmillan's lead the other Western European governments and Japan fol-lowed suit, forcing the United States to agree to an amalgamation of the COCOM and CHINCOM international export control lists.[34]

How did the Soviet Union respond to COCOM? It is evident that the strategic embargo did not have the effect hoped for by the United States. While it is difficult to estimate the real impact of the export control program on the Soviet economy, the embargo did succeed to a certain extent in delaying the Kremlin's access to high technol-ogy and strategic goods. By the late 1960s the Soviet leadership had become concerned about the huge gap that was developing between Moscow and its cold war adversaries. An expansion of East-West trade, they believed, would enable Moscow to procure advanced technology and consumer goods necessary to alleviate bottlenecks in the Soviet economy. The Kremlin's peaceful overtures were received positively in Washington as the United States grappled with the challenges posed by American eco-nomic decline and the diffusion of power across the globe.[35]

In return for trade, however, Washington sought political concessions from Moscow. The deterioration in the American trade position in 1971 alerted the Commerce Department to the benefits that could be derived from opening new markets in the East. More compelling in President Nixon's view was a signal from Moscow that General Secretary Leonid Brezhnev would take part in a summit to discuss relations between the two superpowers. Although the centerpiece of the Summit, which occurred in May

1972, was the Strategic Arms Limitation Talks (SALT) agreement, the two leaders indicated that they would be prepared to explore trade contact in the spirit of détente. On October 18, the two countries signed a historic trade treaty that conferred most-favored-nation (MNF) status on the Soviet Union and committed Washington and Moscow to $2.5 billion worth of bilateral trade.[36] But no sooner had the Nixon and Brezhnev governments secured a new American-Soviet commercial relationship than it came under fire from critics of détente in the US Congress. The (Henry) Jackson-(Charles) Vanik amendment to the Trade Reform Bill 1974, which placed stringent political conditions on the Soviet Union in return for trade, was to sound the death knell for the American-Soviet economic détente. Unwilling to be dictated to by the American legislature, in January 1975 Brezhnev announced that the Soviet Union was abrogating the 1972 trade agreement.[37]

# ECONOMIC ISSUES AND THE END OF THE COLD WAR

There remains a dearth of declassified primary sources conducive to arriving at confident judgments about the factors leading to the demise of the cold war. So far the literature has centered on two lines of inquiry. First, it has been argued that enlightened policies implemented by the West, and especially the United States, forced the Soviet leadership to negotiate an end to the nuclear arms race. Given that the Soviet economy was on the verge of collapse, the Kremlin had no alternative but to seek a permanent truce in the confrontation with the West. The second perspective contends that American policies during the Reagan administration of the 1980s were costly, misguided, and ultimately prolonged the life of the cold war. This hard-line approach diverged sharply from that of its allies and the Soviet Union under the leadership of Mikhail Gorbachev. Gorbachev perceived a future in which Soviet communism could coexist peacefully with capitalism and enjoy the fruits of commercial exchange within an integrated world economy.

For some historians Ronald Reagan was responsible for winning the cold war. In seeking to show the influence of President Reagan's economic defense policies within the overall strategy of defeating the Soviet Union, they argue that the Reagan administration's decision to pursue economic warfare against Moscow brought the Soviet economy to the verge of collapse and compelled the Kremlin to seek negotiations with a view to halting the superpower arms race. Such commentators focus particularly on Washington's adoption in 1981 of a two-pronged economic warfare strategy. First, the United States restricted the Soviet Union's access to hard currency, particularly with respect to its earnings from natural gas. Second, the Reagan administration resumed the comprehensive export control program in COCOM that had been substantially reduced during the 1960s and 1970s. The embargo would specifically target items with a high technology component and raw materials in critically short supply in the Soviet Union. The export prohibitions were also extended to bank credits, which would now be subject to high interest repayments.

The economic warfare strategy was essentially guided by two National Security Decision Directives (NSDD). NSDD 54, signed by President Reagan in September 1982, had as its central goal to break the dependence of Eastern Europe on Moscow and encouraged the splintering of the Soviet bloc through financial, commercial, and diplomatic instruments. NSSD 66 was even more ambitious. Authorized by Reagan in November 1982, this directive provided for more than a strategic embargo on East-West trade. It committed the United States, with the assistance of its allies, to identify economic vulnerabilities and undermine the industrial capacity of the Soviet Union. This was to be achieved through an extensive embargo on critical technologies and equipment, the cancellation of contracts to purchase Soviet natural gas, and wide-ranging restrictions on the provision of government credits to Moscow.[38]

It is debatable whether the Reagan administration's policies amounted to economic warfare against the Soviet Union. Neither the president nor the more moderate officials in the State Department ever spoke publicly about economic warfare. Further, the influence of the hard-line faction on Reagan peaked in 1982, and tapered off as George Shultz succeeded Alexander Haig as secretary of state and began to assert his authority over foreign policy. A critic of economic sanctions, Shultz strongly believed that the COCOM embargo was more a source of disunity in the Western alliance than an effective strategic weapon against the Soviet Union.[39]

Another problem for the historian in determining the effectiveness of the Reagan economic defense strategy is quantitative. Since American-Soviet trade was minimal, it is difficult to discern the extent to which export controls on technology and equipment helped to undermine the Soviet economy. Moscow had achieved high levels of economic growth and managed to achieve parity with the United States during the period in which COCOM had been founded and Washington had operated a strategic embargo on East-West trade. During 1981–3, furthermore, the Reagan administration failed to rally multilateral support behind a campaign of economic warfare against the Soviet Union. The Western European governments refused to consider American proposals for a substantial increase in export controls on East-West trade. They stood firm against American demands for significant extensions to the COCOM lists in exchange for assurances that a $10 billion pipeline project they had previously negotiated with the Soviet Union would not be subject to the embargo. Although Reagan imposed sanctions against the subsidiaries of American corporations in Europe in response to this defiance in July 1982, his more moderate advisors prevailed upon him to remove these punitive measures the following November.[40]

Another more convincing explanation for the end of the cold war focuses on developments in the Soviet Union. Despite high growth rates in the 1950s and 1960s, the Soviet economy experienced a difficult period of stagnation and decline in the 1970s. In fact, by the early 1980s the Soviet economy was growing at a feeble rate of less than 2 percent. Expenditure on military outlays reached 20 percent of GNP and Soviet troops were embroiled in an intractable war in Afghanistan. In March 1985 Gorbachev came to power with radically new ideas on how to deal with these problems. He realized that Moscow could not expect to sustain the arms race with the United States without grave consequences for the future sustainability of the Soviet economy. Gorbachev, therefore, believed that the two superpowers should begin negotiations toward an arms control regime. The Soviet leader was also anxious to dissuade Reagan from embarking on the Strategic Defense Initiative (SDI) as this would force the Kremlin to devote more of its limited financial resources to building an equivalent defense system. Gorbachev, moreover, was convinced that the liberalization of East-West trade would be a panacea for the Soviet Union's economic ills. Diplomatic engagement with the West, he hoped, might yield technologies in critically short supply in the Soviet Union as well as bank credits to enable Moscow to purchase essential manufacturers and consumer goods from the capitalist states.[41]

Together with his ambitious foreign policy objectives, Gorbachev embarked on far-reaching internal reforms in the Soviet Union's political system and economy. In an unprecedented departure from his successors, Gorbachev introduced a policy of glasnost. While stopping well short of establishing a democratic, liberal polity, Gorbachev's reforms partially opened Soviet society by making government more accountable and less corrupt. It was in the realm of political economy, nevertheless, that Gorbachev made a lasting mark. Although he did not want to dispense with the command economy model, Gorbachev concluded that the future economic success of the Soviet Union lay with full integration into the world economy. Thus, his restructuring program, perestroika, revolved around trying to make domestic industries more competitive with their counterparts in the West and preparing the Soviet economy for international trade and, he hoped, export-led growth.

Ironically, Gorbachev's valiant efforts to modernize the economy may have hastened Soviet economic decline. Undeniably, the internal contradictions of the command economy model inhibited the Soviet economy's efforts to adapt to the harsh realities of world trade. As Western states enthusiastically welcomed greater access to Soviet markets, they were rather more reluctant to purchase what they considered the inferior products of the Eastern bloc countries. The net effect was to turn the terms of trade against Moscow, increasing domestic economic malaise and increasing the levels of hardship experienced by the Soviet people.[42] Unwavering in its faith in the command economy model, the Soviet leadership shunned the palpable benefits of trade and foreign capital that economic globalization yielded to the Western nations in the 1960s and 1970s. By refusing to open the economy to international trade and investment, Moscow only succeeded in further isolating the Soviet Union and accelerating the country's economic decline. Keenly aware of the fruits to be derived from economic interdependence, the Eastern European countries began to seek greater engagement with the West and disengagement from the Soviet orbit. Since the late 1970s relations between the Soviet Union and its satellites had deteriorated. The Eastern European governments vehemently opposed the bellicose nature of Soviet Union in its foreign policy and resented Moscow's demands for a 5 percent increase in their military budgets. As their economies began to falter, the Eastern

Europeans looked to open new commercial contacts and sign trade deals with Western Europe.[43]

The contribution of the United States to the final winding down of the cold war should not be underestimated. By the time Gorbachev had assumed the reins of power in Moscow, the moderates had gained the ascendancy in the battle for the control of foreign policy in Washington. President Reagan, too, had a change of heart. Under the astute leadership of Shultz in the State Department, the Reagan foreign policy team responded positively to Gorbachev's peaceful overtures. On his visits to Moscow, Shultz helped to sow the seeds of economic engagement between the Soviet Union and the West by pointing out to Gorbachev the great commercial opportunities open to Moscow in world trade. Shultz was preaching to the converted.[44] After the two superpowers signed the Intermediate-Range Nuclear Forces (INF) Treaty in September 1987, the relationship between the United States and the Soviet Union moved from one of military competition to one of economic cooperation. In 1988, as Gorbachev pulled the remaining Soviet troops out of Afghanistan, the United States agreed to a substantial relaxation of the COCOM embargo. As the Soviet economy teetered on the brink of collapse in the early 1990s, Gorbachev continued to push for MFN status from the United States.[45]

# Conclusion

The first issue that the chapter discussed was the existing literature on the economic dimension of the cold war. It was noted that there is little consensus between historians over the role of economic factors in the cold war. As each of the contrasting perspectives has merit, there is a need for a synthesis which would enable a better understanding of the dynamics of political economy in post-1945 international relations. The world systems model could perhaps be successfully blended with approaches emphasizing national security, economic diplomacy, and corporatism. To this end, economic developments would be studied within a global framework, with greater weight to political and strategic considerations than is currently evident in world systems analyses. Such a synthesis, while acknowledging the primacy of the United States in the international system, would help shed new light on the limits imposed on American hegemony by allies, adversaries, as well as multilateral organizations, central banks, and transnational non-governmental actors such as corporations and trade unions.

Further research is also urgently required on the nature of the economic conflict between the Western alliance and the Soviet bloc. The picture is decidedly clearer on the Western economic order, but less so on the communist one. Given the divergent nature of the two economic systems, it appears that conflict was all but inevitable after the creation of the Marshall Plan. The cold war was thus an ideological confrontation. Future studies should build on the insights of international economic history in explaining how policymakers on both sides of the "iron curtain" conceived, created, and managed their respective capitalist and communist orders over the long haul of the East-West conflict.

The area of East-West trade has been the subject of increasing interest from scholars in recent years. This work has demonstrated the significance of economic statecraft in the cold war. The West, in particular, deployed a strategic embargo as part of its containment strategy against the Soviet bloc throughout the course of the cold war. The embargo was constantly modified, i.e., expanded or reduced, during the conflict in line with Western perceptions of Soviet behavior at a given time period. Yet, the question of the efficacy of economic sanctions will benefit from more sustained reflection. Is it fair to dismiss COCOM as merely an irritant in relations between the United States and its allies or was the embargo a potent strategic instrument in the containment of global communism?

This leads on to the final area addressed by this chapter: economic factors and the end of the cold war. The available evidence suggests that the Reagan administration's campaign of economic warfare in the early 1980s had a minimal impact on the Soviet Union. By the late 1970s the Soviet economy was in a precarious position crumbling under the weight of capacious military spending and the inflexibility of the command economy model. Far from resolving these economic problems, Gorbachev's modernization plans had the adverse effect of hastening the Soviet Union's decline. Had the Kremlin initiated reforms of the command model much earlier and responded positively to the process of globalization, like its communist counterpart the PRC in the late 1970s, it is arguable that, at least in economic terms, the Soviet Union might have survived longer.

## Notes

1. Though it should be noted that Diane B. Kunz, *Butter and Guns: America's Cold War Economic Diplomacy* (New York: Free Press, 1997) provides a history of American foreign economic policy during the cold war.
2. Michael J. Hogan and Thomas G. Paterson, eds., *Explaining the History of American Foreign Relations* (New York: Cambridge University Press, 1991), 1–7.
3. Andrew J. Bacevich, *American Empire: The Realities and Consequences of US Diplomacy* (Cambridge, MA: Harvard University Press, 2002), 11–31.
4. Anders Stephanson, "The United States," in David Reynolds, ed., *The Cold War: International Perspectives* (New Haven, CT: Yale University Press, 1994), 41–3.
5. Thomas J. McCormick, "Drift or Mastery? A Corporatist Synthesis for American Diplomatic History," *Reviews in American History*, 10:4 (December, 1982), 318–30.
6. Michael J. Hogan, "Corporatism," in Hogan and Paterson, *Explaining the History of American Foreign Relations*, 226–36.
7. Michael J. Hogan, *The Marshall Plan: America, Britain and the Reconstruction of Western Europe, 1947–1952* (New York: Cambridge University Press, 1987), 26–54 and 427–45.
8. John Lewis Gaddis, "The Corporatist Synthesis: A Skeptical View," *Diplomatic History*, 10:4 (Fall 1986), 357–62.

9. Thomas J. McCormick, "World Systems," in Hogan and Paterson, *Explaining the History of American Foreign Relations*, 89–98.

10. Bruce Cumings, "'Revising Postrevisionism,' Or, the Poverty of Theory in Diplomatic History," in Michael J. Hogan, ed., *America in the World: The Historiography of American Foreign Relations since 1941* (New York: Cambridge University Press, 1995), 58–9.

11. Thomas J. McCormick, *America's Half-Century: United States Foreign Policy in the Cold War and After*, 2nd ed. (Baltimore: The Johns Hopkins University Press, 1995), 4–7, 43–71, and 237–58.

12. Ian Jackson, "Economics," in Saki R. Dockrill and Geraint Hughes, eds., *Palgrave Advances in Cold War History* (Basingstoke, Palgrave Macmillan, 2006), 167–71.

13. Robert Gilpin, *The Challenge of Global Capitalism: The World Economy in the Twenty-First Century* (Princeton, NJ: Princeton University Press, 2000), 52–88.

14. Robert Gilpin, *The Political Economy of International Relations* (Princeton, NJ: Princeton University Press, 1987), 131–42.

15. G. John Ikenberry, "Rethinking the Origins of American Hegemony," *Political Science Quarterly*, 104:3 (Autumn 1989), 382–91.

16. Michael D. Bordo, "The Bretton Woods International Monetary System: An Historical Overview," in Michael D. Bordo and Barry Eichengreen, eds., *A Retrospective on the Bretton Woods System: Lessons for International Monetary Reform* (Chicago: University of Chicago Press, 1993), 28–47.

17. Harold James, *International Monetary Cooperation since Bretton Woods* (New York: IMF and Oxford University Press, 1996), 148–75.

18. Francis J. Gavin, *Gold, Dollars, & Power: The Politics of International Monetary Relations, 1958–1971* (Chapel Hill, NC: The University of North Carolina Press, 2004), 59–133, and 197–202.

19. James, *International Monetary Cooperation*, 205–28.

20. Mark Kramer, "The Soviet Union and Eastern Europe," in Ngaire Woods, ed., *International Relations Since 1945* (Oxford: Oxford University Press, 1996), 111–12.

21. See, for example, Robert Mark Spaulding, *Osthandel and Ospolitik: German Trade Policies in Eastern Europe from Bismarck to Adenauer* (Providence, RI: Berghahn Books, 1997), 351–9.

22. Barry Eichengreen, *The European Economy Since 1945: Coordinated Capitalism and Beyond* (Princeton, NJ: Princeton University Press, 2007), 131–46.

23. Derek Aldcroft and Steven Mooreword, *Economic Change in Eastern Europe* (Aldershot: Edward Elgar, 1995), 125.

24. Philip Hanson, "The Soviet Union," in Andrew Graham with Anthony Seldon, eds., *Government and Economies in the Postwar World: Economic Policies and Comparative Performance, 1945–1985* (London: Routledge, 1990), 205–11.

25. Robert Bideleux and Ian Jeffries, *A History of Eastern Europe: Crisis and Change* (London: Routledge, 1998), 534–5; Aldcroft and Moorewood, *Economic Change in Eastern Europe*, 156–69.

26. Jeffrey A. Frieden, *Global Capitalism: Its Fall and Rise in the Twentieth Century* (New York: Norton, 2006), 356–9.

27. Jeffrey Sachs, *The End of Poverty: How We Can Make it Happen in Our Lifetime* (London: Penguin, 2005), 47–8.

28. Frieden, *Global Capitalism*, 302–6, and 317–20.

29. Frieden, *Global Capitalism*, 320.

30. Martin Wolf, *Why Globalization Works* (New Haven, CT: Yale University Press, 2004), 201–2.
31. Frieden, *Global Capitalism*, 356.
32. Geir Lundestad, *The United States and Western Europe Since 1945: From "Empire by Invitation" to Atlantic Drift* (New York: Oxford University Press, 2003), 57 and 64.
33. Ian Jackson, *The Economic Cold War: America, Britain and East-West Trade, 1948–63* (Basingstoke, Palgrave Macmillan, 201), 58–72, 111–28, and 159–81.
34. Shu Guang Zhang, *Economic Cold War: America's Embargo Against China and the Sino-Soviet Alliance, 1949–63* (Palo Alto, CA: Stanford University Press, 2001).
35. Mike Bowker, "Brezhnev and Superpower Relations," in Edwin Bacon and Mark Sandle eds., *Brezhnev Reconsidered* (Basingstoke, Palgrave Macmillan, 2002), 91–2.
36. Raymond Garthoff, *Détente and Confrontation: American-Soviet Relations from Nixon to Reagan*, rev. ed. (Washington, DC: Brookings, 1994), 342–6.
37. Henry Kissinger, *Years of Renewal* (New York: Simon and Schuster, 1999), 129–34; Jussi Hanhimäki, *The Flawed Architect: Henry Kissinger and American Foreign Policy* (New York: Oxford University Press, 2004), 342.
38. Paul Kengor, *The Crusader: Ronald Reagan and the Fall of Communism* (New York: Harper, 2006), 117–24.
39. Alan P. Dobson, "The Reagan Administration, Economic Warfare and Starting to Close Down the Cold War," *Diplomatic History*, 29:3 (June 2005), 547–51.
40. Michael Mastanduno, *Economic Containment: CoCom and the Politics of East-West Trade* (Ithaca, NY: Cornell University Press, 1992), 220–66.
41. Dale C. Copeland, "Trade Expectations and the Outbreak of Peace: Détente 1970–1974 and the End of the Cold War 1985–1991," in Jean-Marc F. Blanchard, Edward D. Mansfield, and Norrin M. Ripsman, eds., *Power and the Purse: Economic Statecraft, Interdependence and National Security* (London: Frank Cass, 2000), 43–4.
42. Anders Aslund, *Gorbachev's Struggle for Economic Reform*, rev. ed. (London: Pinter, 1991), 143–5.
43. Valerie Bunce, "The Empire Strikes Back: The Evolution of the Eastern Bloc from a Soviet Asset to a Soviet Liability," *International Organization*, 39:1 (January 1985): 35–41.
44. George P. Shultz, *Turmoil and Triumph: My Years as Secretary of State* (New York: Scribners, 1993), 891–3.
45. George Bush and Brent Scowcroft, *A World Transformed* (New York: Knopf, 1998), 227; James A. Baker III with Thomas M. DeFrank, *The Politics of Diplomacy: Revolution, War and Peace* (New York: Putnam, 1995), 254.

## SELECT BIBLIOGRAPHY

Dobson, Alan P. *US Economic Statecraft for Survival, 1933–1991: Of Sanctions, Embargoes and Economic Warfare*. London: Routledge, 2002.
Eichengreen, Barry. *The European Economy Since 1945: Coordinated Capitalism and Beyond*. Princeton, NJ: Princeton University Press, 2007.
Frieden, Jeffrey A. *Global Capitalism: Its Fall and Rise in the Twentieth Century*. New York: Norton, 2006.
Gavin, Francis J. *Gold, Dollars, & Power: The Politics of International Monetary Relations, 1958–1971*. Chapel Hill, NC: The University of North Carolina Press, 2004.

Gilpin, Robert. *The Challenge of Global Capitalism: The World Economy in the Twenty-First Century*. Princeton, NJ: Princeton University Press, 2000.

Hogan, Michael J. *The Marshall Plan: America, Britain and the Reconstruction of Western Europe, 1947–1952*. New York: Cambridge University Press, 1987.

Jackson, Ian. *The Economic Cold War: America, Britain and East-West Trade, 1948–63*. Basingstoke, Palgrave Macmillan, 2001.

James, Harold. *International Monetary Cooperation since Bretton Woods*. New York: IMF and Oxford University Press, 1996.

Kunz, Diane B. *Butter and Guns: America's Cold War Economic Diplomacy*. New York: Free Press, 1997.

Mastanduno, Michael. *Economic Containment: CoCom and The Politics of East-West Trade*. Ithaca, NY: Cornell University Press, 1992.

McCormick, Thomas J. *America's Half-Century: United States Foreign Policy in the Cold War and After*, 2nd ed. Baltimore: The Johns Hopkins University Press, 1995.

Pollard, Robert A. *Economic Security and the Origins of the Cold War, 1945–50*. New York: Columbia University Press, 1985.

# CHAPTER 5

········································································································

# THE GEOPOLITICS AND THE
# COLD WAR

········································································································

## GEOFFREY WARNER

ON March 12, 1947 President Harry S. Truman, alerting the American people to an alleged communist threat to Greece and Turkey, told Congress, "I believe that it must be the policy of the United States to support free peoples who are resisting attempted subjugation by armed minorities or by outside pressures."[1] More than 21 years later, on September 26, 1968, an article in the Russian newspaper *Pravda* justified the invasion of Czechoslovakia by Soviet-led Warsaw Pact forces the previous month. "Without question," it read, "the people of the socialist countries and the communist parties must have the freedom to determine their own path of development. Any decision they make, however, must not be inimical either to socialism in their own country or to the fundamental interests of the other socialist countries. . . . The sovereignty of individual socialist countries cannot be set against the interests of world socialism and the world revolutionary movement."[2]

Both these statements gave birth to a foreign policy "doctrine": the Truman Doctrine and the Brezhnev Doctrine. Both were couched in ideological terms and represented the cold war as an ideological conflict: "democracy" versus "totalitarianism" on the one hand; "socialism" versus "capitalism" on the other. Ideological differences, nevertheless, were only a part of the conflict known as the cold war. With regard to the threat to Turkey, for example, a joint memorandum from the US Departments of State, War, and the Navy in August 1946 stated that should the Soviets succeed in obtaining control over Turkey, it would be "extremely difficult, if not impossible, to prevent the Soviet Union from obtaining control over . . . the whole Near and Middle East," a region which was "strategically important from the point of view of resources, including oil."[3] In the case of Czechoslovakia, Brezhnev told the Czech leaders "about the sacrifice of the Soviet Union in the Second World War: the soldiers fallen in battle, the civilians slaughtered, the enormous material losses, the hardships suffered by the Soviet people. At such a cost the Soviet Union had gained security, and the guarantee of that security was the postwar division of Europe, and, specifically, the fact that Czechoslovakia was linked with the Soviet Union 'forever.'"[4]

This chapter examines the geopolitics of the cold war. The term "geopolitics" is highly elastic. Originally coined in 1899 by Sweden's Rudolf Kjellen, the German geographer Karl Haushofer eagerly embraced it in the period of Adolf Hitler's ascendancy. Concurrently in the Anglo-American world, geographers like Sir Halford Mackinder and Nicholas Spykman conceptualized a global conflict between an Atlantic-based sea power and a Eurasian land mass dominated first by Germany and then by Russia.[5] Mackinder and Spykman are sometimes cited as inspiring the American doctrine of "containment," and the former is actually quoted in a British cabinet paper of March 1948 that reads, "… physical control of the Eurasian land mass and eventual control of the whole World Island [Europe, Asia and Africa] is what the [Soviet] Politburo is aiming at—no less a thing than that."[6] Contemporary scholars such as Saul Cohen (in the United States), Neville Brown and Colin Gray (in the United Kingdom), and Aymeric Chauprade and Yves Lacoste (in France) continue to publish valuable studies of international relations which develop and move on from the insights of Mackinder and Spykman, but this chapter adopts a broader definition of geopolitics, akin to that set out by Raymond Garthoff, namely, "a synonym for realistic 'power political' factors or approaches. It thus corresponds closely to the traditional term in historical and political science analysis: *Realpolitik*."[7]

The global balance of power changed dramatically during the second half of the 20th century. On the eve of the Second World War, there were seven major powers: the United States, the Soviet Union, the United Kingdom, France, Germany, Italy, and Japan. The League of Nations estimated that, between them, these countries were responsible for just over 80 percent of the world's industrial output in 1936–8.[8] All of them possessed, actually or potentially, sizeable armed forces, and all but the Soviet Union ruled overseas territories. The Second World War was a confrontation between rival, albeit shifting alliances of these powers: the United States, the Soviet Union, the United Kingdom, and France versus Germany, Italy, and Japan.

The end of the war in 1945 saw a new configuration of power. Both Germany and Japan were defeated and occupied countries. Of the five remaining pre-war powers, France and Italy had suffered catastrophic declines, although the former was accorded a permanent seat on the Security Council of the United Nations and an occupation zone in Germany. Despite its own Security Council seat, large armed forces, extensive overseas empire, and Commonwealth, as well as its status as one of the "Big Three" at the wartime conferences of the victorious powers, the United Kingdom was also seriously weakened.

This left the United States and the Soviet Union. Both were powers of continental proportions with more than twice the forces of their nearest rival, the United Kingdom, deployed on land, sea, and in the air. But there the parallel ends. Economically, the United States far outclassed the Soviet Union, and the difference between the two powers had grown as a result of the Second World War (27 million Russians died in the conflict compared to half a million Americans). Soviet GDP, which had been half that of America in 1938, was only 20 percent of it in 1945.[9] It was a similar story with respect to the main sinews of mid-20th-century industrial power. The Soviet Union's steel output was 63 percent of that of the United States in 1938 but only 17 percent in 1945. In the case of coal the proportions were 37 percent and 26 percent and, for oil, 18 percent and 8 percent.[10] These facts and figures signal an extremely uneven rather than bipolar balance of power in 1945.

On the military side, too, there was a considerable imbalance between what became known as the two superpowers. Although postwar demobilization left the United States with much smaller conventional forces than the Soviet Union, an intelligence report presented to US Secretary of the Navy James Forrestal in early 1946 stated, "The present Soviet capabilities may be considered to be restricted to land operations within Eurasia... The Red Fleet is incapable of any important offensive or amphibious operations... [and the] Soviet air effort is confined to ground support; a strategic air force is practically non-existent either in material or concepts."[11] None of these limitations applied to the United States. In addition, of course, as Hiroshima and Nagasaki had demonstrated, the latter possessed the atomic bomb and a means of delivering it.

Why, then, did relations between the United States and the Soviet Union deteriorate so rapidly? One explanation is that the ideologies of the two superpowers were incompatible. Free-market capitalism and communism are polar opposites, and both the United States and the Soviet Union promoted their extension. Looked at from a different point of view, however, the origins of the cold war are much the same as those identified by Thucydides in his history of the Peloponnesian War: "The growth of the power of Athens, and the alarm which this inspired in Sparta, made war inevitable."[12] This war took place within the confines of Ancient Greece. Later, similar rivalries occurred on a broader canvas. The German historian, Ludwig Dehio, brilliantly analyzed the international history of Europe from the 16th century to 1945 in terms of a series of struggles for hegemony in which first Spain, then France, and finally Germany sought overall control.[13] The cold war can be seen as a similar phenomenon.

On the eve of the Second World War the Soviet Union shared borders with seven different European countries: Norway, Finland, Estonia, Latvia, Lithuania, Poland, and Romania. Virtually all these frontiers were fluid, and Russia had attacked or been attacked across them over the previous two centuries. For example, Russian troops reached Berlin in 1760 as well as in 1945, and, as Stalin boasted at the Potsdam conference in 1945, they had got as far as Paris in 1815. On the other hand, Russia had suffered invasion by western powers in 1708, 1812, 1854, 1914, 1918, and 1941.

This to-ing and fro-ing was facilitated by the absence of natural barriers and the weakness and instability of many of the states. Estonia (then a Swedish province) was ceded to Russia as early as 1721. Latvia, Lithuania, and Poland had similarly disappeared from the map between 1772 and 1795 following three successive partitions by more powerful neighbors, namely Prussia, Austria, and Russia. The checkerboard of nation states which appeared following the defeat of Austria-Hungary, Germany, and the Ottoman Empire in the First World War and the collapse of the Russian empire in 1917 was, therefore, unlikely to survive intact once Germany and Russia regained their strength. And so it proved. The entire area—and more—fell under German control by the end of 1941 and, following the German defeat in 1945, the Soviet Union moved in to fill the vacuum.

It reabsorbed the three Baltic states and a large part of Poland, so that its own frontier now abutted those of Czechoslovakia and Hungary. Since Estonia, Latvia, and Lithuania were once more part of Russia, however, the Soviet Union's postwar European boundaries now totaled six instead of the pre-war seven.

The Soviet Union used its victory in 1945 to extend its influence further southwards and westwards into Europe. The states of Eastern Europe (Poland, Hungary, and Czechoslovkia) became Russian satellites, as did the Balkan states of Romania, Bulgaria, Yugoslavia, and Albania, although the last two managed to extricate themselves from this predicament—while remaining under communist rule—in 1948 and 1961 respectively.

The Soviet Union was determined to hold on to its East European "empire." In addition to invading Czechoslovakia in 1968, its forces intervened in Hungary in 1956 and came close to doing so in Poland that same year. Plans were also drawn up to invade Yugoslavia in 1948. Perhaps because of Stalin's caution, they were never implemented. Albania was too small and too far away to merit attack.

What of Germany, the country primarily responsible for the Second World War and the potential economic powerhouse of the whole of Europe? Since 1945 it had been jointly occupied by the four victorious powers (the UK, France, the Soviet Union, and the US), with each allocated a separate zone. Negotiations to establish a unified government faltered because the United States, the United Kingdom, and the Soviet Union could not agree on a formula which ensured that a united Germany could not throw its sizeable weight behind either of the rival power blocs which were already forming. France favored permanent dismemberment. The outcome was the division in 1949 of Germany into the Federal Republic of (West) Germany and the (East) German Democratic Republic.

A geopolitical time-bomb was situated at the heart of Germany in the shape of its former capital, Berlin. Divided, like Germany as a whole, into four "sectors," Berlin was an enclave within the Russian zone of occupation. In 1948 the Russians instituted a blockade of rail, road, and canal traffic into West Berlin in order to remove the embarrassing allied presence from their zone altogether. They even hinted at an exchange of territory which would achieve this peacefully. The Americans, British, and French, however, succeeded in supplying their garrisons and the people of West Berlin by air. Once the winter of 1948–9 ended, the Russians recognized that their tactic had failed and lifted the blockade.

The geopolitical time-bomb remained ticking, nevertheless. Another crisis erupted over Berlin in 1958, when the Russians threatened to hand over control of the access routes to West Berlin to East Germany, which Britain, France, and the United States did not recognize. Its later phase coincided with the desperate step taken by the Russians and their East German ally to build a wall between East and West Berlin in August 1961 to stem the ever-increasing flow of refugees. This move heightened tension and for a few days in October there was a brief stand-off between American and Russian tanks at "Checkpoint Charlie," the main crossing-point between the two halves of the city.

Western Europeans often said after the Second World War that all the Red Army needed to reach the Channel coast was decent boots. Was that the Soviet intention? The United States and its allies thought it was, although they believed that the more immediate threat to Western Europe came from its own communist parties, particularly those of France and Italy. Barriers were soon erected to stem the Red tide: the Marshall Plan of 1947, which was designed to bolster West Europe's economies, and the North Atlantic Treaty of 1949, which was primarily a military alliance. The Soviet Union responded in 1949 with the formation of COMECON, and, after it had failed to prevent the rearmament of West Germany and its integration into NATO in 1955, the Warsaw Pact.

As in Europe there had been a history of great power rivalry in the Middle East. Throughout most of the 19th century "the great game" was played between Britain and Russia over the fate of the Ottoman Empire, Persia (Iran), and Afghanistan. To address their joint anxieties concerning Germany, an agreement between the two countries in 1907 produced a de facto partition of Iran, and during the First World War one of the notorious "secret treaties" had conceded control of the Turkish Straits to Russia, allowing it free access to the Mediterranean.

Both agreements lapsed as a result of the Russian Revolution of 1917. Indeed, the British sought unsuccessfully to secure territorial changes in the Caucasus and Caspian areas, while the Turks seized the provinces of Kars and Ardahan which the Russians had occupied in 1875. The Second World War changed the situation once again. In 1941 Britain and Russia once more partitioned Iran after intervening to put an end to the pro-Axis intrigues of the then Shah, and in 1945–6 the Soviet Union demanded control of the Turkish Straits and the restoration of Kars and Ardahan while refusing to withdraw from northern Iran ostensibly to support Azerbaijani autonomy.

This time oil affected the outcome. The Axis powers had been plagued by a shortage of oil during the Second World War. Although the United States was self- sufficient in oil during the war, its government and industry knew that the situation was not permanent, and they regarded the Middle East as the most potentially productive alternative source. They were right. On the eve of the Second World War, the Middle East produced less than 5 percent of the world's oil supplies. By 1955, however, that proportion had risen to 20 percent.[14] Its reserves, moreover, had grown even faster.

Oil thus figured prominently in American thinking about the Middle East. The Joint Chiefs of Staff pointed out in October 1946 that Iran was "an area of major strategic interest to the United States" because of its oil. It was also an important defensive position against possible attacks upon other oil producing countries in the region. Denial of Middle East oil resources to either side would force it to fight "an oil-starved war;" therefore, it was "to the strategic interest of the United States to keep Soviet influence and Soviet armed forces removed as far as possible from oil resources in Iran, Iraq, and the Near and Middle East."[15]

The Soviet Union was indeed interested in gaining access to Iranian oil. As a result of the destruction brought about by the Second World War, its own output had fallen from 31.1 million tonnes in 1940 to 19.4 million tonnes in 1945. Moreover, the Russians had as much reason to fear the presence of potentially hostile powers in the Middle East as the

Americans, for they knew that during the brief period of the Nazi-Soviet pact (1939–41), Britain and France had drawn up plans to bomb Russian oil fields in the Caucasus from bases in the area. Similar plans were drawn up by Britain and the United States after the Second World War.

Stalin felt too weak to pursue his objectives in the face of American and British opposition. He withdrew his forces from Iran and his threats from Turkey. The latter became a bastion of American influence in the Middle East. The United States sixth fleet was in effect established when President Truman sent the battleship *Missouri* to Turkey in 1946. Turkey joined the North Atlantic Alliance in 1952 and agreed to host American Jupiter intermediate-range ballistic missiles (IRBMs) targeted at the Soviet Union in 1957. Master-minded by the CIA and MI6 in 1953, a military coup overthrew Iran's prime minister, Mohammed Mossadegh, whom the Americans and British considered sympathetic to communism. For the next 26 years Iran was a reliable American ally, becoming a founder-member of what became known as the Central Treaty Organization (CENTO)—an eastern extension of NATO—in 1955.

The key to cold war geopolitics in East Asia was China. The total length of the Soviet Union's land borders was 19,923 km. Almost two-fifths of this length is accounted for by China. Add the length of the frontier with Mongolia (3,441 km) and the proportion comfortably exceeds one-half. Contrast this with the 4,254 km (one- fifth) which the Soviet Union shared with European states, add China's population and size, and its importance becomes clear.

China ended the Second World War in a sorry state. It had been fighting the Japanese since 1937, four years longer than Britain and the United States and almost eight years longer than the Soviet Union. According to one estimate, "[t]he country lost over three million soldiers in combat, and an additional eighteen million civilians as casualties of the war."[16] To make matters worse, the end of the war with Japan did not mean a return to peace. A civil war between the Nationalist government of General Chiang Kai-shek and the Communist People's Liberation Army under Mao Zedong soon broke out and lasted until the victory of the People's Republic of china (PRC) in October 1949.

The Soviet Union was primarily concerned with the possible resurgence of Japan, whose attitude toward both the Czarist regime and its successor had been hostile throughout the first four decades of the 20th century and which failed to join in the German invasion of 1941 only because it was preoccupied elsewhere. Thus Stalin signed a treaty with Chiang Kai-shek's government in August 1945. As the civil war developed, the Russians gave some aid to the Chinese communists, but Stalin remained cautious. There is evidence that he urged the communists not to cross the Yangzi River in 1949, a course of action which could have led to a divided country.[17] The Soviet ambassador remained accredited to the Nationalist regime until after it had withdrawn to the island of Taiwan. Stalin refused to receive Mao until after the official proclamation of the PRC in October 1949, and a new Sino-Soviet treaty, which was signed in February 1950, granted the Russians a privileged position in Manchuria, China's most highly industrialized region, and gave the Chinese no satisfaction in respect to their claim to Mongolia or their desire to "liberate" Taiwan.

In the United States bitter divisions emerged over policy. On the one hand, the Joint Chiefs of Staff argued in a paper of June 9, 1947, that "the military security of the United States will be threatened if there is any further spread of Soviet influence and power in the Far East." Given that Japan was disarmed and occupied, "the only Asiatic government at present capable of even a show of resistance to Soviet expansion in Asia is the Chinese Nationalist Government." The Chiefs recommended, in terms redolent of traditional geopolitical discourse, that "United States assistance to those nations on the periphery of Soviet-controlled areas in Eurasia should be given in accordance with an over-all plan...[which] should take into account the necessity for the maintenance of the Chinese National Government and should eventually provide sufficient assistance to that Government to eliminate all communist armed opposition..."[18]

On the other hand, when Secretary of State George C. Marshall went before Congress in February 1948, he expounded an alternative geopolitical narrative derived from the thinking of one of the most influential US diplomats of the early postwar period, George Kennan. "China," he said, "does not itself possess the raw material and industrial resources which would enable it to become a first-class military power within the foreseeable future. Furthermore...we cannot afford, economically or militarily, to take over the continued failures of the present Chinese Government to the dissipation of our strength in more vital regions...that is, in the vital industrial area of Western Europe with its tradition of free institutions."[19]

Events in neighboring areas of East Asia helped to crystallize positions. Russia and Japan had competed for Korea at the end of the 19th century, and it was annexed by the latter in 1910. Liberated in 1945 by the Red Army and American forces, it was divided into two zones of occupation at the 38th parallel. These two zones soon evolved into separate states, the Communist Democratic People's Republic of Korea (DPRK) to the north and the pro-American Republic of Korea to the south. Both governments desired reunification, albeit on their own terms.

On June 25, 1950, after persuading a wary Stalin that it would be a walkover, the DPRK's leader, Kim Il Sung, launched his forces across the 38th parallel. The US government interpreted the move as a Soviet-inspired attempt to seize the initiative in the cold war and mobilized its allies in the United Nations. In October 1950, after the US/UsN forces halted the enemy advance and rolled it back across the 38th parallel until they approached the Manchurian border, the PRC sent in its own armed forces, eventually totaling 1.45 million "volunteers." The Soviet Union, too, intervened on the side of the DPRK, but clandestinely and on a much smaller scale. After three years of bitter fighting, a ceasefire was concluded on July 27, 1953 on the basis of the status quo ante. The Korean War turned the cold war into an armed conflict, albeit one in which the United States and the Soviets confronted each other through allies and proxies.

The United States and the Soviet Union were thus locked into a confrontation along the Eurasian periphery. In order to gain the advantage, both parties built up huge nuclear arsenals. The Soviet Union had tested its first nuclear device in 1949, four years after the United States. The gap between the two countries' first thermonuclear (hydrogen bomb) tests was less than a year, from October 1952 to August 1953. The number of nuclear weapons held by each superpower rose from 365 (for the United States) and five (for the Soviet Union) in 1950, to 20,434 and 1,605 in 1960.[20] This does not take into account the power of individual weapons or the means of delivery. The latter multiplied from strategic bombers to various kinds of missiles: the land-based medium-range ballistic missiles (MRBMs), intermediate-range ballistic missiles (IRBMs), and intercontinental-range ballistic missiles (ICBMs); and the submarine-launched ballistic missiles (SLBMs) of various ranges. In 1970 it is estimated that the United States possessed 1,054 ICBMs, 656 SLBMs, and 1,710 nuclear warheads to the Soviet Union's 1,465, 229, and 1,694.[21] This relative parity lasted until the end of the cold war.

The Soviet Union and its Warsaw Pact allies enjoyed a continuing superiority on the ground in Europe. In 1989, for example, Warsaw Pact forces in Europe possessed an estimated 58,000 main battle tanks compared to 21,900 in the opposing NATO forces.[22] The Soviet navy also expanded. As early as 1968, its commander-in-chief, Admiral Sergei Gorshkov, was quoted as saying, "The flag of the Soviet navy now proudly flies over the oceans of the world. Sooner or later, the US will have to understand that it no longer has mastery of the seas."[23] Twenty years later the strategic geographer Hugh Faringdon wrote, "By the 1980s the Soviet Union had accomplished an historic breakout from its geopolitical boundaries as a land power, and acquired the capacity to challenge the interests of the west in every corner of the globe."[24] It had bases or port-of-call facilities in Vietnam, South Yemen, Ethiopia, Mozambique, Angola, and Syria. The United States had its third fleet, based in the eastern Pacific, its sixth fleet in the Mediterranean, and its seventh fleet in the western Pacific. Still, the increased Russian naval presence far from home waters was both impressive and threatening.

This maritime expansion must be seen in the context of another cold war dimension: the rise of the Third World. One of the most significant developments in world politics after 1945 was decolonization. While autonomous from the cold war, decolonization is also inextricably linked to it. This was spelled out as early as September 1948 by analysts of the fledgling US Central Intelligence Agency. "The growth of nationalism in colonial areas," they concluded, "which has already succeeded in breaking up a large part of the European colonial system and in creating a series of new, nationalistic states in the Near and Far East has major implications for US security, particularly in terms of possible world conflict with the USSR. This shift of the dependent areas from the orbit of the colonial powers not only weakens the probable European allies of the US but deprives the US itself of assured access to vital bases and raw materials in these areas in time of war. Should the recently liberated and currently emergent states become oriented toward the USSR US military and economic security would be seriously threatened."[25]

There were fifty-one founding members of the United Nations in 1945. By the end of the cold war the organization's membership stood at 159. More than three-quarters of the additional members were former colonial dependencies. Seventeen newly independent African states became members in 1960 alone. What had been an American-dominated world organization in the early postwar period gradually turned into one in which the United States could no longer be sure of getting its own way. The use of the veto in the UN Security Council is revealing in this respect. Although the Soviets cast 117 vetoes to America's seventy-two between 1946 and 1990, the United States cast none before 1972 and the Soviet Union only eight after it. American disillusionment with the UN during the Reagan administration was reflected from 1983 onwards in the withholding of funds from the organization which was seriously damaging to it.

The Soviet Union seized the opportunity to "leapfrog" its opponents by intervening in the developing world, where the process of decolonization, resentment at the arrogance of the western powers, and chronic political instability offered plenty of scope for making mischief. This was doubly so because the United States was instinctively hostile to European colonialism, although its own behavior in the Third World, especially in Latin America, looked to many suspiciously like a form of colonialism. This attitude provided the Russians with a wedge to drive between the United States and its European allies.

Soviet intervention began in the Middle East in the mid-1950s, when the United States and Britain were trying to form an anti-Soviet regional alliance in the area. The Egyptians, who had suffered from British interference in their affairs for three-quarters of a century, turned to the Russians for support. They concluded an arms agreement with Czechoslovakia in 1955, and the anti-Soviet Baghdad Pact had to be restricted to the so-called "northern tier" of Turkey, Iraq, Iran, and Pakistan. Even then the Americans refused to join it because they thought that, without Egypt, the pact had become more a vehicle to extend British and Iraqi influence in the Middle East than a defensive alliance against the Soviet Union.

Syria followed Egypt into the Soviet orbit, and Iraq drifted in and out after the revolution of 1958 got rid of the pro-British monarchy. Since both Egypt and Iraq treated their own communist parties with varying degrees of severity, this new alignment with the Soviet Union was hardly ideological. The existence of the new Jewish state of Israel, established in 1948, further complicated the situation. The Arab countries were implacably opposed to the existence of Israel and the Soviet Union ended up supplying weapons and expertise for the Arabs to engage in three Arab-Israeli wars: the Suez war of October 1956, the Six Day War of June 1967, and the Yom Kippur War of October 1973. The United States, which had been sympathetic toward Israel from the start, became even closer to it the more the Russians sided with the Arabs. Eventually, the Americans succeeded in prising the Egyptians apart from the Russian embrace, and a peace agreement between Egypt and Israel was signed, under American auspices, in 1978.

If the British were something of an embarrassment to the Americans in the Middle East, so were the French in North Africa and Southeast Asia. President Roosevelt had opposed France regaining its overseas empire at the end of the Second World War, but events and the United Kingdom's solidarity with its fellow-colonial power helped it to do so. The tension between the United States and France caused by the long struggle (1954–62) for Algerian independence was nothing compared to that produced in Indochina, where the French fought a war against a communist-led nationalist movement from 1946. While pushing the French to grant the Indochinese colonies (Vietnam, Laos, and Cambodia) some form of independence, the United States extended aid to France in its war. By 1954 it was paying three-quarters of the cost.

There were two reasons for this. The first was France's importance to the defense of Western Europe. The second was a belief in the so-called "domino theory," publicly enunciated by President Eisenhower in April 1954. As Eisenhower explained, "You have a row of dominoes set up, you knock over the first one, and what will happen to the last one is the certainty that it will go over very quickly." In other words, if Indochina fell to communism, the rest of Southeast Asia would likely follow, adding its large population and considerable natural resources (rubber, tin, and tungsten) to those of the communist world. Strategically, it would mean the outflanking of "the so-called island defensive chain of Japan, Formosa, and the Philippines," constituting a danger to Australia and New Zealand. It would also threaten Japan by depriving it of the essential markets it needed. Japan would therefore "have only one place in the world to go—that is, toward the Communist areas in order to live."[26]

This apocalyptic geopolitical vision brought the United States close to intervention in Indochina in 1954. A settlement was, however, reached at Geneva in July, whereby Vietnam was temporarily partitioned and Laos and Cambodia neutralized. The United States, after maneuvering the French out of their former colony, turned Vietnam into an anti-communist bulwark under the aegis of the South East Asia Treaty Organization (SEATO), a hollow counterpart to NATO.

The communist North Vietnamese were dissatisfied with the partition of their country, especially as the promised elections of 1956 to pave the way for reunification never occurred. Guerrilla warfare broke out again toward the end of the decade and spilled over into Laos. The French could not be blamed on this occasion for the weakness of the non-communist governments in South Vietnam or Laos, and the United States once more faced a dilemma over what to do. This time it chose to intervene militarily, first with advisors, then, in 1965, with air power and ground forces. The proximity of China figured prominently in its rationale. As Secretary of Defense Robert McNamara, a principal architect of intervention, wrote in a memorandum to President Johnson on November 7, 1965, "The February decision to bomb North Vietnam and the July approval of Phase I [troop] deployments make sense only if they are in support of a long-run United States policy to contain Communist China. China—like Germany in 1917, like Germany in the West and Japan in the East in the late 30s, and like the USSR in 1947—looms as a major power threatening to undercut our importance and effectiveness in the world and, more remotely but more menacingly, to organize all of Asia against us."[27] By 1968 the United States had over half-a-million troops in Vietnam.

Africa, too, became an arena of geopolitical rivalry. The most serious contests occurred in the former Belgian Congo, which became independent in 1960, in the former Portuguese colony of Angola, which gained independence after the Portuguese revolution of 1974, and in the Horn of Africa, where Marxist or quasi-Marxist regimes in Ethiopia and Somalia battled for supremacy in 1977–8. The Soviet Union was backing both regimes in Somalia and Ethiopia when war broke out between them in 1977, but switched its support to the latter. "Its motives," according to Christopher Andrew and the former KGB archivist Vasili Mitrokhin, "had more to do with realpolitik than with ideology. Ethiopia had ten times the population of Somalia and an even more important strategic location commanding sea-lanes for oil shipments from the Persian Gulf to the West."[28]

Briefing the National Security Council in May 1976 on his return from a visit to Africa, Secretary of State Henry Kissinger may have stressed the need to prevent "the radicalization of Africa," but he was not fussy about America's allies in the region. The United States supported the brutal military dictator Joseph Mobutu, who ruled Zaire (the former Belgian Congo) for over thirty years. "Africa," Kissinger said, "is important to us, many key products—coffee, cocoa, cobalt, chrome, iron ore, diamonds—come from Africa, thirty to sixty percent of our consumption; and for our European allies, the figures are even higher."[29] If any state intervened in Africa for ideological reasons it was Fidel Castro's Cuba, which sent thousands of troops to Angola and Ethiopia.[30] A Caribbean island state only 90 miles from the coastline of the United States, Cuba had undergone a revolution in 1959 which placed in power a regime that quickly adopted communism. This touched a particularly raw US nerve, for as early as 1823 President Monroe had warned other powers "that we should consider any attempt on their part to extend their system to any portion of this hemisphere as dangerous to our peace and safety."[31]

Cuba had already been the victim of a botched American-backed invasion by Cuban exiles in 1961. In October of the following year it was the scene of the cold war's most potentially dangerous crisis when the Russians attempted a daring geopolitical coup by deploying intermediate-range and medium-range ballistic missiles on the island to off-set the intercontinental and submarine-launched missiles with which the United States could at that time attack the Soviet Union with comparative immunity. But the CIA detected the missile sites by aerial reconnaissance. The United States initiated a naval blockade to prevent further weapons from entering Cuba, and proclaimed that it would take any necessary steps to remove those already there. After a tense few days the Russians removed their missiles. The quid pro quo was the removal of some obsolescent American missiles from Turkey and, more important, a US pledge not to invade Cuba, which still remains a thorn in America's side.

Cuba was not the only target of the so-called Monroe Doctrine. Covert and/or overt measures were taken by the United States against several regimes in Central and South America which looked as though they were, or might become, communist. Such interventions occurred in Guatemala (1954), British Guiana (1963), Brazil (1964), the Dominican Republic (1965), Chile (1970–1973), Nicaragua and El Salvador (1981), Grenada (1983) and Panama (1989). President Ronald Reagan spelled out the geopolitical stakes in his memoirs:

"Almost half of US exports and imports, including close to half of our essential petroleum imports, travelled through this region," he wrote. "Two out of three ships transiting the Panama Canal carried goods to or from the US Central America was not only a source of imports, but a customer for our products...If the Soviet Union and its allies were allowed to continue subverting democracy with terrorism and fomenting so-called 'wars of national liberation' in Central America, it wouldn'ts stop there: It would spread into the continent of South America and north to Mexico. Then, as I was told that Lenin once said: 'Once we have Latin America, we won't have to take the United States, the last bastion of capitalism, because it will fall into our hands like overripe fruit...'"[32]

The cold war's climactic Third World conflict, however, occurred in Afghanistan. Britain and Russia had competed for influence in Afghanistan for much of the 19th century and the two great powers came close to war in 1886. The Anglo-Russian Entente of 1907, concluded more with Europe in mind than Asia, temporarily ended the rivalry, but in 1919 the Afghan ruler Amir Amanullah's brief war with the British left Afghanistan free to manage its own foreign affairs. The Afghan government steered a mainly neutral course before, during, and after the Second World War, but the situation changed dramatically in April 1978 when a group of communist army officers seized power. Although not responsible for the coup, the Soviet Union signed a Treaty of Friendship and Cooperation with the new regime in December 1978.

The new Afghan government wasted too much time and effort in political infighting and not enough in consolidating its control over outlying areas. Bands of Islamist rebels soon emerged, and Kabul appealed for Russian support. While willing to supply weapons and advisors, the Kremlin did not wish to get too deeply involved by sending troops. Following another coup in September 1979, Afghan President Noor Mohammad Taraki was killed and his followers ruthlessly purged. Reports began to circulate that the new president, Hafizullah Amin, was secretly cosying up to the Americans. This time the Russians moved. On December 27, 1979 Soviet troops crossed the border and Amin was killed when Russian special forces stormed his palace.

These events occurred in juxtaposition with developments in neighboring Iran. In January 1979 the pro-American regime of the Shah had been overthrown and replaced by an Islamic republic under Ayatollah Khomeini. This might have been a positive development for the Soviet Union, since the new Iranian regime was fiercely anti-American, dubbing the United States "the Great Satan." However, the Iranian Islamists were as opposed to the Russians as to the Americans, and the former feared the influence they might bring to bear on both the Afghan rebels and the millions of Muslims who lived in the Soviet Union.

The Russian invasion of Afghanistan was in fact essentially a defensive move.[33] But that is not how it was perceived in the United States. Describing Soviet behavior as "the greatest threat to peace since the Second World War," in January 1980 President Jimmy Carter, influenced by his geopolitically-minded National Security Advisor, Zbigniew Brzezinski, raised the specter of a Soviet thrust toward the Indian Ocean and even the Persian Gulf, the source of "[m]ore than two-thirds of the total exportable oil that supplies the rest of the world."[34] The Soviet invasion of Afghanistan became the backdrop to the final phase of the cold war, during which the Americans and their Pakistani allies armed and equipped the mujahidin, who tied down the Red Army for the best part of a decade and who spawned both the Taliban and al-Qaeda.

Another power which the Russians accused of supporting the anti-communist Afghan rebels in 1979 was China. This hostility between the two communist powers can be traced to the aftermath of the Korean War of 1950–3 and the Russian denunciation of

Stalin at the 20th Congress of the Soviet Communist Party in 1956. Notwithstanding the progressively more intense ideological disputes that followed Stalin's death, geopolitical dynamics lay at the core of the Sino-Soviet split.

The long frontier between the two countries had been settled over the centuries as much by *force majeure* as by negotiation. One source suggests that no less than 36,000 sq. km remained in dispute, and this did not include the frontier with Mongolia, a Soviet satellite, which involved another 17,000 sq. km.[35]

The Kremlin also conspicuously failed to provide much backing for the Chinese in territorial disputes which did not directly involve them. The Chinese considered Soviet support for a forward policy over Taiwan, which remained under the control of Chiang Kai-shek's Nationalist government, to be lukewarm. When a dispute broke out between the Indian and Chinese governments over their common frontier in the Himalayas in 1959, the Russians "told the Chinese government frankly that the aggravation of the dispute... and the development of this dispute into a large armed conflict was undesirable and fraught with negative consequences, not only for Chinese-Indian relations but for the whole international situation."[36] Worried by these "negative consequences," the Soviet Union cancelled its nuclear cooperation program with China in 1959; the following year it withdrew all its technical advisors. When India actually attacked China in October 1962, the Russians blamed the Chinese for provoking it and for "leaguing together" with Pakistan, India's principal rival, which was also a member of both CENTO and SEATO. Following the public disclosure of their disagreements in 1963 and the explosion of China's first nuclear device in October 1964, relations between the two countries deteriorated further. Soviet forces in the border region were reinforced and strategic missiles were deployed to the area. In the spring and summer of 1969 a number of clashes occurred between Russian and Chinese troops along the Sino-Soviet border, and rumors circulated of a planned nuclear strike against China.

The Sino-Soviet rift arguably made possible the most important geopolitical development of the cold war: the United States' rapprochement with the PRC. It was facilitated by the accession to power in 1969 of perhaps the most geopolitically minded of American presidents, Richard M. Nixon. As he said in a 1972 interview, "We must remember the only time in the history of the world that we have had any extended periods of peace is when there has been balance of power.... I think it will be a safer world and a better world if we have a strong, healthy United States, Europe, Soviet Union, China, Japan, each balancing the other, not playing one against the other, an even balance."[37] It did not matter to Nixon or his closest foreign policy advisor, Henry Kissinger, what the domestic political structures of these various political entities were. What counted were their relations with each other.

Nixon was perfectly willing to "play one against the other" in order to achieve his objective. "We're doing the China thing," he told Kissinger on July 22, 1971, "to screw the Russians and help us in Vietnam and to keep the Japanese in line, get another ball in play. And maybe way down the road to have some relations with China."[38] "The China thing" involved a secret mission to China by Kissinger in July 1971, a public one in the following October and a very public one by Nixon himself in February 1972, following which the two countries embarked upon a gradual process of normalizing their previous glacial relationship.

It is difficult to assess the precise extent of the influence the US rapprochement with China had on the cold war, but a lull in the conflict did attend the Nixon presidency. At the end of 1971 representatives of West and East Germany signed an agreement guaranteeing free access to West Berlin. The following year the United States and the Soviet Union concluded a treaty limiting various kinds of nuclear delivery systems, and in 1975 the Americans succeeded in extricating themselves from Vietnam. Although the Soviet Union reached an agreement with China on frontiers in November 1988, the Chinese leader, Deng Xiaoping, told President George H. W. Bush in February 1989 that the greatest threat to China still came from the Soviet Union and that it was unlikely that Sino-Soviet relations would ever be as close as they were in the 1950s.[39] China had, in fact, become a great power in its own right. By 1989 its GDP had surpassed that of the Soviet Union, whereas in 1970 it had been less than half.

China's position was, of course, made even stronger by the collapse of the Soviet empire in Eastern Europe and the subsequent dissolution of the Soviet Union itself. In 1980–1 a crisis had arisen in Poland when the labor organization, Solidarity, challenged the Communist Party's monopoly of power. In December 1980 the Warsaw Pact powers were poised to intervene, but the Polish leaders begged them not to. "Even if angels entered Poland," one of them said, "they would be treated as bloodthirsty vampires."[40] The Russians relented and urged the Polish communists to solve the problem themselves. A year later the Polish government imposed martial law and requested that the Warsaw Pact powers intervene if its own forces were not strong enough to enforce it. The Russians refused. As Yuri Andropov, who took over as Soviet leader the following year, told his Politburo colleagues: "We do not intend to introduce troops into Poland .... [E]ven if Poland falls under the control of Solidarity, that's the way it will be. And if the capitalist countries pounce on the Soviet Union, and you know they have already reached agreement on a variety of economic and political sanctions, that will be very burdensome for us. We must be concerned above all with our own country and the strengthening of the Soviet Union."[41]

After Mikhail Gorbachev became General Secretary of the Soviet Communist Party in March 1985 he told leaders of the Warsaw Pact countries that "we [the Russians] were in favour of relations on an equal footing, respect for the sovereignty and independence of each country, and mutually beneficial co-operation in all spheres. Recognition of these principles also meant all parties taking full responsibility for the situation in their own countries."[42] This, in effect, sounded the death knell of the Brezhnev Doctrine.

Underlying this shift in Russian policy was the economic weakness of the Soviet Union. Although its output of steel and oil had surpassed that of the United States in 1971 and 1974 respectively, the Soviet economy remained backward; per capita GDP in the Soviet Union was still only 35 percent of that in the United States as late as 1980. The chaotic state of Soviet agriculture presented an even more fundamental problem. Before the First World War Russia had been the world's No. 1 grain exporter. In the 1980s it was the No. 1 importer. Moreover, its efforts to keep up with the United States militarily had become cripplingly expensive. Gorbachev discovered in 1987 that military expenditure accounted for 20 percent of GDP instead of 6 percent as previously believed and that the Soviet Union was spending four times as much on defense as the United States.[43] Thanks to the personal rapport he built up, first with President Reagan and later with President Bush, Gorbachev was able to achieve a reduction in this huge amount. Notable steps included the signature in the December 1987 treaty to eliminate intermediate-range nuclear missiles, the commencement in May 1988 of the withdrawal of Soviet troops from Afghanistan, and a unilateral pledge by the Soviet Union in December 1988 to reduce its armed forces by 500,000 and cut back on conventional weapons.

In the absence of Soviet willingness to enforce the Brezhnev Doctrine, communist rule in Eastern Europe first crumbled and then collapsed. The one-party regime in Poland ended following the election of June 1989 and by the end of the year Hungary, Czecholsovakia, Bulgaria, Romania, and East Germany had followed suit. Except in Romania, the transition was peaceful. In 1991 the Soviet Union itself disintegrated into fifteen separate states, based mostly on ethnic identity. The new states had been conquered during the course of Russia's long period of expansion between the 16th and 19th centuries and three of them—the Baltic states of Lithuania, Latvia, and Estonia—had recently enjoyed a brief period of independence between the two world wars. In all, the Soviet Union lost about one-quarter of its territory and the remainder became the Russian Federation.

In 1989-90, however, it was events in East Germany which posed the most serious threat to the Russians because the likely consequence—the reunification of the two Germanies—could be viewed as tantamount to a reversal of the Soviet victory in the Second World War. The situation looked all the more dangerous since the United States insisted that a reunified Germany should be free to join NATO.

The reason for this insistence was that a united Germany might revert to the "Rapallo politics" of the 1920s, when it had attempted to play off the western powers against the Soviet Union. The latter, on the other hand, was equally concerned about the prospect of a united Germany in the western camp, an outcome it had consistently sought to avoid since 1945. Only after East German elections in March 1990 returned the Christian Democrats with a huge majority did the Russians bow to the inevitable. The pill was sweetened by the West German offer to take over all East Germany's economic obligations to the Soviet Union and a sizeable financial credit. The two Germanies formally became one on October 3, 1990.

Arguments about the extent to which the cold war was based on ideological as opposed to geopolitical factors persisted throughout the conflict. Originally these arguments related mainly to the Soviet Union and studies stressing either the role of Marxism-Leninism or the traditional aims of the Czars regularly rolled off the presses. It sometimes seemed that the United States was far too sophisticated to base its foreign policy on anything as one-dimensional as ideology until scholars like Michael Hunt began to remind us otherwise.[44] The fact is that ideologies change and even disappear altogether, but geopolitical factors remain, or more accurately, change more slowly. The fragmentation of both Eastern Europe and the Soviet Union after the end of the cold war has restored a situation akin to that of the 1920s and 1930s in the case of the former and even earlier in the case of the latter. Regardless of the ideologies of the governments involved, it is more than likely that there will be a contest for influence between larger powers in the areas concerned. For example, even though it is peaceful, the expansion of the European Union into the former Eastern European communist bloc is seen by some as a renewed *Drang nach Osten* on the part of Germany, the most influential power in the EU, and the Russians are perturbed by US plans to erect a missile defense system on Polish soil, even though it is ostensibly intended to deter "rogue" states like North Korea and Iran which might be tempted to develop and employ nuclear weapons.

At the global level the United States remains the single most important power, but there is no guarantee that it will remain in that position. China is generally considered as the most likely candidate for superpower status, and it is significant that the Obama administration in Washington decided in 2012 to move the bulk of the US navy to the Pacific. Russia, too, remains a power to be reckoned with. It is still the world's sixth largest economy, has one of the biggest military establishments, and is still level pegging with the United States in terms of its nuclear arsenal. India, too, can be expected to play a larger part in world affairs in future. The balance of power can and almost certainly will change, but the actions of those involved will continue to be influenced as much by geography, economics, and historical precedent as by the clash of ideologies.

## NOTES

1. Special Message to the Congress on Greece and Turkey, March 12, 1947, *Public Papers of the Presidents: Harry S. Truman, 1948* (Washington, DC: Government Printing office, 1963), 178–9.
2. Cited in Jaromir Navrátil, ed., *The Prague Spring 1968: A National Security Archive Documentary Reader* (Budapest: Central European University Press 1998), 502–3.
3. Acheson telegram, August 15, 1946, *Foreign Relations of the United States: 1946*, Vol. VII (Washington, DC: Government Printing Office, 1969), 840–2.
4. Zdenek Mlynár, *Night Frost in Prague* (London: C. Hurst & Co., 1980), 239–40.
5. Mackinder's seminal essays have been collected in Anthony J. Pearce (ed.), *Democratic Ideals and Reality* (New York: Norton, 1962). Spykman's two key texts are Nicholas J. Spykman, *America's Strategy and World Politics* (New York: Harcourt, Brace, & Co.,1942) and Nicholas J. Spykman, *The Geography of the Peace* (New York: Harcourt, Brace, & Co., 1944). The latter was transcribed by a student from lecture notes and published after his death in 1943.
6. Bevin memo, CP(48) 72, March 3, 1948, CAB 129/25, The National Archives, United Kingdom.
7. Raymond L. Garthoff, *Détente and Confrontation: American-Soviet Relations from Nixon to Reagan* (Washington, DC: Brookings Institution, 1994), 6.
8. League of Nations, Economic, Financial and Transit Division, *Industrialization and World Trade* (Geneva: League of Nations, 1945), 13.
9. Unless otherwise stated, all GDP figures in this chapter come from Angus Maddison, *The World Economy* (Paris: OECD Publishing, 2006), 463, 467, 476–7, 479, and 552. Maddison's estimates are expressed in 1990 international Geary-Khamis dollars in order to eliminate the effects of inflation and changes in exchange-rates, etc.

10. These percentages are calculated from the figures given in Brian R. Mitchell (ed.), *International Historical Statistics: Europe 1750-2005* (London: Palgrave MacMillan, 2007), 469, 475-6, and 509; and Brian R. Mitchell, ed., *International Historical Statistics: The Americas 1750-2005* (London: Palgrave MacMillan, 2007), 328-9, 333-4, and 378.

11. Inglis memo, January 21, 1946, Box 24, Forrestal MSS, Seeley Mudd Library, Princeton University, Princeton, NJ.

12. Robert B. Strassler, ed., *The Landmark Thucydides* (New York: Free Press 1996), 16.

13. Ludwig Dehio, *The Precarious Balance: The Politics of Power in Europe, 1494-1945* (New York: Knopf, 1962).

14. Stephen H. Longrigg, *Oil in the Middle East: Its Discovery and Development*, 3rd edition (London: Royal Institute of International Affairs 1968), 478.

15. Hilldring memo, October 12, 1946, *Foreign Relations of the United States: 1946*, Vol. VII, (Washington, DC: Government Printing Office, 1969), 530.

16. Hi-Sheng Ch'i, "The Military Dimension, 1942-1945," in James C. Hsiung and Steven Levine, eds., *China's Bitter Victory: The War with Japan, 1937-1945* (Armonk: M.E. Sharpe 1992), 179.

17. See Guo Moruo's commentary on Mao Zedong's poem, "The PLA Occupies Nanjing," in *Renmin Ribao*, January 4, 1964, cited in Geoffrey Warner, "America, Russia, China and the Origins of the Cold War, 1945-1950," in Joseph M. Siracusa and Glen St. John Barclay (eds.), *The Impact of the Cold War: Reconsiderations* (Port Washington, New York: Kennikat Press, 1977), 157.

18. Enclosure to Lalor memo, June 9, 1947, *Foreign Relations of the United States: 1947*, Vol. VIII (Washington: GPO, 1972), 461.

19. US Department of State, *United States Relations with China: with Special Reference to the Period 1944-1949* (Washington, DC: Government Printing Office, 1949), 383.

20. National Resources Defense Council, *Table of Global Nuclear Weapons Stockpiles, 1945-2002*, <http://www.nrdc.org/nuclear//nudb/datab.9asp>. Note that these figures refer to all warheads, i.e. including battlefield nuclear weapons.

21. David Miller, *The Cold War: A Military History* (London: John Murray, 1998), 422.

22. International Institute of Strategic Studies, *The Military Balance 1989-1990* (London: Brassey's, 1989), 232.

23. "Russia: Power Play on the Oceans," *Time*, February 23, 1968, <http://www.time.com/time/magazine/article/0,9171,837933,00.html> (accessed September 24, 2009).

24. Hugh Farringdon, *Strategic Geography: NATO, the Warsaw Pact, and the Superpowers*, 2nd edition (London: Routledge, 1989), 109.

25. CIS, ORE 25-48, "The Break-up of the Colonial Empires and its Implications for US Security," September 3, 1948, <http://www.cia.gov./browsedocs.asp> (accessed September 9, 2009).

26. The President's News Conference, April 7, 1954, *Public Papers of the Presidents: Dwight D. Eisenhower, 1954* (Washington: GPO, 1960), 383.

27. Robert S. McNamara (with Brian Van De Mark), *In Retrospect: The Tragedy and Lessons of Vietnam* (New York: Vintage 1996), 218.

28. Christopher Andrew and Vasili Mitrokhin, *The Mitrokhin Archive II: The KGB and the World* (London: Allen Lane, 2006), 458.

29. Minutes of NSC meeting, May 11, 1976, *Foreign Relations of the United States 1969-1976*, Vol. E- 6, <http://history.state.gov/historicaldocuments/frus1969-76ve06>, 2-3 (accessed September 9, 2009).

30. See Piero Gleijeses, *Conflicting Missions: Havana, Washington, and Africa, 1959-1976* (Chapel Hill, NC: University of North Carolina Press 2002).

31. 7th Annual Message to Congress, December 2, 1823, Joint Committee of the House and Senate, *A Compilation of the Messages and Papers of the Presidents*, Vol. II (New York: Bureau of National Literature 1897), 787.

32. Ronald Reagan, *An American Life* (New York: Pocket, 1992), 473–4. There is, in fact, no evidence that Lenin actually said or wrote this and the "quotation" appears to be an invention of anti-communists. See Karl E. Meyer, "The Editorial Notebook: The Elusive Lenin," *New York Times*, 8 October 1985.

33. See "New Evidence on the Soviet Intervention in Afghanistan," Cold War International History Project *Bulletin*, Nos. 8–9, Winter 1996–7: 128–84.

34. State of the Union Address, January 23, 1980, *Public Papers of the Presidents: Jimmy Carter: 1980–81* (Washington, DC: Government Printing Office, 1981), 197.

35. M. Taylor Fravel, *Strong Borders Secure Nation: Cooperation and Conflict in China's Territorial Disputes*, (Princeton, NJ: Princeton University Press 2008), 322, 324. Mongolia had been part of China from the 13th century until 1911, when it broke away following the Chinese revolution of that year and later fell under Russian control. When the Chinese sought to negotiate over these border problems in the 1950s, the Russians balked.

36. Soviet government Statement, September 21, 1963, John Gittings (ed.), *Survey of the Sino-Soviet Dispute: A Commentary and Excerpts from the Recent Polemics, 1963–1967* (New York: Oxford University Press, 1968), 112.

37. "The Nation: An Interview with the President: The Jury is Out," *Time*, January 3, 1972, <http://www.time.com/time/magazine/article/0,9171,879011,00.html> (accessed September 24, 2009).

38. Recording of Conversation between Nixon and Kissinger, July 22, 1971, *Foreign Relations of the United States, 1969–1976*, Vol. XVII, 459, fn. 2.

39. George Bush and Brent Scowcroft, *A World Transformed* (New York: Knopf, 1998), 96.

40. Vojtech Mastny, "The Soviet Non-Invasion of Poland in 1980–81 and the End of the Cold War," Cold War International History Project Working Paper No. 23, September 1998, 15.

41. Minutes of the Soviet Politburo meeting, December 10, 1981, Cold War International History Project *Bulletin*, No. 5, Spring 1995, 136.

42. Mikhail Gorbachev, *Memoirs* (London: Transworld, 1996), 465.

43. Martin McCauley, *Gorbachev* (London: Longman, 1998), 66.

44. Michael H. Hunt, *Ideology and US Foreign Policy* (New Haven, CT: Yale University Press 1987).


## SELECT BIBLIOGRAPHY

Brzezinski, Zbigniew. *The Grand Chessboard*. New York: Basic Books, 1997.

Brown, L. Carl. *International Politics and the Middle East*. Princeton, NJ: Princeton University Press, 1984.

Chauprade, Aymeric. *Géopolitique: constantes et changements dans l'histoire*. Paris, 2007.

Cohen, Saul B. *Geopolitics of the World System*. Lanham, MD: Rowman & Littlefield 2003).

Dehio, Ludwig. *The Precarious Balance: the Politics of Power in Europe, 1494–1945*. New York: Knopf, 1962.

Fairgrieve, James. *Geography and World Power*. London: University of London, 1921.

Faringdon, Hugh. *Strategic Geography: NATO, the Warsaw Pact, and the Superpowers*. London: Routledge, 1989.

Gray, Colin S. *The Geopolitics of Superpower*. Lexington, KY: University Press of Kentucky, 1988.

Jian, Chen. *Mao's China and the Cold War*. Chapel Hill, NC: University of North Carolina Press 2001.

Kennedy, Paul. *The Rise and Fall of the Great Powers*. New York: Random House, 1987.

Kissinger, Henry. *Diplomacy*. London: Simon & Schuster, 1994.

Lacoste, Yves. *Géopolitique: la longue histoire d'aujourd'hui*. Paris: Larousse, 2008.

Lederer, Ivo J. ed., *Russian Foreign Policy: Essays in Historical Perspective*. New Haven: Yale University Press, 1962.

Pearce, Anthony J. ed., *Democratic Ideals and Reality*. New York: Norton, 1962.

Spykman, Nicholas J. *America's Strategy and World Politics*. New York: Harcourt Brace, 1942.

Spykman, Nicholas J. *The Geography of the Peace*. New York: Harcourt Brace, 1944.

Zubok, Vladislav. *A Failed Empire: The Soviet Union in the Cold War from Stalin to Gorbachev*. Chapel Hill, NC: University of North Carolina Press, 2007.

CHAPTER 6

........................................................................

# THE COLD WAR AND THE IMPERIALISM OF NATION-STATES[1]

........................................................................

## PRASENJIT DUARA

I wish to grasp the cold war in terms of the historical forces of imperialism and nationalism that have characterized the globe for over a century. Within that long century the
cold war may be seen as a distinct historical period shaped, as the name suggests, by a
rivalry between two nuclear superpowers or hegemons that threatened global destruction. As a period, the cold war is characterized not only by events, personalities, and
policy decisions, nor even by the paradigm of international relations alone. Rather its
historical significance arises from the re-configuration of long-term historical structures. The cold war rivalry provides the *frame of reference* within which the historical
forces of imperialism and nationalism interact with developments such as decolonization, multiculturalism, and new ideologies and modes of identity formation, thus producing a novel *configuration*. The evolving configuration transforms and is affected by
other historical processes regarding race, gender, class, religion, and rights among others. Of course, we come to recognize the configuration more surely only at the point
when it begins to unravel—at dusk when Hegel's Owl of Minerva takes flight—marking
the end of the period.

While the cold war hardly began or went out with a bang, superpower rivalry is
customarily said to have begun in 1947, when the Truman Doctrine sought to contain communism and the expansion of Soviet influence, and ended with the decline
and fall of the Soviet Union and the Eastern bloc in the late 1980s. I want to view the
period as a heuristic device, a provisional enframing that allows us to make sense of
the events and developments taking place between two dates. Periods in history
always make sense from a particular point of view, especially that of political power,
and there are many areas of life that are relatively untouched by the dominant historical structure. Further, as our historical perspective changes, we may see other
longer-term trends both pre-dating and outliving the cold war that may well be

more significant; if so, we may hope that our hypothesis would have enabled that view. Note also that this enframing provides the terms of reference; it says little about agency regarding whether the two superpowers were the only important actors or whether other powers or subaltern states could not play the system or test its boundaries.

While the equilibrium of cold war rivalry generated an entrenched political and ideological hegemony limiting the realization of political, economic, and imaginative possibilities in much of the world, there were several weak links in the system that contributed to its breakdown. While many look to America and Europe for the causes, I argue toward the end of this essay that the developing world represented significant weak links—or relative autonomy in the system—and played an equally important role in its collapse.

# HISTORICAL CONDITIONS OF THE COLD WAR

The end of World War II is thought to mark the end of an epoch. Not only were ultra-nationalist ideologies of fascism, Nazism, and racism defeated, but 1945 also marked the beginning of the end of imperialism. The last was not fully accepted by European imperialists, who made several last-ditch efforts to retake their colonies, especially in Southeast Asia and Africa. But by 1960 there were few Europeans who believed in the need for colonies.[2] The decolonization movement had triumphed, and the postwar world order was enshrined in the United Nations ideal of national self-determination and global development. Yet whereas the UN world order was enshrined in theory, the real world order was determined by the two superpowers and their rivalry. I turn to the longer-term history in which this real order ought to be seen.

While the nation-state (or at least those that were not ultra-nationalist or fascistic) was deemed in the UN ideal to be a model of self-governance, through most of its history the nation-state had been inseparable from imperialist domination of other peoples and societies. By the 19th century the nation-state was already established in the major imperialist societies of Britain and France. Together with the national capitalists, the nation-state became the principal player in the inter-imperialist rivalry for colonies and resources. British imperialism dominated the world for much of the 19th century, but from the last third of the century this dominance came to be increasingly threatened by the rise of new nation-states with imperialist ambitions, including Germany, Italy, Russia, Japan, and the United States. Most of these states sought to modernize and compete globally by creating and mobilizing the nationalist—even hyper-nationalist—sentiments of its citizenry.

The end of World War I led to yet another change in imperialism undertaken not by the old European imperialist powers but by new powers such as Japan, the United States, and the Soviet Union. This is an imperialism that I call the "imperialism of nation-states," and its first expression may be seen in the Japanese puppet state of

Manchukuo established in northeast China (or Manchuria) from 1932 to 1945. In part responding to the increasing demands for economic and political parity made by the new anti-imperialist movement in the colonies, and in part because of economic competition with and between the new imperialists, imperialists sought to create regional formations or economic blocs. These colonies or subordinate territories were often re-constituted as nominally sovereign nation-states, although they remained militarily in thrall to the metropole. The imperialism of nation-states reflected a strategic reorientation of the periphery to be part of an organic formation designed to attain global supremacy for the imperial power. As Albert Lebrun declared after World War I, the goal was now to "unite France to all those distant Frances in order to permit them to combine their efforts to draw from one another reciprocal advantages."[3]

With the simultaneous rise of rights consciousness in the colonies and dependencies and the increased need for resource and social mobilization within them, it was more efficient for the imperialists to foster *modern* and *indirectly* controlled institutions in them. The aim was to control these areas by dominating their institutions of mobilization, such as banks, the transportation infrastructure, and political institutions, which were created to resemble those of the metropole (such as legislative councils, institutions of political tutelage, and political parties like the communist parties or the Concordia in Manchukuo). In short, unlike British free trade imperialism, several interwar imperialists attended to the modernization of institutions and identities. They often espoused cultural or ideological similarities—including sometimes anti-colonial ideologies—even while racism and nationalism accompanied the reality of military-political domination.

Subordinate states were militarily dependent upon and economically mobilized for the sake of the metropole. Nevertheless, it was not necessarily in the latter's interest to have them economically or institutionally backward. This imperialism thus occasionally entailed a separation of economic and military-political dimensions. In some situations, as in the Japan–Manchukuo relationship (and later, as we shall see, in the Soviet case), massive investments and resources flowed into the *client-states*, thereby breaching the classical dualism between an industrialized metropole and a colony focused on the primary sector common to colonial imperialism.[4]

## IMPERIALISM AND THE COLD WAR

In its ideal expression, the cold war represented a logical culmination of the new imperialism. Two superpowers sought to gain the loyalty of theoretically sovereign nation-states that would be militarily dependent upon the hegemonic power and subject to its political, economic, and ideological strategies. Of course, reality was much messier; first there were rivalries within each camp, and the British did not give up hope of superpower status until the Suez crisis of 1956 and the Taiwan Straits crisis of 1958.[5] In this

respect, the Soviet- People's Republic of China (PRC) split was much more consequential in realigning the balance of power. Second, there was the historical force of nationalism operating not only within each bloc but also outside it through the non-aligned
movement (the rhetoric of which was more powerful than its politics), which resisted
the hegemons and their strategies. Finally, the very polarization of the hegemons themselves permitted a few key players like Hong Kong or Ghana to leverage their status as
intermediaries between the two powers.

During the post-World War II era, the Soviet Union's creation of a regional system
of militarily dependent states in Eastern Europe reflected many features of the new
imperialism. A shared anti-imperialist and anti-capitalist ideology sanctioned a centralized economic and political system. The Soviet Union combined economic leverage and military threat to integrate states that were often more economically developed
than itself into a regional economy. In some ways the imperialism of the Soviet Union
revealed the counter-economic consequences of this logic of empire. Not only were
the client-states of the Soviet Union in Europe often more developed, but also the
USSR may have subsidized their economies by supplying them with cheap oil and raw
materials while importing finished products from their economies. This was the price
paid by the imperial power to create and maintain dependence and assure its
security.[6]

In part because of the consciousness of its own colonial past, and with the exception
of a few places (most notably, the Philippines), the United States had long practiced
imperialism without colonialism. After the Spanish–American War in 1898, the
United States created a system of client-states around the Caribbean basin in Central
America. These nominally independent states became increasingly dependent on the
United States, which accounted for more than three-fourths of the region's foreign
trade as well as the bulk of foreign investment. During the decade of the 1920s, when
Japan was experimenting with indirect imperialism in Manchuria, the United States
too was seeking to develop and refine informal control over Central American countries, especially as it faced revolutionary nationalism in the region. Officials, diplomats, and business groups stressed means such as US control of banking,
communication facilities, investments in natural resources, and the development of
education—particularly the training of elites in American-style constitutions, "free
elections," and orthodox business ideas. But the threat and reality of military intervention remained close at hand.[7]

American imperialism was characterized not only by the Monroe Doctrine but also
by the Open Door policy. Although there were contradictions and tensions between the
two approaches, there were also continuities, most importantly in the practice of using
sovereign or nominally sovereign polities to advance American interests. In 1917
President Woodrow Wilson pointed to the continuities when he declared that the
nations of the world should "with one accord adopt the doctrine of President Monroe as
the doctrine of the world…no nation should seek to extend its polity over any other
nation or people." But this clearly did not exclude using military force upon recalcitrant
nations. Just two weeks before Wilson had sent troops to the Dominican Republic and

committed US military forces in Haiti and Mexico as well.[8] The United States sought to foster an ideological and economic hegemony among its client-states by creating them as reliable emulators subject to external economic and military constraints. Note, however, that this imperialism did not become developmentally oriented until the early 1960s, when it was forced to respond to the Cuban revolution.

The tensions between American interests and global enlightenment were to be contained not only by military power, but perhaps more importantly also by the notion of a *limited* self-determination—the idea of tutelage. As Secretary of Interior Franklin Lane wrote in 1922: "What a people hold they hold as trustees for the world.... It is good American practice. The Monroe Doctrine is an expression of it.... That is why we are talking of backward peoples and recognizing for them another law than that of self-determination, a limited law of self-determination, a leading-string law."[9] Little wonder then that the Japanese representative at the League of Nations hearings on Manchukuo repeatedly insisted on the Asiatic Monroe Doctrine as Japan's prerogative in Asia.

In the post-World War II period, this combination of interest, enlightenment, and military violence developed into what Carl Parrini has called "ultraimperialism." The latter refers to US efforts to maintain cooperation and reduce conflict among imperialist nations who were busily scrambling to create monopolistic or exclusive market conditions in various parts of the world during the first half of the 20th century.[10] "Ultraimperialism" is secured by a chain of military bases around the globe—and structures such as the International Monetary Fund, General Agreement on Tariffs and Trade, and World Bank—to enable the conditions of cooperation among advanced capitalist powers and to facilitate the new (developmental or modernizing) imperialism in the decolonized world. With the cold war, the US developed a global empire employing, in the words of Arrighi, Hui, Hung, and Selden, a vast system of "political and military vassalage" and fostering a "functional specialization between the imperial and vassal (*nation*) states ...." In this respect, the postwar United States represents the apogee of the imperialism of nation-states.[11]

My point is not that the cold war represents the essence of imperialism. Rather, we cannot understand the cold war fully without analyzing how the historical relationship between imperialism and nationalism came to be configured anew in the postwar circumstances. Imperialism no longer emphasized conquest on the basis of innate differences among peoples and their inevitable destinies of superiority and exploitation. As noted, moreover, it was development oriented, and there were considerable opportunities for states and societies to move up the economic ladder. The imperialist factor lay in the imposition of *designs for enlightenment* upon emergent nations by an enormously superior national power backed by military force. These enlightenment designs were shot through with paternalism, national interests, and covert racist prejudices that constantly produced contradictions and tensions. Indeed, one could argue that it was this configuration of national imperialism that led to resistance to both the Soviet Union (contributing to its decline) as well as the United States in many parts of the world.

# THE COLD WAR AND NATIONS

We will explore this cold war configuration through the analysis of the three camps often identified in the literature: the mature capitalist world allied to the US, the socialist camp dominated by the Soviet Union, and the developing world of decolonizing nation-states. Although it was the rivalry between the first two camps that shaped the global landscape, the relations among the first two camps were not symmetrical. The description by Arrighi et al. of the US Empire as "political and military vassalage" indicates a hierarchical coalition around a military hegemon rather than pure clientage. Thus Britain, Japan, France, and Germany developed a close partnership of interests and were important beneficiaries of US strategies and investments.

The reduced power and severe indebtedness of the British as produced by World War II not only increased the dependence of the British upon the US but also renewed its need for empire to service the American debt. The chief mechanism used was to increase the dollar earnings of British colonial and dependent states and exchange these at an imperially mandated, lower than market, pound sterling rate. Although the US was not necessarily keen on the imperialist sterling zone, the onset of the cold war made it much more favorably disposed to maintain the status quo with regard to the old empires. Roger Louis and Ronald Robinson have detailed the ways in which the British Empire was rescued and transformed as part of the Allied front in the cold war, especially in the Middle East and in Southeast Asia.

During the Suez crisis in 1956, the US refused to back British and French military efforts to prevent nationalization of the Canal by Egypt's Nasser. Particularly after a brief exchange of nuclear saber-rattling between the two superpowers, Britain saw the virtue of the American perspective on independence of the colonies. It settled into its role as junior partner to the US in order to maintain its economic interests in Africa, the Middle East, and Southeast Asia by seeking to control the independence movements and keep them away from Soviet influence. Britain and the European powers increasingly began to rely on American finances, investments, and most of all, strategic concerns in Africa to protect their own interests.[12]

US dominance within its camp was characterized first and foremost by a chain of about 1,700 military bases in over a hundred nation-states that had varying degrees of clientelist ties to it. These garrisons were strategic enclaves supervised by the Pentagon and sustained by—as much as they sustained—a vast military industrial complex. The bases were often highly privileged enclaves that frequently fostered arrogant attitudes toward the surrounding population, particularly in the non-European regions.[13] For instance, entire townships or camptowns in the Philippines and Korea composed of the sex trade as the main industry sprung up around the bases.[14]

Economically, the principal client-states in Asia, such as Japan, South Korea, Taiwan, and Turkey, benefited handsomely and grew rapidly from their ties with the US. US economic and military aid to South Korea and Taiwan was among the greatest and undoubtedly contributed to the economic miracle that these two societies performed from the 1960s. For instance, between 1946 and 1979 (although mostly until the mid-1960s), South Korea received about $7 billion in military and $6 billion in economic aid. Taiwan was also the recipient of similar magnitudes of aid. Privileged access to US markets and US tolerance of protected domestic markets made South Korea under military dictator Park Chung Hee, which by the late 1940s had become one of the poorest countries in the world, into the 12th largest economy by the late 1970s. At the same time, this backing strengthened the capacity of authoritarian development and the national security state in most of these client-states.[15]

Thus, while the economies of US allies and client-states in Asia developed rapidly, subservience to US military power and interests did not work out smoothly in the wider society. In Japan, a popular, ethnic nationalism identified with an anti-imperialist stance came to be directed against the US.[16] Here the extent of popular disaffection with US policies and ideology became visible during certain periods, for instance during the renewal of the unpopular 1951 Security Treaty in 1960 and the Vietnam War, but was limited in duration and spread. South Korea, South Vietnam, Taiwan, the Philippines, and other smaller allies were not only heavily garrisoned with military bases, but also suffered local military dictatorships through much of the period. The resistance in Vietnam across a wide spectrum of the population is of course well known. Although the economic strategies and ready access to the consumer markets of the developed world in the West enabled considerable economic growth in some of the other societies, the population became deeply alienated from the highly repressive governments. In Korea and the Philippines (and to a lesser extent in Taiwan), popular resistance contributed to the democratization of these states in the last decade of the cold war.

Solidarity within the socialist camp was much weaker within society and across nations. From the early period, there was considerable disaffection with the tight state controls of life and economy produced by the generalization of the Soviet state's Stalinist model which was built not only in Soviet republics and Eastern Europe but also in Asian countries like China, Mongolia, North Vietnam, and North Korea. There were many outbursts of resistance in these societies, and the severe and violent repression that followed ensured that disaffection would continue to fester. But this did not apply to all areas of society. Socialist revolution had brought large classes of the poor and disenfranchised a better material life, especially in the Soviet Union and China, and the all-pervasive ideology of socialist personhood and moral superiority over capitalism constituted an important source of identity for many people. But socialist egalitarianism and collectivism were not the only ideological instruments fostered to build solidarity. The other powerful ideology of the time developed and utilized by the Soviet state was the idea of nationality rights.

While the idea of national rights goes back to the French Revolution, Bolshevik theorists developed the idea of a federated state of nations in the Soviet Union as an alternative to the imperialist domination of "backward" peoples or races (note, however, the Chinese Republic of Five Nationalities was instituted five years before, in 1912).[17] In the process, what developed was an idea of nationhood as constituted by the cultures of different nationalities and could also be seen in opposition to assimilative ideas of nationhood, such as for instance, in the model of the "melting pot" in the US. Interestingly, the US was to develop its version of this idea—multiculturalism and respect for the variety of national cultures both within and outside the US—only with the advent of the cold war.

In contrast to the European socialists of the Second International, the Bolsheviks, and even Stalin, who would famously work from the 1920s to curtail their autonomy, were theoretically committed to the rights of nations to self-determination based on the right to secede.[18] The Bolshevik position on national self-determination entailed territorial autonomy without party autonomy. Communist parties in the non-Russian territories were not particularly nationalized, and the Soviet goal was to subordinate national loyalties to "proletarian" (i.e., party) interests. Japanese empire builders in the 1930s were quick to study the Soviet model of the multinational state for Manchukuo. To these observers Soviet nationality policy fulfilled the goals of federalism and protected minority rights while at the same time strengthening the power of the Soviet state and the military in relation to separatism. Thus, nationalism was not suppressed but utilized positively for the goals of the state.[19] Although for different reasons, the strategies of utilizing nationality policy for state control failed in both Manchukuo and the Soviet Union.

Of course, the Soviet Union practically prevented secession until the very end. But, according to Rogers Brubaker, it did a great deal to institutionalize territorial nationhood and ethnic nationality as fundamental categories of political and personal understanding. The Soviet strategy was to contain, control, and even harness different sources of dissent by creating national-territorial structures of administrative control and fostering loyal national elites. The Soviet state may have been said to have produced both quasi-nation-states and ethnic nationalities where there were often none before.[20] Ironically, it ended up fostering national consciousness in places where it had been very weak or non-existent, often at the expense of identification with the Soviet Union which never succeeded in generating its own narrative or symbolism of nationhood.

Although official nationalities existed only in the Soviet Union, Yugoslavia, and Czechoslovakia (after 1968), as Katherine Verdery argues, ethnic nationalism intensified and became closely intertwined with socialism in all the other East European socialist republics. Despite the official ideology of trans-ethnic class politics, in the absence of other civic organizations, ethno-nationalism mirrored the monolithic nature of the party-state. Just as the party's image of the "People-as-One" cast all who disagreed with it as enemies of the People, so, too, ethno-nationalists could depict those outside the pure nation as its potential enemy. This kind of politics became particularly nasty with the collapse of the system, when ethnic leaders scrambled to create new states dominated by their group, thus reproducing through still more vicious ways—such as ethnic cleansing—the close connection between (imperialistic) domination and nationalism.[21]

The imperial national configuration in which national culture was utilized in the Soviet republics for purposes of the Soviet state and socialist interests affected many dimensions of social life. For instance, in the Central Asian socialist republic of

Uzbekistan, the Soviet party-state sought to "enlighten" society by seeking the support of Muslim women both to reform such practices as polygamy and bride-price and simultaneously establish the power of the party-state in this region. In turn, these policies generated resistance from Uzbek men. Not surprisingly, Uzbek national identity emerged in their resistance to such enlightenment campaigns, particularly over the symbolism of veiled women. Uzbek women, whose stories are archived by Douglas Northrop, found themselves painfully caught between their patriarchal society and the Soviet state.[22]

The new imperial national configuration in the US—though by no means identical to the Soviet Union—also had important social ramifications within the US and in its attitudes and policies abroad. While the US had distanced itself from European racial imperialism since at least the war, it continued to erect racist barriers to citizenship—for instance against Asian immigrants—until 1942. Moreover, the decolonizing world noted a distinct ambivalence of the US toward the ability of darker-skinned people to govern themselves through the early postwar decades and sometimes also became implicated in the efforts of European powers to restore their imperial claims in the colonies. Once the doctrine of containment became fully developed and anti-communism hit fever pitch –particularly with the McCarthy hearings in the 1950s—the US began to be seen increasingly as a neo-imperial power, especially in the non-aligned nations of the decolonizing world.

In fact, US attitudes toward race and the colonial world in the era of United Nations multi-nationalism underwent a fundamental change. Although the roots of change were probably connected to wartime developments, especially the alliance with China, the postwar attitudes were influenced by the decolonizing movement in the context of the rivalry with the Soviet Union for the allegiance of these nations. In other words, the circumstances of the cold war itself induced many of these changes. Christina Klein has shown in her exploration of "middle-brow culture" in the US how the fear of the loss of Asia to communism, especially after the Korean war and wars in Southeast Asia, led to radical changes in the image of American nationhood as premised upon a multicultural society. She uses the idea of cultural hegemony to show how representations of Asia and the Pacific reinforced the "cold war consensus" which supported US expansion of power across the world through the 1950s. Through these representations, "structures of feeling" were created, which worked to channel ideological configurations into the field of emotions, experience, and consciousness of ordinary people. What Klein calls "Cold War Orientalism" did not merely seek to contain communism; it sought to sentimentally integrate Americans with the Orientals who had not yet been made communist, both within the US and internationally.[23]

The image of the US as "the nation of nations" comes through particularly well in the enormously successful historical novel by James Michener (1959), *Hawaii*. As a land of diverse cultures, Hawaii could emerge as the model of racial utopia with its flows and mingling of Polynesian, Japanese, Chinese, and New England whites. It is perhaps not too surprising that the civil rights movement also began to develop in this environment. At the same time, this new-found appreciation continued to be channeled through the paternalistic designs of enlightenment for the misfortunate and child-like Asians and other backward peoples. Klein also notes that the image of Asians as metaphorical children to American parents—as well as the postwar phenomenon of adoption of many Asian children pioneered by Pearl Buck's organization—justified American intervention in Asia.[24]

Notably, during the Pacific War the Japanese had also appealed to their Asian "brethren" to resist the US and European imperialists. This appeal, which had justified Japanese intervention in East Asia, extended the imperial Japanese metaphor of the family-state to all Asians as part of a family of nations. The Russians also sought to reinforce their solidarity in the second world by appealing to their younger socialist brothers in China and elsewhere during the 1950s. Toward China this kind of patronizing attitude was accompanied by a communist evolutionary narrative of history in which the Chinese were seen as backward and in need of help because they had been caught for so long in the stagnant Asiatic mode of production. Needless to say, these euphemisms of dominance backfired most surely in a newly resurgent and proud China.

## HEGEMONY AND COUNTER-HEGEMONY

In the developing world the hegemonic cold war configuration and decolonizing and anti-imperialist movements came to be shaped by each other. On the one hand, the anti-colonial struggles had a major impact on the nature of the cold war, influencing the responses of the superpowers and their future in some cases. The best example is, of course, the Vietnam War, which strained the financial and moral power of the US and contributed to the relative weakening of US economic strength vis-à-vis Japan and Europe. On the other hand, by and large the cold war had a deeply divisive impact on the developing world, weakening what counter-hegemonic potential it possessed.

One of the cruellest ironies of the cold war was that, while the US and its allies championed democracy and freedom as their goals, more often than not in the developing world they ended up supporting undemocratic military regimes, dictators, and monarchies alienated from the aspirations of the ordinary people. The frequent intervention of Western powers to protect their interests in Africa, the Middle East, and Southeast Asia, and the covert and overt US operations in Latin America, polarized and radicalized large segments of the population in these societies. Driven by the need to secure oil supplies in the Middle East, Anglo-American interests sought to develop the pre-war system of mandates and protectorates by establishing military bases and reliable clients who were both anti-Soviet and anti-democratic. In 1953, the CIA engineered the coup in Iran that overthrew the elected government of Muhammad Mossadeq which had nationalized Iranian oil, and restored the Shah as an American protégé.

Even in South Asia, seemingly quite distant from the lethal cold war rivalries, the US involvement with Pakistan considerably affected the nature of that society. Hamza Alavi has shown that the strong military alliance with Pakistan—including a highly secretive

US military base in Pakistan near the Persian Gulf—did not, contrary to Indian views, have to do with its rivalry with India. Rather it was part of a new Anglo-American strategy for the defense of oil interests in the Gulf. Around the time the CIA overthrew the Mossadeq government in August 1953, there was a flurry of negotiations between the Pakistani government and military and the US and a military alliance between the two countries was concluded in May 1954. In 1955, Pakistan became a signatory to the Baghdad Pact.[25] Through these treaties Pakistan (and Turkey, the other trusted ally in the region) undertook to provide military service whenever an allied regime (such as the Shah's) was threatened internally or externally. The extent of American involvement with the Pakistani military was so great that it completely marginalized the civilian government even before the first military coup in that country in 1959. The US-Pakistan relationship and the deteriorating relations between India and China as well as the Soviet Union and China led India, despite its official non-aligned stand, to tilt toward the Soviet Union. It received considerable military and industrial support from the latter. Although the US has been careful not to overtly support Pakistan in the wars against India, it is nonetheless ironic that it found itself allied with the wrong side when it came to democracy and the national aspirations of Bangladeshis.[26]

The most dramatic intervention in Africa took place after Congo (Katanga) won its independence from Belgium in 1960. Patrice Lubumba, who tried to build an independent nation-state on the socialist model and align his nation with the Soviet Union, was removed from power and finally murdered by his opponents, backed militarily by the Europeans and the Kennedy administration. Congo became a vast client-state of the United States with huge investments in its mineral resources. Similarly the coup directed against Sukarno and the communists in Indonesia, where hundreds of thousands—perhaps even a million—people were killed in 1965, had the tacit backing of the CIA.[27]

As Odd Arne Westad has shown, Soviet intervention in the developing world was not as extensive or committed until the 1970s and 1980s. While the Soviets supported radical movements in Africa, Latin America, and Asia, these were largely home-grown Marxist or leftist movements which sought the support of the Soviet bloc. The early Soviet leadership was not quite convinced that revolution could be truly successful in these societies even though it was important for Soviet superpower status to be influential in the emerging nation-states and utilize them for the goals of Soviet socialism. Communist victory in Vietnam among other developments in the 1970s, however, emboldened the Soviet leadership to intervene more actively in places such as Ethiopia, Angola, and finally, with disastrous effects, in Afghanistan from 1979 to 1989. Afghanistan also represented the spread of Islamist radicalism as an alternative to the ideologies of socialism and capitalism and to the legitimacy of the national unit as the boundary of cold war politics.[28]

Even while the cold war represented a new type of imperialist or hegemonic domination of other nation-states and intervention in nation-states belonging to the other camp, the principle of national sovereignty remained the exclusive basis of legitimate and legal power. The rest was informal, covert, and real. This interface between the national and the imperial was a crucial factor in the cold war configuration. I hesitate to call this interface a "structural hypocrisy," because both parts, the legal/legitimate and the illegal/illegitimate—the imperialism of nation-states—were essential to cold war politics. Born in the circumstances of competition, the nation-state generated and required domination of others for self-fulfillment. "Spy versus spy" was paradoxically only the most visible dimension of the novelty of the cold war.

The importance of the national *form* in the cold war should not be underestimated. The legal charter of nations was sanctioned by the United Nations and other multi-national forums, including the General Agreement on Tariffs and Trade (GATT), which regulated trade ties between sovereign nations in the non-socialist world. The nation was the only bearer of rights in international society, and this recognition was a critical resource for states, whatever their real status. We have already indicated the importance of the national principle in the Soviet camp. But the equilibrium sustained by cold war rivalry tended to congeal the political terrain of nation-states organized in the two camps. The territorial boundaries and the institutional and political arrangements estab-lished to the superpower's advantage in the new nation-states had its military support.

The superpowers sought to preserve or acquiesce in the dominant groups that had formed the client nation-state because any change or destabilization might strengthen the other side. Since these arrangements had often not evolved historically—as they had in the West—but had been hastily put together by urban or military elites (including Eastern and Central Europe) in highly contested terrains, the new states in both camps were frequently repressive and partisan. This often led to an interesting variant of the national-imperial configuration whereby the dominant ethnic group or military leaders or a combination were able to use tacit or overt hegemonic support to suppress other ethnic or subaltern classes within the new nation-state. The number of separatist, irre-dentist, and popular—religious and civic—movements that broke out with the weaken-ing or collapse of the cold war is evidence of this suppression.[29]

Another area in which the cold war affected the decolonizing nations was the pattern of national economic development, which was modeled on those of one or the other superpowers. Even the non-aligned movement, led by countries such as India, which sought to develop a new economic development model, ended up combining elements from the Soviet and free-market system (arguably gaining the advantages of neither). The theories of its founding fathers like Mahatma Gandhi, based as they were on autar-kic, self-sufficient rural communities, were shelved even before they saw the light of day as Nehru sought to develop a Soviet-style planned economy with elements of free enter-prise. Indeed, the non-aligned movement per se was not sufficiently unified or strong to upset the power equilibrium that sustained the cold war.

While patterns of economic development largely followed those of the hegemons, the state form typically adopted in the new nations was the form of territorial (though often military and not civic) citizenship in a centralizing, developmental, and sometimes, redistributive state. To be sure, the origins of the developmental state can be traced to the interwar period, but the dynamics of the cold war reinforced the pattern. Both the socialist state and the welfare state in Europe reinforced the anti-colonial movement's rhetoric of the need for a strong state to achieve the goals of social justice. In Asia, even among nations most influenced by American strategies of economic development, such as the export-oriented strategies of Japan, Korea, and Taiwan—in contrast to the import-substitution strategy of the rest—the centralizing state played an increasingly important role in society. In part, the US concurred with this model of the strong state because of the undemocratic nature of many of its allies and clients, such as Park Chung Hee in Korea and Chiang Kai-shek in Taiwan. Note that while "modernization theory," which represented the academic and developmental paradigm for non-revolutionary and non-socialist economic development, is well-known for minimizing problems of class and stratification, at the same time it did not seek to minimize the role of the state—a phenomenon that was to become much more pronounced in the post-cold war neo-liberal ideology. This kind of state-building and penetration in the new nations also produced a massive societal backlash.

It is important to understand how the developmental state came to play an important role in the cold war configuration. In the roughly hundred-year history of the modern nation-state prior to the cold war, nation-making took place in an external environment driven by competition, imperialism, racism, or ethnic chauvinism and warfare, and domestically by homogenizing populations and developing resources for economic growth. The cold war stand-off permitted decolonizing elites some breathing room to develop their nation-states in somewhat artificially delimited spaces, free from external competitive pressures, but not from internal challenges.

Faced with the challenge of creating a nation from its diverse, sometimes warring communities, state builders in the new nations utilized the prevailing territorial model of the nation-state, which granted equal citizenship to all its inhabitants regardless of ethnicity, gender, or religion, as a means of creating a homogenized citizenry. Other military and administrative means of centralizing power, often sanctioned by the relevant superpower, were more commonly utilized to impose local designs of enlightenment upon an often unwilling population whose life-worlds were being destroyed even as tangible benefits from the changes were not readily evident. James Scott's insights into the high-modernist authoritarian state in the developing and East European "second" world are relevant here. The state which sought to administratively reorder society as "legible" by abstract, measurable, and large-scale scientific and engineering means was responding as much to the perceived backwardness as to the recalcitrance of the population, who often did not cooperate with its centralizing and modernizing projects.[30]

Although economic growth was relatively sluggish outside the zone of US client-states in East Asia, through the development and control of education, media, and cultural policies many of the new states succeeded in controlling the means of identity creation in their societies. Take, for instance, religious policies during the cold war period. Many new Asian states sought to monitor the religious practices of their population by enhancing the visibility of these practices in the eyes of the state. It did so by destroying uncontrollable religious groups, co-opting religious leadership, and segregating religious communities to better control their activities. This seemed to work in large part not only in East Asia but also in regions which had seen religious volatility earlier such as Indonesia and South Asia. It is remarkable that since the end of the cold war this ability to channel or subordinate religious identities to national goals has come rapidly undone in many parts of the world.[31]

We cannot undertake to study the post-cold war world dominated by a single hegemon and ideology here. Suffice it to say that the redistributive state and even the civic territorial state model are considerably weaker than before. With the entrenchment of a global market society, the state is no longer the exclusive creator of identity. Globalization may not have weakened the state per se—and in some areas it may even have strengthened it—but state nationalism is now only one among several identities created by globalization and localization. We see the transition quite clearly in the flourishing of transnational religion. The globalization of Islam, to which I will return below, is the most evident phenomenon. The rise of Hindu nationalism is in fact a transnational phenomenon. It had been largely contained during the cold war but has flourished since, in part as a response to the resurgence of Islam. In China the tremendous growth of religious affiliation and identity is testimony to the vastly changed political and social circumstances since the cold war. While the reasons for its emergence can doubtless be found in the rampant spread of capitalism in China, the transnational and local orientations of religious life are equally significant. Christianity, mostly built around house churches, is the most rapidly growing religion, and native Chinese religions, most famously—but by no means exclusively—the Falungong, also have universalist aspirations.

I have indicated the hegemonic power of the cold war configuration upon much of the developing world by looking at national modes of control (both internally and externally) and statist models of development which also channeled much of the ideological identifications of the period. In these concluding pages I will recount two cases of counter-hegemonic forces emerging from the weak links and the reactions to this domination from the developing world that contributed significantly to the end of the cold war. The first case is the People's Republic of China. After it successfully conducted its nuclear weapons test in 1964, China, which was equally estranged from the United States and the Soviet Union, not only was able to play off each power against the other, but it arguably also contributed to the ultimate collapse of the system. During the ideologically and politically polarized Cultural Revolution (1966–9), the Soviet Union came to be seen as a greater threat than the United States. China's overtures to the Nixon administration were, some argued, a direct response to the fear of Soviet attack—even nuclear attack—in 1969.[32] One could thus argue that the nuclear threat not only acted as a deterrent from first attack but also influenced important shifts in the balance of power that ultimately undermined the principal superpower rivalry itself. The Reagan administration, with its heightened ideological fervor –and emboldened by the neutralization of China—ultimately raised military spending to such high levels that the Soviet Union could no longer match it and continue to supply the consumer needs of its population.

But was it only the acquisition of nuclear power that permitted China to play the relatively independent role it did? Nuclear power was certainly a necessary factor, but it was not a sufficient one. In many ways the Chinese rural revolution, which was independent of the Soviet pattern, produced a mighty party-state that was able to break away early from Soviet dependence. This was a sufficient factor as well as the precondition driving

China to acquire the bomb. There is now debate as to how much the fledgling PRC had to concede to the Soviet Union in the Sino-Soviet Treaty of Friendship of 1950, which enabled cooperation of the two during the Korean War and Soviet aid to China through the 1950s.[33] Although the Chinese gained a great deal, the treaty was also alleged to have perpetrated Soviet imperialist-style special interests in the border regions of Xinjiang, Mongolia, and, to some extent, Manchuria. Whatever the merits of the debate, it is clear that Chinese independence was not compromised for long. The independence and power of the Chinese revolutionary state was the historical condition for the emergence of one of the crucial disequilibrating factors in the cold war. Agency in such hegemonic systems as the cold war emerges not only from the attractive power of consumer capitalism but also from alternative and momentous historical developments.

The second case is the globalization of Islam. Indeed, the globalization of Islam is not simply a post-cold war phenomenon. In many ways it was a result of, even a backlash against, the cold war configuration. From the early 1980s the mujahidin, militarily supported by the US and its Muslim allies, played the major role in driving out the Soviets from Afghanistan and bringing the Taliban to power. In turn the mujahidin were encouraged by the success of the Islamic revolution in Iran. Even though these events preceded the end of the cold war, they represented disenchantment with the two Western options of capitalist and socialist modernity.[34]

It is instructive in this context to explore the writings of a relatively obscure Iranian Marxist turned Islamist Jalal Al-i Ahmad (1923–69), who died a decade before the Islamic revolution but whose work was immensely popular among the youth in Iran at the time of the revolution. Al-i Ahmad's early Marxism furnishes him with a radical critique of the contemporary imperialism of industrialized nations—including Europe, North America, and also Soviet Russia—which not only exploited the people and resources of the rest of the world but also patronized the people as objects of knowledge and "raw material for every sort of Western laboratory." In Al-i Ahmad's view, the socialist camp is no less materialist and greedy and represents "would-be corporate colonists" who can sit quite comfortably at the same table as their capitalist counterparts. What gall him particularly are the hypocritical designs of enlightenment that strip a people of their culture and identity. "Thus only we in our Islamic totality, formal and real, obstructed the spread (through colonialism, effectively equivalent to Christianity) of European civilization, that is, the opening of new markets to the West's industries." (61–2). Note how the Marxist materialist critique is no longer sufficient to counter the outrages against morality and identity.[35]

# CONCLUSION

My argument for figuring the cold war as a period began with the emergence of superpower rivalry as a framework for containment. The effort to contain communism and capitalism (and covertly subvert the other), however, entailed a larger containment or channeling of the flow of possible change in various areas of political, social, and cultural life within its political imagination. The cold war rivalry sustained an equilibrium which tended to congeal not only the power relations between hegemonic and client-states but also the political contours of nation-states in the two camps backed by economic inducements, military power, and nuclear threat. The models of development, structures of clientage and dominance, including designs of enlightenment, and even many gender and racial-cultural relationships followed tracks that were similar within and often between the two camps. This configuration was the hegemonic form that characterized the period.

To what extent was the cold war configuration responsible for the imposition of the nation-state model, in particular, the model of the centralizing, and often authoritarian, developmental state in the developing world? To be sure, many of the features of this state model appeared in the pre-war era. Yet equally, the advantages found by hegemonic powers in the nation form to control, incentivize (key sectors usually of the elite), and mobilize support for the goals of the hegemon played a key role in the spread of the model. Indeed, the end of the cold war appears to have significantly transformed the model of the centralizing, developmental state in favor of the "Washington Consensus," which emphasized state withdrawal and redeployment, privatization of public goods, and the model of the consumer citizen. The displacement of national regulatory frameworks by a relatively unregulated global financial system has produced its own crisis. While the nation-state and nationalism have certainly not gone away, our present crisis reveals the replacement of one configuration by another.

And what about the counter-hegemonic forces that played an important role in bringing changes to the cold war? China's role was disruptive of the rivalry and political order, but it turned out to have been counter-hegemonic only in this limited sense. Indeed, the centrality of capitalism and nationalism in China affiliates it with the victorious capitalist side in which it has become a key player today, albeit with its own developmental path. Whether we like it or not, the role of global Islam may be more powerfully counter-hegemonic. Both of these forces emerged in regions of the non-Western world that were able to recover confidence from their relatively independent historical paths—whether revolutionary or tradition-directed. Does this portend the beginning of the end of a long period of Western hegemony?

## NOTES

1. I develop these themes at further length in "The Cold War as a Historical Period: An Intepretive Essay," *Journal of Global History* 6 (November 2011): 457–80.
2. William Roger Louis and Ronald Robinson, "Empire Preserv'd: How the Americans put anti-Communism before Anti-imperialism," in Prasenjit Duara, ed., *Decolonization: Perspectives from Now and Then* (London: Routledge, 2004), 155–7.
3. As quoted in D. Bruce Marshall, *The French Colonial Myth and Constitution-Making in the Fourth Republic* (New Haven, CT: Yale University Press, 1973), 44. See also Prasenjit Duara, "The Imperialism of 'Free Nations': Japan, Manchukuo and the History of the Present" in

Ann Stoler, Carole McGranahan, and Peter Perdue, eds., *Imperial Formations and their Discontents* (Santa Fe, NM: School of American Research Press, 2007).

4. The OED defines the client in the Roman Empire as, "A plebeian under the patronage of a patrician, in this relation called a patron (*patronus*), who was bound, in return for certain services, to protect his client's life and interests." *Oxford English Dictionary*, <http://dictionary.oed.com>. See also Prasenjit Duara, *Sovereignty and Authenticity: Manchukuo and the East Asian Modern* (Boulder, CO: Rowman and Littlefield, 2003).

5. Steve Tsang, *The Cold War's Odd Couple: The Unintended Partnership between the ROC and the UK, 1950–1958* (London: I.B. Tauris, 2006), 10, 194.

6. See Paul Marer and Kazimierz Z. Poznanski, "Costs of Domination, Benefits of Subordination," in Jan F. Triska, ed., *Dominant Powers and Subordinate States: The United States in Latin America and the Soviet Union in Eastern Europe* (Durham, NC: Duke University Press, 1986), 371–99.

7. Robert Freeman Smith, "Republican Policy and the Pax Americana, 1921–1932," in William Appleman Williams, ed., *From Colony to Empire: Essays in the History of American Foreign Relations* (New York: John Wiley, 1972), 273–5.

8. Andrew J. Bacevich, *American Empire: The Realities and Consequences of US Diplomacy* (Cambridge, MA: Harvard University Press, 2002), 115–16.

9. Quoted in Smith, "Republican Policy and the Pax Americana," 271.

10. Carl Parrini, "The Age of Ultraimperialism," *Radical History Review* 57 (1993): 7–9.

11. Giovanni Arrighi, Po-keung Hui, Ho-fung Hung, and Mark Selden, "Historical Capitalism, East and West," in G. Arrighi, T. Hamashita, and M. Selden, eds., *The Resurgence of East Asia: 500, 150 and 50 Year Perspectives* (London: Routledge, 2003), 259–333; the quote appears on p. 301.

12. William Roger Louis and Ronald Robinson, "Empire Preserv'd: How the Americans put Anti-Communism before Anti-imperialism," in Duara, ed., *Decolonization*. For the nuclear saber-rattling exchange, see p. 157.

13. Chalmers Johnson, *The Sorrows of Empire: Militarism, Secrecy, and the End of the Republic* (New York: Henry Holt, 2004), 23–37.

14. Linda Carty, "Imperialism: Historical Periodization or Present-day Phenomenon?" *Radical History Review* 57 (Fall 1993): 38–45; Katherine H. S. Moon, *Sex among Allies: Military Prostitution in US-Korea Relations* (New York: Columbia University Press, 1997), 17–18.

15. Mark Berger, *Battle for Asia: From Decolonization to Globalization* (London: Routledge, 2004), 225–9.

16. Curtis Anderson Gayle, "Progressive Representations of the Nation: Early Post-War Japan and Beyond," *Social Science Japan Journal* 4 (2001): 9.

17. For the Soviet Union, see Ronald Grigor Suny, "Nationality Policies," in Edward Action, Vladimir Cherniaev, and William G. Rosenberg, eds., *Critical Companion to the Russian Revolution, 1914–1915* (Bloomington and Indianapolis, IN: Indiana University Press, 1997), 659–66. For China, see Edward J. M. Rhoads, *Manchus and Han: Ethnic Relations and Political Power in Late Qing and Early Republican China, 1861–1928* (Seattle, WA: University of Washington Press, 2000), 226–7.

18. J. V. Stalin, *Marxism and the National Question*, transcribed by Carl Kavanagh. *Prosveshcheniye*, Nos. 3–5 (March–May 1913), <http://intersci.ss.uci.edu/wiki/eBooks/Russia/BOOKS/Stalin/Marxism%20and%20the%20National%20Question%20Stalin.pdf>.

19. Tominaga Tadashi, *Manshūkoku no minzoku mondai* (Shinkyō, 1943), 43–5.

20. Rogers Brubaker, *Nationalism Reframed: Nationhood and the National Question in the New Europe* (Cambridge: Cambridge University Press, 1996), 18–24.

21. Katherine Verdery, "Nationalism and National Sentiment in Post-socialist Romania," *Slavic Review* 52 (Summer 1993): 179–203.

22. Douglas Northrop, *Veiled Empire: Gender and Power in Stalinist Central Asia* (Ithaca, NY: Cornell University Press, 2004).

23. Christina Klein, *Cold War Orientalism, Asia in the Middlebrow Imagination, 1945–1961* (Berkeley, CA: University of California Press, 2003), 7–16.

24. Klein, *Cold War Orientalism*, 253–63.

25. Hamza Alavi, "The Origins and Significance of the Pakistan–US Military Alliance," Hamza Alavi Internet Archive, <http://hamzaalavi.com/?p=102>. See also Robert J. McMahon, *The Cold War on the Periphery: The United States, India and Pakistan* (New York: Columbia University Press, 1996), 160–76.

26. Alavi, "Pakistan–US Military Alliance."

27. Jussi M. Hanhimaki and Odd Arne Westad, *The Cold War: A History in Documents and Eyewitness Accounts* (Oxford: Oxford University Press, 2003), 167.

28. Odd Arne Westad, *The Global Cold War: Third World Interventions and the Making of Our Times* (Cambridge: Cambridge University Press, 2007), chapters 7 and 8.

29. For some examples from Southeast Asia, see Anthony Reid, "Cultural Revolution and (Southeast) Asian Cultures," unpublished paper.

30. James C. Scott, *Seeing Like a State: How Certain Schemes to Improve the Human Condition have Failed* (New Haven, CT: Yale University Press, 1998). See also Michael Szonyi, *Cold War Island: Quemoy on the Front Line* (Cambridge: Cambridge University Press, 2008).

31. Richard Madsen, "Secularism, Religious Renaissance, and Social Conflict in Asia," in Martin Marty Center Web Forum, September 1, 2008.

32. This was the view in the CIA and State Department in 1969. See Yukinori Komine, *Secrecy in US Foreign Policy: Nixon, Kissinger and the Rapprochement with China* (Aldershot Ashgate Publishers, 2008), 118, 130.

33. Dieter Heinzig, *The Soviet Union and Communist China 1945–1950: The Arduous Road to the Alliance* (Armonk, NY: M.E. Sharpe, 2004).

34. Steve Coll, *Ghost Wars: The Secret History of the CIA, Afghanistan, and Bin Laden, from the Soviet Invasion to September 10, 2001* (New York: Penguin Press, 2004).

35. Jalal Al-i Ahmad, "Diagnosing an Illness," in Duara, ed., *Decolonization*, 56–63.

## SELECT BIBLIOGRAPHY

Arrighi, G., T. Hamashita, and M. Selden, eds. *The Resurgence of East Asia: 500, 150 and 50 Year Perspectives*. London: Routledge, 2003.

Bacevich, Andrew J. *American Empire: The Realities and Consequences of US Diplomacy*. Cambridge, MA: Harvard University Press, 2002.

Berger, Mark. *Battle for Asia: From Decolonization to Globalization*. London: Routledge, 2004.

Brubaker, Rogers. *Nationalism Reframed: Nationhood and the National Question in the New Europe*. Cambridge: Cambridge University Press, 1996.

Duara, Prasenjit. *Sovereignty and Authenticity: Manchukuo and the East Asian Modern.* Boulder, CO: Rowman and Littlefield, 2003.

Duara, Prasenjit, ed. *Decolonization: Perspectives from Now and Then.* London: Routledge, 2004.

Johnson, Chalmers. *The Sorrows of Empire: Militarism, Secrecy, and the End of the Republic.* New York: Henry Holt, 2004.

Klein, Christina. *Cold War Orientalism, Asia in the Middlebrow Imagination, 1945–1961.* Berkeley, CA: University of California Press, 2003.

McMahon, Robert. *Cold War on the Periphery: The United States, India and Pakistan.* New York: Columbia University Press, 1996.

Northrup, Douglas. *Veiled Empire: Gender and Power in Stalinist Central Asia.* Ithaca, NY: Cornell University Press, 2004.

Scott, James C. *Seeing Like a State: How Certain Schemes to Improve the Human Condition Have Failed.* New Haven, CT: Yale University Press, 1998.

Stoler, Ann, Carole McGranahan, and Peter Perdue, eds. *Imperial Formations and their Discontents.* Santa Fe, NM: School of American Research Press, 2007.

Westad, Odd Arne. *The Global Cold War: Third World Interventions and the Making of Our Times.* Cambridge: Cambridge University Press, 2007.

PART II

REGIONAL COLD
WARS/COLD WAR
CRISES

CHAPTER 7

....................................................................................................

# SOVIET-AMERICAN RELATIONS THROUGH THE COLD WAR

....................................................................................................

## VLADIMIR O. PECHATNOV

SOVIET-AMERICAN relations were central to cold war history and have been studied from many different perspectives. The story is being constantly revised as new documents from both sides become available. Yet despite this ever-expanding sea of literature, there has been little comparative analysis of Soviet and American strategies during this critical period.[1]

One under-explored way to analyze the dynamics of the Soviet-American relationship during the cold war is to compare the evolution of "strategic codes" on both sides: i.e., how each perceived the nature and prospects of this conflict, their respective goals, and means to achieve them. For these purposes one can divide the period of 1945–91 into five distinctive stages: the early cold war (1945–53), competitive coexistence (mid-1950s–late 1960s), détente (1969–76), the late cold war (late 1970s–early 1980s), and the end of the cold war (mid-1980s–1991).

It was during the *first stage* that both sides began to assess the nature and possible prospects of the protracted conflict into which they were descending.

In the United States that assessment was soon fleshed out in the strategy of containment. According to its logic, the conflict was rooted in the nature of a Soviet system that combined deep hostility toward and fear of the West with a huge military potential. Yet the system was also seen as based on distorted principles and thus having basic flaws—economic inefficiency and political disconnection from its own people. Given these vulnerabilities and continued pressure from the West, the Soviet system eventually was likely to collapse or reform itself. Externally, the main weakness of the Soviet "empire by coercion" was considered by Washington to be Moscow's inability to ensure the lasting loyalty of its allies against the pressures of nationalism.

With these calculations in mind, the founders of containment—especially George Kennan and his successors at the State Department—believed that the long-term advantages in this struggle between the two systems favored the West, provided the latter adopted the right strategy. The twofold goals of that strategy were (1) to contain and reverse Soviet expansion; and (2) to force the Soviet leadership into giving up its class-based ideological worldview in dealing with the outside world. In the key documents of American strategy of 1948—NSC 20/1 and NSC 20/4—those goals (which were also the terms of victory in the cold war) were "retraction of Soviet influence" and "basic change in the Soviet approach to international relations."[2] By 1950—following the "loss of China" and the first test of a Soviet A-bomb—a more alarmist and militarized version of containment was articulated in NSC 68. While retaining the previous basic goals, NSC 68 portrayed a more threatening and powerful enemy bent on world conquest. The mission of the "free world" was now seen as disrupting this "grand design" by accumulating a preponderance of power and employing a wide variety of means, with the main emphasis on a huge military build-up. "Without superior aggregate military strength, in being and readily mobilizable," the directive went on to say, "a policy of 'containment' which is in essence a policy of calibrated and gradual coercion, is no more than a policy of bluff."[3]

The requisite change in Soviet behavior could come either through the "mellowing" or "break-up" of the Soviet system (to use Kennan's famous words), the former being preferable from a security point of view. This mellowing was seen as an extended process of de-ideologization in the course of gradual adaptation to diminishing opportunities for growth and expansion. The more hawkish elements in the Truman and the early Eisenhower administrations were very skeptical of this option and thought in terms of a rapid Soviet collapse under intense Western pressure by overt and covert means (the rollback strategy in Eastern Europe and the western part of the USSR).[4] In either case it was presumed that a radical change in Soviet intentions would hardly be possible without a basic change in the nature of the Soviet political regime. In this sense containment became a giant experiment in modification of the enemy's behavior and—ultimately— in regime change. This transformation was also expected to be of fairly short duration with a timeframe of ten to fifteen years.

The main risk of containment implementation was assessed as a possible Soviet overreaction to Western pressure: faced with the prospect of losing its hard-won positions (particularly in Eastern Europe), the Soviet leaders might "slam the door," so to speak, instead of absorbing their defeat and quietly retiring to the "ashbin of history." "The danger exists," the special committee of SWNCC stressed in one of its early reports, "that our successful diplomatic efforts to check Russian expansionism may produce a feeling of intense frustration in the Soviet leadership, leading to an outbreak of war.... If Russia then possesses the A-bomb, the inevitable use of this absolute weapon by both sides will bring at once the holocaust which we are striving to avoid."[5] That risk was to be minimized by a careful calibration of Western pressure combined with an Anglo-American belief in the rationality of Soviet policy and personal behavior of Stalin, known for his inner caution in contrast to Hitler's suicidal risk-taking. Both military and political planners in Washington based their calculations on the flexibility and patience of Soviet policy, its inclination to avoid extreme risks and yield to a superior force.[6]

As for the Soviet leadership, it had not formulated a consistent strategy of waging and winning the cold war primarily because long-term planning in general had never been a part of the Soviet decision-making process. That process was much more personalized and much less institutionalized than in the American case. Consequently, historians have searched Russian archives in vain for a Soviet equivalent of NSC 20/1 or NSC 68. Yet, the Kremlin did develop some general assumptions and guidelines which amounted to a much more primitive and crude version of containment. It had a similar image of the opposite system as inherently hostile and expansionist, but also unstable, generating economic crises and imperialist wars. Moscow likewise had a similar goal of containing and thus allowing for the "mellowing" of the enemy, counting on prospective favorable changes in an overall correlation of forces caused by capitalist crises, "imperialist contradictions," and wars. After all, for Bolsheviks of Stalin's generation the history of the 20th century seemed to have been working in their favor: World War I paved the way for the emergence of the Soviet state, World War II led to the break-up of the colonial empires and the creation of a world socialist system, so that "fighting capitalism has become much more cheerful," as Stalin said in 1952.[7]

A sense of having history on their side did not prevent Kremlin rulers from trying to help its hidden hand by supporting friendly regimes and forces all over the world. Yet, as the more ideologically deterministic and weaker side in the enveloping struggle, they were more patient and flexible in their cold war timetable. Another difference was that the Soviet leadership did not associate its victory in the cold war with a regime change in the US. It simply made a clear distinction between "pacifist" and "aggressive circles" of capitalists, hoping that redressing the power imbalance between the US and the USSR would cut the ground from under the latter, thereby removing the danger of American aggression. Ultimately, "the socialist USA" was seen as the most desirable outcome of the systemic struggle, but that vision was too far beyond the horizon to have any operational meaning.

Both sides had to mobilize all available resources for waging and winning the cold war. But in the Soviet case this task was much more imperative given the preponderance of American power. It was also more natural for a Soviet system based on constant mobilization, militarized priorities, and central planning. Besides, the cold war environment was conducive to preserving the dictatorship at home: the external imperialist threat served to bond the Kremlin with its subjects and could be blamed for economic hardships, thus masking the system's chronic inefficiencies. In short, both Moscow and Washington during the first stage thought in terms of victory over the other—victory in a classical sense, meaning a defeat of the enemy or abandonment of its main goals.

The *second stage* (mid-1950s to late 1960s) was characterized by the growing dynamism and competitiveness of the Soviet system, demonstrated in post-Stalin political liberalization, the rise of living standards, enhanced economic growth, rapid progress in science and technology, and the increased appeal of the Soviet model in the third world. The successful detonation of a Soviet thermonuclear device in 1953 meant the narrowing of the gap between strategic arsenals on both sides and generated increasing nuclear stalemate. Instead of collapsing under the strain of its internal contradictions, the USSR was becoming a more powerful, stable, and increasingly non-revolutionary state. It also became clear that despite outbursts of resistance in East Germany (1953), Poland (1956), and Hungary (1956), the Soviet Union had established control over the region and could not be forced out by the West. That finally put the rollback/liberation option to rest. Coupled with the growing realization of the suicidal nature of a nuclear war, these changes gradually led the US to replace its initial cold war victory goals with a modus vivendi in the spirit of "competitive coexistence."[8]

The Soviet Union, in turn, de facto gave up its early hopes of a collapse of capitalism in the foreseeable future. Instead of a new round of depressions and wars, Western capitalism entered a period of political stabilization and economic boom. At the 20th Congress of the CPSU (February 1956), the Soviet leadership explicitly revised the Stalinist dogmas of the inevitability of world wars and "hostile encirclement," embarking upon "peaceful coexistence" as a safer and more regulated form of competition between the two systems. The Stalinist pattern of total mobilization and Spartan self-sacrifice was also revised in favor of material incentives and consumer needs. To facilitate new budget priorities, between 1955 and 1958 deep cuts were made in conventional forces and the defense budget. A new notion of victory in the cold war emerged: "catching up and overtaking" the United States in per capita production of basic food staples in the process of building up an idealized communist society by 1981 ("we will bury you"). This extension of the cold war competition into mass consumption (albeit Soviet style) had lasting implications: while in the short run it helped to energize the population after the long period of constant mobilization and sacrifice of the Stalin years, it was fraught with the danger of the frustrations and resentment bound to be produced by the system's inability to deliver the promised abundance.

Encouraged by Soviet dynamism and new opportunities for an expansion of the Soviet model created by national liberation movements in Asia, Middle East, Africa, and Latin America, Khrushchev and his colleagues made a breakthrough in the developing world by supporting non-aligned and anti-Western nationalist regimes. This departure from Stalin's, homeland defense strategy was also a way to bypass the SEATO-Baghdad pact ring of hostile blocs around Soviet borders and strike at the rear of "Western imperialism."

The globalization of Soviet ambitions and commitments turned the USSR into a truly worldwide power and widened the scope of Soviet-American competition. Cognizant of this new role, the Kremlin leadership on the one hand felt it was becoming "a member of the world club" (in Khrushchev's words before his colleagues).[9] On the other hand, the Soviet Union became entangled in a new protracted and very expensive rivalry with the United States, the benefits of which ultimately proved far less than its costs and initial expectations.

High hopes for a "socialist orientation" and loyalty on the part of new allies proved to be illusory[10]—in part because of the Soviets' inferiority vis-à-vis the United States in exercising economic and cultural influence over those countries.[11] The intensifying struggle over the developing world poisoned Soviet-American relations and endangered the rest of Khrushchev's foreign policy agenda—détente with the West.

Faced with a lack of reciprocity from skeptical Western capitals and frustrated by continuing US strategic superiority, an impatient Khrushchev resorted to "détente by intimidation."[12] He tried to force presidents Eisenhower and Kennedy into concessions on Berlin (1958–61) and Cuba (1962). But Washington called his bluff, and he had to retreat in both crises. No wonder the Dulles brothers, unnerved by his "deviation from the usual Soviet caution," felt nostalgia about the "chess playing" style of Stalin.[13] Recent research based on newly declassified documents makes it clear that in all those cases Khrushchev had no calculated crisis strategy. He basically relied on Western concessions to Soviet pressure, built according to what he called the "meniscus principle"—"to increase pressure" but stopping short of "liquid flowing over the edge, so that it is kept by the force of surface stretching."[14]

Having approached the brink of nuclear war, both Moscow and Washington chose to improve relations in a short-lived détente of 1963–4. By then the initial optimism of the Khrushchev years had been eroded by growing problems in the socialist world. Soviet allies in East and Central Europe were becoming more of an economic burden than an asset. The Warsaw Treaty Organization and Comecon (Council for Mutual Economic Assistance) structures remained rigid and hierarchical even though Khrushchev admitted privately that "socialist friends" had grown out of their "boy scout pants" and should be freed from "petty supervision."[15] Even more serious in its strategic implications was the Sino-Soviet split. It meant a radical shift in the global geopolitical landscape, led to a schism in the world communist movement, and presented a potential security threat along the vast Soviet-Chinese border.

The main lesson drawn by Khrushchev's successors from his policies was a need to narrow the gap between new Soviet global ambitions and capabilities by building up its strategic potential while avoiding risky brinkmanship and grand promises. Yet there were also considerable continuities: globalism, continued development of economic and cultural ties with the West (leading to new Soviet dependence on imported food and exported fuel), and the emphasis on mass consumption.

The Soviet struggle for the third world likewise continued unabated, albeit in different forms. Following the first round of failed regimes of ambiguous "socialist orientation" (Zaire, Ghana, Guinea, Indonesia, Mali), an emphasis was placed on setting up loyal communist parties and providing military assistance in order to establish more radical and effective regimes able to defend themselves (à la Cuba and North Vietnam).[16] Summing up the results of Soviet expansion in the third world by the end of 1971, CIA analysts wistfully concluded, "The Soviets must feel that, over the past 15 years, they have accomplished a great deal in the third world. They have broken the ring of containment built by the West,... have established the USSR as the most influential great power in most radical Arab states, have gained acceptance of their right to concern themselves closely with the affairs of all the Middle East and South Asia, and have extended their influence into parts of Southeast Asia, Latin America and Africa."[17]

Both sides by then had discovered some additional advantages in the regulated cold war regime. Internally, this rivalry, with its ever looming foreign threat, helped US political elites mobilize public support and material resources for a global foreign policy, while the Soviet *nomenklatura* used it to maintain ideological controls and justify a low standard of living for its people. Externally, a bipolar confrontation made it easier for each power to control its allies, dependents, and spheres of influence. Besides, on both sides of the great divide, there emerged a powerful institutional infrastructure of the cold war—a military-industrial-scientific complex which acquired a huge momentum of its own. A whole new generation of military and civilian cold war managers came on the scene, and for them managing this rivalry became the name of the game even as its initial goals (i.e., liquidation or transformation of the enemy) were forgotten or postponed indefinitely. This process of means becoming ends, described so well by John Gaddis for the US, had its counterpart on the Soviet side.[18]

The *third stage* for the USSR was a period of slackening economic growth and creeping social conservatism, accompanied by a massive military build-up and attainment of rough strategic parity with the US. The latter entered a period of relative decline, caused by the failure in Vietnam, mounting economic difficulties, the Watergate political crisis, and domestic constraints on the use of military power abroad. In this new context, the main initiative in rethinking policies and programs came from the American side. Spurred by German and French rapprochement with the Soviet Union, the team of Richard Nixon and Henry Kissinger undertook a reassessment of US cold war strategy. The USSR was now seen as a "status quo" and even "legitimate" power—a highly stable authoritarian system which had lost its former dynamism and messianic zeal but firmly retained its power status and was here to stay. The old line of isolating and undermining the Soviet Union was now replaced by Franklin Roosevelt-like containment through gradual integration. In more liberal circles there was a rebirth of convergence theory, which envisioned an incremental closing of the political-ideological gap between the two systems and, thus, the end of the cold war itself.

The US and its allies agreed to a long-standing Soviet request to legitimize the post-World War II status quo in Europe (The Helsinki Final Act of 1975) and stabilize the German problem by affirming the USSR-FRG treaty of 1970, the Quadripartite treaty on Berlin of 1971, and the Federal Republic of Germany (FRG)-German Democratic Republic (GDR) treaty of 1972. A new arms control regime was created in the early 1970s to reduce the danger of a nuclear war and make the nuclear arms race more predictable. The ABM Treaty, SALT I and SALT II, and the Agreement on Prevention of Nuclear War laid the ground for strategic stability that lasted into the next century.

In the Soviet Union détente was perceived as a Rubicon if not the end of the cold war. The Soviet leaders felt that they had finally caught up with the US in the key strategic dimension and forced Americans to recognize the legitimate security interests of the USSR. The United States was seen as having abandoned its efforts to destabilize the Soviet system and "undo" the results of World War II. "Our foreign policy," stated Andrey Gromyko at a staff meeting of senior Soviet diplomats in the early 1970s, "is now conducted in a qualitatively new environment of a genuine equilibrium of power. We have really become a world power even though it took hard work of two generations of Soviet people to reach that goal."[19] The new global role of the USSR as a guarantor of national security and superpower status became an increasingly important source of legitimacy for a Soviet system that was facing growing domestic difficulties. The Kremlin leaders sensed this connection well: "We are now clearly bolstered by our foreign policy on a grand scale," said Leonid Brezhnev at a staff meeting of the CPSU Central Committee.[20] A growing security challenge from China was another powerful incentive for cooperation with the US as well as Soviet interest in American trade and economic assistance to alleviate its mounting economic problems.

Yet détente proved to be fragile and short-lived. For the Soviet Union—a weaker side engaged in a catching-up operation—détente as a sort of "draw" in the cold war was close to victory. However, for many in America, which historically led the race, it looked more like a defeat. Recognition of strategic parity with the Soviet Union bordered on moral equivalence with an alien and vicious system. Liberals were insulted by the cynicism of Nixon-Kissinger realpolitik, while conservatives never really accepted strategic parity and regarded détente as a short breathing space in the cold war that worked to the benefit of the Soviets. The American public was incensed by the Soviet restrictions on Jewish emigration and repression of a courageous dissident movement. US policy makers were increasingly concerned about growing Soviet penetration in the third world. The intensifying opposition to détente from both right and left emasculated containment. The administration could no longer offer the Soviets the positive incentives on which its strategy depended. For example, the Jackson-Vanik amendment aborted efforts to extend to the Soviets most-favored nation status in return for its "good behavior."[21]

In the Soviet Union détente was also full of contradictions. Proponents of US-Soviet cooperation were soon outnumbered by those who saw détente as a chance to fill the vacuum left by America's weakening power and expand the sphere of Soviet influence in Africa, the Middle East, and Central America. Key Politburo statements of 1971 directed the Soviet foreign policy apparatus "to seek, without disclosing it publicly, a weakening of USA role in international affairs, including its position in Western military-political alliances, as well as in strategically important regions of the world (Europe, Middle East, Asia), by facilitating manifestations of contradictions between the USA and its allies."[22] This new assertiveness was soon reinforced by the energy/economic crisis in the West and a huge influx of petrodollars into the Soviet treasury, as well as by newly developed power projection capabilities. American diplomats registered concern with the new arrogance of their Soviet counterparts, who advised them "to get accustomed" to the situation in which the Soviet Union had lived for many years—"life under preponderance of the other side."[23]

The developing world remained the main target of the new Soviet assertiveness. As the Soviet model was losing its former attraction, Moscow's policy became increasingly geopolitical and militarized. Soviet military aid to almost thirty developing countries reached $35.4 billion for 1978–82 although this aid brought more losses than profits.[24] Behind this surge was neither internationalist ideology nor security concerns but a reflexive zero-sum game with the United States, which became a self-generating enterprise with little connection with the national interests of either country. "The more that could be taken away from Washington, the better," admitted in retrospect one of the architects of this policy. This way of thinking, natural for the cold war mentality, often prompted acquisitions regardless of their true value or capacity to "digest" them.[25]

Perceived by many Western experts as a consistent "grand strategy," this expansion in reality was little more than an inchoate combination of group, agency, and even personal interests, deprived of "genuine meaning and central goal." "In Latin America and the Third World as a whole the Soviet leadership," continued the former chief analyst of KGB foreign intelligence, Nickolai Leonov, "did not have planned, strategically oriented policy, backed up by sufficient human, technical, and material resources."[26] Domestically the climate of détente created new problems for the Soviet authorities—an erosion of ideological controls in the milieu of expanding contacts with the West and the emergence of a dissident human rights movement.

The *fourth stage* opened with a deepening systemic crisis in the Soviet Union characterized by an economic slowdown, a growing science–technological gap between Russia and the West, negative demographic trends, and socio-political stagnation. This crisis was exacerbated by the extreme militarization of the economy and growing "imperial overstretch" accumulated over the cold war years. The Soviet decline led to growing American optimism about the prospects of bilateral confrontation.

Its first signs became noticeable during the Carter administration, which drifted from accommodation to a more adversarial posture by the late 1970s. This drift was accelerated by new Soviet intervention in the African Horn, support for the Sandinistas in Nicaragua, and Moscow's decision to introduce a new class of IRBMs (SS-20s) in Eastern Europe. This step (which Gromyko would soon call "a grave mistake") reflected more the inertia of a Soviet military-industrial complex in seeking to utilize its accumulated production capacity than a deliberate aggressive posture.[27] Soviet intervention in Afghanistan (December 1979) became the final straw. Washington interpreted the defensive move to save an inept client regime as a strategic offensive aimed at the Persian Gulf. For its part, Moscow was deeply concerned about Carter's human rights policy (seen by the Kremlin as a flagrant interference in its domestic domain), US growing rapprochement with the PRC, decreased influence in the Middle East as a result of the Camp David agreement of 1978, and NATO's "two track" decision of December 1979.

This escalation of tensions buried ratification of a newly signed SALT II treaty in the US Senate and drove the Soviets to walk out of arms control negotiations in Geneva and Vienna. The Americans also instituted an economic embargo on the USSR and a boycott of the 1980 Olympic Games in Moscow. Most ominously, the Carter Doctrine called for repelling Soviet efforts to gain control of the Persian Gulf region "by use of any means necessary, including military force."[28]

The cold war was reviving, but it took a transfer of power to the Republican right, which was never reconciled to competitive coexistence, to resurrect the original maximum goal of containment—destruction of Soviet power. On the rhetorical level this shift was reflected in the negation of the Kremlin's legitimacy and re-consignment of Moscow to the dustbin of history. On the policy level it included rolling back communism in the third world ("Reagan Doctrine") and attriting the Soviet economy through the intensified nuclear arms race and the Strategic Defense Initiative (SDI), popularly known as "Star Wars." Yet even Reaganites did not fully understand how fragile the Soviet system was. Their obsession with the Soviet threat ("window of vulnerability") made the USSR seem stronger than it really was; so conservatives too, despite their subsequent claims to have buried the "evil empire," were poorly prepared for radical changes in the Soviet system.

The initial Soviet reaction to the new surge of the cold war under Leonid Brezhnev's short-lived successors, Yuri Andropov and Konstantin Chernenko, was symmetrical: stepped up military preparations, intensified ideological warfare, tightening the screws at home, and reanimation of the old bogey of the "aggressive nature of imperialism." In the context of new Soviet vulnerabilities, it only enhanced the Kremlin's inferiority complex and widespread fears of a major war with the US. The new Soviet-American confrontation reached its peak in 1983 with the shooting down of KAL 103 and the alarm of the Soviet intelligence network over preparations for a nuclear attack by the US provoked by a misperception of NATO's Able Archer military exercise. The primary Soviet strategic goal was now downscaled to holding the line against the new American offensive.

*Fifth stage.* By the early 1980s a systemic crisis engulfed not only the Soviet Union, but also its European allies. Their economies were stagnant and increasingly dependent on Western loans and credits, and social discontent and anti-Soviet protest were on the rise. The introduction of martial law in Poland in 1981 demonstrated the fragility of Moscow rule—its "intervention limit" (Yuri Andropov's words) was exhausted.[29] The preservation of the residual loyalty of East European regimes required growing economic and financial assistance, further straining the Soviet economy that was increasingly unable to feed its own people.[30] The total costs of the Soviet empire at the beginning of the decade reached 20–25 percent of its GNP, far exceeding the American ratio.[31] The drastic fall of world oil prices (a major source of Soviet hard currency revenues) in 1985–6 sharply aggravated the problem of budget priorities. The crisis demanded urgent action soon provided by a new group in the Kremlin headed by Mikhail Gorbachev.

Gorbachev clearly saw the irrationality of the cold war and its incompatibility with the long overdue domestic reforms, but he did not want to concede defeat in the Soviet-American competition. Gorbachev's grand design was to draw the US and the West into a joint transcendence of the cold war through a radical change in the mode of thinking on both sides. He went much further than Khrushchev in discarding the old Soviet orthodoxy regarding the outside world: universal human values would replace the class-based approach. What is more, a world divided into two antagonistic systems would yield to a holistic, interdependent planet based on the mutual responsibility of capitalism and socialism for global security, development and general disarmament, leading to an end to the arms race and a nuclear-free world. "Balance of interests" and "common security" would supersede the balance of power itself. Borrowing these ideas largely from 1970s liberal internationalism, Gorbachev wanted to co-opt his conservative Western counterparts.[32] In a nutshell, Gorbachev's policies and "new thinking" were desperate attempts to break the vicious circle of the Russian/Soviet security predicament which his predecessors had tried to solve through militarization, authoritarian rule, self-isolation, and "defensive expansion."

On the military level the build-up of nuclear and conventional forces was slowed down and even reversed. Soviet diplomacy came back to arms control negotiations and agreed to unprecedented liquidation of the whole class of IRBM with strict verification procedures. The Soviet Union began to withdraw from regional conflicts and ceased its support of anti-American regimes in the third world. By spring 1989 Soviet forces were finally withdrawn from Afghanistan, leaving behind a doomed pro-Moscow regime. No less important, the Iron Curtain was dismantled and radical democratization was taking place in many aspects of Soviet society. It all amounted to the "basic change" of the Soviet outlook and behavior that had originally been a central goal of the American containment.

The irony was that until the "velvet revolutions" of 1989, the American leadership did not think this change was real. But that disbelief ultimately worked in the US's favor because it pushed Gorbachev to new concessions in order to convince his skeptical Western partners. This escalation came all the more easily because the Soviet leader did not have a realistic strategy of ending the cold war which would be compatible with his domestic reforms. He grossly underestimated the fragility of the Soviet system at home and the weakness of the Soviet bloc abroad. At the same time Gorbachev overestimated Western responsiveness to the Kremlin's "New Thinking" and the chances of a radical reconstruction of the international system based on those ideas.

Gorbachev's task was greatly complicated by the deepening crisis at home. A severe financial crunch, the disorganization of industry, acute food shortages, bloody ethnic conflicts, and separatist trends in national republics were undermining the Kremlin's positions at home and abroad, forcing it to make new concessions and pleas for foreign assistance.[33] Soviet diplomats sensed how the new time of troubles at home was undermining the prospects for an active and independent foreign policy.[34] Western leaders, headed by George H. W. Bush, exploited this situation to conclude the cold war on their own terms. "By behaving in a constructive and sympathetic way, by showering Gorbachev with praise and by giving him many foreign policy 'successes' as opposed to his domestic failures, the West stimulated Gorbachev to make the choices he did," concluded Geir Lundestad. "But in realpolitik terms the job of the West was easy: to cash in on all the concessions Gorbachev made, concessions which resulted in the end of the Cold War."[35]

The dissolution of the Warsaw Treaty Organization, the fall of pro-Soviet regimes in Eastern Europe, and the unification of Germany within the NATO framework liquidated the main Soviet geopolitical asset in the cold war—a massive political-military presence in the heart of Europe won by great sacrifice during World War II. Parting with this Stalinist legacy was all but inevitable considering its organic defects; in this sense Gorbachev had to redeem "the original sin"—the brutal Sovietization of the region after World War II and the failure of his predecessors to transform the alliance into a more equitable and effective system. Perhaps this dismantling could have been handled more prudently. Yet conversely, the liberation could have been much more destructive had Gorbachev resorted to Stalinist or even Khrushchev-Brezhnev type repressions.

Contrary to the fears of containment's founding fathers, Gorbachev "didn't slam the door" upon the Soviet exit from Germany and Eastern Europe.

The Soviet policy reversal in the third world followed the same pattern. Instead of orderly retrenchment and joint Soviet-American resolution of regional crises, there was an abrupt, unconditional, and unilateral disengagement that devaluated all previous investments in former allies and left them to their own salvation. As a result, in the course of two or three years the former superpower lost almost all of its allies, while the dissolution of the Soviet Union itself completed its transformation into a regional power.

Notwithstanding all the talk about "the new world order," the George H.W. Bush administration did not have an exit strategy for the cold war either. For the most part it simply responded to Gorbachev's initiatives, using opportunities presented by his policies, and followed the lead of allied leaders such as Helmut Kohl. But US diplomacy was very skillful in locking in foreign policy gains and gently pushing Gorbachev and Minister of Foreign Affairs Eduard Shevardnadze to new concessions without provoking extreme measures. That pattern was particularly relevant in German reunification and the "velvet revolutions" in Eastern Europe. In this sense the US contributed to the peaceful end of the cold war, although the main credit here belongs to Gorbachev and his policy.

Why did the Soviet-American rivalry end like it did? In retrospect the answer seems to be clear. First, the West had *a better model*. Vladimir Lenin, the founder of the Soviet state, once said that the struggle between socialism and capitalism would ultimately be decided by the productivity each side was able to achieve, not on the battlefield. And he was right in essence, if not in picking the winning side. Capitalism, i.e., markets and democracy, proved to be more productive in guns and especially butter (consumer goods) than Soviet-type socialism. The latter could not adapt to the post-industrial economy; instead of catching up it lagged farther and farther behind the West. This backwardness discredited the Soviet system not only in the outside world but also in the eyes of its own people, who by then could see enough through the porous iron curtain to compare their quality of life with that of the "rotten" West. In political terms the Soviet alliance model was also inferior to the American-led Western alliance. The latter was based largely on consent, mutual interests, and accommodation, while the former relied mostly on coercion and dictate. No wonder the "American empire" survived the end of the cold war while the Soviet one did not.[36]

Second, the *West had much greater resources* at its disposal than the Soviet bloc, especially after China's defection from the Soviet orbit. Even in terms of hard power, the American-led bloc was predominant on the seas, in global military base infrastructure, and power projection capabilities. Economically, the Soviet bloc never was a match for the Western economic powerhouse, and its soft power resources were modest at best. In short, the Soviet Union was largely a one-dimensional military power confronting a multidimensional Western bloc.

Third, this Western preponderance of power also had an important intellectual dimension—the *US possessed a better cold war strategy*. The paradox is that in the centrally planned Soviet state, foreign policy making was much more chaotic, personalized, and improvised than in the pluralist West. There was poor inter-agency coordination, no policy planning mechanism, and little serious discussion at the Politburo level; most decisions were made personally by a party leader or designed to please him. Among those only Stalin was a grand strategist, and he, too, made serious blunders. Khrushchev was basically a gambler, Brezhnev, a cautious bureaucrat, and Gorbachev, a well-meaning idealist. Ideology and the nature of the Soviet political regime made things even worse. Ideology distorted perception and fed leaders' infallibility complex. The Communist Party monopoly on power meant an exclusion of alternative options and an absence of accountability. In combination they opened the gates to arbitrary improvisation from the top, impeded learning from mistakes, and left little room for long-term planning or expert analysis. In short, the reality of Soviet foreign policy making had little in common with the image of a monolithic and focused Kremlin armed with a grand strategy of world domination.

If there was a grand design, it was in Washington rather than Moscow. The strategy of containment in its various incarnations from Truman to Reagan was an effective way of employing a wide range of means to achieve long-term strategic aims. Consistent in its basic thrust, it was also flexible enough to adjust to changing situations. Moscow's version of containment was deeply flawed, distorted by ideological wishful thinking: it drastically underestimated the vitality of the capitalist world, grossly overestimated the anti-Western potential of the third world and the strength of the so-called "inter-imperialist contradictions" for the Kremlin to play upon.

Given these three basic handicaps (in model, resources, and strategy), the overall correlation of forces (to use a favorite Bolshevik term) always favored the West, and the Soviet Union never had a real chance of winning the cold war.[37] At best—with a healthy dose of luck and mismanagement by the West—the Soviet Union could have gained a draw, which seemed to be the case with the détente of early 1970s. But that mirage soon evaporated in the new round of tension and Soviet decline. Yet while the ultimate outcome of that great conflict was largely predetermined (to the extent there is determination in history), neither the specific form of that final stage nor its time framework was.

The stagnation of the late Brezhnev years could have continued at a slow rate. The overextension of Soviet empire could have been handled by a careful retrenchment, and incremental market reforms could have been introduced more effectively à la Deng Xiaoping's China. But accidents of history and human factors intervened to provide for a quick and relatively peaceful dissolution of Soviet power. Gorbachev was not Deng: he unleashed the forces of change and lost control over them, but he preferred to live with the dissolution of Soviet power rather than trying to stop it by force. The Soviet intelligentsia craved freedom and democracy almost at any price. And people of the Baltic states, Eastern Europe, and East Germany refused to wait patiently for an incremental de-Sovietization of their countries or reform of the Warsaw Pact. So, it happened all at once in a velvet revolution way. Overall the process of Soviet disintegration took much longer and was messier than predicted by "Mr X": first, mellowing and then, break-up. But in general Kennan proved to be right.

He was also right in foreseeing the dynamics of a future Soviet collapse. Kennan always thought that the Kremlin masters, whose rule was based on iron discipline and total obedience rather than compromise and mutual accommodation, were so alienated from their own people that in the event of a legitimacy crisis the system would have very few defenders. Hence instead of a civil war there would likely be a swift and bloodless collapse of the regime. But in the wake of that collapse, as Kennan foresaw, there would be no political force capable of running the country effectively, because communist rule had destroyed all capacity for self-organization. So, if the Communist Party was incapacitated, Soviet Russia "would almost overnight turn from one of the mightiest into one of the weakest and miserable nations of the world...."[38]

Even more remarkably, Kennan foresaw a chain reaction between the internal and external dissolution of the Soviet empire. He always considered Eastern Europe to be the most vulnerable part of that empire, ready to run away should Moscow's control seriously weaken. But that loss, he predicted, would deal such a blow to the Kremlin's legitimacy and self-confidence that it would "unleash an avalanche downfall of Soviet influence and prestige which would go beyond satellite countries to the heart of the Soviet Union itself."[39] In short, the US analysis of the prospects for Soviet-American competition was much superior to the Kremlin's.

While immensely costly (in terms of the arms race, wars by proxies, imposition of the Soviet system, superpower interventions in the third world, the corrosion of democratic norms and practices in the US and suppression of them in the USSR, and more),[40] the Soviet-American rivalry had its positive side effects.

*The effect of competition.* This rivalry forced each side to mobilize resources and enhance its attractiveness and competitiveness in order to overtake the main rival and gain new allies. In retrospect it is hard to imagine that just a half-century ago the Soviet model seemed a serious scientific and technological challenge to the US. For the competitive American nation, this challenge became an additional incentive for domestic reforms. The emergence of modern federal support for higher education and sciences, creation of NASA and space exploration programs, and even some social reforms of 1960s were all connected with the cold war competition.[41] The Soviet Union, to use Arnold Toynbee's words, "became a functional equivalent of the Devil that forced us into doing what we should have done anyway."[42] Conversely the disappearance of this competition and America's resultant triumphalism (the "end of history") contributed to the complacency and arrogance which created the context for the economic crisis of 2008–9.

The same mobilizing effect also applied to the Soviet side. It was to the cold war that the Soviet Union owed its greatest technological achievements of those years—launching Sputnik and the first man into space, and reaching strategic parity with the United States.

In the framework of competition between the two blocs, the US had to be more accommodating and generous vis-à-vis its allies, in contrast to the coercive "Soviet empire." Without the unifying "Soviet threat," the Marshall Plan, the unprecedented American efforts to rehabilitate its former mortal enemies Germany and Japan, and the economic and political integration of Western Europe would scarcely have been imaginable. It was this transatlantic cooperation that helped to produce the historic rapprochement between Germany and the rest of Europe, the European economic miracle, and the creation of a true Atlantic community. While the Soviet-American confrontation led to economic and military-political integration on both sides of the iron curtain, only West European integration survived the end of the cold war. In other words, here, too, the Soviet Union played the same role of "functional equivalent of the Devil" that forced the US to pursue more far-sighted and long-term interests rather than purely selfish and short-term ones.

Deterrence based on the danger of escalation of local conflicts into global nuclear war established checks and balances on a global scale. It forced both sides to act with greater restraint and responsibility, thereby keeping emotions and ideological instincts on a leash. It is not difficult to imagine how far the adventurous Khrushchev might have gone during the Berlin and Cuban crises (or even the more cautious Stalin in the Iran and Turkey of 1945–6) without US deterrence. On the other hand, in the absence of the Soviet countervailing power, the US might have resorted to nuclear weapons in Korea or Vietnam, or to escalating other regional conflicts. The US traumatic experience in Iraq is another example of the risks that unchecked American supremacy is fraught with.

Gone are both the cold war and the centrality of Russian-American relations, with both countries now searching for a new role in a much more fluid and pluralistic world. Nostalgia for the days of bipolar conflict and mutual assured destruction is certainly unwarranted. Only time will tell how much of an improvement the subsequent environment of national upheaval, ethnic warfare, and stateless terrorism turns out to be.

## Notes

1. One notable exception is John L. Gaddis, *We Now Know: Rethinking Cold War History* (Oxford: Clarendon Press, 1997), chs. 2–3. Also see his "The Evolution of the US Policy Toward the USSR in the Post-War Era," in Severin Bialer and Michael Mandelbaum, eds., *Gorbachev's Russia and American Foreign Policy* (Boulder, CO: Westview Press, 1988).

2. "US Objectives with Respect to Russia" (NSC 20/1), in Thomas Etzold and John L, Gaddis, eds., *Containment: Documents on American Policy and Strategy 1945–1950* (New York: Columbia University Press, 1978), 176.

3. "United States Objectives and Programs for National Security" (NSC 68), in Etzold and Gaddis, *Containment*, 389.

4. Robert Bowie and Richard Immerman, *Waging Peace. How Eisenhower Shaped an Enduring Cold War Strategy* (New York: Oxford Universitiy Press, 1998), 161–3.

5. "US Policy with Respect to Russia," A Report by a special committee of State War Navy Coordinating Committee (April 1946), National Archives (thereafter NA), Record Group (thereafter RG) 165, ABC 336 Russia (August 22, 1943), Sec. 1-C. See also Rheinhold Niebuhr's remarks at the State Department Policy Planning Staff, November 20, 1950, NA, RG 59, Records of Policy Planning Staff, PPS Meetings, Box 32.

6. George Kennan, "The Long Telegram," in Etzold and Gaddis, *Containment*, 61.

7. *Pravda*, October 15, 1952.

8. Bowie and Immerman, *Waging Peace*, 176–7.

9. *Presidium TsK KPSS, 1954–1964*, Tom 3 (*Presidium of the Central Committee of the CPSU, 1954–1964*, vol. 3) (Moscow: ROSSPEN, 2008), 408.

10. Evgeny M. Primakov, *Konfidentsial 'no. Blizhny Vostok na Stsene I za Kulisami (vtoraya polovina XX–nachalo XXI veka)* (*In Confidence. Middle East on Stage and Behind the Curtain*) (*second half of XX—early XXI century*) (Moscow: Rossiiskaya Gazeta, 2006), 131.

11. For a detailed case study of this policy see: Sergey Mazov, *Politika SSSR v Zapadnoi Afrike, 1956–1964: Neizvestnye stranitsy istorii holodnoi voiny* (*Soviet Policy in Western Africa, 1956–1964: Unknown Episodes of the Cold War History*) (Moscow: Nauka, 2008).

12. John L.Gaddis, *The Soviet Union, and the United States: An Interpretive History* (New York: Wiley, 1978), 240.

13. *FRUS, 1955–1957*, vol. XXIV (Washington: GPO, 1989), 119–20.

14. *Presidium TsK KPSS, 1954–1964*, Tom 1 (*Presidium of the Central Committee of the CPSU, 1954–1964*, vol. 1), 545.

15. From Khrushchev's speech before Communist Party leadership, November 4, 1956, *Istochnik*, 2003, No. 6, pp. 65, 67.

16. Westad Odd Arne, *The Global Cold War: Third World Interventions and the Making of Our Times* (New York and London: Cambridge University Press, 2005), 203–4.

17. "The Uses of Soviet Military Power in Distant Areas" (National Intelligence Estimate 11-10-71), December 15, 1971, *FRUS, 1969–1976*, vol. XIV, Soviet Union, October 1971–May 1972 (Washington, DC: GPO, 2006), 96–7.

18. John L. Gaddis, *Strategies of Containment: A Critical Appraisal of American National Security Policy during the Cold War*, rev. and expanded ed. (New York and London: Oxford University Press, 2005), 92–3.

19. Cited in Yuri A. Kvitsinsky, *A. Vremya I Sluchai: zametki professionala* (*On Time and Accident: Notes by a Professional*) (Moscow: Olma Press, 1999), 278.

20. *Vestnik Arhiva Prezidenta Rossiiskoi Federatsii: Spetsialny vypusk. General'ny Secretar', TsK KPSS Leonid I.Brezhnev, 1964–1982* (Presidential Archive of Russia, Special Issue: Secretary General of the CPSU Leonid I. Brezhnev, 1964–1982), Moscow, 2006, p.133.

21. Henry A. Kissinger, *The Years of Upheaval* (New York: Simon & Schuster, 1999), 111.

22. Cited in Anatoly F. Dobrynin, *Sugubo doveritel'no. Posol v Vasningtone pri shesti prezindah CShA (1962–1986)* (*In Confidence: Ambassador in Washington under Six US Presidents, 1962–1986*), (Moscow: Avtor, 1997), 201.

23. *FRUS, 1969–1976*, vol. XIV, p. 92.

24. Irina V. Bystrova, *Sovetsky Voenno-Promyshlennyi Kompleks: Problemy Stanovlenia I Razvitya* (*Soviet Military- Industrial Complex: Problems of Formation and Development*) (*1930–1980 gody*) (Moscow: Institute of General History, 2006), 373–6.

25. Karen N. Brutents. *Nesbyvshees'ya. Neravnodushnye zametki o perestroike* (*The Unfulfilled: Partial Notes on Perestroika*) (Moscow: Mezhdunarodnye otnoshenia, 2005), 117, 118.

26. Nickolai Leonov, *Likholetie* (*The Woeful Times*) (Moscow: Terra, 1997), 118, 91; also see: Georgy Mirskii, "Soviet-American Relations in the Third World," in Kiron K. Skinner, ed., *Turning Points in Ending the Cold War* (Stanford, CA: Hoover Institution Press, 2008), 176–8.

27. *V Politburo TsK KPSS. Po Zapisyam Anatolia Chernyaeva, Vadima Medvedeva, Georgia Shahnazarova* (*In the Politburo of the Central Committee of the CPSU. As recorded by*

*Anatolii Chernyaev, Vadim Medvedev, Georgy Shakhnazarov (1985–1991)*). Compiled by A. Chernyaev et al. (Moscow: Alpina Business Books, 2006), 86; Georgy Shakhnazarov, *S Vozhdyami I bez nih* (*With and without Leaders*) (Vagrius: Moscow, 2001), 340–2.

28. Jimmy Carter, State of the Union Address, January 23, 1980, <http://www.jimmycarterlibrary.org/documents/speeches/su80jec.phtml>.

29. Shakhnazarov, *S Vozhdyami I bez nih*, 250.

30. Valerie Bunce, "The Empire Strikes Back: The Evolution of Eastern Bloc from Soviet Asset to Liability," *International Organization*, 39 (Winter 1985): 1–46; Mark Kramer, "The Soviet Union and the Eastern Europe: Spheres of Influence," in Ngaire Woods, ed., *Explaining International Relations since 1945* (Oxford: Oxford University Press, 1990), 98–125.

31. Geir Lundestad, "Imperial Overstretch: Mikhail Gorbachev, and the End of the Cold War," *Cold War History*, 1 (August 2000): 5; Henry S. Rowen and Charles Wolf, Jr., eds., *The Impoverished Superpower: Perestroika and the Soviet Military Burden* (San Francisco: Institute for Contemporary Studies Press, 1990), 1–12.

32. For more detail on the intellectual roots of "the new thinking" see: Robert English, *Russia and the Idea of the West. Gorbachev, Intellectuals and the End of the Cold War* (New York: Columbia University Press, 2000); Anatoli Chernyaev, "Gorbachev's Foreign Policy: The Concept," in Skinner, *Turning Points in Ending the Cold War*, 111–40.

33. For more detail see: Egor Gaidar, *Gibel' Imperii: Uroki dlya Sovremennoi Rossii* (*The Death of the Empire: Lessons for Today's Russia*), 2nd ed. (Moscow: Rosspen, 2007), ch. 6.

34. Yuri V. Dubinin. *Vremya Peremen: Zametki Posla v Vashingtone* (*Time of Change: Sketches by the Ambassador in Washington*) (Moscow: Aviarus-XXI, 2003), 330–1, 397; Kvitsinsky, *On Time and Accident*, 553.

35. Lundestad, "Imperial Overstretch," 14–15.

36. For a comparative tale of the two empires, see: Gaddis, *We Now Know*, ch. 2.

37. For a similar argument see Zbigniev Brzezinski, "The Cold War and its Aftermath," *Foreign Affairs* (Fall 1992): 47.

38. George F. Kennan, "The Sources of Soviet Conduct," *Foreign Affairs* (July 1947): 580–1.

39. Cited in: Walter Hixson, *George F. Kennan: Cold War Iconoclast* (New York: Columbia University Press, 1989), 36.

40. For recent literature on this dark side of the Cold War see: Richard Ned Lebow and Janice Gross Stein, *We All Lost the Cold War* (Princeton, NJ: Princeton University Press, 1994); Westad, *Global Cold War*; Melvyn P. Leffler, *For the Soul of the Mankind: The United States, the Soviet Union, and the Cold War* (New York: Hill & Wang, 2007).

41. Robert Divine, *The Sputnik Challenge* (New York: Oxford University Press, 1993); H. W. Brands, *The Strange Death of American Liberalism* (New Haven, CT: Yale University Press, 2001).

42. Arnold Toynbee et al., *The Impact of Russian Revolution 1917–1957* (New York: Oxford University Press, 1967), 17.

## Select Bibliography

Bowie, Robert, and Richard Immerman. *Waging Peace: How Eisenhower Shaped an Enduring Cold War Strategy*. New York: Oxford University Press, 1998.

Dobrynin, Anatoly F. *In Confidence: Moscow's Ambassador to America's Six Cold War Presidents*. New York: Crown, 1995.

Donaldson, Robert H., and Joseph L. Nogee. *The Foreign Policy of Russia: Changing Systems, Enduring Interests*, 3rd ed. London: M.E. Sharpe, 2005.

Fursenko, Alexander A. and Timothy Naftali. *Khrushchev's Cold War: The Inside Story of an American Adversary*. New York: Norton, 2007.

Gaddis, John L. *Russia, the Soviet Union, and the United States: An Interpretive History*, 2nd ed. New York: McGraw-Hill, 1990.

Gaddis, John L. *Strategies of Containment: A Critical Appraisal of Postwar American National Security Policy during the Cold War*, rev. and expanded ed. New York: Oxford University Press, 2005.

Garthoff, Raymond J. *Détente and Confrontation: American-Soviet Relations from Nixon to Reagan*, rev. ed. Washington, DC: Brookings, 1994.

Garthoff, Raymond J. *The Great Transition: American-Soviet Relations and the End of the Cold War*. Washington, DC: Brookings, 1994.

Geyer, David and Douglas Selvage. *Soviet-American Relations: The Détente Years, 1969–1972*. Washington, DC: Government Printing Office, 2007.

LaFeber, Walter. *America, Russia, and the Cold War, 1945–1996*, 8th ed. New York: McGraw-Hill, 1996.

Legvold, Robert, ed. *Russian Foreign Policy in the Twenty-First Century and the Shadow of the Past*. New York: Columbia University Press, 2007.

Zubok, Vladislav M. *The Failed Empire: The Soviet Union in the Cold War from Stalin to Gorbachev*. Chapel Hill, NC: University of North Carolina Press, 2007.

# CHAPTER 8

# CHINA AND THE COLD WAR

## RANA MITTER

THE cold war era in China is inseparable from the political supremacy of one man: Mao Zedong. "Mao's China" and "Cold War China" are interchangeable terms in the minds of many, and the chairman's long tenure in power from 1949 to 1976 had a major influence on the progression of the cold war in Asia and beyond.

Nevertheless, understanding Mao's role is not sufficient to understand the cold war's effect on China. After all, the cold war lasted for over a decade following Mao's death. No less crucially, during the critical period between the end of World War II and the triumph of the Chinese Communist Party (CCP) in 1949, real political alternatives for China were in conflict with one another. Just as 1945–50 was a turning point in the European cold war, so it was in China. And just as in Europe, China inherited the massive displacements of World War II.

China played a pivotal role as the third (albeit shorter) leg of a cold war tripod. If this suggests a certain unsteadiness, that is not inappropriate. The cold war was also the era of decolonization, and China managed to maintain a simultaneous narrative about itself that was highly convincing to many emerging non-Western states. It used the Bandung Conference in 1955 to argue that it was a new, cooperative force in what would become known as the Third World. However, it also proclaimed itself the savior of the revolutionary world, spearheading anti-imperialist liberation. In saying this, it contrasted itself implicitly, then after 1960, explicitly, with the Soviet Union.

## THE ORIGINS OF COLD WAR CHINA: NATIONALIST CHINA IN WORLD WAR AND COLD WAR

When the People's Republic of China (PRC) was officially declared on October 1, 1949, it was the child of a vicious civil war between the CCP and its predecessor, the Nationalists

(Guomindang) under Chiang Kai-shek. That war was, in turn, the immediate successor to a devastating world war. In 1945 Chiang Kai-shek, the Nationalist leader, emerged victorious against the Japanese, although his victory was a pyrrhic one; the capacity of his state had been deeply compromised. The areas of communist control in China during the war had expanded rapidly, with some 100 million (of the total of 900 million) in broadly CCP-dominated areas by August 1945.

The war against Japan transformed China's future. In the 1920s and 1930s it had been riven by militarist violence. Although nominally united under the Nationalist government established by Chiang Kai-shek in 1928, China suffered from poverty, political corruption, human rights abuses, and repeated outbreaks of civil war. Nonetheless, the country progressed, with new railways, roads, and telecommunications established and international assistance from the League of Nations used to develop flood prevention and new crop varieties. By 1936 the CCP was on the run: the "Long March," which became part of the party's foundational myth, was actually a retreat by a party that had been shattered by Nationalist attacks.

The outbreak of war between China and Japan in the summer of 1937 destroyed the fitful modernization of the previous decade. The Nationalist government was forced to retreat to the inland city of Chongqing, while the Japanese occupied most of China's eastern heartland. In the north and east communist control expanded. The Nationalist government nearly collapsed under the strains of the war. By 1945 it was beset by corruption, and its military was profoundly dysfunctional. This breakdown resulted largely from four years of fighting almost alone against Japan, the difficulties of running a government under constant aerial bombardment, dealing with refugee displacement running into millions of people, and being forced into a geographical isolation from the sea. By 1945 the Nationalists were exhausted.[1]

After 1945 mediators, including the American General George C. Marshall, attempted to broker a coalition government between the Nationalists and Communists. Marshall abandoned his effort when it became clear that neither side was willing to compromise. The civil war erupted in 1946 and raged until 1949.[2] It became a deadly ideological conflict. Yet much of Chiang's motivation was similar to the underpinnings of foreign policy under the CCP after 1949. In particular, Chiang's actions portended a cold war phenomenon: decolonization and nation-building among non-European peoples. It was the Nationalists, not the Communists, who negotiated an end to the hated "unequal treaties" with the European imperial powers in the late 19th century. As a result, China emerged from war in 1945 as truly sovereign for the first time since the end of the Opium War in 1842. In addition, Nationalist China had been designated one of the "Four Policemen" by Franklin D. Roosevelt and given a permanent seat on the UN Security Council. The Nationalists and the CCP used significantly different methods in their relationship with the international community, but their aims were not that different, particularly on the question of territorial integrity and sovereignty.

The civil war took place in the middle of a rapidly changing global situation as the cold war took shape. Until 1948 the US and USSR predicated their policies for Asia on the idea that China would be united under the Nationalists. This would have generated a US-oriented East Asia, as Chiang's government would have oriented itself toward the

US, and Japan would also have been an American satellite. Stalin was initially complicit with this assumption, and his relations with the CCP waxed hot and cold as he sought to calculate what side was more likely to win the civil war. Nonetheless, the hardening of the global cold war forced Chiang to choose sides; Stalin would not let him accept support from both the US and the USSR. Chiang chose the US as the lesser of two evils.[3]

The CCP never forgot the way that Stalin had toyed with its loyalty. Their victory, largely a consequence of the collapse of the Nationalist administration, was not long in coming. Chiang's government was too compromised by its own flaws, which had been seriously aggravated by the experience of the war against Japan. Rebuilding state capacity when so much of the country had been destroyed would have been hard enough, but to engage in a major civil war almost immediately afterward was too much. Combined with human rights abuses, corruption, and an unwillingness to compromise on the control of political power, the Nationalists' brief experiment in sovereign government came to an end with the communist victory in autumn 1949.

## Communist victory and the cold war

On October 1, 1949 the chairman of the CCP, Mao Zedong, stood at the Tiananmen Gate in the center of Beijing and announced that the People's Republic of China, the world's most populous state, was now a communist country.

The cold war was central to the shaping of the new state domestically as well as internationally. Militarism had become a major factor as the state atrophied from the late Qing dynasty onward, but the mass dislocations produced by the war against Japan altered society profoundly. Many of the competing regimes within China—the Nationalists in exile in the southwest, the Communists in the north, and Wang Jingwei's collaborationist Nationalists who claimed to have "reorganized" the true Nationalist party in Nanjing—demanded greater contributions from society and offered a wider social vision in return. Although the communist vision proved most compelling, *most* modern political actors in China saw the need for a wider vision of social reform, which was frequently linked to militarization. Mao's years in charge of the PRC were heavily militarized in many ways (the Cultural Revolution is a notorious example). Propaganda stressed this element of social control at all times.[4]

The new divisions imposed by the cold war were visible in the PRC's most pressing domestic issue: the economy. There is much historical evidence that China's economy was improving until 1937. The eight years of war changed that: most of China's fledgling industrialization was in the eastern seaboard cities that Japan took over (with much of the plant destroyed by bombing). The war broke up traditional trade routes and economic networks.[5]

A Nationalist-run China would have drawn on economic assistance from the US. The CCP's victory made that impossible. The United States refused to recognize the new government in Beijing, maintaining that Chiang's government in exile in Taipei was China's legitimate government (in the United Nations Security Council, the "China" seat was also retained by the Republic of China, which held it until 1971). Instead, the country became embedded in the emergent socialist world economy that Stalin's USSR promoted after 1945.[6] Although China never joined Comecon, which controlled trade within the socialist bloc, its economy became highly integrated with the organization's members from 1953, when the PRC's first Five Year Plan began. A common cold war point of contrast was between the command economy of the Eastern bloc and free markets of the West, but in fact both bloc leaders sacrificed short-term economic advantage to strengthen the commitment of the parts of East Asia under their control. The US allowed members of its bloc to obtain an economic advantage in return for support by allowing the East Asian developmental states (Japan, Taiwan, South Korea) to maintain highly protected economies for decades. The USSR offered goods within its bloc at advantageous prices to cement the socialist community: for instance, one ton of Chinese frozen pork became enough to buy five tons of steel products. The importance of cementing bloc alliances also led to strategic trade: during the 1953 riots in East Berlin, China sent 50 million rubles worth of foodstuffs to help shore up the fledgling GDR government.[7] From its origin, China was brought into the fold of the world socialist economy.

# THE KOREAN WAR

The newly established PRC was almost immediately plunged into another brutal conflict: the Korean War. The war confronted the rulers of the new state with a hard choice. On the one hand, the PRC desperately needed time for domestic consolidation: the regime had won a military victory but had not yet secured all China's territory. On the other, the commitment of the party and Mao Zedong in particular to anti-imperialist liberation was genuine. The war in Korea presented an opportunity for the new state to show its credentials and gain ideological influence.

Part of the Chinese motivation to enter the war in Korea came from frustration over their perception that their Soviet partners regarded them as supplicants. CCP Vice-Chairman Liu Shaoqi visited Stalin in the months before the Chinese Communist victory in 1949 to discuss a variety of issues. It became clear that Mao was unhappy with the patronizing flavor of Stalin's demands.[8] The USSR wanted special rights to operate in the parts of China that bordered the USSR (the northeast and northwest). For Mao, Stalin's proposals implied new "unequal treaties."

So the emergence of a crisis on the Korean peninsula, on China's northeastern border, gave Mao a chance to demonstrate his revolutionary credentials. The emergence of new documentation since the early 1990s, however, shows Stalin and Mao were playing a complex game with each other.[9] At stake were ideas about revolutionary anti-imperialism and the leadership of the communist world. The catalyst was the request in April 1950 by Kim Il-Sung, leader of the new communist North Korean state, for approval to invade the south. Stalin eventually acceded. He seems genuinely to have felt that the Western forces were in a position of weakness at that time, and the prospect of success was realistic. However, he was also conscious that he needed to maintain leadership within the communist bloc: having declined the chance to support communist movements in Greece and Indochina, his prestige could have further eroded had he turned his back on the revolution in Korea as well.[10] Mao hesitated. The new People's Republic was deeply unstable in 1950, with pockets of resistance to the CCP still to be found in peripheral areas, and the country reeling from the effects of two major wars in quick succession. Nonetheless, Mao had a vision of spreading anti-imperialist communist revolution, and the opportunity opened up by Kim was hard for him to turn down. To undertake support for the Korean War would make a powerful statement of ideological intent.

Stalin proved an uncertain ally during the Korean War, failing to provide much-desired air cover for Chinese troops at a crucial moment in 1950. He had believed that the West would not force a confrontation over a North Korean invasion and was discomfited by the rapid success of UN forces in recapturing the south. Mao, however, having gambled by entering the war, insisted on sticking by Kim. Stalin ultimately provided support, if not actual Soviet troops, for the war effort. While Mao could not claim complete victory, by 1953 the stalemate allowed the new regime to argue that it had prevented the establishment of a hostile state on its borders.

Mao had also made his campaign of domestic consolidation dependent on mobilizing popular support for the war with the "Resist America, Aid Korea" campaign.[11] This use of the Korean War to influence domestic politics reflected a dynamic that accompanied the CCP's rise to power in the years before 1949: the radicalizing and pragmatic trends in CCP thought were in conflict not only within the party but also within Mao himself. "Marxist-Leninist-Mao Zedong Thought" was often pragmatic, as shown by its turn toward the cross-class alliance of "New Democracy" during the war against Japan and the early PRC period. In 1940 Mao had defined the term "New Democracy" as a means of creating a unified society in which the Chinese Communist Party would be paramount, but also cooperate with other elements in society (such as capitalists and entrepreneurs). This adoption of temporary pragmatic politics by Mao, however, did not mean an abandonment of a radical view of the world and of China's future. Mao's vision revolved around class warfare at home and anti-imperialism abroad in the service of an ever-renewing revolutionary stance. This should have been no secret to those who had observed the Rectification (*Zhengfeng*) movements that marked Mao's radicalization of politics and concentration of it in his own person in the years after 1941. The Korean War became the first test of that commitment in the PRC; by its end society was considerably more radicalized than it had been at the start.

## Taiwan crisis, Bandung cooperation

Wider cold war tensions were reflected in confrontations between Mao and Chiang. After his defeat in 1949, Chiang retreated to the island of Taiwan, maintaining that he remained the legitimate ruler of the Republic of China. Mao, of course, regarded the continued irredentism of his great rival as an affront to his new state. In 1954–5 the PRC military shelled the island of Jinmen (Quemoy) and succeeded in capturing smaller Nationalist- held islands off the coast of Zhejiang province.[12] Just three years later Taiwan's outlying islands once again came under fire from the PRC. This event had more to do with cold war tensions than any particular urgency caused by the situation within Taiwan itself. Mao's relations with Nikita Khrushchev had deteriorated further after 1956, and he was displeased by the Soviet leader's attempts to discredit Stalin, which he (correctly) thought were an oblique way to criticize Mao himself. Mao was also angry that Khrushchev was seeking to ratchet down tensions with the US without consulting him first. Therefore, Mao initiated the bombardment of the islands of Jinmen and Mazu in August 1958 as a means of heightening general tension rather than as a response to a particular political event.[13] Throughout the crisis, as Khrushchev's memoirs attest, the Chinese kept the Soviets in the dark about their intentions.[14] The crisis eventually subsided and was not repeated. However, for the inhabitants of Jinmen memories of the bombardment of their small fishing island, along with the militarization of everyday life, became central to their everyday existence.[15] The offshore islands became a frontier in the cold war world and affected the lives of ordinary inhabitants in many ways, including the greater militarization of society and the development of a mentality that reflected a permanent state of crisis.

Despite the confrontations over Taiwan, China's international behavior during the 1950s also had a cooperative face, symbolized above all by the 1955 Bandung Conference. This was the first grouping of African and Asian countries which would become known as the Non-Aligned Movement. At Bandung, China projected itself as a leading voice of international engagement and development which was not required to follow the path of "modernization" defined by the American or Soviet bloc. During the conference, China's credentials were measured not only as a rival to Moscow or Washington, but also against the newly independent India. Jawaharlal Nehru was pursuing a program of parliamentary democratic socialism. China's ideological radicalism may have been as much a disadvantage as a benefit in this context, and Zhou Enlai's presence as an advocate of the "Five Principles of Peaceful Co-existence" served as a message that the PRC was capable of compromise as well as confrontation. (Zhou used the occasion of his presence at Bandung to announce a halt in the offshore bombing of Taiwan in 1955.) Yet China's closeness to the USSR and radical politics made it an uneasy bedfellow for many of the newly emerging independent states.

# THE SINO-SOVIET SPLIT

Even while it tried to carve out a new status for itself in postwar international society, the PRC remained highly dependent on its relationship with its patron, the USSR. Nevertheless, relations between the two giant communist states led to a split in the early 1960s, which was perhaps the most momentous internal event within the communist bloc during the entire cold war. Although the fissure had been brewing for years, it took many Western observers by surprise. The split was never total, but it was nearly three decades before it was overcome with Soviet leader Mikhail Gorbachev's visit to Beijing in 1989.

Mao and the CCP were wary of Soviet intervention in their revolution from the very earliest days of the PRC. All Chinese nationalists, whether communists or not, had long memories of the "century of humiliation," in which foreign imperialists (including Russia) had occupied large parts of China's territories. In addition, Stalin's demands for special rights in China's borderlands in 1949–50 had angered Mao greatly. The seeds were sown that would eventually lead to the split with the Soviets. On the one hand, Mao's government wanted to stress that its revolution was indigenous, that it had come to power through its own strategic choices, and that it was genuinely rooted in a popular revolution. On the other hand, for reasons of ideological commitment and economic and strategic need, it had to be close to the USSR.

The relationship between Mao and Stalin had always been marked by distrust as well as admiration: Mao believed that much of Stalin's advice to the CCP before 1949 had been mistaken, and Stalin disliked Mao's independence of thought. However, the two had sufficient respect for each other to maintain effective relations between their two countries. Mao had little respect for Stalin's ultimate successor, Nikita Khrushchev. Furthermore, Mao regarded Khrushchev's denunciation of Stalin in the secret speech of 1956 as a coded attack on Mao's own cult of personality, which had been developing since the wartime Rectification movements.

The international and domestic tensions came together during 1956–9, in the wake of the Khrushchev thaw in the USSR. Despite China's involvement with the socialist international economic bloc, Mao was deeply suspicious of the Soviet proposal to intervene by military means in the Polish uprisings of 1956: at a Politburo meeting on October 20, 1956, he observed, "This is serious big-power chauvinism, which should not be allowed under any circumstances."[16] Chinese representatives, including Liu Shaoqi, stressed to Khrushchev their uneasiness about Moscow's intervention in the decisions of other socialist countries. The Chinese position altered during the Hungarian crisis later that year, however. Although its initial response toward intervention was negative, the Chinese leadership became alarmed about the nature of the uprising, which they considered "anti-communist" rather than just "anti-Soviet."[17]

The theoretical questions raised by the 1956 uprisings in Eastern Europe profoundly influenced the development of Chinese domestic policy. Mao took away the message that the Eastern European parties had not been strong enough to combat "reactionary" forces, and that Moscow had also been heavy-handed in its management of those crises.

The effect of this was a contradictory turn within domestic Chinese politics. In 1956–7 Mao supported the Hundred Flowers Movement, which actively called for constructive criticism of the Party from the wider population. He intended that the CCP should glean suggestions on how to reform itself. By 1957, however, Mao had become alarmed at the harsh level of criticism that had emerged through the Hundred Flowers; he launched the Anti-Rightist Campaign in which thousands of people who had criticized the party were arrested.

1956 saw the Chinese more enthused about their efforts to have Beijing replace Moscow as the ideological focal point of world communism. Yet the language that Moscow and Beijing used between themselves over the events of 1956 was shared: language, rhetoric, and political understandings genuinely linked the socialist countries and shaped their understanding of what bound them together against the Western bloc. This disparity, in which the PRC and the USSR shared goals while disagreeing on approaches, was another factor that would lead to their split.[18]

Between 1956 and 1961 relations continued to deteriorate as Mao demanded more radicalism in the face of Soviet attempts to lessen tensions with the Western bloc. Khrushchev had become increasingly disillusioned by what he saw as both Mao's willingness to risk confrontation with the West and his establishment of a cult of personality. Khrushchev was also motivated by a racism that found it hard to take the Chinese seriously. The most symbolic moment was the withdrawal of all Soviet advisors from China in 1960: so sudden was their departure that they left the bridge under construction across the Yangtze at Nanjing half-built. By that stage, the alliance between the two sides was in tatters.

The split with the Soviets meant that China had a new freedom to exercise its influence as a revolutionary actor on the global stage. China projected itself as a role model at a moment when scores of Asian and African countries were decolonizing and seeking to shape their emerging nation-states. While China and the USSR remained allied for the first decade of the PRC's existence, it was clear that China had an authenticity about its rhetoric of anti-imperialist liberation that the Soviet Union lacked (as did the US). Eastern Europe was essentially a colony of Moscow. China's revolution, in contrast, was genuinely indigenous, even if it had received significant Soviet assistance. After the Sino-Soviet split of the early 1960s, China's rhetoric became much more explicitly anti-Soviet, haranguing Soviet "revisionism and social imperialism." In his 1965 declaration "Long Live the Victory of People's War," Lin Biao sneered at the "Khrushchev revisionists," whom he accused of collaborating with the US "imperialists" trying to sabotage the Chinese-led ideas of "people's war."[19]

# THE VIETNAM WAR

The worsening relationship between the PRC and the USSR was also reflected in the Chinese involvement in the war in Vietnam. China provided support for the Vietnamese in their struggle against French colonialism from its earliest days, and then for the North Vietnamese in their war to unify Vietnam under their control. From the early 1950s to the late 1960s, the CCP exploited their long ties with the Vietnamese Communist movement to offer them support. As with Korea, Chinese policy linked an ideological commitment to a more pragmatic mode of operation. The latter was particularly evident in the 1954 Geneva Accords, through which postcolonial Vietnam's borders were defined. These marked one of the major diplomatic successes of Zhou Enlai, China's foreign minister and prime minister. Nonetheless, the Accords did represent an ideological retreat, as Zhou (and the Soviets) pressured Ho Chi Minh not to press for an immediate unification of the two halves of Vietnam but to accept a "temporary" division of the country—something which Mao later came to regret. Chinese involvement in Vietnam would soon intensify significantly.

During much of the 1960s, the North Vietnamese found themselves in the curious position of accepting assistance from both the PRC and the USSR even while hostility between the latter two states increased.[20] Some 320,000 Chinese troops were deployed across the border into North Vietnam between 1965 and 1968. The troops took part in fighting (operating gun positions) and also undertook significant construction work, thereby freeing up Vietnamese soldiers for the assault into South Vietnam. This involvement was never formally acknowledged, nor did the US seek to draw attention to it. Still, it is a marker of the seriousness with which China took its cold war mission. In assisting the North Vietnamese, the Chinese drew attention to their own path for anti-imperialist liberation, which combined allegiance to ideas of radical social change with a strong sense of non-European nationalism. On both these points the USSR was unable to trump China. By intervening in Vietnam, Beijing also made up for those occasions when it had had to draw back from involvement, such as the failure to conquer the south in the Korean War or the inability to prevent a right-wing coup in Indonesia in 1965 against a leadership that seemed to be orienting itself toward Beijing.[21]

However, that nationalism also caused one of the major rifts between China and Vietnam, and illustrated a wider problem—that China continued to have a highly sinocentric attitude toward its neighbors. Mao's comments on the countries of East Asia that "we belong to the same family and support one another" strongly signaled that he considered China to be the "elder brother" in the relationship.[22] Such attitudes and the continuing realization of the Vietnamese that they would have to choose between support from the USSR and from China led to the breakdown of relations between Vietnam and China and the final withdrawal of Chinese troops in 1970.

## THE OPENING TO THE US

The mid-1960s likewise witnessed the most convulsive social change in the whole of Mao's period in power, the Cultural Revolution, which eventually precipitated the biggest ideological shift in China's international behavior: the opening to the United States. The Cultural Revolution was Mao's revolt against his own party: fearing that he was being sidelined and that the PRC as a whole was losing revolutionary fervor, he launched a campaign in 1966 which exhorted China's population to rise up and "bombard the headquarters" of the CCP itself. The result was a massive radicalization of domestic policies for the next three years. However, as the most radical phase of the Cultural Revolution ended, prominent figures in the leadership began to feel China's lack of global allies keenly. By 1969 the relationship between Beijing and Moscow had become so bad that the two sides feared that war might break out over control of territories on China's northeastern border. There were significant reasons for China to reopen relations with its "most respected enemy," particularly as it became clear that the newly elected American president, Richard Nixon, held similar sentiments. As early as 1967 Nixon had written in an editorial, "[W]e simply cannot afford to leave China forever outside the family of nations."[23]

The reasons that Mao's government reversed its ideological strategy and invited the representatives of the greatest capitalist nation on earth to the heart of Beijing were domestic as well as international. The upheavals of the Cultural Revolution were exposing the contradictions in Mao's vision of modernity. After the departure of Soviet advisors in 1960, it no longer had the indigenous capacity to develop technology, particularly as the Cultural Revolution's initial phase was predicated on breaking down any pretensions to high technical knowledge or expertise. Although various areas of scientific endeavor, such as the Chinese atomic bomb program, remained protected from the Cultural Revolution, overall the movement was immensely destructive to the country's knowledge base. It was clear by the early 1970s that some source of external technical knowledge was needed to replace the Soviets.

Mao himself became a strong supporter of the opening to the US, having read and noted what he took as positive signals from Nixon. The latter's inaugural address had made it clear that he would not be bound simply by ideology in his decisions as to which countries to talk to. However, it seems that Mao's putative successor, Lin Biao, was not favorably inclined toward an opening toward the US.[24] The situation changed with Lin's death in 1971. He appears to have been involved in an attempted coup against Mao, and his disappearance from the scene meant that the Chinese leadership became more unified toward the opening toward the US.

After a series of maneuvers and false starts, US National Security Advisor Henry Kissinger arrived under conditions of top secrecy in Beijing in 1971. He was subjected to robust conversations by Zhou Enlai and other Chinese officials, and this helped to clear the way for the visit by Nixon. On February 21, 1972, Nixon arrived in Beijing. His visit was only a week long, but it was highly public (more so to the outside world than within China itself) and demonstrated clearly that the cold war structures had been reoriented. With the emergence of détente in Europe, the US became the only superpower to have active engagement with the other two major powers, the USSR and China.[25]

The myth that "only Nixon could go to China" (that is, only a right-wing Republican could do so without accusations of going soft on communism) is now widely dismissed. Both Kennedy, and more so Johnson, had experimented with greater communication with the PRC. From 1966, however, these efforts were hampered by the outbreak of the Cultural Revolution, which made it difficult to have any meaningful communications with the Beijing government.[26] The rapprochement between the two countries had as much to do with changes in China as did the arrival of a new US president: even Mao realized that his beloved Cultural Revolution had run out of steam and that to continue it risked domestic collapse and even international conflict. Furthermore, Mao was disturbed by the Soviet invasion of Czechoslovakia, and this may well have inclined him toward seeking an ally against a future attack by Moscow.[27]

The odd alliance of convenience between the US and China would last for some two decades. When cold war crises emerged, China would side with the West: China attended the 1984 Los Angeles Olympics when they were boycotted by the USSR and most Eastern European countries, and the West and China both chose to support the Khmer Rouge in 1979 when the Soviet-backed Vietnamese ousted that genocidal regime. The neutralization of China enabled the US to concentrate on the European front of the cold war.

The other government that was most affected by the switch in US policy was the Republic of China on Taiwan, the rump state controlled by Chiang Kai-shek. For much of the high cold war, Taiwan was a major factor in right-wing US politics (in particular the so-called "China Lobby"), but Democratic as much as Republican presidents found it hard to abandon Chiang Kai-shek. Chiang's regime was clearly underpinned by US support; without the US Seventh Fleet in the Pacific, there would have been little to prevent the PRC retaking the island. Chiang had one overriding agenda, which he repeatedly pressed on his American backers: the recapture of the mainland. However, Taiwan under his rule also achieved certain domestic successes that Chiang had failed to gain on the mainland. The major social change that emerged under American pressure was land reform, the issue on which the Communists had won over much of the peasantry on the mainland.[28] Thus Taiwan became a model of a cold war developmental state.

The political constraints of the cold war also allowed Taiwan to maintain a highly protected economy and currency in return for fealty to the US. This enabled it to build a powerful manufacturing base which enabled the island to become a major exporter from the 1970s onward. In political terms, the Republic of China was an authoritarian dictatorship. The Nationalist government committed many human rights abuses. The regime was particularly discriminatory against ethnic Chinese who had been born on the island as opposed to emigrating from the mainland after 1945 or 1949, as well as the island's aboriginal population. Yet it also followed the example of US-backed societies such as authoritarian South Korea and democratic Japan in using its economic policies to drive down income inequality. Chiang's death in 1975 brought his son Chiang Ching-kuo to power, and moves began to legalize the pro-democracy civil society groups, which had started to form on the island. As Taiwan became more diplomatically isolated, it began to use its democratic credentials rather than its anti-communist ones to justify its reluctance to reunify with the mainland.

## The culture of cold war China

The language within which China expressed and understood the cold war was in large part a subset of the period's global linguistic environment: a dispute between two differing versions of the Enlightenment, in which the vocabulary of "freedom" and "democracy" became the terrain of contestation between the two blocs. In China, the local variation of this dispute was linked to two different historical streams. The first was the May Fourth Movement, a liberal and anti-traditional strain of Enlightenment thought which had embraced the ideas of "science and democracy" as the key to combating imperialism and renewing China's politics in the 1910s. The Chinese Communist Party, founded in 1921, was just one product of the period.[29]

The second source was the legacy of the wartime period. China, more than perhaps any belligerent during World War II, had seen the "world war of values" fought on its own soil. The Nationalists and Communists had engaged in a deadly dispute, but they had both sought ownership of the language of democracy. Nationalist China had called itself "Free" China to the outside world, and Mao's major wartime theoretical innovation had been the concept of "New Democracy." During the cold war, Mao's regime continued to speak of itself as being "democratic." In doing so, it drew on the pre-1949 tradition of political reform without openly acknowledging that it was doing so.

China also used another commonplace term of the era, "modernization," to define its own distinctive path. Modernization theory is probably the social scientific phrase most associated with the cold war. It refers to the postwar idea, accepted in the USSR as well as in the West, that technological progress could come through a carefully mapped and defined pathway from "tradition" to "modernity."[30]

China provided an alternative view of modernization that shared much of the desire for progress, as well as the goals of "modernization," but found different pathways to achieve it. For a start, because China remained a less developed and more agrarian country than either the US or USSR, its policies were tied to the countryside more than in the other two countries. Furthermore, Mao's engagement with modernity and progress was always tempered by his dislike of China's "intellectual" classes, which he regarded as insufficiently committed to the revolution and too linked to their Confucian predecessors. Therefore, there were strong elements that ran through the Chinese revolution that differentiated it from the Soviet view. The mobilization of the countryside was central to Mao's view of modernization in the Great Leap Forward of 1958–62.

The Leap was a disaster, leading to a massive famine that killed more than 20 million Chinese. Nonetheless, Mao remained enchanted by the idea of an alternative model of modernization in which the power of rural-dwellers could be unleashed. Other aspects of the Chinese experience did prove inspiring to radical groups and governments as far apart as India and East Africa, and in some cases were assisted by formal Chinese assistance. The TanZam railway, linking Dar es Salaam, Tanzania, to landlocked Zambia, was one of the most prominent projects to use Chinese assistance to construct infrastructure in decolonized Africa as an alternative to Western or Soviet assistance.

One element of China's discourse that was specifically tied to the cold war was the fetish that it made of the atomic bomb. The cold war globally was associated with a romantic view of technology and its possibilities. Of course, this was not unprecedented (Futurism was just one of the artistic trends in the early 20th century which was underpinned by an obsession with technology), but nuclear technology in particular is associated inextricably with the wider trajectory of the cold war. For smaller, post-imperial powers such as Britain and France, acquisition of atomic weapons became symbolic of national prowess. The US and USSR found themselves torn between stressing the power that atomic weaponry bestowed and reflecting on its destructiveness. Japan, in contrast, heavily tied its postwar self-image to having been a victim of the only atomic bombs dropped.

The PRC was unequivocal about stressing the search for an atomic weapon as a powerful symbol of national virility. Attitudes on this issue were shaped at the very top: Mao had shocked Khrushchev by declaring, as the two of them relaxed by a swimming pool in Beijing, that the atomic bomb was a "paper tiger."[31] Lin Biao, China's defense minister, gave a pithy example of the metaphor's power when he spoke of Mao Zedong's thought as being "a spiritual atom bomb of infinite power." This was an image which could never have been used in Japan, or most of postwar Europe. In general, the PRC embraced the romanticism of technology wholeheartedly, and unashamedly combined it with politics.

# A NEW WORLD: FROM NIXON TO THE END OF THE COLD WAR

China tends to fade from the global narrative of the cold war after the Sino-US rapprochement in 1972. After the traumas of the Cultural Revolution, it became clear that China had reversed its policy of international revolutionary intervention. The death of Mao and the arrest of the "Gang of Four," as the leaders of the Cultural Revolution Central Group became known, were further signs of the move away from radical policies. Nonetheless, Chinese policy had begun to change several years before Mao's death. In 1971 the PRC finally replaced Taiwan at the United Nations. This development was a first step toward socializing the country into the wider international community.

The opening to America had been preceded, not followed, by the opening of relations with Japan. This had happened partly as an act of pique; Prime Minister Satô Eisaku had been angered at the "Nixon Shocks" of 1971–2, when the US president had abandoned the Bretton Woods monetary system and opened channels to China without informing Tokyo in advance. Satô's successor, Tanaka Kakuei, visited Beijing in 1972 and signed the Zhou-Tanaka communiqué, which established the first sustained diplomatic relations between a sovereign Japan and the Chinese mainland since 1938. Another important area that showed a real shift by the PRC in the 1970s was its policy toward Southeast Asia. By the early 1970s China's relations with Vietnam had become frostier, as the latter tied its fortunes to the USSR. However, Beijing continued to maintain a stake in the success of the rival Khmer Rouge movement in neighboring Cambodia. Among the last conversations recorded between Mao and foreign leaders was a dialogue with Pol Pot, in which it is clear that Mao's ideological radicalism had remained undimmed. Beijing offered support for the Khmer Rouge during its four years in power, and in 1979, after the Vietnamese had ousted Pol Pot, Beijing allied with the Western powers in continuing to recognize the Khmer Rouge representative at the UN. In addition, in February 1979 China launched an invasion of northern Vietnam, ostensibly to counter discrimination against ethnic Chinese in the area, but also as a wider warning to Vietnam that they could not act against China and its allies with impunity. For Beijing, the war was a disaster; People's Liberation Army (PLA) troops were expelled fast. The Sino-Vietnamese War remains the last occasion that Chinese troops have been deployed in anger outside Chinese territory.

The late cold war also saw significant changes in the Chinese historical memory of the recent past. In 1949 the Mao regime had decreed that the Nationalist government that preceded it should be treated in public pronouncements and educational materials as villains and rogues: corrupt, in thrall to foreign powers, and worst of all, unwilling or unable to fight the Japanese while the CCP led the war effort. After the 1980s this viewpoint changed significantly. Within China there was widespread disillusionment at the chaos wrought by the Cultural Revolution, and it became clear to the post-Mao leadership that a new source of domestic legitimacy, drawing on nationalism, was needed to substitute for ideological radicalism. Then, the death of Chiang in 1975 and Mao in 1976 removed some of the personal venom from the ideological wars of the previous half-century.

In addition, the politics of the Mao years had stressed the danger from Chiang much more than it had paid attention to the memory of the many war crimes committed in China by the Japanese during the years 1937–45. The PRC had wished to detach Japan from the cold war embrace of the US, and this made it less politic to stress past atrocities. However, once the 1972 Shanghai communiqué had been signed, it became politically useful to remind the Japanese of their past record as a stimulant for domestic nationalism. The emphasis in modern history moved away from the Civil War and back to the War of Resistance against Japan (as the Sino-Japanese War was known in China). The new historiographical turn, which was supported at the highest level in government, saw new museums, books, and films appear. One of the most striking aspects was the remembering of Japanese war crimes, most notably the Nanjing Massacre ("Rape of Nanking") of 1937–8; a memorial museum was opened in 1985 on the site of one of the mass murders.

But equally notable was the stark, if unstated, shift in cold war historiography with regard to the Nationalist government's wartime role. The major museum in Beijing commemorating the War of Resistance (opened in 1987) stressed the importance of Nationalist victories such as the Battle of Taierzhuang in 1938, in which the CCP had played no part. The new history still emphasized the leading role of the CCP, but it no longer dismissed the Nationalists as useless or cowardly. Instead, the role of the Chiang regime in resisting the Japanese for eight years was given due seriousness. Even Chiang's old mansions in eastern China were rehabilitated as museums and his role given a respectful description: this would have been unthinkable in the era of Mao.[32]

# UNCERTAIN ENDINGS

From China, the end of the cold war looks different from the view from the West. In the West, a very clear overarching narrative emerged. One side, the West, "won." Key figures—notably Ronald Reagan and Mikhail Gorbachev but also Margaret Thatcher and Helmut Kohl—gave a human face to the narrative. Most importantly, there was a clear shift of regimes from communist to non-communist governance.

This left Asia as a seeming anomaly. The continuing existence of North Korea, Vietnam, and most of all, the People's Republic of China as states still run by communist parties that had no intention of relinquishing power was made to seem like a global outlier. The killings of protestors in Tiananmen Square in Beijing on June 4, 1989, seemed to seal China's fate as a dinosaur of history: the emergent superpower of the early 21st century did not appear that way after the Beijing Spring of 1989 had ended. Yet it may be that the most important shifts that ended the cold war structure emerged first in Asia rather than Europe.

The Nixon visit of 1972 and the rapprochement with Japan marked a re-engagement by the PRC with the non-communist world, even while the Cultural Revolution continued and the cold war remained cold. But it is important not to read these events as they have been understood in retrospect—that is, with the knowledge that the USSR would collapse and that communism would end in Eastern Europe. For even in the last years of the cold war, its structures did not appear to be weakening. To many, the appearance of leaders such as Reagan, Thatcher, Yuri Andropov, and Konstantin Chernenko made the cold war still seem very chilly. It was in this context that China's reforms in the 1980s, leading up to 1989, need to be viewed. At the time, they were seen in Beijing not as a way of overcoming communism but of reinterpreting it for a new world in which the US and USSR would both play a role.

The 1980s, then, have some similarity with the years 1945–50 with which this chapter started. In both cases China's story seems in retrospect to be part of a clearly defined wider global narrative: in 1949, one that ended with the establishment of the PRC and the establishment of a cold war Asia, and in 1989, one that ended with the collapse of Eastern European communism and the discrediting of classic state socialism. Yet the major actors did not make decisions at the time with the knowledge of the end result. In 1945, neither the Nationalists nor Communists knew that the latter would win; in 1978, when the Chinese economic reforms started, nobody in Beijing believed that the Soviet Union had only a decade more of existence left. China's final cold war decade was shaped by an understanding that the world would remain under the influence of the superpowers that had dominated it for thirty years. In practice, it was the implosion of one of those superpowers that allowed China to become the power with the global reach that it had craved for decades. And at the start of the 21st century, the question that exercises at least some analysts in the West is whether the end of the old cold war with the USSR has paved the way for a new one with China instead. In the 1950s, there was real debate over whether the Soviet bloc provided an alternative model of modernization that, in Khrushchev's word, might "bury" the West. As the West is racked in the present day by economic crisis and political self-doubt, one of the key questions of the decades to come is whether a Chinese model may pose an equally important challenge, and whether that alternative may prove more lasting than the failed Soviet model.

## Notes

1. An important revisionist work on the Nationalist record is Hans van de Ven, *War and Nationalism in China, 1925–1945* (London: Routledge Curzon, 2003).
2. Odd Arne Westad, *Decisive Encounters: The Chinese Civil War, 1946–1950* (Stanford, CA: Stanford University Press, 2003).
3. Odd Arne Westad, *Cold War and Revolution: Soviet-American Rivalry and the Origins of the Chinese Civil War, 1944–1946* (New York: Columbia University Press, 1993); Chen Jian, *Mao's China and the Cold War* (Chapel Hill, NC: University of North Carolina Press, 2001), ch. 2.
4. On rival nationalisms, see Timothy Brook and Andre Schmidt, *Nation Work: Asian Elites and National Identities* (Ann Arbor, MI: University of Michigan Press, 2000).
5. On China's pre-1937 economy, see Loren Brandt, "Reflections on China's late 19th and early 20th century economy," *The China Quarterly* 150 (June 1997): 282–308.
6. William C. Kirby, "China's Internationalization in the Early People's Republic: Dreams of a Socialist World Economy," *The China Quarterly* 188 (December 2006): 884.
7. Kirby, "China's Internationalization," 887.
8. Chen, *Mao's China*, 52–3.
9. Chen, *Mao's China*, 89–90.
10. Vladislav Zubok and Constantine Pleshakov, *Inside the Kremlin's Cold War: From Stalin to Khrushchev* (Cambridge, MA: Harvard University Press, 1997), 55, 62.
11. Chen Jian, *China's Road to the Korean War: The Making of the Sino-American Confrontation* (New York: Columbia University Press, 1994).
12. Chen, *Mao's China*, 168–70.
13. Zubok and Pleshakov, *Inside the Kremlin*, 220–1. See also Thomas Christiansen, *Useful Adversaries: Grand Strategy, Domestic Mobilization, and Sino-American Conflict, 1947–1958* (Princeton, NJ: Princeton University Press, 1996).
14. Zubok and Pleshakov, *Inside the Kremlin*, 222–4.
15. Michael Szonyi, *Cold War Island: Quemoy on the Front Line* (Cambridge: Cambridge University Press, 2008).
16. Chen, *Mao's China*, 147.
17. Chen, *Mao's China*, 155.
18. Lorenz M. Lüthi, *The Sino-Soviet Split: Cold War in the Communist World* (Princeton, NJ: Princeton University Press, 2008), 345.
19. Thomas W. Robinson, "Chinese Foreign Policy from the 1940s to the 1990s," in Thomas W. Robinson and David Shambaugh, eds., *Chinese Foreign Policy: Theory and Practice* (Oxford: Oxford University Press, 1994), 558.
20. Qiang Zhai, *China and the Vietnam Wars, 1950–1975*, 135; Chris Connolly, "The American Factor: Sino-American Rapprochement and Chinese Attitudes to the Vietnam War, 1968–1972," *Cold War History* 5/4 (November 2005): 501–527.

21. Peter Van Ness, *Revolution and Chinese Foreign Policy* (Berkeley, CA: University of California Press, 1970).

22. Odd Arne Westad et al., eds., *77 Conversations between Chinese and Foreign Leaders on the Wars in Indochina, 1964–1977*, Cold War International History Project Working Paper 22 (Washington, DC: Woodrow Wilson International Center for Scholars, 1998), 185–6.

23. Chen, *Mao's China*, 245. He Di, "The Most Respected Enemy: Mao's Perceptions of the United States," *The China Quarterly* 137 (1994):144–158.

24. Chen, *Mao's China*, ch. 9.

25. Margaret MacMillan, *Nixon and Mao: The Week that Changed the World* (New York: Random House, 2007).

26. Michael Lumbers, *Piercing the Bamboo Curtain: Tentative Bridge-Building to China during the Johnson Years* (Manchester: Manchester University Press, 2008).

27. Chen, *Mao's China*, 243, 245.

28. John Copper, *Taiwan: Nation-State or Province?* (Boulder, CO: Westview Press, 1996).

29. Rana Mitter, *A Bitter Revolution: China's Struggle with the Modern World* (Oxford: Oxford University Press, 2004).

30. Odd Arne Westad, *The Global Cold War: Third World Interventions and the Making of our Times* (Cambridge: Cambridge University Press, 2006).

31. Zubok and Pleshakov, *Inside the Kremlin*, 219.

32. Rana Mitter, "Old ghosts, New Memories: China's Changing War History in the Era of Post-Mao Politics", *Journal of Contemporary History* 38/1 (2003):117–131; Parks M. Coble, "China's 'New Remembering' of the Anti-Japanese War of Resistance, 1937–1945," *The China Quarterly* 190 (2007):394–140.

## Select Bibliography

Chen Jian. *China's Road to the Korean War: The Making of the Sino-American Confrontation.* New York: Columbia University Press, 1994.

Chen Jian. *Mao's China and the Cold War.* Chapel Hill, NC: University of North Carolina Press, 2001.

Foot, Rosemary. *The Practice of Power: US-China relations since 1949.* Oxford: Oxford University Press, 1995.

Lüthi, Lothar M. *The Sino-Soviet Split: Cold War in the Communist World.* Princeton, NJ: Princeton University Press, 2008.

Qiang Zhai. *China and the Vietnam Wars, 1950–1975.* Chapel Hill, NC: University of North Carolina Press, 2000.

Radchenko, Sergey. *Two Suns in the Heavens: The Sino-Soviet Struggle for Supremacy, 1962–1967.* Washington, DC and Stanford, CA: Woodrow Wilson Center and Stanford University Press, 2009.

Szonyi, Michael. *Cold War Island: Quemoy on the Frontline.* Cambridge: Cambridge University Press, 2008.

Westad, Odd Arne. *Cold War and Revolution: Soviet-American Rivalry and the Origins of the Chinese Civil War, 1944–1946.* New York: Columbia University Press, 1993.

Westad, Odd Arne, ed. *Brothers in Arms: The Rise and Fall of the Sino-Soviet Alliance, 1945–1963.* Washington, DC and Stanford, CA: Woodrow Wilson Center and Stanford University Press, 1998.

...............................................................................................................

# CHAPTER 9

# BRITAIN AND THE COLD WAR, 1945–1990

...............................................................................................................

## KLAUS LARRES

IN the midst of the Second World War, Winston Churchill stood up in the House of Commons and declared: "the British nation is unique in this respect. They are the only people who like to be told how bad things are, who like to be told the worst."[1] Yet, over the following decades even the resilience of the British people was severely tested by the avalanche of bad news they received. The drastic decline of the country's world power status, the end of Britain's far-flung global empire, the economic woes of the 1960s and 1970s, and the country's inability to compete with the cold war superpowers, the United States of America and the Soviet Union, were all too evident. Still, Britain was an active participant in many of the crucial events which shaped the cold war years. The UK remained an important, albeit waning, cold war power.

This essay explores how the UK managed to maintain its global influence during the cold war, despite its decline. London's "soft power" and Britain's reputation as an effective international power broker allowed the country to punch well above its real weight in world politics. The UK's network of global connections that extended back to the days of the Empire, the country's reputation as a trusted ally of the US, its military and foreign policy professionalism, London's impressive intelligence expertise, and not least Britain's high-quality armaments industry decisively contributed to the perception throughout the cold war that the UK was considerably more influential than it really was. Three distinct phases emerge: the early cold war years (1945–56) when Britain benefited from its World War II victor status and was still seen as a real world power; the post-Suez years of the cold war (1957–1970s), when Britain's influence diminished at an accelerating rate; and a period of apparent revival but continuing practical impotence on the larger world stage (1979–90).

The bipartisan foreign policy consensus among British leaders throughout the cold war years, which made any prolonged discussion of national interest questions superfluous, gives credence to Kenneth Waltz's neo-realist theory of international relations, which argues that "structure dictates policy."[2] Among the crucial elements of the cold war structure within which Britain was forced to operate were America's unassailable supervision of the cold war system, the perceived Soviet threat, Britain's ever-declining economy, the nationalistic fervor of many of Britain's imperial subjects, and the influence of such domestic forces as British public opinion and the increasingly important tabloid press. Britain's withdrawal from Palestine and India in the mid-1940s and retreat from east of Suez in the late 1960s were largely imposed by structural forces. This chapter argues that the British state and its leaders, nevertheless, did have choices and exercised them. To cite some examples, the determination to develop a nuclear bomb shortly after the end of World War II, the decision not to participate in the Schuman Plan negotiations of 1950, and the war resolution against Argentina to recapture the Falklands islands in 1982 were not dictated by systemic necessities. They resulted from individual and political decisions.

## A BRIEF SURVEY OF THE LITERATURE

The thirty year rule of the UK National Archives has largely driven the writing of British contemporary history.[3] Thus, notwithstanding a number of valuable popular histories, at present scholarly accounts of cold war Britain extend only to the early 1980s.[4] This scholarship, moreover, has focused on the successive British governments and follows the archival trail. Consequently, there is a rich literature available on the Labour governments of 1945–51, the Harold Macmillan and Harold Wilson years, and Britain's role in the end of the cold war during the Margaret Thatcher era, including the prime minister's strong opposition to German unification. The latter generated the publication of an important volume of Foreign Office documents.[5]

The major developments in British cold war history have also been covered along thematic lines. Much of the historiography addresses Britain's military and defense policies, the challenges of decolonization and "Third World" nationalism, and Britain's role as an awkward and belated partner in the European integration process.[6] Likewise, the country's bilateral relationships, especially with Germany and France, its role in international organizations such as NATO, and its decline from imperial world power have attracted much attention.[7] Recently, moreover, the history of British intelligence during the cold war has proven to be a fruitful area of research.[8]

Britain's status as a junior partner in Anglo-American relations and the nature of the so-called "special relationship" have also produced keen analyses.[9] Indeed, the meager benefits for the UK from its close partnership with President George W. Bush in the context of the post-cold war "Global War on Terror" have led to increasing doubts about whether a "special relationship" with the US ever existed. Along with Britain's declining economic fortunes, it was the United States, after all, which diminished London's cold war role. The forceful and rapid rise of the United States as the global hegemon and its dominating power in international affairs in the West pushed Britain aside.[10]

Throughout the cold war it became obvious that Britain was rapidly sliding down an ever more declining slope. The swinging London of the 1960s and the global importance

of the British popular music industry could hardly make up for the gradual disappearance of Britain's once powerful manufacturing base and the social deprivations and poverty which afflicted many British regions.[11] The rise of crime and violence in London and
the big cities of the north were only surpassed by the outbreak of civil war in Northern
Ireland in the late 1960s. Despite multiple attempts to resolve this conflict, only the Good
Friday Agreement of 1998, negotiated with active American support and participation,
brought about a relatively stable peace.[12] The end of the East-West conflict, and with it
the UK's lack of strategic, economic, and political interest in this small British province
of 1.5 million people in the north of Ireland, proved decisive in overcoming this conflict.

## Phase I:  Britain during the early cold war years (1945–1956)

When World War II in Europe ended on May 8, 1945, the mood in Britain was one of joy
and relief. Nevertheless, as signaled by the defeat of Winston Churchill's Conservative
party in the general election a few months later, there also was a profound desire for
change. The population dreamed of a "new Jerusalem" after all the deprivations of the
war years. As expected, the new Labour government embarked on a program of radical
reform. Within 18 months more than 20 percent of the British economy was nationalized. The Bank of England, the railways, the airports, the road system, and the coal and
steel industries came under public ownership. The state pledged to look after its citizens
from the "cradle to the grave." The enactment of the National Health Service Act in May
1946 and the National Insurance Act established the "welfare state." The government
overhauled Britain's antiquated education system, subsidized housing, and developed a
new state-directed industrial policy.[13]

Similar new departures did not occur in the foreign policy sphere, however. In fact,
there was a pervasive belief in Whitehall that Britain's economic and political predicaments were merely temporary. Most Britons were convinced that the economy would
recover. As reflected by the Foreign Office's Sir Orme Sargent's famous "Stocktaking after
VE-Day" memorandum of July 1945, they were likewise confident that in the meantime
the country's finely-honed diplomatic skills could overcome any international political
setbacks.[14]

The foreign policy of Clement Attlee's government was decidedly conservative and
attached to past lines of thinking. Pundits that initially assumed that a left-wing Labour
government would be more sympathetic to the communist Soviet Union were mistaken.
The "massive, boisterous, shrewd, and vindictive Ernest Bevin," the formidable new
Foreign Secretary, intended to prove "that he would not be hectored by the representatives of the workers' paradise" in Moscow.[15]

The new British government's relations with the Soviet Union never recovered from
the disputes over the future of Germany and Eastern European states such as Poland and
Czechoslovakia. The Foreign Office was alarmed that the Soviet Union had not hesitated
to violate the Yalta agreement of February 1945, as interpreted in London and
Washington, by imposing communist governments on Poland, Czechoslovakia,

Hungary, Bulgaria, Romania, and other countries.[16] Whitehall even took the lead in supporting the royalist faction in Albania. In 1946 joint Anglo-American covert plans for overthrowing the Soviet-backed communist regime were developed, and Albanian guerilla units were trained with Greek support.[17] These small units entered the country in 1949 but were bloodily repulsed. Code-named "Valuable," the operation was "a clinical experience to see whether larger rollback operations would be feasible elsewhere," CIA chief of covert operations, Frank Wisner, cynically explained.[18]

Eastern Europe notwithstanding, Germany remained the potential main enemy in the mind of British officials. Soviet dictator Josef Stalin and the British Foreign Office mandarins shared the belief that the German nation would rise again in the not-too-distant future. Only gradually did British policymakers come to regard Stalin's postwar objectives as irreconcilable with Britain's aims. Indicative of a new anti-Russian direction of British foreign policy was not only Winston Churchill's "iron curtain" speech in March 1946 but also the creation of the "Russia Committee" within the Foreign Office. While Stalin and other influential Soviet politicians interpreted Churchill's speech as the opening shot in the cold war, the top-secret weekly analyses of the "Russia Committee" concluded that Stalin was intent on destroying the British empire and obstructing Britain's objectives in Europe.[19]

Predictably, the joint four-power administration of the occupation zones in Germany and Berlin did not work well. Disputes over reparations and whether or not Germany should ultimately be reunited burdened allied relations greatly. While the British government continued to ration bread and other items at home, its obligation to ship huge quantities of food and heating material to its former enemy created hardship and resentment. Coal production in the UK could not keep up with industrial and private demand. Cuts in electricity and heating services were a daily occurrence. In May 1947 the only way out seemed to be the merger of the British and American zones of occupation into a single unit: "Bizonia."[20]

There also existed plenty of other problems. Britain's still heavy involvement and large military commitments in the Far East were an immense financial and political burden. In the Mediterranean the Communist parties, especially in France and Italy, were not only pro-Soviet but also serious competitors for power. In addition the Soviet Union was pushing for a new agreement with Turkey regarding control over the Dardanelles that would have given the Soviet navy access to the still British-dominated Mediterranean. The Soviet Union also refused to withdraw its troops from oil-rich and strategically important Iran.[21]

Anglo-Soviet confrontations at successive sessions of the Council of Foreign Ministers in the second half of the 1940s persuaded London and Washington to cooperate closely. Still, Britain continued to pursue an independent foreign policy. This climaxed in 1949 when, despite much criticism from Washington, London recognized Communist China following Mao's victory in the Chinese civil war. The British, however, put the blame squarely onto the Americans for their frequent discord. They faulted Washington for underestimating the UK's economic weakness and for under-appreciating the country's global challenges. The Labour government was particularly upset by the McMahon Act, which a reluctant President Harry S. Truman signed in August 1946. This legislation brought to an end Anglo-American cooperation in atomic matters despite Churchill and Roosevelt having signed an agreement for postwar collaboration.[22]

Most important in immediate practical terms was Britain's financial predicament. Its accumulated debt of over 4.7 billion pounds sterling, the abrupt termination of lend-lease in August 1945, the wartime sale of overseas assets valuing £1.1 billion, and the resulting loss of future revenues from these assets became a major problem. Although British negotiator John Maynard Keynes was optimistic that he could persuade the United States to extend a generous interest-free loan to Britain given its wartime sacrifices, the Truman administration proved very stubborn. Eventually in December 1945 the US agreed to offer a loan of $3.75 billion at 2 percent interest and largely forgave Britain's lend-lease debt. But in return it compelled Britain to ratify the 1944 Bretton Woods agreement, which established a new international monetary order characterized by fixed exchange rates pegged to the dollar and other features that ushered in a US-dominated economic order. The British had to agree to make the pound sterling convertible, a condition aimed at eviscerating Britain's imperial preference system. In the event, the effort was aborted in 1947 because the British economy proved too weak to sustain convertibility.[23]

Taking into account Britain's extensive military commitments abroad, that same year the House of Commons voted to continue wartime conscription and even extend the length of service from 12 months to first 18 and then 24 months. This also explains why the Labour government believed it had no choice but to develop a British atomic bomb. Although notions of prestige and international status influenced the top-secret decision, formally taken in January 1947, there was also a "strategic rationale for a British bomb," albeit a highly expensive one which the country could not afford. Even more than in the US, the relationship between Britain's commitments and resources required more bang for the buck.[24]

The receipt of the lion's share of Marshall Plan funds sustained Britain in the early postwar years, but this aid would not last forever. The obvious solution was to reduce Britain's defense expenditure by curtailing its global commitments. Britain significantly reduced its global commitments after May 1948 when the Labour government returned its old League of Nations mandate for Palestine to the new United Nations. Israel was founded soon thereafter. Already on August 15, 1947 London had honored its wartime commitment to grant independence to India in return for Indian support. London withdrew from the subcontinent, unable to prevent the outbreak of civil war, which led to the death of up to a million people, the displacement of 12.5 million more, and the establishment of an independent Pakistan.[25] The withdrawal from India and Palestine was not sufficient, however, to match Britain's diminishing resources more closely with the country's global responsibilities. Sacrifices had to be made in Europe, too.

London gave notice in early 1947 that the British would have to withdraw from Greece. This decision precipitated President Truman's announcement of the Truman Doctrine, pledging the US to support any country confronting communist aggression anywhere. Historians often present Britain's threat to withdraw from Greece as a deliberate ploy designed to cement US involvement in cold war Europe. The evidence suggests otherwise. Britain was a severely overstretched country desperate to cut its commitments.[26]

It was Labour's foreign secretary, Ernest Bevin, who negotiated the Brussels Treaty Organization that created a defensive alliance with the French and the Benelux countries in 1948 to signal to Washington that Britain and the Europeans had begun to organize against a potential military onslaught by the Red Army. Subsequently, the US and Canada began negotiating with the major Western European countries to establish a North Atlantic Treaty Organization (NATO). The NATO treaty, including that important Article 5 that guaranteed mutual military assistance in the case of an attack, was signed in April 1949.[27]

When North Korean forces crossed the 38th parallel into South Korea in June 1950, the Labour government, now fully committed to the principle of collective security, joined the US in a war that was formally conducted under UN auspices. This exhausting and drawn-out conflict proved to be very unpopular at home, generating heated disputes that almost brought down Attlee's government. The economic sacrifices needed for British rearmament made necessary the first cuts in the provisions of the national health service. Prescription charges were introduced on dental care and spectacles that the health service previously provided for free. This, at the time, highly controversial step, led to the resignation of ministers, including Nye Bevan and Harold Wilson, the future prime minister.[28] But Attlee recovered. His dramatic trip to Washington in early December 1950 to consult with Truman when the president was widely rumored to be considering dropping an atomic bomb to break the stalemate in Korea received much positive attention in Britain.[29]

Attlee's evident success in dissuading Truman from crossing the brink notwithstanding, the rumors of US nuclear saber rattling focused the minds of many Britons on the unpalatable fact that Britain was now clearly the junior partner to a reckless American superpower that presided over Britain's fortune, and even survival. If that was not enough, the rearmament of West Germany, which the United States favored and strongly pushed onto its Western allies to strengthen the number of conventional forces at the disposal of the West, caused prolonged controversy and heated debates in both Britain and France.[30]

When Churchill succeeded Attlee as prime minister in the general election of October 1951 with a narrow majority of 17 seats, he largely continued Labour's foreign policy. Despite Churchill's strongly pro-European speeches as leader of the opposition, he confirmed Britain's non-participation in the 1950 European Coal and Steel Community (the Schuman Plan), which would lead to the 1957 Rome treaties. These treaties established the European Economic Community (EEC) and the European Atomic Energy Community (Euratom). Building on the United Kingdom's historic detachment from the continent and seeking to reinforce its special relationship with the United States, Britain had refused to participate in the negotiations. After the sudden death of Stalin in March 1953, however, Churchill's strong anti-communism mellowed significantly. Increasingly fearful of a nuclear Armageddon, he became consumed by attempts to organize a summit meeting with the new American president, Dwight D. Eisenhower, and the new Kremlin leadership. The 79-year-old British prime minister wished to re-open the Potsdam conference and bring it to a successful conclusion by terminating the cold war. He proposed to reunite Germany on a neutral basis and achieve a peaceful all-European settlement of the East-West conflict. However, this came to nothing as Eisenhower and West German Chancellor Konrad Adenauer felt that it was much too dangerous to reunite Germany before the country's western half (the Federal Republic of Germany, FRG) was firmly integrated with the Western camp.[31]

While British leaders and diplomats tended to be less focused on the ideological contest with the Soviet Union than many American policymakers, the vast majority of the British did assess a Soviet invasion and subsequent domination of the European continent by Moscow as a serious threat. This would not only threaten Britain's democratic way of life but also its very survival as a small offshore island dependent on a capitalist economy and vital trading links with the outside world. Churchill's attempt at a rapprochement with the Kremlin in 1953–4 was a unique and even idiosyncratic initiative which was dismissed by most within Britain's political class as an elderly politician's last desperate attempt to shape world events. West Germany gained full membership of NATO in May 1955, and a summit did take place in Geneva that year, in July. It nevertheless had little effect on the by then deep division of the European continent.

An ailing Churchill had been pushed into retirement shortly before the Geneva summit. Within just over a year, his successor as prime minister, Anthony Eden, presided over the most crucial event for British cold war history in October/November 1956. Eden's fateful decision to collude secretly with France and Israel in order to bomb Egypt and recapture the Suez Canal in the wake of Egyptian President Nasser's nationalization of the Anglo-French Universal Suez Maritime company caused a major world crisis. Within a short period of time, however, Britain and France were forced to abandon their invasion. "Anthony, have you gone out of your mind? You've deceived me," Eisenhower shouted at Eden before he broke off all personal contact with the British prime minister and the British embassy in Washington.[32]

Eisenhower was furious. Not only was he in the middle of a re-election campaign, which he fought on a platform of having preserved world peace, but his close ally and World War II comrade had kept him in the dark. Further, the US president feared that Eden's resort to atavistic imperialism would open the strategically vital Middle East to Soviet influence. It had already deflected attention from the Kremlin's almost simultaneous brutal suppression of the popular uprising in Hungary. Reluctantly yet resolutely, Eisenhower applied political and above all financial pressure to coerce America's allies to withdraw from the attempt to subjugate Nasser. The British had intended to re-occupy their once huge military base on the Suez Canal, which London had only vacated in 1954 after prolonged Anglo-Egyptian negotiations. In 1956 Anglo-American relations reached their nadir.[33]

France as well as Britain drew important conclusions from this ill-fated adventure, which have proven to be crucial for the nature of British and French foreign policy until the present day. After Suez the French concluded that the US was a most unreliable and untrustworthy ally and that therefore Paris had to develop its own independent power position in the world. Means to do so included acquiring nuclear weapons and assuming a leadership role in Europe by closely cooperating with the West Germans. The British learned an entirely different lesson. Without a trusting and intimate relationship with the US, London realized, Britain could no longer play a global role. Thus, being on the right side of American foreign relations became the primary if unspoken precept of Britain's foreign policy. As a corollary the Anglo-American "special relationship" needed to be maintained and nurtured to the greatest extent possible. Cooperation with the European continent and countries such as France and West Germany were regarded as secondary and sometimes tertiary considerations.

It was therefore not surprising that only a year after the Suez debacle the new Harold Macmillan government eagerly cooperated with the Eisenhower administration in the crisis in Lebanon. It led to the short-lived deployment of American troops to that country and British paratroops to neighboring Jordan. Nevertheless, any hopes Macmillan had of a more permanent joint Anglo-American Middle East strategy did not materialize.[34] The Suez crisis proved to be a crucial event for Britain's reputation and self-image. The enforced termination of the Anglo-French-Israeli campaign just 24 hours before the invading forces would have recaptured the Suez Canal displayed the new political realities of the cold war world. Without US support or at least agreement, no European power was capable of wielding global power.

## Phase II:  Britain and the cold war in the 1960s

On August 5, 1963 the three nuclear powers—the US, the Soviet Union, and the UK—signed the Nuclear Test Ban Treaty. With the exception of the two-plus-four negotiations which brought about German unification in 1990, it was "the last time," British cabinet minister Lord Hailsham observed, "that Britain appeared in international negotiations as a Great Power."[35] Indeed despite all the pretensions and grandstanding of the Macmillan era, after the late 1950s the cold war world was largely a bipolar one.

The Berlin crisis of the late 1950s and early 1960s, for instance, saw the British only play a marginal role. Prime Minister Macmillan did use the opportunity to embark on a much-publicized visit to Moscow to bolster his election prospects in October 1959. But the US and the West Germans were highly critical of Macmillan's summit diplomacy, and he only narrowly avoided humiliation at the hand of the Soviets. Macmillan's overtures to the Russians not only did not defuse the crisis; they might even have given the Kremlin the impression of Western dissonance and a keenness to find an easy way out.[36] In any case, the Berlin crisis led to the building of the Berlin Wall in August 1961 and the brief but dangerous confrontation between Russian and American tanks at Checkpoint Charlie in Berlin in October 1961.[37] Moreover, Macmillan's attempts to save the Paris four-power summit conference in May 1960 by shuttling between Eisenhower's and Khrushchev's hotel rooms had already proven futile. The Soviet leader exploited the interception of the US U-2 spy plane to wreck the summit by insisting on an apology from Eisenhower, which the American president refused to give. The failure of the summit terminated Macmillan's unrealistic attempts to go down in history as a peacemaker by overlaying the cold war system with regular summits of the major powers. London was hardly consulted during the Cuban Missile Crisis of 1962, although Macmillan did pass on his advice to the White House via Britain's ambassador, a personal friend of Kennedy's. Still, the prime minister's recommendations had no perceptible impact.[38]

The British did not delude themselves about their increasing lack of influence in Washington. This was one of the main reasons why Churchill's peacetime government had already given the go-ahead for the prohibitively expensive development of a British hydrogen bomb. In 1954 Britain had exploded its first atomic bomb, and three years later it successfully tested a thermonuclear device. This put the country firmly back into the nuclear club. In fact, once Britain had exploded its own "superbomb," Congress amended the McMahon Act to again allow Britain access to American nuclear expertise. The "Sputnik shock" of 1957 and the perception of huge Soviet advances in the development of intercontinental missile technology provided Britain with additional leverage. The British White Paper of April 1957, however, implemented severe cuts in London's defense budget. Britain reduced its forces based in Germany by more than 40 percent, conscription was ended in 1960, and both the Royal Navy and Royal Air Force were significantly diminished in size. As an alternative the White Paper foresaw a greater reliance on Britain's nuclear capacity in an effort to gain more bang for the buck. Eisenhower's "New Look" policy of the mid-1950s was being imitated in the UK.[39]

Yet because attempts at developing Britain's own missile, *Blue Streak*, for the country's nuclear warheads proved intolerably expensive, and the design was technologically flawed, London had to rely on American missiles to transport its warheads. Thus, America's cancellation of the Skybolt missile in 1962, which had been promised to Britain, cast doubt on the future of British nuclear capabilities. A humiliated Macmillan had to approach President Kennedy cap in hand during the Bermuda conference of December 1962 to obtain American Polaris missiles for Britain's nuclear warheads. Only after much hesitation and British cajoling did Kennedy offer Polaris missiles to the UK during that conference. Kennedy also offered them to the French, but Paris, set on developing its own capacity, refused. In light of NATO's new "flexible response" strategy, which replaced the "massive retaliation" doctrine of the Eisenhower era, Britain's influence on cold war nuclear strategy, regardless of the Polaris missiles, declined precipitously.[40]

The Macmillan government's application in 1961 to become a member of the European Economic Community (EEC) symbolized Britain's inability to act on a global scale. Washington had repeatedly emphasized to London that it would be a more useful and stronger partner for the United States if the UK became a full member of the EEC.[41] Macmillan likewised realized that for economic and financial reasons joining the EEC was highly desirable. At heart, his government was no more pro-European than its predecessors. But he was more pragmatic and perhaps somewhat less focused on Britain's past imperial grandeurs.

French President Charles de Gaulle, however, viewed Britain's membership application with great suspicion. He perceived London as a Trojan horse for American influence in the EEC and worried that, once inside, the British would attempt to take over the leadership of the EEC. De Gaulle intended to share French dominance of the six-nation club with no one. He had arrived at a good working arrangement with the West Germans, who despite their economic miracle believed that the Nazi legacy precluded their exercising predominant power within the EEC. Moreover, de Gaulle was able to moderate the aging West German chancellor's reflexively pro-American posture. In January 1963 he signed the Elysée treaty with Adenauer shortly after vetoing Britain's entry into the EEC. The original preamble, which the West German parliament ultimately nullified, contained strong anti-American language.[42]

Macmillan was a good actor. With the help of an elegant Edwardian style coupled with intellectual arrogance and considerable personal charm, he had succeeded in persuading many that Britain's global importance had been stabilized and even revived after the Suez disaster. In reality this was not the case. Despite Macmillan's appealing slogan "You have never had it so good," the British economy's sliding course had not been stopped let alone reversed.[43] Britain's importance in the cold war further declined after Macmillan's resignation in October 1963 and replacement by his foreign secretary, Alec Douglas-Home. During the two Labour governments of Harold Wilson (1964–70 and 1974–6), Britain's fall from the ranks of the great powers became so apparent that no Briton could pretend otherwise.

Wilson did stand up to US President Lyndon Johnson's repeated requests for British military assistance in Vietnam. He was deeply convinced that succumbing to Washington's pressure would be folly. While Wilson and the Foreign Office sympathized with America's struggle against communism in Southeast Asia, with virtually no dissent they judged the war unwinnable. Moreover, forced to protect the new Malaysian federation against attacks from Indonesia, Britain had no troops to spare. In addition, Wilson's Labour government only had a majority of three seats, and the left wing of his party would never have allowed him to send troops to Vietnam. Wilson's way out was to attempt to mediate in the conflict. This proved worse than futile; at times Johnson was openly dismissive of Wilson.[44]

In 1967 Wilson's Labour government applied for British EEC membership for a second time; de Gaulle vetoed it again. Wilson doubtless predicted this result; he probably applied primarily in order to appease the United States. Johnson kept urging Britain to give it another try. Wilson may also have wanted to signal to the international financial markets (and his domestic audience) that the government had a clear strategy for overcoming the country's dire economic difficulties. Between late 1964 and the middle of 1966, London had to cope with three currency crises, a continuing significant balance of payments deficit, and a high exchange rate against the dollar. In November 1967 a painful devaluation of the pound sterling by 14.3 percent against the dollar could no longer be avoided. These difficulties drove Wilson's decision to withdraw from the important port of Aden and other British possessions east of Suez. For an explanation as to why Britain's economy nonetheless remained so troubled, Wilson could point the finger at de Gaulle.

After the November 1967 sterling crisis, the up-and-coming Labour politician Roy Jenkins became Chancellor of the Exchequer. Jenkins immediately insisted on further reducing London's overseas obligations and a more concentrated focus on Europe. In January 1968 Wilson announced that by the end of 1971 the British would surrender all their military bases in both the Far East and the Persian Gulf, with the exception of Hong Kong. The forces deployed in the Far East were drawn down significantly, and the remaining troops relocated to Europe. It mattered little that the main cold war theatres had shifted to Asia and the Middle East. The retreat from east of Suez, Sean Greenwood aptly writes, "was an incontrovertible turning point. The fig leaf which had obscured the threadbare British pretensions to globalism fluttered to the ground."[45]

## Phase III:  Britain and the cold war from the late 1960s to the end of the cold war

Despite this withdrawal from its global commitments and a new focus on Europe, Britain's importance to the European cold war theater continued to wane. The British did not play a particularly significant role in the mid- to late 1960s rapprochement in East-West relations, soon to be referred to as détente. It was de Gaulle who traveled to Moscow in June 1966 to lay the groundwork. The West Germans soon followed suit by forging closer commercial, political, and cultural relations with East Germany (GDR) and other Eastern European states. In Washington the new Nixon administration viewed Chancellor Willy Brandt's *Ostpolitik* highly critically.[46]

Prime Minister Wilson and the British did not share the alarm of their American allies. Unlike Nixon and his national security advisor, Henry Kissinger, Wilson did not perceive the West Germans as too pro-Soviet or prepared to trade unification for neutrality and the severance of their links with the West. Wilson's ability to calm American concerns about détente in Europe was modest, however. Only when the Americans felt that they were back in charge of East-West relations, with the negotiation of the 1972 Berlin treaty that stabilized the volatile Berlin situation for good and the development of superpower détente in the context of Nixon's Moscow summit with Brezhnev, did their alarm at West German and French overtures to the East decrease.[47] Except for comparatively modest trade initiatives with the GDR and some other Eastern European states, the British were largely bystanders to these developments.[48]

Confident of victory, Wilson called a snap election in early 1970. To his consternation, the Conservative Edward Heath won. Heath's term in office was notable for two developments. Domestically the country was torn asunder by strikes and economic discontent. Externally, Anglo-American relations grew more distant. Heath became the only British prime minister since World War II to keep America at arm's length. He never used the term "special relationship." Heath almost treated the United States as just one of many allies and devoted his energies almost entirely to negotiating Britain's membership in the EEC. After painful and long-drawn out negotiations, he succeeded in 1973.[49] De Gaulle's resignation in April 1969 and a much more constructive and flexible new French president, Georges Pompidou, were decisive. Pompidou sought to balance the

West Germans, who increasingly dominated the EEC economically and financially. But Heath also enjoyed the support of West Germany's Willy Brandt. Brandt wished to demonstrate his pro-European bona fides to overcome American skepticism about *Ostpolitik*. Moreover, the December 1969 EEC summit in The Hague produced an agreement on a new strategic concept for the future which included British membership.[50]

Counter-intuitively, the admission of Britain to EEC membership in 1973 completed Britain's fall from great power status. The country had to accept its status as one among other European powers, and in an EEC context it was not even the strongest country. Both West Germany and France were more influential, though only the French could match the British in military terms.

Margaret Thatcher, who moved to Downing Street in May 1979, sought to change this. Like all her predecessors except Heath, Thatcher thought in global rather than in European terms. And with the help of her personal friendship with new US President Ronald Reagan, Thatcher believed she could make Britain great again. The goal proved unreachable. Thatcher did obtain at a reasonable price the Trident missile as a successor to Polaris. And albeit not without hesitation, the US did support Britain in the Falklands war against Argentina in 1982.[51] Yet, without minimizing Thatcher's importance to Reagan, the Anglo-American "special relationship" was far from his top priority. He focused much more on the changing Soviet leadership and the ever louder dissenting movements in Poland and other Eastern European countries than on any of the Western European countries, including Britain.[52]

Overcoming massive public protests in both Europe and the United States, in 1983 the Reagan administration, allegedly as a counter to the Soviet SS-20 missiles, deployed its own Pershing II and Tomahawk cruise missiles to its NATO allies. At the 1986 American-Soviet bilateral summit conference in Reykjavik, Iceland, however, Reagan, without consulting the Western Europeans, almost agreed with Gorbachev on the total elimination of all nuclear weapons. Thatcher was outraged—and personally insulted.[53] Reagan did not care. When the Americans and Soviets signed the Intermediate Nuclear Force Treaty (INF) in December 1987, they again ignored the Europeans. With the United States protected by its strategic deterrent an ocean away, Thatcher, as well as West Germany's Helmut Kohl and other European leaders, feared a decoupling of America's commitment to the nuclear and also conventional defense of the European continent. Reagan's response was to bypass them. The two superpowers unilaterally agreed to the so-called "zero option"—the removal from European soil of the American Pershing missiles and cruise missiles as well as the Soviet SS-20s.

By the late 1980s the tide of popular mass protests in Eastern Europe proved to be unstoppable, breaching the Berlin Wall in November 1989. Instead of jumping onto the bandwagon, as US President George H.W. Bush, French President Mitterrand, and ultimately even Soviet leader Mikhail Gorbachev did, Thatcher watched in horror. Remembering all too well the atrocities of the Nazis during her youth, and personally disliking West German Chancellor Helmut Kohl, she recoiled at the prospect of the recreation of a united and even more economically powerful Germany. Thatcher wished to preserve the cold war world. Only after Gorbachev accepted German unification in the summer of 1990 did Thatcher accept the inevitable and reluctantly express her support. However, she continued to speak of an independent but democratic East Germany and believed that unification should come about only after an undefined period of transition.[54]

Thatcher's Euroskepticism was almost as profound as her anti-German feelings.[55] She also balked at Mitterrand's suggested integration of a united Germany into the European Community and the creation of a common European currency, rejecting the Maastricht Treaty of 1991–2 which led to the EC evolving into the European Union (EU). Because of responsibilities dating back to the Potsdam Conference, Britain did join with France in the two-plus-four negotiations which led to German unification in October 1990. But neither played significant roles. The West Germans and the US called the shots.

Britain's marginalization at the end of the cold war reflected the country's global standing by this stage: the empire had disintegrated, the British Commonwealth never developed into a formidable instrument, the country continued to be beset by economic problems, the "special relationship" with the US had evolved into a one-sided affair, and Britain's foreign and economic policy had to a large extent been redirected toward Europe. Yet, the British were never comfortable with limiting their sights to Europe and remained an awkward partner within the EC. The longing for a global role continued to influence British political thinking. Dean Acheson's 1962 statement that Britain had "lost an Empire and not yet found a role" continues to capture the British dilemma.[56]

# Conclusion

Britain played an important if not crucial role during the first ten years of the cold war. By the time of the Suez crisis of 1956, however, much of its international influence had dissipated. The withdrawal from east of Suez, announced in 1968 for economic reasons, effectively ended Britain's role as a world power. Just over twenty years later, when the cold war came to an end, few would have regarded the country as a truly vital player in international affairs. Yet, largely by cooperating closely with the US and milking the legacy of empire as much as possible, Britain continued to punch above its weight in world politics. This was a deliberate bipartisan strategy of Britain's political elite; it was not a policy dictated by the international structures of the cold war system. The economic recovery of the 1990s and the first decade of the 21st century extended this trend. For instance, British Prime Minister Tony Blair's keen cooperation with President George W. Bush in the unprovoked invasion of Iraq in 2003 was not only a clearly illegal but also an entirely "unnecessary war." Furthermore, although initated and mostly paid for by the United States, it was Britain and France which successfully waged the air war that proved decisive in the rebel forces' overthrow of Libyas' dictator Muammar Gaddafi in 2011.

The dire consequences of the "great recession," which began in 2008, and the implementation of a severe austerity program that targeted both domestic and foreign policy in an effort to stave off bankruptcy makes it questionable whether the country can sustain a truly international role. A simultaneous renewed Euroskepticism has become an increasingly pervasive obsession of many British policymakers. It is undermining Britain's standing as a leading power within the European Union and, by implication, in the world at large. Still, similar doubts about the UK's ability to be an important global and European player were expressed in the 1960s and 1970s, and London did manage to hang on to at least moderate international influence. It may well do so again in the coming decades.

## NOTES

1. British Parliamentary Papers, House of Commons (Hansard), June 10, 1941.
2. Kenneth Waltz, *Theory of International Politics* (Reading, MA: Addison-Wesley, 1979). For a good critique, see Robert O. Keohane, ed., *Neorealism and its Critics* (New York: Columbia University Press, 1986).
3. <http://www.nationalarchives.gov.uk/>.
4. Kenneth O. Morgan, *The Oxford History of Britain* (Oxford: Oxford University Press, 1999); Andrew Marr, *A History of Modern Britain* (London: Macmillan, 2007); Sean Greenwood, *Britain and the Cold War, 1945–1991* (New York: St. Martin's Press, 2000); Michael J. Turner, *Britain's International Role, 1970–1991* (New York: Palgrave Macmillan, 2010).
5. Kenneth O. Morgan, *Labour in Power, 1945–1951* (Oxford: Clarendon Press, 1984); Sabine Lee and Richard Aldous, eds., *Harold Macmillan and Britain's World Role* (New York: St. Martin's Press, 1996); D.R. Thorpe, *Supermac: The Life of Harold Macmillan* (London: Chatto & Windus, 2010); Ben Pimlott, *Harold Wilson* (London: Harper Collins, 1992); John Campbell, *Margaret Thatcher* (London: Jonathan Cape, 2000); E.H.H. Green, *Thatcher* (London: Hodder Arnold, 2006); *Documents on British Policy Overseas*, Series III, Vol. VII: *German Unification, 1989–1990* (London: Routledge, 2010).
6. Ritchie Ovendale, ed., *British Defence Policy since 1945* (Manchester: Manchester University Press, 1994); Robert C. Self, *British Foreign and Defence Policy since 1945: Challenges and Dilemmas in a Changing World* (Basingstoke: Palgrave Macmillan, 2010); John Darwin, *The End of the British Empire: The Historical Debate* (Oxford: Blackwell, 1991); John Darwin, *The Rise and Fall of the British World System, 1830–1970* (Cambridge: Cambridge University Press, 2009); Nicholas J. White, *Decolonization: The British Experience since 1945* (London: Longman, 1999); W. David McIntyre, *British Decolonization, 1946–1997: When, Why and How Did the British Empire Fall?* (New York: St. Martin's Press, 1998); Stephen George, *An Awkward Partner: Britain in the European Community*, 3rd ed. (Oxford: Oxford University Press, 1998); David Gowland, et al., *Britain and European Integration since 1945: On the Sidelines* (New York: Routledge, 2010).
7. Klaus Larres, ed., with Elizabeth Meehan, *Uneasy Allies: British-German Relations and European Integration since 1945* (Oxford: Oxford University Press, 2000); Antoine Capet, *Britain, France and the Entente Cordiale since 1904* (Basingstoke: Palgrave Macmillan, 2006); Beatrice Heuser, *NATO, Britain, France and the FRG: Nuclear Strategies and Forces for Europe, 1949–2000* (New York: St. Martin's Press, 1997); Piers Brendon, *The Decline and Fall of the British Empire, 1781–1997* (London: Jonathan Cape, 2007).
8. Richard J. Aldrich, *The Hidden Hand: Britain, America and Cold War Secret Intelligence* (London: John Murray, 2001); Christopher M. Andrew, *The Defence of the Realm: The Authorized History of MI5* (London: Allen Lane, 2009).
9. John Dumbrell, *A Special Relationship: Anglo-American Relations from the Cold War to Iraq*, 2nd ed. (Basingstoke: Palgrave Macmillan, 2006).

10. Donald Cameron Watt, *Succeeding John Bull: America in Britain's Place* (Cambridge: Cambridge University Press, 1984).

11. Nickolas Tiratsoo, *From Blitz to Blair: A New History of Britain since 1939* (London: Weidenfeld & Nicolson, 1997).

12. Conor O'Clery, *Daring Diplomacy: Clinton's Secret Search for Peace in Ireland* (Boulder, CO: Roberts Rinehart Publishers, 1997); Timothy J. Lynch, *Turf War: The Clinton Administration and Northern Ireland* (Aldershot: Ashgate, 2004).

13. Jim Fyrth, *Labour's High Noon: The Government and the Economy, 1945-1951* (London: Lawrence & Wishart, 1993).

14. *Documents of British Policy Overseas.* Series 1, vol. 1. (London: HMSO, 1984), p. 102 (July 11, 1945).

15. Mark Gilbert, "From War to Cold War," in Klaus Larres, *Blackwell Companion to Europe since 1945* (Oxford: Blackwell, 2009), 14.

16. Fraser Harbutt, *Yalta 1945: Europe and America at the Crossroads* (Cambridge: Cambridge University Press, 2010).

17. Stephen Dorril, *MI6: Inside the Covert World of Her Majesty's Secret Intelligence Service* (New York: Free Press, 2000), 372ff.

18. Charles Gati, *Failed Illusions: Moscow, Washington, Budapest and the 1956 Hungarian Revolt* (Washington, DC: Woodrow Wilson Center Press, 2006), 86; John Prados, *Presidents' Secret Wars: CIA and Pentagon Covert Operations since World War II* (New York: W. Morrow, 1986), 46.

19. Fraser Harbutt, *The Iron Curtain: Churchill, America, and the Origins of the Cold War* (Oxford: Oxford University Press, 1986); Ray Merrick, "The Russia Committee of the British Foreign Office and the Cold War, 1946–47," *Journal of Contemporary History* 20 (July 1985): 453–68.

20. Anne Deighton, *The Impossible Peace: Britain, the Division of Germany and the Origins of the Cold War* (Oxford: Clarendon Press, 1990).

21. Bruce Kuniholm, *The Origins of the Cold War in the Near East: Great Power Conflict and Diplomacy in Iran, Turkey, and Greece* (Princeton, NJ: Princeton University Press, 1980).

22. Lawrence Freedman, *Britain and Nuclear Weapons* (London: Macmillan, 1980); Robert H. Paterson, *Britain's Strategic Nuclear Deterrent: From before the V-bomber to beyond Trident* (London: Frank Cass, 1997).

23. Matthias Matthijs, *Ideas and Economic Crisis in Britain from Attlee to Blair* (London: Routledge, 2010).

24. David Reynolds, *Britannia Overruled: British Policy and World Power in the Twentieth Century* (London: Longman, 1991), 161.

25. Erez Manela, *The Wilsonian Moment: Self-Determination and the International Origins of Anticolonial Nationalism* (Oxford: Oxford University Press, 2009); Denis Judt, *Empire: the British Imperial Experience from 1765 to the Present* (New York: Basic Books, 2003); Lawrence James, *The Rise and Fall of the British Empire* (London: Little, Brown, 1994).

26. Robert Frazier, "Did Britain Start the Cold War? Bevin and the Truman Doctrine," *Historical Journal*, 27 (September 1984): 715–27; David Wills, *Greece and Britain since 1945* (Newcastle upon Tyne: Cambridge Scholars, 2010); Athanasious Lykogiannis, *Britain and the Greek Economic Crisis, 1944-1947* (Columbia, MO: Missouri University Press, 2002).

27. Klaus Larres, "North Atlantic Treaty Organization," in Alexander DeConde, et al., eds., *Encyclopedia of American Foreign Relations*, 2nd ed., Vol. 2 (New York: Scribner's, 2002), 573–93.

28. C.A. MacDonald, *Britain and the Korean War* (Oxford: Blackwell, 1990); Till Geiger, *Britain and the Economic Problem of the Cold War* (Aldershot: Ashgate, 2004).

29. Klaus Larres, *Churchill's Cold War: The Politics of Personal Diplomacy* (New Haven, CT: Yale University Press, 2002), 136.

30. Saki Dockrill, *Britain's Policy for West German Rearmament, 1950–55* (Cambridge: Cambridge University Press, 1991).

31. Dockrill, *Britain's Policy*, 174ff.

32. Steven Solomon, *Water: The Epic Struggle for Wealth, Power and Civilization* (New York: Harper, 2010), 242.

33. Keith Kyle, *Suez* (London: Macmillan, 1992); David A. Nichols, *Eisenhower 1956: The President's Year of Crisis* (New York: Simon and Schuster, 2011).

34. Stephen Blackwell, *British Military Intervention and the Struggle for Jordan* (London: Routledge, 2009).

35. Peter Mangold, *The Almost Impossible Ally: Harold Macmillan and Charles de Gaulle* (New York: Routledge; London: I.B. Tauris, 2005), 208; John R. Walker, *British Nuclear Weapons and the Test Ban, 1954–1973* (Farnham: Ashgate, 2010).

36. R. Gerald Hughes, *Britain, Germany, and the Cold War: The Search for a European Détente* (London: Routledge, 2007).

37. Frederick Kempe, *Berlin 1961: Kennedy, Khrushchev, and the Most Dangerous Place on Earth* (New York: G.P. Putnam's, 2011); Kitty Newman, *Macmillan, Khrushchev and the Berlin Crisis, 1958–1960* (London: Routledge, 2007).

38. L.V. Scott, *Macmillan, Kennedy, and the Cuban Missile Crisis* (New York: St. Martin's Press, 1999).

39. Richard Moore, *Nuclear Illusion, Nuclear Reality: Britain, the United States, and Nuclear Weapons, 1958–1964* (Basingstoke: Palgrave Macmillan, 2011).

40. Ian Clark, *Nuclear Diplomacy and the Special Relationship: Britain's Deterrent and America, 1957–62* (Oxford: Oxford University Press, 1994).

41. Guy Arnold, *Britain since 1945: Choice, Conflict and Change* (London: Blandford, 1989), 37.

42. Jacqueline Tratt, *The Macmillan Government and Europe* (New York: St. Martin's Press, 1996); Oliver Bange, *The EEC Crisis of 1963: Kennedy, Macmillan, de Gaulle and Adenauer* (Basingstoke: Palgrave, 2000); Piers Ludlow, *The European Community and the Crises of the 1960s: Negotiating the Gaullist Challenge* (London: Routledge, 2006).

43. Alistair Horne, *Harold Macmillan, 1957–1986* (London: Macmillan, 1989), 236–7.

44. Eugenie Blang, *Allies at Odds: America, Europe, and Vietnam, 1961–68* (Lanham, MD: Rowman and Littlefield, 2011).

45. Greenwood, *Britain and the Cold War*, 174; Tom Pocock, *East and West of Suez: The Retreat from Empire* (London: Bodley Head, 1986).

46. Klaus Larres, "Germany and the West: The 'Rapallo Factor' in German Foreign Policy from the 1950s to the 1990s," in K. Larres and P. Panayi, eds., *The Federal Republic of Germany since 1949: Politics, Society and Economy before and after Unification* (Harlow: Longman, 1996), 278–326.

47. Gottfried Niedhart, "The Federal Republic's Ostpolitik and the United States: Initiatives and Constraints," in Kathleen Burk and Melvyn Stokes, eds., *The United States and the European Alliance since 1945* (Oxford: Berg, 1999), 289–311.

48. Klaus Larres, "Britain and the GDR in the 1960s: The Politics of Trade and Recognition by Stealth," in Jeremy Noakes, et al., eds., *Britain and Germany in Europe, 1949–1999* (Oxford: Oxford University Press, 2002), 187–217; Stefan Berger, *Friendly Enemies: Britain and the GDR, 1949–1990* (New York: Berghahn, 2010).

49. Edward Heath, *Course of My Life* (London: Hodder and Stoughton, 1998).

50. Haig Simonian, *The Privileged Partnership: Franco-German Relations in the European Community, 1969–1984* (Oxford: Oxford University Press, 1985), 78–100; Claudia Hiepel, "The Hague Summit of the European Community Britain's Entry, and the New Atlantic Partnership, 1969–1970," in Thomas A. Schwartz and Matthias Schulz, eds., *The Strained Alliance: US-European Relations from Nixon to Carter* (Cambridge: Cambridge University Press, 2009), 105–25.

51. Richard Thornton, *Falklands Sting: Reagan, Thatcher, and Argentina's Bomb* (Washington, DC: Brassey's, 1998).

52. Nicholas Wapshott, *Ronald Reagan and Margaret Thatcher: A Political Marraige* (New York: Sentinel, 1997); Geoffrey Smith, *Reagan and Thatcher* (London: Bodley Head, 1990); Richard Aldous, *Reagan and Thatcher: The Difficult Relationship* (New York: W.W. Norton, 2012).

53. Margaret Thatcher, *The Downing Street Years* (New York: Harper Collins, 1993).

54. George R. Urban, *Diplomacy and Disillusion at the Court of Margaret Thatcher: An Insider's View* (London: I.B. Tauris, 1996); Percy Cradock, *In Pursuit of British Interests: Reflections on Foreign Policy under Margaret Thatcher and John Major* (London: John Murray, 1997).

55. Klaus Larres, "Margaret Thatcher and German Unification Revisited," in Michael Gehler, Wolfgang Mueller, and Arnold Suppan, eds., *The Revolutions of 1989* (Vienna: Austrian Academy of Sciences, forthcoming).

56. John T. McNay, *Acheson and Empire: The British Accent in American Foreign Policy* (Columbia, MO: University of Missouri Press, 2001), 196.

## Select Bibliography

Andrew, Christopher M. *The Defence of the Realm: The Authorized History of MI5*. London: Allen Lane, 2009.

Cook, Chris, *The Routledge Guide to British Political Archives: Sources since 1945*. London: Routldege, 2006.

Cook, Chris, and David Waller. *The Longmans Guide to Sources in Contemporary British History. Vol 1: Organizations and Societies; Vol. 2. Individuals*. Harlow: Longman, 1994.

George, Stephen. *An Awkward Partner: Britain in the European Community*, 3rd ed. Oxford: Oxford University Press, 1998.

King, Anthony, and Robert J. Wybrow, eds., *British Political Opinion, 1937–2000*. London: Politico, 2001.

Knight, Nigel. *Governing Britain since 1945*. London: Politico, 2006.

Kyle, Keith. *Suez*. London: Macmillan, 1992.

Larres, Klaus. *Churchill's Cold War: The Politics of Personal Diplomacy*. New Haven: Yale University Press, 2002.

Morgan, Kenneth O. *Labour in Power, 1945–1951*. Oxford: Clarendon Press, 1984.

Pimlott, Ben. *Harold Wilson*. London: Harper Collins, 1992.

Reynolds, David. *Britannia Overruled: British Policy and World Power in the Twentieth Century*. London: Longman, 1991.

Robbins, Keith. *A Bibliography of British History, 1914–1989*. Oxford: Oxford University Press, 1996.

Thorpe, D.R. *Supermac: The Life of Harold Macmillan*. London: Chatto & Windus, 2010.

Young, John W. *Britain and the World in the Twentieth Century*. London: Arnold, 1997.

# CHAPTER 10

## WESTERN EUROPE

### ANDREAS ETGES

In a speech before the United Nations General Assembly in New York on October 1, 1990, President George H.W. Bush celebrated the end of the cold war: "The long twilight struggle that for forty-five years has divided Europe, our two nations [the United States and the Soviet Union], and much of the world has come to an end." With regard to the official act of German reunification, scheduled for October 3, 1990, he declared: "Two days from now, the world will be watching when the cold war is formally buried in Berlin."[1] The end of the cold war, like its beginning, cannot be pinned down to a certain day or event. For many contemporaries, nevertheless, among them President Bush, it was the fall of the Berlin Wall, beginning on November 9, 1989.

Whichever date one picks, Europe was the crucial battleground, where the cold war began and ended. Germany and especially Berlin took center stage from start to finish, and not only because of its location in Central Europe. In many ways "the German question," as it came to be called, was the crucial question of the cold war. The defeat of Germany had united the Allies during World War II. Over the subsequent decades, making sure that it would never again start a war remained a main goal for the Soviet Union, for the nations around Germany, and even for the United States.

When examining Western Europe during the cold war, it is important to keep the following points in mind: first, "Western Europe" is not a precise political or geographical entity. It consisted of more than a dozen nation states, of which a large number joined a military, an economic, and a political alliance, while others like Austria, Sweden, and Switzerland—each for different reasons—stayed "neutral."

Second, Western Europe during the cold war can only be understood in the context of its changing internal dynamics and changing relationship with the United States, as well as its relations with the Soviet Union and the countries of Eastern Europe. While observers often regard the cold war as a special period of Western unity, based on common goals and a common enemy, there were a significant number of internal conflicts among the countries of Western Europe and with the United States. Third, even though Europe was often the main battleground of the cold war, developments on the continent cannot be separated from those in other parts of the world, especially the European states' former colonies.

This essay cannot do full justice to all of these issues and to all of the countries of Western Europe during the cold war. Thus it will concentrate on those issues that are most fundamental and illustrative, such as the German question, Franco-German rapprochement and European integration, the military aspects of the Western alliance, European powers and decolonization, détente and *Ostpolitik*, the resurgence of the cold war during the 1980s, and, finally, German reunification and the end of the cold war.

In a political, economic, military, cultural, and ideological sense, Western Europe was a product of the cold war itself. This essay will show how it both shaped and was shaped by the confrontation, with broad international repercussions. Other "battlefields" were much more bloody, but the roots of the cold war and finally also its solution have to be located in Europe.

To contextualize the cold war issues that consumed Europe, it is necessary to discuss briefly how World War II changed the balance of power between the United States and Western Europe as well as the relationship between the two. While much of Western Europe was in ruins at the end of the war, the US emerged not only as the strongest economic and military power but also as one of the most powerful "European" players. This development did not come naturally. The warning of George Washington to "steer clear of permanent alliances with any portion of the free world," echoed by Thomas Jefferson ("entangling alliances with none"), and followed by the Monroe Doctrine in 1823, had dominated US foreign policy into the 20th century. The results of World War I confirmed the view of many Americans that staying out of European conflicts had been a smart policy, which in turn led to a resurgence of isolationist views.

Internationalists like Henry R. Luce, the publisher and editor of *Life* and *Time*, worked hard to convince the American people that it was time they accepted a new international role for their country. His famous essay "The American Century," published in *Life* on February 17, 1941, was a sharp rejection of isolationism and a passionate plea to finally act as "the most powerful and the most vital nation in the world." It turned out to be a prophetic description of the 20th century as an "American Century." Writing several months before the Japanese attack on Pearl Harbor, Luce argued that in order to stay secure, American lines of defense could not be limited to the homeland anymore. Instead, the country had to be defended globally and act as the arsenal of its allies. But American leadership should not end there: it should "defend and even [...] promote, encourage and incite so-called democratic principles throughout the world," use its influence "for such purposes as we see fit and by such means as we see fit," and in general be "the Good Samaritan of the entire world."[2] During World War II, many Americans began to change their outlook on the world and reluctantly agree that their country had become and should be a global power along the lines described by Luce. The early years of the cold war, especially events in Europe, quickly drowned whatever isolationist tendencies were still lingering.

Conflicts among the Allies had become visible during major meetings at Yalta in February 1945 and in Potsdam in July and August of the same year. There was basic agreement regarding policy toward Germany and Austria, which, like their capitals Berlin and Vienna, were each divided into four zones of occupation (Soviet, American,

British, and French). The issue of Soviet domination of Eastern Europe, especially regarding Poland's borders and "free elections" promised in the Yalta "Declaration of Liberated Europe," was much more controversial. It would be wrong, though, to charge Presidents Franklin D. Roosevelt and Harry S. Truman with having "betrayed" Poland and Eastern Europe. Nevertheless, Stalin surely got the upper hand here and later ignored the declaration. In 1946 and 1947 what contemporaries such as Walter Lippmann started to call the "cold war" escalated.

On March 5, 1946, former British Prime Minister Winston Churchill famously deplored the emergence of a Soviet-dominated sphere in Europe: "From Stettin in the Baltic to Trieste in the Adriatic, an iron curtain has descended across the Continent."[3] A speech by Joseph Stalin a month earlier in which he had blamed the two world wars on the capitalist system was read in the West as declaring a state of war as long as capitalism existed. A most important analysis on the American side came from George F. Kennan, the chargé d'affaires at the US Embassy in Moscow. In the so-called "Long Telegram" to Secretary of State James Byrnes of February 22, 1946, he argued that for the Soviet Union there could be "no permanent *modus vivendi*" with the United States. In a follow-up article in *Foreign Affairs*, he suggested a "policy of firm containment designed to confront the Russians with unalterable counterforce at every point where they show signs of encroaching upon the interests of a peaceful and stable world."[4]

The confrontation was not limited to rhetoric. The Soviet Union continuously tightened its grip on Eastern Europe, while the United States, perceiving that stabilizing Western Europe was of utmost urgency, was working on a postwar order of its own. These efforts had political, military, and economic components, most prominently spelled out in the closely-linked Truman Doctrine and in the Marshall Plan. In order to gain Congressional support for military and economic aid worth 400 million dollars to Turkey and Greece in March 1947, Truman and others used an early version of the Domino Theory. They warned that if the United States did not act now, the spread of communism would become unstoppable.[5] Economic hardships and hunger, made worse by an extremely cold winter in Western Europe, might also lead to a political turn to the left. In June 1947 Secretary of State George C. Marshall announced a plan for a European Recovery Program (ERP). Opposition in the US Congress quickly broke down after the communists seized power in Czechoslovakia in February 1948. The United States offered support to all European countries but Spain, which remained a dictatorship. The rejection of the offer by the Eastern European countries and Russia came as no surprise to the Americans. But with the exception of Finland, which feared a Soviet reaction, all the Western European countries, including Austria, Sweden, and Switzerland, profited from the more than 13 billion dollars allotted until 1952. While the Marshall Plan was not solely responsible for the economic recovery of Western Europe during the following years, the funds made a big difference. They also made the American presence in Europe even more visible.[6]

Whether the juxtaposition of the Marshall Plan and the Truman Doctrine was responsible for the formal division, whether it only confirmed a pre-existing division, or whether it should be judged as a positive plan for all of Europe as opposed to a negative one for

Eastern Europe, remain contested questions.[7] In a way, one can answer all three in the affirmative: the danger from the communists in Western Europe was exaggerated and a main goal of the Marshall Plan was to bind Western Europe closer to the United States. The Truman Doctrine and the Marshall Plan no doubt cemented the division that had become apparent before March 1947. In that respect the dynamics caused by decisions and events in the East and in the West should not be underestimated. The coup in Czechoslovakia confirmed fears in the West, as did the Berlin Blockade, which Stalin imposed on June 24, 1948. The latter was itself a reaction both to the Marshall Plan and to the introduction of a new currency by the three Western powers in their zones of Berlin. Blocking rail, road, and waterways to the city, the Soviet Union hoped to prevent the foundation of a West German state. But American and British forces kept West Berlin going by airlifting in supplies. The Soviets finally ended the blockade after more than 300 days without achieving their main goal: on May 24, 1949 the Federal Republic of Germany (FRG) was founded.

The Berlin airlift was a crucial event in the early cold war. In the eyes of many Westerners, the Soviet Union had shown its true face. But, underestimating Western resolve, it had been "contained" in its supposed drive westwards. In addition, the airlift created a new bond between the Western allies and West Germans. The Western victory had long-term consequences, especially for the United States. Committed to defending Berlin in order to insure its credibility, its security interests became even more closely tied to those of Western Europe than before.

Western commitment to West Germany's freedom was only one part of the new security architecture. After the war it was not only the Soviet Union that regarded Germany's potential political, military, and economic power with suspicion. The Western allies all agreed that Germany, like the Soviet Union, had to be contained. For the United States this meant a policy of "double containment": "the containment of the Soviet Union at arm's length, and of West Germany with an embrace."[8] The embrace mostly consisted of binding the FRG to the West through international organizations and treaties even as measures were instituted to constrain Germany's ability to produce weapons and conduct an independent foreign policy.

Beyond their impact on the German situation, events in Eastern Europe led to closer economic ties within Western Europe and to a closer military cooperation between it and North America, giving rise to the European Economic Community and the North Atlantic Treaty Organization (NATO). The idea of a united Europe, which Churchill promoted in 1946, gained urgency with the experience of two major wars and the evolving cold war. While the Council of Europe was founded in May 1949, European integration began largely in the economic sphere. France and the FRG, recognizing that they needed each other in order to achieve their respective national ambitions, took the lead. The first step was the creation of the European Coal and Steel Community on April 18, 1951, based on plans by Jean Monnet and French Foreign Minister Robert Schuman. In the Treaty of Paris, France, Italy, West Germany, and the Benelux States agreed to establish a joint market for their national coal and steel industries. Six years later, on March 25, 1957, the European Economic Community (EEC) was founded by the same group of states through the Treaty of Rome, creating among other things a customs union.

Although the United States feared Europe's emergence as a "third force," it generally preferred European cooperation to European division. Thus Washington lamented that Great Britain was not part of the integration process, and was unhappy about the French veto of British membership in the EEC in both 1963 and 1967. French President Charles de Gaulle saw British entry as endangering French influence and the Franco-German partnership. Americans focused on the danger of Soviet expansion.[9]

Debates about a Western defense alliance began in 1946. On March 17, 1948, only about a month after the Czech coup, representatives of Belgium, France, Luxembourg, the Netherlands, and the United Kingdom signed a treaty of mutual assistance in Brussels, pledging to establish a joint defensive system that included military support in case of an armed attack on one of the partners. After the Berlin Blockade the European initiative became a transatlantic one, involving Canada and the United States as well as Italy, Portugal, Denmark, Iceland, and Norway. The North Atlantic Treaty Organization, America's first military peacetime alliance, was founded on April 4, 1949 in Washington. The members pledged collectively to defend one another in case of an armed attack. But while the containment of the Soviet Union was a driver of NATO's founding, the organization also strove to complement efforts toward European recovery and to bind Western Europe together politically. Notwithstanding NATO's becoming a military alliance dominated by the United States, it grew out of a European initiative which quickly found strong support in North America.

In its first two years NATO was more of a political than a military endeavor. Again it was an external event that gave a decisive push to transforming NATO into a more formal military alliance with an integrated military structure. To Truman and others, the Korean War (1950–3) was a challenge by the Soviets that, if unanswered, would trigger fateful developments in the region and beyond. A year before, the United States had not only lost its nuclear bomb monopoly when the Russians successfully detonated their first plutonium bomb on August 29, 1949, but it had also "lost" China to communism. With the armistice signed in July 1953, for some in the West another part of Asia was "lost" as well.

The Korean War also changed the dynamics of military cooperation in Western Europe and led to a militarization of the cold war. With American forces committed to Korea, the United States, bolstered by British support, demanded a West German contribution to Western defense efforts. The French government, its own troops deployed to Indochina and afraid of an independent German army, suggested a European Defense Community (EDC) in order to envelope German forces within a supranational command. Fearful that the EDC did not provide sufficient security against a resurgent Germany, however, in August 1954 the French National Assembly refused to ratify the treaty. The British resolved the impasse by proposing that West Germany's rearmament come about through membership in the Western European Union (WEU) and NATO. The WEU was founded in October 1954 as an institutional means to add West Germany and Italy to the original signatories to the 1948 Treaty of Brussels. This way France along with Britain and the other European states could carefully monitor its rearmament. The next step was for the FRG to join NATO in May 1955 (Turkey and Greece had joined in 1952).

As members of a collective security organization, the West Germans could now officially rearm and regain general sovereignty. The remaining restrictions on heavy industries were also lifted, although the development of an atomic, biological, or chemical warfare capability was strictly prohibited.

The integration of West Germany into a Western economic and military bloc was answered in similar fashion in the East. Again, the economy came first with the establishment of the Council for Mutual Economic Assistance (Comecon) in January 1949 by the Soviet Union and its East European allies. Five years later, in May 1955, the Warsaw Pact, a political and military alliance, was founded as a counterpart to NATO. The German Democratic Republic (GDR) joined Comecon in 1950 and was a founding member of the Warsaw Treaty organization. A year later the East German National People's Army was created.

By 1955–6 the two opposite blocs at the center of the East-West conflict had been formally established in political, military, and economic ways. There were changes over time, but the basic features remained more or less the same, in some cases even after the end of the cold war. For the Western countries distinct national interests emerged, but they were all bound to and dependent on each other. There was a lot of cooperation, but also competition and struggles among them throughout the cold war.

First, economically, militarily, and to some extent even politically the United States had become a European power. It had given billions of dollars to European recovery and through its military shield—especially nuclear deterrence—guaranteed the security of Western Europe. While the US was the dominant power in the West, it was unable to impose its will on its allies. The populations of its West European allies had largely welcomed or even asked for US support, which is why Geir Lundestad termed the relationship an "empire by invitation."[10] To be sure, the United States did not act purely out of altruism. Believing it was engaged in a deadly struggle with the Soviet bloc, it needed a strong Western Europe both for its own security and so that it could showcase the benefits of being an American ally. Political, military, and economic integration of Western Europe and across the Atlantic also meant that there would be less willingness and opportunity on the part of the smaller Western countries to pursue an independent foreign policy or even think about neutrality, which from the American point of view would have been tantamount to defecting. That was especially true for Germany.

Second, for Chancellor Konrad Adenauer and other FRG leaders, Western integration was a primary goal, for many even more important than unification. Reconciliation with its European neighbors, especially "arch-enemy" France, was crucial for the FRG's economic recovery and largely successful integration into the EEC, NATO, and parallel institutions. All of this in turn helped to stabilize the situation in Europe. What that meant, however, was that reunification with Eastern Germany became more difficult.

Third, like the other West European powers, France and Great Britain needed American assistance after the war not only to rebuild their economies, but also to keep their status as major international powers. Both faced the same dilemma. While their great power status was "enshrined" in their permanent seats and veto power in the United Nation's Security Council, they fought a hard, costly, and ultimately losing battle to keep their colonial empires. Yet they pursued their goals in different ways and often in competition with one another. The French focused on Western European integration as a means to become more independent of the United States. They thought it crucial to control German power, while also using it for French purposes. The British emphasized their special relationship with the US, which made them America's closest ally, not just in Europe. Neither in favor of European integration nor fully opposed, Great Britain stayed on the sidelines in Europe and was twice denied membership in the EEC before joining in 1973. In many ways Britain, which had never defined itself as a continental power, saw the Commonwealth as more important. Furthermore, it understood its role as serving as a bridge between the United States and Europe.

Fourth, like their larger neighbors, the smaller European countries in the EEC and NATO depended militarily on the deterrent against communism provided by the United States even as they regarded American power with distrust. However, they never became pawns of the larger powers, which needed their cooperation. Keeping their own national interests in mind, the smaller European powers were quite successful in shaping European and NATO policy. The latter mandated consultation and empowered the smaller countries through its joint decision-making process.

In the 1950s the cold war became an increasingly global affair. To be sure, the bloc confrontation in Europe remained a dominant feature until the end. Yet, apart from a second major crisis in Berlin that extended from 1958–61, the main crisis spots and the main battlefields were outside of Europe. They often were closely linked to European colonialism, however, especially that of Great Britain and France. Both succeeded in acquiring financial, political, and military support from the US by framing the "colonial" conflicts in cold war terms. Their victories proved pyrrhic ones, though.

With the pronouncement of the Truman Doctrine, the United States pledged to take over the British "burdens" in Greece and Turkey. The Americans directly supported Great Britain in Iran, where the government of Prime Minister Mohammed Mossadegh was nationalizing the Anglo-Iranian Oil Company (AIOC). Some in the Truman administration worried that support for Britain might be seen as neocolonial policy. In the end, the anti-communist trump card won, and the British got the support of the new Eisenhower administration for a coup instigated jointly by the Central Intelligence Agency (CIA) and the British MI6, but executed by the CIA with Iranian support. Mossadegh was overthrown on August 19, 1953, and under Shah Mohammed Reza Pahlavi a pro-Western and anti-communist government was installed. To the chagrin of the British, the Shah steadily distanced himself from London and gravitated toward Washington, signaling the decline of British influence in the Middle East.

American support for France in regaining its empire in Indochina was equally controversial—and produced similar consequences. The State Department's Southeast Asia desk lost to the European desk, which held that because America's most vital interest was the security of Europe, supporting France took priority over supporting independence in Vietnam. The French, moreover, claimed that their colonies in Indochina served as a bulwark against the spread of communism through the region—and beyond. In spite of American financial and military aid, the French lost the Battle of Dienbienphu in May 1954. The Geneva Conference of 1954 began simultaneously with the French surrender and ended with the decision to divide Vietnam at the 17th parallel. By the next year, France abandoned its efforts to retain influence over the government of South Vietnam, ceding responsibility to the United States.[11]

For Britain and France, the balance of power in the Western alliance took a turn for the worse in 1956 with the Suez Crisis. Great Britain and the United States saw Egypt under President Gamal Abdul Nasser as moving ever closer to the Soviet orbit. When the US denied a promised credit to fund the building of the Aswan Dam, Nasser retaliated by nationalizing the Suez Canal on July 26, 1956, in order to use the revenues for the construction. That brought his ongoing dispute with London, which identified the canal as its imperial lifeline and symbol of its glorious past, to a climax. The invasion of Israeli forces via the Sinai Peninsula in late October as well as the British and French invasion that brought a quick military victory a few days later had been both carefully coordinated and concealed from the United States. With the Soviet Union about to crush a revolt in Hungary and American presidential elections just a few days away, Eisenhower responded angrily. The administration submitted a resolution in the UN demanding a ceasefire and withdrawal of all foreign troops. The Suez Crisis meant the end of British and French power in Egypt and the Middle East.[12]

The United States and the Soviet Union filled the vacuum. For Eisenhower, the main goal was to contain both communism and Arab nationalism in a region of major oil-producing countries. Western Europeans were and still are much more dependent on oil from the Middle East than the Americans. But with economic stability of Western Europe and other parts of the West being a central element of US strategy, stability in the Middle East to guarantee the supply of cheap oil was of vital importance.

Beginning in 1963 and even more so in the late 1960s, attempts to find common ground between the two blocs gained support. At the same time, growing divisions inside the Western alliance became visible and sometimes even overshadowed the East-West conflict. When John F. Kennedy visited Europe in June of 1963, divisions with the French government under President Charles de Gaulle, who had returned to power in the summer of 1958 and renewed France's historic emphasis on greatness and autonomy, were growing. One of the main purposes of Kennedy's visit was to reassert the importance of the Western alliance—under American leadership. De Gaulle accused the Americans of asking for burden-sharing while resisting power-sharing. His determination to keep Great Britain out of the common market was also partly based on his view that British membership would mean indirect US membership. But to reduce America's influence, he needed Germany. In January 1963 de Gaulle and West German Chancellor Konrad Adenauer signed the Franco-German treaty of friendship (Elysée Treaty) which included regular consultations between the leaders of both countries. The Americans saw the treaty as a possible Franco-German axis that could even lead to a separate settlement with the Soviet Union. But the Germans were not ready to choose between France and the United States. The German parliament attached a preamble to the friendship treaty, which repeatedly mentioned the United States and emphasized Germany's and Europe's strong Atlantic ties as well as multilateral treaties, so that the emphasis was on both reconciliation and transatlantic consultation.

Another goal of Kennedy's trip was to renew American credibility in Europe, which had suffered during the height of the Second Berlin Crisis in 1961. Already in 1958 Soviet leader Nikita Khrushchev had issued an ultimatum regarding Berlin, demanding a new status for East Germany and Berlin. He wanted the latter to become a "free" and demilitarized city, and threatened to conclude a separate peace treaty with East Germany, which would have terminated the rights of the Western Allies regarding Berlin. The city, 180 kilometers inside the GDR, was used as an escape route by thousands of East Germans, among them many academics, engineers, and doctors. The East German government put increasing pressure on the Soviet Union to find a remedy. At the US-Soviet summit in Vienna in early June 1961, Khrushchev renewed his ultimatum, hoping to scare the young American president, who appeared weak in the wake of the disastrous Bay of Pigs invasion. Kennedy strongly rejected the ultimatum and both leaders threatened war. In a major television address on July 25, 1961, Kennedy declared three essentials about which the United States would not compromise: first, the occupation rights of the Allies in West Berlin; second, free access to West Berlin; third, the freedom of the West Berliners. Western, and especially American, credibility, an essential element of cold war thinking, was at stake. However, when on August 13, 1961, the East German government—after having finally received permission from the Soviet Union—completely closed access to West Berlin by erecting barbed wire barriers (later reinforced with concrete walls), the only American and Western reaction was strong protests.[13]

From the American point of view, Kennedy's essentials had not been violated. No one was ready to go to war, possibly nuclear, for the freedom of the East Berliners and East Germans. And in some ways the building of the wall even promised a relaxation of the tensions around Berlin. In late October 1961, however, a dispute regarding the harassment of members of the US occupation authorities when entering the Eastern part of Berlin—a small but serious infringement of Allied rights in Berlin—quickly escalated until American and Soviet tanks faced each other for sixteen hours at the Checkpoint Charlie border crossing. Back-channel diplomacy between Kennedy and Khrushchev dissolved this most dangerous crisis. The tank confrontation at Checkpoint Charlie was the last major crisis over Berlin during the cold war. The wall helped to stabilize the GDR, even if the political and human costs were high. Marc Trachtenberg even argues that by 1963 the German problem had been turned into a "constructed peace" based on nuclear deterrence and the general acceptance of the status quo in central Europe.[14]

Trachtenberg is right that by 1963 the environment in Europe had changed. It was John F. Kennedy who, after the peaceful end to the Cuban Missile Crisis, began to question the logic of the cold war. The installation of the hotline between the American and Russian government and the Limited Nuclear Test Ban Treaty in the summer of 1963 were early signs of détente. While Adenauer was suspicious of the United States directly negotiating with the Soviet Union, opposition leader Willy Brandt of the German Social Democratic Party felt encouraged to pursue his own détente policy regarding Germany's Eastern neighbors. Ostpolitik, as it became known, was based on similar ideas as those promoted by Kennedy and his successor Lyndon B. Johnson, who spoke about healing the wounds in Europe by "building bridges" between East and West through trade, exchange, aid, and mutual trust. While Johnson was increasingly occupied with domestic problems and the Vietnam War, Brandt and his advisor Egon Bahr kept working hard on their policy of "change through rapprochement." When Brandt became foreign minister of a Grand Coalition in December 1966 and then Chancellor in September 1969, he was able to make real progress. In 1971 he received the Nobel Peace Prize for his policy of rapprochement. The Americans and Germans were not the only ones putting out feelers to the East. In 1966 de Gaulle, who advocated "détente, entente, and cooperation," visited Moscow and started regular consultations with the Soviet government.[15]

But de Gaulle's agenda and objectives differed from those of the United States and the FRG. In March 1966 he announced that France would withdraw from the military command structure of NATO, while remaining part of the Alliance. Although not unexpected, this move created a crisis in the Atlantic Alliance, which had already been divided about nuclear deterrence and nuclear sharing. The deployment of tactical nuclear weapons in Europe to replace more expensive conventional American forces had begun in 1954 as part of Eisenhower's policy of "massive retaliation." Long before "flexible response" became officially the new doctrine in 1967, critics on both sides of the Atlantic expressed reservations about a strategy that threatened "mutually assured destruction" (MAD) even in the case of smaller conflicts. But there was also reluctance among America's West European allies to support the flexible response option because it might lessen America's commitment to the defense of Europe. The fact that the Soviet Union by 1959 had operational intercontinental ballistic missiles (ICBMs) had made the United States vulnerable to nuclear weapons as well. The Vietnam War also weakened the US and caused growing criticism by the European allies, while increasing the pressure to reduce American military expenditures in Europe.

At the same time there were debates over which countries in Europe should be allowed to develop or have nuclear forces. The American proposal of a "multilateral (nuclear) force" (MLF) did not gain much support beyond the Federal Republic, partly because the United States wanted to keep control over nuclear warheads. France developed its own nuclear arsenal, the *force de frappe*, which became operational in 1964. The Eisenhower administration had offered Skybolt air-launched missiles to the British. When Washington cancelled the program unilaterally in late 1962, it created a major problem for Britain, which had abandoned its own development of nuclear weapons. But Kennedy and Prime Minister Harold Macmillan quickly found a face-saving solution in agreeing on the British purchase of American submarine-launched Polaris missiles.[16]

The French move in 1966 put pressure on the Alliance to rethink NATO's purpose. The result was the Harmel Report of December 1967, named after Belgian Foreign Minister Pierre Harmel. The report recognized that the world had changed since 1949. Europe had recovered from the war and had made strides towards unity. The communist bloc had fractured and the idea of "peaceful coexistence" had eased tensions to some degree. Harmel stressed that deterrence and defense against communism must remain a central pillar of NATO. Détente, however, had to become a second pillar. The report determined that the "German question" still needed to be solved before there could be a final settlement in Europe. While détente was to be a joint effort, member states could pursue individual policies (multilateral détente), but they had to do this in close consultation with one another.[17] That was specifically, though not exclusively, targeted toward the Germans. Distrust with regard to an independent West German foreign policy and fears about German readiness to sacrifice Western integration for a separate settlement with the Soviet Union persisted. Perpetuating its non-nuclear status by signing the Non-Proliferation Treaty in late 1969 was an important assurance to the Federal Republic's Western—and also its Eastern—neighbors.

While Germany and the United States would not act in perfect unison, they needed one another in order to pursue a successful policy of détente, inscribed in a number of bilateral and multilateral international treaties. In many respects, it was the Germans who decided on the pace of European détente. In taking the initiative, Brandt had to overcome strong domestic opposition, partly because the new policies meant that rapprochement with countries in Eastern Europe would be a precondition for German unification (not vice versa, as before), even though a reunited Germany remained the ultimate goal of Germany's foreign policy. The "illogical" logic was that change should come through recognition of the status quo.

The first agreement was the Moscow Treaty between West Germany and the Soviet Union on August 12, 1970. The two signatories accepted the "territorial integrity" of all European states "within their present frontiers," which for Germany explicitly meant the acceptance of the Oder-Neisse line which had cut off its eastern territories after World War II. Both countries also renounced the use of force. The treaty was not ratified by the FRG parliament until May 1972, together with the Treaty of Warsaw, which had been signed on December 7, 1970. The latter normalized the relationship between West Germany and Poland. Germany again agreed to recognize the Oder-Neisse line as the western border of Poland.

The long delay in ratifying the treaties was largely because the two treaties were linked to the Four Power Agreement on Berlin—and vice versa—signed on December 3, 1971, by the four victorious powers of World War II. The agreement reconfirmed their rights and responsibilities, which the Soviet Union had repeatedly challenged. It also included measures to improve travel and communication between the western and eastern parts of Berlin and the GDR, respectively.

The signing of the Moscow and Warsaw treaties were important preconditions for the Four Power Agreement. Once that happened, the German parliament could discuss ratification of the treaties, which in turn led to the signing of the final protocol of the Quadripartite Agreement on Berlin in June 1972. All of this opened the door to bilateral negotiations between the two German states. While there was still no full diplomatic recognition between them—instead of ambassadors the two countries exchanged permanent representatives—in 1973 both countries were finally able to join the United Nations.

The bundle of interconnected efforts, treaties, and agreements opened another chapter of détente, embodied in the Conference on Security and Cooperation in Europe

(CSCE). Begun in 1973, the Final Act was signed on August 1, 1975, in Helsinki by the United States, the Soviet Union, and the members of their respective alliances which had pushed for multilateral détente beyond the bilateral agreements in military matters between the two superpowers (like SALT I of May 1972). In addition, neutral European states like Switzerland joined the CSCE, which in some ways resembled a peace settlement after World War II.

While the United States was occupied by the Vietnam War and Watergate, the West European members of the European Community nudged the negotiations forward. The US re-entered the process in 1974, and Secretary of State Henry Kissinger played a key role in reaching a final agreement, which arranged all issues into different "baskets." The first consisted of ten principles covering political and military issues that included territorial integrity and non-intervention in internal affairs, the peaceful settlement of disputes, and the implementation of confidence-building measures. Basket two covered economic issues and scientific cooperation. The third dealt with human rights, cultural exchanges, and freedom of the press.

Initially, it seemed as if the Soviet Union had come out on top. Moscow received Western recognition of its sphere of influence. However, the signatories agreed that the frontiers were "inviolable"—which did not mean "untouchable." That left open the possibility that the borders could be changed in the future in a peaceful process. The Soviet Union, in turn, agreed to respect human rights and basic freedoms, as stipulated in basket three. Eastern European dissidents would later use this pledge domestically, and Western diplomats would point to it in follow-up conferences, to challenge Soviet policy. Overall, the CSCE process was an important element in the non-military and non-violent ending of the cold war in Europe, even if that was an unforeseeable consequence in 1975.[18]

After major progress in the field of détente, the Soviet invasion of Afghanistan in December 1979 and the election of Ronald Reagan revived cold war tensions. The new American president began a rhetorical offensive against communism and charged that détente so far had only been beneficial to the East. Arguing that the Soviet Union had surpassed the United States in the number of nuclear weapons ("window of vulnerability"), Reagan doubled military expenses and ordered many new bombers, nuclear missiles, and submarines. Moscow grew even more worried over the Reagan administration's announcement of a Strategic Defense Initiative (SDI), publicly dubbed "Star Wars." Reagan claimed that the goal of the highly controversial program was to develop a missile defense shield against a possible Soviet nuclear attack. The Kremlin leaders feared that SDI, which in their view violated the Anti-Ballistic Missile Treaty of 1972, was meant to gain first strike capability against their territory.[19]

Reagan became the target of public opposition in the form of large peace movements on both sides of the Atlantic. The European protestors not only opposed Reagan's armament program but also turned against their own leaders who promoted the stationing of new intermediate range nuclear missiles on European soil. In 1976 the Soviet Union had begun to install new medium range nuclear missiles (SS-20s), which could reach Western Europe. The Soviet leaders claimed that this was just a modernization of their land-based nuclear forces. Many in the West disagreed. Led by the German Chancellor Helmut Schmidt, Western European leaders had grown concerned that SALT I and a possible SALT II "decoupled" the United States from and diminished Western nuclear deterrence in Europe.[20] The deployment of SS-20s in their view threatened the strategic balance in a dangerous way. In a speech at the International Institute for Strategic Studies in London in October 1978, Schmidt demanded a European answer. The United States initially had not been in favor of stationing new nuclear missiles, but it caved in to European pressure to avoid a crisis of confidence. On December 12, 1979, NATO agreed on the so-called dual-track decision. The Alliance proposed to station 108 Pershing II missiles, which could reach and destroy targets like Soviet missile sites in less than ten minutes, as well as 464 cruise missiles in Europe. The new missiles would replace 1,000 older nuclear warheads. At the same time, NATO offered negotiations. If the Soviet Union agreed to remove its SS-20s, the Western Alliance would not deploy its missiles. The Germans were ready to have all the Pershing and some cruise missiles stationed in their country, but only if other West European countries were prepared to do the same. Great Britain, Italy, Belgium, and the Netherlands all agreed to do so. Mass protests all over Western Europe turned the planned stationing of the "Euromissiles" into one of the most debated domestic and international issues of the decade.

When negotiations failed in 1983 the missiles were deployed, again accompanied by major protests. No one could know at this point that only four years later both sides would agree to remove the Euromissiles and the SS-20s from European soil. The new Soviet leader, Mikhail Gorbachev, who had assumed power in March 1985, decided to put an end to the costly arms race and to focus on the serious domestic problems inside the Soviet Union. This made a new détente possible. It took a while for Gorbachev and Reagan to build up confidence. At their first summit in Geneva in November 1985, they talked about reducing strategic arms by 50 percent; a year later, in Reykjavik, they discussed the possibility of eliminating all nuclear weapons. Only Reagan's insistence on continuing research on SDI prevented a breakthrough. Many European leaders, while supportive of détente, resented the lack of consultation on the part of their American ally. The "near miss" also revived old fears of a bilateral détente and an end to America's nuclear umbrella. When in 1987 the Intermediate-range Nuclear Forces Treaty (INF) was signed, which included the "zero option" of eliminating all ground-based intermediate missiles, the peace movements celebrated, but Atlanticists grew more worried about the decoupling of America from Europe.

Gorbachev also pursued a new policy toward the communist allies by renouncing the Brezhnev Doctrine, which had been formulated by the Soviet leadership to justify the violent end of the Prague Spring in 1968. Instead of threatening to crush independence movements, the Soviet Union allowed its East European allies to go their own way.[21] Already in May 1988, the Soviets began to withdraw their troops from Afghanistan. West Europeans regarded these developments as very positive signs. But they still left open the question of how the Soviets would deal with the German question.

The opening of the borders between East and West Berlin on November 9, 1989, had not been a deliberate decision of the new East German government or an order by the

Soviet Union. It was as much the result of a confusing message by a leading East German politician during a press conference as it was the result of the pressure on the streets, which would keep sweeping away any plans by politicians in the East or West to move slowly.

The fall of the wall signaled that the cold war was coming to an end. But it also reopened the question of German unification. Taking even his Western allies by surprise, West German Chancellor Helmut Kohl in late November 1989 announced a ten-point plan for unification, which in his view would take up to ten years. But the people in East Germany demanded a faster pace. When even a monetary union beginning in July 1990 could not stop the continuous movement of people to the West, negotiations on German unification began. On October 3, 1990, East Germany joined the Federal Republic. A divided Germany and with it a divided Berlin were things of the past.

Among the Western Allies, US President George Bush had been most supportive and open to this development, as long as the Western integration of Germany remained untouched. British Prime Minister Margaret Thatcher as well as French President François Mitterand had been much more reluctant to see Germany become the largest power in central Europe again.[22] Gorbachev in the end not only allowed unification but also accepted a united Germany remaining in NATO. Both German states, the Soviet Union, the United States, Great Britain, and France discussed German reunification in the so called two-plus-four negotiations. They signed the Treaty on the Final Settlement with Respect to Germany in Moscow on September 12, 1990. Germany would regain its full sovereignty, but it had to reduce its troop levels, continue to commit to non-proliferation, and accept the new borders in the East once and forever. With the East European states free to pursue their own course and the German question answered, the CSCE declared the end of the East-West confrontation in its Charter of Paris for a New Europe on November 21, 1990: "The era of confrontation and division of Europe has ended."[23]

The cold war had started with the "confrontation and division of Europe," and Western Europe had been a major place of confrontation throughout. The end of European division and German unification signaled the end of the cold war. While the bloc confrontation in Europe had an impact far beyond the continent, the cold war also shaped the postwar development of Western Europe, itself a creation of the cold war, by splitting Europe into a clearly demarcated East and West. The containment of Germany and closer cooperation among European powers—as well as decolonization—would have happened without the cold war. But the speed of economic and military cooperation would have been much slower. More importantly, the composition of economic and military alliances like the European Union and NATO would have been different. Without the cold war the United States would not have become the quasi (West) European power that it did. Central and Eastern European countries, which could only join after 1990, would have been much more "natural" members of similar alliances than the US and Canada. In that sense the cold war did prevent the inclusion of countries like Poland and Hungary for several decades, but it did not permanently stop a development that had been deeply rooted in Europe's experience of two devastating wars in the first half of the 20th century. Instead of being defined in political, military, and ideological terms, Western Europe after 1990 has become once more a primarily geographical denotation.

## NOTES

1. George H.W. Bush, "Address before the 45th Session of the United Nations General Assembly in New York, October 1, 1990," in *Public Papers of the Presidents* (Washington, DC: Government Printing Office, 1991), 1330–4.
2. Henry R. Luce, "The American Century," *Life*, February 17, 1941, 61–5.
3. Winston Churchill, "The Sinews of Peace," in Robert Rhodes James, *Winston Churchill: His Complete Speeches 1987–1963* (New York: Chelsea House Publishers, 1974), 7285–93.
4. The "Long Telegram," <http://www.gwu.edu/~nsarchiv/coldwar/documents/episode-1/kennan.htm>. X [George F. Kennan], "The Sources of Soviet Conduct," *Foreign Affairs* 25 (July 1947): 566–82.
5. President Harry S. Truman's Message to Congress, 12 March 1947, <http://www.ourdocuments.gov/doc.php?doc = 81&page = transcript>.
6. Michael J. Hogan, *The Marshall Plan: American, Britain, and the Reconstruction of Western Europe, 1947–1953* (New York: Cambridge University Press, 1987).
7. See the articles in *Journal of Cold War Studies* 7/1 (Winter 2005): 97–181.
8. Wolfram F. Hanrieder, *Germany, America, Europe: 40 Years of German Foreign Policy* (New Haven: Yale University Press, 1989), 6.
9. Jeffrey Glen Giauque, *Grand Designs and Visions of Unity: The Atlantic Powers and the Reorganization of Western Europe, 1955–1963* (Chapel Hill, NC: University of North Carolina Press, 2002).
10. Geir Lundestad, "Empire by Invitation? The United States and Western Europe, 1945–1952," *Journal of Peace Research* 23/3 (September 1986): 263–77.
11. Marc Atwood Lawrence, *Assuming the Burden: Europe and the American Commitment to Vietnam* (Berkeley, CA: University of California Press, 2005); Kathryn C. Statler, *Replacing France: The Origins of American Intervention in Vietnam* (Lexington, KY: University of Kentucky Press, 2007).
12. William Roger Louis and Roger Owen, eds., *Suez 1956: The Crisis and its Consequences* (New York: Oxford University Press, 1989).
13. Michael R. Beschloss, *The Crisis Years: Kennedy and Khrushchev, 1960–1963* (New York: Burlingame Books, 1991).
14. Marc Trachtenberg, *A Constructed Peace: The Making of the European Settlement, 1945–1963* (Princeton, NJ: Princeton University Press, 1999).
15. Arne Hofmann, *The Emergence of Détente in Europe: Brandt, Kennedy and the Formation of Ostpolitik* (London: Routledge, 2007); Wilfried Loth, ed., *Europe, Cold War and Co-existence, 1953–1965* (London: Frank Cass, 2004); Wilfried Loth and Georges-Henri Soutou, eds., *The Making of Détente: Eastern and Western Europe in the Cold War, 1965–75* (London: Routledge, 2008); Frédéric Bozo, *Two Strategies for Europe: De Gaulle, the United States and the Atlantic Alliance* (Lanham, MD: Rowman and Littlefield, 2001).
16. Lawrence S. Kaplan, *The Long Entanglement: NATO's First Fifty Years* (Westport, CT: Praeger, 1999).
17. "Report on the Future Tasks of the Alliance (The Harmel Report), Brussels, December 13–14, 1967," *European Foreign Policy—Key Documents* (London: Routledge, 2000).

18. Conference on Security and Cooperation in Europe: Final Act, Helsinki 1975, <http://www.osce.org/mc/39501>; Andreas Wenger et al., eds., *Origins of the European Security System: The Helsinki Process Revisited, 1965–75* (Milton Park, UK: Routledge, 2008).

19. Raymond L. Garthoff, *Détente and Confrontation: American-Soviet Relations from Nixon to Reagan* (Washington, DC: Brookings Institute, 1985).

20. Geir Lundestad, *The United States and Western Europe since 1945: From "Empire" by Invitation to Transatlantic Drift* (Oxford: Oxford University Press, 2003), 229.

21. Therefore the new policy has sometimes been called the "Sinatra Doctrine."

22. Frédéric Bozo et al., *Europe and the End of the Cold War: A Reappraisal* (Abingdon, UK and New York: Routledge, 2008).

23. Charter of Paris for a New Europe, Paris, November 19–21, 1990, <http://www.osce.org/mc/39516>.

## Select Bibliography

Bozo, Frédéric et al., eds. *Europe and the End of the Cold War: A Reappraisal*. Abingdon, UK and New York: Routledge, 2008.

Garthoff, Raymond L. *Détente and Confrontation: American-Soviet Relations from Nixon to Reagan*. Washington, DC: Brookings Institute, 1985.

Giauque, Jeffrey Glen. *Grand Designs and Visions of Unity: The Atlantic Powers and the Reorganization of Western Europe, 1955–1963*. Chapel Hill, NC: University of North Carolina Press, 2002.

Kaplan, Lawrence S. *The Long Entanglement: NATO's First Fifty Years*. Westport, CT: Praeger, 1999.

Loth, Wilfried, ed. *Europe, Cold War and Coexistence, 1953–1965*. London: Frank Cass, 2004.

Loth, Wilfried and Georges-Henri Soutou, eds. *The Making of Détente: Eastern and Western Europe in the Cold War, 1965–75*. London: Routledge, 2008.

Lundestad, Geir. *The United States and Western Europe since 1945: From "Empire" by Invitation to Transatlantic Drift*. Oxford: Oxford University Press, 2003.

Nuenlist, Christian and Anna Locher, eds. *Transatlantic Relations at Stake: Aspects of NATO, 1956–1972*. Zurich: Center for Security Studies, 2006.

Schulz, Matthias and Thomas A. Schwartz, eds. *The Strained Alliance: US-European Relations from Nixon to Carter*. New York: Cambridge University Press, 2010.

Wenger, Andreas et al., eds. *Origins of the European Security System: The Helsinki Process Revisited, 1965–75*. Milton Park: Routledge, 2008.

# CHAPTER 11

......................................................................................

# EASTERN EUROPE

......................................................................................

## BERND STÖVER

THE history of East Central Europe's cold war began with the gradual dissolution of the anti-Hitler coalition at the end of World War II. Until then the three wartime allies, the Soviet Union, Great Britain, and the United States, sought agreement on the political postwar order. At the Tehran Conference in 1943, Franklin Roosevelt and Winston Churchill accepted the Soviet Union's annexations of the Baltic states and of eastern Poland, which Joseph Stalin had negotiated with Adolf Hitler in 1939. The Soviet dictator was able to hold onto the Baltic states and occupied eastern Poland. At the Moscow meeting in October 1944—this time without Roosevelt—Churchill and Stalin reached the Percentages agreement, in which Churchill had noted by hand on a sheet of paper his vision of dividing up the spheres of influence in Eastern Europe, and Stalin had agreed by making a check mark next to the percentages. Soviet influence was capped at 90 percent in Romania, 75 in Bulgaria, 50 in Hungary and Yugoslavia, and 10 in Greece.[1]

Stalin, too, had accommodated the Western powers in some crucial areas during the war. Among other things, he had agreed to the provisions in the Atlantic Charter of August 1941, which would serve as the underlying principles of the postwar order. These included self-determination, free choice of government, rejection of annexation, acceptance of non-aggression, and free trade. Furthermore, during the Yalta Conference in February 1945, Stalin agreed to the substantially similar "Declaration on Liberated Europe." Breaking with this "Yalta Declaration" during the Soviet occupation of Eastern Europe would become a principal reason for the disintegration of the wartime alliance in 1944–5.

The first serious clash of Western and Soviet interests occurred within the context of the liberation of Poland. Stalin feared the strengthening of the Polish resistance movement, which could complicate his plans for the postwar order. As early as July 1944 he had made it clear that he would only accept politically powerful "parties" within Poland that were pro-Soviet. Poland was an essential link in Stalin's security zone—so essential that he was willing to risk conflict with London and Washington.[2] Finland was the opposite. Stalin was content with Finland's assurance of good will, even though it had waged war against the Soviet Union as an ally of Germany during the war.

Romania, Bulgaria, and Hungary became showcases for how the Soviet Union dealt with countries that were indispensable to the Soviet security cordon yet had fought on Germany's side during the war.[3] In these three countries, the Kremlin imposed a harsh policy of Sovietization. Because of Romania's geostrategic importance, its Sovietization started immediately in 1944, even though Romania had few communists. The Soviets also eliminated known anti-communists in Bulgaria in early 1945, in order to preclude any possible resistance to Soviet dominance. In November 1945 Moscow installed Georgi Dimitrov, the head of the former Comintern, as Bulgaria's prime minister through rigged elections. After that, the country became a dependable part of the security cordon that Stalin had demanded. The story was similar in Hungary, where the Soviet Union proceeded no less heavy-handedly by rigging the 1948 elections to produce a communist majority.

Stalin calculated that the remaining states in the Soviet security cordon, Yugoslavia, Albania, and Czechoslovakia, did not pose an immediate danger to Soviet security. In all three states, reliable left-leaning or communist leaders appeared to be in control: Josip Tito in Yugoslavia, Enver Hoxha in Albania, and Edvard Benes (tightly managed by Moscow-trained party functionaries) in Czechoslovakia. Internal conditions generated distinct developments, nevertheless, as illustrated by the contrasts between Yugoslavia and Albania. Soviet troops left Yugoslavia in March 1945. Even though Tito began a process of "self-Sovietization" from 1946 on, his independent foreign policy concerned Stalin and led to a break between the two countries in 1948. Albania's Enver Hoxha, on the other hand, remained a loyal Stalinist even after the Soviet de-Stalinization of the later 1950s. Albania's leadership relied on the Stalinist model until the opening of the iron curtain in 1990.

Czechoslovakia was of central geopolitical significance to the Soviet Union as well. After 1944 the exiled parties regrouped as Moscow exercised subtle influence on the formation of a postwar government. Yet Czechoslovakia's sympathies were oriented toward the West. Thus the Czech communists used the economic crises starting in 1947 to stage a coup in 1948, which assured Czechoslovakia's transformation into a satellite of the USSR.

Within the Eastern bloc the transition to the officially declared cold war was accompanied by various official statements. In September 1947, Andrej Zhdanov delivered Stalin's answer to Truman's March 12 "declaration of war," the Truman Doctrine. The founding of the Communist Information Bureau, or "Cominform," to replace the defunct Comintern, which had been dismantled in 1943, provided the occasion for Zhdanov to present his so-called "two camp theory"—the "imperialist anti-democratic" camp of the West was irreconcilably opposed to the "anti-imperialist democratic" Soviet camp. Only nine months later, Stalin used the example of Yugoslavia to demonstrate that indeed every deviation from the Soviet "camp"—even and particularly any form of national communism—would result in a break with Moscow. In addition Moscow blocked the wishes of several East Central European states to take part in the European Recovery Program (ERP). After Molotov was unable to push through his demand to grant such loans bilaterally at the Paris meeting in June 1947, the Soviets prohibited all

East Central European parties interested in participating from accepting the offer. Stalin's rejection of the Marshall Plan formed part of his overall policy of withdrawal from the Western economic system. However the Eastern bloc's efforts to create its own economic apparatus, the Council for Mutual Economic Assistance (Comecon), and later a banking system, never gained international traction. Thus by the 1970s, at least part of international trade within the Eastern bloc was conducted in US dollars.

The formation of the Eastern bloc, accelerated by the First Berlin Crisis in 1948 and the Korean War two years later, was completed with the founding of the Warsaw Pact on May 14, 1955. With it, all Soviet-controlled Eastern European states pledged "friendship, cooperation and mutual assistance" to one another in case of an armed attack. Until its dissolution on April 1, 1991, the Warsaw Pact was always headed by a Soviet general. Yet over time some members left. Among them was Albania in 1968, which withdrew in order to signal its protest against the invasion of Czechoslovakia. Furthermore, the escalating Soviet-Chinese rift created discord among Warsaw Pact allies, preventing any joint resolutions on Vietnam after 1966. In these instances bilateral treaties, such as the mutual assistance pact with Finland in 1955, replaced the alliance system. Indeed, because of the questionable reliability as well as capabilities of the Eastern European forces, the credibility of the Warsaw Pact as an instrument of collective security was always suspect.

The cold war escalated further with the Eastern bloc uprisings between 1953 and 1956. In March 1953 the death of Stalin not only produced fear but also hope for an easing of tension. A further thaw occurred as a result of Khrushchev's speech in February 1956 at the Soviet Communist Party's 20th Party Congress, in which he condemned Stalin's crimes and cult of personality. The uprisings in four satellite states, Czechoslovakia, East Germany, Poland, and Hungary, were possible only within the context of Stalin's death and his demythologization, which began well before Khrushchev's secret speech. Each of these uprisings had similar origins. Both Czechoslovakia and the GDR had just undergone an intense period of Sovietization, although the political and economic conditions in Czechoslovakia were quite different from those in the GDR. The increased development of the industrial sector and immense payments for armaments caused Czechoslovakia's budget deficit to soar and propelled the country into a deep economic crisis. The government's response to the crisis, a comprehensive currency reform in 1953, wiped out the savings accounts of millions of citizens. They responded with widespread protests, spontaneous strikes, and finally mass political demonstrations in which even some Communist Party (CP) members and state officials participated. The official crackdown of the so-called Pilsen uprising occurred with no casualties. More than a thousand of the uprising's leaders were arrested, however, and many received lengthy prison sentences.

The events unfolded differently two weeks later in the GDR, where a process of internal political consolidation and Sovietization was under way as a result of decisions made at the 2nd Party Conference of the SED (Sozialistische Einheitspartei Deutschlands) on July 12, 1952. The uprising began at the construction site of the Stalin Allee, in the center of East Berlin on June 16. Joined by thousands of passers-by, the workers of the Stalin

Allee initially demanded economic benefits. As news spread of the protests, they were joined by smaller demonstrations in 560 other cities and towns, and the demands included political changes, among them democracy, freedom, and the unification of Germany.[4] The next day the Soviets declared a state of emergency and deployed tanks. At least 51 people lost their lives during the uprising, many of them youths.[5]

Almost exactly three years later the uprising in Polish Poznan started, directly inspired by Khrushchev's critique of his predecessor at the CPSU's 20th Party Congress. The resulting thaw was an essential precondition for both the Polish and Hungarian uprisings. Unrest started in February 1956 as a workers' demonstration. Collectivization and the crash program of industrialization had created economic problems, particularly a spike in consumer prices without a rise in wages. At the same time dissatisfaction over increased workloads exacerbated the discontent. After negotiations with the Warsaw government broke down, about 100,000 people took to the streets in Poznan on 26 June. The protests escalated into violence that left 53 people dead and about 200 injured.

Nevertheless, at least in the short run, the reformers were able to claim victory. Indeed, the year 1956 put an end to collectivization, and, until 1957, workers could establish their own governing councils in about 60 percent of non-agricultural production sites. The Catholic Church benefited as well: clergy were released from prisons and by mid-December, the government reintroduced religious instruction in state schools. But this liberalization came to an end with the election of Władysław Gomulka as First Secretary of the Communist Party. After 1957 political and cultural activities became ever more restricted.[6]

Following Poland's lead and encouraged by US propaganda that promoted the "liberation" of "captive peoples," latent discontent in Hungary erupted into a bloody uprising in October 1956. Here, too, the population generally despised the Communist Party. A list of demands presented to the party leadership in mid-October 1956, included the return of the reformer Imre Nagy to the post of prime minister, revisions of workloads, a pluralist party system, free elections, civil rights, the re-establishment of economic independence, as well as the reintroduction of Hungarian national symbols and holidays. The Soviet decision to intervene militarily occurred after and in direct relation to the Suez crisis in the Middle East. Until October 29 it seemed as if the Soviets were trying to exhaust all political means before moving to a military option. Yet in the aftermath of the British, French, and Israeli intervention in Egypt, and in conjunction with Imry's declaring his intention to withdraw Hungary from the Warsaw pact a Soviet version of the "domino theory" propelled Moscow toward a draconian response. Starting November 4, the Red Army crushed the Hungarian Revolution mercilessly. Its sympathies notwithstanding, the Eisenhower administration, unwilling to intervene even indirectly in a country of manifestly vital interest to the Soviets, remained on the sidelines. After its defeat on 11 November, the Hungarians reported 300 deaths and about 1,000 injured. The Soviets reported 669 deaths and 1,540 injured.[7] Yet military defeat did not mean the end of all resistance. In the wake of the revolution there were strikes for months to come.[8]

The building of the Berlin Wall on August 13, 1961, represented the main watershed in the history of the Eastern bloc as well as in the evolution of the cold war.[9] The cold war was shut down in Central Europe and the GDR could develop its own socialism as a laboratory experiment. On the other hand, the cold war now found its main battle-ground in the Third World, where the number of small wars increased. In 1968 Moscow showed that its demand for hegemony had not changed at all. By the early 1960s, the Czechoslovak Socialist Republic (CSSR) had moved in a different direction than the one planned in Moscow. An economic crisis created widespread discontent among the population, which resulted in serious doubts about the system. The party leadership began to advocate something like a "socialist market economy," which was supposed to loosen strict state control and allow for non-state trade unions and private enterprises. By 1968 the discontent extended to demanding more cultural and personal freedoms.

Initially, the Czechoslovakian Communist Party reacted in predictable ways. In the fall of 1967, Antonín Novotny, who served as both president and party chief, sought to silence outspoken dissidents like Pavel Kohout and Václav Havel and prohibited any political demonstrations. Yet in January 1968 the party reformers forced Novotny out of office and replaced him with the reform-minded Alexander Dubček. This change of leadership encouraged further popular opposition to Moscow's leadership. Dubček tried unsuccessfully to curb the popular reforming spirit, and the demands for political and economic freedom. He was also unsuccessful in convincing the Soviet leadership that the suggested reforms did not aim to abandon socialism in Czechoslovakia. During the night of August 21, 1968, troops of the Warsaw Pact marched into Czechoslovakia. An estimated 98 Czechs and about 50 Warsaw pact troops died during the invasion. Dubček and others were arrested. On 23 August, his successor Ludvik Svoboda was summoned to Moscow and forced to sign the Moscow Agreement, which put an end to all reforms.[10] The so-called Brezhnev Doctrine, which *Pravda* had already published on July 15, 1968, emphasized: "Such 'self-determination', as a result of which NATO troops would have been able to come up to the Soviet border, while the community of European socialist countries would have been split, in effect encroaches upon the vital interests of the peoples of these countries and conflicts, as the very root of it, with the right of these people to socialist self-determination."[11]

The cold war has to be understood as an internal social and political struggle against alleged or actual supporters of the opposite political camp, which in the Eastern bloc happened uniformly from the top down, even before the challenges of the generation of 1968. Long before the cold war, the persecution of dissidents and deviants as well as the purposeful support of loyalists had become common practice. Increased persecution started with the exclusion of Yugoslavia from the Cominform in 1948. "Nationalist-Titoist" deviants were persecuted by the dozen and accused of being supporters of the West, and sometimes they were convicted in sensational show trials. Such trials occurred regularly in Albania, Romania, Poland, Hungary, Bulgaria, and Czechoslovakia. In many cases judges meted out the death penalty. Those identified as dissidents suffered in prisons or camps, even if they pledged support for Marxism-Leninism, albeit in a more liberal version. Beginning in the 1970s, many were "expatriated."[12]

The emergence of a period of détente represented another pivotal moment in the history of the cold war, one which had unintended consequences for the Eastern bloc. The SALT I agreement, and to a greater extent the series of treaties between West Germany the GDR, Poland, Czechoslovakia, and the USSR, known as the *Ostverträge*, paved the way for a special series of meetings on European security. The first Conference on Security and Cooperation in Europe, initially promoted by the Eastern bloc in 1967, was convened from November 1972 to August 1975 and concluded with the Helsinki Accords. By signing it, the Eastern bloc states agreed to more political tolerance and the observance of human rights. In the following years, the Helsinki Accords encouraged more and more human rights groups in the Eastern bloc, such as Charter 77 in Czechoslovakia, but also emboldened people in the GDR to request emigration by referring to Helsinki.[13]

These concessions on human rights and attendant issues posed serious challenges to the Soviet system of control in Eastern Europe. These challenges intensified in conjunction with supplementary developments over the next few years. Chief among these was the emergence of the Eastern bloc's first non-state, free trade union, Solidarność (Solidarity) in Poland in the summer of 1980. A drastic increase in meat prices, announced in June 1980 by the Polish government under Prime Minster Edward Gierek, immediately resulted in nationwide strikes. One of the largest occurred at the Lenin Shipyard in Gdansk on August 14, in which about 17,000 workers took part. The movement was successful: not only did Gierek resign but also the government in Warsaw accepted an agreement with representatives of the shipyard workers from Gdansk and their spokesman, Lech Walesa. It stipulated that in the future not only an independent trade union but also strikes should be legal—something unprecedented in the history of the Eastern bloc. Shortly thereafter, on September 17, 1980, the shipyard workers founded the Solidarity trade union. Its "action program" expressly declared support for the principles of Western democracy and the traditions of Christendom even as it pledged allegiance to the nation and the socialist idea of society.

Several leaders in the Eastern bloc greeted these developments in Poland with concern. The GDR government feared most of all a spillover into German territory.[14] Its leader Erich Honecker called on Soviet president Leonid Brezhnev and other socialist leaders to "thwart once and for all the counterrevolution in Poland."[15] Moscow was not enthusiastic about the East German demand to apply the Brezhnev Doctrine to Poland. First, the Soviet Union already had more than enough image problems. Second, Moscow had just begun its intervention in Afghanistan, and the situation there was evolving in a way that portended increasingly grave problems. It was becoming increasingly evident that an invasion might well result in a deepening quagmire. Ultimately Poland, with virtually no direct Soviet support, averted the crisis by itself. The ruling Communist Party appointed Secretary of Defense General Wojciech Jaruzelski, known as a hardliner, as prime minister, and then in October 1981 it designated him head of the party as well. The end result was something of a compromise: no Soviet invasion but the imposition of martial law on December 13, 1981. Until the lifting of martial law in July 1983, a "Military Council of National Rescue" ruled the country with a ban on public gatherings, the imposition of a curfew, and the dissolution of the Solidarity trade union, whose leaders were arrested.

Other socialist states likewise suffered political unrest. The GDR, from 1978 on—since the announcement that the "Sozialistische Wehrerziehung" (socialistic defense education) would be part of the regular school curriculum—experienced a boom in peace groups. These opposition groups would almost certainly have remained marginal had it not been for the political revolution under way in the Soviet Union itself. The "New Thinking"—a fundamental "reorganization" (perestroika) of Soviet politics as well as a new "openness" and "transparency" (glasnost)—decreed by the new Soviet Secretary General, Mikhail Gorbachev, in 1985 at first only for the USSR, was the spark that ignited reform movements everywhere in the Soviet sphere of power and which—an unintended consequence politically—turned the entire Eastern bloc upside down.[16]

The internal situation of the Soviet Union at the end of the 1970s and the beginning of the 1980s was much more tumultuous than the West perceived at the time. Brezhnev, after his severe stroke in 1976, was hardly capable of any sustained activity. The decision to march into Afghanistan was made in 1979 by the head of the KGB, Yuri Andropov, who took over after Brezhnev's death on November 10, 1982. However, the leadership crisis continued. Two years after Brezhnev's death, Andropov, who had succeeded him, died. A year later, on March 10, 1985, Andropov's successor Konstantin Chernenko died also. Chernenko's successor became the comparatively youthful Mikhail Gorbachev, born in 1931.

Gorbachev's election in the spring of 1985 initiated a new start after years of political paralysis, not only in the Soviet Union and the Eastern bloc but also in the West. His ideological views had been shaped by Khrushchev's reckoning with Stalinism. This socialization allowed Gorbachev to approach reforms in the realm of foreign policy more flexibly and even to sell the retreat from certain foreign policy positions as a success.[17] In domestic policy, he announced his intention to place particular emphasis on perestroika and glasnost. This "New Thinking" represented an attempt to reform the communist state from the interior, without threatening its entire existence.

Gorbachev did not hesitate to provide the West with evidence of his "New Thinking" on foreign policy. Only a day after his assumption of office on March 12, 1985, he resumed talks on arms control, including the long-debated question of medium-range missiles. The Soviet Union faced a dramatic budget deficit, and Gorbachev hoped to ease the burden through reduced military spending. Up until the successful conclusion of the Intermediate-Range Nuclear Forces (INF) Treaty in 1987, the Soviet Union was spending almost as much on the military as the USA—about $260 billion in comparison with the US's $290 billion.[18]

Gorbachev's foreign policy retreat ultimately provided financial relief for the USSR. Gorbachev explained his shift in foreign policy as a means to further develop socialism in his country. He insisted that this was not an indication of weakness but a means to increase the USSR's reputation. Most of all, however, "New Thinking" broke with the concept of the "restricted sovereignty" of the socialist states, the so-called "Brezhnev Doctrine," and replaced it with what would later be known as the "Sinatra Doctrine."[19] Every socialist country, Gorbachev declared in several speeches after April 1986, had the right to go "its own way." In retrospect, many considered this retreat from the Brezhnev Doctrine the actual beginning of the end of the Eastern bloc.

The Eastern European socialist states reacted to the Soviet change of course with different strategies. Four patterns emerged: unanimous approval in Poland and

Hungary; open rejection in Romania, Albania, and the GDR; a tactical response from Bulgaria and Czechoslovakia, which claimed to lead the reform movement by making their own suggestions for change; and, finally, indifference from bloc-free Yugoslavia, which referred to already existing reforms and rejected any further change.[20]

For decades Poland and Hungary had been the political exceptions within the Soviet sphere of power.[21] In the summer of 1989 both became trailblazers of the revolutions that marked the end of the Eastern bloc. Hungary had long practiced a strategy to allow smaller economic reforms without questioning its fundamental political stability or any Soviet demands.[22] By the beginning of the 1980s, however, the popularly known "goulash communism" under János Kádár had reached the limits of those incremental reforms. The Communist Party and press began openly to discuss changes that previously had been regarded as taboo: economic reforms and closer ties to the European Community. In May 1988 the CP replaced more than half of its politburo members with reformers. Long-time head of both the party and state Kádár was replaced first by Prime Minister Károly Grosz, who belonged to the conservative wing of reformists, and then after only six months by Miklós Németh, a supporter of socialist pluralism.

After the first free elections in the spring of 1990, the communists had disappeared from the Hungarian parliament altogether. Those who held political sway immediately resumed at the point where they had been stopped in 1956: they chose the former chairman of the Revolutionary Committee during the Hungarian Revolution, Jószef Antall, as their new prime minister. The post-communist government marked that continuity with two other events: it posthumously rehabilitated Imre Nagy, the leader of the Hungarian Revolution who had been executed in 1958, by transferring him with great ceremony to an honorary grave on June 16, 1989. Second, on May 2, 1989, Hungary became the first Eastern European country to open its border with the West. The iron curtain had been raised. Almost immediately tourists from the GDR began flocking to West Germany through the Hungarian opening. On October 23, 1989, the anniversary of the 1956 Soviet invasion, Hungary officially declared itself a republic.

In Poland, politically the most unstable state of the Eastern bloc, change happened in a more dramatic way.[23] Partly in response to the challenge posed by Solidarity, Jaruzelski had initiated minor economic reforms, which eventually gained even Gorbachev's approval. In addition, in 1986 he granted political amnesty to members of Solidarity, even though the trade union remained banned until April 1989. By the beginning of that year, the momentum for reform was unstoppable. The government agreed to a phased plan for implementing democratic reform. After semi-free parliamentary elections in Poland in June 1989, the government initiated long-awaited economic and political reforms. The results of the elections were stunning. Solidarity won every one of the 161 seats up for election in the Sejm. This victory spelled the end of Poland's Communist Party. In July 1989 Jaruzelski was elected to the presidency with a bare majority of a single vote. Solidarity advisor Tadeusz Masowiecki became Poland's new prime minister, the first non-communist in the Eastern bloc. On December 30, 1989, Poland declared itself a democratic republic. The People's Republic of Poland ceased to exist as a component of the Soviet orbit. Just a few days later the Communist Party of Poland was dissolved. In December 1990 Lech Walesa, the former leader of Solidarity, became Poland's first freely elected president.

In Bulgaria and Czechoslovakia the communist leadership tried to forestall its own demise by implementing changes according to the Soviet model. Todor Shivkov had been ruling Bulgaria since 1954 and had survived by adapting to all Soviet political reforms. Therefore his response to Gorbachev's shift in governance was to offer his own, reduced version of perestroika, the *preustrojstwo*.[24] Thereafter Shivkov avoided further reforms—until 1989. As a result, relations with the USSR deteriorated until they reached an all-time low. Moscow reacted especially harshly to the Bulgarian policy of forced assimilation and deportation of its Turkish minority. By June 1989 the Soviets were actively supporting regime change. Shivkov was finally forced out of office by a "palace revolt" of two cabinet ministers on November 10, 1989. A new government under former Secretary of State Petar Mladenov rapidly implemented reforms, which averted greater unrest. Government and reform advocates agreed to create a "round table" in January 1990 to discuss further reforms. On March 12, the round table decided, among other things, to introduce a pluralist party system that would facilitate a peaceful transition to democracy. In May 1990 Bulgaria held its first free postwar elections.

Despite the different histories of Bulgaria and Czechoslovakia, the trajectory of the Czech Communist leader, Gustáv Husák, paralleled that of Shivkov. Husák was confronted with a special problem because Gorbachev's reforms were similar to the demands of the "Prague Spring." Adopting those reforms would have rehabilitated the reformer Dubček as well as undermined Husák's own authority. Hence he resisted. In December 1987 Husák was forced to resign, probably, as in the Bulgarian case, with tacit support from Gorbachev. He was replaced by Miloš Jakeš, whose assessment of the situation was the same as Husák's. Jakeš continued Husák's political course, which resulted in huge demonstrations in 1988. These marked the beginning of the "Velvet Revolution."[25] The government resigned after a series of massive demonstrations and a general strike on November 29, 1989. In December, Václáv Havel, the playwright and longtime political dissident, who had only recently been released from prison, was elected the first free president, and, fittingly, Alexander Dubček was elected president of the parliament.

In Romania change did not come as a "peaceful revolution." On December 21, 1989, the despotic Nicolae Ceauşescu was executed in the course of a bloody rebellion against the Romanian state security forces, the notorious Securitate.[26] The revolution started with violent demonstrations in the city of Timisoara, the Hungarian part of the country, which had been suppressed for decades. It began on December 16 with a demonstration in support of the clergyman László Tökes, who in June 1989 had denounced the frequent violations of human rights on Romanian TV. Soon the protest was transformed into a general protest against the despot in Bucharest. From then on events in Romania unfolded in a dramatically different manner than in the neighboring countries. Ceauşescu's offer to step down on December 17 was rejected by the hardliners of his government. The army, which in other countries had exercised restraint, opened fire on demonstrators with hundreds, possibly thousands of casualties. Finally on 22 December enraged demonstrators stormed the building of the Central Committee. Even though

Ceaușescu was able to flee, he was ultimately captured and executed after a summary trial, which probably occurred on December 25, 1989.

Prior to the bloody Romanian revolution Gorbachev had encouraged reforms in Romania, which Ceaușescu rejected. The indigenous opposition under Ion Iliescu probably began planning the overthrow of the dictator with Moscow's backing as early as October 1989. Iliescu was not only considered a supporter of perestroika but knew Gorbachev from their student days. Iliescu was appointed Ceaușescu's successor on December 26, 1989, and became Romania's first freely elected president.

Albania too at first resisted reform. Having served as Albania's head of state since 1946, Enver Hoxha was universally considered one of the most loyal Stalinists. He had evaded de-Stalinization in the 1950s by closing off his country to outside influence, including the Soviet Union itself. The Albanian-Soviet rift had developed along parallel lines to the Chinese-Soviet struggle. The final split occurred at the Moscow World Conference on November 16, 1960, when Hoxha openly supported the Chinese position. A year later, at the CPSU's 22nd Party Congress in October 1961, Khrushchev made clear that he no longer considered Albania part of the socialist camp. China became Albania's biggest supporter. After Hoxha's death in 1985, his successor, Ramiz Alia, continued the fight against Moscow's "revisionists." Alia insisted that Gorbachev's reforms were not appropriate for Albania. However, many Albanians, most of all university students, publicly voiced their disagreement. Demonstrations in the city of Shkoder in 1989 resulted in the government declaring a state of emergency. The government's minimal corrections to the state-run economic system did little to placate the public. Recognizing that popular discontent had reached a level that posed an unprecedented danger, Alia reversed his posture. In May 1989 the government revived the Justice Department, which had been abandoned in 1967, allowed free practice of religion, and restricted the imposition of the death penalty.

Yet pressure from the population continued unabated. In December 1990 the Alia government made an even greater concession. It allowed alternative political parties to be set up. After early elections on March 22, 1992, Albania's first non-communist Democratic Party, founded in February 1991, won a majority of almost two-thirds of all votes. As elsewhere in Eastern Europe, the Communist Party did not survive the pressure of free elections: it dissolved in June 1991.

The destabilization in Yugoslavia that accompanied the end of the cold war was even more dramatic—and more violent—than in Romania. Until Tito's death in 1980, Yugoslavia had been very successful at maneuvering between the blocs. What is more, Tito's unassailable regime combined with Yugoslavia's East-West balancing act to mask intense internal nationalist and religious tensions. These tensions exploded in the post-cold war environment. Yugoslavia's multi-ethnic state, which was dominated by Serbia, was the only one in East Central Europe to react to the reform movement with military force.[27]

It was probably the self-confidence of the Belgrade government due to its independence from both blocs, along with an illusion of invulnerability produced by the implementation of reforms under Tito, that influenced the multi-ethnic state to lag behind its neighbors in initiating both political and economic reforms. The problems that surfaced in the latter part of the 1980s in Yugoslavia dated back to earlier decades and now blended with the transformations brought about by perestroika. When Slobodan Milošević took over the presidency of Yugoslavia in May 1987, he rapidly manifested a form of aggressive Serbian nationalism, which provoked resistance in other parts of the country. In the summer of 1989 Serbia's nationalist mobilization reached a preliminary peak with the celebration of the 600 year anniversary of the battle against the Turks on Kosovo polje (Blackbird Field). Since October 1988, the central government in Belgrade had begun to chip away at the autonomous status of the Kosovo and Vojvodina provinces which had been constitutionally guaranteed.

Questioning the autonomy that had been granted by Tito had an immediate effect on the two republics. Gorbachev's reforms had produced a growing self-confidence among other non-Serbian republics within Yugoslavia. Fearing that Belgrade's behavior toward Kosovo and Vojvodina was establishing a dangerous precedent, they now feared for their own autonomy. In 1989 Slovenia openly offered support to the Kosovan Albanians. Belgrade's answer followed immediately, thereby exacerbating friction. Milošević imposed a trade boycott, to which the forceful Slovenian province responded by stopping its payments to the federal treasury in Belgrade. When in February 1990 the Slovenian communists officially left the confederation at Yugoslavia's party congress, the state crisis reached its climax. After the first free elections in April 1990, on June 25, 1991, Slovenia declared its independence from Yugoslavia.

Notwithstanding sporadic outbreaks of violence, at first, Belgrade's reaction was surprisingly moderate. With European Community mediation, both parties signed a peace treaty two weeks later. Belgrade's accommodating posture soon changed radically, however. During 1990, free elections had occurred in all Yugoslav republics for the first time since World War II. With the exception of Serbia and Montenegro, the communists had been voted out of office everywhere. These elections can be considered the beginning of the end of Yugoslavia as a united state, as a new crop of nationalist-minded politicians took power in each of the republics. When Croatia declared independence on May 19, 1991, the central government in Belgrade retaliated. After isolated gunfire between the Serbian minority and Croatian policemen at the end of March, the conflict escalated into civil war in December 1991, when Serbian-dominated areas within Croatia seceded to Serbia. The developing bloody civil war had nothing to do with the fronts of the cold war and continued well into the post-cold war era. Yugoslavia's federal government, which insisted on keeping Yugoslavia together, waged war against several renegade republics. By April 1992 only Serbia and Montenegro were left in the Federal Republic of Yugoslavia.[28]

In the GDR perestroika had raised widespread hopes among dissidents and reformers. Yet everyone expected long-time party chief and head of state Erich Honecker to block any fundamental change.[29] According to reliable estimates, the number of applications for exit visas had risen to about 250,000 in 1988, about three times as high as at the beginning of the 1980s.[30] When Hungary opened its borders to the West in May 1989, GDR citizens crossed the border to Austria by the thousands, many never to return. In

Prague and Warsaw, East Germans stormed the West German embassy, pleading for exit visas. The GDR leadership resisted reform. It increased pressure on well-known dissidents. As early as 1987 the GDR's chief ideologist, Kurt Hager, had explained the GDR's position on reform during an interview with the West German magazine *Stern*: "Would you, if your neighbor wallpapers his flat, feel obliged to also wallpaper your own flat?"[31] Gorbachev was sharply critical of this attitude, as shown during his state visit in 1989 on the occasion of the GDR's 40th anniversary. He warned Honecker and other GDR hardliners: "Life punishes those who come too late."[32] As a matter of fact, many of the traditional measures for maintaining power were already failing before the fall of the Wall. Neither the brutal clampdown of the security forces during the celebrations of the GDR's anniversary nor rigged votes could keep demonstrators away from their meetings.

The situation of the GDR leadership became critical only when the dissatisfied masses no longer sought to leave the country but allied themselves with the dissident movement. During the 1980s, political resistance in the GDR had coalesced around the Protestant-Lutheran Church. Thus, by the fall of 1989 churches like the Gethsemane Church in East Berlin and the Nikolai Church in Leipzig became centers of the movement for change. Under the banner of peaceful resistance, demonstrators met weekly in ever greater numbers. In Leipzig, the "Monday demonstrations" garnered international attention. In East Berlin, about half a million people demonstrated for democracy on Alexander Square on November 4.

Party leaders attempted to regain control over the situation by replacing Honecker with his "crown prince." Egon Krenz, however, was no alternative in the eyes of those who wanted to reform the GDR. Krenz left in place the GDR's political structure and, worse, the hated state security service.

The precise series of events leading up to the opening of the border between East and West Berlin on November 9 remained an open question for a long time. No one disputed that the immediate catalyst was a misunderstanding at a press conference held by the Secretary of Information designate, Günther Schabowski, at 6 p.m. that day. To everybody's surprise, Schabowski announced that permits for GDR citizens to take private trips abroad would be available at short notice; even permanent exit visas could be obtained without any delay. Within the hour Western stations were broadcasting that the GDR had agreed to open its borders.

Soon the members of the border police in Berlin's center were not able to stem the rush of East Berliners seeking to cross into the western part of the city. After frantic consultations, some of these officials opened the gates at 10 p.m. That night thousands streamed in and out of West Berlin. For practical purposes the border was open—"the Wall had fallen."[33]

Efforts by the East German government to retract the statement the next day proved fruitless. On the evening of November 11, Gorbachev, in conversation with the West German Chancellor Helmut Kohl, stated explicitly that the Red Army would not intervene. In this informal way, Gorbachev gave German unification the Soviet Union's endorsement. The conservative "Alliance for Germany" won the first open post-cold war elections in March 1990. A couple of months later, on May 18, the two Germanys agreed on an "economic, social and currency union" to take effect on July 1. Sanctioned by the former occupying powers, Great Britain, France, the United States, and the Soviet Union, Germany officially sealed its unification on October 3, 1990.[34]

The Soviet Union fell victim to its own reform course and ceased to exist on December 31, 1991. Since the last third of the 1980s Gorbachev had been compelled to defend his reform course against diverse opponents. On one side were the conservatives who adamantly opposed perestroika and glasnost. Indeed, in August 1991 the conservative wing of the CPSU launched a coup against him, charging that Gorbachev had weakened the socialist camp and made it vulnerable to attack from the enemies of the working class.[35] This line was a repeat of the critique against de-Stalinization in 1956 and détente in the 1960s. Arrayed against the conservatives were progressives of varying degrees who thought that Gorbachev's reforms did not go far enough, among them the chairman of the Moscow CPSU, Boris Yeltsin, and other well-known dissidents.

Further, several Soviet Republics faced increasingly powerful independence movements, which eventually threatened the Soviet Union's very existence. The resurgence of regional nationalism was helped significantly by a 1988 ruling by the Supreme Soviet that allowed national flags, hymns, and holidays in the various republics. Non-Russian peoples in particular rediscovered their national traditions and their long suppressed languages. By the same token, almost everywhere Soviet-internationalist symbols disappeared. In some areas national conflicts erupted with renewed fervor, sometimes stirred up by outside forces, among them the dispute between predominantly Muslim Azerbaijan and Christian Armenia over the region of Nagorno-Karabakh.

The first areas to secede from the Soviet Union were the Baltic republics of Estonia, Latvia, and Lithuania, which Stalin had annexed in 1940. They were followed by Moldavia, Armenia, and Georgia. Lithuania was the first to declare its independence on March 11, 1990. From then on the dissolution of the Soviet Union could not be stopped. When on June 12, 1990, the Russian Soviet Federative Socialist Republic (RSFSR), the core country of the USSR, declared its sovereignty, it effectively spelled the end of the Soviet Union.

It also spelled victory for Boris Yeltsin over Mikhail Gorbachev. Gorbachev held extensive power and fought doggedly against the dissolution of the Union. He even employed military force to prevent it. In April 1989 he sent the Red Army into Georgia, causing 19 deaths and about 200 injuries. In January 1990, Soviet armed forces marched into Azerbaijan, resulting in several hundred casualties. The Soviet Union imposed an economic blockade against Lithuania, and in January 1991 it intervened militarily. In Latvia, Soviet forces stormed the building of the Secretary of the Interior. None of these interventions, however, could reverse the dissolution of the Union.

The August 1991 coup against Gorbachev signaled the USSR's weak position to the international community. Then, in the coup's immediate aftermath, Gorbachev resigned as Secretary General of the CPSU. Because of its involvement in the coup, the party was banned from further political activity. Yeltsin succeeded in quickly establishing predominance over Gorbachev. Having been elected president of Russia in June 1990, he spearheaded the annulment of the Union Treaty of the Soviet Republics and, without consulting any other former Soviet Republic, established together with Ukraine and Belarus the Commonwealth of Independent States (CIS). The CIS officially came into being on December 21, 1991. Four days later Gorbachev resigned from the presidency of the USSR. With the Red Army in retreat, the economic and military organization of the Eastern bloc soon dissolved. Shortly after New Year's Day in 1991, member states dissolved the Council for Mutual Economic Assistance. This was followed by the dissolution of the Warsaw Pact at the end of the next month. With this the last instrument of the former Soviet Empire disappeared from Eastern Europe. On December 26, 1991, the Soviet Union ceased to exist—almost exactly 69 years after its foundation. With its breakdown, the cold war officially came to an end.

## NOTES

1. Rolf Steininger, *Deutsche Geschichte seit 1945: Darstellung und Dokumente in vier Bänden*, Vol. I: 1945–1947 (Frankfurt am Main: Fischer, 1996), 29.

2. Stefan Creuzberger and Manfred Görtemaker, eds., *Gleichschaltung unter Stalin? Die Entwicklung der Parteien im östlichen Europa 1944–49* (Paderborn: F. Schöningh, 2002), 15ff, 419ff.

3. Jens Hacker, *Der Ostblock. Entstehung, Entwicklung und Struktur 1939–1980* (Baden-Baden: Nomos, 1983), 125ff.

4. Thomas Flemming, *Der 17. Juni 1953* (Berlin: Landeszentrale für politische Bildungsarbeit, 2003), 78ff.

5. Flemming, *Der 17. Juni 1953*, 78ff; Christian F. Ostermann, *Uprising in East Germany, 1953: The Cold War, the German Question, and the First Major Upheaval behind the Iron Curtain* (Budapest: Central European Press, 2003).

6. Marcin Zaborowski, *Germany, Poland and Europe: Conflict, Cooperation, and Europeanisation* (Manchester: Manchester University Press, 2004), 58–9.

7. Figures according to Peter Gosztony, "Der Volksaufstand in Ungarn 1956: Eine Nation wehrt sich gegen die sowjetische Diktatur," *Aus Politik und Zeitgeschichte* 37/8 (1996), 3–14.

8. Victor Sebestyen, *Twelve Days: The Story of the 1956 Hungarian Revolution* (New York: Vintage, 1956); Charles Gati, *Failed Illusions: Moscow, Washington, Budapest, and the 1956 Hungarian Revolt* (Stanford, CA: Stanford University Press, 2006).

9. Robert Slusser, *The Berlin Crisis of 1961: Soviet-American Relations and the Struggle for Power in the Kremlin, June—November 1961* (Baltimore, MD: Johns Hopkins University Press, 1973).

10. Jiri Valenta, *Soviet Intervention in Czechoslovakia, 1968: Anatomy of a Decision* (Baltimore, MD: Johns Hopkins University Press, 1991); Galia Golan, *Reform Rule in Czechoslovakia: The Dubcek Era 1968–1969* (New York: Cambridge University Press, 2008); Matthew Ouimet, *The Rise and Fall of the Brezhnev Doctrine in Soviet Foreign Policy* (Chapel Hill, NC: University of North Carolina Press, 2003).

11. *Pravda*, July 15, 1968.

12. Kieran Williams, *The Prague Spring and its Aftermath: Czechoslovak Politics, 1968–1970*, (New York: Cambridge University Press, 1997).

13. Daniel C. Thomas, *The Helsinki Effect: International Norms, Human Rights, and the Demise of Communism* (Princeton, NJ: Princeton University Press, 2001).

14. Quoted in Michael Kubina and Manfred Wilke eds., *"Hart und kompromisslos durchgreifen." Die SED contra Polen 1980/81* (Berlin: Akademieverlag, 1995), 122f.
15. Quoted in *Cold War International History Project Bulletin* 5 (Washington, 1995): 121.
16. Archie Brown, *Aufstieg und Fall des Kommunismus* (Berlin: Propyläen, 2009), 648ff.
17. Jerry Hough, *Russia and the West: Gorbachev and the Politics of Reform*, 2nd ed. (New York: Simon & Schuster, 1990); Aurel Braun, ed., *The Soviet-East European Relationship in the Gorbachev Era* (Boulder, CO: Westview Press, 1990).
18. *SIPRI Yearbook* (Oxford: Oxford University Press, 1987), 124.
19. Michael R. Beschloss and Strobe Talbott, *Auf höchster Ebene. Das Ende des Kalten Krieges und die Geheimdiplomatie der Supermächte 1989–1991* (Düsseldorf: ECON, 1993), 176.
20. James F. Brown, *Surge to Freedom: The End of Communist Rule in Eastern Europe* (Durham, NC: Duke University Press, 1991).
21. Charles Gati, *Hungary and the Soviet Bloc* (Durham, NC: Duke University Press 1986); Jane Leftwich Curry and Luba Fajfer, eds., *Poland's Permanent Revolution: People vs. Elites, 1956 to the Present* (Washington, DC: American University Press, 1996).
22 Zoltán Tibor Pállinger, *Die politische Elite Ungarns im Systemwechsel 1985–1995* (Bern: P. Haupt, 1997).
23. Mieczyslaw Rakowski, *Es begann in Polen: Der Anfang vom Ende des Ostblocks* (Hamburg: Hoffmann und Campe, 1995).
24. Wolfgang Höpken, ed., *Revolution auf Raten: Bulgariens Weg zur Demokratie* (Munich: Oldenbourg, 1996).
25. Bernard Wheaton and Zdenek Kavan, *The Velvet Revolution: Czechoslovakia, 1988–1991* (Boulder, CO: Westview Press, 1992).
26. Anneli U. Gabanyi, *Systemwechsel in Rumänien: Von der Revolution zur Transformation* (Munich: Oldenbourg, 1998).
27. Overview: Michael Weithmann, ed., *Der ruhelose Balkan: Die Konfliktregionen Südosteuropas* (Munich: DTV, 1993).
28. Laura Silber and Allan Little, *Yugoslavia: Death of a Nation* (New York: Penguin), 1997.
29. For an overview, see Hannes Bahrmann and Christoph Links, *Chronik der Wende*, 2 vols. (Berlin: Ch. Links, 1994/95).
30. Figures according to Wolfgang Kenntemich, *Das war die DDR: Eine Geschichte des anderen Deutschland* (Berlin: Rowohlt, 1999), 223.
31. Quoted in Kenntemich, *Das war die DDR*, 224f.
32. Quoted in Kenntemich, *Das war die DDR*, 224f.
33. See Hans-Hermann Hertle, "Der Mauerfall," in Konrad Jarausch and Christoph Kleßmann, (eds.), *Mauerbau und Mauerfall* (Berlin: Ch. Links, 2002), 269–84; in particular: 278f.; Frederick Taylor, *Die Mauer, 1. August 1961 bis 9. November 1989* (Bonn: Bundeszentrale für politische Bildung, 2009), 500ff.
34. *Die Verträge zur Einheit Deutschlands* (Munich: DTV, 1990), 43ff.
35. Quoted in Gerhard Simon and Nadja Simon, *Verfall und Untergang des sowjetischen Imperiums* (Munich: DTV, 1993), 62.

## Select Bibliography

Bahrmann, Hannes, and Christoph Links. *Chronik der Wende*, 2 vols. Berlin: Ch. Links, 1994–5.
Brown, Archie. *Aufstieg und Fall des Kommunismus*. Berlin: Propyläen, 2009.

Creuzberger, Stefan, and Manfred Görtemaker, eds. *Gleichschaltung unter Stalin? Die Entwicklung der Parteien im östlichen Europa 1944–49*. Paderborn: F. Schöningh, 2002.

Curry, Jane Leftwich, and Luba Fajfer, eds. *Poland's Permanent Revolution: People vs. Elites, 1956 to the Present*. Washington, DC: American University Press, 1996.

Gati, Charles. *Failed Illusions: Moscow, Washington, Budapest, and the 1956 Hungarian Revolt*. Stanford, CA: Stanford University Press, 2006.

Golan, Galia. *Reform Rule in Czechoslovakia: The Dubcek Era 1968–1969*. New York: Cambridge University Press, 2008.

Jarausch, Konrad, and Christoph Kleßmann, eds. *Mauerbau und Mauerfall*. Berlin: Ch. Links, 2002.

Silber, Laura, and Allan Little. *Yugoslavia: Death of a Nation*. New York: Penguin, 1997.

Simon, Gerhard and Nadja Simon. *Verfall und Untergang des sowjetischen Imperiums*. Munich: DTV, 1993.

Slusser, Robert. *The Berlin Crisis of 1961: Soviet-American Relations and the Struggle for Power in the Kremlin, June—November 1961*. Baltimore, MD: Johns Hopkins University Press, 1973.

Weithmann, Michael, ed. *Der ruhelose Balkan: Die Konfliktregionen Südosteuropas*. Munich: DTV, 1993.

Williams, Kieran. *The Prague Spring and its Aftermath: Czechoslovak Politics, 1968–1970*. New York: Cambridge University Press, 1997.

Zaborowski, Marcin. *Germany, Poland and Europe: Conflict, Cooperation, and Europeanisation*. Manchester: Manchester University Press, 2004.

# CHAPTER 12

········································································

# LATIN AMERICA

········································································

## LARS SCHOULTZ

LATIN America did not play a significant independent role in the cold war. Of course the region's inhabitants were much more than passive pawns, as noted below, but in general Latin America served largely as a symbol—specifically, as an area where the United States enjoyed a long-established primacy and, therefore, where communist adversaries could attempt to tilt the bipolar balance of power. Or, as President Ronald Reagan explained about the subregion that bedeviled his administration:

> If Central America were to fall, what would the consequences be for our position in Asia, Europe, and for alliances such as NATO? If the United States cannot respond to a threat near our own borders, why should Europeans or Asians believe that we're seriously concerned about threats to them?... The national security of all the Americas is at stake in Central America. If we cannot defend ourselves there, we cannot expect to prevail elsewhere. Our credibility would collapse, our alliances would crumble, and the safety of our homeland would be put in jeopardy.[1]

This symbolic role was new, created in the aftermath of World War II. Latin America's modest participation in that war often focuses on Argentina's galling neutrality, but most of the region provided concrete assistance, and its cooperation was captured best by the US ambassador in Havana: "The Cuban Government and people are one hundred percent with us in the war and their measures of cooperation are whole-hearted and complete."[2] Two countries had fought alongside the Allies—Brazil in Italy and Mexico in the Philippines—but Latin America's primary role had been to provide raw materials and to guard against subversion, particularly in the Caribbean sea lanes to ship bauxite from the Guianas and in the countries within striking distance of the Panama Canal. There was nothing symbolic about this concrete assistance.

US officials expected a continuation of this support during the cold war, but now the nature of the challenge was different—*subversion* rather than a frontal attack. It was feared that Moscow-directed local communists would patiently consolidate their strength among important social groups, especially labor unions, and eventually seize power at a propitious moment. Such a seizure might cut off access to a few raw materials or make important sea lanes insecure, but the principal loss would be Washington's credibility, as the National Bipartisan Commission on Central America worried in 1984: "The triumph of hostile forces in what the Soviets call the 'strategic rear' of the United States would be read as a sign of US impotence." Commission chair Henry Kissinger added that "if we cannot manage Central America, it will be impossible to convince threatened nations in the Persian Gulf and in other places that we know how to manage the global equilibrium."[3]

No such threat appeared imminent in the early postwar days, but no one in Washington considered it far-fetched, given commonly held beliefs about Latin Americans and their chaotic political culture. As a member of the State Department's Policy Planning Staff explained, "When candid and not saying what he thinks a visiting American would like to hear, the average Asian or Latin-American laborer, farmer, or businessman will confide: 'We need a strong hand governing us.'" This echoed a long-standing theme expressed perfectly in a pre-war State Department memorandum, which pointed out that in Latin America "the United States supports, legally and financially, such men in power as are widely recognized to be dictators holding their power by force. In the present stage of cultural and political development of some of the republics this is not only inevitable but perhaps the only way toward stability which can be realistically envisaged."[4]

Not everyone thought this way. In April 1946 President Harry S. Truman reminded the Pan American Union (today's Organization of American States) that "the peoples of the Americas have a right to expect of the Pan American system that it show its validity by promoting those liberties and principles which the word 'democracy' implies." Warned in advance that his audience was far more concerned with economic development, Truman threw in a sentence agreeing that "the danger of war will never be completely wiped out until the economic ills which constitute the roots of war are eliminated." He then returned immediately to his central theme: "Democracy is the rallying cry today for free men everywhere in their struggles for a better life."[5]

This early postwar effort to promote Latin American democracy would soon be shelved, as would any significant US contribution to the region's economic development. Yet everyone in Washington understood why Latin America's leaders worried that declining postwar demand for the region's exports would push their economies into a tailspin, just as everyone remembered how the Depression had precipitated the downfall of nearly every one of the region's governments, democratic or not. The pressures were even greater in these early postwar days, for now Latin America was at the dawn of what soon would be called "the revolution of rising expectations." Mexico's Lázaro Cárdenas and Argentina's Juan Perón had led the way, and now, just as the Cold War was beginning, "all across Latin America the ancient oligarchies—landholders, Church, and Army—are losing their grip," wrote a young Arthur Schlesinger, Jr. "There is a ground swell of inarticulate mass dissatisfaction on the part of peons, Indians, miners, plantation workers, factory hands, classes held down past all endurance and now approaching a state of revolt."[6]

Fearful that this mass dissatisfaction could lead to a social revolution (as it had a generation earlier in Mexico) or to populist turmoil (as it had more recently in Argentina),

Latin American elites began pressing for US assistance with economic development. The need was obvious. After surveying pre-war caloric intake in thirteen Latin American countries, in 1946 the Food and Agriculture Organization reported that only five of the thirteen had enough food to provide a minimum level of nutrition. One of the fortunate five was Cuba, where a 1950 World Bank study mission reported that "living levels of the farmers, agricultural laborers, industrial workers, storekeepers, and others, are higher all along the line than for corresponding groups in other tropical countries and in nearly all other Latin American countries." But Cuba's per capita income at mid-century was only about half that of Mississippi, the poorest US state, and while Cuba may have been doing well by Latin American standards, that may have said more about Latin American standards than about Cuba. "Any figure for average *per capita* income is rather fictitious," the World Bank warned, "especially where—as in Cuba—there is a very wide gap between the incomes of a relatively few high-income receivers at the top and the mass of income receivers."[7]

This gap between the haves and the have-nots was especially obvious in the country-side, where a 1956 survey sponsored by Cuba's *Agrupación Católica Universitaria* found that "people are living in conditions of stagnation, misery, and desperation that are difficult to believe." The data reported in Cuba's 1953 census were also discomforting: it was not that an inside toilet was found in only 3 percent of rural homes, but that over half of all rural dwellings had neither an inside *nor* an outside toilet. Two-thirds of rural dwellings had dirt floors, only 9 percent had electricity, and only 2 percent had running water. All this combined to make the Cuban countryside a public health nightmare. The World Bank estimated that between 80–90 percent of rural children were infested with intestinal parasites, generally acquired by walking barefoot in animal feces; the fecal worms then work their way up through the bloodstream to lodge in the intestines, where they live on the food intended to nourish the child.[8]

What made this seem almost hopeless was that education, the primary route to improvement, was closed to most Latin Americans. Less than a quarter of Cuba's rural children attended school, for example, and the World Bank was also concerned about the island's urban children, less than half of whom attended school. It was especially worried about the absence of progress: "The general trend in the school system as a whole has been one of retrogression. A smaller proportion of the school-age children are enrolled today than a quarter of a century ago; the number of hours of instruction has been cut; the quality and morale of the teaching and supervisory force have gone down." The Bank argued that "unless and until drastic improvements are effected, the Cuban people cannot hope effectively to develop their country." It concluded: "It is impossible to be optimistic"—this in a country that was doing well by Latin American standards.

And so at the 1945 Chapultepec conference Mexico's foreign secretary warned a member of the US delegation about the revolution of rising expectations and indicated that "the way to the heart of the masses is through raising the standard of living."[9] While Latin America's economic development was the last topic Washington wanted to discuss, the US goal at the conference was to ensure a united hemisphere at the upcoming

San Francisco conference, and Washington, needing the region's twenty votes, did not want to appear insensitive to Latin American concerns.[10] Hence at Chapultepec the US delegation agreed not only to an Economic Charter of the Americas calling for greater cooperation, but also to the creation of an Inter-American Economic and Social Council (ECOSOC) to promote the region's development. When Latin America's diplomats kept prodding at San Francisco, the United States agreed to a conference before the end of 1945 to implement Chapultepec's Economic Charter.

The pressure of postwar crises in Europe and Washington's time-consuming dispute with Peronist Argentina delayed a conference on this or any other topic until mid-1947, by which time the cold war had seized center stage in US foreign policy and relegated economic development to a secondary role; hence the meeting's title: the Inter-American Conference for the Maintenance of Continental Peace and Security. Traveling to Rio de Janeiro, President Truman gave conferees his "solemn assurances that we in Washington are not oblivious to the needs of increased economic collaboration within the family of American nations and that these problems will be approached by us with the utmost good faith and with increased vigor." Then he let the other shoe drop. At precisely the moment when his advisors were meeting with Europeans to draw up the Marshall Plan, Truman told Latin America's leaders that the United States was obliged "to differentiate between the urgent need for rehabilitation of war-shattered areas and the problems of development elsewhere."[11]

That left only Washington's topic, regional security, on the table at Rio, where the conferees produced the cold war's first mutual security pact, the Inter-American Treaty of Reciprocal Assistance. It specified that "an armed attack by any State against an American State shall be considered as an attack against all the American States and, consequently, each one of the said Contracting Parties undertakes to assist in meeting the attack."[12] By this time George Kennan had sent his Long Telegram from Moscow, Winston Churchill had delivered his iron curtain speech in Missouri, President Truman had gone before a joint session of Congress to request aid for Greece and Turkey, and Kennan, in his widely circulated "X" article in *Foreign Affairs*, had argued for the containment of communism "by the adroit and vigilant application of counter-force at a series of constantly shifting geographical and political points." Soon the assistant secretary of state for Latin America warned that "the basic situation in the hemisphere today is this. The 21 American states together face the challenge of Communist political aggression against the hemisphere."[13]

This was also when the Truman administration gave up any lingering thoughts about promoting democracy in Latin America. The public announcement came from Louis Halle, a member of State Department's Policy Planning Staff, whose 1950 *Foreign Affairs* article, "On A Certain Impatience with Latin America," argued that 19th century Latin Americans had won their independence at a time when they "were quite unready to assume the responsibility of self-government [and] the result was a sordid chaos out of which Latin America has still not finally emerged." Instead of democracy, Latin America had developed "a tradition of political behavior marked by intemperance, intransige-ance [sic], flamboyance and the worship of strong men." The last of these four characteristics made democracy impossible. "Worship of the 'man on horseback' (through self-identification) is another manifestation of immaturity. It is characteristic of adolescence, this admiration for the ruthless hero who tramples down all opposition, makes himself superior to law, and is irresistible to passionate women who serve his pleasure in droves."[14]

Given this perspective, Latin America's military became Washington's vehicle for meeting the communist challenge, and the policy focus therefore turned to military aid. Convincing the public to pay for this aid had not been possible in war-weary 1946, the year Truman asked Congress to pass an Inter-American Military Cooperation Act, and as late as 1949 Congress was still refusing to authorize a penny for Latin America in the $1.3 billion Mutual Defense Assistance Act. The outbreak of the Korean War raised the overall sense of anxiety in Washington, however, and the National Security Council (NSC) had warned even before the shooting began that "Communists in Latin America have the capability of severely weakening any war effort of the United States by interfering with the source and transit of strategic materials, by damaging vital installations, and by fomenting unrest and instability." Then came the punchline: "In the event of war, the main deterrent to execution of this capability is the ability of the security forces of the Latin American nations." Although a young Representative John F. Kennedy still argued that aid was unnecessary because Latin America was "not in the line of the Soviet advance," the 1951 Mutual Security Act contained $38 million in military aid to Latin America; the following year it was $52 million, and for the balance of the 1950s the need for internal stability to deter communist subversion became the cold war ace that trumped both economic development and the promotion of democracy.[15]

This policy of supporting military leaders reflected traditional thinking about Hispanic culture and Latin American reality. Reporting on his 1955 goodwill visit to Central America and the Caribbean, Vice President Richard Nixon observed that "Latinos had shown a preference for a dictatorial form of government rather than a democracy," and similar statements about Latin America's undemocratic culture pervade State Department documents during the Eisenhower years—from a lower-level analysis referring to "the Latin penchant for *personalismo*," to the president telling British Prime Minister Harold Macmillan that "the average Cuban sugar worker wants to receive his earnings in cash and go to the store, buy a white *guayabera*, white shoes, a bottle of rum and go to a dance." Secretary of State John Foster Dulles believed a central task of US diplomats in Latin America was "to pat them a little bit and make them think you are fond of them."[16]

This thinking was reinforced by the prevailing view of Latin America's geostrategic insignificance. In 1946, just weeks after Kennan had sent his Long Telegram and at a time when it seemed probable that Republicans would soon regain the White House, publisher Henry Luce offered Dulles the pages of *Life* magazine to discuss foreign policy. Focusing on the emerging cold war, Dwight D. Eisenhower's future secretary of state accepted Kennan's view of Moscow's relentless effort to expand, adding nuance by dividing the Soviet worldview into three zones—inner, middle, and outer. The Soviets were at the moment consolidating their power in the inner zone surrounding Russia, Dulles argued, while biding their time in the middle zone, which included the oil-rich Middle East and

Western Europe, and avoiding commitments in the outer zone of new nations being created in Asia and Africa, together with Latin America. These outer-zone states needed
Washington's careful watching, however, for they were engaged in "a tremendous surge
in the direction of popular government by peoples who have practically no capacity for
self-government and indeed are like children in facing this problem." To Dulles, "this
presents the Communists with an ideal situation to exploit."[17]

That is what appeared to be occurring in Guatemala when Dulles became secretary of
state in early 1953. International communism "has achieved a high degree of covert control over the reformist regime of President Arbenz," warned Louis Halle. Guatemala
itself was unimportant, but it could serve as a launching pad: "The real and direct threat
that Guatemala poses for her neighbors is that of political subversion through the kind
of across-the-borders intrigue that is a normal feature of the Central American scene.
The danger is of Communist contagion."[18]

That danger was exaggerated. Guatemala's 1944 October Revolution ousting dictator
Jorge Ubico had been led by middle-class reformers, including nationalist, modernizing
elements within the military. They had handed the presidency to Juan José Arévalo, an
educator, and, as Professor Robert Trudeau has demonstrated, "Arévalo's program was
Guatemala's equivalent of the New Deal." He was succeeded by Colonel Jacobo Arbenz
Guzmán, who launched an agrarian reform that affected US corporate interests, most
famously the United Fruit Company, which maintained exceptionally close ties to the
Eisenhower administration and whose lobbyists encouraged Washington to think of the
Arbenz government as communist dominated. The United States then moved to overthrow Guatemala's democratic government, but Trudeau warns that "it is important not
to overestimate the effect of US efforts at the time, nor to underestimate the role of
domestic forces." With its incorporation of the poor into the political system and with its
redistribution of property, the October Revolution challenged Guatemala's *domestic*
structure of privilege, and the privileged fought back. "The success of the counterrevolution is probably due far more to these domestic dynamics than to international pressures," Trudeau concludes.[19]

So what happened? In 1954 US-backed forces commanded by Colonel Carlos Castillo
Armas attacked from a base in Honduras, and President Arbenz capitulated. A few
months later Secretary Dulles explained that "for several years international communism has been probing here and there for nesting places in the Americas. It finally chose
Guatemala as a spot which it could turn into an official base from which to breed subversion which would extend to other American Republics." Fortunately, Dulles continued,
"there were loyal citizens of Guatemala who, in the face of terrorism and violence and
against what seemed insuperable odds, had the courage and the will to eliminate the
traitorous tools of foreign despots."[20]

With that Guatemala moved off the US foreign policy agenda, although President
Eisenhower revived it during the 1954 off-year election campaign by repeatedly pointing
with pride to this Republican victory over communism. An election also occurred in
Guatemala. With all political parties banned, with the military staffing the polling places,
and with the ballot not secret, the results were 486,000 for Castillo Armas, 400 opposed.

Now cast as a democratic leader, the colonel was invited to visit the United States, where he received a hero's welcome, including honorary degrees from Colombia and Fordham universities and an appearance before a subcommittee of the House Select Committee on Communist Aggression, where he warned that "we have merely won the first battle in a long war. Our most complicated and most serious difficulties are still ahead." The State Department added that "what was mistakenly considered in some quarters as a 'local Guatemalan Communist orientation' was in truth a coldly calculated, armed conspiracy of international communism to extend the system of the Soviets to a small and strategically located country in the hemisphere."[21]

Four decades later, a Guatemalan indigenous leader would receive the Nobel Peace Prize for challenging this interpretation—for explaining why everyday Guatemalans opposed the series of savage dictators inaugurated by Castillo Armas and for denouncing the murder of tens of thousands of Guatemalans by US-backed, military-dominated governments between 1954 and the 1990s. In 1999 President Bill Clinton would fly to Guatemala to apologize for underwriting these decades of bloodletting in the name of anti-communism. But after 1954 the primary goal of cold war US policy toward Latin America was to ensure that friends like Castillo Armas held power.[22]

And what about economic development? Supporting repressive military dictators may have been considered necessary, given the global stakes and Latin America's undemocratic political culture, but almost everyone agreed with what Harry S. Truman had said of Greece and Turkey—that the odds favored communism wherever people were destitute. The first sentences of the basic Latin American policy document of the Eisenhower years, NSC 144/1, laid out the problem: "There is an increasing popular demand for immediate improvement in the low living standards of the masses, with the result that most Latin American governments are under intense domestic political pressures to increase production and to diversify their economies. A realistic and constructive approach to this need which recognizes the importance of bettering conditions for the general population is essential to arrest the drift in the area toward radical and nationalistic regimes."[23]

The United States was not up to this challenge in the 1950s. A few State Department officials were beginning to argue that Washington would eventually have to confront the region's underdevelopment in order to avoid future Guatemalas, but any serious attack on poverty would require substantial amounts of money, and that would jeopardize the administration's bedrock commitment to "fiscal responsibility." NSC 144/1 was adopted in early 1953 on the specific understanding that "approval did not constitute an endorsement of any special program of military and economic assistance for Latin America, which will be subject to review in the light of (1) the priority of... Latin America in relation to programs for other foreign areas and to programs for domestic security, and (2) the overall objective of achieving a balanced Federal budget." Instead, NSC 144/1 specified that the State Department "assist in the economic development of Latin America by encouraging Latin American governments to recognize that the bulk of the capital required for their economic development can best be supplied by private enterprise."[24]

While private enterprise kindled economic growth, Washington needed to insure against another Guatemala. Unwilling to attack the disease, the Eisenhower administration focused upon suppressing the symptoms—upon supporting anti-communist dictators who could maintain order. The minutes of a 1954 NSC meeting record Treasury Secretary George Humphrey as asserting that "a strong base for Communism exists in Latin America. He said that wherever a dictator was replaced, Communists gained. In his opinion, the US should back strong men in Latin American governments." One of Eisenhower's special assistants, Nelson Rockefeller, spoke up to challenge this view, and the president registered "his agreement with Mr. Rockefeller that in the long run the United States must back democracies."[25] But given Washington's far more pressing problems elsewhere, a policy of supporting dictators made good sense. Since no one can prove a counterfactual, we will never know whether these authoritarian governments would have existed without US support. All we know for certain is that they had Washington's support, and that supporting a dictator was a rational choice for anyone who believed, as so many in Washington did, that Latin American culture was inclined to authoritarianism—inclined to admire, in Halle's words, "the ruthless hero who tramples down all opposition, makes himself superior to law, and is irresistible to passionate women."

The best example of this policy was Cuba, where Fulgencio Batista's 1952 coup, executed without Washington's knowledge, converted the island from a civilian democracy into a military dictatorship. Three days before the coup, the Pentagon had signed a military aid agreement with Batista's civilian predecessor, and now the Department of Defense acted as if nothing had happened, proposing to send a seven-member Military Assistance Advisory Group to Havana. The embassy protested, noting that thirty-eight US military personnel were already in Cuba and that "every one [sic] is aware of the support which the Cuban armed forces have received from our own armed forces before and since the *coup d'état.*" Ambassador Willard Beaulac, a career foreign service officer, repeatedly emphasized that "the presence of this large number of American military personnel is very noticeable to persons in Cuba," and he reminded Washington that "it is essential that our military help to Cuba be provided in the most discreet manner possible." Another embassy warning came in mid-1953, a few weeks after a group of rebels led by Fidel Castro had assaulted the Moncada army barracks at Santiago: "The arms supplied by the United States to Batista's Government are regarded by a segment of the population as weapons to attack rather than defend democracy and to maintain an oppressive regime in power."[26] Washington ignored every one of these messages.

Meanwhile, in late 1956 Nikita Khrushchev had made his famous "We will bury you" boast to Western diplomats. That was not seen as an idle threat, especially when the Soviets won the race into space a few months later, and Sputnik's success occurred at a time when several of Latin America's reliable military governments were falling. "President Carlos Castillo Armas, of Guatemala, has just died of an assassin's bullet, fired by a palace guard who stood revealed as an acknowledged Communist," announced Representative Gardner Withrow to his House colleagues in mid-1957. "Just previously, President Jose A. Remón, of Panama, was murdered, followed by President Anastasio Somozo [sic], of Nicaragua. These three were not only devoted friends and allies of the

United States, but each was bitterly anti-Communist. The pattern is too widespread to be purely localized political unrest."[27]

It was more than a series of assassinations. From Argentina's replacement of a military junta by civilian Arturo Frondizi, to the fall of Colombia's General Rojas Pinilla and Venezuela's Colonel Pérez Jimenéz, Latin America was in the midst of what journalist Tad Szulc labeled the Twilight of the Tyrants. "Indications are that democracy...is here to stay in Latin America," Szulc predicted. While acknowledging that the dictators' excesses had hastened their own downfall, Szulc argued that "the fundamental factor bringing the dictatorial era toward an end in Latin America was the rapid growth of political consciousness on all class and educational levels in the last decade or so. It accompanied the powerful economic and social ferment of the postwar period."[28]

If this was correct—if dictators were now out of fashion—what did that imply for US policy? One answer came from President Eisenhower's brother, Milton, who after two fact-finding missions confirmed a 1953 NSC report: "Our postwar policies of rebuilding a sound Europe gave rise to [Latin] American charges that the United States, friendly to them only during the war years, was again neglecting them. Latin Americans felt that they should at least have received a larger share of aid."[29] By the beginning of his second term President Eisenhower had been convinced to pursue an active US role in Latin America's economic development, but that ran counter to the view of Treasury Secretary George Humphrey: three years earlier, just after Milton Eisenhower's first report, an NSC staffer had been sent to sound out Humphrey on an aid program, and returned with an adamant "No." "He is utterly convinced that a soft policy and a policy of winning Latin America by spending money on them is not the way to go about it. He believes the way to control Latin America is by a tough hard-hitting policy which would envisage, if necessary, the use of force." Now, three years later, the president wrote Humphrey a personal note underscoring that "*protection of our own interests*" required more than supporting dictators while lecturing about the transformative power of private investment. "We must at the same time understand that the spirit of nationalism, coupled with a deep hunger for some betterment in physical conditions and living standards, creates a critical situation."[30]

Humphrey soon resigned, clearing away the principal obstacle to fresh thinking about Latin America. But while Milton Eisenhower may have convinced his brother to promote economic development, there was little sense of urgency—after all, this was the cold war's outer zone—and in late 1957 Secretary Dulles reported that "we see no likelihood at the present time of communism getting into control of the political institutions of any of the American Republics."[31] No concrete policy change had occurred before Vice President Richard Nixon set out on his 1958 South American goodwill tour. The first stops were uneventful, but the vice president faced a group of protesters in Lima, one of whom, Nixon reported, "let fly a wad of spit which caught me full in the face." Then he flew to Caracas where, five months earlier, Venezuelans had finally been able to free themselves from the decade-long clutch of Colonel Marcos Pérez Jiménez. As a final slap in the face of Venezuela's democrats, the Eisenhower administration had opened the nation's doors to both Pérez Jiménez and his detested secret police chief, Pedro Estrada—"as vicious a man hunter as Hitler had ever employed," to use Hubert Herring's apt characterization.[32]

Within minutes of Nixon's arrival, the Caracas embassy sent Washington the first of several flash cables reporting that "a large and unfriendly crowd met the Vice President and his party at the airport." That was an understatement. Nixon himself recalled that, at the airport, "hundreds of people were there on the balcony spitting down on us as we stood listening to their national anthem." Then, the cables continued, on the way into town Nixon's motorcade was blocked by a group "made up of ruffians and riffraff and it was in an ugly mood. The mob closed in on the vehicles in which the vice president and his party were traveling, and the Venezuelan police escort ran. The windows were broken out of the car in which Mr. Nixon was riding," and a *Life* photographer snapped pictures for next week's cover story: demonstrators spitting on the vice president of the United States of America.[33]

Nixon's driver eventually nudged his limousine across the highway median and raced down the wrong side of a divided highway to the US ambassador's residence. There the vice president remained sequestered until he left for a hero's welcome home and a report to the National Security Council, which began by warning that "we should all get clearly in mind that the threat of Communism in Latin America was greater today than ever before in history." A few years later Nixon acknowledged that "not all the rioters, of course, were Communists. But this misses the major point: there can be no doubt that the riots were Communist-planned, Communist-led, and Communist-controlled." Nearly everyone agreed, with the lower levels of the State Department informing Secretary Dulles that "the pattern of organization and of slogans in all cases points to Communist inspiration and direction."[34]

Then Congress decided to solicit the views of a broader circle, including former Costa Rican President José Figueres, who argued that "people cannot spit on a foreign policy, which is what they meant to do." Of course, he agreed, "spitting is a despicable practice, when it is physically performed. But what about moral spitting? When your Government invited Pedro Estrada, the Himmler of the Western Hemisphere, to be honored in Washington, did you not spit on the faces of all Latin American democrats?" At the same time, Brazilian President Juselino Kubitschek wrote to President Eisenhower to emphasize that "the problem of underdevelopment will have to be solved." His message was reinforced by a third leading Latin American democrat, Argentina's Arturo Frondizi: "The hour of concrete decisions has come," he warned Congress during his 1959 state visit to Washington. "To leave an American country in stagnation is as dangerous as an attack coming from an extra-continental power." Sandwiched between the Nixon trip and the Frondizi visit was a third fact-finding mission by the president's brother. "Now I must add a note of urgency," Milton Eisenhower reported.[35]

By this time the Eisenhower administration was struggling to cope with a new problem: the Twilight of the Tyrants had reached Cuba, where Fulgencio Batista had been ousted on the first day of 1959. A year earlier the embassy had seen no cause for alarm—some urban unrest and a few armed rebels in the eastern mountains, but "the revolutionary elements are disorganized, splintered and lack a program with public appeal."

Perhaps, but as one revolutionary combatant titled a chapter of her memoir, it was "a generation on the march," with the opposition ranging across a wide social, political and economic panorama. Soon these "revolutionary elements" had chased Batista out of the country.[36] Louisiana Senator Allen Ellender saw no reason to worry: "The Cubans are a good people. They are very sensitive and easily aroused, but I have a feeling that they would listen to reason. The Cubans look upon us as big brothers." The US embassy agreed, and so did the Pentagon.[37]

How little Washington understood; how quickly everything changed. Overnight, this Caribbean island went from banana republic to social revolution.[38] "There was something on Cuba every five minutes," complained Dulles's exasperated successor as secretary of state, Christian Herter. While he and President Eisenhower tried at first to accommodate the new revolutionary regime, they soon gave up and authorized preparation for the Bay of Pigs invasion. By early 1960 the revolution's economic reforms had crippled US investors, its non-aligned foreign policy had included an alarming trade agreement with the Soviet Union, and its hostile rhetoric had angered the president. "There is a limit to what the United States in self-respect can endure," Eisenhower explained as he closed the US embassy, and when he handed John Kennedy the keys to the White House three weeks later, he also passed along an admonition: "We cannot let the present government there go on."[39]

That was in 1961. Twenty years later Eisenhower and Kennedy were both dead and buried, yet Castro was boasting that "we will still be here in *another* 20 years." Not if president-elect Ronald Reagan and Secretary of State Alexander Haig had anything to do with it. During the 1980 campaign Reagan had proposed a blockade of Cuba, and now, at the first meeting of his national security team, the new secretary of state suggested going one step further: an invasion. Finding little support for the idea, Haig pulled aside his principal deputy, Robert "Bud" McFarlane, and gave him his first assignment: "I want to go after Cuba, Bud. I want you to get everyone together and give me a plan for doing it."[40] That was in 1981. Twenty years later Ronald Reagan was dying of Alzheimer's disease, Alexander Haig was a semi-retired consultant, the cold war was a fading memory, and Cuba's revolutionary generation was refusing to say "uncle."

The half-century US policy toward revolutionary Cuba is a lengthy story in itself, but the island's broader significance for Latin America defied exaggeration during the final three decades of the cold war. In Washington, the immediate impact of the revolution was to convince any remaining doubters of the need to change the policy of leaving Latin America's economic development to market forces. Now almost everyone agreed that trickle-down development was simply too slow to halt the radicalization of the region's awakening masses.

Something also needed to be done about the region's economic elites, too many of whom remained adamantly opposed to substantial reforms—"Latin America's landed oligarchy does not understand the gravity of its own situation," Arthur Schlesinger, Jr., told JFK. Like other members of the New Frontier, Schlesinger was convinced that the region needed a "*middle-class revolution* where the processes of economic modernization carry the new urban middle class into power and produce, along with it, such necessities of modern technical society as constitutional government, honest public administration, a responsible party system, a rational land system, an efficient system of taxation, mass education, social mobility, etc.... The problem for US policy is to do what it can *to hasten the middle-class revolution*." Castro offered the Cuban alternative—a working-class revolution at home along with a promise that his government would help like-minded Latin Americans to "convert the Cordillera of the Andes into the Sierra Maestra of the American Continent."[41]

A new "development" bureaucracy was required. In 1961 the Mutual Security Act was replaced by the Foreign Assistance Act, and to administer US programs an aptly named Agency for International Development (AID ) replaced what had been an equally aptly named Mutual Security Agency. AID's development work was soon supplemented by a host of cooperative public and government-funded private institutions, ranging from the Peace Corps to the AFL-CIO's American Institute for Free Labor Development. To ensure that communists were kept at bay while the United States helped improve living conditions and defused Latin American radicalism, an already-elaborate set of security institutions was strengthened. The Pentagon dramatically increased the size of its Military Assistance Advisory Groups stationed throughout the region, it expanded the US military schools such as the Army's School of the Americas to accommodate officers and now even enlisted personnel, and it sent "civic action" teams of US military engineers to build roads, to string electrical lines, and to construct health clinics in areas thought vulnerable to insurrection.

These economic and military assistance institutions constitute the enduring legacy of the cold war's second decade; what passed quickly into history was the Kennedy elan. When Latin America's economic progress seemed painfully slow and when the war in Vietnam sapped a generation's optimism, stability once again became the holy grail of the Johnson, Nixon, and Ford administrations. Armed rebel groups were emerging in much of the hemisphere, confronting Washington with the problem identified in 1957 by Representative Gardner Withrow: "It is no longer possible for us to distinguish between quarreling among political groups and what we now know to be international Communism tactics."[42] That conceptual problem faced all cold war administrations, and not one of them could resolve it. Instead, Washington provided both economic aid and military assistance, and simply assumed that someone, somehow could separate the instability caused by rising expectations (the people who deserved economic aid) from the instability caused by communist adventurism (the people who deserved to be shot). The assumption was unrealistic, as the insurgency in El Salvador during the 1970s and 1980s demonstrated: from 1932 to 1979, every Salvadoran president had also been a military officer, and in that country, as in so many others, the separating had been performed by the US-trained and US-armed Salvadoran military. By the time this flaw in the logic of cold war US policy was recognized, tens of thousands of Salvadorans were dead, at least a million displaced, and hundreds of thousands had fled to the United States.[43]

Harkening back to 1950s thinking, many in Washington attributed this lamentable outcome to El Salvador's blood-thirsty political culture. Jeane Kirkpatrick, the architect of the Reagan administration's policy, repeated in the late 1970s and early 1980s what Louis Halle had written in 1950: "El Salvador's political culture…emphasizes strength and *machismo*."[44] While no one could deny the brutality of the Salvadoran military, still today we know very little about that nation's political culture—Professor Kirkpatrick, for one, had never set foot in El Salvador before offering her self-confident assessment. The Salvadoran military might have massacred the peasantry without US support (that was what it did in 1931–2), but all we know for certain is that the United States used its military assistance program to provide more than arms and training; Washington also passed along a rigid bipolar national security mentality to Latin America's militaries reinforced by US *economic* assistance: by 1964 AID had begun training its own personnel at the Army's Special Warfare School at Fort Bragg, and by 1966 AID's police assistance bureau, the Office of Public Safety, was spending 38 percent of the entire economic assistance budget for Latin America to provide counter-insurgency training to police in every country except Cuba.[45]

Washington's cold war fixation on anti-communist stability in Latin America eventually ran aground on the political shoals surrounding the Vietnam debacle, the Watergate scandal, and the destruction of Chilean democracy. Earlier, in the 1950s, no one in Washington raised an eyebrow over US aid to Guatemala, where the United States had only a small Point Four technical assistance program until the overthrow of the Arbenz government; then between 1954 and 1955, at a time when Treasury secretary Humphrey was vetoing aid to the rest of Latin America, Guatemala's aid jumped from $463,000 to $10,708,000. This funding pattern was repeated a decade later in Brazil, immediately after a US-encouraged military coup: from $15 million in the 1964 fiscal year (which ended three months after the coup), AID expenditures jumped to $122 million in 1965 and did not dip below that level until the 1970s. Along with the debacle of Vietnam, that was enough for Senator Frank Church, who captured a growing mood with the title of his 1971 speech: "Farewell to Foreign Aid: A Liberal Takes Leave."[46]

The repressive military government of Brazil was quickly "graduated" from US economic assistance programs, and the Nixon-Ford administration attempted to mollify its critics with AID's "New Directions," which placed a renewed emphasis on assisting the poor. But in practice the focus simply shifted from supporting Brazil's generals, who no longer needed US help, to backstopping the Chilean military. This time the chosen economic aid mechanism was food. Less than a month after the 1973 military coup against the democratic government of Salvador Allende, the Nixon administration gave General Augusto Pinochet a $24 million loan to purchase US wheat, which was eight times the total commodity credit to Chile during all three Allende years. The next year Chile, with 3 percent of Latin America's population, received 48 percent of the region's Food for Peace shipments. As aid to Pinochet skyrocketed, the revelations of US covert action against the Allende government became a well-documented subject of public discussion—revelations such as Henry Kissinger's 1970 remark that "I don't see why we need to stand by and watch a country go Communist due to the irresponsibility of its own people," and Nixon's instruction to CIA Director Richard Helms immediately after Allende's election: "Make the economy scream."[47]

President Nixon's forced resignation left Gerald Ford to answer the questions. With Kissinger serving as his coach, Ford dismissed a reporter's query about covert action against the Allende government by arguing that it was not only good for the United States but also "in the best interest of the people of Chile."[48] By this time—the mid-1970s—the general public's support for cold war US foreign policy had reached rock bottom. The principal problem had been Vietnam, of course, but Vietnam could now be consigned to history, while Chile seemed to be a mortification without end. In 1973 the Senate published its hearings on International Telephone and Telegraph's effort to prevent Allende from assuming office. In 1974 the House surveyed the wreckage, and the following year a Senate select committee (the Church Committee) issued two especially damaging reports. One was titled *Alleged Assassination Plots Involving Foreign Leaders*, which included a revealing discussion of CIA plotting that led to the 1970 murder of the commander-in-chief of Chile's army, General René Schneider, a resolute anti-communist whose only offense had been to oppose a military coup to pre-empt an Allende presidency. The second committee report, *Covert Action in Chile 1963–1973*, began: "Covert United States involvement in Chile in the decade between 1963 and 1973 was extensive and continuous."[49]

In mid-1976 presidential candidate Jimmy Carter promised that his administration would "restore the moral authority of this country in its conduct of foreign policy," and no one was surprised to hear the new president assert that "our commitment to human rights must be absolute," nor to hear his conviction that "human rights is the soul of our foreign policy."[50] In the Kennedy era, dictators such as Nicaragua's Anastasio Somoza had wagered that Washington's fear of communism was stronger than any desire for reform, and they had won; not so in the post-Vietnam era, as Jeane Kirkpatrick observed: "What did the Carter administration do in Nicaragua? *It brought down the Somoza regime.*" The Carter State Department "*acted* repeatedly and at critical junctures to weaken the government of Anastasio Somoza and to strengthen his opponents."[51] Kirkpatrick was correct. While the Nicaraguan people were responsible for Somoza's downfall, since the mid-1930s Washington had helped to keep his family in power while turning a blind eye to its repression of the opposition and its looting of the economy. Meanwhile, wrote Professor John Booth, "the government spent less of its budget on health and education than any other nation in the region."[52]

Then in the late 1970s the Carter administration pulled the plug. All sides in Washington continued to believe, as Theodore Roosevelt had asserted in his 1904 corollary to the Monroe Doctrine, that the United States had an obligation to act against "chronic wrongdoing" in Latin America. The post-Vietnam question was the identity of the wrongdoers. To the Carter administration, the wrongdoers were repressive dictators violating the human rights of their citizens, many of whom were caught up in the revolution of rising expectations. But after four years the Democrats lost the White House to Ronald Reagan, who thought the wrongdoers were communists: "Let's not delude ourselves," Reagan told a 1980 campaign audience, "the Soviet Union underlies all the unrest that is going on. If they weren't engaged in this game of dominoes, there wouldn't be any hot spots in the world." The cold warriors were back for one last stand, elected by a public that rejected

President Carter's 1977 assertion that "we are now free of that inordinate fear of communism which once led us to embrace any dictator who joined us in that fear."[53]

At exactly the time that this battle line was being drawn in Washington, Central American instability was escalating steadily, and the dispute over causality characterized policy debates. Ambassador Robert White spoke for those who attributed the instability to poverty and rising expectations, telling Congress that "the guerrilla groups, the revolutionary groups, almost without exception began as associations of teachers, associations of labor unions, campesino unions, or parish organizations which were organized for the definite purpose of getting a schoolhouse up." In contrast, the Reagan State Department attributed the instability to communist adventurism, asserting that Cuba, Moscow's proxy, "is now trying to unite the radical left, commit it to the use of violence, train it in warfare and terrorism, and attempt to use it to destroy existing governments and replace them with Marxist-Leninist regimes."[54]

Since neither side could prove its case to the satisfaction of the other, US policy became a function of how much money a determined administration could wring out of an ambivalent Congress to prop up anti-communist governments in El Salvador, Honduras, and Guatemala, and to support anti-Sandinista rebels in Nicaragua. This required all the rhetorical skill of President Reagan, who lamented that "many of our citizens don't fully understand the seriousness of the situation, so let me put it bluntly: There is a war in Central America that is being fueled by the Soviets and the Cubans. They are arming, training, supplying, and encouraging a war to subjugate another nation to communism, and that nation is El Salvador. The Soviets and the Cubans are operating from a base called Nicaragua. And this is the first real Communist aggression on the American mainland." In what many considered a prelude to direct military action in Central America, a few months later the United States invaded the Caribbean mini-state of Grenada, and President Reagan again went before the TV cameras to explain why: Grenada, he said, "was a Soviet-Cuban colony, being readied as a major military bastion to export terror and undermine democracy. We got there just in time."[55]

Although the Reagan administration never received the Congressional green light it requested, for eight years it obtained enough support from a hopelessly divided Congress to continue the fight against rebels in El Salvador. But a Congressional ban on the CIA's effort to overthrow Nicaragua's Sandinista government prompted the administration to embark upon an illegal clandestine funding operation that led to the Iran-Contra scandal.[56] In the end the Washington body count was substantial, forcing President George H.W. Bush to grant presidential pardons to the principals. By that time the Soviet Union had disappeared, Cuban adventurism was a fading memory, and Central America's major wars had ended, leaving only the chronic insurgency in Guatemala and a devastated human landscape in El Salvador and Nicaragua, where an estimated 110,000 citizens had been killed in the two conflicts—twice the number lost by the United States in Vietnam. Economic aid quickly fell and military aid declined to virtually nothing, at least until the Pentagon found a new role in combating drug trafficking. With the cold war over, Latin America once again moved off the front pages and out of Washington's consciousness.

# NOTES

1. Address before a Joint Session of the Congress, April 27, 1983, *Public Papers of the Presidents of the United States* (hereafter *PPP*), 605, 607.

2. George S. Messersmith to Spruille Braden, January 15, 1942, Folder "Correspondence Diplomatic 1942 M-R," Box 8, Spruille Braden Papers, Columbia University.

3. *Report of the National Bipartisan Commission on Central America* (Washington, DC: Department of State, January 1984), 93; Kissinger, *Public Opinion* 6 (April–May 1983), 54.

4. John Paton Davies, *Foreign and Other Affairs* (New York: W.W. Norton, 1964), 57; Harley A. Notter to Laurence Duggan, September 12, 1939, 710.11/2417 1/2, Record Group (hereafter RG) 59, National Archives (hereafter NA).

5. Speech to the Pan American Union, Washington, DC, April 15, 1946, *PPP*, 200–2.

6. Arthur M. Schlesinger, Jr., "Good Fences Make Good Neighbors," *Fortune* 54 (August 1946): 167–8.

7. Food and Agriculture Organization of the United Nations, *Proposals for a World Food Board and World Food Survey*, Combined Reprint, Washington, DC, October 1, 1946, unpaginated Figure 1, opposite page 24; International Bank for Reconstruction and Development (IBRD), *Report on Cuba* (Baltimore, MD: Johns Hopkins University Press, 1951), 39–40, 42, 57, 65.

8. Melchor W. Gastón, Oscar A. Echeverría, and René F. de la Huerta, *Por que reforma agraria* (Havana: Agrupación Católica Universitaria, n.d. but probably 1957), typescript, 6. (This unpublished study represents the findings of a sample survey of 1,000 households conducted over a ten-month period beginning in November 1956.) Cuba, Tribunal Superior Electoral, Oficina Nacional de los Censos Demográfico y Electoral, *Censos de población, viviendas y electoral: informe general* (Havana: P. Fernández, 1955), 209, 213; US Department of Commerce, Bureau of Foreign Commerce, *Investment in Cuba: Basic Information for United States Businessmen* (Washington, DC: Government Printing Office, 1956), 187. See also Harry T. Oshima, "A New Estimate of the National Income and Product of Cuba in 1953," *Food Research Institute Studies* 2/3 (November 1961): 214; Juan Felipe Leal, "Las clases sociales en Cuba en vísperas de la revolución," *Revista Mexicana de Ciencia Política* 19/74 (October–December 1973): 99–109; Vladimir Akulai and Domingo Rodríguez Fragoso, "La situación socio-económica del campesinado cubano antes de la Revolución," *Islas* 54 (May–August 1976): 56–80; Lowry Nelson, *Rural Cuba* (Minneapolis: University of Minnesota Press, 1950), esp. ch. 11; *Report on Cuba*, 441.

9. Cuba: *Censos de población, viviendas y electoral*, 99, 143; *Report on Cuba*, 404, 18, 434. Mexico: Memorandum of Conversation with Mexican Foreign Minister Ezequiel Padilla, by Merwin L. Bohan, Technical Officer of the US Delegation, Mexico City, January 29, 1945, *Foreign Relations of the United States* (hereafter *FRUS*), 1945, 9:72–3.

10. Crucial in 1945, Latin America's votes would continue to be important throughout the cold war—in 1955 the permanent US representative to the United Nations worried "that if we did not have the Latins with us in the voting processes in the UN, the United States would simply have to get out." Ambassador Henry Cabot Lodge in minutes of NSC meeting, March 10, 1955, *FRUS* 1955–7, 6:615.

11. *PPP*, September 2, 1947, 431.

12. Inter-American Treaty of Reciprocal Assistance, 62 *Statutes at Large* 1681, September 2, 1947.

13. "X" [pseud. George F. Kennan], "The Sources of Soviet Conduct," *Foreign Affairs* 25/4 (July 1947): 566–82; Edward Miller, speech to the Pan American Society of New England, Boston, April 26, 1950, *Department of State Bulletin* (hereafter *DOSB*), May 15, 1950, 770.

14. "Y" [pseud. Louis Halle, Jr.], "On A Certain Impatience with Latin America," *Foreign Affairs* 28/4 (July 1950): 565–9.

15. "US Policy toward Inter-American Collaboration," NSC 56/2, May 18, 1950, *FRUS* 1950, 1:630; Kennedy: *Congressional Record*, August 17, 1951, 10290.

16. James Hagerty quoting Nixon, diary entry for March 11, 1955, Folder "Hagerty Diary, March 1955," Box 1a, Diary Entries, James C. Hagerty Papers, 1953–61, Dwight David Eisenhower Presidential Library (hereafter DDEL), Abilene, Kansas; "Political Development in Cuba," April 19, 1951, 737.00/4-1951, RG59, NA; Eisenhower to Macmillan, August 8, 1960, *FRUS* 1958–1960, 6:1051; Dulles's Memorandum of Telephone Conversation, February 26, 1953, John Foster Dulles Papers, Seeley Mudd Library, Princeton University.

17. Dulles, "Thoughts on Soviet Foreign Policy and What to Do About It," *Life*, June 3, 1946, 112–26, and June 10, 1946, 118–30 (quotations are 3 June, 114, 118); see also Dulles at NSC meeting, June 19, 1958, *FRUS* 1958–60, 5:29.

18. Halle, "Our Guatemalan Policy," May 28, 1954, *FRUS* 1952–4, 4:1140, 1147.

19. Robert H. Trudeau, *Guatemalan Politics: The Popular Struggle for Democracy* (Boulder, CO: Lynne Rienner, 1993), 21–3. On the counterrevolutionary ties to the United States, see Richard H. Immerman, *The CIA in Guatemala: The Foreign Policy of Intervention* (Austin, TX: University of Texas Press, 1982); Piero Gleijeses, *Shattered Hope: The Guatemalan Revolution and the United States, 1944–1954* (Chapel Hill, NC: University of North Carolina Press, 1991).

20. Dulles's June 30, 1954 speech: *DOSB*, July 12, 1954, 43–5.

21. Castillo Armas: US Congress, House, Select Committee on Communist Aggression, Subcommittee on Communist Penetration of the Western Hemisphere, *Communist Aggression in Latin America*, 83rd Cong., 2nd Sess., 1954, 7. US Department of State, *A Case History of Communist Penetration: Guatemala* (Washington, DC: GPO, April 1957), 70.

22. *I, Rigoberta Menchú: An Indian Woman in Guatemala*, edited and introduced by Elisabeth Burgos-Debray (London: Verso, 1984 translation of 1983 original, *Me llamo Rigoberta Menchú y así me nació la conciencia*); Beatriz Manz, *Paradise in Ashes: A Guatemalan Journal of Courage, Terror, and Hope* (Berkeley, CA: University of California Press, 2004). President Clinton's apology: *PPP*, March 10, 1999, 340; and Sean D. Murphy, "US Promotion of Human Rights Abuses in Guatemala during the Cold War," *American Journal of International Law* 93/3 (July 1999): 658–9.

23. National Security Council, "United States Objectives and Courses of Action with Respect to Latin America," NSC 144/1, March 18, 1953, *FRUS* 1952–4, 4:6.

24. National Security Council, "Memorandum of Discussion at the 137th Meeting of the National Security Council on Wednesday, March 18, 1953," *FRUS* 1952–4, 4:2–6.

25. "Memorandum of Discussion at the 237th Meeting of the National Security Council, Washington, February 17, 1955," *FRUS* 1955–7, 6:4–5.

26. Beaulac to Secretary of State, January 9, 1953, *FRUS* 1952–4, 4:882; Embassy to Department of State, February 19, 1953, 737.5-MSP/2-1953, RG59, NA; Beaulac to Secretary of State, July 15, 1953, *FRUS* 1952–4, 4:895, see also 876–7; Embassy to Department of State, February 19, 1953, 737.5-MSP/2-1953; Embassy to Department of State, February 5, 1953, 737.5-MSP/2-553; "Joint Weeka [*sic*] No. 35 for State, Army, Navy and All Departments from SANA," August 28, 1953, 737.00(w)/8-2853, all RG59, NA.

27. Khrushchev: comment to Western diplomats in Moscow, November 18, 1956, reported in *The Times* (London), November 19, 1956, 8; Withrow: *Congressional Record*, August 8, 1957, 14149.

28. Tad Szulc, *Twilight of the Tyrants* (New York: Henry Holt, 1959), 4, 6.

29. NSC: "Reported Decline of US Prestige Abroad," September 11, 1953, Folder "Miscellaneous (3) (Sept 1953)," Box 5, NSC Series, Subject Subseries, Office of the Special Assistant for National Security Affairs: Records 1952–61, White House Office Files, DDEL. Milton Eisenhower, "Report to the President," *DOSB*, November 23, 1953, 695–717.

30. "Memorandum for the Record," September 17, 1954, Folder "Latin America, US Policy toward (3) 1954–60," Box 12, NSC Series, Briefing Notes Subseries, Office of the Special Assistant for National Security Affairs: Records, 1952–61, White House Office Files, DDEL; Eisenhower to Humphrey, March 27, 1957, Folder "George M. Humphrey (4)," Box 21, Administration Series, Ann Whitman File, DDEL.

31. Dulles news conference, November 5, 1957, *DOSB*, November 25, 1957, 826.

32. Richard Nixon, *Six Crises* (New York: Simon and Schuster, 1990 ed. of 1962 original), 202, 204; Hubert Herring, *A History of Latin America from the Beginnings to the Present*, 2nd ed. (New York: Knopf, 1964), 491.

33. The cables from Caracas are in Folder "Vice President"s South American Tour—April 27–May 15," Box 23, Lot File 61D332, Office Files of Maurice M. Bernbaum, 1954–9, Bureau of Inter-American Affairs, RG 59, NA; Nixon, *Six Crises*, 215; Memorandum of Telephone Conversation, Burrows (Venezuela) and Rubottom and Sanders, May 13, 1958, *FRUS* 1958–60, 5:226–7.

34. Memorandum of Discussion at the 366th Meeting of the National Security Council, May 22, 1958, *FRUS* 1958–60, 5:240; Nixon, *Six Crises*, 219, 231n; William P. Snow to Secretary of State, May 15, 1958, *FRUS* 1958–60, 5:237.

35. Figueres testimony: US Congress, House, Committee on Foreign Affairs, Subcommittee on Inter-American Affairs, *A Review of the Relations of the United States and Other American Republics*, 85th Cong., 2nd Sess., June and July 1958, 12, 70, 76–7; Kubitschek testimony: *DOSB*, June 30, 1958, 1090–1; Frondizi testimony: *Congressional Record*, January 21, 1959, 996–8; Milton Eisenhower: *DOSB*, January 19, 1959, 89–105.

36. Embassy to Department of State, February 10, 1958, *FRUS* 1958–60, 6:21; Gladys Marel García-Pérez, *Insurrection and Revolution: Armed Struggle in Cuba, 1952–1959* (Boulder, CO: Lynne Rienner, 1998), especially chapter 2; Ovidio García Reguiero, *Cuba: raíces frutos de una revolución; consideración histórica de algunos aspectos socio-económicas cubanos* (Madrid: IEPAL, 1970); John Dorschner and Roberto Fabricio, *The Winds of December* (New York: Coward, McCann & Geoghegan, 1980); Ramón L. Bonachea, *The Cuban Insurrection, 1952–1959* (New Brunswick, NJ: Transaction Books, 1974); Julia Sweig, *Fidel Castro and the Urban Underground* (Cambridge, MA: Harvard University Press, 2002).

37. Diary entry for Senator Allen J. Ellender, December 14, 1958, *FRUS* 1958–60, 6: 288; Embassy to Department of State, October 22, 1958, 611.37/10-2258, RG59, NA; Southcom Intelligence Summary, January 2, 1959, available in *The United States and Castro's Cuba, 1950–1970: The Paterson Collection* (Wilmington, DE: Scholarly Resources, 1998).

38. A summary of this exceptionally complex transition is chapter 11 ("Between the Old and the New"), of Louis A. Pérez, Jr., *Cuba between Reform and Revolution*, 3rd ed. (New York: Oxford University Press, 2006); also useful are two early studies: Andrés Suárez, *Cuba: Castroism and Communism* (Cambridge, MA: MIT Press, 1967), and K.S. Karol, *Guerrillas in Power: The Course of the Cuban Revolution* (New York: Hill and Wang, 1970).

39. Herter telephone log, July 11, 1960, Folder "CAH Telephone Calls, 7/1/60 to 8/31/60 (3)," Box 13, Christian Herter Papers, DDEL; President's statement on closing the embassy, January 3, 1961, *PPP*, 388; "Transfer: January 19, 1961, Meeting of the President and Senator Kennedy," January 19, 1961, Folder "Kennedy, John F. 1960–61 (2)," Box 2, Augusta-Walter Reed Series, Post-Presidential Papers, DDEL.

40. Castro speech, Havana, April 16, 1981: <http://www.cuba.cu/gobierno/discursos>, emphasis added; Haig instruction: Robert C. McFarlane with Zofia Smardz, *Special Trust* (NY: Cadell and Davies, 1994), 177–8; Reagan blockade proposal: CBS "60 Minutes" interview with Dan Rather, recorded January 26, 1980, audio CD, Ronald Reagan Presidential Library, Simi Valley, California.

41. Schlesinger to JFK, March 10, 1961, *FRUS* 1961–3, 12:10–12, emphasis in original; Castro speech, Las Mercedes, July 26, 1960: <http://www.cuba.cu/gobierno/discursos>.

42. *Congressional Record*, August 8, 1957, 14149.

43. For a compelling illustration of this approach, see Mark Danner, *The Massacre at El Mozote* (New York: Vintage, 1994).

44. Jeane J. Kirkpatrick, "US Security and Latin America," in Howard J. Wiarda, ed., *Rift and Revolution: The Central American Imbroglio* (Washington, DC: American Enterprise Institute, 1984), 352.

45. David E. Bell, "Memorandum for the President," November 27, 1964, Confidential File, Box 25, Lyndon Baines Johnson Presidential Library, Austin, TX; US Agency for International Development, *FY1966 Annual Report to the Congress* (Washington, DC: AID, 1967), 38. On living conditions in El Salvador, see Edelberto Torres Rivas, *Interpretación del desarrollo social centroamericano* (San José: Editorial Universitaria Centroamericana, 1971); Ricardo Sol, *Para entender El Salvador* (San José: Departamento Ecuménico de Investigaciones, 1980); Enrique Baloyra, *El Salvador in Transition* (Chapel Hill, NC: University of North Carolina Press, 1982), esp. 30–1, 188.

46. *Congressional Record*, October 29, 1971, 38252–8.

47. Kissinger's remark was leaked to the *New York Times*, September 11, 1974, 14; a photocopy of CIA Director Richard Helms' handwritten "scream" note is in US Congress, Senate, Select Committee to Study Governmental Operations with Respect to Intelligence Activities, *Intelligence Activities*, vol. 7, 94th Cong., 2nd Sess., December 4 and 5, 1975, 96.

48. President's news conference, September 16, 1974, *PPP*, 151, 156.

49. US Congress, Senate, Committee on Foreign Relations, Subcommittee on Multinational Corporations, *Multinational Corporations and United States Foreign Policy, Hearings . . . on the International Telephone and Telegraph Company and Chile, 1970–71*, Parts 1 and 2, 93rd Cong., 1st Sess., March and April 1973; US Congress, House, Committee on Foreign Affairs, Subcommittee on Inter-American Affairs, *United States and Chile during the Allende Years, 1970–1973*, 94th Cong., 1st Sess., 1975; US Congress, Senate, Select Committee to Study Governmental Operations with Respect to Intelligence Activities, *Alleged Assassination Plots Involving Foreign Leaders* and *Covert Action in Chile, 1963–1973*, 94th Cong, 1st Sess., 1975.

50. Inaugural Address, January 20, 1977, *PPP*, 3; Remarks on the 30th anniversary of the Universal Declaration of Human Rights, December 6, 1978, *PPP*, 2164.

51. Jeane Kirkpatrick, "US Security and Latin America," *Commentary* 71/1 (January 1981): 36, emphasis in original.

52. John A. Booth, *The End and the Beginning: The Nicaraguan Revolution*, 2nd ed. (Boulder, CO: Westview Press, 1985), 75–7, 85.

53. Reagan: *Wall Street Journal*, June 3, 1980, 1; Carter: Speech, University of Notre Dame, Notre Dame, Indiana, May 22, 1977, *PPP*, 956.

54. White: US Congress, House, Committee on Foreign Affairs, Subcommittee on Inter-American Affairs, *Presidential Certification on El Salvador*, vol. 1, 97th Cong., 2nd Sess., 1982, 228. The Reagan administration's position by Assistant Secretary of State Thomas O. Enders: "The Central American Challenge," *AEI Foreign Policy and Defense Review* 4/2 (1982): 9. On the administration's view of Cuba as a Soviet surrogate, see Reagan press conference, Los Angeles, October 14, 1980, verbatim transcript *New York Times*, October 15, 1980, 24; press conference, Washington, DC, March 31, 1982, *PPP*, 400; speech, Washington, DC, March 10, 1983, *PPP*, 372; speech, Miami, May 20, 1983, *PPP*, 743; speech, Tampa, August 12, 1983, *PPP*, 1153; Ronald Reagan, *An American Life* (New York: Simon and Schuster, 1990), 472, 474.

55. Remarks to International Longshoremen's Association, Hollywood, FL, July 18, 1983, *PPP*, 1044; Address to the Nation, October 27, 1983, *PPP*, 1521.

56. Peter Kornbluh and Malcolm Byrne, *The Iran-Contra Scandal: The Declassified History* (New York: New Press, 1993).

## SELECT BIBLIOGRAPHY

Atkins, G. Pope. *Latin America in the International Political System*, 3rd ed. Boulder, CO: Westview Press, 1995.

Blasier, Cole. *The Giant's Rival: The USSR and Latin America*. Pittsburgh, PA: University of Pittsburgh Press, 1983.

Brenner, Philip et al. *A Contemporary Cuba Reader: Reinventing the Revolution*. Lanham, MD: Rowman and Littlefield, 2008.

Caicedo Castillo, José Joaquín. *El derecho internacional en el sistema interamericano* Madrid: Editorial Cultura Hispánica, 1970.

Coatsworth, John H. *Central America and the United States: The Clients and the Colossus* New York: Twayne Publishers, 1994.

Díaz Albonico, Rodrigo. *Antecedentes, balance y perspectivas del sistema interamericano*. Santiago: Editorial Universitaria, 1977.

Fernández-Shaw, Damián. *La Organización de los Estados Américanos*, 2nd ed. Madrid: Ediciones Cultura Hispánica, 1963.

Gleijeses, Piero. *Shattered Hope: The Guatemalan Revolution and the United States, 1944–1954*. Chapel Hill, NC: University of North Carolina Press, 1991.

Gómez Robledo, Antonio. *La seguridad colectiva en el continente americano*. Mexico: Escuela Nacional de Ciencias Políticas y Sociales, 1960.

Grow, Michael. *US Presidents and Latin American Interventions: Pursuing Regime Change in the Cold War*. Lawrence, KS: University Press of Kansas, 2008.

Herrera, Felipe. *Nacionalismo, regionalismo, internacionalismo: América Latina en el contexto internacional*. Buenos Aires: Banco Interamericano de Desarrollo, 1970.

Immerman, Richard H. *The CIA in Guatemala: The Foreign Policy of Intervention*. Austin, TX: University of Texas Press, 1982.

Jaguaribe, Hélio. *El nuevo escenario internacional*. Mexico: Fondo de Cultura Económica, 1985.

LaFeber, Walter. *Inevitable Revolutions: The United States and Central America*. New York: W.W. Norton, 1983.

LeoGrande, William M. *Our Own Backyard: The United States in Central America, 1977–1992*. Chapel Hill, NC: University of North Carolina Press, 1998.

Núnez del Arco, José, Eduardo Margaín, and Rachells Cherol, eds. *The Economic Integration Process of Latin America in the 1980s*. Washington, DC: Inter-American Development Bank, 1984.

Pastor, Robert A. *Whirlpool: US Foreign Policy toward Latin America and the Caribbean*. Princeton, NJ: Princeton University Press, 1992.

Pérez, Louis A. Jr., *Cuba and the United States: Ties of Singular Intimacy*, 3rd ed. Athens, GA: University of Georgia Press, 2003.

Portales, Carlos, ed. *El mundo en transición y América Latina*. Buenos Aires: Grupo Editor Latinoamericano, 1989.

Prebisch, Raúl. *Nueva política comercial para el desarrollo*. Mexico: Fondo de Cultura Económica, 1964.

Rabe, Stephen G. *Eisenhower and Latin America: The Foreign Policy of Anti-Communism*. Chapel Hill, NC: University of North Carolina Press, 1988.

Rabe, Stephen G. *The Most Dangerous Area in the World: John F. Kennedy Confronts Communist Revolution in Latin America*. Chapel Hill, NC: University of North Carolina Press, 1999.

Rojas Aravena, Francisco and Luis Guillermo Solís Rivera. *Súbdito o aliados? La política exterior de Estados Unidos y Centroamérica*. San José: Editorial Porvenir-FLACSO, 1988.

Schmitz, David F. *Thank God They Are On Our Side: The United States and Right-Wing Dictatorships, 1921–1965*. Chapel Hill, NC: University of North Carolina Press, 1998.

Schwartzberg, Steven J. *Democracy and US Policy in Latin America during the Truman Years*. Gainesville, FL: University Press of Florida, 2003.

Tomassini, Luciano, ed. *Relaciones internacionales de la América Latina*. Mexico: Fondo de Cultura Económica, 1981.

Varas, Augusto. *Jaque a la democracia: orden internacional y violencia política en América Latina*. Buenos Aires: Grupo Editor Latinoamericano, 1990.

Varas, Augusto, ed. *Hemispheric Security and US Policy in Latin America*. Boulder, CO: Westview Press, 1989.

# CHAPTER 13

...........................................................................................

# SOUTH ASIA

...........................................................................................

## ANDREW J. ROTTER

ON February 25, 1954, amid the full frost of the cold war, President Dwight D. Eisenhower announced that the United States would provide military aid, the amount unspecified, to Pakistan. The decision was predicated on the vision of Eisenhower's secretary of state, John Foster Dulles, that Pakistan would anchor an alliance with several Middle Eastern countries, including most significantly Turkey, that would stand in opposition to possible Soviet encroachment into that strategically significant area. Some six weeks later Pakistan and Turkey signed an agreement calling for "mutual cooperation"; on May 19, Pakistan and the United States agreed to a Mutual Defense Assistance Pact, underscoring the US commitment to Pakistan's defense and Pakistan's apparent embrace of its new role as a key link in an American security chain ringing the Soviet Union. These agreements formed the basis for Pakistani participation in the Baghdad Pact, with Turkey, Iran, Iraq, and Great Britain, beginning in 1955—participation bought and paid for by the United States, to the tune of $400 million. Given the relative weakness of the Pact states, this arrangement's benefit to the United States was never clear. Regardless of its strategic merits, it nevertheless established the United States as Pakistan's champion.[1]

The American decision to create a military alliance with Pakistan infuriated Jawaharlal Nehru, prime minister of Pakistan's South Asian rival, India. The February announcement, he said, "created a grave situation for us in India and for Asia," and he declared that "India has no intention of surrendering or bartering her freedom for any purpose or under any compulsion whatever," in pointed contrast to what Pakistan had done. The proposed pact between Pakistan and the Middle Eastern nations threatened to bring the cold war "right to our doors, to the frontiers of India," with implications that were "bound to be unfortunate." Nehru had long bristled at what he considered great power meddling in the affairs of the region. He had also, as a point of pride, resisted any outsider's policy that seemed manipulative or heavy handed; he would not allow the recent colonies of South Asia to continue to be "the playthings of others." In the aftermath of the US decision to bolster Pakistan, Nehru appeared to manifest greater warmth toward the Soviet Union, though in truth he was no more pleased with Soviet involvement in South Asia than with American. In early 1955 the Soviets agreed to build a steel plant at

Bhilai, in central India. Nehru visited the Soviet Union that summer, and at the end of the year Soviet premier Nikita Khrushchev and a retinue of Soviet officials barnstormed through India, hugging *harijans* (outcastes) and promising assistance without strings attached. The cold war had come to South Asia.[2]

The disagreements between Pakistan and India over US military aid and the forging of alliances or attachments during the mid-1950s were indicative of deeper fissures that rent South Asia during the cold war. Nearly from the first—that is, from the independence of India and Pakistan in 1947—Pakistan sought alignment with the United States, in an effort to achieve stability, security, and prosperity in what it considered a hostile world, one made especially so by the resentment toward it of its Indian neighbors, whom Pakistanis believed wished their nation oblivion. Pakistan presumed its own weakness, and thus assumed that it needed a strong patron to help it stand up to New Delhi.

India, on the other hand, wanted to spare the region involvement in the cold war. Nehru, who was both prime and foreign minister of his country from his declaration of its independence in August 1947 to his death in 1964, fought to prevent any of the powers from interfering in South Asian affairs. India presumed its own relative strength, and regarded the possibility of American, Soviet, or Chinese involvement in the region as interference, not incidentally as requiring the possible militarization of India at a time when economic development and domestic reform must have priority. Nehru was not a pacifist. He would threaten Pakistan and mean it, especially when it came to the disputed state of Kashmir. But he believed that taking sides in the great power struggle, and alliance-making in particular, would invite the cold war into the area and unsettle the equation of forces that plainly favored him. He wanted his nation to remain "non-aligned," seeing merit and flaw in both sides' cold war positions, denying that the world was black and white, and trying at nearly all costs to stay clear of imbroglios that would require Indian blood and treasure. By the end of his life, however, Nehru would conclude that he simply could not keep the cold war at bay.[3]

This essay addresses a general question: What was the position of South Asia in the cold war? More pointedly, what were the reasons why Pakistan embraced US help during the period, while India sought to avoid great power alliances and keep the cold war at arm's length? To answer these questions, the essay considers historical, strategic, economic, ideological, and cultural reasons why nations pursued the policies they did. The problems of South Asia, or the stakes raised by disagreements there, were never regarded by the cold war powers as more dangerous than those in Europe, the Middle East, or East Asia. As Dennis Kux has noted, neither Washington nor Moscow was much concerned with affairs on the subcontinent, and while China shared borders with India, East Pakistan (later Bangladesh), and disputed Kashmir, it too tended to regard South Asian issues as annoyances rather than crises if problems arose. Yet the cold war was a totalizing conflict. It left no place out, and even secondary fronts like South Asia could provoke the powers to harsh words and bring them to the threshold of damaging conflict. Gradually, both nations assumed greater strategic weight, especially as both developed nuclear weapons. Insofar as they embraced the likelihood of the cold war being played out in their precincts, the Pakistanis managed to use international rivalries to their advantage and keep the Indians off balance. The Indians, who hoped to resist the cold war's aggravations, were destined for disillusionment—but once forced into the game by events beyond their control, they would demonstrate a capacity to play it nearly as cunningly as their Pakistani counterparts.[4]

# THE LEGACY OF COLONIALISM

India and Pakistan shared a history. In the beginning there was only India, not a nation-state by any modern definition but an amalgamation of ethnic and religious groups—localized, agrarian, and generally ruled from the top down by a prince or powerful clan. Some of these groups might be brought together by conquest, as in 1526 when the Mughal chieftain Babur defeated Ibrahim Lodi at Panipat and established a government that ruled from Delhi. The Mughal heirs of Babur were Sunni Muslims. They extended their empire south, and technically ruled much of India until the mid-19th century. The Mughals were challenged by the Maratha princes of the Western Deccan plateau, and they never mastered the far south. The Europeans, seeking trade and especially the abundant spices of India, began arriving in the late 15th century: first the Portuguese in the south and west; then the British East India Company in Bengal in 1650; and the French, whose Compagnie des Indes Orientales placed a settlement at Pondicherry, in the southeast, in 1674. (The Dutch and Danes had small presences.) The Portuguese were largely limited to Goa, and by the mid-18th century the British had defeated the French militarily in India, reducing them to scattered coastal outposts. On behalf of the East India Company, Robert Clive seized all of Bengal at the Battle of Plassey in 1757. The Company's object was trade, but it became de facto the administrative arm of British rule in India. It used British soldiers and civil servants to extend its control over the declining Mughals and the regional clans. If not quite an empire born in a fit of absent-mindedness, the British presence in India before the mid-19th century was surely no "imperial project." It was undertaken by a business enterprise rather than a government, was inconsistent in its demands, and remained incomplete in its control.[5]

In 1857, Indian soldiers in the Company's army rose in rebellion when rumors spread that the rifle cartridges that they had been issued, which required biting to load them into the chambers of their weapons, had been lubricated with the fat of cows and pigs, outraging Hindus and Muslims respectively. Underlying resentment of British highhandedness broke into the open. "Dark deeds were done on both sides," writes Percival Spear, "on the one side in the abandon of the release of long-suppressed passions, on the other in the rage of reprisal and blind vengeance." Thousands died before the British regained control in the summer of 1858. The Sepoy Rebellion left the British badly shaken. No more would the government in London leave its empire to the haphazard stewardship of the Company. The British replaced the Company's president with a secretary of state for India, seized the levers of finance and land distribution, promoted the development of public works, especially railroads, and reorganized the army, dividing it along religious lines, Hindu versus Muslim versus Sikh. The new regime established government schools and encouraged the growth of private colleges, which attracted more Indian students, mostly men. It had in mind control of a type more complete than that preceding the rebellion. Some in Britain had in mind reform as well, with education providing the benefits of civilization to benighted Asians, "a race debased by three thousand years of despotism and priestcraft," as Thomas Macaulay put it in the House of Commons. These policies ironically spawned the growth of a western-educated intellectual class that came to reject colonialism, however benign its face, and endorse an India for Indians. The great men of the 20th century Indian and Pakistani nationalist movements—Mohandas Gandhi, Jawaharlal Nehru, Mohammed Ali Jinnah, and others—had privileged backgrounds and British educations. The legacy of colonialism was its own undoing.[6]

The trauma and catharsis of independence did not fully erase memories of colonialism, and considerations of the cold war were regarded in both India and Pakistan in the light of their experience of domination. For one thing, the British did not pack up and go home in August 1947. Some officials remained in place, including in both nations' armed forces. Pakistan especially continued to rely on British officers, having been denied by partition an experienced officer corps and a well-trained soldiery. The first commander-in-chief of Pakistan's armed forces was British, and the leading generals and heads of vital military directorates were, too. (No Pakistani would head the military until 1951.) Both nations became dominions of Britain; that is, self-governing members of the British Commonwealth. English remained the language of diplomatic correspondence in both nations. It was English spoken with a British accent; the sons of the elite continued to attend Oxford and Cambridge. Trade followed long-standing patterns that linked South Asia to British producers, merchants, and consumers. Ties of education and culture bound Indians and Pakistanis to their former masters, and many South Asians professed to harbor no hard feelings, unlike, say, those directed at, the French in Vietnam, the Dutch in the East Indies, or the Portuguese in India itself. These persistent bonds inclined India and Pakistan toward the British side in the cold war, even if the Indians did not accept fully the "us against them" division of the world as the British described it.[7]

In one particular way the legacy of colonialism lingered sourly in South Asia, and it had to do with race. Whatever else Indians had felt about the British prior to 1947, they had deeply resented British intimations that Asians were not the equals of Europeans because of the color of their skin. The British casually referred to South Asians as "niggers," a coinage readily adopted by visiting Americans. Colonial India featured separate park benches for "whites" and Indians, and waiting rooms at train stations and railway cars were divided by race. Indians who carried umbrellas against the rain or sun were expected to close them if they met whites on the street. Mohammed Ayub Khan, who would become prime minister of Pakistan in 1958, attended the British Royal Military Academy at Sandhurst in the mid-1920s. "The British did not practise the colour bar in a blatant manner, as in some countries," he recalled, "but they were no less colour conscious. In those days anyone coming from a subject race was regarded as an inferior human being and this I found terribly galling."[8]

Yet it was on India that memories of British racism rested most heavily—Pakistanis were on balance lighter-skinned than Indians—and Jawaharlal Nehru remained highly sensitive to racial slights, intended or perceived. Nehru believed that racism was the foundation of colonialism, and that insofar as the cold war West continued to countenance colonialism in Asia and Africa, it retained the taint of racism. British and especially American discrimination against people of color at home explained their support for colonialism abroad, and their support for colonialism in turn reinforced their racism. Because the Soviets did not practice domestic racism, Indians claimed, their policies in the developing world could not be construed as colonialist. "By reason of its own experience," wrote the US ambassador John Sherman Cooper from New Delhi in 1956, "[India] thinks of colonialism as the rule of an Asian country or a colored people by a Western nation, with the subjugated country having no government or international entity." Nehru thus inscribed race on the cold war.[9]

Nehru's own sense of racial identity was complicated. Unlike Ayub, he did not register any complaint of racism during his years in England (he attended Eton, read law at Cambridge, and for a time was coxswain for the university rowing club). He was relatively light-skinned and passed for white in the higher circles of European society in which he traveled. But in the years after independence, Nehru became a steadily harsher critic of white racism especially in Africa, even at the expense of Indians living in Africa who were in most cases closer to whites than blacks socially, and who over the years had succeeded economically—often, charged blacks, at their expense. Nehru targeted particularly the practice of apartheid in South Africa, a "monstrous evil" in its racism. Nehru's attitudes about race strongly influenced his posture toward the cold war: distasteful as he found Soviet doctrine and practice, and threatening as he found the Chinese after 1949, he could not bring himself to stand with those who were slow to jettison racism and colonialism, their own and others".[10]

## EMBRACING THE COLD WAR: PAKISTAN

Even as the Pakistanis struggled to overcome their colonial past, and even as they contemplated the dangers of the cold war, fear of India dominated their cold war posture and their foreign policy more generally. The British decision to partition the subcontinent into predominantly Hindu and Muslim states had been a triumph for M. A. Jinnah and his followers in the Muslim League, but it had shocked most Hindu nationalists, who had assumed that the British, having made a state (however incomplete) in India, would leave the place intact when they left. Gandhi, Nehru, and the other Hindus in the Indian National Congress had insisted that there was no need to separate Muslims and Hindus: while the British had insidiously tried to divide the communities, there was nothing natural in the division and no inherent reason why religious groups should live in separate states. Gandhi promised special consideration for the Muslim minority in independent India. Jinnah was not reassured.

In the end the British agreed with Jinnah that an independent Pakistan would provide a refuge for Muslims and was a safer, more just, and more expedient solution to the problems associated with their departure, given Jinnah's threats and anti-Muslim challenges from reactionary Hindu nationalists. Many in India wished for an early end to Pakistan, for its absorption into India. Pakistanis were convinced that all Indians felt this way. The horrifying bloodshed that followed independence, in which Muslim, Hindu, and Sikh refugees were murdered on a massive scale by their religious rivals, seemed to confirm Pakistani fears that their nation and India were destined for permanent enmity.

Worse, according to Pakistanis, the balance of power left by the British in their wake was markedly skewed in India's favor. Twenty-one of twenty-nine infantry regiments remained with India. New Delhi also controlled most of the weapons and ordnance; while the British urged India to show good faith and allow the transport north of some of this equipment, the Indians dragged their feet and often substituted non-lethal shipments, in one case several cases of aging prophylactics, for the materiel Pakistan had requested. Pakistan, lacking a political tradition or infrastructure, was governed during its early months by the force of Jinnah's personality. Ethnic strife plagued its provinces. The economy hardly existed—in 1947 there was no such thing as a Pakistani bank, for instance. The foreign office consisted of six men, all without typewriters and using stationery purchased from a store in downtown Karachi. Jawaharlal Nehru's Independence Day speech in India, delivered at midnight on August 15, 1947, is justly remembered for its drama and its hope: India, he said, had "a tryst with destiny." Jinnah's speech to his new nation on the same day was terse; in two of its nine paragraphs he pleaded with the country's "minorities" to "fulfill their duties and obligations" to Pakistan, promising that if they did so, "they [would] have nothing to fear." It was an inauspicious beginning.[11]

Whatever India's intentions regarding Pakistan, as Jinnah's speech implied, the Muslim nation had reason to worry about its stability, and thus reason to cultivate an outside power to help it survive. It was a state divided into two wings, East and West Pakistan, separated from each other by 1,000 miles of India. The difficulty of ruling from West Pakistan 40 million East Pakistani Bengalis, over a quarter of whom were Hindus, across all this space was obvious even in 1947; it would grow even harder over time. The state of Punjab was split between Pakistan and India, a decision responsible for the worst of the violence that followed independence. Pakistan, lamented Jinnah, was "moth-eaten." The groups collected in West Pakistan—Sindhis, Punjabis, Baluchis—had to be persuaded to make common cause. Most contentious was the position of the Pathans, located in the Northwest Frontier Provinces but also in the Punjab and, significantly, across the border in Afghanistan, where they were called Pushtuns. Afghanistan was unhappy about the advent of Pakistan, especially because it divided the Pathans and created a potentially hostile regional power to its southeast. With the quiet support of India the Afghanis demanded the creation of a state of "Pushtunistan" (or "Pakhtunistan") that would encompass the tribes on both sides of the Pakistan-Afghanistan border and reduce Pakistani territory. Hoping to defuse the situation, and badly overstretched given its suspicions of India, the Pakistani military withdrew from the northwestern tribal

areas in late 1947, leaving the locals in charge of their own defense—a decision with resonances some sixty years later.[12]

The issue that seemed to threaten Pakistan existentially concerned the state of
Kashmir. At the time of partition the British Viceroy, Lord Mountbatten, knowing the
potential of Kashmir to create mischief between his offspring, had avoided making a
decision about its future, leaving it to the state to choose its course. Nehru, a descendent
of Kashmiri Brahmins, assumed the state would accede to India. Jinnah, noting that
Kashmir was 78 percent Muslim, assumed otherwise. Some in Kashmir sought union
with India, some hoped for Pakistan, while others, including the head of state (mahara-
jah) Hari Singh, preferred autonomy. In late October 1947 thousands of Muslims, most
of them Pathans, surged into Kashmir to "liberate" their co-religionists. The modern
weapons they carried and the trucks that bore them strongly indicated Pakistani involvement. A panicky Hari Singh signed a letter of accession to India, placed before him by
Indian officials. The Indian military then stopped the attack by airlifting thousands of
troops to Kashmir. Pakistan called for a plebiscite; Nehru replied that Kashmir was now
legally part of India, and that as long as Pakistan continued to stir up Muslims there his
forces would have to stay to protect the Hindu minority and promote stability. The sug-
gestion that the state hold a plebiscite or be divided between India and Pakistan made
Nehru apoplectic. Efforts by the United States and the United Nations to secure a solution to the Kashmir problem were unavailing.[13]

Pakistan did hold a pair of cold war trumps. The first was a key position in the intensified contest for control of the Middle East and its vast reserves of oil. The West's conflict
with the Soviet Union over this part of the globe was nothing new. During the 19th century "Great Game," the Russian tsars had sought determinedly to extend their influence
south, over Afghanistan, Persia, Mongolia, and China, while the British had used their
base in India to try to block their rival—"The Bear that looks like a man," as Rudyard
Kipling called Russia—and even to press north against Russian encroachment, using
what the British players labeled the "forward strategy." The game stopped when the
Russians were defeated by Japan in 1905, but resumed at the end of World War II. Now
the stakes were higher. The cold war was an ideologically charged, constant-sum Great
Game, whereby a gain for the other side was by definition a loss for yours. And in the
areas again sharply contested by the powers, in Iran, Iraq, and the Arabian Peninsula, lay
the oil that Europeans and, increasingly, Americans needed to fuel their economic
recovery and sustain their prosperity. Pakistan, with its extensive borders with
Afghanistan and Iran and its maritime proximity to Saudi Arabia, could be of vital strategic importance in the contest for oil. What exactly the Pakistanis could do for the
West's position in these areas was unclear, given the fragility of Pakistan's unity and the
weakness of its army. But their willingness to play some role in the defense of the Middle
East made them an enticing asset to the practitioners of the new Great Game, cold war
version.[14]

Pakistanis were willing to play this part largely because of their fear of India: enlist the
western powers on their side, solicit western arms with the disingenuous promise to use
them against the Soviets if required, and Pakistan might win itself some protection

against the rival who wished it gone from the earth. Still, the attraction between the West and Pakistan was not wholly opportunistic. The second cold war trump held by the Pakistanis was the long-standing British perception, inherited by the Americans, that Muslims were a martial people: forthright in their relationships, constant in their loyalties, and, significantly, tough and manly in their willingness to stand on principle and fight for it if necessary. It is tempting to label this a myth created by the British following the 1857–8 Rebellion, when they had divided the military and denigrated the Hindus, whom they blamed for the attacks, and elevated Muslims (and Sikhs) to prominence in the armed forces. But the durability of the myth of Muslim loyalty and toughness, and its persistence into the cold war period in Washington as well as London, suggests the presence of many people willing to keep it alive. The most important of these were themselves Pakistanis. British and American policymakers admired Muslims for their monotheism, for it suggested their belief in a single truth. If there could be no atheists in the foxholes of the cold war, then Pakistan's Muslims might well be suitable allies, as long as they believed the right sort of truth—which seemed likely given their presumed hostility to communism. In quest of American military assistance, Pakistani leaders cultivated their image as believers in a single almighty deity. "The people of Pakistan believe in the supreme sovereignty of God," Prime Minister Liaquat Ali Khan told the Truman administration on a visit to the United States in 1950, and thus they believed in "the equality of man"—unlike caste-ridden Hindus.

Western leaders also admired their Pakistani counterparts for their manliness. Liaquat and his successors, many of them military men, showed enthusiasm for the martial virtues, shook hands vigorously, drank alcohol, ate meat, and accepted shotguns as presents from American hosts and visitors. "The only Asians who can really fight are the Pakistanis," Secretary of State John Foster Dulles once told the journalist Walter Lippmann. Chester Bowles, who served two tours as US ambassador to India during the cold war years and sympathized with the Indian position on most things, grumbled at the ease with which Pakistani men seemed to fool Americans into thinking that the parties had much in common. The Pakistanis were "Asians they can really understand, Asians who argue the advantages of an olive over an onion in a martini and who know friends they know in London." All of this was by contrast to the Indians, who connected culturally to westerners far less easily.[15]

The cultural construction of selves and others rested largely on stereotypes based on religion and gender. These stereotypes were false; Muslims were not theologically akin to Christians despite their common belief in monotheism, and Muslim men were not naturally more masculine than Hindus. Culture is never coterminous with the state, especially a state as heterogeneous as Pakistan, India, or the United States, and it changes over time, which makes generalizations about it hazardous in the extreme. And yet, cultural identities of selves and others surely influenced the actions taken by those westerners and South Asians responsible for making policy decisions. Language, perceptions, emotions, attitudes, prejudices—all matter in the conduct of international relations, and all are the products and elements of culture. Beliefs and perceptions about monotheism and manhood predisposed the Pakistanis to side with the Americans in the cold war, and predisposed the Americans to look with favor on the connection. The Eisenhower administration's decision to provide military aid to Pakistan in 1954, and the Pakistani government's decision to accept alliance with the Americans in Asia as payment for the aid, were therefore hardly surprising.

# SHUNNING THE COLD WAR: INDIA

India had external interests during the first years after its independence, but it had little capacity and less appetite for projecting itself into the fray of cold war. It was a regional power, a condition that satisfied Nehru; as long as India could bully Pakistan when needed, consolidate its power over the few remaining princely states and colonial enclaves (among them Goa and Pondicherry) lying within its borders, win Kashmir, and establish itself as an exemplar of development and democracy for other new states, he would be content. Taking a side in the cold war offered no strategic advantage to India. The nation needed some help economically, but Indian planners generally looked inward, concentrating on protecting home markets through centralized planning. Frustrated British and American observers stigmatized Nehru's foreign policy as "neutralist," a label Nehru rejected for its seeming moral detachment; he preferred to say that India was "non-aligned" in the cold war.

The perceptive British diplomat Sir Archibald Nye wrote in 1951 that India could most accurately be seen as "operating in three concentric circles, the principles governing each of which bear little or no relation to the principles followed in the others." In the innermost circle were mainly contiguous states, with which India had "vital" interests. In the second circle out—nations other than the great powers—India had interests in several places (such as Southeast Asia) but virtually none in others (Latin America). The outer ring, consisting of the cold war powers Britain, the United States, the Soviet Union, and China, mainly warranted avoiding: relations with these nations were "to a great extent determined by [India's] passionate desire to keep out of conflict and to stand aside from Great Power struggles." Nye spotted some Nehruvian delusion here, especially regarding Soviet expansionism and Chinese perfidy. But he also recognized the logic in India's resisting cold war affiliations, and noted that the United States had been "isolationist" for many years. He counseled patience.[16]

Nehru did have ideological preferences and dislikes. He admired Britain's parliamentary government and the openness of American democracy. He deplored the racism of whites in both countries, connected, as he saw it, to their continued support for colonialism, abhorred the hypocrisy of societies that claimed to represent justice but allowed their lower classes to live in misery, remained suspicious that the West was inclined to militarism, and found Americans crass, materialistic, and boorish. As a moderate socialist, Nehru expressed solidarity with the Soviet's rhetoric of economic equality and Mao Zedong's affinity for China's peasants. Like the communist powers, India would have Five-Year Plans for economic development that focused on building industry, consolidating agriculture, and relieving poverty. But, though he muted his public criticism, Nehru found appalling the brutalities of the Soviet and Chinese Communist political systems and their utter lack of regard for human freedom. Neither cold war system, in other words, provided a model for India to follow. The fragility of his nation's democracy and the uncomfortable persistence of caste in India confirmed Nehru's resolve to find his own way in the world, free of entanglement in the toxic cold war. India had too many of its own problems to involve itself with others'.

Nehru also felt that India could not afford the frenzied defense spending that came with participation in the cold war. If Pakistan agreed to help the West resume the Great Game through a "forward strategy" aimed at the Soviet Union, India preferred the alternative 19th century British posture known as "masterly inactivity." That way, India would draw the attention of no enemy and be left instead to address its enormous domestic problems, unhindered and unburdened by heavy defense spending. Gandhian nationalism was based partly on economic self-sufficiency. Gandhi believed that it was morally right for people to make modest consumer goods for themselves, and shrewdly noted that Britain's exploitation of his country relied on Indian purchases of British-made textiles, often manufactured with inexpensive cotton furnished by India. He urged his countrymen and women to produce their own cloth, grow their own food, and generally to stay away from large-scale economic enterprise that inevitably meant entanglement in the global trading nexus. Nehru would not go that far; a modern nation, he believed, needed more than millions of household spinning wheels to move forward economically. But he was committed to ambitious, largely self-sustaining economic development. If his plans were to work, it would make no sense to spend large sums on the military.

India had reserves of manganese, monazite, and beryl, all vital to modern industry and especially defense. Given the press of the cold war, the United States sought to buy great quantities of all three. In each case, however, Indian policymakers refused to sell freely, or to sell at what the Americans felt was a reasonable price, or to sell at all. Nehru wanted to move slowly toward trade, particularly with the Americans, whom he considered crafty (the Americans felt the same way about him). He wanted India to build its own industry, and to do so it might be necessary to preserve as much of these resources as possible. Manganese was needed to produce steel. Monazite and beryl had possible applications for nuclear technology. Nehru also wished to sell these goods and others to any party interested, and for the best possible price. If non-alignment meant anything, surely it meant the ability to avoid trade agreements that constrained the amount of a mineral that could be sold to the highest bidder, regardless of ideology. This, at first, was the policy that the Indians followed.[17]

Just as culture, gender, and religion influenced Pakistan's encounter with the world, so these factors helped shape India's external relations during the cold war. Non-alignment was partly a strategic choice. It also flowed naturally from Indian ideas about time and space, from the ways in which others perceived Indian men and Indian men saw themselves, from ideas concerning the maturity of peoples and nations, and from the predilections of Hindus to avoid making stark choices between what they saw as false, binary alternatives. So, for example, Indians traditionally imagined space—that place beyond the known and understood—as threatening. Even as they insisted that others not violate their space in South Asia, they showed no inclination to venture boldly into Archibald Nye's "third ring" of great power dominance. While Americans, British, and others viewed India, the country, as bound stubbornly to tradition and with an ossified infrastructure that frustrated modernization, and Indians, the people, as childishly immature and incapable of reason, Indians saw their nation as representing "an older and wiser civilization" than that made by the "parvenus" of the West, and themselves as fresh and imaginative; as Nehru put it in his Independence Night speech: "At the stroke of the midnight hour, when the world sleeps, India will awake to life and freedom. A moment comes, which comes but rarely in history, when we step out from the old to the new, when an age ends, and when the soul of a nation, long suppressed, finds utterance." India would forge a new way through the world, one untrammeled by the petty jealousies and serious dangers of the cold war. Nehru himself, "graceful" and "beautiful" by westerners' description, wearing perpetually a red rose in the lapel of his flowing *kurta* overshirt, seemed to many in the West effeminate, and thus unable or unwilling to stand up to the communist evil in the cold war. And Hinduism itself, with its many deities and thus multiple versions of truth, was, in the view of men in Washington and London, incapable of discerning right from wrong, unlike the steadfastly monotheistic Muslims in Pakistan. Indians feared "a holy war or crusade" that would involve them. Nehru cultivated both these gendered and religiously-inflected versions of himself and his people in order to keep his country aloof from the dangers of the cold war.[18]

## The cold war powers and South Asia

The advent of the People's Republic of China (PRC) in October 1949 quickly drew the concern of Pakistan and India. Pakistani Prime Minister H. S. Suhrawardy told Chinese Premier Zhou Enlai in 1955, "China would soon be able to occupy Pakistan easily, as the Mongols did in the thirteenth century." (Zhou remonstrated that China had no interest in such a policy.) In reality, the Chinese Communists, for at least the first decade following their triumph, had limited foreign policy goals: they sought unity, which was to include the incorporation of Nationalist-held Taiwan, security, an end to colonial arrangements, and, connected to this, the respect of their neighbors and other nations. They had no intention of invading Pakistan. The Chinese harmoniously settled some boundary differences with Pakistan and, while they were unhappy with Pakistan's military association with the United States and Asian treaty organizations that they regarded as hostile to them, overall they remained ready to provide help to Pakistan if they could do so opportunistically and on the relative cheap—and, after 1960, as long as the Pakistanis were not also accepting aid from the Soviet Union. In their own way, the Chinese, like the Indians, were trying to keep the cold war out of South Asia, or at least to keep the Americans out.[19]

China-India relations were ultimately to prove more delicate, and more perilous. Nehru professed friendship with the leaders of the PRC and would help orchestrate a public relations campaign with the slogan "Hindi-Chini *Bhai Bhai*," meaning that Indians and Chinese were brothers. The chant masked profound anxiety about what might happen if the Chinese, for any reason, found India's policy not to their liking. In pursuit of what it considered China's territorial integrity, in October 1950 the People's Liberation Army entered Tibet, whose residents had long considered themselves citizens of an independent state. The Chinese move worried New Delhi. Nehru feared the growth of Chinese power to his north and the loss of Indian influence in Tibet. Seeking a compromise, he told Parliament that, while he hoped the Chinese would preserve Tibet's "autonomy," he would recognize China's "suzerainty" over the region. In April 1954 Nehru and Zhou Enlai signed an agreement on Tibet, in which Nehru glumly offered (as he put it to legislators) his "recognition of the existing situation there," but which more importantly contained a preamble articulating "five principles (*panchsheela*) of peaceful coexistence" between India and China. These called for "(1) mutual respect for each other's territorial integrity and sovereignty, (2) mutual non-aggression, (3) mutual noninterference in each other's internal affairs, (4) equality and mutual benefit, and (5) peaceful coexistence." "We need not live in a fairy world where nothing wrong happens," said Nehru. He was, as two historians have put it, "bowing to the inevitable" regarding Tibet.[20]

The *panchsheela* attained greater glory when they were incorporated into the final declaration of the conference of non-aligned nations at Bandung, Indonesia, in 1955. The Indo-Chinese agreement on Tibet would fare less well. In March 1959 an uprising broke out in the Tibetan capital of Lhasa. When the Chinese entered to suppress it, the Dalai Lama and thousands of his followers fled to India and requested political asylum, which Nehru granted. This decision upset Beijing; Chinese newspapers attacked Nehru as an American "stooge." Tensions over Tibet, and the disposition of its exiled citizenry in India, fueled a long-standing Sino-Indian dispute over the placement of the nations' border. Nehru argued that India's northern boundaries had been established by the British in the 19th century, and that they extended to the Himalayas. The Chinese considered these borders the relics of imperialism and asked that they be renegotiated. When it became clear that Nehru would not budge, and after Indian military units took up positions north even of the British line of demarcation in the northeast, the Chinese acted. In October 1962 they struck Indian forces on both northern fronts and quickly pushed them back. This was not, as most in India and some in the West feared, the opening assault of a war of conquest but rather "a giant punitive expedition," as one historian has called it. The Chinese were registering their displeasure with Indian arrogance and flexing their muscles, but no more. Relations between China and India remained frosty through the Sino-American détente of the 1970s, which fed Indian fears of great powers ganging up against it; a thaw in Indo-Sino relations came only with the government of Prime Minister Indira Gandhi, Nehru's daughter, in the early 1980s.[21]

Indian relations with the Soviet Union were erratic, though on the whole better than those between India and China. Neither Joseph Stalin nor Nikita Khrushchev was much interested in South Asia, though Khrushchev was eager to portray himself as a champion of anti-colonialism—by contrast, he said, to the ersatz communists in the People's Republic. Throughout much of the cold war the Soviets had little use for the Pakistanis, who were, the Russians thought, in thrall to the Americans, the Chinese, or both, and who were so obsessed with India as to be of little use elsewhere. Toward India the Soviets tried to be friendlier. Khrushchev in particular claimed solidarity with Nehru's spirit of non-alignment, though Nehru always remained suspicious of Soviet support for India's communist parties, the bane of his political existence. The Soviets proclaimed their sympathy for India's position in the dispute over Kashmir, offered, in the wake of Pakistan's acceptance of US military aid in 1954 to build the Bhilai steel mill, and the following year dangled before the Indians the sale of modern fighter jets. Soviet economic aid to India increased throughout the 1960s and 1970s. In 1965, war broke out between India and Pakistan over Kashmir. The Soviets, alarmed that the Chinese might exploit the hostilities and even fan their flames, successfully stepped in to mediate. The Soviets would step in again in 1971, when West Pakistan sent forces into East Pakistan. This eventually brought the Indians into the fighting and led to the establishment of the independent nation of Bangladesh. Though the Russians were shaken by the recklessness of both Pakistani and Indian decisionmaking during the war, they fared better than the Richard Nixon administration in the United States, which cast its lot fully with Pakistan and damaged its reputation with India and most other nations into the bargain.[22]

And what, finally, of the Americans and South Asia? At the time of Indian and Pakistani independence, the United States hoped that Great Britain would continue to take the lead in the region, given Britain's history with the people there and the glaring lack of American expertise about the place. As British power diminished and the all fronts Cold War impinged on South Asia, the Americans were drawn in. The Truman administration actually provided more military equipment to India than to Pakistan but laid the groundwork for this policy to shift after the Korean War broke out. While the Pakistanis sympathized with the US position in Korea and lobbied for it with recalcitrant Arab nations, the Indians, though supportive of the United Nations Security Council resolution that condemned North Korea's attack, were disinclined to play advocate for the Americans and instead served as intermediary between the United States and China, whose representatives would not talk to each other directly. The Americans saw the Korean War as clear evidence that the communist powers were acting aggressively and in concert to expand across the globe, and they worried that South Asia might be the communists' next target. The Pakistanis were willing to adopt this view if it won for them US support, especially in the dispute over Kashmir. Nehru did not accept it, continuing to insist that colonialism and racism were problems worse than expanding communism, and that it would be better to negotiate with an adversary than to fight in a world increasingly filled with nuclear weapons.[23]

The Americans' growing disillusionment with India, along with their greater willingness to embrace Pakistan, culminated in the Eisenhower administration's 1954 decision to provide military aid to Pakistan and involve Pakistan in Asian alliances—the Southeast Asia Treaty Organization and the Middle East Defense Organization—designed to counter predicted communist probes into these areas. The Pakistanis accepted the aid gladly but contributed mostly lip service to the new alliances. Reacting angrily to the introduction of the cold war into the region, India consorted openly with the communist powers, all the while continuing to express its commitment to non-alignment, as at Bandung in 1955. President Eisenhower did not want to lose India, and in meetings with Nehru in the United States in December 1956 managed at least to convince the prime minister of his goodwill and sincerity. (Nehru had also been pleasantly surprised by the firmness with which Eisenhower had condemned the British/French/Israeli attack on Suez the previous October.) Still, these meetings did not produce a significant, favorable shift in US-India relations.[24]

Nehru hoped affairs would improve when John F. Kennedy became president in early 1961. The new president and many of his advisors, including John Kenneth Galbraith, whom Kennedy chose to head the US embassy in New Delhi, admired Nehru and claimed to respect non-alignment. They saw India as a laboratory for democracy in Asia and a likely place for a capitalist economic take-off to occur. But when Nehru came to Washington in late 1961, his meetings with Kennedy and other officials went poorly. The two men sparred about the testing of nuclear weapons. Nehru spoke vaguely about policy issues and seemed frequently distracted. Soon after he returned home, the prime minister authorized a successful Indian invasion of Portuguese Goa, which had stubbornly and singularly resisted incorporation into India. Kennedy expressed dismay; Nehru responded with dismay over Kennedy's dismay.[25]

In October 1962 came India's border war with China. Despite the limited Chinese aims—to punish rather than occupy India—the failure of Indian forces to slow their adversaries even briefly led to fear and recrimination in New Delhi. Nehru fired Krishna Menon, his sharp-tongued defense minister, and was forced to admit that he *had* been living in a sort of "fairy world" regarding his neighbors. "We were," he said, "getting out of touch with reality in the modern world and were living in an artificial atmosphere of our own creation." Nehru looked exhausted; he concluded that he could no longer deny that the cold war had come to South Asia. He chose to accept American military assistance and advice, once anathema to him. US and Indian air forces conducted joint exercises, the Americans agreed to train Indian pilots, and American spy planes were for the first time allowed to land and refuel at Indian air bases. Nehru would not countenance, as Pakistan had, a formal alliance with the United States. But his response to Chinese aggression placed India, however tentatively, on the side of the West in the cold war. The Soviet Union was unreliable, China too threatening, and US aid too much needed, even despite the strings always attached to it.[26]

## Cold war legacies

Following Nehru's death in the spring of 1964 and a brief, unfortunate interregnum government led by Lal Bahadur Shastri, Indira Gandhi became the nation's prime minister. She would hold the position for fifteen of the eighteen years from 1966 to 1984. She did not always get along with the American presidents with whom her time in power coincided. Like her father, Gandhi resented what she considered American condescension, American exploitation of Indian food shortages that inspired humiliating Indian requests for aid (nearly always granted), and the American insistence that there might be two sides to the dispute over Kashmir. In the face of these and other perceived slights, Gandhi returned to her father's original determination that India must go it alone as much as possible. When the Chinese had tested a nuclear weapon in 1964, the Indians had considered whether to develop such weapons of their own. Unable to get from the United Nations a guarantee against a Chinese nuclear attack, Gandhi's government decided that it would not sign the 1968 Nuclear Non-Proliferation Treaty and resolved to move ahead with a nuclear program. The successful test of a nuclear device in the Rajasthani Desert in 1974, no matter how stridently Gandhi construed it as "peaceful," resulted from her conviction that none of the powers had much sympathy for India, especially after Nixon's refusal to see the justice of India's intervention in East Pakistan in 1971. According to Dennis Kux, "India, in Washington's eyes, had become just a big country full of poor people." The perception rankled in India, and the nuclear test was designed, in part, to change it.[27]

It did not work. For the duration of the cold war, and even as Soviet support for India dwindled through the 1980s, Americans continued to regard India as no more than a regional power, and often as a nuisance. There was a bit of a popular craze for India and things Indian during the mid-1980s, coincident with the release in the West of the film *Gandhi* and the celebration of the "Festival of India" in the United States. Rajiv Gandhi, who succeeded his mother as prime minister following Indira's assassination in 1984, began to open the country to trade, investment, and transfers of technology, and this won him points with Washington and London. In general, however, India remained peripheral to the deepest concerns of the powers, and the end of the cold war had little to do with India. Oddly, Indians might have claimed that the world had at last caught up to them: in long rejecting the axioms of the cold war, they had predicted its demise, and though the waiting had been painful, there was some vindication in their having been right: great power conflict was dangerous and ought to be renounced. Like all nations should, India would first cultivate its own garden. That India's nuclear program continued to irritate others (India detonated several devices in 1998), and that India's conflict with Pakistan continued to fester, was of some moment to Indians in the 21st century. So, too, was the considerable energy of the nation's economy, which increased Indian trade and investment and swelled the ranks of the middle class, largely invisible to the world during the cold war. India's quest for respect had, some sixty years after independence, begun to bear fruit.

Pakistan, unlike India, had ridden the cold war as a wave, first siding with the West and earning considerable economic and military aid, then tipping toward China following the 1962 border war—the reward for which, paradoxically, was American gratitude when the Pakistanis served as intermediaries for Richard Nixon's *démarche* to China in 1971. It is common to regard Pakistan's history as that of a nearly-failed state. Throughout, the nation has suffered from domestic instability, humiliation at the hands of its Indian rival, corrupt and authoritarian government, a record of human rights abuses, and actual vivisection following the uprising in East Pakistan and the creation of Bangladesh in 1971. It is tempting to say that Pakistan, having lived by the cold war, is now in steep decline because the cold war has ended.

Yet that judgment may be premature. When the Soviet Union overthrew the government of Afghanistan and invaded that country in 1979, Pakistan became the immediate beneficiary, as the Americans funnelled millions in military aid through Pakistan to Afghanis who were battling the Russians. The Americans were ready to overlook a multitude of Pakistan's sins, including its pursuit of enriched uranium for possible use in a nuclear weapon, in order to torment the Soviets. The last great battle of the cold war ended with the Soviets' retreat from Afghanistan, a blow that contributed significantly to Mikhail Gorbachev's conclusion that ongoing conflict with the United States was no longer sustainable. But the end of the cold war did not signal the end of Pakistan's usefulness to the United States. Having established itself as a force in Afghanistan's political situation, Pakistan became vital to American efforts, after September 11, 2001, to dislodge the Taliban government from Kabul and keep it out. At this writing, Pakistan, its borders utterly compromised by the Taliban and the presence (as ever) of Pathans, who live in both countries and respect the boundaries of neither, is professing its desire to help the Americans defeat evil, even as it pleads for more money and weapons with which to do the job. The cold war has ended, but a familiar conflict continues. India practices masterly inactivity, growing its economy despite a global recession. Pakistan, source of violence and instability (including the terrorist attacks in Mumbai in November 2008), remains as aggravating, and evidently as indispensable, as ever.

## NOTES

1. M. S. Venkataramani, *The American Role in Pakistan, 1947–1958* (New Delhi: Radiant Publishers, 1982), 268; Robert J. McMahon, *The Cold War on the Periphery: The United States, India, and Pakistan* (New York: Columbia University Press, 1994), 172–3.

2. McMahon, *Cold War on the Periphery*, 172–3, 213–14; Andrew J. Rotter, *Comrades at Odds: The United States and India, 1947–1964* (Ithaca, NY: Cornell University Press, 2000), 39, 67–8; H. W. Brands, Jr., *India and the United States: The Cold Peace* (Boston, MA: Twayne Publishers, 1990), 85.

3. South Asia is generally held to include not only India and Pakistan but Bangladesh, Nepal, Sri Lanka, and sometimes Afghanistan. I will treat Bangladesh, an offspring of Pakistan, briefly here. Nepal and Sri Lanka were each visited by Maoist problems during this period, but both were largely dominated by India and thus had little independent standing as cold war states. Afghani problems were unique and demand their own treatment.

4. Dennis Kux, *The United States and Pakistan 1947–2000: Disenchanted Allies* (Washington, DC: Woodrow Wilson Center Press, 2001), 15–16.

5. Romila Thapar, *A History of India: Volume 1* (Harmondsworth, UK: Penguin Books, 1966); Percival Spear, *The Oxford History of Modern India 1740–1975*, 2nd ed. (Oxford: Oxford University Press, 1978); quotation is at p. 8.

6.  Spear, *Oxford History*, 224, 229–37, 274–6; Gauri Viswanathan, *Masks of Conquest: Literary Study and British Rule in India* (New York: Columbia University Press, 1989), 16–17.

7.  Shuja Nawaz, *Crossed Swords: Pakistan, its Army, and the Wars Within* (Oxford: Oxford University Press, 2008), 32, 80; Deepak Lal, "Manners, Morals, and Materialism: Indian Perceptions of America and Britain," in Sulochana Raghavan Glazer and Nathan Glazer, eds., *Conflicting Images: India and the United States* (Glenn Dale, MD: Riverdale Publishers, 1990), 271–88.

8.  Mohammed Ayub Khan, *Friends Not Masters: A Political Autobiography* (Oxford: Oxford University Press, 1967), 10.

9.  See Rotter, *Comrades at Odds*, 150–87; quotation at pp. 170–1.

10. Rotter, *Comrades at Odds*, 178.

11. Nawaz, *Crossed Swords*, 30–2; Brian Cloughley, *A History of the Pakistan Army: Wars and Insurrections* (Oxford: Oxford University Press, 1999), 2–4; Kux, *The United States and Pakistan*, 17–18; Jinnah's speech at <http://forum.chatdd.com/freedom-speech/858-jinnah-s-independence-day-speech.html>.

12. Kux, *The United States and Pakistan*, 12–13, 42–3; Richard Symonds, *The Making of Pakistan* (London: Faber and Faber, 1950), 120–1, 142.

13. McMahon, *Cold War on the Periphery*, 19–22; Rotter, *Comrades at Odds*, 137–44; Mushtaqur Rahman, *Divided Kashmir: Old Problems, New Opportunities for India, Pakistan, and the Kashmir People* (Boulder, CO: Westview Press, 1996).

14. Rotter, *Comrades at Odds*, 48–56; Kux, *The United States and Pakistan*, 45–6.

15. Rotter, *Comrades at Odds*, 196, 217–18; Kux, *The United States and Pakistan*, 72.

16. Rotter, *Comrades at Odds*, 45–8.

17. Rotter, *Comrades at Odds*, 93–115; Dennis Merrill, *Bread and the Ballot: The United States and India's Economic Development, 1947–1963* (Chapel Hill, NC: University of North Carolina Press, 1990), 45–74.

18. Rotter, *Comrades at Odds*, 188–248. Nehru's speech at <http://www.fordham.edu/halsall/mod/1947nehru1.html>.

19. Simei Qing, *From Allies to Enemies: Visions of Modernity, Identity, and US-China Diplomacy, 1945–1960* (Cambridge, MA: Harvard University Press, 2007), 256; Joseph Camilleri, *Chinese Foreign Policy: The Maoist Era and its Aftermath* (Seattle, WA: University of Washington Press, 1980), 80; Kux, *The United States and Pakistan*, 181.

20. Qing, *From Allies to Enemies*, 272; Charles H. Heimsath and Surjit Mansingh, *A Diplomatic History of Modern India* (Bombay: Allied Publishers, 1971), 188–93.

21. Qing, *From Allies to Enemies*, 274–6; Rotter, *Comrades at Odds*, 71–4; Neville Maxwell, *India's China War* (London: Jonathan Cape, 1970), 214; Brands, *India and the United States*, 141, 170.

22. McMahon, *Cold War on the Periphery*, 216–20; William Taubman, *Khrushchev: The Man and his Era* (New York: W. W. Norton, 2003), 354; Heimsath and Mansingh, *Diplomatic History of Modern India*, 448–50; Vladislav M. Zubok, *A Failed Empire: The Soviet Union in the Cold War from Stalin to Gorbachev* (Chapel Hill, NC: University of North Carolina Press, 2007), 194, 217.

23. McMahon, *Cold War on the Periphery*, 123–6; Dennis Kux, *Estranged Democracies: India and the United States 1941–1991* (New Delhi: Sage Publications, 1993), 87–9.

24. Rotter, *Comrades at Odds*, 22–3; McMahon, *Cold War on the Periphery*, 224–9; Kux, *Estranged Democracies*, 140–3.

25. Rotter, *Comrades at Odds*, 24–5; Kux, *Estranged Democracies*, 192–6.

26. Rotter, *Comrades at Odds*, 74–6.
27. Kux, *Estranged Democracies*, 267–8, 314–17. On India's nuclear program, see George Perkovich, *India's Nuclear Bomb: The Impact on Global Proliferation* (Berkeley, CA: University of California Press, 1999).

## Select Bibliography

Brands, H. W. *India and the United States: The Cold Peace*. Boston, MA: Twayne Publisher, 1990.

Camilleri, Joseph. *Chinese Foreign Policy: The Maoist Era and its Aftermath*. Seattle, WA: University of Washington Press, 1980.

Cloughley, Brian. *A History of the Pakistan Army: Wars and Insurrections*. Karachi: Oxford University Press, 1999.

Glazer, Sulochana Raghavan, and Nathan Glazer, eds. *Conflicting Images: India and the United States*. Glenn Dale, MD: Riverdale Publishers, 1990.

Heimsath, Charles H., and Surjit Mansingh. *A Diplomatic History of Modern India*. Bombay: Allied Publishers, 1971.

Isaacs, Harold R. *Scratches on Our Minds: American Views of China and India*. Armonk, NY: M. E. Sharpe, Inc., 1980.

Khan, Mohammed Ayub. *Friends Not Masters: A Political Autobiography*. Oxford: Oxford University Press, 1967.

Kux, Dennis. *Estranged Democracies: India and the United States 1941–1991*. New Delhi: Sage Publications, 1993.

Kux, Dennis. *The United States and Pakistan 1947–2000: Disenchanted Allies*. Washington, DC: Woodrow Wilson Center Press, 2001.

McMahon, Robert J. *The Cold War on the Periphery: The United States, India, and Pakistan*. New York: Columbia University Press, 1994.

Merrill, Dennis. *Bread and the Ballot: The United States and India's Economic Development, 1947–1963*. Chapel Hill, NC: University of North Carolina Press, 1990.

Nawaz, Shuja. *Crossed Swords: Pakistan, its Army, and the Wars Within*. Oxford: Oxford University Press, 2008.

Noman, Omar. *Pakistan: A Political and Economic History since 1947*. London: Kegan Paul International, 1988.

Perkovich, George. *India's Atomic Bomb: The Impact on Global Proliferation*. Berkeley, CA: University of California Press, 1999.

Qing, Simei. *From Allies to Enemies: Visions of Modernity, Identity, and US-China Diplomacy, 1945–1960*. Cambridge, MA: Harvard University Press, 2007.

Rahman, Mushtaqur. *Divided Kashmir: Old Problems, New Opportunities for India, Pakistan, and the Kashmir People*. Boulder, CO: Westview Press, 1996.

Rotter, Andrew J. *Comrades at Odds: The United States and India, 1947–1964*. Ithaca, NY: Cornell University Press, 2000.

Spear, Percival. *The Oxford History of Modern India 1740–1975*, 2nd ed. New Delhi: Oxford University Press, 1979.

Symonds, Richard. *The Making of Pakistan*. London: Faber and Faber, 1950.

Taubman, William. *Khrushchev: The Man and His Era*. New York: W. W. Norton, 2003.

Thapar, Romila. *A History of India: Volume 1*. Harmondsworth: Penguin Books, 1966.

Venkataramani, M. S. *The American Role in Pakistan, 1947–1958*. New Delhi: Radiant Publishers, 1982.

Viswanathan, Gauri. *Masks of Conquest: Literary Study and British Rule in India*. New York: Columbia University Press, 1989.

Zubok, Vladislav M. *A Failed Empire: The Soviet Union in the Cold War from Stalin to Gorbachev*. Chapel Hill, NC: University of North Carolina Press, 2007.

# CHAPTER 14

......................................................................

# THE COLD WAR IN
# SOUTHEAST ASIA

......................................................................

## ANG CHENG GUAN

IN 2008–9, the History Channel, the National University of Singapore (NUS), the Asia Research Institute (ARI), and the National Library Board of Singapore (NLB) organized a series of seminars entitled "The Cold War in Southeast Asia." Its publicity brochure states that "there is much about the cold war in Southeast Asia that still remains shrouded in mystery."[1] This chapter aims to help readers understand the cold war as it was played out in Southeast Asia. It does so by guiding readers through the phases in the historiography of the cold war in the region, while concurrently providing a critical account of the state of the field. It also describes the challenges historians face in writing the international history of the cold war in Southeast Asia and suggests approaches and issues that seem most likely to advance the scholarship.

Why should scholars or general readers be interested in the history of the cold war in Southeast Asia? Why should Southeast Asians themselves appreciate that the cold war is a historical event that has significantly affected the development of their countries? Kwa Chong Guan (Chairman, National Archives Board, Singapore) offered three reasons: (a) it shaped the political development of the nation-states as well as influenced inter-state relations in the region; (b) memories of the cold war continue to loom large in shared memories—the trauma of war, political chaos, violence, riots, and revolutions—all of which have influenced the lives of indigenous people; and (c) there is, as in the US and Europe, a growing interest in rewriting the history of the cold war.[2] To add a last but not least reason, Southeast Asia is part of, and by no means an insignificant dimension of, "the global cold war."[3]

The cold war is certainly more than just an episode in the history of Southeast Asia in the 20th century. Lee Kuan Yew (the last surviving Southeast Asian leader of the cold war era besides Prince Sihanouk) opined that it helped the region in two ways: because of the conflict, the British, Americans, Australians, and New Zealanders "stayed here for some time and provided stability." Second, the threat from the Soviet Union, China, and North Vietnam brought about the formation within the non-communist countries of

Southeast Asia of the Association of Southeast Asian Nations (ASEAN). The cold war was thus "beneficial in consolidating (non-communist) Southeast Asia and providing stability under which development could take place."[4]

Southeast Asia today comprises eleven countries, nine of which attained independence during the cold war years. Indonesia proclaimed independence in August 1945 but only achieved it in December 1949. The Philippines obtained independence in July 1946; Burma (now Myanmar), in January 1948. Cambodia achieved independence in November 1953 but only acquired international recognition of its status at the 1954 Geneva Conference. Laos also achieved independence from the French at the 1954 Geneva Conference but was plagued by a civil war until December 1975, when the People's Democratic Republic of Laos was established. Vietnam, too, went through first a colonial war (First Vietnam War) against the French and then a civil war (Second Vietnam War), before the northern and southern parts of Vietnam were unified under the communists in April 1975. This was formalized as the Socialist Republic of Vietnam in July 1976. The Federation of Malaya achieved independence from the British in August 1957. With the inclusion of the British colonies of Singapore, Sabah, and Sarawak, it became the Federation of Malaysia in August 1963. Singapore separated from the Federation and became an independent state in August 1965. Brunei obtained independence from the British in January 1984. The eleventh and newest Southeast Asian state, East Timor (now known as Timor-Leste), only became a sovereign entity in May 2002. Thailand, an anomaly, was never colonized.

Milton Osborne put it in a nutshell when he wrote that, for all the countries of Southeast Asia, the decades after the Second World War were "dominated by the issue of independence, how it would be granted or resisted, and whether it would be gained by violence or peace."[5] It was a complex period accentuated by the diversity of the region. The histories were "individual" but the goals were common.[6] The preoccupation of the first postwar generation of historians was with the writing of what John Smail terms "autonomous" Southeast Asian history and "national history." Autonomous history was a reaction against history written from the perspective of the European colonial masters.[7] Its emphases were on "nationalism" and "decolonization."[8]

These national histories were essentially written from the perspective of the victors, the incumbent powers, and the Southeast Asian elite. They claim to be the official histories and are generally Whiggish in interpetation. The limitations and linearity of these "national histories" led a new generation of historians to challenge the national narratives by writing what Thongchai Winichakul labels "postnational" histories or "alternative" histories—the versions of history which had been ignored or rejected by the ruling elite. An example is "history from below."[9]

Another, more recent, trajectory is the international history of the cold war in Southeast Asia—the focus of this chapter. In Southeast Asia, the onset of the cold war—the international contest between the United States on the one hand and the Soviet Union and China on the other—coincided with nationalist struggles and decolonization. In the first generation "national" histories, the cold war was the context. For the second generation, the cold war was at the center of the analysis.[10] This is an important difference, and I will return to this point below. The respected historian Wang Gungwu cautions against conflating the history of decolonization with the history of the cold war, even though he acknowledged that some overlap was inevitable. He asks: "does the story of American intervention and commitment not overlap with something that should belong to another story, that of the anticommunist Cold War, of keeping the Soviet bear away and containing the Chinese dragon?"[11] Conflation would dilute the explanatory power of the concept. Not everyone agrees with Wang. Karl Hack for example believes that the approach should be to "hyperlink the various imperial, globalization, colonial records, radical, counterinsurgency, diplomatic, and nationalist strands into a coherent account."[12] Two notable collections of essays attempt (with uneven success) to describe the connection between decolonization and the cold war in Southeast Asia, or, in the words of Nayan Chanda, "the agonizing dilemma faced by Asia's nationalist movements when confronted with the choice between imperialist and colonial powers and the newly rising non-democratic communist movement."[13]

Although the post-World War II period is, as the editor of *The Cambridge History of Southeast Asia* described, "copiously covered in written and printed documents," most do not provide Southeast Asian perspectives on the cold war in the region.[14] Take for instance the early study of the cold war in Asia by Akira Iriye, which aimed to redress the American-centric and European-centric history of the cold war. Although outstanding in many respects, the book, despite its title, focuses on East Asia.[15] Another notable book on the origins of the cold war in Asia, edited by Iriye and Yonosuke Nagai, contains three chapters on Southeast Asia, but principally from the perspectives of Japan, the United States, and the Soviet Union.[16] As Lee Kuan Yew emphasized, "we have to distinguish between Northeast Asia and Southeast Asia."[17] Lee's reminder is timely because the paths to nationhood and the geopolitics of the two regions differed and consequently their responses to the cold war, while overlapping at times, likewise differed. The literature on the cold war in East Asia is more extensive than that on Southeast Asia.[18]

Until as late as 1995 historical writings on US policy and involvement in Southeast Asia, with the exception of Indochina, were limited. In his 1995 survey of the literature of the cold war in Asia, Robert J. McMahon noted the "relative scholarly neglect" of nearly all parts of Southeast Asia outside Indochina.[19] The situation improved by 2003, although I only partially agree with McMahon's later assessment. Reviewing the literature at the beginning of the 21st century, he described the scholarship on US-Southeast Asian relations from World War II to the end of the Vietnam War as "voluminous and richly documented," albeit the historiography of the post-1975 period is "still in its infancy."[20] Recent studies are "richly documented" and multi-archival. Still, the body of literature is at present by no means "voluminous."[21]

Most scholars trace the origins of the cold war to the immediate years after World War II, although the exact point and the causes remain in dispute. What many have labeled the second cold war spans 1979 to 1985. For Southeast Asia, the start of the second phase of the cold war coincides with the Vietnamese invasion of Cambodia in December 1978. But the scholarship with regard to Southeast Asia remains "stuck" on the origins. The debate over whether 1948 was the starting point, given the spate of simultaneous communist-led uprisings that occurred in Burma, India, Indonesia, Malaya, and the Philippines in that year, is not new. The "orthodox" school held that the abandonment of the broad united front strategy of the previous year resulted from directives Moscow issued at the South East Asia Youth and Student Conference (the Calcutta Conference) and the Second Congress of the Indian Communist Party, which took place in February and March 1948 respectively. The "revisionist" school argued that there were no such Soviet instructions and the revolts were all locally induced. Soviet influence was at most extra tinder to the already simmering fire.

While this debate never fully subsided, it was reinvigorated forty years later at a round table marking the sixtieth anniversary of the 1948 uprisings.[22] The most recent scholarship based on new documentation reveals that the situation was more complex and that Soviet influence occurred "at different times and in different ways." In their summary of the proceedings, the convenors of the round table, Karl Hack and Geoff Wade, observed that "The 'Southeast Asian Cold War' was constituted by local forces drawing on outside actors for their own ideological and material purposes, more than by great powers seeking local allies and a proxy theatre of conflict; and that the 'international line' was a more crucial transmission belt between locality and great powers than orders or direct involvement."[23] As for the starting date of the Southeast Asian cold war, it could be 1945–6, 1948, or 1949–50, depending how one defines the term. The answer, as Geoff Wade noted, is "as much a matter of semantics as of evidence."[24]

This judgment is unlikely to be the last word. As Richard Mason maintains, the conclusions are "suggestive... pending alternative interpretations that might be borne out by further research in the relevant archives."[25] My own research shows that it is not the same for each country. In the case of Vietnam, 1948 is not considered a particularly important year compared to 1946, 1950, and 1954. The Calcutta Conference did not immediately affect the Vietminh experience. While the transformation from a purely colonial war against the French into a cold war can be traced to 1948, it only became significant in 1950. Yet as Shawn McHale observes, Vietnam scholars are still "grappling to understand the internal dynamics of Vietnam in this period, not to mention the regional and international contexts of the war."[26]

More salient than Soviet influence, which despite Moscow's efforts never really permeated Southeast Asia, was that of the People's Republic of China (PRC). It was the PRC that substantively affected the perceptions of both communist and non-communist Southeast Asian leaders during the cold war. When examining retrospectively the international history of the cold war in Southeast Asia, to varying degrees a litany of defining events emerge. There was a Chinese element in each: These landmarks include but are not limited to the Malayan Emergency (1948–60), the Vietminh's victory at Dien Bien Phu (1954), the Bandung Conference (1955), the Confrontation/*Konfrontasi* (1963–6), the 1954 Geneva Conference and the Indochina Wars, the Indonesian Communist Party (PKI) coup in Indonesia (1965), and the formation of ASEAN (1967). The concern was not so much the physical intervention of the PRC, which was considered unlikely (albeit there were exceptions, especially in the United States). The greater worry was the Chinese trademark: "People's War." Lee Kuan Yew articulated it well by expressing a view shared by the non-communist Southeast Asian leaders during the cold war. The problem was not so much "Chinese aggression" (meaning: PRC armed soldiers marching down Southeast Asia). If that were to happen, "the problem would be much simpler," because communism would be equated with Chinese imperialism and the rest of Asia would cooperate to fight it. Lee noted that the Chinese were "much more subtle ... They believe in revolution. They are going to help revolution. ... There is not one single Chinese soldier in South Vietnam. There never will be, unless there is massive intervention by the Western powers which justifies their massive intervention .... They are able to get proxies to carry the torch of revolution with tremendous fervor and zeal."[27] As Michael Leifer notes, "the kernel of Domino theorizing is that American disengagement will lead to a measurable increase in China's power within Southeast Asia."[28] This was as true then as it is today. Even Vietnam subscribes to this view, and more openly now than ever. Hanoi is encouraging the US navy to utilize its deep water port at Cam Ranh Bay, which served as the US naval base during the Vietnam War. According to the Pentagon, Vietnam and the United States are developing a "robust bilateral defence relationship."[29]

One significant event in the early cold war years was the inaugural Asian-African Conference, known more commonly as the Bandung Conference. Anthony Reid suggests that the conference, held in Indonesia in 1955, should be considered the major Southeast Asian initiative to transcend the ideological divisions of the cold war.[30] Bandung was the brainchild of the prime ministers of two Southeast Asian countries— Burma and Indonesia—and three South Asian countries—Ceylon (now Sri Lanka), India, and Pakistan. In addition to the sponsors, twenty-four other countries from Asia and Africa (including the Middle East) participated. The Southeast Asian countries were Cambodia, Laos, the Philippines, Thailand, and South Vietnam. (Malaysia, Singapore, and Brunei were then still under British rule.) The contrast between the Bandung experiment and the American-initiated South East Asian Treaty Organization (SEATO) warrants examination. Despite its name and although headquartered in Bangkok, SEATO included only two Southeast Asian countries– the Philippines and Thailand. It therefore cannot be considered truly Southeast Asian. In fact, Indonesia and Malaysia (when it achieved independence) refused to join. Accordingly, despite enveloping other nations, the Bandung Conference was more Southeast Asian than SEATO.

Whereas SEATO was formed in 1954 with the explicit aim of checking the spread of communism in Southeast Asia, the Bandung Conference attempted to persuade Asian and African nations that their advancement could be achieved through "neutralism" and "peaceful coexistence," amongst themselves and with the major powers. The conference provided the platform to introduce China, an emerging and to many a dangerous Asian power, into the community of newly independent countries. Neither SEATO nor Bandung fully realized its objective. As a military force SEATO was hollow, and the success of the Bandung Conference was more apparent than real. It did not end the cold war ideological division in Asia. China, despite its best efforts to project itself at the Conference as benign and conciliatory, failed to convince the Southeast Asian countries.[31] The Chinese government has in recent years declassified archives pertaining to Bandung. Thus, we now know more from the Chinese angle; but the Southeast Asian perspective is still patchy. For example, while PRC premier Zhou Enlai was supportive of peaceful coexistence, Mao was less so.[32] As Jason Parker notes, we still lack an in-depth and multidimensional analysis of Bandung.[33]

Of the events mentioned above, the historiographies of the Malayan Emergency and the Indochina Wars are the best developed, particularly the British side of the "story," and, in the case of the Vietnam Wars, the American dimension. The Malayan Emergency refers to the twelve years of armed uprising by the Communist Party of Malaya (CPM) between 1948 and 1960 to overthrow the British colonial government and establish a Communist People's Democratic Republic of Malaya. The term "emergency" is a misno-mer. Leon Comber, who was then with the Malayan Special Branch, recalled that the British colonial government deliberately described it as an "emergency" so that London's commercial insurance rate would not spiral upwards and adversely affect Malayan business; the connotation of "emergency" was less serious than "war." But, as Comber emphasized, "it was nothing less than an outright war."[34]

Phillip Deery's "Malaya, 1948: Britain's Asian Cold War?" and, more importantly, Karl Hack's review of Deery's article, provide entry points to understanding the "emergency" from the cold war perspective.[35] Both essays revisit its international dimensions in con-nection with the origins of the cold war in the region (as described earlier). In recent years, the publication of memoirs by senior members of the CPM has thrown more light on the thinking and decision-making of the CPM during this period.[36] C.C. Chin, an independent scholar and researcher, has rendered some of the contemporary docu-ments and oral history accounts, most of which are in the Chinese language, into English. The CPM was indeed very much influenced by the Chinese Communist Party (CCP) but was by no means a stooge. While the CPM leadership looked upon the CCP as "the guru for the revolution," they also made strategic and tactical errors of their own in the course of their struggle against the British. In this respect, it was not unlike the relationship between the Vietnamese Communist Party (VCP) and the CCP until around 1975-6. The international dimension of the Malayan Emergency is a potential area for further research. Unlike the Vietnam War, however, Chinese sources on this topic are still unavailable.

Turning to the international history of the Vietnam or Indochina Wars, in the last two decades we have got to know much more about the communist side(s) of the "story"— the decision-making and debates amongst the Chinese Soviet and the Indochinese com-munists—the Vietnamese communists, the Khmer Rouge, and to a lesser extent the Pathet Lao. The literature continues to grow and diversify. In recent years, scholars have also started to focus on the non-communist South Vietnamese perspective, which has for too long been neglected in the historiography of the Vietnam War.[37] What is still very much lacking in the historiography is the non-communist Southeast Asian dimension— Indonesia, Malaysia, Philippines, Singapore, and Thailand—which is ironic given that the vision of falling dominoes in Southeast Asia goes back to as early as 1949, when the Nationalists were forced to withdraw from mainland China. The "Domino Theory" had been expressed in one version or another since 1949, the most well-known being President Dwight Eisenhower's press conference on April 7, 1954, when he described the possible impact of the war in Vietnam on the non-communist Southeast Asian countries. The domino theory remains controversial. While one cannot disagree with the view that the theory was a simplistic shorthand for an extremely complex reality, as states, with their own interests and attributes, are very unlike dominoes, those in positions of power surely appreciated the complexity beneath the "shorthand."[38] It is still premature to pass final judgment on the theory; our knowledge of the debates and decision-making of both the communist and non-communist sides remains too limited.

The most recent study from a non-communist Southeast Asian perspective is Ang Cheng Guan's *Southeast Asia and the Vietnam War*. Ang concludes that it was difficult to generalize the responses of the Southeast Asian countries to the Vietnam War because the war lasted for more than a decade. Each country had distinct characteristics and needs which shaped its commitment to the American cause. But there was one common and consistent goal for all five countries, which was for the US to play a key/dominant role in the regional balance of power. It is true that had it not been for the cold war, the United States would most likely not have interfered in Vietnamese affairs to the extent that it did. What is more, support for the domino theory does not equate to support for the way the Americans fought the Vietnam War. Most of the Southeast Asian leaders were rather critical about the way the war was conducted.[39]

Although the Vietnam War is the most recognizable event of the cold war in Southeast Asia, it is by no means the most significant throughout the period of the First Cold War. At the end of 1960 and early 1961, Laos rather than South Vietnam was the focus of international concern. As President Eisenhower told president-elect John F. Kennedy, if Laos should fall to the communists, then it would just be a matter of time before South Vietnam, Cambodia, Thailand, and Burma would follow. What Eisenhower recommended to Kennedy is ambiguous. What is incontrovertible is that Kennedy's predecessor identified Laos as the key to the entire region of Southeast Asia; Vietnam was in comparison considered less critical.[40] Indeed, in 1960, and particularly from the Kong Lae coup on August 9, 1960, until the summer of 1962, developments in Laos overshadowed the armed struggle in South Vietnam. It was initially in Laos after the Kong Lae coup and not in South Vietnam that Moscow, which had been staunchly opposed to a military solution to the Vietnam problem, became deeply involved. Until Maxwell Taylor's mission to South Vietnam in October 1961, Beijing was also more concerned about the situation in Laos than in South Vietnam. It was only after Laos's "neutralization" following the year-long International Conference on the Settlement of the Laotian Question in Geneva (May 16, 1961–July 23, 1962) that Vietnam became dominant on the radar screen and Laos was cast into, to borrow a phrase from Timothy Castle, "the shadow of Vietnam."[41]

Besides Laos, in the first half of the 1960s, the political situation in Indonesia which brought about the Confrontation, including a military phase between September 1963 and 1965, and the coup that overthrew President Sukarno and denuded the PKI in October 1965, also overshadowed developments in Vietnam. Despite the significance of the Confrontation in the early years of the cold war in Southeast Asia, it is not as well known as the conflict in Vietnam, and its historiography remains meager in comparison. The Confrontation—a major military conflict in maritime Southeast Asia—was essentially brought about by the demand of Indonesian President Sukarno that the British colonies of Sarawak and North Borneo as well as Singapore and Brunei each acquire independence and not be included into the Federation of Malaya.

It was the fear of communism that motivated an initially uninterested prime minister of the Federation of Malaya, Tungku Abdul Rahman, to welcome the inclusion of the predominantly Chinese populated Singapore situated at the tip of the Malay Peninsula into the Federation as a deterrent to the island's turning into "a little China." Tungku warned that if Malaya were invaded by the communists, "the result will be not a local war but a global one."[42]

Sukarno's opposition to the formation of the Federation of Malaysia, in the words of Ralph B. Smith, "created the opportunity for leftist participation in a 'liberation struggle'."[43] Such a struggle could have potentially escalated into another "Vietnam War" had it not been for the unexpected annihilation of the PKI in late 1965. Sukarno's anti-US stance and flirtation with the communists—the PKI, Moscow, and Beijing—led Marshall Green, the US ambassador to Indonesia in 1965, to opine that a "successful Sino-Indonesian alliance would have created a great communist pincer in Southeast Asia, with the largest and fifth largest countries in the world enclosing not only Vietnam but also vulnerable countries of mainland Southeast Asia." Or as then-Under Secretary of State George Ball asked, was it "not true that in size and importance, Indonesia was objectively at least on a par with the whole of Indochina...? Was not a far left, if not totally communist, takeover there, on existing trends, only a matter of time, with immense pincer effects on the position of the non-communist countries of Southeast Asia?"[44] The struggle between the right and the left ended in favor of the former because of the abortive coup of September 30/October 1, 1965, which led to the military takeover of Indonesia under Suharto and the indiscriminate and mass killing of hundreds of thousands of people who had or were presumed to have the slightest connection with the PKI.[45] In March 1967 Sukarno's effective power was formally and completely withdrawn, replaced by the pro-American Suharto regime. Sino-Indonesian relations remained frozen till 1990, and Suharto remained in power through the cold war years. Not until May 1998 was he forced to step down during the Asian Financial Crisis. There is still no hard evidence of Beijing's role in the abortive coup.[46] The Chinese have consistently denied abetting the PKI. Still, Smith's observation and the views of both Marshall Green and George Ball mirror exactly the views held by the non-communist Southeast Asian governments.[47]

The removal of Sukarno, the demise of the PKI, and the ascendency of General Suharto and the military paved the way for the formation of ASEAN in August 1967. It was the shared fear of communism—of Chinese hegemony and the prospect of a Vietnamese communist victory in Indochina—that provided the impetus for the establishment of ASEAN. ASEAN began in 1967 as a sub-regional organization comprising Indonesia, Malaysia, Thailand, the Philippines, and Singapore (separated from Malaysia since August 1965), and joined by Brunei the day it gained independence in 1984.

Indonesian Foreign Minister Adam Malik tried unsuccessfully to impress upon Sihanouk that only by closer cooperation with Southeast Asian countries could Phnom Penh withstand Chinese communist pressure.[48]

The reaction of the communist camp to the formation of ASEAN was predictably hostile. The bloc strongly believed that ASEAN was a creation of the United States and a "Western puppet." The United States naturally benefited from cooperation amongst non- and/or anti-communist countries, but Washington had nothing to do with ASEAN's formation. Indeed, as Thai Foreign Minister and one of the founding fathers of ASEAN Thanat Khoman remarked, while the member states would appreciate "the discreet blessing" of the United States, Washington should "not bestow the kiss of death" on the fledgling organization "by too close an embrace."[49]

ASEAN remained a sub-regional entity for the duration of the cold war, and only when Vietnam joined the Association and Cambodia finally followed suit in 1999 did it achieve its organizational aim, stated in Article 18 of the Founding Charter, of uniting all the nations of Southeast Asia within one entity. Moreover, when ASEAN was formed, most people did not expect it to last long. It went through a rather long "teething decade." ASEAN's achievements or lack thereof must be judged against the history of the difficult relationships between and amongst the member countries prior to 1967. It took ten years and the fall of Saigon before the five countries managed to develop cohesion and direction. After the end of the Vietnam War in April 1975, the ASEAN countries hoped that the region would be free from big power rivalry. ASEAN extended its offer of cooperation to Cambodia, Laos, and Vietnam. But regional amity was not to be. The schism in the communist camp culminated in Vietnam's invasion of Cambodia in December 1978. Between 1978 and 1991 (the second cold war), ASEAN was absorbed by the Cambodian problem. Its success in steering the Cambodian conflict to a peaceful end marked the zenith of ASEAN as a sub-regional unit. In the words of Nayan Chanda, "it is almost an aphorism to say that Vietnam's invasion of Cambodia was a gift to the Association of Southeast Asian Nations (ASEAN)—an organization in search of a cause." In the wake of the Cambodian settlement, there were concerns that ASEAN might lose the solidarity and cohesion gained from the fear of communist expansion.[50]

The cold war was essentially played out on three fronts: political, economic, and cultural. We have discussed the political aspect above. Not much has been written about the economic dimension of the cold war in Southeast Asia, although in the last few years there have been some studies pertaining to Indonesia, albeit more from the US and Soviet perspectives than the Indonesian.[51] It was the involvement of the US in the security of East and Southeast Asia during the cold war that brought about the economic transformation of the region. The cold war drew a clear line of demarcation. The Soviet Union, China, North Korea, and North Vietnam were on one side, and Japan, South Korea, Taiwan, and the ASEAN countries on the other. Washington helped to rebuild Japan as an industrial power in the wake of the Korean War, protected Taiwan against China, and also helped South Korea and Taiwan industrialize. The American strategy was to link Japan (the industrial core) with Southeast Asia, which would serve as both a market and provider of raw materials.[52] In the 1970s, Hong Kong, South Korea, Taiwan, and Singapore came to be known as the "Asian Tigers" because of their economic success. There is a need for further study of how cold war concerns brought the Northeast and Southeast Asian political economies together. But we also have to distinguish between Northeast and Southeast Asia. Driven by American, Japanese, and European multinationals, industrialization in Southeast Asia started in the 1960s, whereas the Northeast Asian countries depended primarily on their indigenous corporations.

In recent years, attention has shifted to the "social and cultural phenomena" of the cold war in the region. In the last two decades or more, much has been written about the impact of cultural dynamics on cold war politics and diplomacy in the West, but comparatively little attention has been paid to Southeast Asia, again with the exception of Vietnam.[53] Thus, the publication of the edited collection, *Dynamics of the Cold War in Asia* is most timely.[54] All except three of the essays in this volume deal with the experiences of the Southeast Asian countries. In contrast, another collection, *The Cold War in Asia: The Battle for Hearts and Minds*, contains just two essays on Southeast Asia—a rare chapter on Burma by Michael Charney and one on Indonesia.[55] Both books attempt to explore the mindsets of the Asian actors and show how they were shaped by, to borrow the words used by Wang Gungwu when endorsing *Dynamics of the Cold War in Asia*, "not only national or developmental concerns" but also "cultural ideals that reflected both their own traditions and their response to universalist and international aspirations."[56]

To cite one example, Michael Charney provides an illuminating account of how a much-publicized Burmese-language play, *Ludu Aung Than (The People Win Through)* written by U Nu, the first prime minister of Burma (1948–62), was used as a propaganda tool by both the U Nu government as well as the United States for their respective interests. The original intent of the play was to promote democracy and to admonish those who attempted to seize power by force. But Nu also wanted the play "to warn the Burmese not to allow themselves to be fooled by self-interested foreign countries," specifically the Soviet Union and the United States. Nu deliberately omitted the PRC in his imagined cold war for a complex set of reasons. Most importantly, he wanted as much as possible to prevent Communist China's intervention in Burma under any pretext. But when the play was subsequently republished with a new and lengthy introduction by Edward Hunter (a former propaganda expert in the Office of Strategic Service, the OSS) for an American audience, Nu, who saw himself as a neutralist in the cold war, was transformed into "a defender of democracy on the frontlines of international communist aggression." This was not complete misinformation because the original Burmese and English introductions by United Nations Secretary-General U Thant, which he wrote for two different audiences, differed in their descriptions of the aggression faced by Burma. Certain quarters within Nu's government had apparently also encouraged it.[57]

While one can learn much from such historical accounts, and while they certainly add to the depth of our understanding of the cold war in the region, we still lack a comprehensive narrative of the cold war in Southeast Asia because historians working on these years in Southeast Asia are limited by the paucity or unavailability of primary documents. Although the cold war ended more than two decades ago, there is no indication that Southeast Asian governments are making the archives easily accessible to scholars. In addition, the writings on the second cold war period have been dominated by journalists and political scientists. That historians have been reticent about venturing into this period is not surprising given that even for the United States, the *Foreign Relations of the United States* (FRUS) volumes pertaining to Southeast Asia end with the Ford Administration. A substantial portion of the Carter administration files have yet to be declassified.[58]

Yet the Southeast Asian dimension, both communist and non-communist, is as significant as the American dimension. A popular cold war analogy illustrates the importance of studying the moves of players and pieces on all sides of the conflict: the history of a game of chess cannot be accurately documented by only recording the moves of the white or the black player, however dominant the player.[59] For a long time and in fact still today, diplomatic historians writing on Southeast Asia depend considerably on Western archival sources, particularly those in the United States and the United Kingdom, and to a lesser extent Australia, where most received their training as historians. Nicholas Tarling, the doyen diplomatic historian of Southeast Asia, noted in his latest book that the newly independent states in Southeast Asia had to develop their own foreign policies. Yet few, if any, have been willing to allow the public to peruse any documentation of their activities.[60]

In May 2009, the National Archives of Singapore (NAS) and that country's S. Rajaratnam School of International Studies (RSIS) jointly organized a conference on "The Role of Archives in Documenting a Shared Memory of the Cold War: Asia-Pacific Perspective," with archivists from Australia, Brunei, Cambodia, Indonesia, Laos, Malaysia, Myanmar, the Philippines, Singapore, South Korea, Thailand, and Vietnam in attendance. Besides the archivists there were a number of Singaporean and Singapore-based historians with an interest in the cold war as well as select Americans. It was the first ever dialogue between Southeast Asian archivists and historians on the archival records of the cold war in the Asia Pacific, in particular Southeast Asia.[61]

The presentations of the archivists revealed that apart from Brunei and Myanmar, the participating archives hold significant primary materials about their countries' involvement in the cold war. Access to them, however, will be difficult, and the archives are not as user-friendly as the repositories in the US or Britain. Also, a command of the indigenous languages will be necessary to fully exploit the potential of the archive(s). From what the archivists explained at the conference, nevertheless, there is surely fodder for scholars interested in social and cultural issues such as gender, race, class, labor, and religion, but less so for historians interested in diplomacy or "high politics." Many questions still await answers: for example, whether Southeast Asians had other reasons for their interests in the war in Indochina besides the fear of falling dominoes. Were there communities in Southeast Asia that looked to the war for political inspiration or lessons for their own countries?

The 2009 conference explored the prospects for cooperation and collaboration between scholars and archivists, and of producing a unified list of materials pertaining to the cold war. Unfortunately there has not been any follow-up action after that first meeting.[62] Historians Ang Cheng Guan and Joey Long are presently trying to resurrect this Cold War International History of Southeast Asia project. Addressing the many unanswered questions depends on their success and that of others committed to unearthing what continues too much to be a hidden history.

The study of the cold war in Southeast Asia is still very much in its infancy. There is unequivocally a growing interest in its history and for giving agency to the Southeast Asian countries. For a balanced history, however, all sides of the conflict need to be heard—the external or exogenous powers as well as the indigenous Southeast Asian countries. Even as we privilege the latter, we must not neglect the former. As noted above, the interactions were complex and it was not as simplistic as great powers manipulating the local parties or the local parties merely acting parochially. In the history of the cold war, Southeast Asian inputs are still lacking. Filling this lacuna will require, in the words of Anthony Reid, more "openness, and even a friendly competition in openness." Given the region's linguistic diversity, it will also need cooperation and collaboration amongst historians.

## NOTES

1. <http://www.historychannelasia.com/coldwar/seminar.aspx>, accessed on September 16, 2008. See Malcolm H. Murfett, ed., *Cold War Southeast Asia* (Singapore: Marshall Cavendish Editions, 2012).

2. *The Role of Archives in Documenting a Shared Memory of the Cold War: Asia-Pacific Perspective, Seminar Proceedings, May 13–14, 2009* (Singapore: National Archives of Singapore, 2010), 8–11.

3. Odd Arne Westad, *The Global Cold War: Third World Interventions and the Making of Our Times* (Cambridge: Cambridge University Press, 2005).

4. Transcript of Senior Minister Lee Kuan Yew's Interview with Yoshinori Imai of NHK, at Istana, (Part 1), December 18, 1999, Document 200010306, <http://stars.nhb.gov.sg/stars/public/>.

5. Milton Osborne, *Exploring Southeast Asia: A Traveller's History of the Region* (Sydney: Allen and Unwin, 2002), 156. Also see, Milton Osborne, *Southeast Asia: An Introductory History* (Sydney: Allen & Unwin, 2010), one of the best one-volume histories of Southeast Asia now in its 10th edition.

6. Osborne, *Exploring Southeast Asia*, p. 156. For a summary, see Nicholas Tarling (ed.), *The Cambridge History of Southeast Asia, Volume 2* (Cambridge: Cambridge University Press, 1992), Part 2: "From World War Two to the Present."

7. See John R.W. Smail, "On the possibility of an Autonomous History of Modern Southeast Asia," *Journal of Southeast Asian History* 2 (July 1961): 72–102.

8. Thongchai Winichakul, "Writing at the Interstices: Southeast Asian Historians and Postnational Histories in Southeast Asia," in Abu Talib Ahmad and Tan Liok Ee, eds., *New Terrains in Southeast Asian History* (Singapore: Singapore University Press, 2003), chapter 1.

9. Winichakul, "Writing at the Interstices."

10. Email correspondence with Long Shi Ruey Joey, May 27, 2011.

11. Marc Frey, Ronald W. Pruessen, and Tan Tai Yong, eds., *The Transformation of Southeast Asia: International Perspectives on Decolonization* (Armonk, NY: M.E. Sharpe, 2003), 270, 272; chapter 17. See also the chapters by Akira Iriye, Prasenjit Duara, and Cary Fraser in this volume.

12. Frey et al., *Transformation of Southeast Asia*, 272; also chapter 7.

13. Christopher E. Goscha and Christian F. Ostermann, eds., *Connecting Histories: Decolonization and the Cold War in Southeast Asia, 1945–1962* (Stanford: Stanford University Press, 2009), p. x. Frey et al., *Transformation of Southeast Asia*.

14. Tarling, *Cambridge History of Southeast Asia*, 327.

15. Akira Iriye, *The Cold War in Asia: A Historical Introduction* (New Jersey: Prentice Hall, 1974).

16. Yonosuke Nagai and Akira Iriye, eds., *The Origins of the Cold War in Asia* (Tokyo: University of Tokyo Press, 1977). The three chapters are: "Who Set the Stage for the Cold War in Southeast Asia?" (Yano Toru); "The United States and the Anticolonial Revolution in Southeast Asia, 1945–50" (George McT. Kahin); and "The Cominform and Southeast Asia" (Tanigawa Yoshihiko).

17. Address by Senior Minister Mr Lee Kuan Yew at the Institute of Strategic and International Studies (ISIS) Malaysia Forum, August 16, 2000, Kuala Lumpur, Document 2000081603, <http://stars.nhb.gov.sg/stars/public/>.

18. See Tsuyoshi Hasegawa, ed., *The Cold War in East Asia 1945–1991* (Stanford, CA: Stanford University Press, 2010).

19. Michael J. Hogan, ed., *America in the World: The Historiography of US Foreign Relations since 1941* (New York: Cambridge University Press, 1995), 524–5; see chapter 17.

20. Robert D. Schulzinger, ed., *A Companion to American Foreign Relations* (Malden, MA: Blackwell Publishing, 2003), 443–4. See Chapter 24.

21. See, for example, S.R. Joey Long, *Safe for Decolonization: The Eisenhower Adminstration, Britain and Singapore* (Ohio: The Kent State University Press, 2011).

22. The papers of the round table are published in: "Asian Cold War Symposium," *Journal of Southeast Asian Studies* 40 (October 2009); and "1948 Insurgencies and the Cold War in Southeast Asia Revisited," *Journal of Malaysian Studies*, 27/1–2 (2009).

23 Karl Hack and Geoff Wade, "The Origins of the Southeast Asian Cold War," *Journal of Southeast Asian Studies* 3 (October 2009): 443.

24. Hack and Wade "Origins of the Southeast Asian Cold War," 448.

25. Richard Mason, "Revisiting 1948 Insurgencies and the Cold War in Southeast Asia," *Journal of Malaysian Studies* 27/1–2 (2009): 9.

26. Ang Cheng Guan, "Vietnam in 1948: An International History Perspective,", *Journal of Malaysian Studies* 27/1–2 (2009): 61–84 n. 62.

27. Transcript of an interview given by the Prime Minister, Mr. Lee Kuan Yew at NZBC House, March 11, 1965, lky\1965\lky0311.doc, <http://stars.nhb.gov.sg/stars/public/>.

28. Michael Leifer, *Dilemmas of Statehood in Southeast Asia* (Vancouver: University of British Columbia Press, 1972), 149.

29. See, for example, "Strategic Interests at Cam Ranh Bay," *The Straits Times*, August 1, 2011.

30. See Seng Tan and Amitav Acharya, eds., *Bandung Revisited: The Legacy of the 1955 Asian-African Conference for International Order* (Singapore: NUS Press, 2008), 23.

31. Ang Cheng Guan, "The Bandung Conference and the Cold War International History of Southeast Asia," in Tan and Acharya, eds., *Bandung Revisited: The Legacy of the 1955 Asian-African Conference for International Order* (Singapore: NUS Press, 2008), 42.

32. Shu Guang Zhang, "Constructing 'Peaceful Coexistence': China's Diplomacy towards the Geneva and Bandung Conferences, 1954–55," *Cold War History* 7 (November 2007). <http://www.wilsoncenter.org/topics/pubs/CWIHPBulletin16_intro.toc.pdf>.

33. Jason Parker, "Third World, First Time Around?" *Diplomatic History* 34 (September 2010): 760.

34. Leon Comber, "The Malayan Emergency: Nothing Less than Outright War," *The Straits Times*, June 27, 2008.

35. Phillip Deery, "Malaya, 1948: Britain's Asian Cold War?" *Journal of Cold War Studies* 9 (Winter 2007): 29–54. The article was reviewed by Karl Hack, published by H-Diplo on June 15, 2007, <http://www.h-net.org/~diplo/reviews/jcws/jcws2007.html>.

36. Most notable are Chin Peng, *My Side of History* (Singapore: Media Masters, 2003); C.C. China and Karl Hack, eds., *Dialogues with Chin Peng: New Light of the Malayan Communist Party* (Singapore: Singapore University Press, 2004). Chin Peng was the CPM's Secretary General.

37. The leading scholars on the non-communist South Vietnamese perspective, particularly on the Ngo Dinh Diem regime are Edward Miller, Phillip Catton, Matthew Masur, and Jessica Chapman. For the Vietnamese communist side, see Christopher E. Goscha, *Thailand the Southeast Asian Networks of the Vietnamese Revolution, 1885–1954* (London: Curzon, 1999), particularly chapters 4ff. The Vietnamese side is better developed in the book than the Thai. Ang Cheng Guan, *The Vietnam War from the Other Side: The Vietnamese Communists' Perspective* (London: RoutledgeCurzon, 2002) and *Ending the Vietnam War: The Vietnamese Communists' Perspective* (London: Routledge, 2004). For more recent studies, see especially Lien-Hang T. Nguyen, "The War Politburo: North Vietnam's Diplomatic and Political Road to the Tet Offensive," *Journal of Vietnamese Studies* 1/1–2 (2006): 4–58; Lien-Hang T. Nguyen, "Vietnamese Historians and the First Indochina War," in Mark Atwood Lawrence and Fredrik Logevall, eds., *The First Vietnam War: Colonial Conflict and Cold War Crisis* (Cambridge, MA: Harvard University Press, 2007), chapter 3; Merle L. Pribbenow II, "General Vo Nguyen Giap and the Mysterious Evolution of the Plan for the 1968 Tet Offensive," *Journal of Vietnamese Studies* 3 (2008): 1–33; Pierre Asselin, *A Bitter Peace: Washington, Hanoi, and the Making of the Paris Agreement* (Chapel Hill, NC: The University of North Carolina Press, 2002); Pierre Asselin, "The Democratic Republic of Vietnam and the 1954 Geneva Conference: A Revisionist Critique" in *Cold War History* 11 (May 2011): 155–95; Robert K. Brigham, *Guerrilla Diplomacy: The NLF's Foreign Relations and the Vietnam War* (Ithaca, NY: Cornell University Press, 1999); Mark Philip Bradley, *Imagining Vietnam and America: The Making of Postcolonial Vietnam, 1919–1950* (Chapel Hill, NC: The University of North Carolina Press, 2000). For the Khmer Rouge and Cambodia, see in particular the writings of David Chandler and Ben Kiernan.

38. Hasegawa, *The Cold War in East Asia*, 23.

39. See Ang Cheng Guan, *Southeast Asia and the Vietnam War* (London: Routledge, 2010).

40. "Memorandum of Conversation on January 19, 1961 between President Eisenhower and President-Elect Kennedy on the Subject of Laos," in United States Department of Defense, *United States-Vietnam Relations 1956–1960*, 1360–4; *The Pentagon Papers, Volume II* (Senator Gravel Edition) (Boston: Beacon, 1971), 635–7; Fred I. Greenstein and Richard H. Immerman, "What Did Eisenhower Tell Kennedy about Indochina? The Politics of Misperception," *The Journal of American History* 79 (September 1992): 568–87.

41. The literature on Laos during the cold war is still thin. A recent study based on British documents is Nicholas Tarling, *Britain and the Neutralization of Laos* (Singapore: NUS Press,

2011). For the communist dimension, see Ang Cheng Guan, *Vietnamese Communists' Relations with China and the Second Indochina Conflict, 1956–1962* (Jefferson, NC: McFarland & Company, Inc., Publishers, 1997), which has substantial chapters on the international situation related to developments in Laos. Se also Timothy Castle, *At War in the Shadow of Vietnam: United States Military Aid to the Royal Lao Government, 1955–75* (New York: Columbia University Press, 1993).

42. Lee Kuan Yew, *Battle for Merger* (Singapore: Ministry of Culture, 1964), Appendix 3, p. 120.

43. R.B. Smith, *An International History of the Vietnam War, Volume II: The Struggle for Southeast Asia, 1961–65* (London: Macmillan, 1965), 136.

44. Marshall Green, *Indonesia: Crisis and Transformation 1965–1968* (Washington, DC: The Compass Press, 1990), pp. xi, 150.

45. The abortive coup of September 30/October 1, 1965 continues to be a subject of historical uncertainty and debate. The most recent reconstruction of the event is John Roosa, *Pretext for Mass Murder: The September 30th Movement & Suharto's Coup d' etat in Indonesia* (Madison, WI: The University of Wisconsin Press, 2006).

46. See Yang Kuisong, "Changes in Mao Zedong's Attitude toward the Indochina War, 1949–1973," Cold War International History Project (CWIHP), Working Paper Number 34, February 2002, <http://www.wilsoncenter.org/sites/default/files/ACFB04.pdf>.

47. See Ang, *Southeast Asia and the Vietnam War*.

48. Airgram from the American Embassy in Singapore to the Department of State, Singapore, September 29, 1967, RG 59, Box 2478, POL 7 Singapore National Archives and Records Administration (NARA), College Park, Md.

49. SEATO Council Meeting, Canberra June 27–9, 1966, ANZUS Ministerial Meeting, Canberra, June 30–July 1, 1966, *Foreign Relations of the United States (FRUS) 1964–1968, Volume XXVII, Mainland Southeast Asia: Regional Affairs* (Washington, DC: United States Government Printing Office, 2000), 190–2.

50. Nayan Chanda, "Vietnam's Withdrawal from Cambodia: The ASEAN Perspective," in Gary Klintworth, ed., *Vietnam's Withdrawal from Cambodia: Regional Issues and Realignments* (Canberra, Australia: Strategic and Defence Studies Centre, Research School of Pacific Studies, Australia National University, 1990), 75.

51. Ragna Boden, "Cold War Economics: Soviet Aid to Indonesia," *Journal of Cold War Studies* 10 (Summer 2008): 110–28; Bradley R. Simpson, *Economists with Guns: Authoritarian Development and US-Indonesian Relations, 1960–1968* (Stanford, CA: Stanford University Press, 2008). See also J. Thomas Lindblad, "Current Trends in the Economic History of Southeast Asia," *Journal of Southeast Asian Studies* 26 (March 1995): 159–68.

52. See William S. Borden, *The Pacific Alliance: United States Foreign Economic Policy and Japanese Trade Recovery 1947–1955* (Madison, WI: Wisconsin University Press, 1984); Andrew J. Rotter, *The Path to Vietnam: Origins of the American Commitment to Southeast Asia* (Ithaca, NY: Cornell University Press, 1987).

53. Perhaps the best known are Frances Fitzgerald, *Fire in the Lake* (Boston, MA: Atlantic-Little, Brown, 1972) and Bradley, *Imagining Vietnam and America*.

54. Tuong Vu and Wasana Wongsurawat, eds., *Dynamics of the Cold War in Asia: Ideology, Identity, and Culture* (New York: Palgrave Macmillan, 2009).

55. Zheng Yangwen, Hong Liu, and Michael Szonyi, eds. *The Cold War in Asia: The Battle for Hearts and Minds* (Leiden: Brill, 2010).

56. Wang Gungwu, blurb for *Dynamics of the Cold War in Asia*, <http://us.macmillan.com/dynamicsofthecoldwarinasia> (accessed August 9, 2011).

57. Michael Charney, "U Nu, China and the 'Burmese' Cold War: Propaganda in Burma in the 1950s," in Zheng et al., *The Cold War in Asia*, chapter 3.

58. The most recent is *1969–1976, Volume E-12, Documents on East and Southeast Asia, 1973–1976*, published online on March 3, 2011. The most up-to-date historical study of the Third IndoChina War is Odd Arne Westad and Sophie Quinn-Judge, eds., *The Third Indochina War: Conflict between China, Vietnam and Cambodia, 1972–79* (London: Routledge, 2006). As the title suggests, the focus is on the origins of that conflict during the Nixon and Ford years.

59. Two path-breaking studies which tap into the indigenous (Filipino and Thai) as well as Western sources must be mentioned: Nick Cullather, *Illusions of Influence: The Political Economy of United States-Philippines Relations, 1942–1960* (Stanford, CA: Stanford University Press, 1994) and Daniel Fineman, *A Special Relationship: The United States and Military Government in Thailand, 1947–1958* (Honolulu: University of Hawaii Press, 1997). However, the use of indigenous source material in these two books is also limited.

60. Nicholas Tarling, *Southeast Asian Regionalism: New Zealand Perspectives* (Singapore: ISEAS, 2011).

61. *The Role of Archives*, 8–11.

62. Notes of Joint National Archives of Singapore (NAS)—S. Rajaratnam School of International Studies (RSIS) Conference on The Role of Archives in Documenting a Shared Memory of the Cold War: Asia-Pacific Perspectives, May 13–14, 2009, at Reflections at Bukit Chandu taken by Joey Long. An attempt in 2007 to apply for a research grant to document the cold war in Asia spearheaded by the Asia Research Institute, National University of Singapore also petered out.

## SELECT BIBLIOGRAPHY

Ang Cheng Guan. *Southeast Asia and the Vietnam War*. London: Routledge, 2010.

Frey, Marc, Ronald Pruessen, and Tan Tai Yong, eds. *The Transformation of Southeast Asia: International Perspectives on Decolonization*. Armonk, NY: M.E. Sharpe, 2003.

Goscha, Christopher E., and Christian F. Ostermann, eds., *Connecting Histories: Decolonization and the Cold War in Southeast Asia, 1945–1962*. Stanford, CA: Stanford University Press, 2009.

Lau, Albert, ed. *Southeast Asia and the Cold War*. London: Routledge, 2012.

Roberts, Priscilla, ed. *Behind the Bamboo Curtain: China, Vietnam and the World beyond Asia*. Washington, DC: Woodrow Wilson Center Press, 2006.

Vu, Tuong, and Wasana Wongsurawat, eds. *Dynamics of the Cold War in Asia: Ideology, Identity, and Culture*. New York: Palgrave Macmillan, 2009.

Westad, Odd Arne, and Sophie Quinn-Judge, eds. *The Third Indochina War: Conflict between China, Vietnam and Cambodia, 1972–1979*. London: Routledge, 2006.

*The Role of Archives in Documenting a Shared Memory of the Cold War: Asia-Pacific Perspective, Seminar Proceedings, 13–14 May 2009*. Singapore: National Archives of Singapore, 2010.

# CHAPTER 15

# THE COLD WAR AND THE MIDDLE EAST

SALIM YAQUB

FOR four-and-a-half decades after the end of World War II, the great powers of the world struggled to shape the geopolitical destiny of the Middle East. They did so mainly because of the region's vast mineral resources and vital strategic location. The Middle East held well over half of the world's known oil reserves, access to which was essential to global industrial development in the postwar era. The region was situated at the cross-roads of Europe, Africa, and Asia and was adjacent to the Soviet Union. In 1945 Britain still dominated the Middle East, but over the following decade it was largely supplanted by the United States, while the Soviet Union gained considerable influence as well. For the remainder of the cold war era, the two superpowers were the main outside parties to the struggle for the Middle East.

All three powers—along with lesser players like France, communist China, and some Eastern European countries—had to contend with indigenous nationalist movements, which were primarily secular in the early postwar decades and increasingly religious (mostly Islamist) thereafter. Middle Eastern nationalists were generally indifferent to the merits of the cold war struggle. They instead sought to achieve or maintain national independence, to attract support from outside powers while avoiding domination by them, to develop their own resources, and to gain advantage in local conflicts. In many of these conflicts, the superpowers lined up behind the opposing parties. Thus, in disputes pitting Israel against the Arab states, Iran against Iraq, and conservative versus radical Arab regimes, the Americans generally supported the first set of antagonists and the Soviets the second. In doing so, the superpowers helped polarize and destabilize the region. But the antagonists needed little encouragement and indeed often resisted their patrons' efforts to restrain them.

At no time was the cold war in the Middle East a contest between equals. The Western powers always enjoyed a decisive advantage. Although they were unable, over the long term, to retain outright control over the oil reserves and strategic positions of the Middle East, they succeeded in preserving access to them, mainly by cultivating cooperative local regimes. The general unpopularity of these regimes, combined with Arab bitterness over Western support for Israel, gave the Soviet Union numerous opportunities to enhance its own position in the region. But Moscow had limited ability to exploit these openings on account of its relative weakness, its outsider position, and its lack of appeal to ordinary Middle Easterners, especially devout Muslims who disdained the atheism of communist doctrine. The Soviets never came close to dislodging the Western powers and exhausted themselves in the effort. Indeed, it can be said that the cold war ended a decade early in the Middle East. As the 1980s began, the Soviet Union presented hardly any impediments to the extension of US power in the region. The main resistance came from local actors, especially Islamists, as it would continue to do in the post-cold war era.

In the period between the world wars, much of the Middle East was under Western European domination. Following its defeat in World War I, the Ottoman Empire lost its non-Turkish holdings and re-emerged as the modern republic of Turkey, mostly confined to Anatolia. The League of Nations awarded France a single mandate over Syria and Lebanon and gave Britain separate mandates over Iraq, Transjordan, and Palestine. Egypt, though not included in the Mandate system, remained subject to British military occupation, as it had been since 1882. Much of North Africa was under French colonial rule, and Britain had protectorates on the Arabian Peninsula. Saudi Arabia and Iran were independent, though the former was subject to heavy-handed British guidance and the latter to economic, military, and diplomatic pressure from both Britain and the Soviet Union. Throughout the interwar Middle East, the experience of European domination aroused powerful nationalist sentiments, which grew even stronger during and after World War II.[1]

From late 1941 to mid-1945, when they were allied against the common Nazi foe, Britain, the United States, and the Soviet Union cooperated in the Middle East in ways that prefigured their postwar rivalry. The Allies agreed on the vital strategic importance of the region, for two main reasons: it contained enormous oil reserves, and it abutted the Soviet Union. The Middle East's oil had to be kept accessible to the Allies and denied to the Axis. Its territory had to serve as a transit route for the shipment of US-supplied war materiel from the Persian Gulf to the Soviet Union. Together and individually, London, Washington, and Moscow labored to ensure that Middle Eastern governments supported or acquiesced in the Allied war effort. Britain forcibly removed pro-Axis cabinets in Egypt and Iraq. The United States extended lend-lease aid to Iran and Saudi Arabia. British, US, and Soviet troops jointly occupied Iran so that Russia could be supplied via the "Persian Corridor."[2]

After 1945 the three powers continued to appreciate the Middle East's crucial importance for the same reasons: its massive oil wealth and its proximity to Soviet territory. Yet now these features were points of conflict, rather than cooperation, between the Soviets on the one hand and the Anglo-Americans on the other. At war's end, most of the oil Americans consumed came from the Western Hemisphere. But the economic recovery of Britain and the rest of Western Europe, in which the United States had a vital stake, overwhelmingly depended on continued access to Middle Eastern oil. European recovery also entailed the revival of Germany's industrial zone, a project anathema to the Soviet Union. Similarly, whereas during the war the Middle East had been an avenue of sustenance for the Soviet Union, it now became a source of potential attack. As intercontinental ballistic missiles had not yet been developed, Anglo-US war plans relied on the ability to conduct short- and medium-range bombing raids against enemy targets. Britain's numerous airbases in the Middle East, along with some American ones, gave both countries the capability to strike Soviet territory.[3] In sum, Britain and the United States wanted to tap Middle Eastern oil for postwar recovery and use the region's territory to target the Soviet Union. The Soviets sought to disrupt these plans.

Although the crux of the cold war lay in Europe, some of the earliest cold war crises occurred in the Middle East. These erupted when Joseph Stalin attempted to create buffer zones between Soviet territory and areas controlled by hostile adversaries, much as he was doing in Eastern Europe. Unlike in Eastern Europe, however, the Red Army was not overwhelmingly dominant in the Middle East, and so Stalin's efforts in the latter area were unsuccessful. At the end of the war, the Soviet Union refused to withdraw its troops from northern Iran, claiming oil-drilling rights in the country. Meanwhile, it demanded disputed territories on the Soviet-Turkish border and pressed for partial Soviet control over the Turkish Straits. With British and US diplomatic backing, Iran and Turkey resisted. In early 1947 the United States assumed financial responsibility for the Turkish and Greek governments (the latter was battling a leftist insurgency) after Britain gave notice that it could no longer bear this burden. In a statement known as the Truman Doctrine, President Harry S. Truman declared that "it must be the policy of the United States to support free peoples who are resisting attempted subjugation by armed minorities or by outside pressures." Moscow, which had already withdrawn its troops from Iran, subsequently eased its pressure on Turkey. In 1949 Turkey applied for membership in the newly formed North Atlantic Treaty Organization (NATO), and in 1951 it was admitted to the alliance.[4]

In the wake of these failed—indeed, counterproductive—attempts to secure a Middle Eastern periphery, Stalin resigned himself to the presence of hostile forces on his southwestern borders. But fears of a resumption of Soviet adventurism, combined with suspicion of local nationalism, kept US and British officials in a state of exaggerated vigilance, as a second crisis in Iran made clear. In 1951 the Iranian parliament voted to nationalize the Anglo-Iranian Oil Company (AIOC) and elected Mohammed Mossadeq, Iran's leading proponent of nationalization, prime minister. Mossadeq began a power struggle with the country's pro-Western monarch, Mohammed Reza Shah Pahlavi. The prime minister occasionally cooperated with the Iranian Communist Party and hinted that he might seek Soviet support. In the summer of 1953 US and British intelligence agencies orchestrated an Iranian military coup that unseated Mossadeq. The Shah, who had fled the country, returned to Iran, and a pro-Shah politician became prime minister. The nationalization of Iranian oil facilities remained formally in effect, but a consortium of foreign oil companies was allowed to control and market Iran's oil, with the AIOC surrendering a large share of its operations to American oil companies. The British were not happy with this result, especially as American oil companies already dominated Saudi oil operations, but they accepted it as the price of ousting the hated Mossadeq.[5]

Back in power, the Shah visited a corrupt and repressive reign on his country, receiving extensive support from a succession of US administrations preoccupied with oil and geopolitics. "American policy between 1953 and 1978," writes the Iran scholar James A. Bill, "emphasized a special relationship with the Shah and his political elite while largely ignoring the needs and demands of the Iranian masses."[6] On both the secular left and the religious right, these circumstances created a mood of simmering resentment toward the Shah and his American patrons that would erupt in revolution in the late 1970s.

If the full potential of Iranian nationalism took a quarter-century to reveal itself, the power of Arab nationalism was already evident in the 1950s. In that decade Arab nationalism posed a formidable challenge to Anglo-US efforts to enlist the Middle East in the cold war, while offering the Soviets a golden opportunity to expand their influence in the region. Although British and US attempts to contain Arab nationalism came to grief, there were limits to Moscow's ability to exploit these openings. By decade's end the Soviet Union had made dramatic inroads into the Arab world without fundamentally challenging Western access to the region's resources and strategic positions.

To a considerable degree, the potency of Arab nationalism grew out of the Arab world's particular experience with Western domination. By 1945 most Arab countries had achieved or were about to achieve national independence. Still, portions of North Africa and the Arabian Peninsula remained under direct French and British control, respectively, while several other Arab countries, like Egypt, Jordan, and Iraq, were subject to informal British domination. These circumstances caused many Arabs to feel victimized by the West, a perception exacerbated by the establishment in 1948 of the state of Israel, which most Arabs saw as an outpost of Western imperialism.[7]

This latter view, of course, was oversimplified. Zionism was an independent force that at times had been aided, and at others hindered, by the great powers. In November 1947 Britain declined to support the United Nations partition plan, which divided Palestine into a Jewish and an Arab state. Although Britain had earlier promoted Zionism, it had retreated from this position in the face of Arab opposition. By contrast, both the United States and the Soviet Union supported partition. Washington saw Jewish statehood as a practical, humane, and politically sensible answer to the plight of Jewish refugees in Europe. Moscow saw it as a device for expelling Britain from the Middle East and possibly extending Soviet influence in the region. Both superpowers recognized Israel immediately after it declared its independence in May 1948. Over the next few years, however, the Soviet Union began endorsing Arab positions in the Arab-Israeli dispute (while continuing to support Israel's existence), Britain established cordial relations with Israel, and Israel generally supported the Western position in the cold war.[8] These facts reinforced the Arab tendency to associate Israel with the West.

Whatever the accuracy of Arab nationalist perceptions, Britain and the United States ignored them at their peril. In the early to mid-1950s, the two governments attempted to organize an anti-Soviet Middle East defense pact to complement similar initiatives in Western Europe and East Asia. The effort drew a sharp response from Egypt, whose charismatic leader, Gamal Abdel Nasser, was emerging as a pan-Arab figure. Although strongly opposed to local communism, Nasser insisted that the Arab states should refrain from aligning with either cold war bloc and instead position themselves to receive assistance from both—a stance similar to that of other "non-aligned" nations, like India, Indonesia, and Yugoslavia. In the fall of 1955 Egypt concluded a barter agreement with the Soviet Union (with Czechoslovakia serving as intermediary) whereby Egypt acquired $225–50 million worth of sophisticated weapons in exchange for surplus cotton.[9]

The arms deal represented the Soviet Union's first major foray into Arab geopolitics and reflected a broader shift in Moscow's attitude toward what would be called the "Third World." After Stalin's death in 1953, the Soviet government abandoned its professed belief in the inevitability of armed conflict between communism and capitalism and began calling instead for "peaceful competition" between the two systems. One way the Soviets hoped to compete was by establishing political, economic, and military ties to regimes and movements they had previously dismissed as "bourgeois nationalist." This approach became especially prominent after Nikita Khrushchev emerged as the Soviet Union's undisputed leader in 1955.[10] Over the next three-and-a-half decades numerous Arab regimes, espousing nationalist ideologies tinged with socialism but pointedly non-communist, benefited from Moscow's pragmatic flexibility. While the availability of Soviet aid did not directly drive the region's decolonization process, it consolidated that transformation by providing alternative diplomatic options to newly independent Arab states.

Nasser's dealings with the Soviet Union antagonized the administration of Dwight D. Eisenhower. In July 1956 it reneged on an offer to help fund the Aswan Dam, a massive Egyptian public works project designed to regulate the flow of the Nile. In response, Nasser announced that Egypt had nationalized the Suez Canal Company, most of whose shares were British- and French-owned, and would use the canal's toll revenues to finance construction of the dam. In the fall of 1956 Britain and France joined Israel in launching a military assault on Egypt.[11] Though hostile to Nasser, President Eisenhower strongly opposed the attack, seeing it as a reckless act that could irrevocably alienate Arab and Muslim opinion from the West. In a remarkable spectacle, the United States and the Soviet Union simultaneously condemned the intervention. Eisenhower then placed extraordinary diplomatic and economic pressure on Britain, France, and Israel, forcing them to halt their operations and withdraw their forces from Egypt.

The Suez crisis revealed to the world that Britain could no longer be considered the primary Western power in the Middle East. Britain would continue for some years to dominate Iraq and portions of the Arabian Peninsula, but its ability to call the shots in a more general sense was severely diminished. France, too, was discredited, though its profile in the region had been lower to begin with. By contrast, the United States and the Soviet Union, both of which had opposed the attack on Egypt, gained considerable prestige in the region. For the next quarter-century the two superpowers would be the primary outside actors in the international politics of the Middle East. Nasser was an even greater beneficiary of the crisis. Having defiantly withstood an attack by great powers, he emerged as a hero in the Arab world. In the coming years Nasser would serve as the standard-bearer of pan-Arab nationalism, preaching a vague but stirring creed of anti-imperialism, anti-Zionism, social justice, and cold war non-alignment.[12]

Recognizing both the opportunities and the challenges that Suez had created, Eisenhower seized the mantle of Western leadership in the Middle East. In 1957 and 1958, pursuing a policy known as the Eisenhower Doctrine, the president sought to discredit Nasser's neutralist program by forging a coalition of conservative Arab regimes willing to side openly with the United States in the cold war. The effort failed. Nearing the peak of his regional acclaim, Nasser convinced Arab audiences that, Suez notwithstanding, the United States remained tethered to Zionism and European imperialism. The conservative regimes could not respond favorably to the Eisenhower Doctrine without jeopardizing their own political standing. In July 1958 army officers who appeared to be acolytes of Nasser overthrew Iraq's pro-Western monarchy, a significant setback for the Western position in the region. Eisenhower responded by sending 14,000 US marines to briefly occupy Lebanon, which seemed in danger of succumbing to a Nasserist rebellion. No sooner had the marines waded ashore, however, than Eisenhower effectively abandoned his doctrine in favor of a less confrontational approach to Nasserism. "Since we are about to get thrown out of the area," he quipped to his advisors, "we might as well believe in Arab nationalism."[13]

Such a conversion became easier to stomach in early 1959, when tensions unexpectedly arose between Nasser and the Soviet Union. The dispute resulted from the Soviets' support for the new Iraqi government, which had allied itself with the Iraqi Communist Party (ICP) in a power struggle with Iraqi Nasserists. Events came to a head in March, when the Iraqi regime, with the help of the ICP, crushed a Nasserist revolt in Mosul. After a few weeks of public recrimination between Nasser and Khrushchev, Cairo and Moscow restored a semblance of cordiality. Still, the episode underscored the Soviet Union's ongoing dilemma in dealing with Middle Eastern polities: whereas cultivating non-communist nationalists usually required abandoning local communists, supporting communists came at the cost of alienating nationalists. For its part, the United States now saw that Nasserism could function as a barrier to, rather than an avenue of, Soviet encroachment on the region. Even the situation in Iraq proved tolerable. Although the new government abandoned its predecessor's alliance with the West and forged close ties to the Soviet Union, it recognized that Western Europe remained the primary market for Iraqi oil and honored existing contracts with Western companies. Eisenhower could bequeath to his successor a more relaxed view of Arab nationalism.[14]

In the early 1960s, cold war tensions in the Middle East were relatively muted. Preoccupied with crises elsewhere on the globe, most notably over Berlin and Cuba, the superpowers showed little interest in confronting each other in the Middle East. They also worked to improve relations with regional powers they had previously shunned; thus the administration of John F. Kennedy sought closer ties to Egypt and like-minded Arab states, while the Soviets mended fences with Turkey and Iran. By the end of the decade, however, the pattern had been inverted. Even as the superpowers pursued global détente, their rivalry intensified in the Middle East. Washington and Moscow became enmeshed in the region's politics to an unprecedented degree.

To some extent, the superpowers' rising activism resulted from decisions made outside the region. In 1962, after a bloody eight-year war, France abandoned its colony in

Algeria, and in 1967 it stopped serving as Israel's primary arms supplier. That same year Britain pulled out of the Aden protectorate in southern Yemen, and in 1968 London announced it would complete its withdrawal from the Persian Gulf region in 1971. These retractions of European power presented Washington and Moscow with opportunities—obligations, they would say—to expand their own involvement in the Middle East, at a time of escalating global demand for the region's oil. Meanwhile, in the aftermath of Khrushchev's ouster from power in late 1964, the Soviet government began pursuing a more targeted foreign policy. Recently thwarted in Cuba and Berlin and facing growing Chinese hostility in East Asia, Soviet leaders apparently concluded that the Middle East offered a more promising field for extending their influence.[15]

A greater catalyst for superpower involvement was the intensification of local disputes that followed a logic of their own, fed on each other, and destabilized the region in ways that made outside intervention more likely. Perhaps most unsettling of all was a set of rivalries that the political scientist Malcolm Kerr called the "Arab Cold War."[16] On one level, the Arab cold war pitted US-allied conservative regimes (like Saudi Arabia and Jordan) against self-proclaimed "radical" regimes (like Egypt, Syria, and Iraq) that were formally non-aligned but increasingly dependent on Soviet support. On another level, the Arab cold war was a struggle for primacy within the radical Arab camp in which each member sought to burnish its revolutionary credentials at the expense of its nominal allies. The first of these rivalries pushed the two Arab camps closer to their respective superpower patrons, especially in the area of arms purchases. Both rivalries, working together, made the Arab states as a whole increasingly reckless in their dealings with Israel. The result was a brief but cataclysmic war that transformed the geopolitical landscape of the Middle East and drew the superpowers more deeply into the region.

For most of the 1960s Nasser scrupulously avoided war with Israel, recognizing that the Arab states were in no position to wage it. Such caution, while sensible, allowed Arab conservatives to charge the Egyptian leader with cowardice. Meanwhile, in the mid-1960s the Syrian military stepped up its resistance to Israel's attempts to acquire three demilitarized zones along the Syrian-Israeli armistice line, and the Palestinian paramilitary group al-Fatah began conducting guerrilla raids into Israel from Syria, Lebanon, and the Jordanian-controlled West Bank. Israel responded by striking Syrian and Jordanian targets. Under growing pan-Arab pressure to enter the fray, and presented with (faulty) intelligence that Israel was preparing to invade Syria, in May 1967 Nasser requested the removal of UN peacekeeping forces stationed in the Sinai Peninsula and replaced them with Egyptian troops. While these moves could be portrayed as measures to deter an Israeli attack on Syria, Nasser's next step—the announced closure of the Strait of Tiran to Israeli shipping—was far more provocative. Evidently, Nasser found it politically impossible to avoid blockading the strait once his forces were logistically positioned to do so. He also seems to have calculated that, although the Israelis would almost certainly answer the blockade with violence, the Arab states could absorb the attack at acceptable cost.[17]

This was a grave miscalculation. In early June 1967 Israel launched a devastating strike against Egypt, moving next against Jordan and Syria when they entered the war on

Egypt's side. In six days Israel seized the Sinai Peninsula and Gaza Strip from Egypt, the West Bank from Jordan, and the Golan Heights from Syria. Unlike the Eisenhower administration, which a decade earlier had demanded a full and immediate Israeli withdrawal from Egyptian land, the administration of Lyndon B. Johnson pushed for a UN Security Council resolution instituting a ceasefire "in place," thereby allowing Israel to remain indefinitely in the territory it had captured. The Soviet Union initially called for an immediate Israeli withdrawal but quickly endorsed the ceasefire in place, seeing it as the best that could be salvaged from the catastrophe.[18]

The 1967 war was a crushing defeat for Nasserist pan-Arabism, which could not avoid responsibility for the catastrophe. Previous Arab setbacks could be blamed on effete politicians who had allegedly betrayed the Arab cause on behalf of Western patrons. This war had been lost by fiery Arab nationalists. It was a blow from which Nasserism would never recover, and Nasser's own death of a heart attack in 1970 signaled the end of an era. The decline of Nasserist Arab nationalism left a vacuum in Arab politics that would, in coming years, be filled by two previously marginalized tendencies: Palestinian nationalism, which sprang up almost immediately after the war, and political Islam, which gathered force more gradually, not emerging into full view until the early 1980s.[19]

In the aftermath of the 1967 war, the Arab states demanded that Israel withdraw completely and unconditionally from all the land it had seized. Israel insisted that the Arab states directly negotiate with Israel over the scope of any withdrawal, which in any event could not be to the pre-war borders. The Soviets endorsed the Arab demand. They also severed diplomatic relations with Israel, while remaining formally committed to its existence. Officially, the United States took an independent stance, calling for indirect negotiations leading to Israel's withdrawal from virtually all of the occupied territory. Unofficially, Washington often indulged the Israeli position, especially on the territorial question.[20]

Militarily, the superpowers became more closely identified with the contending parties. Moscow rebuilt Cairo's shattered military machine, an enormous undertaking that involved the dispatching to Egypt of thousands of military advisors and technicians. The effort was replicated in Syria on a smaller scale. The United States replaced France as Israel's primary arms supplier, providing Israel with state-of-the-art fighter aircraft. Both superpowers justified arms transfers as confidence-building measures that would induce greater diplomatic flexibility in their clients. All too often, however, the availability of arms encouraged the parties to shun compromise and pursue their objectives through force. This situation was annoying to the Americans but truly vexing to the Soviets, whose clients seemed destined to fare poorly in any resumption of full-scale hostilities.[21]

Another new element in the post-1967 Middle East was the rise to international prominence of an independent Palestinian movement. In 1969 the Palestine Liberation Organization (PLO), which the Arab League had created in 1964 to serve as a harmless outlet for mounting Palestinian frustration, emerged as an independent political and military force. Al-Fatah, which had previously operated outside of the PLO framework, joined the organization and became its dominant faction. From bases in Jordan, Syria, and Lebanon, PLO groups launched guerrilla raids into Israel and staged spectacular acts of international terrorism to draw attention to the Palestinian cause. On the political front, the PLO called for the dismantling of Israel in favor of a "secular democratic state" in which Muslims, Christians, and Jews enjoyed equal political rights.[22]

The resurfacing of Palestinian claims, even as some Arab states grew increasingly willing to recognize Israel within its pre-June 1967 borders, complicated the diplomatic situation. Nevertheless, in the late 1960s the Soviets established contact with the PLO and by the early 1970s were furnishing it modest military aid. Still committed to Israel's existence, the Soviets had little use for the PLO's political program, but they saw the value of expanding their ties in the Arab world. They were also determined to prevent communist China, which since the mid-1960s had aggressively courted Palestinian groups, from making further political inroads into the region. The United States, by contrast, shunned the PLO as a lawless organization with unrealizable national aspirations.[23] This was another way in which cold war rivalries were mapped onto the Arab-Israeli dispute.

The Persian Gulf, too, was becoming an arena of greater superpower involvement. By the late 1960s the Soviets were concerned about their ability to produce enough oil to meet their internal consumption needs and foreign export goals. Most of the country's untapped reserves lay in frozen Siberia, accessible only at great trouble and expense. So Moscow moved closer to Baghdad, offering increased military and economic assistance in exchange for access to Iraqi crude oil. Meanwhile, in January 1968 Britain announced that it would complete the withdrawal of its forces from the Persian Gulf region by December 1971, prompting speculation over who would fill the resulting strategic vacuum. The Shah of Iran was only too eager to step into the breach. He was determined to dominate the sea lanes through which Persian Gulf oil was exported and that would be crucial in time of war. He desired the wherewithal to thwart potential challenges to such domination by Iraq or radical insurgents in southeastern Arabia. Shrewdly highlighting Soviet support for these local rivals, the Shah convinced Washington to sell Tehran an ever-expanding arsenal of sophisticated arms.[24]

The Shah's regional ambitions dovetailed with broader changes in US foreign policy. By the late 1960s a relative decline in US global power, combined with the debacle of Vietnam, had convinced many US officials that stricter limits had to be placed on America's future overseas commitments. In a July 1969 speech, President Richard M. Nixon declared that, while the United States remained committed to the defense of its allies, it "cannot—and will not—conceive all the plans, design all the programs, execute all the decisions and undertake all the defense of the free nations."[25] Allies would have to play a much larger role in their own defense. This Nixon Doctrine, initially confined to Southeast Asia, soon provided the conceptual framework for a broader strategic retrenchment, as the United States reduced its forces in Japan, South Korea, and Thailand. The doctrine also came to mean a growing reliance on regional proxies—powerful pro-Western governments that could protect US interests in trouble spots around the globe. Accordingly, in the early 1970s Nixon enthusiastically endorsed the Shah's bid for regional hegemony, agreeing to sell him any conventional weapons he desired. Few US officials, in either Washington or Tehran, paid much attention to the Shah's dismal human rights record and growing unpopularity at home, a failure that would come back to haunt the United States.[26]

Another beneficiary of the Nixon Doctrine was Saudi Arabia. During the first two decades of the postwar period, the world had experienced an oil glut. In the late 1960s, however, global demand for petroleum began to outstrip available supply, boosting the price of oil and elevating the strategic profile of oil-producing states. Holding a fifth of the world's proven reserves, Saudi Arabia was a huge beneficiary of this shift, and in the early 1970s it spent tens of millions of dollars of its expanding oil revenues on US-manufactured weapons, especially in air defense. The Nixon administration warmly encouraged the sales, partly to promote the American defense industry, partly to retain Saudi friendship, and partly to empower Saudi Arabia to cooperate with Iran in combating Soviet and radical influences in the Gulf region. The cultivation of Iran and Saudi Arabia was sometimes called the "twin pillars" strategy, though the Iranian pillar was always the more prominent of the two.[27]

By the early 1970s, then, both the United States and the Soviet Union were deeply entrenched in Middle Eastern geopolitics, lining up behind their respective clients in Arab-Israeli, inter-Arab, and Iranian-Iraqi disputes. In all of these arenas, each superpower had to pursue two separate and often competing goals: retaining influence with its local allies and preventing regional disputes from escalating in ways that damaged its own interests. In retrospect, it is clear that the United States played this game far more successfully than the Soviet Union did. Indeed, the events of the 1970s broke the back of Soviet influence in the Middle East. Although daunting obstacles remained in the path of US hegemony into the 1980s, by that time they were almost entirely indigenous.

The main driver of Moscow's undoing was the asymmetrical manner in which the Arab-Israeli conflict unfolded, both on the battlefield and at the negotiating table. As the 1970s began, Israel and its Arab neighbors remained deadlocked over the consequences of the 1967 war, fortified by their respective cold war patrons. Officially, both superpowers favored a diplomatic settlement involving Israel's withdrawal from occupied land in exchange for Arab recognition of Israel. In practice, both abetted a drift toward renewed hostilities. After 1971 Nixon's national security advisor, Henry Kissinger, stymied the State Department's diplomatic initiatives, seeking to delay any settlement until key Arab countries reduced their ties to the Soviet Union. US military aid to Israel dramatically increased, reinforcing Israel's inclination to sit on its gains. The Soviets continued to build up the arsenals of Egypt and Syria. Although Moscow worried that its clients might rush into another disastrous war with Israel, it seemed even more fearful of losing influence with them. This dilemma took tangible form in July 1972, when Egyptian president Anwar Sadat, who had succeeded Nasser in 1970, expelled thousands of Soviet military personnel from the country, in protest against Moscow's reluctance to furnish the best weapons in its arsenal. The Soviets hastened to conclude a more generous arms agreement with the Egyptians.[28]

In early October 1973 Egypt and Syria launched major offensives against Israeli positions in the Sinai Peninsula and Golan Heights. The attack was surprisingly effective, especially the Egyptian prong, which involved a crossing of the Suez Canal that stunned military experts. The Soviet Union conducted a massive airlift of arms to Egypt and Syria, prompting the United States to do the same for Israel. In mid-October Israel gained the initiative and began pushing Egypt and Syria back to the 1967 ceasefire lines, and even behind them in places. When the conflict ended in late October, Israel held more Arab territory than it had at the start of the war. But if the Soviet Union suffered a setback, so did the United States and its allies. In retaliation for US support for Israel, several Arab states, including Saudi Arabia, imposed an embargo on oil shipments to the West, causing considerable damage to the global economy. The conflict also brought the superpowers to the brink of confrontation: when the Soviets intimated that they might intervene to rescue Egypt from disaster, the United States briefly placed its nuclear forces on heightened alert. As the ceasefire took hold, then, both Washington and Moscow seemed to agree that the Arab-Israeli status quo was untenable.[29]

And so Henry Kissinger, who had become Nixon's secretary of state, hastened to the Middle East to begin his famous "shuttle diplomacy." By now Israel faced growing international pressure to withdraw to the pre-June 1967 lines. Kissinger, however, believed that Israel should be permitted to retain substantial portions of the occupied territories. To facilitate that outcome, he forged an alliance with Sadat, who was extremely eager to end Egypt's conflict with Israel and focus instead on pressing economic needs. Although Sadat insisted that any Egyptian-Israeli agreement be linked to an overall Arab-Israeli settlement, Kissinger suspected that Sadat would accept the former without the latter. With Egypt thus removed from the conflict, the remaining Arab states would find it extremely difficult to resume major hostilities for the purpose of compelling a full Israeli withdrawal. Working with Egypt held the further promise of pulling that country out of the Soviet orbit and into closer association with the United States.[30]

Deftly confining his Soviet counterparts to little more than ceremonial roles, Kissinger launched a bilateral peace process whereby Egypt gradually reduced its state of belligerency against Israel as Israel vacated portions of the Sinai Peninsula. The culmination of Kissinger's diplomacy was the Sinai II Agreement of September 1975. In exchange for Israel's withdrawal from a swath of territory in the western Sinai, Egypt pledged to refrain from the use of force and to grant Israel limited use of the Suez Canal. The United States gave Israel additional military and economic aid and began providing Egypt with modest military assistance.[31] With the most powerful Arab country now under Washington's sway, Moscow had suffered a painful diplomatic setback.

Egypt was not the only Arab country to give the Russians grief; even regimes that remained ostensible clients were evading Soviet influence. In March 1975 Iraq signed a treaty with Iran to end a three-year dispute over Shatt al-Arab, a tidal river bordering the two countries that feeds into the Persian Gulf. The cessation of hostilities made Baghdad less dependent on Soviet assistance and allowed it to broaden its commercial ties to Western Europe, a happy outcome for an oil-rich nation at a time of soaring oil prices. Iraq even began purchasing arms from France. In the summer of 1976 Syria militarily intervened in Lebanon's civil war to prevent a leftist/Muslim/Palestinian coalition from gaining the upper hand. The Soviet Union strongly opposed the intervention, but Syria went in anyway, hoping to deny Israel a pretext for sending its own forces into Lebanon.[32]

The Soviets had an opportunity to recoup some of their fortunes in 1977, when the new US president, Jimmy Carter, supported the convening of an international conference in Geneva, co-sponsored by the superpowers, to achieve a comprehensive settlement of the Arab-Israeli dispute. This was precisely the scenario Kissinger had worked to avoid, for it would generate overwhelming diplomatic pressure for a full Israeli withdrawal to the pre-June 1967 lines, while also restoring some of Moscow's waning influence in the region. Not surprisingly, the Soviet Union and most Arab states endorsed the convening of a Geneva conference, and Israel greeted it with deep suspicion.

Unprepared for the intensity of Israel's objections, Carter watered down his own proposal, drawing the ire of Arab leaders as well. In November 1977, impatient with the politicking over Geneva and eager to recover the remainder of Egypt's territory, Sadat stunned the world by traveling to Jerusalem to meet with Israeli leaders. Sadat's move redirected Arab-Israeli diplomacy to the bilateral track, and Carter had to forgo his international conference. The result was the Camp David process of 1978–9, whereby Egypt, in exchange for Israel's withdrawal from the rest of the Sinai, recognized and made peace with the Jewish state. Israel continued to occupy the Golan Heights, the West Bank, and the Gaza Strip, but Egypt's formal removal from the conflict left the remaining Arab actors with few means to recover their lost territories. Egypt became a full-fledged client of the United States, receiving nearly as much military and economic aid as Israel.[33] Camp David was thus the fulfillment of Kissinger's diplomatic strategy, and a confirmation of the Soviets' diplomatic defeat.

The latter outcome was not immediately apparent, however; in 1978–9 Washington suffered two major reverses in the Middle East that gave Moscow hope of improving its regional position. One setback was the Arab world's sharply hostile reaction to the Camp David peace process. Across the political spectrum, Arab governments denounced Egypt's moves toward a separate peace with Israel. It was selfish and immoral, they argued, for Egypt to conclude an agreement that restored its own territory while leaving other Arab lands under Israeli occupation. The Arab League moved its headquarters from Cairo to Tunis and imposed economic sanctions against Egypt. The anti-Egyptian campaign temporarily united Syria and Iraq, whose mutual enmity had frequently exasperated Soviet officials. Perhaps, these officials now hoped, the Damascus/Baghdad rapprochement could form the nucleus of a revived "anti-imperialist" Arab bloc.

The other setback for the United States was the Iranian Revolution, which forced the Shah from power in early 1979. The revolution shocked the US government, which had scarcely appreciated the extent of the Shah's domestic unpopularity. US officials were especially unprepared for an Islamist opposition movement, preoccupied as they were with the threat of local communism. The Shah's ouster severely damaged America's position in the Persian Gulf, and the subsequent hostage crisis dealt a painful blow to US prestige.[34]

Still, Washington's travails afforded Moscow only limited advantage. Syria and Iraq soon resumed their feuding, frustrating Soviet hopes for a united anti-Western coalition. Iraq further irritated the Soviet Union by cracking down on the Iraqi Communist Party and skirmishing with the People's Democratic Republic of Yemen (aka South

Yemen), the only avowedly Marxist Arab regime. Moreover, despite the Arab world's nearly universal rejection of Camp David, the Soviets were incapable of launching a peace process of their own, largely because they had no diplomatic relations with Israel. As for the Iranian Revolution, it was, at best, a double-edged sword in Soviet hands. The event did seriously harm US strategic interests, and Iranian communists did wield some influence in the early stages of the Revolution. But soon Shiite conservatives gained control of the new Iranian government, purged it of secular and leftist figures, and announced a policy of "equidistance" from the two superpowers—often a euphemism for extreme hostility to both. Worse still, the Iranian Revolution unleashed an Islamic messianism that seemed likely to spread to Muslim populations within the Soviet Union itself.[35]

This latter concern helped to propel Moscow toward disaster. In the spring of 1978, a pro-Soviet Marxist regime had seized power in Afghanistan, Iran's eastern neighbor. The new government's clumsy imposition of economic and social reforms provoked a formidable Islamist rebellion that drew inspiration from the revolution then unfolding in Iran. The fact that the regime was internally divided only increased its vulnerability, a condition Washington exacerbated by providing covert assistance to Afghan rebels. Alarmed by the specters of rising instability and Islamist agitation in a nation bordering its own Central Asian republics, in December 1979 the Soviet Union sent 80,000 troops into Afghanistan to prevent the collapse of the Marxist regime.[36]

The United States reacted extremely harshly to the invasion, interpreting it as the first step in a Soviet drive to take over the Persian Gulf region. The Carter administration imposed economic sanctions against the Soviet Union, got Congress to increase military spending, and stepped up its support for anti-Soviet Afghan rebels, using Pakistan as a conduit for military and logistical aid. In a January 1980 statement that was dubbed the Carter Doctrine, the president warned: "An attempt by outside force to gain control of the Persian Gulf...will be repelled by any means necessary, including military force." That same month Carter hyperbolically called the Soviet invasion "the greatest threat to peace since the Second World War," an act clearly signaling Moscow's aggressive intent.[37]

Actually, the Soviets had plunged into a quagmire. Although Soviet forces held Afghanistan's urban centers, they were incapable of pacifying the surrounding countryside, where a fractious array of local insurgents, supported by the United States, Pakistan, Saudi Arabia, China, and other nations, harassed and bloodied the occupiers. Over the next decade, the commitment in Afghanistan would drain an already depleted Soviet treasury, hampering Moscow's ability to project power elsewhere. The war would tarnish the Soviet Union's international image, especially in the Muslim world, and demoralize the Soviet citizenry.[38]

Thus, by the start of the 1980s, the Soviets had embarked on a venture that would help to ensure their global defeat a decade later. In the Middle East, they had already lost the cold war. Although Moscow continued to cultivate Middle Eastern clients into the 1980s, it grew less and less relevant to the region's politics. Despite continuing Arab disapproval of Camp David, the Egyptian-Israeli agreement held, and the United States remained

central to prospects for future Arab-Israeli peacemaking. The Soviet Union could provide Arab states with arms and rhetorical support, but only the United States had the
ability (albeit largely unrealized) to compel Israel to withdraw from occupied territory.
The 1980s also marked the resumption of direct US military intervention in the Middle
East, a practice generally avoided since the dispatching of US marines to Lebanon in
1958. While these latter-day adventures often entailed considerable risks, military intervention by the Soviet Union was almost never one of them. In a foreshadowing of things
to come, the United States was increasingly vexed by indigenous Middle Eastern adversaries, especially Iranian-backed Shiite militants.

Events in and around Lebanon bear out these patterns. In June 1982 Israel invaded
Lebanon and besieged Beirut, attempting to crush PLO forces headquartered in the city.
The invasion also brought Israel into confrontation with Syria, which had occupied
Lebanon since 1976. In a series of dogfights, the Israeli air force destroyed 85 Syrian
planes without losing a single one of its own. The Soviet Union partially replenished
these losses and called on the United States to restrain its Israeli allies but otherwise took
little action over Lebanon. Nor could Moscow prevent Washington from monopolizing
the diplomacy surrounding the crisis. Later that summer, a special US envoy convinced
Israel to lift its siege of Beirut in exchange for the PLO's relocation to Tunisia. US marines
took part in a multilateral peacekeeping force (excluding the Soviet Union) to help
pacify the country.[39]

The US intervention in Lebanon quickly turned sour. The marines became a target of
some of the country's warring factions, drawing the special ire of Lebanese Shiites who
had borne the brunt of the Israeli invasion. In October 1983 a suicide bomber—apparently a Syrian-backed Lebanese Shiite—drove a truck filled with explosives into the
marines' compound in Beirut, killing 241 servicemen. President Ronald Reagan withdrew the marines in early 1984, but this was not the end of America's troubles in Lebanon.
Over the next couple of years several American residents were taken hostage by Iranian-
supported Lebanese Shiite factions. Secretly, the Reagan administration sold arms to
Iran on the understanding that the latter would pressure its Lebanese allies to release the
American captives. In late 1986 the administration's covert dealings (which were
bizarrely linked to Central American politics) became public knowledge, causing considerable embarrassment in Washington.[40] These were striking reverses for the United
States, but they had nothing to do with Moscow's actions and scarcely redounded to
its gain.

Events elsewhere in the region further underscored and sometimes hastened the
decline of Soviet influence. In April 1986 the United States launched a bombing raid
against Libya, a major recipient of Soviet military aid, claiming that its government was
complicit in international terrorism. The Soviet Union denounced the US operation but
took no concrete action. During the Iran-Iraq War of 1980–8, both superpowers generally tilted toward Iraq while occasionally providing tactical assistance to Iran. But,
whereas the conflict strengthened the US position in the region, it diminished that of
the Soviet Union. The war diverted Arab governments' attention from the Arab-Israeli
conflict, easing Egypt's diplomatic isolation and further obstructing Soviet efforts to

forge an anti-US Arab coalition. The crisis drew conservative Arab Gulf states closer to the United States and permitted a vast expansion of US naval forces in the area. By 1987 US warships were openly skirmishing with Iranian gunboats in the Gulf. Moscow's criticism of Washington's actions angered many Arab governments without doing much to gratify the Iranians.[41]

By now, Soviet foreign policy was in a state of upheaval. Upon assuming leadership of the Soviet Union in 1985, Mikhail Gorbachev had pledged to redouble his government's efforts to keep and gain influence in the Third World, including the Middle East. Over the next few years, however, the deterioration of the Soviet economy made such a posture untenable. The Soviets had fewer resources to devote to Third World ventures, especially as the war in Afghanistan ground on. It was also increasingly clear that the surest route to economic relief was a reduction of cold war tensions, as this would allow Moscow to spend less on arms and improve its trade relations with the West. One of the prices of renewed détente was a scaling back of Soviet activism across the globe. In the late 1980s, therefore, Moscow began retreating from its Third World commitments. In early 1989 it withdrew all of its troops from Afghanistan, despite the absence of firm guarantees that the United States and Pakistan would stop aiding rebel efforts to overthrow the Marxist regime left behind in Kabul. In 1990 the Soviet Union dramatically reduced its foreign aid across the board.[42]

In the Middle East, Gorbachev's "new thinking" amounted to near-total acquiescence to US initiatives. After Iraq invaded Kuwait in August 1990, the Soviet Union abandoned its erstwhile client and supported a UN Security Council resolution implicitly authorizing the use of force against Iraq if it failed to withdraw by a certain date. In early 1991 the Soviets sat on the sidelines as a US-led coalition ejected Iraqi forces from Kuwait. In October of that year the Soviet Union and the United States co-sponsored an international conference in Madrid to seek a resolution of the Arab-Israeli dispute. Moscow had long called for an international conference to achieve, through multilateral negotiations, a comprehensive settlement of the conflict, but the proceedings at Madrid scarcely satisfied those criteria. By prearrangement, after a few days of public speeches the conference broke up into a series of bilateral negotiations, dominated by the United States, in which the Israelis dealt separately with their Syrian, Jordanian, and Palestinian counterparts. These ground rules ensured minimal pressure on Israel to conduct a substantial withdrawal from occupied territory.[43] By year's end the Soviet Union had vanished into history. It thereafter remained for local actors—whether "rogue" states like Iraq and Iran or Islamist movements like Hizbollah and the emerging al-Qaeda network—to mount the principal opposition to the extension of US hegemony in the Middle East.

The cold war accentuated existing patterns in Middle Eastern geopolitics. The great powers enhanced the ability of local actors to pursue rivalries they would have pursued anyway, occasionally restraining the antagonists when their conflicts threatened to spin out of control. Anglo-American support allowed conservative, oil-rich governments to cling to power (thus ensuring Western access to the region's petroleum reserves), while the Soviets offered a leg-up to secular, left-leaning nationalist movements and regimes. In the 1970s secular nationalism lost vitality, eventually giving way to Islamist forms.

This phenomenon followed an internal logic of its own but was reinforced by the simultaneous decline of Soviet influence in the area. And so, a decade before the Soviet Union disintegrated, the post-cold war era dawned over the Middle East. The United States began projecting power directly and unilaterally into the Middle East, facing little opposition from outside the region but no shortage of passionate resistance from within. This pattern has continued into the current era and seems likely to endure for the foreseeable future.

## NOTES

1. Albert Hourani, *A History of the Arab Peoples* (Cambridge, MA: Harvard University Press, 1991), 315–32.

2. Thomas A. Bryson, *Seeds of Mideast Crisis: The United States Diplomatic Role in the Middle East During World War II* (Jefferson, NC: McFarland, 1981), 33–65.

3. David S. Painter, *Oil and the American Century: The Political Economy of US Foreign Oil Policy, 1941–1954* (Baltimore, MD: The Johns Hopkins University Press, 1986), 153–60; Melvyn P. Leffler, "Strategy, Diplomacy, and the Cold War: The United States, Turkey, and NATO, 1945–1952," *Journal of American History* 71:4 (March 1985): 813–14.

4. James A. Bill, *The Eagle and the Lion: The Tragedy of American-Iranian Relations* (New Haven, CT: Yale University Press, 1988), 31–8; Odd Arne Westad, *The Global Cold War: Third World Interventions and the Making of Our Times* (Cambridge: Cambridge University Press, 2005), 60–4; Galia Golan, *Soviet Policies in the Middle East: From World War II to Gorbachev* (Cambridge: Cambridge University Press, 1990), 30–2; George S. Harris, *Troubled Alliance: Turkish-American Problems in Historical Perspective, 1945–1971* (Washington, DC: American Enterprise Institute, 1972), 15–44; Harry S. Truman, Special Message to the Congress on Greece and Turkey, March 12, 1947, *Public Papers of the Presidents of the United States: Harry S. Truman, 1947* (Washington, DC: Government Printing Office, 1963), 178–9.

5. For an account of the Iranian oil nationalization crisis, see Mary Ann Heiss, *Empire and Nationhood: The United States, Great Britain, and Iranian Oil, 1950–1954* (New York: Columbia University Press, 1997).

6. Bill, *The Eagle and the Lion*, 92–7.

7. Hourani, *A History of the Arab Peoples*, 353–65.

8. Ritchie Ovendale, *Origins of the Arab-Israeli Wars* (London: Longman, 1984), 29–71, 92–125; Golan, *Soviet Policies*, 34–43.

9. Steven Z. Freiberger, *Dawn Over Suez: The Rise of American Power in the Middle East, 1953–1957* (Chicago: Ivan R. Dee, 1992), 83–100, 103–4; Oles M. Smolansky, *The Soviet Union and the Arab East Under Khrushchev* (Lewisburg, NJ: Bucknell University Press, 1974), 28–30.

10. Smolansky, *The Soviet Union and the Arab East*, 15–17, 24–5; Aleksandr Fursenko and Timothy Naftali, *Khrushchev's Cold War: The Inside Story of an American Adversary* (New York: W. W. Norton, 2006), 22–3.

11. For accounts of the Suez crisis, see Keith Kyle, *Suez* (New York: St. Martin's Press, 1991); W. Scott Lucas, *Divided We Stand: Britain, the United States, and the Suez Crisis* (London: Hodder & Stoughton, 1991).

12. Salim Yaqub, *Containing Arab Nationalism: The Eisenhower Doctrine and the Middle East* (Chapel Hill, NC: University of North Carolina Press, 2004), 61–5; Robert Stephens, *Nasser: A Political Biography* (New York: Simon & Schuster, 1972), 251–4.

13. Eisenhower quoted in John Lewis Gaddis, *We Now Know: Rethinking Cold War History* (Oxford: Clarendon Press, 1997), 175. For an account of the Eisenhower Doctrine, see Yaqub, *Containing Arab Nationalism*.

14. Yaqub, *Containing Arab Nationalism*, 256–65; Smolansky, *The Soviet Union and the Arab East*, 125–36.

15. Robert O. Freedman, *Soviet Policy toward the Middle East since 1970* (New York: Praeger, 1982), 2224.

16. Malcolm H. Kerr, *The Arab Cold War: Gamal 'Abd al-Nasir and His Rivals, 1958–1970*, 3rd ed. (London: Oxford University Press, 1971).

17. Kerr, *The Arab Cold War*, 107–14; Patrick Seale, *Asad of Syria: The Struggle For the Middle East* (London: I.B. Tauris, 1988), 118–21, 123–9; Donald Neff, *Warriors For Jerusalem: The Six Days that Changed the Middle East* (New York: Simon & Schuster, 1984), 57; Yaqub, "No War, No Peace: Egypt and the Arab-Israeli Conflict, 1952–1973," *Zeitgeschichte* 31:2 (March–April 2004): 73–5.

18. Galia Golan, "The Soviet Union and the Outbreak of the June 1967 Six-Day War," *Journal of Cold War Studies* 8:1 (Winter 2006): 12–15.

19. Adeed Dawisha, *Arab Nationalism in the Twentieth Century: From Triumph to Despair* (Princeton, NJ: Princeton University Press, 2003), 251–9, 278–9.

20. Golan, *Soviet Policies*, 64, 69–72; William B. Quandt, *Peace Process: American Diplomacy and the Arab-Israeli Conflict since 1967*, rev. ed. (Berkeley, CA: University of California Press, 2001), 63–8.

21. Quandt, *Peace Process*, 66, 70–2; Pedro Ramet, *The Soviet-Syrian Relationship since 1955: A Troubled Alliance* (Boulder, CO: Westview Press, 1990), 46–7; Freedman, *Soviet Policy*, 31–3.

22. Helena Cobban, *The Palestine Liberation Organization: People, Power and Politics* (Cambridge: Cambridge University Press, 1984), 28–9, 36–57.

23. Freedman, *Soviet Policy*, 38–9, 69–70; Roland Dannreuther, *The Soviet Union and the PLO* (London: Macmillan, 1998), 36–43; Cobban, *The Palestine Liberation Organization*, 221–4.

24. Freedman, *Soviet Policy*, 35–6; Bill, *The Eagle and the Lion*, 169–82; Douglas Little, *American Orientalism: The United States and the Middle East since 1945* (Chapel Hill, NC: University of North Carolina Press, 2002), 141–3.

25. Nixon quoted in Walter LaFeber, *The American Age: United States Foreign Policy at Home and Abroad*, 2nd ed., *1750 to the Present* (New York: W.W. Norton, 1989 [1994]), 638.

26. LaFeber, *The American Age*, 640; Bill, *The Eagle and the Lion*, 183–202; Little, *American Orientalism*, 144–5.

27. Daniel Yergin, *The Prize: The Epic Quest for Oil, Money, and Power* (New York: Simon & Schuster, 1991), 567–8, 580–7; David Long, *The United States and Saudi Arabia: Ambivalent Allies* (Boulder, CO: Westview Press, 1985), 47–8; Rachel Bronson, *Thicker than Oil: America's Uneasy Partnership with Saudi Arabia* (New York: Oxford University Press, 2006), 109–12.

28. Quandt, *Peace Process*, 92–104; Freedman, *Soviet Policy*, 73–5, 84–91.

29. Quandt, *Peace Process*, 105–24.

30. Yaqub, "The Weight of Conquest: Henry Kissinger and the Arab-Israeli Conflict," in Fredrik Logevall and Andrew Preston, eds., *Nixon in the World: American Foreign Relations, 1969–1977* (New York: Oxford University Press, 2008), 227–8, 235–7.

31. Quandt, *Peace Process*, 130–70; Henry A. Kissinger, *Years of Renewal* (New York: Simon & Schuster, 1999), 355–7, 366–8, 427–9.

32. Golan, *Soviet Policies*, 151–3, 168–70; Freedman, *Soviet Policy*, 249–57; Seale, *Asad*, 280–8.

33. For a comprehensive account of the Camp David process, see Quandt, *Camp David: Peacemaking and Politics* (Washington, DC: Brookings Institution, 1986).

34. Freedman, *Soviet Policy*, 346–52, 370–3; David Farber, *Taken Hostage: The Iran Hostage Crisis and America's First Encounter with Radical Islam* (Princeton, NJ: Princeton University Press, 2005), 72–180.

35. Golan, *Soviet Policies*, 170–3; Freedman, *Soviet Policy*, 357–69; Oles M. Smolansky and Bettie M. Smolansky, *The USSR and Iraq: The Soviet Quest for Influence* (Durham, NC: Duke University Press, 1991), 127–40; John W. Parker, *Persian Dreams: Moscow and Tehran since the Fall of the Shah* (Washington, DC: Potomac Books, 2009), 5–10.

36. Westad, *The Global Cold War*, 299–326, 328.

37. Gaddis Smith, *Morality, Reason, and Power: American Diplomacy in the Carter Years* (New York: Hill and Wang, 1986), 224–30; Ronald E. Powaski, *The Cold War: The United States and the Soviet Union, 1917–1991* (New York: Oxford University Press, 1998), 223–4.

38. Henry S. Bradsher, *Afghan Communism and Soviet Intervention* (Oxford: Oxford University Press, 1999), 196–255.

39. Patrick Tyler, *A World of Trouble: The White House and the Middle East—from the Cold War to the War on Terror* (New York: Farrar Straus Giroux, 2009), 267–90; Golan, *Soviet Policies*, 126–37.

40. Tyler, *A World of Trouble*, 290–302, 304–11, 328–33.

41. Robert O. Freedman, *Moscow and the Middle East: Soviet Policy since the Invasion of Afghanistan* (Cambridge: Cambridge University Press, 1991), 238–41, 267–76; Stephen Page, "'New Political Thinking' and Soviet Policy toward Regional Conflict in the Middle East," in David H. Goldberg and Paul Marantz, eds., *The Decline of the Soviet Union and the Transformation of the Middle East* (Boulder, CO: Westview Press, 1994), 30–6; Parker, *Persian Dreams*, 13–14; Golan, *Soviet Policies*, 195.

42. Westad, *The Global Cold War*, 364–87.

43. Page, "'New Political Thinking,'" 36–44; Kathleen Christison, *Perceptions of Palestine: Their Influence on US Middle East Policy* (Berkeley, CA: University of California Press, 1999), 265–73.

## SELECT BIBLIOGRAPHY

Bill, James A. *The Eagle and the Lion: The Tragedy of American-Iranian Relations*. New Haven, CT: Yale University Press, 1988.

Christison, Kathleen. *Perceptions of Palestine: Their Influence on US Middle East Policy*. Berkeley, CA: University of California Press, 1999.

Freedman, Robert O. *Soviet Policy toward the Middle East since 1970*. New York: Praeger, 1982.

Freedman, Robert O. *Moscow and the Middle East: Soviet Policy since the Invasion of Afghanistan*. Cambridge: Cambridge University Press, 1991.

Golan, Galia. *Soviet Policies in the Middle East: From World War II to Gorbachev*. Cambridge: Cambridge University Press, 1990.

Kerr, Malcolm H. *The Arab Cold War: Gamal 'Abd al-Nasir and His Rivals, 1958–1970*, 3rd ed. Oxford: Oxford University Press, 1971.

Little, Douglas. *American Orientalism: The United States and the Middle East since 1945*. Chapel Hill, NC: University of North Carolina Press, 2002.

Quandt, William B. *Peace Process: American Diplomacy and the Arab-Israeli Conflict since 1967*, rev. ed. Berkeley, CA: University of California Press, 2001.

Westad, Odd Arne. *The Global Cold War: Third World Interventions and the Making of Our Times*. Cambridge: Cambridge University Press, 2005.

Yergin, Daniel. *The Prize: The Epic Quest for Oil, Money, and Power*. New York: Simon & Schuster, 1991.

# CHAPTER 16

································································

# AFRICA

································································

## ELIZABETH SCHMIDT

Of all the cold war battlegrounds, Africa is the least well known. Yet, the United States, the Soviet Union, the People's Republic of China, and Cuba, as well as other nations, became embroiled in the internal affairs of countless African countries in the decades following World War II. Outside interest in Africa was nothing new. From the Arab and Euro-American-dominated slave trades in the 7th through 19th centuries, through the conquest and colonization of Africa by European powers in the late 19th and early 20th centuries, outsiders attempted to control and profit from the continent's people and resources. In many ways cold war interventions were simply a continuation of past imperial practices, with more powerful nations attempting to exploit Africa's riches for their own ends. However, in some instances outside forces helped African liberation movements and struggling new nations to chart independent paths free of imperial control.

Colonial policies during World War II had resulted in major hardships for African populations, as they were forced to provide labor and resources to support the war effort. Wartime exactions, propaganda promoting democracy and self-determination, and the experiences of African military conscripts led to widespread resistance after the war. For many European powers, the costs of colonial rule—both political and economic—increasingly seemed to outweigh the benefits. From the late 1950s, therefore, a growing number of African nations achieved political independence. In the case of colonies with a significant white minority, the solution was neither quick nor easy, and armed struggle often ensued. In other cases, when independence was deemed inevitable, the imperial powers, supported by the United States, attempted to establish moderate, pro-Western regimes that would leave the colonial economic relationships intact. When local actors, supported by socialist countries, challenged these objectives, Africa became a battle-ground in the cold war.

The cold war, like colonialism, affected all regions of the continent, and its legacy has contributed to many of the problems that plague Africa today. Outside interests altered the dynamics of local struggles, as cold war tensions were superimposed on local ones.

The result was unprecedented levels of destruction and widespread instability. The United States, in collaboration with its NATO allies, supported movements and regimes that opposed communism, no matter how corrupt or repressive they might be. Western patronage was based on the willingness of local actors to serve as allies and regional policemen, providing military bases for Western use and thwarting radical nationalist movements and governments among their neighbors. With fewer means at its disposal and less intrinsic interest in the continent, the Soviet Union generally increased its presence in response to intensified Western involvement. It supported movements and regimes that declared themselves in favor of scientific socialism and a Soviet-style model of development—regardless of their internal practices—as well as radical nationalist regimes that were shunned by the West. Although deemed by the United States to be following the Soviet lead, Cuba often took an independent route, not always to the liking of its Soviet ally. China favored African political parties, movements, and regimes that opposed Soviet influence and ideology.

The late 1980s and early 1990s witnessed the economic and political collapse of the Soviet Union and the end of the cold war. Years of war and repression had destroyed the political opposition in many African countries. Thus, as popular forces ousted cold war dictators, in many instances warlords and opportunists moved into the power vacuum. Having "won" the cold war, the United States turned its back on Africa in the 1990s. Foreign aid dwindled to a trickle. In the face of growing poverty and collapsed states, African nations were expected to pay off enormous debts incurred by cold war dictators. Since the dawn of the 21st century, however, the "war on terror" and the struggle to secure the flow of oil and other strategic resources have put Africa back on the map. Increased foreign military presence, outside support for repressive governments in oil-rich nations, and unsavory alliances, purportedly to root out terror, have brought another round of foreign intervention to Africa. Once again, the continent, its resources, and its people have become the object of struggle by outsiders.

This chapter assesses the impact of the cold war on Africa. It investigates the ways in which African actors sought outside assistance to bolster their positions in internal struggles and how their external allies introduced geopolitical considerations into the conflicts. It argues that, while some local actors initially benefited from outside intervention, the increasingly militarized conflicts were decidedly detrimental to civilian populations and their negative impact intensified over time. To explain why foreign powers became embroiled in these conflicts, the chapter examines the ideologies, practices, and interests of the main external actors—the United States, the Soviet Union, the People's Republic of China, and Cuba. It then surveys four major arenas of conflict that are representative of broad trends in cold war intervention in Africa: Nasser's Egypt, which served as a model of radical nationalism and nonalignment for many African countries; the former Belgian Congo, the site of the first cold war crisis in sub-Saharan Africa; the white-ruled countries of Southern Africa, where external powers backed various factions engaged in armed struggle against settler regimes—and sometimes one another; and finally, the Horn of Africa, where shifting alliances and armed conflicts brought regional devastation that has outlasted the cold war.

# THE UNITED STATES

The United States was the most powerful of the external actors whose ideology and interests shaped conflicts in Africa. From the end of World War II until the collapse of communism in the early 1990s, the promotion of free market capitalism and opposition to communism were dominant factors in American foreign policy. As European nations lost their empires after the war, the United States filled the void. Colonialism had restricted free trade; decolonization gave the United States access to the raw materials and markets previously controlled by the colonial powers. Assuming the "white man's burden" of fostering Western civilization and capitalist economic development, the United States also took on the task of fighting communism in the Third World.

Since poverty and instability provided fertile ground for communist ideas, the United States attempted to thwart communism through economic development. From the mid-1950s, the United States engaged in a massive transfer of foreign aid to developing countries that adopted free enterprise models, opened their countries to American investment and trade, and agreed to the export of profits on generous terms. While the United States rhetorically championed freedom, democracy, and self-determination, its opposition to communism often resulted in support for unsavory but anticommunist dictatorships. Hence, in the case of Southern Africa, a region valued for its strategic location and minerals, the United States reinforced, rather than opposed, colonialism and white minority rule.[1]

# THE SOVIET UNION

The Soviet Union's involvement in Africa during the cold war in most instances occurred in response to intensified involvement by the United States and its allies. While the American economy had been bolstered by World War II, the Soviet Union had lost more than 25 million people and almost half its economic capacity. Far from being bent on world conquest after the war, the Soviet Union was primarily concerned with securing its perimeters and surrounding itself with compliant regimes that would forestall future invasions. However, the country also took an interest in Third World decolonization, which offered the possibility of new alliances in the struggle against Western imperialism. Arguing that the "backwardness" of emerging nations was the result of capitalist exploitation, the Soviet Union deemed the removal of colonial capitalism necessary for Third World advancement, and the triumph of national liberation over imperialism a precondition for the victory of socialism. To advance this agenda, the Soviet Union initiated relationships with anticolonial and anti-imperialist regimes in Africa, Asia, and Latin America.

In their competition for Third World allies, the United States and the Soviet Union offered contrasting development models. Promoting the free enterprise capitalist system, the American model depended on the slow accumulation of capital through profits generated by the market. The Soviet model, premised on centralized economic planning, focused on the collectivization of agriculture, the development of heavy industry, the advancement of large infrastructure projects, and a massive redistribution of wealth. Because this model had enabled the Soviet Union to move rapidly from an agrarian to an industrial society, many Third World nationalists found it extremely appealing.[2]

Besides its economic example, the Soviet Union had another advantage. Since the Soviet Union did not have colonial possessions, African countries did not associate it with exploitative colonialism. The United States, however, was closely aligned with the Western European powers that had dominated Africa and Asia. Its continuation of French colonial wars in Indochina and its own history in Latin America provided little reassurance. Thus, many in the Third World associated the United States with the poverty and oppression they experienced within the colonial capitalist system, while the Soviet Union offered an attractive alternative.

Convinced that the victory of socialism over capitalism would be achieved in the Third World, the Soviet Union supported an array of national liberation movements and radical new states. While it established commercial agreements with most African countries and helped to build hundreds of industrial and other facilities, it was in the realm of military assistance to radical regimes and movements that the Soviet contribution was most decisive.

# THE PEOPLE'S REPUBLIC OF CHINA

China, like the Soviet Union, saw the African continent as an arena in which to challenge imperialism. Nevertheless, during most of the cold war, China and the Soviet Union supported rivals in the struggle for power. Despite Soviet support for the Chinese Communist Party during the 1945–49 civil war, and the friendship treaty that provided China with critical Soviet technology and economic assistance, the two countries struggled over both ideology and policy—and competed for allegiances in the Third World.

Although Soviet aid to African liberation movements and nations was more substantial, Chinese ideology often had greater allure. Soviet ideology anticipated a relatively slow progression of societies from feudalism to communism, each stage determined by the level of development of the productive forces. In contrast, China's Mao Zedong believed that societies could skip quickly through stages of material development if the people's consciousness was suitably evolved. While the Soviet Union had little regard for the rural populace, claiming that the urban proletariat would spearhead the socialist revolution, Mao argued that the peasantry, with its innate wisdom and revolutionary consciousness, would lead a country to socialism.[3]

Maoism had significant appeal in emerging African nations, where populations were predominantly rural and colonial powers had done little to develop the productive forces. Maoist ideas were prominent in Zimbabwe African National Union (ZANU) doctrines during the struggle against white minority rule in Rhodesia. In Mozambique, the Front for the Liberation of Mozambique (FRELIMO) benefited from Chinese military training and employed Maoist guerrilla strategies to attain independence from Portugal. However, FRELIMO also welcomed Soviet aid and remained strictly neutral in the Sino-Soviet conflict.

China and the Soviet Union also had major conflicts over foreign policy that had important implications in Africa. Mao considered Khrushchev's turn toward détente and "peaceful coexistence" with the West to be reactionary. In the early 1960s China publicly declared its independence in both domestic and international affairs, and the scramble for allies began. Rivalry with China, as well as the United States, thus became an important stimulus for Soviet involvement in Africa.[4] During the anticolonial struggles of the 1960s–80s, the Soviet Union and China generally supported competing movements. The Soviet Union aided the struggle of the Zimbabwe African People's Union (ZAPU) against white minority rule in Rhodesia, while China assisted ZANU's breakaway movement. In Angola, the Soviet Union supported the Popular Movement for the Liberation of Angola (MPLA), while China supported the National Front for the Liberation of Angola (FNLA) and the National Union for the Total Independence of Angola (UNITA). Ironically, the United States and China supported the same Angolan factions, finding common cause in their mutual opposition to the Soviet Union.

# CUBA

Although considered by the United States to be a Soviet surrogate, Cuba followed an independent foreign policy in Africa, often straining the relationship between the two communist countries.[5] Fidel Castro and his associates believed that Cuba could serve as an example to oppressed peoples in Latin America and Africa. It had thrown off an exploitative dictatorship and stood up to the United States in the process. Africans, in turn, were impressed by Cuba's willingness to donate military, medical, and educational assistance without expectation of future reward. Cuba's focus on Africa stemmed in part from the belief, shared by all the cold war powers, that decolonization provided a new arena for the struggle between socialism and capitalism. Unlike the other external players, however, Cuba also had an emotional link to Africa. About one-third of all Cubans had at least some African blood. Many Cubans were motivated by the desire to liberate their African brothers and sisters from colonialism and imperialism and to share the fruits of the Cuban revolution with them.[6] Thus, tens of thousands of Cuban health, education, and construction workers, and tens of thousands of Cuban soldiers, served in more than a dozen African countries during this period—all expenses paid by the Cuban government.[7]

# EGYPT, RADICAL NATIONALISM, AND THE NON-ALIGNED MOVEMENT

During the postwar period, radical nationalism and the philosophy of neutralism in international affairs threatened America's ability to replace France and Britain as the dominant power in Africa and the Middle East. These factors came to the fore in April 1955, when representatives of twenty-nine African and Asian nations and colonies and numerous liberation movements met in Bandung, Indonesia, to discuss their vision of the rapidly decolonizing world. Voicing their opposition to racialism, colonialism, and imperialism, they pledged economic and cultural cooperation and support for emancipatory movements throughout the Third World. Refusing to take sides in the cold war, the conference participants formed the core of what would become the Non-Aligned Movement. Gamal Abdel Nasser, who had helped to overthrow the Egyptian monarchy in 1952, emerged as a leader at Bandung. He was central to the formulation and promotion of the philosophy of neutralism and nonalignment, which was rapidly embraced by leaders across the African continent and elsewhere in the developing world.

While the United States rebuffed nonalignment, the Soviet Union saw it as an opportunity. Moscow seized the chance to establish political and economic ties to regions that previously had been beyond its reach. No longer holding to the Stalinist creed that only Marxist-Leninist parties were worthy of support, the Soviet Union under Nikita Khrushchev declared that movements for political and economic independence were anti-imperialist by definition and thus deserving of Soviet assistance. The Kremlin actively courted Nasser and other radical nationalists, hoping to further their common goal of undermining Western imperialism.[8] While the United States hesitated, the Soviet Union responded to Egyptian requests for economic and military aid. The United States considered this aid confirmation that Egypt was a proponent of international communism.

In July 1956, following Egypt's recognition of the People's Republic of China, the United States reneged on a promise to help fund Egypt's Aswan Dam project, which would expand arable acreage and provide power for industrialization. In response, Nasser nationalized the French and British-owned Suez Canal Company, asserting that canal revenues would henceforth be used to finance the dam. Despite their common fear of Nasser and his growing influence, Western nations differed in their response. While France and Britain supported direct military intervention, consistent with past imperial practices, the United States worried that such actions could generate anti-Western sentiment in Africa and the Middle East and might provoke a Soviet counterattack. Washington's main concern was access to Middle Eastern oil, which was not necessarily threatened by Egyptian control of the canal. Therefore, when Israel, with French and British support, attacked Egypt and occupied the Sinai Peninsula in late October, the United States introduced a UN Security Council resolution calling on Israel to withdraw and other nations to refrain from military intervention. The Soviet Union was forced into the embarrassing position of supporting the American resolution, while France and Britain vetoed it, then bombed Egyptian military installations and invaded the country by air and sea. France, Britain, and Israel withdrew only after the UN General Assembly and the British-dominated Commonwealth of Nations publicly condemned the invasion.

The denouement of the Suez War was a major victory for Nasser. He had successfully pitted the cold war powers against the imperial ones, promoting Egyptian claims in the process. His prestige among Arab nations, and nonaligned countries in general, grew enormously. Among emerging nations, the Soviet Union and the United States were applauded for their anti-imperialist stance. However, the US quickly squandered this goodwill through its support for repressive anticommunist regimes throughout the Middle East.[9]

# The Congo crisis

The Belgian Congo was the next African cold war battleground. Although the initial conflict focused on inequities that had originated under colonial rule, the dispute assumed a cold war character as local actors appealed to external powers for support. When independence came in 1960, the West was determined to retain control of the country's enormous mineral wealth by installing a moderate pro-Western government. The government of Patrice Lumumba, elected prime minister in May 1960, did not fit the bill. Lumumba's party envisioned economic transformations that would benefit ordinary Africans—but would threaten the unfettered profits of Western mining interests. Moreover, it espoused a nonaligned foreign policy along the lines articulated at Bandung.

On July 5, five days after independence, Congolese soldiers mutinied, having been informed by their Belgian officers that there would be no wage increases, promotions, or African officers in the postcolonial army. Lumumba dismissed the Belgians and promoted Joseph-Désiré Mobutu to army chief of staff. On July 10 the Belgian army intervened, purportedly to protect Belgian lives and property. The following day, Moïse Tshombe, who was closely associated with Belgian settler and international mining interests, instigated the secession of the mineral-rich Katanga province. The secession deprived the new government of more than half of its annual revenue and most of its foreign exchange earnings. The Belgian government, along with powerful Western and regional political and business interests, backed the secessionists.[10]

Convinced that Belgium was attempting to recolonize the country, Lumumba appealed for UN intervention. In 1960 the United States held key positions in the UN hierarchy and paid a disproportionate share of its operating expenses. As a result, the UN generally promoted US policies in the name of international cooperation. While the UN sent troops to the Congo, its mission was to protect white lives and property and to resolve the crisis to the benefit of Western political and economic interests. When the

UN refused to support the elected government and the United States rebuffed his appeals, Lumumba turned to the Soviet Union. The United States concluded that Lumumba was a Soviet stooge who threatened American interests not only in the Congo but in all of Africa.[11] A local conflict with colonial-era roots had been transformed into a sideshow in the broader geopolitical struggle.

In August and September, the American and Belgian governments independently formulated plans to assassinate Lumumba.[12] With CIA and Belgian military support, army chief of staff Mobutu staged a coup d'état, and Lumumba was placed under house arrest. When Lumumba attempted to flee, Mobutu's army, with CIA and Belgian assistance, captured him. High-level Belgian officials ordered Lumumba's transfer to Katanga, where he was turned over to Tshombe's secessionist forces, tortured, and executed.[13]

Lumumba was dead, but the Congo crisis was far from over. The Katanga secession was quelled in January 1963, but a rebellion by Lumumba's partisans threatened governmental authority. In July 1964 Tshombe was installed as Congolese prime minister. Viewed as the strongman needed to restore order and stem the radical tide, Tshombe quickly won Belgian and US government support. Wrongly perceiving Lumumbist rebels as communist insurgents, the United States helped Tshombe to recruit, train, and pay for a 1,000-man mercenary army, composed primarily of white South Africans and Rhodesians. Between 1964 and 1967, the private army killed thousands of Congolese civilians.[14] Communist nations responded with increased support for the rebel cause. The Soviet Union and East Germany joined China in providing military assistance. Cuba sent troops and military instructors.[15] In November 1965 Mobutu, backed by the US government, staged another coup d'état, establishing a notoriously corrupt and brutal dictatorship. He remained in power for more than three decades, serving as a proxy for Western interests in Central and Southern Africa even as he amassed a personal fortune worth billions of dollars. Abandoned by the West at the end of the cold war, he was driven from power by a rebel army in 1997. Rival warlords supported by neighboring governments rushed to fill the power vacuum. Like their colonial and cold war predecessors, they plundered the country's mineral wealth and left devastation in their wake. Between 1998 and 2007, war and war-related hunger and disease took an estimated 5.4 million Congolese lives. The ongoing Congo crisis is one of the most damning legacies of the cold war in Africa and of the colonial system that preceded it.

# White minority rule in Southern Africa

With a staunch American ally ensconced in the Congo, the focus of US anxiety moved to the white-ruled territories in the south. From the 1960s through the early 1990s, cold war concerns were superimposed on local struggles emanating from colonial conditions. In South Africa, Rhodesia, Namibia, and the Portuguese territories of Angola and Mozambique, African liberation movements challenged white minority governments for political control. The white regimes fought back with every means at their disposal, raising the hue and cry of communist aggression both to rally their white constituents and to bolster external support for their cause. It was in this context that the Nixon administration ordered a thorough review of US policy toward Southern Africa. According to the secret 1969 study, key US goals included protecting economic and strategic interests and minimizing "the opportunities for the USSR and Communist China...to gain political influence with black governments and liberation movements." The premise of the new Nixon policy was that "the whites are here to stay and the only way that constructive change can come about is through them. There is no hope for the blacks to gain the political rights they seek through violence, which will only lead to chaos and increased opportunities for the communists." The United States would adopt an attitude of consultation, rather than confrontation, maintaining "public opposition to racial repression but relax[ing] political isolation and economic restrictions on the white states."[16]

For African states and liberation movements, the US government's pronounced tilt toward the white minority regimes was totally unacceptable. The Nixon policy also proved to be extremely short-sighted, underrating African resolve to obtain political equality and overrating the ability of the white minority regimes to hold out indefinitely. Within a matter of years the white regimes were gone and the Nixon policy fell apart. The Portuguese colonies of Angola and Mozambique gained their independence in 1975, followed by Zimbabwe in 1980, and Namibia in 1990. The final chapter ended in 1994, when the racially oppressive apartheid system crumbled and South Africa elected its first majority rule government.

## South Africa

White-ruled South Africa was the cornerstone of US policy toward the region. In the decades following World War II, South Africa's cheap labor economy and mineral wealth attracted billions of dollars in foreign investments. American corporations rapidly expanded their direct investments, which by the early 1980s accounted for 20 percent of South Africa's total foreign investments. While American businesses controlled the most strategic sectors of the economy, US bank loans allowed South Africa to build its military, stockpile oil, and finance major infrastructure projects.[17] In the international arena the United States promoted the interests of the white government, consistently vetoing UN economic sanctions, despite appeals for sanctions from the African National Congress (ANC) and other anti-apartheid organizations.

Although American investments in South Africa continued to grow during the Carter years, and his administration continued to veto sanctions, Carter's emphasis on human rights led to increased public criticism of white-ruled South Africa. Thus, when the Reagan administration announced a new policy of "constructive engagement," it brought relief to apartheid proponents. Much like the Nixon policy, constructive engagement called for cooperation with the white regime. "We must avoid the trap of an indiscriminate attack on all aspects of the [apartheid] system," wrote Chester Crocker, who conceptualized the policy and served as Reagan's assistant secretary of state for African affairs.[18] "It is not our task to choose between black and white," he asserted. "The Reagan Administration has no intention of destabilizing South Africa in order to curry favor elsewhere."[19] The South African government played on cold war fears, using threats of communists on the border to rally both Western and white domestic support. The constant reference to communists as the enemy caused many anti-apartheid activists to view them as allies and to identify the United States and capitalism with apartheid.[20]

The ANC, which led civil rights and the anti-apartheid struggle for more than eight decades, became a target of US anti-communist rhetoric. The organization was founded in 1912—five years before the Bolshevik Revolution and nine years before the establishment of the Communist Party of South Africa. After the institution of apartheid in 1948 and the outlawing of communism in 1950, communists assumed leading positions in the ANC, and following the banning of the ANC in 1960 and the commencement of armed struggle in 1961, communists played key roles in the establishment of the ANC's armed wing. However, the ANC was never a communist organization.[21]

Brushing nuance aside, some US presidential administrations considered the ANC to be a communist-terrorist organization.[22] Following Pretoria's lead, the Reagan administration defined terrorism so broadly that it encompassed the activities of most African liberation movements. In January 1981 Secretary of State Alexander Haig proclaimed that "international terrorism will take the place of human rights in our concern because it is the ultimate abuse of human rights."[23] In 1982 the Republican-led Senate Judiciary Committee's Subcommittee on Security and Terrorism characterized the ANC as a Soviet surrogate and a terrorist organization that acted "in opposition to US security interests."[24] Even the Comprehensive Anti-Apartheid Act of 1986, enacted over President Reagan's veto, suggested that the ANC had engaged in "terrorist activities" and may have been the target of "Communist infiltration."[25]

## The Portuguese colonies: the case of Angola

As the United States increasingly supported the white minority regimes of Southern Africa in the late 1960s and early 1970s, the Soviet Union and its allies countered with support for liberation movements throughout the region, including those in the Portuguese colonies of Angola and Mozambique. When armed resistance began in both colonies in the early 1960s, Portugal sought support from its NATO partners, claiming that it faced a Soviet-backed communist insurgency. NATO members responded with loans that helped finance the war and bolster Portugal's failing economy. The United States supplied fighter and transport planes, bombers, helicopters, and chemical defoliants. It also trained Portuguese soldiers in counter-insurgency techniques. West

Germany provided napalm and jet planes. France furnished armored cars, helicopters, warships, and ammunition.[26] In April 1974 young Portuguese army officers, disenchanted by grueling colonial wars, and poverty and oppression at home, staged a coup d'état. The new Portuguese government quickly disengaged from its colonies. Mozambique was granted independence in June 1975, followed by Angola in November of the same year. Both countries became cold war battlegrounds, targets of foreign invasion, destabilization, and proxy wars that destroyed their infrastructures and economies. In the decades following independence, millions of civilians were maimed, killed, or rendered homeless.

The richest and most strategic of the Portuguese colonies, Angola, attracted the most outside interest. A major producer of oil, industrial diamonds, and coffee, Angola was the site of significant investments by American, British, Belgian, French, and West German firms. The colony bordered Mobutu's Congo (renamed Zaire in 1971) and South African-occupied Namibia, both of which were determined to install a compliant regime on their perimeters. Angola became a cold war battleground when the United States, the Soviet Union, China, and Cuba embroiled themselves in the conflict on the eve of Angolan independence.

Since the 1960s there had been three competing nationalist movements in Angola: the FNLA, UNITA, and the MPLA. Each of the movements was roughly associated with one of Angola's three main ethnic groups, although each had members of different ethnic origins, and the MPLA in particular had a national appeal. The oldest organization, the FNLA, was based in the northwest and was dominated by the Bakongo ethnic group. Its staunchest regional ally was Zaire, which also had a large Bakongo population. Mobutu hoped to use the FNLA to annex Angola's Bakongo areas and the oil-rich Cabinda Enclave, forming a wealthier Greater Zaire. UNITA, which split from the FNLA in 1966, was based primarily among the Ovimbundu in the central highlands. The MPLA's stronghold was among the Mbundu in north central Angola, which included the capital city of Luanda. The MPLA also found strong support among Western-educated Marxist intellectuals, urban workers, people of mixed race (*mestiços*), and a small number of Portuguese settlers. Ideology also distinguished the movements. While the MPLA was avowedly Marxist, the FNLA and UNITA used anticommunist rhetoric to win international backing, but accepted military aid from China. Both the FNLA and UNITA criticized the prominence of whites, *mestiços*, and Western-educated Africans in the MPLA and presented themselves as the only representatives of authentic African nationalism.[27]

From the outset the three liberation movements aroused interest among the key cold war players. During the Kennedy administration, the United States provided significant support to Portugal, but hedged its bets by giving token non-military aid to the FNLA.[28] In the early 1970s China, North Korea, and Romania provided the FNLA with weapons and advisors, while China also supplied UNITA. Initially the recipient of both Chinese and Soviet aid, the MPLA became entangled in the Sino-Soviet conflict and opposing sympathies fractured its leadership. Soviet disenchantment with the MPLA—due primarily to its internal leadership struggles—led to the cessation of all Soviet aid for several months in 1974.[29] After the April 1974 Portuguese coup, China stepped up aid to both the FNLA and UNITA, using Zaire as a conduit to send arms, advisors, and military instructors. The CIA followed suit, funneling support to the FNLA through Mobutu's territory. In December, concerned by the escalating involvement of China and the United States, the Soviet Union again threw its weight behind the MPLA.[30]

Portugal and the three liberation movements signed the Alvor Accord on January 15, 1975. The signatories agreed to form a transitional government that included representatives from all three movements and to hold constituent assembly elections in October, followed by formal independence on November 11, 1975. The Alvor Accord was violated almost immediately. Determined to challenge the MPLA, which the US government viewed as a Soviet proxy, the CIA immediately resumed covert support for the FNLA. In March, with tacit American support, Zairean troops attacked the MPLA in Angola. The Soviet Union responded by resuming weapons shipments to the MPLA. In July Pretoria and Washington shipped weapons and vehicles valued at tens of millions of dollars to the FNLA and UNITA.[31] The South African Defence Force (SADF) launched a massive invasion in mid-October. By the end of the month some 1,000 South African soldiers were entrenched in Angola, while 2,000 more were poised on the border. Together with FNLA, UNITA, and Zairean troops and European mercenaries, the South African army began to advance on the Angolan capital.[32]

Cuban troops then entered the fray—to the Soviet Union's dismay. Unwilling to upset a tenuous détente with the United States, Moscow had refused to supply Soviet troops—or airlift Cuban soldiers—until after independence day.[33] Cuba, however, had a different perspective. After the disintegration of the Alvor Accord, it was clear that whoever controlled the capital on independence day would determine the government. Convinced that South Africa would take Luanda before November 11 unless impeded by outside forces, Havana was unwilling to wait. On November 10 MPLA and Cuban forces held Luanda against an onslaught of FNLA and Zairean soldiers, Portuguese mercenaries, and advisors supplied by South Africa and the CIA. The following day Portugal conferred independence on the "Angolan people," and the MPLA announced the establishment of the People's Republic of Angola.[34]

After independence the Soviet Union embarked on a massive sea-and airlift, transporting more than 12,000 Cuban soldiers to Angola between November 1975 and January 1976. As the CIA's covert operation unraveled, the US Congress cut off further funding. Exposed and isolated, South Africa withdrew most of its forces from Angola in early 1976, but maintained a buffer of several thousand troops near the Namibian border to prevent Angola's use as a rear base by guerrillas fighting for Namibian independence. The victory over South Africa brought a tremendous boost to Cuban prestige in the Third World.[35] Distancing themselves from the movements associated with the apartheid regime, the vast majority of African nations quickly recognized the MPLA government.

Throughout the ensuing decade South Africa engaged in unremitting assaults on southern Angola and provided uninterrupted support for the anti-government insurgency. American aid to UNITA resumed in the mid-1980s, while the number of Cuban troops defending the MPLA government reached 52,000 in 1988.[36] The tide began to turn in March 1988, when Cuban and MPLA soldiers forced South African troops into a stalemate at Cuito Cuanavale, Angola. Pretoria then gave up hope of continuing its decades-long occupation of Namibia and began to negotiate its withdrawal from both Namibia and southern Angola. Perceived as a triumph over the apartheid army, the events at Cuito Cuanavale bolstered Cuban and MPLA reputations in the Third World.

The end of the cold war and the dismantling of apartheid in the early 1990s lessened superpower interest in the Angolan turmoil. Their outside support severed, the MPLA, FNLA, and UNITA agreed to a ceasefire in May 1991 and held elections in September 1992. The MPLA won a solid parliamentary victory and a plurality of the presidential ballots. Soured by his electoral defeat, UNITA leader, Jonas Savimbi, plunged the country back into a war that ended only with his death in 2002. During the twenty-seven year conflict, more than half a million Angolans died, and much of the country's infrastructure and economy were destroyed.

## Rhodesia/Zimbabwe

The cold war also came into play in Rhodesia, where Western powers again mistook indigenous resistance to white minority rule for an externally backed communist insurgency. From 1890 to 1980 European settlers and their descendants dominated the political and economic structures of a territory that was successively called Southern Rhodesia, Rhodesia, and finally, independent Zimbabwe. Rural Africans were dispossessed of their ancestral land and forced into impoverished reserves, restricted to poorly paid jobs, and subjected to intense political repression. The situation in white-ruled Rhodesia was much like that in apartheid South Africa.

In the early 1960s, as Britain began to transfer political power to its African colonies, it pressured the white ruling elite in Rhodesia to share power with the African majority. On November 11, 1965, Rhodesian Prime Minister Ian Smith, who opposed any move toward majority rule, announced a complete break with Britain. The international community refused to recognize the rogue regime, and in May 1968 the UN Security Council imposed comprehensive sanctions, prohibiting any economic or diplomatic relationship with Rhodesia. While ZAPU and ZANU applauded the imposition of sanctions, Rhodesian political and economic leaders engaged in a concerted effort to circumvent the embargo. They found willing partners on several continents.

In flagrant violation of international law, a number of UN member states openly flouted Rhodesian sanctions. South Africa and the Portuguese colonial regime in Mozambique served as conduits for Rhodesian imports and exports, supplying the country with petroleum, military equipment, and foreign exchange. France, Britain, and the United States looked the other way as their oil companies illegally exported petroleum to Rhodesia, and Rhodesian minerals and tobacco found their way into international markets. Between 1971 and 1977, the United States overtly contravened international law by allowing the importation of "strategic and critical materials" from Rhodesia, so long as there was no similar ban on the importation of such materials from communist countries. The American loophole was a major boon to the Rhodesian economy, and the regime's supporters touted it as an act of solidarity in the common struggle against international communism.[37]

From the early 1960s until independence in 1980, ZAPU and ZANU waged a campaign for majority rule, first as nonviolent political parties, then, after their banning, as armed liberation movements. When it became clear that the West was unwilling to enforce sanctions to bring the Smith regime into compliance with international law, ZAPU and ZANU turned to communist countries for assistance. ZAPU, which received military training and financial support from the Soviet Union, followed Soviet military strategy, preparing a conventional army for a cross-border invasion from Zambia.[38] ZANU, backed by China, implemented Mao's strategy of mass mobilization and guerrilla warfare, infiltrating the rural population and relying on the peasantry for food, shelter, intelligence, and protection.[39]

Although the US government sympathized with Smith's assessment that ZAPU and ZANU were "communist terrorist" organizations, Washington hoped that a negotiated settlement would result in a moderate government and thwart opportunities for Soviet and Cuban expansion in the region. Toward this end the United States supported Britain's 1979 initiative that resulted in an agreement on a transitional constitution, followed by elections, and independence in April 1980. Much to the surprise—and dismay—of Britain and the United States, ZANU won fifty-seven out of 100 parliamentary seats, and ZAPU (as the Patriotic Front) won twenty. The United African National Council, favored by Britain and the United States, won only three seats, while the remaining twenty seats, reserved for whites, were won by Ian Smith's party.

The determination of Rhodesian whites to retain a monopoly on political and economic power, and Western fear of radical nationalism-cum-communism, had led to a war that killed some 20,000 to 30,000 people, the vast majority of whom were Africans. Approximately one-quarter of the white population left Zimbabwe within two years of independence. Early efforts at economic restructuring and political reconciliation ended in failure. Zimbabwe's current leaders, who learned their political lessons through war rather than parliamentary democracy, have brought the nation to the brink of another disaster.

## Namibia

Rich in strategic minerals and bordering both South Africa and Angola, Namibia was another critical cold war battleground. Formerly a German colony, Namibia was transferred to South Africa as a League of Nations mandate after World War I. Violating its mandatory responsibility to promote economic and social progress in the territory, South Africa divided Namibia into ethnic reserves, plundered its mineral wealth, and established an apartheid-like system of politically repressive and racially discriminatory laws. In 1966 the UN General Assembly terminated South Africa's mandate and declared that the territory was henceforth a UN responsibility. Three years later, the Security Council endorsed the General Assembly's actions, and in 1971 the International Court of Justice found that South Africa's continued occupation of Namibia was illegal and ordered its immediate withdrawal. South Africa refused to budge.

Meanwhile, the South West Africa People's Organization (SWAPO) had begun an armed struggle for national liberation. Recognized by the UN General Assembly as "the sole and authentic representative of the Namibian people,"[40] SWAPO received economic and humanitarian aid from the UN, Nordic and African countries, and a number of religious organizations. It also received financial and military assistance from the Soviet Union and its allies. After Angola's independence in 1975, the MPLA government allowed SWAPO to establish bases in southern Angola, where its personnel received training and logistical support from Angolan, Cuban, Soviet, and East German military advisors. China supported a smaller rival movement, the South West Africa National Union (SWANU).

In 1978 the UN Security Council adopted Resolution 435, which called for a ceasefire in Namibia, followed by UN-supervised elections and the withdrawal of South African troops and administration. However, the Western powers on the Security Council stalled on the resolution's implementation, consistently vetoing sanctions against South Africa. Privately, SADF officials admitted that the war in Namibia was unwinnable, and officials in Pretoria acknowledged that SWAPO would win any free UN-supervised elections. Therefore, they were determined that such elections would not take place.[41]

The South African position elicited a sympathetic response from the newly-elected Reagan administration. In late January 1981 Washington assured Pretoria that it would not be "steamrolled on Namibia." Assistant Secretary Crocker proposed the adoption of constitutional principles prior to the elections that would enshrine white minority rights, protect private property, and otherwise limit the authority and independence of the future Namibian government. At the end of April the United States vetoed four UN Security Council resolutions that would have imposed sanctions on South Africa for its intransigence on Namibia. A few weeks later Crocker advised Secretary Haig to tell his South African counterpart that "we are willing to work with them toward an internationally acceptable settlement which will safeguard their interests and reflect our mutual desire to foreclose Soviet gains in southern Africa."[42]

In 1982 the Reagan administration introduced a new issue that would delay Namibian independence for another eight years. Arguing that the presence of Cuban troops in Angola constituted a legitimate security concern for South Africa, the administration insisted that Namibian independence be contingent on prior Cuban troop withdrawal from Angola. Embracing the linkage doctrine, South Africa intensified its assaults on southern Angola—ensuring that Cuban troops stayed in Angola and Namibia remained under its control until the waning days of the cold war.

It was only after the military stalemate at Cuito Cuanavale in March 1988 that South Africa accepted the inevitability of Namibian independence. In December South Africa and Cuba agreed to withdraw their troops from Angola, while South Africa agreed to implement the UN plan for Namibian independence. Elections were held in November 1989. As Pretoria and Washington had feared, SWAPO won 57 percent of the vote and led the country to independence in March 1990. While the Reagan administration proclaimed the December 1988 settlement to be a victory for constructive engagement, it was in fact another case of justice delayed. American support for South Africa, as a staunch anticommunist ally and regional policeman, had helped to thwart Namibian independence for more than a decade.

# THE HORN OF AFRICA: ETHIOPIA AND SOMALIA

Simultaneous with the struggle for Southern Africa was the cold war battle for the Horn. Bordering on the critical Red Sea and Indian Ocean sea lanes and in close proximity to Middle Eastern oil, Ethiopia and Somalia were both regional rivals and objects of competition between the United States and the Soviet Union. In the early 1970s, the United States helped to sustain Emperor Haile Selassie's feudal order in Ethiopia, while the nominally socialist military regime of Mohamed Siad Barre in Somalia was supported by the Soviet Union. However, by 1978, after a military coup in Ethiopia brought a self-proclaimed Marxist regime to power and Somalia attempted to annex Somali-inhabited territory in Ethiopia, the Soviet Union and the United States had switched sides. Meanwhile, the collapse of Haile Selassie's regime had resulted in a surge of separatist movements among peoples subjugated by the Ethiopian empire, and the former Italian colony of Eritrea, which had been annexed by Ethiopia in 1962, escalated its war for independence. Although the conflicts in the Horn had deep local roots, they were exacerbated by the cold war intervention of the superpowers and their allies.

Central to US interests in the region was the Kagnew communications station in Asmara, Eritrea. In order to ensure uninterrupted access to the communications station, which was critical to American intelligence gathering in Africa and the Middle East, the United States provided Ethiopia with more than $280 million in military aid between 1953 and 1977 and trained thousands of military personnel.[43] Determined to maintain its longstanding relationship with Ethiopia and to undermine Soviet-backed Somalia, the Ford administration supported the military regime that toppled Selassie in 1974—despite its socialist rhetoric and flagrant human rights abuses. However, when the Carter administration took office in early 1977, it suspended military assistance. By that time, the Kagnew communications station had been rendered obsolete by satellite technology and new American naval facilities in the Indian Ocean.[44]

Meanwhile, in Somalia, the Soviet Union had developed the port of Berbera into a sophisticated military base and provided millions of dollars in military assistance to the Siad Barre regime. By 1976, there were some 1,400 Soviet military advisors in Somalia, which had become the fourth most heavily armed nation in sub-Saharan Africa, surpassed only by Nigeria, Zaire, and Ethiopia.[45] Convinced that the Ethiopian government had stronger Marxist credentials than its Somali counterpart, the Soviet Union began to supply Ethiopia as well as its Somali rival. After Somalia attempted to advance territorial claims by invading the Ogaden region of Ethiopia in July 1977, the Soviet Union threw its full support behind Ethiopia.[46]

In late November, 1977, the regional conflict escalated into a major war. In response to Ethiopian government appeals, the Soviet Union airlifted $1 billion in military supplies and thousands of Soviet and Cuban military personnel to Ethiopia. By March 1978, when Somalia withdrew from Ethiopia in defeat, there were 16,000 Cuban troops in the country.[47] The military operation in Ethiopia had been the Soviet Union's most significant engagement outside Eastern Europe since the Korean War. Following Somalia's departure from Ethiopia, the United States openly backed the Siad Barre regime, replacing its lost assets in Ethiopia with naval, port, and air facilities in Somalia. In return, Washington provided Mogadishu with $500 million worth of military and economic assistance between 1979 and 1986, making Somalia one of the largest recipients of US military aid in sub-Saharan Africa.[48]

As the cold war wound down in the late 1980s, the superpowers proclaimed that they could no longer stomach their allies' human rights abuses. The Soviet Union drastically reduced its aid to Ethiopia, which then abandoned its Marxist rhetoric and turned to the United States for assistance. In May 1991 the Ethiopian regime collapsed under the weight of internal dissent. Meanwhile, the United States had cut its links to Somalia. In January 1991 General Mohamed Farah Aideed and his militia overthrew the Siad Barre government. As the country disintegrated into fiefdoms ruled by warlords and their clan-based militias, Somalia was transformed from a cold war battleground into a free-for-all between local warlords, Islamic militants, and, in the early 21st century, an American and Ethiopian-backed government with little popular support. Once again, foreign intervention during the cold war left a horrific and enduring legacy.

# CONCLUSION

For four decades Africa was the site of multiple cold war conflicts whose origins were in local struggles and the exploitative practices of the colonial past. The United States, the Soviet Union, China, and Cuba jockeyed for influence and advanced their respective political and economic agendas by supporting opposing sides in these disputes. The stage was set in Egypt, where Nasser's promotion of radical nationalism and nonalignment was welcomed by the Soviet Union and greeted with skepticism by the United States. Although the cold war affected all parts of the continent, its impact was most pronounced and its legacy most enduring in the Congo, the white-ruled countries of Southern Africa, and the Horn. As outside powers armed and financed rival movements and states, these regions were engulfed in violence. When the cold war ended, dictators, once propped up by the superpowers and their allies, were cut loose by both East and

West. African nations were left alone to deal with the consequences. In many instances, nascent popular democratic forces were obliterated by a new generation of warlords and dictators who had cut their teeth on the lessons of war and repression. While the conflicts and crises that ravage much of Africa today are rooted in indigenous contests for power and resources, they are also the legacy of colonialism and the devastation wrought by the cold war.

## NOTES

1. Stephen E. Ambrose, *Rise to Globalism: American Foreign Policy since 1938*, 4th ed. (New York: Penguin Books, 1985), 64–5, 81; Odd Arne Westad, *The Global Cold War: Third World Interventions and the Making of Our Times* (New York: Cambridge University Press, 2005), 9–10, 21, 31, 34–6, 38, 110–11.
2. Westad, *Global Cold War*, 67, 92–3, 166–7.
3. Maurice J. Meisner, *Mao's China and After: A History of the People's Republic*, 3rd ed. (New York: Free Press, 1999), 41–4, 192, 200–1, 295–8.
4. Meisner, *Mao's China and After*, 43, 59; Westad, *Global Cold War*, 61, 69, 215.
5. Piero Gleijeses, *Conflicting Missions: Havana, Washington, and Africa, 1959–1976* (Chapel Hill, NC: University of North Carolina Press, 2002), 155, 158, 212–13, 373, 378–9, 391.
6. Gleijeses, *Conflicting Missions*, 29, 34–7, 89, 98, 105, 136, 166–8, 175–7, 186–90, 198–9, 203–4, 213–14, 377–80; Westad, *Global Cold War*, 179–80.
7. Gleijeses, *Conflicting Missions*, 30–1, 34–8, 51, 53–5, 168, 188–9, 203–4, 207, 209, 228, 381, 392.
8. Aleksandr Fursenko and Timothy Naftali, *Khrushchev's Cold War: The Inside Story of an American Adversary* (New York: W. W. Norton, 2006), 64–5.
9. O. M. Smolansky, "Moscow and the Suez Crisis, 1956: A Reappraisal," *Political Science Quarterly* 80/4 (December 1965): 581–605.
10. Stephen R. Weissman, *American Foreign Policy in the Congo, 1960–1964* (Ithaca, NY: Cornell University Press, 1974), 19–20, 24, 66–71.
11. Weissman, *American Foreign Policy in the Congo*, 58–65, 74–84, 103–8; Madeleine G. Kalb, *The Congo Cables: The Cold War in Africa—From Eisenhower to Kennedy* (New York: Macmillan, 1982), 15, 19–22, 24–39, 41–4, 49–70, 78–83, 90–3, 101–3, 128–56, 174–96.
12. Kalb, *Congo Cables*, 54–5, 63–7, 101–3, 128–56, 175–96; United States Senate, *Alleged Assassination Plots Involving Foreign Leaders: An Interim Report of the Select Committee to Study Governmental Operations with Respect to Intelligence Activities* (Washington, DC: US Government Printing Office, 1975), 13–70; Ludo de Witte, *The Assassination of Lumumba* (London: Verso, 2001), 24–6, 46–124.
13. Kalb, *Congo Cables*, 71–5, 81–5, 89–92, 95–7, 103–5, 134–9, 147–9, 157–64, 172–4, 186–97; de Witte, *Assassination of Lumumba*, 22–3, 25, 44–5, 52–124.
14. Weissman, *American Foreign Policy in the Congo*, 234–54; Gleijeses, *Conflicting Missions*, 60–184.
15. Weissman, *American Foreign Policy in the Congo*, 254; Gleijeses, *Conflicting Missions*, 7, 60–76.
16. National Security Council Interdepartmental Group for Africa, "Study in Response to National Security Study Memorandum 39: Southern Africa," December 9, 1969, in Kenneth

Mokoena, ed., *South Africa and the United States: The Declassified History* (New York: New Press, 1993), 209, 211.

17. US companies controlled 33 percent of South Africa's motor vehicles market, 44 percent of its petroleum products market, and 70 percent of its computer market. Even more significant was the transfer of American technology and expertise. Elizabeth Schmidt, *Decoding Corporate Camouflage: US Business Support for Apartheid* (Washington, DC: Institute for Policy Studies, 1980), 59–60.

18. Chester Crocker, "South Africa: Strategy for Change," *Foreign Affairs* 59/2 (Winter 1980–1): 347.

19. Chester Crocker, "Regional Strategy for Southern Africa," *Current Policy*, No. 308 (Washington, DC: US Dept. of State, Bureau of Public Affairs, August 29, 1981): 3.

20. Thomas G. Karis, "South African Liberation: The Communist Factor," *Foreign Affairs* 65/2 (Winter 1986–7), 286.

21. Karis, "South African Liberation," 267–8, 270, 274, 277–8; Christopher Andrew and Vasili Mitrokhin, *The World Was Going Our Way: The KGB and the Battle for the Third World* (New York: Basic Books, 2005), 443.

22. Karis, "South African Liberation," 267–87; Thomas G. Karis, "Revolution in the Making: Black Politics in South Africa," *Foreign Affairs* 62/2 (Winter 1983–4): 378–406; Central Intelligence Agency, Special Report, "Subversive Movements in South Africa," May 10, 1963, in Kenneth Mokoena, ed., *South Africa and the United States: The Declassified History* (New York: New Press, 1993), 188–94.

23. "Excerpts from Haig's Remarks at First News Conference as Secretary of State," *New York Times*, January 29, 1981, p. A10.

24. Quoted in Karis, "Revolution in the Making," 379, 400.

25. Public Law (PL) 99-440, Comprehensive Anti-Apartheid Act of 1986, Sec. 102 (a) and Sec. 509 (a), October 2, 1986.

26. Allen Isaacman and Barbara Isaacman, *Mozambique: From Colonialism to Revolution, 1900–1982* (Boulder, CO: Westview Press, 1983), 104–5.

27. John A. Marcum, *The Angolan Revolution: Exile Politics and Guerrilla Warfare (1962–1976)* (Cambridge, MA: MIT Press, 1978), 2: 46–58, 165–6, 193–5, 239–40, 276.

28. Richard D. Mahoney, *JFK: Ordeal in Africa* (New York: Oxford University Press, 1983), 204–6.

29. Gleijeses, *Conflicting Missions*, 238–9, 242–4; Westad, *Global Cold War*, 226–7.

30. Gleijeses, *Conflicting Missions*, 238–9, 281; Westad, *Global Cold War*, 210, 217–18, 224–7; John Stockwell, *In Search of Enemies: A CIA Story* (New York: W. W. Norton, 1978), 67.

31. Gleijeses, *Conflicting Missions*, 258, 283, 291–7, 304; Westad, *Global Cold War*, 230–2; Stockwell, *In Search of Enemies*, 55, 162, 187–8, 206–7, 218, 229, 258.

32. Gleijeses, *Conflicting Missions*, 300–4; Stockwell, *In Search of Enemies*, 163–4.

33. Gleijeses, *Conflicting Missions*, 260, 307–8, 317–18, 365–72, 381; Andrew and Mitrokhin, *The World Was Going Our Way*, 451–2.

34. Gleijeses, *Conflicting Missions*, 303–11; Westad, *Global Cold War*, 232–6, 439 n. 63.

35. Gleijeses, *Conflicting Missions*, 316–18, 332, 339–46, 380, 393; Stockwell, *In Search of Enemies*, 207, 216–17, 220–6, 231–2.

36. Piero Gleijeses, "Moscow's Proxy? Cuba and Africa, 1975–1988," *Journal of Cold War Studies* 8/4 (Fall 2006): 98.

37. William Minter and Elizabeth Schmidt, "When Sanctions Worked: The Case of Rhodesia Reexamined," *African Affairs* 87/347 (April 1988): 211–18.

38. Andrew and Mitrokhin, *The World Was Going Our Way*, 460–1.
39. David Martin and Phyllis Johnson, *The Struggle for Zimbabwe: The Chimurenga War* (New York: Monthly Review Press, 1981), 11–13.
40. UN General Assembly Resolution 31/146, "Situation in Namibia Resulting From the Illegal Occupation of the Territory by South Africa," December 20, 1976.
41. Elizabeth Schmidt, "'Marching to Pretoria': Reagan's South Africa Policy on the Move," *TransAfrica Forum* 2/2 (Fall 1983): 7.
42. Quoted in Schmidt, "Marching to Pretoria," 8.
43. Bereket Habte Selassie, "The American Dilemma on the Horn," in Gerald J. Bender, James S. Coleman, and Richard L. Sklar, eds., *African Crisis Areas and US Foreign Policy* (Berkeley, CA: University of California Press, 1985), 170; Edmond J. Keller, "United States Foreign Policy on the Horn of Africa: Policymaking with Blinders On," in *African Crisis Areas and US Foreign Policy*, 180–2.
44. Keller, "United States Foreign Policy on the Horn of Africa," 186; Westad, *Global Cold War*, 259–60, 272.
45. Andrew and Mitrokhin, *The World Was Going Our Way*, 449; Westad, *Global Cold War*, 270–3; David D. Laitin, "Somalia's Military Government and Scientific Socialism," in Carl G. Rosberg and Thomas M. Callaghy, eds., *Socialism in Sub-Saharan Africa: A New Assessment* (Berkeley, CA: University of California, 1979), 194; Bereket Habte Selassie, *Conflict and Intervention in the Horn of Africa* (New York: Monthly Review Press, 1980), 143.
46. Selassie, *Conflict and Intervention in the Horn of Africa*, 97–125; Keller, "United States Foreign Policy on the Horn of Africa," 186–7; Andrew and Mitrokhin, *The World Was Going Our Way*, 453, 458; Westad, *Global Cold War*, 260–1, 271–6.
47. Gleijeses, "Moscow's Proxy?," 98, 108; Gleijeses, *Conflicting Missions*, 392.
48. Westad, *Global Cold War*, 277; Mark Huband, *The Skull beneath the Skin: Africa after the Cold War* (Boulder, CO: Westview Press, 2001), 282.

## Select Bibliography

Fursenko, Aleksandr, and Timothy Naftali. *Khrushchev's Cold War: The Inside Story of an American Adversary*. New York: W. W. Norton, 2006.
Gleijeses, Piero. *Conflicting Missions: Havana, Washington, and Africa, 1959–1976*. Chapel Hill, NC: University of North Carolina Press, 2002.
Kalb, Madeleine G. *The Congo Cables: The Cold War in Africa—From Eisenhower to Kennedy*. New York: Macmillan, 1982.
Mahoney, Richard D. *JFK: Ordeal in Africa*. New York: Oxford University Press, 1983.
Mazov, Sergey. *A Distant Front in the Cold War: The USSR in West Africa and the Congo, 1956–1964*. Washington, DC: Woodrow Wilson Center Press; Stanford, CA: Stanford University Press, 2010.
Minter, William. *King Solomon's Mines Revisited: Western Interests and the Burdened History of Southern Africa*. New York: Basic Books, 1986.
Mokoena, Kenneth, ed. *South Africa and the United States: The Declassified History*. New York: New Press, 1993.
Onslow, Sue, ed. *Cold War in Southern Africa: White Power, Black Liberation*. New York: Routledge, 2009.

Schraeder, Peter J. *United States Foreign Policy toward Africa: Incrementalism, Crisis and Change*. New York: Cambridge University Press, 1994.

Shubin, Vladimir. *The Hot "Cold War": The USSR in Southern Africa*. London: Pluto Press, 2008.

Weissman, Stephen R. *American Foreign Policy in the Congo, 1960–1964*. Ithaca, NY: Cornell University Press, 1974.

Westad, Odd Arne. *The Global Cold War: Third World Interventions and the Making of Our Times*. New York: Cambridge University Press, 2005.

# CHAPTER 17

# JAPAN AND THE COLD WAR:

## *An Overview*

### ANTONY BEST[1]

IN the immediate aftermath of the cold war, some American observers noted sardonically that neither of the main protagonists, the United States or the Soviet Union, had actually won the conflict; the real "victor" was Japan.[2] Drawing on contemporary hostility toward Japan's burgeoning balance of trade and Paul Kennedy's recent criticism of American imperial over-stretch in his *The Rise and Fall of the Great Powers*, the Japanese were characterized in this discourse as having had the good sense to distance themselves from superpower rivalry and concentrate instead on developing their economic might.[3] Moreover, observers claimed, the United States had foolishly contributed to Japan's inexorable rise by providing it with a "free ride" in terms of security. Sitting safely under the American nuclear umbrella, Japan had managed to avoid the pressures that the cold war had inflicted on virtually every other country on the planet.

This idea that Japan had somehow "sat out" the cold war is fundamentally flawed. In reality, every aspect of Japanese life—political, strategic, economic, and cultural—was influenced to some extent by that ideological conflict. Indeed, it is difficult to see how it could have been otherwise; Japan was occupied by the United States between 1945 and 1952 and was seen thereafter as a vitally important American ally.

This essay addresses a number of questions relating to Japan and the cold war. In regard to Japan's own evolution, it examines why it consistently allied itself to the "West" rather than the "East"; why it, alone among America's major allies, adopted a low-security posture; and why the United States tolerated its failure to rearm fully. Linked to these questions, it also examines the effect that the cold war had on Japan's supposedly homogenous politics and the extent to which the conflict influenced its economic development. Having established the reasons for its unique cold war stance, the essay then investigates what Japan, given its lack of substantial armed forces, contributed to the Western alliance system. In particular, the chapter focuses on Japan's role in the cold war in Asia and how its economic power was used to fight the spread of communism. In discussing these issues, it emphasizes that, while the cold war was important for Japan, its conduct in that conflict was influenced and constrained by its recent past, for its humiliating defeat in World War II and its sullied reputation had immense ramifications for its domestic politics and its international standing.

# JAPAN IN COLD WAR STRATEGY

The best place to begin in explaining Japan's role in the cold war is to understand how its security came to be seen as a vital Western interest. The first and most obvious point to note, of course, is that at the end of World War II Japan was occupied by the United States and thus temporarily lost control of its own sovereignty.[4] In the initial years of the cold war, therefore, it was the United States that shaped Japan's relationship to that conflict. As the occupying power the Americans had the opportunity to build Japan, with its well-educated population and its significant economic potential, into a bulwark of Western influence in East Asia. At first the occupation concentrated on the development of political pluralism. However, when the first cold war tensions emerged in the region in 1948, the United States, fearing that communism might gain a foothold in Japan, duly shifted its policy to stressing the importance of economic growth and fiscal stability. Furthermore, in pursuing this "Reverse Course" of building a stable and prosperous Japan that could resist the lure of communism and contribute to the international economy, Washington provided sizeable quantities of economic aid in a policy that echoed the Marshall Plan that had been established for Europe. At the heart of this policy was the belief that Japan was one of the five key industrial zones in the world and that, accordingly, it had to be retained within the Western camp.[5]

The stress that the United States put on the geo-strategic importance of Japan is not surprising, for the latter had been an important factor in the Western great powers' containment of Russian expansion ever since the 1890s. Witness, for example, the Anglo-Japanese alliance of 1902, which had been implicitly supported by the United States. In this context, it must also be emphasized that in the interwar period the Soviet Union had acted as a very real threat to regional security. It had financed and armed the anti-imperialist Guomindang in the period between 1923 and 1927, when that party had challenged the West's unequal treaties with China and maintained links with communist parties all across Asia.[6] Consequently, in the 1930s Japan had perceived its actions on the Asian continent, including the Manchurian crisis and the Sino-Japanese War, as pre-emptive blows against communism.[7] Indeed, many commentators during these years had speculated on the likelihood of a new Russo-Japanese war breaking out.[8] In other words, when the United States established itself in Tokyo in 1945, it entered a region in which, arguably, a "cold war" had already existed in the very recent past. Thus, once American-Soviet antagonism in Asia emerged in the late 1940s the policy-makers in Washington adopted the strategic fear of Russia that had previously exercised their

Japanese counterparts. Japan came to be seen as an integral part of an offshore island perimeter in the western Pacific that had to be denied to the Soviet Union.[9]

The American tendency to view Japan as strategically important was further reinforced by the ascendancy of East Asia, especially after the establishment of the People's Republic of China (PRC) in 1949, as the cold war theater second only to Europe in importance. Here, too, the recent past played an important role, for neither the Soviet Union nor China had forgotten nor forgiven the past behavior of Imperial Japan. Nor could either help but view the American attempt to rebuild the Japanese economy with foreboding, fearing that militarism would rise again in its wake. They therefore were keen to influence Japan against taking this path by pointing to the potential dangers of its aligning with the United States. Thus, in January 1950 the Cominform criticized the Japanese Communist Party for its pursuit of power within the parliamentary system and urged it to take up the cause of violent revolution.[10]

Faced with these tensions in Asia, which exploded into conflict with the outbreak of the Korean War in 1950, the United States sought to ensure that Japan was tied to the West. In 1951 the Truman administration convened the San Francisco peace conference to which the PRC was not invited and where the Soviet Union was presented with a fait accompli in regard to the peace treaty, which it duly refused to sign. The peace treaty was on the whole a lenient document, but simultaneously Japan was called upon to sign a security pact with the United States. Under its terms the Americans obtained the right to use naval and air bases in Japan for military operations in East Asia without the need to consult with the Japanese government. Furthermore, the United States retained direct control of Okinawa, which contained a large array of bases.[11] The Japanese archipelago thus became America's "unsinkable aircraft carrier" in the East, mirroring one of Britain's roles in Europe.

Japan's location also held economic significance. Since the start of the 20th century, it had been the leading Asian economic power, whose export of cheap products, such as affordable cotton textile goods, was seen as vital to the regional standard of living. Accordingly, when the Western powers became concerned about conditions in South and Southeast Asia in the late 1940s and early 1950s, they recognized that Japanese economic growth was a potent force that might bring stability not just to Japan itself but also to the region more widely. Thus the West perceived Japan as vital to stemming the tide of communism that thrived on poverty and resentment. Linked to this, Japan also came to be important to the United States because it could be manipulated to appear as a demonstration of what the Western-style liberal-capitalist model of modernization could achieve in practice. In the context of the battle of modernizations that was being played out in the Third World, its success therefore provided an important message.[12] Furthermore, another salient aspect of Japan's position was the fact that, in the early years of the cold war, it was one of the few non-white powers among America's major allies. Its ties to Washington thus communicated, it was hoped, that the United States could understand the non-Western world and that the Western alliance system was not merely another white man's club.

# DOMESTIC POLITICS AND JAPAN'S COLD WAR STANCE

The United States thus saw Japan as a vital asset, but the question the former faced was how to ensure the latter's loyalty to the West once the occupation ended and Japanese sovereignty was restored. There was, after all, no guarantee that Japan would view the world through the American prism. The possibility existed that it might be tempted by neutralism or perhaps even move toward the political extremes represented by communism and right-wing nationalism.

The United States was, however, fortunate in that the conservative political elite that came to dominate Japan throughout the cold war period consistently held views that were not greatly dissimilar to those in Washington. This was, of course, in part because control over the occupation had given the Americans the means to tilt the political process in favor of those who it deemed sympathetic. They had, for example, decided not to abolish the monarchy or engage in a large-scale purge of the bureaucracy and the existing right-wing political parties. In addition, their efforts to decrease the influence of the large economic combines, such as Mitsui and Mitsubishi, had only partially been carried out. Moreover, from 1947 the occupation authorities had become steadily less tolerant of the labor movement, which appeared to act as an obstacle to the development of economic and social stability. The conservative and statist bias in Japanese politics and institutions that had been in evidence since the Meiji restoration of 1868 was thus left largely intact.

In addition, though, the right in Japan, due to its desire to restore the country's shattered prestige and to preserve the domestic political status quo, enthusiastically supported economic reconstruction and greatly feared the rise of the left.[13] In regard to the latter, even with many of the overt warmongers of the 1930s purged from public life, lingering suspicion of the Soviet Union was widespread in Japanese conservative circles. This was exacerbated by the fact that the end of World War II had created a territorial dispute between Japan and the Soviet Union over the latter's permanent occupation of the southern Kurile Islands, and that animosity was also generated by Russian treatment of Japanese prisoners of war.[14] Thus, on the single most important cold war issue—hostility toward the USSR—Japan's rulers were as one with their American backers.

One might expect on this basis that Japan's relations with the United States and its role within the Western alliance system would mirror those of the major Western European members of NATO—that it would maintain large-scale armed forces ready to fight alongside the United States in the region and that it would contribute about 5–10 percent of annual GNP to defense spending. Japan, however, did not move in this direction. Instead it adopted a low-security profile, whereby its forces would only be available for self-defense. And for most of the cold war its military spending was pegged at only 1 percent of GNP.

In part, Japan's reticence can be understood in geographical terms. Unlike Germany it was not partitioned, and it did not share a land border with the Soviet bloc. The threat to its security was thus not as immediate as that to West Germany. The military danger that the Soviet Union did pose was air and missile attack, but this, it was believed, would be deterred by the American nuclear umbrella. In addition, Japanese domestic politics posed major obstacles to rearmament. The key factor to note here is that, while Japan's international image was one of a stable, consensual, and homogeneous society, the reality was different. The catastrophic end of World War II, in particular the dropping of the two atomic bombs, the Tokyo war crimes trial that singled out the Japanese military elite as being responsible for the conflict, and the hunger that marked the early years of the occupation had a powerful effect on sections of the general population, generating a feeling of victimhood and an abhorrence of war.[15] This manifested itself in the postwar belief that Japan should construct a new national identity based on pacifism and opposition to nuclear weapons. The conservatives could only ignore this sentiment at their peril, for any return to militarism might provoke a backlash.[16]

The conservative reluctance to confront the pacifists was, of course, linked to the fear that the latter, who were an amorphous collection of students, women's groups, and labour unions, might become dominated by the political left. This was a real problem. In contrast to most of its Western European counterparts, the largest left-wing grouping, the Japanese Socialist Party (JSP), which consistently polled between 20–35 percent of total votes, was not dominated by social democrats who were prepared to accept a broadly bipartisan pro-Western approach to foreign policy. It leaned toward Marxism and the adoption of a foreign policy platform that included neutralism, opposition to rearmament, and recognition of the PRC.[17] The JSP therefore had in the view of the political right to be prevented from ever gaining a grip on power. Such, indeed, was the importance of this issue that the structure of Japanese politics came to be shaped by this cold war divide.[18] Up until 1955 a number of conservative political parties had vied for power, but fear of the JSP led to their consolidation into the newly minted Liberal Democratic Party (LDP). Despite its members' many disagreements in the ensuing years both over policy and personality, the LDP would remain united and in power until 1993; the alternative—providing the left with an opportunity to rule—being too appalling to contemplate.[19]

Given these circumstances, the policy of adopting a low-security profile made sense. Moreover, it had the added advantage that the money saved by only possessing a small military establishment meant that more government spending could be directed to investment in economic growth. This would lead to prosperity and a better standard of living for the population at large, which would, in theory, reduce the attraction of communism and socialism for those at the poorer end of society.

The decision to adopt a low-security posture is often attributed to Yoshida Shigeru, the prime minister between 1948 and 1954. In 1951, when the Americans pressed Japan to rearm, he refused on the basis that the country should focus instead on economic reconstruction. Some take this as the moment that fixed Japan's future course and argue that Japanese foreign policy can be understood through reference to the "Yoshida doctrine."[20] This interpretation of events is ahistorical; in reality, the move toward permanently adopting this policy was not sealed in 1951. For most of the 1950s the conservatives continued to be engaged in a prolonged debate about what weight should be given respectively to the armed forces and to the economy. Final proof of the importance of avoiding full rearmament only came in 1960, when the government of Prime Minister Kishi Nobusuke manipulated parliamentary procedure to force through ratification of a more equitable security treaty with the United States. This unscrupulous use of power precipitated the most serious political demonstrations of the post-1945 era, in which one person died and a visit to Japan by President Eisenhower was cancelled because his security could not be guaranteed. For the LDP and its backers in industry, this was a turning point. Kishi, who had been indicted but never tried for war crimes and who the left saw as sympathetic to the emperor-centered fascism of the 1930s, was forced to resign. He was replaced by one of Yoshida's protégés, Ikeda Hayato. In his first major policy proclamation in 1960, Ikeda showed his colors by announcing his intention to see Japan double its national income in the next decade. From now on economics would be the priority.[21]

The continued importance of a low-security profile was bolstered in the late 1960s by the large-scale demonstrations that took place against the Vietnam War. This agitation in part mirrored anti-American feeling elsewhere, but in Japan the proximity of the conflict and the fact that American bases on Japanese soil and in Okinawa were seen as key supports for the war effort reinforced the animosity.[22] In part as a result of this unrest, the coming years would see Japan's low-security stance become more formalized. In 1968 Prime Minister Sato Eisaku announced his "three nuclear principles," whereby Japan renounced any intention of developing nuclear weapons. Then in 1975 one of his successors, Miki Takeo, formally proclaimed that Japanese defense spending would never exceed 1 percent of the country's GDP.

# JAPAN'S ROLE IN THE COLD WAR ALLIANCE SYSTEM

At first the Japanese government encountered difficulties in persuading the United States to accept its reading of the domestic political constraints. For example, when faced after the end of the occupation in 1952 with Yoshida's reluctance to rearm, the United States brought considerable pressure to bear on the Japanese government by linking the rearmament issue to American military procurements from Japan. This "carrot and stick" approach worked. In 1954 Japan agreed to establish a Self-Defense Force (SDF) of 150,000, which was an army, navy, and air force in all but name. Over time and particularly after the events of 1960, however, Washington came to accept the necessity of Japan's low-security profile.[23]

Concern about the potential rise of the left was the deciding factor in American acceptance of the low-security posture. There was no wish to push rearmament at the cost of allowing the Soviet Union or the PRC to be able to fish in Japan's troubled waters. Moreover, the perception existed in Washington that Japan was a strongly elitist country which did not fully understand democracy. Accordingly, Americans feared that Japan's public might be easily led astray by the Marxist intellectuals who appeared to dominate academic and public discourse. In reality, both of these concerns were misplaced. Russia's ability to appeal to Japanese public opinion was compromised by the territorial issue, and the development of the Sino-Soviet split only further blunted the ability of the socialist bloc to reach out to the Japanese masses. In addition, while the Marxist intellectuals were undoubtedly vocal, the Americans tended to exaggerate their influence.[24]

Moreover, it is important to see that the American willingness to accept Japan's low-security stance was also linked to its suspicion of the nationalist right, as exemplified by LDP politicians such as Nakasone Yasuhiro. Here too, cultural factors, as well as the past, were important. Believing that "feudal" elements remained embedded in Japanese society and that its recent history displayed dangerous and violent propensities, the Americans feared that Japan's developing a powerful military might tempt the right to introduce a more independent and nationalistic foreign policy.[25] In 1969 this anxiety led the Richard Nixon administration to hesitate to use the Guam (Nixon) Doctrine, which called upon American allies in Asia to devote greater resources to their own defense, to coerce Japan to do more. Moreover, in the 1971–2 talks between Nixon's national security advisor, Henry Kissinger, and the Chinese prime minister, Zhou Enlai, the former openly claimed that the US-Japan alliance existed not merely to contain the Soviet Union but also to ensure control over Japan itself.[26]

These uncertainties about Japan and its future course existed despite the fact that even after the occupation the United States engaged in a policy of cultural diplomacy toward Japan in the hope that Western values might take root in Japanese society. This involved initiatives such as providing subsidies to Japanese publishers to translate key English texts and the financing of American studies as an academic discipline. In addition, in order to demonstrate its progressive values, the United States slowly revised its immigration laws and finally allowed Japanese born in America to naturalize. These efforts to display goodwill had some effect, but mutual misperception continued to be a problem.[27]

While it reluctantly accepted the low-security posture, the United States was nevertheless keen to support the path that Japan was prepared to follow—economic growth. A focus on the economy would not just benefit Japan, but also offered the prospect of Japanese exports bringing a bounty to other non-communist countries in Asia. Indeed, so attractive was this prospect that the United States acted in the 1950s as Japan's sponsor in international trade, lobbying successfully for its membership in the General Agreement on Tariffs and Trade (GATT) in 1955, while simultaneously allowing Japanese industry to develop behind a protectionist tariff shield. Recently scholars have pointed out that without this American assistance the form and scope of Japan's "economic miracle" would not have been the same. There was an irony in this. To the outside world the United States lauded Japan as a free-market, free-trade model for economic development to the Third World; but behind closed doors it tolerated practices, such as high tariffs and barriers to foreign direct investment, that when used elsewhere came in for damning criticism.[28]

As Japan became richer, its potential to help the Western cause grew ever greater. Its most important contribution came in terms of trade with and the provision of international aid to Southeast Asia. This began in the 1950s, when both the United States and Britain did their best to encourage Japanese trade with the region on the grounds that it would assist in the struggle against communism.[29] Japan's economic power proved particularly vital to American strategy during the Vietnam War. From 1966 Washington realized the importance of raising living standards in Southeast Asia as a means of stopping the contagion that had infected Indochina from spreading further. With its own resources dedicated to the battlefield, the United States looked to Japan to assist in this area. Thus in 1966 the Japanese joined with the Americans in establishing the Asian Development Bank (ADB) and proceeded to provide, jointly with the US, the largest sum of capital to the ADB's coffers. By 1969 50 percent of Japan's Overseas Development Aid (ODA) went to Southeast Asia. Japan thus began to follow a path that would later see it become the largest provider of ODA to the Third World.[30]

Japan's ability to act as an effective junior ally was, nevertheless, once more constrained by its recent past. Just as its wartime experience had made its public lean toward pacifism, so its brutal behavior against civilians and prisoners of war in that conflict continued to blight its international image. In addition, memories of Japan's supposedly "unfair" trade competition in the 1930s and fears that cheap Japanese goods might once again drive competitors out of important markets led to resentment. These concerns were particularly prevalent in Southeast Asia, where they were linked to the determination of the newly independent states not to replace their former colonial masters with a new Japanese "co-prosperity sphere." In the period between 1957 and 1960, Kishi's efforts to make Japan the leader in a Southeast Asian development plan met with regional suspicion. Moreover, the United States turned down Kishi's request for financial aid to support his plan, in part because, drawing again on culture and past history, they saw his ideas as a dangerous throwback to the pan-Asian ambitions of the Pacific War era.[31] In the early 1960s Japan's relations with Malaya and Singapore were, in what was referred to as the "blood debt" crisis, disturbed by the discovery of mass graves of murdered Chinese civilians.[32] Then in 1974 a tour of the region by Prime Minister Tanaka Kakuei was met by riots in Thailand, Malaysia, and Indonesia. These incidents had less to do with war memory than with anger about Japanese trading practices, which exploited regional workers and allowed the states that constituted the Association of Southeast Asian Nations (ASEAN) only limited access to the Japanese market. However, even then Japanese behavior had distant echoes of the "co-prosperity sphere."[33] In regard to Western Europe and the British Commonwealth, relations likewise suffered. In 1955 Japan discovered that many of the countries in these blocs were unwilling to extend full GATT rights to Japan, a situation that was not reversed until 1962.[34] Moreover, Emperor Hirohito's visit to Western Europe in 1971 was met with a mixture of sullen indifference and outright hostility.[35]

The greatest problem, however, for the United States was the hostility between the Republic of Korea and Japan. From 1952 to 1965 no formal diplomatic relations existed between the two most important American allies in the region. This was largely a legacy of the period between 1910 and 1945, when Japan had occupied Korea as a colonial power and had attempted to extinguish Korean national identity. There was therefore no love lost between the Korean and Japanese peoples and governments. For the United States this presented a considerable strategic disadvantage. It saw Japanese investment in South Korea as essential in order to help kick-start high-speed economic growth and thus strengthen Seoul in its competition with Pyongyang. After much lobbying the Americans finally achieved their desired result in 1965, when Japan and South Korea agreed to normalize their relations. There was, however, no doubt that this was far from being an amicable arrangement; the Korean people continued to define their national identity in part around enmity toward their former colonial masters.[36] This mutual antagonism meant that it was difficult to contemplate the establishment of a multilateral security structure for East Asia in imitation of NATO. Instead Washington had to rely on a series of bilateral pacts and vague declarations of interest by Japan in the security of South Korea and Taiwan.

Japan therefore emerged as a useful cold war ally in the economic field, but its utility was restricted by its wartime past and its long-term reputation as an industrial jugger-naut that ruthlessly swept aside foreign competitors. Furthermore, the United States also saw another problem arise: the symbiotic relationship that it had hoped to see between Southeast Asia and Japan was slow to develop, for initially the former region was not economically advanced enough to absorb the goods produced by a rapidly industrializing Japan. The unfortunate truth in the first two decades of the cold war was that if the United States put such a premium on Japan's prosperity, then it had to let the latter's goods into its own domestic economy even if this led to criticism of Washington by those such as the American textile lobby who competed with Japanese products. This process began in the 1950s but accelerated in the early 1960s when, following the security treaty crisis, the Kennedy administration dismantled some of the American protectionist trade barriers in order to assist the entry of Japanese exports.[37]

## THE RISE AND IMPACT OF JAPAN'S OMNIDIRECTIONAL DIPLOMACY

Japan's diplomacy and economic activities overseas were, of course, not entirely concentrated on the cold war, and economic growth was not encouraged merely to disarm the potential for communism at home. Japan had its own national interests in terms of developing trade relations, enhancing its international prestige, and espousing its agenda of opposing the possession and testing of nuclear weapons. The question is whether its cold war ties to the United States furthered or inhibited these goals.

The area in which Japan most hoped to prosper in terms of international prestige following the return of sovereignty in 1952 was in acting as a bridge between the West and the Third World. It was encouraged in this aim by the example of Jawaharlal Nehru's India. In

1951 Nehru refused to attend the San Francisco peace conference on the grounds that the United States was coercing Japan into choosing sides in the cold war. In 1952 India signed its own peace treaty with Japan, in which it notably waived its right to reparations.[38] The concept of neutralism and the emergence of a bloc in Asia that sought to distance itself from the cold war clearly appealed to the left in Japan, but in addition, it interested the nationalist right as it fitted into the pre-war tradition of pan-Asianism. In 1955, therefore, Japan's attending the Afro-Asian conference in Bandung, Indonesia, was never in question, although the Japanese delegation was ordered to avoid all controversial issues.[39]

A further stimulus for Japan to pursue a more independent line came in 1956, when it entered the United Nations. Japan was keen to use the international organization as a forum through which it could move on from its past and rebuild its prestige. Accordingly, in 1957 the Kishi government announced the three basic principles of Japanese diplomacy: UN-centrism, "membership" in Asia, and cooperation with the free countries. To further the first two aims, Kishi adopted policies that had hitherto been the property of the Japanese left. His administration called, for example, for a ban on nuclear testing, and in 1958 it publicly criticized Anglo-American intervention in Lebanon and Jordan, respectively.[40] In the same year Japan provided its first international postwar loan of ¥50 million to India, while Kishi also moved ahead with negotiating reparations agreements with states such as Indonesia and the Republic of Vietnam.[41]

There was, however, a limit to just how far Japan could lean toward the Third World. Not wishing to challenge the United States directly on African-Asian issues and unable to decouple itself from the cold war, all it could offer was a mediation channel with the West. But the atmosphere among the newly independent states did not favor compromise. Thus, when Japan abstained in 1959 on a series of UN General Assembly resolutions supporting the National Liberation Front (FLN) in its drive for Algerian independence, its standing with the Afro-Asian bloc plummeted. Further damage was done in the 1960s when Japan refused for economic reasons to join in condemning South Africa and felt that it had no choice but to offer public support for the American cause in Indochina.[42] Japan's attempt to carve out a new role as a mediator was therefore doomed to failure, for its reliance on the United States meant that it could not drift too far from that superpower's orbit. The cold war thus acted as a constraint which reduced Japanese foreign policy options and ironically also undercut Japan's value to the United States as a non-white ally.

The ability of the United States to curb Japanese ambitions was most notable in regard to the PRC. China had always been an important trading partner for Japan, and Tokyo hoped that this could continue to be the case despite the existence of the cold war. The Americans, however, saw the PRC as an implacable enemy that had to be contained at all cost and thus argued that its allies should only engage in very limited trade with China. In the case of Japan, the United States insisted in 1951–2 that it should open diplomatic relations exclusively with the Republic of China on Taiwan, and hinted that the peace treaty might not be ratified if this order was ignored.[43] The severed ties with continental China were a source of great frustration, and at various points Japan sought to push trading links further than the United States wished. This was particularly the case under the Ikeda administration between 1960 and 1964. The Americans though held the whip hand and restrained the Japanese from going too far. In particular, Japan had to contend with the fact that until 1972 the United States remained in possession of Okinawa, which became a hostage to its good behavior.

The early 1970s, however, proved to be a period of flux in which greater independence in foreign policy appeared as a real possibility. In 1971 the Japanese-American relationship began to change due to the "Nixon shocks." The first "shock" came in July when Nixon announced he would visit the PRC, thereby abruptly changing two decades of American policy toward China. Then in August, in the second "shock," Nixon suddenly announced his decision to devalue the dollar. These "shocks" came at a time when Ikeda's 1960 policy of "income doubling" had been achieved beyond his wildest dreams. By the early 1970s Japan had become the Western world's second largest economy. It could therefore afford, if it desired, to adopt a more independent and assertive foreign policy because it now had the financial muscle. With the United States under Nixon foregrounding American interests and the first oil hike taking place in 1973, this ability to behave independently became more of a necessity than a luxury; Japan began to strike out with a new policy termed "omnidirectional diplomacy." This involved defending its economic security by improving its relations with a number of key trading partners.[44]

The first notable move was that Japan in September 1972 opened its own diplomatic relations with the PRC and expanded its economic ties; at the same time it cut formal ties with Taiwan, although trade links remained.[45] Then, in an action which flew directly in the face of American policy, Japan reacted to the oil hike by loosening its ties with Israel and moving closer to the Arab world in an effort to curry favor with the Organization of Petroleum Exporting Countries (OPEC). In addition, Japan's reliance on the maritime trade routes that ran through Southeast Asia added even further to the latter region's significance. In the mid-1970s the Japanese government sought closer relations with the Association of Southeast Asian Nations (ASEAN). This culminated in in the "Fukuda Doctrine," in which Prime Minister Fukuda Takeo announced that Japan rejected the use of military power in regard to Southeast Asia and wished to be an equal partner with ASEAN. These words were then matched by action—a loan of $1 billion for investment in industrial projects.[46]

In addition, a limited attempt at détente was made with the Soviet Union, which was rich in energy resources such as oil and gas. This effort at rapprochement, however, foundered on the territorial issue. Indeed, Soviet ambitions in the late 1970s and early 1980s, as seen in its support for the Socialist Republic of Vietnam in 1978, the invasion of Afghanistan in 1979, and the stationing of SS-20 intermediate range missiles in Asia, revealed that Japan's effort to become more independent could not stretch to the strategic realm. Fear of the Soviets and the application of American pressure led the government of Nakasone Yasuhiro in 1983 to agree to the Maritime Self-Defense Force taking up the new role of patrolling sea lanes up to 1,000 miles from Japan. In addition, mirroring the policy of the United States, Japan moved to establish closer relations with the PRC. In 1978 the latter two countries signed a peace treaty which included an "anti-hegemony" clause directed against Russia.

The escalation of cold war tensions after the collapse of détente did not merely remind the Japanese of the importance of the American connection. It also revealed once again that Japan's political weight in the world was not commensurate with its economic power. In the economic field Japan unambiguously sat at the head table. For example, in 1975 Prime Minister Miki was invited to the Rambouillet summit, which marked the first step in the move toward establishing the annual Group of Five (G-5) economic summits. In 1979, however, Japan was not party to the Guadeloupe summit in which the United States, Britain, France, and West Germany discussed security matters such as the crisis in Iran, SALT II, and the Soviet deployment of SS-20s.[47] For the nationalist wing of the LDP, this was a matter of concern, and in 1982, in the figure of Nakasone, there finally emerged a prime minister who sought to elevate Japan's international political standing. Key to this was Nakasone's thinking that Japan ought to become a "normal state." In other words, it should abrogate article 9 of the constitution and transform the SDF into a "normal" military force that could act overseas if necessary. Nakasone moved cautiously toward this goal by increasing defense spending, fostering the growth of Japanese nationalism through the revision of school textbooks, and visiting the Yasukuni Shrine, where Japan's war dead are commemorated, on the 40th anniversary of the surrender— August 15, 1985.[48]

To the United States, where public and Congressional anger over Japan's burgeoning trade balance was growing, this evidence that Japan was becoming more willing to pull its weight was welcome.[49] Moreover, Japan's willingness in the early 1980s to buy US Treasury bonds, thus helping to fund Ronald Reagan's arms build-up, and its subsequent agreement in the G-5's Plaza Accord in 1985 to let the dollar devalue, also assisted in improving the country's image. However, both within Japan, where Nakasone's policies overtly challenged the postwar consensus, and in East Asia the atmosphere ranged from disquiet to outright opposition. In the PRC and South Korea the governments and public opinion were outraged by Nakasone's apparent effort to rehabilitate Japan's past. Indeed, having largely ignored the Sino-Japanese War as an issue up to this point in order not to alienate the Japanese masses, the PRC suddenly decided to use history to burnish its nationalist credentials.[50] Japan's effort to become a full ally in the cold war thus again revealed that the country was still hemmed in by its wartime past.

In response to this domestic and regional criticism, Takeshita Noboru, Nakasone's successor in 1987, engineered a shift back toward traditional policies. When the United States requested in 1987 that Japan send ships to help to patrol the Persian Gulf, Takeshita refused. Meanwhile, relations with ASEAN, which had been less prominent under Nakasone, were revived with the granting of a $2 billion aid package. Takeshita continued in the same vein by announcing that Japan would double its ODA to the Third World. In addition, in the wake of Mikhail Gorbachev's arrival as the new Kremlin leader and his "rediscovery" of Asia, a slight thaw began in relations with the Soviets. Still, the territorial issue remained an obstacle to whole-hearted rapprochement, and Japan responded less enthusiastically to the era of glasnost than the United States or Western Europe.[51]

# CONCLUSION

As the cold war passed away between 1989 and 1991, Japan was still in an anomalous position. It had over the prior thirty years gained great wealth and been a vital ally of the United States due to its economic power. Indeed, some even argued that Japanese consumer goods had contributed to the dismantling of the Iron Curtain by allowing East Europeans and Russians a glimpse of a life of comfort that the Soviet command economy could never offer. At the same time, however, Japan remained reliant on an American security umbrella and carried relatively little weight as a strategic entity. To assess the influence that the cold war had on Japan and the role that it played in that conflict is therefore difficult. Perhaps the most effective approach is to compare it with that of the other defeated powers from World War II.

The most obvious difference is that, whereas West Germany and Italy were members of both NATO and the European Economic Community, Japan was not involved in a process of regional strategic, economic, and political integration that could, at least in the eyes of its neighbors, dilute its past. Instead, its nearest neighbor, South Korea, was a reborn but newly partitioned state whose national identity was defined by hostility toward its former colonizer. It thus had no interest in any initiative that might produce any merging of its sovereignty with Japan. Japan thus remained a relatively isolated state within its region, a phenomenon which reinforced its timidity in its relations with the United States. In addition, in contrast to West Germany, Japan was not partitioned territorially and politically, and it did not share a land border with the Soviet bloc. The absence of these factors was important. While West German public opinion was on the whole prepared to rearm in order to deter the immediate menace to its national security, Japan lacked an imminent Soviet threat. Consequently, the strong neutralist left that emerged out of the experiences of World War II could afford to play on fears of the past.

In sum, Japan could not play a major military role in the cold war. Instead, its focus turned to economic activity and, with the overt sponsorship of the United States, it emerged as an industrial and financial powerhouse that played its own important part in containing communism and eventually assisting in the collapse of the Soviet Union. While Japan's role was different from that of America's other allies and perhaps more difficult to measure, it was still significant. Moreover, the cold war in turn helped to stimulate the Japanese economy, which benefited greatly from American, and even sometimes British, sponsorship and which prospered from such windfalls as the Korean and Indochinese Wars. Thus, while it can be argued that Japan might very well have moved in the direction of prioritizing economic development as a national goal after World War II no matter what the international circumstances were, it is also arguable that the success that it achieved in practice was considerably boosted by its drive toward high-speed growth in a cold war environment.

Japan's contribution to the West's victory over the Soviet Union came, however, at a price. In the economic field, Japan discovered after 1989 that its statist approach to international trade, which had been tolerated in the cold war, was ill-suited to the new era of "globalization", and it soon lapsed into a prolonged recession. Further damage was done in terms of Japan's regional standing. With its eyes on Japan's utility in the cold war, the United States had not encouraged its ally to reflect deeply on its past. Victimhood rather than war guilt became the major sentiment in Japanese society. As a result Japan's neighbors saw it as failing to come to terms with its wartime past, and this issue came to afflict Japanese foreign policy in the 1990s and 2000s. Thus, while the cold war passed from the scene, the memory of Imperial Japan's disastrous expansion lingered both at home and abroad.

## NOTES

1. I am grateful to Arne Hofmann, Akira Iriye, Tomoki Kuniyoshi, Kristina Spohr Readman, and the editors of this volume for their very useful comments on this chapter. Japanese names are rendered in the Japanese style of putting the family name first except when referring to the Japanese authors of work in English.

2. See, for example, the speech by Paul Tsongas quoted in Timothy P. Maga, "The New Frontier and the New Japan: Kennedy, Ikeda, and the 'End of US Protectionism,' 1961–63," *Diplomacy and Statecraft* 5/2 (July 1994): 371.

3. Paul Kennedy, *The Rise and Fall of the Great Powers: Economic Change and Military Conflict from 1500 to 2000* (London: Unwin Hyman, 1988).

4. Many other states, including the Soviet Union, were represented on the Allied Council for Japan and the Far Eastern Commission, which nominally oversaw the occupation, but in reality the United States through its presence on the ground dominated policy making.

5. Michael Schaller, *The American Occupation of Japan: The Origins of the Cold War in Asia* (New York: Oxford University Press, 1985), 87–90.

6. Alexander Pantsov, *The Bolsheviks and the Chinese Revolution 1919–1927* (Richmond: Curzon, 2000).

7. Sakai Tetsuya, "Nichi-bei kaisen to nichi-so kankei," in Hosoya Chihiro, Homma Nagayo, Iriye Akira, and Hatano Sumio, eds., *Taiheiyo senso* (Tokyo: Tokyo Daigaku Shuppankai, 1993), 133–61.

8. See, for example, Malcolm Kennedy, "Russo-Japanese Friction," *Nineteenth Century and After* 116/692 (October 1934): 380–90.

9. Schaller, *The American Occupation of Japan*, 53–7, 122–4. For Japanese thinking on how it might take advantage of American-Soviet postwar rivalry in East Asia, see Yukiko Koshiro, "Eurasian Eclipse: Japan's End Game in World War II," *American Historical Review* 109/2 (2004): 417–44.

10. Vojtech Mastny, *The Cold War and Soviet Insecurity: The Stalin Years* (Oxford: Oxford University Press, 1994), 91–2.

11. The most recent account of the San Francisco treaties is John Swenson-Wright, *Unequal Allies: United States Security and Alliance Policy toward Japan, 1945–1960* (Stanford, CA: Stanford University Press, 2005), 57–76.

12. For Japan and the modernization debate see, Laura Hein, "Free-Floating Anxieties on the Pacific: Japan and the West Revisited," *Diplomatic History* 20/3 (Summer 1996): 414–19.

13. The most important Japanese-language studies of the occupation are, Iokibe Makoto, *Beikoku no nihon senryō seisaku—sengo nihon no sekkeizu*, 2 vols. (Tokyo: Chuo Koronsha, 1985) and Iokibe, *Nichibei sensō to sengo nihon* (Tokyo: Kodansha, 2005). The best study in English is John W. Dower, *Embracing Defeat: Japan after World War II* (New York: Free Press, 1999).

14. For Japanese-Soviet relations, see Tanaka Takahiko, *Nisso-kokko kaifuku no shiteki kenkyu: sengo nisso kankei no kiten, 1945–1956* (Tokyo: Yuhikaku, 1993); Joseph P. Ferguson, *Japanese-Russian Relations, 1907–2007* (London: Routledge, 2008); and Hiroshi Kimura, *The Kurillian Knot: A History of Japanese Russian Border Negotiations* (Stanford, CA: Stanford University Press, 2008).

15. Dower, *Embracing Defeat*, 33–162 and 443–523.

16. For the growth of the pacifist movement, see James J. Orr, *The Victim as Hero: Ideologies of Peace and National Identity in Postwar Japan* (Honolulu: University of Hawai'i Press, 2001), 36–8 and 43–4.

17. J.A.A. Stockwin, *The Japanese Socialist Party and Neutralism: A Study of a Political Party and its Foreign Policy* (London: Melbourne University Press, 1968).

18. Gerald L. Curtis, *The Logic of Japanese Politics: Leaders, Institutions, and the Limits of Change* (New York: Columbia University Press, 1999), 28–33.

19. Tetsuya Kataoka, *The Price of Constitution: The Origins of Japan's Postwar Politics* (New York: Crane Russak, 1991), 145–7.

20. The idea of the "Yoshida Doctrine" asserts that Yoshida was a realist who consciously exaggerated fear of internal interest in order to manipulate the Americans into accepting Japan's low security posture, thereby allowing Japan to concentrate on economic growth. It is an interpretation that tends to be more popular among political scientists than historians. See, for example, Kenneth Pyle, *Japan Rising: The Resurgence of Japanese Power and Purpose* (New York: Public Affairs, 2007), 31–2 and 229–30.

21. Kataoka, *The Price of Constitution*, 211.

22. For the Vietnam War and Japan, see Thomas R. H. Havens, *Fire Across the Sea: The Vietnam War and Japan, 1965–1975* (Princeton, NJ: Princeton University Press, 1987).

23. Michael Schaller, *Altered States: The United States and Japan since the Occupation* (New York: Oxford University Press, 1999), 143–83.

24. Rodger Swearingen, *The Soviet Union and Postwar Japan: Escalating Challenge and Response* (Stanford: Hoover Institution Press, 1978), 90–117; Takeshi Matsuda, *Soft Power and its Perils: US Cultural Policy in Early Postwar Japan and Permanent Dependency* (Stanford, CA: Stanford University Press, 2007), 142–6.

25. Naoko Shibusawa, *America's Geisha Ally: Reimagining the Japanese Enemy* (Cambridge, MA: Harvard University Press, 2006), 59–73; Matsuda, *Soft Power and its Peril*, 60–3 and 115–16.

26. Liang Pan, "Whither Japan's Military Potential? The Nixon Administration's Stance on Japanese Defense Power," *Diplomatic History* 31/1 (January 2007): 111–43.

27. Yukiko Koshiro, *Trans-Pacific Racisms and the US Occupation of Japan* (New York: Columbia University Press, 1999), 159–200; Matsuda, *Soft Power and its Perils*, 138–213.

28. Aaron Forsberg, *America and the Japanese Miracle: The Cold War Context of Japan's Postwar Economic Revival, 1950–1960* (Chapel Hill, NC: University of North Carolina Press, 2000).

29. On Japanese trade with Southeast Asia in the 1950s, see Suehiro Akira, "The Road to Economic Re-entry: Japan's Policy toward Southeast Asian Development in the 1950s and 1960s," *Social Science Japan Journal*, 2/1 (1999): 66–105; Junko Tomaru, *The Postwar*

*Rapprochement of Malaya and Japan, 1945–61: The Roles of Britain and Japan in South-East Asia* (Basingstoke: Macmillan, 2000); and Nicholas J. White, "'Complementarity', Decolonization, and the Cold War: British Responses to Japan's Economic Revival in Southeast Asia During the 1950s and 1960s," in Antony Best, ed., *The International History of East Asia, 1900–1968: Trade, Ideology and the Quest for Order* (London: Routledge, 2010), 168–81.

30. Dennis S. Yasutomo, *Japan and the Asian Development Bank* (New York: Praeger, 1983); Alan Rix, "ASEAN and Japan: More than Economics," in Alison Broinowski, ed., *Understanding ASEAN* (London: Macmillan, 1982), 175–7; and Suehiro, "The Road to Economic Re-entry," 100–2.

31. Sayuri Shimizu, *Creating People of Plenty: The United States and Japan's Economic Alternatives, 1950–1960* (Kent, OH: Kent State University Press, 2001), 194–8.

32. Tomaru, *Postwar Rapprochement*, 229–30.

33. Rix, "ASEAN and Japan," 181–3.

34. Noriko Yokoi, *Japan's Postwar Economic Recovery and Anglo-Japanese Relations 1948–1962* (London: RoutledgeCurzon, 2003), 115.

35. Kenneth J. Ruoff, *The People's Emperor: Democracy and the Japanese Monarchy, 1945–1995* (Cambridge, MA; Harvard University Asia Center, 2001), 142–4.

36. See Victor Cha, *Alignment Despite Antagonism: The US-Korea-Japan Security Triangle* (Stanford, CA: Stanford University Press, 1999), *passim*.

37. Shimizu, *Creating People of Plenty*; Maga, "The New Frontier," 371–93.

38. P.A. Narasimha Murthy, *India and Japan: Dimensions of their Relations, Historical and Political* (New Delhi: ABC Publishing, 1986), 310–42.

39. Kweku Ampiah, "Japan at the Bandung Conference: An Attempt to Assert an Independent Foreign Policy," in Iokibe Makoto, Caroline Rose, Tomaru Junko, and John Weste, eds., *Japanese Diplomacy in the 1950s: From Isolation to Integration* (London: Routledge, 2008), 79–97. The best account in Japanese is Miyagi Taizō, *Bandon kaigi to nihon no ajia fukki: amerika to ajia no hazama de* (Tokyo: Sōshisha, 2001).

40. Liang Pan, *The United Nations in Japan's Foreign and Security Policymaking, 1945–1992* (Cambridge, MA: Harvard University Press, 2005), 34–51.

41. Sueo Sudo, *The Fukuda Doctrine and ASEAN: New Dimensions in Japanese Foreign Policy* (Singapore: Institute of Southeast Asian Studies, 1992), 44–6.

42. Pan, *The United Nations*, 54–6.

43. Swenson-Wright, *Unequal Allies*, 87–92.

44. Shiro Saito, *Japan at the Summit: Its Role in the Western Alliance and in Asian Pacific Co-operation* (London: Routledge/RIIA, 1990), 38–42 and 46–54.

45. Sadako Ogata, *Normalization with China: A Comparative Study of US and Japanese Processes* (Berkeley, CA: University of California Press, 1988).

46. Sudo, *The Fukuda Doctrine and ASEAN*, 162–80.

47. Saito, *Japan at the Summit*, 60–4.

48. Pyle, *Japan Rising*, 270–7.

49. Thomas W. Zeiler, "Business is War in American-Japanese Economic Relations, 1977–2001," in Akira Iriye and Robert Wampler, eds., *Partnership: The United States and Japan, 1951–2001* (Tokyo: Kodansha, 2001), 223–38.

50. Yinan He, "Remembering and Forgetting the War: Elite Mythmaking, Mass Reaction, and Sino-Japanese Relations, 1950–2006," *History and Memory* 19/2 (2007): 43–74.

51. Kimura, *The Kurillian Knot*, 92–102.

## Select Bibliography

Dower, John, *Embracing Defeat: Japan after World War II*. New York: Free Press, 1999.

Ferguson, Joseph P. *Japanese-Russian Relations, 1907–2007*. London: Routledge, 2008.

Forsberg, Aaron. *America and the Japanese Miracle: The Cold War Context of Japan's Postwar Economic Revival, 1950–1960*. Chapel Hill, NC: University of North Carolina Press, 2000.

Iokibe, Makoto, ed. *The Diplomatic History of Postwar Japan* (London: Routledge, 2010).

Kataoka, Tetsuya. *The Price of Constitution: The Origins of Japan's Postwar Politics*. New York: Crane Russak, 1991.

Orr, James J. *The Victim as Hero: Ideologies of Peace and National Identity in Postwar Japan*. Honolulu: University of Hawai'i Press, 2001.

Pyle, Kenneth. *Japan Rising: The Resurgence of Japanese Power and Purpose*. New York: Public Affairs, 2007.

Saito, Shiro. *Japan at the Summit: Its Role in the Western Alliance and in Asian Pacific Co-operation*. London: Routledge/RIIA, 1990.

Schaller, Michael. *Altered States: The United States and Japan since the Occupation*. New York: Oxford University Press, 1999.

Sudo, Sueo. *The Fukuda Doctrine and ASEAN: New Dimensions in Japanese Foreign Policy*. Singapore: Institute of Southeast Asian Studies, 1992.

Swenson-Wright, John. *Unequal Allies: United States Security and Alliance Policy toward Japan, 1945–1960*. Stanford, CA: Stanford University Press, 2005.

# PART III

## WAGING THE COLD WAR

# CHAPTER 18

# COLD WAR STRATEGIES/POWER AND CULTURE—EAST

## Sources of Soviet Conduct Reconsidered

### VLADISLAV ZUBOK

THE aftermath of the cold war has generated fresh approaches and themes in the study of its history. Cold war scholars have looked to post-colonial studies, the sociology of mass consumption and tourism, cultural and intellectual history, and other areas to make sense of the period. Cold war history has benefited greatly from innovative scholarship on the Soviet "side." It is now transdisciplinary in character—not unlike the literature produced by the first generation of Soviet experts in the West.[1]

This essay addresses themes that emerged from this rapprochement. First, it discusses the root motives behind the Soviet struggle against the West: "persistent factors," including imperialist expansion and ideology, and "supporting factors," such as the generational experience of Soviet elites.[2] Then it assesses the effects of decolonization on Soviet behavior in the Third World and on the further expansion of the cold war. Finally, it examines the domestic, regional, and global developments from the 1960s to the early 1980s that eroded the Soviet cold war consensus, weakened the Soviet imperial will, and contributed to the sudden and unilateral Soviet "exit" from the cold war.

## THE PARADIGM OF SOVIET INTERNATIONAL BEHAVIOR

Alfred J. Rieber wrote about persistent factors that shaped Imperial Russia's international behavior, including economic backwardness; porous frontiers, a multinational society, and cultural alienation. The Bolsheviks at first seemed to create an antidote to

Russia's historic empire and to its "persistent factors." They promoted an intoxicating vision of a global proletarian revolution that would destroy borders and states themselves. Yet, the realities of the imperial space and Russian history and culture returned. After the hopes for a revolution in Germany and other European countries faded, Stalin adopted the doctrine of "socialism in one country." Imperial ambitions re-emerged under the rubric of revolutionary Bolshevik internationalism, producing a *revolutionary-imperial paradigm*. This paradigm responded to some of the same "persistent factors" of Russian (and now Soviet) weakness. At the same time, it would be a mistake (committed by George Kennan, among many others) to equate Russian and Soviet international behavior. In fact, the tsars and Stalin approached "persistent factors" in radically different ways. The leaders of the old empire sought to overcome insecurity and backwardness by emulating European great powers and affirming Russia's place in the concert of these powers. The Bolsheviks' paradigm identified the Soviet Union as the vanguard of a new modernity, a global transformation from capitalism into socialism.[3]

Soviet leaders wore two mantles: world statesmen and leaders of "progressive mankind's" march toward communism. As Odd Arne Westad explains, "The Soviet elites saw their mission as part of a world-historical progression.... Their view of their own role in that process was conditioned not just by Marxist-Leninist political theory but also by Russian exceptionalism and by the experiences of the Soviet leadership since 1917."[4] Stalin was concurrently a shrewd advocate of realpolitik. Any alliance, even with the Nazis in 1939–41, was justified because it was a temporary device designed to serve the Soviet Union and its security, and thereby the future of communism.

George F. Kennan simplified this phenomenon. He concluded that Soviet foreign conduct was defined by insecurity, tyranny, and only in the last instance by the rhetoric of Marxism-Leninism. Kennan did not think that the Kremlin rulers really believed in the communist ideology they preached. Rather, they had to justify the Marxist-Leninist dogmas that validated their power. He failed to see a crucial distinction, however, between the factors of the Russian imperial behavior and the revolutionary-imperial paradigm, between the antiquated authority of the Tsar and the modern anti-liberal phenomenon of Stalinism.[5]

Stalin's conduct misled many, including Kennan. More than Lenin, the Soviet dictator could do whatever he wanted, violating "ideological correctness" as well as law and morality. Some historians even surmised that Stalin was tempted to join the concert of great powers after Yalta. His pragmatism confused them. In Melvyn Leffler's judgment, for Stalin "there were certain constants, but never clear strategies. There would always be fear and suspicion, a lust for power and a craving for security." Leffler found "Marxist-Leninist thinking" lurking behind Stalin's actions, but concludes that it was "no blueprint for a cold war."[6] Tsyuoshi Hasegawa goes farther in rejecting an ideological motive: "Stalin's policy [in 1945] was motivated by expansionist geopolitical designs. The Soviet leader pursued his imperialistic policy with Machiavellian ruthlessness, deviousness, and cunning."[7]

Both arguments are reductionist. Stalin could temporarily suspend the revolutionary component of the paradigm of Soviet international behavior. But he could not shed it. He used the Yalta framework as a cover to promote his agenda. Indeed, Stalin imagined himself as a great realist statesman who could expand the Soviet Union by acting in tandem with some "imperialists," the leaders of Great Britain and the United States.[8]

One should never confuse Stalinist logic with the logic of European balance of power. In January 1948 Stalin told the Bulgarian and Yugoslav communists, "The correlation of forces is the thing. You should strike if you can win and avoid the battlefield if you cannot. We will join the battle when the circumstances favor us, rather than when the enemy wants us to."[9] His concept of "correlation of forces" envisioned not simply a balancing act, but also, influenced by Soviet power, a fundamental transformation of entire societies. Stalin exploited the ideas and cultural images borrowed from the arsenal of the Russian empire to justify the Soviet Union's hegemony in Eastern Europe and the "historical rights" to the territories from Romania to Manchuria and Japan. Yet because those ideas and images were antiquated and tactical, he returned to communist sources of imperialist expansionism in order to reaffirm Soviet claims on the spheres of influences in Europe and Asia. The more resistance Stalin encountered from the United States and Britain, the more he revalidated the communist component of the international paradigm. As early as in 1945, Stalin began to prepare for a policy of confrontation against Western powers based on the Leninist concepts. By 1947 in Europe and after 1949 in the Pacific, Stalin resorted to ideological proselytism and open support for communist forces.

No ambitious foreign policy can be pursued without a strong ideological component. Leninism and Stalinism arose from the most radical European strand of thought and generated a mindset that rejected liberal democracy, repudiated free markets and trade, and proclaimed that the future belongs to the Soviet form of modernity. Nigel Gould-Davies correctly observes that Stalin's conceptual world included assumptions that were "fundamentally different from our own" (i.e., British and American).[10] These were inextricable from the violent nature of the Soviet regime and its society, its anti-capitalist structures, and the propaganda bubble within which Soviets lived. To preserve this regime and society, Stalin needed isolation from the capitalist world. Before and after Yalta, Stalin's thinking and behavior were consistent.[11]

Above all, Stalin and other Soviet policy-makers believed in the Leninist postulates about the inevitability of wars as long as capitalism existed. The premise of Stalin's policies in 1945–53 was the need to remobilize Soviet society for another, even more terrible conflict. Subsequent phases of the cold war reveal that any openness, trade, and cultural interaction with the West were dangerous to the stability of Stalin's "socialist empire."

# Factors supporting Soviet cold war behavior

Stalin dragged Soviet elites and people into the cold war—one of the most striking revelations of the Soviet archives. Soviet elites, nevertheless, quickly followed Stalin's trumpet in lockstep. What helped Stalin were "supporting factors" rooted in Soviet collective identity, culture, and history. The most important was the traumatic experience of World War II. Historians demonstrate that the war experience replaced the memories of the Russian revolution and the Civil War as the defining moment for collective identities, Soviet patriotism, and worldview. The German invasion smashed Soviet armies and almost defeated the Soviet state. The road from defeat to triumph required the exertions of the entire people; this bolstered the Russian national pride; by 1943 the war had become the Great Patriotic War. Tens of millions of Russians and non-Russians fought for their "socialist motherland" and liberated half of Europe from Nazism. The defeats of 1941–2 justified the feeling of vulnerability and insecurity that the regime could manipulate. The victory created a special "entitlement": for secure borders, for the geostrategic glacis against former enemies, and for a special role in the postwar international order. Soviets felt both physically and morally superior to the Eastern Europeans whom they "liberated," not to mention the Germans and their allies. Later this triumphalism led the Soviets to consider East Germany and Eastern Europe as an essential glacis for the Soviet Union and natural target for spreading "socialism." Joseph Rothschild aptly remarked, "The hegemony over East Central Europe...became the most visible and palpable prize of the great Soviet victory and therefore functioned as a powerful moral bond between the regime and its peoples and among the various sectors of the Soviet elite."[12]

Some observers hoped the war experience would weaken the regime. Before the "Iron Curtain" descended, millions of Soviet war veterans visited other lands and glimpsed a freer life. Comparisons between the Soviet regime and life abroad awakened anti-Stalinist sentiments among Russian peasants and urban intellectuals, arousing hopes for ideological transformation. Stalin, however, used the two primary effects of the war, vulnerability and great power entitlement, to suppress the trend toward liberalization. He convinced the exhausted and decimated people that the United States and "capitalist encirclement" endangered Soviet security.[13]

Vital to Stalin's schemes was molding the feelings of the Soviet people into a "socialist-nationalist" consensus. The struggle against the Nazis taught Stalin to respect the power of nationalism even more. He counted on Russian nationalism having historically developed in an imperial form; Russians never claimed their own nation-state. Therefore, Soviet state-sponsored identity could be "Russified" without provoking an immediate danger of nationalist separatism. During the war the Russians became the "senior brother" to other nationalities of the Soviet Union. After 1945 Stalin continued to rely on this chauvinist and patriotic legacy.[14] In his response to Churchill's Iron Curtain speech, he chose the language of "Anglo-Saxon" to challenge "the slavs," not the language of Marxist-Leninist ideology. In fact, Stalin appealed not only to Russian but also to Ukrainian, Georgian, Armenian, and Azeri nationalisms to expand and consolidate his "socialist empire."[15] His use of nationalist and patriotic themes bolstered the revolutionary-imperial paradigm through the mobilization not only of communist elites and intellectuals, but also millions of people from the ethnic majorities in the countries of the Soviet bloc and beyond. Especially when compared with Tsarist Russia, Stalin's success is incontrovertible. Placing Russian imperial patriotism at the service of the Tsar's agenda was ineffective. Stalin later resurrected it and built it into the postwar Soviet identity. He also projected the cold war against the West as a continuation of the Great Patriotic War.[16]

The third supporting factor was militarism. Violence infused the structures and beliefs of Soviet elites and society. World War II confirmed the danger of an enemy coming from the West and the high cost of military unpreparedness.[17] Such prominent features of the Soviet worldview as reliance on force, permanent military preparedness, expectations of high casualties, and the glorification of sacrifice became even more pronounced after 1945. In October 1947 Stalin, in an unusual gesture, circulated to the top Soviet hierarchy a transcript of his meeting with a group of pro-Soviet British Labour Party MPs. Contemporary international life, Stalin said, is governed by "feelings of personal profit," not "feelings of sympathy." If a country realizes it can seize and conquer another country, it will. "Nobody pities or respects the weak. Respect is reserved only for the strong."[18]

The cataclysmic experience of World War II made Stalin's Hobbesian vision of international relations appear as the only credible way to interpret confrontation with the West. Marxism-Leninism, as well as the Russian-Soviet version of history propagated by the regime, translated the cult of force into the zero-sum concept of the struggle between the Soviet "progressive" camp and the "reactionary" camp of imperialism. Soviet propaganda excoriated "abstract humanism" and "pacifism" as naïve illusions at best and ideological fallacies at worst.

Western containment of the Soviet Union after 1946 validated the militarism that pervaded postwar Soviet elites. The Anglo-American alliance loomed as a formidable enemy—with global reach and the military bases around the Soviet borders. Those Soviets who might have questioned official propaganda could not ignore the American bombing of Hiroshima and Nagasaki and its determination to retain its atomic monopoly. The creation of NATO and the Marshall Plan, and talk of rearming West Germany, persuaded Soviet leaders and followers to believe Stalin: without military force the Soviet Union could be crushed.

Hence, Soviet recovery from the war transformed rapidly into remobilizing for another. The construction of a giant military-industrial complex, an extension of the 1930s industrialization drive, became the patriotic duty and a lifetime project for Soviet scientists and engineers. Participants in Soviet atomic and missile projects harbored no qualms about building the weapons of mass extermination; only after Stalin's death did they begin to consider the dangers of a thermonuclear arms race. Soviet writers and artists helped build a firewall against pacifism and other influences that could "soften" Soviet society.[19]

# DECOLONIZATION AND SOVIET OVEREXTENSION

The process of decolonization contributed to globalizing the cold war. The precipitous decline of British, French, and other European colonial empires in the 1950s created irresistible temptations for the Kremlin to intervene in parts of the globe previously beyond

Soviet reach. The initial refusal of Stalin to capitalize on decolonization in Asia and else-where can be explained by the Soviet dictator's preference for great power diplomacy and total control. Also, Stalin, a self-taught Marxist-Leninist "realist," refused to provide Soviet assistance to those countries where he estimated that the "correlation of forces" could not guarantee victory in case of war. Stalin's decision to ally the Soviet Union with Mao Zedong's regime in China was the first major breakthrough of Soviet policies beyond the ideo-geostrategic periphery of the USSR. The establishment of the People's Republic of China (PRC) changed the course of the cold war.

After Stalin's death, the new Kremlin leaders moved to recalculate the "correlation of forces." They reframed the map of the cold war according to a new definition of allies and partners. The evolution of Soviet policies resulted from the emergence of the Third World as contested terrain between the cold war blocs and the growing salience of the non-communist, nationalist, and radical military forces in the post-colonial countries. In the Kremlin, Stalinist geostrategic caution and a penchant for total control gave way to more flexible and ambitious policies.

1955 marked a breakthrough in Soviet ideological views and practical policies. The restoration of relations with Tito's Yugoslavia opened ideological and political room for a rapprochement with non-aligned and neutral elements that Stalinist dogma had con-sidered "bourgeois" and unworthy of trust and support. The participation of India, China, and Indonesia in the Bandung conference attracted great attention in the Kremlin. And the trip of Khrushchev's protégé Dmitry Shepilov to Syria and Egypt revealed to the Soviet leadership the power of anti-British and anti-French Arab nation-alism in the Middle East.

Nikita Khrushchev's ascendency coincided with spectacular victories of national-lib-eration movements in Asia, the Middle East, and Africa. His new look at the Third World began with China. While Stalin treated China as a junior partner in his "socialist empire" and during the Korean war sold arms to the PRC for US dollars, Khrushchev provided China with generous economic, technological, and military assistance. Chinese indus-trialization became almost an extension of the Soviet five-year plan: the PRC was the first to receive Soviet-produced machines and industrial tools. Supporting decolon-ization and national liberation forces around the globe was also congruent with Khrushchev's double-barreled effort to replace Stalin's cult with the "back to Lenin" campaign. In December 1955 former Soviet ambassador to Britain Ivan Maisky wrote to Khrushchev that "the next act of the struggle for global domination of socialism will unfold through the liberation of colonial and semi-colonial people from imperialist exploitation." Repeating the basics of Leninist teaching, Maisky concluded: "The loss of colonies and semi-colonies by the imperialist powers must accelerate the victory of socialism in Europe, and eventually in the USA."[20] Khrushchev's policies demonstrated that he concurred.

Soviet policies in the Third World during the late 1950s radically improved its geostra-tegic positions. In 1957 the Third World "came" to Moscow, when the youth from Asia, Africa, and Latin America participated in the 7th World Youth Festival in the Soviet cap-ital. This festival became a cultural event of tremendous importance for the delegates from the Third World, but even more so for the people of Moscow. With the festival and the launch of Sputnik a few months later, Soviet "soft power" in the Third World soared. At the same time, collaboration with a different set of leaders and movements profoundly affected Soviet conduct. "Romancing the Third World" altered the worldview and political culture of Soviet elites. Thousands of Soviet technicians, engineers, doctors, and military personnel traveled to and worked in China, Indonesia, India, Burma, Egypt, Syria, Iraq, Ghana, and other countries that allied with the Soviet Union or professed their "socialist" and "progressive" orientation. The exposure to the countries where people lived in even greater poverty than in the Soviet Union validated Soviet ideological convictions and generated faith in a bright socialist future.[21]

While the experience of World War II and the Soviet victory fueled the "imperial" component of the paradigm, decolonization and the emergence of anti-imperialist, anti-Western regimes boosted the "revolutionary" aspects. The willingness of Third World radicals and intellectuals to emulate Soviet experiences and welcome Soviet assistance produced a euphoric effect among the Soviet leaders. Many came to regard the countries of Asia, Africa, and the Middle East as new frontiers for the communist experiment. This phenomenon climaxed with the Soviet infatuation with the Cuban revolution. Fidel Castro, Che Guevara, and other "barbudos" became more popular among Soviet people than was Khrushchev himself. The head of the Communist Youth League rhapsodized in January 1961: "Any time other Latin American countries may follow after Cuba. Americans are literally sitting on the powder keg in Latin America." Soviet cultural elites saw in Cuba "socialism with a human face." Cuba's defiance of its US neighbor and its defeat of the Bay of Pigs invasion buttressed Soviet optimism about the worldwide triumph of their model.[22]

The spillover from the Third World affected Soviet conduct in many ways. An ambitious, almost reckless global projection of Soviet influence replaced Stalin's cautious calculation of the "correlation of forces." Evidence suggests that developments in Iraq and China influenced Khrushchev to ignite the Berlin crisis in November 1958. Vyacheslav Molotov, already in retirement, even drafted in 1959 a project establishing a future "confederation of socialist states," beginning with the USSR and the PRC.[23]

Changes in Soviet international behavior caused by global decolonization and the rise of the developing world produced greater risks and ultimately imperial overextension. Dealing with radical allies in the Third World meant accepting a new level of unpredictability in Soviet foreign policy. The Kremlin could not even control its allies and clients. This became painfully clear in Sino-Soviet relations, where the PRC threatened twice, in 1954–55 and 1958, to unleash a war in East Asia by shelling offshore islands occupied by the Nationalists. Notwithstanding the Kremlin's displays of solidarity with the Chinese, personal tension erupted between Khrushchev and Mao Zedong. The Kremlin was slow to recognize that national liberation impulses might turn not only against the West but also against the Soviet Union.

The expansion of Soviet commitments in the Third World led to the increasing vulnerability of its empire's boundaries. The Kremlin worried about its ability to protect weak yet adventurous allies and clients. This fear propelled Khrushchev's decision to send nuclear missiles to Cuba in 1962. The forced and humiliating withdrawal of the Soviet missiles contributed to Khrushchev's downfall two years later. Khrushchev's successors even questioned the entire Soviet course of extending their influence in Third World countries. Leaders "of those countries," stated one critic, "ate what we gave them, and then turned away from us. Capitalists laugh at us and they have reason to do so."[24] Yet, they stayed the course.

Soviet overextension in the post-colonial world turned out to be a lasting factor in Soviet cold war behavior. Khrushchev's successors expected the victory of "progressive forces" in the Third World to have a decisive effect on the "correlation of forces." The fall of Sukarno's pro-communist regime in Indonesia in 1966 and the crushing defeat of the Egyptian-Syrian armies in the 1967 Arab-Israeli war plunged the Kremlin into doom and gloom. After the Soviets "lost" Egypt in 1970–4, they sought revenge. The US defeat in the Vietnam war and the collapse of Portugal's African empire incentivized Moscow, together with its Cuban ally, to fill the power vacuum first in Angola and Mozambique and then in the Horn of Africa. The future of the Third World, once a booster to the revolutionary component of the Soviet foreign policy paradigm, was turning into a drain on its resources and a source of geopolitical insecurity.

Yet the Soviets persisted. Support for radical movements in the Third World remained an index of the regime's self-validation. Soviet propaganda constantly promoted the image of the "march of socialism and progress." Pilgrimages of Third World radicals to Moscow, in search of armaments and loans, became a ritual that reconfirmed the centrality of the Soviet Union in the world. Finally, there was a powerful coalition of group interests, uniting the military, the KGB, the ideologists in the apparatus, and external operators in the Third World itself.[25]

Brezhnev and other Kremlin leaders threw "good money" after "bad." By the end of the 1970s, the Soviets funded sixty-nine regimes, clients, and movements—most of them in the Third World. Because the survival of these regimes became the primary support for theorizing about the inevitable "victory of socialism," no one in the Soviet leadership had the political will to cancel the investments in them.[26]

## SOVIET COLD WAR CONSENSUS ERODES

The revolutionary-imperial paradigm could continue to engender a Soviet cold war consensus as long as Soviet elites and the populace adhered to two tenets: (1) that the future belonged to the Soviet version of modernity; and (2) that the West was inherently aggressive, determined to destroy the Soviet Union and its "socialist empire" by force. Both of these tenets became suspect in the 1960s and 1970s, as domestic, regional, and global developments contributed to the erosion of ideological and experiential certainties. The Soviet cold war consensus began to crumble.

At the core of these developments was a generational and cultural change among Soviet elites. During the 1960s–70s new cohorts of highly educated men and women, with diverse cultural needs and material interests, replaced the aging Stalinist cohorts. The cold war competition in education, science, and technology accelerated this change. The logic of this competition compelled the Soviet leadership to sponsor science and technology, to expand higher education, and to grant more freedom—and influence—to scientific and engineering elites. From 1928 to 1960 the number of college students grew twelve-fold and reached 2.4 million. The number of college-educated professionals increased from 233,000 to 3.5 million.[27]

The post-Stalin rulers also wanted to demonstrate that the Soviet model produced a contented society of creative and highly educated people. Khrushchev and later Brezhnev sharply reduced work hours and taxes and increased investments in public housing, education, mass culture, and the health system. They also undertook to establish modern urban infrastructures and consumer-oriented industries, neglected or sacrificed during Stalin's years.[28] By the end of the 1960s Soviet society was bursting with young professionals and managers.

Jeremi Suri argues that the rise of these groups in the Soviet Union was part of a global "counter-culture" rebellion against the cold war consensus during the 1960s.[29] In fact, something different and even more significant was going on in Soviet society. The younger cohorts matured at a time when state terror abated, the gulag system eroded, the leaders debated Stalin's crimes publicly, and cultural influences began to penetrate Soviet society from abroad. With the improvements in mass communications, diverse and complex cultural production reached tens of millions in the Soviet Union. Western movies, jazz, and Elvis Presley, then Beatles-mania and rock produced a parallel and distinctly "un-Soviet" culture among Soviet students, particularly the children of Soviet elites. Travel and tourism outside the Soviet Union mushroomed; millions of foreigners began to visit the Soviet Union. In 1957 over 700,000 Soviet citizens traveled abroad as state employees as well as tourists, and this number expanded in subsequent decades.[30]

This growing openness of the Soviet society to the outside world had a huge impact on the new educated elites' sense of historical superiority of Soviet "socialism" and on the enemy image of the West. The partial opening of the Soviet Union to the West coincided with fundamental changes, economic and social, in Western countries. During the 1950s and beyond, they experienced unprecedented economic boom, created impressive social programs, and expanded mass consumption beyond the expectations of earlier generations. As the laissez-faire capitalism of the cartoonish upper classes and miserable workers in Western Europe gave way to new realities, Soviet visitors confronted an ever-growing cognitive gap between what the propaganda told them at home and what they could see with their own eyes.

Nevertheless, the paradigmatic components of Soviet cold war consensus proved resilient. The new cohorts of Soviet educated elites became neither an anti-socialist generation, nor a "counter-culture" generation, as in the West. Even after Khrushchev's denunciation of Stalin's cult, the vast majority remained devotees of the revolutionary-imperial paradigm. A movement toward cultural liberalization that emerged after 1965 ("dissidents") was at first generally socialist in its worldview.[31] The dominant trend among educated Soviets was not "return to capitalism" but improvement and perfection of the Soviet system—perhaps at some point "converging" with the increasingly humane Western capitalist democracies. It was especially true of the highly positioned group of "enlightened apparatchiks" who worked as consultants and speech-writers to the top political leadership. Among them were the future "new thinkers" of the Gorbachev era: Georgy Arbatov, Anatoly Chernyaev, Fedor Burlatsky, Nikolai Inozemtsev, and Georgy Shakhnazarov. Although influenced by European ideas and culture, they remained staunch Soviet patriots and unwilling to accept the superiority of America's "way of life."[32]

1965–8 was the peak of this reformist-technocratic momentum in Soviet educated elites: economic reforms were under way, and the scientific-technical revolution seemed to augur imminent political changes. Then came the invasion of Czechoslovakia. The onslaught of Soviet tanks was a brutal reality check for the reformist vanguard of the younger Soviet elites. The ghost of the Prague Spring continued to haunt the "enlightened apparatchiks" into the 1980s. Len Karpinsky, one of the intellectual leaders of communist reformism, wrote that the Soviet tanks could not kill ideas, and these ideas "are percolating into the apparatus and forming a layer of party intellectuals, an arm of the intelligentsia within the administrative structure." When Gorbachev became the leader of the Soviet Union, his reformist advisors recalled 1968 as the year of missed opportunity for socialism.[33]

With the erosion of the communist idealism and millenarian faith after 1968, alternative views began to emerge in Russian society. The old divide between Westernizers and Slavophiles became replicated among cultural elites in Moscow in the form of a ferocious polarization between the liberal "left" and the neo-Stalinist "right." The "left" began to regard the democratic and liberal West as a natural ally against the Soviet bureaucracy—this trend found its complete expression in the alliance between human rights defenders in Moscow with Western journalists stationed there. During the 1970s thousands of Soviet/Russian intellectuals emigrated to the West, thanks to the "Jewish emigration" sanctioned by the Kremlin in the name of détente.[34] The "right" continued the traditions of Stalinist glory and Russian imperial nationalism. They viewed the cold war as a stage in the historic struggle between the West and the Russian superpower in the shape of the USSR.

A number of Soviet educated elites continued to work inside the system but felt alienated and bitter. The murder of the Prague Spring shattered their belief in the Soviet version of modernity. The "New Left" in the West and even West European communists relegated the USSR to the ranks of anti-modern, reactionary forces, an obstacle to progress.

1968 marked the beginning of a sharp decline of another supporting factor of Soviet cold war behavior: the predominance of the culture of violence. The anti-militarist trend evolved after Stalin's death and intensified during the 1960s. The emergence of transnational scientific networks, authorized by the Soviet state, promoted this phenomenon among Soviet intellectuals.[35] During the early 1970s, the anti-militarist tendencies in Soviet elites gained unexpected support from Leonid Brezhnev, who was horrified by Khrushchev's nuclear brinkmanship. Brezhnev's vision of "European Security and

Cooperation" was a prequel to Gorbachev's new thinking: it involved rapprochement with NATO and disavowing the force or the threat of force.[36] Brezhnev's policies helped erode the "enemy image" of the West. Soviet propaganda touted strategic parity with the United States and the successes of Brezhnev's agreements with West Germany and the Helsinki Final Act. Cohorts of Soviet youth grew up assuming that peace, not war and militarism, was a natural state of life.

Toward the end of 1970s, optimism in the Soviet Union evaporated, a victim of Western economic superiority and the growing gap between consumerist expectations and the failure of the Soviet economy to meet those expectations.[37] The post-Stalin leadership had to downsize the military and redirect resources toward civilian consumption, beginning with prefabricated housing and household durables. Khrushchev's faith in the superiority of the Soviet model led him to authorize and promote policies that had unintended consequences. To replace terror as an instrument to mobilize the population, the Soviet leader launched the campaign to "catch up and surpass America" in economics, consumerism, and culture. He explained to Walter Ulbricht, "The Americans believe that the Soviet people, looking at their achievements, will turn away from the Soviet government. But the Americans do not understand our people. We will tell our people: look, this is what the richest country of capitalism has achieved in one hundred years. Socialism will give us the opportunity to achieve this significantly faster."[38]

Khrushchev's bragging had the effect of undermining Soviet anti-American propaganda. Czech reformer and former communist Zdenek Mlynar rightly observed: "Stalin never allowed the comparison of socialism with capitalist realities because he insisted that here we build an absolutely new world, comparable to nothing." Khrushchev's slogan fundamentally changed the perception of the West for the average Soviet person. Over the following years people became accustomed to comparing their lives to Americans' and developed an inferiority complex. One generation after another recognized that American living standards remained much higher than theirs. And, Mlynar continued, those who looked for explanations concluded that the main obstacle that prevented them from achieving an American-style life was the existing economic and political system.[39] One may add that comparison between East Germany and West Germany was even more painful: both sides of the country, destroyed during World War II, demonstrated the economic-consumerist triumph of the Western ways over the "socialist" ways.

The unfavorable comparison, however, took years to sink in. At the end of the 1960s millions of Soviets seemed for the first time since the Russian revolution to benefit from the communist system. Pensions, free education, healthcare, maternity leave, paid vacations, childcare, and other services made Soviet life better and less stressful. Yet, the growth of the "social state" came at a cost. After food riots in 1962, the Soviet leadership had to import grain and fix artificially low "stable" prices for basic goods. Under Brezhnev, food and consumer imports kept increasing, the list of subsidized goods grew, and costs spiraled out of control. The Soviet state became a hostage to its social commitments. During the 1970s it became clear that the Soviet model had serious structural problems. The economic reforms initiated in 1965 failed or were ended by the conservative Brezhnev leadership. Also, the system of fixed low prices in conjunction with central planning produced hidden inflation, creeping inefficiency, and declining incentives to work. The destabilization of Soviet finances made goods disappear from the shelves and reappear on the black market. Consumer frustration escalated—Khrushchev's vision of Soviet abundance became the subject of cynical jokes. Western visitors to the Soviet Union during this time were stunned to discover that the Soviet Union resembled a stagnating society, with people desperate to find a slice of beef or milk for their children. These consumer problems undermined belief in the superiority of Soviet modernity.[40]

Normally empire-builders expect to enjoy higher living standards than those whom they conquer, protect, or dominate. The situation in the Soviet Union was the opposite: Russians, the ethnic backbone of the Soviet Union, received the worst economic deal. Russians could see first-hand that they lived worse than Georgians, Armenians, Azeris, most Ukrainians, and the Balts. Russia's natural wealth was used to buy the allegiance of non-Russian "republics." The state redistributed resources from the Russian-Ukrainian region to subsidize underdeveloped Central Asia. The same scenario was replicated on a global scale. The countries of Eastern Europe, especially East Germany, Hungary, and Czechoslovakia, enjoyed a much more comfortable lifestyle than Soviet citizens. While the United States during the 1980s profited enormously from a global financial system dominated by the US dollar, the Soviet Union became a giant "cow" for those countries that pledged allegiance to its "socialist empire" in return for oil, gas, and other subsidies.

This paradox could only survive with the help of systematic terror, total isolation, and ideological indoctrination. But none of these factors remained by the end of Brezhnev's rule. While contradictions intensified inside the Soviet Union and between the USSR and its partners and clients, the economic competition with the West turned into a rout. The success of the Western European "social state" and the emergence of a prosperous middle class in the 1960s and 1970s impressed Soviet visitors more and more. Tourism and travel to the West, increasingly accessible during the 1970s, made Soviets painfully aware that the consumer paradise Khrushchev promised in the future already existed in the West. In the early 1970s Gorbachev and his wife Raisa rented a car and toured Italy. Raisa Gorbachev, a sociologist, was surprised by the contrast between the images of poverty and unemployment that she had seen in the films of Italian neorealism in her youth and the new reality. At one point she asked her husband: "Misha, why do we live worse than they do?"[41] Feelings of Soviet patriotism gave way to a sense of personal and national humiliation.

The mass emigration from the Soviet Union during the 1970s was another stark sociological and ideological phenomenon. Studies reveal that many of the émigrés were highly educated professionals from Moscow, Leningrad, and other Soviet cities. They did not leave only because of anti-Semitism and persecution of their Jewish identity; the vast majority of them did not care much about their Jewishness. A growing segment of them began to think of their future outside the Soviet and communist framework.[42]

# MIKHAIL GORBACHEV AND THE DISMANTLING
## OF THE PARADIGM

The first half of the 1980s was painful for the generation of Soviet rulers who had come of age during Stalinism and World War II. This generation had internalized what George Kennan had prematurely applied to Stalinist leadership in February 1946: if Kremlin leaders repudiated their revolutionary ideology, "they would stand before history, at best, as only the last of that long succession of cruel and wasteful Russian rulers who have relentlessly forced country on to ever new heights of military power in order to guarantee external security of their internally weak regimes." [43] In 1985, when the young Mikhail Gorbachev was elected Soviet leader by the politburo, the mood of pessimism and loss of direction was endemic. A year later Gorbachev and his lieutenants launched glasnost to illuminate publicly what thwarted Soviet progress. Then in 1986–8 Gorbachev and a small group of "new thinkers" began to dismantle the structural foundations of Soviet cold war behavior. Beginning in 1988 they began to dismantle the foundations of the Soviet Union as a superpower.

Careful analysis reveals that the Gorbachevian dismantling of the revolutionary-imperial paradigm was intentional. Yet the evidence also shows that Gorbachev and the new thinkers proceeded without a clear strategy, without anticipating the consequences, and without control over the process.[44] Gorbachev's years became a time of historic revenge for those who had prepared the reformist-technocratic "socialism with a human face" and supported the Prague Spring in 1968. It became the dismantling of the Stalinist mentality, structures, and historical legacy—which stood as the real and imagined target of the policies of perestroika and glasnost. Gorbachev himself relied on the educated elites of his generation. He preserved the ingenious historical optimism of the bygone era, boosted by his remarkable personal self-confidence.

The self-image of Gorbachev is vital for understanding his determination to "exit" the cold war. He posed and acted as "anti-Stalin," in terms of both his domestic reforms and international behavior. The creator of the Soviet state and empire, Stalin conflated his personality with his creations. Gorbachev did not feel a personal association with the Soviet state that he inherited. Later he claimed that he did everything "to preserve the Union." In reality, he sought to create a new state according to the principles that had emerged among the Soviet intellectuals during the 1960s. Gorbachev's conversations with foreign leaders reveal that Western statesmen became a crucial reference group for him. Gorbachev liked and respected Western statesmen; he regarded even conservative anti-communists like Thatcher, Reagan, and Bush as personal friends. While Stalin always suspected the worst from the West, Gorbachev assumed Western good faith, honesty, integrity, and fealty to agreements. Trust in the "goodness" of the West can be seen in the transformation of Gorbachev's "common European Home." This concept, first used in 1985–6 as a tool to drive a wedge between the US and other NATO countries, became by 1989 shorthand for "return to Europe" and rejection of Stalinist closed society.

Gorbachev's determination to solidify Soviet-German cooperation as a foundation for a future "common European home" influenced his 1990 talks on German unification and its membership in NATO.[45]

Gorbachev's Westernism must be situated in the context of long-term societal and cultural changes that had accumulated in Soviet elites after Stalin's death. For many Soviet intellectuals who grew up during the 1950s and 1960s, the image of the West as an enemy was gradually replaced by the image of the West as a successful model of modernization and progress. For Stalin's regime the image of a hostile West was pivotal to justifying the Bolshevik "dictatorship of development." Europe was, as historian Mark Mazower writes, a "dark continent." [46] Competing nation-states, selfish imperialism, racism, and, of course, fascism and Nazism were inherent pathologies of Western societies. Post-Stalinist propaganda continued to exploit Russian phobias about the West.

But during the 1950s and 1960s, Western countries began to embrace international liberalism and economic integration as alternatives to their past. They designed new transnational projects of cooperation, from NATO to the European Community. Much of Western Europe adopted Social Democracy, implementing social welfare programs. Japan, Taiwan, South Korea, and others were incorporated into a global system of international economic liberalism, where zero-sum logic no longer predominated. This transformation of the West affected Russian public opinion. Within this framework Gorbachev's Westernism was a resurrection of the Russian tradition: leaning to the West to pull the country out of systemic backwardness. Before Gorbachev, Andrei Sakharov and the dissidents spoke about a "convergence" between Soviet "socialism" and the West. After Gorbachev, Boris Yeltsin and the "Russian democrats" appealed to the United States and Western countries for advice and assistance.[47]

The rejection of Stalin's legacy meant the rejection of his cult of force and militarism. From the beginning Gorbachev manifested a genuine interest in nuclear disarmament. Later events showed Gorbachev's profound aversion to the use of force. Western politicians understood that feature of Gorbachev's statesmanship. This understanding was particularly useful during the talks about German reunification. Helmut Kohl, George H. W. Bush, and James Baker knew that the Soviet Union still had troops in East Germany, but they were convinced that Gorbachev would never use them as a bargaining chip to influence negotiations. Gorbachev agreed that a reunified Germany could become a member of NATO without even obtaining a formalized agreement that NATO would not expand to Soviet borders.[48]

Gorbachev's renunciation of the use of force as a matter of principle was a remarkable development, which reflected trends among the generation of Soviet educated elites who came of age in the decades after Stalin's death. In 1988–9 the supporters of Gorbachev's reforms inside the party apparatus expressed their profound convictions when they argued that the Soviet Union should under no circumstances intervene militarily in Eastern Europe.[49] The KGB, the military, and the provincial party apparatchiks never shared Gorbachev's anti-militarism. At the same time, Gorbachev's rejection of force was supported by numerous Soviet intellectuals and became one of the main themes of glasnost and the campaign for "de-Stalinizing" and democratizing the Soviet Union.

The comparison between "Stalinist" and "Gorbachev" elites highlights the spectacular cultural and ideological change in the USSR between 1945–8 and 1985–8. Stalin dragged Soviet elites and society into the cold war. Four decades later, Gorbachev convinced his generation of party elites, the KGB, the military, and the military-industrial complex of the need to escape the superpowers' confrontation. The majority within these institutions did not seek the destruction of the great power status of the Soviet Union. They wanted limited cultural and economic liberalization. Yet Gorbachev and a few new thinkers were able to impose a new course on the enormous party bureaucracy and military because of the elite's changing character. During the three decades after Stalin's death, many Soviet elites began to value high culture, scientific degrees, and knowledge of languages. Even cold warriors who were stationed in outposts around the world ended up sharing with Western adversaries a culture of materialism and consumerism. And above all, they universally chose a better life for themselves over the preservation of the Soviet empire.

Consequently, the "exit" of the Soviet Union from the cold war was a remarkable case of peaceful dismantling of the revolutionary-imperial paradigm with minimal resistance from the power structures and vested elite interests. This essay has analyzed the paradigmatic factors behind Soviet cold war behavior. After World War II the paradigm had found huge support in post-war vulnerabilities, triumphalism, nationalist pride, and the reliance on militarism and force. The demise of these factors was linked to dramatic social, cultural, and ideological changes inside the Soviet Union and within the Soviet bloc. With the partial opening of Soviet societies to outside influence after Stalin's death, international developments also became major "players" in the drama of Soviet change. From the second half of the 1950s, Soviet elites were affected by transnational factors and increasingly torn between growing engagement with the wider world and imperial xenophobia and arrogance. Ultimately, in a remarkable explosion of historical serendipity represented by Mikhail Gorbachev, the former prevailed over the latter.

## NOTES

1. David C. Engerman, *Know Your Enemy. The Rise and Fall of America's Soviet Experts* (New York: Oxford University Press, 2009); Rosa Magnusdottir, Review Essay, *Kritika: Explorations in Russian and Eurasian History* 11/1 (Winter 2010): 201–11.

2. Alfred J. Rieber, "How Persistent are Persistent Factors," in Robert Legvold, ed., *Russian Foreign Policy in the Twenty-First Century and the Shadow of the Past* (New York: Columbia University Press, 2007), 205–78.

3. Vladislav Zubok and Constantine Pleshakov, *Inside the Kremlin's Cold War* (Cambridge, MA: Harvard University Press, 1996).

4. Odd Arne Westad, *The Global Cold War: Third World Interventions and the Making of Our Times* (Cambridge: Cambridge University Press, 2006), 72.

5. Nicholas Thompson, *The Hawk and the Dove: Paul Nitze, George Kennan, and the History of the Cold War* (New York: Henry Holt and Co, 2009), 59–60.

6. Melvyn Leffler, *For the Soul of Mankind: The United States, The Soviet Union, and the Cold War* (New York: Hill and Wang, 2007), 38, 81.

7. Tsuyoshi Hasegawa, *Racing the Enemy: Stalin, Truman, and the Surrender of Japan* (Cambridge, MA: Belknap Press, 2005), 300.

8. Zubok and Pleshakov, *Inside the Kremlin's Cold War*, 3.

9. *Istoricheskii Arkhiv* 4 (1997), 102–3.

10. Nigel Gould-Davies, "Rethinking the Role of Ideology in International Politics during the Cold War," *Journal of Cold War Studies* 1 (Winter 1999): 92.

11. S.M. Plokhy, *Yalta: The Price of Peace* (New York: Viking, 2010).

12. Joseph Rothschild and Nancy M. Wingfield, *Return to Diversity: A Political History of East Central Europe since World War II*, 3rd ed. (New York: Oxford University Press, 2000), 73.

13. Vladimir Pechatnov, *Stalin, Rusvelt, Trumen: SSSR i SshA v 1940-kh godakh. Dokumentalnye ocherki* (Moscow: TERRA, 2006).

14. Geoffrey Hosking, *Rulers and Victims: The Russians in the Soviet Union* (Cambridge, MA: Belknap Press, 2006).

15. Jamil Hasanly, *SSSR-Iran. Azerbaidzhanskii krizis I nachalo kholodnoi voiny (1941–1946)* (Moscow: Geroi Otechestva, 2006); also ibid., *SSSR-Turtsiia: ot neitraliteta k kholodnoi voine, 1939–1953* (Moscow: Tsentr Propagandy, 2008).

16. Hosking, *Rulers and Victims*.

17. P.H. Vigor, *The Soviet View of War, Peace and Neutrality* (London: Routledge and Kegan Paul, 1975).

18. "Zapis besedi tov. Stalina s gruppoi angliiskikh leiboristov—deputatov parlamenta," October 14, 1947, Georgia's Central State Archive of Contemporary History, Tbilisi, f. 1206, op. 2, d. 326d, l. 16.

19. Vladislav M. Zubok, *Zhivago's Children: The Last Russian Intelligentsia* (Cambridge, MA: Belknap Press, 2009), 80.

20. Westad, *The Global Cold War*, 39–67; Vladislav Zubok, *A Failed Empire: The Soviet Union in the Cold War from Stalin to Gorbachev* (Chapel Hill, NC: University of North Carolina Press, 2007), 247.

21. Zubok, *Zhivago's Children*, 118.

22. Zubok, *Failed Empire*.

23. Alexandr Fursenko and Timothy Naftali, *Khrushchev's Cold War: The Inside Story of an American Adversary* (New York: Norton, 2006); Zubok, *Failed Empire*.

24. *Istochnik* 2 (1998), 114–20.

25. Westad, *Global Cold War*.

26. Zubok, *Failed Empire*, 249–50, 268.

27. S.V. Volkov, *Intellektualnyi sloi v sovetskom obschestve* (Moscow: Fond Razvitie, 1999), 30–1, 126–7.

28. Elena Zubkova, *Russia after the War: Hopes, Illusions, and Disappointments, 1945–1957* (Armonk, NY: M.E. Sharpe, 1998), 175.

29. Jeremi Suri, *Power and Protest: Global Revolution and the Rise of Détente* (Cambridge, MA: Harvard University Press, 2003).

30. David Caute, *The Dancer Defects: The Struggle for Cultural Supremacy during the Cold War* (Oxford: Oxford University Press, 2003); Walter L. Hixson, *Parting the Curtain: Propaganda, Culture, and the Cold War, 1945–1961* (New York: St. Martin's Press, 1997); Ann E. Gorsuch and Diane P. Koenker, eds., *Turizm: The Russian and East European Tourist under Capitalism and Socialism* (Ithaca, NY: Cornell University Press, 2006).

31. Zubok, *Zhivago's Children*.

32. Robert E. English, *Russia and the Idea of the West: Gorbachev, Intellectuals, and the End of the Cold War* (New York: Columbia University Press, 2000); Zubok, *Zhivago's Children*.

33. Len Karpinsky, "Words Are Also Deeds," in Stephen F. Cohen, ed., *An End to Silence: Uncensored Opinion in the Soviet Union* (New York: Norton, 1982), 306–10.

34. Victor Zaslavsky and Robert J. Brym, *Soviet-Jewish Emigration and Soviet Nationality Policy* (Hong Kong: Macmillan Press, 1983).

35. Matthew Evangelista, *Unarmed Forces. The Transnational Movement to End the Cold War* (Ithaca, NY: Cornell University Press, 2002).

36. Vojtech Mastny, "The Warsaw Pact as History," in Vojtech Mastny and Malcolm Byrne, eds., *A Cardboard Castle? An Inside History of the Warsaw Pact, 1955–1991* (Budapest: Central European University Press, 2005), 42–3.

37. John Bushnell, "The 'New Soviet Man' Turns Pessimist," in Stephen F. Cohen, Alexander Rabinowitch and Robert Sharlet, eds., *The Soviet Union Since Stalin* (Bloomington, IN and London: Indiana University Press, 1980), 179–85.

38. Short Summary of the Talks with the GDR Party-Governmental Delegation on June 9, 1959, AVP RF, f. 0742, op. 4, papka 31, d. 33, l. 86–7, translated and published by Hope Harrison in *Cold War International History Project Bulletin* (*CWHIP*) 11 (Winter 1998): 212.

39. Mikhail Gorbachev and Zdenek Mlynar, *Conversations with Gorbachev* (introduction by Archie Brown) (New York: Columbia University Press, 2001).

40. Egor Gaidar, *Collapse of an Empire: Lessons for Modern Russia* (Washington, DC: Brookings Institution Press, 2007).

41. Mikhail Gorbachev, *Zhizn i reformi*, vol. 1 (Moscow: Novosti, 1995), 155–68; Andrei Grachev, *Gorbachev's Gamble. Soviet Foreign Policy and the End of the Cold War* (Boston, MA: Polity, 2008), 56.

42. Yuri Slezkine, *The Jewish Century* (Princeton, NJ: Princeton University Press, 2004).

43. George Kennan, The Long Telegram, at: <http://www.gwu.edu/~nsarchiv/coldwar/documents/episode-1/kennan.htm>.

44. Zubok, *Failed Empire*, 301–302, 313.

45. Marie-Pierre Rey, "'Europe is our Common Home': A Study of Gorbachev's Diplomatic Concept," *Cold War History* 2 (January 2004): 33–65.

46. Mark Mazower, *Dark Continent: Europe's Twentieth Century* (New York: Vintage, 2000).

47. Dmitry Furman, "Fenomen Gorbacheva," *Svobodnaia Mysl* 11 (1995), 68, 70–1; Zubok, *Failed Empire*, 316–8.

48. Mary Elise Sarotte, *1989: The Struggle to Create Post-Cold War Europe* (Princeton, NJ: Princeton University Press, 2009).

49. A. Cherniaev, A. Veber, and V. Medvedev, eds., *V Politburo TsK KPSS…Pso zapisiam Anatolia Cherniaeva, Vadima Medvedeva, Georgiia Shakhnazarova (1985–1991)* (Moscow: Alpina Biznes Books, 2006), 61; Vladislav M. Zubok, "New Evidence on the 'Soviet Factor' in the Peaceful Revolutions of 1989," *CWIHP* 12/13 (Fall–Winter 2001): 10.

## SELECTED BIBLIOGRAPHY

Arbatov, Georgy. *The System: An Insider's Life in Soviet Politics*. New York: Times Books, 1992.

Dobrynin, Anatoly. *In Confidence. Moscow's Ambassador to America's Six Cold War Presidents (1962–1986)*. New York: Random House, 1995.

English, Robert D. *Russia and the Idea of the West: Gorbachev, Intellectuals and the End of the Cold War*. New York: Columbia University Press, 2000.

Fursenko, Alexander and Naftali, Timothy. *"One Hell of a Gamble." Khrushchev, Castro and Kennedy 1958–1964*. New York: W.W. Norton, 1997.

Harrison, Hope. *Driving the Soviets Up the Wall: Soviet-East German Relations, 1953–1961*. Princeton, NJ: Princeton University Press, 2003.

Kramer, Mark. "The Soviet Union and the Founding of the German Democratic Republic: 50 Years Later—A Review Article," *Europe-Asia Studies* 51/6 (1999), 1093–106.

Levesque, Jacques. *The Enigma of 1989: The USSR and the Liberation of Eastern Europe*. Berkeley, CA: University of California Press, 1997.

Taubman, William. *Khrushchev. The Man and His Era*. New York: W.W. Norton, 2003.

Zubok, Vladislav, *A Failed Empire. The Soviet Union in the Cold War from Stalin to Gorbachev*. Chapel Hill, NC: University of North Carolina Press, 2007.

Zubok, Vladislav. *Zhivago's Children. The Last Russian Intelligentsia*. Cambridge, MA: Belknap Press, 2009.

# CHAPTER 19

..................................................................................

# POWER AND CULTURE IN
# THE WEST

..................................................................................

## CHRISTOPHER ENDY[1]

THE phrase "cold war culture" conjures images of repression and fear: Joseph McCarthy waving a list of supposed communists in the US government, nervous filmmakers testifying on "un-American" activities in Hollywood, and suburbanites building bomb shelters. Each image captures a certain truth but fails to convey the full relationship between the cold war and domestic society in the West. After all, few homeowners in the United States or elsewhere built fallout shelters, and Hollywood never fully succumbed to anti-communist hysteria. A focus on McCarthyism also tells us little about the relationship between culture and the cold war outside the United States, particularly among those US allies with communist and socialist movements that were too powerful to persecute.

Taking a broader approach, this essay argues that scholars should recognize three major forms of western cold war culture. First, and most familiar to historians, was a cold war culture of anti-communist repression. This culture revolved around a transnational network of anti-communist elites, most notably US government officials, who sought to combat allegedly dangerous forms of political and cultural expression. The second form was a cold war culture of progressive reform and inclusion. Red Scare fears, to be sure, marginalized leftist radicals, but anti-communism also solidified progressive social reforms, especially in North America and Western Europe. The cold war's emphasis on international alliances also made the United States more cosmopolitan and diverse, in ways that many anti-communists never anticipated. Finally, this essay highlights a third form, a cold war culture of popular resistance to elite-driven cold war mobilization. Cold war culture in the West consisted of two battles. On the surface, it was a struggle between anti-communists and their ideological rivals. At a deeper level, it was a battle waged by a relatively small and often elite group of anti-communists (and by an even smaller number of communists) who wanted to prioritize cold war strategies over more private concerns. Yet western citizens often shirked geopolitical duty and pursued private lives free from cold war intrusions. Anti-communism in particular proved a fragile bond that could break down when challenged by private priorities such as household consumption, business profit, or religious ethics.

By viewing western cold war culture as a struggle to mobilize societies, historians can construct a new narrative of culture's role in the cold war. Most analyses of cold war culture, focused on Red Scare repression, conclude in the late 1950s. By that moment, one historian writes, "the culture of the cold war" apparently "decomposed."[2] While anti-communist repression did decline, this model provides little help for understanding the Cold War's inclusive side, and it omits the long stretch of the cold war after 1960.

An expanded narrative of western cold war culture must start in the mid-1940s with a surge in leftist politics that led moderate and conservative elites across the West to pursue appeasement, repression, or a combination of both. These social pressures in turn exacerbated geopolitical tensions. To marginalize leftist rivals, anti-communists exaggerated the threat of Soviet expansionism. In this polarizing environment, both anti-communists and communists enjoyed great success mobilizing western societies. Still, popular resistance to politicization remained significant. By the 1960s and 1970s, those western societies that had achieved stable compromises between social welfare policies and market economics experienced even greater public resistance to cold war mobilization. Increasing disenchantment with the cold war pressured western politicians to negotiate with communist nations, contributing to cold war détente. Growing resistance and apathy frustrated anti-communists, but it posed bigger challenges to the West's faltering communist movements, particularly in France and Italy.

Domestic social pressures elsewhere in the West also shaped geopolitics. Those western societies that failed to reach stable compromises between socialism and the free market, such as Guatemala, Chile, and Greece, witnessed increasing societal mobilization along ideological lines. The intensification of the cold war in 1970s Latin America even contributed to a revival of US cold war consciousness in the 1980s. However, the revival failed to endure, in part because of Mikhail Gorbachev's reforms in the Soviet Union, but also because many westerners had decided to limit the superpower rivalry's intrusion into their own societies. Westerners' resistance to domestic cold war mobilization thus helped bring the geopolitical cold war to an end. Paradoxically, the West's long record of private resistance and indifference also provided a reason why the West outlasted the Soviet bloc.

Before proceeding further, two terms require definition: culture and the West. The word "culture" here carries two senses. First, it refers to the creative output of artists, musicians, writers, filmmakers, and others engaged in arts and entertainment. In this usage, cold war culture describes those aspects of the arts and popular culture that became entwined with the rivalry between communists and anti-communists. This essay also employs a second, anthropological definition of culture: the contested customs, codes, discourses, and practices that people use to make meaning of the world.[3] In this sense, cold war culture refers to struggles to control the meaning of words and ideas, not just in the arts but also in economic and political life.

Definitions of "the West" became a cold war cultural battleground. Anti-communists spoke of saving "Western Civilization," a phrase one historian called "the cultural equivalent of the Marshall Plan."[4] Yet communism itself was a western invention; the *Communist*

*Manifesto* was published by two Germans living in London. While recognizing the term's tangled heritage, this essay takes as western any nation in Europe and the Americas that allied with the United States during the cold war. Latin America deserves inclusion because it shared important patterns with North America and Western Europe. European colonization brought to both Americas Christianity, slavery, and then republican revolutions that struggled to reconcile new ideals of universal citizenship with pre-existing social and racial hierarchies. During the cold war, this common heritage contributed to shared political patterns and facilitated the movement of transnational actors, particularly religious leaders, throughout an Atlantic world. The inclusion of Latin America also highlights how Catholicism, often depicted as solidly anti-communist, played a more complicated role in cold war culture.

# THE ANTI-COMMUNIST INTERNATIONAL

A pivotal feature of cold war culture in the West was campaigns to repress communism and other forms of leftism. Political conflict between bourgeois and radical causes had long shaped western politics, particularly in nineteenth-century battles over industrialization. The cold war intensified these pre-existing struggles. Thanks to the cold war, each nation's internal politics acquired new geopolitical importance. Anti-communist activists, led by the US government, thus created transnational networks of government and private organizations designed to contain or even co-opt leftist radicalism.

There is no small irony in anti-communism's transnational nature. Anti-communists often cited the universal aspirations of the Communist International to prove communism's threatening nature. In this view, international communism, propelled by Moscow, violated individual nations' freedom. Yet anti-communists proved equally adept with international movements. Just as actual communist internationalism took different forms, what this essay calls anti-communist internationalism also lacked a single center. The US government was the most important hub, but conservative religious and business organizations and the British government also played key roles. Although every country displayed unique political conditions, each national experience bore the mark of a shared set of ideas and funds promoted by border-crossing anti-communist activists and diplomats.

In the anti-communist international's most influential base, the United States, a post-1945 Red Scare intensified earlier patterns of anti-radical repression. The House Committee on Un-American Activities (HUAC), created in 1938 by enemies of Franklin Roosevelt's liberal New Deal, attacked leftist radicals, whether communist or not. HUAC's investigations convinced many American leftists to refrain from overt political organizing. In its four investigations of Hollywood between 1947 and 1958, HUAC found no clear evidence of communist subversion. Yet studio executives responded by generating a "blacklist" that excluded about 2,000 screenwriters and other creative figures from studio work through the 1960s.[5]

While HUAC garnered media attention, the Federal Bureau of Investigation (FBI) quietly built a surveillance network with thousands of new agents monitoring potential subversives. Under J. Edgar Hoover's direction, the FBI even helped write, produce, and publicize a 1951 spy movie, *Walk East on Beacon*, which depicted the FBI as a bulwark against Soviet espionage.[6] To insulate his social programs from anti-communist accusations, Democratic President Harry S. Truman added to the Red Scare by supporting the 1947 Federal Employee Loyalty Program, intended to root out subversives from government positions. The Red Scare contributions of Truman and Hoover's FBI facilitated the rise of Senator Joseph McCarthy, who held unusual influence between 1950 and 1954. Although textbooks often refer to the early cold war as the "age of McCarthy," the senator's reckless accusations and smear tactics provided just one episode in a Red Scare that originated before and continued after his turbulent moment in the spotlight.[7]

More enduring than McCarthy were the many private organizations that carried anti-communist messages into everyday life. The American Legion and the Boy Scouts promoted anti-communism for ordinary Americans at small-town parades and ceremonies. Religious leaders, from the Catholic Church to evangelical and mainline Protestantism, found the cold war useful for asserting the centrality of spirituality in American life. Meanwhile, the Advertising Council, a business-funded "public service" organization, linked the cold war to free enterprise in magazine and television advertisements.[8]

This public-private campaign created obstacles for leftist politics in the United States. Anti-communism did not preclude all social welfare reform in the United States, but it did impose constraints on leftist radicals and on the Democratic Party's more progressive members. Congress's 1947 Taft-Hartley Act required union leaders to sign statements disavowing communist affiliations. Meanwhile, numerous progressive policy goals—including price controls, public housing, and universal healthcare—floundered amidst charges that they could lead to communism.[9]

The Red Scare also reduced freedom for American women, gays, and lesbians. Truman's loyalty program uncovered few communists but succeeded in driving from government service thousands of men and women suspected of being gay or lesbian. Homosexuals, the theory went, posed a security risk because of weak moral character and vulnerability to blackmail. For women in the United States, fear of communist subversion created pressure to remain at home. As housewives, women could raise patriotic children with the moral and physical strength needed to fight communism. Moreover, because the Red Scare discouraged public protest, many middle-class women addressed their frustrations through private methods, such as therapy and doctor-prescribed tranquilizers.[10]

The United Kingdom and Canada shared much with US cold war culture, even if their Red Scares were less intense. British anti-communists contributed key ideological concepts, most famously in Winston Churchill's "Iron Curtain" speech. Labor Party leaders proved equally invested in anti-communism. Laborites had first-hand experience of battling British communists for control of labor unions. With a strong anti-communist coalition, the British government employed their own Red Scare tactics.

The Foreign Office covertly spread anti-communist news stories through the British and international media. British agents also quietly promoted George Orwell's novels, *Animal Farm* and *1984*, through Western and Eastern Europe. Orwell aided his government by providing names of potentially subversive artists, writers, and journalists who warranted government monitoring.[11] The Canadian government, which had banned Canada's communist party during World War II, subjected leftists in the early cold war to surveillance and harassment. The government's movie production agency, the National Film Board, underwent purges to root out radicals. Yet in both the United Kingdom and Canada, political leaders exerted tighter control over government institutions, which minimized the wilder forms of anti-communism that marked the US Red Scare.[12]

Elsewhere in the West, cold war culture took more diverse forms. In France and Italy, where the communist parties drew a quarter of national voters after World War II, geopolitical tensions helped conservative and moderate politicians exclude communists from governing coalitions. This political marginalization might have happened without a cold war, but the specter of Soviet aggression, alongside pressure from US diplomats, encouraged in both countries the formation of anti-communist coalitions by 1947. At the same time, French and Italian communists retained strong influence in unions, universities, and other cultural institutions. For instance, France's most famous post-1945 intellectual, Jean-Paul Sartre, advanced Marxist ideas and at times even associated himself with French communists.[13]

West Europeans did not pursue American-style Red Scares for another, more subtle reason: many European anti-communists distrusted the United States' growing power. Anti-Americanism, as much as anti-communism, defined cold war culture in Western Europe. For many Europeans, rising US influence threatened European sovereignty and cultural traditions. As a result, West Europeans often refused to see the cold war in binary terms of good versus evil.[14] These complex fault lines appeared most clearly among conservative nationalists. Cultural conservatives such as 1950s French populist Pierre Poujade denounced both the United States and the Soviet Union as purveyors of stultifying cultural standardization. Meanwhile, more forward-looking conservatives responded to the superpower rivalry by arguing that Europeans needed to modernize to remain independent. Charles de Gaulle exemplified how cold war anti-Americanism could promote a modernizing impulse. From French-designed nuclear reactors to gleaming high-rises, Gaullists trumpeted modernization projects as proof that France would remain free from US and Soviet domination.[15] Even British Labour leader Clement Attlee, a reliable US ally, spoke of creating a "Third Force" between Soviet communism and what he described as American "laissez-faire capitalism."[16]

Compared to European leaders, Latin American anti-communists faced greater pressure to adhere to the binary logic of good versus evil. Latin American societies suffered deeper social and racial inequalities, which often contributed to polarized politics well before the cold war. More than in Western Europe, Latin American anti-communist leaders also depended on the US government or American corporations for economic investment. Just as in France and Italy, however, many leading Latin

American intellectual and artistic figures, such as Chilean poet Pablo Neruda, maintained loyalty to communist parties or other leftist causes.[17]

Many Latin American societies, therefore, experienced both the Manichean anti-communism of the United States and the pro-communist subculture of France and Italy. The results could be violent. In Brazil, for instance, anti-communists associated leftist politics with sexual deviancy and promiscuity, much as US anti-communists did. Yet Brazil's more polarized politics resulted in the country's right-wing military dictatorship using the ideology of cold war domesticity in the 1960s to justify the imprisonment and torture of female leftists.[18]

The West's diversity of attitudes toward communism led anti-communists, especially the US government, to form transnational networks promoting strong cold war alliances. Throughout the cold war, US propagandists produced magazines, films, and traveling displays to defend US diplomacy and convince fellow westerners of the superiority of the American way of life. Cold war propaganda continued programs already under way in Latin America, where the US government had spent World War II trying to keep Latin Americans from sympathizing with the Axis powers. By the 1950s, the US government had developed new bureaucracies, most notably the US Information Agency (USIA), to expand its cultural offensive.[19]

Although most USIA projects took place in public, US propaganda frequently relied on clandestine tactics. Continuing London's promotion of George Orwell, Washington covertly funded movie versions of *1984* and *Animal Farm*.[20] In Mexico, the USIA secretly produced one of the country's leading newsreels, bringing Mexican audiences favorable coverage of the United States and of Mexico's pro-US politicians.[21] The Central Intelligence Agency (CIA) funneled money to the Congress for Cultural Freedom (CCF), an organization of anti-communist intellectuals from Western Europe and the Americas. CIA funding allowed the CCF to organize high-profile conferences in which intellectuals warned of the perils of communism, at least until public exposure of the CIA's role in 1967 derailed the congress. The CIA even promoted abstract expressionist painting as a symbol of Americans' cultural freedom, after learning that Soviet leaders viewed the avant-garde style as threatening to communist values.[22]

The US government's cultural campaign benefited from enthusiastic collaboration with private organizations and citizens. The discovery of CIA funding behind the CCF and abstract expressionism has led some scholars to treat anti-communist politics as a byproduct of government planning. A better perspective is to emphasize the genuine appeal of anti-communism among intellectuals and politicians in the West.[23] For example, in 1948 the US government, the Catholic Church, and private Americans helped Italy's center-right Christian Democratic party outpoll Italy's Communist party. While the CIA worked covertly to aid the Christian Democrats, Italian-American organizations conducted a grassroots campaign writing letters to their ancestral homeland. Italian-American celebrities such as Frank Sinatra added their own public endorsements.[24]

Other American social groups contributed to longer-term anti-communist projects. In part to deflect Red Scare accusations, the major US labor confederations, the

American Federation of Labor and Congress of Industrial Organizations, sent advisors to Western Europe and Latin America to preach the virtues of moderate, non-communist labor activism.[25] Conservative women's organizations also forged transnational partnerships, stressing the common interest of mothers in resisting communism. The Committee of Correspondence exchanged letters and visits with women in seventy-three countries, a project aided by covert CIA funding. Anti-communist women's groups also helped marginalize those leftist women's groups that stressed mothers' interest in disarmament and peace.[26]

# COLD WAR CULTURE'S INCLUSIVE SIDE

The repressive side of cold war culture, although significant, should not obscure how the cold war also helped secure progressive and inclusive reforms. Disadvantaged groups and progressive reformers could benefit from cold war tensions, if they were willing and able to cast their cause in anti-communist terms. The cold war also increased conservatives' willingness to accept expansions in social democracy, especially when those reforms promised to contain or co-opt calls for more radical change. In this way, the cold war helped make many western societies more democratic, inclusive, and even socialistic than they might have been otherwise.

In the United States, Washington's global propaganda battle against communism provided African Americans with an important tool in their struggle for political rights. As African and Asian peoples broke free from European colonialism, US policymakers feared that images of white racism at home would send the new nations into the communist camp. This logic led the State Department to argue on behalf of school integration in the Supreme Court's 1954 *Brown* decision. US diplomats even deployed such jazz musicians as Duke Ellington and Louis Armstrong on goodwill tours to show foreigners America's racial equality. The tours further helped African Americans claim status as true Americans.[27]

Anti-communism also allowed marginalized religious groups to enter the mainstream of American life. The cold war gave American Catholics common cause with the United States' largely Protestant social and political elite. Thanks to the cold war, American Catholics could be loyal to the Vatican and to the American flag simultaneously. Within Protestantism, anti-communism brought evangelical denominations like Southern Baptists closer to circles of power. The rise of Baptist preacher Billy Graham, who held rallies in Washington and frequently visited the White House, embodied the new-found respectability that anti-communism gave evangelicals.[28]

The superpower struggle also made the United States more ethnically diverse. At the cold war's outset, the United States maintained a racist quota system from the 1920s. The quotas restricted immigration from Asia, Africa, and the Middle East and limited entries from less "desirable" European countries, particularly those with large Jewish populations. Much as with African American civil rights, US policymakers' desire for non-white allies undermined discriminatory policies. After the Korean War, Congress relaxed immigration restrictions and allowed Americans to adopt babies from South Korea. By 1965, the need for allies, especially in Asia, contributed to the Hart-Cellar Act, which ended the 1920s immigration quotas and gave identical allotments to each nation in the world.[29]

Refugee policy further increased US diversity. Among the first cold war refugee arrivals were dissidents, often Jewish, from Hungary and the Soviet Union, precisely the social groups blocked by the 1920s quotas. Later refugee movements brought Southeast Asians, Cubans, and Central Americans to US shores.[30] In this perspective, Vietnamese fishing communities on the US Gulf Coast and Hmong communities in Minnesota represent a legacy of cold war culture. So, too, do American restaurants serving Cuban sandwiches and Salvadoran pupusas.

Another integrative feature of cold war culture came in its ability to promote cosmopolitanism within the West. Historians often overlook how cold war geopolitics required Americans and other westerners to see themselves as part of a shared community. While the cold war reduced western cultural and economic ties with communist nations, it intensified ties *within* the West. Western nations reduced tariffs, increased multinational corporate investment, and promoted academic exchanges and other border-crossing measures that laid the groundwork for post-1989 global integration. The US government even subsidized the construction of luxury hotels among cold war allies so that westerners could forge tighter economic and cultural bonds. Cold war geopolitics also sent millions of American men and women to military bases. The experience of life abroad often turned Americans into supporters of cross-cultural understanding and multilingual "world citizenship." Many even formed interracial or bi-cultural families.[31]

The cold war likewise facilitated the rise of a cosmopolitan film culture, in which movie-makers and actors from western countries collaborated on border-crossing projects. Although these filmmakers did not typically define themselves as cold warriors, their multinational films projected what historian Vanessa Schwartz has called a "triumphant Occidentalism." The popular 1956 movie, *Around the World in Eighty Days*, for instance, drew together the on-screen talents of Englishman David Niven, Mexican comic actor Cantinflás, and US television journalist Edward Murrow.[32]

A major integrative feature of the cold war came in the form of increased social democracy and welfare policies. While the cold war hurt leftist radicals, it also provided few victories for advocates of laissez-faire economics. Ideological rivalry with the Soviet Union made political moderates, and even some conservatives, eager to rebut communist accusations of capitalism's inherent flaws. The cold war thus created political space for the entrenchment of social welfare policies, or what West Germans called the "social-market economy." Only in the 1970s and 1980s, when fears of communism subsided, did more radical free-market advocates gain a stronger foothold.

The rise of social-market economies originated largely in a wave of leftist populism that swept through the West in the 1940s. In Europe, communists had played leading roles in the underground anti-fascist resistance. In Europe and the Americas, wartime mobilization and Allied rhetoric on freedom generated popular expectations that the postwar world would offer economic benefits for average citizens. From Guatemala and Bolivia to the United States and France, workers and peasants in the mid-1940s went on strike and rallied around progressive causes. To steer this populist surge in moderate directions, many western politicians experimented with socialism. Canada's postwar conservative government pursued left-wing projects such as social security and full employment.[33] In West Germany, France, and the United Kingdom, conservatives such as Ludwig Erhard and Charles de Gaulle endorsed their governments' nationalization of large industries. West Germany also established a system in which labor unions earned seats on corporate boards.[34] In the United States, politicians expanding social welfare programs argued that "a full stomach and a trained mind will never embrace either Nazism or communism." Republican President Dwight Eisenhower, for all his warnings against big government, approved significant expansions of the 1935 Social Security Act.[35]

Typically, social-market compromises thrived only when a western nation's political landscape allowed for alliances between leftists and centrists. In countries with anti-communist center-left coalitions, US policymakers tolerated and even subsidized socialist reforms as a bulwark against communism. For instance, a center-left government in Bolivia nationalized the country's tin mines in 1953, with support from the Eisenhower administration. When centrists and leftists chose not to align, however, leftist reformers often turned to communists and other radicals for support. In Guatemala, President Jacobo Arbenz looked to Guatemala's small communist movement to help advance his otherwise moderate land reform program in 1952. Arbenz's leftward turn brought Eisenhower to authorize a CIA coup, even though the reforms were no more radical than Bolivia's. Chile's Popular Unity movement, led by Salvador Allende and overthrown in 1973 by a coalition of Chilean conservatives and US anti-communists, provided another example of how the cold war hindered reforms conducted without center-left alliances. Yet the examples of Guatemala and Chile stand alongside many other countries in which anti-communist politics proved conducive to substantial social reform.[36]

Anti-communism's egalitarian side was more consistent and pronounced in its support of mass consumption. Western societies had been developing consumer societies well before the cold war, but the superpower rivalry amplified the symbolic value of mass consumption. Indeed, the cold war often made western consumerism more egalitarian than it might have been otherwise. Beginning with the Marshall Plan, the US government deployed "productivity" experts to help Europeans produce goods more cheaply, so that average Europeans could consume more. US public diplomacy programs often targeted socialists and moderate leftists. Under its Foreign Leader program, the US State Department brought non-communist Europeans on tours of the United States. When the programs worked, Europeans returned home impressed by American workers' consumer abundance.[37] US diplomats even pressured the French government to shift more of its tax burden onto the wealthy, so that French workers would have more to spend. With a new refrigerator, Americans argued, a worker would be less likely to vote communist.[38]

Anti-communists' emphasis on consumerism and capitalist growth had another egalitarian, long-run effect: it undermined the ideology of female domesticity. Anti-communist leaders typically preached traditional family values, but in reality their economic programs encouraged women to leave the home and enter the wage labor force. Chile and the United States provide examples of how cold war culture could, over time, erode domesticity. In Chile, the ideal of the male breadwinner had long been a staple of left-wing politics. While fathers earned a fair wage, mothers stayed home to inculcate working-class consciousness in their families. When socialist governments led Chile, household consumption ran through institutions controlled by men. Chileans often received radios and cars through labor unions and state farms. In contrast, it was right-wing dictator Augusto Pinochet, seeking to expand Chilean export industries in the 1970s, who pushed Chilean women out of the home and into wage labor. Concurrently, the Pinochet dictatorship helped justify its repressive rule by cultivating consumerism among Chile's working class. Even if Pinochet himself espoused conservative gender values, his promotion of women's wage labor and consumerism encouraged Chilean women to exert more independence in their daily lives and in household finances.[39]

A similar, if less deliberate, process occurred in the United States. US labor unions, like Chilean socialists, had long emphasized male workers' "family wage." Yet for many middle- and working-class families, a single paycheck from the husband failed to sustain consumer dreams. Increasingly, women who had been stay-at-home housewives ventured into wage labor, often in part-time jobs meant to augment household consumption. Women's participation in the labor force would have likely increased without a cold war, but anti-communists' emphasis on consumer abundance accelerated the decline of domesticity as both ideal and reality.

# EVERYDAY RESISTANCE TO THE COLD WAR

The most ardent anti-communists hoped that all features of western society, including family life, could support their struggle. Yet this vision never appealed to all westerners. Some leftists explicitly opposed it. More commonly, westerners accepted anti-communism in principle but did not want to sacrifice private pursuits for the sake of waging cold war. Private resistance began at the very outset, grew in the 1960s and 1970s, and eventually contributed to the decline in superpower tensions. For anti-communist leaders, private defiance posed a dilemma. Personal freedom represented a key rationale for battling communism, but too much freedom could render the West weak and disorganized. For their part, western communists struggled to harness westerners' everyday lives to their cause. In this light, cold war culture in the west should not be seen as a coherent set of anti-communist values. Rather, it represented a struggle by both anti-communists and communists to combat popular indifference.

Throughout much of the West, ordinary citizens gave little attention to the cold war in their daily lives. Even during the height of the Red Scare, US civil defense officials

hoping to prepare the nation for nuclear war floundered against widespread public apathy.[40] Americans who interacted with foreigners when traveling or living abroad showed
little interest in representing their government's foreign policies. American teachers,
including government-trained Peace Corps volunteers, often expressed doubts about
the superiority of American values when interacting with their foreign hosts. American
tourists visiting Western Europe frequently developed sympathy for European neutralism, a position directly at odds with US diplomacy.[41]

When forced to choose between personal economic interests and policymakers' specific cold war goals, westerners normally prioritized their private interests. Among the
first to defy cold war demands were West Berliners, who defied anti-communist propaganda in the early postwar years and exchanged currency and goods in the less expensive Soviet-occupied zone of Germany. American tourists displayed a similar geopolitical
nonchalance in the 1960s by ignoring President Lyndon Johnson's request to postpone
overseas vacations, a move Johnson saw as necessary to retain dollars needed for his war
in Vietnam. On a larger scale, British and French exporters led their governments into
frequent battle with US diplomats over what goods they could sell to the Soviet Union
and Communist China. US businesses increasingly followed suit in pushing for greater
access to communist nations.[42]

Like multinational corporations, the Catholic Church proved to be an important but
not always a reliable ally of the United States' anti-communist campaign. Certainly, the
Church and most of its faithful rejected communism and its atheist principles. In 1949,
Pope Pius XII even excommunicated all Catholics who advanced communist causes.
Still, Catholics could disagree with US cold war policies. The two most important tensions concerned poverty and nuclear weapons, which many Catholics saw as pressing
moral problems in their own right. Catholic concerns that the United States' militant
foreign policies failed to address both moral dangers help explain why even Pius XII had
by the late 1950s moved the Vatican closer to cold war neutrality, a shift continued by his
successor, John XXIII.[43]

Catholic dissent against the cold war took sharpest form in the transatlantic travels of
Catholic priests and missionaries. Inside a seminary in 1950s Belgium, a Latin American
study center cultivated the leftist social ideas that later crystallized into liberation the-
ology. Spanish, German, and US missionaries then helped spread liberation theology in
Central America. The socialist revolutionary movements in 1970s Guatemala, El
Salvador, and Nicaragua drew many leaders from progressive Catholic organizations.
By one estimate, half of the Nicaraguan Sandinistas' *comandantes* had participated in
Catholic study groups. Similar Catholic roots sustained Guatemala's Committee for
Peasant Unity (CUC). While Guatemala's US-backed military government killed thou-
sands of peasants to crush the CUC, early CUC meetings took place in church spaces,
and leaders in the peasant movement, such as future Nobel Prize winner Rigoberta
Menchú, had experience in Catholic organizations.[44]

Hollywood likewise proved only a partial ally in the anti-communist crusade. The
ultimate arbiters of film content were ticket-paying audiences, not HUAC, and movie-
goers throughout the West showed little desire to fight the cold war in theaters.

Hollywood's most explicit Red Scare movies, with titles such as *I Married a Communist*, fared poorly at the box office. When Hollywood blockbusters endorsed anti-communist values, the message usually came disguised in historical parable, as in Biblical-era epics such as *Spartacus* and *The Ten Commandments*. The creators of the James Bond movies learned their lesson. While the original Bond novels pitted Agent 007 against a Moscow-backed organization known as SMERSH, the movies replaced SMERSH with a mere crime syndicate, SPECTER.[45]

Movies and television shows revealed particular independence in their representations of nuclear weapons. As early as 1953, US television networks aired apocalyptic stories that contradicted official assurances on civilians' prospects for surviving a nuclear war. West European audiences displayed a similar fascination with nuclear nightmares. By the late 1950s, Hollywood caught up with television and produced science fiction movies that challenged US government statements on nuclear weapons. 1959's *On the Beach* led the Eisenhower White House to launch a public relations counterattack in hopes of limiting the film's impact on domestic and international opinion.[46]

Popular anxiety over nuclear weapons contributed to a major cold war turning point, the emergence of détente in the late 1960s and 1970s. In Western Europe, a rising generation of students and youth questioned anti-communists' Manichean rhetoric. Rather than spend entire lives in the shadow of nuclear annihilation, they pushed for cooperation with communist nations. The United States' unpopular war in Vietnam increased the urgency with which many Europeans sought resolution of the cold war. In part to co-opt these youthful protestors, policymakers such as the United States' Richard Nixon and West Germany's Willy Brandt scrambled to claim the mantel of "peace" and forge cooperative ties with their communist counterparts.[47]

Westerners' increasing rejection of cold war binaries weakened not just the culture of anti-communism but also the culture of communism. "Neither Ford nor Lenin," proclaimed one student slogan popular during France's May 1968 student and worker revolt. Student leaders like West Germany's Rudi Dutschke imagined European youth as allies of Third World nationalists, fighting a common struggle against both superpowers. To many leftist youth, personal freedom required leaving behind the rigid institutions of both capitalism and traditional communism. After May 1968, the French Communist party suffered a steady and steep decline, in contrast to its status as France's largest party during the early cold war. In the United States, a rock and folk music counterculture, fueled by Vietnam War protest, similarly emphasized personal freedom over rigid political doctrine. In Latin America, where rock music often sounded like Yankee cultural imperialism, youth created a folk genre, *nueva canción*, which provided the soundtrack for the region's non-communist leftist movements in the late 1960s and early 1970s. West Germany's counterculture, aware of how the Nazis had exploited German folk traditions, instead gravitated toward avant-garde "Krautrock" and electronica to proclaim their freedom from the cold war.[48]

While cultural binaries faded in much of the West during the 1970s, the mobilization of culture to wage cold war intensified in parts of Latin America. Some Latin American countries such as Mexico forged social-market democracies, even if their level of prosperity and political openness failed to match West European levels. Elsewhere, especially in Central America, the failure of centrist politics fueled political struggles that often turned violent. In Guatemala, a series of repressive right-wing governments encouraged Mayan peasants to fuse indigenous beliefs with Marxism. This combination of indigenous and communist culture, aided by the leftward turn of ocean-crossing Catholics, helped propel Guatemala's guerilla movement.[49]

Along with the Soviet invasion of Afghanistan, leftist insurgencies in Central America inspired in US conservatives a renewed commitment to militant containment. To a degree, Hollywood played along, offering anti-communist fare such as 1984's *Red Dawn*, in which Soviet, Cuban, and Nicaraguan armies invade the Midwest.[50] Yet this anti-communist revival carried much less force than the earlier Red Scare. In the wake of the Vietnam War, Hollywood produced movies that went beyond atomic anxiety and explicitly criticized US cold war policies, especially in Latin America. During the Reagan era, for every *Red Dawn*, movie-goers could also watch movies such as Oliver Stone's *Salvador*, a 1986 critique of the US-backed right-wing government in El Salvador.[51]

Further evidence of anti-communism's weakening grip came with the "nuclear freeze" movement. Led by German Protestants, 300,000 West Germans rallied in Bonn in 1981 to protest against the deployment of US missiles in their country. A year later, close to a million Americans marched in New York City to call for "freezing" nuclear stockpiles at current levels. By 1983, the US-based National Conference of Catholic Bishops endorsed a freeze and called for abolishing nuclear weapons. The mass media reflected and amplified popular dissent with graphic depictions of nuclear war, such as the 1983 television drama, *The Day After*. Just as nuclear stalemate and the Vietnam War fueled youth protest in the 1960s, Reagan's nuclear build-up helped popularize new forms of non-communist leftism such as West Germany's Green Party. Grassroots protest against nuclear weapons also pressured Reagan to accept Mikhail Gorbachev's overtures in the mid-1980s to engage in superpower negotiations.[52]

As Reagan discovered, the West's promise of cultural freedom at times challenged militant anti-communism, but in the end that freedom proved even deadlier to communism. Many of the cultural innovations that most alarmed cold warriors turned out to be assets. At one point, militant anti-communists expressed fear that student protest, jazz, rock, abstract expressionism, and an excessive devotion to material comforts would render western citizens unfit for resisting communism. Yet each of these cultural trends convinced many on both sides of the Iron Curtain that western societies offered more freedom and happiness than their Soviet-bloc counterparts. West German elites, for example, at first feared jazz and rock as threats to conservative gender values. In time, however, West German adults saw American-inflected youth culture as a healthy release valve for young Germans. In contrast, communists proved less capable of accepting mass culture. East Germany's communist leaders never developed the same therapeutic interpretation of jazz and rock, and they spent much of the cold war battling American-style youth culture within East Germany. West European communists suffered further from Soviet filmmakers' inability to match Hollywood's popularity with western consumers.[53]

The Italian Communist party exemplified communist failures in adapting to consumerism and mass media. Rather than embrace mass culture, Italian communists envisioned a vibrant subculture in which members could share proletarian values in social clubs and even in communist-oriented vacation villages. Party leaders prioritized relations with artists and intellectuals and sought to uplift Italian workers by democratizing high-culture traditions. Yet in an age of television and movies, those strategies proved increasingly ineffective. Hobbled by an ill-suited cultural program, the Italian Communist party managed to survive into the 1970s before experiencing a precipitous decline in the 1980s.[54]

Meanwhile, US propaganda proved most effective when government officials exercised the least control over its content. African-American jazz "ambassadors" frequently worried their State Department handlers by adopting a populist message on tour. Yet this free spirit impressed foreign audiences with Americans' cultural freedom and creativity. US propagandists showed equal nimbleness with blacklisted Hollywood writers. Once blacklisted, leftist screenwriters such as Dalton Trumbo won popular followings in Western Europe and Latin America for their critical attention to racism, colonialism, and nuclear peril. In time, that popularity led US policymakers to reverse course and promote their work overseas.[55]

To be sure, the unruly freedom of westerners, especially western consumers, sometimes created liabilities for anti-communists. American gamblers and tourists flocking to Cuba helped fuel the popular revolution that put Fidel Castro in power in 1959.[56] Consumer appetites in the United States, and the importance of satisfying that demand with low prices, gave US policymakers an additional reason to distrust leftist social reform in Latin American countries that produced bananas, coffee, and other staple crops or raw materials.[57] In most cases, however, the vibrancy of the US consumer model won admirers in the West. From Mexico to West Germany, consumers and business leaders saw Sears, Coca-Cola, and other US brands as proof that American-style modernity could help their nation achieve a more prosperous future.[58]

# CONCLUSION

Anti-communists in the West dedicated substantial energy and resources to winning the loyalty of ordinary citizens. In part, they desired popular support to inoculate western societies against subversive influences. They also needed support to convince western citizens to accept the substantial costs required to wage a global cold war. Anti-communists thus repressed radicals, circulated propaganda, promoted books and movies, fostered transnational citizens' exchanges, and altered domestic social and economic policies. To a large extent, this mobilization of cultural and social resources worked. Nonetheless, western culture and society never became mere auxiliaries of the anti-communist crusade. Movie-makers, consumers, business executives, students, and religious believers provided inconsistent support for cold war aims. This independent streak within western societies in turn shaped the geopolitical cold war, by pressuring western politicians toward negotiation with communist nations, and also by helping discredit less vibrant communist social models. Far from a side show, the struggle to maintain popular loyalty in the West proved to be one of the driving forces in the cold war's entire history.

## NOTES

1. For help in preparing this essay, the author thanks Cora Granata, Michael H. Hunt, Laura McEnaney, Alan McPherson, Enrique Ochoa, Carole Srole, Angela Vergara, and *Handbook* editors Richard Immerman and Petra Goedde.
2. Stephen J. Whitfield, *The Culture of the Cold War* (Baltimore, MD: Johns Hopkins University Press, 1991), 205.
3. Naoko Shibusawa, "Ideology, Culture, and the Cold War," Chapter 3 in this volume.
4. Silvia Federici, ed., *Enduring Western Civilization: The Construction of the Concept of Western Civilization and its "Others"* (Westport, CT: Praeger, 1995).
5. Ellen Schrecker, *Many Are the Crimes: McCarthyism in America* (Boston, MA: Little, Brown and Company, 1998), 90–1, 317–33.
6. Tony Shaw, *Hollywood's Cold War* (Amherst, MA: University of Massachusetts Press, 2007), 52–64.
7. Schrecker, *Many Are the Crimes*, 201, 209.
8. Richard M. Fried, *The Russians are Coming! The Russians are Coming! Pageantry and Patriotism in Cold-War America* (New York: Oxford University Press, 1998).
9. Lizabeth Cohen, *A Consumer's Republic: The Politics of Mass Consumption in Postwar America* (New York: Alfred A. Knopf, 2003), 130.
10. David K. Johnson, *The Lavender Scare: The Cold War Persecution of Gays and Lesbians in the Federal Government* (Chicago, IL: University of Chicago Press, 2004); Elaine Tyler May, *Homeward Bound: American Families in the Cold War Era* (New York: Basic Books, 1988).
11. Marc J. Selverstone, *Constructing the Monolith: The United States, Great Britain, and International Communism, 1945–1950* (Cambridge, MA: Harvard University Press, 2009), 34; Paul Lashmar and James Oliver, *Britain's Secret Propaganda War 1948–1977* (Stroud: Sutton, 1998).
12. Reg Whitaker and Gary Marcuse, *Cold War Canada: The Making of a National Insecurity State, 1945–1957* (Toronto: University of Toronto Press, 1995), 19.
13. Ian H. Birchall, *Sartre Against Stalinism* (New York: Berghahn, 2004).
14. Marc Lazar, "The Cold War Culture of the French and Italian Communist Parties," *Intelligence and National Security* 18 (Summer 2003): 213–24; Pierre Grosser, "L'Éntrée de la France en guerre froide," in Serge Berstein and Pierre Milza, eds., *L' Année 1947* (Paris: Presses de Sciences Po, 2000), 167–88.
15. Gabrielle Hecht, *The Radiance of France: Nuclear Power and National Identity after World War II* (Cambridge, MA: MIT Press, 1998); Richard Kuisel, *Seducing the French: The Dilemma of Americanization* (Berkeley, CA: University of California Press, 1993); Kristin Ross, *Fast Cars, Clean Bodies: Decolonization and the Reordering of French Culture* (Cambridge, MA: MIT Press, 1995).
16. Selverstone, *Constructing the Monolith*, 79.

17. Gilbert M. Joseph and Daniela Spenser, eds., *In From the Cold: Latin America's New Encounter with the Cold War* (Durham, NC: Duke University Press, 2008).

18. Victoria Langland, "Birth Control Pills and Molotov Cocktails: Reading Sex and Revolution in 1968 Brazil," in Joseph and Spenser, *In From the Cold*, 308–49.

19. Kenneth Osgood, *Total Cold War: Eisenhower's Secret Propaganda Battle at Home and Abroad* (Lawrence, KS: University of Kansas Press, 2006); Laura A. Belmonte, *Selling the American Way: US Propaganda and the Cold War* (Philadelphia, PA: University of Pennsylvania Press, 2008).

20. Shaw, *Hollywood's Cold War*, 94.

21. Seth Fein, "Producing the Cold War in Mexico: The Public Limits of Covert Communications," in Joseph and Spenser, *In From the Cold*, 171–213.

22. Hugh Wilford, *The Mighty Wurlitzer: How the CIA Played America* (Cambridge, MA: Harvard University Press, 2008).

23. For an account emphasizing government influence, see Frances Stonor Saunders, *The Cultural Cold War: The CIA and the World of Arts and Letters* (New York: The New Press, 2000). For a critique, see Tony Shaw, "The Politics of Cold War Culture," *Journal of Cold War Studies* 3 (Fall 2001): 59–76.

24. Scott Lucas, *Freedom's War: The American Crusade against the Soviet Union* (New York: New York University Press, 1999), 43–6.

25. Federico Romero, *The United States and the European Trade Movement, 1944–1951*, trans. Harvey Fergusson II (Chapel Hill, NC: University of North Carolina Press, 1992).

26. Helen Laville, *Cold War Women: The International Activities of American Women's Organisations* (New York: Manchester University Press, 2002).

27. Mary L. Dudziak, *Cold War Civil Rights: Race and the Image of American Democracy* (Princeton, NJ: Princeton University Press, 2000); Penny M. Von Eschen, *Satchmo Blows Up the World: Jazz Ambassadors Play the Cold War* (Cambridge, MA: Harvard University Press, 2004).

28. Whitfield, *The Culture of the Cold War*, 77–82, 92.

29. Mae M. Ngai, *Impossible Subjects: Illegal Aliens and the Making of Modern America* (Princeton, NJ: Princeton University Press, 2004), 221, 243; Christina Klein, *Cold War Orientalism: Asia in the Middlebrow Imagination, 1945–1961* (Berkeley, CA: University of California Press, 2003), 175–9.

30. Carl J. Bon Tempo, *Americans at the Gate: The United States and Refugees during the Cold War* (Princeton, NJ: Princeton University Press, 2008).

31. Annabel Wharton, *Building the Cold War: Hilton International Hotels and Modern Architecture* (Chicago: University of Chicago Press, 2001); Dennis Merrill, *Negotiating Paradise: US Tourism and Empire in Twentieth-Century Latin America* (Chapel Hill, NC: University of North Carolina Press, 2009); Donna Alvah, *Unofficial Ambassadors: American Military Families Overseas and the Cold War, 1946–1965* (New York: New York University Press, 2007), 210. On globalization, see Akira Iriye, "Historicizing the Cold War," and Hyung-Gu Lynn, "Globalization and the Cold War," Chapters 2 and 3 in this volume.

32. Vanessa R. Schwartz, *It's So French! Hollywood, Paris, and the Making of Cosmopolitan Film Culture* (Chicago: University of Chicago Press. 2007), 197.

33. Whitaker and Marcuse, *Cold War Canada*, 11, 16, 22.

34. William I. Hitchcock, *The Struggle for Europe: The Turbulent History of a Divided Continent, 1945–2002* (New York: Doubleday, 2002), 141–7.

35. Susan Levine, *School Lunch Politics: The Surprising History of America's Favorite Welfare Program* (Princeton, NJ: Princeton University Press, 2008), 82.

36. Greg Grandin, *The Last Colonial Massacre: Latin America in the Cold War* (Chicago: University of Chicago Press, 2004), 188; Kenneth Lehman, "Revolutions and Attributions: Making Sense of Eisenhower Administration Policies in Bolivia and Guatemala," *Diplomatic History* 21 (Spring 1997): 185–213.

37. Giles Scott-Smith, *Networks of Empire: The US State Department's Foreign Leader Program in the Netherlands, France and Britain, 1950–1970* (New York: Peter Lang, 2008); Reinhold Wagnleitner, *Coca-colonization and the Cold War: The Cultural Mission of the United States in Austria after the Second World War*, trans. Diana M. Wolf (Chapel Hill, NC: University of North Carolina Press, 1994).

38. Irwin Wall, *The United States and the Making of Postwar France, 1945–1954* (Cambridge: Cambridge University Press, 1991), 168.

39. Heidi Tinsman, "Politics of Gender and Consumption in Authoritarian Chile, 1973–1990," *Latin American Research Review* 41 (October 2006): 7–31.

40. Laura McEnaney, *Civil Defense Begins at Home: Militarization Meets Everyday Life in the Fifties* (Princeton, NJ: Princeton University Press, 2000); Peter Filene, "'Cold War Culture' Doesn't Say it All," in Peter J. Kuznick and James Gilbert, eds., *Rethinking Cold War Culture* (Washington, DC: Smithsonian Institution Press, 2001), 156–74.

41. Jonathan Zimmerman, *Innocents Abroad: American Teachers in the American Century* (Cambridge, MA: Harvard University Press, 2006); Christopher Endy, *Cold War Holidays: American Tourism in France* (Chapel Hill, NC: University of North Carolina Press, 2004), 122–3.

42. Paul Steege, *Black Market, Cold War: Everyday Life in Berlin, 1946–1949* (New York: Cambridge University Press, 2007), 285; Endy, *Cold War Holidays*, 182–202; Alan P. Dobson. *US Economic Statecraft for Survival, 1933–1991: Of Sanctions, Embargoes, and Economic Warfare* (London: Routledge, 2002).

43. Stephen Gundle, *Between Hollywood and Moscow: The Italian Communists and the Challenge of Mass Culture, 1943–1991* (Durham, NC: Duke University Press, 2000), 44; Diane Kirby, "The Religious Cold War," Chapter 31 in this volume.

44. Dirk Kruijt, *Guerillas: War and Peace in Central America* (New York: Zed Books, 2008), 40–53.

45. Shaw, *Hollywood's Cold War*, 112–26; James Chapman, *Licence to Thrill: A Cultural History of the James Bond Films* (New York: Columbia University Press, 2000).

46. Andrew J. Falk, *Upstaging the Cold War: American Dissent and Cultural Diplomacy, 1940–1960* (Amherst and Boston, MA: University of Massachusetts Press, 2010), 161–3; Shaw, *Hollywood's Cold War*, 135–66.

47. Jeremi Suri, *Power and Protest: Global Revolution and the Rise of Détente* (Cambridge, MA: Harvard University Press, 2003).

48. Suri, *Power and Protest*; Ross, *Fast Cars*; Eric Zolov, *Refried Elvis: The Rise of the Mexican Counterculture* (Berkeley, CA: University of California Press, 1999), 225–32; Alex Seago, "The 'Kraftwerk Effekt': Transatlantic Circulation, Global Networks and Contemporary Pop Music," *Atlantic Studies* 1 (2004): 86–106.

49. Grandin, *The Last Colonial Massacre*, 120.

50. Derek N. Buckaloo, "Carter's Nicaragua and Other Democratic Quagmires," in Bruce J. Schulman and Julian E. Zelizer, eds., *Rightward Bound: Making America Conservative in the 1970s* (Cambridge, MA: Harvard University Press, 2008): 246–64; Shaw, *Hollywood's Cold War*, 269–76.

51. Shaw, *Hollywood's Cold War*, 255–62, 302–3.

52. Lawrence S. Wittner, *The Struggle Against the Bomb*, Vol. 3, *Toward Nuclear Abolition: A History of the World Disarmament Movement, 1971 to the Present* (Stanford, CA: Stanford University Press, 2003), 146, 180.

53. Uta G. Poiger, *Jazz, Rock, and Rebels: Cold War Politics and American Culture in a Divided Germany* (Berkeley, CA: University of California Press, 2000), 109–11, 213, 217; Marie-Pierre Rey, "Le Cinéma dans les relations franco-soviétiques. Enjeux et problèmes à l'heure de la détente (1964–1974)," in Jean-François Sirinelli and Georges-Henri Soutou, eds., *Culture et guerre froide* (Paris: Presses de l'Université Paris-Sorbonne, 2008), 159–72.

54. Gundle, *Between Hollywood and Moscow*; Ellen Furlough, "Making Mass Vacations: Tourism and Consumer Culture in France, 1930s to 1970s," *Comparative Studies in Society and History* 40 (April 1998): 247–86.

55. Von Eschen, *Satchmo Blows Up the World*; Falk, *Upstaging the Cold War*.

56. Merrill, *Negotiating Paradise*, 103–76.

57. Richard Tucker, *Insatiable Appetite: The United States and the Ecological Degradation of the Tropical World* (Berkeley, CA: University of California Press, 2000).

58. Julio Moreno, *Yankee Don't Go Home! Mexican Nationalism, American Business Culture, and the Shaping of Modern Mexico, 1920–1950* (Chapel Hill, NC: University of North Carolina Press, 2003); Jeff R. Schutts, "Born Again in the Gospel of Refreshment? Coca-Colonization and the Re-making of Postwar German Identity," in David F. Crew, ed., *Consuming Germany in the Cold War* (New York: Berg, 2003), 121–50.

## Select Bibliography

Gundle, Stephen. *Between Hollywood and Moscow: The Italian Communists and the Challenge of Mass Culture, 1943–1991*. Durham, NC: Duke University Press, 2000.

Hitchcock, William I. *The Struggle for Europe: The Turbulent History of a Divided Continent, 1945–2002*. New York: Doubleday, 2002.

Joseph, Gilbert M. and Daniela Spenser, eds. *In From the Cold: Latin America's New Encounter with the Cold War*. Durham, NC: Duke University Press, 2008.

Kuznick, Peter J. and James Gilbert, eds. *Rethinking Cold War Culture*. Washington, DC: Smithsonian Institution Press, 2001.

Schrecker, Ellen. *Many Are the Crimes: McCarthyism in America*. Boston, MA: Little, Brown and Company, 1998.

Shaw, Tony. *Hollywood's Cold War*. Amherst, MA: University of Massachusetts Press, 2007.

Suri, Jeremi. *Power and Protest: Global Revolution and the Rise of Détente*. Cambridge, MA: Harvard University Press, 2003.

Wilford, Hugh. *The Mighty Wurlitzer: How the CIA Played America*. Cambridge, MA: Harvard University Press, 2008.

# CHAPTER 20

·······································································

# THE MILITARY

·······································································

## DAVID R. STONE

ALTHOUGH the cold war fundamentally revolved around a potential East-West military clash in central Europe, military aspects of the cold war have been strangely divorced from the mainstream of scholarship, echoing a divide between military and diplomatic historians across regions and periods. Scholars of diplomatic history, international history, and US foreign relations have normally occupied "compartments" separate from military historians, studying in different programs, attending different conferences, and publishing in different journals. To the extent that military concerns have penetrated the literature on the cold war, they have centered around nuclear weapons and nuclear strategy, not conventional forces, their structure, and their employment.[1] Bookshelves buckle under the weight of literature on Korea, Vietnam, and Afghanistan (to name only the most significant armed conflicts the two superpowers faced) in addition to the dozens of limited wars, insurgencies, interventions, and civil wars connected in some degree to the broader cold war and superpower intervention in some form.[2] But those military histories of individual conflicts tend not to be tied to diplomatic studies of how those wars began and ended, and there are relatively few efforts to synthesize the military side of the cold war into a comprehensive whole.[3]

Though in part the relative separation of military history from broader issues of the cold war has to do with academic specialization, the conventional military side of the cold war can in addition seem peripheral, an epiphenomenon. The cold war became hot only at its margins, not on the central battlefield of Europe. In forty-five years of potential great power war, direct military clashes between the great powers are striking in their rarity: Chinese troops and Soviet pilots fighting American, British, and French soldiers in Korea, and Soviet and Chinese border forces clashing on the Ussuri River more or less exhaust the list. If what really mattered in the cold war were the tens of thousands of nuclear warheads that maintained a balance of terror, then infantrymen, tanks, artillery pieces, and fighter planes seem relatively unimportant. The actual conduct of the Vietnam War on the ground, say, matters to those who care about revolutionary warfare and counter-insurgency, and to the American and Vietnamese publics, and perhaps to the military institutions which might learn from those experiences, but the actual military history of that conflict is treated in scholarship as largely separate from the diplomacy of the war and from the policies and ideologies that shaped the broader cold war.

Moreover, examining general questions of the military history of the cold war, as opposed to the particular history of individual conflicts, means studying the painstaking preparations for an apocalyptic confrontation which never occurred. Military institutions devoted the bulk of their time and treasure for forty-five years preparing for a massive clash in central Europe that never came, but spent the bulk of their blood fighting under very different circumstances. The NATO and Warsaw Pact militaries trained for a war that did not happen while actually fighting limited wars (Korea, the Falklands, the first Gulf War) or counter-insurgencies (Malaya, Vietnam, Afghanistan). The Chinese People's Liberation Army, torn between a revolutionary doctrine of people's war and the demands of modernization to fight a great power war, after Korea fought instead brief demonstrative campaigns against India (1962), the Soviet Union (1969), and Vietnam (1979), none of which had much to do with Mao Zedong's theories of warfare.

The disruption of training one way and fighting another was amplified by the need to adapt to a nuclear battlefield. Cold war militaries had to overhaul their organization and doctrine to cope with the prospect of nuclear war: first, through the early 1950s, with the mere existence of nuclear weapons, and, subsequently, with the spread of tactical nuclear weapons as well as the increasing destructive power of strategic weapons and the seeming obsolescence of conventional arms. The cultural impact was equally significant. The self-identification of military officers with virtues such as honor, professionalism, personal bravery, and regard for civilian life were at odds with push-button warfare that could kill hundreds of millions. At the other end, counter-insurgency constantly pulled militaries away from a relatively clean clash of professionals into the dirty business of separating indistinguishable combatants and civilians. Those common constraints—preparation for total war while waging limited war, and the disruptive effects of the nuclear revolution—together mean that there are striking parallels in the military history of the cold war on both sides of the iron curtain.

Our understanding of those parallel developments has been obscured by our highly unbalanced knowledge of how precisely cold war militaries dealt with their challenges. The American military in the cold war is the subject of an enormous literature, particularly for the early decades of the cold war, less so for more recent administrations. Much of it is of high quality and produced in substantial proportion by the military itself. Even the constraints of classification have not prevented a broad and deep understanding of many questions. It is easier, for example, to classify the sources, methods, and impact of intelligence, say, than to hide organizational and doctrinal changes affecting hundreds of thousands of servicemen and women. The situation for Britain is nearly as good, though the British military has put less emphasis on the study of military history than the American.[4] The literature, particularly literature in English, is much thinner for other Western allies.

For the other side of the iron curtain, limited knowledge of Russian has prevented many Western scholars from tackling the dynamics of the post-1945 Soviet military.

More seriously, strict secrecy over military affairs in the Soviet Union (which kept even Soviet civilian leadership ignorant of key military questions) has decreased only slightly with the collapse of the Soviet Union and the resultant opening of much of the Soviet archival record. While materials dating from before World War II are in the hands of Russian civilian archivists, cold war-era military records remain with the Russian Ministry of Defense, which has proven unwelcoming to scholarly inquiry. Much of what scholars do know about the Soviet military has come through the materials of former Warsaw Pact allies, far more willing to release archival material. Given the way in which the Soviet Union dominated the Warsaw Pact to a far greater degree than the United States dominated NATO, this dearth of Soviet sources is still a substantial handicap. Even with these limitations, certain topics are now far better understood today than during the cold car, including, say, the particulars of alliance dynamics, the fall of Marshal Georgii Zhukov, and Soviet participation in the air war in Korea.[5] China is the least studied of the great powers, with archival and language obstacles even more severe than for the Soviet Union.[6]

Despite these limitations, the military history of the cold war is still an enormous subject. In order to cope, this essay must necessarily be selective, both in the subjects it covers and the literature it discusses. Rather than emphasizing individual conflicts, it will focus on how military institutions dealt with the changing environment of the cold war. The nature of the available literature means that this essay will look most closely at the United States, but at the same time it will bring in comparative cases wherever possible. In particular, it will explore the central dynamics mentioned above: the changes in mission and means produced by the global nature of the cold war itself, as well as the impact and implications of the cold war's nuclear dimension (though a focus on nuclear weapons and the nuclear balance will be left to this *Handbook*'s chapter specifically devoted to nuclear weapons). The essay aims to reintegrate military force into the overall history of the cold war, re-establishing the historical nexus between force and statecraft. Theorist Carl von Clausewitz famously asserted that war is the continuation of politics by other means. While the advent of the nuclear age seemed to make war no longer a rational tool of statecraft, a closer look at the military history of the cold war reveals the ongoing connection between military power and international history.

At the most basic level of national strategy and military structure, the cold war was profoundly disruptive for the United States, and somewhat less so for other powers. For the United States, the cold war's global commitments were not new in its requirement of extended deployment abroad; indeed, the US Army and Marine Corps had spent much of their history up to 1941 as a frontier constabulary and imperial police and defense force. Similarly, the US Navy had been a tool of American global power projection at least since its Great White Fleet circled the globe under President Theodore Roosevelt. The fundamental changes that the cold war brought to the traditional American peacetime model of a small and weak regular army and more powerful navy were, first, a long-term expansion of American military commitments from Latin America and the Pacific to Europe as well, and, second, the substantial and permanent peacetime expansion of a standing army, particularly after the 1950 outbreak of the Korean War.

Britain faced similar structural changes, though altered by the context of the aftermath of World War II. While the war had transformed the United States into a financial and industrial power without rival, it had exhausted British resources and forced retrenchment in British foreign commitments. The British withdrawal from Palestine, India, and Pakistan in 1947–8 reduced imperial commitments but produced an equal reduction in imperial capabilities. The British Indian Army had provided much of the manpower that defended and policed the British empire throughout the world. Despite those differences, Britain's political culture and geographic isolation, both shared with the United States, had combined to produce a historical tradition of a large and powerful peacetime navy, and a small peacetime army largely devoted to imperial defense. The cold war brought Britain, as it had the United States, a permanent commitment of forces to the European continent: the British Army of the Rhine. What changed much more slowly was the British military maintenance of an active role in policing the British empire. The British counter-insurgency campaigns in Malaya and Kenya, for example, differed in detail but not in essence from numerous such campaigns dating back to the 19th century. To be sure, the relative British commitment to imperial policing dropped steadily in lockstep with Britain's continuing withdrawal from empire.[7]

Other militaries found that the cold war brought less alteration to basic national patterns of military policy. France, for example, had always had a military split between continental defense and imperial policing. French military efforts to maintain control in Vietnam and Algeria were not qualitatively different from what French soldiers had done before World War II, though the increased importance of world opinion and France's relative decline produced quite different results.[8] France's ultimately successful efforts to acquire an independent nuclear force were part of a general shift in relative emphasis from colonial security in the aftermath of World War II to European defense in the 1950s.[9] The Soviet Union before World War II had committed itself, like its imperial Russian predecessor, to a large, mass army, and that remained the case throughout the cold war. Though the Soviet military establishment had shrunk to a relatively insignificant 562,000 men during the lean years of the 1920s, the Soviet Union built an army of three million men by 1939, and could of course draw on the imperial Russian tradition of massive armed forces. What did fluctuate dramatically was the relative commitment to naval power. While the tsarist regime had been forced to abandon its naval pretensions after the disastrous 1904–5 Russo-Japanese War, and the new Soviet regime had neglected its navy as a matter of economy, Joseph Stalin had begun rebuilding a blue-water navy in the 1930s and 1940s, until Nikita Khrushchev abandoned that effort in the 1950s.[10]

In the immediate aftermath of World War II, however, the slow emergence of political confrontation between East and West was, for military institutions, initially outweighed in significance by the much greater disruption from massive demobilization. In the United States, overwhelming political pressure to bring soldiers home overcame growing disquiet among military leaders about America's ability to defend its newly-acquired global commitments, even though the postwar army remained several times larger than its pre-war ancestor. The Soviet Union also demobilized rapidly, though Soviet policy was driven by the need for reconstruction of its devastated territory, not political pressure from below. Despite the reduction in force on both sides of the emerging iron curtain, the more rapid and complete American demobilization left military officials deeply alarmed. By 1947, almost all combat capability was gone from American troops in Europe, who served not as a serious fighting force but instead as a trip-wire for the employment of atomic weapons in any potential war against the Soviet Union. After the expiration of Selective Service, the US Congress did reintroduce the draft in 1948. The draft remained highly unpopular, however, and the armed forces resorted to deliberate public relations campaigns to make military service more attractive and steel the American public for the rigors of the emerging cold war.[11]

The US military, particularly the army, remained alarmingly small in the view of American officials. Down to ten divisions on the eve of the Korean War, the army could maintain that number only by shrinking its constituent units. As a result, American war plans were pessimistic, anticipating the loss of continental Europe, the Middle East, and the Far East in any war with the Soviet Union. Early NATO strategy was heavily reliant on nuclear weapons, and ultimate victory against the Soviet Union would require a long and grinding campaign of atomic bombing from bases in Britain or elsewhere around the periphery of Europe. In Britain, the Army's desire to maintain Mideast bases for this atomic campaign against the Soviet Union clashed directly with the Labour government's desire to wind up its imperial commitments. The 1949 NATO treaty added the complication of a commitment to the defense of continental Europe, not merely the abandonment of the continent as indefensible. In 1950, the US government rejected Greece and Turkey's appeals to join NATO on the grounds that the alliance could make no meaningful contributions to their defense.[12]

In 1949, the Soviets broke the American nuclear monopoly. With nuclear weapons now in the hands of both sides, militaries had to cope with the wrenching transformation created by the very existence of nuclear weapons. Both sides had to reckon with both the employment of and the defense against atomic bombs, a problem made more acute by the rapid introduction of the far more powerful hydrogen bomb. Without exclusive American control of atomic weapons and with economic recovery in Western Europe, the precise nature of the Soviet threat as perceived in the West shifted from political subversion to an increased likelihood of Soviet military attack on Western Europe. The changes imposed by nuclear weapons in the early years of the cold war were less radical than might have been expected, given that the atom bombs of the 1940s and early 1950s were quite different in quantity and destructive power from what became available later in the cold war. Even decades later, armored vehicles provided a substantial degree of protection from nuclear attack.[13] This both increased military reliance on tanks and armored personnel carriers on a nuclear battlefield, and reduced the potential impact on actual battlefield conditions.

Despite the limited numbers and power of early atomic weapons, their general impact and more importantly their implications were nonetheless particularly dire for traditional branches of the military. Unprotected infantry were terribly vulnerable to nuclear attack, and capital ships and air bases made excellent targets. This existential threat to military traditions was worsened when it was combined with the budget strictures of the lean years from 1945–50. The so-called revolt of the admirals in the United States Navy was a direct consequence of these two interacting trends: shortages of money and the need to adapt to the nuclear age. In 1947, the United States combined its War and Navy Departments, together with the newly independent Air Force, under a single Secretary of Defense. While this reform was intended to produce more rational national strategy and reduce duplication of effort, in practice the individual services resented dictates from above. While the first Secretary of Defense, James Forrestal, was a navy man, his replacement, Louis A. Johnson, lacked a naval connection and was deeply committed to cost-cutting. This led to his approval of the Air Force's B-36 strategic bomber, intended for nuclear strikes on the Soviet Union, and simultaneous cancellation of the USS *United States*, the first flush-desk supercarrier. Naval leadership perceived this as a threat to the Navy's very existence: if American security could be assured by atom bombs delivered by relatively cheap aircraft (though an individual B-36 was itself quite expensive), why spend scarce tax dollars on expensive and vulnerable capital ships? Strong attacks on Johnson cost a number of high-ranking naval officers their careers, but the ultimate outcome was a victory for the Navy. Johnson was forced out as Secretary of Defense as a result of the disastrous first few months of the Korean War, and the Navy did win the prize of developing nuclear-capable aircraft carriers, guaranteeing itself a place in the new nuclear environment.[14]

The US Army and Marine Corps had different experiences than the Air Force and Navy. Until the development of nuclear munitions like the "Davy Crockett" (a fission warhead fired from a recoilless rifle with an effective range of 1–2 miles), both services served solely as potential targets and trip-wires in the nuclear age, and even the acquisition of tactical nuclear weapons did not restore their ability to serve as a decisive arm. The Marine Corps was particularly vulnerable to losing a distinct role. It had reinvented itself in the interwar period as a branch specializing in amphibious warfare. In the new environment of the cold war, the continued relevance of that mission was difficult to imagine. Not only was the usefulness of traditional infantry under question, but it was hard to imagine a more lucrative target for a nuclear strike than a narrow and crowded beachhead. Even the Marines' spectacular success in the amphibious landing at Inchon that decisively turned the tide of the Korean War was managed with the hasty assembly of World War II veterans, not new capabilities. Over time the Marines shifted their role away from amphibious landings on beaches to helicopter-borne, vertical assaults, as well as to a more general role as light infantry. Britain's Royal Marines likewise had to reinvent themselves in a new era as an elite commando force, quite different from their origins as seagoing infantry and bodyguards to naval officers.[15]

In the early postwar period, the Soviet bloc followed a similar pattern of demobilization, though it was not nearly as complete, and then renewed expansion. Our knowledge of the process is not as clear for the Soviet Union as it is for the Eastern bloc satellites, but Soviet military manpower dropped from approximately six million combat troops at the end of World War II to approximately three million men in the late 1940s.[16] East European militaries were controlled by Soviet advisors, by bilateral agreements, by the presence of Soviet occupation forces, and even the direct transfer of Soviet personnel. Soviet Marshal Konstantin Rokossovskii, for example, became Polish Defense Minister in 1949. In Hungary, the military bottomed out at 5,000 soldiers in 1948, but the Soviet leadership then insisted on rapid expansion in parallel with total Sovietization of doctrine and equipment. Stalin redirected the Eastern European economies to heavy industry at the expense of consumer goods, and in January 1951 he proclaimed to the leaders of the Soviet Union's satellites that they should prepare their societies and economies for imminent war with the West.[17] Indeed the 1953 anti-communist uprisings in East Germany were the indirect result of Stalin's policies of crash industrialization.

The nuclear revolution, however, had a much slower impact on the Soviet military than the American. Part of this was Stalin's deliberate effort to downplay the impact of nuclear weapons, but it was also a result of Stalin's startlingly slapdash approach to policymaking in the last years of his life. The Soviet occupation regime in Germany was chaotic and fragmented, and when Stalin implemented the Berlin blockade in 1948, he had instituted no military preparations for the very real possibility of a Western armed response: no contingency planning, and no troops put on alert. For Soviet ground forces generally, the immediate postwar period was dominated by the lessons and experience of World War II, though with the addition of massive numbers of armor and artillery. Soviet doctrine continued to follow the lessons of World War II, as perfected in the final drive to Berlin, quite closely. During Stalin's lifetime, organizational and doctrinal innovation was limited. Only his death in 1953, and the increasing importance of nuclear weapons, forced changes in Soviet military thinking. Some organizational changes did take place even during the period of intellectual stagnation: Soviet aviation grew much faster than the rest of Soviet armed forces and air defense became its own independent branch of the armed forces in 1948.[18]

In the United States, growing official disquiet at the military threat from the Soviet Union, combined with the perception of the global and intractable nature of communism, produced in 1950 the highly-ambitious NSC 68, a policy prescription for the massive expansion of the American military to support a worldwide confrontation with the Soviet Union. Though the American military naturally favored such an expansion of its resources, the expense of such a commitment prevented its implementation. Without the budgetary appropriations to pay for new ships and aircraft, NSC 68 was a dead letter. Only the June 1950 North Korean invasion of the South, which post-cold war evidence shows took place only with Joseph Stalin's express permission, galvanized American opinion into funding a massive military build-up. Not only did the Korean War permit the financial support of a major procurement campaign, but it also overcame American public resistance to the notion of a large peacetime army. The US Army went from ten to twenty-one divisions; the Navy from seven to sixteen carrier groups. By the end of the Truman presidency, American defense spending reached its highest point from 1945 to the present as a percentage of gross domestic product (13–14 percent).[19]

1950 thus marks a key moment in the transformation of the cold war from a political struggle into an immanent military confrontation. The turn towards a post-Korea conventional build-up had deep implications for military institutions. NATO gained a real command hierarchy, defense strategy, and logistical infrastructure, going far beyond the essentially political organization that had been created in 1949. American bases in Europe became permanent institutions, a transition marked by steadily-growing numbers of dependents. A NATO meeting in Lisbon in 1952 set ambitious targets for basing divisions in Europe. These escalating demands for manpower and equipment naturally raised the question of West German rearmament. If American soldiers were defending the West German border, the Eisenhower administration saw no reason why West Germans ought not to participate in that process. The failure of a French proposal to head off German rearmament through the creation of a European Defense Community of integrated, multinational units, combined with the burden of defending Western Europe east of the Rhine River, brought West Germany's membership in NATO in May 1955.[20] In response, the Soviet Union created the Warsaw Pact, a multilateral organization of its East European satellites to replace the previous bilateral arrangements and direct controls that had ensured Soviet control of satellite militaries.

German rearmament could only take place with German rehabilitation in the eyes of other Europeans, a process hastened by the Berlin blockade, but also the rehabilitation of the soldiers themselves who had served in Hitler's *Wehrmacht*. Building a West German *Bundeswehr* without the participation of German veterans was unthinkable. From soon after the war, Western officers faced with the possibility of fighting the Soviets had turned to the men with extensive experience of doing just that: former *Wehrmacht* officers. Within West Germany, the prospect of rearmament meant a de-emphasis on war crimes trials for *Wehrmacht* generals and an end to Western involvement in the trials that did take place. Over succeeding decades, West Germany would continue to wrestle with the proper balance between repudiating Germany's Nazi past and at the same time celebrating the traditions vital to military *esprit de corps*.[21]

The simultaneous post-Korea nuclear and conventional build-up proved unsustainable on both sides of the iron curtain. On taking office in 1953, President Dwight Eisenhower sought to reduce the military burden on the American economy by strengthening the Secretary of Defense in order to enforce inter-service cooperation, expanding reliance on European partners (including the possibility of providing Europeans, including West Germans, with nuclear weapons) and more broadly implementing the "New Look," replacing conventional deterrence with strategic deterrence: reliance on massive nuclear retaliation against any communist aggression, a stance that became official NATO strategy in 1956. In essence, the New Look sought to replace expensive conventional forces with cheaper nuclear weapons that the Truman administration had already begun to stockpile. The 1952 Lisbon targets were substantially reduced as part of the general reduction of burdens.[22]

For the US Air Force, this emphasis was almost entirely an unmixed blessing, with the mainstays of massive retaliation, both strategic bombers and the rapidly-developing ballistic missiles, in its hands. General Curtis LeMay, head of Strategic Air Command from 1948–57, turned it into the central implement of the New Look. The Navy, driven by Admiral Hyman Rickover, found that nuclear propulsion removed the traditional logistical constraints imposed by coal or oil. In addition, submarine-launched nuclear missiles, first the relatively crude Regulus in the 1950s and then the Polaris in the 1960s, gave the Navy a secure position in America's nuclear arsenal. Conventional surface war-ships suffered by comparison to submarines and aircraft carriers as guided missiles seemed to make them increasingly irrelevant.[23]

Other American services continued to struggle to find an effective defense of their institutional interests and their proper place in a nuclear era. The effort to carve out mis-sions and space in the increasingly-nuclear environment went to absurd lengths. In an effort to acquire a strategic role for itself to compete with the Air Force's Minuteman ICBMs and the Navy's Polaris SLBMs, the Army proposed in 1960 the Iceworm IRBM system. Six hundred missiles would travel through tunnels carved under Greenland's ice cap, using mobility and the ice itself for defense, but easily capable of reaching targets within the Soviet Union. Engineering difficulties soon wrecked the plan. In addition, if conventional forces were deliberately weakened, any clash had the potential of provok-ing a devastating nuclear exchange. This in turn forced restraint on military contingency planning. Though the Army was sidelined in the development of strategic systems, it did experiment with nuclear power as a means around the logistical complications of pro-viding heat and electricity in far-flung locations.[24]

As for the US Army's key mission of fighting the Soviets in central Europe, in the late 1950s under General Maxwell D. Taylor it experimented with an overhaul of its organ-ization to better cope with the nuclear battlefield: the pentomic division. This broke the three-regiment organizational structure that the infantry division had inherited from World War II into five independent battle groups, each self-sufficient and containing its own integral artillery. Though perhaps inspired by Taylor's World War II experience with five-regiment airborne divisions, this structure was intended to enable more flexi-ble deployment and, more importantly, dispersion, reducing the destructive impact of any individual nuclear strike and presenting less attractive individual targets. The exper-iment proved a substantial failure, as the command and control mechanisms necessary to coordinate five separate battle groups and other divisional formations proved beyond the capability of the division commander. Unit cohesion and effective rotation between Europe and the United States were also terribly difficult. John Kennedy's administration cancelled the experiment as part of a general retreat from Eisenhower's exclusive reli-ance on nuclear weapons.[25]

Wherever possible, the military services attempted to incorporate new systems in a way that extended and complemented their existing institutional culture, whether the Air Force's strategic bombing or the Navy's capital ships. The case of the cruise missile is a particularly good illustration of military institutions' resistance to weapons and sys-tems that threatened to undermine their interests, or even their self-image of why and how to fight. The cruise missile—an unmanned one-way aircraft carrying an explosive warhead—originated with the World War II German V-1. Though the US military experimented with cruise missiles after the war, they could not compete with ballistic missiles until the 1960s, when fusion bombs, more accurate guidance systems, and smaller jet engines improved their effectiveness. Despite cruise missiles' accuracy and cheapness, the Air Force did not want competition with its manned bombers, and blamed the cruise missile for killing the B-1 bomber program and unduly extending the lifespan of the ancient B-52 bomber. The Navy was shocked into exploring cruise missiles by the 1967 sinking of an Israeli destroyer, but missile-launching submariners saw the cruise missile as a threat to their purpose, while attack submariners saw a dilution of their mission. The cruise missile also threatened to take away the aircraft carrier's deep strike mission while rendering the carriers themselves far more vulnerable. The Navy took on the Tomahawk cruise missile only as a newer and better Harpoon surface-to-surface missile. In the end, it took vigorous leadership by civilians in the Department of Defense, away from the particular loyalties of the service branches, to bring the cruise missile to fruition.[26]

The Soviet incorporation of nuclear weapons appears to have been less problematic and fraught with inter-service rivalry than the American, perhaps because of the centralizing role of the General Staff within the Soviet military system. This perception may, however, merely be a result of our continuing ignorance of the high politics of the Soviet military, where a great deal of additional research remains to be done. Contrary to the American system, which evolved toward three redundant means of delivering nuclear weapons—bombers, land-based missiles, and submarine-launched missiles, the Soviets were ultimately content to remain substantially dependent on land-based missiles alone, with a much smaller role for bombers and submarines. This judgement may be again a result of a more centralized Soviet system less dependent on assuaging the concerns of individual service branches; it may also come from the maritime geography of the Soviet Union, with relatively limited access to the open sea and a correspondingly more vulnerable submarine force. As opposed to American intercontinental missiles, which remained under the authority of the Air Force, the Soviets in 1959 created a separate branch, the Strategic Rocket Forces, to handle nuclear missiles as part of an overall five-branch structure (the others being army, navy, air force, and air defense).[27]

The role and place of nuclear weapons in the Soviet military fluctuated dramatically over time. In the initial years of the cold war, Stalin from either braggadocio or ignorance downplayed the importance of nuclear weapons. After Stalin's death, however, that appraisal changed. Khrushchev's views fluctuated: he dismissed the idea that nuclear war might mean the end of world civilization, but he was at times terrified of the destructive power of the hydrogen bomb and horrified by Mao Zedong's cavalier comments about nuclear war and the death of half the world's population.[28] On the other hand, Khrushchev was intrigued by nuclear weapons' capability to provide defense on the cheap. In a striking parallel to Eisenhower's New Look, Khrushchev implemented deep cuts to Soviet conventional forces (though they remained far larger than their Western equivalents) in order to emphasize nuclear weapons and reduce military expenditures. Soviet ground forces temporarily lost their independent status in 1964. Like Eisenhower, Khrushchev faced resistance from military men unhappy about the cuts they suffered. The generals who had defended him in 1957 against a palace coup by the so-called "Anti-Party Group" did not lift a finger to defend him when he was ousted in 1964.[29]

After Stalin's death loosened some of the constraints on military reform, the widespread introduction of nuclear weapons required substantial changes to the organization and make-up of Soviet forces, such as the general introduction of armored personnel carriers and an offensive doctrine of echeloning offensives, allowing successive waves of attackers to move dispersed, but re-concentrate upon reaching the front lines. In the late stages of World War II, Soviet doctrine had emphasized mass, with a rifle battalion attacking on a frontage of only 125–50 meters, and this approach had carried through into the postwar period. The implications of a nuclear battlefield made dispersion more important. By the 1960s, mechanization had permitted the breadth of a battalion attack to spread to 2 km. Quite similarly, a World War II rifle battalion was typically tasked with defending a sector of front 2 km in breadth, but by 1960 that frontage had widened to 5 km. The sacrifice of mass was compensated for by the use of nuclear firepower to force gaps and of vehicle-mounted infantry to exploit those gaps more quickly. Speed became vital—to close with the enemy and to move onto enemy territory in order to limit nuclear attack or seize enemy nuclear weapons, as well as to exploit the temporary breaches in enemy defenses made possible by nuclear detonations. Soviet thinking even anticipated dropping paratroopers onto the site of nuclear detonations to seize key objectives in the shortest possible time.[30]

The fact that both sides in the cold war by the 1950s found themselves compelled to alleviate their military burdens by turning to nuclear weapons suggests some of the impact of the cold war on domestic society. Though this burden appears to have peaked in the early 1950s for the United States and the Soviet Union (though our conclusions for the Soviets are provisional at best), there were key differences. Both superpowers and their European allies had conscription for some or all of the cold war. While this was historically an aberration for the United States and the United Kingdom, it had been the norm since the 19th century for continental Europe. Generally, the Soviet bloc states, given their far smaller economies, spent a much greater proportion of their national income to achieve rough military parity with the West. In addition, the Soviet bloc devoted far more time and effort to civil defense and the active preparation of society for war than did Western states. For a whole host of reasons, not least the absence of meaningful prices in Soviet-style planned economies, a precise figure for Soviet defense spending is impossible to name. By any calculation, nevertheless, the relative burden was far greater for the communist bloc. Though Eisenhower warned against the establishment of a military-industrial complex upon leaving the presidency, that term is far better applied to the Soviet Union, which had established the institutional foundations for a military-dominated economy in the early 1930s, and lacked any of the moderating influences present in the West—not least, tax-averse voters.[31] The result of the spending disparity was a substantial Soviet quantitative advantage in most weapons systems.

Much Western literature on the Soviet military during the cold war, particularly that focusing on nuclear weapons and deterrence theory, has presumed that Soviet thinking on deterrence and the relative roles of conventional and nuclear war was fundamentally the same as the way American deterrence theorists conceived of such matters. This is not self-evidently true; as Edward Katzenbach wrote in 1960, "Both the doctrine of graduated deterrence and that of limited nuclear war demanded Soviet cooperation for their fulfillment....United States doctrine has not always been based on the realities of Russian strategy, but rather on a forgetful version of a hoped-for response."[32] Generally speaking, Soviet military thinking treated nuclear weapons as an inseparable part of an integrated system of weapons. Contrary to American deterrence theory, which saw an enormous break between conventional and nuclear weapons, Soviet thinkers saw the purpose of weapons as to be used (as suggested in part by the Soviet preoccupation with civil defense). This tendency reached its height under Marshal Vasilii Sokolovskii, Chief of the General Staff from 1952 to 1960. His 1962 textbook *Military Strategy* outlined a view of future war that was entirely nuclear. He emphasized surprise, the destructive potential of nuclear weapons, and the superiority of strategic nuclear forces to conventional. He stressed that nuclear weapons had not altered military theorist Carl von Clausewitz's classic claim that war was an instrument of policy, and dismissed notions of deterrence and limited war as capitalist inventions. The next war, Sokolovskii confidently asserted, would be nuclear and would bring the victory of socialism.[33]

On both sides of the front lines in Europe, military men found nuclear weapons to be both exhilarating, in the sense that they offered the tantalizing prospect of quick and decisive victory, and horrifying, in that they seemed to remove all sense of honor from the military profession. Soviet Rear Admiral K. I. Derevianko wrote Khrushchev in August 1961 to complain of the "excessive, I would even say irrational passion for the use of nuclear weapons in front conditions...and a clear diminution of the significance of conventional means of defeating the enemy with non-nuclear weapons." Derevianko condemned the allegiance to "trite clichés" which had led military men "to think only in nuclear categories." He was not opposed to the use of nuclear weapons by any means, supporting their application against "the most important strategic objects on the European continent threatening our country and troops—the rocket and air bases of the enemy." He only objected to the complete nuclearization of military thinking.[34]

The emergence of détente in the 1960s reduced tensions in central Europe, especially as the United States became distracted by conflict in Vietnam. In both the United States and the Soviet Union, the exclusive reliance on nuclear forces of the Eisenhower-Khrushchev period disappeared. The result was steady and continuing growth in Soviet nuclear and conventional forces while American resources were directed elsewhere. Under Leonid Brezhnev's system of governance, key interest groups received all the resources they required to keep them happy, and the military was no exception. The Soviets continued to develop a strategic nuclear force, but built conventional forces with the same alacrity. The gradual ascendancy of the Soviet military-industrial complex culminated in Dmitrii Ustinov's appointment as Minister of Defense in 1976. Ustinov waged successful bureaucratic turf fights against all opposition to broad and continuing military build-up. By the time Mikhail Gorbachev came to power in 1985, Soviet defense spending amounted to 15–25 percent of gross domestic product, compared to 6–7 percent of GDP in the United States at the height of Ronald Reagan's defense build-up. The Soviet Navy grew substantially as well. Though Stalin had begun to expand the Soviet navy from its small beginnings, Khrushchev's stress on economy had left it starved of resources. After Khrushchev's 1964 ouster, Admiral Sergei Gorshkov, who ran the Soviet

Navy for nearly forty years, steadily built up a fleet capable of protecting Soviet missile submarines in the Arctic and even challenging NATO's mastery of the North Atlantic and imperiling resupply in the event of general war.[35]

The Soviet return to conventional weapons coincided with the John Kennedy and Lyndon Johnson administrations' efforts to move away from the nuclear-centered policies of New Look, continuing a process of rethinking that had already begun in the late years of the Eisenhower administration. The new doctrine of "flexible response" aimed at providing a range of options, including full-scale nuclear war: this period saw the first "Single Integrated Operational Plan," or SIOP, for use of nuclear weapons in the event of war. But flexible response also incorporated conventional war, and limited war or counter-insurgency as well. Even under Eisenhower, the US government had grown increasingly concerned over the revolutionary potential of the developing world, where nationalism and Marxism might combine into an explosive force. Though the details of events might differ, the mix of nationalism and socialism in places as diverse as Guatemala, Egypt, and Iran presented a threat that was quite different from either conventional or nuclear war. This same concern led Kennedy to expand the US Army's Special Forces, created under Truman, and eventually to deepen America's commitment to war in Vietnam, culminating in full intervention under his successor Johnson in 1965. While flexible response avoided the all-or-nothing extremes of Eisenhower's New Look, it presumed a capability of careful and calculated calibration of means and ends. While appealing to bright, confident technocrats like Secretary of Defense Robert McNamara, it ran afoul of complex reality and notably came apart in Vietnam. As Carl von Clausewitz famously remarked in *On War*, "everything in war is very simple, but the simplest thing is difficult. The difficulties accumulate and end by producing a kind of friction that is inconceivable unless one has experienced war."[36]

While the intricacies of Vietnam are covered in a literature far too voluminous to summarize here, what is worth noting is the parallel difficulty the American and Soviet militaries faced in waging unconventional war. Both were designed and built to fight an apocalyptic war between superpowers: the tens of thousands of tanks, combat aircraft, artillery pieces, and nuclear warheads existed in preparation for a war that never took place. Instead, both militaries were forced into duties far different from those which officers and soldiers on both sides saw as their reason for being: imperial policing, counter-insurgency, and limited war.

In the Soviet case, the army was used on multiple occasions for the suppression of rebellion inside the empire—East Germany in 1953, Hungary in 1956, Czechoslovakia in 1968. On at least two other occasions (Poland in 1956 and 1980–1), the threat of Soviet military intervention was an important factor in the ultimate political resolution of the crisis. Even the intervention in Afghanistan, which became a counter-insurgency, was initially conceived of as the use of military force to bring an unruly ally back within the fold. For other militaries, the dichotomy between convention and unconventional roles was less stark. The British and French, for example, had always understood a major imperial policing role for their soldiers, and British soldiers in numbers peaking at nearly 30,000 spent decades policing Northern Ireland, in what was essentially a counter-insurgency, to say nothing of the French travails in Vietnam and Algeria. For all militaries, the experience of counter-insurgency and pacification was difficult and frustrating, even for those which had long traditions of such activities.[37]

The United States and Soviet Union alike faced substantial difficulty in adapting conventional military establishments to the demands of unconventional warfare and counter-insurgency. Part was simple lack of preparation. Indeed, the 1952 creation of the Green Berets, more formally the 10th Special Forces Group, was intended primarily as a force multiplier: a small number of American soldiers training indigenous forces for combat against the Soviets and Soviet allies, not primarily for the repression of anti-American guerrillas. In effect, the purpose of American special forces was more to promote anti-Soviet insurgencies, not to repress pro-Soviet insurgencies. As a result, numerous scholars have argued that the US military, focused on conventional warfare, found itself intellectually and organizationally unprepared for counter-insurgency in Vietnam.[38]

The Soviets were no different. A detailed Russian staff study of the war in Afghanistan reveals how the Soviets were handicapped by their preparation for war in Europe. Geography and the very nature of the war made Soviet conventional tactics utterly unworkable, especially once the Afghan resistance abandoned its early attempts at conventional fighting and moved fully to guerrilla warfare. The Soviet system was poor at developing the initiative in its lower-ranking officers and men that the fluid nature of counter-insurgency demanded. In quite concrete ways, preparation for European war hurt performance in Afghanistan. For example, given the short lifespan of equipment in the horrific violence of European war, Soviet designers had made no provisions for providing needed spare tires and treads for the extended distances of Afghanistan. Soviet boots were unsuitable for mountainous terrain, and soldiers swapped them for track shoes.[39]

The deep unpopularity of the Vietnam War with the American public, and the resolution it produced in the American military to avoid such conflicts in the future, had significant effects on subsequent developments. During the 1968 election campaign, Richard Nixon pledged to end the draft, and once in office as president appointed a commission to study the possibility of shifting to an all-volunteer force against substantial military opposition. When the US Congress declined to renew conscription, it ended in July 1973. The resultant transition to an all-volunteer force was not easy, as living conditions and military culture had to be adjusted to new realities. Though military leadership was not thrilled with the change, it recognized the all-volunteer force as a political necessity, and soon came to embrace the virtues of a professional military.[40]

Rejecting counter-insurgency, the leadership of the US Army refocused its attention on central Europe. Alarmed by increasing Soviet superiority in conventional forces and the decline of détente over the course of the 1970s, a whole series of technical and doctrinal innovations sought to restore the conventional balance. In 1973, the Army created its Training and Doctrine Command to rethink how to fight a war. Under first General William Dupuy and then General Donn Starry, it reformulated tactics to deal with the increasing lethality of the modern battlefield, as revealed by the use of anti-tank guided missiles in the 1973 Yom Kippur War. The essence of the reforms, both in the form of AirLand Battle (US doctrine from 1982) and NATO's parallel Follow-on Forces Attack, was to use precision deep-strike weaponry and highly-skilled soldiers and officers (a necessity in the post-conscription US Army) to disrupt Soviet offensives by flexible and unpredictable counter-attacks, while at the same time using cruise missiles and aircraft to stop Soviet reinforcing echelons from reaching the battlefield. Soviet doctrine for the next war depended on a vast feat of coordination and control; NATO intended to use the same friction that had undone McNamara's war in Vietnam to bring a Soviet offensive to a halt. The introduction of the M1 Abrams tank (1980) and M2 Bradley infantry fighting vehicle (1981) provided the material means of implementing this highly demanding doctrine.[41] As these were the result of the Gerald Ford and Jimmy Carter administrations, the military build-up of the Reagan administration thus harvested intellectual and material seeds planted in previous years. These developments were complemented by parallel shifts in Britain well before the advent of Thatcherism, as Prime Minister Harold Wilson's withdrawal of British power from "east of Suez," particularly Malaysia and Singapore, led to a renewed focus on European defense in the 1970s.

To the Soviets, AirLand Battle and the technological developments that made it possible were highly alarming. For the Soviet high command, they required substantial efforts at research and procurement to enable the Soviets to catch up in the technical arms race and develop precision deep-strike capabilities of their own. When combined with a draining war in Afghanistan, economic stagnation at home, and the accelerating pace of the Reagan military build-up, Soviet civilian leaders began to challenge for the first time the military's response to Western military innovation, exploring the option of political solutions to European conflict and even the institution of a military doctrine that aimed only at sufficient means to defend, not the massive forces capable of pushing through to the English Channel.[42]

The military side of the cold war, though too often divorced from its international history, has played a major role in debates on the cold war's end. A common triumphalist narrative of Western victory stresses how the Reagan military build-up (begun in the final years of the Carter administration) forced the Soviets to spend themselves into bankruptcy. An equally prevalent counter-narrative suggests that Reagan's military policies, particularly his attachment to missile defense, delayed and almost derailed the improvement in US-Soviet relations in the late 1980s. Both are flawed. There is little evidence that Reagan's policies were intended to produce moderation in the Soviet leadership, and until Gorbachev's ascent to power Soviet policy was more hostile and confrontational than it had been previously. On the other hand, the briefest look at the Soviet leadership's deliberations in the 1980s reveals their preoccupation with economic stagnation, and their deep conviction that any improvement in Soviet economic performance had to come in part from reducing the defense burden, which required in turn better relations with the United States. As a result, while the collapse of the Soviet Union had many antecedent causes, it is undeniable that at least one trigger for new thinking in the Soviet leadership was the decay of Soviet military superiority and the increasing burden of defense spending. Mikhail Gorbachev's reforms, impelled in part by this debate over Soviet military spending and the proper response to the West, produced an end to the cold war and, as an utterly unintended consequence, the disintegration of the Soviet Union itself.

## NOTES

1. See, for example, the classic John Lewis Gaddis, *Strategies of Containment: A Critical Appraisal of Postwar American National Security Policy* (New York: Oxford University Press, 1982).

2. Odd Arne Westad, *The Global Cold War: Military Interventions and the Making of Our Times* (Cambridge: Cambridge University Press, 2005).

3. The most comprehensive narrative history of military aspects of the Cold War is Norman Friedman, *The Fifty-Year War: Conflict and Strategy in the Cold War* (Annapolis, MD: Naval Institute Press, 2000); David J. A. Stone (no relation to this author), *Wars of the Cold War: Campaigns and Conflicts, 1945–1990* (London: Brassey's, 2004) covers exactly what its subtitle indicates; David Miller, *The Cold War: A Military History* (New York: Thomas Dunne Books, 1999) focuses on weapons systems. Vojtech Mastny, "The New History of Cold War Alliances," *Journal of Cold War Studies* 4/2 (Spring 2002): 55–84, though nominally focused as its title suggests on alliance politics, in fact has much to say about military aspects of the cold war.

4. For brief and recent introductions, see Jeremy Black, *A Military History of Britain* (Westport, CT: Greenwood, 2006) and Hew Strachan, ed., *Big Wars and Small Wars: The British Army and the Lessons of War in the Twentieth Century* (London: Routledge, 2006).

5. Vojtech Mastny and Malcolm Byrne, eds., *A Cardboard Castle? An Inside History of the Warsaw Pact, 1955–1991* (Budapest: Central European University Press, 2005); V. Naumov, ed., *Georgii Zhukov: Stenogramma oktiabr'skogo (1957 g.) plenuma TsK KPSS i drugie dokumenty* (Moscow: MFD, 2001); Xiaoming Zhang, *Red Wings over the Yalu: China, the Soviet Union, and the Air War in Korea* (College Station, TX: Texas A&M Universtiy Press, 2002).

6. Among the noteworthy exceptions are Bruce A. Elleman, *Modern Chinese Warfare, 1795–1989* (London, 2001); Mark A. Ryan, David M. Finkelstein, and Michael A. McDevitt, eds., *Chinese Warfighting: The PLA Experience since 1949* (Armonk, NY, 2003); Peter Worthing, *A Military History of Modern China: From the Manchu Conquest to Tienanmen Square* (Westport, CT: Praeger, 2007); and Xiaobang Li, *A History of the Modern Chinese Army* (Lexington, KY: University of Kentucky Press, 2007).

7. Malaya's status as a successful counter-insurgency has made it a celebrated historical case. See, for example, John Nagl, *Learning to Eat Soup with a Knife: Counterinsurgency Lessons from Malaya and Vietnam* (Westport, CT: Praeger, 2002), which leapt into public debate in the wake of the 2003 Iraq War, and a 2009 special issue of the *Journal of Strategic Studies* 32/3: "British Counter-Insurgency from Malaya to Iraq."

8. On France as a hybrid power, see Paul Kennedy, *The Rise and Fall of the Great Powers: Economic Change and Military Conflict from 1500–2000* (New York: Random House, 2000), 88–90, 169, 219; Matthew Connelly, *A Diplomatic Revolution: Algeria's Fight for Independence and the Origins of the Post-Cold War Era* (New York: Oxford University Press, 2002).

9. Sten Rynning, *Changing Military Doctrine: Presidents and Military Power in Fifth Republic France, 1958–2000* (Westport, CT: Praeger, 2001).

10. Jürgen Rohwer and Mikhail S. Monakov, *Stalin's Ocean-Going Fleet: Soviet Naval Strategy and Shipbuilding Programmes, 1935–1953* (London: Frank Cass, 2001); S. G. Gorshkov, *The Sea Power of the State* (Annapolis, MD: Pergamon Press, 1979); Robert Waring Herrick, *Soviet Naval Doctrine and Policy, 1956–1986*, books I–III (Lewiston, NY: Edwin Mellen Press, 2003).

11. Mark R. Grandstaff, "Making the Military American: Advertising, Reform, and the Demise of an Antistanding Military Tradition, 1945–1955," *Journal of Military History* 60/1 (April 1996): 299–323; Lori Lyn Bogle, *The Pentagon's Battle for the American Mind: The Early Cold War* (College Station, TX: Texas A&M Press, 2004).

12. Julian Lewis, *Changing Direction: British Military Planning for Post-War Strategic Defence, 1942–47* (London: Frank Cass, 2003); Steven T. Ross, *American War Plans, 1945–1950* (New York: Garland, 1988); David R. Stone, "The Balkan Pact and American Policy, 1950–1955," *East European Quarterly* 28/3 (Fall 1994): 393–407.

13. See, for example, William E. Odom, *The Collapse of the Soviet Military* (New Haven, CT: Yale University Press, 1998), 72 and 436 n. 27.

14. George Watson, *The Office of the Secretary of the Air Force, 1947–1965* (Washington, DC, 1993); Jeffrey G. Barlow, *The Revolt of the Admirals: The Fight for Naval Aviation, 1945–1950* (Washington, DC: Naval Historical Center, 1994); Michael Palmer, *Origins of the Maritime Strategy: American Naval Strategy in the First Postwar Decade* (Washington, DC: Naval Historical Center, 1988); Jeffrey G. Barlow, *From Hot War to Cold: The US Navy and National Security Affairs, 1945–1955* (Stanford, CA: Stanford Universtiy Press, 2009).

15. Joseph H. Alexander and Merrill L. Bartlett, *Sea Soldiers in the Cold War: Amphibious Warfare, 1945–1991* (Annapolis, MD: Naval Institute Press, 1995); Julian Thompson, *The Royal Marines: From Sea Soldiers to a Special Force* (London: Sidgwick & Jackson, 2001).

16. V. A. Zolotarev, ed., *Istoriia Voennoi Strategii Rossii* (Moscow: Kuchkovo Pole, 2000), 412.

17. Zoltan D. Barany, "Soviet Control of the Hungarian Military under Stalin," *Journal of Strategic Studies* 14/2 (June 1991): 148–64; Mikhail Heller and Aleksandr M. Nekrich, *Utopia in Power* (New York: Summit, 1986), 504–5.

18. Norman Naimark, *The Russians in Germany* (Cambridge, MA: Belknap Press, 1995), esp. chap. 1; Victor Gobarev, "Soviet Military Plans and Actions during the First Berlin Crisis, 1948–49," *Journal of Slavic Military Studies* 10/3 (September 1997): 1–24; M. Cherednichenko, "Razvitie teorii strategicheskoi nastypatel'noi operatsii v 1945–1953 gg.," *Voenno-istoricheskii zhurnal* (hereafter *VIZh*) no. 8 (1976): 38–45; P. Altukhov, "Razvitie vzgliadov na organizatsiiu upravleniia voiskami v obschevoiskovom boiu v poslevoennoi period," *VIZh* no. 11 (1979): 31–3.

19. Ernest May, ed., *American Cold War Strategy: Interpreting NSC 68* (New York: Bedford, 1993); David R. Fautua, "The 'Long Pull' Army: NSC 68, the Korean War, and the Creation of the Cold War US Army," *Journal of Military History* 61/1 (January 1997): 93–120; Raymond P. Ojserkis, *Beginnings of the Cold War Arms Race: The Truman Administration and the US Arms Build-Up* (Westport, CT: Praeger, 2003).

20. Christopher Sandars, *America's Overseas Garrisons: The Leasehold Empire* (New York: Oxford Universtiy Press, 2000); Kevin Ruane, *The Rise and Fall of the European Defence Community: Anglo-American Relations and the Crisis of European Defence, 1950–55* (Basingstoke: Palgrave, 2000); William I. Hitchcock, *France Restored: Cold War Diplomacy and the Quest for Leadership in Europe, 1944–1954* (Chapel Hill, NC: University of North Carolina Press, 1998).

21. Donald Abenheim, *Reforging the Iron Cross: The Search for Tradition in the West German Armed Forces* (Princeton: Princeton University Press, 1988); Jay Lockenour, *Soldiers as Citizens: Former Wehrmacht Officers in the Federal Republic of Germany, 1945–1955* (Lincoln, NE: University of Nebraska Press, 2001); Alaric Searle, *Wehrmacht Generals, West German Society, and the Debate on Rearmament, 1949–1959* (Westport, CT: Praeger, 2003); James A. Wood, "Captive Historians, Captivated Audience: The German Military History Program, 1945–1961," *Journal of Military History* 69/1 (January 2005): 123–47; Kerstin von Lingen, *Kesselring's Last Battle: War Crimes Trials and Cold War Politics, 1945–1960* (Lawrence, KS: Universtiy Press of Kansas, 2009).

22. Robert R. Bowie and Richard H. Immerman, *Waging Peace: How Eisenhower Shaped an Enduring Cold War Strategy* (New York: Oxford University Press, 1998); Gerard Clarfield, *Security with*

*Solvency: Dwight D. Eisenhower and the Shaping of the American Military Establishment* (Westport, CT: Praeger, 1999); Marc Trachtenberg, *A Constructed Peace: The Making of the European Settlement* (Princeton: Princeton University Press, 1999), esp. chaps. 5–6.

23. Francis Duncan, *Rickover and the Nuclear Navy: The Discipline of Technology* (Annapolis, MD: Naval Institute Press, 1990); Malcolm Muir, Jr., *Black Shoes and Blue Water: Surface Warfare in the United States Navy, 1945–1975* (Washington, DC: Naval Historical Center, 1996); Barlow, *Hot War to Cold.*

24. James D. Marchio, "Risking General War in Pursuit of Limited Objectives: US Military Contingency Planning for Poland in the Wake of the 1956 Hungarian Uprising," *Journal of Military History* 66/3 (July 2002): 783–812; Lawrence H. Suid, *The Army's Nuclear Power Program: The Evolution of a Support Agency* (New York: Greenwood, 1990); Erik D. Weiss, "Cold War under the Ice: The Army's Bid for a Long-Range Nuclear Role, 1959–1963," *Journal of Cold War Studies* 3/3 (Fall 2001): 31–58.

25. A. J. Bacevich, *The Pentomic Era: The US Army between Korea and Vietnam* (Washington, DC: National Defense University Press, 1986); Kalev I. Sepp, "The Pentomic Puzzle: The Influence of Personality and Nuclear Weapons on US Army Organization, 1952–1958," *Army History* no. 51 (Winter 2001), 1–13.

26. Kenneth P. Werrell, "The Weapon the Military Did Not Want: The Modern Strategic Cruise Missile," *Journal of Military History* 53/4 (October 1989): Kenneth P. 419–38; Werrell, *The Evolution of the Cruise Missile* (Maxwell, AL: Air University Press, 1985).

27. Iu. A Iashin and N. K. Monakhov, "O razvitii teoreticheskikh osnov boevogo primeneniia i ekspluatatsii raketnykh system pervykh pokolenii," *Voennaia mysl'* no. 2 (1995): 74.

28. David Holloway, *Stalin and the Bomb: The Soviet Union and Atomic Energy, 1939–1956* (New Haven, CT: Yale University Press, 1994), 338–40; Sergei Goncharenko, "Sino-Soviet Military Cooperation," in Odd Arne Westad, ed., *Brothers in Arms: The Rise and Fall of the Sino-Soviet Alliance, 1945–1963* (Washington, DC: Woodrow Wilson Center Press, 1998), 157–8.

29. On the Chinese question, see Westad, *Brothers in Arms*, and Lorenz Lüthi, *The Sino-Soviet Split: Cold War in the Communist World* (Princeton, NJ: Princeton University Press, 2008); on military cuts, see "Sokrashchenie vooruzhennykh sil SSSR v seredine 50-x godov," *Voennye Arkhivy Rossii* (Moscow, 1993): 271–308.

30. L. Korzun, "Razvitie taktiki oboronitel'nogo boia motostrelkovykh i tankovykh podrazdelenii v poslevoennye gody," *VIZh* no. 10 (1980): 34–41; P. Tsygankov, "Razvitie taktiki nastupatel'nogo boia strelkovykh (motostrelkovykh i tankovykh podrazdelenii v poslevoennye gody,") *VIZh* no. 7 (1977): 37–45; P. Tsygankov, "Razvitie taktiki nastupatel'nogo boia noch'iu v poslevoennyi gody," *VIZh* no. 10 (1978), 53–61; Z. Shutov, "Rabota komandirov chastei i podrazdelenii pri organizatsii nastupleniia na podgotovlennuiu oboronu protivnika (1946–1980gg.)," *VIZh* no. 5 (1981): 27–32.

31. On the origins of the Soviet military-industrial complex, see David R. Stone, *Hammer and Rifle: The Militarization of the Soviet Union, 1926–1933* (Lawrence, KS: University of Kansas Press, 2000); for the social impact of the Soviet military, Ellen Jones, *Red Army and Society: A Sociology of the Soviet Military* (Boston, MA: Harper Collins, 1985); Aaron L. Friedberg, *In the Shadow of the Garrison State: America's Anti-Statism and its Cold War Grand Strategy* (Princeton: Princeton University Press, 2000).

32. Edward L. Katzenbach, "Russian Military Developments," *Current History* 39/231 (December 1960): 264; see also Mastny, "Cold War Alliances," 63–4; Odom, *Collapse*, 66–71.

33. V. D. Sokolovskii, *Soviet Military Strategy* (Englewood Cliffs, NJ: Prentice Hall, 1963).

34. Derevianko to Khrushchev, August 1, 1961, in Rossiiskii Gosudarstvennyi Arkhiv Noveishei Istorii, f. 5, op. 30, d. 372, ll. 203–12.

35. I. V. Bystrova, *Voenno-promyshlennyi kompleks SSSR v gody kholodnoi voiny* (Moscow: Institute rosiiskoi istorri RAN, 2000); Dale Herspring, *The Soviet High Command, 1967–1989*

(Princeton: Princeton University Press, 1990); on naval matters, see Rohwer and Monakov, *Stalin's Ocean-Going Fleet*, Gorshkov, *Sea Power of the State*, and Robert Herrick, *Soviet Naval Doctrine and Policy*.

36. Carl von Clausewitz, *On War*, trans. Michael Howard and Peter Paret (Princeton: Princeton University Press, 1976), 119.

37. A British Army history of its campaign in Northern Ireland is "Operation Banner: An Analysis of Military Operations in Northern Ireland" (2006), prepared under the direction of the Chief of the General Staff; available at <http://www.vilaweb.cat/media/attach/vwedts/docs/op_banner_analysis_released.pdf> (accessed June 3, 2012). On the trying experience of British soldiers, see Charles Allen, *The Savage Wars of Peace: Soldiers' Voices, 1945–1989* (New York: Viking Penguin, 1990).

38. For a charming memoir of the early days of the Green Berets, see Chalmers Archer, Jr., *Green Berets in the Vanguard: Inside Special Forces, 1953–1963* (Annapolis, MD: Naval Institute Press, 2001). On intellectual shortcomings in Vietnam, see Andrew F. Krepinevich, Jr., *The Army and Vietnam* (Baltimore, MD: John Hopkins University Press, 1986); Christopher M. Gacek, *The Logic of Force: The Dilemma of Limited War in American Foreign Policy* (New York: Columbia University Press, 1994) explores the broad tension between total war and limited war approaches in American policy; H. R. McMaster, *Dereliction of Duty: Lyndon Johnson, Robert McNamara, the Joint Chiefs of Staff, and the Lies that Led to Vietnam* (New York: Harper Collins, 1997) emphasizes excessive service loyalty; C. Dale Walton, *The Myth of Inevitable US Defeat in Vietnam* (Portland, OR: Frank Cass, 2002) pulls together a variety of different strategic critiques.

39. *The Soviet-Afghan War: How a Superpower Fought and Lost* (Lawrence, KS: University of Kansas Press, 2002).

40. Robert K. Griffith, Jr., *The US Army's Transition to the All-Volunteer Force, 1968–1974* (Washington, DC: Center for Military History, 1997).

41. Saul Bronfeld, "Fighting Outnumbered: The Impact of the Yom Kippur War on the US Army," *Journal of Military History* 71/2 (2007): 465–98; Robert A. Doughty, *The Evolution of US Army Tactical Doctrine, 1946–1976* (Leavenworth, KS: Fort Leavenworth Combat Studies, 1979).

42. Kimberly Marten Zisk, *Engaging the Enemy: Organizational Theory and Soviet Military Innovation, 1955–1991* (Princeton: Princeton University Press, 1993), chap. 5.

## SELECT BIBLIOGRAPHY

Friedman, Norman, *The Fifty-Year War: Conflict and Strategy in the Cold War*. Annapolis, MD: Naval Institute Press, 2000.

Gaddis, John Lewis, *Strategies of Containment: A Critical Appraisal of Postwar American National Security Policy*. New York: Oxford University Press, 1982.

Herspring, Dale, *The Soviet High Command, 1967–1989*. Princeton: Princeton University Press, 1990.

Mastny, Vojtech, "The New History of Cold War Alliances," *Journal of Cold War Studies* 4/2 (Spring 2002): 55–84.

Mastny, Vojtech, and Malcolm Byrne, eds., *A Cardboard Castle? An Inside History of the Warsaw Pact, 1955–1991*. Budapest: Central European University Press, 2005.

Odom, William E., *The Collapse of the Soviet Military*. New Haven, CT: Yale University Press, 1998.

Stone, David J. A., *Wars of the Cold War: Campaigns and Conflicts, 1945–1990*. London: Brassey's, 2004.

Trauschweizer, Ingo, *The Cold War US Army: Building Deterrence for Limited War*. Lawrence, KS: University of Kansas Press, 2008.

........................................................................................................

# CHAPTER 21

# THE NUCLEAR REVOLUTION

*A Product of the Cold War, or Something More?*

........................................................................................................

## CAMPBELL CRAIG

NUCLEAR weaponry plays a starring role in our common memory of the cold war. The United States' atomic bombardment of Hiroshima and Nagasaki stands as a vivid and brutal starting point to that struggle, however one evaluates President Harry S. Truman's motivations for dropping the two bombs. The Korean War—the first real military campaign of the cold war—did not evolve into a general third world war, as someone mindful of recent history might have predicted. Rather, it descended into a limited-war stalemate in large part due to fears of escalation to the atomic level. The Cuban missile crisis remains the climactic event of the cold war, an intense showdown between the two superpowers that can hardly be understood without reference to nuclear weaponry. And above all of this, especially during the latter three decades of the cold war, loomed the specter of mutual assured destruction (MAD), the novel prospect of a war that could exterminate the human race.

Indeed, nuclear weaponry and the widespread fears that a war waged with them could destroy the planet appear to us today as *intrinsic* to our historical understanding of the cold war, as problems literally inseparable from the larger political confrontation between the United States and the Soviet Union. Just as barbed wire and machine guns stand not simply as the inanimate means of waging World War I but also as deeper symbols of the inescapable carnage of trench warfare, so do nuclear weapons represent something essential about the cold war, something that distinguishes it fundamentally from other conflicts.[1] A cold war without nuclear weapons seems unthinkable. And had several of them gone off, it would be all we would think about.

Yet on another level the cold war can be readily analysed apart from the nuclear factor. In other words, had the bomb never been invented—had scientists around the world repeatedly failed to build a workable bomb until governments eventually gave up trying—many scholars would contend that something basically similar to the cold war would have taken place nevertheless. "Neorealist" scholars of international relations have argued that the basic structure of the postwar system is what really defined the cold war: the emergence of the two continental superpowers in the aftermath of World War II was inevitable, or close to it, once Germany and Japan were beaten, and that would have happened whether the bomb was around or not. Systemic factors, particularly the bipolar geopolitical rivalry between the Soviet Union and the United States, maintain Kenneth Waltz and like-minded theorists, essentially shaped the cold war. In the final analysis, it differed from previous international great-power conflicts only in terms of the number of actors involved rather than the weapons they deployed.[2]

Scholars who emphasize ideology also play down the nuclear factor. For them, the cold war was about the contest between capitalism and communism, or between democracy and totalitarianism; it was this struggle that really underlay the half-century after World War II. Marxist scholars argue, or did argue, that the cold war represented less a rivalry between states than a stage, some claimed a final stage, of late capitalism; conversely, conservative theorists in the West regard the cold war not so much as a battle between nation-states as between political ideologies, a stage, some likewise claim a final stage, of the struggle between democratic liberalism and its many statist and autocratic enemies. For these scholars, nuclear weapons again remain secondary, important to be sure as a means of cold war contention, but subordinate to the larger story of grand ideological struggle.[3]

Finally, a more recent liberal analysis of modern international relations, represented by the work of the political scientist John Mueller, suggests that nuclear weapons were not that important to the cold war no matter how one regards its larger political meaning. While scholars from Realist or ideological viewpoints would admit that nuclear weapons played a key part in determining how the cold war proceeded, only arguing that the larger processes are more important in explaining its essence, Mueller contends that the common perception that nuclear weapons and nuclear fear shaped cold war confrontations is itself incorrect. The Western world, he maintains, has come to regard warfare as barbaric and obsolete, and so the two superpowers would have likely refused to go to war at any time even had nuclear weapons never been invented. The importance of nuclear weapons in dissuading American and Soviet leaders from risking war in places like Korea and Cuba, or in general in the age of mutual assured destruction, he insists, has been vastly overstated.[4]

The United States and the Soviet Union would have likely emerged as the two leading superpowers after World War II had the bomb never existed, and they would probably have contended with one another over a war-torn Europe. It is equally likely that China would have had its revolution in any event and emerged as a new third power regardless of the nuclear arms race. So, too, the two superpowers would have begun to confront one another not only in Europe but also for the allegiance of decolonizing countries in the third world, and they would have done so in the name of their respective ideologies.[5] On the other hand, several signal features of the cold war—nuclear showdowns over Berlin and Cuba, various arms control agreements, anti-nuclear and disarmament movements, to name a few of the most obvious—were so singularly shaped by the bomb that they would never have emerged in anything like their actual form without it.

My goal in this essay is not to drill down deeper into the conventional debates but to step back from them. I will argue, in three suggestive historical sections, that the development of nuclear weapons affected the cold war between the United States and the Soviet Union in ways that went beyond the obvious crises and arms races.[6] The simple existence of the bomb affected the cold war in fundamental respects: without it the rivalry between the US and the USSR might have begun more slowly; the military confrontation between them would surely have been radically altered, and, finally, the cold war would almost certainly have ended in a much different way, if it ended at all. I will focus upon three large historical developments: the role of the atomic bomb in dooming basic forms of postwar cooperation between the United States and the USSR; the role of mutual assured destruction in pushing the superpowers away from direct confrontation and toward war in the third world and senseless military overproduction at home; and finally, and most important, the role of nuclear fear in invalidating the programmatic ideology of Marxism-Leninism in the USSR.

# THE ATOMIC BOMB AND THE ONSET
# OF THE COLD WAR

Some kind of postwar confrontation between the United States and the Soviet Union was on the cards after 1945. From a strictly structural perspective, the very fact that these two nations emerged from the war as by far the two most militarily powerful regimes left standing (though in almost all respects the US was considerably stronger) made a great-power rivalry between them predictable—some theorists would say inevitable. Balance-of-power systems always emerge after major wars, most Realist scholars contend, and the cold war represented another example of this timeless pattern.

Added to these structural forces was the clear fact that the United States and the Soviet Union stood for radically different political orders. Although these differences were played down during the war, and although there were some in the West (most notably Franklin D. Roosevelt) who believed that this wartime cooperation could lead to some kind of grand political compromise afterward, it remained inescapable that America was committed to capitalism and liberal democracy; the USSR, to communism and the dictatorship of the proletariat. What was more, many Soviet leaders and citizens retained their ideological belief in the dream of global communist revolution, and their conviction that its attainment could arrive after another war started by the capitalist imperialists.[7]

History, of course, is not just driven by "factors"; actual people were in a position to shape events. And leaders on both sides were primed after the war to err on the side of insecurity and mistrust. Joseph Stalin, not the trusting type in the first place, acquired an even more cynical attitude toward international cooperation following the Nazi abrogation of the 1939 peace treaty and the near-subjugation of his nation to German conquest in 1941 and 1942. He also was bitter toward his major wartime allies, Great Britain and the US, for having delayed opening a major second front until the middle of 1944. Indeed, it could be said that few leaders in all of history were less likely to put their trust in serious international cooperation than the Joseph Stalin of 1945. Like many of his fellow citizens, the new American president, Harry S. Truman, regarded World War II as proof that the United States was no longer protected from the old world, and that to remain secure Americans would have to confront aggression there at an early stage. Truman came from an utterly different world than Stalin, and surely believed, at least in an abstract sense, in the possibility of maintaining the "Grand Alliance." But he was determined that the United States would not make the same mistakes it had committed in the 1930s.[8]

For all of these reasons, the emergence of some kind of a rivalry between the two nations was close to inevitable after the war, atomic bomb or not. What the bomb did was create new political problems for both sides that had the effect of accelerating, intensifying, and raising the stakes of their mutual enmity. That was a great irony, for it was the solemn belief of many (in the West at least) that the weapon that obliterated Hiroshima and Nagasaki made US-Soviet cooperation an absolute moral imperative if the world was to avoid an atomic holocaust.[9]

Three aspects of US-Soviet atomic diplomacy during the pivotal years of 1945 and 1946 show how the simple existence of atomic weaponry aggravated tensions between the two nations. The first was Stalin's decision during the war to pursue a bomb for himself, a policy that attracted modest resources during the war and then, following the US bombardment of Hiroshima and Nagasaki, became nothing less than "Problem Number One" for Stalin and his associates in the Kremlin, and thus for the nation as a whole. Stalin put his most ruthless henchman, Lavrentii Beria, in charge of the Soviet atomic project, and—at a time of unimaginable deprivation throughout the Soviet Union—told Beria to commit as many resources and allocate as many funds as necessary to the scientists so as to build a bomb as quickly as possible.

Stalin took this course of action because he believed that America's unwillingness to inform him about the atomic project and its ruthless destruction of Hiroshima and Nagasaki indicated that the Americans meant to use their monopoly to intimidate the Soviet Union and perhaps actually attack it. But he also chose this path because he was convinced that the *only* way to repel such American pressure was to develop a Soviet atomic capability as soon as possible, rather than to respond to American overtures about international atomic control or, even further, to work with the United States in the name of comprehensive international order. In other words, Stalin decided early on to pursue the bomb single-mindedly, and after the war was even more determined to get it even at the expense of forgoing deals with the United States.[10]

It is crucial to see how the bomb shaped Stalin's decision-making in a way that previous kinds of weaponry would not have done. Had the United States been in sole possession of some kind of advanced ship, or tank, or airplane, Stalin could have gone along with initiatives to restrict a postwar arms race, confident that if talks fell apart his nation would have the time to catch up with the Americans. No ships or tanks or airplanes could by themselves imminently threaten the vast Soviet Union and its victorious Red

Army. But an atomic bomb could. Stalin had received detailed information about the destruction wrought at Hiroshima and Nagasaki.[11] He knew that a United States wielding a monopoly of even a handful of atomic bombs could, over the long term, threaten and intimidate the USSR. In the event of war, moreover, it could lay waste to several Soviet cities. To make sure that could not happen, Stalin had to get a bomb to deter the Americans. It was understandably of little consequence to him, therefore, if this project killed off grand plans of international atomic control and cooperation in the cradle.

A second consequence of the politics of the bomb that hardened US-Soviet enmity in the immediate postwar period stemmed from the Soviet espionage program in the United States. During the war, dozens of American (and British and Canadian) citizens spied on the atomic project, channeling important scientific and technological information about the new weapon back to Moscow. Historians are now in broad agreement not only about the impressive scope of the espionage program, but they also almost universally hold that the material the atomic spies passed on to the USSR substantially enhanced Stalin's efforts to obtain a bomb as quickly as he could.[12] Indeed, Soviet espionage had been so effective that Stalin learned of the atomic project long before Truman, who had been a US Senator during most of the war, did.

Despite the White House's best efforts to conceal the successful Soviet program from the public, news leaked out, most spectacularly in the form of syndicated columnist Drew Pearson's radio address in early February 1946. These revelations of atomic spying by America's wartime ally had a dramatic effect upon American public opinion, and it led to a vociferous campaign, led by Republicans in Congress, to accuse prominent Democrats of communist sympathies and even outright treason. Indeed, the espionage scandal provided the justification that virulent American anti-communist politicians, such as Richard Nixon and Joseph McCarthy, needed to launch a general Red Scare (one that had little to do with prosecuting atomic spies) in the late 1940s and early 1950s.[13]

In such a political environment, Truman came quickly to realize that continued attempts to pursue better relations with the USSR were going to put the political prospects of his party and his own career in serious jeopardy. But that was nothing compared to the ongoing American efforts to establish international atomic control, namely the Acheson-Lilienthal report put forward by the US State Department in early 1946 and then presented to the world in the (modified) form of the Baruch Plan later that year. If Truman could understand that serious talks with the Soviet Union of any kind had now become politically dangerous, then what would happen to him if he announced to the American people a plan to transfer the US atomic arsenal to an international agency while newspapers screamed of spies working for the USSR having stolen the bomb from under his nose? It would be an act of political suicide. Truman gave up on the "Grand Alliance" and the prospect of international control by early 1946, even as Stalin had done so long before; the Baruch Plan, heralded at the time as a bold initiative to secure a permanent world peace, was actually a scheme designed to fail.[14]

Finally, the atomic bomb exacerbated US-Soviet hostility in the immediate postwar period because it made the alternative to superpower rivalry—serious and sustained international cooperation—so obviously unattainable. It is here where the unique nature of the bomb was most telling. Veteran scientists and statesmen in the West, such as Niels Bohr, the Danish physicist who worked on the bomb, and Henry Stimson, secretary of war under Roosevelt and Truman, understood what serious cooperation meant in the atomic age. Because, as Stalin had discerned, the bomb is so devastating even if a nation possesses only a few of them, major powers (such as the USSR) would want to obtain one if they were to avoid eventual defeat on the global stage. What could possibly dissuade them from doing so? The only conceivable answer was the establishment of an exceedingly powerful international agency that could assume possession of all atomic bombs and provide air-tight assurance that no individual nation could ever build its own arsenal.

Such an agency, accordingly, would not only have to take control over all atomic weaponry; it would also have to command the vast power and resources necessary to inspect all nations suspected of trying to build a bomb (such as the USSR) and forcefully prevent them from doing so. Worded differently, the agency would have to have more power than any state on earth; it would have to become a kind of world government with the authority to punish, by means that would include military force, any renegade or outlier.

Establishing such an institution would require the political leaders of the United States and the Soviet Union, at least, to come together and form a global regime that would be acceptable to both sides. In 1945 and 1946, few political leaders in the United States could even entertain such a notion, much less advocate it as a foreign policy priority. But Americans were dreamy idealists compared with Stalin and his regime, for whom the idea of deeply cooperating with the United States to establish a powerful international agency that would immediately inspect the entirety of the USSR for atomic facilities was utterly beyond conception.

In the atomic age, the alternative to power politics as usual was (and is), effectively, world government. The starkness of that choice made it easy for American and Soviet leaders to settle for the former straight away.

## Military competition under MAD

A second general effect of the bomb upon the cold war is the most apparent one: its radical alteration of the way both superpowers conceived of and planned for war. The main and most obvious effect, of course, was that the advent of MAD led leaders on both sides, beginning with Dwight D. Eisenhower and Nikita Khrushchev and continuing until the end of the cold war, to regard major war as catastrophic and make it a primary interest to prevent one from occurring. We shall also, however, look at some side effects of this transformation.

During the middle of the 1950s, both the United States and the Soviet Union began to develop intercontinental missiles capable of delivering thermonuclear warheads to the major cities of the other side. While the United States was far ahead of the Soviet Union in this field (despite the alarmist Washington "missile gap" politics of the late 1950s), the fact remained that sooner rather than later each side would be able to annihilate the other in the space of a few hours. A total war fought in the absolute manner of, say, World War II would lead to the deaths of hundreds of millions and the destruction of the governments and societies involved. The term "nuclear revolution" refers to this condition, when all-out war means the effective death of all of the nations fighting it. As the legendary French statesman Charles de Gaulle put it in 1960, after a nuclear war the nations involved would have "neither powers, nor laws, nor cities, nor culture, nor cradles, nor tombs."[15]

While it is easy to see in hindsight the logic of MAD, leaders at the time could not be so sure, especially because its overriding implication—that it was no longer acceptable to wage major war—flew in the face of the timeless political tenet that it is always better to fight than to accept defeat. And indeed, there was no guarantee that American and Soviet leaders would not resist the logic of MAD, that they would not try to find ways of waging and winning war even in the thermonuclear era. Many political leaders and strategic thinkers on both sides (though particularly in the US) did just that, refusing to believe that technology had made war unwinnable.[16] However, the leaders of the two superpowers at the dawn of the nuclear revolution, Eisenhower and Khrushchev, both recognized in the middle of the 1950s that major war was becoming an absurdity, and they began to develop foreign and military policies to reflect that fact. By the end of that decade, both leaders had transformed their basic security policies so that the aim of *deterring* a third world war with their most powerful weapons replaced the aim of *winning* one with them. Nuclear deterrence governed de facto the military policies of both superpowers with respect to major war until the end of the cold war.[17]

The most obvious cold war consequence of the system of MAD that Eisenhower and Khrushchev initiated, to repeat, was its acutely sobering effect upon decision-makers in the US and the USSR when the mere possibility of armed conflict with the other side emerged. This is not the place to recount in any detail the great nuclear crises of the late 1950s and early 1960s, but certain salient decisions might be highlighted. For example, during the second Quemoy-Matsu crisis in 1958, the Eisenhower administration responded to Communist China's threats against this offshore island chain held by Taiwan not by darkly hinting at a nuclear attack, as it did over the exact same issue in 1954–5, but rather by striking a deal with the Chinese in the face of massive protests by not only the Taiwanese leader Jiang Jieshi [Chiang Kai-shek] but also much of the US military. During the Berlin ultimatum crisis of 1958–9, Eisenhower agreed to meet Khrushchev in a summit on the status of Berlin, despite the fact that he was negotiating under an ultimatum; Khrushchev, for his part, simply cancelled his decision to turn over Berlin to East Germany despite having received no concrete reciprocation from the West. When East Germany made the fateful decision to erect the Berlin Wall in 1961, Khrushchev approved and saw it as a way to eliminate an impossible political problem peacefully. President John F. Kennedy, in turn, was privately relieved by the act, despite furious demands from many in the US military that the wall must be destroyed.

And then there was the Cuban missile crisis, the final act of the 1958–62 play. Those who doubt the unique effects of the fear of nuclear war upon decision-making need only study cursorily the repeated efforts made in the White House and in the Kremlin to find a way to back down from this showdown, to reach a deal, any deal, that would allow both sides to save some face. Kennedy, despite America's overwhelming military superiority both on the scene and in strategic nuclear capabilities, gladly pledged that the US would never invade Cuba (a promise that has been kept) and to dismantle intermediate-range missiles in Turkey. Khrushchev in turn agreed to dismantle the missiles in Cuba and bring them back to Russia, a humiliating step that Cuban leader Fidel Castro and other third world figures regarded as a cowardly betrayal of the revolution, and that soon cost him his leadership of the USSR.[18]

It is important here again to specify how the nuclear specter altered the way the two leaders dealt with the crisis. It is not as though they refused to take any risky steps that might increase the possibility of a nuclear war—Khrushchev, after all, decided to send the missiles to Cuba, knowing that it might trigger a serious American response. Rather, once it became clear that the US was responding and that further steps might lead to armed conflict, both leaders shrank away from further confrontation and grasped at any diplomatic solution to the crisis that seemed feasible. In an earlier time, a similar show-down might have led to a minor war between the US and the USSR, one that might have quickly escalated into a general conflagration, as the regional conflicts in Europe during the summer of 1914 led to World War I. In the nuclear age, however, *any* armed conflict between the two sides was too dangerous for fear that it could escalate into an uncontrollable nuclear exchange. Once nonviolent forms of offensive action and posturing were exhausted, military conflict of any kind was off the table and it was time to deal. That was the new reality which Eisenhower, the father of MAD, had perceived several years earlier.[19]

After Cuba, both superpowers accepted the logic of MAD for the ensuing three decades of the cold war. There were two events that might have triggered a nuclear war between them during this period—Nixon sounding a nuclear alert during the Yom Kippur War in 1973 and the Soviet misinterpretation of the Able Archer exercise as a NATO preparation for a first strike a decade later—but neither of these was a direct political showdown between the US and the USSR, and neither was probably anywhere close to as dangerous as Berlin and Cuba, though work remains to be done on these questions. For the most part, leaders on the two sides were content to accept the paradox that they remained in a geopolitical rivalry of global stakes that could never be resolved by war. Yet vast military and political bureaucracies in both nations had been built with the mission of defeating the other side on the field of battle. This tension led to secondary aspects of the cold war during its last three decades which, I would suggest, also can be attributed to nuclear weaponry and the stubborn durability of MAD.

One "secondary aspect" of the latter part of the cold war, though it was hardly secondary for the poor nations involved, was the propensity of both superpowers to wage limited and proxy wars in the third world. For the United States, the major such war was its decade-long campaign in Vietnam, and for the Soviet Union, it was the grisly war in

Afghanistan that lasted a similar duration. Both nations, moreover, funded and trained proxy armies around the globe to wage irregular warfare in third world nations torn between the American and Soviet models. It hardly needs to be stated that in both cases the superpowers had plausible reasons to wage these limited wars (though with Vietnam it is difficult to identify them), and that, *ceteris paribus*, in the absence of nuclear weapons they would surely have intervened in these third world theaters or ones like them.[20]

What gives these wars their "nuclear" flavor was their exclusively remote locations and the intensity with which the two superpowers waged them. Great powers routinely waged limited wars throughout the modern period in places near and far, even at the risk of igniting a larger war (think, for example, of Bismarck's limited campaigns of the 1860s and 1870s). After 1962, both the United States and the Soviet Union realized that waging war on a nation that had close ties with the other superpower had become too dangerous, especially in Europe but also in East Asia and Latin America, as well as select allies in the Middle East, Africa, and Australasia. War was only possible in nations which were far removed from major cold war theaters and did not have close ties to the other side.

A striking feature of these wars was also the way leaders described them and the armies fought them. Vietnam, to take the most salient case, was routinely characterized by American politicians and military officials throughout the 1960s and into the 1970s as a vital stake in the struggle with communism, as a war upon which ultimate cold war victory or defeat might have hinged, even though such was manifestly not the case—as many American leaders admitted privately and, sometimes, publicly, especially as the war began to turn sour.[21] Correspondingly, the United States poured hundreds of thousands of troops into Vietnam, spent hundreds of billions of dollars on the war, and bombed much of the country into desolation, killing perhaps as many as a million Vietnamese, all to prevent a relatively popular and nationalist left-wing regime from taking power (as it eventually did in 1975, with no important further cold war effects).

To be sure, there were key proximate explanations for the American decision to escalate its war in Vietnam, above all the domestic political calculations of President Lyndon Baines Johnson, and this essay does not mean to underplay them.[22] But the nuclear context loomed above. Denied a chance to wage a military campaign directly against the cold war enemy, American political and military leaders were primed to turn their energies toward a war that was unlikely to lead to nuclear escalation. What is more, MAD perversely allowed the United States to wage a costly war it did not need to win, because its campaign in Vietnam did not seriously erode its military ability to contend with the Soviet Union. In a previous era, a great power would have been much less likely to spend so many resources on a peripheral war such as Vietnam for fear that its ability to keep up with major rivals would be weakened. In an era of easy nuclear deterrence, this was not a danger.[23]

The tension created by the novel reality that a bipolar superpower struggle for global preponderance could not be decided by arms led both the US and the USSR to inflate the importance of its peripheral wars. Another consequence of this tension is best described as the advent of the "Military-Industrial Complex," a term introduced to the world by President Eisenhower in his 1961 farewell address.

The military forces and the vast bureaucracies attending to them in both superpowers had attained massive institutional power by the end of the 1950s, as the prospect of general war seemed to require the construction of elaborate conventional and nuclear capabilities. Politicians, strategists, and military officials on both sides incessantly argued that if the cold war ever went hot, it would be necessary to deploy the most advanced and overpowering military armaments to avoid the catastrophe of losing World War III. And because this contest depended upon cutting-edge technological innovation, it would be necessary as well to devote billions of dollars or rubles to research and development, a process that benefited not merely the military but also civilian science and (especially in the US) major research universities. As a result, huge and influential constituencies stood to gain from an eternal arms race between the two superpowers.[24]

MAD undermined this, as both Eisenhower and Khrushchev immediately understood. Deterrence required the deployment of invulnerable second-strike forces, enough nuclear missiles (10? 100?) that could survive an all-out attack and deliver a massive nuclear retaliation that could destroy the major cities of the other side. It was based upon the premise that leaders in the US and the USSR (or any putative nuclear state) would never come to believe that an attack on the other side, no matter how comprehensive, was worth the obliteration of one's cities, the deaths or maiming of millions of one's fellow citizens, and the political and social breakdown that would follow. Therefore, a large military force prepared to wage World War III was not really needed, as long as one could maintain and cultivate a basic retaliatory arsenal. It would be possible to cut military spending radically without putting the security of the nation at any risk. Khrushchev and, with less success, Eisenhower tried to force this way of thinking upon their respective military bureaucracies by the end of the 1950s.[25]

The response to this strange condition in both nations, though more vividly (given the more open political system) in the US, was also uniquely "nuclear." In pre-nuclear eras, the military and civilian bureaucracies dependent upon ever-higher spending had a much easier argument to make. Put bluntly, more was always better. All things being equal, it would undeniably be preferable to have more tanks and ships than one's adversaries, and so the argument for building weapon X or Y had to be answered on strategic grounds (will it be effective?) and/or fiscal ones (can we afford it?).

The political scientist Robert Jervis has aptly described the response by the military and scientific bureaucracies in both the US and the USSR whom MAD threatened with obsolescence as the attempt to "escape" the logic of the nuclear revolution.[26] Arms industrialists, military officials, and civilian strategists on both sides created an industry of sorts, one which lasted throughout the cold war, dedicated to the single proposition that deterrence was unstable, that nuclear wars were winnable, and that therefore it was necessary to continue to build new nuclear weapons systems and to maintain an arms parity with the other side. The uniqueness of this process when compared with pre-nuclear eras can be easily illustrated by the arsenals each side ended up building during the last two decades of the cold war. Both the US and the USSR deployed, by the middle of the

1980s, tens of thousands of nuclear weapons, most of which were capable of leveling an entire city.[27] US war planning stipulated targeting Moscow in the event of all-out war with dozens of nuclear missiles, even though after the first one or two got through the rest would only "make the rubble bounce," as Winston Churchill nicely put it. Strategists on both sides soberly developed war plans in which the destruction of one's economy and elimination of basic government functions for decades and estimated civilian casualties in the tens of millions was characterized as "victory." MAD constituted an acute crisis for the military-industrial complexes of both superpowers, and the ironic result was the spending of hundreds of billions of dollars and rubles on weaponry that served no identifiable military purpose whatsoever, and which, had it been used, would have resulted in the defeat of both sides and the destruction of civilization.[28]

# THE OBSOLESCENCE OF THE SOVIET EXPERIMENT

The unique effects of nuclear weaponry on the practice of international politics during the cold war shaped the policies of both sides, though as we have seen in the first two cases the United States often experienced the effects more profoundly.[29] The top-down, authoritarian nature of Soviet politics, even in its milder form after Stalin, always meant that political and cultural resistance to the novel ramifications of the bomb would be muted and less influential. For instance, Khrushchev decreed in 1959 and 1960 that the Soviet Union would adopt a policy of basic deterrence and cut military spending substantially, the very same objectives that Eisenhower sought in Washington. While Khrushchev did not succeed wholly in his aims, he encountered far less resistance than did his American counterpart, who found himself at times overwhelmed by the military-industrial complex and its allies in Congress.

For the Soviet Union, the most important effects of the nuclear revolution were systemic—they altered the very nature of its political program. The USSR was founded upon the Marxist-Leninist doctrine that the new regime would act as a vanguard of global revolution, that it would use its power as a nation-state to foment working-class rebellion. Central to this doctrine was the assumption that the imperialist great powers would find themselves going to war over and over again in their struggle for markets and colonies. Thus it was the mission of the Soviet state not only to survive these wars but also to capitalize upon the discord and misery they caused to advance the communist cause. War would be the catalyst of sweeping political change, just as the conservative diplomats of the 19th century feared it would be.

Stalin, it is true, had come to reject his rival Leon Trotsky's demand that the USSR dedicate itself immediately to "permanent" revolution, turning instead to the policy of "socialism in one country," whereby the Soviet Union would build up its power first before spreading it elsewhere. But that hardly foretold a future of peace. He continued to believe that the capitalist powers would go to war with one another, and that this would threaten Soviet existence: for him, World War II represented this danger at its pinnacle.

He further understood that the imperialist powers would not be likely to accept their historical destiny peacefully, and that the revolution would unfold in conditions of violence, reaction, and international tumult, just as his predecessors Trotsky and Lenin believed.[30]

When Stalin died in early 1953, therefore, his successor would inherit a political tradition in which the prospect of great war remained at the heart of the Soviet experiment, not only as a means of national survival in a hostile world but also as a central component of its programmatic ideology. The question of whether this could be sustained in the face of thermonuclear weaponry divided the three main contenders for the leadership after Stalin's death: Khrushchev, Georgi Malenkov, and the venerable foreign minister Vlacheslav Molotov.[31] David Holloway's fine account of the initial debates about this decision, especially between Khrushchev and Molotov in 1954 and 1955, deserves an extensive quotation:

> If imperialism and socialism could keep to themselves, [argued Molotov] then "pray, what are we living for?" It was an illusion to think that communism could be reached by way of peaceful coexistence: "we ought to preserve peace, but if we, besides fighting for peace and *delaying* war, if we also believe that it is possible to get to communism that way, then that is deception from the point of view of Marxism, self-deception, and deception of the people."

Nevertheless a Kremlin committee devised a study later in 1954 which stipulated that a thermonuclear war could eventually destroy the Soviet Union and perhaps "all life on earth." On this study Holloway simply points out

> This remarkable document is open and explicit about the consequences of nuclear war. There is nothing here about the destruction of capitalism and the victory of socialism.[32]

Responding to this report, Molotov objected that the Soviet Union should not be focusing upon the dangers of nuclear war but rather on "the need to prepare and mobilize all forces against the bourgeoisie."

By 1955 Khrushchev had taken power, and in 1956 he famously declared that the Soviet Union would pursue a policy of "peaceful coexistence" with the West, whereby the worldwide triumph of socialism would come about not by means of violent revolution and war, but rather by the USSR providing to the world's masses a more attractive model of political and economic development. For Khrushchev, the nuclear revolution had made the old model of violent political change, one that Lenin, Trotsky, and Stalin all took for granted, simply too dangerous, and even absurd. How could a thermonuclear war that destroyed the USSR advance the cause of socialism? It was this logic that led the Soviet premier to develop the policies of minimum deterrence and war avoidance that we have seen above.[33]

Khrushchev's new policies were of world-historical importance, not only because they permitted the two superpowers to avoid World War III, but also because of their deep impact upon the political determination of the communist world. For at one stroke

Khrushchev removed major war from the Marxist-Leninist program, acknowledging that the avoidance of a thermonuclear holocaust superseded the objective of violent international upheaval, *and* determined that the only way for communism to defeat capitalism now was by means of a peaceful competition to see who could provide the people with a more pleasant material life, something wholly removed from the Marxist-Leninist playbook.

It is not difficult to imagine how these decisions then helped to undermine the Soviet experiment. Since 1918 the vast majority of Soviet citizens had endured terrible suffering and privation. Many of course lost their faith in the regime, especially those with direct experience of Stalin's genocidal repressions of the 1930s, but many others retained their belief in the USSR as an agent of history. Indeed, given the hard life that the Soviet people had experienced, it was hardly surprising that many would justify, or rationalize, their miseries by taking a pride in the feeling that their country was on the side of historical destiny. The citizens of the West enjoyed a more comfortable material life—who could deny that?—but they were not part of something greater, of a political project that went beyond mere consumer gratification. During and immediately after the war, this belief pervaded much of Soviet society and indeed societies in Eastern Europe, China, and elsewhere where Marxism was on the march.

As Molotov anticipated, Khrushchev's peaceful coexistence policy, his war avoidance during the 1958–62 crisis years, and his successor Leonid Brezhnev's acceptance of MAD thereafter all combined to shatter the premise that the Soviet Union remained committed to revolutionary and global transformation. By ruling out war with the West, deploying Soviet forces only in lands far removed from any industrial proletariat, and, perhaps above all, declaring that the great struggle with the imperialists would now be waged in fields like technological innovation and consumer satisfaction, leaders in the Kremlin deprived their citizens and those in other communist lands of the solace that they could live to see the day of global revolution and the triumph of the system they had suffered so much for. This was precisely the reason why committed revolutionaries in places like China and Cuba were so virulently critical of Khrushchev's cautiousness.

The collapse of political meaning causes disillusionment and cynicism, and one sees throughout the Eastern bloc in the 1960s and 1970s the collapse of political enthusiasm at all levels of society, a remarkable increase in corruption and fraud, ossification of central political and economic institutions, and pervasive public apathy.[34] By the time of the appearance of Mikhail Gorbachev in 1985, it is probably accurate to say that throughout the USSR and the other major member nations of the Warsaw Pact (the situation was different in China, other newly communist states, and perhaps a couple of smaller Eastern European nations like Albania and Bulgaria), a small and dwindling percentage of the populace still really believed in the communist dream; among the younger generations, it had almost completely disappeared. Indeed, Gorbachev was forced to resort to radical measures to reform the system, measures that instead led to its collapse, precisely because Soviet society had become so corrupt and listless.[35]

Are we claiming here that the nuclear revolution, and the decisions by Khrushchev and Brezhnev to respect it by avoiding war with the West, explain the degeneration of

Soviet bloc society by itself? Of course not. The legacy of Stalinism tainted the communist experiment throughout Eastern Europe from the outset, and the dysfunctional nature of communist command economies could be tolerated for only so long, especially during a long stretch of peacetime. The development of new communication technologies that conveyed images of Western luxury and political freedoms to Eastern bloc citizens in the 1970s and 1980s surely played a key role as well. But the disappearance of the prospect of war, revolution, and world-historical political change allowed these political dissatisfactions to intensify and ferment during the last decades of the Soviet experiment, as Molotov precisely predicted. In a great irony, one of Gorbachev's last-gasp measures to sustain his dying empire was to embrace the cause of nuclear peace, placing it against the apparent nuclear aggressiveness of the American president Ronald Reagan and his notorious "Star Wars" project, in the futile hopes that this would increase the USSR's attractiveness to a Western public fearful of nuclear holocaust.[36] That was a long way from Marxism-Leninism, and can be characterized as a desperate act by a dying empire. By the end of 1991, the Soviet Union was no more.

The three effects of the nuclear revolution outlined here were, in many ways, particular to the cold war. The prospect of nuclear war shaped US-Soviet relations and affected the political cultures of both countries in the context of a bipolar geopolitical confrontation that gave the possibility of nuclear war specific connotations.

One of the great questions facing scholars and policymakers in the post-cold war era is whether the lessons taken from the nuclear confrontations during the cold war, confrontations that never escalated into war, can be applied to our present international order. One of the aims of this essay is to suggest that while the actual crises and political confrontations between East and West were indeed specific to the cold war, and hence have a limited relevance to our unipolar and globalized order today, there was a larger phenomenon, one caused by the logic of the nuclear revolution, that will always apply as long as there are sovereign states and some of them have nuclear arsenals. This is the reality that large-scale war between nations in possession of thermonuclear arsenals has become irretrievably absurd, and that the future of international politics in the 21st century will hinge upon whether leaders accept this reality or whether they try to overcome it.

## NOTES

1. See the introduction to Paul Fussell, ed., *Norton Book of Modern War* (New York: Norton, 1990).
2. Kenneth Waltz, *Theory of International Politics* (Reading, MA: Addison-Wesley, 1979); John Mearsheimer, *Tragedy of Great Power Politics* (New York: Norton, 2001); Dale Copeland, *Origins of Major War* (Ithaca, NY: Cornell University, 2001); Robert Gilpin, *War and Change in World Politics* (Princeton, NJ: Princeton University, 1983).
3. See Immanuel Wallerstein, *After Liberalism* (New York: Norton, 1995); Fred Halliday, *Rethinking International Relations* (Basingstoke: Macmillan, 1994); Francis Fukuyama, *The End of History and the Last Man* (New York: Free Press, 1992); John Lewis Gaddis, *The Cold War: A New History* (New York: Penguin, 2006).

4. John Mueller, "The Essential Irrelevance of Nuclear Weapons," *International Security*, 13/2 (Autumn 1988); Idem., *Atomic Obsession: Nuclear Alarmism from Hiroshima to Al-Qaeda* (Oxford: Oxford University Press, 2009).

5. Robert Jervis, "Was the Cold War a Security Dilemma?" *Journal of Cold War Studies*, 3/1 (Winter 2001).

6. For reasons of space and focus this essay concentrates on the effect of nuclear weaponry upon the policies and attitudes of the two superpowers, leaving aside the important, but fundamentally different, question of nuclear proliferation to other states during the cold war.

7. For an important recent examination of this question, see Geoffrey Roberts, *Molotov: Stalin's Cold Warrior* (Washington, DC: Potomac Books, 2011).

8. See John Lewis Gaddis, *The Long Peace: Inquiries into the History of the Cold War* (Oxford: Oxford University Press, 1987), chapter 2.

9. The following section draws heavily on Campbell Craig and Sergey Radchenko, *The Atomic Bomb and the Origins of the Cold War* (New Haven, CT: Yale University Press, 2008). See also Gregg Herken *The Winning Weapon: The Atomic Bomb in the Cold War, 1945–1950*, 2nd ed. (New York: Knopf, 1988), and Wilson Miscamble, *The Most Controversial Decision: Truman, the Atomic Bombs, and the Defeat of Japan* (Cambridge: Cambridge University Press, 2011).

10. David Holloway, *Stalin and the Bomb: The Soviet Union and Atomic Energy, 1939–1956* (New Haven, CT: Yale University Press, 1994), chapter 15.

11. See Craig and Radchenko, *Atomic Bomb*, chapter 4, and Tsuyoshi Hasegawa, *Racing the Enemy: Stalin, Truman, and Surrender of Japan* (Cambridge, MA: Harvard University Press, 2005).

12. Many historians used to argue that the effect of espionage was minimal, but this view has been discredited. See Richard Rhodes, *Dark Sun: The Making of the Hydrogen Bomb* (New York: Simon and Schuster, 1996) and Katherine Sibley, *Red Spies in America: Stolen Secrets and the Dawn of the Cold War* (Lawrence, KS: University of Kansas Press, 2007). For a vivid critique of historians who downplayed or completely denied the existence of espionage for ideological reasons, see John Earl Haynes and Harvey Klehr, *In Denial: Historians, Communism, and Espionage* (New York: Encounter, 2005).

13. On this point, see Campbell Craig and Fredrik Logevall, *America's Cold War: The Politics of Insecurity* (Cambridge, MA: Harvard University Press, 2009), chapters 2–3.

14. Craig and Radchenko, *Atomic Bomb*, chapter 5.

15. De Gaulle is quoted in Robert Jervis, *The Illogic of American Nuclear Strategy* (Ithaca, NY: Cornell University Press, 1984). As Jervis and others have stressed, the development of the atomic bomb, while fantastically destructive, did not constitute a revolution, because large nations like the US and the USSR could survive an all-out attack of manned bombers and atomic weaponry. It was only with the advent of thermonuclear and intercontinental ballistic missile technology in the 1950s that all-out war became unsurvivable. For a powerful theoretical discussion, see Daniel Deudney, "Nuclear Weapons and the Waning of the Real-State," *Daedalus* 124 (Spring, 1995): 209–31.

16. See for example Henry Kissinger, *Nuclear Weapons and Foreign Policy* (New York: Harper and Brothers for the Council on Foreign Relations, 1957), and, for a more intellectually honest work, Herman Kahn, *On Thermonuclear War* (Princeton, NJ: Princeton University Press, 1960).

17. See McGeorge Bundy, *Danger and Survival: Choice's About the Bomb in the First Fifty Years* (New York: Random House, 1988); Craig and Logevall, *America's Cold War*; Timothy Naftali and Aleksandr Fursenko, *Khrushchev's Cold War* (New York: Norton, 2006).

18. On the crisis, see Timothy Naftali and Aleksandr Fursenko, *One Hell of a Gamble: Krushchev, Castro, and Kennedy, 1958–1964: The Secret History of the Cuban Missile Crisis* (New York: Norton, 1998); Michael Dobbs, *One Minute to Midnight* (London: Hutchinson, 2008).

19. Campbell Craig, *Destroying the Village: Eisenhower and Thermonuclear War* (New York: Columbia University Press, 1998); Robert Jervis, *The Meaning of the Nuclear Revolution* (New York: Cornell University Press, 1989).

20. Odd Arne Westad, *The Global Cold War: Third World Interventions and the Making of Our Times* (Cambridge: Cambridge University Press, 2006).

21. See Lien-Hang T. Nguyen, "Waging War on All Fronts: Nixon, Kissinger, and the Vietnam War, 1969–1972," in Fredrik Logevall and Andrew Preston, eds., *Nixon and the World: American Foreign Relations, 1969–1977* (New York: Oxford University Press, 2008).

22. See Fredrik Logevall, *Choosing War: The Last Chance for Peace and Escalation of War in Vietnam* (Berkeley, CA: University of California Press, 1999), and his introduction to *The Origins of the Vietnam War* (New York: Longman, 2001).

23. Kenneth Waltz, *Foreign Policy and Democratic Politics: The American and British Experience* (Boston, MA: Little, Brown, 1967).

24. Craig and Logevall, *America's Cold War*; Julian Zelizer, *Arsenal of Democracy: The Politics of National Security—From World War II to the War on Terrorism* (New York: Basic Books, 2010); Richard Rhodes, *Arsenals of Folly: The Making of the Nuclear Arms Race* (New York: Knopf, 2007).

25. Naftali and Fursenko, *Khrushchev's Cold War*; Christopher Preble, *John F. Kennedy and the Missile Gap* (DeKalb, IL: Northern Illinois Press, 2004).

26. Robert Jervis, *The Illogic of American Nuclear Strategy*, chapters 1–2.

27. See David Rosenberg, "The Origins of Overkill," *International Security* 7 (Spring 1983): 3–71.

28. Rhodes, *Arsenals of Folly*.

29. The effects of nuclear weapons also shaped the policies of other nuclear and even non-nuclear effect. Moreover, anti-nuclear movements in many states affected both international and domestic politics.

30. See Margot Light, *The Soviet Theory of International Relations* (Brighton, Sussex: Wheatsheaf, 1988), chapters 1–2; Karel Kara, "On the Marxist Theory of War and Peace," *Journal of Peace Research* 5 (March 1968): 1–27.

31. Holloway, *Stalin and the Bomb*; Naftali and Fursenko, *Khrushchev's Cold War*; Vladislav Zubok, *A Failed Empire: The Soviet Union in the Cold War from Stalin to Gorbachev* (Chapel Hill, NC: University of North Carolina Press, 2007).

32. Holloway, *Stalin and the Bomb*, 336–9.

33. Light, *Soviet Theory of International Relations*, chapter 3.

34. Westad, *Global Cold War*; Zubok, *Failed Empire*; James R. Millar, "The Little Deal: Brezhnev's Contribution to Acquisitive Socialism," *Slavic Review* 44/4 (Winter 1985): 694–706.

35. Archie Brown, *The Gorbachev Factor* (Oxford: Oxford University Press, 1997); Gaddis, *The Cold War: A New History*.

36. Daniel Deudney and G. John Ikenberry, "International Sources of Soviet Change," *International Security*, 16/3 (Winter 1991–2): 74–118.

## SELECT BIBLIOGRAPHY

Amis, Martin. *Einstein's Monsters*. New York: Vintage, 1990.

Bundy, McGeorge. *Danger and Survival: Choices about the Bomb in the First Fifty Years*. New York: Random House, 1988.

Craig, Campbell. *Destroying the Village: Eisenhower and Thermonuclear. War* New York: Columbia University Press, 1998.

Craig, Campbell and Fredrik Logevall. *America's Cold War: The Politics of Insecurity.* Cambridge, MA: Harvard University Press, 2009.

Craig, Campbell and Sergey Radchenko. *The Atomic Bomb and the Origins of the Cold War.* New Haven, CT: Yale University Press, 2008.

Holloway, David. *Stalin and the Bomb.* New Haven, CT: Yale University Press, 1994.

Jervis, Robert. *The Meaning of the Nuclear Revolution.* Ithaca, NY: Cornell University Press, 1989.

Naftali, Timothy, and Aleksandr Fursenko. *Khrushchev's Cold War.* New York: Norton, 2005.

Preble, Christopher. *Kennedy and the Missile Gap.* DeKalb, IL: Northern Illinois University Press, 2008.

Rhodes, Richard. *The Making of the Atomic Bomb.* New York: Simon and Schuster, 1986.

Rhodes, Richard. *Dark Sun: the Making of the Hydrogen Bomb.* New York: Simon and Schuster, 1995.

Rhodes, Richard. *Arsenals of Folly: the Making of the Nuclear Arms Race* New York: Knopf, 2008.

Scott, Len. *The Cuban Missile Crisis and the Threat of Nuclear War: Lessons from History.* London: Continuum, 2008.

# CHAPTER 22

························································································

# INTERNATIONAL
# INSTITUTIONS

························································································

## AMY L. SAYWARD[1]

INTERNATIONAL institutions during the cold war operated both within and outside of the traditional narrative of East-West superpower conflict. They provided arenas for states large and small to raise questions outside the bipolar power contest; they promoted their own agendas for global action that sometimes competed with those of the superpowers; they acted as mitigators in international conflicts and promoted international consensus; they were frequently more preoccupied with North-South issues (especially development) than East-West conflicts; they handled crises and challenges that no single nation could; and they worked with a broad spectrum of governmental and nongovernmental actors to accomplish their mission. Their histories are therefore integral to understanding the complexities of the cold war, even though their role in international society often preceded the advent of the cold war and has persisted and expanded since its end. Most significantly and primarily outside the traditional East-West drama of the cold war, international institutions have largely succeeded in changing the lens through which people and national governments view, think about, and interact with the world. At the center of the cold war universe of international institutions was the United Nations system, which seemingly touched upon all aspects of the international community. Building on the foundations of the League of Nations, the United Nations included six principal organs (the General Assembly, the Security Council, the Economic and Social Council, the Secretariat headed by the Secretary-General, the Trusteeship Council, and the International Court of Justice) and incorporated both new and previously established specialized agencies. From its beginning, it also served as a center for the work of nongovernmental organizations (NGOs) the world over. This chapter therefore primarily uses examples drawn from the international institutions that make up the United Nations system.

The United Nations and its specialized agencies built upon eighty years of international organizing. Starting in the mid-19th century, countries had worked together to coordinate issues that threatened burgeoning international trade and had grown too complex to be effectively handled by binational or even regional conventions. For example, to prevent the spread of epidemic disease without unduly hindering the flow of trade through restrictive quarantines, countries created the intergovernmental Conseil Supérieur de Santé de Constantinople (established 1849), Egypt's Sanitary, Maritime, and Quarantine Council (est. 1893), the Pan American Sanitary Bureau (PASB, est. 1907), and the Office International d'Hygiène Publique (OIHP, est. 1908). The International Meteorological Organization (est. 1873 and renamed the World Meteorological Organization in 1950) monitored and reported global weather phenomena and standardized national weather reporting. The International Telecommunications Union (ITU) similarly aimed to facilitate international trade and communications by standardizing equipment, creating uniform operating procedures, and establishing a common rate structure first for telegraphs (1865), then for telephony (1885), radio transmissions (1906), and television (1927). The origins of the Universal Postal Union were similar, as countries in 1875 decided to create an international framework to standardize postal rates and regulations and to replace an increasingly complex set of national and regional agreements. At the dawn of the new century, growing international trade led to the first (1899) Hague Peace Conference; the 26 states attending included European countries, the United States, Mexico, Japan, China, and Persia. The resulting Permanent Court of Arbitration established a standard set of rules and procedures to govern international arbitration and issued several landmark rulings in the development of international law, including the 1913 *Carthage* and *Manouba* cases regarding the seizure of vessels. Rationalizing international agricultural commodity markets by gathering and disseminating global agricultural statistics and technical studies was the initial charge of member governments to the International Institute of Agriculture (est. 1908).[2] The 19th and early 20th centuries confronted the governments of the world with issues that increasingly seemed outside their ability to control and led them to turn to international forms of organization—a trend that accelerated significantly with the catastrophe of the Great War.

In the wake of World War I, the international community created the League of Nations (whose health and cultural work scholars have largely overlooked), the International Labour Organization (also established by the Treaty of Versailles), and the Permanent Court of International Justice at the Hague (which grew out of Article 14 of the League Covenant). The League of Nations Council created a commission to combat the epidemics that spread through Eastern Europe (especially Poland) in the upheaval that followed the war. Building on this work, the League established its Health Organization (LNHO) in September 1923, as part of the League Secretariat. It created a truly global system of epidemiological surveillance by incorporating Asia and the Pacific with the work already being done by the PASB and OIHP, conducted educational initiatives, served as an international clearing house for medical information, standardized health and vital statistics, and developed international standards for biological products used in the diagnosis, treatment, and prevention of disease. In addition to preventing disease, the Health Section of the League of Nations worked toward establishing global standards in nutrition. Its 1935 study, which found pervasive malnutrition around the world, led to a three-day discussion in the League Assembly and the creation of a technical committee on nutrition that established a set of universally applicable minimum dietary standards. The League of Nations Mixed Committee on Nutrition then created national nutrition committees to report annually on their countries' efforts to improve nutrition both at home and in their colonies. Just as it was working to establish international standards in nutrition and the understanding of common human needs, the League also promoted international understanding and cross-cultural artistic and educational exchange through its International Institute for Intellectual Cooperation and International Educational Cinematographic Institute. However, the beginning of World War II cut this work short.[3]

Like the League, the International Labour Organization (ILO) pursued "the establishment of universal peace." The Treaty of Versailles explicitly linked such peace to social justice and the conditions of labor. To carry out this work, the ILO had a permanent staff (the International Labour Office) as well as a tripartite system of representatives, in which each member country sent a representative of its government, organized labor movement, and business community. In its first International Labour Conference in 1919, the ILO established six international labor conventions dealing with hours of work in industry, unemployment, maternity protection, minimum age for employment, and night work for women and young people in industry. Such conventions served as models for national legislation as well as global standards. Also working to craft international standards was the Permanent Court of International Justice, created by the First Assembly of the League of Nations in 1920. The court's judges were to "represent the main forms of civilization and the principal legal systems of the world." From its first sitting in 1922 until the advent of World War II, it issued rulings on 29 contentious international cases and 27 advisory opinions based on a fixed body of procedure and international law. During this period, it also became the declared jurisdictional body for several hundred treaties, conventions, and declarations, testifying to the legitimacy that the court had developed through its increasingly representative nature.[4] In pursuit of universal peace in the aftermath of World War I, the nations of the world experimented with a variety of organizational methods and focused on health, law, nutrition, education, and employment, which promised to root out the underlying causes of the war. This work laid the foundation for the United Nations, which followed an even more devastating global conflagration.

Indeed, the need to plan for a new international order following World War II seemed so urgent that several international conferences established new specialized agencies even before the creation of the United Nations Organization proper, including the 1943 Hot Spring Conference that established the Food and Agriculture Organization (FAO) and the 1944 Bretton Woods Conference that established the International Monetary Fund and the International Bank for Reconstruction and Development (more commonly called the World Bank). At the 1945 San Francisco Conference on International Organization, those considered to be outside the realm of the great powers worked assiduously to ensure that the functions that they had most appreciated from the League would have a prominent role in the new United Nations Organization. They lobbied successfully to have the Economic and Social Council (ECOSOC) elevated to the status of a principal organ of the United Nations and whole-heartedly supported the motion that led to the 1948 International Health Conference and the creation of the World Health Organization (WHO).[5] But much of the optimism generated by these wartime conferences quickly dissipated as the cold war took form.

In the early cold war, the United Nations—especially the General Assembly—became an arena of sorts where the superpowers and their allies squared off against one another, each trying to score points against its adversary and earn the allegiance of the global audience. In the 1950s, the UN Security Council first sent troops into an international conflict in support of the South Koreans under the leadership of US General Douglas MacArthur, but the Soviet Union used the brand new UN Human Rights Commission and later the General Assembly to highlight African-American civil rights organizations' claims of pervasive racial discrimination and violence in the United States. During the next decade, iconic images of cold war drama included Nikita Khrushchev's dramatic response (whether he actually banged his shoe or not) in October 1960 to a delegate from the Philippines referring to the peoples of Eastern Europe being "swallowed up ... by the Soviet Union," and US ambassador to the UN Adlai Stevenson's internationally televised Security Council presentation, which featured enlargements of American intelligence photos of missile silo sites in Cuba and his belligerent questioning of Soviet Ambassador Valerian Zorin. In the 1970s and 1980s, the United States complained about the "politicization" of several UN specialized agencies and withdrew from the International Labour Organization (November 1977–February 1980), the International Atomic Energy Agency (September 1982–February 1983), and the United Nations Educational, Scientific, and Cultural Organization (UNESCO, December 1984–October 2003). The Soviet Union during the Stalinist era had employed similar tactics—for example, never joining the International Monetary Fund and World Bank (though it had played an important role in the creation of both organizations) and withdrawing from the World Health Organization (February 1949–May 1957), taking the rest of the Soviet bloc with it.[6]

But not all of the great theater of the United Nations revolved around the bipolar agenda of the superpowers. Newly independent countries openly challenged the cold war paradigm in the United Nations as well as the persistence of imperialism, racial discrimination, and unequal terms of global trade. The Non-Aligned or Neutralist Movement emerged under the philosophical leadership of Indian Prime Minister Jawaharlal Nehru through a series of conferences starting in 1947 to facilitate communication and joint action between non-aligned nations. In December 1950, twelve states from Asia and Africa joined together to establish their own bloc within the United Nations, expressing a common stand that differed significantly from the superpower agenda then playing out on the Korean peninsula. These states worked cooperatively to pass a December 1952 General Assembly resolution condemning South African apartheid in solidarity with the Indian and African Defiance Campaign then taking place in that country. South Africa's Nationalist government believed that this UN action provided a major impetus to the nonviolent campaign and was a grave trespass on its domestic affairs. When a diverse set of twenty-nine Asian and African nations gathered in Bandung, Java, Indonesia, in April 1955, they shared a common vision (despite ideological differences and regional conflicts) of cooperative action to influence, if not control, the actions of the superpowers through the collective body of the United Nations and to reorient the priorities of that organization away from the superpower contest in order to better reflect their own concerns. At roughly the same time, advocates for and supporters of independence for the French colony of Algeria began actively to work through the United Nations to "internationalize" the question of Algerian independence. This gave the Non-Aligned Movement a platform from which to advocate for the decolonization of all areas. By 1961, when the French negotiated Algerian independence at Evian, the Non-Aligned Movement had largely succeeded in making decolonization, racial equality, and the development of these newly independent nations the focus of the UN agenda and a standard trope of international discourse. Subsequently, the UN General Assembly created a Special Committee against Apartheid in 1962, adopted an International Convention on the Suppression and Punishment of the Crime of Apartheid in 1973, and by globally publicizing and condemning such actions, played an important role in ending apartheid in South Africa before the end of the century. Indeed, the Non-Aligned Movement succeeded throughout the cold war in undermining the dominant paradigm of white supremacy across the globe.[7]

In many ways, the United Nations was most intensely involved in the Middle East during the cold war, where many countries seemed to have vital interests—whether related to oil, religion, national security, trade, refugee settlement, territorial boundaries, or all of the above. From the Mediterranean Sea to the Persian Gulf, the United Nations sought to resolve conflicts by engaging in diplomacy, suggesting international borders, passing Security Council Resolutions, dispatching peacekeeping forces, and aiding refugees. Not only did the United Nations help resolve the Iran-Iraq War (1980–8), but it also played a key role in resolving conflicts in Lebanon and between Iraq and Kuwait. In particular, the United Nations sought to address the region's most intractable problem, the Arab-Israeli dispute. When its initial plan to partition Britain's Palestinian mandate failed and war erupted in 1948, the United Nations issued ceasefire resolutions and dispatched a UN mediator, who sought to win Arab acquiescence to the existence of the state of Israel, Israeli repatriation of Palestinian refugees, and the internationalization of Jerusalem. After none of these measures worked, the UN Security Council in 1949 created the United Nations Relief and Works Agency for Palestine Refugees in the Near East (UNRWA) to care for more than half a million Palestinian refugees displaced by the conflict. More than a half-century later, UNRWA remains a temporary agency, although it has provided four generations of Palestinian refugees with education, health care, and other vital social services. Following the 1956 Arab-Israeli War, the United Nations helped to defuse an explosive situation by negotiating a ceasefire resolution and by deploying peacekeepers to serve as a buffer between Israel and Egypt. A decade later, the United Nations passed Security Council Resolution 242, which called on Israel to withdraw from Arab territories occupied in 1967 in exchange for peace and Arab recognition of the Jewish state. This formula, often known as "land for peace," was the foundation for subsequent diplomatic agreements, including the 1979 Camp David Accords between Israel and Egypt, along with the 1993 Oslo Accords between Israel and the Palestinian Liberation Organization. It is exceedingly difficult to judge whether the ongoing conflicts in the Middle East were part of the cold war or explosive regional conflicts that would have taken shape regardless of the structure of post-World War II international relations. Nonetheless, it is clear that the threat of superpower conflict made the stakes in the Middle East higher than in many other regions of the world and required an active presence by the United Nations, which could assume the mantle of impartial mediator.[8]

Those working for the United Nations embraced their identity as impartial, international civil servants and frequently promoted their own agendas, which sometimes differed significantly from those of the superpowers. The Food and Agriculture Organization's first Director-General, Sir John Boyd Orr of Scotland, was an independent-minded, outspoken, world-renowned nutritional scientist whose 1945 candidacy for the organization's highest office had been opposed by his national government. Orr, building on the earlier work of the League of Nations, believed that the majority of the world's people were suffering from malnutrition and that, in the face of the projected growth in global population, a gargantuan increase in agricultural production was needed. He believed this expansion would require a stabilization of commodity prices as well as modernization of Third World agriculture. Additionally, Orr sought to transform global distribution networks in order to help the world's poor break out of malnutrition and poverty, which in turn would buoy the global economy and serve as a stepping stone to a better world order. But his vision of an agriculturally centered economic development model quickly ran aground in the face of Anglo-American opposition. FAO Director-General B. R. Sen of India, who took the helm in 1956, built on Orr's vision of agricultural development with his Freedom From Hunger Campaign of 1959–63, which redirected the focus of agricultural development work toward rural and human development activities (with the active support of a wide range of NGOs). This focus differed significantly from US efforts at the same time to promote the "Green Revolution"—an effort to increase agricultural productivity by introducing high-yield strains of grains, more effective pesticides and fertilizers, and new management techniques that greatly favored commercial agriculture.[9]

A more dramatic example of UN civil servants' independent agency was Secretary-General Dag Hammarskjöld's initiative in the Congo crisis, which ultimately claimed his life. This second UN peacekeeping operation (known as ONUC), which involved some 20,000 troops and civilians, was the UN's most complex and protracted operation to date. UN actions contributed, against the odds, to holding the Congo together, decreasing the level of civilian hardship, and preventing another proxy war between the superpowers. Hammarskjöld's policy of strict political neutrality, however, ensured that at one time or another during the crisis all sides were discontented with the UN Secretary-General and his policy. Nevertheless, his push for intervention helped transform the image of the UN (from perceived agent of US policy to mediator) and make it a prominent forum for the forces of decolonization.[10]

Like Hammarskjöld, the leaders of the UN specialized agencies frequently sought to mitigate international conflicts (related and unrelated to the cold war) in order to accomplish their work, and also like Hammarskjöld, their efforts to maintain political "neutrality" often produced mixed results. To illustrate, the World Bank under President Eugene Black was most successful in negotiating an amicable sharing and development of the resources of the Indus River, divided after the 1947 partition of the subcontinent between India and Pakistan. The Indus Waters Treaty of 1960 removed a source of great friction between the two contentious neighbors and established a more stable basis for further economic development in both countries. However, the World Bank failed in its effort to negotiate a settlement of the Anglo-Iranian oil crisis that would allow Iranian and regional development efforts to move forward. The bank had hoped to serve as a neutral broker that would operate Iran's Abadan oil refinery and keep the resulting profits in escrow until an Anglo-Iranian agreement was reached. Yet its efforts quickly ran aground on the twin shoals of Iranian suspicion and British hopes for an International Court of Justice decision that would reverse Iranian nationalization. Black similarly sought and failed to promote Egyptian and Middle Eastern development by assembling a consortium of funders to construct the Aswan High Dam. Although the World Health Organization's Malaria Eradication Program (1955–69) was also ultimately a failure, it was singularly successful in facilitating cooperation between contentious neighboring countries, because the mosquitoes spreading malaria stubbornly refused to recognize even contested borders. Focused on this goal of malaria eradication, the WHO was able, for example, to unite the countries of southeastern Africa (Mozambique, Southern Rhodesia, Bechuanaland, Swaziland, and the Union of South Africa) in 1958 into a single regional malaria eradication program whose multinational coordination board established, supervised, and evaluated the coordinated DDT-spraying program. While UN development agencies sought to mitigate conflict in order to accomplish their work, several of the UN specialized agencies found their very mission in the midst of conflict.[11]

In 1950, the Office of the UN High Commissioner for Refugees (UNHCR) received a three-year mandate to complete the mission of the UN Relief and Rehabilitation Administration (UNRRA) in caring for World War II refugees in Europe. Throughout the cold war, UNHCR worked with many millions around the globe, including refugees from the 1956 Hungarian Revolution, the Algerian war for independence in the 1950s, Bangladesh's 1971 war for independence from Pakistan, the decades-long clashes between Greeks and Turks on Cyprus, the famines in Ethiopia in the 1980s, and civil wars in Namibia, Vietnam, Cambodia, Nicaragua, Mozambique, and Afghanistan.[12] These conflicts, like the earlier Palestinian refugee crisis, quickly overtaxed the hospitality and resources of neighboring countries, threatened to become humanitarian crises, and therefore required an international response.

The primary focus of the UN's cold war work was the promotion of development, which both superpowers used to further their own foreign policy agendas and which the newly independent countries eagerly sought. In pursuing the elusive goal of development, the United Nations created several agencies dedicated exclusively to this task, among them the World Bank (est. 1944), the UN Conference on Trade and Development (UNCTAD, est. 1964), the United Nations Development Program (UNDP, est. 1965), the International Fund for Agricultural Development (IFAD, est. 1974), and the United Nations Industrial Development Organization (UNIDO, est. 1975). With the creation of the United Nations Program for Technical Assistance in 1948, the UN had begun to move development to the very center of its work, a move that newly independent countries warmly welcomed and determinedly pushed forward in the coming decades, including the Development Decades of the 1960s and 1970s. These developing nations preferred multilateral aid through the UN and its specialized agencies to bilateral aid, which seemed to come with more "strings" attached and seemed to threaten their independence.[13]

Development was among the many problems that the UN tackled because no single country could deal with such problems independently, as they affected entire continents or even the world as a whole. Much of this work, though it is vital to the effective functioning of the world system, took and still takes place without much public awareness. The specialized agencies of the United Nations have been the source of important global standards and international norms. The International Telecommunications Union, the Universal Postal Union, the International Maritime Organization, the International Civilian Aviation Organization, and the World Health Organization all set international standards that allow mail, radio, television, medicines, vaccines, ships, and planes to cross international borders daily with few problems. In many ways, this technical work closely knits the nations of the world together.[14] More controversial have been the standards that the UN system has defined in terms of the rights of workers, children, women, and human beings in general. Even in these areas, however, the United Nations has succeeded in establishing global norms that have shaped international discourse and that have the potential to deter human rights abusers, to hold such people accountable for their actions, and to pave the way for future improvements.

The field of human rights has been one of the primary areas of contestation between the idea of universal standards and the rights of sovereign nations. While countries have frequently defined and defended their right to treat their own citizens in a way that sustains their national security, the United Nations and its organizations have repeatedly established international rights and norms for a variety of people. In the wake of the World War II Holocaust of the Jews, banning discrimination based on racial prejudice seemed particularly imperative and was written into Article 55c of the United Nations Charter, embodied in ECOSOC's Commission on Human Rights, and more clearly defined by the 1948 Universal Declaration of Human Rights. Subsequently, the ILO and UNESCO similarly passed conventions banning racial discrimination in employment (1958) and education (1960) respectively. By 1985, the UN's 1969 International Convention on the Elimination of All Forms of Racial Discrimination had more countries adhering to it than any other human rights instrument. However, the fact that most countries have condemned racial discrimination in the international arena has not prevented such discrimination within national boundaries; the postwar period has witnessed a number of racially motivated genocides. Additionally, UN human rights work during the cold war often became a battleground between the two superpowers: the Americans emphasized individual civil and political rights and therefore condemned the communist nations for their lack of free elections and freedom of speech, press, assembly, and religion; while the Soviet Union emphasized collective economic, social, and cultural rights, condemned capitalist nations for their failure to guarantee employment, and especially criticized the US for its treatment of African Americans during the Jim Crow era.[15]

Eventually, the UN framework of human rights became a platform for the assertion of ethnic rights, prisoner rights, women's rights, and indigenous rights as categories of human rights. Although the guaranteeing of such rights varies from country to country even now, the establishment of a universal standard has served as a rallying point for these groups and catalyzed the creation and work of international NGOs (such as Amnesty International). By contrasting international standards with governmental practices, NGOs have often been able to gain global media attention and public support on a range of human rights issues, including racially motivated genocidal practices and the treatment of political prisoners, women, and indigenous and tribal peoples. The UN Commission on the Status of Women, which operates under ECOSOC and whose creation was opposed by both the United States and the United Kingdom, drafted the Convention on the Political Rights of Women (accepted by the General Assembly in 1952), worked with the ILO on crafting conventions on equal pay and employment discrimination, and organized the 1975 Mexico City conference. Although that conference exposed the different priorities of First World and Third World women (with the former focusing on legal equality while the latter focused on economic development), it did help to identify the global problems facing women and served as the launching point for the International Decade of Women. The Mexico City conference also mobilized the General Assembly to adopt the Convention on the Elimination of All Forms of Discrimination against Women in 1979 and to launch a series of international conferences on women's global issues (Copenhagen 1980, Nairobi 1985, Beijing 1995). Similarly, the United Nations hosted an International NGO Conference on Discrimination against Indigenous Populations in the Americas in 1977 in recognition of the developing Fourth World Movement that grew out of grassroots indigenous movements. Subsequently, this network helped coordinate the formulation and communication of the needs and demands of indigenous peoples throughout the world. Formal milestones in this movement have included "The International Year of the World's Indigenous People" (1993) and creation of a permanent forum on indigenous issues within ECOSOC in May 2002.[16]

Another area in which claims of national sovereignty have collided with the needs of the global community is the environment. As each country sought to advance its own economic standing through trade and development, the question arose, what are the rights of neighboring countries that share migratory animals, air, water, and soil? International debates about environmental concerns began with efforts to protect wildlife in the early 20th century and resulted in the 1916 Treaty for the Protection of Migratory Birds between Canada and the United States, the 1933 Convention relative to the Preservation of Flora and Fauna in their Natural State (which focused specifically on Africa), and a series of postwar conventions related to oceanic fishing that included the creation of the International Whaling Commission in 1946. Increased concern over pollutants (especially oil), realization that airborne pollutants were causing acid rain and depleting the ozone layer, and concern that deforestation was affecting global climate change all accelerated international environmental discussions, resulting in the 1969 UN General Assembly Resolution that convened the first UN Conference on the Human Environment. The resolution instructed the participants of the June 1972 Stockholm Conference to provide "a framework for comprehensive consideration within the United Nations of the problems of the human environment." The objective was "to focus the attention of Governments and public opinion on the importance and urgency of this question and also to identify those aspects of it that can only or best be solved through international co-operation and agreement." Conference delegates discussed the future of the human race within the context of its global environment under the motto "Only One Earth." Although the entire Soviet bloc abstained from participation, 113 governments were represented. They drafted a Declaration on the Human Environment that created the UN Environment Program (UNEP) as a special body within the UN Secretariat and established 26 "Principles" that helped to focus international attention on key environmental issues. Headquartered in Nairobi, Kenya, UNEP was able to sidestep many prevailing cold war issues and focus on key North-South development issues. Its conventions on marine pollution (1973), international trade in endangered species (1975), and long-range air pollution (1979) helped to establish the principle that, although there is a recognized right of sovereign nations to exploit their natural resources, there is also an attendant responsibility to ensure that no significant damage is suffered by others in the community of nations.[17]

When the UN convened the 1972 Stockholm Conference on the Human Environment, international environmental NGOs organized a parallel forum that attracted some 400 NGO representatives, facilitated their meetings with the governmental representatives attending the conference, provided opportunities for demonstrations, and created a global platform for these NGOs to promote their issues alongside and in conjunction with the UN representatives. This arrangement showed the growing political clout of non-governmental organizations and set a precedent for future UN conferences. At the 1975 UN Conference on the Status of Women in Mexico City, an unofficial forum of NGOs, called the Tribune, garnered as much international media attention as the main conference. The Tribune pushed for a more progressive feminist agenda and helped establish an international network of feminists. Leading up to the 1985 Nairobi Conference, NGOs with consultative status in ECOSOC participated in the formulation of the "Forward Looking Strategy for the Advancement of Women to the Year 2000."[18]

In many ways the United Nations and international NGOs developed a thriving symbiotic relationship during the cold war that again complicates a state-focused view of this period. Under the guidance of Article 71 of the UN Charter, the Economic and Social Council granted forty-one NGOs formal consultative status in 1946. Subsequently, consultative status was divided into general and special consultative status, recognizing that some NGOs are interested and involved in most of ECOSOC's areas of work, while others are more specialized. Once accorded such status, NGO representatives gained access to UN meetings, information, and conferences as well as the right to add items to ECOSOC's agenda.[19] The UN actively recruited and officially recognized NGOs, because it needed their resources to carry out its ambitious mission, their voices to enrich a conversation dominated by official government positions, and their prodding to move the organization forward and make it more responsive to the needs of the world's people. In turn, the NGOs received an international bully pulpit, a locus for the development of international networks of activists, the legitimacy that came with official UN recognition, and some ability to shape international policies.[20]

NGOs not only reflected the interests of international actors outside and occasionally independent of the nation-state but they also exposed both different viewpoints within single governments and agreements across state and even cold war divides. When FAO Director-General Orr floated his World Food Board proposal in 1946, the State Department was vociferously opposed, but the US Department of Agriculture saw great merit in the idea. International organizations often dealt with federal bureaucrats specializing in agriculture, the postal service, telecommunications, international shipping, and public health among other fields, and these became areas in which the superpowers could and did cooperate. The World Health Organization's global Smallpox Eradication Program, which was launched in January 1967 and celebrated eradication in 1980, brought the two superpowers together to cooperate in a campaign whose primary soldiers were a global "epistemic community" of epidemiologists and health officials. Indeed, the founders of the World Health Organization initially created an advisory executive board whose medical experts were to act on their professional standards rather than their national allegiances. However, only the International Labour Organization has been able to maintain an organizational structure in which governments, labor, and business are each independently represented.[21]

The people who worked for and with these international organizations began to see the world in a different way. The health and cultural work of the League of Nations had begun to define people in human terms—their caloric and nutritional needs, their ability to create valuable artistic and intellectual products—that transcended national borders and racial categories. The League of Nations effectively integrated Asian, Latin American, and African countries as equal members, and Asians, Africans, and Latin Americans during the interwar period became increasingly active in international organizations of all sorts. This reflected larger intellectual trends of the 20th century that used social science to break down the immovable dichotomy between "savagery" and "civilization." Although Western nations had used this dichotomy extensively in the 19th century to rationalize and legitimate imperialism, it had also accorded a different status, especially in international law, to those nations, such as Japan and Thailand, which adopted some of the accepted norms of "civilization." With the advent of the 20th century, such countries were increasingly invited to participate in international conferences and organizations (such as the 1899 Hague Peace Conference, the League of Nations, and the Permanent Court of International Justice). Additionally, the horrors of the

Holocaust exposed the fallacy of Western "civilization," and the decolonization and civil rights movements of the postwar era helped to establish a more universal discourse for the second half of the 20th century by undermining the dominant paradigm of the previous century that had divided nations into "civilized" and "savage" along racial lines. "Development"—the idea that all countries defined as poor and traditional could become affluent and modern by following a historically derived model—embodied these new ideas and sought to make them a reality.[22] The international civil servants charged with implementing UN development projects shared this liberal ideology of development, seeing only global problems and believing that with the help of expertise and resources that all could enjoy the fruits of modern society, including good health, gainful employment, quality education, equality, and access to the global consumer economy.[23]

Indeed, the preamble to the UN Charter began "We the peoples of the United Nations" and focused on the fundamental purposes of the new organization: "to reaffirm faith in fundamental human rights, in the dignity and worth of the human person, in the equal rights of men and women and of nations large and small." In pursuit of these goals, the peoples of the United Nations committed themselves "to practice tolerance and live together in peace with one another as good neighbours...and to employ international machinery for the promotion of the economic and social advancement of all peoples." In other words, the United Nations established a new standard and goal for the international community. That it has not always succeeded in attaining those standards and goals has made it the rightful target for criticism or even charges of hypocrisy, but this should not obscure the fact that such standards and expectations were largely absent before the United Nations and have transformed the expectations of the peoples of the world.

During the cold war, something began to develop that sociologists have variously called "world society" and "world culture," which political scientists have termed "international society" or "functionalist epistemic communities," and which some historians have called a "global community" or just plain "globalization." Regardless of its nomenclature, the United Nations system has helped to craft an era of global expectations and conventions that do not fit neatly into the still-dominant paradigm of nation-states. Indeed, during the cold war the superpowers expended a great deal of diplomatic energy on avoiding criticism in the United Nations and on criticizing the other side by utilizing the new UN standards on human rights and its efforts to promote development throughout the Third World. Despite the centrality of the UN in the cold war narrative, the end of the cold war brought no noticeable diminution of the United Nations' global work and role. Indeed, the need for economic development in the former Soviet bloc, the environmental dangers created by the nuclear program of the USSR, and the ethnic and national conflicts between and within the former Soviet Republics seem to indicate, if anything, a greater need for an international organization that can address these additional challenges.[24] As long as there continue to be large numbers of refugees from conflicts like those in Kosovo, East Timor, and Rwanda; as long as human rights, indigenous rights, and women's rights remain issues that transcend national boundaries; as long as global epidemics threaten the world's peoples; as long as rising population and unsustainable natural-resource use seem to threaten the environment and climate of the globe; as long as an earthquake in one part of the world threatens another with a catastrophic tsunami; as long as the trafficking of human beings and narcotic drugs crosses national boundaries; and as long as the countries of the world trade and fight with one another, it seems likely that international institutions will continue to be vital to the life of the planet and its peoples.[25]

## NOTES

1. The author thanks Sean Foley, Rowly Brucken, Petra Goedde, and Richard Immerman for their comments on earlier drafts of this chapter.
2. Norman Howard-Jones, *The Scientific Background of the International Sanitary Conferences, 1851–1938* (Geneva: World Health Organization, 1975); Morley K. Thomas and W. J. Maunder, *Sixty-Five Years of International Climatology: The History of the WMO Commission for Climatology, 1929–1993* (Downsview, Ontario: Environment Canada, 1993); Moussibahou Mazou and Sribhumi Sukhanetr, *The Universal Postal Union: Past, Present and Future* (Paris: Maisonneuve & Larose, 2004); Luciano Tosi, *Alle Origini della FAO: Le relazioni tra l'Instituto Internazionale di Agricoltura e la Società delle Nazioni* (Milan: Franco Angeli, 1989); Michla Pomerance, *The Advisory Function of the International Court in the League and UN Eras* (Baltimore, MD: Johns Hopkins University Press, 1973); International Telecommunication Union, *International Telecommunication Union: Celebrating 130 Years, 1865–1995* (London: International Systems and Communications, 1998); Robert N. Wells Jr., ed., *Peace by Pieces—United Nations Agencies and their Roles: A Reader and Selective Bibliography* (Metuchen, NJ: Scarecrow Press, 1991).
3. Paul Weindling, ed., *International Health Organisations and Movements, 1918–1939* (Cambridge: Cambridge University Press, 1995); Michael Worboys, "The Discovery of Colonial Malnutrition between the Wars," in David Arnold, ed., *Imperial Medicine and Indigenous Societies* (Manchester: Manchester University Press, 1988), 208–23; F. P. Walters, *A History of the League of Nations*, 2 vols. (London: Oxford University Press, 1952); Norman Howard-Jones, *International Public Health between the Two Worlds Wars: The Organizational Problems* (Geneva: World Health Organization, 1978); Jean-Jacques Renoliet, *L'UNESCO Oubliée: La Société des Nations et la Coopération Intellectuelle, 1919–1946* (Paris: Publications de la Sorbonne, 1999); League of Nations, *International Institute of Intellectual Co-operation* (Paris: League of Nations, 1933).
4. Antony Alcock, *History of the International Labor Organization* (Los Angeles, CA: Octagon Books, 1971); Victor Yves Ghebali, *The International Labour Organisation: A Case Study on the Evolution of U.N. Specialised Agencies* (Dordrecht, Netherlands: Martinus Nijhoff, 1989).
5. Georg Schild, *Bretton Woods and Dumbarton Oaks: American Economic and Political Postwar Planning in the Summer of 1944* (New York: St. Martin's, 1995); Walter R. Sharp, *The United Nations Economic and Social Council* (New York: Columbia University Press, 1969).
6. Carol Anderson, *Eyes Off the Prize: The United Nations and the African American Struggle for Human Rights, 1944–1945* (Cambridge: Cambridge University Press, 2003); Caroline Pruden, *Conditional Partners: Eisenhower, the United Nations, and the Search for a Permanent Peace* (Baton Rouge, LA: Louisiana State University Press, 1998); David L. Bosco, *Five*

*to Rule Them All: The UN Security Council and the Making of the Modern World* (Oxford: Oxford University Press, 2009); Mark F. Imber, *The USA, ILO, UNESCO and IAEA: Politicization and Withdrawal in the Specialized Agencies* (New York: St. Martin's Press, 1989); John Farley, *Brock Chisholm, the World Health Organization, and the Cold War* (Vancouver: University of British Columbia Press, 2008).

7. Thomas Borstelmann, *Apartheid's Reluctant Uncle: The United States and Southern Africa in the Early Cold War* (New York: Oxford University Press, 1993); Matthew Connelly, *A Diplomatic Revolution: Algeria's Fight for Independence and the Origins of the Post-Cold War Era* (Oxford: Oxford University Press, 2002); Kweku Ampiah, *The Political and Moral Imperatives of the Bandung Conference of 1955: The Reactions of the US, UK and Japan* (Kent Global Oriental, 2007).

8. Anthony Curnow, *Palestinian Refugees: The Role of UNRWA in Fulfilling an International Responsibility for their Welfare* (Christchurch, New Zealand: Australiasian Middle East Studies Association, 1987); Edward H. Buehrig, *The UN and the Palestinian Refugees: A Study in Nonterritorial Administration* (Bloomington, IN: Indiana University Press, 1971); Peter L. Hahn, *Crisis and Crossfire: The United States and the Middle East since 1945* (Washington, DC: Potomac Books, 2005).

9. Nick Cullather, "Miracles of Modernization: The Green Revolution and the Apotheosis of Technology," *Diplomatic History* 28 (April 2004): 227–54; Sergio Marchisio and Antonietta di Blase, *The Food and Agriculture Organization (FAO)* (Dordrecht, Netherlands: M. Nijhoff, 1991).

10. William J. Durch, ed., *The Evolution of UN Peacekeeping: Case Studies and Comparative Analysis* (New York: St. Martin's Press, 1993); Odd Arne Westad, *The Global Cold War: Third World Interventions and the Making of Our Times* (Cambridge: Cambridge University Press, 2007).

11. Edward S. Mason and Robert E. Asher, *The World Bank since Bretton Woods: The Origins, Policies, Operations, and Impact of The International Bank for Reconstruction and Development and the Other Members of the World Bank Group* (Washington, DC: Brookings Institution, 1973); Arthur Eyffinger and Arthur Witteveen, *The International Court of Justice, 1946–1996* (The Hague: Kluwer Law International, 1996); Javed Siddiqi, *World Health and World Politics: The World Health Organization and the UN System* (Columbia: University of South Carolina Press, 1995); Amy L. S. Staples, *The Birth of Development: How the World Bank, Food and Agriculture Organization, and World Health Organization Changed the World, 1945–1965* (Kent, OH: Kent State University Press, 2006).

12. Gil Loescher, *The UNHCR and World Politics: A Perilous Path* (Oxford: Oxford University Press, 2001); Mark Cutts, *The State of the World's Refugees, 2000: Fifty Years of Humanitarian Action* (New York: Oxford University Press, 2000).

13. Craig N. Murphy, *The United Nations Development Programme: A Better Way?* (Cambridge: Cambridge University Press, 2006); Shigehisa Kasahara, Charles Gore, and Rubens Ricupero, *Beyond Conventional Wisdom in Development Policy: An Intellectual History of UNCTAD, 1964–2004* (New York and Geneva: United Nations, 2004); Digambar Bhouraskar, *United Nations Development Aid: A Study in History and Politics* (New Delhi: Academic Foundation, 2007).

14. Samir Mankabady, *The International Maritime Organisation* (London: Croom Helm, 1984); Hendrik Gerrit Cannegieter, *The History of the International Meteorological Organization, 1872–1951* (Offenbach: Selbstverlag des Deutschen Wetterdienstes, 1963); David MacKenzie, *ICAO: A History of the International Civil Aviation Organization* (Toronto: University of

Toronto Press, 2009); James Schwoch, *Global TV: New Media and the Cold War, 1946–69* (Urbana, IL: University of Illinois Press, 2008); Fred Brown, *A Celebration of 50 Years of Progress in Biological Standardization and Control at WHO* (Basel and New York: Karger, 1999).

15. In addition to the contribution by Barbara Keys and Roland Burke to this *Handbook*, see Robert F. Drinan, *The Mobilization of Shame: A World View of Human Rights* (New Haven, CT: Yale University Press, 2001); Rowland Brucken, "A Most Uncertain Crusade: The United States, the United Nations, and Human Rights, 1941–1954," dissertation, Ohio State University, 1999; Jean-Marc Coicaud, Michael W. Doyle, and Anne-Marie Gardner, *The Globalization of Human Rights* (New York: United Nations University Press, 2003).

16. Elissavet Stamatopoulou, "Women's Rights and the United Nations," in Julie Peters and Andrea Wolper, eds., *Women's Rights Human Rights: International Feminist Perspectives* (New York and London: Routledge, 1995), 36–48; Hilkka Pietilä and Jeanne Vickers, *Making Women Matter: The Role of the United Nations* (London: Zed, 1990); George Manuel, *The Fourth World: An Indian Reality* (New York: Free Press, 1974); S. James Anaya, *Indigenous Peoples in International Law*, 2nd ed. (Oxford: Oxford University Press, 2004); Bice Maiguashca, "The Transnational Indigenous Movement in a Changing World Order," in Yoshikazu Sakamoto, ed., *Global Transformation: Challenges to the State System* (Tokyo: United Nations University Press, 1994), 356–82.

17. Richard Tucker's essay in this volume; Mostaffa Kamal Tolba and Iwona Rummel-Bulska, *Global Environmental Diplomacy: Negotiating Environmental Agreements for the World, 1973–1992* (Cambridge, MA: MIT Press, 1998); Kurkpatrick Dorsey, *The Dawn of Conservation Diplomacy: US-Canadian Wildlife Protection Treaties in the Progressive Era* (Seattle, WA: University of Washington Press, 1998); Kurk Dorsey, "International Environmental Issues," in Robert D. Schulzinger, ed., *A Companion to American Foreign Relations* (Malden, MA: Blackwell, 2006), 31–47.

18. Jutta M. Joachim, *Agenda-Setting, the UN, and NGOs: Gender Violence and Reproductive Rights* (Washington, DC: Georgetown University Press, 2007); Peter Willetts, ed., *"The Conscience of the World": The Influence of Non-Governmental Organisations in the UN System* (Washington, DC: Brookings Institution, 1996).

19. The number of NGOs in consultative status with ECOSOC in 1992 was more than 700 and in 2009 stood at more than 3,000.

20. Michele Merrill Betsill and Elisabeth Corell, *NGO Diplomacy: The Influence of Nongovernmental Organizations in International Environmental Negotiations* (Cambridge, MA: MIT Press, 2008); John Boli and George M. Thomas, eds., *Constructing World Culture: International Nongovernmental Organizations since 1875* (Stanford, CA: Stanford University Press, 1999); Volker Heins, *Nongovernmental Organizations in International Society: Struggles over Recognition* (New York: Palgrave Macmillan, 2008).

21. Erez Manela, "A Pox on Your Narrative: Writing Disease Control into Cold War History," *Diplomatic History* 34 (April 2010): 299–323; R. E. Riggs, "FAO and the USDA: Implications for Functionalist Learning," *World Politics Quarterly* 33 (September 1980): 314–29; Ernst B. Haas, M. P. Williams, and D. Babai, *Scientists and World Order: The Uses of Technical Knowledge in International Organizations* (Berkeley, CA: University of California Press, 1978).

22. Although historians and critics of development have rightly pointed out that the idea of "development" still enshrined the Western experience and labeled "others" as "less than," such critiques ignore the ways in which this idea was an improvement over previous

hierarchical and deterministic views that identified most people of color as "inferior" and destined to remain in such a state due to immutable, racial realities. Additionally, it ignores the fervor with which new nations sought such development during the early cold war period.

23. Carol C. Chin, *Modernity and National Identity in the United States and East Asia, 1895–1919* (Kent, OH: Kent State University Press, 2010); Nick Cullather, *The Hungry World: America's Cold War Battle against Poverty in Asia* (Cambridge, MA: Harvard University Press, 2010); Leila J. Rupp, *Worlds of Women: The Making of an International Women's Movement* (Princeton, NJ: Princeton University Press, 1997); Bernard Semmel, *The Liberal Ideal and the Demons of Empire: Theories of Imperialism from Adam Smith to Lenin* (Baltimore, MD: Johns Hopkins University Press, 1993); Robert A. Packenham, *Liberal America and the Third World: Political Development Ideas in Foreign Aid and Social Science* (Princeton, NJ: Princeton University Press, 1973); Robert Latham, *The Liberal Moment: Modernity, Security, and the Making of Postwar International Order* (New York: Columbia University Press, 1997); Michael E. Latham, *The Right Kind of Revolution: Modernization, Development, and US Foreign Policy from the Cold War to the Present* (Ithaca, NY: Cornell University Press, 2011); David Ekbladh, *The Great American Mission: Modernization and the Construction of an American World* Order (Princeton, NJ: Princeton University Press, 2010); David C. Engerman, Nils Gilman, Mark H. Haefele, and Michael E. Latham, eds., *Staging Growth: Modernization, Development, and the Global Cold War* (Amherst and Boston: University of Massachusetts Press, 2003); Garrit W. Gong, *The Standard of "Civilization" in International Society* (Oxford: Oxford University Press, 1984); Hedley Bull and Adam Watson, eds., *The Expansion of International Society* (Oxford: Clarendon, 1984); Arturo Escobar, *Encountering Development: The Making and Unmaking of the Third World* (Princeton, NJ: Princeton University Press, 1995); Nils Gilman, *Mandarins of the Future: Modernization Theory in Cold War America* (Baltimore, MD: Johns Hopkins University Press, 2003); Frederick Cooper and Randall Packard, eds., *International Development and the Social Sciences: Essays on the History and Politics of Knowledge* (Berkeley, CA: University of California Press, 1997).

24. Hyung-Gu Lynn's essay in this volume; Leslie Sklair, *Sociology of the Global System*, 2nd ed. (Baltimore, MD: Johns Hopkins University Press, 1995); John W. Burton, *World Society* (Cambridge: Cambridge University Press, 1972); Boli and Thomas, *Constructing World Culture*; Akira Iriye, *Global Community: The Role of International Organizations in the Making of the Contemporary World* (Berkeley, CA: University of California Press, 2002); Alfred E. Eckes Jr. and Thomas W. Zeiler, *Globalization and the American Century* (Cambridge: Cambridge University Press, 2003).

25. National Intelligence Council, "Global Trends 2025: The National Intelligence Council's 2025 Project," <http://www.dni.gov/nic/NIC_2025_project.html>, predicts a revolution in the entire international system that has developed since 1945 that will be marked by an unprecedented transfer of wealth from West to East, unprecedented economic and population growth, and an increased potential for conflict.

## Select Bibliography

Diehl, Paul F. *The Politics of Global Governance: International Organizations in an Interdependent World*. Boulder, CO: Lynne Rienner, 1997.

Iriye, Akira. *Cultural Internationalism and World Order*. Baltimore, MD: Johns Hopkins University Press, 1997.

Jolly, Richard, Louis Emmerij, and Thomas G. Weiss. *UN Ideas that Changed the World*. Bloomington, IN: Indiana University Press for the UN Intellectual History Project, 2009.

Kennedy, Paul. *The Parliament of Man: The Past, Present, and Future of the United Nations*. New York: Random House, 2006.

Luard, Evan. *International Agencies: The Emerging Framework of Interdependence*. London: Macmillan, 1977.

Ostrower, Gary B. *The United Nations and the United States*. New York: Twayne, 1998.

Simons, Geoff. *The United Nations: A Chronology of Conflict*. New York: St. Martin's Press, 1994.

Zweifel, Thomas D. *International Organizations and Democracy: Accountability, Politics, and Power*. Boulder, CO: Lynne Rienner, 2006.

# CHAPTER 23

## TRADE, AID, AND ECONOMIC WARFARE

### ROBERT MARK SPAULDING

FOR both sides in the cold war, trade, aid, and economic warfare were important global activities conducted with allies inside each bloc, with clients in the non-aligned world, and with rivals belonging to the other bloc. Trade, aid, and economic warfare were consequential arenas of economic competition between communist and capitalist economies and governments. The difficulty of the Soviet bloc economy in these fields is an indispensable component in any serious account of the ultimate collapse of Soviet power and the cold war's end.

The terms trade, aid, and economic warfare were already employed during the initial decades of the cold war and have been widely used by scholars since that time. Economic warfare during the cold war has been subjected to penetrating scholarly debate, and we now have a much better understanding of most of the important activities in this area, even if disagreements on salient points remain. In contrast, work on understanding the growth of developmental aid and its role in the evolving political economy of the cold war is just beginning. Between those two points lies our understanding of trade itself. The enormity of the subject leaves much work to be done connecting the cold war to shifting patterns of global trade and in tying those patterns to the lived experiences of many millions of people around the world. Subsequent scholarship might also provide greater insight into how some cold war patterns of trade transcended the cold war framework by contributing to a new wave of economic globalization in the late 20th century.

These three activities are often tightly intertwined. Subsidized trade with client states was a form of aid, but embargoed trade between the blocs became a type of economic warfare; foreign aid programs were a form of East-West competition that was also seen as a variety of economic warfare. Similarly, all these economic activities went hand-in-hand with geopolitical and cultural strategies of competition between rival powers. Communist and capitalist governments often deployed trade, aid, and economic warfare to reinforce other incentives and dissuasions designed to influence foreign behaviors. Indeed, many states and governments found positive and negative trade manipulations to be among the most useful tools of statecraft throughout the cold war.

Exploration of each of these topics centers on the following three analytic tasks. First, we can assess how these economic activities shaped the cold war, highlighting how foreign economic policies influenced global strategies and foreign relations on both sides of the East-West divide. We can also indicate how such assessments might move beyond macroeconomics and high politics to describe the impact of global movements of food, consumer goods, equipment, and energy supplies on everyday lives. A second, closely related, task is to evaluate the importance of each of these activities within larger strategies of cold war competition. As the cold war evolved into a rough military stalemate, economic competition moved to the fore; yet economic activities remained only single elements in complex equations about foreign relations. In broad strokes we can identify compromises, sacrifices, and trade-offs made by several parties to keep policies on trade, aid, and economic warfare compatible with other foreign policy goals. A third, larger, task is connecting cold war developments in these three areas to the more expansive economic history of the modern world. Some cold war economic policies remained confined to the era of the cold war proper, but other practices and structures that originated during the cold war period survived past 1989 and continue as important pieces of global regimes. Distinguishing between transient, period-specific practices and more enduring structures that persisted after the end of the cold war is a crucial step in refining our understanding of the long-term historical significance of the cold war and its legacy for the development of the global political economy.

# TRADE

Merchandise trade flows, and the structures and policies that determined them, shaped the cold war in four important ways. First, altered trade flows and new international trade organizations helped define and solidify the rival politico-economic blocs. Second, trade helped determine levels of prosperity and economic performance within the two competing portions of the global economy as intra-bloc trade produced sharply divergent welfare gains within capitalist and communist systems. Third, growing trade between East and West became the primary form of economic interaction between the two systems, which gave East-West trade a dual economic-political function as both a vehicle for moving billions of dollars in merchandise around the globe and as a barometer of political relations between the two systems. Fourth, as the primary form of economic exchange between communist and capitalist economies, trade also became the primary forum for policies of economic warfare.

Trade flows were important enough to influence non-economic portions of the East-West relationship, but Eastern and Western goals in trade were never so significant that either side pursued its trade agendas without internal and external compromises. Finally, we can connect a number of trade patterns and trade structures that emerged during the cold war to larger, more enduring trends in the global economy.

In the early years of the cold war, trade and international trade organizations precipitated the division of the world economy into capitalist and communist spheres and helped consolidate those spheres into economic blocs with distinct patterns and mechanisms of trade. In the West, GATT (General Agreement on Tariffs and Trade) emerged in 1947 as an important international institution that facilitated the great rise in trade in the reconstructed capitalist order.[1] GATT also became "a forum in which to wage the cold war," and Francine McKenzie has recently shown how Western political and economic calculations shaped the development of GATT in its first decade as the trade institution became "a pillar of the 'free world.'"[2] In Western Europe the Committee of European Economic Cooperation, which coordinated Marshall Plan aid beginning in 1947, also originated important trade liberalizing practices. The European Coal and Steel Community (1951), and the European Economic Community (1957) expanded these practices, facilitated by the terms of the European Payments Union (1950).

Deliberate Soviet choices created a communist trade and payments system separated from the larger and more successful liberal capitalist order. Redirected trade flows helped define the communist sphere. With fateful long-term consequences, Stalin chose not to participate in the structures that reconstructed the international and European economies: the International Monetary Fund and the World Bank (1944), the Marshall Plan (1947), and GATT (1948). Further, Soviet leadership insisted that Soviet satellites in Eastern Europe make parallel decisions both to impose state control over foreign trade and to preclude participation in global structures.[3] In Asia, the People's Republic of China (PRC) used trade and aid agreements with the Soviet Union in early 1950 to create a communist economic alliance rather than move toward cooperation with the capitalist world.[4]

Stalin redirected East European trade toward the Soviet Union with bilateral trade and economic agreements, reinforcing these ties in 1949 with the multilateral Council for Mutual Economic Assistance (CMEA) which included the Soviet Union and its East European satellites (the EE Six).[5] Trade among member states remained on a bilateral basis until Nikita Khrushchev attempted to use the CMEA for genuine multilateral trade coordination among members. However, Stalin's decisions to maintain limited contact with the global economy were not fundamentally reversed.

Within the capitalist economy, rapid increases in trade, foreign investment, personal contacts, and technology transfers were important factors in achieving unprecedented Western prosperity during the cold war era.[6] In the East, restricted external contact and unwieldy practices prevented intra-bloc trade from producing continuing welfare benefits for its members.[7] Trade structures and patterns in the planned economies greatly reduced contact, trade, and technology transfer from the West, which exacerbated the Soviet system's own structural failures in developing and deploying technical innovations that could boost productivity.

The burdens of self-contained Soviet bloc trade profoundly affected both Soviet-East European relations and external relations between Soviet bloc states and the global economy. Randall Stone shows that, by sending overpriced machinery and equipment to the Soviet Union in exchange for energy and raw materials, "the European members of the CMEA were receiving a substantial subsidy by the late 1950s," transferred from the Soviet Union through intra-bloc trade.[8] Over the following decades global trends increased the size of the Soviet subsidy: commodity prices rose, increasing the Soviets' opportunity costs in sending energy supplies to Eastern Europe rather than into the world market for higher prices in hard currencies; meanwhile the quality gap widened between East European machinery and similar Western products, reducing the value of East European goods sent to the Soviet Union. In analyses of Soviet bloc trade, both Charles Maier and Philip Hanson discuss Soviet "subsidies" and "transfers."[9] Repeated Soviet attempts to create a more equitable distribution of trade benefits with programs such as a "Socialist Division of Labor" (1962) or "Socialist Economic Integration" (1971) failed as the EE Six deliberately thwarted decades of proposed Soviet trade reforms.[10]

The Soviets and the East Europeans complained to each other about a trade pattern of subsidized backwardness which inspired both partners to seek alternatives in trade with the West. The inability to solve chronic problems of low agricultural productivity or to produce for themselves the advanced tools, machinery, and equipment needed for a genuine modernization of the economy forced the Soviet bloc states, including the Soviet Union, to expand trade with the non-communist world. In the course of the 1960s, as communist growth rates slowed, the idea of using Western imports to raise production levels grew.

By the early 1970s all of the Soviet bloc states were increasing Western trade to reinvigorate economic growth at home. These economic motives were a major factor in Soviet policies that fostered the political context for détente. Yet East-West trade created as many problems, both economic and political, as it solved. From the late 1950s to the late 1980s, communist governments struggled futilely to weave economically viable and politically safe relationships between their economies and larger global trade patterns.[11]

Throughout the cold war period, trade occupied center stage in the variable but growing economic relationship between East and West; for most communist governments, trade with the West did not lead to additional forms of economic contact such as foreign investment.[12] In the 1960s larger and longer-term Western credits required specific forms of import purchases by communist borrowers. Even after Hungary became the first communist state to join the IMF in 1982, its currency remained inconvertible. In short, trade, including trade based on Western credit, remained the most important form of economic contact between East and West.

Political considerations and economic factors determined the flow of East-West trade during the cold war. The best known and most controversial political deliberation was the Western "embargo" or strategic export control program, discussed below. Among the economic factors, the communist economies' limited ability to pay for Western products remained the central problem throughout the period. Beneath the more visible political restrictions of Western export controls, this economic limitation of communist economies served as a recurring barrier to expanded trade between East and West.

Generally, our knowledge about the global history of East-West trade during the cold war remains fragmented between in-depth studies that cover individual national experiences.[13] We still need analyses of multidirectional merchandise trade flows which examine the economic, political, social, and cultural implications of East-West exchange from the 1950s to the 1980s. Cold war policies initiated movements of food, consumer goods, industrial equipment, and energy resources that affected the daily lives of millions of people around the world. We have yet to link the macroeconomic developments and high politics of East-West trade with its impact on diet, consumption, status, working conditions, and social transformations in the many countries involved. A broad economic history could show how high-level trade policy decisions shaped the lived experience of citizens on both sides of the East-West divide as well as in the developing world.[14]

Three broad phases of East-West trade co-determined the larger trends in overall political relations during the cold war. First, severed trade was an integral part of dividing the globe into rival politico-economic blocs. Beginning in 1948, Stalinist trade policies and Western export controls cut short immediate postwar plans for restoration of East-West trade. European and American planners had envisioned Western Europe importing millions of tons of East European coal, grain, potash, and timber, worth between $5 and $6 billion.[15] In 1947 and 1948 US authorities in Western Germany began restoring traditional German trade patterns with Poland and Czechoslovakia. Thereafter, trade-reducing pressures from both sides constricted merchandise flows. These pressures peaked during the Korean War as West European imports from and exports to Eastern Europe reached respective low points in 1952 in 1953. Severing centuries-old patterns of commerce running between Eastern and Western Europe contributed powerfully to the effective division of the continent and to the isolation of populations in Eastern Europe which historically had been linked to the West through webs of exchange.

Second, beginning in the late 1950s, expanded trade worked toward gradually improving the relationship between the Soviet bloc and the West. Khrushchev's use of increased Western imports to alleviate systemic agricultural and technical shortcomings in the Soviet economy stimulated a slowly accelerating increase in trade. Increased imports were made possible by expanded trade contacts with the West, such as the 1958 long-term trade treaty with the Federal Republic of Germany and contracts for Soviet oil sales to Italy in 1960 and 1961. The Soviets placed orders for complete factory infrastructures and large "turn-key" projects such as the 1965 deal with Italian car-maker Fiat to design, build, and begin operation of a production facility for small cars at Tolyattii in Russia. From 1960 to 1963 the Soviets also bought significant quantities of wheat in Western markets, almost $1 billion from Canada alone, in order to compensate for failed Soviet harvests. In the shadow of these Soviet practices, East European countries also began to experiment with increased trade and imports from the West.

The Chinese communists did not follow suit. The PRC did make purchases in the global grain market to reduce famine levels caused by Mao's misguided Great Leap Forward. Nevertheless, the Chinese refused to rethink economic strategy to include increased trade with the West.

In the 1960s and 1970s these trends accelerated. New Soviet leader Leonid Brezhnev presided over annual increases in imports of Western machinery and equipment above 11 percent for the years 1966–70, and gigantic purchases of Western wheat to make up for unreliable Soviet grain harvests. Imports were financed by a combination of Soviet energy, mineral, and metal exports, Western credits for industrial and agricultural sales, and Soviet sales of gold. The gas pipeline deal negotiated with West German banks and steel producers in 1970 brought Western energy delivery technology into the Soviet Union, to be repaid with natural gas deliveries to Western Europe. The normalization of trade relations on an MFN (most-favored-nation) basis with the United States in October 1972 was another milestone along this path, as was the so-called "second basket" of economic arrangements in the Helsinki Agreements in 1975.[16]

In Eastern Europe, Poland and Hungary embarked on aggressive strategies of import-led growth by buying Western capital goods and production licenses. They financed these imports by borrowing from the West, and foreign debt in both countries reached dangerous levels by the end of the 1970s. In the German Democratic Republic (GDR), Western imports also rose significantly, and even the special benefits arising from "inner-German trade" could not prevent an unsustainable rise in foreign debt.[17] By 1978 the Soviets and East Europeans were $50 billion in debt to the West, with no clear strategy for debt reduction.[18] Unlike the Soviets, the Chinese were not yet interested in coupling an emerging political détente with the United Stated to an expansion of trade; they rejected Kissinger's attempts to negotiate a resolution of outstanding claims and assets questions as a first step to better business relations.

Among Western countries, increased trade with Soviets was invariably part of improving relations in this period. For the Soviet leadership, particularly in the Brezhnev years, Western imports were material proof that the Soviet Union could benefit from reducing tensions with the West. For these reasons, every serious analysis of Eastern and Western policies in the "détente" period includes some treatment of the role that successful trade deals played in underpinning other agreements and improving the political climate between the two blocs. Similarly, beginning in the 1980s, increased trade between the PRC and the West solidified the political understandings of earlier years.

A third phase of trade relations emerged in the early 1980s as intractable economic problems in the communist economies and renewed political tension brought about by the collapse of détente and the arrival of the Reagan administration combined to reverse the trend of growing trade. Mounting foreign debt moderated Soviet import demands, as domestic oil production stagnated at around 12.5 million barrels per day and oil prices collapsed in late 1985. Gorbachev decentralized control over foreign trade and allowed joint ventures with 49 percent foreign ownership. The Soviet leadership focused its reform efforts on internal economic restructuring, however, and neglected foreign trade as a "peripheral" issue.[19]

In the late 1970s, Western lenders grew increasingly nervous about high levels of global foreign debt and the risk of default among developing countries, particularly in Latin America. These concerns called attention to unsustainable foreign debt levels in Eastern

Europe. Western alarm about the creditworthiness of Soviet bloc states brought reductions in East European imports even as debt levels continued to rise. The resulting austerity measures and declining living standards provoked the 1980 Solidarity protests in Poland. For the GDR, credits from West Germany could not address the core problem of rising debt. By 1987 popular discussion in East Germany centered on reduced availability of imported food and consumer goods.

The root causes of stagnating trade lay in the economic fortunes of the Soviet bloc countries themselves. Yet the refusal of Western exporters, banks, and governments to extend economic relief to distressed Soviet bloc states may also have been a significant element in their demise and cannot be detached from the larger political climate of disappointment that followed the end of détente.[20]

Economic problems likewise inspired a reversal of previous Chinese policies. After the normalization of diplomatic relations with the United States in 1979, the Chinese government began its historic economic opening to the West. The Shenzhen "special economic zone," which began in 1980 as a laboratory for new forms of economic interaction with the West, is now the world's primary assembly point for electronic consumer equipment. The creation of significant pockets of capitalist activity within the Chinese economy encompassed a range of international economic and financial opportunities that included more than trade. This accelerating integration of the Chinese and global economies underpinned a Chinese relationship to the outside world that went beyond a mere short-term détente with the West.

Ironically, East-West trade might be most important for what it did *not* accomplish during the cold war—the resuscitation of the Soviet economic model. After Stalin, every constellation of Soviet leadership counted on imported Western machinery and equipment to help rescue a gradually sinking economy. Yet it was precisely when trade with the West increased most rapidly, during the Brezhnev years, that the Soviet economy fell irretrievably behind the West's. Similarly, it was during the phase of large-scale energy exports in the 1980s that Soviet foreign debt soared.[21] The consensus view is that "the Soviet system impeded the assimilation and diffusion of imported technology, just as it limited the effectiveness of domestic research, development, and innovation."[22] Expanded trade and imported technology did not affect communist economies in the way that Soviet leaders hoped and Western cold warriors feared.

If trade was a significant long-term driver of cold war relations, how do we assess the importance of trade policies to each side? In the initial years of the cold war, trade policies were central to each side's vision of the post-World War II order. A reconstructed liberal-capitalist global economy was pivotal to American, and with some reservations British, postwar visions, and remained a centerpiece of all planning. These Western efforts were too important to be compromised regardless of their effect in widening an emerging division of Europe. In fact, the cold war intensified American reconstruction efforts as the Marshall Plan and other aid programs purchased widespread international cooperation. A parallel determination was visible on the Soviet side. Control of Eastern Europe required a state monopoly on foreign trade as part of the Soviet economic model notwithstanding the trade disruptions and inefficiencies that resulted.

In the longer period from the mid-1950s to the early 1980s, East-West trade grew dramatically, implying a significant commitment by both sides. For Soviet leaders, trade with the west had "high symbolic and material value," as Vladislav Zubok points out.[23] But desires for expanded trade did not overwhelm the larger political goals of the Soviet government. Khrushchev's ambitious plans for importing foreign technology did not restrain his destabilizing political thrusts involving Berlin and Cuba, which provoked an intensified US embargo of oilfield pipes in late 1962 and temporarily slowed trade expansion. The Soviets abandoned wheat purchases from the United States because of Lyndon Johnson's Vietnam escalation. Soviet negotiators repeatedly rejected West German efforts to include West Berlin in economic agreements despite the delays and cancellations this caused. Most famously, in January 1975, the Kremlin unilaterally set aside the Trade Agreement signed with the United States in October 1972 after the Jackson-Vanik amendment connected US approval to Soviet emigration policy for Jews. Soviet leaders would not tolerate that sort of "interference in internal affairs," the costs in foreign trade notwithstanding.[24]

The West's overwhelming productive advantage over the communist economies allowed trade to be subordinated to larger political goals for most of the cold war. In the 1970s the Soviet market could be important to individual Western firms, and high-profile deals sometimes received a misleading amount of publicity. Only after 1980, however, did Western Europe begin to acquire a truly substantial material stake in East-West trade as Soviet natural gas joined Soviet oil in the West European energy palette. For the United States and Japan, the material aspects of this East-West trade never approached its political significance.

Because the Soviets valued trade with the West and because Western economies were generally not dependent on trade with the Soviets, Western governments found trade useful in devising the broad range of incentives and disincentives they employed across the East-West divide. By facilitating or impeding trade Western governments incentivized some behaviors, punished others, and signaled communist governments about the overall state of relations. Trade manipulations were more nimble and easily scalable than other tools of statecraft. Western regulations covering trade with communist countries were generally anchored in the ministerial or executive bureaucracy, and slight alterations usually did not require legislative action. Quick trade responses to communist actions around the world sent clear signals to all foreign governments. Also Western trade responses could be finely calibrated, for example by raising or lowering import quotas on specific East European or Soviet commodities, and they could be appropriate rejoinders to communist strategies that sometimes amounted to "a policy of pinpricks" as Adenauer once described it.[25]

Because of their utility, trade manipulations, both large and small, were widely used by Western governments. Some type of trade response in almost every Western capital accompanied every significant development in East-West relations from the death of Stalin in 1953 to the ascension of Mikhail Gorbachev in 1985. Manipulated trade flows were central to virtually every Western government when engaging communist states. Consequently, vigorous debates about the best ways to use various degrees of "economic warfare" were endemic to the Western alliance for most of the cold war.

Four outstanding themes connect these patterns of East-West trade to larger and more durable developments in the global economy. First, East-West trade widened the historical gap between Eastern and Western European levels of technology, productivity, and prosperity. Inadequate physical infrastructure, under-capitalized dwarf farms in Poland, and manufacturing sectors that struggle to compete globally are manifestations of East European backwardness exacerbated by cold war patterns of trade. The EU's attempts to ameliorate these problems have raised continued East European backwardness from a regional problem to a wider continental issue.

Three other developments that emerged during the cold war period have continued into the subsequent post-cold war decades of intensified globalization. Western trade organizations created during the cold war have been expanded and transformed into truly global trade organizations since 1989. In 1995 GATT became the World Trade Organization (WTO). Since that time China and many other former communist states have joined. GATT's history demonstrates how cold war pressures stimulated the development of an institution that continues to set global trade rules. In that way the long-term impact of the cold war on (now truly) global trade practices is still with us. In its original form the European Union (EU) is another organization created by the pressures of the cold war that acquired an independent life of its own and continuing importance. Many features and structures of our contemporary international trade regime are direct extensions of Western practices and institutions created during the cold war that have come to envelope some of the states that sought "non-aligned" status during the cold war and even some of the former Soviet bloc states.

The integration of China into the global economy on a hitherto unknown scale is another development of the cold war era that constitutes a monumental development in the history of the modern global economy. The Chinese path to modernization through integration into the global capitalist economy was rooted in the quintessentially cold war developments of the Sino-Soviet split and the subsequent Sino-American détente. The repercussions of cold war developments, in the form of China's global economic presence, will resonate far into the future.

A final consequence of East-West trade that has emerged as an important element of the global economy is Russia's role as a major exporter of hydrocarbon energy. Western technology and markets were essential for developing Soviet exports of oil and gas during the cold war. Recent Russian exercises in energy-based economic statecraft directed against the Ukraine and elsewhere have had material implications for Western Europe. These developments are a direct legacy of East-West trade.

# AID

Trade and economic warfare each had long traditions before the cold war, but foreign aid as we think of it now, i.e., as development aid, was a product of the cold war era.[26] Aid was a product of the cold war itself, deployed by communist and capitalist governments as a new instrument of statecraft in the peculiar circumstance of global rivalry unfolding simultaneously with the emergence of newly independent, but underdeveloped, nations around the world. Carol Lancaster states flatly that "foreign aid as we know it began as an instrument of cold war diplomacy."[27]

Despite the enormous sums spent in rival programs of foreign aid during the cold war (some $50 billion annually by 1988), historians have only very recently begun to write full-length explanatory accounts of the most important foreign aid programs. Because developmental aid did not achieve prominence until the 1960s, we have only recently come to see it as an enduring element of international relations that influenced the lives of hundreds of millions of donors and recipients around the world. The fragmented nature of foreign aid deliveries, involving many governments, multiple large international organizations, and myriad smaller religious and non-religious non-governmental organizations (NGOs), may have obscured the cumulative impact of aid. Finally, only recently have we acquired access to institutional records for significant periods of foreign aid activity.

Two recent complementary trends in cold war research bring attention to the vast new field of developmental aid. One is the increasing awareness of the global cold war outside of Europe, reflected in research over the past decade. A second trend has been the importance attached to competing communist and capitalist plans for modernization in the less developed world, particularly in the 1960s and 1970s. Recent studies of government modernization programs and their relationship to larger cold war strategies are important steps in exploring the larger fields of governmental, international, and non-governmental developmental aid.[28] Yet investigations of governmental aid programs have only begun. For example, we need a new history of Public Law (PL) 480, (the extensive US "Food for Peace" program), we have no treatments of Soviet or Chinese government foreign aid programs equivalent to those of Western aid programs, and we should examine how subsidized trade served as a form of aid without always being acknowledged as such. A new appreciation of how international institutions affect the contemporary world is just now resulting in well-researched studies of some of the largest international aid programs.[29] Placing government programs in this larger context and explicating the role of international and non-governmental developmental aid programs will be an exciting new frontier in cold war research.

With archival research into international and non-governmental aid programs just beginning, we can offer but preliminary observations about how aid programs helped shape the cold war and the significance of aid programs in the East-West competition. By the late 1950s developmental aid had become an important means for both sides in the cold war to support client states and influence non-aligned governments. Foreign aid expanded the cold war arena by extending political and economic competition from Europe into Asia, Africa, and South America. Many non-aligned states that accepted governmental and international aid would not have allowed an overt political or military presence by either side. With their ambiguous mixture of instrumental and humanitarian motives, aid programs were more acceptable to recipient governments than other forms of influence and were therefore more useful to donor states. By 1970 almost every government in the world was involved in foreign aid as either a donor or a recipient. Thus foreign aid became the most pervasive means of conducting the cold war in every corner of the globe.

Perhaps because of its pervasive nature and the complicated multilateral and multi-layered nature of foreign aid delivery, it became increasingly challenging for any single government to deploy aid in a straightforward manner as an effective political tool. For that reason it is difficult to determine if or how foreign aid spending worked to the advantage of particular countries during the cold war. This uncertainty sparked recurring questions in both the United States and the Soviet Union about whether governmental aid and donations to international aid projects were "worth it" politically.[30]

By the late 1950s the field of donors had become crowded: Britain and France had aid programs for their former colonies, the European Nordic countries had small programs, the Soviet Union concluded a major aid package with India in 1953, East Europeans offered token programs, and Japan had entered the field. Almost every government channeled some funding to NGOs and used these organizations to provide global services. The United Nations offered programs on health and agriculture; the World Bank created an International Finance Corporation in 1953, the new OECD joined the mix in 1961 with its Development Assistance Commission.[31] By the late 1960s the Chinese had become aid donors, as had some Middle East oil producers. Even developing countries such as India, Nigeria, and Brazil offered small amounts of aid in order to obtain regional influence. In the late 1970s aid sums increased rapidly as did the number of governments, international institutions, and NGOs involved.

Many aid initiatives were extensively modified by negotiation and compromise. Aid policies were subjected to debate between realists who advocated the use of aid to advance the national interest, especially in the cold war environment of global competition, and humanitarians who saw aid's purpose as relieving human suffering. Americans were concerned that governmental or international aid might crowd out commercial opportunities overseas. Because developmental aid, particularly from Western donors, became enmeshed in complex webs of delivery and was subject to conflicting ideologies and motivations, it is not clear how, or even if, aid contributions were producing advantages for any party in the cold war.[32] At present historians "know far more about modernization as an intellectual framework than about modernization on the ground."[33] We are still accumulating a critical mass of local studies that can tell us how foreign aid was deployed and the impact of those programs on recipients and donors.

With characteristic cold war mentality, participating governments pursued aid as a form of economic competition despite the ambiguous material and political benefits. By the mid-1960s West European aid donors had established ministries for "Cooperation" or "Development" that oversaw national aid strategies. The Kennedy administration's well-publicized commitment to developmental aid was perceived as integral to the global economic competition with communism. In June 1963 US Ambassador Foy Kohler reported on Soviet perceptions that "increasing [US] foreign economic aid in hope the Soviets would be obliged to do the same" was seen as part of a US "policy of attempting to bring Soviet Union to its knees."[34] These competitive fears helped fuel a tripling of worldwide foreign aid expenditures in the 1970s, from $8 billion to $24 billion, and a doubling of aid spending again in the 1980s.

In 2004 worldwide foreign aid expenditures topped $120 billion. The continuation and growth of global foreign aid beyond 1989 is one of the most important and happiest legacies of cold war economic competition. During the 1960s, the multiplicity of foreign aid actors, networks, and motives gave aid a justification beyond its instrumentality in the cold war. Aid became an international expectation for donors, providers, and recipients, a routine element of foreign policy, and a "norm" of international relations that would not be undone after 1989. As we unpack the history of aid programs that have transformed the lives of hundreds of millions of humans over the past half-century, we should remember that "without the Cold War, aid would likely not exist today."[35]

# Economic warfare

Perhaps no issue in the cold war produced such vexing policy quarrels as did questions about Western policies of "economic warfare" toward communist economies. The issue plagued Western political leaders from Stalin's early cold war actions through Gorbachev's struggles with perestroika. Eisenhower's "great impatience and exasperation" with the subject was probably shared by many others who tackled the problem.[36] The troublesome nature and enduring persistence of the issue have made it a subject of extensive scholarship.

The limited scope of interaction between communist economies and the larger world economy prescribed the forms of economic statecraft that Western states could employ. The inconvertibility of communist currencies precluded any Western attempts at "monetary statecraft." Western efforts were largely confined to manipulations of merchandise trade, primarily by restricting Western exports of strategic commodities.

The centerpiece of Western activities was a set of joint export controls on trade with communist states that were loosely referred to as the "strategic embargo." Western policy debates repeatedly returned to the same fundamental question: How extensively and intensively should Western governments apply controls on exports to communist states? An embargo of military equipment was easily agreed to, but controls on items with dual civilian and military use and items that had high economic, but not military, value aroused intense controversy. Negotiators struggled to reconcile the economic and political requirements of the many participants. Common answers emerged only painfully, if at all, and the question was re-addressed frequently as the Western powers sought to modify controls as the East-West relationship evolved.

Evolving Western policies on trade with communist economies shaped the cold war more by their political consequences than their material impact. From 1950 to 1953 a relatively high degree of Western unity, which included Japan, facilitated a rigorous export control regime overseen by the multilateral Coordinating Committee (COCOM) and the Chinese Committee (CHINCOM), but the material impact of these controls remains unclear. Stalinist trade policies were a greater factor in the early decline of East-West trade. Loosening Western restrictions on trade with the Soviet bloc in 1954, with the PRC in 1957, and with both in 1958, along with revisions on ship and steel exports in 1955 and energy equipment in 1957, failed to produce the surge in trade that many Europeans had anticipated, indicating that communist economies had internal trade-limiting factors.

Nor were Western controls effective in their original purpose of reducing communist economic potential for war. Even hawkish members of the Eisenhower administration admitted that Western export controls had not seriously eroded Soviet industrial growth or military capabilities. The results were no better in subsequent decades: the November 1962 Western embargo of wide-diameter pipes did not prevent the rise of Soviet oil exports, an array of Western trade sanctions imposed after the Soviet invasion of Afghanistan "had little effect" on the Soviet economy, and the 1981–3 US embargo on oil and gas equipment to the Soviet Union produced no conclusive results.[37]

With little material impact, Western export control policies were primarily political signals to communist governments, as the Americans came to realize. The Eisenhower administration re-conceived export controls as a political tool rather than an economic endeavor.[38] Major decisions about trade with communist countries, such as Kennedy's 1963 wheat sale to the Soviets, Nixon's 1972 normalization of trade relations, and Reagan's 1983 resumption of energy equipment sales were far more important as political signals than as economic policies. Evaluating export controls by their material impact misses the more essential portion of Western, especially US, thinking.

The Soviets also initiated policies of economic warfare, which fell into three broad categories. First were Soviet efforts to undermine Western cooperation on export controls by touting the vast possibilities of the Soviet market if trade restrictions were lifted. Soviet statements about additional billions in potential Western exports received extensive publicity and occasionally created short-term political problems for West European governments, but experienced East-West traders understood the Soviet bloc's economic limitations and administrative rigidities that limited trade. Most Western businesses preferred non-communist markets to communist ones and would not trade the one for the other.[39]

In the mid-1950s Western governments perceived a second avenue of Soviet economic warfare in rapidly rising Soviet bloc trade with the developing world. Khrushchev aggressively expanded trade and foreign aid to build political relations with non-aligned nations. Just a decade later, however, a new Soviet leadership more attuned to Soviet economic limitations placed economic advantage above political considerations when evaluating trade deals. Despite absolute growth in trade volumes over these two decades, Soviet bloc economies were largely unable to expand their relative market share of Third World trade. In 1975 the global demand for Soviet bloc heavy machinery and transportation equipment began to shrink. Although commercial transactions for military equipment continued to grow, the relative importance of Soviet-Third World trade declined from the mid-1970s through the early 1980s.[40] A third line of Eastern economic warfare was industrial espionage, at which the East Germans excelled. Ultimately the

economic impact of espionage was small because command economies could not diffuse and deploy stolen technology any more successfully than imported technology.[41]

Western export control practices had weighty material and political repercussions
inside the Western alliance. Scholarly opinion differs in assessing the material sacrifices
required by controlling exports. Jeffrey Engel uses the civilian aircraft industry to demonstrate how Western rules closing off potential markets in communist countries disadvantaged British aircraft manufacturers, who needed a large export market to justify
development costs, in competition with American producers less dependent on foreign
sales.[42] In contrast, Jacqueline McGlade points to US national rules that were consistently more restrictive than COCOM's common Western program as the reason that US
manufacturers lagged behind European competitors when opportunities in communist
countries did arise, leaving the Americans with little more than the agricultural portion
of communist markets.[43] Additional work may confirm this picture of results highly differentiated by sector.

At the macroeconomic level the West Europeans, Japanese, and Americans suffered
little under export controls. The peak of restrictions in the 1950s coincided with high
rates of growth and low levels of unemployment in most of the Western world. Japan's
rise as a global exporter in the 1960s and 1970s did not depend on trade with China;
record West German trade surpluses of 1986–9 received almost no contribution from a
sputtering market in the Soviet bloc.

Within the alliance the political burden of export controls outweighed the material
sacrifices. Divergence between liberal West European views on trade and more restrictive American views burdened the alliance throughout the cold war. In May 1953 the
NSC Planning Board reported that US-European negotiations over export controls were
"a source of constant irritation" for both sides, a characterization that applied to most of
the cold war period.[44] Europeans particularly resented extraterritorial application of US
laws which produced two well-known conflicts and several lesser-known incidents. In
1962 the US government prevented Italian export of wide-diameter oil pipes produced
with technology licensed from American companies. In June 1982 US pipeline sanctions
were extended to cover foreign affiliates and subsidiaries of US companies, provoking
furious public criticisms in Europe and Japan and the most serious alliance crisis over
export controls. The US government retreated, abandoning plans for countersanctions
against participating French, Italian, British, and West German companies and cance-
ling the extraterritorial rules sixteen months later.[45]

American use of trade controls primarily as political signals made it difficult to revise
policy in a way that could meet European thinking partway. Attaching psychological,
diplomatic, and political considerations to the embargo made export controls "sticky."
Restricted items were not de-controlled when they lost strategic value, as the Europeans
advocated, because strategic value no longer guided American thinking. For the
Americans, embargo reductions were guided by a desire to send the right political signal
at the right time to the target country. In this view, the proper intersection of international developments and American domestic politics produced few opportunities for
improving trade with communists. West European impatience could reach dangerous

levels. In 1957 the British unilaterally reduced controls on exports to China after two years of fruitless discussions with US counterparts, who would not send a positive signal while the Chinese were making mischief in the Taiwan Strait. Mutual dissatisfaction by West European governments and successive US administrations was chronic. The issue irritated the Western alliance for forty years and remains a curious failure in a general pattern of sophisticated transnational management.

Governments of the Western economies endured this intra-alliance debate precisely because trade manipulations were perceived as useful vehicles for managing communist regimes. Explicating these struggles has been a dominant theme of historical investigations since Gunnar Adler-Karlsson's seminal work appeared forty years ago.[46] Two questions in particular have endured. First, what was the nature of the US-West European negotiations for a common export control program? Adler-Karlsson emphasized the coercive element in these negotiations, specifically the role of "American threats" in obtaining European cooperation for an embargo.[47] Some scholars maintain that view, while other interpretations emphasize West European co-agency in producing a compromise policy.[48] US negotiators held some sharp weapons in congressional legislation that tied US aid for Western Europe to European compliance on export controls, especially section 117 (d) of the 1948 Marshall Plan authorization and the Battle Act of 1951. Neither Truman nor Eisenhower supported such blunt tactics, but the existence of such language focused European attention on finding workable agreements with the United States. Alan Dobson's thorough treatment of US policies concludes that the Americans placed great value on voluntary cooperation by allies, that US "pressure" was "selective, muted, and restrained," and that the export control lists emerged as a "gradual compromise" between US and European positions.[49] In short, US actions in this issue closely resemble the subtle exercise of hegemonic influence that steered the reconstruction of many other areas of the global economy as well.

A second enduring issue has increasingly defined the set of Western trade policies directed against communist economies during the cold war. In the 1940s and 1950s, Western policymakers generally used the terms economic warfare, export controls, and strategic embargo. Since that time a wide-ranging scholarly discussion has offered terms such as "economic containment," "cold economic warfare," and "economic cold war." Scholarship has pursued two intertwined themes. First is the distinction between various stripes of economic statecraft as ideal categories, total economic warfare vs. economic warfare vs. cold economic warfare, for example. A second theme is determining which among these labels best describes Western policies pursued during the cold war. Dobson's recent work offers the most sophisticated discussion of both issues. He points out that US policy "went beyond a pure military-strategic embargo" because it was "designed to condemn Soviet behavior or to send messages," but that legal, domestic, and international "constraints" moderated policy development. He proposes "cold economic warfare" as the best term to describe the resulting policies.[50]

US policies of restricting Soviet access to important Western commodities were always only part of larger containment strategies. Even during relatively intense embargo pressures in the early 1950s, Americans tolerated a substantial volume of trade with the East; in 1982–3 the Reagan administration made significant concessions in its export control program that allowed increased European exports of pipes and turbines to the Soviets. Alliance cohesion was always more central to Western efforts than specific export rules.

Although the global anti-communist strategic embargo did not survive the end of the cold war, many of its lessons are relevant to the contemporary world. Multilateral export control regimes, such as the Nuclear Suppliers Group and the Missile Technology Control Regime, remain vital to global security. Multilateral sanctions are among the most useful foreign policy tools and are currently employed against troublesome regimes around the world. Part of the cold war legacy is that sanctions will remain an indispensable and frequently used element in addressing security problems for the foreseeable future. Even if specific forms of sanctions change over time, their successful use will require adroit political management of multilateral coordination. The historical record of cold war actions will remain a rich field from which we will draw lessons about sanctions management, as the best recent literature demonstrates.[51]

# Epilogue

Communists and capitalists both invested enormous material and political efforts in trade, aid, and economic warfare during the cold war. Our current understanding of the cold war confirms the important role played by economic competition in these three spheres, even as additional tasks remain in more fully explaining how these economic activities helped form the changing contours of the cold war. A comprehensive global history that analyzes how trade was managed across the East-West divide and assesses its impact on millions of daily lives is an important next step in the research agenda. Further explicating the dynamics of foreign aid, particularly the relationship between donor states' political goals and the impact of international aid as delivered around the world, appears as one of the most important frontiers in global cold war research.

Trade, aid, and economic warfare co-determined the outcome of the cold war struggle, but we are also interested in assessing these activities in a longer context, beyond the confines of the cold war. The full importance of these economic activities during the cold war lies in their repercussions lasting beyond the era itself. Exploring these trends beyond 1989 will be indispensable in assessing the historic significance of the cold war in the development of the modern world economy. Although it may be too soon to draw firm conclusions about the relationship between the trends of the period 1945–90 and developments thereafter, we can hypothesize on the basis of observations from the twenty year period 1989–2009.

Most fundamentally, it appears that the trends of the cold war did not slow the progress of previous centuries in moving toward a globalized economy. On the contrary, several key developments of the cold war period are important components of contemporary globalization: patterns of export featuring Russian energy and Chinese electronics, the current international trade regime, the global web of foreign aid, and the ubiquity of economic sanctions as foreign policy tools.

Cold war economic competition and the failures and successes of the rival states in that competition helped prepare the way for a new wave of globalization that began in the 1980s and expanded after 1989. The very nature of cold war economic competitions in trade and aid stimulated the processes of globalization by driving both the capitalist West and the communist East to use foreign aid and development programs around the world to establish global networks of allies and clients. Both systems assaulted traditional peasant societies, undermined the economic independence of previously isolated regions, and brought new territories into standing contact with larger global patterns of exchange and investment. Over the forty years of its existence, the competitive nature of the cold war international system surely increased the reckless pace and far-reaching extent of these globalizing processes.

The decline and fall of the Soviet economic model also stimulated globalizing forces. The inability of the Soviet system to deliver satisfactory living standards discredited economic policies and systems that were based on limited contact with the outside world of global exchange. The Soviet system could not advance in fully autarkic isolation, yet the leadership never developed the ability to manage a highly controlled trade relationship with the outside world in a successful manner. As these Soviet dilemmas became increasingly clear by the 1980s, the governments of many developing countries, including China and India, began to see participation in a global economy as an unavoidable component of economic development. East European countries rushed to join the global economy and integrative institutions such as the EU as soon as the restraining influence of Soviet power was withdrawn. In Russia itself the most successful economic sector—energy— remains that branch of the economy most closely integrated into world markets. The argument for generating economic growth through closer integration into the global economy appears to have been greatly strengthened by the failed Soviet experience.

During the cold war international economic institutions created an increasingly global economy that helped secure capitalist prosperity. That success has been a major impetus for the expansion of globalizing institutions since 1989. Most economists hold a deep appreciation for the impressive welfare gains produced by growing volumes of exchange in a progressively more liberal global setting, even as they acknowledge that globalization has not been and cannot be a universally beneficial development. Perhaps in the longer run we will reach the ironic conclusion that trade, aid, and economic warfare during the cold war proved Karl Marx correct in his early characterization of capitalism: that it "draws all nations" into its orbit, that it "compels them" to adopt capitalist forms of production, and that it "creates a world after its own image."[52]

## Notes

1. Within the voluminous multidisciplinary literature on GATT, cold war scholars might begin with Douglas Irwin's "The GATT in Historical Perspective," *American Economic Review* 85/2 (May 1995): 323–8.
2. Francine McKenzie, "GATT and the Cold War: Accession Debates, Institutional Development, and the Western Alliance, 1947–1959," *Journal of Cold War Studies* 10/3 (Summer 2008): 86, 106.

3. Only Czechoslovakia was a member of GATT throughout the cold war; Poland joined GATT in 1967 and other East European countries followed in the 1970s.

4. On these developments, Shu Guang Zhang, "Sino-Soviet Economic Cooperation," in Odd Arne Westad, ed., *Brothers in Arms: The Rise and Fall of the Sino-Soviet Alliance, 1945–1963* (Stanford, CA: Stanford University Press, 1998), 189–225.

5. W. Brus, "Postwar Reconstruction and Socio-Economic Transformation," in M.C. Kaser and E.A. Radice, eds., *The Economic History of Eastern Europe, 1919–1975. Volume II: Interwar Policy, the War, and Reconstruction* (Oxford: Clarendon Press, 1986), 579–84; and Paul Marer, *Soviet and East European Foreign Trade, 1949–1969: Statistical Compendium and Guide* (Bloomington, IN: University of Indiana Press, 1972).

6. Angus Maddison, *The Contours of the World Economy, 1–2030 AD* (Oxford: Oxford University Press, 2007), 81.

7. The 1950s did see some technical transfer from the more industrialized members of the bloc to the less industrialized. Alan Smith, *The Planned Economies of Eastern Europe* (New York: Holmes & Meier, 1983), 205.

8. Randall Stone, *Satellites and Commissars: Strategy and Conflict in the Politics of Soviet-Bloc Trade* (Princeton, NJ: Princeton University Press, 1996), 30.

9. Charles Maier, *Dissolution: The Crisis of Communism and the End of East Germany* (Princeton, NJ: Princeton University Press, 1997), 63–4; Philip Hanson, *The Rise and Fall of the Soviet Economy: An Economic History of the USSR from 1945* (London: Pearson, 2003), 156–7.

10. Stone, *Satellites and Commissars*, 22, 26.

11. Maier's *Dissolution*, chapter 2, offers a masterful analysis of the ideologies, structures, and personalities involved in one important case.

12. Joint ventures with up to 49 percent foreign ownership were first allowed in Hungary and Romania in the mid-1970s, in the Soviet Union in January 1987.

13. E.g. Philip Funigiello, *American-Soviet Trade in the Cold War* (Chapel Hill, NC: University of North Carolina Press, 1988); Julia von Dannenberg's *The Foundations of Ostpolitik: The Making of the Moscow Treaty between West Germany and the USSR* (Oxford: Oxford University Press, 2008) indicates that new work remains confined to national or bilateral accounts.

14. For example, Timothy Brook's *Vermeer's Hat: The Seventeenth Century and the Dawn of the Global World* (New York: Bloomsbury Press, 2008).

15. Committee of European Economic Cooperation, technical reports, vol. 2, July–September 1947 (Department of State Publication 2952); Report by the ad Hoc Subcommittee of the Advisory Committee of the Secretary of Commerce, *FRUS*, 1948, IV: 536.

16. The Helsinki Final Act addressed three broad sets of issues, often referred to as "baskets." The second basket concerned economic, scientific, technological, and environmental cooperation.

17. The peculiarities of inner-German trade have been the subject of a number of specialty studies in German, most recently Peter Krewer, *Geschäfte mit dem Klassenfeind: Die DDR im innerdeutschen Handel 1949–1989* (Trier: Kliomedia, 2008).

18. Paul Marer and John Montias, "Theory and Measurement of East European Integration," in Marer and Montias, eds., *East European Integration and East-West Trade* (Bloomington, IN: Indiana University Press, 1980), 31.

19. Hanson, *Rise and Fall*, 200, and the literature cited there.

20. Celeste Wallander, "Western Policy and the Demise of the Soviet Union," *Journal of Cold War Studies* 5/4 (Fall 2003): 137–77.

21. Anders Aslund, *Russia's Capitalist Revolution* (Washington, DC: Peterson Institute, 2007), 70.

22. Hanson, *Rise and Fall*, 63.

23. Vladislav Zubok, *A Failed Empire: The Soviet Union in the Cold War from Stalin to Gorbachev* (Chapel Hill, NC: Univeristy of North Carolina Press, 2007), 233. Zubok applies this assessment to Brezhnev's leadership. I have extended it to the longer period under discussion here.

24. TASS statement cited in Raymond Garthoff, *Détente and Confrontation*, rev. ed. (Washington, DC: Brookings, 1994), 512.

25. The utility of Western trade responses, rather than their effectiveness, runs throughout Shu Guang Zhang's *Economic Cold War: America's Embargo against China and the Sino-Soviet Alliance, 1949–1963* (Stanford, CA: Stanford University Press, 2001).

26. Developmental aid is distinguished from relief aid, which is not treated here. Hence the omission of the Marshall Plan from this discussion. For the Marshall Plan debates and its voluminous literature, begin with "Special Forum: The Marshall Plan and the Origins of the Cold War Reassessed," *Journal of Cold War Studies* 7/1 (Winter 2005).

27. Carol Lancaster, *Foreign Aid: Diplomacy, Development, Domestic Politics* (Chicago: University of Chicago Press, 2007), 25. Figures on foreign aid used here are taken from Lancaster, *Foreign Aid*, chapter 2.

28. The field is surveyed in *Diplomatic History* 33/3 (June 2009), a special issue devoted to "Modernization as a Global Project." See also Burton Kaufman's pioneering study *Trade and Aid: Eisenhower's Foreign Economic Policy 1953–1961* (Baltimore, MD: Johns Hopkins University Press, 1982).

29. E.g. Amy Staples, *The Birth of Development: How the World Bank, Food and Agriculture Organization, and World Health Organization Have Changed the World 1945–1965* (Kent, OH: Kent State University Press, 2006).

30. On Soviet dissatisfaction with Khrushchev's foreign aid commitments, see Elizabeth Valkenier, *The Soviet Union and the Third World* (New York: Praeger, 1983), 11–13.

31. The emergence of foreign aid was noted by George Liska, *The New Statecraft. Foreign Aid in American Foreign Policy* (Chicago: University of Chicago Press, 1960) and Hans Morgenthau, "A Political Theory of Foreign Aid," *American Political Science Review* 56 (June 1962): 301–9.

32. See for example Matthew Connelly's conclusion that "the international politics of population control did not fit into cold war categories," *Social Engineers Run Amok: The International Politics of Population Control* (Cambridge, MA: Belknap Press, 2008), 152.

33. David Engerman and Corinna Unger, "Introduction: Towards a Global History of Modernization," *Diplomatic History* 33/3 (June 2009): 380.

34. Embassy Moscow (Kohler) to the Secretary of State, May 31, 1963, National Archives and Records Administration, College Park, MD, Record Group 59, State Department Central Foreign Policy File, 1963, POL US-USSR, 611163.

35. Lancaster, *Foreign Aid*, 25.

36. 188th meeting of the National Security Council, March 11, 1954, *FRUS*, 1952–4, 1: 1109–10.

37. Hanson, *Rise and Fall*, 161; Douglas Reynolds and Marek Koldziej, "Former Soviet Union Oil Production and GDP Decline," *Energy Economics* 30 (2008): 278.

38. Funigiello, *American-Soviet Trade*, 86; Alan Dobson *US Economic Statecraft for Survival, 1933–1991: Of Sanctions, Embargoes, and Economic Warfare* (London: Routledge, 2002), especially 133–48.

39. Volker Berghahn, "Lowering Soviet Expectations: West German Industry and Osthandel during the Brandt Era," in Berghahn, ed., *Quest for Economic Empire: The European Strategies of German Big Business in the Twentieth Century* (Providence, RI: Berghahn Books, 1996), 145–57.

40. These trends are summarized in Valkenier, *Soviet Union and Third World*, 3–26.

41. Kristie Macrakis, Thomas Wegener Friis, Helmut Mueller-Enbergs, eds., *East German Foreign Intelligence: Myth, Reality, and Controversy* (London: Routledge, 2010) contains several contributions on this theme.

42. Jeffrey Engel, *Cold War at 30,000 Feet: The Anglo-American Fight for Aviation Supremacy* (Cambridge, MA: Harvard University Press, 2007).

43. Jacqueline McGlade "CoCom, Western Relations, and the Containment of World Trade," in Jari Ojala and Jari Eloranta, eds., *East-West Trade and the Cold War* (Jyväskylä: University of Jyväskylä Press, 2005).

44. May 25, 1953, *FRUS*, 1952–4, 1: 975.

45. Bruce Jentleson, *Pipeline Politics: The Complex Political Economy of East-West Energy Trade* (Ithaca, NY: Cornell University Press, 1986).

46. Gunnar Adler-Karlsson, *Western Economic Warfare, 1947–1967* (Stockholm: Almqvist & Wiskell, 1968).

47. Adler-Karlsson, *Western Economic Warfare*, 45.

48. See Ian Jackson, *The Economic Cold War: America, Britain and East-West Trade, 1948–63* (New York: Palgrave, 2001), 2–3 and the literature cited there.

49. Dobson, *US Economic Statecraft*, 94, 96.

50. Dobson, *US Economic Statecraft*, 87.

51. Richard Haass, ed., *Economic Sanctions and American Diplomacy* (New York: Council on Foreign Relations, 1998); Gary Hufbauer and Jeffrey Schott, *Economic Sanctions Reconsidered: History and Current Policy*, 3rd ed. (Washington: Peterson Institute, 2007).

52. "The Communist Manifesto," in *Marx/Engels Collected Works*, vol. 6 (New York: International Publishers, 1976), 488.

## Select Bibliography

Dobson, Alan. *US Economic Statecraft for Survival, 1933–1991: Of Sanctions, Embargoes and Economic Warfare*. London: Routledge, 2002.

Hanson, Philip. *The Rise and Fall of the Soviet Economy: An Economic History of the USSR from 1945* London: Longman, 2003.

Jentleson, Bruce. *Pipeline Politics: The Complex Political Economy of East-West Energy Trade*. Ithaca, NY: Cornell University Press, 1986.

Kaufman, Burton. *Trade and Aid: Eisenhower's Foreign Economic Policy, 1953–1961*. Baltimore, MD: Johns Hopkins University Press, 1982.

Lancaster, Carol. *Foreign Aid: Diplomacy, Development, and Domestic Politics*. Chicago: University of Chicago Press, 2007.

Lippert, Werner D. *The Economic Diplomacy of Ostpolitik: Origins of NATO's Energy Dilemma*. New York: Berghahn, 2010.

Stone, Randall. *Satellites and Commissars: Strategy and Conflict in the Politics of Soviet-Bloc Trade*. Princeton, NJ: Princeton University Press, 1996.

Zhang, Shu Guang. *Economic Cold War: America's Embargo against China and the Sino-Soviet Alliance, 1949–1963*. Washington, DC: Woodrow Wilson Center Press, 2001.

# CHAPTER 24

# COLD WAR INTELLIGENCE HISTORY

## JOHN PRADOS

THERE are at least four ways in which intelligence operations directly affected the evolution of the cold war. Most familiar are covert operations: either efforts to exert political influence by secret means or attempts to transform situations by means of actual military interventions carried out clandestinely. Because this is a controversial area and includes several aspects, it will be covered only indirectly here and dealt with separately in the next section. The arena of technical intelligence collection, the effort to gather photographic or electronic information about an adversary, is a second avenue. Such efforts often included naval or airborne missions that could provoke the adversary. A third is the provocative aspect inherent in the discovery of foreign espionage activities. The data collected by these and other means had a role in cold war crises, and this is relatively well understood—treatments of crises feature coverage of intelligence inputs as a matter of course. Finally, national interests in maintaining intelligence capabilities and platforms have driven foreign policy in concrete ways. Because the last element is dimly appreciated, this discussion begins with the foreign policy of intelligence.

There *is* a foreign policy of intelligence; the creation and maintenance of intelligence capabilities has had implications for national policies. This is not simply a matter of collaboration between intelligence agencies in different countries (termed "intelligence liaison"). For the US this has meant preserving friendly relations with governments, encouraging alliances, extending foreign and military aid, and other forms of cooperation. Both the mechanisms for technical intelligence collection and those for covert operations have led to these kinds of measures, because their characteristics and requirements demand the assistance of other nations. The foreign policy measures entailed, in turn, have affected general international relations as well as the specific evolution of the cold war.

Consider the case of the radio intercepts necessary to derive communications intelligence. Due to the nature of radio waves, the phenomena of radio propagation over distance, and the requirements for large antenna arrays for effective interception, United

States efforts to collect Soviet radio traffic were best served by constructing bases around the Soviet Union and its allies. It was relatively easy to establish bases of this type on allied territory. But problems could arise even in those cases. For example, US relations with Japan were complicated for almost three decades of the cold war by the question of recognition of Japanese sovereignty over the island of Okinawa, where the US maintained radio listening stations and other bases. Moreover, the American-Japanese alliance difficulties had implications for the separate radio listening post the US maintained at Misawa, in Japan itself.[1]

Difficulties like these were a piece of the larger issues of American foreign military bases and alliances. Each of these bases entailed status of forces arrangements, long-term aid agreements, and other appurtenances of bilateral relations. Likewise spy facilities usually involved intelligence liaison agreements. There are cases where the communications facilities and radio intercept stations—or other intelligence bases—were the main or even sole US national security interest. In Ethiopia an American base at Kagnew played such a role. Maintaining it was a key consideration in US foreign aid to Ethiopia, which was greatly curtailed after the US facility closed in early 1977. Pakistan is another example. The original US relationship with Islamabad evolved after Pakistan joined the Southeast Asia Treaty Organization (SEATO) and the British-sponsored Baghdad Pact. It coalesced around several intelligence radar facilities placed to observe Soviet guided missile tests. The Pakistani cold war role also featured granting use of airfields to US reconnaissance aircraft flying along the periphery of the Soviet Union. Peripheral flight programs will be discussed below, but a pair of US aircraft lost on these missions during the late 1950s were en route to Pakistan when they went down. The ill-fated U-2 aircraft flown by Francis Gary Powers and destroyed within the USSR had refueled in Pakistan before penetrating Russia. That plane formed part of a detachment actually based in Turkey, which also hosted several other intelligence bases that observed Soviet missile tests and intercepted communications. Use of and access to intelligence bases were incontrovertibly major considerations in US policy toward Pakistan and Turkey throughout the period.[2]

After the United States lost access to the Pakistani bases in the late 1960s, it established substitutes in Iran under the Shah, using even more sophisticated technology. US reluctance to entertain thoughts of threats to those facilities factored in Washington's inability to perceive the fundamentalist challenge that ended with the Shah's overthrow and the Iranian hostage crisis. In the mid-1970s American interest in a satellite control facility in Australia that helped manage the constellation of US reconnaissance satellites led Washington to pressure the British government to overturn the result of an Australian election. Meanwhile, *Soviet* perceptions of the utility of the US intelligence bases in Africa became a factor in Russian backing for Marxist forces that overthrew the Ethiopian government, and for a government in Somalia that permitted Moscow to establish bases, including a communications intelligence facility, at Berbera. Those Soviet interventions were a major element in making Africa a cold war cockpit in the 1970s and 1980s. These were real foreign policy impacts.[3]

The need for bases to execute US covert operations has also had foreign policy implications. A pro-American ruler in Nicaragua, which the CIA used as a base for operations into Guatemala in 1953–4, was able to force the US to provide certain aircraft and military equipment in aid. A few years later, protecting base access in Guatemala prior to the Bay of Pigs operation necessitated supporting a coup d'état against its government. In the mid-1970s a CIA covert operation in Angola meant support for a dictatorial regime in Zaire and a racist one in South Africa. Resumption of Angolan operations during the Reagan administration extended US policy problems in both adjoining countries. Also in that period the Reagan administration's efforts to unseat the government of Nicaragua required support for military, then oligarchic rulers in Honduras. All these covert operations were cold war activities.

Of course, bases and access are often subsumed within broader cooperative frameworks, such as the US "special relationship" with the United Kingdom or the NATO and SEATO alliances. So these cannot be evaluated primarily as intelligence costs in foreign policy. But preserving the capability to mount operations, as well as intelligence liaison relationships, should be viewed as components of foreign policy goals. CIA covert operations into Albania, Eastern Europe, and the Soviet Union between 1949 and 1957 would have been impossible without British, Italian, and NATO facilities and, in several cases, bilateral cooperation. South Vietnam and Thailand were crucial to CIA operations in Southeast Asia during the American war of the 1960s and 1970s. And only Pakistani cooperation made possible the CIA Afghan war against Russia in the 1980s.[4]

References to bilateral cooperation open the door to intelligence liaison. For America the relationship with Great Britain is central.[5] The CIA and Britain's MI6 mounted numerous joint operations, including Albania (1949–52), the Soviet Union (1950–3), Iran (1953–4), Afghanistan (1980s), and an abortive attempt in Syria in the middle 1950s. Saudi Arabia was a notable collaborator with CIA Afghan operations in the 1980s. The Afghan operation in fact involved additional allies, including the People's Republic of China and Egypt. Similarly France participated in the CIA operation in Angola in 1975, and that in Nicaragua enveloped the Saudis, Argentina, Honduras, and El Salvador. The Soviet Union obtained help from its Eastern European satellites and Cuba. Liaison relationships never figured as the main elements of superpower policy interests. Nevertheless, they broadened and reinforced the content of international connections, enhanced covert operations, and made possible certain espionage operations in the first place.

Cold war intelligence agencies also played important roles in foreign policy in terms of how they conditioned the perceptions of leaders and catalyzed events. Probably the best-known case of the direct influence of intelligence operations upon diplomacy is the U-2 Affair. On May 1, 1960, the CIA's U-2 photographic reconnaissance aircraft, overflying the Soviet Union, was lost and its pilot captured. At the time the Soviets were poised for a summit conference in Paris that had been carefully prepared and held a promise of reducing East-West tensions. The US clung to a cover story denying the intelligence mission of the U-2, and President Dwight D. Eisenhower permitted himself to become implicated in the clumsy fabrication. Soviet leader Nikita Khrushchev cancelled the summit. Direct assessment of the impact depends on the imponderables of how serious the sides really were about introducing détente, the actual level of tension, and the degree to which

Moscow felt itself forced to posture in the context of the emerging Sino-Soviet split. Nevertheless the aftermath of the U-2's loss made it impossible even to test the possibilities.[6]

Two years later, during the Cuban missile crisis, other U-2 incidents exacerbated the tension. One of these planes blundered into Soviet airspace, while another was shot down over Cuba. Evidence shows Soviet nuclear forces went to their highest state of alert, while US officials of the Kennedy administration considered retaliation against Cuba ranging from bombing to an invasion, either of which could have led to general war.[7]

Incidents at sea involving naval intelligence collectors likewise held potential for triggering conflict. The paradigm case is the Gulf of Tonkin incident in 1964, when the Johnson administration actually retaliated against the Democratic Republic of Vietnam on the basis of an assumed North Vietnamese response to a US intelligence mission. Tonkin Gulf even became a core element of the US justification for its Vietnam War. A pair of incidents off the North Korean coast in 1968, in which the American intelligence trawler *Pueblo* and its crew were captured, and in 1969 when another collection aircraft was shot down, both led to US consideration of military action which could have escalated into hostilities. These episodes show that intelligence activities in the cold war could and did produce diplomatic and military consequences.[8]

Beyond these sorts of events intelligence could condition international agreements. Data is still lacking on the extent to which espionage and technical collection provided diplomats with vital information on the goals of their counterparts in negotiations, but the role was a real one. Intelligence also conditioned the kinds of agreements that could be obtained. Nuclear arms control is the most prominent example. Soviet-American negotiations on nuclear weapons testing in the late 1950s foundered over doubts that underground blasts could be detected. Arguments over "on site inspection" were important because, on the US side, technical studies showed that scientific intelligence could not reliably establish the power of underground tests. The 1963 test ban prohibited atmospheric nuclear testing only—precisely because of the verification difficulties. The 1972 agreement limiting intercontinental ballistic missiles, submarine-launched missiles, and nuclear-armed bombers was framed in that way because reconnaissance satellites could count missile launchers but not weapons. Later agreements that constrained numbers of weapons were made possible by coupling technical intelligence collection on weapons testing with explicit rules on counting a launcher as embodying a certain number of weapons depending upon its test history.[9]

Espionage also was an irritant in international relations. In 1963 the Soviet arrest of an American academic in Moscow, Frederick C. Barghoorn, created political complications for President Kennedy at a moment when he was attempting to reduce tensions. An embarrassing spy scandal in the United Kingdom that same year brought about the fall of the prime minister. In 1971 the British government, in the wake of another espionage affair, ordered a mass expulsion of Soviet diplomats and intelligence operatives. The French took similar, though less extensive, action a decade later in a different spy case. At a minimum, mass expulsions poisoned diplomatic activity. In Moscow, Soviet intelligence had long had listening devices planted in the United States embassy and contrived other means of extending technical surveillance to the US and Western embassies. Soviet diplomacy profited from the knowledge thus gained, though specific benefits remain unknown. However, in the 1980s, with a new US embassy under construction in Moscow, Soviet efforts to embed listening devices in the very structure of the building were discovered. This Soviet espionage manifestly affected superpower diplomatic relations.[10]

One instance in which espionage had a clear impact on diplomatic relations occurred in 1986 when Nicholas Daniloff, an American journalist in Moscow, was apprehended by Soviet intelligence in retaliation for the arrest of a Russian spy who had worked for the United Nations and had been caught trying to buy US secrets. Daniloff's "espionage" was simply his contact with Soviet dissidents, but in reality the Soviets hoped to use him as a bargaining chip to trade for their captured intelligence officer. The superpowers exchanged increasingly shrill charges over both arrests for a month until suddenly the Soviet press agency announced that President Ronald Reagan and Soviet leader Mikhail Gorbachev would meet for a summit at Reykjavik. Within minutes of the announcement the Soviet spy was released, and within hours Daniloff arrived back in the United States. Though Washington denied any deal, the connection was unmistakable. And Reykjavik became one of the most important meetings of the cold war era.[11]

So there was a foreign policy of intelligence during the cold war. Partly driven by national security interests in gaining and preserving access to bases from which intelligence could be collected or intelligence operations conducted, and partly from the need to establish and maintain alliances among different nations' spy agencies, intelligence considerations played a role in setting policy goals. In addition, intelligence conditioned the possibilities for international agreements, while events in the intelligence arena directly influenced international relations, catalyzing developments as diverse as threatening or starting wars and precluding or encouraging summitry.

## COVERT OPERATIONS

If asked about the importance of intelligence in international relations, observers most frequently refer to covert operations. The next association is typically to crises or wars. There might also be an expressed appreciation for the ways in which demands for intelligence information drove the powers. But covert operations retain primacy when it comes to elucidating the impact of intelligence on the cold war.[12]

There are several reasons for this. First, covert operations, especially paramilitary action in which intelligence agencies arm local allies and engage in proxy wars, are obvious enough and violent enough to threaten the peace. Second, these covert operations have or have threatened to directly implicate the powers' foreign policy objectives, most notably by potentially shifting the loyalties of third countries. In addition, the crises created by such operations have provided occasions for the powers themselves to intervene, raising the stakes or changing the calculus of interests in a given situation.

However, there are other considerations which complicate determining the impact of a covert operation. In a substantial number of cases, the countries in which covert operations took place were not themselves important theaters of cold war confrontation. Guatemala and Chile, to take two examples, whether or not they were led by Marxist governments, made little difference to the cold war balance. Laos is another illustration: the 1960 confrontation between a CIA-supported pro-Western faction, Laotian neutralists, and North Vietnamese-supported communists furnished an occasion for Soviet intervention, almost making Laos a cold war crisis, but international negotiation led to agreements in Geneva in 1962. Thereafter a proxy war continued in Laos for over a decade without effect on the cold war proper. In the Congo there were CIA operations and Soviet airlifts over a period of years that collectively did little more than fuel tribal strife in the name of the cold war. In Nicaragua in the 1980s the US intervened against a Marxist government supported by the Soviets and Cubans. The ensuing stalemate masked the probability that had that country changed sides it would have made no difference. In Angola from 1975 on, a CIA operation intended to unseat a Marxist government put the US in the position of intervening alongside white supremacist allies (from South Africa) and led to tribal warfare that outlasted the cold war itself, pulling in not only the CIA but Soviets and Cubans as well.

Early cold war covert operations launched by the United States and its allies into the Soviet Union and its Eastern European satellites were among the least effective and were progressively curtailed. Subsequently, the arena of covert conflict largely moved to South and Southeast Asia, Africa, and Latin America, lands not central to cold war confrontation. During the final decade of the conflict more covert activities were initiated in Europe, mainly supporting dissident movements or attempting to influence political attitudes, but their impact was indeterminate because they occurred in a context in which major economic, ideological, and cultural influences had already attained great momentum.

Within the genre of covert operations of a paramilitary nature, one can identify at least six "campaigns": sets of activities following a particular doctrine or dedicated to a specific goal. Notwithstanding some overlap in time, the campaigns are distinct enough to enumerate independently. These campaigns, mostly American, rise to the level of strategy and therefore influenced the evolution of the cold war.

The first of the campaigns followed from President Eisenhower's "New Look" national security policy, which minimized the utility of conventional military forces in limited war situations. Thus Eisenhower made CIA covert operators his contingency intervention force. The Eisenhower covert campaign included, but was not limited to, operations carried out in Iran, Guatemala, Tibet, Indonesia, the Middle East, the Dominican Republic, and the Congo.[13]

Eisenhower also initiated the second campaign—against Cuba—but that initiative would extend through the Johnson administration and come to include not just CIA actions against Cuba itself but also activities carried out in Africa and Latin America. The abortive Bay of Pigs invasion of 1961 had a visible impact on the cold war by inducing Fidel Castro to appeal for Soviet security guarantees, hence leading to the Soviet decision to deploy nuclear weapons to Cuba and the Cuban missile crisis. By itself this episode displays the relevance of intelligence studies for cold war history writ large.

Another CIA covert campaign took place in Southeast Asia in conjunction with the American war in Vietnam. The array of individual activities in Vietnam, Laos, Cambodia, and Thailand amounted to a secret war and is best conceptualized that way. Enduring from the mid-1950s into the mid-1970s, the CIA operations were among the most effective in the long sweep of its history, whatever the judgment of their ultimate success. Because of the Vietnam War's place in cold war annals, this CIA campaign must be taken into account.

The closest thing to a Soviet covert operations campaign was Moscow's decision under Nikita Khrushchev to adopt a stance in support of national liberation movements. The Soviets supported a range of movements in many countries of Africa and Latin America, and some in Asia, over a period extending into the 1970s. This support included money and arms, technical experts, and advocacy in such international forums as the United Nations. It is debatable whether Moscow's approach amounted to a foreign policy, and its support assumed a shape different from a CIA-style covert operation. Still, American officials persistently characterized Soviet actions as subversion.

Under President Ronald Reagan the CIA conducted a liberation-support operation of its own that involved help to Eastern European and Soviet dissidents, plus active covert operations in Angola, Mozambique, the Horn of Africa, Cambodia, Nicaragua, and elsewhere. The range of these activities certainly makes them a strategic campaign in the classic sense. One initiative, the CIA operation in Afghanistan, became significant enough in its own right to be considered a separate campaign. Indeed some analyses maintain that the proxy war in Afghanistan between Russian forces and CIA-backed tribal and religious rebels had a primary role in the Soviet Union's demise. While this argument remains contested, that the Afghan war became a major focus of cold war activity for both sides is not.

Covert operations that did not usually involve violence were secret efforts to influence opinion. The CIA took the lead as a surreptitious opinion-maker, owning newspapers and journals, using friendly journalists or even agency assets to place articles, investing in ideologically slanted movies, and so on. The CIA was an invisible backer of the National Committee for a Free Europe, and Radio Free Europe (RFE) amounted to a CIA proprietary. Dispute surrounds the degree to which the dissemination of CIA-made opinion played a role in the Hungarian uprising and other disquiet among the Soviet satellite states in 1956, but these events attest to the impact of CIA propaganda on world-shaking events. For their part the Soviets held the lead in supporting and exploiting youth organizations for their own ideological purposes. Although ultimately unsuccessful, in the 1980s Moscow's "agents of influence" made every effort to intensify the already significant Western political opposition to the NATO plan to deploy intermediate range nuclear-armed missiles in Western Europe.[14] In summary, although many covert operations related to superpowers' bilateral or regional interests, and though the impact of certain ones is hard to distinguish amid co-existing trends, some covert activities were important from the perspective of the cold war, and a few had directly identifiable effects. Moreover, covert action campaigns were artifacts of the powers' foreign policies that clearly must figure in any overall assessment.

# SPIES IN THE MIST

Even more than the contributions of covert operations to international relations, the impact of intelligence collection is extremely difficult to discern. In combination, the zealousness of authorities to protect their "sources and methods" and the wide range of the possible sources make any judgments about the impact of intelligence collection problematic. How important must an intelligence discovery be to be significant to the cold war as a whole? Which spies or other sources rise to that level?

It is impossible to estimate precisely the number of spies recruited by the sides in the cold war, much less specify their contributions. No doubt agents number in the thousands, if not tens of thousands. Only a handful of them—that we know about—furnished information of vital importance. Even the technical collection mechanisms—the vaunted satellites that photographed the adversary or listened in to their communications, the ships and aircraft that circulated around the Soviet Union or entered it, and the ground stations that were intelligence bases—gathered far more material than was useful or was ever, in fact, looked at. Separating the chaff from the wheat will always pose a central problem in evaluating the contributions of intelligence.

Throughout the cold war all the intelligence services were critically alert to the opposition's ability to capture agents, mislead them, turn their loyalties, or fabricate information in the first place. These were spy games. Cynics might argue that the only importance of spies was to each other. For example, the most controversial recent cases of Americans spying for the Soviet Union (Aldrich Ames and Robert Hansen in the 1980s and 1990s) are both known to have furnished substantial intelligence about US security services and agents the Americans had recruited in Russia but are not known to have provided much data on US national security plans or forces. Earlier (in the 1960s), Soviet intelligence officer and defector Anatoli Golytsin made a virtual career out of embroidering a Soviet conspiracy to delude the US by means of false agents and defectors. Both sides could play at that. In Vietnam the longest-running US spy game was the CIA and military effort to make North Vietnam doubt its own security or believe in national resistance forces that did not exist. Defectors were primarily sources on the opposition security services and grist for the mills of those who engaged in spy games.

The sides did realize significant intelligence "coups" during the cold war. A distinction must be made between "grades" of information, however. Much of what was collected concerned specifics—the details of troop movements or imminent diplomatic declarations, the characteristics of weapons systems. Some of this material was tactical; much of it was ephemeral. Even the enduring consequences of appreciating the adversary's weapons, enabling designers to craft countermeasures, occupied a middle rung on the intelligence spectrum. Truly high grade information pertained directly to the adversary's strategic planning and calculations, or to technological innovations so important as to create whole new types of weapons. For each of the high grade sources, there were countless agents or collection channels reporting lesser information.

This point can be made with greater precision through examples. One of the first (and very valuable) CIA agents in the Soviet Union, an army officer named Pyotr Popov, was an active source through the middle and late 1950s. It was from Popov that the CIA, in addition to material on Soviet intelligence operations, gained its first hard data on the organization of Soviet ground forces and certain new types of equipment. These were intelligence breakthroughs, but they essentially concerned low grade information. Oleg Penkovskiy, the Soviet agent who worked for the CIA in the early 1960s, furnished important information on Soviet missile systems, down to operating manuals for systems. By this schema, Penkovskiy's intelligence was medium grade. It is true that Penkovskiy's data enabled US intelligence analysts in the Cuban missile crisis to reach key conclusions about Soviet deployments to Cuba, and the CIA to make prescient predictions, but those observations were value added by intelligence analysis, not data furnished directly. Both these agents are hailed as heroes of the espionage war without regard to the grade of the data they provided.[15]

Similarly, the espionage of Robert Lee Johnson, a courier with access to NATO document vaults in 1962–3, supplied copies of alliance war plans to the Soviets. This was top secret information but also ephemeral. The Walker spy ring, active from the late 1960s through 1985, disclosed key data about US naval operations, warships, and encryption procedures. The latter data may have enabled the Soviets to decrypt US naval communications for an extended period, though there is no material from the Soviet side to show what Moscow gained from the Walker ring. Regardless, data on US naval movements would have been low grade information, and that on weapons characteristics and codes of medium value.

A high grade source was one that gave insight into a new universe of weapons or the adversary's inner decision making circle. Some penetrations of this order are known. The atomic spies who revealed details of the design of nuclear weapons to the Russians through the end of World War II and into the early cold war period are probably the best example. Less known sources were the East German recruitment of West German officials, including one who functioned as a key aide to national leader Willy Brandt. The American side also had its achievements. One was the acquisition, by means still unknown, of a copy of the actual Soviet five-year plan of the late 1960s, along with other hard data on the Soviet economy. Another was the interception by technical means of telephone conversations among Soviet leaders in the period 1972 and after. Technical penetrations were an American (and British) forte. Soviet telephone trunk cables were breached in Vienna and Berlin in the 1950s, outside Moscow in the 1980s, and at sea in the Soviet Far East during that same timeframe. These were important sources of data— but they could also be spoofed or fed misinformation in a different kind of spy game. Among important spies who worked for the CIA were Arkady Shevchenko, an official of the Soviet Foreign Ministry, and Colonel Ryzard Kuklinski of the Polish General Staff. Kuklinski's key contribution, along with data on Warsaw Pact war plans, was intelligence on Soviet intentions to invade Poland, then to impose martial law, in the 1980–1

Solidarity crisis. A crucial British agent was Soviet intelligence officer Oleg Gordievskiy, whose information about Soviet fears of war in 1983 was vital to establishing that a nuclear crisis was impending or had occurred.[16]

Intelligence collection *was* important to the cold war. The Soviets' path to acquiring a nuclear weapon was shortened by spies' contributions. Interpretation of adversary moves in several crises relied on spy data. In the Cuban missile crisis a spy helped the United States interpret what the Russians were doing. Interception of Soviet leaders' conversations helped the Nixon administration in its 1972 negotiations with the Soviet Union. During the Solidarity crisis the Carter and Reagan administrations virtually set their policies based on espionage information. These instances alone establish the value of intelligence collection.[17]

# INTELLIGENCE AND PERCEPTIONS

The value of intelligence lies not simply in the information collected but also in the use given that data, and the skill with which it was melded into broader interpretations of the decisions and actions of cold war competitors. Those analyses, in turn, affected the perceptions of the leaders of the powers engaged in the cold war. Perceptions influenced foreign policy choices, national security decisions, and military programs. The impact intelligence had on the cold war is an amalgam of the direct policy consequences discussed earlier plus its effect on leaders' perceptions of the evolving conflict.

Assessing the impact of intelligence is not the same as determining whether the interpretations and data furnished by the spy agencies were correct. Nor is impact a question of asking whether leaders relied on intelligence or even believed what they were given. American presidents differed in the degree to which they had confidence in the CIA and its analyses, and also in the extent to which they brought pressure on intelligence agencies to deliver information to please. Presidents Eisenhower, Kennedy, and Johnson probably had the highest regard for US intelligence. Richard Nixon had the lowest. Agencies experienced the most pressure on their analyses under Nixon and Ronald Reagan. Yet intelligence influenced every cold war president.[18]

The United States has a particular way of handling this function, termed intelligence analysis. In the US there are analytic units in most intelligence agencies, capped by a Directorate of Intelligence at the CIA and a mechanism dedicated to producing all-service and all-source reports called National Intelligence Estimates (NIEs), housed within the CIA until after the end of the cold war, when it moved to the office of the Director of National Intelligence. Other powers have different approaches. In the British system there are similar analytic units, with the capstone element located within the Cabinet Office and called the Joint Intelligence Committee. The Soviets worked at a major disadvantage, with intelligence services supplying raw information directly to leaders, who might or might not select some of this material and ask the Central Committee Secretariat to do interpretive reports. The following discussion focuses on the US case.

American intelligence analysis on Soviet military capabilities varied in quality. At the dawn of the CIA, the agency had not established its value in this area, while US military intelligence lacked hard data. Thus in the period of the Czech Coup and the Berlin Blockade, aside from CIA political and diplomatic reporting, US leaders were left to act mostly on instinct. In 1950 intelligence reporting on Chinese and Soviet military deployments, redeployments, and other measures after the start of the Korean War demonstrate that the CIA had achieved some expertise. By the beginning of the Eisenhower administration, a regular series of NIEs on the Soviet Union had been initiated, "Kremlinology" had been developed as a technique for analyzing Soviet politics, the CIA was striving to understand the Soviet economy, and, courtesy of agent Popov and other sources (especially signals intelligence), the NIEs exhibited a new depth of knowledge on the Soviet Union and its military.[19]

The intelligence community's reporting and analyses of current events served the Eisenhower administration well in crises over Berlin with the Soviets and the Taiwan Straits with the Chinese. This valuable service continued through the Kennedy and Johnson administrations; the Cuban missile crisis was a paradigm case. Although a Special NIE on Cuba in the summer of 1962 made a wrong prediction—an intelligence failure—more estimates and reports gave the Kennedy administration a correct appreciation, while current reporting provided the president a margin of warning before the Soviets could bring their plans to fruition. Intelligence misinformed President Lyndon B. Johnson on an alleged communist threat in the Dominican Republic, but it was largely accurate and prescient on Vietnam, except where pressures were exerted on analysts, and on the Middle East, where the CIA correctly predicted the Six Day War and the emergence of Israel as a nuclear power.[20]

The observation about pressures on analysts opens the door to a fruitful area for exploring the "politics" of intelligence. Vietnam estimates provide a good example. In the spring of 1963 the community drafted an NIE that concluded, correctly, that the Saigon regime faced a worsening situation of military stagnation and mushrooming political instability. The CIA's own director forced a rewrite of the paper to reflect the views of Washington officials rather than the agency's own intelligence. The final NIE was much more optimistic, but shortly after its release the Saigon regime encountered precisely the difficulties the original draft NIE had observed.[21] Similarly, during the Reagan administration there were pressures on US intelligence to craft NIEs that projected a significant international threat from Nicaragua's Marxist government. Officials' preferences for an activist US policy in El Salvador, and support for CIA covert operations in Nicaragua itself, hinged on estimates like these. In short, political maneuvering introduced or encouraged estimative inaccuracy.

Estimates were worth fighting over because they carried weight—again political. In the American system, presidents do not want to be seen as acting contrary to the intelligence. When presidents do so, they accept a political cost. At lower levels, officials want the intelligence to come out a certain way because it bolsters their policy preferences or programmatic goals. The result is the prevalence of maneuvers to affect information.

Colonel Penkovskiy might report a certain thing, but whether that information turns up in a certain year's NIE is a function of considerations in addition to espionage trade-craft. Penkovskiy is a good example, for his reporting began at the height of what was known in the US as the Missile Gap. Russia first launched an intercontinental ballistic missile (ICBM) in 1957—ahead of the United States—and made that fact visible to the world by orbiting the Sputnik I space satellite. Thereafter the sufficiency of ICBM programs became a staple of US defense budgeting—and the size of the Soviet ICBM threat a constant measure of adequacy. The U-2 aircraft was not capable of photographing the entire Soviet land mass, and imagery satellites did not become a reality until the summer of 1960. During the interval, projections of Soviet ICBM production were based entirely on assumptions, estimates of Soviet factory space, and comparisons to American industrial experience. Driven by US Air Force contributions to the NIEs, the projections of Soviet ICBM strength were huge—the lowest considerably higher than the actual—and far ahead of US missile deployment programs. The difference between the (asserted but imaginary) Soviet numbers and the actual US strength became the "Missile Gap." John F. Kennedy even argued in his 1960 presidential campaign that if elected he would end the Missile Gap.[22] Meanwhile, the spy Penkovskiy reported that the Soviets had *no* ICBMs save for four on their test facility launch pads. Penkovskiy's number never appeared in the NIEs, though after Kennedy was elected the Missile Gap disappeared, with the NIE projections reduced to a low number (twenty-five), and approved US ICBM deployment programs, already providing for more than five hundred missiles, on their way to a thousand.

Some observers choose to focus primarily on "intelligence failures," instances where the estimates were clearly wrong or can be presented as in some way inaccurate. The boundary case in estimative failure is the argument that the CIA failed to predict the disintegration of the Soviet Union. But there are multiple sources of estimative failure, ranging from a thing not being knowable (and therefore not predictable), to inability or failure to collect necessary information, to the possibility that analysts accurately appreciated the reality but their views were edited out of the final papers, to actual estimative failure. There is also the possibility that lower level elements or different intelligence agencies were reporting correctly but their information did not appear in the NIEs. Further, intelligence analysis often operates under conditions of uncertainty, at times having to predict the results of decisions the adversary has yet even to make. The case of estimates of the Soviet future on the eve of disintegration contains elements of several of these factors.[23]

The great intelligence disputes of the cold war era reflect maneuvers to affect information. Overestimates in the Missile Gap NIEs gave way to underestimates of the number of missiles the Soviets eventually deployed—in a situation where Secretary of Defense Robert McNamara sought to curtail US ICBM deployment, the CIA wanted to avoid a repetition of the Missile Gap error, and the assumption that prevailed was that the Soviets would seek to match US numbers, not exceed them. Meanwhile, McNamara advocated deploying a ballistic missile defense—and early NIEs on Soviet missile defenses endowed them with unreal capabilities. Later, the Nixon administration sought a missile defense reoriented to protect ICBM bases—and the CIA came under pressure to prematurely credit the Soviets with a capability for independently targeting multiple ICBM warheads. Debates in the 1970s and 1980s over the level of Soviet defense spending projected in the NIEs occurred at times of demands that Congress maintain or increase US military spending. Urgings that the CIA of the 1980s produce estimates that judged the Soviets rushing forward on laser and particle beam weaponry took place in the context of the Reagan administration push for its Strategic Defense Initiative program. All these weapons programs were significant elements in cold war arms racing, and intelligence disputes formed integral parts in each of them.

None of this is to say that intelligence agencies did not develop their own parochial views. The Air Force's intelligence view of the Missile Gap is but one example. In general each of the US armed services had its own view, less or more pessimistic depending on the subject and its institutional interests. The CIA adopted a less militarized institutional view, which invited attack from other intelligence units when the core values of their parent services were implicated by an issue. Secretary McNamara took the initiative to create a Defense Intelligence Agency (DIA), with the idea that the voices of the service intelligence units might be softened thereby, but the net result was simply to add one more military intelligence point of view. One need go no further than to compare the NIEs of the 1980s—as manipulated as they may have been—with the glossy, publicly released DIA annual threat compendiums titled *Soviet Military Power*, to see that these differences persisted through the end of the cold war. In fact, in 1991, with Richard Cheney serving as secretary of defense as the Soviet Union tottered on the brink of disintegration, the DIA produced one more edition of its glossy publication in which the Soviet threat appeared scarcely less ominous than before.

For all the politics of intelligence and the maneuvers, leaks, and other devices employed, and the weaknesses of the estimative process, possession of a capability of this sort was a major advantage for the West. Cold war military theoreticians could refer to a large body of work that sought to understand Soviet capabilities in elaborating countervailing doctrine. War planners benefited from that work and in depth studies of actual Soviet force postures. Government officials had access to reams of tightly focused analyses of Soviet intentions. Presidents stood at the apex of the system. The value added by analysis was to bring integrated intelligence to leaders rather than leave them to wade through the raw data, both saving time and suggesting lines of action congruent with events.

# CONCLUSION

A topology of cold war events would include aspects of ideological struggle, an arms race, wars along the periphery, and a central story punctuated by intense crises, in which periods of hostility alternated with those of détente, plus social and economic developments that culminated in the collapse of the Soviet Union. Intelligence forms one piece of that story. Simply listing the set of conflicts and crises in which intelligence had some involvement suggests the centrality of this element. Intelligence contributions figured in the Korean War; the Indochina crises in 1954–5; unrest in Eastern Europe in 1956; Chinese communist difficulties in consolidating control over the People's Republic; the Congo and Laos crises, starting in 1960; Fidel Castro's alignment with the Soviet Union and his internal security problems from 1960 on; the Cuban missile crisis; the Vietnam War; superpower proxy struggles in Africa, Latin America, and South Asia from the 1960s through the 1980s; the Solidarity crisis in Poland from 1980 on; the political crisis over NATO deployment of intermediate-range nuclear forces in the 1980s; the Afghan insurgency against Soviet occupiers; and the social and cultural crisis of communism that successively brought down Moscow's Eastern European satrapies and then the Soviet Union itself. Intelligence platforms were themselves central to crises in the Gulf of Tonkin and in the *Pueblo* affair, and fear of intelligence platforms figured in the crisis that surrounded the 1983 Soviet shootdown of the Korean Airliner KAL-007. Moreover, with the periodic emergence of new evidence, the story is still evolving.

In addition the maintenance of intelligence bases, capabilities, and alliances figured directly as a factor in determining the foreign policies of the powers. Covert action contributed to ideological and cultural struggles and covert operations campaigns became elements in policy over certain periods or against certain enemies. In some cases covert operations furnished occasions for superpower intervention. Intelligence was important to the powers' perceptions of each other, and consequently the sides' willingness to reduce tensions. Intelligence capabilities conditioned the kinds of arms control agreements that could be negotiated, and played a still shadowy role in the progress of negotiations themselves. Espionage cases occasionally disrupted diplomatic initiatives and even posed political difficulties that brought down governments. In at least one instance an espionage case played a direct role in catalyzing one of the most important summit conferences of the cold war. Intelligence estimates contributed to the arms race by projecting an adversary force which defense programs would have to take into account, and were used by officials and politicians as clubs in national politics, driving defense budgets or supporting covert operations. Intelligence failures contributed to leaders' inaction at key passages. The amalgam of these influences makes it necessary to conclude that intelligence activity played a major part in the course of the cold war.

Spying has been called "the second-oldest profession," and writing on espionage dates back to the Bible. But intelligence history as a discipline is very recent, indeed younger than the cold war is old. Observers wrote of espionage, or of codes, or put pen to biographies of famous (or infamous) practitioners, or spies contributed their own memoirs, but all this was largely dismissed as a variety of popular history. It is difficult to pinpoint when this changed. Perhaps the appearance of official records of intelligence organizations and activities, beginning in the 1970s, influenced the emergence of this variety of historical analysis as a systematic endeavor. Many of the early record releases concerned World War II or even earlier, so it is not surprising that historians focused on those periods. Even today intelligence history is strongest through the period ending in 1945, and thereafter falls off rapidly in scope and amplitude.

A number of developments are combining to make possible a more concerted approach to recent intelligence history. Spy memoirs are as legion as ever, and there are even some official or semi-official treatments of intelligence officers or operations. Political controversies sparked by intelligence operations, at least in the US, have resulted in detailed congressional investigations of intelligence work that put a baseline of authoritative information in the hands of historians. In the United States and the United Kingdom, Freedom of Information laws are bringing intelligence records at least theoretically within reach. At the same time the cold war itself is receding into the past, weakening rationales for maintaining the secrecy of the documentary record. With costly top secret vaults bursting with older material, and new secret documents being added at an unprecedented rate, the logic of cost and benefit is going to open the files.

Whither intelligence history? In its early days the discipline focused primarily on accounts of individual covert operations on several continents, of spy networks, or intelligence officers and chieftains. Other works focused on "intelligence instrumentalities," whether the U-2 or SR-71 aircraft or the development and use of the single-side band radar. A fresh element is a layer of increasingly sophisticated studies of institutions, in the American context ranging from the CIA to the National Reconnaissance Office or the National Security Agency.

Much of this literature contains observations on the impact of particular intelligence instrumentalities, operations, officers, or agents. Historians are reaching toward aggregation of these elements but have as yet barely scratched its surface. There is no major study that brings together all of the elements mentioned earlier in this essay. Without an articulated literature it is too soon to survey schools of thought on cold war intelligence history or draw conclusions as to which analysis seems the most appropriate.

Intelligence historians thus face an enormous task. Stories of spies, operations, and gambits need to be assembled into a bigger picture, integrated into nations' institutional frameworks, and related to events and trends of the cold war as a whole. This needs to be done not just for the United States, but for the Soviet Union, United Kingdom, France, Germany, the People's Republic of China, and other actors in these events. Aggregated overview histories also have to be compiled. And—government secrecy being what it is—historians must remain alert for the spy or endeavor that, once revealed, may unlock the door to explaining more cold war mysteries. This is a considerable challenge, but facing it will bring intelligence history to its maturity. The day when historians can debate contending schools' views on the contributions of cold war intelligence will be the day the discipline comes of age.

## Notes

1. Nicholas Sarantakes, *Keystone: The American Occupation of Okinawa and and US-Japanese Relations* (College Station, TX: Texas A&M University Press, 2000).
2. John Sorensen, *Disaster and Development in the Horn of Africa* (New York: Palgrave Macmillan, 1995), 50–1; Robert McMahon, *Cold War on the Periphery: The United States, India, and Pakistan* (New York: Columbia University Press, 1996).

3. Two decades after the end of the cold war there is still no standard work on what is described here as the foreign policy of intelligence. For a study of US communications intelligence that touches on some aspects of the base problem see Matthew M. Aid, *The Secret Sentry: The Untold History of the National Security Agency* (New York: Bloomsbury Press, 2009).

4. On covert operations see John Prados, *Safe for Democracy: The Secret Wars of the CIA* (Chicago: Ivan R. Dee Publisher, 2006).

5. Again there is no standard source. The most detailed work has been done in the context of cooperation on communications intelligence, and on the Anglo-American relationship as it blossomed to include additional British Commonwealth nations. See Jeffrey T. Richelson and Desmond J. Ball, *The Ties That Bind: Cooperation between the UKUSA Countries* (London: Allen & Unwin, 1985).

6. Michael R. Beschloss, *Mayday: Eisenhower, Khrushchev, and the U-2 Affair* (New York: Harper & Row, 1986). Gary Powers's own account (with Chris Gentry) is in *Operation Overflight: A Memoir of the U-2 Incident* (Washington: Brassy's, 2004). Possibly the best operational historian of the U-2 is Christopher Pocock. Consult any of his works. The CIA has declassified its own official history monograph on the U-2, Gregory W. Pedlow and Donald E. Welzenbach, *The CIA and the U-2 Program, 1954–1974* (Washington, DC: Central Intelligence Agency, Center for the Study of Intelligence, 1998).

7. The huge literature on the Cuban crisis has been supplemented, most recently, by Michael Dobbs, *One Minute to Midnight: Kennedy, Khrushchev, and Castro on the Brink of Nuclear War* (New York: Knopf, 2008).

8. For the Gulf of Tonkin incident see Edwin Moise, *Tonkin Gulf and the Escalation of the Vietnam War* (Chapel Hill, NC: University of North Carolina Press, 1996). For the *Pueblo* see Mitchell B. Lerner, *The Pueblo Incident: A Spy Ship and the Failure of American Foreign Policy* (Lawrence, KS: University Press of Kansas, 2002). Again there is no general history of naval intelligence incidents and their relation to the cold war. I have not mentioned the *Liberty* incident of 1967 because it is most properly viewed in the context of Middle East history.

9. A substantial literature on what became known as "verification" evolved during the Soviet-American arms control negotiations from about 1975 to 1990. Many of these sources are cited in the work of Raymond L. Garthoff, particularly in his book *Détente and Confrontation: American-Soviet Relations from Nixon to Reagan*, rev. ed. (Washington, DC: Brookings Institution, 1994).

10. There is a vast literature on individual spy cases but no overview history that takes a specific cold war perspective. A broader general account that includes the cold war period is in Jeffrey T. Richelson, *A Century of Spies: Intelligence in the Twentieth Century* (New York: Oxford University Press, 1997).

11. For his personal account, see Nicholas Daniloff, *Of Spies and Spokesmen: My Life as a Cold War Correspondent* (Columbia, MO: University of Missouri Press, 2008).

12. This discussion draws upon my own work *Safe for Democracy*, which makes the first sustained effort to identify the impact of covert operations upon diplomatic history.

13. Christopher Andrew, *For the President's Eyes Only: Secret Intelligence and the American Presidency from Washington to Bush* (New York: HarperCollins, 1995), 199–256.

14. On the CIA front organizations, see, most receny, Hugh Wilford, *The Mighty Wurlitzer: How the CIA Played America* (Cambridge, MA: Harvard University Press, 2008).

15. Tim Weiner, *Legacy of Ashes: The History of the CIA* (New York: Doubleday, 2007).

16. Christopher Andrew and Oleg Gordievksy, *KGB: The Inside Story of its Operations from Lenin to Gorbachev* (New York: HarperCollins, 1992).

17. Richelson, *A Century of Spies*.

18. This section draws upon my book *The Soviet Estimate: US Intelligence Analysis and Soviet Strategic Forces* (Princeton, NJ: Princeton University Press, 1986).

19. In addition to my *Soviet Estimate*, see Robert Bowie and Richard H. Immerman, *Waging Peace: How Eisenhower Shaped an Enduring National Security Strategy* (New York: Oxford University Press, 1998).

20. Richard J. Kerr, "The Track Record: CIA Analysis from 1950–2000," in Roger Z. George and James B. Bruce, eds., *Analyzing Intelligence: Origins, Obstacles, and Innovations* (Washington, DC: Georgetown University Press, 2008), 35–54.

21. Harold P. Ford, *CIA and the Vietnam Policymakers: Three Episoides, 1962–1968* (Washington, DC: Central Intelligence Agency, Center for the Study of Intelligence, 1998).

22. Christopher Preble, *John F. Kennedy and the Missile Gap* (Dekalb, IL: Northern Illinois University Press, 2004).

23. Richard Betts, *Enemies of Intelligence: Knowledge and Power in American National Security* (New York: Columbia University Press, 2007); Thomas Fingar, *Reducing Uncertainty: Intelligence Analysis and National Security* (Stanford, CA: Stanford University Press, 2011).

## Select Bibliography

Aid, Matthew M. *The Secret Sentry: The Untold History of the National Security Agency*. New York: Bloomsbury Press, 2009.

Bamford, James. *Body of Secrets: Anatomy of the Ultra-Secret National Security Agency*. New York: Doubleday, 2001.

Betts, Richard. *Enemies of Intelligence: Knowledge and Power in American National Security*. New York: Columbia University Press, 2007.

Prados, John. *The Soviet Estimate: US Intelligence Analysis and Soviet Strategic Forces*. Princeton, NJ: Princeton University Press, 1986.

Prados, John. *Safe for Democracy: The Secret Wars of the CIA*. Chicago: Ivan R. Dee Publisher, 2006.

Ranelagh, John. *The Agency: The Rise and Decline of the CIA from Wild Bill Donovan to William Casey*. New York: Simon & Schuster, 1983.

Richelson, Jeffrey T. *A Century of Spies: Intelligence in the Twentieth Century*. New York: Oxford University Press, 1997.

Treverton, Gregory. *Covert Action: Central Intelligence Agency and the Limits of Intervention in the Postwar World*. New York: Basic Books, 1988.

Weiner, Tim. *Legacy of Ashes: The History of the CIA*. New York: Doubleday, 2007.

Wilford, Hugh. *The Mighty Wurlitzer: How the CIA Played America*. Cambridge: Harvard University Press, 2008.

PART IV

CHALLENGING
THE COLD WAR
PARADIGM

# CHAPTER 25

....................................................................................................

# INTERNAL CHALLENGES
# TO THE COLD WAR

*Oppositional Movements*

*East and West*

....................................................................................................

## PHILIPP GASSERT

IN retrospect the cold war looks like an era of remarkable stability. In Europe, the superpower stalemate led to the most prolonged period of peaceful coexistence in modern history. After the post-World War II civil wars ended in the Balkans, Europe did not see a major military confrontation within or between states for more than forty years. The situation differed markedly elsewhere. Particularly in Asia, Africa, but also in Latin America, decolonization and superpower rivalry produced violent confrontations, some smoldering for decades. Yet even here, the cold war period was notable for the absence of large-scale hot wars, if we exclude the military conflagrations that saw direct superpower involvement: Korea, Vietnam, and Afghanistan. Even the simmering Arab-Israeli conflict was largely contained. Compared to what came after the end of the cold war in places like Rwanda, the Congo, Bosnia, Afghanistan, and Iraq, the 1947–90 period has attained the nostalgic tinge of a long peace.[1]

This was not the prevailing sentiment at the time. The cold war "order" was always contested, especially in divided Europe. There, as well as in similarly divided East Asia, the consolidation of the two superpower empires meant that century-old lines of communication were severed, families were torn apart, and people were prevented from going about their businesses across newly erected borders. That was most visible in places like Berlin or the Korean Demilitarized Zone (DMZ), situated a few miles from Korea's historical capital. What used to be in the center found itself at the margins. As the Czech writer Milan Kundera lamented in a famous essay, the city of Prague, once a proud cultural, economic, and political crossroads of Europe, was now relegated to the place of a provincial capital of an isolated Russian-dominated East, of which it never had felt to be a part.[2]

Europeans, East Asians, and even Americans and Russians frequently contested this "unnatural" situation at the ancient centers of European and Asian civilizations. While West Europeans and the people of Japan (as well as later the South Koreans, Taiwanese, Hong Kong Chinese, Greeks, Portugese, and the Spanish) were now living in relative prosperity, those North and East of the border were punished for cold war stability, as were those living in "Third World" countries, where the superpowers fought "proxy wars." Moreover, many perceived the situation along the geopolitical faultlines as a dangerous powder keg that could detonate at any moment. Cold war popular culture is ripe with imaginations of accidental or not so accidental nuclear armageddons.[3] Millions took to the streets in the 1950s and again in the 1980s to protest against impending nuclear doom. The "struggle against the bomb" became one of the most prolonged social movements in history and found supporters across the globe.[4]

This chapter focuses on internal challenges to the cold war in East and West.[5] Therefore, the Non-Aligned Movement (NAM), which was founded outside the two blocs in 1961 in opposition to superpower dualism, had to be excluded. It is part of international relations. Moreover, domestic challenges to the cold war should not be confused with domestic opposition to the political status quo. Given the pressing importance of superpower rivalry and the all-encompassing nature of the cold war, internal challenges and domestic opposition often intersected with each other. Nevertheless, this essay underscores the importance of the cold war paradigm as a catalyst for domestic opposition to the geopolitical status quo.

The challenges to the cold war paradigm can be divided into societal challenges and those carried out by governments. Societal challenges often emanated from social movements, which frequently transcended national borders and which rallied against state authorities. Examples include the anti-Vietnam protests and the 1956 Hungarian uprising. They also took the form of an intellectual critique. In Western countries these challenges often surfaced within parliaments. Government-led opposition to the cold war order as part of "domestic foreign policy" was not unusual either. Examples include de Charles Gaulle's France, Nicolae Ceauşescu's Romania, or Mao Zedong's China during the 1960s and 1970s. The leadership of the two superpowers at times tried to overcome the cold war stalemate, too: witness the US drive toward détente during the 1960s (which met resistance among continental European allies) and the Soviet policies under Mikhail Gorbachev during the "endgame" of the 1980s (which were disliked by many Eastern European leaders). West German Ostpolitik of the 1970s likewise was designed to overcome cold war divisions. Yet in contrast to de Gaulle's dealings with Eastern Europe, West German Chancellor Willy Brandt strove to stay within the alliance consensus.[6]

I will focus on five core periods: first, the early days of the cold war including the Korean War, when the "division of the world" had yet to become universally accepted. The second period runs from the mid-1950s to the early 1960s, the apex of the nuclear arms race. The 1954 US testing of the hydrogen bomb on Bikini Atoll led to the first large-scale nuclear peace movement; then the 1962 Cuban missile crisis seemed barely to avert Armegeddon. Eastern challenges to the status quo during the 1950s and 1960s will be dealt with in a separate section of this essay, because at that time Eastern dissidents eagerly sought alternatives to both the prevailing Eastern and Western models. The third period covers the late 1960s rebellions against the Vietnam War as part of the anti-imperialist challenge of the new left and its search for a "third way." The fourth period begins with the renewal of cold war tensions during the second half of the 1970s leading to huge anti-war and anti-nuclear protests in 1982–3. At that point superpower dominance had become much reduced. Europeans and East Asians now often behaved independently of the superpowers. Neither Ronald Reagan's efforts to reconstruct American superiority nor Gorbachev's reform program could stem the demise of the cold war order during the fifth and final period of the second half of the 1980s, which culminated in the peaceful revolutions of 1989–90. The cold war therefore ended where it had started: in Central Europe.

As is evident from this brief overview, the cold war order almost never went uncontested in the years between 1947–8 and 1989–90. One could argue that the eerie stability along its borders made the challenges to it all the more revealing. The cold war would not have been the cold war had it not been contested. To tell this story, one can draw on a wide variety of expressions of "cold war dissent," which permeated the culture of that period as much as did anti-communism in the West or anti-capitalism in the East. Cold war dissent was expressed in political speeches and manifestos. It ran through intellectual treatises. It also manifested itself in pulp fiction such as the popular *James Bond* series or Italy's *Don Camillo et Pepone* film series.[7] It was highly present in movies, music, the visual arts, and the theatre. Even though dissent had to be hidden from the authorities, especially in the East but sometimes in the West, too, it was part and parcel of the cold war. And it played its part in bringing it to an end.

# REFUSING TO ACCOMMODATE TO THE COLD WAR: THE LATE 1940S AND EARLY 1950S

Even though realists think of the rivalry between the Soviet Union and the United States as a natural outcome of the power vacuum opened up in Central Europe and Northeast Asia after the fall of Germany and Japan, the cold war was not a historical given. Sure, it had been predicted for a long time, beginning with Alexis de Tocqueville's famous 1835 prophecy that the United States and Russia were destined to rule half of the globe.[8] Furthermore, an impending conflict between the two future superpowers had been the staple of Nazi propaganda during the final years of World War II.[9] At war's end it seemed imminent to conservative observers such as Winston Churchill. His 1946 Fulton speech, therefore, became an early cold war rallying cry. The ousted prime minister helped push the idea that a prolonged conflict between the two most powerful countries on earth was dawning. Given Soviet concepts of ever-expanding power, the West would be well advised to resist it.

While a dramatic re-ordering of European and East Asian spaces took place during the late 1940s, efforts to create clear lines of demarcation still met with robust intellectual and political resistance. In the United States, prominent members of the liberal "New Deal" establishment, such as former Vice President and Secretary of Commerce Henry Wallace, became highly critical of President Harry S. Truman's tough stance on Russia. They observed with unease the growing anti-communism as well as the string of political measures such as the Truman Doctrine and the Marshall Plan designed to shore up Western defenses against the Soviet Union. Although Wallace condemned Moscow's policies in Eastern Europe, his 1948 third party presidential campaign became notable for his unwillingness to accept force as the ultimate arbiter. Wallace dubbed the European Recovery Program the "Martial Plan."[10]

In the United States, challenges to the cold war paradigm and the growing militarization of US foreign policy dissipated during the late 1940s. Wallace's disappointing showing in the 1948 presidential elections took the steam out of the peace movement, of which Wallace had become the most illustrious proponent. It had found considerable resonance among prominent civil rights activists and labor leaders such as A. Philip Randolph and A. J. Muste, and among intellectuals and scientists such as Albert Einstein. But Soviet policies in Eastern Europe further helped to push less belligerent alternatives to the margins of US politics. As Lawrence Wittner has written, the 1948 Czech coup and the 1948–9 siege of Berlin drove many in the peace movement to take a more bellicose stance toward the Soviets. The outbreak of military hostilities in Korea then "dealt the final hammer-blow to the fragile postwar peace movement."[11] By the early 1950s the peace movement had reached a nadir. Given the anti-communist hysteria of the McCarthy years, alternative views met dwindling audiences. While an intellectual critique of cold war confrontationism was never completely muted, politically it barely mattered in the early 1950s.

In British and American occupied Western Europe, the cold war was more immediately present on the ground than in North America, while at the same time it was less easily accepted. In semi-sovereign Germany, even the most principled anti-communists like the West German Social Democratic Party (SPD) leader, Kurt Schumacher, mounted a strong political and intellectual challenge to a worldview in which there seemed to be no middle ground between two opposing ideological and military camps.[12] To Schumacher and other representatives of a "third force" between East and West, such as the French Socialist Party leader and former prime minister, Léon Blum, cold war antagonism was neither inevitable nor necessary. They did not accept the notion that Europe and Germany needed to be divided for the sake of freedom. And they were distrustful of the motives of both superpowers.[13]

European conservatives, too, were initially divided over how to best deal with the redrawn European map. In France, with its large Communist party and its fear of a German economic and military resurgence, conservatives, despite their resistance against cultural Americanization, were mostly pushing plans to keep the US involved in Europe.[14] Within the dominating continental Christian Democratic parties of Italy, the Netherlands, Belgium, and Germany, those opposing cold war antagonisms soon found themselves in a minority. West Germany's Konrad Adenauer and Italy's Alcide de

Gasperi benefited from American protection and, in the latter case, secret CIA money.[15] As the leaders of two of the major defeated European powers of World War II, they understood that in order to regain trust with the world, their countries needed to be pro-NATO and pro-American. To get Germany back on track, Adenauer gave long-term Western integration and security a higher priority than short-term tinkering with the German problem. He deemed Stalin's 1952 offers for a unified, but neutral Germany highly dubious, giving it little chance of realization.[16]

Given the ideological and political divisions of the late 1940s, 1950s, and early 1960s in Western Europe, conservative challenges to the cold war order were pushed to the margins. Historically, continental conservatives (to a much greater extent than British Tories) had opposed both liberalism and socialism. During the cold war the US and the USSR most prominently represented these 19th century ideologies. Building on their interwar European networks, which had been geographically centered on the old Habsburg empire, and now partially supported by postwar Fascist Spain, these so-called "Occidentalists" were both reliably anti-American and anti-communist. Despite a great deal of personal and even institutional overlap with pro-American Christian Democracy, they would not accept the dominance of either of the two warring "materialist brothers"—Soviet communism and Americanism—over Europe.[17]

In countries like Poland, Hungary, and Romania, neither communism nor the Soviet Union were popular. Given the military situation on the ground, internal political challenges against the cold war had to be even more muted than in the staunchly anti-communist 1950s West. As the Soviets imposed their model on Eastern Europe (in part as a reaction to the US consolidation of its European empire), chances of a third way diminished fast. Poland's most popular party, the Peasant Party, was eviscerated through a combination of Red Army pressure and communist ruthlessness. The Polish filmmaker Andrej Wajda, an intellectual antagonist of the cold war order, memorialized the losing battle of the non-communist Poles in *Ashes and Diamonds* (1958).[18] Some Poles waged guerrilla warfare until the late 1940s. Yet the Polish state no longer stood for an alternative to either East or West. Even the Czechs, who had welcomed Soviet liberation in 1945, had to abandon their balancing act between maintaining a foreign policy friendly to Moscow while keeping a liberal domestic sphere. Only Finland succeeded—in part because of the shock over the Prague coup in 1948. Conversely, in Yugoslavia a radical form of socialism ruled on the domestic front, leading to Tito's split with the Soviet Union in 1948.[19]

# RESISTING THE BOMB: WESTERN CHALLENGES DURING THE 1950S AND EARLY 1960S

On March 1, 1954, the US testing of a hydrogen bomb at the Bikini atoll in the South Pacific led to rising public concern over the long-term health effects of nuclear radiation. When nuclear fallout contaminated 28 Americans, 239 Marshall Islanders, and 23 crew members of a Japanese fishing boat, the "Lucky Dragon," the Bikini tests made international headlines and alarmed the US public. American domestic and international peace organizations, such as War Resisters' International (WRI), the International Fellowship of Reconciliation (IFR), and the Women's International League for Peace and Freedom (WILPF), renewed demands for nuclear disarmament. While anti-nuclear activism did not perceive itself as either pro- or anti-communist, it clearly questioned the underlying paradigm of an arms race borne out of superpower rivalry.[20]

By no means were these concerns limited to the United States. The Japanese reacted to the Bikini tests with universal fury. Memories of Hiroshima and Nagasaki were marshaled as a means to reject military "nuclearism." Initially, the "Japan Council Against Atomic and Hydrogen Bombs" (Gensuikyô) had been critical of both US and Soviet armaments. From 1959 onwards, however, the Japanese peace movement came under the sway of socialist and communist groups and limited its criticism to the weapons of the US and its allies.[21] In West Germany, the stationing of the first US nuclear weapons in 1953 as well as reports of NATO military exercises that simulated the dropping of 335 atomic bombs, with the immediate result of 5.2 million Germans wounded or killed, evoked demands to ban the bomb.[22] In the Federal Republic protests against nuclear weapons were inextricably linked to opposing plans to rearm the country. Like the Japanese, Germans opposed to the cold war, and nuclear arms, reminded their audiences about the lessons learned from World War II.[23]

In the mid-1950s polls throughout Western and Northern Europe showed that, despite significant mistrust of the Soviet Union, many supported a test ban treaty as well as the prohibition of nuclear arms. Early on scientists were prominent in these struggles. Britain's anti-nuclear activists urged their government not to develop the hydrogen bomb as early as 1950. A key figure was the British mathematician and philosopher Bertrand Russell, whose December 23, 1953, BBC radio address attracted international attention. It led to the creation of the Pugwash Movement that was supported by a number of leading physicists, including several Nobel laureates on both sides of the cold war barrier. Influenced by Western colleagues, Soviet physicists such as Andrei Sakharov apparently warned their government of the dangers of nuclear weapons.[24]

When nuclear testing programs accelerated during the late 1950s, a first wave of mass protests to "ban the bomb" erupted in Western countries. Britain took the lead with the formation of the Campaign for Nuclear Disarmament (CND). The first march from London to Aldermaston on Easter 1958 adopted the symbol that has become the emblem of peace movements ever since: a circle encompassing a broken cross.[25] The West German Easter March Movement, which originally grew out of opposition to NATO's decision to arm West German forces with US nuclear weapons, copied CND.[26] Although the 1963 Test Ban Treaty fell short of the expectations of peace activists, protesters could claim that they had contributed to growing pressure, forcing US and Soviet governments to achieve a breakthrough at the negotiating table. By politicizing a generation of young people and developing new forms of political action, the anti-nuclear campaign set the stage for the protests against the Vietnam War.

# Eastern challenges during the 1950s and 1960s

In the Soviet empire, challenges to the cold war order more directly translated into questioning the existing form of government. Already during the early 1950s, when communist rule remained fragile and people remembered a life before Stalinism, protests and demonstrations endangered the domestic status quo. Stalin's death in 1953 raised hopes throughout the Eastern bloc. Yet, the Plzeň demonstrations of May 1953 and the East Berlin workers' uprisings in June 1953 were easily crushed. Similar strikes could be observed in Hungary, Bulgaria, Romania, and even the USSR itself.[27] The crackdown was swift, but costly. East Germans were voting with their feet. Until the erection of the Berlin wall in 1961, about 2.7 million left for the West.[28] In Hungary, the 1953 strikes blazed a path for economic liberalization, which fueled the 1956 revolution.

While in 1953 Czechs, East Germans, and Hungarians primarily demanded better living and working conditions, in 1956 opposition groups confronted the cold war order more directly. Albeit not a challenge to the basic tenets of Soviet rule (only of Stalin's ruthless "digressions"), Khrushchev's repudiation of Stalinism in his February 1956 "Secret Speech" at the 20th CPSU Party congress set Poland and Hungary firmly on the path of reform communism. In Poland, according to the historian Paweł Machcewicz, the Communist party went through its most profound crisis of the cold war period, even eclipsing the heyday of Solidarity in 1980–1. The government averted a complete meltdown of communist rule by bringing back Władysław Gomułka, a high-ranking member of the communist nomenclatura who had fallen out of favor with Stalin and now represented both communism and Polish nationalism. Gomułka abandoned Sovietization, including the collectivization of agriculture; most Russian advisors left the country. Crucially, because the Catholic Church gained more breathing space, it could build a parallel society.[29] In Hungary, workers' councils (consciously modeled on the 1917 Russian Revolution) briefly realized alternative visions of socialism in 1956, when they gained considerable influence. Imre Nagy's "reform communism" provided a template for later reform efforts. Given the prevailing mood in Moscow and the rigidity of the East-West conflict, however, the 1956 Hungarian challenge to the cold war order did not stand the test of political reality.[30]

Northeast Asia also had its 1956. It was a little known but fascinating chapter of cold war history that Khrushchev's secret speech prompted a group of North Korean communist reformers to challenge Kim Il-Sung's orthodox Stalinism. What became known as the "August plot" evolved into a serious leadership crisis.[31] Ultimately, Pyongyang students, intellectuals, and party cadres failed to overthrow the domestic cold war order. Like their Hungarian counterparts they were brutally suppressed by the regime. The repercussions were far-reaching, nevertheless. The 1956 events in Hungary, Poland, North Korea, and the Soviet Union itself pushed Mao and the Chinese Communists to incrementally disassociate themselves from Moscow. China adhered to a Stalinist model for two more decades. After going through the cataclysm of the Cultural Revolution, it developed its own alternative to the bipolar cold war order. It also became an inspiration during the 1960s for Western revolutionaries who did not know much about China but were searching for leftist ideas beyond orthodox cold war communism. It was during the 1970s and 1980s that China, in part prompted by the 1968 Soviet crackdown in Prague, would open up toward the West, thus helping to penetrate cold war boundaries.[32]

The 1953 and 1956 movements failed politically. Yet, they set in motion processes which culminated a decade later with the 1968 Prague Spring and the 1968–9 Sino-Soviet military skirmishes. In Poland following 1956, for example, the young Marxist philosopher Leszek Kołakowski abandoned orthodox Marxism and became one of the standard bearers of what came to be known as "revisionism." Unlike their Western peers, who after 1956 left their Communist parties in droves, Eastern reform communists still tried to work through the party. They were not yet ready to replace communism with Western liberal democracy. They sought a "third way" outside the rigid cold war system, As Tony Judt observed, during the 1960s reform communism afforded "a brief window of optimism about an alternative Socialist future."[33]

In 1965, Jacek Kuroń and Karol Modzelewski, two young Polish communists, published a manifesto in which they sketched their vision of a socialism "with a human face."[34] Their "Open Letter to the Party" struck a chord among their Polish peers. It also became an important inspiration for those West European and North American students of the "1968" generation, who solicited ideas beyond the orthodox communist and liberal models.[35] Kuroń and Modzelewski were not supporters of Western liberal democracy. They adamantly opposed "parliamentary regimes" and favored the liberation "of a large group of countries from capitalist domination." Yet they also advocated a "workers' democracy" that gave autonomy to the local and factory level, allowed unions independent of the state, and channeled more resources from heavy industry into consumption (a conventional goal that had been on the agenda of many Eastern regimes since the mid-1960s). In addition, they demanded an end to the political police, the standing army, censorship, and one-party rule. In a similar fashion, the resolution passed by the Fourth Czechoslovak Writers' Congress in the summer of 1967, which became one of the rallying cries of the "Prague Spring," paralleled Czech party chief Alexander Dubček's "third way." It did not argue for a sweeping "counter-revolution," as Leonid Brezhnev later alleged. Rather, it challenged the cold war order in both its Eastern and Western incarnations.

"Prague" and "Warsaw" 1968 were by no means direct precursors to 1989. East Central European intellectuals such as the Czech writer Vaclav Havel and his Polish counterpart Adam Michnik were still a long way from becoming adherents of Western-style democracy.[36] It was only during the 1970s and 1980s, mostly in reaction to the Prague crackdown, that reform communism became suspicious to younger generations of East Europeans and Northeast Asians. Yet, during the 1980s concepts like "freedom" and "democracy" could be perceived outside the post-1989 triumphalist Western notion of these terms. Even among the members of the dissident Polish labor union Solidarity, these terms were imbued with a socialist meaning. In fact, it was precisely because Dubček tried to square the circle by envisioning a less centralized, open, and liberal form of socialism that the Prague Spring turned out to be so contagious all across the Eastern bloc, including the German Democratic Republic (GDR).[37]

Whereas communist regimes managed to suppress civic unrest for almost two more decades, its critics lost faith in communism's ability to reform itself. After Prague 1968, working through the established Communist parties was no longer an option. In 1989 during the Czech "Velvet Revolution," Dubček received a hero's welcome on Wenceslas Square. Yet it was obvious that not he, the failed leader of the Prague Spring and proponent of "Socialism with a human face," but the most prominent speaker among the 1970s dissidents, Vaclav Havel, would lead his country into the post-communist era. Even though the democratic impulse of 1968 had not led to an immediate overthrow of the existing orders, its long-term consequences were nevertheless remarkable. In 1989 Havel, Kuroń, Michnik, and other intellectual protagonists of 1968 would become driving intellectual forces behind the peaceful revolutions in East Central Europe.[38]

# Against imperialism: anti-Vietnam protests and "1968"

In Western countries, too, 1956 was a turning point. The failed Franco-British invasion of Suez highlighted the extent to which the international system had become a bipolar one. Little political space was left for meddling mid-size powers (and former colonial masters at that) still mired in dreams of European greatness.[39] While Britain sought to reinforce its "special relationship" after Suez, throwing in its lot with the Americans, the French government consented to the next step of European integration with the founding of the European Economic Community (EEC) in Rome 1957. It also developed its own alternative vision of the cold war, which culminated in President Charles de Gaulle's quixotic campaigns of the 1960s. He was unable to reconcile his effort to establish "great power" relations with Moscow with his simultaneous encouragement of Polish emancipation. His policies toward Western Europe were similarly inconsistent. While he promoted Western European "independence" from the US, he could not overcome suspicions among the West Germans, Dutch, and Italians that his program aimed purely toward French "grandeur."

For Western left-wing intellectuals, the brutal crushing of the Hungarian revolution was at least as important as Suez was for the decolonization process in Africa. Many deserted the traditional Communist parties and worked toward the establishment of a "new left," which laid the intellectual groundwork for the 1960s protest movements.[40] New left challenges to the cold war differed markedly from anti-nuclear activism. First, the anti-nuclear campaign had been closely linked to the "old left" of established social democratic parties and labor unions, whereas the new left did not organize in traditional ways at all. Second, its social basis was not workers, but young people and intellectuals.

Third, while the anti-nuclear campaign had been mostly limited to Western Europe, the United States, and Japan, the new left developed real and imagined ties to postcolonial revolutionary movements.[41] Fourth, the new left was less about the cold war as such. Although critical of both the USSR and the US, it by and large subordinated the nuclear threat to what it considered more fundamental North-South issues. The new left hoped to turn the direction of the world's main political axis from East-West to North-South.[42]

By the late 1960s Vietnam had come to replace concerns over nuclear armament as the main reason for peace-related activities. In Europe, Vietnam came to crowd out the legacies of earlier struggles against colonialism such as the Algerian War of the late 1950s and early 1960s. In the US, worries over the Vietnam War intensified even before President Lyndon B. Johnson began to dispatch combat troops in 1965. Developing parallel to and often in close association with the African-American civil rights, feminist, student, and environmental movements, leftist protest in part turned into a more elemental critique of the cold war order. Taken together with these other challenges to the status quo, the domestic and international impact was huge. It accelerated the demise of the liberal ("New Deal") consensus, undercut American economic pre-eminence, left the US military in its deepest crisis, fed into the Sixties "counter-cultural" challenges, and ultimately came to symbolize the end of the era of great dreams of the early 1960s.[43]

The anti-Vietnam protests were a global phenomenon. Beginning in 1966, simultaneous anti-war rallies were staged in several Western countries. In October 1967, for example, the march on the Pentagon that was organized by US peace groups was closely coordinated with solidarity demonstrations against American military installations in West Berlin and with anti-war rallies in Amsterdam, London, Oslo, Paris, Rome, and Tokyo.[44] In Britain and West Germany, student protests, originally organized over issues of college discipline, escalated into mass demonstrations with more than 100,000 participants in 1968. The greatest mobilization was seen in Japan, where anti-Vietnam protests rallied almost 800,000 people in 1970. In many other Western as well as non-Western countries such as Mexico, the Philippines, Thailand, and Zambia, opposition to the American engagement in Vietnam led to student radicalization.[45] The anti-Vietnam protests challenged cold war doctrines in new and different ways. Anti-imperialism, which in principle was directed at both superpowers, superseded anti-nuclearism as the main oppositional rallying cry.

Like its anti-nuclear predecessor during the 1950s and to a more limited extent the 1953-6 East Central European movements, the Vietnam protests saw the emergence of transnational networks of rebellion. The close ties between American, West German, and other European protesters matched their governments' cold war cooperation. Important figures of the German new left, for example, had become acquainted with their American counterparts as exchange students during the early 1960s. After their return to Germany they helped organize protests against the American war in Vietnam using methods they copied from the US civil rights movements, such as "sit-ins," or following their American campus peers by organizing "teach-ins" at German universities.[46] Similar cross-pollination could be observed in many other countries.[47]

Anti-Vietnam protests evolved into a more systemic anti-imperialist and anti-capitalist critique of Western democracy that envisioned a world beyond the cold war. The revolutionary rhetoric and violent methods of "1968" often alienated middle-class voters who had been broadly sympathetic to the anti-nuclear cause. On its extreme fringes it also spawned left-wing terrorist groups, which took lives in the name of overcoming the established order. While often grounded in particular local grievances, this Western terrorism, which found only a limited measure of support among the majority of the 1960s movements, focused on domestic political targets as well as on US military installations. Particularly in Italy, Japan, and West Germany—the three successor states of the 1930s aggressors—terrorist groups targeted US military installations. Here, the challenge to the cold war became increasingly one-sided, anti-American, and lethal.[48] Yet, in the United States, too, the radical left Weather Underground brutally opposed the cold war order and carried out bombings in the name of anti-imperialism and anti-capitalism.[49]

# The rise of Europe and East Asia: challenging the "second cold war"

When the thaw in superpower relations was giving way to new tensions during the second half of the 1970s, East Asians, West Europeans, and to a lesser extent North Americans were at first not prepared to accept renewed cold war belligerence. Several developments helped revive the peace and anti-nuclear campaigns. First, beginning in the early 1970s, NATO started to modernize its nuclear arsenal through the testing of advanced weaponry such as cruise missiles. It also upgraded its air and ground arsenal with new generations of tanks and bombers. Second, the Soviet Union likewise modernized its nuclear forces by introducing SS-20 medium range missiles and "Backfire" bombers. From NATO's point of view this tilted the military balance toward the Warsaw Pact organization. Third, the Soviet invasion in Afghanistan in late 1979, NATO's December 1979 "Dual track decision," and finally Ronald Reagan's election to the American presidency in November 1980 elicited mounting fears of nuclear armageddon in East and West.[50]

The fourth and most important game changer, however, was the reduction of the dominance of the superpowers. During the 1960s and 1970s, allies of both the US and to a more limited extent the USSR had made headway vis-à-vis the hegemonic powers. Western Europe, in particular, was much less dependent on the United States. West Germany, France, and Japan, but also smaller allies like the Netherlands and South Korea, were flexing their economic muscles, while the US seemed to be in economic decline. The Federal Republic especially made a huge military, economic, and increasingly political contribution to the Western alliance. With regard to the NATO dual-track decision, West European leaders like Prime Minister James Callaghan of Britain,

Chancellor Helmut Schmidt of West Germany, and President Valéry Giscard d'Estaing of France exercised leadership, while US President Jimmy Carter seemed to lack the resolve to lead the West.[51]

New protests against the cold war exploded with NATO's decision to deploy a new generation of intermediate-range ballistic missiles in December 1979.[52] This second great anti-nuclear campaign in postwar history achieved most domestic support in Belgium and the Netherlands, where governments agreed to delay the NATO deployment schedule.[53] In Britain, where CND was rejuvenated, nuclear weapons became an important political issue as well. In October 1980, 80,000 marched to Trafalgar Square. In Germany the same year anti-nuclear demonstrations reached 100,000. The high point occurred in October 1983 just before the deployment of NATO's new missiles began. Up to an estimated one million demonstrators protested in West Germany, 600,000 in Rome, and 400,000 in London. New York City witnessed the largest demonstration in US history with almost a million taking to the streets in June 1982.[54]

Unlike the first anti-nuclear campaigns of the 1950s and the protests against the Vietnam War, the 1980s peace movement did not originate in the United States. While supported by American peace groups (such as the National Freeze Campaign), the European peace movements of the 1980s developed independently. Their focus was the Pershing II and cruise missiles, which concerned the balance of power in Europe. This was a lesser worry among US peace activists, whose outlook was more global and who focused on intercontinental weapons such as the MX missiles.[55] Japanese activists also re-emerged during the 1980s, when 27 million Japanese signed anti-nuclear petitions.[56] While the transnational protests of the 1980s continued older traditions, they also had their roots in the ecological and feminist movements. In several European countries, this led to the founding of new parliamentary groups such as the Green parties, which made challenging the cold war order a central plank of their platform.

The 1980s saw the emergence of a growing sense of inner-European solidarity vis-à-vis the two superpowers. Europeans and East Asians became more distrustful of both the United States and the Soviet Union, who seemed to have re-ignited the cold war in order to stay on top of their respective alliance systems. Eastern bloc peace activists shared many concerns with their Western peers. East German peace groups, for example, which were mostly anchored in the Protestant churches, found much common ground with peace-minded Dutch and German church representatives. The British-based peace group European Nuclear Disarmament (END) created a network that sought to bring together activists from both sides of the iron curtain.[57] In addition, unlike Margaret Thatcher and the British Tories, continental European conservatives were less willing to return to the sharp anti-communism of the 1950s. In West Germany, Helmut Kohl and his staunchly conservative arch rival, the Bavarian premier Franz-Josef Strauß, continued to work on improving relations with the GDR and preserving the hard-won gains of *Ostpolitik*. Kohl even spoke of a "German-German coalition of reason."[58]

In East Asia, too, the old order was crumbling. From the time of the invasion of Czechoslovakia in the late 1960s, China, now under its new post-Maoist leadership, had ceased to view the US within the framework of an ideologically driven cold war competition. South Korea went through a phase of domestic turmoil beginning in the late 1970s that resulted in the overthrow of the US backed anti-communist military dictatorships and a gradual transition to democracy. While US-Soviet relations deteriorated in the early 1980s, especially after the shooting down of a Korean airliner (KAL flight 007) in September 1983, South Korea's external relations vis-à-vis China and Japan relaxed. As part of the domestic "thaw" in South Korea and China, trade began to crowd out former ideological and military conflicts.[59] Japan's economic miracle, like Europe's, had been built on exports to the United States, which provided cheap defense and thus took a big burden off the shoulders of the Japanese. By the late 1980s, however, the East-West conflict seemed to have been replaced by an epoch of trilateral global economic competition among Western Europe, East Asia, and North America.[60]

# The final years: challenging the cold war becomes consensus

By the mid-1980s challenging the cold war order was de rigeur. That consensus was now so broad that it was shared by conservative and progressive politicians alike. Ronald Reagan astonished friend and foe when he famously reversed his position on the arms race in early 1984.[61] The Reagan reversal together with the 1985 ascendancy of Mikhail Gorbachev to the post of CPSU general secretary helped pave the way toward nuclear abolition and détente . The final challenge to the cold war thus started in the halls of government, although the ground had been prepared by Solidarity in Poland and the large-scale West European and North American peace movements of the 1980s.

Solidarity merits its own chapter in a history on challenges to the cold war. Given the central strategic and political importance of Poland to the Soviet empire, Solidarity's success was critical to the fall of the Soviet Union in 1990–1. Beginning in 1976 Poland had been in a state of almost continuous economic crisis. After the 1976 strikes, the Workers' Defense Committee (KOR) was founded, which included March 1968 veterans like Adam Michnik and Jacek Kuroń. It was soon joined by other groups that openly challenged the party monopoly. Karol Wojtyła's election to the papacy confirmed the church's role as a societal organization. John Paul II's triumphal visit to Poland in June 1979 demonstrated that the Church could mobilize millions without having to ask for the consent of the state.[62]

With the economic situation going from bad to worse in early 1980, the austerity measures of the Polish government led to an explosion of strikes that soon engulfed the country. Solidarity came into being in the summer of 1980. Within a year it had millions of members. The striking workers were able to extract considerable concessions from the regime. This time the Poles were lucky. Since late 1979 the Soviet Union had been embroiled in a costly war in Afghanistan. On its eastern border it was challenged by a westward looking China. The Polish government could not spend its way out of trouble as had been the case during the 1960s and 1970s. It (as well as the GDR, the CSSR, and Hungary) depended on a continuous flow of Western cash. A 1953, 1956, or 1968 "solution" was thus out of the question. The government declared martial law in 1981, but continued to face an impasse.[63]

The cold war ended in Poland in the fall 1988. The establishment of a "round table" brought the various parties and groups together. The government also had to accept the legalization of Solidarity, which was registered in April 1989. Even as Western politicians struggled to grasp the seriousness of these Polish moves toward an uneasy coexistence between a communist government and non-communist organizations, Poland slipped into the new post-cold war order. In September 1989, Tadeusz Mazowiecki was appointed the first non-communist prime minister since World War II.[64] When the East German "embassy crisis" emerged during the summer of 1989, Poland provided an example that could be copied by other Soviet satellites. Gorbachev declared the cold war to be over when he came up with the "Sinatra Doctrine" that the Eastern Europeans could have it their own way.

In the decades between World War II and the 1980s, the history of the world was shaped by the competition between the two superpowers. In a divided Europe in particular, but also in East Asia and North America, throughout the forty years of the cold war this state of the world was almost constantly challenged. As much as anti-communism in the West and anti-capitalism in the East, rejecting the cold war order was part and parcel of the East-West conflict. In Eastern Europe, these challenges often turned violent because the domestic cold war order was originally imposed by the Soviet Union. In the West, the cold war also permeated the political culture. Yet within democratic systems challenges to the prevailing international order such as those expressed by the peace movements of the 1950s and 1980s or the anti-imperialist critique of the 1960s often helped to create a new consensus. Here, in the long run, challenging the cold war turned out to be a means of integration and building a democratic consensus. While we cannot overlook the fundamental differences between East and West, challenging the cold war created (imagined) communities of protest across national borders and thus helped to bring people on both sides of the iron curtain together.

## NOTES

1. See John Lewis Gaddis's iconic essay, "The Long Peace: Elements of Stability in the Postwar International System," in John Lewis Gaddis, *The Long Peace: Inquiries into the History of the Cold War* (New York: Oxford University Press, 1987), 215–45.

2. Milan Kundera, "Die Weltliteratur: How We Read One Another," *The New Yorker*, January 8, 2007 (originally published 1983 as part of *Un occident kidnappé*).

3. Jerome Shapiro, *Atomic Bomb Cinema: The Apocalyptic Imagination on Film* (London: Routledge, 2002); Gerard J. DeGroot, *The Bomb: A Life* (Cambridge, MA: Harvard University Press, 2005).

4  Lawrence S. Wittner, *The Struggle against the Bomb*, 3 vols. (Stanford, CA: Stanford University Press, 1993–2003).

5. East and West are ideological markers, not geographical distinctions. Obviously, cold war East Asia was divided between a communist North and a capitalist South.

6. Jeremi Suri, *Power and Protest: Global Revolution and the Rise of Détente* (Cambridge, MA: Harvard University Press, 2003), 216–26; Carole Fink and Bernd Schaefer, eds., *Ostpolitik, 1969–1974: European and Global Responses* (New York: Cambridge University Press, 2009).

7. This may seem surprising because the Bond novels and movies are the staple of any class on cold war culture. Early volumes, however, stress British and French cooperation, often at the expense of a good laugh about the ineptitude of Soviet and American spies.

8. Alexis de Tocqueville, *Democracy in America* [1835/40], translated by Gerald E. Bevan, with an Introduction and Notes by Isaac Kramnick (London: Penguin Books, 2003), 485.

9. Philipp Gassert, "Defending Europe Against Bolshevism, Liberalism, and Americanism: Right Wing Images of the West, 1930–1950," in Riccardo Bavaj and Martina Steber, eds., *German Images of "the West": The History of a Modern Concept* (New York: Berghahn Books, forthcoming).

10. J. Samuel Walker, *Henry A. Wallace and American Foreign Policy* (Westport, CT: Greenwood Publishers, 1976).

11. Lawrence Wittner, *Rebels Against War: The American Peace Movement, 1933–1983* (Philadelphia, PA: Temple University Press, 1984), 201.

12. David Calleo, *The German Problem Reconsidered: Germany and the World Order, 1870 to the Present* (Cambridge: Cambridge University Press, 1978), 172.

13. Léon Blum, "La Trosième Force internationale. Éditorial in Le Populaire" (January 1948), <www.europa.clio-online.de/site/lang__en-US/mid__11373/ItemID__13/40208215/default.aspx> (April 15, 2011).

14. Irwin M. Wall, *The United States and the Making of Postwar France, 1945–1954* (Cambridge: Cambridge University Press, 1991), 127–57.

15. Paul Ginsborg, *A History of Contemporary Italy: Society and Politics 1943–1988* (New York: Palgrave Macmillan, 2003), 157–60.

16. Ronald Granieri, *The Ambivalent Alliance: Konrad Adenauer, the CDU/CSU, and the West, 1949–1966* (New York: Berghahn Books, 2003), 49–56.

17. Vanessa Conze, *Das Europa der Deutschen: Ideen von Europa in Deutschland zwischen Reichstradition und Westorientierung, 1920–1970* (Munich: Oldenbourg, 2005).

18. John Orr and Elzbieta Ostrowska, *The Cinema of Andrzej Wajda: The Art of Irony and Defiance* (London: Wallflower, 2003).

19. Tony Judt, *Postwar: A History of Europe since 1945* (New York: Penguin, 2005), 140–5.

20. Lawrence S. Wittner, *Resisting the Bomb: A History of the World Nuclear Disarmament Movement 1954–1970* (Stanford, CA: Stanford University Press, 1998), 10–14.

21. Volker Fuhrt, "Peace Movements as Emancipatory Experience—Anpo Tôsô and Beiheiren 1960s' Japan," in Benjamin Ziemann, ed., *Peace Movements in Western Europe, Japan, and the USA during the Cold War* (Essen: Klartext, 2009), 77–90.

22. Alice Cooper Holmes, *Paradoxes of Peace: German Peace Movements since 1945* (Ann Arbor, MI: University of Michigan Press, 1996).

23. It should be pointed out that in the British case opposition to nuclear arms was in part also motivated by memories of the Blitz. Dietmar Süß, "Memories of the Air War," *Journal of Contemporary History* 43 (2008), 333–42.

24. Joseph Rotblat, *Scientists and the Quest for Peace: A History of the Pugwash Conferences* (Cambridge, MA: MIT Press, 1972); Paul Rubinson, "'Crucified on a Cross of Atoms': Scientists, Politics, and the Test Ban Treaty," *Diplomatic History* 35: 2 (April 2011), 283–319.

25. Richard Taylor, *Against the Bomb: The British Peace Movement, 1958–1965* (Oxford: Clarendon Press, 1988).

26  Holger Nehring, "Searching for Security: The British and West German Protests against Nuclear Weapons and 'Respectability', 1958–1963," in Ziemann, *Peace Movements*, 167–87.

27. Geoff Eley, *Forging Democracy: The History of the Left in Europe, 1850–2000* (Oxford: Oxford University Press, 2002), 330.

28. Mary Fulbrook, *Anatomy of a Dictatorship: Inside the GDR 1949–1989* (Oxford: Oxford University Press, 1995), 177–87.

29. Paweł Machcewicz, "The Polish 1956," in Carole Fink, Frank Hadler, and Tomasz Schramm, eds., *1956: European and Global Responses* (Leizpig: Leipziger Universitätsverlag, 2006), 141–65.

30. Peter Kenez, "Khrushchev and Hungary in 1956," in Fink et al., *1956*, 105–18; Eley, *Forging Democracy*, 333–4.

31. Andrei Lankov, *Crisis in North Korea: The Failure of De-Stalinization, 1956* (Honolulu, HI: University of Hawai'i Press, 2004).

32. See Nancy Bernkopf Tucker, "China under Siege: Escaping the Dangers of 1968," in Carole Fink, Philipp Gassert and Detlef Junker, eds., *1968: The World Transformed* (New York: Cambridge University Press, 1998), 193–216.

33. Judt, *Postwar*, 427.

34. Jerzy Eisler, "March 1968 in Poland" in Fink et al., *1968*, 243.

35. George Lavan Weissman, ed., *Revolutionary Marxist Students In Poland Speak Out (1964–1968)* (New York: Merit Publishers, 1968), 2.

36. Paul Berman, *A Tale of Two Utopias: The Political Journey of the Generation of 1968* (New York: Norton, 1996), 224–30.

37. Philipp Gassert and Elisabeth Piller, "East Germany: Solidarity with Red Prague," in Philipp Gassert and Martin Klimke, eds., *1968: Memories and Legacies of a Global Revolt* (Washington, DC: German Historical Institute, 2009), 159–61.

38. Timothy Garton Ash, *The Magic Lantern: The Revolution of '89 Witnessed in Warsaw, Budapest, Berlin, and Prague* (New York: Random House, 1990).

39. William R. Keylor, "The Wind of Change in 1956," in Fink et al., *1956*, 235–43.

40. Madeleine Davis, "The Origins of the British New Left," in Martin Klimke and Joachim Scharloth, eds., *1968 in Europe: A History of Protest and Activism* (New York: Palgrave Macmillan, 2008), 45–56.

41. Gassert and Klimke, *1968*; Samantha M.R. Christiansen and Zachary A. Scarlett, eds., *1968 and the Global South* (New York: forthcoming).

42. Cynthia Young, *Soul Power: Culture, Radicalism, and the Making of a US Third World Left* (Durham, NC: Duke University Press, 2006); Quinn Slobodian, *Foreign Front: Third World Politics in Sixties West Germany* (Durham, NC: Duke University Press, forthcoming).

43. David Farber, *The Age of Great Dreams: America in the 1960s* (New York: Hill and Wang, 1994).

44. Ronald Fraser, *1968: A Student Generation in Revolt* (New York: Pantheon, 1988).

45. Andreas W. Daum, Lloyd C. Gardner, and Wilfried Mausbach, eds., *America, the Vietnam War, and the World: Comparative and International Perspectives* (New York: Cambridge University Press, 2003).

46. Martin Klimke, *The Other Alliance: Global Protest and Student Unrest in West Germany and the US, 1962–1972* (Princeton, NJ: Princeton University Press, 2010).

47. See the various contributions in Fink et al., *1968*; Klimke and Scharloth, *1968 in Europe*; Gassert and Klimke, *1968*.

48. Dorothea Hauser, "Terrorism," in Klimke and Scharloth, *1968 in Europe*, 269–80; Philipp Gassert, "Anti-Amerikaner? Die deutsche Neue Linke und die USA," in Jan C. Behrends, Árpád von Klimo, and Patrice G. Poutrus, eds., *Anti-Amerikanismus im 20. Jahrhundert: Studien zu Ost- und Westeuropa* (Bonn: Dietz, 2005), 250–67.

49. Jeremy Varon, *Bringing the War Home: The Weather Underground, the Red Army Faction, and Revolutionary Violence in the Sixties and Seventies* (Berkeley, CA: University of California Press, 2004).

50. Leopoldo Nuti, ed., *The Crisis of Détente in Europe: From Helsinki to Gorbachev, 1975–1985* (London: Routledge, 2009).

51. Matthias Schulz and Thomas A. Schwartz, eds., *The Strained Alliance: US-European Relations from Nixon to Carter* (New York: Cambridge University Press, 2010).

52. Philipp Gassert, Tim Geiger, and Hermann Wentker, eds., *Zweiter Kalter Krieg und Friedensbewegung. Der NATO-Doppelbeschluss in deutsch-deutscher und internationaler Perspektive* (Munich: Oldenbourg, 2011).

53. Alfred van Staden, "To Deploy or Not to Deploy: The Case of the Cruise Missiles," in Philipp P. Everts, ed., *Controversies at Home: Domestic Factors in the Foreign Policy of the Netherlands* (Dordrecht: Martinus Nijhof Publishers, 1985), 133–57.

54. April Carter, *Peace Movements: International Protests and World Politics since 1945* (London: Longman, 1992), 121.

55. David Cortright, Ron Pagnucco, "Limits to Transnationalism: The 1980s Freeze Campaign," in Jackie Smith, Charles Chatfield, and Ron Pagnucco, eds., *Transnational Social Movements and Global Politics: Solidarity beyond the State* (Syracuse, NY: Syracuse University Press, 1997), 159–74.

56. Lawrence S. Wittner, *Toward Nuclear Abolition: A History of the World Nuclear Disarmament Movement, 1971–Present* (Stanford, CA: Stanford University Press, 2003), 203–4, 227.

57. Rudolf Bahro et al., *The Dynamics of European Nuclear Disarmament* (Nottingham: Spokesman for European Nuclear Disarmament, 1981).

58. Timothy Garton Ash, *In Europe's Name: Germany and the Divided Continent* (London: Jonathan Cape, 1993).

59. Francis Pike, *Empires at War: A Short History of Modern Asia since World War II* (London: I.B. Tauris, 2010), 527–31.

60. See, for example, Lester Thurow, *Head to Head: The Coming Economic Battle among Japan, Europe, and America* (New York: Time Warner Books, 1992).

61. Beth A. Fischer, *The Reagan Reversal: Foreign Policy and the End of the Cold War* (Columbia, MO: University of Missouri Press, 1997).

62. Olga A. Narkiewicz, *Eastern Europe 1968–1984* (London: Croom Helm, 1986).

63. Norman Davies, *Heart of Europe: A Short History of Poland* (Oxford: Oxford University Press, 1986).

64. Ash, *Magic Lantern*.

## SELECT BIBLIOGRAPHY

Ash, Timothy Garton. *In Europe's Name: Germany and the Divided Continent*. London: Jonathan Cape, 1993.

Fink, Carole, Philipp Gassert, and Detlef Junker, eds. *1968: The World Transformed*. New York: Cambridge University Press, 1998.

Fink, Carole, Frank Hadler, and Tomasz Schramm, eds. *1956: European and Global Responses*. Leizpig: Leipziger Universitätsverlag, 2006.

Gassert, Philipp. "The Anti-American as Americanizer: Revisiting the Anti-American Century in Germany," *German Politics and Society* 27:1 (Spring 2009): 24–38.

Judt, Tony. *Postwar: A History of Europe since 1945*. New York: Penguin, 2005.

Klimke, Martin and Joachim Scharloth, eds. *1968 in Europe: A History of Protest and Activism, 1956–1977*. New York: Palgrave Macmillan, 2008.

Nuti, Leopoldo, ed. *The Crisis of Détente in Europe: From Helsinki to Gorbachev, 1975–1985*. London: Routledge, 2009.

Pike, Francis. *Empires at War: A Short History of Modern Asia since World War II*. London: I.B. Tauris, 2010.

Schulz, Matthias and Thomas A. Schwartz, eds. *The Strained Alliance: US-European Relations from Nixon to Carter*. New York: Cambridge University Press, 2010.

Suri, Jeremi. *Power and Protest: Global Revolution and the Rise of Détente*. Cambridge, MA: Harvard University Press, 2003.

Wittner, Lawrence S. *The Struggle against the Bomb*, 3 vols. Stanford, CA: Stanford University Press, 1993–2003.

Ziemann, Benjamin, ed. *Peace Movements in Western Europe, Japan, and the USA during the Cold War*. Essen: Klartext, 2009.

# CHAPTER 26

........................................................................................

# LOCATING THE
# TRANSNATIONAL IN THE
# COLD WAR

........................................................................................

## PENNY VON ESCHEN

In November 2005 the first monument to martial arts expert and film star Bruce Lee was unveiled in Mostar, Bosnia Herzegovina (a second monument was displayed in Hong Kong a day later). Honoring Lee as a symbol of "loyalty, skill, justice, and friendship," the organizers also intended the life-sized bronze statue "as a rebuke to the ongoing use of public spaces to glorify the country's competing nationalisms." In a city that had been divided over identities and boundaries and had been torn apart in the 1992–3 war that largely destroyed the 15th and 16th century Bosniak (Bosnian Muslim) west side, it was critical to the monument's planners that Lee was neither Serb, nor Croatian, nor Muslim, and that his statue faced north, favoring neither East nor West.

Moreover, the organizers explained, Bruce Lee, who had emerged as a transnational screen icon of anti-imperialism in the 1970s, fighting European and Asian colonizers alike, reminded them of the hope of their childhood. For young audiences across the globe, from Mostar, to Los Angeles, Zagreb, Bombay, and Hong Kong, Lee embodied a vision of a future free from poverty and political repression, and the armed conflict that raged through the Asian, African, and Central American continents during the era we still refer to, perhaps inescapably for our generation, as the "cold war." Sadly, a mere statue of the famed martial artist was hardly a deterrent for vandals. Within hours after the dedication, desecrators stole the nunchucks and defaced the statue. The statue was quickly removed and stored for repair.[1]

As I read reports of Lee monuments in 2005, I recalled a conversation a decade earlier with a colleague from Budapest. As we discussed the triumphalism that dominated western accounts of the end of the cold war, he grew nostalgic for the camaraderie of drinking with friends on Budapest's Lumumba Street. That street, of course, enshrined the memory of Patrice Lumumba, post-independence Prime Minister of the short-lived republic of the Congo, assassinated by Belgian authorities with CIA complicity in 1961.

Despite his limited prospects and frustrations under Hungarian communism, nonetheless my colleague mourned a vanished world of anti-imperialism and hopes of global justice that had always seemed larger than his own circumstances. Lumumba Street, he explained, no longer existed. It had been renamed after the fall of the socialist government, when practically overnight streets commemorating revolutionary icons were rechristened after monarchs and elites. Friends had trouble meeting each other because they didn't know the names of familiar streets. In time, I would discover that Budapest's Lumumba Street had been renamed Rona Utca. There had been dozens of Lumumba Streets in cities throughout the former eastern bloc. Most no longer exist: as in Budapest they were renamed after the fall of the communist regimes. The contested legacies of Lee and Lumumba reveal an ongoing struggle over cold war memory. The incarnation of Lee and the erasure of Lumumba as global symbols attest to the power as well as the fragility of the transnational projects and aspirations of the cold war era.

In this essay, I take up three central and related issues. First, to address my specific charge to consider ways in which transnational actors and groups permeated the East-West divide, I argue that we must first consider cold war transnationalism as a highly specific political and ideological formation. Much of the recent scholarly discussion on transnationalism has focused on analytic and methodological questions, but to begin to grasp the promise and fragility of transnational formations in the cold war era, it is imperative that one does not conflate transnationalism as methodology and analytic category with transnationalism as political, material, and ideological formations. Only by considering cold war transnationalism as a historically specific political and ideological formation can we grasp the frame of the possible, as well as the limitations of such transnational projects as those reflected in the Bruce Lee and Patrice Lumumba examples.[2] Following Prasenjit Duara's essay in this volume on nation/empire and the cold war, I suggest that these projects were triangulated with the dominant structures of nations and empires on the one hand, and the universalizing aspirations of the superpowers on the other. Indeed, transnationalism could only have achieved its centrality during the cold war because these projects laid bare and mediated between the core contradictions and tensions of the era, as the cold war's superpowers, each with considerable imperial baggage, sought to legitimize universalizing projects.

Cold war era transnational projects generated sites for political negotiation and leverage in conditions of extraordinarily unequal global power relations amidst war, shifting empires, and decolonization. I will discuss a range of transnational formations, attempting to account for the ubiquity and power of these formations. In doing so, I explore a realm of what Svetlana Boym has called "critical nostalgia," a theme that has emerged in the burgeoning literature on cold war memory as an expression of loss: not necessarily for a particular political formation of the cold war, but for a sense of vanished hope itself.[3] As suggested above, far from a simple celebration of transnationalism as an alternative to cold war formations, I emphasize the contradictions and conundrums of cold war transnationalism. Throughout the cold war era, multiple transnational actors challenged, but also intersected with, the projects of states, including cold war superpowers. Both western and eastern bloc states advocated and sponsored extensive transnational projects. The socialist bloc sponsored a host of aid projects, labor and international peace and friendship conferences, and financed cultural diplomacy and anti-imperialist projects. The US sponsored transnational networks of modernization and development, and related educational, cultural, and religious projects; taken together these were rich sites of political formation for the arena of transnational anti-communism. To understand the significance of transnational actors during the cold war, and the fragility as well as the power of transnational formations, we need to delve into possibilities enabled by this moment.

Second, I suggest that attention to transnational formations as well as the movement of peoples across nations and multiple histories illuminates this volume's concern to show the interconnectedness of the cold war with national and transnational histories that predated the particular policies/crises of the cold war. The cold war recast some of the transnational networks that predated it, including evangelical Christianity and a range of missionary projects as well as transnational circuits in the performing arts. The cold war also resituated a range of consumer commodities, long circulated in far-flung circuits of exchange, as not simply the mechanisms or conditions for power, but as the very face of state power, as shown in such examples as blue jeans and plastics, in what Eli Rubin has called "synthetic socialism."[4]

Cold war remappings of the trajectories of anti-colonial movements stretched to nearly every part of the globe. From 1945 onward, the violent imposition of cold war geographies on colonial and decolonizing landscapes produced multiple wars and a massive displacement of people who were then forced to imagine a global political landscape where they would be visible—legible in the emerging international order as peoples with rights—and safe. From the arbitrary division of Korea at the 38th parallel on the night of August 10–11 in 1945; to the brokering of US administrative control of the Pacific Trust Territories and newly drawn Italy/Yugoslavian borders; through the division of Vietnam at the 13th parallel at the 1954 Geneva conventions and the securing by Jan Smuts of effective control of Southwest Africa at the United Nations, borders redrawn in the murky transition from World War II to the cold war generated an explosion of global anti-colonial and non-aligned as well as transnational anti-communist projects that dominated international politics for years to come.[5] For a global non-aligned movement, transnational alliances heralded a potent challenge to the prerogatives of superpowers. Here, I will consider the example of the intersection between transnational protests that followed Lumumba's death and non-alignment.

Third, I suggest that attention to transnational movements and formations raises fundamental questions about the archive of the cold war. Who gets to tell the story of the cold war? Emphasizing the limits of state archives for telling the story of the cold war and as a frame for following transnational actors under the radars of states, I turn to Kamila Shamsie's critically acclaimed 2009 *Burnt Shadows*. This work of historical fiction begins with the 1945 bombing of Nagasaki, and follows an arc through 1947 Delhi at the moment of partition, to CIA infused Pakistan, and finally to Afghanistan, New York City, and by implication Guantanamo. Probing intersections between cold war policies and historical trajectories of decolonization once viewed as independent of the cold war,

Shamsie further illuminates the emergence of what we might view as "blowback" transnationalism, calling attention to two of the most powerful transnational formations
spawned by the cold war: al-Qaeda on the one hand, and a vast network of mercenaries
and private military corporations made up primarily of former national security and
intelligence officers from every part of the globe on the other.[6] Yet, as I argue in concluding reflections on the afterlife of cold war transnationalism and the significance of contemporary commemorations of Patrice Lumumba, the transnational remains a powerful
dream space, a space for imaging alternatives to the present precisely because it beckons
past current formations of power, and the states and nations that have so badly failed the
people they purport to represent and protect.

# THE HISTORICAL MOMENT: NATION, EMPIRE, AND TRANSNATION

Scholars, including historians Ronald Suny, Terry Martin, Odd Arne Westad, and the
philosopher Susan Buck-Morss, have reminded us of how deeply and fundamentally
problems of nationalism and empire were woven into the very fabric of the cold war. To
appreciate the power and ubiquity of transnational formations as well as the conundrums of the transnational in the cold war era, it is necessary to revisit the World War
I-era formulations of Leninist and Wilsonian transnationalism. Indeed, tensions
between nations, empires, and new global formations had forcefully emerged much earlier. From the age of European, American, Haitian, and Latin revolutions on the cusp of
the 18th and 19th centuries, and cascading throughout the 19th century in anti-slavery,
workers', and women's movements, new media and circuits of exchange enabled and
emboldened global narratives. Here I take a page from earlier diplomatic historians as
well as global historians and recent scholarship on the Soviet Union to revisit the ways in
which the internationalism of the early Soviet and Wilsonian systems developed in relation to one another. To borrow a phrase from Carol Gluck and Anna Tsing, we might
speak of a "global lexicon" of the cold war shaped by a shared vision of the good life for
the masses and shared languages of egalitarianism, democracy, and modernization.[7]

The philosopher Buck-Morss and the historian Westad have asked us to consider the
shared assumptions and discursive worlds of the 20th century across the cold war divide.
Buck-Morss argues that the dream of mass utopia defines the 20th century: both capitalist and socialist forms of industrial modernity were characterized by a "collective dream
that dared to imagine social world in alliance with personal happiness."[8] Her emphasis
on the ubiquity of utopian visions is critical to understanding the abiding allure of the
transnational movements and icons of the cold war era, as well as the era's unexpected
and often fragile alliances. Indeed, what we might think of as the equally outlandish
promises and betrayals of communism and capitalism, along with the jarring experience of the celebration and violations of ideals, set the stage for interconnections and

alliances between those with similar aspirations and grievances that characterized many transnational movements.

Like Buck-Morss, Westad frames the US and Soviet projects as competing universalizing responses to the break-up of older empires and colonialism: both wrestling with their own legacies of empire.[9] In World War I, with the collapse of the Romanov (tsarist Russia), Habsburg, and Ottoman empires, the Bolsheviks inherited an empire in which over seventy ethnic groups spreading from Norwegian to Korean borders outnumbered Russians. Likewise, for Westad, the "origins of American interventions in the Third-World" are consonant with the very origins of the American state, from continental westward expansion, slavery, and colonial conflict with Native Americans, to the late 19th century occupation and annexation of Hawaii and turn of the century interventions and occupations of the Philippines and Cuba. Moreover, Westad adds, Africa had been at the heart of US policies both at home and abroad for the first hundred years.

In the case of the Soviet Union, recent scholarship has demonstrated the breadth and depth of the Bolshevik project of cultivating forms of ethno-nations as a counter to statehood. Historians Ronald Suny and Terry Martin noted the crowning irony of Soviet history: A "radical socialist elite that proclaimed an internationalist agenda that was to transcend the bourgeois nationalist phase of history in fact ended up by institutionalizing nations within its own political body."[10] Lenin viewed nationalism as dangerous because it could promote cross-class alliances, or in the 1918 words of Stalin: "the national flag is sewn on only to deceive the masses, a cover-up for the counter-revolutionary plans of the bourgeois."[11]

Despite their deep suspicion of nationalism, Lenin and Stalin adopted wildly ambitious ethno-nationalist projects. On the rationale that with modernization class divisions would naturally emerge which would allow the Soviet State to recruit proletarian and peasant support for the socialist project, in the 1920s the Soviets sponsored programs that at their most far-reaching involved not only the creation of ethnically specific cultural institutions from the opera to the press, but also the creation of written languages where none had previously existed.[12] This wishful belief in an evolution from nationalism to socialism might be compared to Wilsonianism and the US post-1945 foreign policy premise that democracy must yield to the needs of capitalism, because democracy will naturally emerge from capitalism. Such logic seemed to justify the overthrow of democracies in the short run. Indeed, Westad and Buck-Morss are astute in their recognition of the structural contradiction in both the US and Soviet systems as the avowed universalist ideologies of each came up against national interests and imperial entanglements.

Western tensions between local, national, and transnational projects also had antecedents in World War I. Wilson asserted his vision of internationalism in 1917, when he championed the right of self-determination as the central principle of legitimacy in the new international order and defined the self-determining nation state as the sole legitimate entity in international relations. Wilson presented his Fourteen Points, foremost among which was self-determination, as a response to the Bolshevik revolution and Lenin's call for worldwide anti-imperialism. As Wilson advocated national self-determination as an alternative to class conflict, in what Erez Manela has elegantly described as the "Wilsonian Moment," Afro-Asian colonial nationalists appropriated and interpreted the principle as a challenge to imperialism in international relations that required the recognition of the equality and sovereignty of hitherto "dependent" peoples.[13]

The Paris Peace Conference of 1919 became a focal point for anti-colonial aspirations. These anti-colonial activists quickly became disillusioned by Wilson and turned to the more vigorous support of Lenin, buoyed by the Communist International, founded in 1919 to promote world revolution. Wilson's failure notwithstanding, the stage had been set for a vigorous nation-building anti-communism that would be mobilized on behalf of anti-communist regimes in the post-1945 era. And more significantly in the short term, the left-inflected independence movements of the mid-20th century were bitterly opposed by an increasingly US dominated western bloc. While the Wilsonian vision proposed a world of nations modeled after US institutions, transnational aspirations were fundamental in both blocs.

Transnational projects that were in varying degrees related to identifiable ideological blocs in the cold war existed alongside and sometimes intersected with other transnational initiatives. In the case of Soviet bloc transnationalism, it is tempting to cynically dismiss the obvious failings of the Comintern and Soviet internationalism; Stalin obviously withdrew support for communist movements during and after World War II. As Westad observes in reference to Korea in particular and postwar intervention generally, "It was as if Stalin, having started up the ladder to socialism in one country, was deliberately kicking away the ladder for others to follow."[14]

But the opportunities afforded and relationships forged through the extensive Soviet international infrastructure of aid and solidarity organizations developed over the decades of the cold war can no more be reduced to crude projections of Soviet power than the US jazz ambassadors, of whom I have written elsewhere, can be reduced to agents of US imperialism.[15] One of the more striking examples of this can be seen in the Soviet support for South Africa's African National Congress. In 1953, well before the Soviet Union through Communist Party channels returned to a vigorous support of anti-imperialist movements with Khrushchev, Walter Sisulu traveled to London, Eastern Europe, and Moscow, holding meetings with any Africans present in an attempt to organize a Pan-African meeting on the continent of Africa.[16] After the Soviet rediscovery of the Third World (1955–60), Soviet sponsorship of conferences, camps, and global anti-imperialism projects expanded, with a flurry of activities sponsored by the Soviet Afro-Asian Solidarity Committee (founded in 1956); along with the World Federation of Trade Unions (WFTU), the World Federation of Democratic Youth (WFDY), created in London in 1945 by Communist youth groups; the Women's International Democratic Federation (1945); and the World Peace Council (WPC), created in 1949.

The fragility of the alliances enabled by these organizations, as they rapidly vanished after 1991, is striking. But does that necessarily imply that these expressions were superficial, artificially manufactured, and propped up by the state? Perhaps in some cases, but recent studies by historians and anthropologists working on the former Soviet bloc suggest otherwise. Their scholarship recovers the socialist idealism shared by many citizens of the Soviet Union and eastern bloc countries. As the anthropologist Alexei Yurchak argues: "What tends to get lost... is the crucial and seemingly paradoxical fact that, for great numbers of Soviet citizens, many of the fundamental values, ideals, and realities of socialist life (such as equality, community, selflessness, altruism, friendship, ethical relations, safety, work, creativity, and concern for the future) were of genuine importance, despite the fact that many of their everyday practices transgressed, reinterpreted, or refused certain norms and rules expressed in the official ideology of the socialist state."[17]

Indeed, like perestroika and glasnost, the 1989 revolutions took hold as movements to reform socialism, for "socialism with a human face," *not* for capitalism. And as the Mostar monument to Bruce Lee attests, anti-imperial liberation for the world's colonized peoples was part and parcel of that vision. Yurchak argues further that: "An undeniable constitutive part of today's phenomenon of 'post-Soviet nostalgia,' which is a complex post-Soviet construct, is the longing for the very real humane values, ethics, friendships, and creative possibilities that socialism afforded—often in spite of the state's proclaimed goals—and that were as irreducibly part of the everyday life of socialism as were the feelings of dullness and alienation."[18] Thus, we might suggest that the rapid collapse of transnational solidarity networks after the collapse of the eastern bloc states had less to do with cynicism than the fact that solidarities previously enabled through state mechanisms simply had no routes of circulation after the state collapsed. Though dependent on state infrastructures, such solidarities were not defined by them.

While the US had no counterpart to the Cominform, scholars have traced what we might think of as a complex transnational anti-communism, an area at the forefront of new developments in cold war historiography. Extensive US covert support for intellectual and cultural institutions, and US sponsored research by social scientists, educators, and the private sector in US modernization projects, buttressed but also stretched beyond US support for anti-communist regimes. Building on initial projects in the western hemisphere and the colonial Philippines, such networks fanned out through postwar occupations and military bases in a burgeoning global anti-communist network.[19]

## Transforming transnational circuits

Melani McAlister argues that during the cold war, Christian evangelicals recast the story of missionaries as symbols of altruistic sacrifice. In seeking to combat Godless communism, missionaries were now participating in the same kind of martyrdom as that undergone by the early Christians. An international evangelicalism cast as the "suffering church vs. communism" thrived in the cold war era through newspaper accounts and popular culture media in concert with "the occasional congressional hearing" such as a 1959 meeting of the House on Un-American Activities Committee with ministers from China and Korea. Later, as McAlister demonstrates, the Romanian Jewish convert

Richard Wurmbrand, in his 1967 *Tortured for Christ*, and the organization Voice of Martyrs, married "the iconography of Christian martyrdom to the larger project of universal rights."[20] Along with the Catholic Marians, with practices and theology based on veneration of the Virgin Mary, and who drew on Polish, Russian, and Lithuanian Marian exiles to fan out through Southeast Asia, Africa, and South America during the cold war, these state-supported non-state actors recast the language and aims of Christianity in cold war terms. Historians have long recognized the evangelical Protestant language of the cold war—depicted as a spiritual battle between good and evil—but along with Dianne Kirby's essay in this volume, the historian Axel R. Schäfer further explores the deep entanglements of Protestantism and the cold war state's subsidization of churches. "The [US] federal government's efforts to strengthen the anti-communist training of army recruits, support for the military chaplaincy and evangelical campaigns, and the promotion of church building on military sites were decisive factors in furthering the evangelicals and establishing contacts between church and state."[21]

Schäfer's important exploration of "the public/private networks that underlay US Cold War state building" exemplifies new scholarship on the cold war that unsettles the categories of state and non-state actors as it uncovers hitherto unexplored reaches of the state.[22] In the case of evangelical projects, their major protagonists were neither defined by nor direct agents of US anti-communism; nor were they *independent*. Indeed, we need to consider state, non-state, and transnational formations and actors as intersecting and rarely, if ever, entirely independent entities.

Given the intersection of state and non-state actors, it is hardly surprising that state-sponsored transnational projects often yielded unexpected consequences, as seen in the case of cultural diplomacy. After World War II the United States and the Soviet Union competed for the political allegiances and resources of peoples emerging from decades of colonialism. The superpowers joined such countries as Mexico and France that had long made the promotion and export of their arts a central part of their diplomacy. While the Soviets sent classical orchestras and ballet companies across the world, and also promoted folk cultural expressions, the United States responded with modern performing arts, sending such jazz musicians as Dizzy Gillespie, Louis Armstrong, Duke Ellington, and Dave Brubeck, and such dancers and choreographers as Martha Graham, Alvin Ailey, Paul Taylor, and Jose Limon, on world tours. Not to be outdone by Soviet sponsorship of classical music, Washington also sent classical orchestras, often to entertain elites in pro-western Latin American dictatorships. If jazz was the pet project of the State Department, based on that form's salience for promoting a racially integrated American modernism, state sponsorship had perhaps the most significant impact on the dance world; the fortunes of the companies of Martha Graham and Alvin Ailey became inextricably bound with their State Department sponsorship. These international tours brought artists to places that often would not have been commercially profitable or logistically viable.

Yet, such sponsorship had unintended consequences. In the case of jazz and the US State Department, musicians brought their own agendas, promoting civil rights, black militancy, and challenging State Department priorities. Moreover, their desire to connect with musicians in other countries and to learn new musical styles accentuated a globalization of popular music that belied the purported distinctiveness of national cultures promoted by state sponsorship in this era. Indeed, scholars have pointed to the importance of transnational performance in challenging the authority of colonial powers, as transnational cultural exchanges provided a source of alternative cultural capital for all parties involved.

## Non-aligned and anti-colonial transnationalism

Decolonization and non-alignment have been explored at length by scholars and are treated elsewhere in this volume, but it is impossible to account for the power and ubiquity of transnationalism without placing these dynamics at the center.[23] Non-aligned movements defied cold war blocs, and anti-colonial movements were at odds with the superpowers, including the Soviet Union and China, far more than is commonly acknowledged. But they also intersected with superpower interests. The consistently socialist-leaning character of the non-alignment movements and the strength of the global/transnational anti-imperialism of the 1960s and 1970s can in part be understood by US responses to non-aligned positions from the late 1940s through the 1960s.

US officials were contemptuous of the non-aligned politics advocated by Jawaharlal Nehru in India, Gamal Abdel Nasser in Egypt (and the short-lived United Arab Republic), and Kwame Nkrumah in Ghana.[24] From the time that Truman and Stalin declared cold war on one another in 1946 and 1947, nations around the globe announced with growing frequency that they would not be subjugated by either the West or the East and declared their intentions to be neutral, "non-aligned states," forming their own "Third World." Even before India's independence, Nehru held an Asian Relations Conference in Delhi in March of 1947. Coinciding with the announcement of the Truman Doctrine, the conference addressed general concerns of the decolonizing world, but was followed up by another conference responding to Dutch attempts in 1948 to re-colonize Indonesia. This later conference also passed resolutions on World Peace and dangers of nuclear weapons. US hostility toward India and non-alignment crystallized during the Korean War, when the US chafed at India's refusal to acquiesce to US directives. Krishna Menon, the Indian representative to the United Nation, was elected chairman of the UN Commission on Korea in 1947 and appealed to the great powers to let Korea be united. When North Korea invaded the South in 1950, Korea joined the US in the UN Security Council in condemning North Korea as the aggressor and calling for a ceasefire; but India infuriated US officials by abstaining from another resolution calling for assistance to South Korea and the establishment of a united command.[25]

In 1954 when the United States established the anti-communist Southeast Asian Treaty Organization (SEATO) and sought to include all the states in the region, India, Burma, Ceylon, and Indonesia resisted and asserted their resolve to remain "neutral" in the cold war.[26] The 1954 Asian Leaders Conference in Colombo was followed by the gathering of Asian and African nations in Bandung, Indonesia in 1955. The West, as Paul

Gordon Lauren has observed, reacted with "silence, vacillation, or opposition." US Secretary of State John Foster Dulles condemned the meeting as "an obsolete, immoral, and short-sighted conception."[27] As the insistence on independence from superpowers and the promotion of the interests of decolonizing countries drew the ire of the western bloc, such non-aligned efforts drew critical attention and inspired a generation of world-wide communities of intellectuals of African and Asian descent. In addition to political forums, artists and writers gathered in such venues as the 1956 First World Congress of Negro Writers and Artists in Paris, which brought together African, Caribbean, and black American artists and writers, including George Lamming, Leopold Senghor, James Baldwin, and Richard Wright.

Building on these earlier efforts, the founding meeting of the Non-aligned Movement opened in Belgrade on September 6, 1961, just as the Berlin crisis was peaking. For Westad, the fact that participants all sent letters to Kennedy and Khrushchev "lecturing superpowers on proper conduct in international relations" constituted a significant shift.[28] The heady promise of this moment is perhaps better appreciated in the context of the international outpouring of protest over the assassination of Lumumba on January 17, just seven months before the Belgrade Conference. As documented by the historian Leo Zeilig, after the news was officially announced on February 13, "as many as 30,000 smashed their way into the Belgian Embassy in Belgrade." The Yugoslav demonstrators shouted, "Lumumba will live forever." President Tito argued that the murder "had no precedent in [recent] history."[29]

Outrage over the Lumumba murder was widespread. An estimated one-half million people demonstrated in Shanghai. Belgium's Embassy was attacked in Warsaw, and the Ambassador fled for his life. In Syria students and workers took to the streets, and demonstrations occurred in London and Paris as well.[30] As African American protestors at the United Nations in New York held signs declaring that "The Murder of Lumumba Exposes the Nature of Colonialism," Kwame Nkrumah observed from Ghana that Lumumba's murder was "the first time in history that the legal ruler of a country has been done to death with the open connivance of a world organization on whom that ruler put his trust."[31] According to Zeilig, "a potent sense of shame and seething anger" clouded the meeting rooms of the UN. Journalist Philip Deane reported that "the Afro-Asian delegates... swallow their drinks as if there was a bitter taste in their mouths... [I]n the lobbies and corridors and bars of the United Nations' glass palace, you can hear growing almost hour by hour, a menacing myth that could destroy the world organization itself."[32]

UN complicity in Lumumba's assassination proved not to be myth. The covert intrigue surrounding Lumumba's assassination and civil war in the Congo has been told at length. Of special concern here is how the crisis gave a powerful impetus to the Non-aligned Movement. Its founding meeting later that year was a venue for reasserting independence at a moment when the United Nations had acted brazenly as the instrument of colonial and neo-colonial interests.

Lumumba's assassination reverberated across the globe, literally changing the cold war landscape, as streets were named after him in cities including Jakarta, Belgrade,

Tehran, Budapest, Algiers, Santiago de Cuba, Łódź, Kiev, Rabat, Maputo, Leipzig, Lusaka, Tunis, Fort-de-France, and Montpellier. In Moscow, the Peoples' Friendship University had been established by the Soviet Union on February 5, 1960. Already conceived as a university for the education and training of foreign students from decolonizing regions, on February 22, 1961, it was renamed "Patrice Lumumba Peoples' University." In the first year, 539 foreign students from 59 countries were enrolled (plus 57 Soviet students).

The resurgent anti-imperialism and non-alignment of that moment was by no means simply a result of renewed Soviet support for the Third World. The Soviet Union had been dilatory in its support for Lumumba until Lumumba finally asked for assistance after being betrayed by the United Nations. Only two months after Che Guevara's scathing indictment of the United States in his December 11, 1964, speech at United Nations, in which he also charged the United Nations with complicity in the assassination of Lumumba and declared his allegiance with non-alignment, Che notably took the Soviet Union to task in a speech in Algiers on February 24, 1965.[33] As Piero Gleijeses writes in his exploration of Cuba and the United States in Africa, Che charged that the USSR and other socialist countries were "to a certain extent accomplices to the imperialist exploitation of the third world ... and have a moral duty to liquidate their tacit complicity with the exploiting countries of the west."[34] While the public admonishment of the Soviets did not sit comfortably with Castro, Castro approved Che's return to Africa with Cuban troops to intervene in Zaire (Congo) on behalf of the beleaguered guerilla army of Laurent-Désiré Kabila, made up of Lumumba's former supporters. Che's campaign ended in despair and disillusionment, and four days after Che and the Cuban group departed on November 21, 1966, General Joseph-Désiré Mobutu, a close ally of the US since 1960, consolidated his power in a coup, beginning his thirty-two year dictatorship. Che's failed campaign in the Congo illustrates tensions between radical anti-imperialists and the Soviet Union. Transnational projects exceeded and were not defined by the superpowers.

# Transnationalism and locating the archive of the cold war

Che's efforts in the Congo marked only the beginning of Cuba's increasing commitments in Africa, and Gleijeses' masterful account is based on vast multilingual and transnational archival research. But other scholars have demonstrated that the genesis of momentous transnational formations cannot be adequately understood from the papers of diplomats alone. For example, social history beyond the purview of state archives reveals the ways in which transnational religious organizations such as global Christian missionary societies and global Islamic formations such as the Muslim Brotherhood have filled the breach when states cannot respond to famine in the Sudan, broken levees in New Orleans, or floods in Pakistan. Such formations benefited from the deep entanglement of state and religion from 1947 onward and the later cold war CIA funding of Islamic fundamentalists in Afghanistan. While an exploration of such formations is beyond the scope of this essay, transnational movements that claim a religious impetus are among the most significant legacies of the cold war.

Historical fiction also offers an important vehicle for recovering the complex, multiple global histories engendered or transformed by the cold war. Kamila Shamsie's *Burnt Shadows* is woven through with cold war dynamics, from the 1945 bombing of Nagasaki, to CIA permeated Karachi, to late 20th and early 21st century wars in Afghanistan. The novel opens in 1945 Nagasaki with 19-year-old Hiroko Tanaka tutoring Konrad Weiss, a German man who has spent the war years in Japan and finds himself in an awkward position after Germany's surrender to the Allies. Just as the young couple have fallen in love, Konrad is incinerated in the atomic blast. Hiroko survives, with the images of the birds and, indeed, the fabric of the kimono she wore at the time of the explosion, indelibly etched into her back, forever a part of her body.

Proscribed as a bomb victim, Hiroko makes her way to Delhi in 1947 to find Konrad's British half-sister, whose husband serves in the British Foreign Service, along with Konrad's boyhood friend, Sajjad Ashad. As Sajjad tutors Hiroko in Urdu, once again language study leads to love. Honeymooning in Istanbul to escape the violent upheavals of partition, the couple is denied re-entry into India when officials claim that Sajjad left voluntarily and, as a Muslim, has no right to return. Exiled from Dilli, Sajjad's home in the Muslim heart of Delhi, they settle in Karachi, where after decades of building a life and raising a son, Raza, their lives are overtaken by cold war perils: the threat of nuclear war between India and Pakistan; the growing repression under the US-backed Pakistani military dictatorships; and the shadowy but ubiquitous presence of the CIA and its alliance with Pakistan's ISI (Inter-Services Intelligence). As the agencies police the Pakistan/Afghanistan border, reaching into the border camps and far beyond, Raza is drawn into the intrigue, deceit, and divided loyalties of private military corporations.

Shamsie's rendering of global postwar history imagines developments that were independent of, yet fatefully affected by, bipolar rivalry. Following Shamsie's example, to consider the interconnectedness of the cold war with other developments, historians must at once recover the projects and dreams of those whose lives were hijacked by cold war dynamics, without evading the violence imposed on those lives. This call for an integrated history immediately raises the question of archives and, mostly simply put, who gets to tell the story of the cold war?

As the cold war reinforced the partition of India and Pakistan after the US swept Pakistan into its Northern Perimeter Defense Zone after partition, and vexing questions of repatriation arose from multiple new borders, problems of the transnational were fundamentally woven into the fabric of the cold war. Where do people belong; and with millions left without recourse to *any* governmental body that recognized the legitimacy of their political aspirations and subjectivity, to what possible (or overlapping) jurisdictions could one appeal for justice or the adjudication of disputes?

While Hiroko's story is fictional, the story of lives shattered by the bomb and partitions, the story of displaced people forced to rebuild lives and dreams again and again, are barely glimpsed in state archives. Yet the stories of the everyday displaced are urgently critical to any comprehension of the 20th century. In the novel, as Hiroko left Japan for India, and then Pakistan, and later for New York after her husband was killed by a trigger-happy CIA driver, we see the complex ways in which the deformities of colonialism hardened and were reified under the pressures of cold war geopolitics. If partition was a product of colonial policies, the military hostilities between India and Pakistan are inseparable from the US cold war alliance with Pakistan and its cold war hostility toward the non-aligned policies of India. Without the US arming of Pakistan and support of military dictatorships, along with extensive CIA presence in Pakistan and Afghanistan, Hiroko would not have lost her husband to an assassin, nor would she have found herself in Karachi, living in fear of yet another nuclear explosion, or lost her beloved son to the CIA's secret prison complex.

Had Hiroko stayed in Japan, she might have faced another version of the intersection of colonialism and nuclear warfare, perhaps discovering that 30 percent of Hiroshima's bomb victims were Korean, and that at the end of the US-Japanese conflict, 18–20 percent of the Korean population was living outside of Korea, conscripted in Japanese war efforts. Scholars such as Lisa Yoneyama have challenged the erasures of the 30,000 Korean victims of Hiroshima from history and have created a frame for understanding movement and displacement, where borders crossing peoples and states conscripting peoples are as significant as people crossing borders.[35] From the newly drawn borders of Korea, India/Pakistan, Yugoslavia/Italy, Germany, Poland, the Congo, to the 1948 Apartheid consolidation of "homelands" carved outside of the mineral wealth of the region, the transnation is imbricated through every fabric of the cold war world.

# THE AFTERLIFE OF COLD WAR TRANSNATIONALISM

The Johannesburg-born and Cape Town-based photographer Guy Tillum says of his 2009 exhibit *Avenue Patrice Lumumba*, a haunting document of the post-colonial urban African landscape:

> [T]hese photographs are not collapsed histories of post colonial African states or a meditation on aspects of late-modernist-era colonial structures, but a walk through avenues of dreams. Patrice Lumumba's dream, his nationalism, is discernible in the structures, if one reads certain clues, as is the death of his dream, in these de facto monuments. How strange that modernism, which eschewed monument and past, for nature and the future, should carry memory so well.[36]

Over the past two decades, and reaching a crescendo with the 50th anniversary of Lumumba's assassination in January 2011, film and theater productions on Lumumba's death represent resistance to efforts to erase this sordid episode. The Haitian-born filmmaker Raoul Peck followed his 1992 documentary *Lumumba: Death of a Prophet* with the 2000 feature film, *Lumumba*, recounting Lumumba's demise and the consolidation of Mobutu's dictatorship. More recently, Michel Noll's *Death Colonial Style: The Execution of Patrice Lumumba* has incorporated interviews with Larry Devlin, the CIA station chief in Leopoldville, as well as with Belgian officials. Although the CIA failed to carry out its orders to assassinate Lumumba, it worked extensively with Belgian authorities to ensure his removal. The documentary unearths a grisly tale involving the destruction of Lumumba's body in acid and secret body-part trophies retained by the murderers. Most recently, Gayatri Spivak's 2009 translation of the Martiniquean poet and writer Aime Cesaire's 1966 play about the death of Lumumba, *Une Sai au Congo* (*A Season in the Congo*) opened in September 2010 for a limited run at the Lion Theatre in New York City, through Rico Works Production, producers Jackie Jeffries and Rico Speight.[37]

Projects exploring Lumumba and his memory challenge superpowers' erasure of Third World movements and insist on telling the story of the cold war in terms of the violent disruptions of fledgling democratic projects and the horrific legacy of superpower-armed dictatorships in the Congo and elsewhere in southern Africa.

Fifty years after the assassination of Lumumba, his legacy remains for many a focal point for contesting the legacy of the cold war. As noted above, Lumumba Streets have disappeared from many eastern bloc cities. On February 5, 1992, Patrice Lumumba Peoples' University was renamed and officially re-founded as the Peoples' Friendship University of Russia, as part of the State Institute of Higher Education of the government of the Russian Federation. Yet the embassy rows in many African capitals still bear Lumumba's name, and one can still find in Tehran, Port-au-Prince, and other cities that Lumumba's memory endures. The revival of interest in Lumumba has significance beyond symbolism and iconography.

Like the organizers of the Bruce Lee monument in Mostar who spoke of the screen icon as embodying the *hope* of their childhood, anthropologist and filmmaker Maple Razsa, in his 2010 film *Bastards of Utopia*, recalls the sense of empowerment once felt by people in his native Yugoslavia that they could choose a path not defined by cold war superpowers and make a difference in the world. Exploring the democratic projects of a younger generation, Razsa explains: "I was not nostalgic for the object of Yugoslav socialists' political hopes—the socialist state and economy—but for political hope itself."[38] In the burgeoning literature on post-cold war memory, a current trope is that of hope itself: hope of surmounting crippling economic inequalities, reductive nationalisms, superpower blocs, wars, violence, and despair. For Buck-Morss, it was not the dream of bringing the good life to the masses itself that was flawed so much as the unaccountable and terrifying "wild zones of power" that developed within state structures, whatever their avowed ideological commitments. The tension of universalizing utopian visions on the one hand, and state and political structures that not only failed to deliver on their promise, but committed murderous betrayals of their ideals on the other, gave rise to the potent alternative utopias. The Bosnian monument to Bruce Lee, along with

Razsa's film, echo the contemporary revival of interest in Patrice Lumumba, and speak to the resilient appeal of the era's transnational projects.

Just as the Mostar organizers of the Bruce Lee monument see in Lee's memory the embodiment of the anti-imperialist ideals that were the more positive memory of the Yugoslavia of their youth, so Lumumba's image as an icon of global liberation has survived the post-Soviet abandonment of Third World liberation movements. In marking a political moment that also transcended a bipolar divide, Lumumba Street named and continues to evoke a democratic and oppositional imagination that could not be contained by the Soviet and eastern bloc states, or the superpower struggle of the cold war era. Recovering the transnational power of Lumumba shows us how an identification and solidarity with the decolonizing world was part of the imagination of the cold war, affirming the basis for community and solidarity in imperfect worlds.

## NOTES

1. Alexander Zaitchik, "Mostar's Little Dragon: How Bruce Lee Became a Symbol of Peace in the Balkans," *Reason Online*, April 2006, <http://www.reason.com/0604/cr.az.mostars.shtml>; on the vandalism, see, <http://www.artfagcity.com/2009/08/24/img-mgmt-turbo-sculpture/>; on the global importance of Bruce Lee, see, Vijay Prashad, "Bruce Lee and the Anti-imperialism of Kung Fu," *Positions: East Asia Cultures Critique* 11 (Spring 2002): 51–90.

2. For an example of a historically situated discussion of transnationalism, see Prasenjit Duara, "Transnationalism and the Challenge of National Histories," in Thomas Bender, ed., *Rethinking American History in a Global Age* (Berkeley, CA: University of California Press, 2002). See also, Heonik Kwon, *The Other Cold War* (New York: Columbia University Press, 2010).

3. Svetlana Boym, *The Future of Nostalgia* (New York: Basic Books, 2002). See also Charity Scribner, *Requiem for Communism* (Cambridge, MA: MIT Press, 2005).

4. See, Uta Poiger, *Jazz, Rock, and Rebels: Cold War Politics and American Culture in a Divided Germany* (Chapel Hill, NC: University of North Carolina Press, 2000); Eli Rubin, *Synthetic Socialism: Plastics and Dictatorship in the German Democratic Republic* (Chapel Hill, NC: University of North Carolina Press, 2008).

5. Mark Mazower, *No Enchanted Palace: The End of Empire and the Ideological Origins of the United Nations* (Princeton, NJ: Princeton University Press 2009); Samuel Moyn, *The Last Utopia: Human Rights in History* (Cambridge, MA: Belknap/Harvard University Press, 2010); Pamela Ballinger, "Borders of the Nation, Borders of Citizenship: Italian Repatriation and the Redefinition of National Identity after World War II," *Comparative Studies in Society and History* 49:3 (2007): 713–41; S. James Anaya, *Indigenous Peoples in International Law* (New York: Oxford, 2004).

6. Chalmers Johnson, *Blowback: The Cost and Consequences of American Empire*, with post 9–11 introduction (New York: Henry Holt, 2004). For one of many examples of recent coverage of this phenomenon, see Mark Mazzetti, "Former Spy with Agenda Operates Own Private C.I.A." *New York Times*, January 22, 2011.

7. Carol Gluck and Anna Lawenhaupt Tsing, eds., *Words in Motion: Towards a Global Lexicon* (Durham, NC: Duke University Press, 2009).

8. Susan Buck-Morss, *Dreamworld and Catastrophe: The Passing of Mass Utopia in East and West* (Cambridge, MA: MIT Press, 2002).

9. Buck-Morss, *Dreamworld*; Odd Arne Westad, *The Global Cold War: Third World Interventions and the Making of our Time* (New York and Cambridge: Cambridge University Press, 2006).

10. Ronald Grigor Suny and Terry Martin, eds., *A State of Nations: Empire and Nation-Making in the Age of Lenin and Stalin* (New York: Oxford University Press, 2001), 16. See also Terry Martin, *The Affirmative Action Empire: Nations and Nationalism in the Soviet Union, 1923–1939* (Ithaca, NY: Cornell University Press, 2001).

11. Martin, *Affirmative Action Empire*, 69.

12. Martin, *Affirmative Action Empire*.

13. Erez Manela, *The Wilsonian Moment: Self-Determination and the International Origins of Anticolonial Nationalism* (New York: Oxford University Press, 2007).

14. Westad, *The Global Cold War*, 66.

15. Penny Von Eschen, *Satchmo Blows Up the World: Jazz Ambassadors Play the Cold War* (Cambridge, MA: Harvard University Press, 2004).

16. Penny Von Eschen, *Race against Empire: Black Americans and Anticolonialism, 1937–1957* (Ithaca, NY: Cornell University Press, 1997).

17. Alexei Yurchak, *Everything Was Forever, Until It Was No More: The Last Soviet Generation* (Princeton, NJ: Princeton University Press, 2006); Rubin, *Synthetic Socialism*, 8. See also, Katherine Pence and Paul Betts, eds., *Socialist Modern: East German Everyday Culture and Politics* (Ann Arbor, MI: University of Michigan Press, 2008); Rubin, *Synthetic Socialism*.

18. Yurchak, *Everything Was Forever*, 8.

19. Satoshi Nakano, "South to South across the Pacific: Ernest E. Neal and Community Development Efforts in the American South and the Philippines," *The Japanese Journal of American Studies* No. 16 (2005): 181–202; Bruce Cummings, *Dominion from Sea to Sea: Pacific Ascendancy and American Power* (New Haven, CT: Yale University Press, 2009), chapters 14–16.

20. Melani McAlister, "The Persecuted Body: Evangelical Internationalism, Islam, and the Politics of Fear," in Michael Laffan and Max Weiss, eds., *Facing Fear: The History of an Emotion in Global Perspective* (Princeton: Princeton University Press, forthcoming 2012).

21. Axel R. Schäfer, "The Cold War State and the Resurgence of Evangelicalism: A Study of Public Funding of Religion since 1945," *Radical History Review*, Issue 99 (Fall 2007): 25–6.

22. Schäfer, "The Cold War State." For antecedents, see James Sparrow, *Warfare State: World War II Americans and the Age of Big Government* (New York: Oxford University Press, 2011).

23. See Cary Fraser in this volume.

24. On US views of Middle Eastern non-alignment, see Douglas Little, *American Orientalism: The United States and the Middle East since 1945* (Chapel Hill, NC: University of North Carolina Press, 2002); on US diplomacy and views of non-alignment in Ghana and Africa, see Kevin K. Gaines, *American Africans in Ghana: Black Expatriates in the Era of Civil Rights* (Chapel Hill, NC: University of North Carolina Press, 2006).

25. Mridula Mukherjee, "Situating India in the Nehru Years," paper presented at Tokyo University, Slavic Department, symposium of Working Group on Regional Powers and the Cold War in Asia, March 8–9, 2010. On the US hostility to India and non-alignment and the sharp contrast with Pakistani military support from the United States that reached back

to partition, see Mahmood Mamdani, *Good Muslim, Bad Muslim: The Cold War and Roots of Terror* (New York: Pantheon, 2004). See also Westad, *The Global Cold War*, and David F. Schmitz, *The United States and Right Wing Dictatorships, 1965–1989* (New York and Cambridge: Cambridge University Press, 2006).

26. The signatories of the SEATO treaty were the United States, Britain, France, Australia, New Zealand, the Philippines, Pakistan, and Thailand. See Von Eschen, *Race against Empire*, 168–73; Paul Gordon Lauren, *Power and Prejudice: The Politics of Diplomacy and Racial Discrimination* (Boulder, CO: Westview Press, 1988), 209.

27. Lauren, *Power and Prejudice*, 214: Von Eschen, *Race against Empire*, 170–1.

28. Westad, *The Global Cold War*, 107.

29. Leo Zeilig, *Patrice Lumumba: Africa's Lost Leader* (London: Haus Publishing, 2008), 131–3.

30. Zeilig, *Lumumba*, 133.

31. Quoted in Gaines, *American Africans in Ghana*, 122.

32. Quoted in Zeilig, *Lumumba*, 133.

33. <http://www.youtube.com/watch?v=a8p0840sCl8&feature=related>; 1964 speech at the United Nations with English translation. On the 1965 Algiers speech, see, Piero Gleijeses, *Conflicting Missions, Havana, Washington, and Africa* (Chapel Hill, NC: University of North Carolina Press, 2002), 79.

34. Gleijeses, *Conflicting Missions*, 79.

35. Lisa Yoneyama, *Hiroshima Traces: Time, Space, and the Dialectics of Memory* (Berkeley, CA: University of California Press, 1999).

36. Guy Tillum, *Avenue Patrice Lumumba*, with texts by Robert Gardner and Guy Tillum (Cambridge, MA: Prestel and Peabody Museum of Archaeology and Ethnology, Harvard University, 2008).

37. See: A Season in the Congo YouTube—trailer from New York production; <http://www.youtube.com/watch?v=HtzfCMHXIYg>. Other recent commemorations include the Argentinean reggae band "Lumumba," featuring Fidel Nadal and Pablo Molina; and an April 2009 commemoration of the late 1960s naming-struggle at UC San Diego when students from the Black Student Council and Mexican-American Youth Association of the University of California, San Diego attempted to name the newly established Third College, "Lumumba-Zapata College." Unable to obtain permission for the administration, the college went without a name for two decades until it was christened "Thurgood Marshall College."

38. In a forthcoming book of the same name, Razsa is currently writing an ethnography of transnational cooperation among radical activists in Europe based on work with radical anarchist youth in Zagreb, Croatia.

## Select Bibliography

Boym, Svetlana. *The Future of Nostalgia*. New York: Basic Books, 2002.

Buck-Morss, Susan. *Dreamworld and Catastrophe: The Passing of Mass Utopia in East and West*. Cambridge, MA: MIT Press, 2002.

Duara, Prasenjit. "Transnationalism and the Challenge of National Histories," in Thomas Bender, ed. *Rethinking American History in a Global Age*. Berkeley, CA: University of California Press, 2002.

Gleijeses, Piero. *Conflicting Missions, Havana, Washington, and Africa*. Chapel Hill, NC: University of North Carolina Press, 2002.

Kwon, Heonik. *The Other Cold War*. New York: Columbia University Press, 2010.

Mamdani, Mahmood. *Good Muslim, Bad Muslim: The Cold War and Roots of Terror*. New York: Pantheon, 2004.

Manela, Erez. *The Wilsonian Moment: Self-Determination and the International Origins of Anticolonial Nationalism*. New York: Oxford University Press, 2007.

Moyn, Samuel. *The Last Utopia: Human Rights in History*. Cambridge, MA: Belknap/Harvard University Press, 2010.

Schäfer, Axel R. "The Cold War State and the Resurgence of Evangelicalism: A Study of Public Funding of Religion since 1945," *Radical History Review* No. 99 (Fall 2007), 19–50.

Suny, Ronald Grigor and Martin, Terry, eds. *A State of Nations: Empire and Nation-Making in the Age of Lenin and Stalin*. New York: Oxford University Press, 2001.

Westad, Odd Arne. *The Global Cold War*. Cambridge: Cambridge University Press, 2007.

Zeilig, Leo. *Patrice Lumumba: Africa's Lost Leader*. London: Haus Publishing, 2008.

# CHAPTER 27

........................................................................................

# DECOLONIZATION AND
# THE COLD WAR

........................................................................................

## CARY FRASER

THE decolonization of the pre-war empires—American, Belgian, British, Dutch, French, Japanese, and Portuguese—has stimulated an extraordinary range of scholarship on the processes of imperial disengagement from the colonies in Asia, Africa, and the Caribbean. The scholarship has focused on: (a) the dynamics of nationalist struggle in the colonies; (b) the shifting dynamics of policy at the level of the imperial capitals; (c) the role of international organizations such as the United Nations (UN) and the Non-Aligned Movement (NAM) in various cases of decolonization; and (d) the ways in which the competition between the members of the North Atlantic Treaty Organization (NATO) and the Warsaw Pact and their allies influenced the processes and outcomes of the decolonization process. Some of the studies provide detailed explorations of the process of decolonization in individual instances, while others seek to synthesize the dynamics of decolonization in regional, comparative, and global contexts.[1]

The myriad contexts that shaped the decolonization process, the complexity of issues that emerged as the process unfolded, and the proliferation of nationalist sentiment and struggles all contributed to the fascination with decolonization and its role in reshaping the international order after 1945. Decolonization marked a phase in the globalization of politics that ended the intellectual and political legitimacy of colonial rule and eroded the hierarchies of race that underpinned the centuries-old colonial order. In effect, the globalization of European imperial projects after 1492 was reversed by the decolonization process in the second half of the 20th century.

Decolonization was thus both a response to the globalization of European influence and a process of globalization that paved the way for the dismantling of the North Atlantic-centered international system. It was driven simultaneously by imperatives of imperial deconstruction and the constitution/reconstruction of sovereignty in the former colonies. However, scholars also need to give greater thought to the ways in which decolonization was both reflective of the rise of nationalist sentiment and a process that was larger than the relationship between the imperial powers and their respective colonies. Future scholarship will need to be attentive to the international and transnational dimensions of decolonization as a global process. There is much to be said about the ways in which the diplomatic initiatives of new nations such as India, Indonesia, and Egypt that emerged after 1945 helped to mobilize resources and develop strategies to accelerate and expand the opportunities for the decolonization process by way of the United Nations, the Non-Aligned Movement, the Commonwealth Group of Nations linking the former British colonies, and other multilateral fora. Similarly, the role of the Soviet Union, the People's Republic of China, and Cuba in providing military supplies, military advisors, and, on occasion, combat units to nationalist movements challenging the colonial powers helped to accelerate the decolonization process after 1945. Decolonization was part of the shifting terrain of international relations and a factor in the calculus of the global balance of power.

In addition, the decolonization process helped to create avenues of political mobilization within the imperial centers which opened opportunities for coalitions supportive of decolonization to engage and influence policy at home and in the wider international system. In Britain, the Labour Party became a major factor in pushing the process of decolonization, while the Communist and Socialist parties played similar roles in France. The rise of the American civil rights movement, which challenged the domestic racial regime, had a catalytic effect upon the national liberation struggles in various African countries. In turn, the rise of independent states in Africa forced American policymakers to recognize the paradox of its claim to "leadership of the Free World." As a consequence, the American racial regime became a casualty of the cold war and decolonization after 1945.[2] This interactive effect between the struggle for national liberation in colonies across the international system and the impetus for social and political change in other societies is, perhaps, best represented in the ways in which Gandhi's advocacy of nonviolence to challenge both South African race policies and British colonial rule in India helped to frame the civil rights struggle in the United States.[3]

The transnational activism that shaped the decolonization process had a "domino effect" that required new avenues of collaboration among the colonial powers for policies aimed at preventing, slowing, and/or defining the process of decolonization during the cold war. The North Atlantic Treaty Organization was not simply about a mutual security pact that provided an American commitment to the defense of Western Europe—it was also a mechanism used to develop coordinated strategies for dealing with the decolonization process in the non-European world. In the 1950s, America helped France contain the communist insurgency in Vietnam as a way to maintain a French commitment to the containment of the Soviet Union in Europe. Similarly, America premised its support for the Portuguese colonies in Southern Africa on the need to maintain access to military bases in the Azores for American military operations within the NATO alliance. NATO represented an alliance of the European colonial powers with the United States that influenced the process of decolonization after 1945. As a consequence NATO, as one of the major alliance systems in the cold war, became a vehicle for the expansion of America's "informal empire" on the global stage and symbolized the Western Alliance's commitment to maintaining the politics of racial supremacy that had underpinned the pre-1945 global order.[4]

The successful Japanese military and ideological assault on the European and American imperial holdings in Asia during World War II seriously discredited the legitimacy of colonialism. The Japanese military successes in the Asia-Pacific region during the war exposed the vulnerabilities of Western colonial rule and created the political space for the rise of nationalism in Asia.[5] As the Asian power that demonstrated its immunity to the spread of European imperial rule in the nineteenth century, Japan became an independent industrial and military power capable of defeating Russia in the 1905 Russo-Japanese War. Japan also established its own colonies in Korea, Taiwan, and in mainland China. Japan in the early 20th century became a symbol of Asian modernization and industrialization that could withstand European imperial ambitions.

If Japan's success provided an alternative vision to Western imperial rule, it was the genocidal tragedies unleashed by Nazi Germany in Europe that shattered the idea of Western imperial rule as sustainable. The Nazi regime demonstrated through genocide the ultimate logic of Western civilization's politics and ideology of racial supremacy. All the colonial powers, including the Japanese and the United States, had less than stellar records in their treatment of their colonial subjects, and Nazi Germany's treatment of the Jewish populations of Europe followed the earlier pursuit of genocidal policies against the Herero population in its colony in South West Africa. This convergence of the domestic and colonial politics of race in the German experience provided powerful insight into the dangers of the ideology of racial supremacy. In the wake of World War II, racial supremacy was progressively relegated to the margins of serious political debate. The complicities of European colonial rule in the non-European world with the trajectory of Nazi Germany could not be avoided after 1945.[6]

In effect, the anti-colonial struggle and decolonization were catalysts in the creation of an alternative moral universe in which colonial rule was repudiated by its challengers as antithetical to the ideas of a global society based upon the principle of human equality. The course of decolonization was more than a process of political transformation of countries and peoples. It was also a symbol of moral regeneration leading to the birth and reinvigoration of "nations." Simultaneously, it represented a search for international redemption from the historical embrace of the "civilizing mission," and its corollary, racial supremacy, on the part of the colonial powers.[7] It was this dual thread of the decolonization process that helped to fuel and constrain the cold war in the post-1945 era.

The cold war was driven by the search for a security architecture in Europe that would prevent a return to the destabilizing nationalisms that had wracked Europe in the first half of the 20th century. The rise of non-European nationalism, however, limited the appeal of the major alliances to the emergent nationalist elites. Unless the alliances showed themselves disposed to support the challenge to colonial rule by nationalists and demonstrated a willingness to distance themselves from the commitment to imperial rule by the colonial powers, their claims to leadership within the international system were contested. Decolonization represented the search for a new international order in which nationalism and ideological pluralism—as opposed to bipolarity—were constituent elements. Decolonization was thus project, process, and outcome of the search for a replacement for the quest for North Atlantic hegemony that had shaped the imperialism that preceded 1945 and the bipolar vision of the leaders of the North Atlantic Treaty Organization and the Warsaw Pact that emerged after 1945.

The intersection of the cold war and decolonization produced a sustained engagement global in its reach. In the aftermath of World War II, the decolonization of the Philippines, followed by the transfer of power from Britain in India, Pakistan, Ceylon (Sri Lanka), and Burma, and the Dutch decision to leave Indonesia, were early indications of the momentum building for decolonization. However, the US decision to extend its colonial possessions by acquiring the Pacific territories that had been held by Japan under the League of Nations' Mandate, and France's decision to reoccupy Indochina and reassert its colonial rule, sent an alternative message. When the Chinese Communist party won the civil war in 1949, establishing the People's Republic of China (PRC), it became evident that the geopolitics of Asia had shifted against the colonial powers. It was also evident that the struggle over Asian independence would become a catalyst for the expansion of the cold war into Asia. For the United States, the "loss of China" illustrated the limits of its strategy of containment directed against the Soviet Union. The creation of the PRC extended communist influence into the heart of Asia, confronting America with a new challenge. Two of the world's largest states which straddled much of the Eurasian landmass were now both communist powers.

The competition for influence in the changing Asian context triggered a military confrontation that superimposed the cold war struggle on a civil war on the Korean peninsula in 1950. The Korean War provided the venue for the United States and the PRC to deploy resources to engage in mutual containment on the Asian mainland as they clashed over the future of the former Japanese colony. The war was about both the struggle for control over the entire country between the pro-American and pro-communist nationalist factions and the confrontation between the United States and the communist powers in the strategic competition for influence in Asia.[8] The first large-scale military conflict of the post-1945 era symbolized the integration of the decolonization processes into the cold war conflict. The insurgencies in Malaya, the Philippines, and Vietnam that emerged during the late 1940s provided further evidence that the politics of decolonization and communism were intimately linked at the level of the internal politics of the Asian nationalist movements.[9] Korea signaled the emerging struggle for influence among the Western alliance, the Soviet Union, and a resurgent China in the post-1945 politics of Asia.

Even as the Korean War settled into a protracted military stalemate, the Vietnamese insurgency escalated. French military weakness provoked a major crisis. American support for the French military effort to defeat the insurgency by the Vietnamese communist forces proved to be inadequate. The Eisenhower administration discussed the possibility of direct American intervention, but there was little enthusiasm for another misadventure on the Asian mainland following Korea. The possibility of the use of American nuclear weapons against the Vietnamese communist forces was considered briefly but failed to gain traction.[10] Nevertheless, the issue indicated that the nuclear genie unleashed by the cold war in Europe was beginning to influence the calculus of the shifting Asian balance of power. The growing realization that the Western powers lacked the military capacity to win a decisive victory against Chinese military forces and Chinese-backed insurgents in countries directly bordering the PRC created the conditions for the negotiated settlements and geographical division in both the Korean War and the French war in Vietnam. The cold war had become a determinant of the contours of the Asian decolonization process and the boundaries of the post-colonial states in Korea and Vietnam. Just as important, the divisions among the United States, France, and Great Britain that emerged around the issue of the French military failures in Vietnam reflected the tensions that decolonization had provoked within the heart of the NATO alliance over strategy in both Europe and Asia.[11]

This process involved both the former Japanese colonies and the European colonies occupied during the war by Japanese forces. The Japanese conquests of the Philippines, Vietnam, Malaya, and Indonesia during World War II had shattered the legitimacy of American, French, British, and Dutch colonial rule in each colony. The Americans acknowledged independence for the Philippines in 1946. The unsuccessful Dutch campaign—with support from the British—to reassert colonial rule in Indonesia led to the Hague's acceptance of the independence of its colony in 1949.[12] The British faced an insurgency led by the Communist party in Malaya from 1948 to 1960, which albeit unsuccessful, paved the way for Malayan independence under a pro-Western government.[13] For the French, however, imperial disengagement from Vietnam came only after a decisive military defeat at Dien Bien Phu in 1954.[14] The surrender of Japan in 1945 had also led to the loss of its pre-war colonial possessions in Taiwan and Korea, which resulted in a confrontation between China and the United States over the future of these former colonies after the 1949 communist victory in the Chinese civil war. China was determined to reassert its sovereignty over Formosa/Taiwan while the United States sought to protect the nationalist regime on the island from the consequences of the political and military ineptitude of its leaders.[15] Similarly, the Korean War laid the basis for the escalation of Sino-American tensions over the unresolved status of the former Japanese colonies. Thus, the decolonization process in Asia had provoked the imposition of cold war tensions in the former colonies of both the European and Japanese empires.

In response to the expansion of the cold war into Asia, the newly independent countries of the region sponsored the Bandung Conference of 1955 that sought to create support for Asian nationalism and the space for a negotiated end to colonial rule. Signaling that a "Colored Curtain" had been drawn against the European alliances in the affairs of the non-European world, invitations were extended to the PRC and Japan, but the United States, the Soviet Union, and the Western colonial powers were excluded. The conference articulated a vision of neutrality that sought to decouple the struggle for decolonization in Asia and the non-European world from the cold war. It marked the emergence of the Non-Aligned Movement as a factor in post-1945 international politics that would complicate the efforts of the major alliance systems to consolidate their influence outside of Europe. Just as important, the pursuit of neutralism under the umbrella of the NAM by the new states stimulated the growth of ideological pluralism that contested the bipolar order that defined the North Atlantic region over the course of the cold war. Yet, Bandung also represented an early indication that the bipolar system in Europe was less stable than it appeared. Yugloslavia's Josip Broz "Tito" proved to be an early harbinger of European disaffection with the bipolar order as he became a founding member of the Non-Aligned Movement.[16]

The emergence of the NAM created the "Third World"—a term used to define countries that sought to avoid being trapped by the major alliance systems in Europe. This strategy of distancing themselves from the bipolar conflict provided these states with the room to manipulate that conflict for their own individual and collective aims. It also allowed them to bring to the international agenda their concerns about the legacies of colonial rule and "underdevelopment" that perpetuated their relative poverty within the international political economy. Thus, the NAM served member states as both a device for escaping the pressures of the cold war and a framework for coordination on trade and economic issues that could become articulated through the United Nations and other international organizations. For newly independent states which had limited economic and military resources, the NAM was a mechanism for enhancing their autonomy vis-à-vis the major military alliances, a diplomatic tool to advance the goals of national self-determination and economic development, and a forum for legitimizing the idea of ideological pluralism as a counter to the competing theologies of communism and capitalism. The fact that the largest Asian states were represented at the Bandung Conference was a powerful statement of the ideological (and religious) pluralism that shaped the Third World challenge to the agendas of the major European alliances. As a consequence, by the mid-1950s the process of decolonization in Asia had begun to reshape the contours of the international system and to establish limits upon the capacity of the major powers to enforce ideological conformity.[17]

This challenge to ideological conformity represented by the NAM also had an enormous impact upon the relationships among the major powers. In the wake of the Soviet Union's successful launch of its Sputnik satellites, signaling the sophistication of its space exploration technology and its development of an intercontinental-range ballistic missile (ICBM) launch system, the United States and the Soviet Union began to explore the possibilities of détente in an effort to negotiate mechanisms for stabilizing their relationship and limiting the possibility of nuclear war. The development of intercontinental nuclear missiles elevated the status and power of both the United States and the Soviet Union. In 1956 both had been motivated to use their considerable leverage to "limit" the autonomy of their alliance partners. The Hungarian challenge to Soviet orthodoxy in 1956 had resulted in a Soviet-led invasion and the installation of a loyal regime in Budapest. Simultaneously, Britain, France, and Israel had invaded Egypt in an effort to seize control over the Suez Canal, which had been nationalized by the Egyptian government led by Gamal Abdel Nasser.[18] Soviet support for Nasser's nationalization policy, as well as its willingness to supply Egypt with arms and financing for the Aswan Dam project, had helped to trigger the actions by Britain, France, and Israel. The Eisenhower administration used its economic leverage and its influence at the United Nations to force the withdrawal of its partners from Egyptian territory and accept Nasser's nationalization policy.[19]

Each superpower demonstrated the limits of its willingness to accord autonomy to its alliance partners. For the Soviets, ideological orthodoxy was a primary concern in maintaining their control over the Warsaw Pact, and their determination to prevent the emergence of another Yugoslavia in Eastern Europe was manifest in their intervention in Hungary. For the United States, Eisenhower was signaling America's willingness to support non-European nationalism for reasons of grand strategy in limiting the expansion of Soviet influence in the non-European world even if it required humiliating its NATO partners, As the Dutch had discovered in Indonesia, the United States was prepared to concede political independence to nationalists in the non-European world if required to "contain" communism. In the Suez crisis and the Hungarian uprising, actions by allies of the superpowers had escalated international tensions, and the superpowers pursued initiatives that signaled their control of their respective partners. With the emergence of ICBM systems on both sides of the iron curtain, the superpowers confronted the dilemma of preventing their allies from triggering crises that could precipitate escalation of conflicts because of treaty commitments. The cold war had crossed a critical threshold.

Several of America's partners in NATO were colonial powers, and this was a matter of concern as the growth of nationalism and decolonization in the non-European world gained momentum. In 1962, the increasing Cuban-American antipathy that followed upon the Cuban revolution in 1959 and the American-backed Bay of Pigs invasion aimed at toppling the revolutionary regime was a trigger for the major post-1945 superpower confrontation over non- European nationalism. While Cuba was no longer an American colony in constitutional terms, the American military base at Guantanamo and American investment in Cuba had compromised Cuban sovereignty since the end of the American occupation in 1903. The Soviet decision to deploy nuclear missiles, and the threat of a major confrontation between the two nuclear powers over the issue, provided a stark glimpse into the possibilities which could result from unrestrained competition between the two major alliances over their influence in the non- European world.[20] The increasing globalization of the decolonization process—spreading from Asia to Africa and thence to the Caribbean—had undermined the ability of the superpowers to assert control over the international order.

As the Suez crisis likewise demonstrated, the United States and its European partners diverged on the issue of decolonization as a symptom of the relative decline of the influence of the European colonial powers in the international system. The process of decline also had a significant impact upon the domestic politics of the colonial powers. Great Britain's prime minister in 1956, Anthony Eden, resigned and departed from politics, opening the way for a new generation of political leaders. In 1960 his successor, Harold Macmillan, delivered his speech on "The Wind of Change" in South Africa, acknowledging that the age of European empire was on the wane.[21] Later that year the UN General Assembly passed its Declaration on the Granting of Independence to Colonial Countries and Peoples which stipulated:

> Immediate steps shall be taken, in Trust and Non-Self-Governing Territories or all other territories which have not yet attained independence, to transfer all powers to

the peoples of those territories, without any conditions or reservations, in accordance with their freely expressed will and desire, without any distinction as to race, creed or colour, in order to enable them to enjoy complete independence and freedom.[22]

A similar process of colonial disengagement occurred after France's failures in Vietnam, at Suez, and in Algeria. The collapse of French imperial influence led to a loss of legitimacy for the Fourth Republic and the return to power of Charles De Gaulle. De Gaulle conceded independence to Algeria and decided to negotiate independence for France's other African colonies.[23] More than a decade later, with the collapse of the fascist-era Estado Novo regime under Marcelo Caetano in Portugal, the successor regime in Lisbon divested the country of its colonies in Africa.[24] As the individual European empires in the non-European world disintegrated, the project aimed at deepening and widening the integration of the European states gained momentum. European integration provided a focus for the energies of European leaders who sought to have the continent remain a major player in international politics. Decolonization was a catalyst for increasing pluralism in the international order. As a consequence, the former imperial powers sought to forge bonds that would allow the continent to compete more effectively with the superpowers. They even became part of the search for ways to limit the capacity of the superpowers to define the limits of sovereignty.[25] A major step in this direction began under the Willy Brandt government in West Germany with the adoption of *Ostpolitik*, a policy intended to create alternative forms of constructive engagement across the iron curtain.[26] The search for sovereignty that underpinned the decolonization process in the non-European world opened the way for the search for a new European order that would revive Europe after the tragedies of two world wars and the division of Europe into competing ideological and military blocs.

As Anthony Hopkins argues, the decolonization process also triggered a recalibration of the relationship between Britain and its colonies in Canada, Australia, New Zealand, and South Africa, which had become self-governing dominions with considerable prerogatives in domestic and foreign policies. During the cold war, these former colonies moved to reshape the constitutional relationship with Britain to expand the scope of their sovereignty and to develop greater latitude in foreign policy.[27] This search for enhanced sovereignty among these former colonies revealed the centrality of nationalism in reshaping the post-1945 international order even as the superpowers had sought to secure greater control over the international order. Of considerable importance in this process was the way in which these former British colonies became increasingly tied to the global strategy of the United States and the Anglo-American alliance. While Canada was a member of NATO, the others were not—yet they emerged as strategic partners for both Great Britain and the United States in the Asia-Pacific, the South Atlantic, and Indian Ocean regions. This redefinition of the imperial connection among the former British colonies and the creation of a new alliance system among the "Anglo-Saxon" countries were indicative of subtle shifts in the international political order triggered by the cold war's decolonization process.

The expansion of American influence by way of American penetration of the European empires and, on occasion, for the displacement of the colonial powers' influence in specific colonies during and after the transfer of power paved the way for the United States to redefine the priorities of the various countries. One early example of this process was the creation of Israel in part of the Palestine Mandate. The Truman administration's recognition of Israeli independence in 1948 opened the way for American influence to expand in the country over succeeding decades; British influence became increasingly marginal.[28] America's role in South Vietnam followed a similar path until the unification of the country by the Vietnamese communist forces in 1975.[29] An analogous process occurred in the Belgian Congo, which became an American client state in Central Africa after its independence from Belgium amid a protracted violent struggle among the country's political factions.[30] This process of American displacement of British influence during the decolonization process was also evident in British Guiana during the country's struggle for independence.[31] The expansion of American influence in parts of the non-European world resulted in the transformation of formal European colonial rule into informal American empire.[32]

The case of Diego Garcia in the Indian Ocean suggests how the pursuit of American strategic goals also subverted and delayed the process of decolonization. In 1971 the American government leased Diego Garcia from the British government. As part of the arrangement, the British systematically removed and relocated the indigenous people of the islands in order to facilitate the American occupation. In return, the United Kingdom received American-subsidized Polaris submarine-launched nuclear missiles from the United States to support its goal of becoming a military nuclear power.[33] Diego Garcia illustrates that the continuation of European colonial rule facilitated the expansion of American containment strategy in a global context. Some colonies were trapped by the imperatives of the cold war conflict, which provided the communist states with the opportunity to pillory the Western alliance for perpetuating colonial rule.[34]

In response to the American integration of the European colonies and ex-colonies in the containment of Soviet and PRC influence in the non-European world, the two communist states embraced anti-colonialism as a strategy for limiting Western influence. Insurgents in Vietnam, Algeria, and Angola among others received military and diplomatic support from the communist powers. This support for the decolonization of the European empires, and the identification of the United States with the European colonial powers, illustrated the ways in which decolonization became an integral factor in the evolution of the cold war and the strategic calculus of the superpowers and their respective alliance partners. America's perception of itself as a superpower capable of guaranteeing the survival of an allied regime in South Vietnam was key to its pursuit of a futile war. In 1975 South Vietnam collapsed despite more than two decades of American military and financial support.

The longest war of decolonization during the cold war was the terrain of the shifting fortunes of the major powers and the recalibration of the relationship among them. The People's Republic of China's support for Vietnamese reunification did little to enhance its relationship with the Vietnamese Communist party. The two countries fought a brief war in 1979 and competed for influence in Laos and Cambodia,[35] The reunification of Vietnam likewise exacerbated the Sino-Soviet split as both Vietnam and the Soviet Union were clearly interested in containing China and its growing engagement with the United States.[36] The United States found itself increasingly isolated from its European allies as it escalated its involvement in Vietnam, and both China and the Soviet Union competed for influence over the Vietnamese Communist party, while the latter manipulated both in pursuit of its goal of national reunification. The outcome was the reorientation of priorities that resulted from the negotiations over ending the war. The Soviet Union and the United States moved toward détente, while the United States and China opened an era of strategic engagement that would result in increasing collaboration between them to contain the growth of Soviet-bloc influence.

If the Vietnam War proved to be a catalyst for the relaxation of cold war tensions by way of détente and the US-PRC rapprochement, it was the decolonization of the Portuguese empire in Africa that signaled that détente between the superpowers was ephemeral. As the Estado Novo regime under Marcel Caetano collapsed in Portugal, the nationalist movements in Angola, Guinea-Bissau, and Mozambique moved to take control of these territories. The disintegration of Portuguese rule triggered an effort by the Gerald Ford administration to encourage the South African government to intervene in Angola and Mozambique. Following South African military intervention in Angola, the Cuban government responded to the request by the MPLA faction of the nationalist movement for support. Cuban troops routed the South African military forces, and the Soviet Union subsequently provided even greater support for the Cuban military forces in Angola as the MPLA sought to consolidate its authority against an insurgency supported by South Africa and the United States.[37]

The Cuban military success, and the Soviet decision to support the Cuban effort, reflected the shifting strategic balance in the international system. The Soviets displayed an unprecedented, and decisive, long distance force-projection capability that was critical in accelerating the end of colonial rule in Southern Africa. The demise of Portuguese colonialism posed a direct threat to the survival of the apartheid regime in South Africa, its control over Namibia, and the white supremacist regime in Rhodesia. The United States and the United Kingdom had supported South Africa and Rhodesia in their pursuit of policies that systematically deprived the black majority populations of political rights and economic opportunities. In 1976 South Africa's military defeat was followed by the Soweto uprising, led primarily by students. These protests laid the basis for more than a decade of escalating confrontation that eventually produced a democratically elected multiracial government in 1994. In 1980 the new country of Zimbabwe emerged after the Rhodesian white minority regime was removed through an insurgency and growing international pressure.[38] By 1988 the country of Namibia had achieved its political independence as the domestic crisis within South Africa undermined the apartheid regime's legitimacy and regional influence.[39] In Rhodesia-Zimbabwe, Namibia, and South Africa, the communist states provided support for the victorious nationalist factions against the white supremacist regimes. Decolonization continued to be a catalyst for increasing conflict between the superpowers even in an era of détente, and the decolonization process in Southern Africa further eroded the influence of NATO and its allies as the cold war was coming to an end. The end of apartheid in South Africa and Namibia was the ultimate acknowledgment that the politics of white supremacy that had underpinned the Euro-American colonial order had been discredited. Soviet-Cuban intervention in Southern Africa contributed to the revival of the cold war in the 1980s, and the end of the cold war in Europe resulted in the unraveling of the apartheid regime in South Africa. The collapse of the Soviet Union and the repeal of apartheid both occurred in 1991. These historical convergences in the politics of Europe and Africa in the post-1945 era offer useful insights into the ways in which the politics of white supremacy and European colonial rule were at the heart of the cold war. For both the Eastern and Western blocs, decolonization became a surrogate battlefield in their struggle to expand or retain their influence. For the Western alliance, continued colonial rule was a critical component of a grand strategy to maintain the pre-eminence of the capitalist order at home and abroad. For the communist powers, the end of colonialism was an effective strategy for undermining the Western alliance and its historic control over the international political economy. Decolonization was integral to the cold war confrontation and the struggle for ideological supremacy in the wider world.

However, decolonization also raised salient questions about human equality and citizenship within the imperial states. As the legitimacy of white supremacy was increasingly questioned in the post-1945 era, the status of colonial subjects within the imperial framework forced open new avenues of debate and struggle. As colonial subjects and members of "inferior races" within the colonial dispensation, the inequality of citizenship was taken for granted. However, wartime service in the imperial armies by colonial subjects, and the postwar challenge to notions of racial supremacy that defined the colonial order, raised the issue of whether colonial subjects would be content to remain second-class citizens within the imperial project. The rise of the nationalist movements in the colonies offered one route to first-class citizenship in a country free of colonial rule for many colonial subjects. However, for those interested in seeking citizenship within the imperial state, the problem of the color line and the politics of citizenship became increasingly contested terrain as the imperial centers struggled with the idea that "alien" populations would constitute an indelible part of their post-colonial ideas of national community.

Integrating the human "fruits of empire" within the post-colonial North Atlantic context has been a fundamental predicament of the post-1945 international order and a dimension of the decolonization process that requires exploration by scholars in greater depth and breadth across the post-imperial order in Europe, North America, and their surrogates in the wider world. Given the population losses in Europe due to war and its consequences in the first half of the 20th century, postwar reconstruction through the recruitment of labor from the colonies to work in the imperial center increasingly became a strategy for addressing the demographic deficit within Europe. In addition, the reliance upon military recruits from the colonies during World War II and to support the efforts to reassert/maintain colonial rule after 1945 posed the problem of how to deal with populations of colonial subjects who sought imperial citizenship as an alternative to returning to their places of origin.

For these societies, most of which were democracies in the cold war, integrating former colonial and other "alien" subjects as citizens was critical to their creation of an alternative to the politics of white supremacy. In this project of integrating "alien" populations, the United States had to address its own problem of second-class citizenship for African Americans and other minorities in the post-1945 period. As the United States sought to exercise leadership in the cold war, it found its credibility challenged by its politics of racial inequality and segregation. In 1944 Gunnar Myrdal, with support from the Carnegie Corporation, published *The American Dilemma*, advocating an end to its racial regime. It was the first major domestic effort to articulate an alternative to the politics of white supremacy in the post-1945 international order.[40] As the cold war intensified, and as the NATO alliance and its championship of democracy as a system of government superior to communism was refurbished, the gap between the rhetoric of democracy and the reality of an exclusionary politics that targeted "alien" populations became a problem that could not be wished away. Further, the Nazi regime provided a powerful incentive to find a way out of the morass of ideologies and policies based upon the absurdity of "racial supremacy" and its corollary, color-coded citizenship.

In the case of the United States, this search for a vision of citizenship that transcended race eventually converged around both its domestic history of color-coded citizenship and its own policies as a colonial power. The *Brown v. Board of Education* decision by the Supreme Court in 1954 invalidated the constitutional sanction of segregated education and citizenship. The decision was a major catalyst for the escalating civil rights struggle in the United States. Further, Martin Luther King, Jr. and other civil rights leaders pushed the process of racial reform that culminated in the passage of the Civil Rights Act in 1964 and the Voting Rights Act of 1965. These acts removed the legal impediments to the exercise of citizenship by the historically disadvantaged racial/ethnic groups in the United States. As Mary Dudziak argues, the politics of racial reform in the United States was driven by the sensitivity of American policymakers to the contradictions of their espousal of democracy as superior to communism while continuing segregation.[41] In the post-1945 era, similar problems were faced by other Western democracies, including Britain, France, and the Netherlands, which had become a destination for immigrants from the former colonies, many of them people of color. These new arrivals were responding to political changes in the colonies and the growing demand for labor in Europe as a result of the postwar reconstruction process.[42]

However, a little noticed aspect of American domestic political reform during the cold war was the transformation of Alaska and Hawaii from colonial possessions into non-contiguous states in the American union. American colonial rule had become, like domestic racial segregation, a liability in the cold war conflict. By undertaking its own process of colonial reform, the United States was burnishing its credentials as leader of the "Free World." With the accession of Hawaii and Alaska to statehood, the US provided an example of its commitment to ending colonial rule by including its former colonial subjects in the American body politic as citizens. The importance of this step was underlined by the fact that Hawaii had become a state despite the non-white, multi-ethnic identity of the majority of its inhabitants even before the mid-1960s.[43]

A similar strategy was adopted by the Netherlands with regard to its colonies in the Caribbean, by France in relation to its own Caribbean and Pacific colonies, and Britain for some of its colonies in the Caribbean, which were recognized as lacking the economic viability to obtain independence. In the United States similar approaches were adapted to Puerto Rico, the Virgin Islands, and the Pacific territories, where the inhabitants of these territories had representative government based on universal suffrage and citizenship but were hostage to limited economic opportunities. These former colonies were transformed into units where their inhabitants were citizens but with limited economic options and dependent upon the largesse of the imperial country. As a consequence, colonial reform did not lead to decolonization in legal terms but rather mitigated the perpetuation of a colonial politics of racial disadvantage and color-coded citizenship. Just as important, these arrangements made it possible for the inhabitants of the dependent territories to migrate to the imperial countries and exercise citizenship rights there—effectively creating a shift in the demographic composition of these societies and leading them to grapple, like the United States, with the implications of multicultural democracy during, and after, the cold war. The American dilemma during the cold war became part of a larger problem of equal citizenship within the North Atlantic world and in other areas of the former colonial world. Any area settled by Europeans who had displaced indigenous populations during the colonial period, including the United States, Australia, New Zealand, Canada, and South Africa, had to confront the issue of equal citizenship rights for the disadvantaged populations.

As the American civil rights struggle unfolded in 1954 after the landmark *Brown v. Board of Education* decision, the politics of race and equal citizenship within the democracies became intimately linked to the issue of decolonization. In a very evocative insight into the ways in which these processes were linked, Martin Luther King, Jr. observed in April 1957—after his return from Ghana's independence celebrations—that:

> ...Ghana tells us that the forces of the universe are on the side of justice...That night when I saw that old flag coming down and the new flag coming up, I saw something else. That wasn't just an ephemeral, evanescent event appearing on the stage of history, but it was an event with eternal meaning, for it symbolizes something. That thing symbolized to me that an old order is passing away and a new order is coming into being. An old order of colonialism, of segregation, of discrimination is passing away now, and a new order of justice and freedom and goodwill is being born.[44]

King's observation was remarkably prescient. He understood the linkages that were driving the processes of change in both the United States and in the wider international system and recognized that his generation of leadership would play a critical role in that transition. Decolonization in Africa became a catalyst for empowering King as a civil rights leader who saw African decolonization as a stepping stone for the advancement of the African American struggle for full citizenship in the United States. African independence, like Gandhi's advocacy of nonviolence in the Indian nationalist struggle, offered King valuable insights about the development of a strategy for promoting change within the United States.

In the final analysis, decolonization during the cold war was about more than either the "end of empire" or the "transfer of power." It was also about the rethinking of the nature of the global order and the role of race and citizenship therein. In very fundamental terms, it was a process that was transformative for both the colonies and the imperial powers. It also represented the emergence of a global process that was both international—as in the relationships among states, and transnational—as in the relationships among individuals and groups at the level of sub-national strategies of engagement. In addition, decolonization marked a shift in global consciousness from notions of racial hierarchy as a fundament of human society to the search for human community by transcending race. The study of decolonization as a global process featuring a range of actors within multiple arenas provides a multifaceted prism through which the post-1945 history of international relations can be reconceptualized. Decolonization constituted a constant reminder that the bipolar order pursued after 1945 by the superpowers and their alliance partners was never a stable framework for the management of international relations.

## Notes

1. See, among others, Franz Ansprenger, *The Dissolution of the Colonial Empires* (New York and London: Routledge, 1989); Frederick Cooper, *Colonialism in Question: Theory, Knowledge, History* (Berkeley, CA: University of California Press, 2005); D. LeSueur, ed., *The Decolonization Reader* (New York and London: Routledge, 2003); Wm. Roger Louis and Roger Owen, eds., *Suez 1956: The Crisis and its Consequences* (Oxford: Clarendon Press; New York: Oxford University Press, 1989); Rudolf von Albertini, *Decolonization* (New York: Doubleday & Co. 1971); and Yves Collart, "Limites à la décolonisation," *Relations Internationales* no. 18 (1979): 115–30.

2. Thomas Borstelmann, *The Cold War and the Color Line: American Race Relations in the Global Arena* (Cambridge, MA: Harvard University Press, 2001); Mary Dudziak, *Cold War Civil Rights* (Princeton, NJ: Princeton University Press, 2000); Azza Salama Layton, *International Politics and Civil Rights in the United States, 1941–1960* (New York: Cambridge University Press, 2000); Brenda Gayle Plummer, ed., *Window on Freedom: Race, Civil Rights, and Foreign Affairs, 1945–1988* (Chapel Hill, NC: University of North Carolina Press, 2003).

3. Sudarshan Kapur, *Raising Up a Prophet: The African-American Encounter with Gandhi* (Boston, MA; Beacon Press, 1992).

4. Cary Fraser, "Understanding American Policy towards the Decolonization of European Empires, 1945–1964," *Diplomacy & Statecraft* (March 1992): 105–25; and Wm. Roger Louis and Ronald Robinson, "The Imperialism of Decolonization," *Journal of Imperial and Commonwealth History* 22 (1994): 462–511.

5. Eri Hotta, *Pan-Asianism and Japan's War, 1931–1945* (New York: Palgrave Macmillan, 2007); Akira Iriye, *Power and Culture: The Japanese-American War, 1941–1945* (Cambridge, MA: Harvard University Press, 1981); and Christopher Thorne, *The Issue of War: States, Societies, and the Far Eastern Conflict of 1941–1945* (New York: Oxford University Press, 1985).

6. Paul Gordon Lauren, *Power and Prejudice: The Politics and Diplomacy of Racial Discrimination* (Boulder, CO: Westview Press, 1996).

7. The Nazi genocidal policies had already stimulated strong sentiment among the colonial powers to abandon the politics of racial supremacy. By 1950, UNESCO published a report which asserted: "Racial Doctrine is the outcome of a fundamentally anti-rational system of thought and is in glaring conflict with the whole humanist tradition of our civilization. It sets at nought everything that UNESCO stands for and endeavors to defend." (UNESCO, *The Race Concept: Results of an Inquiry,* Paris: UNESCO, 1950, 5).

8. William Stueck, ed., *The Korean War in World History* (Lexington, KY: University Press of Kentucky, 2004).

9. Marc Frey, Ronald W. Pruessen, and Tan Tai Yong, eds., *The Transformation of Southeast Asia: International Perspectives on Decolonization* (Armonk, NY: M.E. Sharpe, 2003).

10. George C. Herring and Richard H. Immerman, "Eisenhower, Dulles, and Dienbienphu," *Journal of American History* 71 (September 1984): 343–63.

11. Herring and Immerman, "Eisenhower, Dulles, and Dienbienphu"; and George McT. Kahin, *Intervention: How America Became Involved in Vietnam* (New York: Alfred A. Knopf, 1986), 34–65.

12. Robert J. McMahon, *Colonialism and Cold War: The United States and the Struggle for Indonesian Independence, 1945–1949* (Ithaca, NY: Cornell University Press, 1981); Andrew J. Rotter, *The Path to Vietnam: Origins of the American Commitment to Southeast Asia* (Ithaca, NY: Cornell University Press, 1987).

13. Simon C. Smith, *British Relations with the Malay Rulers from Decentralization to Malayan Independence, 1930–1957* (New York: Oxford University Press, 1995).

14. Mark Atwood Lawrence and Fredrik Logevall, eds. *The First Vietnam War: Colonial Conflict and Cold War Crisis* (Cambridge, MA: Harvard University Press, 2007).

15. Gordon H. Chang, *Friends and Enemies: the United States, China, and the Soviet Union, 1948–1972* (Stanford, CA: Stanford University Press, 1990).

16. William Zimmerman, *Open Borders, Nonalignment, and the Political Evolution of Yugoslavia* (Princeton, NJ: Princeton University Press, 1987).

17. J.W. Burton, ed., *Nonalignment* (New York: James H. Heinemann, Inc., 1966).

18. On the relationship between the two crises, see Brian McCauley, "Hungary and Suez, 1956: The Limits of Soviet and American Power," *Journal of Contemporary History* 16 (October 1981): 777–800.

19. Peter L. Hahn, *The United States, Great Britain, and Egypt, 1945–1956* (Chapel Hill, NC: The University of North Carolina Press, 1991); Diane B. Kunz, *the Economic Diplomacy of the Suez Crisis* (Chapel Hill, NC: The University of North Carolina Press, 1991).

20. Raymond L. Garthoff, *Reflections on the Cuban Missile Crisis,* rev. ed. (Washington, DC: Brookings Institution Press, 1989).

21. Ritchie Ovendale, "Macmillan and the Wind of Change in Africa, 1957–1960," *The Historical Journal* 38 (1995): 455–77.

22. UN Declaration on Granting Independence to Colonial Countries and Peoples, 1960—United Nations General Assembly Resolution 1514 (XV), December 14, 1960.

23. Tony Chafer, *The End of Empire in French West Africa: France's Successful Decolonization* (New York: Berg, 2002).

24. Stewart Lloyd-Jones and Antonio Costa Pinto, eds., *The Last Empire: Thirty Years of Portuguese Decolonization* (Bristol, UK and Portland, OR, USA: Intellect, 2003); Norrie MacQueen, *The Decolonization of Portuguese Africa* (New York and London: Longman, 1997).

25. See Robert Bidelux, "Introduction," in Robert Bidelux and Richard Taylor, eds., *European Integration and Disintegration: East and* West (London and New York: Routledge, 1996), 1–21.

26. Arne Hoffman, *The Emergence of Détente in Europe: Brandt, Kennedy and the Formation of Ostpolitik* (New York: Routledge, 2007).

27. Anthony G. Hopkins, "Rethinking Decolonization," *Past and Present* 200 (August 2008): 211–47.

28. See Douglas Little, *American Orientalism: The United States and the Middle East since 1945* (Chapel Hill, NC: The University of North Carolina Press, 2002).

29. Marilyn Young, *The Vietnam Wars, 1945-90* (New York: Harper Collins, 1991); Daniel Ellsberg, *Secrets: A Memoir of Vietnam and the Pentagon Papers* (New York: Viking Penguin, 2002).

30. Peter J. Schraeder, *United States Foreign Policy toward Africa: Incrementalism, Crisis and Change* (New York: Cambridge University Press, 1994).

31. Cary Fraser, "The 'New Frontier' of Empire in the Caribbean: The Transfer of Power in British Guiana, 1961–1964," *The International History Review* 22 (September 2000): 583–610.

32. Fraser, "Understanding American Policy;" Louis and Robinson, "The Imperialism of Decolonization."

33. Christian Nauvel, "A Return from Exile in Sight? The Chagossians and Their Struggle," *Northwestern Journal of International Human Rights* 5 (2006), 22.

34. The Cuban government after 1960 used the continued presence of an American naval base at Guantanamo to excoriate "Yankee Imperialism." Its decision to ally with communist powers proved to be a major embarrassment for American policy in the non-European world since Cuba embarked upon a policy of lending material support to nationalist movements in Africa and elsewhere. See Piero Gleijeses, *Conflicting Missions: Havana, Washington, and Africa, 1959–1976* (Chapel Hill, NC: The University of North Carolina Press, 2002).

35. Bruce Elleman, *Modern Chinese Warfare, 1795–1989* (New York: Routledge, 2001), 284–97.

36. Raymond Garthoff, *The Great Transition: American-Soviet Relations and the End of the Cold War* (Washington, DC: The Brookings Institution, 1994), 670–75.

37. Raymond Garthoff, *Détente and Confrontation: American-Soviet Relations from Nixon to Reagan* (Washington, DC: The Brookings Institution, 1985); and Gleijeses, *Conflicting Missions*.

38. M. Tamarkin, *The Making of Zimbabwe: Decolonization in Regional and International Politics* (London: Frank Cass, 1990).

39. According to George Shultz, Namibian Independence meant "the colonial era in Africa had ended." George P. Shultz, *Turmoil and Triumph* (New York: Charles Scribner's Sons, 1993), 1129.

40. Gunnar Myrdal, *An American Dilemma* (New York: Harper & Row, 1962). Myrdal observes: "If America in actual practice could show the world a progressive trend by which the Negro became finally integrated into modern democracy, all mankind would be given faith again—it would have reason to believe that peace, progress and order are feasible. And America would have a spiritual power many times stronger than all her financial and military resources—the power of the trust and support of all good people on earth." ( Myrdal, *An American Dilemma*, 1021–2.)

41. Dudziak, *Cold War Civil Rights*.

42. Carl-Ulrik Schierup, Peo Hansen, and Stephen Castles, eds., *Migration, Citizenship, and the European Welfare State: A European Dilemma* (New York: Oxford University Press,

2006), 24–8; and Kathleen Paul, *Whitewashing Britain: Race and Citizenship in the Postwar Era* (Ithaca, NY: Cornell University Press, 1997).

43. Rostow argues that Lyndon Johnson's advocacy of civil rights was influenced by the Hawaiian statehood campaign in the 1950s. See W.W. Rostow, "The Case for the Vietnam War," *Parameters* 26 (Winter 1996–7): 39–50.

44. Martin Luther King, Jr., "The Birth of a New Nation," a sermon delivered at the Dexter Avenue Baptist Church on April 7, 1957, in Clayborne Carson, ed., *The Papers of Martin Luther King, Jr., Vol. 4. Symbol of the Movement, January 1957–December 1958* (Berkeley, CA: University of California Press, 2000).

## Select Bibliography

Baudet, Henri. *Paradise on Earth: Some Thoughts on European Images of Non-European Man.* New Haven, CT: Yale University Press, 1965.

Hopkins, A. G. *Global History: Interactions between the Universal and the Local.* Basingstoke: Palgrave Macmillan, 2005.

Memmi, Albert. *The Colonizer and the Colonized.* New York: Orion Press, 1965.

Robinson, Ronald Edward, and John Gallagher. *Africa and the Victorians: The Official Mind of Imperialism.* London: Macmillan, 1967.

Trouillot, Michel Rolph. *Silencing the Past: Power and the Production of History.* Boston, MA: Beacon Press, 1997.

von Albertini, Rudolf. *Decolonization: The Administration and Future of the Colonies, 1919-1960.* New York: Africana Publishing Company, 1982.

# CHAPTER 28

···········································································································

# HUMAN RIGHTS

···········································································································

## BARBARA KEYS AND ROLAND BURKE[1]

IN stark contrast to the cold war's division of the world into two antagonistic blocs, ideas about universal human rights brooked no global divides: they were predicated on a belief that the most important identity was a common humanity. Such ideas predated and outlasted the cold war and, while the conflict persisted, became powerful enough to play a role in ending it. As Akira Iriye writes in this volume, the cold war "can be considered to have been a footnote to human rights history, not the other way around."[2] Though often used by both sides as a vehicle for propaganda battles, developments in the field of human rights were never more than partly subsumed by the bipolar political struggle. Along with other forces to which they were closely tied—the rise of nongovernmental organizations, globalization, a growing sense of interdependence, and changes in technology and communications—issues of human rights often transcended cold war dynamics, and when they became a mass movement it was as an alternative to cold war politics.

Chronicling attempts to define, codify, and protect human rights during the cold war is best conceived not as a linear and unitary narrative of progress in the face of resistance but rather as a series of discontinuities, intersections, and appropriations in which the scope and content of the term itself was always an area of contestation. A kaleidoscope of state and nonstate actors, at different times and in different forums but always with political motives, picked up the mantle of human rights and invested the concept with varied meanings. At times used domestically to combat repression, universal human rights were more often a program for export: a means of restraining abuses elsewhere. The United States played a central role in the first phase of defining human rights at the United Nations, where an emphasis on the civil and political rights of individuals prevailed and measures were limited to codifying, rather than enforcing, norms. By the 1950s the main movers behind a revised human rights agenda were Third World countries advocating collective rights such as self-determination. A new phase began at the end of the 1960s, as leftist disillusionment with socialist reformism after the failure of the Prague Spring and the Vietnam War's undermining of the cold war consensus created an opening for new ideas to take hold. In this environment, human rights seemed to offer a compelling, politically neutral moral calculus that transcended cold war issues as the organizing principle for international affairs. A mass movement arose, spearheaded by a new cohort of nongovernmental organizations (NGOs) engaged in information-gathering and publicity campaigns against individual countries, often focusing on sensationalist integrity-of-the-person abuses. By the end of the cold war, when human rights emerged as the world's dominant moral language, it did so partly because the term had become so capacious that it could support a wide array of political agendas.

The cold war shaped these diverse human rights projects in several important respects. The eagerness with which both East and West at times used human rights language to wage the conflict—and to justify its existence and magnitude—raised the profile of human rights. Cold war competition endowed world public opinion with great significance, an effect that could sharpen the pressures on each side to adhere to human rights standards. When worldwide press attention, fanned by Soviet propaganda, turned the spotlight on US racial discrimination in the 1950s and 1960s, for example, the cold war imperative pushed the executive branch toward reforms at home.[3] In similar fashion, dissidents in the Soviet bloc harnessed global public opinion in their successful efforts to give meaning to the human rights provisions of the 1975 Helsinki Final Act. More often, the influence of the cold war worked to undermine the promotion of human rights in practice. Communist bloc regimes used Western hostility to legitimize their own suppression of human rights. In the West, many believed that the struggle against communism was, at its core, a struggle for human rights that superseded all others and justified overlooking human rights violations committed by anticommunist allies.

One of the few areas of superpower consensus on human rights was a mutual desire to avoid genuine supranational oversight. Most postwar human rights advocacy aimed at empowering the individual against the state. All states, whether East or West, North or South, had a level of shared interest in protecting state power. While eager to trade accusations across the floor of the General Assembly, neither the United States nor the Soviet Union was willing to endow the UN with powers that infringed on state prerogatives. As both sides fought propaganda battles against each other on human rights questions, they simultaneously mounted a less conspicuous rearguard action against the diminution of untrammeled, unsupervised state sovereignty.[4] This defensive campaign was overt and brutal in the case of the Soviet bloc, and more contradictory and subtle in the West. Neither approach succeeded in halting the limited and uneven shift toward international accountability that gained momentum in the 1970s.

## CONTESTATION AND CODIFICATION

Horrified by the Second World War's record of carnage, many policymakers and intellectuals seized on human rights and democratization as means of preventing another such conflagration. The interwar rights machinery had centered on protecting the rights of collective minorities, but in the wake of the destruction wrought by fascist dictator-ships, a new consensus arose that the rights most in need of protection were the rights of individuals.[5] Already during the war, the Allies had begun to use human rights language in describing their war aims. In the 1942 Declaration by United Nations, for example, representatives of twenty-six Allied and twenty-one other nations declared their intent "to preserve human rights and justice in their own lands as well as in other lands."[6]

None of the war's victorious great powers, however, was eager to see human rights embedded in the Charter of the new United Nations. It was the weight of public opinion and pressure applied by nongovernmental organizations, about forty of which were offi-cial consultants to the US delegation at the San Francisco conference of 1945, that con-vinced US policymakers to press for human rights provisions as part of the new body's mandate.[7] The result was the inclusion of more than a half-dozen references to human rights in the Charter, including in Article 1 setting forth the principal purposes of the organization: "to achieve international cooperation in...promoting and encouraging respect for human rights and for fundamental freedoms for all." Articles 55 and 56 com-mit members to take "joint and separate action" to promote "universal respect for, and observance of, human rights."[8] The Charter thus became the first international treaty to refer to human rights in general, rather than to the rights of specific groups.[9]

Contrary to popular myth, the new attention to human rights did not stem from revulsion at the horrors of the Holocaust, as the marginal attention paid to genocide shows.[10] Rather, the human rights references in the UN Charter were largely cosmetic. If they pointed to a new reading of international relations, one in which states have a duty to promote universal respect for human rights, such a reading was contradicted by pro-visions that shielded states from attempts at enforcing rights. Article 2(7) of the Charter reads: "Nothing contained in the present Charter shall authorize the United Nations to intervene in matters which are essentially within the domestic jurisdiction of any State...."[11] During the cold war, states accused of human rights violations commonly cited Article 2(7) as protection against international action.

Advocates of human rights within the United Nations originally intended to draft a legally binding "international bill of human rights." The delays that beset this project, though often blamed on the cold war, owed more to superpower condominium than to superpower rivalry. In 1947 (and again later) both the United States and the Soviet Union, against the wishes of many smaller states, worked hard to forestall any document that might have enforcement powers.[12] It was principally at their insistence that the first UN human rights document was a nonbinding declaration rather than a binding treaty. Signed in 1948 in the shadow of the Eiffel Tower in Paris and then passed by the General Assembly in New York, the Universal Declaration of Human Rights (UDHR) is the foundational document of the postwar human rights regime and a reference point for all subsequent discussions of human rights. Drafted by a commission headed by Eleanor Roosevelt, it has often been criticized as embodying Western values, despite its drafters' care in drawing on many political and cultural traditions.[13] Billed as "a common stand-ard of achievement for all peoples and all nations," it contains civil and political rights—such as the right to life, liberty, and security of the person, to fair trial, property, and freedom of movement and religion, and prohibitions on slavery, torture, and arbitrary arrest—as well as economic and social rights, including the right to work, to education, and to an adequate standard of living.[14]

The Soviet Union, which abstained from the vote on the UDHR, opposed it on the grounds that it undercut the principle of state sovereignty.[15] The Soviet conception of rights differed sharply from Western, liberal notions of rights as a protection from state power. According to the Soviet view, the interests of state and individual were coterminous. Rights did not inhere in individuals by virtue of their humanity but derived from the state and reflected its stage of development.[16] Andrei Vyshinsky, the veteran prosecutor of the Stalinist show trials, lectured the UN that rights "could not be conceived outside the state" and that in the Soviet Union, "the state and the individual were in harmony with each other."[17] As internal repression moderated after Stalin's death in 1953, however, the Soviet Union came to see benefits in the propaganda value of embracing elements of the UN human rights program.[18] Not surprisingly, the Soviet bloc, which systemically violated almost the entire corpus of civil and political rights, discounted them in international forums. It emphasized instead social and economic rights, where the communist track record could be presented somewhat more favorably.

Having passed the UDHR, the United Nations turned to the drafting of binding human rights treaties. The cold war had a major impact on this process, as the United States succeeded in splitting what had initially been intended as a single human rights covenant into two separate ones. The Eisenhower administration argued that there was a fundamental distinction between civil and political rights, on the one hand, and social and economic rights, on the other, in that only the first group were legally enforceable. Fearing that a split into two sets of rights would relegate social and economic rights to a secondary status, many countries, including the Soviet Union, argued unsuccessfully for a single covenant.[19] Cold war maneuvering, and the complexities and difficulties inherent in writing documents with enforcement power, delayed the drafting for nearly two decades: it was not until 1966 that the General Assembly approved the International Covenant on Civil and Political Rights (ICCPR) and the International Covenant on Economic, Social, and Cultural Rights (ICESCR).[20]

Although the initial postwar efflorescence of rights owed much to US NGOs, often working in concert with an activist Truman administration, the leadership role of the United States was soon subordinated to cold war concerns and remained submerged until the 1970s. In the early 1950s, fearing that human rights treaties would undermine US sovereignty and mandate such radical social and economic programs as desegregation, the Senate very nearly passed a Constitutional amendment sponsored by Ohio Republican John Bricker to overturn the provision that made treaties the supreme law of the land. Bricker claimed to see a "similarity between the Soviet Constitution and the proposed Human Rights Covenants" then being drafted at the UN: both, in his view, were antithetical to American values.[21] President Eisenhower, who opposed the amendment's limitations on executive power, succeeded in preventing its passage, but at the cost of withdrawing from genuine participation in the drafting of the UN covenants. In 1953 Secretary of State John Foster Dulles announced that the administration would "favor methods of persuasion, education and example rather than formal undertaking which commit one part of the world to impose its particular social and moral standards upon another part of the world community."[22]

Codification and, to a lesser extent, enforcement of human rights standards also occurred in regional forums. Within Europe, human rights became embedded in the process of European reconstruction and integration.[23] West European governments acceded to a steady accretion of legal and multilateral human rights policies, creating a system in which participants surrendered a degree of sovereignty to regional human rights institutions. The Council of Europe, founded in 1949 to facilitate European integration, made respect for human rights a condition of membership. The European Convention for the Protection of Human Rights and Fundamental Freedoms, limited to civil and political rights, entered into force in 1953. It granted strong monitoring powers to the European Human Rights Commission and authoritative decision-making powers to the European Court of Human Rights, formed in 1959. Under this regional regime, European governments allowed individuals and NGOs to bring complaints for binding decisions.[24] Latin American countries adopted the American Declaration of the Rights and Duties of Man in 1948, and, drawing on the European model, ratified an American Convention on Human Rights in 1978 and established an Inter-American Court of Human Rights in 1979.

Despite erecting an impressive edifice of conventions, covenants, and declarations, the United Nations in its first decades effectively ignored actual human rights violations. Enthusiasm for linking the soaring rhetoric of abstract rights with the miserable reality of specific violations was scarce on both sides of the cold war divide. Nowhere was the relative importance of state and individual more apparent than in the treatment of the thousands of complaints from individuals alleging violations of human rights that poured in to the UN Human Rights Commission from across the world beginning in 1945. In 1947 the Commission formally renounced any power to investigate the correspondence, creating instead a system for filing complaints, in place until 1967, that one participant called "the most elaborate wastepaper basket ever created."[25]

Throughout the 1950s and 1960s, a loose coalition of Asian, Arab, and African states took the initiative in human rights, as decolonization created an agenda that often bypassed the conventional cold war divide. Newly independent states from across Asia in the 1950s, and Africa in the 1960s, radically re-ordered rights priorities around anti-racism, development, and self-determination. The growing Third World pioneered aggressive new methods that implied vastly less respect for assertions of domestic jurisdiction—that is, unless the jurisdiction in question was their own. Beginning at the 1955 Asian-African Conference in Bandung, Indonesia, when the Third World emerged as a political force, delegates showed an obvious engagement with human rights, which were often incorporated into the demands of the broader anti-colonial liberation movement.[26] As early as 1949, in negotiations on a draft Convention on Freedom of Information, these states disrupted any notion of a bipolar cold war dynamic with initiatives that were incompatible with both the legalistic liberalism of the West and the uncompromising totalitarian positivism of the communist bloc.[27]

The Third World crusade to add a right to self-determination to the pantheon of rights that had been agreed to in 1948 exemplified the changing configuration of the debate. Proposals for the right to self-determination were met with unsurprising hostility from European colonial powers, but the United States and the Soviet bloc scrambled to find friends and advantage. US delegates sought to co-opt self-determination as a weapon against Soviet imperialism. Conversely, Soviet representatives sought a narrow definition replete with anti-colonial condemnation and "respect for sovereign rights...without exception."[28] Yet in the boldest statement of self-determination, the landmark 1960 Declaration on Colonialism—the most cited resolution in UN history—African and Asian states rejected the overtures of both sides, refusing Soviet and Western amendments. Given their growing numbers in the General Assembly, the imperative for compromise on the part of the "South" was rapidly receding by the 1960s. Increasingly, the reality of UN human rights diplomacy for Western and communist delegations alike was session after session of reactive measures and marginalization.

Third World dominance changed the order and emphasis of the rights being promoted. It also shifted the means permitted for monitoring and protection.[29] A core issue was the treatment of petitions by individuals; they begged the question of whether individuals were proper subjects under international law, which had previously been limited to states. Third World countries ensured that the 1965 International Convention on the Elimination of Racial Discrimination (ICERD), for example, included an optional petition system, a precedent that strengthened the case for petition in the 1966 ICCPR, where a petition system was included as an optional protocol.[30] Under ICERD states could opt in to the jurisdiction of a monitoring Committee on the Elimination of Racial Discrimination (CERD), which could investigate the complaints of individuals once all domestic remedies had been exhausted. For the first time individuals could appeal to a UN human rights body that stood above their states. Similar monitoring and investigating provisions were granted to committees on colonialism and apartheid, which began to target the pariah states of Portugal, Rhodesia, and South Africa.[31] A more radical move in the Commission on Human Rights came in 1967. Building on the logic that made colonialism and apartheid allowable topics for review, an alliance of Western, African, and Asian delegates extended the criteria to allow the study of *all* petitions "which reveal a consistent pattern of violations of human rights."[32]

Only on paper, however, was the right of petition a major step toward enforcement of the UN's human rights instruments; as a means of redress for real individuals, it was entirely ineffective. CERD, for example, did not hear its first petition until 1984 and did not issue its first ruling until 1988—two decades after the General Assembly adopted the convention—and only a small minority of states recognized its competence.[33] Even within the rarefied world of UN debates, Third World espousal of human rights soon devolved into farce. In 1968, Nigeria spoke in favor of a legally impressive petition procedure, even while Federal Nigerian forces were waging a ruthless campaign against secessionist Biafra that created arguably the worst humanitarian emergency since 1945. On the 20th anniversary of the UDHR, an assembly of dictatorships gathered, appropriately, in Shah Reza Pahlavi's Tehran for the UN World Conference on Human Rights.

Led by the Shah's sister, a number of delegates openly questioned the universal validity of the UDHR that they were ostensibly celebrating and exalted instead the primacy of economic development. The remainder of the program was consumed by ritualistic denunciation of friendless regimes: Israel, South Africa, and Portugal. As the 1960s closed, absolute monarchs and Soviet clients allied to diminish the status of civil and political rights as second-order freedoms subordinated to modernization, an agenda that would evolve into the authoritarian New International Economic Order of the 1970s. The same climate of "Southern" dominance that enabled a right to petition also facilitated the passage of the notorious 1975 UN Resolution 3379 declaring Zionism "a form of racism."[34]

# INTERNATIONAL MOBILIZATION AND THE HUMAN RIGHTS "BOOM"

Defining and codifying human rights at the United Nations, in regional forums, and in corridors of state was a quiet process that rarely affected the lives of individuals and attracted little public interest before the 1960s. The rise of social protest movements in the 1960s, however, changed the international terrain. During the 1970s, a transnational mass movement rose to prominence by appropriating human rights as its central rallying cry, and stories of human rights abuses became common features in Western media. The term "human rights," little used even by a nascent cohort of activists in the 1960s, became a ubiquitous watchword. Whereas earlier NGOs had focused their efforts on the UN or on private pressure on governments, the movement that emerged at the end of the 1960s adopted new tactics: gathering detailed information on individual cases, publicizing it in ostensibly neutral reports, and generating public and government pressure on offending states. Like states, NGOs approached human rights with their own agendas, shining a spotlight on some abuses while ignoring or downplaying others.[35] Many Western NGOs, for example, focused in the 1970s on emotionally resonant abuses such as the state-sponsored torture and disappearance of young middle-class men and women suspected of political subversion in Brazil, Uruguay, Chile, and Argentina or the release of political prisoners in Indonesia, while other kinds of violence—such as killings and abuses during the Indonesian invasion of East Timor—fell off the radar screen.[36]

By the early 1970s Western governments and the Soviet bloc had moved toward a less ideological approach to fighting the cold war, one that entailed greater tolerance by the West of internal repression in the Soviet bloc. The architects of East-West détente emphasized non-interference in the internal affairs of sovereign states as the basis for cooperation. The transnational human rights movement emerging at the same time challenged this premise, arguing that global security and internal affairs, in the form of respect for human rights, were intertwined. Alexander Solzhenitsyn encapsulated this sensibility in his 1972 Nobel Lecture. "No such thing as INTERNAL AFFAIRS remains on our crowded Earth," he declared. "Mankind's salvation lies exclusively in everyone's making everything his business, in the people of the East being anything but indifferent to what is thought in the West, and in the people of the West being anything but indifferent to what happens in the East."[37]

Solzhenitsyn, physicist Andrei Sakharov, and other Soviet dissidents created a human rights movement behind the iron curtain that eventually affected the nature and course of the cold war. The dissident movement was a distinctly Soviet phenomenon that sprang from internal sources but harnessed the cold war's competition for global public opinion to its own ends—and in a twist that surprised almost everyone, thereby helped to bring the conflict to a close. The Brezhnev-era dissident movement originated in the years after Stalin's death in 1953, when Soviet Premier Nikita Khrushchev set in motion de-Stalinization and a cultural "thaw" that allowed an extraordinary intellectual ferment, including public discussion of some of Stalin's crimes. In 1964 Khrushchev's successor Leonid Brezhnev instituted a "re-Stalinization," signaling the end of the thaw with the arrest and trial of writers Andrei Sinyavsky and Yuli Daniel for publishing "anti-Soviet" stories abroad. The protest against the trial by over a hundred intellectuals in Moscow's Pushkin Square in December 1965 marked the birth of the Soviet human rights movement.[38]

Civil rights activists in the United States had adopted civil disobedience—defiance of laws—as a primary tactic in the struggle to secure domestic human rights. The distinctiveness of the Soviet movement lay in its embrace of civil *obedience*: the demand that the government adhere to its own laws.[39] Some dissidents, the so-called *politiki*, argued that the system had to be overturned. But the most influential strain of thinking in the Soviet human rights movement was represented by the *zakonniki*: those who tried to persuade the Soviet government to respect its own laws and the international agreements it had signed. Thus, the signs that the Pushkin Square demonstrators carried in 1965 called for an open trial and respect for the Soviet constitution, and the petitions that human rights activists sent to the Soviet regime routinely referred to the Soviet constitution and Soviet laws.[40]

The cold war served as a lever for the *zakonniki* in that Western public opinion soon became their main audience. Appealing to Western publics was an integral part of dissident strategy: the goal was to generate external pressure that would impel the Soviet regime toward reform. The best-known dissident organizations—the Initiative Group for the Defense of Human Rights, formed in 1969; the Moscow Committee for Human Rights, formed by Sakharov, A. N. Tverdokhlebov, and Valerii Chalidze in 1970; and the activists who published the *Chronicle of Current Events*, the chief human-rights-related samizdat serial—all had extensive ties with Western media and nongovernmental organizations. Though shaped by internal factors, the movement was also influenced by international ideas about human rights. From its beginning on April 30, 1968, for example, each issue of the *Chronicle* began by reprinting the UDHR's Article 19 on freedom of opinion and expression, using the international document to legitimize its propagation of information.

The environment of the cold war magnified the international salience of the dissident movement. Solzhenitsyn's *The Gulag Archipelago*, a massive, meticulously researched chronicle of torture, forced labor, and deprivation in Soviet prison camps, profoundly affected Western views of the Soviet Union when it was published abroad in 1973. Solzhenitsyn, Sakharov, and other dissidents became household names because many in the West viewed them as moral beacons, willing to suffer harassment, arrest, exile, and imprisonment, including in brutal psychiatric facilities, for criticizing the Soviet regime. Their courage renewed the Western public's interest in the internal affairs of the Soviet Union, an interest signaled by Solzhenitsyn's 1970 Nobel Prize in Literature and Sakharov's 1975 Nobel Peace Prize. Though sometimes greeted with a caution that amounted to cowardice—in 1969, for example, UN General Secretary U Thant instructed UN offices not to accept petitions from Soviet dissidents—the Soviet human rights movement discredited détente's marginalization of human rights.

Soviet-bloc dissidents aligned with and reinforced other trends that recast human rights with new international force in this period. In 1967 a military junta seized power in Greece, claiming to save the country from communism. The establishment of a military dictatorship in "the cradle of democracy" and the junta's widespread use of torture against political opponents caused public revulsion in Europe and the United States and led to important changes in international human rights law. For the first time countries party to the European Human Rights Convention lodged a case against another government when no clear national interest was at stake. An investigation by the European Commission concluded that the Greek government had violated the Convention, and Greece withdrew from the Council of Europe rather than face expulsion.[41]

The European response to the Greek coup d'état, coming at a time when the European Community was making its first appearance on an international stage, brought the issue of European values to the fore. It was partly for this reason that Western Europeans began to push hard for the inclusion of human rights and human contact provisions as part of the Conference on Security and Cooperation in Europe (CSCE). The Soviet Union proposed this multilateral European conference, which began in 1972 and involved thirty-three European countries along with the United States and Canada, as a means to obtain formal recognition of the territorial status quo in Eastern Europe. West European governments urged that "respect for human rights and fundamental freedoms" be included as a basic principle of relations among European states.[42] The Soviet Union opposed these efforts, and the Nixon and Ford administrations, viewing human rights as an obstacle to East-West détente and a destabilizing factor in international affairs, were at best indifferent.

It was primarily due to the insistence of West European governments that the CSCE's final product, the Helsinki Accords of 1975, included a set of provisions on humanitarian cooperation endorsing the view that protection of human rights was linked to international security. The Helsinki Final Act's Basket I, Principle VII stated: "The participating States will respect human rights and fundamental freedoms.... They will promote and encourage the effective exercise of civil, political, economic, social, cultural and other rights and freedoms." All parties further agreed to act in conformity with the UDHR and to fulfill obligations in the human rights covenants and other instruments to which they were signatories.[43] The Helsinki Final Act represented a further shift in the status of international human rights from purely internal matters to legitimate subjects of international action.

The Soviet regime signed the accords in the expectation that the value of what they gained—recognition of the status quo in Eastern Europe—outweighed the disadvantages imposed by human rights provisions that they intended to ignore.[44] In the United States the potential significance of the human rights provisions was also largely unrecognized. Critics charged President Gerald Ford with "selling out" Eastern Europe in a "new Yalta," and dissatisfaction with the trade-offs of the Helsinki Accords contributed to his loss in the 1976 election. Ultimately, however, the Accords paid extraordinary dividends, sparking an unprecedented campaign of mobilization within the Soviet bloc.[45] In 1976 physicist Yuri Orlov formed the first Helsinki Watch Group in Moscow, aimed at monitoring Soviet compliance; similar groups were soon formed in Czechoslovakia and Poland and in the West. The result was far greater public mobilization in both East and West around human rights issues in the Soviet bloc. By 1978 Brezhnev would lament that human rights constituted the West's "main line of attack against socialist countries."[46]

Like the Helsinki Accords, the rapid growth of domestic and international NGOs devoted to human rights was both a manifestation of the human rights "boom" that occurred in the 1970s and a major catalyst for it. While NGO activities were influenced by the cold war, their rise—both in the field of human rights and more generally—was largely independent of the superpower conflict. The 1970s saw the rise of human rights NGOs that harnessed the media and created an "information revolution" to achieve their aims.[47] The few older NGOs devoted to human rights, such as the New York-based International League for the Rights of Man, had operated largely behind the scenes, investigating abuses, compiling reports, and then lobbying the UN. The deliberate use of publicity gave the new groups greater power to influence policy and shape global opinion, in particular through the dissemination of ostensibly apolitical reports on abuses around the world. Amnesty International, founded in London in 1961, was a major global organization by the mid-1970s. It garnered significant global respect—it was awarded the Nobel Peace Prize in 1977—and published reports on abuses in many countries that became required reading for diplomats.[48] Although Amnesty received the most media attention, it was just the tip of a pyramid of local, regional, and transnational networks, comprised of activists, academics, émigrés, lawyers, church groups, and others. It was typically the work of local people on the ground in collecting and disseminating information about abuses that laid the basis for the extraordinary growth in the global public's interest in human rights issues.[49]

The Vietnam War's crumbling of the cold war consensus in the United States, coupled with the Watergate scandal's weakening of executive authority, opened the door for unprecedented human rights activity by the US Congress. Spurred by dissatisfaction with the realpolitik of the Nixon and Ford administrations, many Americans saw an urgent need to return to traditional American values such as promotion of democracy and human rights. A coalition of liberal Congressmen worked to institutionalize human rights considerations in the executive branch, pressing the State Department first to create a Bureau of Human Rights in 1975 and then in 1976 to upgrade the Bureau head to an Assistant Secretary whose appointment was subject to Congressional approval. These liberals, augmented by conservatives who opposed foreign aid, also ushered in a series of unprecedented laws that mandated reductions or cut-offs in aid to governments that violated human rights. Their focus was on "integrity of the person" rights, against torture and arbitrary arrest and imprisonment.[50] Because cut-offs in foreign aid targeted US allies, the legislation roused the ire of conservatives, who saw it as undercutting right-wing dictatorships whose support for the United States was critical to the cold war while ignoring the more serious violations of the Soviet bloc.

A second major strand in the Congressional revolt against Nixon and Kissinger's détente fixed on the Soviet Union as the major human rights violator. Henry "Scoop" Jackson, a conservative Democratic critic of détente, took the lead in attempting to use legislation to bring about changes in the Soviet domestic system, specifically to permit more emigration of Jews. Soviet Jews, subject to discrimination at home and offered a welcome in Israel, tried to leave in large numbers. When the government placed a highly restrictive emigration tax on prospective Jewish émigrés, Jackson demanded that a new US-Soviet trade agreement be linked to emigration. The 1974 Jackson-[Charles] Vanik Amendment denied trade benefits to any country that restricted emigration. It was passed over the strong objections of the Nixon administration in its waning days. US Secretary of State Henry Kissinger raged that the amendment's supporters were trying to "destroy détente" by proclaiming a "moral obligation to change Soviet policies." Even more furious, Soviet Premier Leonid Brezhnev denounced it as "tantamount to interference in our internal affairs."[51]

These Congressional initiatives laid the ground for President Jimmy Carter's elevation of human rights to a guiding principle of US foreign policy. In his 1977 inaugural address, Carter promised to restore morality to a central place in foreign policy. Human rights, however, was only one factor in policymaking, and other interests sometimes took precedence. Where cold war security and economic interests were marginal, as in Uganda and Paraguay, the administration was a strong critic of abuses. Where such interests were significant, the administration's willingness to subordinate human rights considerations invited charges of hypocrisy. A year before, a revolution ousted Iran's repressive ruler, Carter toasted the Shah for support of "the cause of human rights," even as Iran's brutal secret police incarcerated and tortured political opponents.[52] Carter criticized the Soviet bloc for cracking down on dissenters in violation of the Helsinki Accords and spoke up in defense of Sakharov, but Carter prioritized the pursuit of arms control in the form of the Strategic Arms Limitation Treaty (SALT II).

The Reagan administration made the repudiation of Carter's modest pressure on pro-US dictatorships a defining element of its foreign policy. Reagan embraced the ideas of an academic specialist, Jeane Kirkpatrick, who was among the most vehement and articulate critics of Carter's vision. Her highly influential 1979 article "Dictatorships and Double Standards" argued that the United States should support friendly "right-wing autocracies" because they, unlike communist dictatorships, "sometimes evolve into democracies."[53] Reagan's Assistant Secretary of State for Human Rights, Elliott Abrams, built on Kirkpatrick's vision by fashioning a philosophy that conflated human rights advocacy and anti-communism almost entirely, declaring that "we [the Reagan administration] consider anticommunism to be a human rights policy."[54]

Against the countervailing pressures of increasingly influential NGO activism, the Reagan administration downplayed integrity-of-the-person abuses; under the logic of the Abrams position, such abuses would always exist unless there was democratization and would increase if communism proliferated. For critics, such as the Carter administration's human rights chief, Patricia Derian, this policy corrupted human rights into little more than "a counter in a geopolitical struggle, like a hotel in a game of Monopoly."[55] The catalogue of abusive right-wing regimes backed by the Reagan presidency, including those in El Salvador, South Africa, the Philippines, Argentina, and Chile, gave ample basis for this critique, particularly in the first term.

Yet the Reagan administration, while partial to right-wing allies, still used "quiet diplomacy" to pursue the fate of individual cases in right-wing regimes, and Reagan was personally involved in some of these overtures. There was also a marked distinction between the Kirkpatrick doctrine as theoretically elaborated and what the administration practiced. In particular, Reagan did not share Kirkpatrick's pessimism about democratization in East Europe. In his oft-cited 1982 speech to the British Parliament, Reagan directly contradicted the notion that right-wing regimes were the only dictatorships that held the prospect of democratic reform. Reagan was thus inclined to respond favorably when a new kind of Soviet leadership emerged with Mikhail Gorbachev in 1985.

Ultimately, it was Gorbachev's moves, including critical steps in the realm of human rights, that made a decisive contribution to ending the cold war. Pressure from a dissident movement empowered by the Helsinki Final Act played a key role: in this sense, the international human rights movement helped catalyze the process that led to the collapse of communism.[56] Dissident ideas about glasnost, human rights, and the rule of law had a strong influence on Gorbachev's domestic reform agenda.[57] The new Soviet premier initially hoped to improve relations with the West through arms control, but, as one advisor later recalled, Gorbachev eventually "became convinced that without a solution to the human rights problem the cold war could not be brought to an end, a new relationship with the United States could not be built."[58]

It was a sign of just how significant human rights had become as a factor in international relations that it ranked alongside arms control—and a sign of just how well-established ideas of universal civil and political rights had become that Gorbachev eventually repudiated virtually all of the positions Vyshinsky had so vigorously expounded in the 1940s. He released Sakharov from internal exile in 1986 and freed hundreds of other imprisoned dissidents. He publicly acknowledged that not only social and economic rights but also civil and political rights had to be actively promoted and protected. And he reversed the position so steadfastly maintained by his predecessors that the implementation and enforcement of international human rights guarantees were matters solely of domestic jurisdiction. In the end the Soviet Communist Party's endorsement of civil and political rights proved incompatible with maintaining its hold on its East European satellites—and with maintaining communism at home.

At the end of the cold war, the West, and its liberal vision of universal human rights, seemed the undisputed victor. One observer suggested that human rights seemed to fill the vacuum once occupied by the cold war, replacing anticommunism as an organizing principle for international action in the 1990s.[59] Having for decades declined meaningful action against human rights violations, the United Nations began to directly confront some abuses, though these were usually committed by politically vulnerable countries without significant allies. In the face of major human rights violations during the disintegration of Yugoslavia, the great powers in the United Nations agreed in 1993 that Chapter VII could override Article 2(7)—in other words, that the Security Council's mandate to secure international peace, including through the protection of human rights, could override provisions about non-interference in domestic affairs.[60] The UN also took steps to prosecute violators under international jurisdiction, most notably in 2002, when sixty countries established an independent body, the International Criminal Court, as the first permanent, treaty-based international court to try "perpetrators of the most serious crimes of concern to the international community," such as genocide, crimes against humanity, and war crimes.[61]

Yet the dynamics of human rights had operated largely outside the cold war, and the end of the conflict did not resolve the core tensions and debates over the term's content and implications. Defining what should properly be seen as international human rights remained sharply contested. Resolution of the fault line in human rights between East and West had no effect on divisions between North and South, which escalated into a bitter international debate in the early 1990s, as assertive East Asian leaders resurrected earlier Third World claims. Unlike the representatives who had assembled in Tehran in 1968, leaders such as Singapore's Lee Kuan Yew and Malaysia's Mahathir Mohamed were backed by economic success. Proclaiming a distinctive set of "Asian values," they disputed the established set of universal human rights as a Western construction. Tensions over issues of sovereignty also remained acute. The end of the cold war rendered the US Senate only marginally less suspicious of UN challenges to US sovereignty than it had been in Bricker's time. After decades of inaction on UN human rights instruments, in 1992 the US Senate ratified the Covenant on Civil and Political Rights, but with so many qualifications—five reservations, four declarations, and five understandings—that some observers called the ratification nothing more than a cosmetic gesture.[62] The outcome of the US war against Iraq—a war fought partly under the guise of humanitarian intervention and initially embraced by many liberal human rights advocates—suggested to critics that human rights had become a screen for brutality, militarism, and imperialism.[63]

The victory of human rights after the cold war, then, was mostly illusory. Although international pressure over abuses had unquestionably helped some individuals, the overall effectiveness of international human rights law in changing state behavior remained in doubt. Many of the rights proclaimed in the Universal Declaration—including access to education and adequate food and housing—remained starkly out of reach for billions of the world's poor. If, in the words of one leading activist, the discourse of human rights had become "a universal set of manners, a worldwide book of etiquette," it was still a book more honored in the breach than in the observance.[64]

## NOTES

1. The authors would like to thank Carl Bon Tempo, Mark Bradley, Jan Eckel, and Sarah Snyder for helpful comments on an early draft of this essay.
2. Akira Iriye, "Historicizing the Cold War," Chapter 2, p. 19, in this volume.
3. Mary L. Dudziak, *Cold War Civil Rights: Race and the Image of American Democracy* (Princeton, NJ: Princeton University Press, 2000).
4. See e.g. Iain Guest, *Behind the Disappearances: Argentina's Dirty War against Human Rights and the United Nations* (Philadelphia, PA: University of Pennsylvania Press, 1990).
5. See Mark Mazower, "The Strange Triumph of Human Rights, 1933–1950," *Historical Journal* 47 (June 2004): 379–98.
6. Available at <http://avalon.law.yale.edu/wwii/washco16.asp> (accessed June 8, 2012).
7. On the NGOs' role, see Elizabeth Borgwardt, *A New Deal for the World* (Cambridge, MA: Harvard University Press, 2005), 190–1.
8. Charter of the United Nations, at <http://www.un.org/en/documents/charter/> (accessed June 8, 2012). The Covenant of the League of Nations, the UN's predecessor organization, did not mention human rights.
9. A. H. Robertson and J. G. Merrills, *Human Rights in the World*, 3rd ed. (Manchester: Manchester University Press, 1989), 19–21.
10. Samuel Moyn, *The Last Utopia: Human Rights in History* (Cambridge, MA: Belknap/ Harvard University Press, 2010), 47, 82.
11. Charter of the United Nations, Chapter 1.
12. Johannes Morsink, *The Universal Declaration of Human Rights: Origins, Drafting, and Intent* (Philadelphia, PA: University of Pennsylvania Press, 2000), 14–16; Roger Normand and Sarah Zaidi, *Human Rights at the UN: The Political History of Universal Justice* (Bloomington, IN: University of Indiana Press, 2008), 196.
13. Susan Waltz, "Universalizing Human Rights: The Role of Small States in the Construction of the Universal Declaration of Human Rights," *Human Rights Quarterly* 23 (February 2001): 44–72; Mary Ann Glendon, "The Forgotten Crucible: The Latin American Influence on the Universal Declaration of Human Rights Idea," *Harvard Human Rights Journal* 16 (Spring 2003): 27–39, esp. 31.
14. Universal Declaration of Human Rights, at <http://www.un.org/en/documents/udhr/> (accessed June 8, 2012).
15. The eight abstentions included Saudi Arabia, apartheid South Africa, and members of the communist bloc.
16. Morsink, *The Universal Declaration*, 21–4; Hans von Mangoldt, "The Communist Conception of Civil Rights and Human Rights under International Law," in Georg Brunner, ed., *Before Reforms: Human Rights in the Warsaw Pact States, 1971–1988* (New York: St. Martin's Press, 1990), 27–57.
17. Quoted in Morsink, *The Universal Declaration*, 22.
18. Jennifer Amos, "Embracing and Contesting: Soviet Diplomacy on the Universal Declaration of Human Rights, 1948–1958," in Stefan-Ludwig Hoffman, ed., *Human Rights in the Twentieth Century* (New York: Cambridge University Press, 2011), 147–8.

19. For an excellent account of this complicated process, see Daniel J. Whelan, *Indivisible Human Rights: A History* (Philadelphia, PA: University of Pennsylvania Press, 2010), 112–35.

20. Natalie Kaufman Hevener, "Drafting the Human Rights Covenants," *World Affairs* 148 (1986), 234–7.

21. Quoted in Robert David Johnson, *Congress and the Cold War* (New York: Cambridge University Press, 2006), 58.

22. *New York Times*, April 7, 1953, 14.

23. On the appropriation of human rights as a project of Christian conservativism in Europe, see Moyn, *Last Utopia*, 73–81.

24. Kathryn Sikkink, "The Power of Principled Ideas: Human Rights Policies in the United States and Western Europe," in Judith Goldstein and Robert Keohane, eds., *Ideas and Foreign Policy: Beliefs, Institutions, and Political Change* (Ithaca, NY: Cornell University Press, 1993), 148–9. See also Jan Eckel, "Utopie der Moral, Kalkül der Macht. Menschenrechte in der globalen Politik seit 1945," *Archiv für Sozialgeschichte* 49 (2009): 446–9.

25. John P. Humphrey, "The Memoirs of John P. Humphrey, The First Director of the United Nations Division of Human Rights," *Human Rights Quarterly* 5 (1983), 402–3. This comment refers only to individual right of petition to the Human Rights Commission.

26. Roland Burke, "The Compelling Dialogue of Freedom: Human Rights at the 1955 Bandung Conference," *Human Rights Quarterly* 28 (November 2006): 947–65.

27. Kenneth Cmiel, "Human Rights, Freedom of Information, and the Origins of Third World Solidarity," in Mark Bradley and Patrice Petro, eds., *Truth Claims: Representation and Human Rights* (New Brunswick, NJ: Rutgers University Press, 2002), 107–30.

28. "Draft Declaration on the Granting of Independence to Colonial Countries and Peoples, submitted by the Chairman of the Council of Ministers of the USSR," September 23, 1960, *Official Records of the General Assembly, Plenary Meetings*, UN Document A/4502.

29. Roland Burke, *Decolonization and the Evolution of International Human Rights* (Philadelphia, PA: University of Pennsylvania Press, 2010), 59–91.

30. See John Humprey et al., *On the Edge of Greatness: The Diaries of John Humphrey, First Director of the United Nations Division of Human Rights, volume 4, 1958–1966* (Montreal, Quebec and Kingston, ON: McGill-Queen's University Press, 2000), 151.

31. T. J. M. Zuijdwijk, *Petitioning the United Nations: A Study in Human Rights* (New York: St. Martin's Press, 1982).

32. ECOSOC Resolution 1235 (XLII), June 6, 1967, in *The International Law of Human Rights in Africa: Basic Documents and Annotated Bibliography*, compiled by M. Hamalengwa, C. Flinterman, and E. V. O. Dankwa (Boston, MA: Nijhoff, 1988), 377–8.

33. Office of the High Commissioner for Human Rights, "Statistical Survey of Individual Complaints Considered under the Procedure Governed by Article 14 of ICERD," 2004, at <http://www2.ohchr.org/english/bodies/cerd/stat4.htm> (accessed June 8, 2012).

34. Available at <http://www.un.org/documents/ga/res/30/ares30.htm> (accessed June 8, 2012).

35. As Samuel Moyn suggests, focusing on "visible" forms of cruelty such as torture can obscure "structural wrongs" that may also cause bodily suffering, as with hunger or overwork. Moyn, "The Genealogy of Morals," *The Nation* 284 (April 16, 2007): 25–31.

36. On the 1970s, see the excellent accounts in Moyn, *Last Utopia*, 120–75, and Eckel, "Utopie der Moral," 458–64. On East Timor, see Brad Simpson, "Denying the 'First Right': The United States, Indonesia, and the Ranking of Human Rights by the Carter Administration," *International History Review* 31 (December 2009): 798–826.

37. Alexander Solzhenitsyn, "Nobel Lecture," translated by F. D. Reeve, at <http://www.colum-bia.edu/cu/augustine/arch/solzhenitsyn/nobel-lit1970.htm> (accessed June 8, 2012).

38. Ludmila Alekseyeva, *Soviet Dissent: Contemporary Movements for National, Religious, and Human Rights* (Middletown, CT: Wesleyan University Press, 1985), 269.

39. Benjamin Nathans, "The Dictatorship of Reason: Aleksandr Vol'pin and the Idea of Rights under 'Developed Socialism,'" *Slavic Review* 66/4 (Winter 2007): 630–4.

40. Emma Gilligan, *Defending Human Rights in Russia* (New York: Routledge, 2004), 10, 89.

41. Mark W. Janis, Richard S. Kay, and Anthony W. Bradley, *European Human Rights Law: Text and Materials* (Oxford: Clarendon, 1995), 62–3.

42. Daniel C. Thomas, *The Helsinki Effect: International Norms, Human Rights, and the Demise of Communism* (Princeton, NJ: Princeton University Press, 2001), 27–53.

43. The Final Act of the Conference on Security and Cooperation in Europe, August 1, 1975, 14 ILM 1292 (Helsinki Declaration), available at: <http://www1.umn.edu/humanrts/osce/basics/finact75.htm> (accessed June 8, 2012).

44. On whether the CSCE did ratify borders, see Richard Davy, "Helsinki Myths: Setting the Record Straight on the Final Act of the CSCE, 1975," *Cold War History* 9/1 (February 2009): 1–22; on Soviet views of the CSCE, see Svetlana Savranskaya, "Unintended Consequences: Soviet Interests, Expectations and Reactions to the Helsinki Final Act," in Oliver Bange and Gottfried Niedhart, eds., *Helsinki 1975 and the Transformation of Europe* (New York: Berghahn, 2008), 176, 181.

45. See Sarah B. Snyder, *Human Rights Activism and the End of the Cold War: A Transnational History of the Helsinki Network* (Cambridge: Cambridge University Press, 2011).

46. Quoted in G. S. Ostapenko, *Bor'ba SSSR v OON za sotsial'no-ekonomicheskie prava cheloveka, 1945–1977 gg.* (Moscow: Nauka, 1981), 5–6.

47 Kenneth Cmiel, "The Emergence of Human Rights Politics in the United States," *Journal of American History* 86 (December 1999): 1240–5.

48. Ann-Marie Clark, *Diplomacy of Conscience: Amnesty International and Changing Human Rights Norms* (Princeton, NJ: Princeton University Press, 2001).

49 See e.g. James Naylor Green, *We Cannot Remain Silent: Opposition to the Brazilian Military Dictatorship in the United States, 1964–85* (Durham, NC: Duke University Press, 2010).

50. Barbara Keys, "Congress, Kissinger, and the Origins of Human Rights Diplomacy," *Diplomatic History*, 34/4 (November 2010): 823–51.

51. Jussi Hanhimäki, *Flawed Architect: Henry Kissinger and American Foreign Policy* (Oxford: Oxford University Press, 2004): 343–4.

52. Quoted in David F. Schmitz, *The United States and Right-Wing Dictatorships, 1965–1989* (Cambridge: Cambridge University Press, 2006), 177.

53. Jeane Kirkpatrick, "Dictatorships and Double Standards," *Commentary*, November 1979.

54. Quoted in Eric Alterman, "Elliott Abrams: The Teflon Assistant Secretary," *Washington Monthly* 19 (1987): 19–26.

55. Patt Derian, "How to Make Dictators Look Good: Ronald Reagan's Lack of a Human Rights Policy," *The Nation* (February 9, 1985): 129–31.

56. For the argument that the Helsinki Accords played a key role in the downfall of communism, see Thomas, *The Helsinki Effect*.

57. Robert Horvath, *The Legacy of Dissent: Dissidents, Democratisation and Radical Nationalism in Russia* (London: Routledge, 2005), 8–10, 50–4.

58. Anatoly Chernyaev, quoted in William C. Wohlforth, ed., *Witnesses to the End of the Cold War* (Baltimore: Johns Hopkins University Press, 1996), 95.

59. David Rieff, "A New Age of Liberal Imperialism?" *World Policy Journal* 16 (Summer 1999), 1–10.
60. Geoffrey Robertson, *Crimes against Humanity: The Struggle for Global Justice* (New York: Norton, 2006), 25.
61. "About the Court," at <http://www.icc-cpi.int/Menus/ICC/About+the+Court/> (accessed June 8, 2012).
62. See e.g. Kenneth Roth, "The Charade of US Ratification of International Human Rights Treaties," *Chicago Journal of International Law* 1 (2000), 349.
63. Stephen Holmes, "The War of the Liberals," *The Nation* (November 14, 2005).
64. William F. Schultz, *Tainted Legacy: 9/11 and the Ruin of Human Rights* (New York: Thunder's Mouth Press, 2003).

## Select Bibliography

Borgwardt, Elizabeth. *A New Deal for the World: America's Vision for Human Rights*. Cambridge, MA: Belknap/Harvard University Press, 2005.

Burke, Roland. *Decolonization and the Evolution of International Human Rights*. Philadelphia, PA: University of Pennsylvania Press, 2010.

Hoffmann, Stefan-Ludwig, ed. *Human Rights in the Twentieth Century*. Cambridge: Cambridge University Press, 2010.

Keck, Margaret E. and Kathryn Sikkink. *Activists Beyond Borders: Advocacy Networks in International Politics*. Ithaca, NY: Cornell University Press, 1998.

Korey, William. *NGOs and the Universal Declaration of Human Rights: A Curious Grapevine*. New York: St. Martin's Press, 1998.

Lauren, Paul Gordon. *The Evolution of International Human Rights: Visions Seen*. Philadelphia, PA: University of Pennsylvania Press, 1998.

Morsink, Johannes. *The Universal Declaration of Human Rights: Origins, Drafting, and Intent*. Philadelphia, PA: University of Pennsylvania Press, 1999.

Moyn, Samuel. *The Last Utopia: Human Rights in History*. Cambridge, MA: Harvard University Press, 2010.

Normand, Roger and Sarah Zaidi. *Human Rights at the UN: The Political History of Universal Justice*. Bloomington, IN: Indiana University Press, 2008.

Schoultz, Lars. *Human Rights and United States Policy toward Latin America*. Princeton, NJ: Princeton University Press, 1981.

Sikkink, Kathryn. *Mixed Signals: US Human Rights Policy and Latin America*. Ithaca, NY: Cornell University Press, 2004.

Simpson, A. W. Brian. *Human Rights and the End of Empire: Britain and the Genesis of the European Convention*. New York: Oxford University Press, 2001.

Thomas, Daniel C. *The Helsinki Effect: International Norms, Human Rights, and the Demise of Communism*. Princeton, NJ: Princeton University Press, 2001.

# CHAPTER 29

........................................................................

# RACE AND THE COLD WAR

........................................................................

## BRENDA GAYLE PLUMMER

US foreign affairs have always included a racial dimension that even today remains masked in many historical accounts. How leaders thought about racial difference, and the practices they enacted because of their perceptions, characterized policy making from colonial times to the present. Racial thought was not always entirely conscious, but it influenced how Americans conceived their place in the world even before the War of Independence. This history includes the cold war, which took place against the backdrop of a global society in which racism helped to construct frameworks of domination and resistance. The alarm with which US authorities viewed Soviet expansionism in Europe in the late 1940s had a racial component. Washington policy makers perceived the Soviets as not only the captives of an alien totalitarian ideology, but also as racial aliens. The perspective predated cold war hostilities and derived from longstanding western European notions about "Asiatic hordes." Secretary of the Navy James Forrestal thus mistrusted the Soviets because he saw them as "essentially Oriental in their thinking." For Secretary of State Dean Acheson, "the threat they posed to Europe" was comparable to "that which Islam had posed centuries before."[1] These views rehearsed a very old Orientalist trope. George F. Kennan, author of the containment doctrine that underlay much of US cold war policy, shared this perspective. He believed that some nations and peoples would always be subordinate. Improvements in status, where possible, should come only gradually. Kennan endorsed white rule in South Africa and believed that anti-colonial insurgencies normatively derived from outside interference. He favored reform in US race relations so as to assure American leadership of the world's democratic forces, but believed it impolitic to "frighten the South." The opinions of these officials on race suggest the limits of their ability to remove it as a cold war obstacle for the United States.[2]

Racism became part of a cold war framework in which states marshaled ideological and political resources against the threat of dissolution and subversion from within as well as from without. The cold war inherited centuries-old rationales for imperialist rule and led to an early British and American postwar discourse that championed racial domination. When Winston Churchill delivered his "Iron Curtain" speech in Fulton, Missouri in February 1946, he appealed to the racial as well as cultural solidarity of Anglo-Saxons. When the United States developed the Marshall Plan in 1948 to shore up the faltering economies of war-devastated Europe, it yielded to the European insistence that recovery would not be possible without empire, which brought in its train the concomitant ideological and political burden of racism and colonialism. In fashioning a global security blanket for the postwar world, US military officials relied on perpetuating American control of Pacific islands formerly held by the Japanese. Independence for Italy's former colonies in Africa, now UN mandates, was similarly postponed. Cold war priorities led Washington to abstain from challenging Portuguese colonialism in Africa because of American reliance on the strategic military base in the Azores.

One of the seminal cold war documents was the 1947 Truman Doctrine; it warned of "armed minorities" poised to seize power and impose communist rule on embattled fledgling democracies.[3] The white settler regimes in southern Africa, however, did not figure into this caveat. South Africa, the most prosperous of these societies, in 1950 had passed the Suppression of Communism Act, a law it used to ban black South African political activity. The timing of the legislation echoed similar anti-communist initiatives in the United States. South Africa continued to occupy Southwest Africa, now Namibia, a United Nations (UN) trust territory.

Yet the coupling of security with racial domination could not be sustained. African Americans, critical of Churchill's appeal to Anglo-Saxonism, and others, still adhering to the wartime alliance with the Soviets, rejected Churchill's speech. Even President Harry S. Truman at first expressed ambivalence, leading to speculation that he wanted to revive Soviet-American amity.[4] The desire for national sovereignty in Asian and African territories during the war set in motion an unstoppable drive for independence that led most policy makers to acknowledge that colonialism's days were numbered and that any endorsement of it could not be easily squared with the United States' own history of anticolonial revolt.[5]

By 1946, policy elites were challenging white supremacist beliefs. Some members of the US policy elite, defined here as including both elected and appointed officials and selected members of the military and the intelligentsia, proved susceptible to arguments for the reform of race relations. Yet the decentralized nature of the federal system created a situation in which certain initiatives, such as President Truman's desegregation of the armed forces, were coupled with actual increases in segregation in government-sponsored housing and urban development.[6] Real change was at best incremental throughout the 1940s and 1950s, with resistance to racial equality expressed on all levels of government.

The horrific results of Nazi race doctrine had demonstrated the consequences of racist thought. Worldwide revulsion abetted a continuing trend in the social sciences to displace previous biological explanations of human inequality. The older social science had accompanied and rationalized colonialism and racial discrimination, however, which entailed a host of practices that were difficult to abandon. The UN Sub-Commission on Prevention of Discrimination and Protection of Minorities faced obstacles when such countries as the United States and the Soviet Union refused to permit international oversight of their treatment of national minorities. Cold war competition led the respective powers to exploit instances of oppression perpetrated by the other.[7]

In the United States black Americans used the United Nations as a forum to air grievances and court world opinion, in spite of federal efforts to condemn such tactics as unpatriotic. In 1946 the National Negro Congress (NNC), with the endorsement of fraternal organizations, veterans' groups, and trade unions, petitioned the UN on behalf of beleaguered African Americans, then experiencing a postwar increase in lynching and other violent crimes. The NNC presented its petition during a period when numerous groups appealed to the UN. Indonesians addressed the body in their effort to shed Dutch colonialism. The Ewe-speaking peoples of Togo, a mandate under joint British and French authority, asked the Trusteeship Council to clarify their status. Other petitions came from western European Jews, now largely in diaspora; Somalis, and residents of the British Caribbean colonies. In 1946 the UN General Assembly condemned South African abuse of East Indian residents in that country.[8]

Heartened by these developments, the National Association of Colored People (NAACP) drafted its own petition in 1947. The document, compiled largely by W. E. B. Du Bois, called for an investigation of American racial practices by the UN Commission on Human Rights. The NAACP was more conservative than the NNC, which was increasingly condemned by conventional opinion because of the communist affiliations of some of its members. Its petition attracted the support of many African American organizations, political leaders and groups in Africa and the Caribbean, and foreign labor federations. The NAACP also secured cautious endorsements from Belgium, China, Egypt, Ethiopia, Haiti, India, Norway, and Pakistan, although UN rules did not permit nongovernmental organizations to formally bring petitions. The NNC effort had been largely symbolic, but it was noticed. This time, the NAACP document, enjoying as it did the prestige of its originating group, found a sponsor. The Soviet Union introduced the petition in October 1947. While the appeal had wide support, the Sub-Commission on Prevention of Discrimination and Protection of Minorities tabled it to prevent alienating the United States, on whom UN fortunes rested. Washington officials applied pressure to NAACP leaders, who were eager to avoid the opprobrium that Soviet endorsement implied.[9]

The belief that African American agitation for civil rights was prompted by outsiders rather than stemming from their own aspirations fed into cold war discourse about subversives. Watchdogs of political orthodoxy cast a wide net in linking those who maintained interracial friendships with un-Americanism. Racists were further aided by the tendency of leading American politicians to present foreign affairs as a contest between good and evil and to portray communism as a force determined to upset the natural order of things, which for white supremacists was continued black subordination. In corresponding fashion, the habit of linking black political objectives with communism engendered considerable skepticism about the cold war among African Americans who did not believe that loyalty was inconsistent with equal rights. This sentiment produced some black support for the most left-leaning presidential candidate in 1948, former Secretary of Commerce Henry Wallace, who campaigned on the Progressive Party ticket. Wallace took a forthright stand against Jim Crow and would not address segregated southern audiences. While Progressive ranks undoubtedly embraced many communists, Wallace backers also included those whose radicalism had been shaped by independent labor and civil rights struggles. These individuals opposed the growing international tension between Washington and Moscow, and espoused a continuation of wartime Alliance policy. Black leaders who did not support Wallace nevertheless expressed doubts about such key aspects of US foreign policy as the Truman Doctrine and the Marshall Plan. Howard University president Mordecai Johnson believed funds allocated to save Greece and Turkey from communist takeover could be better spent promoting democracy in the American South. The Marshall Plan, the *Courier* asserted, was a program whose unintended effect was to further strengthen the colonial powers' ability to retain their control of territory in Africa and Asia.[10]

As cold war tensions mounted in the late 1940s, the African American electorate as a whole assumed a pragmatic stance toward East-West issues. Truman had broken through the impasse that had situated civil rights advocacy and anti-communism against each other. Seizing the anti-communist initiative from Republicans, the White House instituted a loyalty program for federal employees and endorsed internal security investigative procedures. It simultaneously made important gestures toward racial equality through the integration of the armed forces and through such executive actions as support for fair employment practices. The administration drafted a document, "To Secure These Rights," which came to be seen as a milestone in federal support for civil rights. The promise of equality and the threat of punishment helped turn black voters toward Truman, the incumbent, in 1948. Thereafter conventional African American organizations distanced themselves from the Soviets and from communism, but continued to pointedly hold US race relations up to global scrutiny. Activists created an agenda of international political work to this end as well as for the purposes of eradicating colonialism and its racist manifestations.[11]

The collapse of the European and Japanese economies during World War II and revolutionary conditions in China had propelled the United States into global political and economic leadership and pitted it against the Soviet system. Racial violence was not only a threat to the role Americans felt called upon to play in world affairs, but also a potential source of internal instability. Increasingly, policy makers and the policy-aware public began taking racial reform seriously. Representatives from the media, State Department representatives, US politicians, educators, and United Nations officials participated in a conference called by the NAACP in September 1950 to deliberate the problems racism posed for US cold war aims. Many began to understand that minority oppression hampered efforts to extend American interests and values. In June 1951 the solicitor general of the United States, Philip Perlman, filed an amicus curiae brief in an appellate court case that concerned segregation in public accommodations. The solicitor general connected racial reform to the national interest in his claim that Jim Crow damaged the American image abroad.[12]

The fear of subversion provided powerful motivation for the United States to keep dissidents, including civil rights activists, in line. Surveillance of African Americans, ostensibly for communist affiliations, long predates the cold war and appears in intelligence community records as early as the 1910s. During World War II, the FBI sought to uncover pro-Japanese activity among blacks in the United States. Scrutiny of African Americans dates to the era of the slave trade regardless of contemporaneous ideology. Black resistance to oppression had always been perceived as inherently subversive.[13] In the late 1940s President Truman proved an innovator by coupling the racial reform necessary to ensure US credibility abroad with the repression of communists, thus separating civil rights from radicalism. Those working for civil rights could now enjoy legitimacy as long as they divorced themselves from association with the left.

Those who would not disavow their beliefs, such as the author of the NAACP's 1947 petition, scholar W. E. B. Du Bois, became the subjects of congressional investigation and legal prosecution. Liberals who had accepted Truman's formula purged them from organizations. Persons who had belonged to leftist organizations or espoused radical views, including academics, entertainers, and political activists, were threatened with the loss of jobs, passports, and, in some cases, freedom.[14] Fears exacerbated by the Korean conflict (1950–3) provided even greater incentives to crack down on dissidents.

Black troops stationed in Korea bore the brunt of residual resentment of Truman's armed forces desegregation order. Military brass blamed black soldiers for the consequences of the United States' poorly thought out political and military tactics and lack of preparation. The 24th Infantry Regiment, still intact as an all-black outfit in 1950, achieved the first victory in the Korean War at Yechon on July 20.[15] This did not spare the unit from relentless criticism, mass court-martial, and disbandment in October 1951. The presence of large numbers of African Americans in the armed forces in the early 1950s attested to lack of opportunity in the civilian economy.

Congress failed to pass proposed fair employment practices legislation which Dixiecrats and red baiters succeeded in labeling as communist-inspired. Korea led Truman to de-emphasize civil rights initiatives as the nation proceeded to war. Authorities renewed their attacks on dissent. Presidential advisor Clark Clifford believed that the public had to accept the "stern policies which Soviet activities make imperative and which the US government must adopt."[16] Even Americans living abroad, like writer Richard Wright, were under surveillance by US authorities. Actor and singer Paul Robeson was the first American subjected to television censorship when the National Broadcasting Company refused to air a program on which he had appeared. The revision of history through the banning of books by African American authors in US libraries overseas also characterized the period. In the southern states, governments took the Internal Security Act of 1950 as a model for laws to repress civil rights organizations, forcing them to reveal membership lists and persecuting their leaders. Regulations allowed local governments to fire public employees who belonged to civil rights organizations, which legislatures had decided were communist organizations.[17]

As a result, many African Americans remained unconvinced when two of the most widely and tragically condemned spies of the era went on trial for their lives in 1953.

Support among blacks for clemency for Julius and Ethel Rosenberg came from black trade unionists, newspapers, and fraternal organizations, not all of them on the left.[18] The same year, black trade unionist A. Philip Randolph introduced a resolution at an American Federation of Labor national convention that condemned McCarthyism and its author by name. Union officials, fearful of the consequences, blocked its passage.[19] Resentment of anti-communist politics did not necessarily mean that blacks endorsed the US Communist Party or Soviet politics. Out of 15 million African Americans in 1950, only 4,000 belonged to the Communist Party. The Soviets were remembered for their sale of oil to fascist Italy during Mussolini's war against Ethiopia. American communists, while claiming to represent an indigenous grassroots movement, had also demonstrated their dependence on the vicissitudes of Soviet foreign policy in the political reversals they made during the interwar period. Much African American coolness toward anti-communist zeal was instead prompted by recognition of how closely linked the red smear was to maintaining the racial status quo.

The Truman era reformulation of liberalism made it possible for officials to talk of colonialism as part of an international order which supported the ultimate welfare of subjugated populations. Early Africa policy linked the prevention of communism on the continent with facilitating economic development. US policy makers understood that American racism had made a bad impression on Africans and that Africans resented US assistance to the colonial powers as propping up an imperial domination they hoped to escape. Colonized peoples also recognized the easy access to strategic minerals and other natural resources that American enterprise derived through European contacts. The colonial powers tried hard to persuade Americans that independence should not be extended to colonial subjects across the board. Some were not ready for freedom, colonialists maintained, and were susceptible to communist influence.[20]

During the early cold war years of 1946–53, US policy makers largely accepted these claims. They reconciled an historical predisposition against colonialism with European arguments by invoking the desirability of gradual change. There was accordingly no need to move colonized people along the path to independence quickly, especially at the expense of orderly transition. Order and stability had more immediate importance than democracy. The United States ultimately washed its hands of direct responsibility for African affairs. Instead, it saw its role as cooperating with the colonial powers to advance the future African trade and investment that would result from the restoration of European economies. Prosperity would trickle down to African peoples while some assistance from the United States was available through the Economic Cooperation Agency, the UN, and various exchange programs. In line with this program of inaction, Washington advocated peaceful coexistence between Africans and white settlers in parts of Africa where white minority regimes had installed themselves. No concern for the civil or human rights of Africans in these territories disturbed the relationships between the United States and the colonial powers.[21]

A somewhat different dynamic operated with regard to sovereign states outside Africa that peoples of color governed. For generations, stereotypes had dominated US perceptions of Latin America and the Caribbean on both the popular and policy making levels.

From the days of the early republic, racial mixture in societies south of the US border troubled Washington officials, who often portrayed these populations as irrational, childlike, incompetent, and intemperate. Such representations helped justify exploitative economic relationships and armed interventions. Racism was soft-pedaled after 1945, when communism appeared to present an ideological threat in the region. Official diplomatic correspondence nonetheless indicated that certain key officials still thought of Latin Americans in disparaging terms.[22]

If US hegemony remained fundamentally unchallenged in the western hemisphere for the first half of the 20th century, in Asia and the Middle East, American dominance was less assured. Areas that occupied the prime nexus of Soviet-American conflict also provided strategic minerals for the industries and war machines of the great powers. Asian and Middle Eastern countries had nevertheless experienced racial domination as an accompaniment to colonized or dependent status. Orientalist preconceptions warped understanding of these diverse societies, and dark-skinned Asian visitors to the United States sometimes experienced bias first-hand when denied service at "whites-only" facilities.[23]

It became necessary for the State Department to dispatch an officer to help African, Caribbean, and Asian envoys cope with prejudice and shield them from common racial customs, such as denial of service in public accommodations and housing discrimination in northern as well as southern states. Such incidents that occurred could damage fragile relations with emerging countries. In August 1961, the White House created a commission consisting of federal and state government representatives from the Washington, DC metropolitan area to address the issue of racial discrimination in the region. The State Department had hoped at first to keep foreign blacks from sharing the negative experiences common to African Americans. It became clear, however, that businesses were unable or unwilling to distinguish between African Americans and foreign blacks. Consequently, international imperatives required the desegregation at least of public facilities in the District of Columbia and Maryland. The arrival of African diplomats in Washington also occasioned alterations in capital society. The State Department's chief of protocol felt compelled to resign in 1961 from an elite social club with no black members. In the wake of decolonization, the club had furthermore suspended its erstwhile practice of automatically accepting foreign envoys.[24]

Given racist logic, difference contributed to cold war anxieties about national security and provided a rationale for perpetuating patterns of exclusion. The arms race constituted a major aspect of preparations for possible conflict, whether it was the capacity for apocalyptic nuclear destruction or the streamlined, mobile military of Eisenhower's choice. Soviet-American competition involved heavy investment in atomic research. This accelerated in 1953 after the Soviet test of its first hydrogen bomb. New infrastructure and the ingress of new populations consequently transformed nuclear facilities in rural areas. In rural Georgia and Tennessee African Americans were uprooted by the weapons labs and nuclear power plants but received few benefits from the modernization of their communities. The NAACP and the National Urban League pursued cold war arguments in urging the desegregation of employment in nuclear facilities. Ending bias in defense employment, they claimed, neutralized disaffection and ultimately strengthened national security. Others used the argument to other ends. The Atomic Energy Commission, the Pentagon, and such government contractors as the Du Pont Corporation paid lip service to desegregation, but claimed that national security concerns tied their hands. African Americans who did secure jobs were generally relegated to janitorial posts or those that exposed them to excessive radiation. In its Hanford, Washington, atomic facility, defense contractor Du Pont faced a labor shortage but would not recruit Mexican American workers, claiming it would require a third set of separate eating and toilet facilities, for Mexicans were neither black nor white.[25]

The Bomb also invoked race with regard to civil defense, a major conundrum in the early 1950s when experts still based ideas about the best civil defense practices on World War II era constructs. Historians have suggested that postwar suburbanization was occasioned in part by the desire to disperse population in order to minimize deaths in the case of an atomic explosion. African Americans were clearly at a disadvantage in the event of an attack as residents of thickly populated urban neighborhoods that lacked suitable air raid shelters.[26]

The paucity of black personnel in foreign affairs-related government employment had concerned civil rights activists as early as World War II. Any campaign to present the United States as a racial democracy foundered on the absence of an integrated foreign service. Critics called on federal agencies to address the problems of employment discrimination and American self- representation overseas simultaneously. While African Americans had held unimportant political appointments as consuls and ministers to minor countries under Republican administrations before World War II, the numbers of career black foreign service officers and consular officials remained negligible. The State Department had imbibed the culture of Washington, DC, until the 1960s a segregated southern city. Calls for the integration of the department and, more generally, the appointment of a cadre of officials that more closely mirrored the actual demographics of a changing America, did not yield immediate results. According to Secretary of State John Foster Dulles, one problem the State Department had with blacks in 1953 was FBI security clearance. Few African Americans could pass through the bureau's exacting filter because reds had supposedly infiltrated all black organizations.[27]

Other ethnic-racial US minorities did not share this particular problem because the crowning feature of their experience with American racism was the denial of citizenship. Many of their civil rights struggles focused on this issue. Chinese and Japanese exclusion laws, Supreme Court decisions denying landownership rights to Asians, and policies of segregating Mexican Americans and disputing their racial identity as well as their nationality meant that the full participation of these groups in US politics, including national office-holding, was delayed. While they engaged in civil rights struggles, their populations were heavily concentrated in specific areas, such as Texas and the West Coast, which gave a regional cast to their activism. After the Chinese Revolution of 1949, which coincided with heightening cold war tensions, the loyalties of Chinese Americans came under suspicion, making them unlikely candidates for diplomatic appointments. By the late 1960s many Latinos and Asian Americans had begun challenging prevailing models of passive assimilation and projected their struggle for equality and inclusion beyond local boundaries.[28]

The end of the Korean War and the death of Stalin in 1953 resuscitated postponed concerns about racial justice. President Dwight D. Eisenhower, like his predecessor, realized that American cold war victory necessitated amelioration on the racial front. While Ike personally opposed coerced public school desegregation,[29] he upheld the Supreme Court's decision in *Brown v. Board of Education*, and endorsed the limited civil rights act of 1957.[30] During both Eisenhower administrations, US policy gradually continued to retreat from overt racism but remained both ambivalent and ambiguous about forthright endorsement of desegregation in all aspects of American life. There were exceptions to this changing picture. One of them was South Africa, where US representatives continued a comfortable friendship with the apartheid regime. While uranium, diamonds, and other precious ores shielded South Africa from strong criticism, mounting protest among black Americans and global shifts in attitudes toward racial difference made support for discrimination increasingly difficult to sustain. Officials found themselves giving lip service to democratic ideals while continuing to court the Pretoria regime. US authorities tried to mitigate the deleterious effect of the mixed messages they were communicating by sending black American artists to perform in South Africa. This practice later became controversial when pressure against the apartheid regime accelerated in the 1980s.[31]

Ambivalence also characterized the policy of Secretary of State John Foster Dulles. Dulles appeared to think in racial stereotypes, having once notoriously remarked to a Chinese ambassador that "the Oriental mind, particularly that of the Japanese, was always more devious than the Occidental mind."[32] While he supported decolonization as a matter of principle, he doubted the capacity of emerging nations to maintain democratic regimes. In April 1955 a group of ostensibly nonaligned states convened in Bandung, Indonesia, to discuss issues that affected them as neutrals in a world increasingly divided by bilateralism. The Afro-Asian Conference delegates expressed concern about the problems of development, colonialism, nuclear deterrence, and the pressure placed on them to declare allegiance to one or the other party in the cold war. Washington policy makers viewed the Bandung conference with alarm because of their difficulty in separating the nationalist aims of the participants from anti-white racism and a call to arms for worldwide revolution. The People's Republic of China (PRC) used the Afro-Asian Conference to carve out its own position on race. Adopting a stance that the Japanese had used in the run-up to World War II, the PRC simultaneously and advantageously represented itself as independent of the Soviet Union, as a leader of the Asian peoples, a friend of those still struggling against colonial domination, and a foe of all forms of racial discrimination.[33]

The United States found itself unwilling and unable to clearly distinguish between communism and nationalism in the Third World. In a November 1958 speech in Cleveland, Dulles warned of the "danger that newly granted independence may turn out to be but a brief interlude between the rule of colonialism and the harsh dictatorship of international communism."[34] This was not the only possible perspective on the relationship between decolonization and the "red menace." The NAACP's position, articulated years before, maintained that "independence is the best answer to communist intrigue." Suppressing the aspirations of colonized peoples drained the energies needed for the real fight for freedom, the Association asserted.[35]

In spite of his narrow perspective on racial domination in the context of colonialism, Dulles proved unequivocal in his consternation over the international fallout from the Little Rock crisis in 1957 when Eisenhower sent troops to integrate a high school in defiance of the segregationist governor of Arkansas. The secretary of state regarded it as a public relations disaster that the Soviets and other critics readily exploited. He impressed the gravity of the situation upon Eisenhower and other key officials.[36] When employees of a Delaware restaurant refused to serve the Ghanaian finance minister, President Eisenhower invited the official to breakfast at the White House, and he received an apology from Vice President Richard Nixon.[37]

In other respects, Eisenhower administration policy toward Africa did little to remove the fear that the newly independent states would veer toward the Soviet bloc. Washington's practices did not model its democratic rhetoric. US racial minorities had no significant employment in the State Department, or other agencies responsible for foreign affairs. Protocol officers evaded the question of segregation and discrimination by limiting contacts between African visitors and African Americans prepared to brief them in detail on US racial customs. Curious breaches of protocol when Africans made state visits increased the level of suspicion among those African states inclined to shape their own foreign policies independently of East-West ideological quarrels. Eisenhower named a black ambassador to Guinea, a country with which the United States had prickly relations. Ambassador John H. Morrow found himself undermined by his own subordinates in Conakry and by the skepticism surrounding his appointment.[38]

Just as the focus on communism at home tended to derail other objectives, including the achievement of civil rights for all and the creation of a representative foreign service, it threatened peace abroad. While nonaligned countries pursued their specific interests as individual states, they acted as a group in trying to persuade the United States and the Soviet Union to enter talks. Late in September 1960, Ghana, India, Yugoslavia, Egypt, and Indonesia submitted a resolution to the General Assembly calling for a meeting between Eisenhower and Soviet premier Nikita Khrushchev. They viewed defusing cold war tensions as in the interests of their own development and prosperity. Ike rejected the move, characterizing it as "at best . . . totally illogical; at worst . . . an act of effrontery."[39] US pressure led to the resolution's defeat, especially as the USSR had its own reasons for rejecting talks with the Americans. The maneuver nevertheless alienated the states that had proposed it.

President John F. Kennedy, who assumed office in 1961, had campaigned on a promise of a foreign policy that would take account of changes in the global environment. Kennedy and liberals initially close to him in the first months of his administration endorsed Algerian independence and better relations with India. They advanced the view that promoting the American way of life to foreigners depended on achieving progress in inter-group relations at home. New communications technology meant that adverse news about the United States, including reports of murders, race riots, and brutal treatment of civil rights demonstrators, would reach international audiences. The press in Warsaw Pact countries played up negative stories. Even audiences generally in tune with the American worldview questioned the continuing pattern of violence and discrimination. Bad press dogged American news from Copenhagen to Delhi. Even opinion in Portugal, which still retained its African territories, denounced US hypocrisy for claiming to oppose colonialism while featuring a racial system the Portuguese considered more oppressive than their own. Decolonization increased disapproving voices. It became clear that the color bar was out of date in a diverse world that now contained sovereign Asian and African states. In ironic contrast to the widespread condemnation of racial segregation and discrimination, South Africa's media approvingly reported stories of white resistance to black civil rights.[40]

The desegregation of official Washington proceeded only in tandem with heightened criticism. Presidential initiative and continued pressure from African American leaders prompted most of the desultory changes that did occur. These included eliminating the practice of confining black diplomats to Africa and Caribbean countries or remote posts elsewhere. The Kennedy administration responded creatively to the desire to court black opinion on foreign policy matters. Officials discovered that through invitations for White House visits by African heads of state, they could create the illusion of receptiveness to black demands. This combined effectively with a few well-advertised diplomatic appointments for African Americans. Washington hoped through gestures of friendship to persuade neutral African countries to orient themselves more closely to the United States and distance themselves from the Soviet Union and its allies.[41]

Government action against negative racial publicity became part of an expanded cold war cultural outreach program mounted by the State Department and the United States Information Agency (USIA). Carefully managed news for dissemination abroad, information libraries that contained optimistic material about African American life, and tours by black lecturers, artists, and entertainers who delivered upbeat presentations about US racial difficulties played important roles in this effort, even at the risk of overstating both the changes that had taken place and the national will involved in making them. International expositions and fairs provided another venue for the dissemination of an alternative discourse to the bleak one of Jim Crow. The government's official position did not contradict the realities of a racism that all could see. Instead, propagandists stressed the gradual improvements made to date through peaceful evolution.[42]

The Congo crisis disrupted the pattern of US responses to racial challenges during the cold war. The cold war penetrated Africa as the United States and the Soviet Union took different sides in the Congolese civil war that began shortly after that country's independence in 1960. Worldwide anti-western demonstrations followed upon the 1961 assassination of Congolese premier Patrice Lumumba. The subsequent Kennedy administration stance toward the Congo resulted from the conflicting views of foreign policy analysts who were divided between "Europeanists," who believed that the United States should make its relationships with its strategic European partners paramount, and "Africanists," who placed greater emphasis on decolonization, opposing racism, and courting the new republics. The "Europeanists" prevailed and the United States remained a weak opponent of colonialism and apartheid.[43]

The beginning of Cuban military support for African revolutionaries and the endorsement of Marxism by national liberation fronts in southern Africa shook the United States out of its complacency and quickened its impulse to quell leftist revolts. Independently of the Soviets, Cubans had shouldered the responsibility of a worldwide struggle against imperialism, which they based partly on their own national history, and the perceived affinities of many Cubans with Africa.[44] In 1964, planes piloted by anti-Castro Cuban refugees and financed by the Central Intelligence Agency flew missions against Congolese insurgents in an operation aided also by Belgium. Mirroring views in some western circles, *Time* magazine on December 4, 1964 described a revolt in the Congo's Shaba province as led by "a rabble of dazed ignorant savages."[45] Erstwhile secessionist leader Moïse Tshombe had become prime minister of the Congo. His regime was marked by his distrust of other Congolese and his habit of surrounding himself with white foreigners. Until deposed in late 1965, Tshombe secured mercenary support and the approval of US conservative politicians and Dixie segregationists.[46]

Racialism proved challenging for US policy throughout Africa. In another development, the stirrings of nationalism had troubled white settlers in Rhodesia. Determined to prevent black majority rule, they declared their independence in 1965 and abandoned the British Commonwealth. The Johnson administration worried that American civil rights activists, who were increasingly addressing foreign policy issues, would develop an interest in Rhodesia. Johnson's advisors did not want their hands tied in southern Africa by the domestic electoral constituencies. The White House was, moreover, increasingly involved in Vietnam and hoped to rely on Europeans to suppress African radicalism.[47]

Vietnam was not the only hotspot in US military activities during the Johnson years. In 1964 US troops fired on a Panamanian demonstration and killed two people, whereupon Panama suspended diplomatic relations with the United States. Relations were resumed within the week upon a US promise to review the Canal Zone treaties. The following year, US forces toppled a popular government in the Dominican Republic because of fears of communist infiltration and popular radicalism. Neither the Panamanian nor the Dominican incidents were racial conflicts per se, even though they involved the engagement of US forces against people of color. Instead, they reflected a deep-seated pattern of cultural and racial arrogance that could mask itself as cold war-driven.

The Vietnam War originated in a colonial conflict between a white power and subjugated Asians. US plans for the modernization of Vietnam contained discourse that implied that Americans were on a civilizing mission to improve the backward Vietnamese. The violent and racist manner of prosecuting the war evoked international protest. The United States had failed to adequately address racial oppression within its own borders and now deployed disproportionate numbers of front-line black troops. In the southern states draft boards frequently conscripted civil rights activists. Outspoken comment on the racial implications of the Vietnam War emanated from liberals who no longer felt beholden to President Johnson. Some major figures were reluctant to voice their criticisms for fear of being accused of communist sympathies, and concern about squandering the civil rights movement's political capital by alienating the president. Others believed it inappropriate for civil rights leaders to take stands on foreign issues.

By the mid-1960s, unwillingness to oppose the war was breaking down, even as the Johnson administration struggled to contain the emergence of an African American foreign policy audience. Johnson held to a universalist approach to US citizenship, in which all groups belonged to a national society with shared goals at home and abroad. Anti-war statements nevertheless issued from such organizations as the Mississippi Freedom Democratic Party and the Student Non-violent Coordinating Committee. In 1967, Martin Luther King, Jr., privately an anti-war critic for some time, formally announced his dissidence in a sermon at a New York church. King condemned "the giant triplets of racism, extreme materialism, and militarism" that characterized a war he deemed "dishonorable and unjust."[48] The assassination of King in April 1968 was the capstone to a period of domestic disorder that favored presidential candidate Richard M. Nixon's claims that he could restore law and order to the fractious nation. Following his accession to the presidency in 1969, Nixon created a massive intelligence and police system aimed at identifying and repressing domestic radicals and uncovering any networks they had established abroad. The administration and the intelligence agencies were especially concerned with identifing Cuban influence on the Black Power movement in the United States. In spite of their best efforts, FBI and CIA investigators ultimately could not prove that American unrest had any cause except local opposition to the war in Vietnam and to racial injustice.[49]

When Nixon came to power, he ordered the National Security Council to produce an overall review of Africa policy by December 1969. At the NSC meeting, Vice President Spiro Agnew echoed right-wing opinion in comparing the Rhodesian white settlers' Unilateral Declaration of Independence to the US Declaration of Independence and calling for an end to the ban on importing Rhodesian chrome. National Security Advisor Henry Kissinger counseled less activism for the United States at the UN and retrenchment in any effort to abolish apartheid and Portuguese colonialism. These conservative positions could be offset, Kissinger believed, by a modest increase in aid to black African nations. In the end, the United States continued to follow an Africa policy blueprint from which it had not substantially departed since the early days of the Kennedy administration. Nixon and his closest advisors put African issues on the backburner, to be handled by Secretary of State William Rogers, an outsider in the administration, as they focused on Europe and Asia. "We'll leave the niggers to Bill," the president notoriously recommended.[50]

A counterpoint to White House policy was located in Congress. Michigan Democrat Charles C. Diggs, an African American, became chair of the House Subcommittee on Africa and vigorously used it as a platform to air opinion on African issues that differed from those of the White House and State Department.[51] The subcommittee gave voice to numerous opponents of apartheid, advocates of continued sanctions against the minority white regimes, and critics of US investment in southern Africa. Diggs called for testimony from human rights advocates, academic Africanists, and representatives of liberation organizations. As a congressional representative, he led his own fact-finding missions. If policy critics lacked clout with the administration, they gained influence with the public as opposition to colonialism and racism continued to mount during the decade.

Popular energies that had originated in the civil rights movement found new expression in protests against the minority regimes in Africa and US policy toward them. A handful of workers at the Polaroid plant in Massachusetts objected to the use of the company's equipment in the manufacture of passbooks in South Africa and launched a campaign to force the company to divest its holdings in that country.[52] While civil rights activists had linked US racism to apartheid by the 1960s, the emergence in 1972 of the short-lived African Liberation Support Committee (ALSC), a mass mobilization organization, newly publicized African issues to students, church societies, and black community groups through demonstrations and marches. Certain trade unionists took the initiative in organizing waterfront actions in which dockworkers refused to unload Rhodesian chrome or South African exports. These gestures were more symbolic than effective, but they demonstrated how the roots of domestic opposition to colonial domination lay entwined in struggles for reform in the United States. In 1976, strengthened by the growing numbers of blacks elected to Congress and other offices, a set of activists interested in international issues founded the African American lobby TransAfrica to influence federal policy regarding Africa.[53]

Just as the Cuban démarche in 1964 had led the Johnson administration to pay more attention to events in Africa, the gains made by Marxist-oriented national liberation forces in the Africa of the 1970s and their supporters outside the continent forced modifications in the agendas of Nixon and his successor. Following the death of Portuguese dictator Antonio Salazar in 1970, the Portuguese army withdrew from Angola without designating a successor government from among the three national liberation organizations that strove for power. The Marxist Popular Movement for the Liberation of Angola (MPLA) seized the initiative, taking control of the capital city in the summer of 1975 and expelling adversaries. The other organizations mounted attacks on the capital but could not withstand the victors and Cuban forces sent to defend MPLA holdings even though they called on South Africa for support.

Stunned by these developments, Kissinger, who had become secretary of state in 1973 and now served in that capacity under President Gerald Ford, approached Congress to unblock funds for the CIA to assist the non-Marxist liberation fronts. The Senate refused. Kissinger found that the inertia bred of racism had backfired and set back the anti-communist cause in Africa.

American voters elected Democrat Jimmy Carter to the presidency in 1976. Carter was a Georgian who owed his victory to substantial support from minority voters but would enact conservative economic policies that did not favor most of them. Carter revised Kissinger's stance on Africa. His secretary of state, Cyrus Vance, was more attuned to the aspirations of developing countries than Kissinger had been.[54] Soon after the inauguration, Congress passed White House-sponsored legislation, to repeal a law permitting the import of Rhodesian chrome, the Byrd Amendment. Carter did little about apartheid, choosing to concentrate instead on Rhodesia. Secretary Vance instructed UN ambassador Andrew Young to veto UN resolutions that would ban foreign investment and nuclear cooperation with South Africa or prevent it from developing a domestic arms industry. In spring 1978 Carter made the first visit to sub-Saharan Africa by any US president, traveling to Liberia and Nigeria and making known his opposition to anything but unconditional independence for the black majority in Rhodesia.[55]

In spite of these departures, the Carter administration continued to tolerate repressive government in the Congo, now called Zaire and led by Sese Seko Mobutu. Congressional conservatives also attacked Carter's foreign policy. The segregationist Jesse Helms and Senator Robert Dole invited Rhodesian leader Ian Smith to the United States. Carter refused to see Smith and withstood GOP pressures to lift sanctions against Rhodesia. Right-wing orientations toward African issues soon resurfaced, however, as conservatives gathered electoral strength and were poised to win significant political victories in the 1980s. The brand of conservatism associated with Helms, Ronald Reagan, and others had deep roots in the Jim Crow South, a reality reflected in the policies Reagan pursued as president.[56]

The Reagan administration planned to help the minority regime in South Africa achieve international respectability without forcing it to abandon apartheid. The quid pro quo was South African help in extinguishing communism in southern Africa and coming to an agreement on the future of Southwest Africa, now Namibia. Assistant Secretary of State Chester Crocker was the author of this policy, called "constructive engagement."[57] The breach between professed American ideals and the desire to leave South Africa intact to preserve the strategic and economic advantages that apartheid bestowed on elites enlivened rather than destroyed the anti-apartheid movement. The Congressional Black Caucus in March 1981 issued a statement calling for a US foreign policy that recognized multilateral interests in the modern world. "We reject as unrealistic and potentially disastrous to American global interests," the representatives wrote, "the Reagan Administration's notion that foreign policy issues, especially in the developing world, must be seen primarily in the context of a purely East-West confrontation."[58] The Caucus opposed efforts to destabilize and overthrow the governments of developing states and inhibit reform in the name of ideological orthodoxy.

The studied hostility of Reagan officials to the aims of both civil rights activism in the United States and national liberation in Africa pushed TransAfrica away from its staid preoccupation with lobbying and into the direct action campaigns that had characterized the ALSC. Anti-apartheid activism in the 1980s became more militant and focused on such programs as divestment and exposure of the flaws in such dilatory solutions as constructive engagement. They launched campaigns to isolate South Africa, planning boycotts of entertainers who performed there. Activist pressure contributed to the passage of the Comprehensive Anti-Apartheid Act of 1986, a package of sanctions that withstood Reagan's veto.

While racism persisted in American life, by the late 1980s it could not be as readily espoused as in the past. As immigration from Asia, Africa, and Latin America to Europe as well as North America grew substantially in the late 20th century, racism was revealed as a problem in countries other than the United States. In Warsaw Pact states and China, violence against African students and visitors demonstrated that parts of the local population had not absorbed the official message of tolerance. Those communist regimes began to experience intense pressures for liberalization during the era. Lessened restrictions in Poland, Hungary, and Czechoslovakia, and the dramatic breach of the Berlin Wall foreshadowed the dismantling of the Soviet Union. Advocates of the status quo in southern Africa had used the Soviet threat as a rationale to delay change. With that state disintegrating, in February 1990, South African President F. W. de Klerk at last bowed to world opinion and released the African National Congress leader Nelson Mandela from his twenty-seven-year imprisonment.

Racial consciousness served a dual purpose during the cold war years. Those who advocated racial equality used democratic ideology to argue that all forms of discrimination should be abandoned in order to bring US practices in harmony with American ideals and aspirations to global leadership. Proponents of segregation used the cold war to argue that altering time-honored usages was inherently subversive, degraded civil society, and endangered national security.

These contrasting positions persisted after the cold war, as discourse about race increasingly entered the realm of cultural and symbolic politics.[59] Those wishing to enlarge the participation of people of color in national life and those who were skeptical about change continued to disagree about the meaning and extent of democracy. While the election of Barack Obama as the first black president of the United States seemed to signal a watershed in race relations, Obama received only 43 percent of the white Christian vote, in spite of a gravely troubled economy and the ideological incoherence associated with the incumbent party. At the turn of the 21st century, race continued to figure in US conflicts at home and abroad, including wars in the Middle East, the status of undocumented immigrants, and the nitty-gritty of partisan politics. The cold war had provided race with one of its most trenchant national expressions, but the end of hostilities did not eliminate it as a major factor in American life.

## Notes

1. Forrestal and Acheson quoted in Matthew Connelly, "Taking Off the Cold War Lens: Visions of North-South Conflict during the Algerian War for Independence," *American Historical Review* 105/3 (June 2000): 753. See also Dean Rusk, *As I Saw It* (New York: W. W. Norton, 1990), 422.

2. Thomas Borstelmann, "Jim Crow's Coming Out: Race Relations and American Foreign Policy in the Truman Years," *Presidential Studies Quarterly* 29/3 (September 1999): 552.

3. President Harry S. Truman's Address before a Joint Session of Congress, March 12, 1947, published by the Yale University Law School Avalon Project, <http://avalon.law.yale.edu/20th_century/trudoc.asp>.

4. Borstelmann, "Jim Crow's Coming Out," 550; Wilson D. Miscamble, *From Roosevelt to Truman: Potsdam, Hiroshima, and the Cold War* (Cambridge: Cambridge University Press, 2007), 282; Lynn Boyd Hinds and Theodore Otto Windt, Jr., *The Cold War as Rhetoric: The Beginnings, 1945–50* (New York: Praeger, 1991), 91.

5. Odd Arne Westad, *The Global Cold War: Third World Interventions and the Making of Our Times* (Cambridge: Cambridge University Press, 2005), 112–13.

6. Michael Omi and Howard Winant, *Racial Formation in the United States*, 2nd ed. (London and New York: Routledge, 1994), 79–82.

7. See, for example, UN ambassador Harlan Cleveland's remarks on managing international opinion as transcribed in *Foreign Relations of the United States, 1961–63*, vol. XXV: *Organization of Foreign Policy; Information Policy; United Nations; Scientific Matters* (Washington, DC: US Government Printing Office, 2001), 347, 663, 625.

8. Report by the Chairman of the Sub-Committee Appointed to Study the Question of These Communications, January 24, 1946, pp. 51, 52, in UN General Assembly, Official Records, Committees, 1st sess., 1st pt., January 13–February 14, 1946.

9. Gerald Horne, *Black and Red: W. E. B. Du Bois and the Afro-American Response to the Cold War* (Albany, NY: SUNY Press, 1986), passim.

10. Mark Solomon, "Black Critics of Colonialism and the Cold War," in Thomas G. Paterson, ed., *Cold War Critics* (New York: Quadrangle Books, 1971), 219–20. See also Penny Von Eschen, *Race against Empire: Black Americans and Anticolonialism, 1937–1957* (Ithaca, NY: Cornell University Press, 1997), 107–8.

11. Donald R. McCoy and Richard T. Ruetten, *Quest and Response: Minority Rights and the Truman Administration* (Lawrence, KS: The University Press of Kansas, 1973).

12. Mary L. Dudziak, "Desegregation as a Cold War Imperative," *Stanford Law Review* 41/1 (November 1988): 61–120.

13. Theodore Kornweibel, *Seeing Red: Federal Campaigns Against Black Militancy, 1919–1925* (Bloomington, IN: University of Indiana Press, 1998); Mark Ellis, *Race, War, and Surveillance: African Americans and the United States* (Bloomington, IN: University of Indiana Press, 2001).

14. Carole Boyce Davies, "Deportable Subjects: US Immigration Laws and the Criminalizing of Communism," *The South Atlantic Quarterly* 100/4 (Fall 2001): 949–66.

15. "Colored Troops Win First Victory for US in Korea," *Baltimore Afro-American* (July 29, 1950): 1–2.

16. Quoted in Arthur Krock, *Memoirs* (New York: Funk & Wagnalls, 1968), 582.

17. Martin B. Duberman, *Paul Robeson* (New York: Ballantine, 1990), 385.

18. Duberman, *Robeson*, 390.

19. David M. Oshinsky, *Senator Joseph McCarthy and the American Labor Movement* (Columbia, MO: University of Missouri Press, 1976), 128–9.

20. George C. McGhee, "United States Interests in Africa," *Department of State Bulletin* 22 (June 19, 1950): 1003; Memorandum of Discussion at the 456th Meeting of the National Security Council, August 18, 1960, in *Foreign Relations of the United States, 1958–1960*, vol. XIV: *Africa* (Washington, DC: United States Government Printing Office, 1992); Cary Fraser, "Understanding American Policy toward the Decolonization of European Empires, 1945–64," *Diplomacy & Statecraft* 3/1 (March 1992): 105–25.

21. George C. McGhee, "United States Interests in Africa," *Department of State Bulletin* 22 (June 19, 1950): 1000–3.

22. See, for example, George Kennan's memorandum, "Latin America as a Problem in US Foreign Policy," *Foreign Relations of the United States, 1950*, 2 ( March 20, 1950): 600–1.

Transcript, Thomas C. Mann interviewed by Joe B. Frantz, November 4, 1968, Lyndon B. Johnson Presidential Library, p. 9.

23. For the Asian experience with western racism, see Gerald Horne, *Race War! White Supremacy and the Japanese Attack on the British Empire* (New York: New York University Press, 2004); Horne, *The End of Empires: African Americans and India* (Philadelphia, PA: Temple University Press, 2008); Melani McAlister, *Epic Encounters: Culture, Media, and US Interests in the Middle East, 1945-2000* (Berkeley, CA: University of California Press, 2001); Robert G. Lee, *Orientals: Asian Americans in Popular Culture* (Philadelphia, PA: Temple University Press, 1999).

24. Renée Romano, "No Diplomatic Immunity: African Diplomats, the State Department, and Civil Rights, 1961-1964," *Journal of American History* 87/2 (September 2000): 546-79.

25. Deborah J. Holland, "Steward of World Peace, Keeper of Fair Play: The American Hydrogen Bomb and Civil Rights, 1945-1954," Ph.D. dissertation, Northwestern University, Evanston, Ill., 2002, pp. 5, 25, 217, 259.

26. Lizabeth Cohen, *A Consumers' Republic: The Politics of Mass Consumption in Postwar America* (New York: Alfred A. Knopf, 2003), 177.

27. Michael L. Krenn, *Black Diplomacy: African Americans and the State Department, 1945-1969* (Armonk, NY: M. E. Sharpe, 1999), 126.

28. Angelo N. Ancheta, *Race, Rights, and the Asian American Experience*, 2nd ed. (Rutgers, NJ: Rutgers University Press, 2006); Lorena Oropeza, *Raza si!, Guerra No!: Chicano Protest and Patriotism during the Viet Nam War Era* (Berkeley, CA: University of California Press, 2005); Lee, *Orientals*; Linda K. Kerber. "The Meanings of Citizenship," *The Journal of American History* 84/3 (December 1997): 833-54.

29. Stephen E. Ambrose, *Eisenhower: Soldier and President* (New York: Simon and Schuster, 1991), 367; but see David A. Nichols, *A Matter of Justice: Eisenhower and the Beginning of the Civil Rights Revolution* (New York: Simon & Schuster, 2007), 104.

30. Steven F. Lawson, "Debating the Civil Rights Movement: The View from the Nation," in Steven F. Lawson, Charles M. Payne, and James T. Patterson, eds., *Debating the Civil Rights Movement, 1945-1968* (New York: Rowman & Littlefield, 2006), 14.

31. Thomas Borstelmann, *Apartheid's Reluctant Uncle: The United States and Southern Africa in the Early Cold War* (New York: Oxford University Press, 1993), 24, 94, 51.

32. Borstelmann, "Jim Crow's Coming Out," 553.

33. Amitav Acharya, *Whose Ideas Matter?: Agency and Power in Asian Regionalism* (Ithaca, NY: Cornell University Press, 2009); George McTurnan Kahin, *The Asian-African Conference, Bandung, Indonesia, April 1955* (Port Washington, NY: Kennikat Press, 1972); Richard Wright, *The Color Curtain: A Report on the Bandung Conference* (New York: World, 1956).

34. *State Department Bulletin* (December 8, 1958): 897.

35. John N. Popham, "N.A.A.C.P. Demands Curb on Red Aims; Convention Calls for Wide Action in World and Assails Communist-Ruled Unions," *New York Times* (July 4, 1954): 16.

36. Mary Dudziak, "The Little Rock Crisis and Foreign Affairs: Race, Resistance, and the Image of American Democracy," *Southern California Law Review* 70/6 (September 1997): 1641-716.

37. William Sutherland and Matt Meyer, *Guns and Gandhi in Africa* (Trenton, NJ: Africa World Press, 2000), 42-4.

38. Krenn, *Black Diplomacy*, passim; Romano, "No Diplomatic Immunity, 546-79; John H. Morrow interview, Phelps-Stokes Fund Oral History Project on Black Chiefs of Mission,

New York Public Library; John H. Morrow, *First American Ambassador to Guinea* (Rutgers, NJ: Rutgers University Press, 1968), 45–7, 77, 82–3.

39. Dwight D. Eisenhower, *Waging Peace, 1956–1961: The White House Years* (New York: Doubleday, 1965), 586.

40. Michael Curtin, *Redeeming the Wasteland: Television Documentary and Cold War Politics* (New Brunswick, NJ: Rutgers University Press, 1995), 52–4.

41. Krenn, *Black Diplomacy*, 126.

42. Penny Von Eschen, *Satchmo Blows up the World: Jazz Ambassadors Play the Cold War* (Cambridge, MA: Harvard University Press, 2004); Michael L. Krenn, "'Unfinished Business': Segregation and US Diplomacy at the 1958 World's Fair," *Diplomatic History* 20/4 (October 1996): 591–612.

43. Lise A. Namikas, "Battleground Africa: The Cold War and the Congo Crisis, 1960–1965," Ph.D. dissertation, University of Southern California, Los Angeles, 2002, 306.

44. Piero Gleijeses, *Conflicting Missions: Havana, Washington, and Africa, 1959–1976* (Chapel Hill, NC: University of North Carolina Press, 2002), 29.

45. "The Congo Massacre," *Time* (December 4, 1964): 28–32.

46. David N. Gibbs, *The Political Economy of Third World Intervention: Mines, Money, and US Policy in the Congo Crisis* (Chicago: University of Chicago Press, 1991), 122.

47. Memorandum from Ulrich Haynes to Walt Rostow, April 18, 1966, *Foreign Relations of the United States, 1964–1968*, vol. 26: *Africa* (Washington, DC: Government Printing Office, 1999), 902.

48. Adam Fairclough, "Martin Luther King, Jr. and the War in Vietnam," *Phylon* 45/1 (Spring 1984): 19–39.

49. US Department of State memorandum, Summary of data collected on Cuban and Chinese involvement in the promotion of anti-goverment violence and demonstrations by African-Americans, July 26, 1967, Declassified Documents Reference System, online; US Congress, House Un-American Activities Committee (HUAC), *Subversive Influences in Riots, Looting, and Burning* (Washington, DC.: Government Printing Office, 1968), pt. 4; Jeff Woods, *Black Struggle, Red Scare* (Baton Rouge, LA: Louisiana State University Press, 2003), 252.

50. Quoted in Seymour M. Hersh, *Kissinger: The Price of Power* (New York: Summit Books, 1983), 111.

51. Francis Njubi Nesbitt, *Race for Sanctions: African Americans against Apartheid, 1946–1994* (Bloomington, IN: Indiana University Press, 2004), 35.

52. William Minter, Gail Hovey, and Charles E. Cobb, *No Easy Victories: African Liberation and American Activists over a Half Century, 1950–2000* (Trenton, NJ: Africa World Press, 2007), 25.

53. Cedric Johnson, "From Popular Anti-Imperialism to Sectarianism: The African Liberation Support Committee and Black Power Radicals," *New Political Science* 25/4 (December 2003): 477–507; on TransAfrica, Randall Robinson, *Defending the Spirit: A Black Life in America* (New York: Dutton, 1998).

54. David F. Schmitz and Vanessa Walker, "Jimmy Carter and the Foreign Policy of Human Rights: The Development of a Post-Cold War Foreign Policy," *Diplomatic History* 28/1 (January 2004): 113–43; Robert A. Strong, *Working in the World: Jimmy Carter and the Making of American Foreign Policy* (Baton Rouge, LA: Louisiana State University Press 2000); Douglas Brinkley, "The Rising Stock of Jimmy Carter: The 'Hands on' Legacy of Our Thirty-Ninth President," *Diplomatic History* 20/4 (October 1996): 505–29.

55. Andrew DeRoche, *Black, White, and Chrome: The United States and Zimbabwe, 1953–1998* (Trenton, NJ: Africa World Press, Inc., 2001), 244–64.

56. DeRoche, *Black, White, and Chrome*, 265, 271.

57. Chester Crocker, *High Noon in Southern Africa: Making Peace in a Rough Neighborhood* (New York: W. W. Norton & Co, 1992), 255.

58. Quoted in Locksley Edmondson, "Black America as a Mobilizing Diaspora: Some International Implications," in Gabriel Sheffer, ed., *Modern Diaspora in International Politics* (London and Sydney: Croom Helm, 1986), 164–211.

59. Nikhil Pal Singh, "Culture/Wars: Recoding Empire in an Age of Democracy," *American Quarterly* 50/3 (September 1998): 471–522.

## SELECT BIBLIOGRAPHY

Anderson, Carol. *Eyes off the Prize: The United Nations and the African American Struggle for Human Rights, 1944–1955*. Cambridge: Cambridge University Press, 2003.

Borstelmann, Thomas. *Apartheid's Reluctant Uncle: The United States and Southern Africa in the Early Cold War*. New York: Oxford University Press, 1993.

Dudziak, Mary L. *Cold War Civil Rights: Race and the Image of American Democracy*. Princeton, NJ: Princeton University Press, 2000.

Gleijeses, Piero. *Conflicting Missions: Havana, Washington, and Africa, 1959–1976*. Chapel Hill, NC: University of North Carolina Press, 2002.

Horne, Gerald. *Black and Red: W. E. B. Du Bois and the Afro-American Response to the Cold War*. Albany, NY: SUNY Press, 1986.

Krenn, Michael L. *Black Diplomacy: African Americans and the State Department, 1945–1969*. New York: M. E. Sharpe, 1999.

Minter, William, Gail Hovey, and Charles E. Cobb. *No Easy Victories: African Liberation and American Activists over a Half Century, 1950–2000*. Trenton, NJ: Africa World Press, 2007.

Nesbitt, Francis Njubi. *Race for Sanctions: African Americans against Apartheid, 1946–1964*. Bloomington, IN: Indiana University Press, 2004.

Oropeza, Lorena. *Raza sí!, Guerra No!: Chicano Protest and Patriotism during the Viet Nam War Era*. Berkeley, CA: University of California Press, 2005.

Westad, Odd Arne. *The Global Cold War: Third World Interventions and the making of Our Times*. Cambridge: Cambridge University Press, 2006.

Woods, Jeff. *Black Struggle, Red Scare: Segregation and Anti-Communism in the South, 1948–1968*. Baton Rouge, LA: Louisiana State University Press, 2004.

# CHAPTER 30

# GENDER AND WOMEN'S RIGHTS IN THE COLD WAR

### HELEN LAVILLE

Nixon: In America, we like to make life easier for women.

Khrushchev: Your capitalistic attitude toward women does not occur under Communism.

Nixon: I think that this attitude towards women is universal. What we want to do is make life more easy for our housewives.

(US National Exhibition, Moscow, 1959)

FOR many historians the 1959 kitchen debate between US Vice President Richard M. Nixon and Soviet Premier Nikita Khrushchev at the opening of the American National Exhibition at Sokolniki Park, Moscow, was testament to the centrality of gender in the cold war. In an exchange, which was at times tense and at times aggressive, the two leaders debated the quest for peace, the meaning of communism, censorship, and rival efforts at space exploration. As the competing merits of the USSR and the USA bounced back and forth, the debate took inspiration from the surroundings of the American suburban show kitchen, and the two leaders compared the home life of the average Soviet worker with that of his American counterpart. The quality and availability of domestic goods served in the debate as a measure of progress and quality of life. These were terms on which Nixon felt confident, prompting him to ask if it would not be better to compete on the merits of washing machines rather than the strength of rockets. While the kitchen debate was shaped by disagreements and airings of vast ideological, economic, and social differences between the two systems, Nixon and Khrushchev found common ground on their understanding of heterosexual masculinity. Khrushchev noted Nixon's admiring glances at the hostesses at the exhibition, joking, "You are for the girls too!" Later that day, as the two men raised a glass of wine, Nixon urged, "Let's drink to talking, not fighting!" Unwilling to concede so much diplomatic ground, Khrushchev suggested, "Let's drink to the ladies!" Nixon quickly agreed: "We can all drink to the ladies!"[1]

On the surface the kitchen debates focused on the cutting edge of the modern technological world. Underneath the shiny new Formica surfaces, however, was an older theme of masculine authority and feminine vulnerability. Narratives of international relations have long drawn upon gender roles to measure and express national progress and civilization, with gender differentiation serving as a sign of progress. Civilized and advanced societies were those which relieved women of the burden of work; uncivilized and backwards societies were those which exacted hard labor from their women.[2] The kitchen debate offered nothing new in terms of its assertion that the progress and superiority of the nation-state was best measured by the status of its women—reflecting what Emily Rosenberg succulently summarizes as an "our-women-are-better-off-than-your-women-no-they-aren't-yes-they-are kind of masculine debate."[3]

This chapter critically examines the early cold war use of the status of women as a measure of national progress. First, it examines the way in which the US promoted the measurement of the status of women according to what it argued were universal gender roles, which prioritized domesticity and consumerism. The US asserted that its ability to fulfill these desires and the USSR's failure to do so demonstrated American national superiority in the cold war contest. Second, this essay examines how the USSR sought to contest these terms, maintaining that the measure of women's status was her equality to men; an equality that should be measured by economic and political markers such as state protection of equal pay and the number of women in the workforce. The Soviet Union regarded domesticity, however technologically assisted, as a burden. Working through the new institutions of the United Nations, the USSR attacked the US for what it castigated as a backward approach to women's status, pointing to the lack of women in political office and the failure of Americans to endorse equal pay and equal rights legislation as evidence of their lack of commitment to women's equality. Finally, this essay discusses the breakdown of early cold war paradigms for women's rights, explaining how the efforts of newly liberated and non-aligned countries, together with pressure from increasingly influential women's non-governmental organizations, successfully challenged the early cold war agenda and demanded a more nuanced approach to the global improvement of women's status.

While Americans proudly celebrated the contribution of their women to the Second World War, this was tempered by constant reminders of the temporary nature of their service. In an article that sought to defend the rights of women to work after the war, Mary Anderson, the director of the Women's Bureau, wryly quoted a letter from a male union activist whose industry had been largely dominated by women during the war. The man wished Anderson every success, but added that he was "hoping for the day when women may relax and stay in her beloved kitchen, a loving wife to some man who is now fighting for his beloved country."[4] He was not alone in making the connection between wartime upheaval and postwar domestic bliss. An editorial in *Life* magazine explained, "[T]he trials and separations of war have made real to millions of Americans the beauties and contentment of home. As a sentimental notion, the home today is a great success."[5] Once the war ended, the American embrace of the domestic ideal for women was swift and, for many women, inexorable. The postwar celebration of domesticity evolved into a cold war consensus on the importance of the American housewife to the political, cultural, social, emotional, and sexual stability of the United States.[6] Domestic histories of postwar America have revealed the ways in which this focus on the domestic role of American women served national needs.

Clear and stable gender roles were crucial in offering, or at least seeming to offer, stability in a dangerous world.[7] Some of these dangers were physical, such as the threat of atomic attacks on American homes and families. Efforts to counter the atomic danger quickly became identified with gendered roles, and, in particular, the domestic role of the American woman. Katherine Howard, special advisor to the Federal Civil Defense Administration (FCDA), told the Ladies Auxiliary of Foreign Wars in stark terms the new threat to the American home: "It is my duty...to tell you today that the traditional safeguards upon which we have always relied are no longer enough to save our homes and families from harm." As atomic weaponry rendered traditional, masculine forms of defense obsolete, women and the home became the new battlefront. Howard explained, "It is in the hands of the American housewife and mother that the defense of our home front must lie...Far from being helpless bystanders, the housewives and mothers of this country have become as one with the wearers of our proud uniforms."[8] Indeed this identification was so strong that in 1956 knowledge of civil defense was made one of the requisites in the judging of the Miss American pageant.[9] The strategies which women were encouraged to deploy in this new era of defense drew from traditional housewifery. Campaigns such as "Grandma's pantry" harked back to the skills and abilities of pioneer women, encouraging housewives to stockpile the essential groceries they would need to provide for their families in the event of an atomic attack.[10] Elaine Tyler May concludes that "a major goal of these civil defense strategies was to infuse the traditional role of women with new meaning and importance, which would help fortify the home as a place of security amid the cold war."[11]

As well as ensuring that the American home had the physical capacity to withstand atomic attack from the Soviet Union, American housewives had an ideological role to play in shielding the American home from communist attack. Strongly defined gender roles served as a bulwark against internal subversion and dangerous political ideologies. Domestic cold war strength rested on the emotional, psychological, and social conditioning provided by family life as a defense against political subversion. American popular culture frequently explained political instability and consequent vulnerability to communist subversion with reference to weak or abnormal family structures. Not infrequently, fears of vulnerability to communist subversion as a result of weak domestic structures went hand in hand with fears of sexual "abnormalities" such as homosexuality or oedipal desires. American housewives then had an important role to play in ensuring the establishment of strong family relationships in order to defend against political or sexual subversion, which threatened American strength and purpose.[12]

Alongside these important ideological, cultural, and social functions, the post-Second World War cult of the housewife had a crucial economic function. As housewife-consumers, American women played a public role in the propagation of mass consumerism and thus the promotion of national security.[13] In a context where *Fortune* editor William

H. Whyte could confidently declare "thrift is now un-American," the spending power of the American housewife served a broader purpose than individual satisfaction and pleasure.[14] It is instructive to note that as domestic consumption became a public activity, it was increasingly men, rather than women, who were identified as the holders of the household purse. The 1950s saw an increasing role for men at the decision-making level of domestic consumption. One marketing study reported that "the middle class husband serves as the 'architect of the family's fiscal policy,'" with women serving as the "purchasing agent" for low expense items.[15] This model, which established the male role as the provider, not only of the funds for domestic consumption but also of the expertise and authority necessary to make purchasing decisions, pre-staged the public/private gendered divisions of the kitchen debate. While women's influence in purchasing decisions may have weakened in the face of the growing involvement and expertise of their husbands, their role in driving private demand for domestic consumption was undiminished. Marketing campaigns targeted the desires of housewives as the driving force behind American mass consumption.

American policymakers in the international field actively promoted the central role played by women as housewives in the creation of modern capitalist systems. US foreign aid to India, for example, supported the Community Development Program (CDP) launched by Nehru in 1952 and modeled upon US agricultural extension programs. CDP sought to bring about the transition of agricultural units from subsistence-based units, in which all family members worked, to for-profit production directed by the male head of family. At the same time, women were instructed in vital home science methods and goals, which created consumer demand and the need for private capital. A 1958 Ford Foundation report on the program explained American conceptions of the importance of the housewife in moving the Indian economy to a system of mass domestic consumption: "[I]f rural women learn new ways of sewing and knitting, if they become enthusiastic about better stoves, or about courtyard drains or mosquito nets, or filters for drinking water, the desire to have more money to spend for these is an incentive to change agricultural practices in the hope of a higher income."[16]

Alongside this economic development agenda, the domestic fulfillment of women became a central component in American narratives of ideological cold war rivalry. In internationally trumpeting the contentment of American housewives, the US was making an implicit (and sometimes explicit) connection between women's gendered roles and the success of the US economic, social, and cultural way of life. If the aim of civilized nations was the protection of women from lives of toil, the kitchen debate posited that the US had surpassed all other nations, and that this victory had been achieved, and could be measured, through the superiority and easy availability of the technological accoutrements of private domestic life.

Yet the use of the domestic comfort of women as a measure of American progress was not without its dangers. US information campaigns suggested that the ease of American housewives was, in part, secured by the willingness of the American husband to help out with domestic chores. A Voice of America reporter told Chinese audiences approvingly that, "Nobody thinks it beneath him to push a lawn mower, to paint a wall or to wash dishes," while a United States Information Agency (USIA) survey revealed that at least 68 percent of American men helped their wives with the grocery shopping.[17] This domestic role of the American male risked courting suggestions of unmanliness, or worse, effeminate traits. Within the US, anxiety about the impact of men's willingness to help out around the house on their ability to pursue manly cold war aims was endemic— Arthur Schlesinger Jr., for example, worried that the decline of the American male might be blamed on his eagerness to take on feminine roles around the home, "performing a whole series of what once were considered female duties."[18] In recent years scholars such as Kyle Cuordileone, Robert Dean, and Robert Corber have uncovered the extent to which anxiety over masculinity permeated American cold war culture and politics.[19] In his presidential debate with John F. Kennedy, Nixon found himself being called to account for his interest in domestic technology. "Mr. Nixon might be very experienced in kitchen debates," Kennedy quipped, "So are a great many other married men I know." Focus on the domestic sphere, Kennedy argued, weakened, rather than strengthened, the American position: "Does anyone think for one moment that Mr. Khruschev's determination to 'bury' us was slowed down one iota by all these arguments and debates?"[20] Kennedy asserted that in order to win the real battles of the cold war, American men should eschew domestic comfort and ease in favor of tough lives of struggle and competition; "I would rather take my television black and white," Kennedy manfully offered, "and have the largest rockets in the world."[21]

Anxiety about the relationship between men's role in the promotion of American domesticity and their ability to steel themselves for the tough challenge of facing down the Soviets should not just be seen as a cultural concern, but rather a significant factor in the direction of the cold war. Diplomatic and strategic decision-making processes and steely brinkmanship reflected the need to demonstrate masculine toughness and a repudiation of feminine weakness. "For Kennedy and his national security managers," Dean argues, "self- conceptions of masculine toughness were inseparable from calculations concerning for instance, the threat of communism in Latin America or the strategic dangers of appeasement in Vietnam."[22] This need to demonstrate strength drew not only from masculine rivalry with the leaders of the USSR, but also from the correlation drawn between "soft" masculinity, political weakness, communist subversion, and homosexuality during the early cold war. The "Lavender Scare" of the period, fueled in part by the efforts of Senator McCarthy, posited a relationship between effeminacy and homosexuality, and either diplomatic weakness or political subversion. Men who failed to stand up to the Soviet Union were suspect, not only politically, but sexually, as anti-communist hysteria went hand in hand with homophobic witch hunts.[23] To be too closely aligned to domesticity, for American men, risked identification with 'soft' masculinity, homosexuality, and political weakness.

The more equitable distribution of household chores between men and women suggested by USIA propaganda campaigns was, therefore, dangerous ground. The method of relieving American women of their housekeeping burdens highlighted by the kitchen debate was instead labor-saving consumer technology, made possible by the scientific advances of the American state, afforded by the economic miracle of mass consumption and judiciously selected and provided by the man of the house. This understanding of the relationship between feminine domesticity, technological skill, and mass consumption was not confined to the kitchen debate. In 1945 an advertisement for gas-fueled kitchens in *Life* magazine articulated the relationship between domestic technology, consumerism, and freedom. "More than just a Beautiful Kitchen!" the advertisement gushed to American housewives, "You want a new type of kitchen. Where everything is scientifically arranged to save time and steps ... Your 'New Freedom Gas Kitchen.'"[24]

Katherine Howard, serving as the deputy director of the American section at the 1958 Brussels International exhibition, put the economic and technological miracle of the American kitchen at the center of an ideological struggle, asserting, "[I]t is one of the wonders of the world that Americans in every economic strata have kitchens with labor-saving devices which free the American women from drudgery."[25] The idealized domestic role of the American women was used to demonstrate the civilized desires of American men to secure the comfort of their wives, the scientific expertise and technological skill of American corporations, the ability of a non-centralized, mass-consumer economy to produce a wide choice of products, and the affluence of American workers of all classes who could afford to buy these products.

In contrast, American information campaigns represented the inability of the Soviet Union to either allow the expression of private consumer desires and choices or to fulfill such desires through their centrally organized economy as predictive of the inevitable failure of their way of life. In 1951 American sociologist David Riesman put forward a satirical strategy for winning the cold war. The so-called "Nylon War," or "Operation Abundance," aimed to demonstrate the superiority of capitalism through its ability to fulfill the desires of its citizen-shoppers. Its premise was that "if allowed to sample the riches of America, the Russian people would not long tolerate masters who gave them tanks and spies instead of vacuum cleaners and beauty parlours."[26] Riesman predated the kitchen debate by eight years in his positioning of housewives at the center of the cold war struggle, arguing that "as Soviet housewives saw with their own eyes American stoves, refrigerators, clothing and toys, the Kremlin ... [would be] ... forced to change its line." Historian Susan Reid concludes that the American housewife served an important ideological function in the cold war, asserting, "[T]he happy housewife ... did service in the global politics of the cold war as an advertisement for the benefits of 'people's capitalism'. Her sister in the communist bloc, meanwhile, was constructed by Western observers as a poor, dowdy, work-worn antithesis of the American housewife."[27]

Recent scholarship on consumption in the Soviet Union in the cold war has shown the degree to which communist states responded with determined efforts to improve the domestic lives of their own women. Reid has traced the efforts of the Soviet Union to respond to the consumer demands of its population, particularly women, by increasing the production of consumer goods and domestic technology.[28] However, while the Soviet Union to some extent tacitly accepted the goal of easing the domestic toil of women, the way it sought to achieve this was radically different from the US. With already over-committed economic capacity and existing architectural limitations, the Soviet Union could not promise its housewives the individual ranch-style kitchen displayed by the Americans. Instead it sought to trumpet assistance to women through communal provision of domestic services such as state-run child care. If the American housewife in her kitchen embodied the American values of individual consumption, her Soviet counterpart embodied communist values of collectivization, communal effort, and shared ownership. In asserting a preference for the communal provision of household services, Moscow argued that the individual domestic appliances of American women were nothing less than the accoutrements of a gilded cage. One Soviet journalist explained,

> The countless domestic conveniences of the Americans...anchor to [a] woman in perpetuity her mission as "housewife" wife and cook. They make this role easier for her, but the very process of alleviating individual housework, as it were, eternalizes this way of life, turning it into a profession for the woman. But we love innovations that actually emancipate women—new types of houses with public kitchens with their canteens for everyone living in the house; with laundries where the vast machines wash clothes not just for one family alone.[29]

The means by which the burdens on women should be lifted, therefore, reflected opposing cold war ideologies and economic systems. Moreover, the Soviet Union went beyond the competition over how best to ease the lives of women by asking what their lives were being eased for. The domestic labor-saving devices and collective provision promised by the Soviet Union were intended not just "to make easier the lives of our housewives" but also to free them to spend time pursuing other, implicitly more important, interests, such as work and political participation. The Soviets suggested that it was the communist system that best served the interests of its female citizens by giving women political, economic, and civic equality with men. The Kremlin argued that if the status of women was indeed a barometer of the progress of a nation, then this status should be understood by her place in politics, economics, and society, not her place in the home. It interpreted the US vision of the domestic life of women as a demonstration of the lack of equality available to women in the west as opposed to the fulfillment of women's natural roles.

The arena in which the Soviet sponsorship of women's equality as a measure of their status took place was the new forums of international governance, specifically those established at the United Nations, such as the United Nations Economic and Social Council (ECOSOC), the Commission on the Status of Women (CSW), and the Commission on Human Rights (CHR). With the establishment of these bodies, the use of women's status as a measure of the progress and prestige of the nation-state became enshrined in the institutions of internationalism, wherein the measure of women's status was no longer a vague reference to women's protected status and lives of ease but hard statistical evidence on economic and political equality. If Nixon felt confident that the US could win the battle for women's status in the kitchen, the Soviets felt confident that they could win the battle in the CSW, where hard facts and resolutions took the place of beguiling pictures of washing machines and range stoves. Discussions of women's status in the early years of ECOSOC, the CSW, and the CHR were dominated by rival claims to national superiority. *The New York Times* reported on an ECOSOC resolution of August 7, 1948, which called on members to take measures to give women equal rights in everything concerning "employment and remuneration thereof, leisure, social insurance and professional training." The paper reported that "Russian speakers conducted a campaign to prove that women in the US and other western countries lived underprivileged lives under the tutelage of men. By contrast... women in Russia live independent lives, have equal rights with men and get special consideration in industry when they are taking care of babies." The article determined that the resolution itself was meaningless in terms of prompting countries to take action but concluded, "It is quite clear... that the Russians regard the subject as a highly useful propaganda subject with which to 'needle' the US."[30]

The status of women quickly became a cold war battleground at the United Nations. The position of the Soviet Union on the issue constituted a challenge to US attempts to measure the status of women by the protection of domesticity. Delegates to the UN from the USSR and its satellites attacked the lack of political and economic equality guaranteed to women in the USA, contrasting it with the political and economic equality enjoyed by women in communist states. At a debate in the CHR in 1952, Mr. Morozov (USSR) asserted, "In the United States, despite what that country's representative [Eleanor Roosevelt] has affirmed, inequality between men and women was not confined to important posts alone. The United States Congress had refused ever since 1923 to adopt a bill to ensure equality between men and women... [Statistics show] that in the USSR many important posts, particularly judicial ones, were held by women who also served as representatives of the people, held the highest decorations and had distinguished themselves in agronomy, science, literature and the arts."[31]

The CSW bore the brunt of Soviet criticism of women's roles under capitalism. At the second session of the Commission, in 1948, the Kremlin's delegate, Nina Popova, quoted from articles of the Soviet constitution that guaranteed its citizens equal treatment for men and women. Popova argued that Soviet women, "could and did hold the highest positions... [T]he economic position of women in other countries left much to be desired... The position of women was a true measure of the democracy of any country and... the Union of Soviet Socialist Republics was an inspiring example to all democratic countries." Evdokia Uralova of Byelorussian Soviet Socialist Republic chimed in with her support; "The question of political, economic and social rights of women was always a true yardstick of democracy in any country."[32]

These contributions reveal the eagerness of the Soviet Union to establish a framework for measuring women's status that differed dramatically from that of the US. As with their promotion of collective redress in order to elevate women's domestic burden, the USSR sought to connect political and economic equality between the sexes with the collectivist ethos of the communist state. At a CSW discussion in January 1948, Popova asserted that "the approach to the problem of greater use of the franchise by women had been successfully solved in her country where every effort had been made to ensure that the economic situation of women and their cultural and social development was such as to enable them to make full use of the franchise." Popova asserted that the state provision of child care was a key factor in ensuring that women were able to exercise their equality.

She explained that "nursing homes provided to take care of children [gave] ... women the free time necessary to take part in public life."[33] The Soviet Union submitted a resolution to the CSW in 1948 which recommended that "women [should be] granted equal rights with men to employment and remuneration thereby, leisure, social insurance and education. These rights must be guaranteed by the law of the land and also by the State protection of the interests of mother and children, by state assistance for mothers of large families and mothers living alone, by granting women paid maternity leave, and by the development of a comprehensive network of maternity homes, day nurseries and kindergartens." The Byelorussian delegate supported the proposal and added that "in Byelorussia the equality of women with men was safeguarded. Women were economically equal with men. The State provided them with help for their children so that domestic duties should not interfere with their exercise of political rights."[34]

The USSR derided the doctrine of domesticity for women as an expression of women's imprisonment and lowly status, an approach which was particularly noticeable in the Soviet bride debates at the UN. In 1947 Moscow outlawed marriages between Soviet citizens and foreigners, putting a series of impossible hurdles in the way of Soviet citizens who sought to leave the USSR in order to join their spouses. While the US routinely attacked the lack of freedom of movement in the communist world, these efforts to "legislate affairs of the heart," as one journalist termed it, became a cause célèbre in the western world.[35] In the face of constant pressure from the West, the Soviets argued that their refusal to grant exit visas to Russian brides was not a reflection of their imprisonment; on the contrary, they were saving their women from lives of domestic drudgery in the West; UN delegate Alexei Pavlov claimed that the Soviet government was protecting these women from a future as "kitchen slaves."

These competing interpretations of the measurement of the status of women constituted a new cold war battleground—one which the US was anxious not to lose. A meeting of the State Department's subcommittee on Human Rights and the Status of Women in October 1948 acknowledged: "Each and every item on the Status of women ... must be conceived as part of a hard fought program which can be used by the eastern bloc for any audience to point up possible weaknesses in other nations, attract support from disaffected groups ... [and] ... influence people behind the Iron Curtain and those elsewhere likely to respond to USSR leadership."[36] The US response in the UN was to prioritize the domestic role of women over their formal political role. When *United Nations News* asked US delegate to the CSW, Lorena Hahn, what subjects debated at the Commission most interested her, she replied, "I think it is family relationships, those in the normal or happy family."[37] Furthermore, the US asserted that the relatively low figures of women in public office should be seen as a reflection of American women's freedom of choice and their preference for a domestic role. In response to the accusation by the Polish delegate to the Commission that in the United States "the granting of equal rights to women in public life is still a question for the future," the US Women's Bureau advised that "this is the result of free choice on the part of most women, who evidently prefer the comfort and privacy of their own homes to the grilling experiences of political campaigns and the responsibility of major public office."[38]

While defending the domestic role of the American women, the US also sought to discredit Soviet claims of women's equality under communist rule. In widely reported comments to the New York Women's Press Club, Dorothy Kenyon, the first US delegate the CSW, questioned Soviet claims for women's political equality, pointing out "that there had never been a woman member of the Politburo and that there was now none either on the central committee of the communist party." *The New York Times* reported Kenyon's assertions that "the Russians made much propaganda of the fact that twenty one percent of the Supreme Soviet is made up of women." Kenyon remarked that "this was of no significance, as the body sits only a few days a year for unanimous approval of government proposals." Furthermore, she continued "[I]n newspaper pictures of Moscow celebrations [...] there are not even women used as window dressing. Paper participation in government is too flimsy a foundation to advance the principles of democracy or of women's rights."[39]

Alongside these public pronouncements on the status of women, the US also funded information campaigns to counteract what they saw as a Soviet propaganda offensive on the issue of women's rights. Campaigns by the USIA described the contented lives of American women, stressing their interest in family life and community work. Covertly, the CIA siphoned funding to a women's group, the Committee of Correspondence, which used its contacts with women's groups across the world to challenge Soviet propaganda, which suggested that women's lives would be improved by communism.[40]

US/USSR rivalry dominated early cold war debates on the status of women in a manner that frustrated campaigns for international women's rights. The work of the CSW was hampered by cold war intransigence and the repetitive incantation of rival claims on women's status. International women's associations, which had long served as advocates for the advancement of women's rights, found their work complicated by the global politics of the cold war, with national loyalties and diplomatic alliances complicating international organization and activism. While the ideological positions of the US and the USSR on the status of women limited discussion on the causes and cures of women's discrimination, narrower cold war strategic alliances also had a notable impact on the advance of international women's rights. The 1975 Mexico City conference on women, which has been recognized by many historians as ushering in a new era of women's international activism, was itself the result of cold war rivalries. The proposal for a UN International Women's Year came from the Women's International Democratic Foundation, a communist-dominated organization whose consultative status at the CSW had been suspended between 1954 and 1967 as a result of cold war wrangling. Once the plan for the IWY had received UN approval, Warsaw Pact countries planned to mark the occasion with a women's conference in East Berlin. In an effort to ensure that the cause of women's rights was not dominated by communist nations, the US State Department gave its support to a UN sponsored conference for women in Mexico City. The conference in Mexico City was designed to develop plans to promote the equal rights of women. Although many participants resented what they saw as the intrusion of politics into efforts toward the global improvement of women's status, current affairs inevitably directed some of the proceedings at

Mexico City. The issue of the US sponsored overthrow of the Allende government in Chile, for example, caused a mass walkout of delegates.[41]

While the cold war thus continued to influence women's international rights, the Mexico City conference highlighted some of the significant ideological and institutional challenges to the early cold war framing of international women's rights as a choice between US and USSR visions of women's roles. By the mid-1960s, multiple challenges had emerged to these binary positions, which represented the USSR as promoting women's public role and the US defending her private role. Within the US itself in the early 1960s, cracks were beginning to appear in the ubiquitous idealization of the housewife. Betty Friedan's 1963 work *The Feminine Mystique* ruthlessly interrogated the American promotion of the housewife role. Ironically echoing many of the criticisms that Soviet journalists and politicians had made, Friedan argued that the American housewife was less a contented role model and more a frustrated captive. Friedan's work was hugely significant in sparking the second wave feminist movement in the US, which would demand government support for American women's public roles as workers, politicians, athletes, scientists, students, and more. Women who had been politically active in the civil rights and New Left movements swelled the ranks of American feminism still further. As women who had protested against these social injustices became increasingly aware of the sexism both of mainstream society and of the very protest movement in which they were participating, they took their experience and insight into campaigns for women's equality and an end to discrimination on account of sex.[42]

By the early 1960s groups within the United States were questioning the concentration on women's domestic role and moving toward an acknowledgment of the role of government in protecting the rights and equality of women. The time was ripe for such a challenge. The launching of the Sputnik in October 1957 had sent shockwaves through the US, convincing many that misguided pursuit of mass consumption and leisure on the part of the American people had given the Soviets the opportunity to shoot ahead. For some Americans the ability of the USSR to make such dramatic scientific breakthroughs was testament not to the achievements of their men but to their willingness to utilize female talent. The 1963 USSR's launching of the first woman astronaut, Valentina Vladimirovna Tereshkova, appeared to offer further proof that the national successes of the Soviet Union were the result of their willingness to develop the public potential of both men and women.[43]

While one set of cold war demands, therefore, had promoted the need for American women to pursue private roles as a housewife, a different set of demands required support for her public role. Further pressure on the federal government came from the American labor movement and the feminist movement, both of which had worked throughout the 1950s for government support for American women as workers. The Equal Pay Act of 1963 and the removal of statutory restrictions on the number of women serving as officers in the military represented significant steps in the US government's recognition of American women's public role.[44] While the US government still overtly promoted the importance of American women's role as a homemaker, legal and institutional frameworks were gradually but inexorably shifting toward government protection of woman's public, rather than her private, role.

While challenges were appearing within the US to the housewife model, in the international arena a significant shift occurred in the approach to the cause and cure of women's inequality. Since its establishment in 1946 the dominant focus of the UN Commission on the Status of Women had been on legal and political methods for ensuring women's rights. Its early work concentrated on securing women's rights through declarations, conventions, and treaties such as the Convention on the Political Rights of Women (1952), the Convention on the Nationality of Married Women (1957), and the Convention on the Consent to Marriage (1962).[45] This approach had facilitated the imposition of cold war paradigms on the women's rights agenda by fostering an understanding of women's rights as an expression of the relationship between the nation-state and its women citizens. Within this framework debates over whether US or USSR leadership offered the best chance to secure women's equality seemed appropriate responses to the challenge of improving women's status. By the mid-1960s, however, the influence of two emerging groups challenged this state-centered approach. First, the emergence of both the non-aligned movement (NAM) and of newly independent, post-colonial states meant that women from outside the east-west coalitions of the cold war were able to bring a new understanding of women's rights to international forums. The inclusion of non-aligned and post-colonial nations in formal international organizations resulted in a dramatically different agenda on women's rights than that which had prevailed during the early phase of the cold war. As Davaki Jain and Shubha Chacko argue, "In contrast to the conceptualization of issues relating to women's status as social or cultural phenomenon and that predominated in other bodies in the early 1960s... [the NAM's] analysis of women in development was sharper and reflected a more complex understanding of the interconnection between trends in women's role and status in their societies and the nature and pattern of development processes."[46]

Second, the growing influence of the international women's movement was instrumental in challenging cold war paradigms on women's status. Expectations of cold war national conformity undoubtedly had a stifling impact on the efforts of women's international associations in the early cold war period, as women's groups struggled to organize and unite across the iron curtain.[47] As international NGOs grew in size, authority, and expertise throughout the 1950s and 1960s, however, they played an increasingly influential role in setting the global agenda.[48] The emerging role of women's NGOs forced the fracturing of the early cold war binary dynamic, wresting control of the direction of international women's rights from state-led efforts, and encouraging a more grassroots approach to identifying the cause of and solution to women's inequalities. The growing importance of women's NGOS can be tracked through their participation in the international conferences of women organized by the UN in the decade for women 1975–85. Six thousand women participated as NGO representatives at Mexico City in 1975, 7,000 in Copenhagen in 1980, and 14,000 at Nairobi in 1985. Bitter differences of opinion were evident, as women from different regions disputed questions of ideology and approach. The question of reproductive rights, for example, central to women's liberation movements in Western Europe and North America, was seen as less important to feminists from the global South than issues of economic exploitation. Despite profound differences, however, women's groups were able to develop strong international networks, which have taken a radically different approach to women's rights than that which was contained within early cold war paradigms. Their advocacy served to redirect the agenda on women's international rights to issues such as women's rights as human rights, the impact of development policies on women's lives, reproductive rights, and violence against women.[49]

The influence of these two groups resulted in a move away from cold war alliances and strategies as the framework for women's international rights and toward an agenda more in tune with UN trends. Debates over whether US or USSR leadership offered the best chance to secure women's equality, through their espousal of different models of women's roles, were replaced by far more complex approaches to women's rights. The declaration of the United Nations that the 1960s would be the "decade of development" directed the agenda of the CSW in new ways, making the old dichotomies of the early cold war period seem outdated and overly dogmatic. New critiques of discrimination against women focused, not on legal or political inequality, but on the impact of colonialism, poverty, development policy, and cultural prejudices on women's status. In 1962, the General Assembly firmly directed the CSW toward the development agenda, requesting that they direct their attention to plans for a long-term strategy to address the advancement of women in the developing world.

While work on legal regulation of women's rights continued apace, with the General Assembly requesting in 1963 that the CSW begin work on what would become the Convention on the Elimination of All Forms of Discrimination against Women (CEDAW), the development agenda was becoming increasingly central to the work of the UN. Former UN Secretary-General Boutros Boutros-Ghali has argued that the expansion of the UN in the 1960s and 1970s to include newly independent nations had a profound impact on the direction of women's rights, as "[t]he role of economic relations between developed and developing nations, which directly and indirectly affected the lives of women, increasingly overshadowed debates over women's legal equality."[50] The influence of newly independent states, the burgeoning international feminist movement, and the emerging agency of women of the global South ensured that the narrow paradigms of the early cold war could no longer dominate discussions on international women's rights.

Nixon and Khrushchev's jovial invitation to "drink to the ladies" reflected a world in which women's rights were understood as the gift of overwhelmingly male-led nation-states. The confidence of the nation-state in its ability to both define the cause of women's inequality, and to deliver the solution, was embodied in the swagger of Nixon and Khrushchev during the kitchen debate. This confidence, however, was undermined as new conceptual and structural frameworks on women's rights emerged in the 1970s. As both newly independent states and increasingly confident women's international associations challenged the narrow cold war approach to the global challenge of women's rights, more complex understandings of the difficulty in securing the status of women emerged. Emily Rosenberg has categorized this new approach as representing "a tradition of trans-national networks which emphasize both global issues and locally specific concerns related to human welfare and women's empowerment."[51] Its emergence has not rendered redundant the old approach which promotes and celebrates the role of what are still overwhelmingly male-led nation-states in protecting women; Rosenberg has drawn our attention to the powerful narratives of male rescue that accompanied the US-led inter-vention into Afghanistan in 2001, for example. What we see in the challenge to early cold war paradigms on women's rights, then, is not a transition from one approach to another, but a bifurcation of approaches.

The nuanced and complex understanding of the relationship between discrimination against women and issues such as globalization, cultural prejudices and expectations, and family structure which emerged in the 1960s and 70s challenged the relationship between women's rights and state power which had allowed women's rights to become a cold war battlefield. In the future, while celebrations of the role of nation-states in the protection of women could and did continue, such celebrations would be contested by those who sought to promote the rights of women as a matter of global justice, not a manifestation of national benevolence.

## Notes

1. Karal Ann Marling, *As Seen on TV: The Visual Culture of Everyday life in the 1950s* (Cambridge, MA: Harvard University Press, 1994), 280.
2. See for example Antoinette Burton, ed., *Gender, Sexuality and Colonial Modernities* (London: Routledge, 1999); Anne McClintock, *Imperial Leather: Race, Gender and Sexuality in the Colonial Contest* (London: Routledge, 1995).
3. Emily S. Rosenberg, "Consuming Women: Images of Americanization in the American Century," *Diplomatic History* 23/3 (Summer 1999): 479–97, at 481.
4. Mary Anderson, "The Post-war Role of American women," *The American Economic Review* 34/1 (March 1944): 237–44.
5. *Life*, January 22, 1945, 63.
6. See Elaine Tyler May, *Homeward Bound: American Families in the Cold War Era* (New York: Basic Books, 1988).
7. See May, *Homeward Bound*; Paul Boyer, *By the Bomb's Early Light* (Chapel Hill, NC: University of North Carolina Press, 1994); Laura McEnaney, *Civil Defense Begins at Home: Militarization meets Everyday Life in the Fifties* (Princeton, NJ: Princeton University Press, 2000).
8. Katherine Howard, "Address before the National Encampment of the Veterans of Foreign Wars," Milwaukee, August 5, 1953. Katherine Graham Howard papers, Schlesinger Library, Radcliffe College, Boston, box 1, folder 3.
9. Federal Civil Defense Administration Newsletter, 16, 1956, Jean Wood Fuller papers 1954–6, Schlesinger Library, Radcliffe College, Boston, file 1.
10. See May, *Homeward Bound*, 104–5.

11. May, *Homeward Bound*, 105.

12. Miriam G. Reumann, *American Sexual Character: Sex, Gender and National Identity in the Kinsey Reports* (Berkeley, CA: University of California Press, 2006); Geoffrey Smith, "National Security and Personal Isolation: Sex, Gender and Disease in the Cold War United States," *International History Review* 14/2 (May 1992): 307–37; Jane Sherron De Hart, "Containment at Home: Gender, Sexuality and National Identity in Cold War America," in Peter J. Kuznick and James Gilbert, eds., *Rethinking Cold War Culture* (Washington, DC: Smithsonian Institution Press, 2001); Michael Rogin, "Kiss me Deadly: Communism, Motherhood and Cold War Movies," *Representations* 6 (Spring 1984): 1–36.

13. See Lizabeth Cohen, *A Consumer's Republic: The Politics of Mass Consumption in Post-War America* (New York: Vintage, 1998).

14. Cohen, *A Consumer's Republic*, 121.

15. Cohen, *A Consumer's Republic*, 148.

16. Cited in Kim Berry, "Lakshmi and the Scientific Housewife: A Transnational Account of Indian Women's Development and Production of an Indian Modernity," *Economic and Political Weekly* 38/11 (March 2003): 1059.

17. Laura Belmonte, *Selling the American Way: US Propaganda and the Cold War* (Philadelphia, PA: University of Pennsylvania Press, 2008), 149.

18. Arthur Schlesinger Jr., "The Crisis of American Masculinity" (1958), in *The Politics of Hope and The Bitter Heritage: American Liberalism in the 1960s* (Princeton, NJ: Princeton University Press, 2008), 291.

19. See for example Kyle A. Cuordileone, *Manhood and American Popular Culture in the Cold War* (New York: Routledge, 2005); Robert Corber, *Homosexuality in Cold War America: Resistance and the Crisis of Masculinity* (Durham, NC: Duke University Press, 1997), Robert Dean, *Imperial Brotherhood: Gender and the Making of Cold War Foreign Policy* (Boston, MA: University of Massachusetts Press, 2001).

20. Robert Dean, "Masculinity as Ideology: John F. Kennedy and the Domestic Politics of Foreign Policy," *Diplomatic History* 22/1 (Winter 1998): 29–62, at 45.

21. Dean, "Masculinity as Ideology," 46.

22. Dean, "Masculinity as Ideology," 30.

23. See David K. Johnson, *The Lavender Scare: The Cold War Persecution of Gays and Lesbians in the Federal Government* (Chicago, IL: University of Chicago Press, 2004).

24. *Life*, February 12, 1945, Advertisement for Gas, 111.

25. Rosenberg, "Consuming Women," 488.

26. David Riesman, "The Nylon War" (1951), in *Abundance for What? And other Essays* (London: Chatto and Windus, 1964), 63.

27. Susan E. Reid, "'Our Kitchen is Just as Good!' Soviet Responses to the American Kitchen," in Ruth Oldenziel and Karen Zachmann, eds., *Cold War Kitchen: Americanization, Technology and European Users* (Cambridge, MA: MIT Press, 2009), 83–112, at 83.

28. Susan E. Reid, "Cold War Kitchen: Gender and the De-Stalinization of Consumer Taste in the Soviet Union under Khruschev," *Slavic Review* 61/2 (Summer 2002): 211–52.

29. Mariette Shaginian, cited by Reid, "'Our Kitchen is just as Good,'" 104.

30. "UN Council Votes Equal Rights for Women," *New York Times*, August 7, 1948.

31. UNESCO, Commission on Human Rights Meeting, New York, May 20, 1952 (E/CN.4/SR.301). *National Women's Party Papers 1913–1974* (Microfilming Corporation of America, 1979), series VII, reel 146.

32. Commission on the Status of Women, second session, New York, January 7, 1948. The National Women's Party Papers 1913–1974, (NWP papers hereafter), series VII, reel 145 Microfilming Corporation of America (1979, Sanford, North Carolina).

33. Resolution submitted by the delegation of the Union of Soviet Socialist Republics, January 1948. *NWP papers*, series VII, reel 145.

34. Commission on Status of Women, second session, New York, January 8, 1948. *NWP papers*, series VII, reel 145.

35. Susan L. Carruthers, *Cold War Captives: Imprisonment, Escape and Brainwashing* (Berkeley, CA: University of California Press, 2009), 43.

36. Meeting of the Subcommittee on Human Rights and Status of Women, October 4, 1948, Division of Special Services and Publications, General records, 1918–62, Records of the Women's Bureau 1892–1972: Records of the International Division, (WB papers hereafter), box 12 National Archive's and Records Administration (NARA), College Park, MD).

37. "A Delegate from the Great Plains of the USA," *United Nations News for Women Broadcasters*, 1953, *NWP papers*, series VII, reel 145.

38. Office memo to Miss Miller from Sara Buchanan, September 29, 1949, Status of Women: Replies to Points of Criticism raised by Polish and USSR representatives, WB papers, box 3.

39. *New York Times*, December 16, 1948.

40. See Helen Laville, *Cold War Women: The International Activities of American Women's Organisations* (Manchester, Manchester University Press, 2002).

41. See Jocelyn Olcott, "Globalizing Sisterhood: International Women's Year and the Politics of Representation," in Niall Ferguson, Charles S. Maier, Erez Manela, and Daniele J Sargent, eds., *The Shock of the Global: The 1970s in Perspective* (Cambridge, MA: Belknap Press, 2010), 281–93.

42. See Sara Evans, *Personal Politics: The Roots of Women's Liberation in the Civil Rights Movement and the New Left* (New York: Vintage Books, 1980).

43. See Petra Goedde, "World Cultures since 1945," in Akira Iriye *Global Interdependence: The World Since 1945. Vol. 6 of The History of the World* (Cambridge, MA: Harvard University Press, 2013).

44. Cynthia Harrison, "A 'New Frontier' for Women: The Public Policy of the Kennedy Administration," *Journal of American History* 67/3 (December 1980): 630–46.

45. A notable exception to this approach was the early work of the Commission on the issue of customs and traditions that harmed women, such as widow burning, genital mutilation, and childhood marriage.

46. Davaki Jain and Shubha Chacko, "Walking Together: The Journey of the Non-Aligned Movement and the Women's Movement," *Development in Practice* 19/7 (2009): 895–905, at 898.

47. Francisca de Haan, "Continuing Cold War Paradigms in Western Historiography of Transnational Women's Organisations: The Case of the Women's International Democratic Federation (WIDF)," *Women's History Review* 19:4 (September 2010): 547–73.

48. See Peter Willetts, "From Consultative Arrangements to Partnership: The Changing Status of NGOs in Diplomacy at the United Nations," *Global Governance* 6 (April-June 2000): 191–212.

49. See for example Margaret E. Keck and Kathryn Sikkink, *Activists beyond Borders: Advocacy Networks in International Politics* (Ithaca, NY: Cornell University Press, 1998).

50. Boutros Boutros-Ghali, "Introduction," *The United Nations and the Advancement of Women*, United Nations Blue Book Series, Vol. VI (New York: Department of Public Information, United Nations, 1995), 26.

51. Emily Rosenberg, "Rescuing Women and Children," *The Journal of American History* 89/2 (September 2002): 465.

## SELECT BIBLIOGRAPHY

Belmonte, Laura. *Selling the American Way: US Propaganda and the Cold War*. Philadelphia, PA: University of Pennsylvania Press, 2008.

Cuordileone, Kyle A. *Manhood and American Popular Culture in the Cold War*. New York: Routledge, 2005.

de Haan, Francisca. "Continuing Cold War Paradigms in Western Historiography of Transnational Women's Organisations: The Case of the Women's International Democratic Federation (WIDF)", *Women's History Review* 19/4 (September 2010): 547–73.

Laville, Helen. *Cold War Women: The International Activities of American Women's Organisations*. Manchester: University of Manchester Press, 2002.

Marling, Karal Ann. *As Seen on TV: The Visual Culture of Everyday life in the 1950s*. Cambridge, MA: Harvard University Press, 1994.

May, Elaine Tyler. *Homeward Bound: American Families in the Cold War Era*. New York: Basic Books, 1988.

Meyerwitz, Joanne, ed. *Not June Cleaver: Women and Gender in Post-War America 1945–1960*. Philadelphia, PA: Temple University Press, 1994.

Oldenziel, Ruth and Karen Zachmann (eds). *Cold War Kitchen: Americanization, Technology and European Users*. Cambridge, MA: MIT Press, 2009.

Rosenberg, Emily. "Foreign Affairs after World War II: Connecting Sexual and International Politics," *Diplomatic History* 18 (Winter 1994): 59–70.

Weigand, Kate. "The Red Menace: The Feminine Mystique, and Ohio Un-American Activities Commission: Gender and Anti-communism in Ohio, 1951–54," *Journal of Women's History* 3 (Winter 1992): 70–94.

# CHAPTER 31

# THE RELIGIOUS COLD WAR

## DIANNE KIRBY

THE tendency of the popular imagination to carve out reassuring patterns and continuities from the historical record has cast the cold war as one of history's great religious wars, between the godless and the god-fearing, certainly, but above all, between good and evil. The reality, however, was far more complex—more about lesser and greater evils, about predominant power more than universal ideals; and religion, rather than the champion of one side and the victim of the other, could be both a willing accomplice or a fervent opponent either side of the ideological divide. The religious, of course, had their own agendas, be it survival and some sort of role in the communist bloc or influence and a voice in the corridors of power in the western world. In the global South, religion often proved a bulwark of the status quo, but there were also elements that joined local struggles, from basic land reform to national independence. Although the responses varied tremendously, organized religion was accorded a notable role in the cold war drama that was to have profound consequences for the nature and the conduct of the conflict and the legacy it bequeathed.[1]

When John Foster Dulles heard that Jawaharlal Nehru had refused to sign the 1951 Treaty of Peace with Japan, partly because it omitted the Soviet Union and China, he told Nehru's sister, Ambassador Vijay Lakshmi Pandit, "I cannot accept this. Does your Prime Minister realise that I have prayed at every stage of this treaty?" Pandit was "at a loss for words." Dulles was not challenging the notion that a secular society is a basic element of a democratic one. He was simply revealing the significance religion had assumed in the American approach to cold war politics. In the competition with the Soviet Union, Americans presented religion as the cornerstone of their democracy, whilst they accorded Soviet atheism, contrasted with US religiosity, a central role in defining the nature of the conflict. The US made religion the measure not simply for a nation's morality and justice, but, above all, for democracy and freedom. These, of course, were the very qualities the Soviet Union supposedly lacked and the US held in surfeit. It was an approach that severely undermined traditional modes of diplomacy, with serious consequences for dialogue and negotiation in the international arena, and the conduct of the cold war. It also had global implications for the ongoing contest between secularization and religion.[2]

What I have termed the "religious cold war," can be seen as supporting J.L. Segundo's contention that "… the most common and perhaps primitive function of explicit and recordable religions has been 'ideological'… they have served as instruments for any and every class of values." Another perspective derives from the contested politics of secularism. A socially constructed form of political authority that emerged out of a profoundly Christian Westphalian moral order, secularism influenced ways of organizing religion and politics East and West. The US and the Soviet Union had each in their different ways experienced "a public struggle over authoritative, historically contingent, and often state enforced divisions between the secular, the sacred and the political." Secularism, a social, historical, and political construct, exists in a variety of different forms, the boundaries of which are constantly subjected to ongoing negotiation and mediation.[3]

Today it is clear that there was never anything inevitable about the inexorable forward march of secularism as the companion to modernization, as many scholars once assumed. The uneasy peace between Europe's Catholics and Protestants in the 17th century initially precipitated what eventually became the transformation of Europe into a religiously pluralistic continent. Religion, moreover, despite the secularizing tendencies of the 19th century, always remained part of the "dominant ideology," as illustrated during both world wars when all Christian belligerents invoked it as part of their respective war efforts. The existing nexus between religion, politics, and the global arena was reinforced by the cold war as each side proclaimed universal values and sought religious legitimation. On a global level, the cold war highlighted the extent to which secularist divisions between religion and politics were far from stable and frequently contested.[4]

Cold war divisions presented the world's societies with two competing models of modernization: the communist-socialist, represented by the Soviet Union, versus the liberal capitalist, represented by the US. They also offered two competing trajectories of secularism: laicism and Judeo-Christian secularism. Elizabeth Shakman Hurd outlines critical distinctions between the two rival strategies for managing the relationship between religion and politics. The former represents a separationist narrative in which religion is excluded from politics. The latter is a more accommodationist narrative that presents the Judeo-Christian tradition as the unique basis of secular democracy. Whilst each trajectory defends the separation of church and state, they do so in different ways and with different justifications and political effects. Laicism is portrayed as pretending to neutrality with regard to the assumption that it is both possible and desirable to achieve a fixed and final separation between religion and politics. Although seemingly above and beyond the separation debate, the politics of laicism is in fact profoundly complex.

In contrast, rather than repudiating religion Judeo-Christian secularism sees itself as the basis for secular public order and democratic political institutions. It perceives its dispositions and cultural instincts as having culminated in and contributed to the unique western achievement of the separation of church and state, one that allows political order in the West to remain firmly embedded in a common set of core values derived from Latin Christendom. A set of values that western cold war propaganda insisted were threatened by the Soviet Union, designated the vehicle of a godless and aggressive ideology that sought the destruction of western civilization and Christianity.[5]

When the world of sovereign states that followed the 1648 Peace of Westphalia removed the historical tendency of polities to intervene within other polities to change religious beliefs and practices, it challenged the notion of universal and transcendent values. Two hundred years later the *Communist Manifesto* articulated a secular system of values that challenged both the Wesphalian settlement and religion itself. Yet, in October 1917 the Bolsheviks declared the new Soviet State to be non-religious, not anti-religious. In 1903, the Second Congress of the Russian Social Democratic Labor Party had demanded separation of church and state and church and school, whilst insisting on unrestricted freedom of conscience. The Bolshevik decree of 1918 "on freedom of conscience and religious societies" theoretically safeguarded "Free practice of religious customs," and religious believers were not denied admission to the party because opposition to religion was subordinated to the class struggle. Still, N.I. Bukharin and E.O. Preobrazhensky's *ABC of Communism*, which popularized the party program of 1919, advocated attacking religious institutions and popular religious prejudices. Nonetheless, some religious bodies, Christian and Muslim, flourished under the new regime. Indeed, the Roman Curia welcomed the Bolshevik separation of church and state. This blow to Russian Orthodoxy revived Vatican aspirations to convert Russia to Roman Catholicism. The 1922 Conference of Genoa witnessed the Bolshevik Foreign Minister, Georgi Chicherin, and the Pope's representative, the Archbishop of Genoa, toasting one another in public. However, the Vatican was less pleased that the change in church–state relations was also an opportunity for various Protestant bodies. Evangelical Christians increased their adherents from about 100,000 to over a million in the first decade of Soviet rule.[6]

Arto Luukkanen's research into attitudes toward religion amongst the Bolshevik elites has shown not only the degree to which there was a notable failure to understand Russian religion in all its manifestations, but also how there was not even an agreed religious policy. All levels of the party contained fierce opponents of religion along with moderate sympathizers toward it, and even believers. Wider political and economic considerations usually mattered more than ideological imperatives. Rather than a single office that oversaw religious policy, there arose a series of overlapping initiatives and commissions, all subject to wide local and regional variations, as well as bureaucratic confusion. Under-resourced policies that vacillated between repression and concession, marked by compromise and confusion, were inevitably ineffective and indeed counter-productive. Moreover, the enthusiastic implementation of campaign-like initiatives often produced outcomes at variance with what was intended by central planners. The defects and contradictions of anti-religious institutions such as the Central Standing Commission on Religious Questions (CSCRQ) and the League of the Militant Godless (LMG) reveal the extent to which the Soviets lacked a coherent, intelligible plan to construct an atheist state. Moreover, the low value placed on the work of such institutions, their under-resourcing and lack of direction, suggests that the eradication of religion was far from a government priority. Nonetheless, although the March 1919 Communist Party program, in order not to strengthen religious fanaticism, had warned against offending religious sentiments, religious harassment and persecution, however ad hoc and inconsistent, marked the history of the post-revolutionary years. Moreover, Stalin's more militant anti-religious policies, linked to five year plans, meant an alienated population and a weaker state that was to have significant repercussions in the confrontation with Hitler.[7]

On the very first day of the Nazi invasion, Stalin, responsible for taking the Russian Orthodox Church to the verge of institutional elimination in Russia, was violently confronted by the extent to which his attitude toward and treatment of the church had weakened his regime. It proved to be easing Hitler's way and hindering potential Western support against him. It is notable, therefore, that the Russian Orthodox Patriarch's voice was the first to rally the people against the Nazis. Religion subsequently became a crucial consideration in defeating Hitler, maintaining the wartime Alliance, securing the territories newly incorporated into the Soviet sphere, and in strategically spreading Soviet influence. Stalin had had emphatically impressed upon him the extent to which authoritative cultural and religious systems of belief and practice were powerful determinants that he could neither ignore nor overcome, but which he could use to his advantage. Throughout the Soviet bloc, the nexus between religion and national identity, the congruence, at times, of church–state interests, not to mention the importance of religion in the rest of the world, meant it had to be given consideration by Soviet policy-makers. Kremlin policies toward religion evolved according to changing circumstances. In the cold war battle for hearts and minds, Western policy-makers, far from having a monopoly of religious sentiment, had to reckon with Stalin's fundamental pragmatism, bolstered to some extent by the basic propositions of Marxist philosophy toward religion, plus the long-standing practice of compromise in Soviet–church relations. In the postwar period Stalin's need to reduce anti-Soviet hostility within and without the communist bloc, as well as his desire to improve his regime's image abroad, militated against the crude anti-religious policies that had previously helped the West promote a negative, indeed demonic, image of communism and the Soviet leadership.[8]

Unable to eradicate religious faith and confronted with its power and persistence, Stalin came to see the potential advantages of accommodating to and working with it. Marx, after all, had emphasized religion's progressive aspects before his reference to its narcotic effects, stating that: "Religious suffering is, at one and the same time, the *expression* of real suffering and a *protest* against real suffering." Progressive, radical, and even revolutionary movements can and have taken religious form, as well as being led and supported by those of religious faith. Neither Marx nor Engels in their various discussions of religion treated it as simple folly or deception, but "always as distorted reflections and expressions of real social needs and interests." It was not, however, Marxist considerations that dictated Stalin's behavior toward religion. The persecution to which Stalin subjected religion in the interwar period ignored Engels' observation that "persecution is the best means of promoting undesirable convictions." In a Stalinist environment that suppressed all opposition, real, potential, and imagined, it was inevitable that religion would be persecuted—not simply as an undesirable conviction, or even for faith or doctrine, but because it was a potential Trojan horse, a focal point for counter-revolution and dissent.[9]

Stalin's new support for religion was as much at odds with Marxist philosophy as was its repression. Marxism insists that religion should be a private matter in relation to the state, with complete freedom of religion. In 1905 Lenin clarified the stance a state should adopt:

> Religion must be of no concern to the state, and religious societies must have no connection with governmental authority. Everyone must be absolutely free to profess any religion he pleases, or no religion whatever.... Discrimination among citizens on account of their religious convictions is wholly intolerable.[10]

Marxism opposes the establishment of state churches or any state privileges for religion. Yet Stalin implemented links and structures intended to secure compliant religious institutions responsive to top-down authoritarian policies. Moreover, Stalin's version of authoritarian modernity precluded any possibility of the gradual withering away of religion owing to the disappearance of its underlying causes, identified by Marxists as alienation, exploitation, oppression, and so forth.

Evidence indicates that during the war both Roosevelt and Stalin considered religion a potential bridge that would help ease the wartime alliance into postwar cooperation. For example, Roosevelt considered the joint declaration of Allied Unity a supplement to the Atlantic Charter, "particularly in reference to the real purposes for which we fight." In signing the declaration the Soviet Union committed itself to the stated purposes and principles of the Atlantic Charter as well as to the defense of religious freedom and the preservation of human rights and justice in its own and other lands. George Kennan, a Soviet expert, observed that the reported relaxation in Soviet hostility toward religion was in the best interests of the regime, in Soviet controlled territories and abroad. Kennan, very significantly from the man who was to become known as the father of containment, indicated that once the war was over, "if the Kremlin could be induced to tolerate religion at home and to receive the proffered cooperation of western religious movements in the spirit of friendliness and confidence, I believe one of the greatest barriers to a sound future peace would have been removed."[11]

Using Russian archival sources, Vladislav Zubok and Constantine Pleshakov show how Stalin, aware of the Soviet Union's relative weakness at the end of the war, understood the necessity of maintaining wartime cooperation, with its promise of American loans and reparations. They state that, albeit a ruthless tyrant, Stalin sought neither "unbridled unilateral expansionism" nor confrontation with the West. Indeed, cooperation with the Western powers was a preferable option on which to build his influence and resolve international disputes. Religion seemingly offered Stalin a ready and relatively easy means of reducing the gulf that remained between him and his allies. Whether or not that meant any more than religion as a mobilizing device for transformational purposes that could eventually be transcended, Soviet generals and local communist leaders honored Greek Orthodox clergy in the Balkans and courted Roman Catholic clergy in Poland. Albeit by maladroit means, Stalin even attempted reconciliation with the pope in the spring of 1944. In the 1930s the institutional Catholic Church in the Soviet Union had been crushed. But with the war's end bringing more than 50 million Catholics into the Soviet sphere of influence, it also brought overtures to the Vatican offering a deal: "Potential enemies could be neutralized in return for concessions which would permit Catholics to exercise their faith without molestation." Pope Pius XII and his principal advisors resolutely opposed an agreement, a hard-line stance that proved unwelcome to bishops, clergy, and laity who thought church interests could best be protected by cooperation. This was the situation in Poland, Hungary, Czechoslovakia, Romania, and Bulgaria, where the church was initially treated relatively well.[12]

The Vatican, however, seemingly worried that the crucible of war might merge the Orthodox conception of a messianic Russia with the Marxist conception of a messianic proletariat. Fear that a fusion of such ideas would have incalculable consequences for a postwar world of power vacuums and peoples seeking a new social and political order, the Vatican would not risk any seeming legitimization of Soviet power. Notable statesmen, including John Foster Dulles and Winston Churchill, shared Vatican fears as they observed a world disillusioned with and critically questioning the system that had delivered slump, fascism, and war. Adding to concerns that Stalin might not remain content with his allotted "security zone" were worries about the appeal of a creed that promised "from each according to his ability, to each according to his need," particularly should it be complemented by a religious dimension.[13]

As Anglo-American efforts to construct a Western doctrine with which to counter communism proved futile and unwelcome, anti-communism came to serve in its stead. The religious roots of popular anti-communism endowed it with a pseudo-doctrinal status, reinforced by the potency of religious themes, symbols, and metaphors in public discourse. Anti-communism rested on two fundamental contentions: that communism was a supreme and unqualified evil, and that its purpose was world domination. With religious values placed at its core, anti-communism served the West as a rhetorical device that suggested shared fundamental beliefs, ethics, and interests. It provided a moral framework for "containment" that also facilitated alliances with otherwise unpalatable and undemocratic regimes.[14]

Harry S. Truman inherited from Franklin Roosevelt a policy based on cooperation with the Soviet Union and a public anxious for the peace dividends it promised. He found himself leading a nation that without a discernible threat was divided not simply over what its global role should be, but even over whether or not it should have a global role. Confronting postwar economic realities that required the nation to move from its traditional isolationism toward globalism and world leadership, the US oversimplified Soviet intentions. Because this process applied particularly to the Soviet treatment of and attitude toward religion, the conflict with the Soviet Union was transformed into a politico-religious enterprise. Following the example of his Democratic presidential predecessors, Woodrow Wilson and Roosevelt, Truman called upon the righteous nation narrative to engender national unity in support of an interventionist foreign policy. The notion of divine chosenness that has informed American history, and indeed the very concept of America, from its colonial beginning, required not simply the idealization of America, but the demonization of the "other." Truman dramatically accomplished this process on the world stage by openly allying himself with Pius XII, at that time one of the world's most respected spiritual leaders. He was also the locus of ideo-logical opposition to and avowed enemy of Soviet communism at a time when the Roman Catholic Church was deeply implicated in a range of anti-Soviet activities, as policy-makers East and West well knew.[15]

During the Anglo-Soviet cold war of 1945–6, the Foreign Office recognized and acted upon "the potential importance of organised religion in combating the spread of com-munism." Indeed, the British can be seen as forerunners for the religious cold war. A more cautious and covert affair reflecting traditional Anglo-Russian rivalry, it aimed to counter Soviet attempts to use its religious capital, especially the Russian Orthodox Church, as a conduit for international influence. The Foreign Office preferred to support the Vatican indirectly by "inconspicuous means," feeling "that the Pope's anti-communist propaganda would be more convincing if he had a more positive line to show as regards the Nazis and Fascists, their heirs and assigns and all those who collaborated with them." Therefore, when Truman deliberately affected a highly publicized letter exchange between himself and Pius XII in August 1947, a critical moment in the evolution of the cold war, it was deliberate and symbolic. It demonstrably confirmed the policy of con-tainment implicit in the Truman Doctrine and the Marshall Plan. Dominated by images of the Soviet potential for evil, it stood in stark contrast to the latter, which, it should be emphasized, had been carefully constructed not to omit all hope of future collaboration with the Soviet Union. As the Anglo-Soviet cold war of 1945–6 became a US-Soviet con-flict, Truman enrolled Pius XII into the Western alliance, albeit an essentially symbolic gesture. In doing so he figuratively repudiated accommodation and negotiation, signal-ing the irreconcilable nature of the conflict, as was made resoundingly clear by Pius XII stating there could be no compromise with an avowed enemy of God.[16]

As well as conferring its worldwide moral and spiritual authority onto US leadership of the free world, the Vatican provided intelligence material at a time when US intelli-gence services were in their infancy and mobilized Catholics to defeat communists in electoral contests. The Vatican and the US together became arbiters of Italy's fate in the immediate postwar period. Through the defeat of Europe's largest communist party and the success of Italy's Christian Democrats, the Vatican and the US demonstrated how potent was the combination of spiritual and moral power with that of material wealth, political influence, and military strength. Presented as a crusade against evil, the cold war became the means through which America arrogated the spiritual and moral power associated with organized religion as it transformed containment into a religious enter-prise with itself as the champion of the free world against a demonized Soviet Union.[17]

In addition to its practical application in securing conformity to the cold war consen-sus within America, the religious dimension also helped consolidate transatlantic rela-tions and European integration. The economic health and stability of Europe and the US were interdependent, with transatlantic commercial and financial ties critical to the well-being of American capitalism. Adapting to the way in which the US presented itself and projected its power, European governments offered calculated responses that illus-trated their appreciation of how important ideology was to the US. In addition to pre-senting the basic division between their democracies and the totalitarian states as a conflict between religion and communism, Europe formulated the basis for a theory of totalitarianism that raised the question of the structural similarities between National Socialism and Stalinism. It provided a useful taxonomy of repressive regimes that justified the postwar switch from one enemy to another. Anti-communism provided a powerful ideological basis of agreement between the governing conservative forces in the US and their Social and Christian Democratic counterparts in Western Europe. The latter played a vital role in legitimizing the cold war, in enrolling labor movements into the anti-communist crusade, and in bringing to fruition a form of social reformism that did not threaten the established order. West German Chancellor Konrad Adenauer's Christian Democratic Union, for example, was founded to combat nationalism, materialism, and atheism. The "godless Soviet bogey" was perhaps the key construction facilitating the European nations, united since the Treaty of Versailles in their determination to halt Soviet influence, putting aside their differences and supporting America's cold war leadership.[18]

Truman's apparently successful alliance with the Vatican encouraged him to try to construct an international anti-communist religious front that theoretically embraced Buddhists, Hindus, Muslims; indeed, anyone who believed in God. It was to be not only directed against the Soviet Union, but it also aspired to include religious elements throughout the Soviet bloc, including the Russian Orthodox Church. Although meant to embrace all religious and moral leaders, the focus was largely on influential American and European Christians, with the Vatican as the representative of the Roman Catholic world and the World Council of Churches representing non-Roman Christianity. In the same period, there was a significant degree of Anglo-American collusion to effect the election of the Archbishop of North and South America as the Orthodox Patriarch of Constantinople. Truman again dramatically highlighted what he clearly perceived as another victory in the religious sphere by having Patriarch Athenagoras flown in his personal presidential plane to Istanbul to assume his new position in 1949. The appointment of an American citizen to the primary position in the Orthodox world was intended as a direct challenge to the influence of the Moscow patriarchate, important in the Middle East as well as Eastern Europe.[19]

Roman Catholicism and Eastern Orthodoxy were each closely connected to the national identity, history, and sentiment of key countries in the Soviet bloc. Truman therefore identified himself with a combination that would be regarded with alarm by the new communist regimes. The equation of religious unity with political unity and national identity was the motivational force behind autocephaly in the Orthodox world, considered a key element in the drive toward statehood. At the same time, the CIA established the National Committee for a Free Europe, a front organization explicitly dedicated to mobilizing dissent within the Soviet bloc by exploiting Eastern Europe's spiritual and moral resources. In 1942 Kennan had warned that foreign interference, especially in the realm of religion, would arouse the suspicion and fear of the insecure Soviets. He noted that Soviet violence toward the church derived from the conviction that it was a stronghold of conservatism and political opposition, as well as a spiritual rival. Returning to Moscow in 1944, the first time in seven years, Kennan thought "the spiritual life of the

Russian people" the most important development. In the spring of 1945, following Germany's defeat, Kennan reported that the religious feelings of the Russian masses represented a potentially incalculable danger to the Soviet government. Kennan was to become one of the leading advocates of covert action in the Soviet bloc, lending considerable significance to his observation that the Russian Orthodox hierarchy "may some day prove to be politically a match for the people in the Kremlin."[20]

Given Stalin's Marxist-Leninist background, the overt mobilization of religion by the West could only confirm his gravest suspicions about organized religion and Western hostility. The Soviets knew that religion remained the focus for dissent against them; hence the attempt to rally the religious into a global anti-Soviet crusade played to Stalin's fears about its subversive potential. Stalin responded in kind by seeking to rally believers everywhere behind what the West referred to as the "Soviet-inspired" peace movement. From within the Soviet bloc, many religious communities and organized groups indicated their support for and adherence to socialist values. Nonetheless, the potential power of religion to compromise and challenge communist power, particularly with Western support, meant vacillating and contradictory policies toward religion. Harsh measures by communist regimes against clerics considered to be involved in anti-state activities were invariably reported in the West as evidence of religious persecution, serving to confirm Western propaganda that the intent was to destroy religion, Christianity in particular.

Religion confronted Soviet leaders with a range of policy problems, including domestic and foreign affairs, state security, issues related to ethnicity and nationalism, not to mention ideological differences. In each case the fate of churches and religious institutions in the Soviet bloc was dictated by a complex play of factors. These included historical attributes, political cultures, the calibre and attitudes of religious leaders, and their interaction with their political counterparts. The evolving policies of the different communist regimes were additional factors. Whilst it was inevitable that there would always be tension between religion and a government that adhered to Marxist principles, the degree of outright persecution varied tremendously between different countries, time periods, and denominations. Certainly all religious groups in the Soviet bloc confronted difficulties that included imprisonment, surveillance, censorship, and other means of oppression and control. However, as "modernizing" regimes, East European countries were inherently inclined toward some degree of experiment, change, and adaptation, a process that to some churchmen seemed to offer no more than a means of survival; for others it was a chance for the church to realize a far more meaningful place in communist societies.[21]

Designating the Soviet Union the "evil other" precluded validation or explanation and repudiated accommodation, negotiation, and compromise as evidence of weakness and corruption. It allowed the Truman administration to shift America into permanent military, political, and economic intervention on a world scale despite the tremendous cost. The conviction within the Truman administration among figures such as Dean Acheson and George Kennan was that absolutist anti-communism was a temporary device that America would shed as it matured into its world role. However, when

Eisenhower and Dulles took over the reins of power, the "Soviet threat" was proving sufficiently crucial to effective management of Congress and public opinion, not to mention the Western alliance, that they rejected Soviet overtures following the death of Stalin. They were equally resistant to Winston Churchill's summitry. Their insistence that the basic situation and danger remained unchanged reflected the extent to which the image of an aggressive, evil Soviet regime dedicated to world conquest—the godless Soviet bogey—had become a crucial cold war asset.[22]

Dwight D. Eisenhower, elected president by an America in the throes of a religious revival encouraged by society's core institutions as essential to winning the cold war, fully understood the power of ideological language to advance pragmatic ends and to have pragmatic interests serve ideological commitments. As the cold war exacerbated the popular patriotism and civic religion that marked the postwar revival, Eisenhower oversaw the transformation of Truman's initiative. Rather than a state alliance with organized religion, the nation moved toward a more direct identification with, if not embodiment of, religion itself. Religion and Americanism were brought together in a consensus that personal religious faith reflected proper patriotic commitment. With a variety of groups promoting civic religion, churchmen began to worry about the instrumentalization of religion and the way in which the American Way of Life had been assigned the status of religion. But it was too late. In 1954, the phrase "under God" was added to the Pledge of Allegiance, and Congress required all US coins and paper currency to bear the slogan "In God We Trust." Two years later that became the official US motto without a dissenting voice in House or Senate. Although Eisenhower only joined a church on becoming president, he mandated that all Cabinet meetings begin with a prayer. In actions and words he illustrated the extent to which America identified itself with religious faith. In 1955 Eisenhower notably declared: "Recognition of the Supreme Being is the first, the most basic, expression of Americanism. Without God, there could be no American form of government, nor an American way of life."[23]

Notably, a "Christian amendment" to the Constitution was easily defeated: "Adhesional religious symbolism was what Congress wanted, not invidious distinctions among the God-fearing." In 1952 the Supreme Court, which in 1931 used the word *Christian* to describe the nation, switched to the term *religious*: "We are a religious people whose institutions presuppose a Supreme Being." The global competition for non-white, non-Christian peoples required an affirmation of religious values rather than a Christianity closely identified by former and existing colonies with imperialism. It was a distinction Eisenhower clumsily confirmed in his 1954 declaration that: "Our government makes no sense unless it is founded on a deeply felt religious faith—and I don't care what it is."[24]

The cultivation of popular perceptions about US moral leadership and benign use of power meant that religious values were increasingly represented in secular forms. It reflected a process of assimilation and translation of a religious system of values into secular ethics. Such a process accords with Van Kersbergen's view of secularization as representing "the condensation or transference of religious morality into secular ethics. Secularization may be looked upon as comprising a transformation of religious contents into worldly substance." A similar process was discernible in Europe with the electoral success of Christian Democracy, a postwar phenomenon that remained a significant force in European politics for the rest of the century. The cold war also eased the development toward the now relatively accommodative relationship between the Catholic Church and modern liberal democracies. The Vatican's support for democracy has, however, remained varying and complex.[25]

In the US the seemingly real possibility of nuclear war in the context of the worldview induced by Manichaean cold war rhetoric reduced the distinctions that had separated secular and evangelical America. The cold war climate provided evangelicals with the chance to merge with mainstream culture to generate a political-religious power base for the new Christian right. Despite the considerable disparities between different groupings of evangelicals, the religious cold war, underpinned by the threat of nuclear annihilation, which made foreign relations important for everyone, allowed evangelicals of all stripes to construct a closer relational identity with the rest of the US than had previously been the case. While pre-millennial dispensationalists conceptualized history as time partitioned into certain ages and with a definite end, secular critics of nuclear weapons postulated global annihilation. More importantly, however, the demarginalization of evangelicals during the early cold war that helped them assimilate into mainstream culture meant political participation.[26]

It also meant evangelicals embedded born-again Christianity into America's cultural landscape, with telling implications for the rise of the religious right in the 1970s and early 1980s. Conservative evangelicals were able to move from a tangential to a central subculture owing to the emergence of a new patriotic evangelicalism during the cold war and the way in which cold war discourse intensified strands of pre-millennialism. Reinforced by key historical events with portentous significance for those of faith, such as the nuclear potential for global destruction and the creation of Israel, evangelicals were able to renegotiate and redefine their place in American political culture. The strengthening of this proselytizing element of American Christianity facilitated its outreach into the developing world. It was a process that inevitably excited suspicion that the US was using Christianity to spread American influence as had once the old European imperial powers.[27]

America's cold war policies of encouraging religion and destroying the left also facilitated the rise of political Islam. In the early cold war period the CIA gathered evidence suggesting that religion was an important consideration in communist bloc policies of outreach. As both China and the Soviet Union had sizeable Muslim populations, concern existed about communist mobilization of religious leaders and institutions to appeal to their co-religionists in strategic areas, including the Middle East. Islamic delegations from communist regimes that visited their co-religionists in Muslim countries appeared to validate Sino-Soviet claims of coexistence and cooperation between communism and religion. And indeed there were historical precedents for cooperation between Islamists and communists. Early Bolshevik policies toward Islam in Central Asia and the Caucasus, including agreements that allowed some aspects of sharia law to operate, facilitated alliances with a variety of Islamic groups and movements. Under Lenin and Trotsky "some major Muslim organizations joined the Communist parties in their entirety or joined with the Bolsheviks to defend the revolution." Muslim support for the Bolsheviks was intimately connected to their demands for national rights. As similar demands subsequently fired the Middle East's Muslim populations, there were obvious concerns within American administrations that saw the hand of Moscow at every turn amid worry about the relationship between Islam, communism, and nationalism.[28]

By the 1950s the direction of Islam was of some concern to the Americans. The rise of anti-Americanism in the region was fueled by the support the US accorded the establishment of Israel in 1948, America's ties with the region's colonial powers, Britain and France, plus the perception that "the British tail is all too successfully wagging the American dog." The principal threat to US interests was viewed as "anti-Western" nationalism, with the currents of neutralism and nationalism regarded as "intimately related to Islam." State Department responses to pan-Islamic unity movements suggested a preference "to limit Islam as a political force in the early 1950s." But Truman, followed by Eisenhower, saw Islam as a counter to Soviet moves in the Middle East and the influence of the radical, secular forces aligned with the left. In June 1951 the consul general in Dhahran, William A. Eddy, discussed progress toward a "possible strategy of the Christian democratic West joining with the Muslim world in a common moral front against communism." The secretary-general of the Arab league, Abdul Rahman Pasha, had discussed the idea with high-ranking officials of the US Army and Navy in Washington in December 1950. It was also discussed with Pope Pius XII, who had himself first suggested a religious front against Soviet communism during a visit to the US in 1936 when he was a cardinal. The pope welcomed Muslim participation, as well as Muslim diplomatic representatives at the Vatican "contrary to Vatican policy of the past which required Muslim countries to designate a Christian."[29]

The Saudi leadership, with its system of state Islam as well as its guardianship of Medina and Mecca, was perceived as having the potential to become "Islam's Vatican." Eisenhower, concerned that the Soviet Union might be able to build up Egyptian president Nasser as the "head of an enormous Moslem confederation," explored the possibility of using King Saud as "a counter weight to Nasser." Saud's religious position and his "professed anti-Communism" made him the "logical choice." As relations with Egypt worsened during spring 1956, Eisenhower revealed in his diary that he thought the king could be built up as a spiritual leader, after which "we might begin to urge his right to political leadership." He put the same proposition to British defense minister Duncan Sandys the following year, subsequently reminding Saud of his "special position." Support for Saud's religious leadership meant support for the excessively conservative Wahhabi pan-Islamic movement. Allen Dulles, head of the CIA, even encouraged Saudi Arabia to support the Muslim Brotherhood, widely regarded as a terrorist organization, fanatically religious, nationalist, and anti-Western.[30]

Western propaganda in the region used Soviet atheism and repression of religion to suggest that the Christian West and the Muslim East confronted a common global foe opposed to religious faith. In Iran, for example, in order to convey the sense of a "common moral front," the American embassy distributed a brochure entitled *The Voices of*

*God*. Suggesting a nexus between various faiths and American values, the brochure, with a mosque on its cover, contained quotations from the Koran, Muslim poetry, Jesus Christ, Isaiah, Chinese philosophy, the Buddha, the Sanskrit Bhagavad-Gita, Abraham Lincoln, and Mahatma Gandhi.[31]

However, it was the intellectuals not the ulama that pioneered the development of Islamist political movements, concerned with contemporary political and social issues rather than spiritual. Islamist intellectuals encountered both Marxism and western liberalism. Political Islam can be emancipatory and authoritarian. Moderate political Islam fought for reforms within the system. Radicals sought power, convinced no meaningful social reform was possible without state control. As the radicals were the most stridently anti-communist, anti-Soviet, and conservative representatives of Islam, American support gravitated toward them. Indeed, the support of America and its allies in the region, most notably Saudi Arabia, helped create a situation in which otherwise unpopular and unrepresentative versions of Islam were able, over time, to secure a power and influence they otherwise would have been unlikely to attain. Despite some deep reservations, American officials were impressed by the capacity of this strand of Islam to counter the left. Pakistan's Islamic Student Society (ITJ), for example, influenced by Egypt's Muslim Brotherhood, battled the left relentlessly and effectively, especially on university campuses, an important factor for US officials concerned about the attraction of the left for the Arab intelligentsia.[32]

The dangers of playing the Islamic card were insufficiently considered, especially by American officials fired by a sense of mission who wanted not only to impress on Muslim populations that communism was their common enemy, but also to make Islam serve as a potential fifth column inside the Soviet bloc. Western policy-makers failed to understand the complexity and power of Islam. Too many remained wedded to the view that third world nationalism was a Soviet tool and political Islam an ally to be used against presumed pro-Soviet nationalist leaders. The situation was exacerbated by the fact that the West's Middle East allies shared assumptions that Islam would provide a local buffer against secular nationalism. Subsequently, conservative Arab regimes sheltered and aided militant Islamists, whilst Israel was to allow Hamas to operate unhindered during the first intifada.[33]

For Truman, Eisenhower, and their successors, dealing with Islam meant dealing with often oppressive and corrupt Middle Eastern regimes that lacked popular support and for whom Islam was as much a tool as it was for the Americans. Consequently, much of America's Middle East cold war agenda was mediated through regimes and religious movements that would inevitably prioritize their own political agendas. These were naturally concerned with consolidating and/or extending their own power bases. In addition, US cold war policies that eroded the left and progressive nationalism in the Middle East further helped the rise of right-wing political Islam. By removing what American officialdom regarded as their common foes on the left, the US assisted the growth of a constituency that turned to political Islam in a quest for reform throughout the region, albeit as a default option. US officials, worried by the strength of the anti-Western sentiment harbored by some of their Islamist allies, possibly drew some reassurance from thinking that the religious extremists lacked a popular base. Most Muslims rejected their ideology and their modes of operating. However, the weakening and discrediting of the left in the Muslim world empowered political Islam, making it the main ideological and organized means through which popular discontent and dissent could be expressed. The subsequent lack of progress and reform and the continuation of oppressive regimes allied with and supported by the West inflamed anti-Western sentiments. In the absence of secular left-liberal alternatives, this further galvanized support for the Islamists as the most ardent opposition to the status quo.[34]

Right-wing Islamism had been an ideological tendency with small and scattered numbers. Out of power, it had neither the aspiration of drawing strength from popular organization nor the possibility of marshaling strength from any alternative source. This changed following the Soviet military intervention in Afghanistan. National security advisor Zbigniew Brzezinski saw an opportunity to export a composite ideology of nationalism and Islam to the Muslim majority Central Asian republics with a view to destroying the Soviet system. Little thought was given to how the religious can and will transgress the boundaries between the sacred and profane to assert their own political, social, and economic influences. In the portrayal of the Afghan War as an international jihad, bringing together volunteers from Muslim populations all over the world, there are resonances of Truman's international anti-communist religious front concept. The legacy of the religious cold war lingers around the "Global War on Terror." It is presented as an extremist religious challenge to the legitimacy of the modern international system, a system designated as separate from, and yet the defender of, religion.[35]

All religions, modern and ancient, have been confronted with questions about relations with political power and attitudes toward the poor and vulnerable. The religious cold war naturally brought such questions to the fore, especially in the late 1950s when striking changes in global affairs tore apart the post-World War II anti-communist consensus. As the 1955 Bandung Conference articulated the aspirations of the underdeveloped world and new types of authoritarian and repressive governments stimulated the growth of popular opposition movements, Western policies and practices came under increasing scrutiny and criticism. The depiction of the East-West confrontation as between good and evil became less and less tenable. The concept was increasingly challenged, even within theology, where Marxist analysis of social reality was increasingly used in certain quarters as a frame of reference for the reading of the Bible. By the end of his pontificate in 1958, even the obsessively anti-communist Pius XII sought to move from his alliance with the West toward non-alignment. In the US itself, the political culture of the early cold war, based on apocalypticism and anti-communism, eroded under the impact of first the civil rights movement and then the Vietnam War.[36]

Reinhold Niebuhr, one of cold war America's most influential theologians, viewed communism as "a secularized Hebraic and Christian Messianism with a 'holy nation' in the Soviet Union." At the end of the Eisenhower administration he declared that the West had been successfully inoculated against communism "by the historical dynamism of the Judeo-Christian tradition." However, like many churchmen who worried about a military cold war confrontation and potential nuclear holocaust, Niebuhr was not averse to some sort of accommodation between the US and the Soviet Union and urged American leaders to respond to international developments "with mature empiricism and realism." Like Pius XII, he was a cold warrior who became an advocate of coexistence. The Vietnam War caused Niebuhr, as it did many other clergy, to reconsider the way in which the West conducted the cold war. Niebuhr expressed shame for his nation and was moved to activism, becoming a founding member of Clergy and Laymen Concerned About Vietnam (CALCAV). He began to question if the two superpowers were radically different and wondered whether they had not each revealed "similar imperialist impulses."[37]

The election of John XXIII proved a turning point for the Vatican's attitude toward the Soviet bloc and the cold war. Seeing communism as an outgrowth of modernity, John XXIII transformed what was meant to be a transitional papacy into a revolutionary one by seeking better relations with the communist world. That the cold war was a key factor in his thinking was illustrated by the 1963 encyclical, *Pacem in terris*, tellingly composed in the aftermath of the Cuban missile crisis that brought the world to the brink of nuclear warfare. The pope not only repudiated the concept of a just war in a nuclear world, he drew a notable distinction between unchristian Marxist philosophy and the positive practices to which it could give rise. His statement that the time had come for Catholics to cooperate in good causes with non-Christians began the "opening to the East" that led to the *Ostpolitik* that permitted the "opening to the left" in Europe.[38]

Religious attitudes were further influenced by notable outcomes in the developing world, Eastern Europe included, that derived from the application of the two competing political and economic models of modernization represented by the two superpower rivals. In the Soviet Union the communist-socialist model delivered economic and social security but at the cost of political and personal freedoms. Elsewhere in the developing world the liberal capitalist model also led to repression and often right-wing dictatorial regimes, marked as well by glaring and growing inequality. By the 1960s both models were subject to severe criticism by religious and moral leaders, not least from within Christianity, the religion whose own relationship with power and poverty was historically ambiguous and compromised. But, as illustrated by the relationship between the discourse of liberation theology and power struggles in Latin America, Africa, Asia, and Europe, religion serves oppressed and oppressor.[39]

Within mainstream Christianity divisions were exacerbated by the anti-war, anti-imperialist, socio-political concerns of its youth. They were widened further by the increasing numbers of participants from the developing world, and in some cases the Soviet bloc, who became more involved and active in the high level church affairs that had once been dominated by West European and American churchmen. Whilst religious groups and organizations remained engaged with international issues, there was often little consensus. This allowed each side in the cold war to promote those voices of which they approved, ignoring those that were critical, or else undermining them through accusations of being naïve or even disloyal. The realpolitik that characterized the period following the Cuban missile crisis and the uneasy period of détente seemingly diminished the cold war role of religion in the international arena. However, the election of

Jimmy Carter, followed by that of Ronald Reagan, demonstrated that religion retained significance. Reagan, a self-proclaimed born-again Christian, found religion a useful electoral tool before he began to wield it as a weapon against the "evil empire." Reagan resurrected the Truman-Eisenhower morality play presentation of the cold war as a Manichaean struggle.[40]

Notable irony had resided in the way in which the religious cold war developed in the 1960s. In the heartland of communist power, the Soviet Union and Eastern Europe, the religious moved increasingly toward an accommodation with their respective regimes, whilst in the backyard of the "free world," South America, liberation theology challenged free market ideology and US supported power structures. However, the hopes of communist regimes that the accommodation between themselves and the churches would help their legitimacy and popularity provided the space for religion to facilitate a process by which diverse constituent elements in society used the church to bring into question the legitimacy of communist rule. Glasnost and perestroika meant further opportunities for the churches. Regarded as distinct from the Soviet imposed system, religious values were perceived as part of pre-Soviet European civilization. In addition, many churches were viewed as linked to nationalist sentiments and movements and "in some ways, yielding to the demands of local religious believers rather than those of the nationalists was an easy option for the communists." The religious revivals that followed the demise of the communist regimes were often closely connected with national independence movements. Notably, they proved notoriously short-lived as churchmen and nationalists looked for an idealized world that supposedly existed before communism.[41]

It was, of course, in Poland that the importance of Catholicism in defining national identity, strengthened by the Catholic Church's monopoly in representing civil society against the totalitarian state, proved crucially important. Pulitzer prize-winning investigative journalist Carl Bernstein joined forces with the dean of Vatican journalists Marco Politi to "expose" the degree of collaboration between the Reagan administration and John Paul II's Vatican during the 1980s, especially in supporting Solidarity. Equally important was the seeming papal support for the Reagan administration's anti-Marxist activities in Latin America and the rationale for the US military build-up, despite the objections of Catholic bishops and clergy throughout the Americas. The extent to which either religious or US activities, together or alone, contributed to the demise of communism in Eastern Europe remains to be determined. The scholarly consensus is that the collapse of the Soviet bloc had more to do with internal rather than external pressures. Certainly John Paul II shared the American interest in supporting human rights in Poland, yet he and the Polish bishops opposed America's call for economic sanctions. His 1987 encyclical, *Sollicitudo rei socialis*, accused both East and West of betraying "humanity's legitimate expectations."[42]

The collapse of the communist bloc was preceded by the decreasing ideological persuasiveness of socialism as it departed from its own claims and objectives and failed to deliver material benefits, ultimately destroying its own legitimacy. Far from proving a victory over modernity for the Christian Church, no new Christian order emerged from the failure of Soviet communism. Ironically, the failure of Soviet-type systems, supposed threats to Christianity, weakened the churches. The advance of deregulated market relations as a renewed feature of market capitalism caused John Paul II to lament, "The exploitation produced by inhuman capitalism was a real evil, and that's the kernel of truth in Marxism." Only months later there was deep poignancy in his admonition that: "These seeds of truth (in Marxism) shouldn't be destroyed, shouldn't be blown away by the wind.... The supporters of capitalism in its extreme forms tend to overlook the good things achieved by communism: its effort to overcome unemployment, its concern for the poor."[43]

Within the US the opposition to and eventual "triumph" over "godless" Soviet communism consolidated the link between Christian superiority and American exceptionalism that informed its national identity. It reinforced the narrative of destiny and mission on which American leaders draw, certainly eclipsing a historical record that shows how nearly all the notable personalities in the founding generation harbored grave doubts as to the long-term viability of the Republic. Above all, it was a triumph for the American model of modernity that further reinforced the nation's deep religiosity and opened the door for America's religious market place to extend its global reach. In the immediate aftermath of the cold war, the scholarly tendency was to approach religion as either an obstacle to secular democracy or as evidence of embedded cultural and civilizational differences. Subsequently, the secularization hypothesis with its teleology of modernity was challenged by what seemed a "resurgence" of religion to those who had neglected to notice its persistent significance. In the fundamental reappraisal of previous paradigms now taking place, some suggest the relationship was not as once thought between secularization and modernization, but between modernization and religious pluralism. As these deliberations progress and 20th century history is reassessed, the contribution of the religious cold war must be considered, particularly in the context of Thomas Friedman's observation of the post-1989 international system that whilst the cold war didn't shape everything, it shaped many things.[44]

# CONCLUSION

There were conflicting and deeply complex attitudes toward religion on either side of the iron curtain. Popular Protestant suspicion of the Vatican, mixed with a significant degree of anti-Catholicism, complicated US–Vatican relations. Despite widespread religiosity, traditional reverence for the US Constitution required that the wall between church and state be kept secure. Within the Soviet bloc church leaders were divided between those who advocated cooperation and those who preferred resistance and active opposition. Communist hierarchies were also divided by the question of religion. Marshall Tito and his Foreign Minister Vladimir Velebit had very different solutions for dealing with the problem of Cardinal Stepinac. Shortly after Stepinac's arrest and prior to his 1946 trial, Velebit advised: "Shoot the Archbishop." As the trial grew to a close with a guilty verdict seemingly inevitable, Tito reassured the British ambassador that: "We are not such fools as to kill an Archbishop."[45]

Religion is a significant contributor to, as well as a recipient of, culture; a shaper of, as well as being shaped by, dominant ideas. The religious cold war can be placed in a growing corpus of work exploring the influence of ideas, culture, and norms now complementing material explanations and enhancing causal debates within the fields of international relations. Communist regimes throughout the cold war were keenly aware of the revulsion invoked in the West by mistreatment and oppression of the faithful, not to mention the alienation it could also cause at home. Religion offered the West a stick with which to beat, and a means of subverting, the new communist regimes. The prominence of religious themes and rhetoric in anti-communist propaganda and covert operations that used the religious exacerbated the suspicion of communist leaderships, at times inflicting high costs and unfortunate repercussions on the faithful and the religious organizations to which they adhered. The religious cold war also impacted in a variety of ways on religion in the West and the developing world. And it left an indelible imprint on the US in terms of a reinforced and reinvigorated belief in a universal mission, the religious element of which was notably evident in the post 9/11 Bush administration, which interpreted the lessons of the Reagan administration to be that power harnessed to ideals vanquished evil.[46]

As new historians tackle the question of religion in US foreign policy and the cold war, it is important not to neglect the work of an older generation of historians who experienced some of those crucial decades. The reflections of one particular doyen, William Appleman Williams, are worth recalling:

> If you get too much power, you are tempted to persuade or force other people to do things that even you know are wrong. You act against your own integrity, as well as against the public welfare and public virtue. This is in truth the ultimate corruption. You begin to play at being God.[47]

Williams wrote in 1986, during the Reagan era, concerned yet again by the way in which his nation exercised power. He had previously dismissed the question of who started the cold war as neither intelligent nor rewarding. For him, more important was which side "hardened the natural and inherent tensions…into bitter antagonisms and inflexible positions." In most areas, this still remains a contested question. Today, with reference to the religious cold war, more important than the answer, which would seem to be the US, is the legacy it bequeathed the post-cold war world.[48]

## NOTES

1. In his 1997 book, *We Now Know: Rethinking the Cold War* (Oxford: Oxford University Press), John L. Gaddis, one of the best-known cold war historians, not only notes this truism but also suggests it reflects a crucial dimension of the conflict that historians have been reluctant to address. In a challenging review of the book and other literature that emphasizes idealism over realism, Melvyn P. Leffler, an equally pre-eminent cold war scholar,

cautioned that, in responding to the new master narrative Gaddis was offering, it was important not to confuse the ending of the cold war with its origins and evolution. *American Historical Review*, 104/2 (April 1999), 501–24. Dianne Kirby, "Christian Co-operation and the Ecumenical Ideal in the 1930s and 1940s," *European Review of History* (Spring 2001), 37–60.

2. Dennis Kux, *India and the United States: Estranged Democracies 1941–1991* (Washington, DC: National Defense University Press, 1992), 77; cited in Praveen Chaudhry and Marta Vanduzer-Snow, eds., *The US and India: A History through Archives: The Formative Years* (London: Sage, 2008). Seth Jacobs has shown how religion contributed to Eisenhower's Vietnam policy. Presented to the public as a conflict of religious and irreligious forces, with religious freedom and the persecution of religion as key propaganda themes, the American public thought Vietnam was a Roman Catholic country. Jacobs, " 'Our System Demands the Supreme Being: America's Religious Revival and the Diem Experiment, 1954–1955," *Diplomatic History*, 25/4 (Fall 2001), 589–624.

3. J.L. Segundo, *Faith and Ideologies* (New York: Orbus Books, 1984), 38; Elizabeth Shakman Hurd, *The Politics of Secularism in International Relations* (Princeton, NJ: Princeton University Press, 2008), 137; Olivier Roy, *Secularism Confronts Islam* (New York: Columbia University Press), 2007.

4. Kirby, "The Archbishop of York and Anglo-American relations during the Second World War and early Cold War, 1942–55," *The Journal of Religious History*, 23/3 (October 1999): 327–45.

5. Shakman Hurd, *Secularism*, 6; Kirby, "Divinely Sanctioned: The Anglo-American Cold War Alliance and the Defence of Western Civilisation and Christianity, 1945–48," *Journal of Contemporary History*, 35/3 (July 2000), 385–412.

6. Ralph Carter Elwood, ed., *Resolutions and Decisions of the Communist Party of the Soviet Union, Vol. I: The Russian Social Democratic Labour Party 1898–October 1917* (Toronto: University of Toronto Press, 1974), 42–3; N.I. Bukharin and E.O. Preobrazhensky, *The ABC of Communism* (Harmondsworth: Penguin, 1969), 299–301; A. Manhattan, *Vatican Imperialism in the Twentieth Century* (Michigan: Zondervan Publishers, 1965); Paul D. Steeves, *Keeping the Faiths: Religion and Ideology in the Soviet Union* (New Jersey: Holmes & Meier, 1989), 85–6.

7. Arto Luukkanen, *Party of Unbelief: The Religious Policy of the Bolshevik Party, 1917–1929* (Helsinki: Studia Historica, 1994). In the official 1937 Soviet census, more than half the respondents declared themselves believers to the authorities. Assuming that many preferred not to disclose such sensitive information to the communist state, there must have been many more actual believers. Nor is it without significance that so many felt able to confess their faith to state officials. Daniel Peris, *Storming the Heavens: The Soviet League of the Militant Godless* (New York: Cornell University Press, 1998). The revulsion expressed abroad for its religious activities was very often a powerful deterrent, not least from 1933 when priority was given to building popular anti-fascist fronts. During this period, the CSCRQ assumed the role of defending the churches against local communist officials seeking requisition of their buildings for secular purposes.

8. A. Dickinson, "Domestic and Foreign Policy Considerations and the Origins of Post-war Soviet Church-State Relations, 1941–46," in Kirby, ed., *Religion and the Cold War* (Basingstoke: Palgrave Macmillan, 2003), 23–36; Kirby, "Anglican-Orthodox Relations and the Religious Rehabilitation of the Soviet Regime during the Second World War," *Revue d'Histoire Ecclésiastique*, 96/1–2, (January–June 2001), 101–23; William Van Den Bercken, "Holy Russia

and the Soviet Fatherland," *Religion in Communist Lands*, 15/3 (1987): 264–77; S.M. Miner, *Stalin's Holy War: Religion, Nationalism, and Alliance Politics, 1941–1945* (Chapel Hill, NC: University of North Carolina Press, 2003); Dimitry Pospielovsky, "The 'Best Years' of Stalin's Church Policy (1942–1948) in the Light of Archival Documents," *Religion, State & Society*, 23/2 (1997): 139–62.

9. Tatiana A. Chumachenko, *Church and State in Soviet Russia: Russian Orthodoxy from World War II to the Khrushchev Years* (New York: M.E. Sharpe, 2002); Karl Marx, *Introduction to a Contribution to the Critique of Hegel's Philosophy of Right*, 1970; Marxists Internet Archive, <http://www.marxists.org/archive/marx/works/1843/critique-hpr/intro.htm>; John Molyneux, "More than Opium: Marxism and Religion," *International Socialism*, 119 (June 2008); Karl Marx and Frederick Engels, *On Religion*, 1957; Marxists Internet Archive, <http://www.marxists.org/archive/marx/works/subject/religion>.

10. Vladimir Lenin, "Socialism and Religion," in *Collected Works*, vol. 10, 1965; Marxists Internet Archive, <http://www.marxists.org/archive/lenin/works/1905/dec/03.htm>.

11. Roosevelt to Secretary of State, December 27, 1941, *Foreign Relations of the United States*, (henceforth *FRUS*), I, 1941, 370; Declaration by United Nations, *FRUS*, I, 1942, 25; George Kennan to Myron C. Taylor, October 2, 1942, "Memorandum," PSF Diplomatic Box 52, Taylor Papers, Franklin Roosevelt Library.

12. Vladislav Zubok and Constantine Pleshakov, *Inside the Kremlin's Cold War: From Stalin to Khrushchev* (Cambridge, MA: Harvard University Press, 1996), 275–6; I. Deutscher, *Stalin* (Harmondsworth: Penguin, 1972), 506–7; Kirby, "Truman's Holy Alliance: The President, the Pope and the Origins of the Cold War," *Borderlines: Studies in American Culture*, 4/1 (1997): 1–17. For a detailed account of the different experiences of churches in the Soviet bloc in the early cold war, see Peter Kent, *The Lonely Cold War of Pope Pius XII* (Montreal: McGill-Queen's University Press, 2002).

13. The *Tablet*, September 18, 1943, 138; Kirby, "John Foster Dulles: Moralism and Anti-Communism," *Journal of Transatlantic Studies*, 6/3 (2009): 279–89; At the Potsdam conference, Secretary of State James Byrnes initially refused reparations, before concessions that historian Marc Trachtenberg has interpreted as a policy of "amicable divorce" by which the Americans demonstrated their willingness to tolerate a Soviet "security zone." *A Constructed Peace: The Making of the European Settlement 1945–63* (Princeton, NJ: Princeton University Press, 1999), 34–49.

14. Kirby, "The Cold War, the Hegemony of the United States and the Golden Age of Christian Democracy," in Hugh McLeod, ed., *World Christianities c.1914–c.2000*, 9 (Cambridge: Cambridge University Press, 2006), 285–303. For a wide range of articles addressing anti-communism, see Ralph Miliband, John Saville, and Marcel Liebman, eds., *Socialist Register 1984: The Uses of Anti-Communism* (London: Merlin Press Ltd., 1984).

15. Walter Russell Mead, *Special Providence: American Foreign Policy and How it Changed the World* (New York: Routledge, 2002); this is a well-explored theme in American history books. See Conrad Cherry, ed., *God's New Israel: Religious Interpretations of American Destiny* (Chapel Hill, NC: University of North Carolina Press, 1998). NSC 68 is a compelling example of how the Truman administration subsequently used the concept of an evil "other" to secure a cold war consensus and strengthen nationalism. The reputation of Pius XII, which since the 1960s has been subjected to severe attacks, was at that time akin to the reputation today associated with John XXIII. The scholarly attack on Pius XII began in 1963 with Rolf Hochhuth's play *Der Stellvertreter*, about the Pope and the Jewish holocaust. Michael Phayer, *Pius XII, the Holocaust and the Cold War* (Bloomington, IN: Indiana University Press, 2008).

16. Anne Deighton refers to Britain's "dual policy": "the appearance of great power cooperation was publicly maintained, but the remorseless focus of British policy was directed
toward securing an effective Western alliance to contain Soviet might in Germany, in
Europe, and throughout the world." *The Impossible Peace: Britain, the Division of Germany,
and the Origins of the Cold War* (Oxford: Oxford University Press, 1990), 6–7. In *The Politics
of Continuity: British Foreign Policy and the Labour Government 1945–46* (London: Verso,
1993), John Saville meticulously details how the Foreign Office under Ernest Bevin vigorously encouraged and then collaborated with America in the pursuit of cold war policies.
For a detailed examination of the British mobilization of religion during World War II and
early cold war, see Kirby, "The Church of England in the Period of the Cold War, 1945–56,"
Ph.D., Hull University, 1991. For how an ecclesiastical ally of the Foreign Office was trans-
formed into a crusading cold warrior, see Kirby, *Church, State and Propaganda: The
Archbishop of York and International Relations, A Political Study of Cyril Forster Garbett,
1942–1955* (Hull: Hull University Press, 1999). Kirby, "The Church of England and the early
Cold War," International Research Conference "Christian World Community and the Cold
War," The Evangelical Theological Faculty of the Comenius University, Bratislava, Slovakia,
September 5–8, 2011. Public Record Office, (henceforth PRO), FO 371/56885, May 14, 1946.
PRO, Oliver Harvey to D'Arcy Osborne, FO 371 67917, February 26, 1947. Kirby, "Truman's
Holy Alliance."

17. Charles R. Gallagher, S.J., *Vatican Secret Diplomacy* (New Haven, CT: Yale University Press,
2008), provides a detailed examination of US–Vatican covert intelligence gathering in
Yugoslavia in the early cold war; John Pollard, "The Vatican, Italy and the Cold War," in
Kirby, *Religion and the Cold War*, 103–17.

18. Alessandro Brogi, "'Competing Missions': France, Italy, and the Rise of American
Hegemony in the Mediterranean," *Diplomatic History*, 30/4 (September 2006): 741–70.
Hitler's mobilization of religion, as part of his "crusade" against the Soviet Union, was
disregarded.

19. W.A. Visser't Hooft, *Memoirs*, (London: SCM Press Ltd, 1973), 207; Kirby, "Harry S.
Truman's International Religious Anti-Communist Front, the Archbishop of Canterbury
and the 1948 Inaugural Assembly of the World Council of Churches," *Contemporary
British History*, 15/4 (Winter 2001); Demetrios Tsakonas, *A Man Sent by God: The Life of
Patriarch Athenagoras of Constantinople* (Brookline, MA: Holy Cross Press, 1977).The
extent to which Patriarch Athenagoras continued to regard himself as a "special agent of
the US Government," as well as the degree of manipulation between it and the Turkish
government in effecting his election, is discussed in a report sent to Washington by the
US Consul in Istanbul on March 28, 1967. NARA declassified NND 969000, March 9,
2004.

20. Dennis J. Dunn, ed., *Religion and Nationalism in Eastern Europe and the Soviet Union*
(London: Lynne Rienner Publishers, 1987); Pedro Ramet, ed., *Eastern Christians and
Politics in the Twentieth Century* (London: Duke University Press, 1988); David S.
Foglesong, "Roots of 'Liberation': American Images of the Future Russia in the Early Cold
War, 1948–1953," *International History Review*, XXI (March 1999) 61; George Kennan to
Myron C. Taylor, October 2, 1942, "Memorandum," PSF Diplomatic Box 52, Taylor Papers,
Franklin Roosevelt Library; Kennan, *Memoirs, 1925–1950* (Boston, MA: Little Brown,
1967), 510–11; "Russia's International Position at the Close of the War with Germany," May
1945, reproduced in Kennan, *Memoirs*, 541–2; W.Scott Lucas, *Freedom's War: The US
Crusade Against the Soviet Union, 1945–56* (New York: NYU Press, 1999); Foglesong, *The*

*American Mission and the "Evil Empire"* (Cambridge: Cambridge University Press, 2007), 91–2. Foglesong addresses Kennan's religious thinking within the context of the American drive from the 1880s to liberate and re-make Russia.

21. L.N. Leustean, *Orthodoxy and the Cold War: Religion and Political Power in Romania, 1947–65* (Basingstoke: Palgrave Macmillan, 2009); Kirby, "The Churches and Christianity in Cold War Europe," in Klaus Larres, ed., *A Companion to Europe since 1945* (Oxford: Blackwell, 2009), 203–30.

22. Lloyd Gardner, "Poisoned Apples: John Foster Dulles and the 'Peace Offensive'," Klaus Larres and Kenneth Osgood, eds., *The Cold War After Stalin's Death* (New York: Rowman & Littlefield, 2006).

23. James Baughman, *Henry R. Luce and the Rise of the American News Media* (Boston, MA: Twayne Publishers, 1987). Ira Chernus, "Operation Candor: Fear, Faith, and Flexibility," *Diplomatic History*, 29/5 (November 2005): 785–9. See also Chernus, *Apocalypse Management: Eisenhower and the Discourse of National Insecurity* (Stanford, CA: Stanford University Press, 2008). Will Herberg, *Protestant, Catholic, Jew: An Essay in American Religious Sociology* (Garden City, NY: Doubleday, 1955). The organization "Religion in American Life" stressed "the importance of all religious institutions as the foundations of American life." "Spiritual Mobilization" identified American religion with anti-communism and the defense of free enterprise capitalism. M.E. Marty, *Modern American Religion: Under God Indivisible, 1941–1960* (Chicago IL: University of Chicago Press, 1996), 291. "The Foundation for Religious Action in the Social and Civil Order" was established in 1953. One of its promoters was Elton Trueblood, the US Information Agency's chief of religious policy. It had two major aims: "to stress the importance of religious truth in the preservation and development of genuine democracy; and to unite all believers in God in the struggle between the free world and atheistic Communism, which aims to destroy both religion and liberty." M. Silk, *Spiritual Politics: Religion and America since World War II* (New York: Simon & Schuster, 1988), 96–7. *New York Herald Tribune*, February 21, 1955.

24. Silk, *Spiritual Politics*, 107. "President Elect Says Soviet Demoted Zhukov Because of their Friendship," *New York Times*, December 23, 1952; "Text of Eisenhower Speech," *New York Times*, December 23, 1952. For a detailed analysis of what Eisenhower said and the way in which it was reported and subsequently used, see Patrick Henry, "'And I Don't Care What it is': The Tradition-History of a Civil Religion Proof-Texts," *Journal of the American Academy of Religion*, 49/1 (March 1981): 35–49.

25. S. Kalyvas, *The Rise of Christian Democracy in Europe* (Ithaca, NY: Cornell University Press, 1996), 261; Daniel Philpott, "The Catholic Wave," *Journal of Democracy*, 15/2 (April 2004): 36, 43.

26. For a detailed analysis of this process, see Angela M. Lahr, *Millennial Dreams and Apocalyptic Nightmares: The Cold War Origins of Political Evangelicalism* (New York: Oxford University Press, 2007).

27. Paul Freston, *Evangelicals and Politics in Asia, Africa and Latin America* (Cambridge: Cambridge University Press, 2001).

28. Kirby, "Islam and the Religious Cold War," in D. Howell, D. Kirby, and K. Morgan (eds.), *John Saville, Commitment and History: Themes from the Life and Work of a Socialist Historian* (London: Lawrence & Wishart, 2011), 91–112; Robert Dreyfus, *Devil's Game: How the US Helped Unleash Fundamentalist Islam* (New York: Henry Holt & Co., 2005); A. Bennigsen and S. Winbush, *Muslim National Communism in the Soviet Union: A Revolutionary*

*Strategy for the Colonial World* (Chicago: University of Chicago Press, 1979), 222–3; A. Khaleed, *The Politics of Muslim Cultural Reform: Jadidism in Central Asia* (Berkeley, CA: University of California Press, 1998); Dave Crouch, "The Bolsheviks and Islam," *International Socialism*, 110 (Spring 2006): 55. "Inventory," OCB, May 3, 1957, NARA II, RG59, Box 40.

29. Stephen Penrose to State Dept., "The Soviet Challenge in the Near East," June 2, 1951; George Cameron to Edward W. Barrett, "Propaganda Activities in Iraq," October 24, 1951, NARA II, RG 59, DF 1950–4; Burton Berry to Henry Byroade, "Secretary of State's Understanding of Middle Eastern Problems," July 23, 1953, NARA II, RG 59, Lot File (LF) 57 D 298; Jacobs, "The Perils and Problems of Islam: The United States and the Muslim Middle East in the Early Cold War," *Diplomatic History*, 30/4 (September 2006): 705–39; Eddy to Thompson, June 7, 1951, NARA II, RG 59, LF 57 D 28.

30. Dwight Eisenhower, *The White House Years, Vol II: Waging Peace* (Garden City, NY: Doubleday, 1965); *FRUS, 1955–57*, XV, 425; *FRUS 1955–57*, XIII, 444–5, 645–6; Paul Kesaris, (ed.), *CIA Research Reports: The Middle East, 1946–76*, Microfilm Collection, 7.

31. Loy Henderson to State Department, "Report on the Use of Anti-Soviet Material," May 29, 1953, NARA II, Record Group 59, Decimal Files 1950–4.

32. Seyyed Vali Reza Nasr, *The Vanguard of the Islamic Revolution* (Berkeley, CA: University of California Press, 1994).

33. Nathan J. Citino, *From Arab Nationalism to OPEC* (Bloomington, IN: Indiana University Press, 2002), 96; Ziad Abu-Amr, *Islamic Fundamentalism in the West Bank and Gaza* (Bloomington, IN: Indiana University Press, 1994), 17; Shaul Mishal and Avraham Sela, *The Palestinian Hamas* (New York: Columbia University Press, 2000), 17–18.

34. Gilbert Achcar, *The Clash of Barbarisms: September 11 and the Making of the New World Disorder* (New York: Monthly Review Press, 2002).

35. Mahmood Mamdani, *Good Muslim, Bad Muslim* (New York: Pantheon, 2004), 129–30; Hiro Dilip, *War Without End: The Rise of Islamist Terrorism and Global Response* (New York: Routledge, 2002), 210.

36. Hanjakob Stehle, *Eastern Politics of the Vatican* (Athens, OH: Ohio University Press, 1981), 299.

37. Leo P. Ribuffo, "Moral Judgements and the Cold War: Reflections on Reinhold Niebuhr, William Appleman Williams, and John Lewis Gaddis," in Ellen Schrecker, ed., *Cold War Triumphalism: The Misuse of History After the Fall of Communism* (New York: The New Press, 2004), 33, 35 38; Silk, *Spiritual Politics*, 107.

38. P. Hebblethwaite, *John XXIII: Pope of the Council* (London: Geoffrey Chapman, 1984).

39. Philip Berryman, *Liberation Theology: Essential Facts about the Revolutionary Movement in Latin America and Beyond* (London: I.B. Tauris, 1987); Christian Smith, *The Emergence of Liberation Theology: Radical Religion and Social Movement Theory* (Chicago: University Press, 1991); Gustavo Gutiérres, *A Theology of Liberation: History, Politics and Salvation*, trans. Sister Caridad Inda and John Eagleson (New York: Orbis, 1973); L. Boff, *Church: Charism and Power: Liberation Theology and the Institutional Church* (London: SCM Press, 1985).

40. Kirby, "Ecclesiastical McCarthyism: Cold War Repression in the Church of England," *Journal of Contemporary British History*, 19/2 (June 2005): 185–201.

41. Marite Sapiets, "The Baltic Churches and the National Revival," *Religion in Communist Lands*, (1990): 155–68.

42. Carl Bernstein and Marco Politi, *His Holiness: John Paul II and the Hidden History of Our Time* (New York: Doubleday, 1996). In 1982–3 alone, the CIA spent about $8 million

sustaining Solidarity as an underground movement, 381. For more recent scholarship that moderates the Bernstein-Politi perspective, see Marie Gayte, "The Vatican and the Reagan Administration: A Cold War Alliance?" *Catholic Historical Review*, 97/4 (October 2011); see also Andrea di Stefano, "Stati Uniti-Vaticano: Relazioni Politiche e Aspetti Diplomatici, 1952–1984," doctoral dissertation, University of Teramo, 2008; David Marples, *The Collapse of the Soviet Union, 1985–1991* (New Jersey: Pearson Education, 2004). *Sollicitudo rei socialis*, December 30, 1987, no 14.

43. Bernstein and Politi, *His Holiness*, 497.

44. Conor Cruise O'Brien, *First in Peace: How George Washington Set the Course for America* (Cambridge: Da Capo Press, 2009). One notable legacy is, of course, the Office of International Religious Freedom, established by Congress in 1998 within the State Department. Its basic claim that promoting religious freedom is essential for US interests and security is questioned by its critics, who fear it is a vehicle for Christian right influence on US foreign policy. See Thomas F. Farr, *World of Faith and Freedom: Why International Religious Liberty is Vital to American National Security* (New York: Oxford University Press, 2008). For a discussion of the Christian right and the global arena, see Kirby, "Elephants in the Room," *H-Diplo*, March 2007, <http://www.h-net. org/reviews/showrev.php?id=12960>. For the most famous proponent of embedded differences, Samuel P. Huntington, secular democracy was deeply rooted in Protestant Christianity, a commonly held assumption amongst America's political elites. For secularization debates see Peter L. Berger, *The Desecularization of the World* (Grand Rapids, MI: Wm. B. Eerdmans, 1999); Berger and Samuel P. Huntington, *Many Globalizations: Cultural Diversity in the Contemporary World* (New York: Oxford University Press, 2003). Thomas Friedman, *The Lexus and the Olive Tree* (New York: Anchor Books, 1999), 7.

45. Informal Notes, National Catholic Welfare Conference Papers, Office of the General Secretary, series 10, box 26, file 20, "Communism: Yugoslavia," Catholic University of America, Washington, DC; Kirby, *Church, State and Propaganda*, 163.

46. Melvyn P. Leffler, "9/11 and American Foreign Policy," *Diplomatic History*, 29/3 (June 2005): 395–413.

47. For Elizabeth Edwards Spalding, cold war origins, early decisions, and policies cannot be satisfactorily explained without reference to religion; *The First Cold Warrior: Harry Truman, Containment, and the Remaking of Liberal Internationalism* (Lexington, KY: University Press of Kentucky, 2006), 9. William Inboden accords religion significant weight as a causal factor, stating that the various arguments previously put forward to explain the origins of the cold war are insufficient because: "They ignore God." *Religion and American Foreign Policy, 1945–1960: The Soul of Containment* (New York: Cambridge University Press, 2008), 4. See also Andrew Preston, "Bridging the Gap between the Sacred and the Secular in the History of American Foreign Relations," *Diplomatic History*, 30/5 (2006): 783–812; Mark Edwards, "'God Has Chosen Us': Re-Membering Christian Realism, Rescuing Christendom and the Contest of Responsibilities during the Cold War," *Diplomatic History*, 33/1 (2009); R.A. Schroth, *Bob Drinan* (New York: Fordham University Press, 2011); J.P. Herzog, *The Spiritual Industrial Complex* (New York: Oxford University Press, 2011). Henry W. Berger (ed.), *A William Appleman Williams Reader: Selections from His Major Historical Writings* (Chicago: Ivan R. Dee, 1992), 377–8.

48. William Appleman Williams, *The Tragedy of American Diplomacy* (New York: Delta, 1959; 2nd rev. ed., 1972), 297.

## Select Bibliography

Boff, L. *Church: Charism and Power: Liberation Theology and the Institutional Church*. London: SCM Press, 1985.

Dreyfus, Robert. *Devil's Game: How the US Helped Unleash Fundamentalist Islam*. New York: Henry Holt & Co. 2005.

Dunn, Dennis J. ed., *Religion and Nationalism in Eastern Europe and the Soviet Union*. London: Lynne Rienner Publishers, 1987.

Kirby, Dianne ed., *Religion and the Cold War*. Basingstoke: Palgrave Macmillan, 2003.

Lahr, Angela M. *Millennial Dreams and Apocalyptic Nightmares: The Cold War Origins of Political Evangelicalism*. New York: Oxford University Press, 2007.

Peris, Daniel. *Storming the Heavens: The Soviet League of the Militant Godless*. New York: Cornell University Press, 1998.

Silk, M. *Spiritual Politics: Religion and America Since World War II*. New York: Simon & Schuster, 1988.

# CHAPTER 32

# THE INTERNATIONAL ENVIRONMENTAL MOVEMENT AND THE COLD WAR

RICHARD P. TUCKER

THE environmental dimension of the cold war lurked for the most part on the fringes of strategic rivalries, though in terms of resource depletion, dislocation of ecosystems, and accumulation of toxic and radioactive pollution, it held some of the most fundamental global legacies of the years 1948–90. Hence a review of the cold war's dynamics and legacies must include environmental questions. Did the cold war shape the priorities and evolution of environmental movements in the Soviet and Western blocs? In the many national and international environmental organizations and grassroots movements, when and to what effect did East-West links develop? And crucially, did environmental movements challenge the guiding institutions and ideological assumptions of the cold war?

When we look back over the emergence of environmental movements around the world during the years before 1990, we can see that two largely separate movements—the environmental movement and the peace movement—shared the burden of defending the biosphere. This essay will concentrate on the emergence of and tenuous collaboration between the environmental and anti-nuclear movements.

During the cold war environmental movements were largely organized in individual countries, and focused on issues of natural resource depletion and accelerating pollution in each country.[1] They were slow to confront transnational environmental troubles relating to the cold war, even around the North Atlantic industrialized region. Until the late 1980s, moreover, they had few connections with organizations in the Soviet bloc where tight bureaucratic control of information flows and freedom of movement stifled public debate. Yet even in Western Europe and the United States, public movements struggled constantly against bureaucracies' attempts to suppress or manipulate scientific information about environmental damage. Environmental organizations also emerged in non-aligned countries, with a primary focus on local and national issues such as deforestation, water resources, and industrial pollution.[2] The few environmental organizations that operated transnationally soon recognized that they shared many of the concerns of the international peace and anti-nuclear movements.

Yet each tended to operate in its own sphere, and relations between the two were often distant or awkward.

## THE EARLY ANTI-NUCLEAR MOVEMENT

American testing of nuclear weapons in the South Pacific began within a year of its bombing of Hiroshima and Nagasaki in 1945. In July 1946 Operation Crossroads detonated the first of a series of bombs on Bikini and Enewetak Islands. The United States proceeded to initiate the world's first thermonuclear (hydrogen) bomb test in 1954. Codenamed Castle Bravo, it registered at 15 megatons, nearly three times its predicted power.[3] A Japanese tuna fishing boat, the *Lucky Dragon*, was downwind from the blast. Its crew and catch were severely irradiated, and within six months one crew member was dead; others died of cancer in the following years. Although the Atomic Energy Commission (AEC) tried to suppress information about the blast and the fallout, news of the disaster and concerns about nuclear contamination spread around Japan and the world, sparking the international movement against atomic fallout.[4] The incident struck a particular nerve in the United States, where alarm over fallout from blasts in Nevada had already begun to spread.[5]

Anti-nuclear activists struggled against a public atmosphere in which critics of American strategic policies were derided as pro-communist or as fools playing into Moscow's hands. But in the 1956 presidential campaign, Democratic candidate Adlai Stevenson legitimized public debate by warning against cancer dangers from nuclear fallout. Distinguished scientists publicized nuclear dangers, thus providing a basis for environmental activism. In the United States prominent public figures, led by *Saturday Review* editor Norman Cousins, founded the Committee for a Sane Nuclear Policy (SANE) in 1957.[6] That same year British intellectuals founded the Committee for Nuclear Disarmament (CND).

SANE and CND were complemented in 1958 by the St. Louis Committee for Nuclear Information (CNI), which organized a survey of Strontium-90 in babies' teeth, demonstrating radioactive concentrations far higher than the AEC's claims had indicated. Led by Barry Commoner, one of the country's most influential environmental publicists, CNI organized the dissemination of scientific information on a wide variety of environmental issues.[7] The fallout protest bore fruit when in 1958 Khrushchev announced that the Soviets were halting atmospheric tests, a unilateral ban that lasted three years. When John F. Kennedy entered the White House in 1961, Norman Cousins became an influential lobbyist, before long carrying messages between Kennedy and Khrushchev over a possible test ban treaty. By 1962, when American tests went underground, the AEC had conducted 232 atmospheric tests in the Pacific and Nevada Proving Grounds.

The Limited Nuclear Test Ban Treaty between the US, Britain, and the Soviet Union came about in 1963 in the aftermath of the Cuban Missile Crisis, which in October 1962 brought the superpowers to the brink of war. The signatories pledged a permanent cessation of above-ground nuclear weapons tests. Although this was a significant victory for the anti-nuclear movement, the treaty had two severe limitations. First, France and China, both determined to join the nuclear club, refused to sign. Second, the treaty allowed underground nuclear weapons testing to continue, and both the US and USSR proceeded. So American peace activists concentrated their attention on the US underground test site in southern Nevada, and organized intensive efforts to improve verification systems.

By the late 1960s protest movements in the US and Western Europe were intensifying, especially in opposition to the American conduct of the Vietnam War. In 1969 Henry Kendall and a group of MIT faculty and staff, several of whom were security-cleared consultants to the Department of Defense, founded the Union of Concerned Scientists (UCS). It soon became the most prominent American scientific lobby against the proliferation of nuclear, chemical, and biological weapons and the Vietnam War.[8]

A more militant grassroots anti-nuclear environmental activist group, Greenpeace, emerged in Vancouver, British Columbia, after protests against a planned American nuclear explosion, the Milrow blast, on Amchitka Island off the Alaskan coast in 1969, where 10,000 people participated. After the organizers planned another protest against the Cannikin blast two years later, the explosion was cancelled. Consequently, Greenpeace was established as an international voice against both nuclear weapons and nuclear energy.[9]

# THE EMERGENCE OF THE INTERNATIONAL ENVIRONMENTAL MOVEMENT

The environmental movements of the 1950s and 1960s were largely oblique to the cold war and generated little international awareness. The exception was the wildlife protection network, especially the International Union for the Conservation of Nature (IUCN), accompanied by the World Wildlife Fund founded in 1961.[10] Both were linked to the United Nations, and both encompassed scientists from both West and East. Like all official UN activities throughout the cold war, they had to be extremely discreet in discussing any issue that was politically sensitive in East/West terms.

In the United States, wildlife and wilderness protection gained momentum, in parallel with civil rights protests, feminism, the anti-war movement (largely in opposition to the Vietnam War), and resistance to rampant pollution. As a first step toward internationalization, David Brower expanded the Sierra Club's scope to global issues in the late 1960s, with personal energy that characterized the period's sense of urgency. But he ventured into controversial issues beyond the club's wildlands defense tradition, when he began pressing the club to take an official position against nuclear power. He lost the policy battle, and with finances overstretched and his authority overreached, Brower was fired as executive director. He responded by founding Friends of the Earth, as an explicitly international (at first transatlantic) network of activists. Its politically more provocative work on a broad range of global environmental issues played an important role in the campaigns of the late cold war years. The birth of Friends of the Earth reflected the new militancy and internationalism that produced Earth Day in 1970, a breakthrough in the American environmental movement and at least a temporary merging of the anti-war and environmental movements.[11]

The anti-war movement became environmentally oriented in the late 1960s, when the US Air Force began dropping chemical defoliants on the hill forests of Vietnam to deprive insurgent forces of cover. This was the first use of chemical warfare since 1918; it elicited a growing international outcry of protest—an important stage in the growth of environmentalist resistance to the spectrum of cold war ecological damage.

By the early 1970s the anti-war movement placed the US military's use of Agent Orange and other defoliants in Vietnam at the center of the struggle.[12] But reliable scientific information was not easy for the public to obtain in the face of stonewalling by the strategic command in Washington and its corporate allies. The most important monitoring and publicizing of Agent Orange and other chemical weapons came from the Stockholm International Peace Research Institute (SIPRI), especially its leading American specialist, Arthur Westing.

When the Americans withdrew from Vietnam in 1975, some activists turned their attention to peacetime environmental problems, especially air and water pollution, while others focused on the threat of nuclear disaster from both weapons and power plants. Meanwhile, more conventional environmental issues had assumed some international recognition.

## THE STOCKHOLM CONFERENCE OF 1972

The UN Conference on the Human Environment, held in Stockholm in June 1972, marked the official recognition that environmental challenges must be addressed globally. The Stockholm Conference brought together environmental movements from various countries that stretched back more than a decade. Environmental issues had been circulating within the UN since its inception, but without an identifiable agency to pursue them. By the late 1960s many leading conservationists saw the need to address this deficiency on an international stage. Canadian Maurice Strong was appointed organizer of a conference intended to address both global issues and institutional need. Neutral Sweden served as host.

The diplomatic preparatory meetings for Stockholm included Soviet and East European scientists. But the diplomacy entailed complex and sometimes acrimonious discussions. In addition, the Soviet Union tried to use the conference as leverage to force the West to recognize East Germany by insisting that unless East Germany was formally recognized as a member of the United Nations, it would withdraw from the conference, taking its satellite countries with it.

In Washington, President Richard Nixon had come to appreciate the political value of supporting environmental legislation. He gave his environmental advisor, Russell Train, chairman of the Council on Environmental Quality, support for working toward the conference. Acutely aware of the competition with the USSR on all fronts, Nixon and especially Train were committed to global environmental cooperation. "In the President's view, environmental advocacy could advance his policy of détente. It also could burnish the administration's environmental credentials without burdensome regulations or alienating its conservative base."[13]

The severe political constraints on discussing any politically sensitive issue within the cold war context were vividly evident at the conference. First, the West refused to muddle the conference with the "German Question," so the Soviet bloc withdrew from formal participation. Then, in his introductory speech Swedish Prime Minister Olaf Palme explicitly charged the United States with ecocide in Vietnam.

In the resulting official documents the only reference to military impacts (in itself the only explicit cold war issue) was in the proposed Principles for the Declaration on the Human Environment: "Man and his environment must be spared the serious effects of further testing or use in hostilities of weapons, particularly those of mass destruction." The French in particular resisted this, because France was about to test a nuclear device at Mururoa in the Pacific. The final text read: "Man and his environment must be spared the effects of nuclear weapons and all other means of mass destruction. States must strive to reach prompt agreement, in the relevant international organs, on the elimination and complete destruction of such weapons."[14]

It was again clear that the UN was able to address cold war environmental issues only obliquely. Nevertheless, the conference succeeded in enhancing international scientific and activist networks on environmental issues. It gave official standing to NGOs, granting them an institutionalized role on the international stage. The Sierra Club and Friends of the Earth had lobbied intensively at UN headquarters in New York for this, and in the aftermath the Sierra Club set up an international program office in New York, whose specific purpose was lobbying for environmental reforms.[15]

On the intergovernmental level, later UN conferences were segmented—population, women, appropriate technology, etc.—partly to make conference organization and planning manageable and coherent, and partly to reflect turf control by specialists in each subject area. Above all, subjects that were hypersensitive to member governments were at best marginalized—notably questions of national security.

Environmental movements in the North Atlantic industrialized world were beginning to recognize regional and global environmental issues and create international networks, despite disagreements over priorities and tactics. In 1978 Brower, head of Friends of the Earth, expressed the need for those networks with reference to Vietnam: "The present era of nuclear roulette poses a far greater threat to all living things than the Vietnam War did, because proliferation could stumble us into the final war."[16] There was no activist liaison with the Eastern bloc yet, as there was little public space in the Soviet countries for that sort of discussion.

# Neutral Northern Europe and cold war environmental politics: The Helsinki Convention on the Baltic, 1974

But environmental diplomacy could also be used to bridge the chasm between East and West, as the negotiations over the pollution of the Baltic Sea showed. The Baltic bordered on seven countries: the USSR, Finland, Sweden, Denmark, West and East Germany, and Poland. Because of its shallowness and very slow water exchange with the Atlantic through narrow straits by the southern coast of Sweden, it was highly vulnerable to urban and industrial pollution, affecting some 80 million people in the region. By the 1960s there was rising public alarm, and increasing scientific cooperation among Sweden and Finland (cold war neutrals) and the USSR. Work proceeded toward a formal international convention as basis for gradual clean-up. But the "German Question" stood in the way: the Federal Republic of Germany (FRG, or West Germany) and Denmark were members of NATO, while the German Democratic Republic (GDR, or East Germany), Poland, and the Soviet Union were members of the Warsaw Pact. Neither West nor East Germany officially recognized the other, and Sweden did not recognize the GDR; Finland recognized neither state. Moscow's strategic goal was to hold international environmental cooperation hostage until the West formally recognized the GDR.

Finland's close scientific ties to the Soviet Union, enshrined in a 1968 agreement on scientific cooperation on the Baltic Sea and the normalization of inner-German relations in December 1972, helped overcome the impasse. All seven Baltic countries formally participated in the 1974 Convention on the Protection of the Marine Environment of the Baltic Sea Area. This provided for gradual clean-up of all identified toxics, including industrial pollutants—a highly sensitive issue for the Russians, because it related to their military industries. The Soviets insisted that each country be solely responsible for monitoring its 12-mile coastal waters. Sweden and Finland had to relent on that issue, though it weakened long-term implementation of the treaty. All seven states ratified it by 1980, despite a difficult process of organizing HELCOM (the Helsinki Commission) to administer the treaty, and defining such terms as "pollution." Worse, its findings were nonbinding recommendations. "Power politics still prevailed over environmental politics."[17] Through the 1980s progress in the clean-up was painfully slow.

## The ultimate environmental issue: resisting nuclear war

Most environmental organizations were concentrating on wildlands protection and becoming concerned with urban and industrial pollution, unwilling to become entangled with controversial issues of war and militarization. Another set of organizations had been campaigning on the ultimate ecological crisis: the imminent threat of global disaster by nuclear war. In the West most anti-nuclear campaigns criticized both sides of the nuclear arms race but focused on demanding demilitarization by their own governments. They sought to cooperate with Eastern European peace organizations. This proved largely fruitless, because Eastern bloc peace organizations were government-run and tightly controlled. These organizations consistently denounced the West, especially the United States, for escalating the nuclear arms race without holding their own governments accountable. They offered no space for open dialogue or public dissent.

Internationally Greenpeace, developing a brilliant knack for gaining international publicity, led the way by expanding its agenda to protest against all nuclear blasts... The fledgling organization, in cooperation with the New Zealand branch of CND, targeted French nuclear explosions on Moruroa atoll in the Tuamotu Archipelago for a protest action.[18] In October 1982 David McTaggart sailed to Moruroa, in the Greenpeace ship, the *Rainbow Warrior*. Greenpeace also protested against at Soviet nuclear tests on the Novaya Zemlya Islands in the Arctic, negotiating with the Soviet Peace Committee (SPC) to sail their ship *Sirius* to Leningrad. But the SPC changed its position, halting the *Sirius* in Kronstadt harbor, and the Greenpeace agenda was stymied.

Activists in New Zealand concentrated on the French government's insistence on continuing its nuclear weapons tests on Moruroa. In 1985 French agents destroyed the *Rainbow Warrior* in Auckland harbor. This outrage resulted in major international publicity for Greenpeace and a rapid rise in its membership.[19] Greenpeace maintained close liaison with the governments of New Zealand and Australia in the movement to create a nuclear-free zone in the South Pacific. In 1984 New Zealand banned all nuclear-armed or nuclear-powered ships from its waters. Australia, New Zealand, and the Pacific Island States declared the south Pacific a nuclear-free zone, in order to stop French tests.[20] They finally succeeded when Paris declared an end to testing in the late 1980s.

From 1981–89 both the American peace and environmental movements accelerated, as public fears became focused on the "nuclear winter" debate—the omnipresent danger that a major nuclear war would destroy not only human civilization but profoundly disrupt the entire biosphere.[21] The Reagan administration's saber rattling revitalized SANE, and a Nuclear Weapons Freeze Campaign emerged. The two groups combined forces in 1987 but did not address environmental issues beyond the threat of nuclear winter.

Many citizen activists recognized the link between the peace and environmental movements but groped for strategies. David Brower had declared as early as 1969 that "the Vietnam war and the subsequent proliferation were triggered by the deepening global addiction to exponential growth in material wants, in energy consumption, and in the build-up of military-industrial strength of the nations competing to secure those wants—to preempt the resources essential for dominance.... Vietnam was the stimulus for Earth Day, which worked."[22] In Brower's old organization, the Sierra Club, a nuclear policy committee attempted to strengthen the policy plank on both nuclear war and nuclear energy (especially after the Three Mile Island nuclear crisis in 1979). Yet the club as a whole was unwilling to expand its commitment to anti-war activism.

In Great Britain elite voices challenged the British place in the nuclear arms race from early on in the cold war, protesting British nuclear bomb tests in 1952 on the Monte Bello

Islands off Australia's west coast, and from 1957 to 1962 on Malden and Christmas islands in the Pacific.[23] The debacle of the British and French invasion of Suez and the Soviet military occupation of Hungary led the British left to reconsider both communist society and the nuclear arms race. In 1957 Julian Huxley, Bertrand Russell, Kingsley Martin, the editor of the influential *New Statesman*, and other intellectuals organized the Campaign for Nuclear Disarmament (CND). CND demanded that Britain initiate unilateral nuclear disarmament and withdraw from NATO. People from a wide political spectrum organized direct action campaigns in 1960–1. After the 1962 Cuban missile crisis and the signing the next year of the Limited Nuclear Test Ban Treaty, the antinuclear campaign subsided. New left activists turned their attention to the American conduct of the war in Vietnam.

After a hiatus in the 1970s, the British anti-nuclear movement re-emerged in 1979, when NATO announced a twin track policy: to place medium-range nuclear missiles in Western Europe if disarmament talks broke down. Then the Soviet army invaded Afghanistan. The result was an end to a short decade of partial détente. The election of Ronald Reagan in 1980 further polarized the cold war.[24] Many in the British movement were specifically anti-American, demanding removal of US bases from Britain. CND publications also highlighted the effects of British uranium mining in Namibia and radiation's impacts on Navajos in New Mexico and islanders in the Pacific.

CND leaders were among the founders of the new 1980 organization, European Nuclear Disarmament (END), which stressed the importance of forging an alliance with Russian and East European groups opposing the Warsaw Pact. In October 1981 a major peace demonstration was held in Bonn, mobilizing 200–300,000 participants, with considerable clandestine support from East Germany. "The unifying theme was opposition against war and militarization, rather than support for a clearly defined alternative."[25] But END criticized the Warsaw Pact as well, resulting in the Soviet Peace Committee's rejecting cooperation. END held a second convention in Berlin in May 1983, with 3,000 participants from twenty-five countries, but none from the East. Effective East-West cooperation was not yet possible; it was to emerge rapidly after 1985.[26]

# THE GREEN MOVEMENT IN WESTERN EUROPE

Western Europe's concern over transboundary air pollution (acid rain or sulfur dioxide and nitrogen oxide) dated from the 1960s, when Swedish scientists became concerned about acidification of Swedish lakes from foreign upwind sources. Coordinated international scientific monitoring began in 1972 as an OECD (Organisation for Economic Co-operation and Development) project. The work was broadened in 1977 under the Economic Commission for Europe (ECE), which included East European members. By the late 1970s concern was rising throughout Europe over Waldsterben or forest dieback, the withering of large stands of coniferous forests, especially in mountain zones.

Intensive atmospheric pollution, from both the industrial complex and automotive economy of Western Europe and the highly polluting industrialization of the East, caused this accelerating disaster.[27]

In the early 1980s the movement became increasingly identified with Greenpeace Germany, which was organized in 1980 and grew rapidly into the most prominent activist organization in the country. Its members worked judiciously but with determination to forge links with their East German counterparts. Greenpeace and other West German Greens organized a major protest against forest decline in 1981, blaming West German polluters. But by then many West Europeans understood that the forced industrialization east of the iron curtain was playing a major role in crippling forest resources.

For the most part these discussions addressed pollution as an industrial menace, not specific to the military-industrial complex. Thus it downplayed the significance of the cold war's industrial militarization, in part so as to keep the door open for cooperation with Eastern counterparts. The 1984 Munich Conference on Transboundary Air Pollution included an unprecedented number of East Europeans. It created the "30 Percent Club" of countries vowing to reduce sulfur dioxide production to 30 percent of 1980 levels by 1990. The East European countries did not join the club, insisting on the urgency of industrial development, but the conference showcased a rare moment of East-West dialogue.[28]

## The campaign against nuclear energy

In marked contrast to their largely conservative conservationist predecessors of pre-World War II Germany, the newer protest movements of the 1960s and 70s included a very wide social and ideological spectrum of activists, including young people, new leftists, and anarchists.[29] Through the 1970s activities centered on protests against proposed nuclear power plants. Demonstrations at Wyhl, Kalkar, and Brokdorf mobilized up to 50,000 participants from throughout West Germany, the Netherlands, and France. Those three plants were cancelled, but confrontations with police split the movement, as most of its participants rejected violent tactics. A more decentralized movement closely allied with the Green Party continued through the 1980s.[30]

The West German anti-nuclear-power movement gained new strength after the Ukraine's Chernobyl disaster in 1986. It had a strong ally in Britain, but only weak support in France. In Britain CND was ambivalent about nuclear energy. Its statements stressed the dangers of shifting plutonium to making bombs, and the consequent dangers of proliferation. But many members felt that "CND is and should remain a single-issue organization, and that concern over nuclear energy, although shared by most in CND, is best expressed through environmental groups such as Greenpeace and Friends of the Earth."[31] Uncertainty and disagreement over the division of labor within the movement(s) remained characteristic.

In France the anti-nuclear-power movement in the 1970s achieved minor success in resisting the locations of new power plants. But political power in France was much more centralized than in Germany, and less susceptible to public pressure. Hence grass-roots movements were less able to achieve political leverage than in Germany.[32] This situation was reflected in the futility of public efforts to challenge French nuclear weapons testing in the Pacific.

Across Western Europe, the peace and anti-nuclear movements varied widely in their priorities, political settings, and relations to the left. As one observer commented, "The relationship between the indigenous peace movements on the one hand, and the international front organizations and the domestic Communist parties on the other, between the critics and the adversaries, differs from country to country."[33] This resulted in constant uncertainty in their stance toward Soviet nuclear weapons and energy policy, as well as toward potential allies in the East.

# ENVIRONMENTAL CONTROVERSIES IN THE SOVIET UNION

Throughout the Soviet era a tradition of nature conservation, with roots extending to tsarist times, defended wildlife preserves as a source of romantic national pride. Soviet authorities rarely saw any threat to their power or their economic objectives in this movement, especially since it was supported and even led by prestigious members of the Soviet Academy of Sciences, who were allowed to participate in international conservation organizations such as the semi-governmental IUCN, and bilateral meetings with their American counterparts under the 1972 Moscow Agreement.

The military-industrial complex was an entirely different matter. Stalin's rush to industrialize, much of it for military armaments, had created massive industrial pollution. The problem was evident early on in the controversy over pollution of the world's greatest freshwater lake, Lake Baikal in Siberia. In the 1950s pollution from severe deforestation, as well as untreated sewage from Irkutsk and its factories, began to compromise the lake's unique and fragile ecosystem. Then came proposals for two new pulp mills, which were to produce cellulose for rayon for airplane tires; thus the mills had a strategic purpose. This process required highly pure water. An intense protest arose in 1965–6, led by writers and leading members of the Academy of Sciences, with wide press coverage.[34] The controversy was tolerated by the regime in Moscow, which soon agreed to build waste treatment facilities. Implementation moved slowly, and other military production facilities were located subsequently in the region.[35] With this partial exception, through the early 1980s Moscow, followed by the satellite regimes, squelched any rumbling of protest in the press or by local dissidents concerning issues that would challenge the military-industrial complex.

One of the most dramatic examples of the unfolding crisis happened in Chelyabinsk, a region on the upper Ob River in western Siberia. The Mayak Chemical Combine had been a plutonium plant for nuclear weapons since 1948 (analogous to the Hanford,

Washington site in the United States). Like the rest of the Soviet nuclear weapons complex, it was kept highly secret.[36] In 1957 a high-level nuclear waste tank exploded. The world's worst nuclear accident to that date poisoned a wide area of land and caused many cancers. After that, nuclear wastes were dumped into nearby shallow Lake Karachai. Emitting radiation twenty-four times the intensity of the 1986 Chernobyl disaster, it soon became the most radioactive site in the world. During a 1967 drought, dry winds scattered highly toxic lake-bed sediments, poisoning a vast area. Despite the Kremlin's attempts to control the flow of information, major Western publications, first in Sweden, West Germany, and Britain, and then in America, exposed the pollution.[37] However, the facts of the Chelyabinsk disaster began leaking out to the world only in the late 1970s.[38] Meanwhile, radioactive pollution continued to accumulate at many sites, as the world was to learn in the early 1990s.

Then came the meltdown at the Chernobyl nuclear complex outside Kiev on April 26, 1986, seven years after the Three Mile Island accident in America. Chernobyl constituted the undeniable crisis in Soviet nuclear energy strategy, despite elaborate efforts in Moscow to suppress public and international discussion of the disaster. The nightmare became a major element in undermining the foundations of the Soviet system, demonstrating the technically and politically unmanageable scope of environmental pollution. "The nuclear accident at Chernobyl in 1986 did not just shock Westerners with the immediate and dangerous impacts of nuclear waste and radioactive fallout. It also provided the most striking portrait of a system whose leaders were not only negligent in terms of safeguarding against major environmental health threats, but also determined to misrepresent the extent of these maladies for political reasons."[39] Chernobyl exposed the gross negligence and incompetence of the reigning political and ideological system.[40]

# THE SOVIET BLOC UNDER PERESTROIKA AND GLASNOST, 1985–90

Even before the Chernobyl crisis, Mikhail Gorbachev had opened the door to environmental public debate. In his first foreign policy speech as Soviet leader in May 1985, Gorbachev emphasized the urgent need for effective arms control, especially of nuclear weapons, and invited greater public debate on environmental issues. From that moment a tsunami of grassroots anguish arose over industrial pollution and especially nuclear radiation. The issue itself was hot, since it challenged the heart—and the secrecy—of the Soviet system.

In August 1987 former student nature reserve activists founded the Social-Ecological Union (SEU). In 1988 they held their first open conference in Moscow, with inspiration from Western environmental radicals. SEU developed ties with Greenpeace, Friends of the Earth, the Earth Island Institute, the Nature Conservancy, the Natural Resources

Defense Council in the United States, the Swedish and Finnish Green Parties, IUCN, and others. Moving quickly, they formed the Russian Green Party, demanding a more open system and massive environmental clean-up.[41]

As the grassroots environmental movement in Russia emerged, protests against environmental pollution and its public health risks proliferated throughout the Eastern bloc.[42] East Germany saw the earliest and strongest variety of environmental protests, mostly sheltered by the Protestant churches. Their discontent emphasized both disarmament and environmental issues—in the context of pressing for broader space for civic action. In the early 1980s East German activists developed both official and personal links with West German Greens. Indeed, the country's new leader, Erich Honecker, met with West German Green leaders in October 1983. Nevertheless, repression ensued in the following month. But by early 1986 it became easier for West Germans to get permits to meet with counterparts in Berlin. Contacts and degree of ease varied until 1989.[43] Meanwhile, East Germans gained ready access to information about international environmental controversies and activist politics in the West through West German television.[44]

Poland, like Russia, had a long tradition of protecting nature reserves as an expression of national pride. Under communist rule the League for the Protection of Nature (LOP) was a governmental organ, but its agenda was limited. When the Solidarity movement produced cracks in the regime's façade in 1980, environmental protest became possible. Until then both government and public had been firmly committed to rapid industrialization, and the government suppressed evidence of widespread industrial pollution. Before its suppression in 1981, nevertheless, Solidarity opened the floodgates of public discussion of pollution crises and public health disasters. Even the LOP joined in, publishing a detailed report in 1981.[45] The force of the change was evident that year, when the Skawina aluminum plant outside Cracow, which produced half of Poland's entire aluminum supply, was compelled to close, having polluted 230 sq km with fluorides.

Soon the Academy of Sciences and National Planning Commission began openly discussing the environmental costs of rapid industrialization. And many semi-spontaneous local protests arose against severe pollution of water supplies, including rivers.[46] But there was a pervasive dilemma: as the closing of Skawina plant exemplified, tightening environmental controls threatened to retard economic development. Environmental scientists and government administrators wrestled with the far stronger agency for industrial development. By 1989, when Solidarity was officially recognized again, environmental controversies were central to the full-scale struggle over the political life of the country.

In other Eastern bloc countries environmental movements were often closely linked to ethno-nationalism, as those societies struggled for autonomy from Moscow in the late 1980s. The Slovak segment of Czechoslovakia went through an upheaval that linked environmental protest with ethnic nationalism. As in Russia the Communist regime had tolerated (even integrated) a movement to protect nature reserves and traditional rural architecture. In Bratislava, Slovakia's capital, the Slovak Union of Nature and Landscape Protectors became bolder in its denunciation of rampant pollution in the urban region.

Then, on international Earth Day in April 1989, the Union issued a statement demanding full public debate and an overhaul of environmental management. Within months the Velvet Revolution overturned the Communist regime, pursuing basic institutional change through environmental protest campaigns. In that heady but brief period, tens of thousands of people joined the environmental movement.

In Latvia environmental protest emerged in a different form, an ethno-nationalist defense of family farms against Soviet collectivization. After 1945 "much of the rural mosaic landscape gave way to the flattened and drained tracts of large-scale mechanized collective farming, and half of Latvia's traditional isolated farmsteads, surrounded by decorative trees, were bulldozed."[47] When Gorbachev's glasnost opened the door for public movements, a massive protest was organized in late 1986 against a planned hydro dam on the Daugava River. The protest gained a decisive victory when the Latvian Soviet government cancelled the dam.

In neighboring Baltic republics as well, environmental protest was linked to the anti-Soviet independence movement. In Lithuania environmental dissidents organized a national protest against untreated sewage in its rivers. In October 1986 a petition with 600,000 signatures (16 percent of the national population!) demanded that the Ignalinos nuclear plant, which had been badly damaged by fire, be closed entirely. A newly installed and sympathetic national government closed the existing plant and cancelled an additional planned unit. The movement went international in September 1988, when 15,000 people demonstrated along the Baltic shore of Lithuania, coordinating with others in Latvia, Estonia, Finland, and Denmark, to accelerate the lagging clean-up of the Sea.[48]

In other countries, especially Kazakhstan, environmental protest movements were internationally oriented from the start. In contrast to East European republics, this did not represent ethnic nationalism, since Kazakhs had been reduced to 39 percent of Kazakhstan's population after a history of deportations of Kazakh people under the tsars and Stalin, mass starvation in the 1930s, and the import of many Slavs during Khrushchev's Virgin Lands program of the 1950s, which irrigated wide reaches for cotton, draining the Aral Sea. Kazakh protests against the Aral Sea disaster were muted, because this was a complex multi-republic problem, and Kazakhs wanted to avoid criticizing agricultural expansion.

In contrast, protesting nuclear tests' health disasters drew large numbers on to the streets in 1989, in what became the Nevada-Semipalatinsk movement. Soviet bomb tests had been conducted in the semi-barren steppe since 1949, first above ground until 1963, then underground. In February 1989 toxic gases escaped from containers, poisoning a wide area. A grassroots movement, uniting ethnic Russians and Kazakhs, collected one million signatures in support of closing the site and banning nuclear weapons worldwide. The movement called itself Nevada-Semipalatinsk, sometimes adding Moruroa, as a reminder of ongoing French bomb testing on that Pacific island. Nevada-Semipalatinsk forged new international contacts, especially in France and the US, and with Japanese survivors of the Hiroshima and Nagasaki bombings in 1945. The 1990 elections brought to office a legislature which strongly favored closing the site. In August 1991 President Nazarbayev responded by ending operations.

# OTHER INTERNATIONAL ENVIRONMENTAL LINKS
## IN THE LATE 1980S

In America the anti-nuclear campaign focused on the belligerence of the Reagan admin-istration, emphasizing the apocalyptic fear of nuclear winter, and more broadly, of esca-lating military budgets. David Brower, who had again seen his organization split, in 1986 founded the Earth Island Institute in San Francisco, which continued the campaign against the nuclear establishment West and East.

One of the Sierra Club's International Programs Committee's founding members, the environmental lawyer Nicholas Robinson, had long been active in US-USSR relations. Robinson was a key member of US delegations to the annual meetings of the May 1972 Soviet-American Agreement to Protect the Environment, which immediately preceded the Stockholm Conference. Over the last two decades of the cold war, bilateral meetings held under this agreement produced an impressive record of agreements on environ-mental law, and sustained working contacts among lawyers and scientists.[49]

Conversely, contacts for American environmental NGOs were possible only through the State Department's links with the official All-Russia Society for the Conservation of Nature. In 1979 Michael McCloskey headed an American delegation to Russia. Because the Sierra Club lobbied with its government, however, whereas the Russian Society was largely official, he found little in common with his Soviet counterparts. There was little further cooperation until a 1988 visit by the Russians, and then an American delegation to Russia reciprocated in 1990. But all was lackluster. McCloskey concluded, "While Russia needed environmental help in all sorts of ways, we were not in a position to pro-vide it, nor could it be done effectively through the All-Russia Society." [50]

As perestroika advanced in the Soviet bloc in the late 1980s, communication among nuclear scientists improved, especially after Chernobyl. The fact that Soviet scientists had trouble connecting with each other was not lost on their international colleagues. Another illustration of the new opportunities was the IUCN, which had consistently tried to keep its door open to East Europe, but with only formal success. Delegates from those countries had been to many IUCN meetings, partly because of the high prestige and social-political position of scientists, including biologists, in those countries. But little of substance had been possible until the late 1980s. At its General Assembly in 1988, IUCN launched an East European Programme (EEP). Its first work was to publish sev-eral national environmental status reports in 1990, though even then the authors took political risks, because their work was inherently critical of the Soviet era. But IUCN's Czech representative noted that they "in some modest way even contributed to those [great political] changes."[51] At a meeting in Moscow in February 1990, it changed its name to the IUCN East European Programme Advisory Group. Its agenda now included organizing national and regional environmental monitoring, Danube basin environmental clean-up, and evaluating the environmental impact of intensive agriculture—all of them devastatingly critical of the Soviet era. As this example demonstrates, times had changed rapidly and radically. But the long-term benefit of the transformation after 1990 would prove to be deeply disappointing.

# THE AFTERMATH

By 1990 the environmental victims of the Soviet system and the cold war had won their struggle to open the political process. In that year elections were held throughout East Europe, and many protest movement leaders ran successfully. But the environmental clean-up itself was a far more difficult matter. As one leading observer concluded, "Environmental degradation was seen as the legacy of the former regimes, and regeneration of the environment was seen as part of the establishment of a new and more humane order. It was also a subject of internationally recognized legitimacy and popularity. While virtually every party included sections on the environment in its manifesto, in the great majority of cases the references represented no more than a symbolic indictment of the previous regime."[52]

In Russia by fall 1990 several hundred chemical plants and other factories were closed on environmental grounds, but the loss of jobs and incomes produced an untenable situation. As Feshbach and Friendly note, "Expensive ecological controls would have been hard to institute in a buoyant setting. In the midst of economic disintegration, they fed the gathering backlash against Gorbachev's reform drive in general and Green campaigners in particular."[53]

Throughout the former Soviet region environmental priorities were marginalized, as environmental protest declined precipitously.[54] In Chelyabinsk, for example, where some one million people were victims of radiation exposure from the Mayak complex, activists new to political organizing formed the Movement for Nuclear Safety in 1990, attracting some 2,000 members. Establishing a local Green Party a year later, they attracted 300,000 signatures for a petition to close the region's nuclear industry. But as elsewhere in Russia, old-regime scientists and bureaucrats competed with the newcomers for leverage. The high point of the movement was an international conference on nuclear pollution, hosted by the environmental leaders of Chelyabinsk city in May 1992. For a week scientists, physicians, administrators, environmentalists from around the former Soviet republics, Western Europe, North America, and Japan compared notes and generated policy strategies. But thereafter the systemic economic crisis in Russia and its neighbors drained the movement's energies.[55]

As environmental leaders shifted from impassioned protest to pragmatic management, they faced the imperative to reconstruct their economies (along free market lines). Environmental clean-up was seen as either too expensive or a major impediment to that urgent rebuilding. As the command economies fell apart, funds were unavailable for industrial retrofitting or pollution cleanup. And the struggle for economic employment and income forced many participants in the protests of the late 1980s to abandon hope for short-term environmental improvements. In an unfortunate irony, resurgent nationalism in former Soviet republics worked against international environmental liaison. As one observer writes, "with the fall of communism in Slovakia, not only did greens lose a clear target, but the return of nationalism to the political arena unexpectedly refigured some forms of environmentalism as foreign concepts and as challenges to cultural and political independence."[56]

Internationally, the 1990s saw only marginal progress toward a truly global environmental movement, though rising awareness of global warming gave the potential for understanding the interconnections of environmental damage throughout the biosphere. Each nuclear power, through its rapid militarization, had poisoned its own lands far more severely than those of its adversary. Yet even now there is a pervasive lack of public awareness of the environmental impacts of militarization, reflecting an inchoate resistance to confronting such controversial and sensitive issues. This is in spite of the cold war's devastating ecological consequences. This lack of recognition also reflects the varied and fragmented evolution of the many environmental action groups—West, East, and international—over the course of the cold war. Lacking any consensus on the relations between environmental and strategic challenges, they understandably were unable to establish any lasting focus for public awareness.

## Notes

1. Christof Mauch, Nathan Stoltzfus, and Douglas R. Weiner, eds., *Shades of Green: Environmental Activism around the Globe* (Lanham, MD: Rowman & Littlefield, 2006).
2. N. Patrick Peritore, *Third World Environmentalism: Case Studies from the Global South* (Gainesville, FL: University Press of Florida, 1999).
3. Ralph H. Lutts, "Chemical Fallout: Rachel Carson's Silent Spring, Radioactive Fallout, and the Environmental Movement," *Environmental Review* 9:3 (Fall 1985): 210–25; Mark D. Merlin and Ricardo M. Gonzalez, "Environmental Impacts of Nuclear Testing in Remote Oceania, 1946–1996," in John R. McNeill and Corinna R. Unger, eds., *Environmental Histories of the Cold War* (Cambridge: Cambridge University Press, 2010).
4. Ralph A. Lapp, *The Voyage of the Lucky Dragon* (New York: Harper, 1958).
5. Robert A. Divine, *Blowing on the Wind: The Nuclear Test Ban Debate, 1954–1960* (New York: Oxford, 1978), 262–80.
6. Lawrence S. Wittner, *Confronting the Bomb: A Short History of the World Nuclear Disarmament Movement* (Palo Alto, CA: Stanford University Press, 2009); Milton S. Katz, *Ban the Bomb: A History of SANE, 1957–1985* (New York: Greenwood, 1986).
7. Barry Commoner, *The Closing Circle: Nature, Man & Technology* (New York: Bantam Books, 1972), 51–2.
8. Henry W. Kendall, *A Distant Light: Scientists and Public Policy* (New York: Springer-Verlag, 2000), 1–7.
9. Frank Zelko, "'Make It a Green Peace': The History of an International Environmental Organization," Ph.D. dissertation, University of Kansas, 2003.
10. Martin Holdgate, *The Green Web: A Union for World Conservation* (London: Earthscan, 1999).
11. Frank Zelko, "Challenging Modernity: The Origins of Postwar Environmental Protest in the United States," in Mauch et al., *Shades of Green*, 13–40; Adam Rome, "'Give Earth a

Chance': The Environmental Movement and the Sixties," *Journal of American History* 90:2 (September 2003): 525–54; Frank Uekoetter, "A Twisted Road to Earth Day: Air Pollution as an Issue of Social Movements after World War II," in Michael Egan and Jeff Crane, eds., *Natural Protest: Essays on the History of American Environmentalism* (New York and London: Routledge, 2009),163–84.

12. Barry Weisberg, *Ecocide in Indochina: The Ecology of War* (San Francisco: Canfield, 1970); David Zierler, *The Invention of Ecocide* (Athens, GA: University of Georgia Press, 2011).

13. Barbara Ward and Rene Dubos, *Only One Earth: The Care and Maintenance of a Small Planet* (New York: Norton, 1972); J. Brooks Flippen, *Conservative Conservationist: Russell E. Train and the Emergence of American Environmentalism* (Baton Rouge, LA: Louisiana State University Press, 2006), 121; Russell E. Train, *Politics, Pollution, and Pandas: An Environmental Memoir* (Washington, DC: Island Press, 2003), 133–9.

14. Peter B. Stone, *Did We Save the Earth at Stockholm?* (London: Earth Island, 1973), 73, 151.

15. Michael McCloskey, *In the Thick of It: My Life in the Sierra Club* (Washington, DC: Island Press, 2005), 159–62.

16. David R. Brower, *Work in Progress* (Salt Lake City, UT: Peregrine Books, 1991), 174.

17. Tuomas Rasanen and Simo Laakkonen, "Cold War and the Environment: The Role of Finland in International Politics in the Baltic Sea Region," *Ambio* 36:2 (April 2007): 229–36, 233.

18. Bengt and Marie-Therese Danielsson, *Poisoned Reign: French Nuclear Colonialism in the Pacific*, 2nd rev. ed. (New York: Penguin Books, 1986).

19. Jim Bohlen, *Making Waves: The Origins and Future of Greenpeace* (Montreal: Black Rose Books, 2001); Michael Brown and John May, *The Greenpeace Story* (Scarborough: Prentice-Hall Canada, 1989).

20. Stewart Firth, *Nuclear Playground* (Honolulu, HI: University of Hawaii Press, 1987), x–xii, 12–13.

21. Philip Shabekoff, *A Fierce Green Fire: The American Environmental Movement* (New York: Hill and Wang, 1993), 186–202.

22. Brower, *Work in Progress*, 174.

23. Lorna Arnold and Mark Smith, *Britain, Australia and the Bomb: The Nuclear Tests and their Aftermath*, 2nd ed. (London: Palgrave, 2006).

24. Paul Byrne, *The Campaign for Nuclear Disarmament* (London: Croom Helm, 1988), 42–53, 111–23.

25. Frank Uekoetter, "Peace with Nature and the World: Environmental and Anti-War Activism in the Two German States," in McNeill and Unger, *Environmental Histories*, 343–51.

26. Clive Rose, *Campaigns Against Western Defence: NATO's Adversaries and Critics* (London: Macmillan, 1985), chap. 9.

27. Frank Zelko and Carolin Brinkmann, eds., *Green Parties: Reflections on the First Three Decades* (Washington, DC: Heinrich Böll Foundation, 2006), online at <http://www.ghi-dc.org>; Arvid Nelson, *Cold War Ecology: Forests, Farms, and People in the East German Landscape, 1945–1989* (New Haven, CT: Yale University Press, 1905), 141–70.

28. William T. Markham, *Environmental Organizations in Germany: Hardy Survivors in the Twentieth Century and Beyond* (New York: Berghahn Books, 2008), 234–41; Stanley J. Kabala, "The History of Environmental Protection in Poland and the Growth of Awareness and Activism," in Barbara Jancar-Webster, ed., *Environmental Action in Eastern Europe* (Armonk: M. E. Sharpe, 1993), 124.

29. Sandra Chaney, *Nature of the Miracle Years: Conservation in West Germany, 1945–1975* (New York: Berghahn Books, 2008); Brian Doherty, *Ideas and Actions in the Green Movement* (London and New York: Routledge, 2002), 39–43.

30. Dorothy Nelkin and Michael Pollak, *The Atom Besieged: Extraparliamentary Dissent in France and Germany* (Cambridge, MA: MIT Press, 1981), 60–8, Horst Mewes, "A Brief History of the Germany Green Party," in Margit Mayer and John Ely, eds., *The German Greens: Paradox between Movement and Party* (Philadelphia: Temple University Press, 1998), 29–48.

31. Byrne, *Campaign*, 123.

32. Gabrielle Hecht, *The Radiance of France: Nuclear Power and National Identity after World War II* (Cambridge, MA: MIT Press, 1998).

33. Rose, *Campaigns*, 157.

34. Philip R. Pryde, *Conservation in the Soviet Union* (Cambridge: Cambridge University Press, 1972), 147–51.

35. Thane Gustafson, *Reform in Soviet Politics: Lessons of Recent Policies on Land and Water* (Cambridge: Cambridge University Press, 1981), 39–51.

36. John M. Whiteley, "The Compelling Realities of Mayak," in Russell J. Dalton et al., *Critical Masses: Citizens, Nuclear Weapons Production, and Environmental Destruction in the United States and Russia* (Cambridge, MA: MIT Press, 1999), 29–58.

37. Philip R. Pryde, *Conservation in the Soviet Union* (Cambridge: Cambridge University Press, 1972); Marshall I. Goldman, *The Spoils of Progress: Environmental Pollution in the Soviet Union* (Cambridge, MA: MIT Press, 1972).

38. Zhores Medvedev, *Nuclear Disaster in the Urals* (New York: Norton, 1979); Boris Komarov, *The Destruction of Nature in the Soviet Union* (Armonk, NY: M. E. Sharpe, 1980).

39. Edward Snajdr, *Nature Protests: The End of Ecology in Slovakia* (Seattle, WA: University of Washington Press, 2008), 16.

40. Murray Feshbach and Alfred Friendly, Jr., *Ecocide in the USSR: Health and Nature Under Siege* (New York: Basic Books, 1992); Murray Feshbach, *Ecological Disaster: Cleaning up the Hidden Legacy of the Soviet Regime* (New York: Twentieth Century Fund, 1995).

41. Douglas R. Weiner, *A Little Corner of Freedom* (Berkeley, CA: University of California Press, 1999), 433–4.

42. Duncan Fisher, "The Emergence of the Environmental Movement in Eastern Europe and its Role in the Revolutions of 1989," in Barbara Jancar-Webster, ed., *Environmental Action in Eastern Europe* (Armonk, NY: M. E. Sharpe, 1993), 89–113.

43. Volker Gransow, "A Greening of German-German Relations?" in Eva Kolinsky, ed., *The Greens in West Germany: Organisation and Policy Making* (Oxford and New York: St. Martin's Press, 1989), 141–58.

44. Nathan Stoltzfus, "Public Space and the Dynamics of Environmental Action: Green Protest in the German Democratic Republic," *Archiv für Sozialgeschichte* 43 (2003): 385–403.

45. Stanley J. Kabala, "The History of Environmental Protection in Poland and the Growth of Awareness and Activism," in Jancar-Webster, *Environmental Action*, 114–33.

46. Jacek Purat, "The Woe of Zelazowa Wola," *Earth Island Journal* (Fall 1987): 18–19.

47. Katrina Z. S. Schwartz, *Nature and National Identity after Communism: Globalizing the Ethnoscape* (Pittsburgh, PA: University of Pittsburgh Press, 2006), 81.

48. Gale Warner, "Eco-Politics in the Soviet Baltic Republics," *Earth Island Journal* (Winter 1988–9): 27.

49. Nicholas Robinson and Gary Waxmonsky, "The US-USSR Agreement to Protect the Environment: 15 Years of Cooperation," *Environmental Law* 18 (Spring 1988): 403–47; Train, *Politics*, 125–33.

50. McCloskey, *In the Thick*, 167–8, 317–18.

51. Jan Cerovsky, "IUCN and Eastern Europe," *IUCN Bulletin* 21:4 (December 1990): 27–8.
52. Fisher, "Emergence of the Environmental Movement," 103.
53. Feshbach and Friendly, *Ecocide in the USSR*, 248.
54. Matthew R. Auer, ed., *Restoring Cursed Earth: Appraising Environmental Policy Reforms in Eastern Europe and Russia* (Lanham, MD: Rowman & Littlefield, 2004); Jürg Klarer and Bedrich Moldan, eds., *The Environmental Challenge for Central European Economies in Transition* (Chichester: John Wiley & Sons, 1997).
55. Paula Garb and Galina Komarova, "A History of Environmental Activism in Chelyabinsk," in Dalton et al., *Critical Masses*, 165–80.
56. Snajdr, *Nature Protests*, 6.

## Select Bibliography

Byrne, Paul. *The Campaign for Nuclear Disarmament*. London: Croom Helm, 1988.

Dalton, Russell J., et al. *Critical Masses: Citizens, Nuclear Weapons Production, and Environmental Destruction in the United States and Russia*. Cambridge, MA: MIT Press, 1999.

Feshbach, Murray. *Ecological Disaster: Cleaning up the Hidden Legacy of the Soviet Regime*. New York: Twentieth Century Fund, 1995.

Jancar-Webster, Barbara, ed. *Environmental Action in Eastern Europe*. Armonk: M. E. Sharpe, 1993.

Markham, William T. *Environmental Organizations in Germany: Hardy Survivors in the Twentieth Century and Beyond*. New York: Berghahn Books, 2008.

Mauch, Christof, Nathan Stoltzfus, and Douglas R. Weiner, eds. *Shades of Green: Environmental Activism around the Globe*. Lanham, MD: Rowman & Littlefield, 2006.

McNeill, John R., and Corinna R. Unger, eds. *Environmental Histories of the Cold War*. Cambridge: Cambridge University Press, 2010.

Nelkin, Dorothy, and Michael Pollak. *The Atom Besieged: Extraparliamentary Dissent in France and Germany*. Cambridge, MA: MIT Press, 1981.

Rasanen, Tuomas, and Simo Laakkonen. "Cold War and the Environment: The Role of Finland in International Politics in the Baltic Sea Region," *Ambio* 36:2 (April 2007): 229–36.

Weiner, Douglas R. *A Little Corner of Freedom*. Berkeley, CA: University of California Press, 1999.

Wittner, Lawrence S. *Confronting the Bomb: A Short History of the World Nuclear Disarmament Movement*. Palo Alto, CA: Stanford University Press, 2009.

Zierler, David. *The Invention of Ecocide*. Athens, GA: University of Georgia Press, 2011.

...............................................................

# CHAPTER 33

# GLOBALIZATION AND
# THE COLD WAR

...............................................................

## HYUNG-GU LYNN

In the 1990s "globalization" became a buzzword, promising the launch of a thousand new projects to map and conquer the new neo-liberal political and economic realities that were sweeping the globe. Evidence of globalization, perhaps because of the multiple spaces and forms covered by the term, seemed visible and tangible everywhere—the cornucopia of goods made in China or Vietnam stacked in North American retail stores, Thai and Sri Lankan sapphire merchants amassing in boom towns built around makeshift mines in Madagascar's interior, or advertisements for South Korean conglomerates stenciled on the uniforms of powerhouse soccer teams in the English Premier League.

These and various other developments stuffed under the rubric of globalization provoke questions regarding connections between the cold war and globalization. Did globalization only manifest itself after the end of the cold war, or was the cold war part of a longer trajectory toward globalization? In other words, did the cold war stifle, inhibit, or delay the process of globalization? This chapter answers these questions by arguing that globalization did not succeed or supersede the cold war, but emerged from it through the rapid increase in the speed, scale, and scope of transnational linkages, fueled largely by developments in communications, transportation, and international agreements that occurred during the years 1945 to 1989.

The argument that the cold war was the cradle of globalization runs counter to prevailing tendencies in studies of globalization. The most dominant of these is the argument that the unipolar or multipolar globalization order displaced the bipolar cold war world order. Given the plentiful evidence of transborder trade and flows in earlier periods of history, however, any assertion that globalization is a profoundly new phenomenon requires evidence of significant difference in either the speed, scale, intensity, or patterns of global flows in capital, goods, people, and ideas from these previous interactions.[1] This chapter confronts this challenge first, by parsing the various assumptions that are packed into the concept of globalization, and second, by analyzing cold war innovations in three interlinked areas of globalization—communications, transportation, and international agreements. These innovations were essential in enabling the speed, scale, and scope of transborder interactions.

# DEFINING GLOBALIZATION

The word "globalization" has seeped into the academic lexicon throughout the world; however, it has encompassed a spectrum of subjects and practices without sufficient clarification of the boundaries and processes it contains. It is imperative to distinguish at least five broad ways in which the term is used—empirical, normative, temporal, spatial, and paradigmatic. The most common usage of the term is *empirical*. At the apex of the globalization discourse in the 1990s, Arjun Appadurai distinguished the interplay of economic, cultural, and political transborder flows in five fields: technoscape (science and technology), mediascape (popular culture and media), ideoscape (ideas and norms), ethnoscape (the flow of people), and financescape (currency, investments).[2] These are doubtless useful categories for thinking about the different areas in which such flows have been occurring in the post-1989 world. Nevertheless, this framework does not address the causal dynamics driving globalization. The actual growth in scale, speed, and scope of these different types of flows has been fueled not merely by parallel developments in the various scapes, but also through specific innovations in three areas over the course of the cold war: communications, transportation, and international agreements. More specifically, the speed and scale of diffusion and circulation of information has accelerated immeasurably through the use of computers, the internet, and email in the technoscape, mediascape, and ideoscape. Furthermore, the growth in the scale and speed of commercial mass transportation has facilitated migration and travel in the ethnoscape. Lastly, the proliferation of multilateral, regional, and bilateral international agreements has enabled rapid and large transactions of foreign currency, stocks, commodities futures, and direct investments in the financescape.

Second, globalization *normatively* includes multiple sets of policies, practices, and effects that are discussed at cross-purposes. For instance, globalization has led to the diffusion of diseases; at the same time, it has promoted the worldwide use of medicines. If some animal and plant species were successfully transplanted as food sources, others have become pests. The important point is to start with the presumption of the multivalent intentions, effects, and interpretations of globalization and trace specific origins into the cold war.

Third, globalization often has a *temporal* meaning, pegged to a specific post-cold war paradigm that allegedly emerged after the fall of the Berlin Wall. Early globalization theorists claimed that qualitative changes in the post-cold war era were so profound that they constituted a new age of "globality," an "epochal transformation" that required new paradigms. Initially, observers cited the establishment of the World Trade Organization (WTO) in 1995 and the International Criminal Court (ICC) in 2002 as examples of a fundamentally new era of international integration. The focus on distinctions between a bipolar Cold War period and a multipolar or unipolar globalization period, however, overlooks important continuities between the two periods.

Fourth, globalizations' *spatial* implications converge around sources of global flows, the high tide of its reach, and the tidal interplay between the global and the local. In its most reductionist formulation, globalization is treated merely as a synonym for any transborder flow. At the next level of conceptualization, Westernization, McDonaldization, and Americanization are seen as equivalents of globalization.[3] While useful in drawing attention to the systemic inequalities fueling or exacerbated by globalization, such approaches can underplay the fact that globalization is often highly differentiated in its effects, mediated by the array of factors such as wealth, class, gender, age, location, and mobility.

While I agree with George Ritzer's characterization of globalization as encompassing both "glocalization" (local adaptations of the global) and "grobalization" (profit-oriented hegemonic ambitions of nations, corporations, and organization), there are serious problems with his insistence on locating the primary source of globalization in the West, considering the significant role non-Western countries such as Japan, South Korea, China, and Singapore have played in propelling globalization in various fields.[4] The spatial dynamics and directional flows of globalization do not consolidate all localities into a global monoculture, or merely export the "West" into a previously isolated "local."

Fifth, the *paradigmatic* view of globalization in the 1990s requires reconsideration. What began with bold predictions of the atrophy of the state has evolved into the position that although the nation-state and its institutions have not dissipated, a fundamental shift has occurred in spatial and temporal organization of administrative units, which require new social science approaches that overcome the limitations of the territorialist assumptions of existing frameworks. Deterritorialization, according to this view, has also altered individual identities by transforming people's sense of collective belonging, the experience of place and of self in relation to place.[5] The "historicist" counterargument is that global economic integration occurred on a large scale from 1850 to 1914, followed by a period of deglobalization from 1914 to 1960, which was eventually displaced by a "second wave" of globalization starting around 1960, albeit with considerable regional variation.[6]

Claims of a fundamental paradigm shift, on the one hand, do seem exaggerated. For example, the persistence of notions of ethnicity and nationalism in shaping individual and collective subjectivities has been constant despite the alleged possibilities of more flexible subjectivities under globalization.[7] Global economic integration in trade proceeded at similar levels in 1938 as in 1990, with the East Asian trading region actually registering twice as high levels of economic integration in 1938 than in 1990, according to one calculation.[8]

On the other hand, there are major differences in the routes, types, and speed of the diffusion and circulation of goods, people, money, and ideas. One significant difference is that the value of financial transactions has been exponentially greater in the post-1960 years than in the pre-1914 years. After the end of the fixed rate exchange regimes in the early 1970s, global foreign exchange transactions increased from around $4.6 trillion in value in 1977 to $400 trillion in 1998, or 3.5 times the value of trade in goods in 1977 to 68 times the value by 1998. The introduction and spread of electronic funds transfer and trading systems throughout the 1990s propelled even larger volumes of inter-bank and individual trading, so much so that, in 2010, the average *daily* value of foreign exchange rate was around $4 trillion.[9] Another is that much of the pre-1914 trade was driven by exchange in primary goods between imperial metropoles and their colonies, rather than the equal or unequal trade between sovereign nations that characterizes the post-1960 activities.[10]

Therefore, I would argue that, even if globalization did not signal an epochal shift, a new *genus* of empirical phenomena, its specific characteristics, such as speed, scale, scope, and form, clearly distinguish it from previous forms of transnational flows, rendering globalization a new *species*. Thus, speaking of different waves of globalization throughout history is misleading. Such a view of globalization infused with clear parameters as to what it does and does not include, and what the core components are, provides the essential foundation for the argument that the cold war period was the immediate origin of globalization as we have defined it.

## COMMUNICATIONS, COLD WAR, AND GLOBALIZATION

The primary developments that gave rise to the information and communications technology (ICT) revolution occurred during the cold war. These include the global spread of electrical generation; the proliferation of communications satellites; commercial application of integrated circuits, fiber optics, and microprocessors; and the explosive growth of home/personal computers, the Internet, and the World Wide Web.

Previous technological innovations had compressed space and time. Telegraphs, telephones, and radio spawned regional, national, and transnational networks of infrastructure, and these in turn fostered new notions of collectivity, instantaneity, and punctuality.[11]

These technologies and media, nonetheless, did not have the same impact on the scale and speed of flows as the digital ICT revolution. One study by Morgan Stanley, for example, estimated that it took radio nearly forty years to reach 50 million users in 1960 in the US; it took only five years for the Internet to reach the same mark (in 1994).[12] One of the key preconditions of the ICT revolution was the diffusion of electricity to power research and production equipment, as well as end-use technologies throughout the world after 1945. World electricity generation increased from 5,000 terawatt (TWh) hours in 1970 to 11,000 TWh in 1989, with the share of OECD (Organisation for Economic Co-operation and Development) countries declining over the same period from 69 percent in 1970 to 58 percent in 1989. This expansion in developing countries was propelled by the diffusion of rural electrification, hydroelectric water pumps for agricultural irrigation, electrical household appliances, growth of manufacturing and electricity-intensive industries, and, in some countries, the growth of nuclear energy. In particular, economic growth in Asia was reflected in its increase in total output and percentage of electricity generation—from 7 percent of the world total in 1950 to 20 percent by 1990.[13]

In addition to burgeoning generation and use of electricity, the cold war years also fueled ICT innovations via the space race. The Soviet launch of the Sputnik satellite in October 1957 spurred US development of the space program and eventually led to the US liberalization of satellites for commercial communications purposes. The 1962 Communications Satellite Act created COMSAT (Communication Satellite Corporation), which oversaw the use of satellite communications and then in 1964 INTELSAT (International Telecommunication Satellite Organization). INTELSAT was replaced by more permanent structures that expanded the number of member states to over one hundred by 1973, although it was unsuccessful in persuading the Soviet Union to participate. The Soviets instead chose to form a much smaller rival network, Intersputnik, in 1971.[14]

Cold war military development also fostered innovations in transistors and computers. The early electronic computers of the 1950s were used largely for military purposes, such as decoding messages and designing missiles and aircraft. The US and the UK were the frontrunners in the development of digital computers, holding a virtual monopoly into the mid-1950s. However, the technology quickly grew from military and scientific applications to commercial ones in the latter half of the 1950s, prompting East Germany, France, Italy, Japan, the Soviet Union, Sweden, and West Germany to join the group of computer producers by 1961.[15]

The broadening applications of computers for scientific and commercial use resulted in nearly concurrent breakthroughs in integrated circuits in 1958 by Jack Kilby at Texas Instruments and in 1959 by Robert Noyce at Fairchild Corporation. Intel, a spin-off from Fairchild founded in 1968, collaborated with Busicom, a Japanese manufacturer of calculators, to develop the first commercial microprocessor chip, released to the market as the Intel 4004 in 1971.[16] The increasingly smaller and more powerful microprocessors in turn spurred the growth of personal or home computers that have been crucial to the everyday and widespread application of ICT innovations that has been one of the characteristics of globalization.

Likewise, the Internet was initially driven by the US military's desire to improve strategic communications and networking capacities in the 1960s. While various applied and basic research streams fed into it, the earliest incarnation of the Internet was developed within the US Department of Defense to generate technology for military applications such as ballistic missiles guidance systems.[17] Even if the World Wide Web's history, usually traced to 1990, is significantly shorter than that of the Internet, the underlying hardware and networks were developed under the aegis of the cold war.

## Transportation, cold war, and globalization

If the ICT innovations during the cold war formed the basis for virtual exchange of information, funds, and ideas, the concurrent mass transportation revolution expanded the speed and scope of the movement of people and goods, and through them, ideas and images. In 1960, there were an estimated 75 million transnational migrants; by 2000, this number had risen to 175 million. The increase in speed and scale of migration and trade was greatly aided by greater access to information, communication, and new forms of mass transportation.[18]

The transport of goods did not result in higher levels of trade integration compared to the pre-1914 period, but the speed and scale of transport increased. One of the main reasons for this was the increase in size, capacity, and speed of cargo ships, and the introduction of containers for shore-side operations that reduced the number of days ships waited in port to have their cargo removed. The exponential growth in shipbuilding volume is also reflected in the fact that it took fifty years for ships to evolve from a maximum carrying capacity of 300 tons in 1884 to 10,000 tons, but it took only five years for the supertanker designation to increase from ships with at least 50,000 deadweight tons (dwt: carrying capacity plus the weight of ship's fuel) to 100,000 dwt in 1959, and then just another six years (1966) to double to 200,000 dwt vessels. The development of the standard containers for maritime transport stemmed from entrepreneurial innovation and cold war military priorities. During the Vietnam War, the US government deputized entrepreneur Malcolm McLean to improve shipping efficiency between the US and Vietnam. McLean had developed the container for his long-haul trucking business in 1956, and he applied the same principles to great effect in maritime transport in Vietnam. By the mid-1960s, the standardized shipping container was used on virtually all large-scale maritime transport ships and port cities.[19]

Another factor driving the acceleration and escalating volume of global trade was the decrease in the cost of air transportation through the 1960s. New jet technology reduced air travel time by an estimated 50 percent.[20] Not until regulatory changes and the advent of air traffic computer technology did air travel become affordable and safer. The US set the initial trend when Congress passed the Airline Deregulation Act of 1978, and thereby liberalizing domestic air transport markets for passenger and cargo flights, paving the way for bilateral agreements on international routes to and from the US. These and the development of charter flights led to increases in tourism and longer-term migration, as people were able to travel further and more cheaply at faster speeds than before.[21]

Ground transportation also expanded rapidly. Automobiles replaced railroads as the primary means of land transportation, especially in North America. President Eisenhower's 1956 Federal-Aid Highway Act aimed to support the expansion and improvement of the inter-state highway system. National defense served as one of the main justifications for investing in a super-highway system to accommodate the quick and efficient movement of military equipment and personnel and defend against possible atomic attacks.[22]

The US actively promoted the automobile in Western Europe in the 1950s. The culture of cars and highways had existed in Europe before World War II but road-building projects proliferated in West Germany, Turkey, Sweden, France, and Italy under the auspices of the American IRF (International Road Federation) and the Marshall Plan.[23] Japan, too, developed highways after 1952 based on US models, but the high-speed train Shinkansen became the focus of public attention and use upon its debut in 1964.[24]

While these developments increased the speed and scale of movement of people and goods, they did not lead to a universal compression of time-space: in fact, there were instances of space-time divergence. Increased mobility produced new forms of immobility. The new patterns of suburban residences in North America established during the cold war meant more mobility along fixed routes for many men as they commuted from home to work, but they isolated women from public spaces in which they could interact with others. Homes in essence served as fortresses to shield families from the dangers of the cold war.[25]

On a more practical level, traffic jams on roads meant that in some locales the trip from home to work could be longer than a flight to an international destination. Cities with international hub airports were more intimately connected to foreign cities than domestic areas that were closer in distance. And the conversion of military technology to commercial application was not always successful, as demonstrated by the operational challenges faced by the supersonic commercial plane Concorde.[26]

# INTERNATIONAL AGREEMENTS, COLD WAR, AND GLOBALIZATION

The expectations in the 1990s of greater international cooperation were left unfulfilled by the continued strength of national sovereignty as the primary unit of political action. Nonetheless, globalization has affected not just inter-state relations, but also transformed state control over its own territories through international agreements, diasporic politics, and multiple layers of governance. In fact, multilateral, regional, and bilateral relations and agreements grew exponentially and complicated the picture of a politically bipolar or tripolar cold war well before the fall of the Berlin Wall.

At first glance, the cold war significantly impeded the flow of goods and people beyond the capitalist and communist blocs. The face-off in security affairs between NATO and the Warsaw Pact, and in trade relations between OECD and GATT (General Agreement on Trade and Tariffs) on one side and Comecon (Council for Mutual Economic Assistance) on the other, underscored the limitations of globalization in the cold war era.

But various bilateral relations prior to 1989 undermine a neat division between a bipolar cold war order and a unipolar or multipolar globalization order. For example, Japan and the Soviet Union had normalized relations in 1956, eventually leading to Prime Minister Tanaka Kakuei's visit to Moscow in 1973 and the signing of a bilateral joint energy exploration agreement in 1974.[27] Relations remained volatile in the face of continuing territorial disputes over the Kuril Islands, however, and Soviet wariness of Japan's improved relations with China. The Soviets also sent large quantities of development aid to Indonesia and other non-aligned countries in Asia in the 1950s and 1960s in order to offset SEATO (Southeast Asia Treaty Organization), an anti-communist Asian regional body that included the United States, Australia, New Zealand, France, the United Kingdom, the Philippines, Thailand, and Pakistan. Japan, in turn, was the largest provider of official development aid to Burma from the 1960s through the 1980s, when Burma was officially a socialist country under General Ne Win. Burmese relations with China prior to Ne Win's coup in 1962 were complicated by the presence of Nationalist Guomindang troops on the Sino-Burmese border, but a 1961 agreement that allowed Chinese Communist soldiers to enter Burmese territory to engage with the Guomindang set the stage for a more stable relationship, at least for most of the 1960s.[28]

Another example of cross-bloc bilateral relations was Canada's relationship with Cuba after its revolution in 1959. Despite US pressure, Canadian cabinets hewed to an autonomous approach in its dealings with Cuba. For Cuba's part, there were advantages to maintaining good relations with a North American power, especially one active in NATO and willing to oppose American calls for sanctions against Cuba.[29]

By the late 1960s, the superpowers were moving toward a policy of détente, which opened new avenues of cross-bloc economic and political relations. Among the most prominent was West Germany Chancellor Willy Brandt's Ostpolitik, which included a series of friendship treaties in 1970 with communist countries and the Basic Treaty with East Germany in 1972.[30]

China and the Soviet Union came to rely on economic linkages with capitalist countries as early as 1960. China began importing wheat from Canada and Australia starting in 1960–1, after the failure of the Great Leap Forward caused famines.[31] The Soviet Union, in the mid-1960s, signed on to the Paris Convention for the Protection of Industrial Property in 1965 to establish a legal framework for the acquisition of international intellectual property and technology. By the early 1970s, both China and the Soviet Union, while remaining hostile to each other, had moved toward a more integrated understanding of the world economy, thus preparing the ground for rapprochement with the US. China became a key player in this process by extending an invitation to the US table tennis team to visit China. The "ping-pong diplomacy" as it became known, together with Richard Nixon's visit to China in 1972, spurred détente between the US and the Soviet Union. But it also, as Leonid Brezhnev feared, spurred a Sino-US alliance.[32]

Détente also opened up new possibilities for East-West trade. According to one estimate, in 1960, 22 percent of the countries in the world, representing 21 percent of the global population, had open trade policies; by 2000, this had increased to 73 percent of the countries in the world, representing 46 percent of the world population.[33] This shift was facilitated by the growth of multilateral trade organizations and various trade agreements. The most prominent of these, GATT, was established in 1947 with twenty-three contracting countries, including then pre-communist China and Cuba. In its first two decades GATT focused on reducing tariffs and import quotas. The success of this push resulted in the growth of non-tariff trade barriers, such as duties for antidumping and countervailing, product safety, quality standards, and others.[34] China and the Soviet Union joined GATT later, in 1986 and 1987 respectively, even though the Soviet Union's trade with Western Europe had increased steadily through the 1960s and the 1970s.[35] They followed Yugoslavia, Poland, Romania, and Hungary. These four countries had joined GATT in the 1960s and 1970s even though each retained its membership—observer status in Yugoslavia's case—in Comecon.

Other multilateral organizations and agreements that facilitated East-West trade include the ISO (International Organization for Standardization), which helped unify, among other things, shipping containers' dimensions around the world in 1967. Travel and trade through different time zones was also facilitated in part by standardization of time and weights, agreed upon through international instruments such as the 1956 revised Universal Time set by the IAU (International Astronomical Union) and the International System of Units (SI), a modernized metric system, adopted in 1960 by the CGPM (General Conference on Weights and Measures).[36] The Soviet Union joined the UCC (Universal Copyright Convention), a multilateral agreement to adhere to the protection of international intellectual property rights in domestic markets, in 1973. While China did not accede to the UCC until 1997, it did join a similar international entity, the World Intellectual Property Organization, in 1980.[37]

All this is not to suggest that there was linear, inexorable progression toward a universal, liberalized trade regime. Indeed, East-West trade experienced a sharp decline starting around 1976. Internal rivalries and competition, especially early in the cold war, led to difficult negotiations over Japan's accession to GATT in 1955. Also, although GATT had since 1961 encouraged access for developing countries to the markets of developed countries, non-aligned nations, led by charismatic figures such as Indonesian president Sukarno and Tanzanian president Julius Nyerere, criticized the slow pace and called for a "New International Economic Order" that addressed the unequal terms of trade between the global North and South. Import substitution policies and protectionism became the order of the day, and non-aligned countries, through the Group of 77 in the UN and the formation of UNCTAD (UN Conference on Trade and Development), pressured industrialized nations to reassess the terms of trade.[38] The Lomé Convention signed between the European Community and ACP (African, Caribbean, and Pacific countries) in February 1975 was intended to be another venue through which to address concerns over North-South inequities via a combination of preferential trade terms and aid packages. The results were limited despite renewals in 1981 and 1986.[39]

Nevertheless, trans-bloc trade agreements and multilateral standardization organizations facilitated world trade. The proliferation of bilateral, regional, and bloc trading arrangements was, in fact, not antithetical to the development of global trade frameworks. Bilateral and regional preferential trade agreements essentially constituted a hedging strategy for countries in case multilateral agreements produced unfavorable terms. This strategy was reflected in the rapid increase in the numbers of *both* multilateral and regional/bilateral trade agreements after 1958 and 1977, followed by a period of relative decline, until exponential growth from 1993 on.[40]

There were some exceptions to the long-term move toward lower tariffs and trade-facilitating agreements. The US successfully pushed for the formation of COCOM (Coordinating Committee for Multilateral Export Controls) in 1950 to restrict the flow of technology, capital, and goods to the Soviet Union and its allies. However, the number of technologies and commodities restricted from export to communist states decreased from over 300 in 1950 to around 150 by 1976. Further, the number of applications for individual exceptions received by the committee did not change during the 1970s (approximately 800 applications annually), while the value of the approved exceptions grew larger, from US$11 million in 1967 to US$214 in 1977, indicating that higher-end technologies were being exported.[41]

Regional organizations that were not focused on security issues also grew in number and influence during the cold war. Some of the more prominent examples include: OECC (Organization for European Economic Cooperation) established in 1948, which became OECD in 1961; OAS (Organization of American States) in 1948; Comecon (Council for Mutual Economic Assistance) founded in 1949; EEC (European Economic Community) in 1957; LAFTA (Latin American Free Trade Association) in 1960; the Non-Aligned Movement in 1961; OAU (Organization of African Unity) in 1963; CARIFTA (Caribbean Free Trade Association) in 1965; ASEAN (Association of Southeast Asian Nations) in 1967; and ACP (African, Caribbean and Pacific Group of States) in 1975. Many of these organizations were formally established during the cold war and maintained their organizational structures and mandates into the post-1989 period.[42]

In finance, another Nixon policy shock, the unilateral withdrawal of the US dollar from the gold exchange standard in August 1971, combined with transnational negotiations mediated through organizations such as the World Bank and the International Monetary Fund (IMF), created the underpinnings for the globalization of financial activity. As noted previously, electronic trading systems were instrumental in the exponential growth in the value of foreign exchange; nevertheless, a necessary precondition was the end of the gold standard and the diffusion of free-floating currency. The gold exchange standard had been established under the 1945 Bretton Woods system of international monetary controls that tied currencies to the US dollar, and the US dollar to gold. Both the World Bank and the IMF, now associated with financial liberalization, were initially tasked with helping governments manage monetary policy so as to control the transnational flows of capital and contain them within national bounds. The decline of Keynesian economics and US domestic inflation, balance of payment and trade deficits, continuing expenditures from the Vietnam War, and depletion of the US gold reserve had already triggered a limited floating exchange rate, moderated by the introduction of Special Drawing Rights, a virtual or paper gold, held by the IMF in 1969. Nixon's announcement of the divorce of the US dollar from gold triggered a cascade of defections from gold, eventually rendering all major currencies floating by 1976.

While multilateral, bilateral, and regional agreements that emerged during the cold war framed trade and monetary policies, it was mainly bilateral agreements in combination with international and customary law that governed FDI (foreign direct investment) during the cold war and beyond. Data for FDI prior to the 1970s are imprecise, but one estimate places the world outward stock of FDI in 1938 at $14.6 billion (with 1900 prices as the base year), in 1960 at $15.7 billion, in 1971 at $29.4 billion, in 1980 at $41.9 billion, and 1990 at $102.9 billion, indicating that real growth in FDI through to the 1980s was steady but not comparable to the post-1989 years.[43] But the key point is that BIT (bilateral investment agreements) that currently serve as the framework for FDI inflows and outflows first emerged in 1959 and took root in the 1960s, acting as a complement or replacement when it became clear that customary and international law could not always prevent nationalizations and expropriations. Among the more prominent expropriations in the 1950s that indirectly helped give birth to BITs were Iran's nationalization of British oil facilities and the nationalization of the Suez Canal by Egypt in 1956. Expropriations continued to rise in number through the 1960s and peaked in the mid-1970s, leading to several lawsuits by the affected transnational corporations (TNC).[44] Expropriations declined steadily after 1975. Although the explosion in the number of BITs did not occur until the late 1980s, the spread of the mechanism through the 1960s and 1970s, even at a moderate pace of twenty per year, combined with long-term declines in tariff rates and transportation costs to form the basis of the growth of FDI in the 1990s.[45]

International agreements also helped push environmental concerns to the forefront of the global agenda in the 1970s. The 1972 United Nations Conference on the Human Environment held in Stockholm was the first official world conference on environmental issues and facilitated linkages of non-governmental organizations (NGOs) and established an action plan on paper through the Declaration of the United Nations Conference on the Human Environment. Environmental policies and movements had of course existed before 1972. But while the activities of environmental groups such as Greenpeace and the first Earth Day of April 1970 augured an avalanche of domestic environmental regulations in the US, such organizations and events, notwithstanding globalist rhetoric, did not initially register significant transnational resonances. The Stockholm Conference, despite various political constrictions and substantive problems, provided an official platform for international environmental action, launching the first UN organ dedicated to environmental issues, the United Nations Environment Programme, and leading to a host of other multilateral environmental agreements over the next twenty years, including accords on ocean pollution, acid rain, climate change, the ozone layer, trade in endangered species, biological diversity, hazardous waste trade, and environmental protection of Antarctica.[46]

A similar pattern of international agreements occurred regarding human rights. The 1948 UN Universal Declaration of Human Rights became a touchstone document, encouraging other international agreements on non-discrimination through the 1960s. The language of racial equality and social justice in the Universal Declaration informed civil rights and decolonization movements throughout the world, including those in the US. Another landmark event was the signing of the Helsinki Accords of 1975 by thirty-five largely European countries from both sides of the iron curtain. The signatories agreed on territorial boundaries in Europe, but, just as importantly, on the protection of human rights as a global concern. The Accords gave rise to a host of Eastern European human rights organizations, among them the Moscow Helsinki Watch Group, Charter 77 (disbanded in 1992), and the Helsinki Watch (Human Rights

Watch after 1988), who used these official agreements to exert public pressure on their governments. Nonetheless, human rights violations continued, indicating the limitations of the Helsinki Accords.[47]

The ever-expanding global networks of activists and international non-governmental organizations (INGOs) has been cited as a hallmark of globalization, and occasionally bundled together with anti-globalization demonstrations under the label "globalization from below."[48] INGOS have indeed been prominent in fields such as the environment, human rights, gender rights, health policy, and labor rights, formulating policy proposals, even if at times clashing with local NGOs. Leaving aside whether these transnational networks actually form a medium for globalization from below, the striking fact is that the number of NGOs and INGOs has exploded since the 1960s, outpacing the number of TNCs over the same time by large margins.[49]

# CONCLUSION

The exuberance with which globalization was hailed as a new phenomenon and globalization theory as a conceptual innovation has dissipated since the halcyon days of the 1990s. Part of the loss in momentum can be explained by the definitional opacity of the term. Even recent academic "post mortems" on globalization and globalization theory can end up speaking at cross-purposes due to divergent definitions of what globalization actually means.[50]

Consequently, we need a clear, multidimensional, and analytical conceptualization of globalization. As an empirical phenomenon and spatial process, globalization is certainly not new in terms of its *genus*, since global movement of people, goods, and ideas has obviously been occurring since the start of history. Yet there are clearly differences in the substance of such flows, in terms of speed, scale, and scope, between globalization and its predecessors that make globalization a new *species* in degree if not in kind.

The speed, scale, and scope of transborder flows associated with globalization stem from cold war developments in ICT, transportation, and international agreements at multilateral, regional, and bilateral levels. The ICT revolution owes its existence to the diffusion of private use electricity, breakthroughs in microprocessors, computers, and early versions of the Internet, all of which sprung from military and commercial uses developed during the cold war. Innovations in engines, fuels, and engineering generated greater speed and volume in the transportation of people and goods over air, sea, and land. And international agreements paved the way for sustained increases in trade and the number of TNCs. These agreements also spotlighted issues such as the environment and human rights, and these in turn created opportunities for the proliferation and increase in influence of INGOs. While technological change, international trade, and multilateral agreements certainly existed prior to 1945, the specific technologies, infrastructures, and practices that emerged during the cold war carried within them the primary seeds of globalization.

## NOTES

1. David Armitage, "Is There a Pre-History of Globalization?" in Deborah Cohen and Maura O'Connor, eds., *Comparison and History: Europe in Cross-National Perspective* (London: Routledge, 2004), 165–76.

2. Arjun Appadurai, *Modernity at Large: Cultural Dimensions of Globalization* (Minneapolis, MN: University of Minnesota Press, 1996), 16–47.

3. George Ritzer, ed., *McDonaldization: The Reader* (Thousand Oaks, CA: Pine Forge, 2002), 20–2; Helena Norbert-Hodge, "The March of Monoculture," *Ecologist*, 29/2 (1999): 194–7; and Louise Amoore, ed., *The Global Resistance Reader* (London: Routledge, 2005).

4. George Ritzer, "Rethinking Globalization: Glocalization/Grobalization and Something/Nothing," *Sociological Theory*, 21/3 (2003): 193–209; Koichi Iwabuchi, *Recentering Globalization: Popular Culture and Japanese Transnationalism* (Durham, NC: Duke University Press, 2002); and Tony Day and Maya H. T. Liem, eds., *Cultures at War: The Cold War and Cultural Expression in Southeast Asia* (Ithaca, NY: Southeast Asia Program, Cornell University, 2010).

5. John Tomlinson, *Globalization and Culture* (Chicago, IL: University of Chicago Press, 1999), 20; Ulf Hannertz, *Cultural Complexity* (New York: Columbia University Press, 1992); and Saskia Sassen, *Territory, Authority, Rights: From Medieval to Global Assemblages* (Princeton, NJ: Princeton University Press, 2006).

6. Jeffrey Williamson, "Globalization, Convergence, History," *Journal of Economic History*, 56/2 (June 1996): 277–306; Jürgen Osterhammel and Niels Petersson, *Globalization: A Short History* (Princeton, NJ: Princeton University Press, 2005); and Göran Therborn, "Globalizations: Dimensions, Historical Waves, Regional Effects, Normative Governance," *International Sociology*, 15/2 (June 2000): 151–79.

7. Rogers Brubaker, "The 'Diaspora' Diaspora," *Ethnic and Racial Studies*, 28/1 (January 2005): 1–19; and Pnina Werbner, "Theorising Complex Diasporas: Purity and Hybridity in the South Asian Public Sphere in Britain," *Journal of Ethnic and Migration Studies*, 30/5 (2004), 895–911.

8. Peter Petri, "The East Asian Trading Bloc: An Analytical History," in Jeffrey Frankel and Miles Kahler, eds., *Regionalism and Rivalry: Japan and the US in Pacific Asia* (Chicago, IL: University of Chicago Press, 1994), 24.

9. Bank for International Settlements, *Triennial Central Bank Survey: Report on Foreign Exchange Market Activity in 2010* (Basel: Bank for International Settlements, 2010), 6; and Michael King and Dagfinn Rime, "The $4 trillion question: What Explains FX growth since the 2007 Survey?" *BIS Quarterly Review*, 8/4 (December 2010): 27–42.

10. Frederick Cooper, *Colonialism in Question: Theory, Knowledge, History* (Berkeley, CA: University of California Press, 2005), 105; and John Dunning, "Changes in the Level and Structure of International Production: The Last One Hundred Years," in Mark Casson, ed., *The Growth of International Business* (London: Allen & Unwin, 1983), 9.

11. Lisa Gitelman and Geoffrey Pingree, eds., *New Media, 1740–1915* (Cambridge, MA: MIT Press, 2003); and Vaclav Smil, *Creating the Twentieth Century: Technical Innovations of 1867–1914 and their Lasting Impact* (New York: Oxford University Press, 2005).

12. The diffusion rates for television were comparable according to one estimate, however. See Gisle Hannemyr, "The Internet as Hyperbole: A Critical Examination of Adoption Rates," *Information Society*, 19/2 (April–June 2003): 111–21.

13. Mark Levine et al., "Electricity End-Use Efficiency: Experience with Technologies, Markets, and Policies throughout the World," *Energy*, 20/1 (January 1995): 37–61; James Williams and Navroz Dubash, "Asian Electricity Reform in Historical Perspective," *Pacific Affairs*, 77/3 (2004), 418–20; and Kim Sŏng-chun, "1950-nyŏndae Han'guk ŭi yŏn'guyong wŏnjaro toip kwajŏng kwa kwahak kisuljadŭl ŭi yŏkhal" (Development of Science over Nation: Scientists in South Korea's 1950s Nuclear Program), *Han'guk kwahak sahak hoeji* (Journal of the Korean History of Science), 31/1 (2009): 139–66.

14. Hugh Slotten, "Satellite Communications, Globalization, and the Cold War," *Technology and Culture*, 43/2 (April 2002): 315–50; Marcellus Snow, *International Commercial Satellite Communications: Economic and political issues of the first decade of INTELSAT* (New York: Praeger, 1976); and John Downing, "The Intersputnik System and Soviet Television," *Soviet Studies*, 37/4 (October 1985): 465–83.

15. Paul Ceruzzi, *A History of Modern Computing* (Cambridge, MA: MIT Press, 1998); Slava Gerovitch, "'Mathematical Machines' of the Cold War: Soviet Computing, American Cybernetics and Ideological Disputes in the Early 1950s," *Social Studies of Science*, 31/2 (April 2001): 253–87; and Honghong Tinn, "Cold War Politics: Taiwanese Computing in the 1950s and 1960s," *IEEE Annals of the History of Computing*, 32/1 (February 2010): 90–2.

16. Christophe Lécuyer and David Brock, *Makers of the Microchip: A Documentary History of Fairchild Semiconductor* (Cambridge, MA: MIT Press, 2010); and Shigeru Nakayama and Kunio Goto, eds., *A Social History of Science and Technology in Contemporary Japan: High Economic Growth Period, 1960–1969* (Melbourne: Trans Pacific Press, 2006).

17. Arthur Norberg, and Judy O'Neill, *Transforming Computer Technology: Information Processing for the Pentagon, 1962–1986* (Baltimore, MD: Johns Hopkins University Press, 1996) 12; and Jane Abbate, *Inventing the Internet* (Cambridge, MA: MIT Press, 1999).

18. United Nations Department of Economic and Social Affairs, *2004 World Survey on the Role of Women in Development: Women and International Migration* (New York: United Nations, 2005), 3–4, 8–10; and OECD, *International Migration Outlook: Annual Report 2007* (Paris: OECD, 2007), 350.

19. Marc Levinson, *The Box: How the Shipping Container Made the World Smaller and the World Economy Bigger* (Princeton, NJ: Princeton University Press, 2006), 220; Frank Broeze, *The Globalisation of the Oceans: Containerisation from the 1950s to the Present* (St. John's: International Maritime History Association, 2002); and Vaclav Smil, "The Two Prime Mover of Globalization: History and Impact of Diesel Engines and Gas Turbines," *Journal of Global History*, 2/3 (November 2007): 382.

20. David Hummels, "Transportation Costs and International Trade in the Second Era of Globalization," *Journal of Economic Perspective*, 21/3 (Summer 2007): 131–54; and Xander Olsthoorn, "Carbon Dioxide Emissions from International Aviation: 1950–2050," *Journal of Air Transport Management*, 7/2 (March 2001): 87–93.

21. David Gillen, Richard Harris, and Tae-Hoon Oum, "Measuring the Economic Effects of Bilateral Liberalization on Air Transport," *Transportation Research Part E*, 38/3–4 (2002), 155–75; and Marc Dierkx, *Clipping the Clouds: How Air Travel Changed the World* (Westport, CT: Praeger, 2008).

22. Kathleen Tobin, "The Reduction of Urban Vulnerability: Revisiting 1950s American Suburbanization as Civil Defence," *Cold War History*, 2/2 (January 2002): 1–32; and Mark Rose, "Reframing American Highway Politics, 1956–1995," *Journal of Planning History*, 2/3 (August 2003): 212–36.

23. Frank Schipper, "Changing the Face of Europe: European Road Mobility during the Marshall Years," *Journal of Transport History*, 28/2 (Summer 2007): 211–28; Martin Trevor Wild, *Urban and Rural Change in West Germany* (London: Croom Helm, 1983), 130–8; Axel Dossmann, *Begrenzte Mobilität: Eine Kulturgeschichte der Autobahnen in der DDR* (Limited Mobility: A Cultural History of the Highways of the GDR) (Essen: Klartext, 2003); and Georges Reverdy, *Histoire des routes de France* (History of the Roads of France) (Paris: Presses Universitaires France, 1995).

24. John Black, and Peter Rimmer, "Japanese Highway Planning: A Western Interpretation," *Transportation*, 11/1 (March 1982): 29–49; and Yuji Murayama, "The Impact of Railways on Accessibility in the Japanese Urban System," *Journal of Transport Geography*, 2/2 (June 1994): 87–100.

25. Elaine Tyler May, *Homeward Bound: American Families in the Cold War Era* (New York: Basic Books, 1988); and Joanne J. Meyerowitz, ed., *Not June Cleaver: Women and Gender in Postwar America, 1945–1960* (Philadelphia, PA: Temple University Press, 1994).

26. Andrew James, and Phil Judkins, "Chute libre avant le décollage: le programme GVFA d'avion à géométrie variable franco-anglais, 1965–1967" (Freefall before Takeoff: The GVFA Aircraft Program and Franco-British Variable Geometry, 1965–67), *Histoire, économie & société* (History, Economy & Society), 29/4 (June 2010): 51–73; and Guillaume de Syon, "Consuming Concorde," *Technology and Culture*, 44/3 (July 2003): 650–4.

27. Disputes over the Sakhalins constantly plagued Matsumoto Shunichi's efforts to negotiate the establishment of diplomatic relations with the Soviets in 1956. See Matsumoto Shunichi, *Moscow ni kakeru niji: Nit-So kokkō kaifuku hiroku* (Rainbow to Moscow: The Secret History of Japan-Soviet Normalization) (Tokyo: Asahi shinbunsha, 1966); Sheldon Simon, "The Japan-China-USSR Triangle," *Pacific Affairs*, 47/2 (Summer 1974): 128; and Kimie Hara, *Japanese-Soviet/Russian Relations since 1945: A Difficult Peace* (New York: Routledge, 2003).

28. Ragna Boden, "Cold War Economics: Soviet Aid to Indonesia," *Journal of Cold War Studies*, 10/3 (Summer 2008): 110–28; Fan Hongwei, "Lengzhanshiqi Zhong-Mian guanxi yanjiu: yi Wajiaobu jiemi dangan wei zhongxinde kaocha" (Relations between China and Burma during the Cold War, 1955–1966: Based on the Ministry of Foreign Affairs Archives), *Nanyang wenti yanjiu* (Southeast Asian Affairs), no. 2 (2008): 35–43; and Nagano Shinichirō, *Nihon no sengo baishō: Ajia keizai kyōryoku no shuppatsu* (Japan's Postwar Compensations: The Start of Asian Economic Cooperation) (Tokyo: Keisō shobō, 1999).

29. John Kirk and Peter McKenna, *Canada-Cuba Relations: The Other Good Neighbor Policy* (Gainesville, FL: University Press of Florida, 1997); and Humberto Manuel Palacios Barrera, "Cuba-Canadá: Colaboración, amistad y respeto mutuo en la era de la globalización" (Canada-Cuba: Collaboration, Friendship, and Mutual Respect in the Era of Globalization), *Santiago*, no. 116 (2008): 15–33.

30. William Glenn Gray, *Germany's Cold War: The Global Campaign to Isolate East Germany, 1949–1969* (Chapel Hill, NC, University of North Carolina Press, 2003); Carole Fink, and Bernd Schaefer, eds., *Ostpolitik, 1969–1974: European and Global Responses* (Cambridge: Cambridge University Press, 2009); and Julia Von Dannenberg, *The Foundations of Ostpolitik: The Making of the Moscow Treaty between West Germany and the USSR* (Oxford: Oxford University Press, 2008).

31. Chad Mitcham, *China's Economic Relations with the West and Japan, 1949–79: Grain, Trade and Diplomacy* (London: Routledge, 2005), 61–73; Shu-Guang Zhang, *Economic Cold War: America's Embargo against China and the Sino-Soviet Alliance, 1949–1963* (Washington, DC:

Woodrow Wilson Center Press, 2001); and Li Jie-chuan, "20-shiji 60-niandai Zhong-Jia xiaomai maoyi dui Zhongguode zhongyao yiyi" (Importance of 1960s China-Canada Wheat Trade), *Dangdai Zhongguoshi yanjiu* (Contemporary Chinese History Studies), 12/2 (2005): 88–94.

32. Morris Bornstein, *The Transfer of Western Technology to the USSR* (Paris: OECD, 1985); Stanislaw Gomulka, *Growth, Innovation, and Reform in Eastern Europe* (Madison, WI: University of Wisconsin Press, 1986); Zhaohui Hong, and Yi Sun, "The Butterfly Effect and the Making of 'Ping-Pong Diplomacy,'" *Journal of Contemporary China*, 9/25 (2000): 429–48; and Evelyn Goh, "Nixon, Kissinger, and the 'Soviet Card' in the US Opening to China, 1971–1974," *Diplomatic History*, 29/3 (June 2005): 475–502.

33. Roman Wacziarg, and Karen Horn Welch, "Trade Liberalization and Growth: New Evidence," *World Bank Economic Review*, 22/2 (June 2008): 187–231.

34. Thomas Zeiler, *Free Trade, Free World: The Advent of GATT* (Chapel Hill, NC: University of North Carolina Press, 1999).

35. Still, East-West trade constituted only a small percentage of Soviet total trade throughout these decades. Angela Stent, *From Embargo to Ostpolitik: The Political Economy of West German-Soviet Relations, 1955–1980* (Cambridge: Cambridge University Press, 2003), 138, 245.

36. Craig Murphy and JoAnne Yates, *The International Organization for Standardization (ISO): Global Governance through Voluntary Consensus* (London: Routledge, 2009), 58–9; and Barry Taylor and Amber Thompson, *The International System of Units* (Washington, DC: National Institute of Standards and Technology, 2008).

37. Michael Newcity, *Copyright Law in the Soviet Union* (New York: Praeger, 1978), 38–41; and Deli Yang, "The Development of Intellectual Property in China," *World Patent Information*, 25/2 (June 2003): 136.

38. Akaneya Tatsuo, *Nihon no Gatto kanyū mondai* (Japan's GATT Accession Problem) (Tokyo: Tokyo daigaku shuppankai, 1992); Robert Rothstein, *Global Bargaining: UNCTAD and the Quest for a New International Economic Order* (Princeton, NJ: Princeton University Press, 1979); and Craig Murphy, *Emergence of the NIEO Ideology* (Boulder, CO: Westview, 1984).

39. John Ravenhill, *Collective Clientelism: The Lomé Conventions and North-South Relations* (New York: Columbia University Press, 1985); and Jeffrey Herbst, "Theories of International Cooperation: The Case of the Lomé Convention," *Polity*, 19/4 (Summer 1987): 637–59.

40. Edward Mansfield and Eric Reinhardt, "Multilateral Determinants of Regionalism: The Effects of GATT/WTO on the Formation of Preferential Trading Arrangements," *International Organization*, 57/4 (November 2003): 829–62.

41. Yoko Yasuhara, "Myth of Free Trade: The Origins of CoCom 1945–1950," *Japanese Journal of American Studies*, no. 4 (1991): 127–48; Michael Mastanduno, *Economic Containment: CoCom and the Politics of East-West Trade* (Ithaca, NY: Cornell University Press, 1992); Pál Germuska, "Conflicts of Eastern and Western Technology Transfer Licenses, Espionage, and R&D in the Hungarian Defense Industry during the 1970s and 1980s," *Comparative Technology Transfer and Society*, 7/1 (April 2009): 43–65; and Stephen Kelly, "Curbing Illegal Transfers of Foreign-Developed Critical High Technology from CoCom Nations to the Soviet Union: An Analysis of the Toshiba-Kongsberg Incident," *Boston College International & Comparative Law Review*, 12/1 (Winter 1989): 181–223.

42. James Mittelman, "Rethinking the 'New Regionalism' in the Context of Globalization," in Björn Hettne, András Inotai, and Osvaldo Sunkel, eds., *Globalism and the New Regionalism* (New York: Palgrave, 1999), 25–53; and Mark Beeson, "Rethinking Regionalism: Europe and

East Asia in Comparative Historical Perspective," *Journal of European Public Policy*, 12/6 (2005): 969–85.

43. Harold James, *International Monetary Cooperation since Bretton Woods* (New York: Oxford University Press, 1996); Robert Solomon, "The History of the SDR," in Michael Mussa et al., eds., *The Future of the SDR in Light of Changes in the International Financial System* (Washington, DC: International Monetary Fund, 1996), 25–40; Michael Twomey, *A Century of Foreign Investment in the Third World* (New York: Routledge, 2000), 33; and UNCTAD, *World Investment Report 1995* (New York: UNCTAD, 1996), 34.

44. Stephen Kobrin, "Expropriation as an Attempt to Control Foreign Firms in LDCs: Trends from 1960 to 1979," *International Studies Quarterly*, 28/3 (September 1984): 329–48; Michael Minor, "The Demise of Expropriation as an Instrument of LDC Policy, 1980–1992," *Journal of International Business Studies*, 25/1 (1st Quarter 1994): 177–88; and Patrick Rimbaud, "Les suites d'un différend pétrolier: l'affaire LIAMCO devant le juge français" (The Consequences of an Oil Dispute: The LIAMCO case before the French Judge), *Annuaire français de droit international* (French Yearbook of International Law), 25 (1979): 820–34.

45. Zachary Elkins, Andrew Guzman, and Beth Simmons, "Competing for Capital: The Diffusion of Bilateral Investment Treaties, 1960–2000," *International Organization*, 60/4 (October 2006): 811–46; and Tagi Sagafi-nejad and John Dunning, *The UN and Transnational Corporations: From Code of Conduct to Global Compact* (Bloomington, IN: Indiana University Press, 2008), 22.

46. John McCormick, *Reclaiming Paradise: The Global Environmental Movement* (Bloomington, IN: Indiana University Press, 1991); Ken Conca, "Greening the United Nations: Environmental Organisations and the UN System," *Third World Quarterly*, 16/3 (September 1995): 441–57; and Denis Cosgrove, "Contested Global Visions: One World, Whole Earth, and the Apollo Photographs," *Annals of the Association of American Geographers*, 84/2 (June 1994): 270–94.

47. Roland Burke, "From Individual Rights to National Development: The First UN International Conference on Human Rights, Tehran, 1968," *Journal of World History*, 19/3 (September 2008): 275–96; Daniel Thomas, *The Helsinki Effect: International Norms, Human Rights, and the Demise of Communism* (Princeton, NJ: Princeton University Press, 2001); Emilie Hafner-Burton, and Kiyoteru Tsutsui, "Human Rights in a Globalizing World: The Paradox of Empty Promises," *American Journal of Sociology*, 110/5 (March 2005): 1373–411; and David Cingranelli and David Richards, "Respect for Human Rights after the End of the Cold War," *Journal of Peace Research*, 36/5 (September 1999): 511–34.

48. Alejandro Portes, "Globalization from Below: The Rise of Transnational Communities," in Don Kalb et al., eds., *The Ends of Globalization: Bringing Society Back In* (Lanham, MD: Rowman & Littlefield, 2000), 253–72; and Donatella Della Porta, *Globalization from Below: Transnational Activists and Protest Networks* (Minneapolis, MN: University of Minnesota Press, 2006).

49. Edward Turner, "Why Has the Number of International Non-Governmental Organizations Exploded since 1960?" *Cliodynamics*, 1/1 (2010): 81–91; and Ann Marie Clark, Elisabeth Friedman, and Kathryn Hochstetler, "The Sovereign Limits of Global Civil Society: A Comparison of NGO Participation in UN World Conferences on the Environment, Human Rights, and Women," *World Politics*, 51/1 (October 1998): 9.

50. See Justin Rosenberg, "Globalization Theory: A Post-Mortem," *International Politics*, 42/1 (March 2005): 2–74, and interlocutors in the same issue.

## Select Bibliography

Appadurai, Arjun. *Modernity at Large: Cultural Dimensions of Globalization.* Minneapolis, MN: University of Minnesota Press, 1996.

Ceruzzi, Paul. *A History of Modern Computing.* Cambridge, MA: MIT Press, 1998.

Della Porta, Donatella. *Globalization from Below: Transnational Activists and Protest Networks.* Minneapolis, MN: University of Minnesota Press, 2006.

James, Harold. *International Monetary Cooperation since Bretton Woods.* New York: Oxford University Press, 1996.

Levinson, Marc. *The Box: How the Shipping Container Made the World Smaller and the World Economy Bigger.* Princeton, NJ: Princeton University Press, 2006.

Norberg, Arthur, and Judy O'Neill. *Transforming Computer Technology: Information Processing for the Pentagon, 1962–1986.* Baltimore, MD: Johns Hopkins University Press, 1996.

Ritzer, George, ed. *McDonaldization: The Reader.* Thousand Oaks, CA: Pine Forge, 2002.

Sassen, Saskia. *Territory, Authority, Rights: Frome Medieval to Global Assemblages.* Princeton, NJ: Princeton University Press, 2006.

Snow, Marcellus. *International Commercial Satellite Communications: Economic and political issues of the first decade of INTELSAT.* New York: Praeger, 1976.

Thomas, Daniel. *The Helsinki Effect: International Norms, Human Rights, and the Demise of Communism.* Princeton, NJ: Princeton University Press, 2001.

Tomlinson, John. *Globalization and Culture.* Chicago, IL: University of Chicago Press, 1999.

Zeiler, Thomas. *Free Trade, Free World: The Advent of GATT.* Chapel Hill, NC: University of North Carolina Press, 1999.

# PART V

# THE END OF THE COLD WAR

# CHAPTER 34

·····································································································

# THE END OF THE
# COLD WAR

·····································································································

## NICHOLAS GUYATT

IN the popular imagination, the cold war divisions between East and West were swept away on November 9, 1989, when Berliners began to demolish the wall that had scarred their city for nearly three decades. A few weeks later at a superpower summit in Malta, Mikhail Gorbachev's spokesman Gennady Gerasimov obligingly told the press that the cold war was over. The conflict had stretched "from Yalta to Malta," he quipped, though this student-friendly tagline has not crept into textbooks and survey courses. Some historians argue that the cold war effectively ended a year earlier, when Gorbachev told the United Nations that the Soviet Union would no longer use its military to subdue the satellite states of the Warsaw Pact. Some posit the reunification of Germany in October 1990. And others remind us that the old Soviet Union was still alive even after the loss of Eastern Europe, a fact that was made alarmingly clear to the West by the attempted military coup of August 1991. During these years, a triumphalism in some quarters of Western opinion was balanced by anxiety about what would follow. George H. W. Bush was notoriously reluctant to accept the spoils of victory, though the pummeling of Iraq (and, to a lesser extent, Panama) with Soviet acquiescence eventually persuaded American policymakers that a new world order had arrived.[1]

It is worth recalling the fuzzy end of the cold war because politicians, journalists, and even some historians would soon coalesce around a simpler version of events: the cold war ran from 1945 to 1989; it was ended decisively by the ordinary people of Eastern Europe and the universal desire for freedom. While debate within the American foreign policy community raged in 1989 about the significance of what was taking place, one signal contribution—Francis Fukuyama's essay on "The End of History"—was later taken to represent a more general euphoria about the American victory. After 2001, in a clever piece of branding, journalists talked about the era from "11/9 to 9/11": a moment of unchallenged American supremacy (if not innocence) which began with the fall of the Berlin Wall and was rudely terminated by the terrorist attacks on Washington and New York.[2]

Within a few years of 1989 a gulf opened between the actual process by which the cold war had ended and the place of these events in the Western imagination. Historians of the USSR have argued convincingly that the Soviet collapse was rooted in Gorbachev's misguided zeal for a reformed and revived version of socialism. Soviet observers saw an opportunity to challenge the United States during the 1980s, in spite of the quagmire in Afghanistan, but Gorbachev's efforts to overhaul a dysfunctional economic system accelerated its demise. There was substantial opposition within the Soviet Union to both the effects of Gorbachev's reforms and the path they had unwittingly marked out toward a free-market economy; Gorbymania, after all, seemed to surge overseas in inverse proportion to Gorbachev's popularity at home. But it soon became clear to Russian officials that they could neither roll back the process of reform nor suspend it at the point of small-scale entrepreneurialism that Gorbachev had initially glimpsed. The Soviet Union might have continued in much the same form for several more decades; its sudden transformation owes much to the failure of its institutions, but more to the belief of one of its devotees that it might yet be perfected.[3]

Unsurprisingly, this view of the Soviet collapse proved unappealing to Western observers. In the United States, the historian John Lewis Gaddis and a host of conservative think tanks embraced a vision of systemic change. In their view, the world had been remade by American actions and a series of triumphantly vindicated universalisms. The fall of the Soviet Union was a tribute to American persistence, and particularly the conviction of Ronald Reagan that the world could be changed through toughness rather than the accommodations of liberals. But forces even greater than the United States had brought the cold war to a close: the universal desire for freedom and democracy, and the refusal of people to accept subjugation by foreign governments and military dictatorships. Gaddis himself made much of the fact that, militarily at least, the Soviet Union had not been defeated. But instead of emphasizing the possibility of a leaden Soviet domination under a less dynamic leader than Gorbachev, Gaddis argued that the forces of history had themselves turned against the USSR. As historian Melvyn Leffler later noted, Gaddis had emerged as the "scholarly diplomatic counterpart" of Francis Fukuyama.[4]

During the 1990s, as the "end of history" proved more interesting than Fukuyama implied, this vision of the cold war as an elemental struggle with an uplifting conclusion became more entrenched. The essays in this book tell a different story. The cold war was dangerous and complex. It brought devastation to tens of millions of people and, on several occasions, it threatened to decimate nations or the world entire. Policymakers on both sides were frequently baffled or scared by what was happening, and irrational decisions were at least as common as reasonable ones. Against the image of a long attritional struggle in which the United States slowly overhauled its rival, we now know that Western powers were frequently clueless about Soviet intentions and the respective positions of the superpower rivals. Arguably the best example of American detachment from reality was the failure of the US intelligence community to anticipate that the Soviet Union would collapse as quickly and completely as it did.

The idea of the cold war as a titanic and globe-spanning confrontation between the United States and the USSR also distorted a more intricate international history. The processes of decolonization, democratization, and economic development had their own trajectories and logic that could not easily be subsumed within the battle between the Soviet Union and the West. Scholars have now recovered many of these stories, exposing the extent to which the simple dualism of capitalism and communism (or "freedom" and "tyranny") misses the vitality and persistence of local struggles. The traditional rendition of the cold war, skipping from American or Soviet engagement in Vietnam, Angola, Korea, or Chile, reads like a diary of superpower one-night stands: the rest of the world comes into focus only when the Soviets or the Americans deign to bankroll, harass, or attack a particular regime. When we remove the cold war lens, we can see more clearly that the struggles for independence, autonomy, and economic progress in the Third World were not simply proxy battles between superpower sponsors; and that the cold war itself was rooted in larger struggles over development.[5]

These more nuanced perspectives were largely overlooked in the 1990s, as American policymakers debated the world order that should succeed the cold war. The simple assumption of American omnipotence served to distort both the past and the present, but the defining feature of this winnowed understanding was the impression that world history since 1945 had been cold war history—and that American policymakers were now facing a global vacuum into which they would have to insert themselves. To frame America's victory in this way was to accept burdens as well as opportunities in the new world order, as the events of the 1990s made clear.

For Western commentators trying to make sense of events, the late 1980s and early 1990s produced tantalizing hints of a global shift toward freedom. In Eastern Europe the effect of the Soviet collapse was immediate and far-reaching. But change was hardly limited to those areas that had formerly languished under communism. In South Korea four decades of dictatorship were brought to a close in 1987 by the election of Roh Tae-Woo. In Algeria the following year, mass demonstrations against the leadership of the National Liberation Front began a process of democratization which, by 1991, promised the first free elections in Algeria's independent history. The minority white government in South Africa was finally forced to loosen its grip on power. And, in the most prominent example of an apparent "demonstration effect," the visit of Mikhail Gorbachev to Beijing in May 1989 catalyzed student protests against Chinese communism and resulted in a highly visible confrontation between the students and a rattled leadership.[6]

Against this backdrop, Francis Fukuyama's argument seemed appealing and empirically sound. Fukuyama's witty essay held not that the world would embrace free-market democracy or American leadership, but that liberal capitalism no longer faced a challenge from rival ideologies with global aspirations. Other commentators were bolder, promising that the post-cold war era would see unprecedented democratization throughout the world. Reagan's successor in the White House, George H.W. Bush, was not naturally inclined to this way of thinking. But a combination of Pentagon pressure and foreign intransigence led Bush toward a more expansive definition of America's role. The touchstone for this was the US response to Saddam Hussein's invasion of Kuwait in August 1990.[7]

The first US war in Iraq should be bracketed with the fall of the Berlin Wall as a defining moment in the ending of the cold war. Saddam's aggression toward Kuwait produced the first full-blown international crisis since the Soviet redeployment from Eastern Europe. The USSR, consumed by its own difficulties, stood aside to allow an American-led response to the invasion. In marshalling that response, President Bush (somewhat reluctantly) established two precedents which were applied throughout the 1990s to international affairs: the United States would be regarded as the world's policeman, or at least as a kind of authority-of-last-resort when nations attacked each other or collapsed; and the US would equate its own interests with the interests of the "international community," seeking to confirm this congruence of purpose through the United Nations and other international bodies. In the afterglow of the war, Bush delivered an expansive speech to a joint session of Congress. The international community might now rejoice, the president suggested, because the "world divided" by the cold war had been replaced by a "new world order." Bush lauded the American military, the leaders of the international coalition in the Gulf, and even Winston Churchill; but, as he mapped out a happy future for international relations, he omitted the Soviet Union entirely.[8]

The Gulf War also put Iraq's neighbors on notice that the United States would project power in the Middle East without its traditional qualms about the Soviet response. In spite of the disastrous decision of the Palestinian Liberation Organization to back Saddam rather than the US-led coalition, Iraq's defeat created an opening for diplomacy and the resolution of Israel's many disputes with its neighbors. Some American commentators speculated about the spread of democratic ideas among even the oil-rich autocracies of the Gulf. For his part, Bush dusted off the missionary rhetoric that caused Woodrow Wilson such trouble after World War I. "We went halfway around the world to do what is moral and just and right," he told Congress and the watching world in his victory speech of March 1991. "We lifted the yoke of aggression and tyranny from a small country that many Americans had never even heard of, and we ask nothing in return."[9]

There is considerable evidence to support the view of George H.W. Bush as a cautious, essentially reactive figure. But his foreign policy anticipated many of the priorities and predicaments of the coming decades. At one end of the scale, Bush sanctioned the US invasion of Panama in December 1989, a high-tech assault that recalled some of the grubbiest unilateral operations of the cold war and anticipated the picaresque interventions of his son after 2001. In responding to Saddam Hussein, on the scale's other end, Bush gathered a coalition of nations and worked hard to achieve the formal sanction of the UN.[10]

Nevertheless, Bush's decision to leave Saddam Hussein in power (and to abandon the Shia uprising in southern Iraq) said more about the limits of US power than about America's commitment to the letter of its UN mandate. When Yugoslavia began to disintegrate, State Department spokespeople were peppered with questions about an American response: if US soldiers had crossed the world to do the right thing in Kuwait, in spite of a broader American ignorance of the region, could they now be expected to muster in Dubrovnik or Sarajevo? Although Bush managed to avoid committing troops in the former Yugoslavia, in the dying days of his presidency he sent more than 30,000 soldiers on a relief mission to Somalia. The complexity of the Somali political situation quickly defeated the comprehension of the US military, and Somalia would become the first overseas embarrassment of Bill Clinton's presidency.[11]

If Bush was himself a little suspicious both of the extent of America's power and of its likely duration, even Francis Fukuyama was more cautious than many of his readers acknowledged. He speculated that history would eventually resume its course and interrupt this moment of American ascendancy. The same point was made by the pundit Charles Krauthammer. Writing in the fall of 1990, as American soldiers were massing in the Gulf, Krauthammer announced the arrival of a "unipolar moment" in which the United States would project power without a serious rival. Krauthammer perceptively identified Saddam Hussein as the unhappy discoverer of this moment: "Iraq, having inadvertently revealed the unipolar structure of today's world, cannot stop complaining about it." He dismissed "pious talk about a new multilateral world" and predicted that American policymakers would find a use only for "pseudo-multilateralism," paying lip service to the UN without accepting constraints on its actions. Revealingly, he imagined that pseudo-multilateralism would be useful not to keep up appearances overseas but to co-opt that "large segment of American opinion [that] doubts the legitimacy of unilateral American action." Finally, Krauthammer urged American policymakers to make the most of their power in the "generation or so" before serious rivals emerged once again.[12]

Krauthammer's identification of the end of the cold war as a lull in great power rivalry rather than a liberal millennium was unusual in 1990–1. The Soviet Union appeared to many Western observers to be heading toward obsolescence: wracked by centrifugal nationalisms, hammered by the global economic slump and the subsequent fall in energy prices, and disoriented by political chaos, the USSR broke into more than a dozen states. With American and European economists clambering over the wreckage of command economies throughout the old Soviet Union, it seemed to many in the West that the only option for their erstwhile adversary was to embrace liberal democracy and an American-led vision of global security.

Clearly this was not the case. In their efforts to overturn the old communist economies, Western advisors promoted a form of "shock therapy" for Russia and its neighbors which allowed for the creation of a new class of kleptocrats from the old Soviet *nomenklatura*. The scale of wealth transfer during the 1990s in Russia alone was staggering: according to one estimate, nearly 50 percent of the Russian economy was controlled by just seven men by 1997. The political and economic effort required to pull off this heist necessitated a less expansive engagement with the world beyond Russia's borders; Russia's major conflict of the decade was in its own breakaway province of Chechnya, a reminder of the challenge of holding together even the new Russian republic after the shocks of 1989–91. Russia seemed willing to wave through America's foreign policy ambitions (including the enlargement of the North Atlantic Treaty Organization (NATO)), and even to act as supplicant while American and European scholars prepared exultant narratives on how the West had won the cold war. Sharp-eyed observers pointed to the Chechen debacle, or to Russia's erratic opposition to the Kosovo War of 1999, and questioned the extent of Moscow's liberal awakening. But during the 1990s, it was easy for Western politicians to feel complacent about Russia's subordinate status, and to exploit Charles Krauthammer's "unipolar moment" while it lasted.[13]

Although there were differences of emphasis between the administrations of George H.W. Bush and of Bill Clinton, both presidents operated within a similar set of assumptions and parameters. The sudden collapse of the Soviet Union created an unprecedented space for American involvement in the world. But American policymakers were constrained by two major factors, neither of them perfectly understood. First, there was a tension between American hyperpower and any meaningful definition of an international community: no matter how much Bush or Clinton might have wanted the world's assent, the reality of American interests and influence worked against both a binding multilateralism and a meaningful regime of international law. Second, in spite of this hyperpower or the dazzling humiliation of Saddam Hussein, the world was considerably less amenable to American directions than many policymakers imagined. Wedded to a rhetoric of unipolarity, and (mostly) keen to avoid the impression of wanton capriciousness or self-interested selectivity, American commentators and policymakers alternately boasted that they could shape the world and insisted that they could not assume its many burdens. This contributed to an atmosphere in which, in some domestic quarters and especially overseas, the United States was blamed for virtually everything.

For the rest of the world the end of the cold war had three principal effects. It accelerated the onset of "globalization," especially in the economic sphere; it forced governments to think carefully about the international orders, regional and global, that might succeed the cold war framework; and it encouraged the growth of non-state actors and challenges. None of these developments was entirely new, and the legacies of the pre-1989 period were evident in the problems and opportunities that they presented to governments and peoples around the world. The common feature that linked all three was the erosion of the nation state; or, more precisely, the increasing challenge to the idea of the nation state as the building block of world politics. Both the cold war and the process of decolonization had, for different reasons, placed a great emphasis on the usefulness of the nation state in the decades between 1945 and 1989. After 1989 this was no longer the case, and the consequences of this shift warrant close consideration.

Globalization was not invented in the 1990s, and the challenge for historians is to determine whether the cold war really made much difference to a centuries-long narrative of international exchange and cultural interpenetration. Even if we focus solely on the economic dimensions of globalization, 1989 was not the most obvious watershed. The International Monetary Fund (IMF) and the World Bank, which had been created at the end of World War II principally to manage European recovery, gradually diversified their activities to bankroll development in what became known as the Third World. But it was the collapse of the Keynesian consensus in the 1970s, and especially the debt crisis following Mexico's near-default in 1982, that brought the language of neoliberal economics into the mainstream.[14]

After 1989, the effective discrediting of communism allowed the proponents of neoliberalism to champion their economic model without serious challenge; it is perhaps this unbounded enthusiasm that most thoroughly characterizes the globalization of the 1990s. At the end of the long Keynesian consensus, Margaret Thatcher and Ronald

Reagan had insisted that there was no alternative to the harsh medicine of neoliberalism: privatization, "fiscal discipline," and deregulation were all implemented in the United States and Britain. The IMF and World Bank applied harsher versions of the same policies to indebted countries around the globe, and were particularly insistent on "opening up" the developing world to foreign investment and speculation. In 1990 John Williamson of the World Bank provided a name for the international version of this economic prescription: the "Washington Consensus." Williamson intended merely to acknowledge the fact that the IMF and World Bank were headquartered in the American capital, but his coinage provided an easy target for opponents of these strictures.[15]

The continuing rise of neoliberalism after 1989 depended partly on the acceptance and promotion of these economic ideas by leaders of the major Western powers. But it was also facilitated by the emergence of political and economic interest groups around the world who benefited from these policies. Elites in the global South have long made common cause with the wealthy and powerful in the North, but the magnitude of economic change in developing countries after 1989 turned the local beneficiaries into much more than compradors or go-betweens for Western corporations. From Russia to China to Latin America, the widespread privatization of public utilities, services, and natural resources created instant billionaires and gave a local face to the "Washington Consensus." Disgruntled majorities from the Philippines to Sierra Leone, however, looked on angrily as the spoils of globalization were unevenly divided, and their frustration deepened pre-existing divisions of class and ethnicity.[16]

Although neoliberal globalization's most vocal proponents—like the *New York Times* journalist Thomas Friedman or President Bill Clinton—boasted that it would secure prosperity and political freedom around the world, the evidence for this was mixed. While Clinton and others praised the progress of democracy in Africa and Latin America during the 1990s, some countries—especially China—doggedly rejected political reform. In the Chinese example, this refusal was problematic not only because of China's great size, but because the communist leadership actually endorsed many of the economic policies trumpeted by neoliberalism's proponents. In some respects the two decades between the Tiananmen protests and the Beijing Olympics were a long waiting game for globalization advocates who insisted that, eventually, the fruits of economic liberalization would translate into demands for political reform. As the world gathered in China in 2008, their promises remained unfulfilled.[17]

Conversely, some Western observers noted with alarm that the democratic process in the developing world did not always produce leaders who were committed to neoliberalism. Initially, this outcome was presented as a problem of ethnic or religious extremism, with European and American governments lamenting the triumph of Slobodan Milošević in Serbia or the Islamic Salvation Front in Algeria. But later in the 1990s the democratic challenge became more economic in its orientation: Hugo Chavez wrested power from a neoliberal regime in the Venezuelan elections of 1998; Luiz Inácio da Silva was elected as president of Brazil in 2002; more populist forms of government which were openly skeptical of neoliberalism followed in Argentina and Bolivia as well.[18]

By the early 2000s it was apparent that globalization and neoliberalism had converged for only a brief period. A significant number of countries were already developing economic models that combined a continued engagement with the global economy and a greater role for government. Moreover, the evidence from China suggested that the universal assumptions on which neoliberal globalization had been based required revision. Middle-class Chinese were clamoring for consumer goods, foreign holidays, and bourgeois trappings that would have seemed uncannily familiar to American observers. But there was little evidence that the new middle class was becoming politicized or demanding democratic reform.

This disconnect between economic and political reform had been glimpsed, albeit through a glass darkly, by the Harvard scholar Samuel Huntington in his 1993 essay "The Clash of Civilizations." Huntington warned that non-Western nations might choose to "modernize but not to Westernize," and he predicted a future of ethno-cultural conflict and civilizational struggle between "the West and the Rest." In reality, the challenges facing globalization advocates were more prosaic: How "unipolar" was a world in which China pursued liberal economics without liberal politics? How should the Western champions of neoliberalism engage with a nation that was profoundly undemocratic? Regardless of one's answer to these questions, the course of Chinese history continued to thwart the hopes of Francis Fukuyama and others that liberalism's global triumph was just around the corner.[19]

A full accounting of neoliberalism must await the result of the deep global downturn that began in 2008. Some of globalization's cheerleaders initially saw a silver lining to the crisis: it would bring down oil and gas prices, thus stranding many of the energy-rich challengers to the Washington Consensus in the developing world. But the extent of the crash quickly challenged neoliberal orthodoxy itself. As President Barack Obama and other Western leaders pushed through unprecedented stimulus packages to resuscitate their moribund economies, developing countries that had been ordered to accept "austerity" programs during their own financial crises could hardly miss the double standard. Then, as the crisis moved from commercial banking to sovereign debt in 2010 and 2011, developed nations made a panicked dash toward deficit reduction. This only highlighted the intellectual crisis that underpinned the recession. Should governments be cutting or spending to escape from the downward spiral? Consensus on this basic question was unnervingly elusive.[20]

As the economic crisis spread outward to threaten regional and global stability—and the project of European economic and political integration in particular—it was hard to forget that the problems had started with widespread malfeasance by banks and investment firms during the long speculative boom of the 1990s and 2000s. (The two elements of the crisis were directly linked, given the hair-raising exposure of Europe's biggest commercial banks to the debts of the most insolvent EU member nations.) The terrible reckoning laid bare the bargain that Tony Blair, Gordon Brown, and Bill Clinton had struck with the financial services industry. In the 1990s, center-left governments agreed to relax their traditional commitment to regulation. Banks and traders pursued riskier activities and unprecedented profits, while tax revenues from unbridled corporations were channeled into social programs. As these unregulated firms responded to government largesse by capsizing the economy, a central premise of "Third Way" thinking was destroyed. Neither the right nor the left had a successful model for economic activity in a global age.[21]

A second major consequence of the end of the cold war was a renewed search for international order and cooperation. Since 1945 the Soviet Union and the United States had provided (or imposed) mechanisms for economic development, the resolution of security crises, and the organization of regional blocs. After 1989 the need for international cooperation continued in the absence of this bipolar framework. Nations in the developed and developing worlds explored the possibility of currency unions, trade agreements, political leagues, and a revamping of international law. At the apex of this process was a debate about the purpose and potential of the United Nations.

In the aftermath of the 1991 Gulf War, George H.W. Bush and his advisors encouraged the idea that the UN might now be released from the shackles of the cold war. Brent Scowcroft, Bush's National Security Advisor, later claimed that the Bush administration had tried to realize "the hopes of the world of 1945" by agreeing to accept United Nations resolutions. Historians of the UN's founding might raise an eyebrow at this: the events leading up to the San Francisco conference in 1945 suggest that Franklin Roosevelt and Harry S. Truman viewed the new international body principally as a means of extending American leadership. Having invited the Soviet Union to join the IMF the previous year, US policymakers envisaged the United Nations not as an instrument of world democracy but as an American-led body offering junior partnership to Britain, France, China, and the USSR.[22]

Fortunately for the United Nations, its failings in the cold war era were largely blamed on superpower rivalry rather than the contradiction between American predominance and meaningful multilateralism. After 1989 the UN and its personnel were not so lucky. Boutros Boutros-Ghali, who served as secretary general from 1992 to 1997, may have been naive in taking seriously the multilateral commitments made by Bush and by Bill Clinton. With his strong ties to Francophone countries and flair for the limelight, Boutros-Ghali may also have been unsuited to the kind of plaintive maneuvering that would be required in New York and Washington. He pushed hard for a more assertive role for the United Nations, clashing with George H.W. Bush and especially with Clinton. A vocal and involved secretary-general was a thorn in the side of American diplomats who were keen to pick and choose their foreign interventions. American officials soon began to brief against the United Nations, and to suggest that the occasional paralysis of the organization could be explained by internal problems rather than by an inconstant United States.[23]

The idea of the United Nations as hopelessly unable to tackle the challenges of the post-cold war world was forged in three places: Somalia, where the UN operation was taken over by the American military in 1993 and transformed into something that bore little resemblance to relief work; Rwanda, in which the United States quietly facilitated a wider abdication of responsibility on the part of the international community; and Yugoslavia, where the civil war claimed more than 150,000 lives until the US and NATO took over from a faltering UN in the fall of 1995. Both the Bush and Clinton administrations placed a low priority on political and humanitarian crises that had little effect on America's core strategic interests. But the United States was hardly the only nation to demonstrate apathy toward ethnic conflict, genocide, and "failed states" during the 1990s. (Merely the most powerful one.) The stumbling involvement of the European Union in the Yugoslav conflict suggested that the alternatives to American leadership could be just as mercurial or feckless.[24]

In the two decades that followed the fall of the Berlin Wall, the European Union made considerably more progress toward economic than political integration. Governments and electorates across Europe embraced a common currency even as they trumpeted their national sovereignty. The Eurozone debt crisis eventually exposed the weakness of this selective approach. Given that the health of the Euro appeared to require a common fiscal as well as monetary policy, Europeans seemed only to have postponed a difficult choice between ever closer political integration or the death of the common currency. Even as the Euro was adopted across the continent, defense ministers responded to crises in Bosnia, Kosovo, and Afghanistan by reviving a relic of the early cold war—NATO—rather than creating a bespoke European army. Meanwhile, economic agreements deterred political and social convergence in North America. The North American Free Trade Agreement (NAFTA) bound together the tariff regimes of Canada, Mexico, and the United States without bringing into force the environmental and labor protections that might have encouraged a broader unity between the countries. But the new World Trade Organization (WTO) struggled to find a framework for a global deal on tariffs and development, and WTO meetings from Seattle to Hong Kong were stalked by thousands of protesters challenging the premise of "free trade."[25]

The search for political and economic cooperation among nations was more successful regionally than globally. The difficulties of creating a genuinely effective and representative global body should not be underestimated, nor should the United States be blamed exclusively for the failures of the United Nations after 1989. But what seems troubling is the growing American conviction that the world might be a better place without significant multilateral constraints. George W. Bush was the main offender here, but his predecessors had marked out the path he would blaze down after 2001. George H.W. Bush launched an assault on Panama in December 1989 in the face of international criticism. Bill Clinton ordered the American withdrawal from the negotiations that created the Kyoto Protocol on Climate Change and the International Criminal Court; in the war in Kosovo in 1999, he established a precedent for George W. Bush's unsanctioned war with Iraq in 2003. American officials after 1989 berated the United Nations for its supposed inefficiency or incompetence, while craving the legitimacy it might confer on their selective engagements overseas. The end of the cold war, in this regard, recalled the contradictions that shaped the founding of the League of Nations and the United Nations after the two world wars. If it was hard to imagine a global regime of law and security without active American participation, it was impossible to secure one in the face of American hyperpower.

Like globalization, the proliferation of non-state actors after 1989 was not a new development. International corporations came to prominence in the early modern world, and
their extensive overseas dealings had more of an impact on many early European
empires than armies or bureaucrats. From the Catholic Church to the Communist
International, non-state actors survived the rise of nationalism in the 19th and 20th centuries. They also played a significant role during the cold war. But in the post-1945 era,
the idea of the nation state strengthened considerably: partly because the creation of
new nations was one of the principal mechanisms of decolonization, and partly because
both the United States and the Soviet Union found it useful to work through states and
national governments. Where necessary, as in South Vietnam, South Korea, or
Afghanistan, the superpowers were willing to invent or prop up a state that had little historical or internal logic.[26]

In the immediate aftermath of the cold war, the number of new states actually
increased. The retreat of the Soviet Union in Eastern Europe allowed for the peaceful
breakup of some artificial nations (Czechoslovakia) and the violent death of others
(Yugoslavia), while the Soviet collapse in 1991 created a dozen more states in place of the
USSR. But the birth of these nations coincided with an increase in the movement of people, ideas, and money across national borders. Technological advances encouraged
international travel, cheap communications, a diversified global economy, and the rise
of truly transnational corporations. Some commentators fretted that the corporation
would usurp the nation state in international affairs, but the problems that stymied
agreements on world trade also restrained the political ambitions of the corporation.
Other shifts were more pronounced. Television and the Internet accelerated cultural
exchange. Major cities became more hybridized and diverse, and the promise of closer
links between the world's distant corners upset previously established patterns of migration. In many industrialized countries, first- and second-generation immigrants from
developing countries watched with amazement as their children and grandchildren
rediscovered the culture and religion that they had left behind. This forced new debates
about multiculturalism, which tacked between alarm and excitement about yet another
process of hybridization.[27]

If technology rather than the superpower thaw was principally responsible for these
cultural and demographic shifts, the end of the cold war directly influenced two troubling international phenomena: organized crime and terrorism. The mafia networks of
the 1990s made full use of improved communications and cheaper forms of travel, and
they thrived in the political and social chaos of the "transition" in Eastern Europe and
Russia. The difficulties in establishing the rule of law throughout the former Soviet
Union allowed for the creation of mafia fortunes and the entrenchment of criminal
methods and markets that would make the eventual eradication of this activity even
harder.[28]

Terrorism was also spurred by technological advances, and it found a new lease of life
in the changed geopolitical climate after 1989. Although the 1990s saw the effective resolution of the violent struggle in Northern Ireland, and the co-optation of the Palestine
Liberation Organization (PLO) into the political process in Israel-Palestine, a series of

brazen attacks by Islamic radicals suggested that terrorism would play a major role in the "new world order." Radical Islam emerged during the cold war period in response to local political failures. Political Islamists gained momentum by portraying rulers like the Sauds, Anwar Sadat in Egypt, Mohammed Reza Pahlavi in Iran, and Babrak Karmal in Afghanistan as corrupt, decadent puppets of the great powers. These were leaders who rejected democracy and meaningful political opposition but found it necessary to reach some accommodation with Islam. Inadvertently, they allowed the mosques to become a refuge for resistance to their rule. Given the ossification of these societies, it is hardly surprising that Islam would become politicized and that political Islamists would employ violence to advance their ends.[29]

Although radical Islamists caught the attention of Western media on a number of occasions during the cold war, the biggest successes of political Islam appeared to be in the effective capture of states: Iran in 1979, and Afghanistan in 1996. During the 1990s, political Islamists engaged in a debate over the scope and methods of their political projects. Some groups, like the FIS (Islamic Salvation Front) in Algeria and Hamas in the Palestinian territories, fused a commitment to Islam with a determination to continue the national struggle. Others, including the loose alliance of jihadis who would eventually form al-Qaeda, agitated for change on a much broader scale: the Islamic world should be brought under religious rule in its entirety, from North Africa (or even Spain) to the Philippines. These supranational goals were not formulated in a vacuum of religious zealotry or "fundamentalism." The radical Islamists who eventually called for a restored Caliphate developed a critique of both democracy and national borders as Western impositions. Many had been schooled in Afghanistan, a museum of great-power chicanery and a monument to the vainglory of the nation state.[30]

Political Islam might have faltered without the enormous encouragement offered by the Iranian Revolution and the mujahidin success in Afghanistan; the toppled regimes in both countries had owed their existence to the superpower realpolitik that prevailed during the cold war. It was revitalized by the mistakes made by the United States in the aftermath of 1989, when American policymakers were slow to acknowledge either the weaknesses of cold war Middle East policy or the dangers of continuing on the same course. Although the United States was now prepared to allow former clients to fall in Africa and Asia, from Mobutu in Zaire to Suharto in Indonesia, policymakers continued to support the Saudi regime and the discredited Mubarak government in Egypt. American presidents also became closely involved with a peace process in Israel-Palestine that failed to restrain the settlement expansion at the heart of the conflict. Finally, the US decision to leave Saddam Hussein in power in Iraq after 1991 led policymakers to embrace a clumsy combination of air strikes and economic sanctions; the Iraqi leader was kept "in his box" at the expense of considerable suffering on the part of Iraqi civilians. The cold war had ended, but the awkward calculus that had shaped Middle East policy during the 1960s and 1970s escaped serious reassessment.[31]

This created resentment throughout the region, and the lack of political alternatives to the dictates of unelected leaders gave a fresh wind to the proponents of violent extremism. Western governments could hardly claim to be ignorant of the risks. A ragtag group of Islamists made a serious attempt to destroy the World Trade Center eight years before al-Qaeda's attack, citing America's unequivocal support for Israel as their justification. Meanwhile, the Algerian military's decision to annul the results of elections in December 1991 demonstrated the dangers of shutting Islamist voices out of the political process. In the orgy of violence that followed the abortive victory of the Islamic Salvation Front, radical Islamists outmaneuvered moderates and emphasized both the emptiness of democracy and the limitations of a merely national struggle. Algerian terrorists came to France, to England—even to the Canadian border in the final days of 1999, as a nervous jihadi named Ahmed Ressam was apprehended on his way to blow up Los Angeles International Airport. The problem was not that these warning signs were invisible, but that the danger they suggested was too diffuse and nimble for nation states to comprehend. Policymakers and strategists in Europe and the United States were more concerned with missile defense and rogue states during the 1990s, debates that affirmed the traditional definition of international relations and familiar ideas about the application of power.[32]

Even the attacks of 9/11 failed to force a proper accounting of the threats facing the post-cold war world. The Bush administration attacked al-Qaeda's safe haven in Afghanistan. Then the president turned away from the complex problem of countering America's most elusive enemies and confronted Saddam Hussein. Assistant secretary of defense Paul Wolfowitz identified Iraq as a desirable target within days of 9/11 because unlike Afghanistan, Iraq would "break easily." This turned out to be true, though not in the way that Wolfowitz expected. The attack on Saddam Hussein was not only a piece of misdirection, which led Americans away from the perpetrators of 9/11; it also encouraged the Islamic radicalism and political despair that the "War on Terror" was supposed to defeat. The American government had an enormous stake in imagining that its adversaries were state-based: hence the "axis of evil" and the saber-rattling toward Iraq, Iran, and North Korea. But the truth was more troubling. The most indelible challengers to American power had concluded that nation states were an ineffectual means of challenging the hegemony of the United States. This made them considerably harder to identify, and more dangerous than the "rogue states" that the Pentagon had readied itself to counter.[33]

Liberal Americans, and the rest of the world, placed the blame for the Iraq debacle squarely at the feet of George W. Bush and his advisors. But the problems that led to 9/11, and which dogged the American effort in Afghanistan and Iraq, have deeper roots. The United States emerged in the 1990s as a "lonely superpower," in Samuel Huntington's phrase. In the Middle East American policymakers retained many of their policies from the cold war era in spite of the demise of the Soviet threat. Meanwhile, aggrieved individuals and groups realized that American power might be challenged most effectively not by political mobilization or by appeals to international law, but by creating chaos and bloodshed. Part of the problem facing the United States was the unraveling of decades of misguided policy in the Middle East and central Asia. In this respect, the end of the cold war produced not a new order but a working out of grievances and injustice that had long been overlooked. But the deeper issue was the visibility of the United States after

1989. Where the elixir of economic globalization did not take hold, the United States seemed more mountebank than messiah. In the Middle East, meanwhile, the costs of American influence and "stability" had paradoxically increased in the absence of the Soviet Union: partly because America was now held principally accountable for the region's underlying problems, and partly because the growing sophistication and destructiveness of terrorist groups made American soldiers and civilians more vulnerable than they had ever been.[34]

When change came to the Middle East in the spring of 2011, Western politicians and media reached instinctively for 1989: this was a Berlin Wall moment in which the peoples of the region had confirmed freedom's universal appeal. The reality was more complex. Policymakers in Europe and the United States were completely surprised by the grassroots movements in Tunisia and Egypt. Initially, they clung to familiar certainties and offered scant support to the uprisings. (Client regimes had, after all, been a mainstay of Western policy since the imperial era.) After Egyptian protesters succeeded in toppling their government without Western assistance, the situation changed. The Obama administration, which had been non-committal on the future of Hosni Mubarak, supported a NATO intervention against Muammar Gaddafi in Libya. The resulting conflict had echoes of the Kosovo bombing of 1999. It was much messier and more protracted than Western governments had envisaged, and it stretched the provisions of international law to breaking point. The collapse of the Gaddafi regime in August 2011 confirmed the triumph of the rebels and the arduousness of the task ahead. As in Tunisia and Egypt, there was enormous uncertainty about the shape of the regime that would succeed the long years of dictatorship. Since the United States and its Western allies had created or colluded with the region's scurrying despots, could American and European leaders now be relied upon to support a genuinely democratic future for the Middle East?[35]

The "Arab spring" of 2011 recalled 1989 in two important respects: it reminded the world that the most entrenched political realities could be remade with astonishing abruptness, and it embarrassed the clairvoyance of the United States. In the short term, observers wondered if the revolutions in North Africa would spread eastwards: perhaps even to Saudi Arabia, the kingpin of the old American order in the region. (Violent repression in Yemen and Syria suggested a darker outcome.) In the longer term, the successful challenge to Western-backed dictatorships suggested an alternative to the rhetoric and methods of al-Qaeda and its affiliates. The American execution of bin Laden in Pakistan in May 2011, between the fall of Mubarak and Gaddafi, wrote its own headlines: terrorism was in retreat, liberal democracy had proved its resilience. But the continuing spate of terrorist attacks from Baghdad to Kabul, and the growing involvement of al-Qaeda affiliates in the domestic politics of Yemen, made this conclusion seem more hopeful than persuasive. Political atrophy and a lopsided projection of power continued to define American involvement in Iraq and Afghanistan. (Ten years after 9/11, more than 140,000 American troops remained in those countries.) If the Arab spring vindicated self-determination in parts of the Middle East, the reality of American imperium endured elsewhere.[36]

John Lewis Gaddis's point about the Soviet Union in 1989—that its military power counted for little in the face of popular resistance—found an ironic analogue in the American predicament after 9/11. Although the United States continued to enjoy a vast military superiority over any other nation state, the proliferation of non-state challenges and threats presented an open rebuke to the idea of a unipolar world. Iraq and Afghanistan were unwinnable wars, in spite of the hundreds of thousands of soldiers and years of occupation, because the hopes that these states might be pacified or democ-ratized began to vanish as soon as foreign troops entered the country. The prospect of terrorist groups gaining possession of weapons of mass destruction remained merci-fully hypothetical by the tenth anniversary of the September 11 attacks, but this allowed most Americans to postpone the serious recalculation of both the national interest and the balance of world politics that apocalyptic terrorism would demand. (That task was left instead to Strangelovian thinkers like Dick Cheney.) By the end of George W. Bush's two terms, the president could boast that he had protected the "homeland" from serious attack for more than seven years. Some high-ranking officials had predicted a rolling campaign of bombings that would kill thousands of Americans before Bush left office. Instead, terrorists targeted foreign cities—London, Madrid, Mumbai—and the memory of 9/11 became more distant. Perhaps the most pressing questions in world affairs were how long this relative calm would endure, and what the American government would do after another attack.[37]

When Francis Fukuyama mischievously suggested that the end of the cold war meant the end of history, he warned his readers to prepare for a "very sad time." A world of liberal capitalism would be tedious in the extreme: its inhabitants would make money, but they would forego the really exciting qualities—"daring, courage, imagination, and idealism"—that were only inspired by serious ideological struggle. (There was more than a dash of Theodore Roosevelt in this nostalgia for "competition and conflict.") Perhaps history would start again, Fukuyama surmised, when ordinary people glimpsed the "prospect of centuries of boredom" and decided to fight one another once more. Although some commentators might find a way to vindicate this prediction, referring to the rudderless 1990s and the new American resolve after 9/11, the reality is more straightforward. History neither ended in 1989 nor resumed in 2001. Instead the end of the cold war greatly reduced one enormous danger—a nuclear exchange between the superpowers—but revealed many others that had previously seemed less urgent.[38]

Although the fault lines of the post-cold war world remain to be mapped, we now have a more measured perspective on the Western self-congratulation that accompa-nied the Soviet collapse. The end of the superpower conflict created numerous chal-lenges for policymakers, and brought a long-delayed reckoning of struggles that had been sidelined or dismissed. The illusions of American omnipotence or a liberal millen-nium largely evaporated within two decades of the fall of the Berlin Wall, but the new thinking required to make sense of a turbulent world was not immediately apparent. Perhaps some of the answers lie in a past which is more accessible now than it was in the halcyon days of the 1990s. Seeing beyond the cold war framework and rewriting world history after 1945 may provide us with a fuller understanding of the convulsive forces that shape our present.

## NOTES

1. Jim Hoagland, "From Yalta to Malta," *Washington Post*, November 9, 1989, A23. John Lewis Gaddis, *The Cold War: A New History* (New York: Penguin, 2006), 256–7; and Melvyn Leffler, *For the Soul of Mankind: The United States, the Soviet Union, and the Cold War* (New York: Hill and Wang, 2007), 439–48.

2. Francis Fukuyama, "The End of History?" *National Interest* 16 (Summer 1989): 3–18. Thomas Friedman coined the "11/9 to 9/11" era in *The World is Flat: A Brief History of the Twenty-First Century* (New York: Farrar, Straus and Giroux, 2006).

3. Stephen Kotkin, *Armageddon Averted: The Soviet Collapse, 1970-2000*, updated ed. (New York: Oxford University Press, 2008); Vladislav M. Zubok, *A Failed Empire: The Soviet Union in the Cold War from Stalin to Gorbachev* (Chapel Hill, NC: University of North Carolina Press, 2007).

4. Gaddis, *The Cold War*, 263–6. Melvyn Leffler, "The Cold War: What Do 'We Now Know'?" *American Historical Review* 104/2 (April 1999): 501–24, 523; Peter Schweizer, *Reagan's War: The Epic Struggle of His Forty-Year Struggle and Final Triumph over Communism* (New York: Doubleday, 2003).

5. Odd Arne Westad, *The Global Cold War: Third World Interventions and the Making of Our Times* (Cambridge: Cambridge University Press, 2005); Matthew Connelly, "Taking Off the Cold War Lens: Visions of North-South Conflict During the Algerian War for Independence," *American Historical Review* 105/3 (June 2000): 739–69.

6. George Lawson et al., eds., *The Global 1989: Continuity and Change in World Politics* (Cambridge: Cambridge University Press, 2010); Padraic Kenney, *1989: Democratic Revolutions at the Cold War's End* (New York: Bedford/St. Martin's, 2010).

7. Fukuyama, "The End of History"; Tony Smith, *America's Mission: The United States and the Worldwide Struggle for Democracy in the Twentieth Century* (Princeton, NJ: Princeton University Press, 1994), 311–45.

8. Lawrence Freedman and Efraim Karsh, *The Gulf Conflict 1990-1991: Diplomacy and War in the New World Order* (Princeton, NJ: Princeton University Press, 1992); George H.W. Bush, "Address before a Joint Session of the Congress on the Cessation of the Persian Gulf Conflict," March 6, 1991, in *Public Papers of the Presidents of the United States: George H.W. Bush, 1991, Book I* (Washington, DC: Government Printing Office, 1992), 218–22.

9. Bush, "Address before a Joint Session of Congress," 222.

10. Derek Chollet and James Goldgeier, *America between the Wars: From 11/9 to 9/11* (New York: Public Affairs, 2008), 1–28; Stephen Kinzer, *Overthrow: America's Century of Regime Change from Hawaii to Iraq* (New York: Times Books, 2006), 239–59, 305–7.

11. David Halberstam, *War in a Time of Peace: Bush, Clinton and the Generals* (New York: Scribner, 2001), 9–17, 24–100, 128–56; transcripts of the State Department daily press briefings for May 19, May 27, June 3, August 5, and August 6, at <http://dosfan.lib.uic.edu/ERC/briefing/daily_briefings/1992/index.html> (September 12, 2011).

12. Fukuyama, "The End of History," 11. Charles Krauthammer, "The Unipolar Moment," *Foreign Affairs* 70/1 (Winter 1990/1): 23–33.

13. Stephen Lovell, *Destination in Doubt: Russia since 1989* (London: Zed Books, 2006), 89–112, 136–59; David Hoffman, *The Oligarchs: Wealth and Power in the New Russia* (New York:

Public Affairs, 2004); Anatol Lieven, *Chechnya: Tombstone of Russian Power* (New Haven, CT: Yale University Press, 1998).

14. See Hyung-Gu Lynn, Chapter 33 in this volume.

15. Joseph E. Stiglitz, *Globalization and its Discontents* (New York: Norton, 2002), 16, 53–88. On whether or not the "Washington Consensus" was a synonym for neoliberalism, see Williamson, "A Short History of the Washington Consensus," in Narcís Serra and Joseph E. Stiglitz, eds., *The Washington Consensus Reconsidered: Towards a New Global Governance* (Oxford, UK: Oxford University Press, 2008); 13–30; and Stiglitz, "Is There a Post-Washington Consensus Consensus?" in Serra and Stiglitz, *The Washington Consensus Reconsidered*, 41–56.

16. See Leslie Sklair, *The Transnational Capitalist Class* (Oxford: Blackwell, 2001); Amy Chua, *World On Fire: How Exporting Free Market Democracy Breeds Ethnic Hatred and Global Instability* (New York: Doubleday, 2002).

17. Thomas Friedman, *The Lexus and the Olive Tree: Understanding Globalization* (New York: Farrar, Straus and Giroux, 1999); Friedman, *The World is Flat*; James Mann, *The China Fantasy: How Our Leaders Explain away Chinese Repression* (New York: Viking, 2007).

18. Allister Sparks, *Beyond the Miracle: Inside the New South Africa* (Chicago: University of Chicago Press, 2003), 202–19. Nivedita Menon and Aditya Nigam, *Power and Contestation: India since 1989* (London: Zed Books, 2007), 61–102; Greg Grandin, *Empire's Workshop: Latin America, the United States, and the Rise of the New Imperialism* (New York: Metropolitan Books, 2006), 198–222; Fareed Zakaria, *The Future of Freedom: Illiberal Democracy at Home and Abroad* (New York: Norton, 2003).

19. On the political and cultural orientation of the emerging middle class, see Timothy Cheek, *Living with Reform: China since 1989* (London: Zed Books, 2007), 83–4, 87–9, 91–2, 122. Samuel Huntington, "The Clash of Civilizations?" *Foreign Affairs* 72/3 (Summer 1993): 22–49.

20. Tina Rosenberg, "The Perils of Petrocracy," *New York Times Magazine*, November 4, 2007, 42–9, 78–80; "Ten Mostly Wasted Years," *The Economist*, February 7, 2009, 11; Andrew Ross Sorkin, *Too Big to Fail* (New York: Viking, 2009); Gillian Tett, *Fool's Gold* (New York: Free Press, 2009).

21. Ha-Joon Chang, *Bad Samaritans: The Guilty Secrets of Rich Nations and the Threat to Global Prosperity* (London: Bloomsbury Press, 2007); Joseph E. Stiglitz, *The Roaring Nineties* (New York, 2003), 202–40; John R. MacArthur, *The Selling of Free Trade: NAFTA, Washington, and the Subversion of American Democracy* (New York: Hill and Wang, 2000); Alistair Darling, *Back from the Brink: 1000 Days at Number 11* (London: Atlantic Books, 2011).

22. Chollet and Goldgeier, *America between the Wars*, 11; Stephen C. Schlesinger, *Act of Creation: The Founding of the United Nations* (New York: Basic Books, 2003); Edward M. Bernstein, "The Soviet Union and Bretton Woods," in Michael D. Bordo and Barry J. Eichengreen, eds., *A Retrospective on the Bretton Woods System: Lessons for International Monetary Reform* (Chicago IL: University of Chicago Press, 1993), 195–8.

23. Boutros Boutros-Ghali, *Unvanquished: A US—U.N. Saga* (New York: Random House, 1999); David Hannay, *New World Disorder: The UN after the Cold War, an Insider's View* (London: I.B. Tauris, 2008).

24. Nicholas Guyatt, *Another American Century? The United States and the World since 9/11* (London: Zed Books, 2003), 74–95; Halberstam, *War in a Time of Peace*, 248–92; and Hannay, *New World Disorder*, 119–96.

25. Tony Judt, *Postwar: A History of Europe Since 1945* (New York: Penguin, 2005), 713–36; Stephen Clarkson, *Uncle Sam and Us: Globalization, Neoconservatism, and the Canadian State* (Toronto: University of Toronto Press, 2002), 347–53; Jeffry Frieden, *Global Capitalism: Its Fall and Rise in the Twentieth Century* (New York, 2006), 457–72; Robert Gilpin, *Global Political Economy: Understanding the International Economic Order* (Princeton, NJ: Princeton University Press, 2001), 221–33.

26. See Penny Von Eschen, Chapter 26 in this volume.
27. Stephen Castles and Mark J. Miller, *The Age of Migration: International Population Movements in the Modern World*, 4th ed. (Houndmills: The Guildford Press, 2009); and Jan Nederveen Pieterse, *Globalization and Culture: Global Mélange*, 2nd ed. (Lanham, MD: Rowman & Littlefield, 2009).
28. Misha Glenny, *McMafia: A Journey through the Global Criminal Underworld* (New York: Knopf, 2008), 3–97.
29. Douglas Little, *American Orientalism: The United States and the Middle East since 1945*, 3rd ed. (Chapel Hill, NC: University of North Carolina Press, 2008); Salim Yaqub, "Imperious Doctrines: US-Arab Relations from Dwight D. Eisenhower to George W. Bush," *Diplomatic History* 26/4 (Fall 2002): 571–91; Steve Coll, *Ghost Wars: The Secret History of the CIA, Afghanistan, and Bin Laden, from the Soviet Invasion to September 10, 2001* (New York: Penguin, 2004); Lawrence Wright, *The Looming Tower: Al-Qaeda and the Road to 9/11* (New York: Knopf, 2006).
30. James D. Le Sueur, *Algeria since 1989: Between Terror and Democracy* (London: Zed Books, 2009); Shaul Mishal and Avraham Sela, *The Palestinian Hamas: Vision, Violence, and Coexistence*, 2nd ed. (New York: Columbia University Press, 2006); Wright, *The Looming Tower*, 129–37.
31. Westad, *Global Cold War*, 289; Yaqub, "Imperious Doctrines."
32. Le Sueur, *Between Terror and Democracy*; Michael Klare, *Rogue States and Nuclear Outlaws: America's Search for a New Foreign Policy* (New York: Hill and Wang, 1995).
33. Bob Woodward, *Bush at War* (New York: Simon and Schuster, 2002), 82–3.
34. Samuel Huntington, "The Lonely Superpower," *Foreign Affairs* 78/2 (March–April 1999): 35–49.
35. Roger Cohen, "Tehran 1979 or Berlin 1989?" *International Herald Tribune*, February 8, 2011, 6. David E. Sanger, "Obama Presses Egypt's Military on Democracy," *New York Times*, February 12, 2011, A7. For an early indication that even liberals would be loath to ditch US-friendly autocrats in the region, see Jeffrey Goldberg, "Danger: Falling Tyrants," *Atlantic*, June 2011, 46–53.
36. Thomas L. Friedman, "Farewell to Geronimo," *New York Times*, May 4, 2011, A29; Fouad Ajami, "Osama Bin Laden, Weak Horse," *Wall Street Journal*, May 3, 2011, A17; "War by the Numbers," *New York Times*, September 8, 2011.
37. Richard A. Clarke, "Ten Years Later," *Atlantic*, January/February 2005, 61–77.
38. Fukuyama, "The End of History," 18.

## SELECT BIBLIOGRAPHY

Cheek, Timothy, *Living with Reform: China since 1989* (London, 2007).
Chollet, Derek, and James Goldgeier, *America between the Wars: From 11/9 to 9/11* (New York, 2008).
Halberstam, David, *War in a Time of Peace: Bush, Clinton and the Generals* (New York, 2001).
Lawson, George, et al., eds., *The Global 1989: Continuity and Change in World Politics* (Cambridge, 2010).
Sorkin, Andrew Ross, *Too Big to Fail* (New York: Viking, 2009).
Stiglitz, Joseph E., *The Roaring Nineties* (New York, 2003).
Traub, James, *The Best Intentions: Kofi Annan and the UN in the Era of American World Power* (London, 2006).
Wright, Lawrence, *The Looming Tower: Al-Qaeda and the Road to 9/11* (New York, 2006).

# Index